Florida Gulf Coast University
Planning and Evaluation

Assessment and Program Evaluation

Edited by
Joan S. Stark
and
Alice Thomas

ASHE READER SERIES
Barbara Townsend, Series Editor

SIMON & SCHUSTER
CUSTOM PUBLISHING

SIMON & SCHUSTER CUSTOM PUBLISHING
160 Gould Street/Needham Heights, MA 02194
Simon & Schuster Higher Education Publishing Group

COPYRIGHT ACKNOWLEDGMENTS

Grateful acknowledgment is made to the following sources for permission to reprint material copyrighted or controlled by them:

"Five Evaluation Frameworks: Implications for Decision Making in Higher Education," by Don E. Gardner. Reprinted from *The Journal of Higher Education*, Volume 48, Number 5, September/October 1977.

"Program Evaluation: A Historical Overview," by George F. Madaus, et al. Reprinted from *Evaluation Models*, Daniel L. Stufflebeam and Michael S. Scriven, eds. Copyright ©1987 by Kluwer Academic Publishers.

"To Capture the Ineffable: New Forms of Assessment in Higher Education," by Peter T. Ewell. Reprinted from *Review of Research in Education*, Volume 17, 1991. Washington, D.C.: American Educational Research Association.

"Demystifying Assessment: Learning from the Field of Evaluation," by Barbara Gross Davis, from *New Directions for Higher Education,* Volume 16, Number 67. Published by Jossey-Bass, Inc.

"The Movement to Assess Students' Learning Will Institutionalize Mediocrity in Colleges," by Ernst Benjamin, from *The Chronicle of Higher Education,* July 5, 1990.

"Assessment Is Doing More for Higher Education than Any Other Development in Recent History," by James H. Daughdrill Jr., from *The Chronicle of Higher Education,* January 27, 1988.

"Assessment and Evaluation: Knowing and Judging Results," by Lion F. Gardiner, reprinted from *Planning for Assessment: Mission Statements, Goals and Objectives.* Courtesy of the New Jersey Department of Higher Education: Office of Learning Assessment.

"Trends in Evaluation," by Ernest R. House, from *Educational Researcher,* April 1990, Volume 19, Number 3.

"Assessing Assessment," by Reid Johnson, Joseph Prus, Charles J. Anderson, and Elaine El-Khawas. Excerpts from The American Council on Education Panel Report, Number 79.

"Assessment and Accreditation: A Shotgun Marriage?" by Ralph A. Wolff. Reprinted from *Assessment 1990: Accreditation and Renewal.* Washington D.C.: The American Association of Higher Education Assessment Forum.

"Creating a Context Where Institutional Assessment Yields Educational Improvement," by Marcia Mentkowski, reprinted from *The Journal of General Education*, Volume 40, 1991.

"'But How Do We Know It'll Work?': An Assessment Memoir," by Barbara Wright. Reprinted from *The American Association for Higher Education Bulletin*, April 1990.

"Assessment Through the Major," by Mark I. Applebaum. Reprinted from *Performance and Judgement: Essays on the Principles and Practices in the Assessment of College Student Learning*, 1988, C. Adelman, ed. U.S. Department of Education: Office of Educational Research.

"In Their Own Words: What Students Learn Outside the Classroom," by George D. Kuh. Reprinted from *American Educational Research Journal*, Volume 30, Issue 2.

Excerpt from *Assessing Institutional Effectiveness in Community Colleges*, Don Doucette and Billie Hughes, eds. Laguna Hills, CA: League for Innovation in the Community College.

"The Blind Alley of Value Added," by Jonathan Warren. Reprinted from *The American Association of Higher Education Bulletin*, September 1984.

"Cognitive Measures in Assessing Learning," by Jonathan Warren. Reprinted from *Implementing Outcomes Assessment: Promise and Perils—New Directions for Institutional Research*, Number 59, 1988. Published by Jossey-Bass, Inc.

"An Analysis of Alternative Approaches to Evaluation," by Daniel L. Stufflebeam and William J. Webster. Reprinted from *Educational Evaluation and Policy Analysis*, May/June 1980.

"A Map of Postsecondary Assessment," by Leonard L. Baird. Reprinted from *Research in Higher Education*, Volume 28, Issue 2, 1988.

"Approaches to Outcomes and Outcome Assessment," Joannne M. Alexander and Joan S. Stark. Reprinted from *Focusing on Student Academic Outcomes: A Working Paper*. National Center for Research to Improve Postsecondary Teaching and Learning, 1986.

"Learning Outcomes and Their Effects: Useful Categories of Human Peformance," by Robert M. Gagne. Reprinted from *American Psychologist*. Copyright © 1984 American Psychological Association. Reprinted with permission.

"College Student Outcomes Assessment: A Talent Development Perspective," by Maryann Jacobi, Alexander Astin, and Frank Ayala, Jr. The Association for the Study of Higher Education: ASHE/ERIC Higher Education Report Number 7.

"Assessing the Departmental Major," by Bobby Fong. Reprinted from *Assessing Students' Learning-New Directions for Teaching and Learning*, J. Mcmillan, ed. Number 34, Summer 1988. Published by Jossey-Bass, Inc.

"Assessing Critical Thinking Across the Curriculum," by C. Blaine Carpenter and James C. Doig. Reprinted from *Assessing Students' Learning- New Directions for Teaching and Learning*, Number 34, Summer 1988.

"Linking Program Reviews to Institutional Assessment, Accreditation, and Planning," by Robert J. Barak and Barbara E. Breier. Reprinted from *Successful Program Review*, San Francisco: Jossey-Bass Publishers, 1990.

"Principles of Good Practice in Assessment," Reprinted from *Achieving Institutional Effectiveness Through Assessment*. April 1992. Oakland, CA: Western Association of Schools and Colleges.

"Criterion Three and the Assessment of Student Academic Achievement," by Austin Doherty and Gerald W. Patton. Reprinted from *NCA Quarterly*, Volume 66, Issue 2, 1991.

"Principles of Good Practice for Assessing Student Learning," Washington, D.C.: The American Association for Higher Education, the AAHE Assessment Forum, 1992.

"Meta-Assessment: Evaluating Assessment Activities," by John C. Ory. Reprinted from *Research in Higher Education*, Volume 33, Issue 4, 1992.

"Explorations with Students and Faculty about Teaching, Learning, and Student Life," by Richard J. Light. Reprinted from *The Harvard Assessment Seminars, First Report: Explorations with Students and Faculty About Teaching, Learning, and Student Life*. Cambridge, MA: Harvard University, Graduate School of Education, 1990.

"TQM and Assessment: The North Dakota Experience," by Alice T. Clark and Daniel R. Rice. Reprinted from *A Collection of Papers on Self-Study and Institutional Improvement*. Chicago: North Central Association of Colleges and Schools, 1992.

"Implementing and Maintaining a Classroom Research Program for Faculty," by Nancy E. Stetson. Reprinted from *Classroom Research: Early Lessons from Success-New Directions for Teaching and Learning*, Number 46, 1991. T. A. Angelo, ed.

Contents

Acknowledgments

Each of the editors has recently developed and taught a course about evaluation, assessment, and program review. Our thoughts about developing a reader on these topics were reinforced by a panel we organized at the annual Forum of the Association for Institutional Research in May 1992. A great deal of interest was demonstrated in the topic at the Forum; the symposium attracted between 150 and 200 people, and elicited much discussion. A subsequent meeting to evaluate the Forum included a lengthy discussion of the assessment and evaluation skills needed in the future by those in institutional research. Thus, while the reader is primarily intended for use in higher education programs, we knew that interest extended beyond ASHE membership and that it might have a broader audience. We have been assisted by an Advisory Board of persons with expertise in evaluation and assessment. These individuals hold diverse positions and perspectives; some took issue with our original topic organization. They helped us formulate topic areas more clearly, generate lists of possible readings, and select the best from among them. Some shared work in progress or syllabi for their own courses. We thank them for their considerable help, but we take responsibility for errors of inclusion or omission in the reader.

Thomas Angelo
Trudy Banta
Todd Davis
Peter Gray
George Kuh
Yvonna Lincoln
Marcia Mentkowski
Patricia Murrell
Michael Nettles
Patrick Terenzini
Richard Wilson

We also thank Lisa R. Lattuca, Doctoral Candidate and Research Assistant, and Linda C. Stiles, Executive Secretary, at the University of Michigan for their assistance in various phases of this project. From the vantage point of a student who had taken Professor Stark's course in its formative stages, Lisa reviewed and rated over 100 different volumes and articles. Most selections in the reader (and many others that are not) were used in classes taught by Professors Stark and Thomas in 1992 and 1993. Our work profited from the effort students made to comment on each article.

Introduction

JOAN S. STARK, ED.D., PROFESSOR, UNIVERSITY OF MICHIGAN
ALICE M. THOMAS, PH.D., ASSISTANT DEAN,
ST. CLOUD STATE UNIVERSITY

Educators who attended conferences on assessing student outcomes in the 1980s may remember a spirit of revivalism. Those leading what became known as the assessment bandwagon" encouraged their followers in many ways with sessions on "why do assessment" and "how to get started at assessment." At one concluding conference session the assembly sang "A Battle Hymn of Assessment," with appropriate words obtained through a contest among attendees. The actual battle was never engaged on conference grounds, of course, because opponents of assessment, both faculty and administrators, were not in attendance. The battles over the advantages and disadvantages of assessment were held on some campuses and in some states between committed advocates and equally committed opponents of assessment.

In nearly all of higher education, however, assessing student outcomes is becoming "the ordinary course of business" in the 1990s. Educators have responded—some eagerly, others reluctantly—to demands from statehouses, the public, and accreditors that they validate student learning. Between 1985 and 1995, most faculty and college administrators have voiced their opinions about the advantages and disadvantages of assessment and the debate has subsided. The emphasis now is on "what to assess," "how to assess," and "how to use assessment results." Depending on the specific state and institution, assessment results may be used for accountability, for self-improvement, or both.

Expertise Needed

Many educators responded cautiously to assessment ideas at first simply because they lacked critical knowledge such as: assessment frameworks to adapt in their college context, guidelines on how to measure student outcomes, ways to analyze and present the results, and strategies to ensure use that the information is used. Gradually, however, assessment specialists are emerging; some home-grown and self-taught, others prepared in departments of higher education. These specialists may work on the campus generating data and implementing policy, or in state agencies receiving data and developing policy.

On campus, those responsible for assessment and related evaluation activities may hold leadership positions in the office of a dean, as chair of a faculty committee, in an office of institutional research, or, increasingly, as head of a new office of educational assessment. Colleges are assigning a wide range of administrative personnel to conduct a plethora of instructional studies, and to take responsibility for convincing diverse audiences to collaborate. A majority of colleges surveyed believe their staff lacks expertise to assume the planning and evaluation processes outlined by the Southern Association of Colleges and Schools to assess institutional effectiveness (Rogers and Gentemann 1989). Since those responsible for assessment studies are being recruited from many parts of collegiate institutions, new training is being sought by teaching faculty and academic administrators as well as institutional researchers and others.

A few graduate programs in higher education have developed specific courses in educational assessment and more will surely do so in the next few years. Demonstrably, the theoretical roots of learning about assessment are in evaluation research and, even more basically, in research design. Thus, the topic is a natural one for such programs. According to one expert who has taught such a course for many years, assessment is really "applied research in education and the social sciences" and "Good assessment is good research" (Astin 1991, p. xii).

Even with origins in research design, emphasis on evaluation in colleges and departments of education has waxed and waned. When federal funding for educational and social programs increased after World War II (and particularly in the 1960s), a cadre of evaluation experts emerged to provide accountability for use of federal funds. At that time, most education students took at least one course in evaluation, and often another in testing and measurement. Then, as requirements were loosened in the 1970s and as new issues demanded attention, inclusion of evaluation courses and theories in education studies became less common. For graduate students in elementary and secondary education, as well as those in higher education, assessment has brought a resurgence of evaluation research under a new name and with goals and strategies adapted to new contexts.

Yet, evaluation activities are not dependent upon formal training. Effective curriculum development has always included an evaluation component designed to inform developers about success and to flag needed adjustments in the curriculum design. Good instructors have always sought evidence of student academic growth and used it to refine courses and academic programs. Clearly, evaluation is not a foreign concept to most educators. The current assessment movement, however, includes several new issues: new terminology for evaluation, new demands that institutions be more systematic about evaluative efforts, and possible emphasis on accountability rather than improvement. Assessment techniques for student achievement have expanded to include many strategies besides achievement testing. The development of longitudinal data bases to track student progress raises ethical and privacy issues. These varied issues might be addressed in formal courses, as well in workshops and conferences.

What Might a Course in Assessment, Evaluation and Program Review Include?

We believe, and our advisory committee agreed, that a course in evaluation and assessment taught to higher education graduate students should include evaluation theories, historical and philosophical context, political context, research strategies, and specific applications in educational evaluation. It should apply these theories and strategies in both (1) assessment of outcomes; and (2) program review. Students should be able to use these strategies as an evaluator working within the enterprise being reviewed, or as an external evaluator not directly involved in the enterprise. The course should address the assessment of an institution's educational resources and processes, as well as its educational outcomes. The student outcomes considered should reflect the diverse types of cognitive outcomes in which an institution might be interested: for example, acquiring general education abilities, achieving in an academic major field, demonstrating competence in a career preparation program, acquiring leadership skills, and developing cross-cultural and global understandings. Non-cognitive outcomes, possibly acquired in college life outside the classroom, should be considered too, for example value development and increases in social, emotional, and moral maturity. Ideally higher education students would gain some knowledge in evaluating all of these aspects of students and programs and know where to go to get more knowledge.

Such a broad emphasis is necessary because most higher education programs enroll students with differing backgrounds and professional experiences, as well as diverse career plans. The course may prepare some students who take additional related courses to be evaluators themselves while others become evaluation clients as both faculty members or administrators. We believe that the context in which evaluation is undertaken is very important but we cannot easily specify that context for higher education students who may end up in accrediting or state agencies as well as on campuses. Ellen Faith, who co-taught a course with Todd Davis at Memphis State University emphasized the value of individuals headed for diverse roles taking such a course together and spending time "in each others' shoes." We agree, but in some cases professors may wish to tailor assignments to specific student interests and expertise. We hope this reader will help the instructor in this task.

Based on these overall goals, the specific objectives of a course in evaluation and assessment might include at a minimum:

1. To examine the historical, political, organizational, and administrative origins of evaluation and assessment, including recent debates and perspectives.

2. To examine the commonalties that tie assessment research with institutional research and evaluation research, as well as the distinctions among these different forms of inquiry.

3. To build upon foundational training in research methods by considering varied models and specific applications to the context of assessment and program review in higher education.

4. To help students acquire a balance of skills, attitudes, and knowledge necessary to conduct and supervise assessment studies and program reviews, and to adapt their skills to specific contexts in which they are working.

5. To undergird studies of assessment techniques with discussion of philosophies and purposes of education in order to ensure that assessment supports, rather than detracts from, the educational process.

6. To consider interpersonal and group leadership skills necessary to provide leadership in assessment and program review.

7. To develop professional and ethical sensitivity to the human aspects of assessment and program review by considering sets of applicable standards and guidelines for educational evaluation and assessment, fair testing practice, and use of human subjects in research.

8. To consider the multicultural issues and sensitivities that should be addressed when conducting assessment studies.

9. To consider the links between (1) assessment and development of more effective teaching and learning processes, (2) assessment and effective administration.

10. To deal with the following themes and tensions: accountability versus improvement purposes, centralized versus decentralized models, standardized measures versus locally designed measures, quantitative versus qualitative information, norm-referenced versus criterion-referenced standards, comprehensive versus intrusive programs, confidential versus need/right-to-know information.

Some Basic Definitions

Just as they will have varying objectives for a course in assessment and program review, observers will differ on the definitions of the major terms in this reader such as: evaluation, program review, assessment, and self-study. In fact, unavoidably, we have included selections from authors who use the terms in different ways. To help clarify the basis on which we chose articles, we provide our own definitions here.

Evaluation is a broad term meaning the examination of an enterprise and implies some eventual judgment or decision. In education, evaluation is a multi-faceted endeavor which encompasses more specific types of evaluation like assessment and program review. Evaluation may be formative or summative in type. Formative evaluation is used to make decisions about a continuing enterprise; summative evaluation is used to make decisions about whether the enterprise should continue or draw conclusions about its worth.

Program review most often means a review initiated, undertaken, or required by an authority at a higher organizational level than the enterprise being evaluated. Often the initiating agency is a college or university administration or a state agency. When faculty or staff within an educational unit initiate and undertake their own review of their enterprise it is more typically called a *self-study*. Because of the types of responsibility centered at various organization levels, self-studies most often center on educational questions, whereas program reviews also involve questions of economy, accountability, and cost-effectiveness. Program reviews may be either formative or summative. Although some writers consider assessment to be a broader term than evaluation, we use assessment in the specific definition it has recently acquired in education. It refers to the collection of data about student change (and often factors affecting such change) including, but not limited to, academic achievement resulting from courses and academic programs. Other common uses of assessment are assessment for determining student placement in courses, assessment for determining teaching effectiveness, assessment of effectiveness of various offices and functions, and assessment of future employees to assist in hiring or retention. Some of the authors of articles we have selected may use these additional meanings as well as the primary one of student change.

Available Materials

We feel an ASHE reader can help consolidate selected materials and thereby enable courses in assessment and evaluation to become more effective. Since 1980, assessment tools and resources for higher education have increased rapidly and now include a newsletter, a set of "principles for good practice" and several books discussing specific models or viewpoints. Despite the recent consolidation of material into book form, some early materials that are more difficult to obtain can help students understand the assessment contexts, the roots of the movement, the reasons for the extensive debate, and its advantages and disadvantages. Many early assessment papers were either published by the American Association for Higher Education or in the various *New Directions* quarterly sourcebooks published by Jossey Bass. Although some of these articles became outdated rapidly, others are enduring in the perspectives they bring to assessment and program evaluation. In teaching courses on evaluation, program review, and assessment, both of the editors (and many colleagues) found themselves spending far too much time locating, selecting, collecting, indexing and getting permissions to reprint these enduring materials. We hope the reader will remedy this.

The reader presents a variety of viewpoints, not a unified position. Thus, it is intended to serve as a supplement to other materials, not as the single textbook for an assessment and evaluation course. Since 1990 the teaching task has been made easier by the appearance of two new books: *Assessment for Excellence: The Philosophy and Practice of Assessment and Evaluation in Higher Education*, by Alexander Astin (New York: MacMillan, 1991), and *Assessing Student Learning and Development* by T. Dary Erwin (San Francisco: Jossey-Bass, 1991). Each of these excellent volumes takes a specific perspective and both are extremely readable. An edited volume by Trudy W. Banta and Associates, *Making a Difference*, (Jossey-Bass, 1993) provides reports of actual practice over the last decade which will be helpful to those interested more in analyzing practice than in theoretical discussions. We particularly welcomed the publication of Banta's book because most practical studies involve single institutions and are not easily located. Another recent book, *A Practitioner's Handbook for Institutional Effectiveness and Student Outcomes Assessment Implementation*, by James O. Nichols and others is probably more useful to practitioners in specific contexts than for a course.

Other useful books include *Successful Program Review* by Robert Barak and Barbara E. Brier, (San Francisco: Jossey Bass, 1990); and *Self Study Processes* by Herbert R. Kells, (New York: MacMillan ACE Services, 1988). Including readings from these volumes extends the assessment and evaluation perspective to the state accountability level, on the one hand, and to the faculty of specific departments and colleges, on the other hand. The self-improvement strategies called "classroom research" or "classroom assessment techniques" also should be understood by those hoping to increase faculty involvement. We recommend *Classroom Assessment Techniques (Second Edition)* by Thomas A. Angelo and K. Patricia Cross (Jossey-Bass, 1993). Ideas in Angelo and Cross' book are designed to be scanned, sampled, and used rather than read.

Just as research is the ancestor of evaluation, we see evaluation as the ancestor of assessment. Ideally, someone trying to understand assessment needs a background in research design, and then some knowledge of its specific application to educational evaluation. Unfortunately, available materials on evaluation are often targeted either at evaluation of social programs generally, or at K-12 educational programs, more specifically. Nevertheless, we have found that the text, *Educational Evaluation: Alternative Approaches and Practical Guidelines* by B. R. Worthen and J. R. Sanders (Longman Press, 1991), is adaptable to the teaching and learning of evaluation and assessment in higher education. It is especially helpful for those who may become consultants helping colleges and universities plan their evaluations, or, reciprocally, those who will be in positions to choose, hire and work with consultants.

Organization of the Reader

The reader is divided into seven sections. It begins with a historical perspective and policy debates about assessment and program review. It then discusses the primary audiences for assessment and program evaluation both in and out of colleges and universities. It provides sources of models and techniques for planning, doing, analyzing, presenting, and using assessment and program review, as well as some examples to examine. This organization has been useful to us in our teaching but we recognize that others may wish to use other organizational schemes. In a nascent field of literature, most authors write with multiple purposes. Thus, many of the articles cover a great deal of ground. Some could have been placed in sections different from the one we chose and many are pertinent to several discussions and should be read more than once. We have tried to provide sufficient introductory material to make the content of each set of readings apparent and facilitate appropriate choices for professors, students, and evaluators.

In selecting readings, we have tried to choose articles that include all types of colleges and that illustrate varied objects of evaluation from students to organizational functions. We made special efforts to find materials featuring the unique role of community colleges, but we did not attempt to include materials concerning proprietary schools and specialized colleges. We have also included illustrations of both quantitative and qualitative techniques in assessment and program review. We tried to consider assessment of both cognitive and non-cognitive student outcomes and to include materials concerning the relation of assessment initiatives to minority students. We felt it was particularly important to include ethical considerations and guidelines for conducting assessment and program review.

Even while using this reader, professors teaching higher education courses will need to be alert for new and important materials developing. Accrediting agencies are revising standards annually, state agencies are adopting new regulations rapidly, and colleges are learning from their experiences daily. We encourage faculty members and students to remain abreast of new materials that may keep the reading list up to date. One way is to subscribe to *Assessment Update* published by Jossey-Bass, Inc. which carries news of events, instruments, examples, and publications.

References

Astin, Alexander W. *Assessment for Excellence: The Philosophy and Practice of Assessment and Evaluation in Higher Education*, New York: MacMillan, 1991.

Rogers, B. H. and K. Gentemann. "The Value of Institutional Research in the Assessment of Institutional Effectiveness." *Research in Higher Education* 30 (3) (June 1989), pp. 345–355.

PART I

ASSESSMENT AND PROGRAM EVALUATION: DEFINING THE NEED AND THE SCOPE

Introduction

Traditionally the term assessment was used to describe the gathering of information about an individual, usually through multiple tests and other procedures, for purposes of placement or guidance. In contrast, the term assessment as currently used has a broader meaning that generally applies to the gathering of information to indicate the extent to which an institution or unit within the institution is achieving what it purports to do, that for which it is accountable (see general introduction for definition of terms).

The current concept of assessment in higher education rose to the forefront through national attention on accountability and quality in higher education. Public officials expressed uncertainty about the worth of higher education and asked institutions to demonstrate their educational effectiveness. Quality assessment was viewed by many as a means of promoting accountability in higher education; others emphasized its value as a tool for improvement.

Since the mid-1980s increased demands for accountability have been made by audiences external to universities including national and regional accrediting agencies and state and national governmental policy makers. Such audiences ask accountability questions about the extent to which students are growing in dimensions included in the institutional mission and reflected in the course work or other learning experiences. Audiences within an institution or unit have long used self-study to provide direction for needed program changes.

Literature in this section was selected to provide a basis for understanding the activities known as assessment, evaluation, and program review. The selections provide an introduction to the history of such activities and their evolution to the current focus on the activity known as assessment. A framework for thinking about these activities is necessary to plan and conduct assessments.

History and frameworks of evaluation: A foundation for assessment. The literature in this section provides frameworks for thinking about the purposes of assessment and program evaluation, the questions to be asked, and the decisions that can appropriately be made.

House provides an analysis of the original expectations for evaluation and the evolution of the current pluralistic concept of evaluation that includes multiple methods, measures, criteria, perspectives, audiences and interests. The history of evaluation provided by **Madaus, Stufflebeam and Scriven** illustrates that the current assessment activities are not new and that evaluation can contribute valuable frameworks, tools and lessons for the practice of assessment. Madaus et al. also examine the parallels between the development and history of evaluation and the current assessment debates and changes. They trace various common tensions within evaluation and assessment: the purpose of the activity, the type of acceptable data or information, and the use and users of the information.

Insight into the basis for the wide diversity found among evaluation and assessment programs is gained from the discussion of five evaluation frameworks and models by Gardner. The analysis of each model includes its basic assumptions, focus, examples, advantages, and disadvantages; the models promote general understanding and conceptualization of the disparate evaluation and assessment programs.

3

Assessment history and debate. The historical and political context of the demands for account-ability in higher education and of the role played by assessment in meeting those demands is provided by **Ewell.** The discussion also notes how assessment has evolved during its brief history in conceptual models, measurement, and role of authentic methodologies.

While much of the early debate about assessment has subsided, the higher education commu-nity is not yet in agreement about the overall potential of assessment. In some contexts, allegations about the possible negative effects of such activity still receive attention. The variety of positions reflects the range of success experienced among institutions. Some institutions have designed and conducted effective programs that provide valuable information about quality and direction for improvement and have used the information in a responsible manner for accountability purposes. Other programs, however, illustrate the continuing need to recognize the limitations of assessment and to attend to potential dangers from misuse of information.

Two opinion pieces are provided regarding faculty views and involvement. **Daughdrill** pro-vides an optimistic view of the opportunities assessment can bring to faculty to improve the quality of learning at the institution. In contrast, **Benjamin** offers the opinion that assessment will diminish the quality of teaching and learning.

Current emphasis on assessment and program evaluation. Present assessment activity is rooted both in its historical and political context and in existing frameworks and understandings that inform practice. Insights about the latter are provided by **Davis,** who discusses the parallels between the new, broad definition of assessment and the traditional activity of program evaluation addressed in the above articles. In answering ten questions about assessment, Davis notes the utility of existing evaluation understandings and practices to inform the conduct of assessment.

While much of the early assessment activity focused on outcomes for accountability purposes, educators have increasingly recognized and valued assessment activity designed to provide infor-mation for the purpose of improvement. Understanding student growth and development only identifies a general problem area; specific information may be needed in order to make changes and improvements. Assessment is also increasingly considered an iterative process rather than an episodic activity. It is a way of doing business on an ongoing basis to provide specific helpful data for any needed change and improvement.

Consistent with the focus on "assessment for improvement," **Gardiner** discusses continuous improvement of outcomes based on a performance improvement cycle; a cycle that monitors inputs, processes and outcomes. Continual evaluation of the processes that promote the assessed outcomes provide valuable information for modifying the processes for the improvement of outcomes.

Johnson, Prus, Andersen and El-Khawas provide the results of a study that describe the current assessment activity. They report the purposes, roles of faculty and administrators, models, assessment methods, and challenges of the assessment programs in institutions of higher education.

Additional Core Readings

Conrad, C. F. and Blackburn, R. T. "Research on Program Quality: A Review and Critique of the Literature.n In *Higher Education: Handbook of Theory and Research Volume 1* edited by J. C. Smart. New York: Agathon Press, 1985, pp. 283–308.

Conrad, C. F. and Eagan, D. "Achieving Excellence: How Will We Know?" In *Improving Undergradu-ate Education in Large Universities, New Directions for Higher Education, No. 66* edited by C. H. Pazandak. San Francisco: Jossey-Bass, Summer 1989, pp. 51–63.

Hutchings, Patricia. *Behind Outcomes: Contexts and Questions for Assessment.* Washington, D.C.: American Association of Higher Education, The AAHE Assessment Forum, 1989.

Resnick, D. P. "Expansion, Quality, and Testing in American Education." In *Issues in Student Assessment, New Directions for Communit Colleges No. 59* edited by D. Bray and M. Belcher. San Francisco: Jossey-Bass, Fall 1987, pp. 5–14.

Tyler, R. W. "Educational Assessment, Standards and Quality: Can We Have One Without the Other?" *Educational Measurement: Issues and Practice* (Summer 1983), pp. 14–23.

Willingham, W. W. "Research and Assessment: Tools for Change." In *Improving Undergraduate Education in Large Universities, New Directions for Higher Education No. 66* edited by C. H. Pazandak. San Francisco: Jossey-Bass, Summer 1989, pp. 27–40.

Five Evaluation Frameworks: Implications for Decision Making in Higher Education

DON E. GARDNER*

The author identifies a need for greater understanding of alternative evaluation approaches available in higher education. Five basic definitions of evaluation are identified: (1) evaluation as measurement, (2) evaluation as professional judgment, (3) evaluation as the assessment of congruence between performance and objectives (or standards of performance), (4) decision-oriented evaluation, and (5) goal-free/responsive evaluation. Their basic assumptions, distinguishing characteristics, principal advantages, and disadvantages are presented. Criteria for selecting an evaluation methodology appropriate to specific circumstances, are summarized in the concluding paragraphs.

The accountability crisis has had profound effects on the implementation of evaluative studies in higher education. In the not too distant past, decisions affecting all phases of university operations were routinely made on the basis of unchallenged assumptions regarding benefits (the "assumed good") or the unquestioned judgments of key administrators. Today, those same administrators are often constrained to produce evaluative data to support even the most basic kinds of decisions—to the extent that the cost of collecting the required information is often suspected of rivaling the cost of the course of action ultimately chosen.

The effects of the clamor for evaluative data have been pervasive. For example, in the first issue of the Jossey-Bass *New Directions for Institutional Research* series, *Evaluating Institutions for Accountability* [4] the authors discussed the need for evaluation as it relates to: the ultimate benefits of higher education to society, institutional goals, educational cost-effectiveness, measurement of educational outcomes, the development of management information systems, the implementation of "quantitative fixed effectiveness models," evaluating student performance, evaluating resources and processes, evaluating faculty performance, program review, and evaluations by external agencies. Other examples of current evaluation topics include hiring practices, salary determination and tenure policies, and program cost/benefit.

Correspondingly, there is a rapidly expanding body of literature on different theories, models, and techniques in educational evaluation. Although there have been several notable attempts at categorizing and defining the array of evaluation models and methodologies that has emerged (of particular importance are the works by Stufflebeam, et al. [15], Worthen and Sanders [19], and Anderson, et al. [3]), these are generally unfamiliar to individuals outside the ranks of the "expert" evaluator. Unfortunately, it is most often "nonexpert" evaluators—higher education administrators—who are ultimately responsible for the implementation of evaluation studies and their consequences.

In many situations, lack of familiarity with the basic options available for structuring an evaluation is not a key issue. For example, the kinds of evaluative data needed to satisfy the requirements of an affirmative action report are generally dictated by the requesting agency. Even where the type of evaluation to be conducted is not mandated, common practice or a conspicuous precedent may determine the type of methodology employed, as for example, when the accrediting team approach is used by a college or department for purposes of internal program review. However, where an administrator has a choice with regard to the type of evaluation to be conducted—even if that choice will be expressed only in the selection of the particular expert evaluator who will conduct the study—that individual should be fully aware of the fundamentally different assumptions and outcomes that obtain when a particular type of strategy is selected.

The most prominent educational evaluation models, methodologies, or techniques can be generally classified within five major frameworks corresponding to five different basic definitions of evaluation. Stufflebeam, et al., identified three of these before introducing a fourth, new definition [15, pp. 9–16, 40]; a fifth category is required to accommodate the goal-free type of evaluation proposed by Scriven [12, 13]. In real life situations it would appear that distinctions between the five definitions of evaluation are often blurred by practical considerations. However, the principal focus of any particular evaluation effort—from evaluation of student progress in the classroom to the evaluation of competing academic programs by statewide governing boards—is almost always identifiable as falling within the boundaries of one or another of the frameworks described below.

The premise of this paper is that because the selection of an evaluation methodology is so often determined by latent political or convenience factors, many evaluations are destined to fail before they begin. The selection of a particular evaluation framework always entails certain consequences and constraints. In this light, the administrator faced with the responsibility to evaluate should carefully consider the following question: "Is the selected methodology appropriate to the circumstances?" or, put another way, "What is the probability that this type of strategy will produce results effectively serving the need that prompted the evaluation?"

This article is divided into three main sections: (1) a brief review and analysis of the five basic frameworks or definitions of evaluation (summarized in chart form in Figure 1), (2) discussion of some of the negative and positive consequences that are likely to result from application of the frameworks (summarized in chart form in Figure 2), and (3) a summarization of basic criteria for selecting a methodology appropriate to specific circumstances.

Five Definitions of Evaluation

The five definitions of evaluation that establish the general framework for most evaluations in education today are: (1) evaluation as professional judgment, (2) evaluation as measurement, (3) evaluation as the assessment of congruence between performance and objectives (or standards of performance), (4) decision-oriented evaluation, and (5) goal-free/responsive evaluation. As was noted earlier, in actual practice hybrid types are abundant, but the principal *emphasis* or *focus* of a particular effort will almost always be identifiable as belonging to one of these categories.

The review and description of the five frameworks is presented using the following outline as a guide:[1]

(a) Statement and explanation of the principal focus of the definition

(b) Examples of the definition in current practice

(c) Basic premises and assumptions

(d) "Advance organizers"—variables that structure the evaluation process:

1. Basic value perspective of the approach

2. Nature of typical evaluation designs

3. Typical evaluator roles

4. Nature of typical methodologies

5. Types of communication and feedback

(e) Nature of expected outcomes and mode of interpretation.

Evaluation as Professional Judgment

Evaluation as professional judgment is a well-known concept requiring only a brief description here. The utility of this definition is evidenced in the numerous situations where a qualified professional is asked to examine the thing to be evaluated and then render an expert opinion regarding its quality, effectiveness, or efficiency. In this case, the resulting statement of relative worth *is* the evaluation.

Examples of the use of this model in education include reliance on the judgment of teams of professionals by the various accrediting associations, the use of peer review panels to evaluate funding proposals, use of expert referees in the process of selecting manuscripts for publication, and the passing of judgment on candidates for promotion or tenure by faculty committees [19, pp. 126–27; 15, pp. 13–16].

This approach is obviously based on the assumption that the best judge of worth is an expert in the area of the thing to be evaluated. Values or criteria which form the basis for judgment of the professional is accepted on the basis of that individual's assumed association with a commonly shared value system, or on the basis of assumed superior knowledge which accompanies stature in the particular field in question. In other cases, some type of compromise mechanism is used to deal with differences in point of view, as, for example, in the case where committee meetings are held to arrive at a consensus before a group judgment is delivered.

Basically, the evaluation design based on this definition provides for some type of personal contact between the evaluator and the thing to be evaluated (or its products or effects) structured in accordance with the expectations of the individuals to be served by the evaluation. The outcome may be of little personal concern if the evaluator is an outsider called in to evaluate some aspect of a program or institution; in this case, the values brought to bear might be said to be relatively objective. On the other hand, if the evaluator has a personal stake in the process—as, for example, in the case of the fellow faculty member on the tenure review committee—the needs of the department, college, and personalities involved (as perceived by that individual) will undoubtedly have a bearing on the values that are applied in the evaluation process.

In this type, the evaluator is seen as an information processor whose job is to assimilate and judge relevant data. Skill in synthesizing and weighing facts is assumed, in addition to expertise in the domain of the thing being evaluated. The evaluator's methodology may include personal observation, interviews, component tests, and review of documentation; in short, whatever kind of experiential contact is deemed necessary and agrees with client expectations. However, the assimilation of the data collected is internal—i.e., the final report (whether formal or informal) will emanate from the evaluator's thought processes. The desired outcome is, of course, the educated opinion of the evaluator/judge; interpretation is expressed generally in the form of a pronouncement.

Evaluation as Measurement

This definition is based on a commonly recognized traditional (but narrow) view which simply equates evaluation with measurement. To evaluate means to measure results, effects, or performance using some type of formalized instrument which produces data that can be compared to some sort of standardized scale.

Examples of this definition in practice include such varied applications as the use of SAT or GRE scores to evaluate academic aptitude, and instructional cost analysis studies based on data collected from faculty activity analysis questionnaires.

Measurement experts such as Thorndike [16] and Ebel [6, 7] admit that true evaluation involves a judgment of merit which extends beyond the collection of measurement data, but the focus of this approach is clearly on those data and the instruments used to collect them [15, pp. 9–10]. The instrumental focus of this definition is not difficult to understand since it is based on observations and practices which are common throughout our experience. For example, to evaluate the merits of one metal alloy relative to another, experts *measure* various attributes (strength, flexibility, etc.) using the sophisticated instruments which are available for that purpose, and then compare the resulting figures.

The basic constructs of this approach include assumptions that phenomena to be evaluated have significant measurable attributes, and that instruments can be designed which are capable of measuring them. Misapplication of this type of evaluation—and resulting failures—can generally be traced to the violation of these assumptions: either the thing to be evaluated does not possess significant measurable attributes, or the design of application of the instrument (test, questionnaire, etc.) does not effectively measure the attribute desired. The continuing debate over measurement of the outcomes of higher education is a conspicuous example of the controversy which has resulted, at least in part, from attempts at applying this type of evaluation technique in the field of higher education.

Values in this type of evaluation approach are established in reference to standardized scales, or on the basis of comparability of the results of multiple applications of the same instrument or test under controlled conditions on like objects. The use of SAT or GRE percentile scores is a good example of such norm-referenced values, while the comparison of numbers of degrees granted as an institutional outcome measure is a crude example on a larger scale.

Although some test and measurement technology is highly complex and sophisticated, an evaluation design based on this definition is conceptually quite simple: first, the attributes to be measured are identified; second, an appropriate instrument is designed and tested (validated); third, the instrument is applied to the thing to be evaluated (under controlled conditions to insure reliability); and, fourth, the results are compared to a standard (which may be the results of a pretest specific to the particular person or thing or established norms for groups of that kind of person or thing).

The evaluator in this type of effort must be, of necessity, an expert in the design and/or use of the measurement instruments which are to be employed, including an understanding of how results should be analyzed and interpreted. Measurement methodologies are almost as varied as the phenomena people attempt to measure, ranging from the use of the previously mentioned standardized tests for evaluating academic aptitude to simple information systems in the registrar's office that routinely collect data on students; the latter are generally not thought of as being instruments of evaluation, but where the resulting information is taken as measures of institutional success or failure, the analogy applies.

Measurement technology is formal and systematic, and focuses on the use of instruments that provide results which can be replicated. In an evaluation project, communication between the evaluator and a "client" administrator is likely to be limited to a discussion of the measurement goal; for example, the desired outcome of a questionnaire on faculty attitudes toward tenure policies. Being the expert, the evaluator is generally responsible for selecting or designing an appropriate instrument. Feedback to the administrator will probably come in the nature of a formal report which may even be limited to a simple display of the results of the application of the instrument; e.g., the number of responses in each of the various question categories.

The expected outcome from the measurement type of evaluation is a number or set of numbers which can be compared and interpreted with reference to another number or set of numbers, or a generally accepted standard scale. The number of professors or assistant professors who favor or disagree with a proposed change in tenure policy would be one example—although care must be exercised to insure that the questions were phrased in such a way that they actually measured the attitude intended.

The Assessment of Congruence Between Performance and Objectives

Theories or methodologies that fall into this category basically define evaluation as the process of specifying or identifying goals, objectives, or standards of performance; identifying or developing tools to measure performance; and comparing the measurement data collected with the previously identified objectives or standards to determine the degree of discrepancy or congruence which exists.

Perhaps no other type of evaluation has received more attention in recent higher education literature; competency-based teacher education, the success of institutions in meeting the goal of equal educational opportunity or in preparing students for meaningful careers are familiar goal-oriented evaluation topics.

Evaluation models based on this definition assume that the most important decisions regarding the thing to be evaluated are contingent on its objectives and the criteria established for judging relative success or failure in the attainment of those objectives. The Provus [10] model emphasizes that evaluations of this type are not solely interested in whether or not an objective has been met (i.e., the attainment of a level of performance equal to a minimum standard) but in describing performance whatever the level reached and in determining the reasons for relative success or failure. Furthermore, Scriven has pointed out that this type of evaluation process can play two basic kinds of roles: a *formative* role (evaluation used to improve an ongoing process or project by providing feedback to the administrator in charge), and a *summative* role (evaluation of a completed product) [19, pp. 61–65]. In any case, formal evaluation methodologies are required if rational decisions are to be made as to whether the program or thing should be maintained, improved, expanded, or terminated [10, pp. 183–92].

Evaluation designs based on the congruence between performance and objectives definition may vary from the simple application of a pretest-treatment-posttest technique (as is commonly used to evaluate student learning) to a wide range of more complicated processes and techniques. However, a generalized approach would undoubtedly contain the following elements: (1) identification of goals or objectives of the project, program, or thing to be evaluated; (2) clarification of the variables which affect performance; (3) identification of the criteria (standards) by which performance will be judged; (4) development or identification of tools, techniques, and procedures for collecting information regarding performance; (5) collection of the performance data; (6) comparison of the information regarding performance with the pre-established standards (resulting in a judgment of worth); and (7) communication of the results of the comparison to appropriate audiences.

Several important distinctions between evaluator roles are proposed by the authors of evaluation models falling into this general framework. For example, Scriven argues that in a formative (process oriented) evaluation the evaluator should be prepared not only to clarify or identify objectives, but should make an assessment of the worth of the objectives themselves. Stake carries this a step further by suggesting that expert evaluators should be involved from the beginning of any program or project and should be instrumental in defining its objectives—thereby *insuring* their worth and the feasibility of collecting relevant performance data. Where a summative (end-product oriented) evaluation is desired, the evaluator's primary function will most likely be an after-the-fact determination of the previously defined goals of the project (and pertinent criteria of performance) through interaction with participants and a review of documentation.

In addition to the evaluator's interactive role with administrators in identifying, developing, or judging objectives, this type of evaluation demands that the evaluator be expert in measurement methodology relative to the performance of the thing to be evaluated, the analysis of the performance data, and the formulation of meaningful descriptive reports. Both Scriven and Stake have added that the evaluator should be a capable judge, able to provide educated professional opinion regarding the worth or effectiveness of the thing evaluated in addition to the descriptive information upon which the judgment is based [19, pp. 83–86, 103, 109].

The methodologies used in the implementation of an evaluation design such as the one described above will contain the following specific elements: examination of documentation which describes the thing to be evaluated in detail; small group interaction between evaluation staff and key personnel to further define variables, objectives, and performance standards; rigorous analysis of processes and relationships; identification of the tools or instruments which will be used to obtain performance data; collection and processing of performance data; analysis of the performance data compared to objectives and standards; formulation of judgments and reports; and, finally, communication of reports.

The nature of the outcome expected from this type of evaluation has been alluded to several times in the preceding discussion. To summarize, the intended results of an evaluation of this sort are *judgments of worth* regarding the institution, program, process, or thing based on interpreted comparisons between performance data and objectives (or standards of performance). The judgments themselves may be arrived at by the evaluator, or by administrators based on information supplied by the evaluator. If the evaluation conducted is of the formative type, judgments may be made on an ongoing basis to control and shape performance (as for example, where intermediate results are reviewed in the light of the stated goals of a residential learning project in the early stages of implementation). If the evaluation is summative only, it will focus on products or end results as compared to intended outcomes (i.e., the final impact of the residential-learning project on a group of students who just completed the program as compared to stated objectives).

Decision-Oriented Evaluation

There are currently two major evaluation models which are primarily decision oriented in nature: The CIPP [Context, Input, Process, Product] Evaluation Model developed by the Phi Delta Kappa (PDK) National Study Committee on Evaluation and a model developed at the University of California at Los Angeles Center for the Study of Evaluation. The two models are practically identical in their essential characteristics; the CIPP model is based on a definition of evaluation as, "the process of delineating, obtaining, and providing useful information for judging decision alternatives," [15, p. 40] whereas the UCLA definition is stated as, "Evaluation is the process of ascertaining the decision areas of concern, selecting appropriate information, and collecting and analyzing information in order to report summary data useful to decision-makers in selecting among alternatives" [1, p. 107]. Building on the work of the PDK committee, Dressel has recently proposed a definition of evaluation in the service of decision making that focuses primarily on assumptions and values as they relate to anticipated procedures and goals compared to actual processes and results [5, p. 12].

The essence of the CIPP model is an institutionalized feedback mechanism which provides for a continuous assessment of decision-information needs and the obtaining and providing of information to meet those needs. Efforts at implementing PPBS and Integrated MIS principles in higher education are examples of attempts to institutionalize systematic, decision-oriented, evaluation mechanisms. Also, the WICHE/NCHEMS Costing and Data Management System, and the Higher Education Planning System (HEPS) marketed by Education and Economic Systems, Inc. (EES) are examples of packaged systems (including procedures, input documents, and report producing computer software) which support CIPP-like institutionalized decision-oriented evaluation with at least one important difference: the initial determination of decision-information need has been made by NCHEMS and EES—although admittedly with input from the higher education community—and individual user institutions are constrained to accept and live with assumptions about institutional goals and processes which may or may not be totally appropriate in a particular setting. Also, these systems are more or less rigid in terms of their ability to produce new types of decision information based on feedback from administrators. In contrast, the CIPP model proposes maximum flexibility as an essential ingredient.

Four of the basic assumptions underlying the CIPP model have been stated by Stufflebeam [19, pp. 129–30]: (1) Evaluation is performed in the service of decision making, hence, it should provide information which is useful to decision makers; (2) Evaluation is a cyclic, continuing process and, therefore, must be implemented through a systematic program; (3) The evaluation process includes the three main steps of delineating, obtaining, and providing. These steps provide the basis for a methodology of evaluation; (4) The delineating and providing steps in the evaluation process are interface activities requiring collaboration between evaluator and decision maker, while the obtaining step is largely a technical activity which is executed mainly by the evaluator.

Another basic concept underlying the CIPP model is that different types of decisions require different types of informational inputs. Four basic types of decisions are identified and discussed at length in the PDK book [15, pp. 80–84; 5, pp. 12–15]. Fulfillment of information needs of the four types of decisions is the principal value orientation of the approach. To accomplish the goal of service to decision makers, the CIPP model proposes four different kinds of evaluation activities: *context evaluation* (to assist decision makers in the determination of objectives); *input evaluation* (to clarify decisions regarding the different ways resources might be used to achieve project goals); *process evaluation* (to provide periodic feedback to the persons responsible for decisions during implementation); and *product evaluation* (for the purpose of assessing and interpreting project attainments, whether at the end of a project cycle or at intermediate points through its life, as they relate to decisions regarding whether the activity should be continued, modified, terminated, or repeated). The UCLA model was conceived along the same general lines although the terminology used is different [1, p. 109].

Stufflebeam has provided a logical structure of evaluation design which he has asserted is the same for all of the four primary evaluation activities (context, input, process, and product) encompassed by the CIPP model [19, p. 144]. The proposed design structure includes the following basic elements: focusing the evaluation (identifying the specific decision situations to be served and defining the criteria to be used in the judgment of alternatives), and the collection, organization, analysis, and reporting of information.

With regard to evaluator roles, on a large scale, Guba and Stufflebeam [9, pp. 7–13] have proposed the creation of an evaluation unit within the organization, which might include the following: individuals engaged in research aimed at providing a "dynamic baseline" of descriptive information about the "decision arena" of the institution; persons skilled in identifying alternative ways of determining institutional needs and the criteria by which processes and outcomes will later be judged; a unit which systematically maintains records of the process or thing to be evaluated and measures and interprets attainments relative to both intermediate and final objectives; individuals engaged in the development and implementation of instruments for collecting data; an information office comprised of persons skilled in data reduction, storage, retrieval, and analysis techniques; and a reports section containing individuals skilled at highlighting information in terms of its "relevance, scope, and importance to the decision process."

In real life, the functions described above are typically carried out by offices of institutional research, MIS development teams, systems analysts and programmers, and research and evaluation units—with varying degrees of coordination depending on the situation. The CIPP model provides a useful framework for structuring the tasks that must be assigned to someone if systematic decision-oriented evaluation is to occur.

Regarding evaluation methodology, the authors of the CIPP model stated that, "The methodology of evaluation is the methodology of an information system designed to provide information for project, program, and system decisions" [15, p. 136]. As was pointed out earlier, the general evaluation design of the CIPP model includes three major areas: delineation of information needs, a plan for obtaining the information, and a plan for providing the information. Within those general categories, examples of specific methodological tasks and techniques include: systems analysis, construction of a model of decision paths within the organization, identification or report requirements, identification of policies with regard to data access, identification of information sources, selection of appropriate instruments, and designing an effective combination of media and personal resources for presenting information to decision makers in timely and meaningful ways.

In summary, the desired outcomes of an evaluation of this kind are a continual exchange between evaluators and administrators regarding information needs associated with critical decisions, and a continuous flow of systematically collected, timely, and relevant information to satisfy those needs. Final interpretation of data is generally assumed to be the responsibility of the administrator(s) served, as, for example, when the final report on grade statistics is placed in the hands of the academic vice-president who is looking for evidence of grade inflation. The evaluator's interpretive skills are brought to bear more on issues related to data reduction and extraction (synthesis) than on meaning as it relates to decisions affecting institutional policy.

Goal-Free/Responsive Evaluation

The goal-free concept is a relatively recent definition of evaluation which has been proposed and developed by Scriven [12]. The central theme of this approach is critical examination of the institution, project, program, or thing irrespective of its goals. In other words, the intent of goal-free evaluation (GFE) is to discover and judge actual effects without regard to what the effects were supposed to be. All of the evaluation approaches discussed earlier depend on some kind of preordained establishment of goals, standards, or decision information needs. However, it is often the case that an evaluator turns up information about unintended side effects of the project or program which may be more important in some regard than the information relative to project goals or preidentified decisions.

For example, an evaluator may find that an educational program designed to improve employment opportunities for underprivileged minorities (by providing free special training to persons who meet certain criteria) has succeeded admirably in its efforts to achieve that goal, but has unintentionally resulted in an undesirable intensification of racial hostilities among persons who do not qualify for the program. Many evaluative reports include information about this kind of side effect along with the information regarding intended effects. However, the side effect information may have been acquired merely by accident, and other important information of this type may have been overlooked completely. Scriven has argued [13] that if the main objective of the evaluation is to assess the worth of the outcomes, why make any distinction at all between those that were intended, as opposed to those that were not?

In addition to the concept of GFE proposed by Scriven, an evaluation approach called "responsive evaluation" has recently been proposed by Stake [14]. Responsive evaluation is an iterative process of acquiring information about an institution, program, or project; defining issues of importance to constituencies; and describing strengths and weaknesses relative to those issues. Stated objectives may or may not be centrally important to the issues identified; all aspects of the thing being evaluated are taken into consideration initially, but no single element (whether goals, resources, processes, or participants) is preconceived as being necessarily more important to the evaluator than another.

As mentioned, one of the basic premises of GFE is that an evaluation effort may produce valuable results if it is unencumbered by preordained linkages to goals or standards. However, GFE is not goal free in an absolute sense; an evaluation involving a judgment of merit involves some kind of comparison with a standard, and the evaluator must have some basis for selecting only certain information about a project or program out of the total information pool. What is proposed in GFE is allowing the evaluator to select wider-context goals as opposed to only those prespecified in mission statements, statements of objectives, or the project design [2]. In other words, the evaluator may collect information relevant to project effects as they relate to accepted societal norms (e.g., the evidence of increased racial hostilities produced by the hypothetical employment opportunity program described above is important because of a generally accepted need for decreasing antagonisms of this kind in our society) or some other type of generally recognized standard. In the responsive evaluation model these standards emerge in the identification of the issues that the evaluator has discovered are important to concerned constituencies.

The Scriven concept of GFE calls for an evaluation design centered around the collection of information with regard to actual outcomes or performance. At some point the evaluator will undoubtedly make some assumptions regarding standards by which an outcome or effect might be judged, but Scriven has emphasized that the evaluator should be free to choose those standards for comparison from a wide range of possibilities. Once the information has been collected and analyzed the evaluator then makes the report.

Stake has been more explicit in providing a guiding framework for conducting a responsive evaluation. He has proposed the following cycle of prominent events to guide the evaluation process: (1) talk with clients, staff, and audiences; (2) identify program scope; (3) overview program activities; (4) discover purposes and concerns; (5) conceptualize issues and problems; (6) identify data needs (according to identified issues); (7) select observers, judges, and formal instruments (if any); (8) observe selected antecedents, transactions, and outcomes; (9) "thematize"—prepare portrayals and case studies; (10) match issues to audiences; and (11) prepare and deliver presentations and formal reports (if any) [14, p. 12]. These events do not necessarily occur in sequence, but take place as the result of a series of negotiations and interactions which proceed more or less informally.

In GFE the evaluator is conceptualized as an investigator skilled in identifying important relationships and outcomes. Stake has called for the responsive evaluator to operate informally (though systematically) in the environment of continual interaction with people, drawing conclusions and descriptive information out of the observations and reactions of the persons involved. Obviously, this requires that the evaluator be skilled in social interaction, eliciting honest comments and opinions, and in capturing and recording conversations. Stake further suggests that although a formal report may be a part of a responsive evaluation, much might be accomplished through the use of portrayal and holistic communication techniques [14, pp. 15–19] which may be entirely communicated through verbal means, for example, in informal discussion settings.

The final outcome of GFE should be accurate descriptive and interpretive information relative to the most important aspects of the actual performance, effects, and attainments of the institution, program, or thing evaluated. Interpretation of results by the evaluator should be responsive to the concerns of the individuals affected whether they are simply program participants or those who commissioned the study. While it is probably not yet possible to identify many specific situations where this approach to evaluation has been formally applied, it has potential appeal to a wide range of individuals who have long felt that other methods of evaluation were inappropriate to their particular area, such as evaluating educational programs in the arts. In effect, by including informal investigation and personal testimony as valid tools for evaluation, this approach may help legitimize methods that have had intuitive appeal in many circumstances but have previously received little formal support.

Implications for Decision Making

The basic assumptions and distinguishing characteristics of the five evaluation frameworks described above are summarized in chart form in Figure 1. The chart suggests several implications that might affect decisions to evaluate based on the different approaches.

For example, when the five definitions are arrayed as in Figure 1, a more or less well-defined outline of evolution in educational evaluation thought is apparent: the professional judgment approach being a legacy from earlier times; followed by the appearance of measurement technology in the wake of empiricism; focused after World War II on performance vs. objectives by the work of Tyler [17] and others; further enhanced in the sixties by the application of the system approach and computer technology to the problems of educational decision making; and, most recently, expanded by individuals such as Scriven [12, 13] and Stake [14] as they have attempted to responsively evaluate in situations where earlier approaches have been less than successful.

In view of this evolutionary pattern, administrators concerned with taking advantage of new developments might be tempted to look toward the goal-free/responsive approach as being the most up-to-date solution to their evaluation problems. Obviously, such an assumption could be dangerously misleading. As displayed in Figure 1, each of the frameworks has distinguishing characteristics that make it potentially useful depending on the circumstances. Stufflebeam et al. [15, pp. 9–16] provided a point of departure for determining potential utility in their discussion of the advantages and disadvantages of three of the five approaches. A brief summary of just a few positive and negative aspects, expanded to include all five of the evaluation definitions, is presented in Figure 2.

Advantages vs. Disadvantages

An administrator faced with the question, "Will an evaluation study based on the 'professional judgment' approach effectively serve the need?" will undoubtedly be aware that the results of such studies are often criticized on the basis of their subjectivity and noncomparability. In matters of high constituent interest such as, "Should X department be abolished because its programs no longer serve valid educational purposes?" if one expert in the field says "yes," it is almost always possible to find another who will return an emphatic "no"—often after reviewing the same body of evidence. That politicians (both on and off campus) use this situation to advantage is certainly no secret.

On the other hand, it is common knowledge that the simplest method, at least conceptually, of evaluating an activity or thing is to hire a consultant, a definite advantage where time is of the essence and the nature of the problem does not require a more objective approach. Furthermore, the worship of objectivity should not obscure the fact that individuals "uniquely qualified to judge" (because of their experience and expertise) do exist, and that the human mind can function as a complex mechanism for assimilating and integrating rich bodies of data.

The negative aspects of measurement evaluations are familiar topics. Two common questions related to this subject are: "Did the student achievement test really measure the knowledge or skills supposedly taught in the course?" and, "Are 'student credit hour production' and 'number of degrees granted' valid surrogate measures of the true outputs of higher education?" Measurement experts are frequently accused of measuring only those attributes for which an instrument (test, questionnaire, computerized system, etc.) is readily available and which produces results that are easily quantifiable. As a result, variables that are not easily measured, such as the personal enrichment a person may receive from going to college, continue to be treated by measurement experts as intangibles and/or relatively unimportant.

On the positive side, if a particular measurement instrument has demonstrated some reliability or validity, for example, as is claimed for the SAT, GRE, and certain IQ tests, comparability for certain purposes may be assumed. Also, if procedures are consistently applied, results may be legitimately termed "objective," and may be generalizable in the sense that what is true for one group is probably true for a similar group under identical (or nearly identical) conditions. For administrators who are comfortable with quantitative methods, another advantage of this approach is that results generally will be mathematically manipulable and may be conducive to sophisticated statistical analysis.

The congruence between performance and objectives approach has been criticized as being too narrow in focus in many educational situations. Detractors point out that goal clarification may be a useful exercise where a mission is well defined and where effectiveness and efficiency in pursuit of that mission are primary concerns. But they are quick to point out that academicians are concerned with highly complex activities with ambivalent goals and standards of performance. Also, servicing a pluralistic society makes simple goal statements relatively hard to come by and, in some cases, perhaps even counterproductive. Furthermore, proponents are often accused of focusing on those goals for which measurement data are readily available while disregarding more important objectives in areas where performance is more difficult to assess. Another major criticism is its frequent focus on end results, i.e., after the program, project, class, or cycle of activity (on an institutional scale) is terminated. Where this is the case, intermediate benefits which might have accrued from an evaluation in process would not be realized.

The disadvantages described above represent only a few of the problems that are often associated with the goal-oriented approach to evaluation. Dressel has provided a much more detailed account in his *Handbook of Academic Evaluation* [5, pp. 27–52]. However, he also has highlighted some of the advantages of goal-oriented evaluation. For one, where it is possible to identify clear, stated goals, an objective base is automatically established for the purposes of evaluation; assuming that the goals are generally accepted, it becomes only necessary to devise measures of performance relating to those goals, instruments to collect data, and procedures for comparing the results with the previously established standards of performance. Obviously, this can be a very difficult task in some situations, but—conceptually, at least—the task is relatively well defined. Also, criteria for making value judgments regarding the actual performance of the persons or thing evaluated will be suggested by the nature of the goals and the measurement data collected.

One of the major disadvantages of the decision-oriented approach is its assumption of rationality in decision-making, and that systematically produced decision information will be used, at least to the extent of justifying the cost of collection. Unfortunately, this does not seem to be the case. For example, on the basis of extensive work in this area, Weathersby has recently affirmed what many institutional researchers and systems analysts have long suspected: "The application of rational analysis in public decision making appears to be rather limited" [18, p. 98]. The assumption that a great many important decisions are so cyclic in nature that they can be supported by programmed algorithms and systematic processes appears to be open to question as well.

One of the main advantages of the decision-oriented approach is the impetus it provides for institutional self-study, and analysis of decision processes. Further, by focusing on the specific decisions to be served by evaluation, the decision-oriented approach assures that whatever data are collected will be relevant to specific issues and questions. Also, in the case of the CIPP model (discussed earlier), all aspects of the decision setting may be appropriate for analysis, including administrative relationships, decision types, objectives, processes, and outcomes.

One of the disadvantages of the goal-free and responsive models is their lack of emphasis on formal measurement techniques, which may result in relatively subjective outcomes. However, in contrast with the professional judgment approach, in goal-free/responsive evaluations more emphasis is placed on the evaluator's expertise as an *evaluator* (skilled in goal-free/responsive techniques) as opposed to superior knowledge in the discipline of the thing to be evaluated.

The positive appeal of the goal-free/responsive frameworks lies clearly in their flexible, open-minded approach to the identification and assessment of human concerns. By accepting the potential relevance, at least initially, of all outcomes, effects, and participant attitudes, evaluators may come closer to assessing the true worth of an educational program or activity in some cases than if they were tied to the necessity of finding measurable effects that relate to narrowly defined goals or objectives. Also, if the evaluator is truly responsive, potential acceptance of the evaluation results should be relatively high.

Conclusion

While this review and analysis has been relatively brief, it is designed to highlight some of the principal differences between the major evaluation frameworks in higher education today. Based on this discussion, a number of basic criteria can be identified for selecting an evaluation approach appropriate to specific circumstances. These might be expressed as follows: in situations where a high degree of objectivity is not required, where time is short, where a relatively simple evaluation design is desired and an expert human resource is available, the professional judgment approach may be most appropriate. In situations where high objectivity and reliability/comparability are required, where mathematically manipulable results are desired, where relevant measurable attributes can be identified and valid instruments can be designed and implemented to measure them, the measurement approach is probably indicated. If goals are a primary concern, if specific objectives or standards of performance can be identified, if valid ways to assess performance can be devised and applied, and effects unrelated to stated goals are of little or no importance, then a goal-oriented evaluation framework should be selected. Where systematic evaluation is desired in a relatively cyclic decision environment, where information is likely to be used as an important input to policy decision making, and where a dynamic understanding of decision processes is desired, a decision-oriented information systems approach may be successful. Finally, if all observable effects are potentially relevant, if human concerns are uppermost, if a relatively high degree of objectivity is not required, and if the situation is highly fluid and lacking well-defined goals and/or traditional measurement data, a goal-free or responsive approach may be beneficial.

Literature Cited

1. Alkin, Marvin G. "Evaluation Theory Development." In *Evaluating Action Programs: Readings in Social Action and Education*, by Carol H. Weiss. Boston: Allyn and Bacon, 1972.

2. ———. "Wider Context Goals and Goal-Based Evaluators." *Evaluation Comment*, 3 (December 1972), 5–6.

3. Anderson, Scarvia B., et al. *Encyclopedia of Educational Evaluation*. San Francisco: Jossey-Bass, 1975.

4. Bowen, Howard R., ed., *Evaluating Institutions for Accountability*. New Directions for Institutional Research, No. 1. San Francisco: Jossey-Bass, 1974.

5. Dressel, Paul L. *Handbook of Academic Evaluation*. San Francisco: Jossey-Bass, 1976.

6. Ebel, Robert L. "Educational Tests: Valid? Biased? Useful? *Phi Delta Kappan*. 57 (October 1975), 83–88.

7. ———. *Measuring Educational Achievement*. Englewood Cliffs, N.J.: Prentice Hall, 1965.

8. Guba, Egon G. "The Failure of Educational Evaluation." In *Evaluating Action Programs: Readings in Social Action and Education*, by Carol H. Weiss. Boston: Allyn and Bacon, 1972.

9. Guba, Egon G., and Daniel L. Stufflebeam. "Strategies for the Institutionalization of the CIPP Evaluation Model." Paper presented at the Eleventh Annual PDK Symposium on Educational Research, June 24, 1970, at Ohio State University. Mimeographed.

10. Provus, Malcolm. *Discrepancy Evaluation*. Berkeley, Calif.: McCutchan Publishing Corp., 1973.

11. Salasin, Susan. "Exploring Goal-Free Evaluation: An Interview with Michael Scriven." *Evaluation*. 2 (1974), 9–16.

12. Scriven, Michael. "Goal-Free Evaluation." In *School Evaluation: The Politics and Process*. edited by Ernest R. House. Berkeley, Calif.: McCutchan Publishing Corp., 1973.

13. ———. "Prose and Cons about Goal-Free Evaluation." *Evaluation Comment*, 3 (December 1972), 1–4.

14. Stake, Robert E. "Responsive Evaluation in the Arts and Humanities: To Evaluate an Arts Program." Xeroxed. Urbana, Ill. August 26, 1974.

15. Stufflebeam, Daniel L. et al., *Educational Evaluation and Decision Making*. Itasca, Ill.: F. E. Peacock Publishers, 1971.

16. Thorndike, Robert L., ed. *Educational Measurement*, 2nd Ed. New York: John Wiley & Sons, 1971.

17. Tyler, Ralph W. *Basic Principles of Curriculum and Instruction: Syllabus for Education 360*. Chicago: The University of Chicago Press, 1950.

18. Weathersby, George B. "The Potentials of Analytical Approaches to Educational Planning and Decision Making." In *Proceedings of the 1976 National Assembly* of the National Center for Higher Education Management Systems, edited by William Johnston. Boulder, Colorado: NCHEMS/WICHE, 1976.

19. Worthen, Blaine R., and James R. Sanders. *Educational Evaluation: Theory and Practice*. Worthington, Ohio: Charles A. Jones Publishing Co., 1973.

---

* The author wishes to express special appreciation to Egon G. Guba for thoughtful criticism and insights offered during the preparation of this article.

1. The categories of the outline represent a combination of considerations suggested by Worthen and Sanders [19], and a framework developed by Guba, "Comparison of Preordinate with Responsive Evaluation (after Stake)," presented at the American Educational. Research Association convention, Chicago, April 16, 1974.

Figure 1 Basic Assumptions and Distinguishing Characteristics

	"Professional Judgment"	"Measurement"	"Congruence Between Performance and Objectives"	"Decision Oriented"	"Goal-Free Responsive"
Principal Focus	Expert opinion of qualified professional(s)	Measurement of results, effects, or performance, using some type of formal instrument (test, questionnaire, etc.).	Comparison of performance or product with previously stated standards of performance, goals or objectives.	"Delineating, obtaining and providing useful information for judging decision alternatives."	Identification and judgment of actual outcomes (irrespective of goals, standards, etc.) and/or the "concerns of constituents."
Examples	Accreditation teams. Doctoral Committees. Peer review of grant proposals. Referees for selection of manuscripts for publication/promotion/tenure decisions.	GRE scores. Faculty activity questionnaires. Attitude surveys. Teaching effectiveness questionnaires.	Teacher certification based on achievement of prescribed competencies. Evaluation of academic departments on the basis of stated goals. Behavioral objectives. Contract learning.	Management Information Systems. NCHEMS Costing and Data Management System. HEPS (Higher Education Planning System).	Evaluation reports of "program side effects." "Holistic" evaluation of educational programs in the arts.
Basic Assumptions	Best evaluation is the expert opinion of a qualified professional. There is a commonly shared value system in the "arena" of the program or thing to be evaluated and/or, A "compromise mechanism" exists for accommodating differences in professional opinion.	Best evaluation is obtained from measurement data. Thing to be evaluated has measurable attributes. Instrument effectively measures attributes selected.	Best evaluation is based on an examination of achievement in light of goals or objectives. Goals or objectives exist and are identifiable. Attributes exist (and can be measured) that indicate relative success in achieving goals.	Best evaluation is one that serves decision makers in specific decision situations. Decision making processes are rational. Different types of decisions require different information. Many decisions may be cyclic; systematic processes can be devised to support them.	Best evaluation highlights actual outcomes and/or concerns of constituents and sponsors. The "real" effects of a program or thing can be identified (as can the concerns of affected individuals). The most effective approach is "openminded" and "sensitive."
"Advance Organizers"	Values may or may not be explicitly defined. Evaluator expected to be an information collector, synthesizer and judge.	"Norm-referenced," quantitative values. Formal setting required for application of the measurement instrument. Instrument must be validated, reliable, etc. Evaluator must be a measurement expert.	"Criterion-referenced" (goal oriented) values. Measurement technology commonly used within the context of performance vs. goal assessment. Evaluator may be expected to "judge" as well as measure.	"Decision-oriented" values. Information system methodology. Evaluator should be an information system specialist.	"Wider-context" values (selected by evaluator). "Holistic approach" (all contributive elements, etc. considered as they relate to each other). Evaluator must be skilled in human interaction and identification of concerns.
Nature of Outcome/ Interpretation	Educated, personalized opinion (judgment of worth) of a qualified judge or panel of judges. Interpretation in form of a "pronouncement."	Number of set of numbers which can be compared to other numbers or a standardized scale; data; descriptive statistics. Interpretation in reference to norms.	Judgment of worth based on comparisons between performance data and objectives or standards of performance. Interpretation based on relative discrepancy or congruence.	"Continuous," timely, and relevant information for administrators to assist in judging decision alternatives. Interpretation an administrative function; evaluator concerned with extraction and reduction of data.	Descriptive information regarding "actual" outcomes. Interpretation responsive to constituent concerns.

Figure 2 Advantages vs. Disadvantages

	"Professional Judgment"	"Measurement"	"Congruence Between Performance and Objectives"	"Decision Oriented"	"Goal-Free Responsive"
Advantages	Easily implemented. Uses assimilative and integrative capabilities of human intellect. Recognizes outstanding expertise.	Proper validation and consistent application results in high comparability and replicability. Data mathematically manipulable. Generalizable results.	"Goal-orientation" provides objective basis for evaluation. Judgment criteria pre-established by objectives vs. performance measures selected. Relevant to current societal concerns.	Increased understanding of decision setting and information requirements. Focus on decision information needs assures relevancy of data. Encourages analysis of all factors affecting important decisions.	Flexible, adaptive approach. Useful in complex, relatively unstructured situations. All outcomes, etc. potentially relevant. "People-oriented"—high acceptance potential.
Disadvantages	Results criticized as non—replicable, non-comparable and overly subjective. Generalizability difficult or impossible.	Many variable difficult or impossible to measure. Often anappropriate and/or inflexible—serving available measurement tools instead of the problem. Measurement attributes often irrelevant.	Focus may be too limited—not worthy goals easily identified. Important side-effects may be overlooked. Tendency toward over-emphasis on end-product evaluation.	"Rational decision making" not predominant model in most real-life situations. In practice, frequent inability to cope with changing decision information needs. Inflexibility of "packaged" systems.	Relatively unstructured approach may be difficult to focus an manage. Results criticized as non-replicable, non-comparable and overly subjective. Questionable credibility if an evaluator non-expert in area of thing evaluated.

Program Evaluation: A Historical Overview

GEORGE F. MADAUS, DANIEL STUFFLEBEAM, AND MICHAEL S. SCRIVEN

Program evaluation is often mistakenly, viewed as a recent phenomenon. People date its beginning from the late 1960s with the infusion by the federal government of large sums of money into a wide range of human service programs, including education. However, program evaluation has an interesting history that predates by at least 150 years the explosion of evaluation during the era of President Johnson's Great Society and the emergence of evaluation as a maturing profession since the sixties. A definitive history of program evaluation has yet to be written and in the space available to us we can do little more than offer a modest outline, broad brush strokes of the landscape that constitutes that history. It is important that people interested in the conceptualization of evaluation are aware of the field's roots and origins. Such an awareness of the history of program evaluation should lead to a better understanding of how and why this maturing field has developed as it did. As Boulding (1980) has observed, one of the factors that distinguishes a mature and secure profession from one that is immature and insecure is that only the former systematically records and analyzes its history. Therefore since program evaluation continues to mature as a profession, its origins and roots need to be documented.

Where to begin? For convenience we shall describe six periods in the life of program evaluation. The first is the period prior to 1900, which we call the *Age of Reform*; the second, from 1900 until 1930, we call the *Age of Efficiency and Testing*; the third, from 1930 to 1945, may be called the *Tylerian Age*; the fourth, from 1946 to about 1957, we call the *Age of Innocence*; the fifth, from 1958 to 1972, is the *Age of Expansion* and finally the sixth, from 1973 to the present, the *Age of Professionalization*.

The Age of Reform 1800–1900

This period in the history of program evaluation encompasses the nineteenth century. It was the Industrial Revolution with all of its attendant economic and technological changes, which transformed the very structure of society. It was a period of major social changes, of cautious revisionism and reform (Pinker, 1971). It was a time of drastic change in mental health and outlook, in social life and social conscience, and in the structures of social agencies. It was when the laissez-faire philosophy of Bentham and the humanitarian philosophy of the philanthropists was heard (Thompson, 1950). It was a period marked by continued but often drawn out attempts to reform educational and social programs and agencies in both Great Britain and the United States.

In Great Britain throughout the nineteenth century there were continuing attempts to reform education, the poor laws, hospitals, orphanages, and public health. Evaluations of these social

23

agencies and functions were informal and impressionistic in nature. Often they took the form of government-appointed commissions set up to investigate aspects of the area under consideration. For example, the Royal Commission of Inquiry into Primary Education in Ireland under the Earl of Powis, after receiving testimony and examining evidence, concluded that "the progress of the children in the national schools of Ireland is very much less than it ought to be."[1] As a remedy, the Powis Commission then recommended the adoption of a scheme known as "payment by results" already being used in England, whereby teachers' salaries would be dependent in part on the results of annual examinations in reading, spelling, writing, and arithmetic (Kellaghan & Madaus, 1982). Another example of this approach to evaluation was the 1882 Royal Commission on Small Pox and Fever Hospitals which recommended after study that infectious-disease hospitals ought to be open and free to all citizens (Pinker, 1971).

Royal commissions are still used today in Great Britain to evaluate areas of concern. A rough counterpart in the United States to these commission are presidential commissions (for example, the President's Commission on School Finance), White House panels (e.g., the White House Panel on Non Public Education), and congressional hearings. Throughout their history royal commissions, presidential commissions and congressional hearings have served as a means of evaluating human services programs of various kinds through the examination of evidence either gathered by the Commission or presented to it in testimony by concerned parties. However, this approach to evaluation was sometimes merely emblematic or symbolic in nature. N.J. Crisp (1982) captures the pseudo nature of such evaluations in a work of fiction when one of his characters discusses a royal commission this way: "Appoint it, feel that you've accomplished something, and forget about it, in the hope that by the time it's reported, the problem will have disappeared or been overtaken by events.[2]

In Great Britain during this period when reform programs were put in place, it was not unusual to demand yearly evaluations through a system of annual reports submitted by an inspectorate. For example, in education there were schools inspectors that visited each school annually and submitted reports on their condition and on pupil attainments (Kellaghan & Madaus, 1982). Similarly the Poor Law commissioners had a small, paid inspectorate to oversee compliance with the Poor Law Amendment Act of 1834 (Pinker, 1971). The system of maintaining an external inspectorate to examine and evaluate the work of the schools exists today in Great Britain and Ireland. In the United States, external inspectors are employed by some state and federal agencies. For example, the Occupational Safety and Health Administration (OSHA) employs inspectors to monitor health hazards in the workplace. Interestingly, the system of external inspectors as a model for evaluation has received scant attention in the evaluation literature. The educational evaluation field could benefit from a closer look at the system of formal inspectorates.

Two other developments in Great Britain during this period are worthy of note in the history of evaluation. First, during the middle of the nineteenth century a number of associations dedicated to social inquiry came into existence. These societies conducted and publicized findings on a number of social problems which were very influential in stimulating discussion (for example, Chadwick's Report on the Sanitary Condition of the Laboring Population of Great Britain in 1842 [Pinker, 1971]). Second, often in response to these private reports, bureaucracies that were established to manage social programs sometimes set up committees of enquiry. These were official, governmentsponsored investigations of various social programs, such as provincial workhouses (Pinker, 1971). Both these examples are important in that they constitute the beginnings of an empirical approach to the evaluation of programs.

In the United States perhaps the earliest formal attempt to evaluate the performance on schools took place in Boston in 1845. This event is important in the history of evaluation because it began a long tradition of using pupil test scores as a principal source of data to evaluate the effectiveness of a school or instructional program. Then, at the urging of Samuel Gridley Howe, written essay examinations were introduced into the Boston grammar schools by Horace Mann and the Board of

Education. Ostensibly the essay exam, modeled after those used in Europe at the time, was introduced to replace the *viva voce* or oral examinations. The latter mode of examination had become administratively awkward with increased numbers of pupils and was also seen as unfair because it could not be standardized for all pupils. The interesting point in terms of program evaluation was the hidden policy agenda behind the move to written examinations: namely, it was the gathering of data for inter-school comparisons that could be used in decisions concerning the annual appointment of headmasters. Howe and Mann attempted to establish differential school effects and used these data to eliminate headmasters who opposed them on the abolition of corporal punishment. This is an interesting early example of politicization of evaluation data.

Between 1887 and 1898, Joseph Rice conducted what is generally recognized as the first formal educational-program evaluation in America. He carried out a comparative study on the value of drill in spelling instruction across a number of school districts. Rice (1897), like Mann and Howe before him, used test scores as his criteria measures in his evaluation of spelling instruction. He found no significant learning gains between systems which spent up to 200 minutes a week studying spelling and those which spent as little as ten minutes per week. Rice's results led educators to re-examine and eventually revise their approach to the teaching of spelling. More important from the point of view of this history of program evaluation is his argument that educators had to become experimentalists and quantitative thinkers and his use of comparative research design to study student achievement (Rice, 1914). Rice was a harbinger of the experimental design approach to evaluation first advanced by Lindquist (1953) and extended and championed by Campbell (Campbell & Stanley, 1963; Campbell, 1969) and others in the 1960s and 1970s.

Before leaving this very brief treatment of what has been characterized as the age of reform, another development should be mentioned. The foundation of the accreditation or professional judgment approach to evaluation can be traced directly to the establishment of the North Central Association of Colleges and Secondary Schools in the late 1800s. The accreditation movement did not, however, gain great stature until the 1930s when six additional regional accrediting associations were established across the nation. Since then the accrediting movement has expanded tremendously and gained great strength and credibility as a major means of evaluating the adequacy of educational institutions. (Cf. chapter 15 by Floden for a treatment of the accreditation approach to evaluation.)

The Age of Efficiency and Testing 1900–1930

During the early part of the twentieth century the idea of scientific management became a powerful force in administrative theory in educational as well as in industrial circles (Biddle & Ellena, 1964; Callahan, 1962; Cremin, 1962). The emphasis of this movement was on systemization; standardization; and, most importantly, efficiency. Typifying this emphasis on efficiency were the titles of the fourteenth and fifteenth yearbooks of the National Society for the Study of Education (NSSE), which were, respectively, *Methods for Measuring Teachers' Efficiency* and the *Standards and Tests for the Measurement of the Efficiency of Schools and School Systems*.

Surveys done in a number of large school systems during this period focused on school and/or teacher efficiency and used various criteria (for example, expenditures, pupil dropout rate, promotion rates, etc.). By 1915, thirty to forty large school systems had completed or were working on comprehensive surveys on all phases of educational life (Kengall, 1915; Smith & Judd, 1914). A number of these surveys employed the newly developed "objective" tests in arithmetic, spelling, handwriting, and English composition to determine the quality of teaching. These tests were often developed in large districts by a bureau or department set up specifically to improve the efficiency of the district. For example, the Department of Educational Investigation and Measurement in the Boston public schools developed a number of tests that today would be described as objective references (Ballou, 1916). Eventually tests like those in Boston took on a norm-referenced character as the percentage of students passing became a standard by which teachers could judge whether their classes were above or below the general standard for the city (Ballou, 1916). In addition to these locally developed tests there were a number of tests developed by researchers like Courtis, Ayers, Thorndike, and others, which were geared to measuring a very precise set of instructional objectives. These tests by famous researchers of the day had normative data that enabled one system to compare itself with another (Tyack & Hansot, 1982).

Many of these early twentieth-century surveys were classic examples of muckraking, "*often* initiated by a few local people who invited outside experts to expose defects and propose remedies."[3] Another problem associated with these early surveys—a problem not unknown to evaluators today—was that the "objective" results obtained were often used as propaganda "to build dikes of data against rising tides of public criticism."[4] However, researchers at the time did recognize that such surveys could and should avoid muckraking and public relations use and should indeed be constructive, be done in cooperation with local advisors, and be designed to produce public support for unrecognized but needed change (Tyack & Hansot, 1982).

With the growth of standardized achievement tests after World War I, school districts used these tests to make inferences about program effectiveness. For example, May (1971) in an unpublished paper on the history of standardized testing in Philadelphia from 1916 to 1938 found that commercially available achievement tests, along with tests built by research bureaus of large school districts, were used to diagnose specific system weaknesses and to evaluate the curriculum and overall system performance, in addition to being used to make decisions about individuals. Throughout its history, the field of evaluation has been closely linked to the field of testing. Test data have often been the principal data source in evaluations; this use of tests has been a mixed blessing as we shall see presently.

During the late 1920s and 1930s, university institutes specializing in field studies were formed and conducted surveys for local districts. The most famous of these institutes was the one headed by George Stayer at Teachers College (Tyack & Hansot, 1982). These institutes could be considered the precursors of the university centers dedicated to evaluation that grew up in the 1960s and 1970s.

It is important to point out that studies of efficiency and testing were for the most part initiated by, and confined to, local school districts. In contrast to the national curriculum development projects of the late 1950s and early 1960s, curriculum development before the 1930s was largely in the hands of a teacher or committee of teachers. It was natural, therefore, that evaluations of that period were addressed to localized questions. This focus or emphasis on local evaluation questions continued into the 1960s despite the fact that the audience for the evaluations was statewide or nationwide; this resulted in many useless educational evaluations being carried out during the 1960s. It was only in the 1970s that educators and evaluators recognized and began to deal with this problem of generalizability.

The Tylerian Age 1930–1945

Ralph W. Tyler has had enormous influence on education in general and educational evaluation and testing in particular. He is often referred to, quite properly we feel, as the father of educational evaluation. Tyler began by conceptualizing a broad and innovative view of both curriculum and evaluation. This view saw curriculum as a set of broadly planned school-experiences designed and to implemented to help students achieve specified behavior outcomes. Tyler coined the term "educational evaluation," which meant assessing the extent that valued objectives had been achieved as part of an instructional program. During the early and mid-1930s, he applied his conceptualization of evaluation to helping instructors at Ohio State improve their courses and the tests that they used in their courses.

During the depths of the Great Depression, schools as well as other public institutions, had stagnated from a lack of resources and, perhaps just as importantly, from a lack of optimism. Just as Roosevelt tried through his New Deal programs to lead the economy out of the abyss, so too John Dewey and others tried to renew education. The renewal in education came to be known as the Progressive Education Movement, and it reflected the philosophy of pragmatism and employed tools from behavioristic psychology.

Tyler became directly involved in the Progressive Education Movement when he was called upon to direct the research component of the now-famous Eight-Year Study (Smith & Tyler, 1942). The Eight-Year Study (1932–1940), funded by the Carnegie Corporation, was the first and last large study of the differential effectiveness of various types of schooling until well after World War II. The study came about when questions were asked in the early 1930s about the efficacy of the traditional high school experience relative to the progressive secondary school experience. As a result of these questions, leading colleges began to refuse progressive-school graduates admittance because they lacked credits in certain specific subjects. To settle the debate, an experiment was proposed in 1932 in which over 300 colleges agreed to waive their traditional entrance require-ments for graduates from about 30 progressive secondary schools. The high school and college performance of students from these secondary schools would be compared to the high school and college performance of students from a group of traditional secondary schools.

The Eight-Year Study introduced educators throughout America to a new and broader view of educational evaluation than that which had been in vogue during the age of efficiency and testing. Evaluation was conceptualized by Tyler as a comparison of intended outcomes with actual out-comes. His view of evaluation was seen by advocates as having a clear-cut advantage over previous approaches. Since a Tylerian evaluation involves internal comparisons of outcomes with objectives, it need not provide for costly and disruptive comparisons between experimental and control groups, as were required in the comparative experimental approach that Rice had used. Since the approach calls for the measurement of behaviorally defined objectives, it concentrates on learning *outcomes* instead of organizational and teaching *inputs*, thereby avoiding the subjectivity of the professional judgment or accreditation approach; and, since its measures reflect defined objectives, there was no need to be heavily concerned with the reliability of differences between the scores of individual students. Further, the measures typically cover a much wider range of outcome vari-ables than those associated with standardized norm-referenced tests.

Clearly by the middle of the 1940s Tyler had, through his work and writing, laid the foundation for his enormous influence on the educational scene in general and on testing and evaluation in particular during the next 25 years. (A more detailed treatment by Tyler of his rationale for program evaluation can be found in chapter 4.)

The Age of Innocence 1946–1957

We have labeled the period 1946–1957 as the *Age of Innocence*, although we might just as well have called it the *Age of Ignorance*. It was a time of poverty and despair in the inner cities and in rural areas, but almost no one except the victims seemed to notice. It was a period of extreme racial prejudice and segregation, but most white people seemed oblivious to the disease. It was when exorbitant consumption and widespread waste of natural resources were practiced without any apparent concern that one day these resources would be depleted. It was a period of vast develop-ment of industry and military capabilities with little provision for safeguards against damage to the environment and to future generations.

More to the point of this review, there was expansion of educational offerings, personnel, and facilities. New buildings were erected. New kinds of educational institutions, such as experimental colleges and community colleges, emerged. Small school districts consolidated with others in order to be able to provide the wide range of educational services that were common in the larger school systems, including: mental and physical health services, guidance, food services, music instruction, expanded sports programs, business and technical education, and community education. Enrollments in teacher-education programs ballooned, and, in general, college enrollments increased dramatically. Throughout American society, the late 1940s and 1950s were a time to forget the war, to leave the depression behind, to build and expand capabilities, to acquire resources, and to engineer and enjoy a "good life."

This general scene in society and education was reflected in educational evaluation. While there was great expansion of education, optimism, plenty of tax money, and little worry over husbanding resources, there was no particular interest on the part of society in holding educators accountable. There was little call for educators to demonstrate the efficiency and effectiveness of any developmental efforts. Educators did talk and write about evaluation, and they did collect considerable amounts of data (usually to justify the need for expansion or for broad, new programs). However, there is little evidence that these data were used to judge and improve the quality of programs or even that they could have been useful for such a purpose. During this period there was considerable development of some of the technical aspects of evaluation; this was consistent with the then-prevalent expansion of all sorts of technologies. This was especially true of the testing approach to evaluation, but was also true of the comparative experimental and "congruence between objectives and outcomes" approaches. Chief among these developments was the growth in standardized testing. Many new nationally standardized tests were published during this period. Schools purchased these tests by the thousands and also subscribed heavily to machine scoring and analysis services that the new technology made available. The testing movement received another boost in 1947 when E.F. Lindquist, Ralph Tyler, and others helped establish the Educational Testing Service.

By the 1950s, the practice of standardized testing had expanded tremendously, and the professional organizations concerned with testing initiated a series of steps designed to regulate the testrelated activities of their members. In 1954, a committee of the American Psychological Association prepared *Technical Recommendations for Psychological Tests and Diagnostic Techniques* (APA, 1954). In 1955, committees of the American Educational Research Association and the National Council on Measurements Used in Education prepared *Technical Recommendations for Achievement Tests* (AERA and NCMUE, 1955). These two reports provided the basis for the 1966 edition of the joint AERA/ APA/NCME *Standards for Educational and Psychological Tests and Manuals* (APA, 1966) and the 1974 revision entitled, *Standards for Educational and Psychological Tests* (APA, 1974). The latter report recognized the need for separate standards dealing with program evaluation. (At this writing a joint committee is at work revising the 1974 Standards.)

This rapid expansion of testing was not the only technical development related to program evaluation during this period. Lindquist (1953) extended and delineated the statistical principles of experimental design. Years later, many evaluators and educators found that the problems of trying to meet simultaneously all of the required assumptions of experimental design (for example, constant treatment, uncontaminated treatment, randomly assigned subjects, stable study samples, and unitary success criteria) in the school setting were insurmountable.

During the 1950s and early 1960s there was also considerable technical development related to the Tylerian view of evaluation. Since implementing the Tyler approach in an evaluation required that objectives be stated explicitly, there was a need to help educators and other professionals to do a better job articulating their objectives. Techniques to help program staffs make their objectives explicit, along with taxonomies of possible educational objectives (Bloom et al., 1956; Krathwohl, 1964), were developed to fill this need. The Tyler rationale was also used extensively during this period to train teachers in test development.

During this period evaluations were, as before, primarily within the purview of local agencies. Federal and state agencies had not yet become deeply involved in the evaluation of programs.

Funds for evaluation that were done came from either local coffers, foundations, voluntary associations such as the community chest, or professional organizations. This lack of dependence on taxpayer money for evaluation would end with the dawn of the next period in the history of evaluation.

The Age of Expansion 1958–1972

The age of innocence in evaluation came to an abrupt end with the call in the late 1950s and early 1960s for evaluations of large-scale curriculum development projects funded by federal monies. This marked the end of an era in evaluation and the beginning of profound changes that would see evaluation expand as an industry and into a profession dependent on taxpayer monies for support.

As a result of the Russian launch of Sputnik I in 1957, the federal government enacted the National Defense Education Act of 1958. Among other things, this act provided for new educational programs in mathematics, science, and foreign language; and expanded counseling and guidance services and testing programs in school districts. A number of new national curriculum development projects, especially in the areas of science and mathematics, were established. Eventually funds were made available to evaluate these curriculum development efforts.

All four of the approaches to evaluation discussed so far were represented in the evaluations done during this period. First, the Tyler approach was used to help define objectives for the new curricula and to assess the degree to which the objectives were later realized. Second, new nationally standardized tests were created to better reflect the objectives and content of the new curricula. Third, the professional judgment approach was used to rate proposals and to check periodically on the efforts of contractors. Finally, many evaluators evaluated curriculum development efforts through the use of field experiments.

In the early 1960s it became apparent to some leaders in educational evaluation that their work and their results were neither particularly helpful to curriculum developers nor responsive to the questions being raised by those who wanted to know about the programs' effectiveness. The best and the brightest of the educational evaluation community were involved in these efforts to evaluate these new curricula; they were adequately financed, and they carefully applied the technology that had been developed during the past decade or more. Despite all this, they began to realize that their efforts were not succeeding.

This negative assessment was reflected best in a landmark article by Cronbach (1963; cf. chapter 6). In looking at the evaluation efforts of the recent past, he sharply criticized the guiding conceptualizations of evaluations for their lack of relevance and utility, and advised evaluators to turn away from their penchant for post hoc evaluations based on comparisons of the normreferenced test scores of experimental and control groups. Instead, Cronbach counseled evaluators to reconceptualize evaluation—not in terms of a horse race between competing programs but as a process of gathering and reporting information that could help guide curriculum development. Cronbach was the first person to argue that analysis and reporting of test item scores would be likely to prove more useful to teachers than the reporting of average total scores. When first published, Cronbach's counsel and recommendations went largely unnoticed, except by a small circle of evaluation specialists. Nonetheless, the article was seminal, containing hypotheses about the conceptualization and conduct of evaluations that were to be tested and found valid within a few years.

In 1965, guided by the vision of Senator Hubert Humphrey, the charismatic leadership of President John Kennedy, and the great political skill of President Lyndon Johnson, the War on Poverty was launched. These programs poured billions of dollars into reforms aimed at equalizing and upgrading opportunities for all citizens across a broad array of health, social and educational services. The expanding economy enabled the federal government to finance these programs, and there was widespread national support for developing what President Johnson termed the Great Society.

Accompanying this massive effort to help the needy came concern in some quarters that the money invested in these programs might be wasted if appropriate accountability requirements were not imposed. In response to this concern, Senator Robert Kennedy and some of his colleagues in the Congress amended the Elementary and Secondary Education Act of 1964 (ESEA) to include specific evaluation requirements. As a result, Title I of that Act, which was aimed at providing compensatory education to disadvantaged children, specifically required each school district receiving funds under its terms to evaluate' annually—using appropriate standardized test data—the extent to which its Title I projects had achieved their objectives. This requirement, with its specific references to standardized-test data and an assessment of congruence between outcomes and objectives, reflects the state-of-the-art in program evaluation at that time. More importantly, the requirement forced educators to shift their concern for educational evaluation from the realm of theory and supposition into the realm of practice and implementation.

When school districts began to respond to the evaluation requirement of Title I, they quickly found that the existing tools and strategies employed by their evaluators were largely inappropriate to the task. Available standardiized tests had been designed to rank order students of average ability; they were of little use in diagnosing needs and assessing any achievement gains of disadvantaged children whose educational development lagged far behind that of their middle-class peers. Further, these tests were found to be relatively insensitive to differences between schools and/or programs, mainly because of their psychometric properties and content coverage. Instead of measuring outcomes directly related to the school or to a particular program, these tests were at best indirect measures of learning, measuring much the same traits as general ability tests (Madaus, Airasian & Kellaghan, 1980).

There was another problem with using standardized tests: such an approach to evaluation conflicted with the precepts of the Tylerian approach. Because Tyler recognized and encouraged differences in objectives from locale to locale it became difficult to adapt this model to nationwide standardized-testing programs. In order to be commercially viable, these standardized-testing programs had to overlook to some extent objectives stressed by particular locales in favor of objectives stressed by the majority of districts. Further, there was a dearth of information about the needs and achievement levels of disadvantaged children that could guide teachers in developing meaningful behavioral objectives for this population of learners.

The failure of attempts to isolate the effects of Title I projects through the use of experimental/control group designs was due primarily to an inability to meet the assumptions required of such designs. Further, project-site visitation by experts—while extensively employed by governmental sponsors—was not acceptable as a primary evaluation strategy because this approach was seen as lacking the objectivity and rigor stipulated in the ESEA legislation. When the finding of "no results" was reported, as was generally the case, there were no data on the degree to which the "treatment" had in fact been implemented; the evaluator had overlooked the messy "black box" that constituted the "treatment." Further, we encased the word treatment in quotes advisedly since the actual nature of the treatment rendered to subjects was generally unknown. The technical description was nothing more than a vague description of the project. For example, the term Title I itself was often used to describe an amorphous general treatment. In any event, the emphasis on test scores diverted attention from consideration of the treatment or of treatment implementation.

As a result of the growing disquiet with evaluation efforts and with the consistent negative findings, the professional honorary fraternity Phi Delta Kappa set up a National Study Committee on Evaluation (P.D.K., 1971). After surveying the scene, this committee concluded that educational evaluation was "seized with a great illness"; and called for the development of new theories and methods of evaluation as well as for new training programs for evaluators. At about this same time many new conceptualizations of evaluations began to emerge. Provus (1969 & 1971), Hammond

(1967), Eisner (1967), and Metfessel & Michael (1967) proposed reformation of the Tyler model. Glaser (1963), Tyler (1967), and Popham (1971) pointed to criterion-referenced testing as an alternative to norm-referenced testing. Cook (1966) called for the use of the systems-analysis approach to evaluate programs. Scriven (1967), Stufflebeam (1967 & 1971, with others), and Stake (1967) introduced new models of evaluation that departed radically from prior approaches. These conceptualizations recognized the need to evaluate goals, look at inputs, examine implementation and delivery of services, as well as measure intended and unintended outcomes of the program. They also emphasized the need to make judgments about the merit or worth of the object being evaluated. (Overviews of these developments can be found in chapters 2 and 3.) The late 1960s and early 1970s were vibrant with descriptions, discussions, and debates concerning how evaluation should be conceived; however, this period in the history of program evaluation ended on a down note. A number of important evaluations resulted in negative findings. First, Coleman's famous study, *Equality of Educational Opportunity* (1966, with others), received considerable notice. Particular attention went to his famous conclusion that "schools bring little influence to bear on a child's achievement that is independent of his background and general social context."[5] Title I evaluations (Picariello, 1968; Glass et al., 1970; U.S. Office of Education, 1970) argued against the efficacy of those programs. The Westinghouse/Ohio University Head Start investigation (Cicirelli et al., 1969) turned up discouraging results. Likewise, the results of the evaluation of *Sesame Street* (Ball & Bogatz, 1970; Bogatz & Ball, 1971)—when critically analyzed (Cook)—were discouraging. These disheartening findings raised serious questions about evaluation in general and certain methodologies in particular. For many supporters of these programs, this set the stage for our next period which we call the Age of Professionalization.

The Age of Professionalization 1973–Present

Beginning about 1973 the field of evaluation began to crystallize and emerge as a distinct profession related to, but quite distinct from, its forebears of research and testing. While the field of evaluation has advanced considerably as a profession, it is instructive to consider this development in the context of the field in the previous period.

At that time, evaluators faced an identity crisis. They were not sure whether they should try to be researchers, testers, administrators, teachers, or philosophers. It was unclear what special qualifications, if any, they should possess. There was no professional organization dedicated to evaluation as a field, nor were there specialized journals through which evaluators could exchange information about their work. There was essentially no literature about program evaluation except unpublished papers that circulated through an underground network of practitioners. There was a paucity of pre-service and in-service training opportunities in evaluation. Articulated standards of good practice were confined to educational and psychological tests. The field of evaluation was amorphous and fragmented—many evaluations were carried out by untrained personnel; others by research methodologists who tried unsuccessfully to fit their methods to program evaluations (Guba, 1966). Evaluation studies were fraught with confusion, anxiety, and animosity. Evaluation as a field had little stature and no political clout.

Against this backdrop, the progress made by educational evaluators to professionalize their field during the 1970s is quite remarkable indeed. A number of journals, including *Educational Evaluation and Policy Analysis, Studies in Evaluation, CEDR Quarterly, Evaluation Review, New Directions for Program Evaluation, Evaluation and Program Planning,* and *Evaluation News* were begun; and these journals have proved to be excellent vehicles for recording and disseminating information about the various facets of program evaluation. Unlike 15 years ago, there are now numerous books and monographs that deal exclusively with evaluation. In fact, the problem today is not trying to find literature in evaluation but to keep up with it. The May 12th Group,[6] Division H of the AERA, the Evaluation Network, and the Evaluation Research Society have afforded excellent opportunities for professional exchange among persons concerned with the evaluation of education and other human service programs.

Many universities have begun to offer at least one course in evaluation methodology (as distinct from research methodology); a few universities—such as the University of Illinois, Stanford University, Boston College, UCLA, the University of Minnesota, and Western Michigan University—have developed graduate programs in evaluation. Nova University was perhaps the first to require an evaluation course in a doctoral program. For seven years the U.S. Office of Education has sponsored a national program of inservice training in evaluation for special educators (Brinkerhoff et al., in press), and several professional organizations have offered workshops and institutes on various evaluation topics. Centers have been established for research and development related to evaluation; these include the evaluation unit of the Northeast Regional Educational Laboratory, the Center for the Study of Evaluation at UCLA, the Stanford Evaluation Consortium, the Center for Instructional Research and Curriculum Evaluation at the University of Illinois, The Evaluation Center at Western Michigan University, and the Center for the Study of Testing, Evaluation and Educational Policy at Boston College. The Evaluation Institute of the University of San Francisco briefly expanded evaluation out into the product and personal areas. The state of Louisiana has established a policy and program for certifying evaluators (Peck, 1981), and Massachusetts is currently working on a similar certification program for evaluation. Recently Dick Johnson (1980) issued a first draft of a directory of evaluators and evaluation agencies.

Increasingly, the field has looked to meta evaluation (Scriven, 1975; Stufflebeam, 1978) as a means of assuring and checking the quality of evaluations. A joint committee (Joint Committee, 1981a), appointed by 12 professional organizations, has issued a comprehensive set of standards for judging evaluations of educational programs, and materials Joint Committee, 1981a), and has established a mechanism (Joint Committee, 1981b) by which to review and revise the Standards and assist the field to use them. (Cf. chapter 23 for an overview of these standards.) In addition, several other sets of standards with relevance for educational evaluation have been issued (cf. Evaluation *News,* May 1981).

During this period, evaluators increasingly realized that the techniques of evaluation must achieve results previously seen as peripheral to serious research; serve the information needs of the clients of evaluation; address the central value issues; deal with situational realities; meet the requirements of probity; and satisfy needs for veracity. While the field has yet to develop a fully functional methodology that meets all these requirements, there have been some promising developments, including: goal-free evaluation (Scriven, 1974; Evers, 1980); adversary-advocate teams (Stake & Gjerde, 1974; cf. chapters 11-13); advocate teams (Reinhard, 1972); meta analysis (Glass, 1976; Krol, 1978); responsive evaluation (Stake, 1975; cf. chapter 17); and naturalistic evaluation (Guba & Lincoln, 1981; cf. chapter 18). Under the leadership of Nick Smith (1981a; 1981b), a large number of writers have examined the applicability to evaluation of a wide range of investigatory techniques drawn from a variety of fields (cf. chapter 22). Eisner (1975) and his students have explored and developed techniques for applying the techniques used by critics in evaluating materials from the arts (cf. chapter 19). Webster (1975) and his colleagues have operationalized Stufflebeam's CIPP model within the context of a school district (cf. chapter 7). Stake (1978; cf. chapter 17), has adapted case study methods for use in evaluation. Roth (1977; 1978), Suarez (1980), Scriven & Roth (1978), Stufflebeam (1977) and others have begun to make both conceptual and operational sense of the crucial yet elusive concept of needs assessment. Personnel of the Toledo Public Schools, in collaboration with Bunda (1980) and Ridings (1980), have devised catalogs of evaluative criteria and associated instruments to help teachers and administrators tailor their data collection efforts to meet their information requirements. Finally, a great deal of work has been done to encourage the use of objective-referenced tests in evaluation studies. A particularly fruitful application of this latter technique is seen in curriculum-embedded evaluations, which provide teachers and students with an ongoing assessment of attainment in relation to the sequential objectives of a curriculum (Chase, 1980; Bloom, Madaus, & Hastings, 1981).

This substantial professional development in evaluation has produced mixed results. First, while there is undoubtedly more, and certainly better, communication in the field, there has also been an enormous amount of chatter (Cronbach, 1980). Second, while progress has been made in improving the training and certification of evaluators to ensure that institutions obtain services from qualified persons, some observers worry that this development may result in a narrow and exclusive club (Stake, 1981). Third, the cooperation among professional organizations concerned with educational evaluation, fostered by the Joint Committee on Standards for Educational Evaluation, is a promising but fragile arrangement for promoting the conduct and use of high-quality evaluation work. Finally, while the creation of new professional organizations has increased communication and reduced fragmentation in the evaluation field, there, unfortunately, remains a fairly sharp division between Division H of the AERA, the Evaluation Network, and the Evaluation Research Society of America.

Even though there has been increased communication between those advocating positivistic/quantitative approaches to evaluation and proponents of phenomenological/qualitative approaches, there is a present danger of a polarization developing between those camps. The roots of this polarization are not primarily methodological, but instead reflect ideological differences. Madaus & McDonagh (1982) describe the dangers of this polarization:

> In both cases, the evaluator, if not careful, could become a priest class which gives warning and advice, but does not take it, a class which practices on the one hand in the name of science and on the other through charismatic personality.[7]

Finally, in spite of growing search for appropriate methods, increased communication and understanding among the leading methodologists, and the development of new techniques, the actual practice of evaluation has changed very little in the great majority of settings. Clearly, there is a need for expanded efforts to educate evaluators to the availability of new techniques, to try out and report the results of using the new techniques, and to develop additional techniques. In all of these efforts, the emphasis must be on making the methodology fit the needs of society, its institutions, and its citizens, rather than vice versa (Kaplan, 1964).

Conclusion

Evaluators need to be aware of both contemporary and historical aspects of their emerging profession—including its philosophical underpinnings and conceptual orientations. Without this background, evaluators are doomed to repeat past mistakes and, equally debilitating, will fail to sustain and build on past successes.

We have portrayed program evaluation as a dynamic, yet immature, profession. While the profession is still immature, there can be no doubt that it has become increasingly an identifiable component of the broader governmental and professional establishment of education, health, and welfare. The prediction commonly heard in the 1960s that formalized program evaluation was a fad and soon would disappear proved false, and there are strong indications that this field will continue to grow in importance, sophistication, and stature. The gains over the past 15 years are impressive, but there are many obvious deficiencies, and we still lack sufficient evidence about the impact of evaluations on education and human services. There is a need to improve research, training, and financial support for program evaluation. Leaders of the evaluation profession must ensure that efforts to improve their profession are geared to the service needs of their clients, not merely designed to serve their private or corporate needs. Ultimately the value of program evaluation must be judged in terms of its actual and potential contributions to improving learning, teaching and administration, health care and health, and in general the quality of life in our society.

All of us in the program evaluation business would do well to remember and use this basic principle to guide and examine our work.

Notes

1. Ireland. Royal Commission of Inquiry into Primary Education, 1870.

2. N.J. Crisp, 1982, p. 148

3. D. Tyack and E. Hansot, 1982, p. 161.

4. D. Tyack and E. Hansot, 1982, p. 155.

5. J.S. Coleman, E.Q. Campbell, C.J. Hobson et al., 1966, p. 325

6. In the early 1970s a group of evaluators met on May 12th to discuss issues in evaluation. The group, with added members continues in existance and meets annually to discuss current issues and problems in the field.

7. G.F. Madaus and J.T. McDonagh, 1982, p. 36.

References

American Educational Research Association and National Council on Measurements Used in Education. *Technical Recommendations for Achievement Tests*. Washington, D.C.: Author, 1955.

American Psychological Association. *Technical Recommendations for Psychological Tests and Diagnostic Techniques*. Washington, D.C.: Author, 1954.

American Psychological Association. *Standards for Educational and Psychological Tests. and Manuals* Washington, D.C.: Author, 1966.

American Psychological Association. *Standards for Educational and Psychological Tests*. Washington, D.C.: Author, 1974.

Ball, S., and Bogatz, G.A. *The First Year of Sesame Street: An Evaluation*. Princeton, New Jersey Educational Testing Service, 1970.

Ballou, F.A. "Work of the Department of Educational Investigation and Measurement, Boston, Massachusetts." In G.M. Whipple, (ed.), *Standards and Tests for the Measurement of the Efficiency of Schools and School Systems*. National Society for the Study of Education, Fifteenth Yearbook Part I. Chicago: University of Chicago Press, 1916.

Biddle, B.J., and Ellena, W.J. (eds.) *Contemporary Research on Teacher Effectiveness*. New York: Holt, Rinehart & Winston, 1964.

Bloom, B.S.; Englehart, M.D.; Furst, E.J.; Hill, W.H.; and Krathwohl, D.R. *Taxonomy of Educational Objectives Handbook 1: The Cognitive Domain*. New York: David McKay Co., 1956.

Bloom, B.S.; Madaus, G.F.; and Hastings, J.T. *Evaluation to Improve Learning*. New York: McGraw-Hill Book Co., 1981.

Bogatz, G.A., and Ball, S. *The Second Year of Sesame Street: A Continuing Education*. 2 vols. Princeton, New Jersey: Educational Testing Service, 1971.

Boulding, K.E. "Science, Our Common Heritage." *Science*, no. 4433, 207 (1980), 831-36.

Brinkerhoff, R. "Evaluation Technical Assistance: Reflections on a National Effort." *CEDR Journal,* forthcoming Assessment and Program Evaluation: Defining the Need and the Scope 33.

Bunda, M.A. *Catalog of Criteria for Evaluating Student Growth and Development.* Toledo: Toledo, Ohio Public Schools and the Western Michigan University Evaluation Center, 1980.

Callahan, R.E. *Education and the Cult of Efficiency.* Chicago: University of Chicago Press, 1962.

Campbell, D.T. "Reforms as Experiments." *American Psychologist,* no. 4, 24 (1969), 409-29.

Campbell, D.T., and Stanley, J.C. "Experimental and Quasi-Experimental Designs for Research on Teaching." In: N.L. Gage (ed.) *Handbook of Research on Teaching,* Chicago: Rand McNally, 1963.

Chase, F. *Educational Quandries and Opportunities.* Dallas, Texas: Urban Education Studies, 1980.

Cicirelli, V.G.. et al. *The Impact of Head Start: An Evaluation of the Effects of Head Start on Children's Cognitive and Affective Development.* Study by Westinghouse Learning Corporation and Ohio University. Washington, D.C.: Office of Economic Opportunity, 1969.

Coleman, J.S.; Campbell, E.Q.; Hobson, C.J. et al. *Equality of Educational Opportunity.* Washington, D.C.: Office of Education, U.S. Department of Health, Education, and Welfare, 1966.

Cook, D.L. *Program Evaluation and Review Technique Applications in Education.* Washington, D.C.: Government Printing Office, 1966.

Cremin, L.A. *The Transfonnation of the School.* New York: Knopf, 1962.

Crisp, J.J. *The Brink.* New York: Viking Press, 1982.Cronbach, L.J. "Course Improvement through Evaluation." *Teachers College Record.* 64 (1963): 672-83.

Cronbach, L.J. *Toward Reform of Program Evaluation.* San Francisco: Jossey-Bass Publishers, 1980.

Eisner, E.W. "Educational Objectives: Help or Hindrance?" *The School Review.* 75 (1967): 250-60.

Eisner, E.W. *The Perceptive Eye: Toward the Reformation of Educational Evaluation.* Stanford, California: Stanford Evaluation Consortium, December 1975.

Evaluation News. Sponsored by the Evaluation Network, Sage Publications, no. 2, 2 (1981).

Evers, J.W. "A Field Study of Goal-Based and Goal-Free Evaluation Techniques." Unpublished doctoral dissertation, Western Michigan University, 1980.

Glaser, R. "Instructional Technology and the Measurement of Learning Outcomes: Some Questions." *American Psychologist 18* (1963): 519-21.

Glass, G.V. "Primary, Secondary, and Meta Analysis of Research." *Educational Researcher,* no. 10, 5 (1976), 3-8.

Glass, G.V. et al. *Data Analysis of the 1968-69 Survey of Compensatory Education, Title 1. Final Report on Grant No. OEG8-8-961860 4003 (058).* Washington, D.C.: Office of Education, 1970.

Guba, E.G. *A Study of Title III Activities: Report on Evaluation.* Indiana University, National Institute for the Study of Educational Change, October 1966.

Guba, E.G. and Lincoln, Y.S. *Effective Evaluation.* San Francisco: Jossey-Bass Publishers, 1981.

Hammond, R.L. "Evaluation at the Local Level." Address to the Miller Committee for the National Study of ESEA Title III, 1967.

Ireland, Royal Commission of Inquiry into Primary Education. *Report of the Commissioners.* (H.C. 1870, xxviii, part i).

Johnson, R. *Directory of Evaluators and Evaluation Agencies.* New York: Exxon Corporation 1980.

Joint Committee on Standards for Educational Evaluation. *Standards for Evaluations of Educational Programs, Projects, and Materials.* New York: McGraw-Hill Book Co., 1981a.

Joint Committee on Standards for Educational Evaluation. *Principles and By-Laws.* Western Michigan University Evaluation Center, 1981b.

Kaplan, A. *The Conduct of Inquiry.* San Francisco: Chandler, 1964.

Kellaghan, T. and Madaus, G.F. Trends in Educational Standards in Great Britain and Ireland. In G.R. Austin & H. Garber (eds.), *The Rise and Fall of National Test Scores.* New York: Academic Press, 1982.

Kendall, C.N. "Efficiency of School and School Systems." In *Proceedings and Addresses of the Fifty-third Annual Meeting of the National Education Association,* 389–95, 1915.

Krathwohl, D.R.; Bloom, B.S.; and Masia, B.B. *Taxonomy of Educational Objectives: the Classification of Educational Goals. Handbook 11: Affective Domain.* New York: David McKay Co., 1964.

Krol, R.A. "A Meta Analysis of Comparative Research on the Effects of Desegregation on Academic Achievement. Unpublished doctoral dissertation, Western Michigan University, 1978.

Lindquist, E.F. *Design and Analysis of Experiments in Psychology and Education.* Boston: Houghton-Mifflin, 1953.

Madaus, G.F.; Airasian, P.W.; and Kellaghan, T. *School Effectiveness.* New York: McGraw-Hill Book Co., 1980.

Madaus, G.F., and McDonagh, J.T. "As I Roved Out: Folksong Collecting as a Metaphor for Evaluation. In N.L. Smith (ed.), *Communicating in Evaluation: Alternative Forms of Representation.* Beverly Hills, California: Sage Publications, 1982.

May, P. "Standardized Testing in Philadelphia, 1916–1938." Unpublished manuscript, 1971.

Metfessel, N.S. and Michael, W.B. "A Paradigm Involving Multiple Criterion Measures for the Evaluation of the Effectiveness of School Programs." *Educational and Psychological Measurement* 27 (1967):931–43.

National Society for the Study of Education. *Methods for Measuring Teachers' Efficiency.* Fourteenth Yearbook. Part II. Chicago: University of Chicago Press, 1916.

Peck, H. "Report on the Certification of Evaluators in Louisiana." Paper presented at the meeting of the Southern Educational Research Association, Lexington, Kentucky, Fall 1981.

Phi Delta Kappa Commission on Evaluation. *Educational Evaluation and Decision Making.* Itasca, Illinois: Peacock Publishers, 1971.

Picariello, H. *Evaluation of Title 1.* Washington, D.C.: American Institute for the Advancement of Science, 1968.

Pinker, R. *Social Theory and Social Policy.* London: Heinemann Educational Books, 1971.

Popham, W.J. *Criterion-referenced Measurement.* Englewood Cliffs, New Jersey: Educational Technology Publications, 1971.

Provus, M. *Discrepancy Evaluation Model, 1969.* Pittsburgh, Pennsylvania: Pittsburgh Public Schools, 1969.

Provus, M. *Discrepancy Evaluation.* Berkeley, California: McCutcheon Publishing Co., 1971.

Reinhard,D."Methodology Development for Input Evaluation Using Advocate and Design Teams." Unpublished doctoral dissertation, Ohio State University, 1972.

Rice, J.M. "The Futility of the Spelling Grind." *The Forum* 23 (1897):163-72.

Rice, J.M. *Scientific Management in Education*. New York: Hinds, Noble & Eldredge, 1914.

Ridings, J. *Catalog of Criteria for Evaluating Administrative Concerns in School Districts*. Toledo: Toledo, Ohio Public Schools and the Western Michigan University Evaluation Center, 1980.

Roth, J. "Needs and the Needs Assessment Process." *Evaluation News* 5 (1977):15-17.

Roth, J.E. "Theory and Practice of Needs Assessment With Special Application to Institutions of Higher Learning." Unpublished doctoral dissertation, University of California, Berkeley, 1978.

Scriven, M.S. "The Methodology of Evaluation." In *Perspective of Curriculum Evaluation*. AERA Monograph Series on Curriculum Evaluation, no. 1. Chicago: Rand McNally, 1967.

Scriven, M.S. "Pros and Cons about Goal-Free Evaluation." *Evaluation Comment* 3 (1974):1-4.

Scriven, M.S. *Evaluation Bias and its Control*. Occasional Paper Series no. 4. Western Michigan University Evaluation Center, 1975.

Scriven, M. and Roth, J.E. "Needs Assessment." *Evaluation News* 2 (1977):25-28.

Scriven, M. and Roth, J.E. "Needs Assessment: Concept and Practice." *New Directions for Program Evaluation* 1 (1978): 1-11.

Smith, E.R., and Tyler, R.W. *Appraising and Recording Student Progress*. New York: Harper, 1942.

Smith, H.L., and Judd, C.H. *Plans for Organizing School Surveys*. National Society for the Study of Education, Thirteenth Yearbook, Part II. Bloomington, Illinois: Public School Publishing Co., 1914.

Smith, N.L. *Metaphors for Evaluation: Sources of New Methods*. Beverly Hills, California: Sage Publications, 1981a.

Smith, N.L. *New Techniques for Evaluation*. Beverly Hills, California: Sage Publications, 1981b.

Stake, R.E. "The Countenance of Educational Evaluation." *Teachers College Record* 68 (1967):523–40.

Stake, R.E. "Setting Standards for Educational Evaluators." *Evaluation News* no. 2, 2 (1981),148–52.

Stake, R.E. "The Case-Study Method in Social Inquiry." *Evaluation Researcher* 7 (1978):5–8.

Stake, R.E. "Setting Standards for Educational Evaluators." *Evaluator News* no. 2, 2 (1981),148–52.

Stake, R.E., and Gjerde, C. *An Evaluation of T-City, the Twin City Institute for Talented Youth*. AERA Monograph Series in Curriculum Evaluation, no. 7. Chicago: Rand McNally, 1974.

Stufflebeam, D.L. "The Use and Abuse of Evaluation in Title III." *Theory into Practice* 6 (1967):126-33.

Stufflebeam, D.L. *Needs Assessment in Evaluation*. Audio-tape of presentation at the American Educational Research Association Meeting, San Francisco, September 1977. Published by the American Educational Research Association.

Stufflebeam, D.L. "Meta Evaluation: An Overview." *Evaluation and the Health Proffessions*, no. 2.1. (1978).

Stufflebeam, D.L. et al. *Educational Evaluation and Decision-Making*. Ithaca, Illinois: Peacock Publish-

Suarez, T. "Needs Assessments for Technical Assistance: A Conceptual Overview and Comparison of Three Strategies." Unpublished doctoral dissertation. Western Michigan University, 1980.

Thompson, D. *England in the Nineteenth Century (1815–1914)*. Baltimore: Penguin Books, Inc., 1950.

Tyack, D., and Hansot, E. *Managers of Virtue*. New York: Basic Books, Inc., 1982.

Tyler, R.W. "Changing Concepts of Educational Evaluation." In R.E. Stake (ed.), *Perspectives of Curriculum Evaluation. vol. 1,* New York: Rand McNally, 1967.

U.S. Office of Education. *Education of the Disadvantaged: An Evaluation Reporton Title: Elementary and Secondary Education Act of 1965. Fiscal Year 1968.* Washington, D.C.; Author, 1970.

Webster, W.J. *The Organization and Functions of Research and Evaluation Units in a Large Urban School District.* Dallas, Texas: Dallas Independent School District, 1975.

To Capture the Ineffable: New Forms of Assessment in Higher Education

PETER T. EWELL

Assessment in higher education has become, by any estimate, a curious phenomenon. Begun modestly as a series of isolated institutional experiments in the late 1970s, assessment has become, for many institutions, a condition of doing business. A concomitant result has been the conversion of a scholarly measurement technology into a major and controversial tool of public policy. Thus, on one hand, assessment in higher education has the characteristics of a social movement—driven by political forces and constrained by societal demands (Ewell, 1989). On the other hand, through its language, symbolism, and technology, it is equally rooted in measurement practice. Any attempt to come to terms with it, therefore, must equally partake of both.

In this review, I attempt to do so in the following manner. First, in order to fully understand current assessment practice, it is critical to establish its historical and political context. Regardless of its technical guise, assessment in higher education cannot be divorced from a visible reform agenda. I begin by laying out this background with particular emphasis on the evolution and origins of assessment's contradictory imperatives: academic improvement and external account-ability. Interaction between these two imperatives has produced a bewilderingly complex pattern of "assessment" activities on college and university campuses. Indeed, the term itself has rapidly acquired multiple meanings, each of which carried with it a particular referent and history. In the second portion of the review's initial section, therefore, I attempt to sort out some of these complexities in terms of a commonly applied taxonomy of assessment approaches.

This preliminary discussion sets the stage for the second section: a critical review of current practice. Like many other areas of applied research, assessment in higher education has rapidly moved from a sophisticated measurement technology emphasizing prediction and precision to-ward a field approach centered on robustness and utility. Three recent developments, in particular, demand attention. First, demands for better information about group performance have led to important (and controversial) new approaches to test making. Not only are these developments in measurement technology important in their own right, but they rekindle ongoing debates about the existence and nature of such claimed generic cognitive outcomes of college as critical thinking, creativity, and problem solving. Second, notable changes have taken place in the conceptual basis of assessment measurement, particularly in the model of student learning and development grounding inquiry. Early linear developmental conceptions (e.g., the popular notion of "added value") have been replaced by more complex formations demanding truly longitudinal research designs and a theoretical foundation based on complex integrated abilities. One result has been a growing number of institutional studies that, although intended as action research, can provide useful field verification for more carefully designed studies of collegiate learning and development. Third, as in evaluation more generally, the practice of assessment is increasingly naturalistic. Single-purpose research tools applied under carefully controlled conditions are rapidly being discarded in favor of multimethod approaches embedded in existing classroom or campus settings. Like naturalistic inquiry in other settings, assessments of this kind raise important issues about whether the authenticity gained in such settings is worth the apparent sacrifice of methodological rigor. I treat each of these trends in turn as the review's center core.

Beyond their immediate interest, these trends raise important epistemological issues about research on collegiate learning. Are traditional concepts of validity and reliability fundamentally altered, as some assessment practitioners are claiming, when the unit of analysis becomes an individual performance rather than an estimated group trait? Should the distribution of stakeholders and the size of the stakes associated with the use of any assessment become an integral part of the research effort itself? As assessment practitioners debate such critical questions, they echo earlier voices in the wider testing and evaluation communities (e.g., Guba & Lincoln, 1981; Messick, 1988b). In a final section, I summarize these emerging issues in terms of three general questions that must be posed of any assessment: "What's the construct?" "What's the context?" and "What's the use?" Although assessment practitioners have yet to reach consensus on their answers, the issues raised by these questions are capable of informing all aspects of research on cognitive development.

As a prominent feature of higher education's landscape, assessment appears here to stay. But beyond the attention that comes from emerging prominence, a critical examination seems compelling in at least three ways. First, assessment is by no means the first reform movement of its kind to affect higher education. Examining its origins, dynamics, and probable future can potentially add to our more general understanding of such phenomena. Second, as a technology in use, the evaluation of assessment has much in common with other fields of action research—raising familiar issues of method, politics, and ethics. Treatment of their latest manifestation may provide new insights into how such issues can arise, develop, and possibly be resolved. Finally, the techniques of assessment, though intended to inform practice, are breaking new ground for research on student learning and development. As a clinical counterpart to more formal inquiry, both its methods and its findings are of scholarly interest. A review of this kind, of course, is never complete, and I freely acknowledge the inevitable errors of omission or conclusion that infect the activities of a participant observer. If trends and issues are clear, however, my central purpose is attained.

Higher Education Assessment: Defining the Ground

Assessment's Roots: Two Agendas for Reform

Any appraisal of the current assessment movement in higher education requires recognition of both its recent history and its two quite different origins. One ancestral theme, signaled by a series of prominent reports on undergraduate education in the mid-1980s, lies firmly within the academy. A second, marked by steadily growing state interest in accountability in the same period, is rooted externally. Both involve a multifaceted reform agenda in which assessment plays a key role and without which its current practice cannot be fully understood. Interaction between them, moreover, yields a bewildering array of activities that, despite a common label, are different in both technology and intent.

The Internal Agenda: The Undergraduate Reform Reports of 1984–1985

The internal agenda for reform, may observers claim, is grounded in a periodic swing of fashion regarding the structure and content of the undergraduate curriculum (e.g. Edgerton, 1987). Much as the discipline-based "germanic" curricula of the emerging 20th century spawned in reaction a rediscovery of general education in the 1930s, a curricular swing toward greater coherence in the early 1980s arose in part in opposition to the unstructured, choice-based curricula of the 1960s (Grant & Riesman, 1978). Student assessment is an integral part of this dynamic of curricular reaction. Resnick and Goulden (1987), for example, argue that an "assessment movement" was similarly present with the reemergence of general education in the 1930s, and ascribe this phenomenon historically to a natural period of consolidation following the end of enrollment growth.

The emergence of assessment as an explicit ingredient of reform was clearly signaled by four major reports on undergraduate education, all published in 1984–1985 and all stimulated in part by prior inquiries into national deficiencies in elementary and secondary education (U.S. Department of Education, 1983). Each report, in its own way, made a basic connection between assessment and undergraduate reform. For one of the first of these reports, *Access to Quality Undergraduate Education* (Southern Regional Education Board, 1985), a key linkage lies in the need to identify and address growing basic skills deficiencies among incoming college freshmen. Rather than an exclusionary view of admissions testing, entering basic skills assessment is coupled with improved remediation and directed placement in a comprehensive strategy aimed at recapturing a lost generation of college students let down by the failures of earlier schooling. More than any other, this report signaled the reemergence of widespread basic skills testing in higher education, foreshadowed by New Jersey's statewide program and by a range of integrated testing/placement programs in community colleges (Richardson, Fisk, & Okun, 1983).

For perhaps the most comprehensive of the four reports, *Involvement in Learning* (National Institute of Education, 1984), the linkage lies in the last of its three major themes—high standards, active student involvement in the learning process, and explicit feedback on performance. Notions of feedback through assessment contained in this report strongly echo the views of two of its major authors (Astin, 1977; Bowen, 1977) and contain two quite different propositions. The first, supported by substantial research, is that individual student learning can be significantly enhanced through frequent communication about performance (Astin, 1985). The second, advanced despite the apparent prior failure of large-scale program evaluation based on the methods of social sciences to effect significant organizational change throughout the 1960s and 1970s (Shapiro, 1986), is that institutions can also "learn" through information about results and can make continuous improvements in response (Ewell, 1984). Themes apparent in the two remaining reports—*Integrity in the College Curriculum* (Association of American Colleges, 1985) and *To Reclaim a Legacy* (Bennett, 1984)—are similar, though both are more traditionally focused on curricular content and structure. Here, the curricular connection to assessment lies largely in the felt need for intensive, integrative demonstrations of student knowledge and capacities (similar in structure to the comprehensive examinations typical of earlier undergraduate liberal arts curricula) to complete and certify the process of undergraduate instruction. In addition, both reports sounded a new note by insisting that higher education institutions were substantially (and unhealthily) unaccountable to their major constituents for their educational product. A primary target here was not, however, the kind of public mandate for outcomes testing then emerging in K-12 education. Rather, the intent was to move such existing accountability mechanisms as institutional accreditation away from their traditional reliance on input as the sole hallmark of quality.

Although the actual kinds of assessment called for in these reports remained relatively unspecified, their general requirements were clear. First, for institutional feedback, the results of assessment must be immediately useful in guiding intervention. One implication is that results be provided in sufficiently desegregated form that distinct dimensions of performance can be identified or clear differences among types of students can be adequately diagnosed. At minimum, the framers of these reports recognized, this required different forms of testing than those then available: Most postsecondary assessment instruments at that time existed only in the form of standardized instruments used for college and graduate school admissions, advanced placement, or certification, for which no subscores or item profiles were typically available. For individual feedback, an equal requirement was for developmental measures—usually involving integrative or stimulated performance—using expert assessor judgments (Gamson & Associates, 1984; Grant & Kohli, 1979). In both cases, however, a substantially new (though equally rigorous) technology was required. Indeed, what made these reports different from similar curricular reexaminations in prior decades was that developing such new technologies was *itself* a major premise of reform.

The Accountability Movement in State Governance

Comprehensive though it was, the internal stimulus for higher education assessment did not function long in isolation. By late 1986, responding to state government had clearly supplanted internally sponsored academic reform as the primary reason for most institutional action (El-Khawas, 1987). What was responsible for this major shift of attention? One component is an escalating public policy concern with the effectiveness of funds invested. This is, in part, a function of rising costs and increasing complexity. Both legislators and governors have become unusually sensitive (especially in tight budget years) to the fact that they know very little about the actual impacts of investments in postsecondary education that can consume from a quarter to a third of state general fund revenues each year. At the same time, state higher education leaders have become more sophisticated in their claims about public benefit (Folger & Berdahl, 1987). As a result, explicit links between proposed investments in public higher education and return on investment through economic development—particularly visible in areas such as high technology—have become more salient recently than in prior decades. Both trends have fused in a markedly new pattern of accountability for public higher education (Ewell, 1990): Like their counterparts in business and industry, state leaders appear willing to trade off as the substance of accountability detailed auditing and reporting requirements in such areas as expenditures and personnel decision making in return for much broader performance information. The champions of such reforms, moreover, are not those in legislatures and statehouses that wish to cut higher education funding, but those instead who constitute higher education's traditional political allies.

In the mid-1980s, shifting public policy concerns also spawned a series of national reform reports—prominent among them *Transforming the State Role in Undergraduate Education: Time for a Different View* (Education Commission of the States, 1986) and *Time for Results* (National Governors' Association, 1986). Consistent with prior academic improvement reports, these documents highlighted the use of assessment as a tool of reform. Like the public K-12 assessment tradition that informed them, however, these reports also had a strong accountability flavor: Both maintained that information on college student performances should be publicly available and comparable across institutions, should be used to inform policy and resource allocation decisions at the state level, and should be appropriate to inform consumer choice on the part of students and their parents in the decision of which college to attend.

Like their academic counterparts, these reports also unmistakably signaled what kinds of assessments were required. First, to be maximally credible, assessment techniques should be easily understood and should, if possible, result in quantitative indicators of institutional or program performance. Although academic improvement remains a goal, it is to be achieved primarily through the action of external market forces informed by assessment results and through the unilateral responses of institutions to incentives or sanctions applied through their appointed governing or regulatory bodies. Above all, the process should emphasize demonstrable return on investment in the form of aggregate student performance (Kean, 1987). A popular policy alternative, prominent in state discussions at the time, was "performance funding" as practiced in Tennessee (Banta, 1986): Those institutions best demonstrating their effectiveness through assessment should derive commensurate rewards in the form of additional resources. An alternative available policy choice was directed investment, as practiced in New Jersey, Florida, and Virginia (Berdahl & Studds, 1989): Here the imperative is that marginal resources be directed toward particular institutions and programs specifically to address designated problems or deficiencies that assessment might help to reveal.

Action in response to these reports was unusually prompt. In 1982 there were only 3 or 4 states with recognizable state policy initiatives in higher education assessment; by 1986, however, the number had grown to 15 (Boyer, Ewell, Finney, & Mingle, 1987). Currently, some 27 states have established such programs through board resolution, executive directive, or statute (Ewell, Finney, & Lenth, 1990; Paulson, 1990). Further initiatives are expected or planned in additional dozen states over the next 5 years. Current state approaches vary widely because of differing resource climates, structure of governance, and political circumstances (Ewell & Boyer, 1988). A few include common statewide testing of the basic skills of incoming college freshmen; a much smaller number require periodic statewide testing of college students (usually at the sophomore or senior years) to determine program effectiveness. But by far the majority of current state initiatives require that each institution submit and receive approval for a local assessment plan consistent with institutional mission. Here, in some cases, only one institutional sector is involved; however, in many cases plan approval by a state governing or coordinating board is in some way linked to institutional funding. States also have exhibited widely varying levels of investment in such programs. Frequently, no new dollars are associated with the mandate, as legislators argue that this is an activity that colleges and universities should have been involved in all along. In other states, categorical grant programs have been used to support demonstration projects at individual institutions. Finally, in a few cases substantial new dollars have been invested in direct support of the initiative. . . .

Demystifying Assessment: Learning from the Field of Evaluation

BARBARA GROSS DAVIS

The challenge confronting those undertaking assessment efforts is to make use of the extensive body of knowledge and good practices developed within the field of evaluation.

In the last four years since the assessment movement began, the following developments have occurred: (1) All but fourteen state legislatures have taken action to consider or begin campus assessment programs (National Governors' Association, 1988). Some forty states now require assessment by state law or policy (Blumenstyk, 1988). (2) Accreditation agencies are requesting assessments of student achievement as critical elements in the accrediting process. (3) The Fund for the Improvement of Postsecondary Education (FIPSE) has awarded assessment-related grants to over twenty institutions and organizations. (4) Three national conferences have been held on assessment, the most recent attracting over 1,000 people. (5) Special issues of professional journals have been devoted to assessment; in the last three years, four Jossey-Bass sourcebooks have appeared on this topic (Banta 1988; Bray and Belcher, 1987; Ewell, 1985; Halpern, 1987). (6) Offices of assessment have sprung up at colleges and universities across the country. (7) The testing industry has been aggressively developing new instruments to measure students' cognitive growth and personal development.

As others have pointed out (Ewell, 1988), there is nothing terribly new about higher education's attempt to assess itself. For decades, higher education has assessed student learning and demonstrated institutional effectiveness to external agencies. So, why the flurry of activity at this time?

Observers (Rossman and El-Khawas, 1987; Westling, 1988) have speculated on how economic, social, and political concerns have converged to create a welcome climate for assessment. First, the public perceives that college students often lack basic skills on entry and at graduation. New demands in the workplace for greater sophistication in writing, reading, and computing may have magnified college graduates' weakness. Second, the perceived failings of higher education, as documented by several books and national reports, have credited a crisis of confidence and led to calls for improving the educational system. And education, critics argue, should be judged by assessment; traditional measures of student achievement, such as course grades and retention and graduation rates, do not satisfy these critics' standards for reliability and interpretability across programs and institutions.

Political pressures have also played a role. State legislators know that "creating better schools" is a popular campaign theme, and tight budgets lead public officials to demand accountability and proof of cost effectiveness. Assessment thus becomes the lever helping states to meet their economic and social goals: "It is essential that states maintain the pressure to access despite the many vocal arguments against it" (National Governors' Association, 1988, p. 42).

In the rush to meet external demands for assessment, those involved in assessment have overlooked what the field of evaluation can contribute to their endeavors. To bring some order to the diverse literature of the assessment, this chapter analyzes assessment using the conceptualization of educational evaluation put forth by Stufflebeam (1974) and expanded by Nevo (1986). Ten questions provided the framework for this analysis:

1. What does the term *assessment* mean?

2. What is the purpose of assessment?

3. What can be assessed?

4. What kinds of questions can be asked in assessment?

5. What criteria can be used to judge the merit or worth of what has been assessed?

6. Who should be served by assessment?

7. What are the procedures for conducting an assessment?

8. What methods of inquiry can be used in assessment?

9. Who should do an assessment?

10. By what standards is assessment judged?

What Does the Term Assessment Mean?

Despite increasing nationwide attention to the topic of assessment, there is not consensus on exactly what topics and processes assessment comprises. Is the primary concern to be assessment of the performance of individual students or groups of students, the effectiveness of instructional practices, or the functioning of departments or the institution itself? Various definitions are in widespread use.

Some writers (Boyer and Ewell, 1988; Bray and Belcher, 1987; Eison and Palladino, 1988) approach assessment broadly, describing it as encompassing general activities of testing, evaluation, and documentation. For example, Boyer and Ewell (1988) define assessment as "processes that provide information about individual students, about curricula or programs, about institutions, or about entire systems of institutions." Others equate *assessment* and *evaluation*, using the terms interchangeably.

Still others view assessment narrowly, as specifically tied to student learning, knowledge, skill, and outcomes (Marchese, 1987; Jacobi, Astin, and Ayala, 1987; National Governors' Association, 1988). For this group, assessment encompasses various procedures that determine the extent to which students have met curricular goals, mastered the prescribed subject matter, and acquired the skills and characteristics essential to an educated person (Chandler, 1986). Recognizing the confusion in terminology, some researchers speak about outcomes assessment (Banta, 1988) or assessment of student learning (Adelman, 1988) when referring to assessment and student performance. But many writers simply use the term *assessment* as shorthand notation for measuring student achievement and development.

The problems in defining assessment are similar to those encountered in defining evaluation in the early years of the development of the field. Many definitions of evaluation have been proposed and used (Nevo, 1986). For example, in the 1950s evaluation was defined as the process of determining the extent to which educational objectives are being met. (Note the similarity to Chandler's definition of assessment as the extent to which individual students meet curricular goals.) In the 1960s and early 1970s, evaluation was defined as the process of providing information for decision makers (Note the similarity to Boyer's and Ewell's definition of assessment as the process of providing information about students, curricula, programs, and institutions.) More recently, a broader definition has been adopted by evaluators: Evaluation is the process of determining the worth or merit of an activity, program, person, or product (Joint Committee, 1981). The special features of evaluation, as a particular kind of investigation, include concerns with needs, description, context, outcomes, comparisons, costs, audience, utilization, and the supporting and making of sound value judgments.

It may be that the field of assessment will evolve in much the same manner. But the assessment movement seems to be making little use of what is known about evaluation. For example, a glossary of assessment terminology (Boyer and Ewell, 1988) does not include an entry for "evaluation," and few writers in assessment make reference to the body of evaluation theory and practice.

Given the lack of consensus on what constitutes assessment, we cannot be surprised that there is little agreement on the relationship between the terms *assessment* and *evaluation*. Prior to the growth of the assessment movement, those in the evaluation field sometimes used assessment as a synonym for evaluation. Even then, however, there was a sense that the two were not completely interchangeable. As Scriven (1981) points out, assessment tends to focus more on quantitative or testing approaches, as exemplified by the National Assessment of Educational Progress.

Today, one finds three stances: that evaluation is a subset of assessment, that assessment is a subset of evaluation, that evaluation and assessment are converging. The first is proffered by some in the assessment movement who consider evaluation to be the program or curricular evaluation component of assessment. But this is an inaccurate view, since evaluation encompasses more than programs and curricula.

The second view relies on a narrow definition of assessment focusing on student achievement and development. In fact, "outcome evaluation," or "impact assessment," is an accepted component of evaluation (Rossi and Freeman, 1985; Posavac and Carey, 1985), investigating the results, impact, or outcomes of a program or intervention.

If a broad definition of assessment is adopted, then assessment and evaluation begin to merge into a common effort to understand and judge the merit and worth of teaching and learning within a course, curriculum, educational program, sequence of study, department, unit, or institution.

What Is the Purpose of Assessment?

In the assessment literature, one tends to find statements of wide ranging purposes. For example, Ewell (1988) cites the following: to evaluate curricula, to demonstrate external accountability, to recruit students, to raise funds for institutions, and to change the way teaching and learning occur in individual classrooms. Jacobi, Astin, and Ayala (1987) identify these purposes of assessment: to provide information about students' change and development, to establish accountability for external agencies, to evaluate programs, to analyze cost-effectiveness, and to set goals.

From the field of evaluation comes a more meaningful, less complex, conceptually clearer way to think about the purposes of assessment. A major distinction is made between formative and summative evaluation. Formative evaluation is undertaken for the purpose of improving and developing an activity, program, person, or product. Summative evaluation is undertaken for the purposes of accountability or resource allocation (in the case of programs), for certification, selection, and placement (in the case of students), or for decisions about merit increases and promotions (in the case of faculty). Similarly, we can say that institutions undertake assessments to improve what they are doing (formative) or to make decisions about resources, institutions, programs, faculty, or students (summative). Some writers (Ewell and Boyer, 1988) have grasped the importance of the distinction, but others have overlooked it and therefore have also ignored how the purpose of an assessment influences aspects of its design and analysis.

By borrowing concepts from evaluation, we have highlighted key differences between formative and summative assessment in Figure 1.

Figure 1 Formative Versus Summative Assessment

Feature	Formative Assessment	Summative Assessment
Purpose	Improvement or development of activities, programs, products, people	Accountability, resource allocation; selection, placement, certification; pay and promotion decisions
Audience	Internal decision maker: program or department administrators; individual faculty	External decision maker: central administrators; government officials; accrediting bodies; public
Scope	Diagnostic, detailed, specific assessments	Global assessments
Procedures	Informal; narrow; specialized	Formal; comprehensive
Timing	Ongoing or during a program or sequence of study	Before and after or simply at the completion of a program or sequence of study
Sources of Information	One or more	Multiple and diverse
Emphasis	Suggestions for improvement	Overall judgments

What Can Be Assessed?

Those who adopt a broad view of assessment see all aspects of higher education as subjects for assessment: students, educational and administrative personnel, curricula, programs, departments, and institutions. Under this broad definition, assessment includes the many program reviews, self-studies, faculty evaluations, special-project evaluations, and so on that institutions routinely conduct to gather data about their effectiveness. Here are examples of such regularly scheduled activities at the University of California at Berkeley:

- Peer reviews (including student and faculty surveys as well as interview data) of all undergraduate and graduate programs conducted on a regular review cycle

- Peer reviews of the quality of teaching of every faculty member as part of the regular merit and promotion process

- Annual surveys of entering freshmen regarding students' backgrounds, interests, aspirations, and attitudes

- Placement tests in mathematics and composition used to determine students' skill levels

- Surveys of students in every class each semester about the effectiveness of the course and the teaching performance of the instructor

- Department, college, and campuswide surveys conducted periodically of graduating seniors and alumni regarding their opinion of the education they have received

- Occasional surveys of employers of graduates conducted by individual departments

- Exit interviews with students who leave the campus before graduation

- Review of ethnic diversity of applicants, enrollees, graduates, and dropouts

- Review and analysis of retention rates for students in aggregate and by various subgroups

- Formative and summative evaluation of individual support units and student services, such as the counseling center.

One would think that such information would interest public and state legislatures concerned about assessment. But these data are often overlooked, and special assessment reports are sought instead. The institutions are partly to blame in that they sometimes provide so much data in such detail, without a framework for interpreting their significance, that legislators dismiss the information as just another numbing report. There is also the problem with self-reports: If an institution prepares a negative report, its credibility is usually not questioned. But, for many external audiences, positive self-reports are highly suspect or simply not believed. The final blow against data from routine reviews and surveys is precisely that they are routine. Legislators and the public want to know what is new. The same high levels of accomplishment, reported year after year, may not satisfy external audiences. This demand for news challenges institutions that have been regularly reporting routine data to recast the information and present it as special assessment data.

Those who adopt a narrow view of assessment focus on the student outcomes of higher education. Even with such a view, there are still many possible outcomes. Virtually every human characteristic can be assessed (Baird, 1988a): knowledge, skills, attitudes, values, and behaviors. The problem, then, is not deciding what to assess but deciding how to select the outcomes to be examined. These choices depend on the values and priorities of those commissioning the assessment and those who will actually or potentially use the results (called "stakeholders" in evaluation terminology), as well as on the practical constraints of time, resources, and tools to measure outcomes.

What Kinds of Questions Can Be Asked in Assessment?

The best place to begin any investigation is to define the questions of most interest to the stakeholders—the potential users and audience. In evaluation, emphasis is placed on identifying and asking questions of most interest to decision makers, program participants, and the audiences for the evaluation. A wide range of questions are generated, refined, and narrowed down to those that can be answered given the resource constraints, the interest of the stakeholders, and the circumstances for the evaluation.

This same approach can be used to generate assessment questions. Here are some examples of questions generated, in part, by faculty members of the University of California at a conference called "Assessing the Lower Division," held at the University of California at Los Angeles, in February 1989:

1. *Who applies to and enrolls in the university, and how well prepared are these students?* For summative assessment, information about applicants and new students is a measure of an institution's quality—whether it can recruit and enroll high-ability students— and also a measure of how well the institution is enrolling underrepresented minority students. For formative assessment, information about new enrollments is critical in giving faculty an understanding of the abilities and preparation of the students they will be teaching. Measures that help answer this question include demographic characteristics of students' standardized test scores and high school performance, percentage of students in the upper 5 percent or 10 percent of their graduating class

who apply and enroll in the university, number of valedictorians and number of National Merit Scholars, and pass rates on campus freshmen placement exams in composition and mathematics.

2. *What do students learn?* The specific aspects of learning to be investigated will depend on the values and priorities of individual institutions. Here are some components of student learning, with an indication of data sources for answering the question:

   • *What type of education is represented by the courses students take?* Do the courses students take exemplify the university's concept of a good education? Source: analysis of students' transcripts to identify course-taking patterns.

   • *Does the undergraduate experience develop qualities valued in educated persons?* Such qualities might include critical thinking, problem solving, mastery of general skills, and an understanding of the contemporary world. Sources: transcript analysis; review of course syllabuses; senior theses or projects; comprehensive exams, if available; survey of faculty and students.

   • *Have students developed aesthetic interests and an appreciation of the arts?* Sources: transcript analysis; student attendance at campus museums and performing art events; number of submissions to campus arts award programs; use of campus arts facilities such as darkrooms and pottery studios; student participation in arts clubs.

   • *To what extent can students communicate in writing with clarity and style?* Sources: transcript analysis; junior-level writing exams, if offered; portfolios or collections of students' written work; student journals.

   • *What is the course withdrawal rate?* Measures: percentage of total course registrations that result in withdrawals; percentage of individual student with at least one withdrawal.

   • *How knowledgeable are graduating seniors?* Sources: Graduate Record Examination (GRE), Law School Admission Test (LSAT), and Medical College Admission Test (MCAT) test scores; senior theses, projects, comprehensive exams; external awards and recognition of students.

3. *What do students value?* Again, the priorities and values of each college and university will determine what is measured within this area. Here are some examples:

   • *To what extent do students show interest in and respect for different cultures and different points of view?* Measures: analysis of racial, ethnic, and religious incidents that indicate bias, prejudice, or stereotyping; enrollments in courses dealing with ethnic, gender, and cultural diversity; number of applicants and enrollments in study-abroad programs.

   • *To what extent are students socially responsible and involved in the community?* Measures: student participation in volunteer groups, charitable work, and the like; transcript analysis of field study courses and internships.

4. *Who is dropping out?* Through exit interviews or surveys, on e can identify the reasons students withdraw: transfer to another institution, involuntary withdrawal (health or financial reasons), voluntary withdrawal (job, marriage), or academic dismissal. Rates of attrition and retention can be calculated by major, gender, ethnicity, grade point average, and transfer status.

5. *What is the quality of undergraduate teaching?*

   • *Who teaches undergraduate courses, particularly in the lower division?* Measures: percentage of faculty who teach at least one undergraduate course per term; percentage of lower-division courses taught by faculty at each rank; percentage of undergraduate students by year in school who have had at least three regular faculty members during each term; differences among departments in allocating faculty to the lower division.

   • *How effective is undergraduate teaching?* Sources: student ratings by size of course, discipline, instructional method; alumni surveys; peer judgments of deans and faculty committees reviewing personnel cases.

   • *To what extent are faculty interested in undergraduate teaching?* Sources: course assignments by faculty teaching load and rank; faculty survey; faculty participation in instructional improvement activities.

   • *To what extent do lower-division students have opportunity for quality contact with professors?* Sources: student and faculty surveys; transcript analysis; use of office hours; number of faculty involved in advising.

   • *What is the level, nature, and quality of attention given by departments to the training of teaching assistants (TAs)?* Sources: percentages of departments that offer training for TAs; surveys of faculty and TAs.

   • *How effective are services provided to faculty and TAs for teaching improvement?* Source: evaluation of support services.

6. *What is the quality of the curriculum?*

   • *What reform efforts have taken place or are under way?* Sources: task force reports; changes in policy; comparison of catalogues before and after curriculum revision.

   • *How accessible are lower-division courses? Can students get into the courses that they need or want?* Sources: demands for enrollment; transcript analysis; student surveys.

   • *What is the effectiveness of the lower-division curriculum in satisfying students' needs to explore a diversity of subjects and to pursue a major?* Sources: materials available describing different through transcript analysis; length of drift before declaring a major; number of students who change majors; student performance in upper-division courses; student surveys.

   • *What is the quality of departments with large undergraduate enrollments?* Sources: academic program reviews; alumni surveys; surveys of faculty and current students.

   • *What are the class-size experiences of students?* Measures: percentage of lower-division students who have had at least one course each term that enrolled fifty or fewer students; percentages of lower-division students who have had all courses in their first year enrollment 100 or fewer students; percentage of lower-division students who have had at least one seminar class.

7. *How effective is the advising that students receive?* Who advises students about academic issues (selecting courses and programs of study), career options (career choices and opportunity for further education and training), and personal development (partici-

pation in extracurricular activities or job experiences)? Sources: student and alumni surveys on advisers' knowledge, availability, and rapport.

8. *How do students feel about their undergraduate experiences?* Sources: surveys of junior or seniors; counseling reports on student problems; and ombudsman reports of students' experiences and complaints.

9. *How effective are support services?* Sources: surveys of students and faculty who use particular services.

10. *What happens to students after they graduate?* Sources: alumni surveys; graduate school admissions; job placements; follow-up surveys of employers of graduates.

What Criteria Can Be Used to Judge the Merit or Worth of What Has Been Assessed?

The assessment literature is largely silent on judging worth or merit. In contrast, in evaluation a variety of criteria has been offered for judging merit, and the evaluation literature stresses the importance of using multiple criteria for judging any program, activity, service, person or object. Criteria may include the extent to which the entity being evaluated responds to identified needs of actual and potential clients; achieves national goals, ideals, or social values; meets agreed on standards and norms; outdoes or outperforms alternative objects; or achieves important stated goals (Nevo, 1986).

Judging merit does surface in discussion of value-added or talent-development assessment, which attempts, through pre- and post-testing, to estimate the portion of students' growth or development that can be reasonably attributed to specific educational experiences (the value added by particular in higher education). The assessment asks how a college education has changed students' knowledge, skills, and values, and those institutions that report greater changes are considered more successful. As Ewell (1988) points out, however, students may change greatly but still fall below acceptable standards: Are institutions to be judged primarily in terms of the amount of change or the levels students finally attain? Too, the pre-and posttest model betrays a reductive premise, the education is "addictive" rather than synergistic, multifaceted, and multicausal.

At heart, value-added and talent-development assessments are new terminology for an old fundamental issue in educational research: What are the net effects of an educational experience on students' cognitive and noncognitive development? This question has also been phrased more complexly as "What kinds of students change in what ways when exposed to what kinds of educational experiences?" (Pascarella, 1986). Yet, as the literature shows (Halpern, 1987; Pascarella, 1986; Warren, 1984; McMillan, 1988; Hanson, 1988; Baird, 1988b), reliable, meaningful value-added assessment is difficult to implement. The technical problems include the difficulties (such as regression effects, maturation effects, cohort incomparability, and so on) of measuring change and of unbundling the influence of education from other influences on student growth; the absence of reliable, valid, standardized instruments to measure meaningful educational outcomes beyond content knowledge; and the challenge of developing instruments sensitive enough to measure subtle changes in noncognitive areas.

Finally, even if we had the measures, there are the difficulties of attributing changes to the institution, its students' aptitude or prior achievements, or the quality of students' learning efforts. Research indicates that the largest effects on student growth and change are due to maturation, followed by, in order, effects due to attendance at any college, effects due to attendance at a particular college, and specific college experiences (Baird, 1988b).

Given these conceptual and technical problems, those in the assessment movement may wish to adapt the criteria used in evaluation to judge merit and worth (Nevo, 1986): fills a critical need; achieves universally recognized goals, ideals, or values; meets agreed-on standards and norms; outperforms competitors; achieves important stated goals.

Who Should Be Served by Assessment?

Many in the field of evaluation have adopted Guba and Lincoln's (1981) term *stakeholders* to refer to all the groups of persons having some actual or potential stake in the performance of the entity being evaluated. Stakeholders for an assessment might include the decision makers commissioning the investigation, policy makers with some interest in the result, state and federal officials, campus administrators, program participants, faculty, students, parents, taxpayers, and the public at large.

Baird (1988a) lists examples of the kinds of assessment questions different audiences might post about a college or university:

1. *Parents:* How likely is my child to be admitted? What is the curriculum like? What programs or facilities are available to meet my child's interests? What are the chances a student will drop out, get A's, or go on to graduate school? What is the daily experience of this college like? Is there a sense of community and a strong intellectual climate?

2. *Taxpayers:* What are the costs to the taxpayers of this institution? Is this college meeting the current and future needs of the state in the training it is providing students? Are there provisions for excellence and equity? Can students from families with limited means attend and graduate from this college? Does this college make a difference to the economy and culture of the state?

3. *Faculty:* What are the implications for the curriculum and for students of a rise in student careerism and concern for wealth? What conditions promote research among the faculty? How good is the teaching?

Baird's examples reinforce three important points stressed in the evaluation literature (Nevo, 1986) that are directly applicable to assessment: (1) An investigation can have more than one client, audience, or stakeholder; (2) different audiences may have different information needs; (3) since the questions important to different audience will affect the kind of information collected, the level of data analysis, and the form of reporting the results, the specific audiences and their specific needs must be identified at the early stages of planning the study.

What Are the Procedures for Conducting an Assessment?

Case studies of how to conduct an assessment are widely reported in the literature (Bray and Belcher, 1987; Banta, 1988; Ewell, 1985; Halpern, 1987). Typical advice includes: start small, develop incrementally, use existing data when possible, use multiple measures rather than single test scores, stress formative aspects, ensure support of top leadership, involve faculty during all phases of development and implementation, recognize and incorporate the institution's unique mission and history. In addition, descriptions of activities at the University of Tennessee, Alverno College, and Northeast Missouri State University are available (Halpern, 1987). But the assessment movement as a whole lacks a specific methodology, models, or theoretical perspectives to inform practice.

In contrast, over the last four decades the field of evaluation has evolved detailed methodologies and various models that describe processes for conducting evaluations. Though the specific steps in an evaluation may depend on the evaluator's theoretical bent, evaluators agree on the following general steps:

1. Focus the evaluation problem by defining the charge from the client and the constraints.

2. Identify various stakeholders and audiences.

3. Generate questions of interest to stakeholders.

4. Refine and limit questions through negotiation with vested parties so the questions can be addressed.

5. Determine the methodology: Specify for each question the instrument or data source (new or existing), the sample from whom data have been or need to be collected, the time frame for data collection (if gathering new date), the methods of analysis, and the intended use of the results.

6. Communicate the findings to stakeholders in ways that they can use the results.

What Methods of Inquiry Can Be Used in Assessment?

Both the evaluation field and the assessment movement make use of traditional educational research methods: tests, surveys, interviews, and observations using experimental and quasi-experimental designs. The assessment movement has concentrated primarily on these methods. In contrast, the evaluation field has developed and popularized a range of naturalistic methods and qualitative approaches (Guba and Lincoln, 1981; Lincoln and Guba, 1986; Patton, 1987) and has explored unusual methods of inquiry: jury trials, art criticism applied to educational evaluations, and modus operandi (Smith, 1981a, 1981b).

As Hutchings (1988) notes, there is a growing interest in assessment methods that give more qualitative and complete pictures of what students learn under what conditions. Here, the vitality in evaluations methodology can provide useful models.

Who Should Do an Assessment?

The assessment literature (Ewell, 1988; Mentkowski, 1988; Miller, 1988) stresses the importance of faculty involvement in each step of the assessment process. Researchers also recommended that assessment activities elicit the support and advocacy of influential opinion makers on campus. For conducting an assessment, Ewell recommends that a small separate office of assessment be set up, reporting to high-level policy makers.

Appelbaum (1988) advocates a team approach to assessment. The team must be collectively knowledgeable about relevant instructional goals, current directions in the area under study, and basic evaluation principles and practices. From the evaluation literature, one might add that the team should also include collective expertise in administration to plan and manage the effort, as well as strong interpersonal and communication skills (Davis, 1986).

By What Standard Is Assessment Judged?

The literature on evaluation utilization and evaluation standards has direct implications for assessment, but the findings have not been widely applied. For example, evaluators have developed a set of thirty standards for judging an evaluation (Joint Committee, 1981). These standards are divided into four major categories: utility (does the evaluation serve practical information needs?), feasibility (is the evaluation realistic and prudent?), propriety (does the evaluation conform to legal and ethical standards?), and accuracy (is the evaluation technically adequate?).

Regarding the utilization of evaluation, the literature (Alkin, Daillak, and White, 1979; Braskamp and Brow, 1980; Patton, 1985) identifies general conditions that promote the use of evaluation results. These include involving potential audiences in the process from the beginning; providing opportunities for ongoing discussion of findings between client and evaluator; garnering support of key administrators; ensuring that the data are valid, reliable, and credible; offering explicit recommendations; preparing brief reports that address the client's concerns; releasing results in a timely manner; and identifying one or more concerned individuals who will provide the leadership to ensure that the findings are acted on.

Conclusion

As this review has shown, evaluation has much to offer assessment. The challenges confronting those in assessment is to become familiar with and make use of the extensive body of knowledge and good practices developed within the field of evaluation. For example, from work in evaluation utilization, those facing assessment can learn how to gather information that is likely to be used, and evaluation methodology can provide models for expanding the repertoire of assessment methods in order to gain richer insights and greater understanding of the workings of higher education.

In addition, by reference to evaluation, the assessment movement may be able to defuse some of its critics who tend to view assessment as focusing solely on student outcomes. By linking evaluation and assessment, the two may merge into a common broad-based effort to understand and judge the merit and worth of higher education.

References

Adelman, C. (ed.). *Performance and Judgment*. Washington, D.C.: Superintendent of Documents, U.S. Government Printing Office, 1988.

Alkin, M. C., Daillak, R., and White, P. *Using Evaluations: Does Evaluation Make a Difference?* Newbury Park, Calif.: Sage, 1979.

Appelbaum, M. I. "Assessment Through the Major." In C. Adelman (ed.), *Performance and Judgment*. Washington, D.C.: Superintendent of Documents, U.S. Government Printing Office, 1988.

Baird, L. L. "A Map of Postsecondary Assessment." *Research in Higher Education*, 1988a, 28 (2), 99–115.

Baird, L. L. "Value-Added: Using Student Gains as Yardsticks of Learning." In C. Adelman (ed.), *Performance and Judgment*. Washington, D.C.: Superintendent of Documents, U.S. Government Printing Office, 1988b.

Banta, T. W. (ed.). *Implementing Outcomes Assessment: Promise and Perils*. New Directions for Institutional Research, no. 59. San Francisco: Jossey-Bass, 1988.

Blumenstyk, G. "Diversity Is Keynote of States' Efforts to Assess Students' Learning." *Chronicle of Higher Education*, July 20, 1988, pp. A17, A25-A26.

Boyer, C. M. and Ewell, P. T. *State-Based Approaches to Assessment in Undergraduate Education: A Glossary and Selected References*. Denver, Colo.: Education Commission of the States, 1988.

Braskamp, L. A., and Brown, R. D (eds.). *Utilization of Evaluative Information*. New Directions for Program Evaluation, no. 5. San Francisco: Jossey-Bass, 1980.

Bray, D., and Belcher, M. J. (eds.). *Issues in Student Assessment*. New Directions for Community Colleges, no. 59. San Francisco: Jossey-Bass, 1987.

Chandler, J. W. "The Why, What, and Who of Assessment: The College Perspective." In Educational Testing Service, *Assessing the Outcomes of Higher Education*. Princeton, N.J.: Educational Testing Service, 1986.

David, B. G. (ed.). *Teaching of Evaluation Across the Disciplines*. New Directions in Program Evaluation, no. 29. San Francisco: Jossey-Bass, 1986.

Eison, J., and Palladino, J. "Psychology's Role in Assessment." *APA Monitor*, September 1988, p. 31.

Ewell, P. T. (ed.). *Assessing Educational Outcomes*. New Directions for Institutional Research, no. 47. San Francisco: Jossey-Bass, 1985.

Ewell, P. T. "Implementing Assessment: Some Organizational Issues." In T. W. Banta (ed.), *Implementing Outcomes Assessment: Promise and Perils*. New Directions for Institutional Research, no. 59. San Francisco: Jossey-Bass, 1988.

Ewell, P. T., and Boyer, C. M. "Acting Out State-Mandated Assessment." *Change*, July/August 1988, pp. 40–47.

Guba, E.G., and Lincoln, Y. S. *Effective Evaluation: Improving the Usefulness of Evaluation Results Through Responsive and Naturalistic Approaches*. San Francisco: Jossey-Bass, 1981.

Halpern, D. F. (ed.). *Student Outcomes Assessment: What Institutions Stand to Gain*. New Directions for Higher Education, no. 59. San Francisco: Jossey-Bass, 1987.

Hanson, G. R. "Critical Issues in the Assessment of Value Added in Education." In T. W. Banta (ed.), *Implementing Outcomes Assessment: Promise and Perils*. New Directions for Institutional Research, no. 59. San Francisco: Jossey-Bass, 1988.

Hutchings, P. "Report on Third National Conference on Assessment in Higher Education." *AAHE Bulletin*, October 1988, pp. 3–5.

Jacobi, M. Astin, A., and Ayala, F. *College Student Outcomes Assessment: A Talent Development Perspective*. ASHE-ERIC Higher Education Report, no. 7. Washington D.C.: Association for the Study of Higher Education, 1987.

Joint Committee on Standards for Educational Evaluation. *Standards for Evaluations of Educational Programs, Projects, and Materials*. New York: McGraw-Hill, 1981.

Lincoln, Y. S. and Guba, E.G. *Naturalistic Inquiry*. Newbury Park, Calif.: Stage, 1985.

McMillan, J. H. "Beyond Value-Added Education." *Journal of Higher Education*, 1988, 59 (5), 564–579.

Marchese, T. J. "Third Down, Ten Years to Go." *AAHE Bulletin*, December 1987, pp. 3–8.

Mentkowski, M. "Faculty and Student Involvement in Institutional Assessment." Paper presented at the American Evaluation Association meeting, New Orleans, October 1988.

Miller, R. I. "Using Change Strategies to Implement Assessment Programs." In T. W. Banta (ed.). *Implementing Outcomes Assessment: Promise and Perils*. New Directions for Institutional Research, no. 59. San Francisco: Jossey-Bass, 1988.

National Governors' Association. *Results in Education: 1988*. Washington, D.C.: National Governors' Association, 1988.

Nevo, D. "The Conceptualiztion of Educational Evaluation: An Analytic Review of the Literature." In E. R. House (ed.), *New Directions in Educational Evaluation*. Philadelphia: Falmer Press, Taylor and Francis, 1986.

Pascarella, E. T. "Are Value-Added Analyses Valuable?" In Educational Testing Service, *Assessing the Outcomes of Higher Education*. Princeton, N.J.: Educational Testing Service, 1986.

Patton, M. Q. *Utilization-Focused Evaluation*. (2nd ed.) Newbury Park, Calif.: Sage, 1986.

Patton, M. Q. *Creative Evaluation*. (2nd ed.) Newbury Park, Calif.: Sage, 1987.

Posavac, E. J., and Carey, R. G. *Program Evaluation Methods and Case Studies*. (2nd ed.) Englewood Cliffs, N.J.: Prentice-Hall, 1985.

Rossi, P. H. and Freeman, H. E. *Evaluation: A Systematic Approach*. (3rd ed.) Newbury Park, Calif.: Sage, 1985.

Rossman, J. E., and El-Khawas, E. *Thinking About Assessment*. Washington, D.C.: American Council on Education and the American Association for Higher Education, 1987.

Scriven, M. *Evaluation Thesaurus*. Pt. Reyes, Calif.: Edgepress, 1981.

Smith, N. L. (ed.) *Metaphors for Evaluation*. Newbury Park, Calif.: Sage, 1981a.

Smith, N. L. (ed.) *New Techniques for Evaluation*. Newbury Park, Calif.: Sage, 1981b.

Stufflebeam, D. L. "Metaevaluation." Occasional paper, no. 3. Kalamazoo: Evaluation Center, Western Michigan University, 1974.

Warren, J. "The Blind Alley of Value-Added." *AAHE Bulletin*, September 1984, pp. 10–13.

Westling, J. "The Assessment Movement Is Based on a Misdiagnosis of the Malaise Afflicting American Higher Education" *Chronicle of Higher Education*, October 19, 1988, pp. B1–B2.

The Movement to Assess Students' Learning Will Institutionalize Mediocrity in Colleges

Ernst Benjamin

Despite the increasing adoption of assessment programs aimed at making colleges and universities more accountable for their students' learning, many faculty members believe that assessment will diminish the quality of teaching and learning.

Proponents of assessment acknowledge that poorly designed tests imposed by state mandates may have this effect, but they express confidence that appropriate programs, if developed and administered by faculty members, will prove beneficial. I am not reassured, because I believe the assessment movement misdiagnoses the problem and distracts attention from effective solutions.

Many faculty members might endorse standardized testing of basic skills or of knowledge in the student's major. But faculty support of basic-skills tests reflects disdain for the teaching of basic skills more than acceptance of the tests themselves. Faculty members, as well as most administrators and legislators, believe that students should master basic skills before college, but that if college students need instruction in such skills, it should be offered without college credit. Thus, assessment of basic skills through entrance exams, for example, is more likely to result in colleges' restricting access for the underprepared than in improving their learning.

Using entrance exams as diagnostic tools to assess students' basic skills is a better idea but of no more value than existing placement exams unless state legislatures support, and institutions and faculty members provide, instruction in basic skills. However, the state legislatures that mandate assessment rarely commit the resources needed to implement it, much less to remedy the problems assessment may identify. Worse, some who do offer increased resources say that they will increase budgets if scores improve; they don't offer funds to improve preparation. Such assessment schemes reward institutions that restrict access for those disadvantaged students who would lower average achievement levels.

Although some faculty members support using standardized exams to test students' knowledge in their majors, this would encourage instruction in only the generally agreed-upon core knowledge in the major. Hence, it would encourage students' tendency toward excessive specialization and vocationalism and diminish the opportunity the major provides for independent and analytical inquiry.

An alternative might be a standardized general-education test, which some assessment proponents have sought as a way to force faculty members to pay attention to general education. However, the use of standardized testing to compel general education would confirm the worst fears of general-education proponents and opponents alike. Such testing would encourage revision of curricula toward a "testable" general education that would sacrifice intellectual breadth and imagination in favor of rote learning.

More sophisticated assessment advocates propose that we forestall externally mandated standardization by encouraging faculty-developed and administered assessment, based on faculty-developed curricula and objectives. But that, of course, is what we already have. No undergraduate students in the world are tested as often as American students are. What, then, is the difference between assessment and our existing system of testing?

According to advocates, assessment provides a measure of learning "outcomes" or a "value added" measure based on a comparison of each student's test performance before and after instruction. But having faculty members, rather than outside agencies, design and implement the standardized tests necessary for such measures would not necessarily protect students or faculty members from the intrusive rigidity of the tests.

Some fairly reliable, less intrusive measures of achievement do exist. These include records of job placements, graduate- and professional-school placements, employer-satisfaction surveys, compilations of students' scores on such tests as the Graduate Record Examination and the Law School Admissions Test, and even graduate or alumni surveys. None of these measures is inherently objectionable; each has a specific valid use. They become objectionable, however, when their relative reliability, which grows out of their specificity, is used to validate them as measures of overall curricular and instructional achievement. Where assessment measures have a regulatory, budgetary, or even a public-relations purpose, they are likely to develop this disproportionate influence.

To avoid this danger, the most sophisticated institutions and proponents of assessment have responded to state mandates by using procedural rather than outcome measures—for example, papers, performances, exhibitions, and oral presentations that encapsulate undergraduate students' learning in their major.

But we need to know whether these student activities or "capstone" experiences are appropriate in the context of a specific program, rather than whether they satisfy an external demand for assessment. If we are going to increase the use of "capstone" activities, we ought to do so because they have educational merit, not because they are the least undesirable response to state-mandated assessment.

Finally, proponents of assessment argue that faculty-designed and administered assessment may contribute to improved teaching performance. My principal objection to this argument is the same as it is to that of the overall assessment movement: Assessment promotes a misdiagnosis of the problems of undergraduate instruction. The deficiencies of undergraduate instruction are not due primarily to poor teaching and will not be remedied by improving the teaching of individual instructors. Rather, the problems of undergraduate instruction are systemic and are best summarized as inadequate "involvement in learning."

Our students are inadequately prepared, marginally motivated, and increasingly part time not only in attendance but in attention. Some faculty members' teaching is undermined by their part-time or non-tenure-track status, by excessive teaching loads in community and some four-year colleges, and by too much emphasis on research at universities. Also, in most universities and many colleges, the lower-division undergraduates who need the most faculty involvement receive the least.

Consequently, the assessment movement threatens academic integrity in three ways. The first is budgetary. State governments demand evidence of student achievement to justify increasing higher-education budgets. Yet they ignore the erosion of instructional funding that has contributed substantially to our current deficiencies. For example, as long as inadequate financial aid causes students to work longer hours and study less, they will learn less. And as long as inadequate instructional support increases institutions' reliance on part-time and overloaded instructors, faculty members will teach less well.

The fact is, we have expanded students' access to higher education without providing the learning opportunities and instructional resources necessary to protect the integrity of the learning experience. We need to focus attention on how best to restore support for quality education, not on how to establish an assessment system that will institutionalize mediocrity in the universities as it has in the schools.

Second, the fact that many faculty members find mandated assessment offensive affects the quality of teaching and learning. Those faculty members who participate in innovative assessment programs may find the process stimulating, but those who inherit or must conform to another's test, text, and curricula will not. Ultimately, assessment requires conformity in curricula and instruction to achieve comparability.

Those who are unwilling to conform—that is, to teach to the test—include many of the most able faculty members and many whom we must recruit to the profession at a time of anticipated shortage. In making the profession less attractive to imaginative and innovative teachers, assessment will do far more to diminish student learning than to assist it.

Third, by emphasizing educational outcomes, state governments shape university curricula and priorities. As government becomes increasingly responsible for academic direction, colleges and universities will become more vulnerable to public demands and thus to additional intrusion.

The reformers who encourage us to accept state-mandated assessment so that we may shape it fail to understand this slippery slope. Governing boards and independent accrediting bodies, not state legislatures, should address institutions' need to be accountable for the quality of education they provide. State-mandated assessment is dangerous not because the requirement that universities demonstrate their quality in politically acceptable or popular terms—unmediated by the expertise of an accrediting body or the systematic procedures of a governing board—deprives universities of the safeguards that insure a balance between academic expertise and democratic direction.

The willingness of educators and politicians to overlook this serious and indefensible consequence may proceed from the laudable goal of improving students' learning. But they have turned to assessment after failing to achieve desired reforms through collegial persuasion. They have made a deliberate decision to impose on universities—using outside political support—programs and policies that had been unacceptable to administrations and faculties.

If assessment truly could remedy the inadequacies of undergraduate instruction, one might accept the intrusion as ultimately reasonable. But even at its best, assessment is only a way to diagnose known ills, not cure them. In the meantime, the preoccupation with assessment distracts attention from the real problems of how to enhance teaching and learning.

Assessment Is Doing More for Higher Education than Any Other Development in Recent History

James H. Daughdrill, Jr.

The academic assessment movement has grown out of widespread dissatisfaction with higher education. Americans want to know how much young people are actually learning in college—in short, if we are getting our money's worth. As a consequence of increasing skepticism about their effectiveness, public colleges throughout the country are under pressure from the public and state legislatures to demonstrate that they are worth the hefty investment of tax dollars.

Tennessee, for example, will spend more than $636-million on higher education during this academic year. With outlays of that magnitude, it's no wonder that some years ago the legislature decreed that a portion of the funds allotted to public institutions would be contingent on performance. Today, state institutions are able to "earn" up to 5 per cent more than their regular share of state funds by showing improvement in areas ranging from student performance (as measured by standardized tests) to alumni satisfaction (as shown by surveys).

Private institutions, though not directly tied to government purse strings, have not been exempt from accountability. Tuition increases and a series of education-bashing reports (both extensively covered by the news media) have helped make students and their families more value-conscious when it comes to choosing a college.

There are two very good reasons for institutions, especially private liberal-arts colleges, to begin developing assessment plans. First, assessment will enable them to find out whether what they're doing in the classroom is really working. Second, by having their own plans, they may escape the disastrous consequences of a national assessment program, which would subject all institutions—no matter how different—to the same standardized testing procedure.

My personal leap onto the assessment bandwagon was prompted not only by those reasons but also by the belief that assessment—even now, in its infancy—is already doing more for education, for institutions, and for faculty members than any other development in recent history.

In the first place, it is bringing the focus of higher education back where it should be—not on management or marketing or development, but on education. Professors and administrators and trustees are once again talking about teaching and learning, about how and what students learn and retain. For the first time in decades, the bottom line is education.

Since we cannot measure results until we have established what those results should be, assessment will force colleges to wrestle individually with the questions of what it is they seek to impart to their students and how they expect the students to synthesize and apply the knowledge they acquire.

63

My own institution began such a self-examination in 1986, when the board appointed a committee of faculty members, trustees, administrators, and students to develop a statement of educational goals. After meeting for more than a year, the committee concluded that, during their four years at Rhodes College, students should gain "an informed understanding of the world, cultivate an appropriate set of dispositions and sensibilities, and develop a comprehensive personal philosophy." By the time they graduate, the committee said, students should be able to think critically and creatively, communicate effectively, do research and evaluate the results, and synthesize what they learn. In addition, they should have developed a capacity for empathy and aesthetic expression. Once those goals were defined, a second committee began the task of examining each individual course to see whether the curriculum in fact imparts the agreed-upon knowledge, skills, and attributes, and if not, what to do about it. That step, as crucial as the first, will be completed by the end of this academic year.

Another argument in favor of assessment is that it will re-emphasize the critical role of the faculty in the process of education. In the mid-1960's, faculties became politicized and factionalized. Community spirit crumbled. The motto for everyone on campus—students, faculty members, and administrators alike—was "Do your own thing." Accountability was out of fashion. Professors were neither blamed nor given credit for the learning that took place. Ignored was the eternal verity that the essential ingredient in education is good teaching.

Teachers are the most important factor in learning; yet over the last couple of decades their role has been overlooked in the ratings system. Quantifiable "input" measures—the number of volumes in the library, S.A.T. scores, admission figures—are easy to get and handy to use. College guidebooks count them, institutions tout them. But the truth is, what matters is what comes out of the college experience, not what goes in, and the faculty has the primary responsibility for that outcome.

Every 10 years or so, academe shifts gears. The 1950's were the decade of the faculty, a time when there were fewer Ph.D.'s than available teaching jobs. The 1960's were the decade of the student, a time of campus unrest and open classrooms. the 1970's were the decade of the administration, a time when budgeting, planning, and management were dominant. So far, the 1980's have been the decade of the trustee, a time when competition for support has been the primary concern. I predict that the 1990's will be a time when faculty members and teaching will return to their rightful places at the heart of higher education.

Finally, I am enthusiastic about assessment because I believe it will serve to define and differentiate institutions. Grab a box of cornflakes off the supermarket shelf and you can find out immediately what you're getting. In academe, however, there are no labeling laws, no lists of ingredients that distinguish one institution from another. Scan the descriptions in several different college catalogues, and you will see what I mean.

Academic assessment will not be easy or inexpensive, particularly for the liberal-arts colleges. It is one thing to test a student's ability to type or to solve mathematical equations. It is quite another to measure his or her ability to communicate, create, or synthesize. Standardized tests administered at intervals during the four college years will be insufficient. The real proof of a college's effectiveness is to be found in its graduates. How are they using the knowledge they acquired? What are their values? How do they live their lives? Do they spend their leisure snacking on television sitcoms or feasting on good books? Are they responsible citizens, returning to the community as much as they take out of it?

My hope is that faculty members will view assessment not as a threat but as an opportunity. They will be indispensable to the whole process—from deciding what to measure and how to measure it to designing the measurement tools and evaluating the results.

If accountability is the impetus for reform, assessment will be the means for accomplishing it. By assessing the outcome of our educational programs, we will discover what is needed to improve the quality of learning for students and the quality of life for faculty members.

Assessment and Evaluation: Knowing and Judging Results

Lion F. Gardiner

Since learning is Alverno's "product," after all, the college has to assess it everywhere—just as a manufacturer applies quality control at every step.

The Volunteer Assessor at Alverno College, 1979.

This handbook is intended first of all for those college and university faculty members, administrators, and others who are charged with implementing programs of outcome assessment in their institutions or programs. Although these professionals are experienced in one or more of the academic disciplines or professions, they have not necessarily been introduced to the technical literature of educational assessment and evaluation. The primary focus of this book is on statements of intent—of missions, goals, and objectives. It is not a handbook on specific techniques of assessment and evaluation, and concepts relating to assessment and evaluation are used throughout. Therefore it is the purpose of this short chapter to help lay a brief conceptual foundation for readers unfamiliar with the important concepts.

The discussion below distinguishes among different types of assessment and evaluation and relates these processes to goals and objectives. Readers familiar with assessment and evaluation in education may choose to proceed directly to Chapter Four.

Assessment and Evaluation

The terms measurement, assessment, and evaluation in education have been used in various, often contradictory ways, and have frequently been confused. Anderson, Ball, Murphy, and Associates (1975, pp. 2–27) distinguish among the three concepts these terms represent as they are conventionally, although not universally, used in education. The usage in this handbook follows that of these authors.

Assessment is conceived as broader than simple, undimensional measurement. For example, one "measures" ability to read time from a watch, understanding of spatial relations (relationships among objects), ability to classify objects into groups, and simple computational facility (e.g., to add a column of numbers).

Assessment, however, is often considered to involve multiple traits and multiple methods. Assessment must respond to the complex realities of colleges and universities. Simple measurements are often inadequate to the task. Assessment:

. . . focuses on a number of variables judged to be important and utilizes a number of techniques to assay them. . . . Its techniques may also be multisource (data on the same variable may be collected from trainers, instructors, and course records . . .) and/or multijudge (ratings of the same trainee performance may be obtained from several assessors, whose judgments are then pooled or averaged). (p. 27)

Assessment includes not only the *collection of data,* but also "fashioning them into an interpretable form" (p. 27)—the *generation of information.*

Examples of variables that might be assessed are the among of student involvement and quality of effort on campus, the capacity of students to engage in spontaneous high-level ethical reasoning, the quality and quantity of the scholarly production of college faculty members when preparing study guides for students, student satisfaction with college, and the economic impact of an institution on its local community.

Assessment methods appropriate to the disparate goals of colleges and universities must be equally diverse: quantitative and qualitative, standardized national instruments and those developed locally by the faculty, paper and pencil tests and performances, to mention only a few.

Assessment precedes a second stage of the Study and Control process of the management cycle (Figure 1, Chapter One), evaluation. Evaluation is where judgments—value-based decisions—are made about the adequacy with which a goal or objective has been achieved (e.g., to improve, expand, or add a program; to permit progression by a student to the next course; to admit more students to a program). During the evaluation process, assessment results are judged for adequacy against prespecified standards of attainment associated with or contained in statements of goals or objectives. Is the institution (or program) achieving its goals and objectives at a satisfactory level? What changes in institutional activities should be made to permit a more nearly acceptable level of organizational results? Does a student's, or group of students', achievement represent adequate "mastery" of a skill?

Of course, assessment design should consider the evaluative decisions that will eventually be made on the basis of data collected if the data are to be capable of supporting those decisions. For example, the choice of populations to be sampled; sample number, composition, and size; standards of adequacy; and related issues should be determined carefully before actually carrying out assessment.

An important concern in any assessment is the possibility of "teaching to the test." This condition permits the "needs" of assessment to distort curriculum and instruction or other organizational activities. However, properly used, tests—and other kinds of assessments—should be based on pre-set goals and objectives that are appropriate for colleges and universities and their programs. One teaches to the *goals,* not the test. Similarly, one "tests"—or assesses—to the *goals.* It is the function of the assessment to determine goal achievement.

Technical Characteristics of Assessments

Two important technical concepts relating to the quality of assessments are used in this handbook, validity and reliability.

Validity

Validity, as traditionally understood, refers to the capacity of an *instrument* or *process* to assess a quality or variable and thus to produce data relevant to a decision. For example, a test that is *claimed* to assess students' ability to analyze a problem situation may or may not actually have the *capacity* to do so. The test may merely require for success memory of facts and not analytical skill. An *assessment* procedure that does tap the desired quality is said to be valid; one that does not lacks validity.

A second usage of validity is current today with experts in the field of assessment and evaluation. In this sense validity is a characteristic of *interpretations* placed on data derived from assessments. Is the interpretation of the data appropriate and legitimate, given the characteristics and capabilities of the assessment process employed? For example, a classroom test that exclusively asks questions requiring responses such as knowledge (involving memory alone) or low-level comprehension (see Appendix J) cannot yield information to support inferences about students' critical-thinking ability. Using this understanding of vitality, reasonable, appropriate *inferences* made about behavior on the basis of an assessment are said to be valid; unreasonable, inappropriate interpretations lack validity.

Reliability

Reliability generally refers to the capacity of an assessment instrument or process to produce *consistent* results repeatedly when used at different times or with different groups of people. A reliable assessment produces *stable* results; its results are *reproducible*. For example, given a stable level of student satisfaction with their college, a questionnaire that assesses satisfaction and that consistently produces similar results semester after semester can be said to be reliable. An assessment that critiques the performance of violinists at their senior recital by means of the ratings of three judges is unreliable if the different judges frequently disagree substantially among themselves on the quality of the performances.

Reliability is prerequisite to validity.

For more information about these and other important technical qualities of assessments refer to Anderson et al. (1975), Dressell (1976), and textbooks on assessment and evaluation. See the **Annotated Bibliography (General References and Basic Textbooks on Measurement, Assessment, and Evaluation).**

Some Important Types of Assessment and Evaluation

This handbook alludes to various types of assessment and evaluation. The sections below explain several important terms and concepts as they are used in this handbook. These descriptions should serve both to simplify understanding of the handbook and to help readers as they explore more widely in the literature on assessment and evaluation. There are many other ways of thinking about or classifying types of assessment and evaluation in education. Their description is beyond the scope of this book. Readers who wish to learn more should consult Anderson et al., 1975; Dressell, 1976; or other works described in the Annotated Bibliography under Assessment and Evaluation.

Distinctions Based on Type of Decision to be Made

Formative evaluation. Formative evaluation is evaluation made one or more times on the basis of assessment data collected *during the active life* of a program, project, or course. The purpose of formative evaluation is to provide timely feedback that can be used to modify or "form" the ongoing program and thus improve its outcomes.

> *EXAMPLE 1A:* All students participating in a new developmental academic advising program are surveyed, and a sample interviewed one month after their fall, pre-semester orientation, to assess the degree of their satisfaction with the college's (or department's) academic advising thus far. The students are specifically asked about their perceptions of the quantity and quality of their interactions with their advisors. An inadequate amount or quality of advising might be addressed with an eye toward reaching a suitable standard.

EXAMPLE 2A: A major, year-long program to develop more sophisticated writing skill among undergraduates than in the past is evaluated at the end of its first semester. The faculty want to know, compared witli the traditional writing program, how much writing the participants are doing, how many of the themes are ones they care about, what the quality is of the writing being produced, what the level is of student motivation to write, and to what degree the students perceive their experience in the program as important to their lives. On the basis of the evaluation, changes may be made to "tune" or adjust the program so its results more closely approach the standards the faculty have set.

Summative evaluation. Summative evaluation is evaluation conducted *at the conclusion* of a program, project or course. The purpose of summative evaluation is to make judgments about the adequacy, effectiveness, quality, or worth of the activity just concluded. The evaluation "sums up" the value of the activity. Summative evaluation results in decisions, for example, to continue or discontinue programs, or to certify. If the activity is to be repeated at some time in the future, however, summative evaluation may also play a useful *formative* role during the succeeding iteration.

EXAMPLE 1B: All college seniors are surveyed, and a sample interviewed, one month before graduation, to determine their perceptions of the quality of their relationships with their academic advisors and the effects of the advising program on their lives. The results may help determine whether from a student's perspective this program has had its intended effect. The evaluation results will be used to determine whether to continue the program.

EXAMPLE 2B: At the end of its two-year trial period the writing program is again evaluated and its results compared with those of the traditional program. In addition to the kinds of information developed in the formative assessment above, the experience in other, later courses of students who have completed each of the programs may be compared with an eye toward continuing and institutionalizing the program.

Note: Attributions of *causality* to actions or educational processes, based on assessment results, are underpinned by assumptions and should be made with care. See Attributing Causality to Processes below.

Distinctions Based on Type of Goal or Objective Being Assessed

Input, process, and outcome assessment and evaluation are important concepts when one is attempting to understand the quantity and quality of an institution's or program's *resources, activities,* and *results* and to determine their adequacy. The discussion below relies chiefly on Anderson et al. (1975).

Inputs into an institution are its human and non-human resources. Students, faculty members, library books, and buildings, together with their specific qualities, are all inputs. **Processes** are the activities that are chosen or designed because they are believed to be capable of achieving desired results. Processes include courses, academic advising, department meetings, a student government hearing, a swimming competition. Processes are institutional activities that use inputs to produce results, the ways and means employed to achieve desired ends. **Outcomes** are consequences, the results that are produced by processes. Among many other results, outcomes can include new student competencies developed, new knowledge produced and service to the community rendered by the faculty, university press publications, and the number of local citizens using college facilities. **Intended outcomes** are desired and planned for by the institution; **actual outcomes** are its achievements. Outcomes can be both intended—planned—and unintended. Unintended outcomes can be highly desirable, or undesirable. (See Unintended Outcomes in Chapter Five.) Sometimes outcomes become inputs and recycle through an institution. For example, knowledge of andinterest in the world, increased thinking capacity, and maturation of ethical reasoning on the part of enrolled students all become valuable inputs that can improve the campus climate and positively affect other students. A furtherbetween output and impact outcomes is made in chapter five.

There are *three* mutually supportive systems of assessment and evaluation central to effective management of institutions and programs (Figure 2).

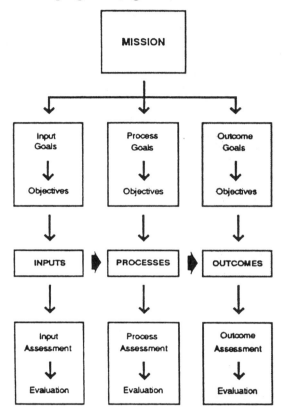

FIGURE 2   Three systems of assessment and evaluation that contribute to academic management. Simplified representation; shaded portions are included in the outcome assessment and evaluation process. Arrows show only major directions of flow.

Input assessment and evaluation collects data and analyzes it to provide information about resources—students, faculty members, non-academic staff members, physical plant—needed or being used to achieve an institution's outcomes. Input assessment and evaluation can, among other things, help (1) to identify the resources necessary to achieve desired outcomes, (2) to identify the resources actually available and their most effective use with respect to costs and benefits, (3) to determine the feasibility of outcome goals, given the resources available, and (4) to develop a process design adequate to achieve the outcomes with the available resources. Common examples of input assessment would include assessing the basic verbal and mathematical skills of incoming freshmen, determining students' learning styles, tracking the monetary gifts received by the institution, and determining patterns in the price paid for fuel.

Process assessment and evaluation can provide several types of feedback on activities during the life of a program, project, or course. (1) Process assessment can provide regular information that can permit close monitoring of institutional activities and detection of flaws in their design or implementation. In other words, process assessment and evaluation can reveal whether the *actual* processes are adequately close to the *intended* processes. (2) Process assessment can *be formative*. That is, it can provide information relatively early in a program, that may be required before decisions can be made concerning later aspects of process design. For example, a teacher may, on the basis of tests of mastery (outcomes) given early in a course, change his instructional objectives more effectively. Or a college may take a variety of actions to improve its campus intellectual climate (a process) following a process assessment that indicates to the faculty and administration a need for change. (3) Collecting data systematically as a project progresses may provide the basis for a *summative* understanding of the causes that led to, or prevented the achievement of, important outcomes.

Outcomel assessment and evaluation determine the degree to which outcome goals and objectives have been achieved. Outcome evaluation makes judgments about the adequacy of the *actual* outcomes produced compared to the outcomes *intended* and analyzes reasons for any discrepancy between the two (Dressell, 1976).

Outcome assessment and evaluations are often *summative* in nature. They help answer the question: Have the program's outcome goals been reached? Outcome assessment and evaluation can, however, also serve important formative purposes. For example, outcome assessment and evaluation can determine whether intermediate goals are being reached during the course of a program.

Although an outcome assessment process may serve an important accountability function, its primary use should be to help faculty members, administrators, and others improve their professional effectiveness. Thus, outcome assessment methods should be developed to provide, wherever possible, *both formative and summative* information. Using these methods *coupled* with process assessments can enable institutions to control the quality of their outcomes more effectively. (See Coupling; Process and Outcome Assessment below.)

Self-Study and Needs Assessment

Self-study refers to an input, process, or outcome assessment and evaluation, or some combination of these, by an institution or program of any aspect of itself. For example, self-study might examine fiscal income, programs, services, courses, cocurricular activities, student skills, or faculty scholarship. Most institutions are familiar with the self-study concept from their experiences with the regional accreditation process. A common type of self-study is a **needs assessment.** The purpose of a needs assessment is to identify systematically institutional needs or problems that interfere with goal achievement and for which fulfillment or solutions are required. Self-study information is integral to the planning process.

Of course, the aggregate of activities, forces, and influences affecting the self-study process is actually far more complex than suggested by the simple assessment-evaluation chains depicted in Figure 2. Kells' (1988) representation of an institution (Figure 3) adds to inputs, processes, and outcomes such important variables as external, environmental forces that can powerfully affect institutions, and feedback from outcome assessment that can be used to improve processes and inputs. Self-study is shown providing information to help improve institutional processes through problem solving.

Moving down through the organization to the departmental level, Figure 4 expands Figure 3 to add departmental goals, processes, and outcomes. The relationships among these components are shown as they interact with each other at their own level, but also with their corresponding institution-level components. Departmental goals and objectives should flow from institutional; departmental processes interact with those outside the department; departmental outcomes contribute to the achievement of institutional goals.

The assessment and evaluation of outcomes is a form of self-study and can be employed to reveal needs and call attention to important problems for which solutions should be sought. Kells

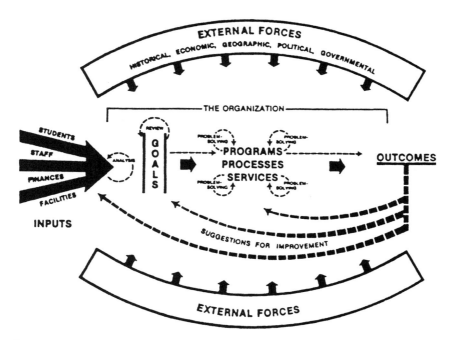

FIGURE 3 A linear systems model showing the institution (organization) and its environment. Broken lines illustrate the self-study components, including goal review and outcome assessment and evaluation. From *Self-Study Processes: A Guide for Postsecondary and Similar Service-Oriented Institutions and Programs* (p. 19) by H.R. Kells, 1988, New York: American Council on Education-Macmillan. Copyright 1988 by American Council on Education and Macmillan Publishing Company. Reprinted by permission.

(1988) provides a self-study manual that can be of considerable assistance to institutions and programs involved in outcome assessment. Kaufman and English (1979) and Witkin (1984) describe the needs-assessment process in detail. See the **Annotated Bibliography (Self-Study, Needs Assessment).**

Attributing Causality to Educational Processes

A major justification for the national interest in outcome assessment is to help institutions develop better information about themselves and thereby understand and improve their results. That is, colleges and universities can use assessment data to modify their processes and thus improve the quality and quantity of their outcomes. However, outcome assessment, and evaluation based upon it, is only one component of the Study and Control phase of academic management (Figure 1, Chapter One). Outcome assessment reveals *whether* and *how much* of a desired outcome is being produced, not *why*. A next step in the self-improvement effort is to attempt to identify *why* results are (or not) being produced.

If outcome assessment data are to be fully useful in improving institutional performance, the institution (or program) should understand as specifically as possible how its activities or processes produce their effects. **Causality** should be assigned to specific processes wherever possible. However, attributing causality to educational processes can at times be difficult indeed. Consider as an example undergraduate education. Colleges are complex organizations composed of many different people who engage in quite dissimilar tasks and interact with students in diverse ways. Many of the effects of these interactions are unobserved and even unintended. Some changes in students

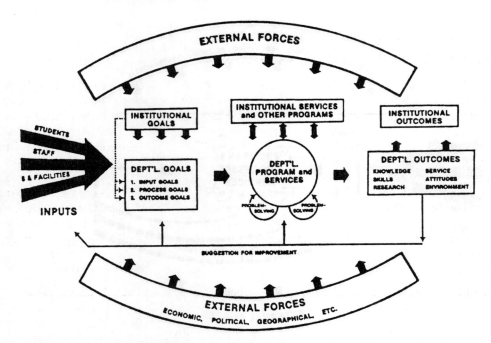

FIGURE 4 A linear systems model of a department of program. Diagram shows interactions between the department or program and other departments, together with some components of the self-study process. From *Self-Study Processes: A Guide for Postsecondary and Similar Service-Oriented Institutions and Programs* (p. 97) by H.R. Kells, 1988, New York: American Council on Education-Macmillan. Copyright 1988 by American Council on Education and Macmillan Publishing Company. Reprinted by permission.

result from natural, age-related maturation; many derive from the pre-college effects of home and school; still others result from employment or other off-campus experiences. Is the curriculum having it's desired effects or is the assessed level of student development due to other, possibly unknown factors?

To be fully confident that a particular educational process is responsible for a specific outcome one would in many cases need to conduct a controlled study. A controlled study is an experiment that incorporates in its design pairs of samples containing both "experimentals," samples in which conditions are special and *experimental*, and "controls" in which the process is *conventional* and unaffected in any way by the experimental "treatment." The pairs of samples are *equivalent* in all significant aspects except for the presence (in the experimentals) or absence (in the controls) of the special experimental treatment. For example, to evaluate the effects of a special thinking-across-the-curriculum program on the problem-solving abilities of graduates, one group, or set of groups, of students should experience the new curriculum and another, *equivalent* group, or set of groups, should go through the educational process of the regular curriculum. By comparing the assessed outcomes of these two possibly quite-different processes, experimental and conventional, one may be able to assign to the new process responsibility for superior outcomes produced in the experimental group or groups, or decide that the experimental process has no effect or even negative effects.

Process assessment should be as specific as necessary and, whenever possible, solidly based on education theory that suggests what activities or process might reasonably be expected to produce the outcomes desired, and how these activities should be structured. Needless to say, theory should also have guided the original design of the educational process during the planning stage when activities were first being selected.

Coupling the Assessment and Evaluation of Processes and Outcomes

Assessment and evaluation of actual institutional outcomes can reveal the extent to which results match intentions as described in an institution's (or department's or program's) outcome objectives. Outcome assessment reveals *what* results and *how much* of them the institution has. However, as observed in the previous section, outcome assessment cannot reveal *what* these results have been achieved. Which processes are responsible for the outcomes? Is the institution itself responsible for the outcomes or are they due to other factors?

By routinely *coupling* outcome assessment with process assessment an institution or program can attempt to link more effectively its existing processes to its actual outcomes. Process assessment and evaluation can indicate whether the intended processes, developed to produce the outcomes, have been implemented properly and are functioning as desired. A discrepancy between intended and actual outcomes may indicate that they are not. On the other hand, such a discrepancy may also indicate inadequacy in the design of the intended process: the design may depart from good practice in education as suggested by theory, or the theory itself may be inadequate.

> A recognition of the critical need for process information to help explain an outcome(s) represented a landmark in the professional development of evaluators. Program effects could not be evaluated in the absence of data which described explicitly the program character. Without any hard data on the character and intensity of program delivery, the only input which will serve as process is program inclusion, and there is no reason to believe that mere inclusion leads to change. . . . (Halasa, 1977, p. 56)

In making the case for combining from the start of planning outcome and process assessments and evaluations, Judd (1987, p. 24) has this to say:

> . . . Some (Cronbach et al., 1980; Cronbach, 1982) have argued that the most important function of evaluation research is to modify treatments [(processes)] so that they achieve their desired goals more efficiently and effectively. If this is a primary evaluation goal, them process evaluations are a necessary addition to outcome evaluations. Ideally, both outcome and process evaluations would be combined in a single research endeavor.

As demonstrated in the previous section, establishing a tightly linked chain of causality for specific educational outcomes is often difficult or impossible. For example, a student's achievement of certain knowledge or skills is dependent upon a number of factors. Involved may be the quality of instruction, prerequisite knowledge or skill upon entry into the institution or program, student attitude toward learning, quality of the psychological and physical environment, and probably Clearly, some of these-variables lie beyond the institution's control. However, some factors, such as instructional quality *can* be under the institution's control and are known on the basis of empirical studies (e.g., Bloom, 1976) to affect learning strongly. Therefore, if an institution's *actual* student learning outcomes do not match its intentions, it makes sense to examine the instructional processes (e.g., classroom instruction, academic advising, cocurricular experiences) with an eye toward possibly modifying them. Are students attending classes? Are instructional methods appropriate to the curricular goals? How many students visit their own advisors each semester? How many times do they visit? How much time do they spend on an average visit? What happens during these meetings?

Taken together with an *input* assessment that can reveal important qualities of both the students and the faculty, and a comprehensive *outcome* assessment that demonstrates results in adequate detail, *process* assessment can provide a faculty administration with a powerful base of the management information it needs to plan effectively for change.

Process assessment, like outcome assessment, can be of many types. It may involve, for undergraduate education, studying faculty or student opinions of what is happening on campus. It may also require a careful look at how closely the characteristics of the curriculum, instruction, academic advising, and other important activities compare to what is considered by experts to be good professional practice today. Expert opinion is in many cases easily accessible by consulting general review works such as *The Modern American College* (Chickering and Associates, 1981—student development in college, among other things); *Developmental Academic Advising* (Winston, Miller, Enders, Grites, and Associates, 1984—academic advising); *Handbook on Undergraduate Curriculum* (Levine, 1978—undergraduate curriculum); *Student Services: A Handbook for the Profession* (Delworth, Hanson, and Associates, 1989—student services) and *Increasing Student Retention* (Noel, Levitz, Saluri, and Associates, 1985—retntion of undergraduate students in the institution). In addition, one might read the series of critical national reports on higher education that have appeared in the last several years, such as *Integrity in the College Curriculum: A Report to the Academic Community* (Project, 1985) and *Involvement in Learning: Realizing the Potential of American Higher Education* (Study Group, 1984). These publications enumerate many of the qualities shown to be important for, for example, effective classroom learning, academic advising, or campus psychological climate ("campus ecology"), qualities that can motivate to learning and persistence in college, and thus to significant change in students.

These desirable institutional qualities can provide the raw materials from which a process assessment can be designed that can probe the educational activities of the institution. The assessment should be sufficiently detailed if it is to produce useful information. For example, a questionnaire that asks students to rate by means of a single item the quality of the instruction they have received may be appropriate as a general, global indicator of their perceptions. However, such a question can do little to inform the faculty of the degree to which their instructional process conforms to accepted professional practice. The students doubtless have little knowledge of such things. If the students rate instruction highly on this single, broad question, one does not know if this result is merely due to their perception that the instruction is superior to that which they received in high school or, although instruction is pedestrian, it conforms to what they are familiar with. If they rate their instruction less highly, one still does not know what, if anything, is wrong and should be changed. Student respondents may be reacting negatively to sophisticated but unfamiliar modes of instruction that require them to think rigorously and do not permit easy solutions to difficult problems.

Instead of asking only one broad, general question about instruction, a series of questions about perceptions could be asked. These questions might explore, for example, the perceived presence in courses and clarity of written goals and specific, instructional objectives; relative emphasis placed on, for example, thinking-skill development, as contrasted with memory of factual content alone; amount of active student involvement in learning; amount of out-of-class contact with instructors; and demonstration by instructors of both the theoretical and practical value of what is to be learned. Other, "hard," supporting data about courses might also be collected.

These and other questions could emerge from the literature on instruction. Taken together with student responses to questions about other important areas, faculty and administrator perceptions, and hard data collected on actual practices, a valuable integrated base of information about actual institutional processes can become continuously accessible. Systematically examining, along with instruction, a series of other areas may enable one to paint a vivid picture, with adequate resolution of detail, to help the members of a faculty or administration to understand the educational experiences of their students.

The primary purpose of this handbook is to assist in laying the foundation for the design of effective outcome assessments and evaluations. However, the **Annotated Bibliography (Assessment and Evaluation)** lists references that can help in developing other types of assessments as well.

Using Assessment and Evaluation to Improve Outcome Achievement

In any organization results are what count. Inputs of high quality—for example, students, faculty members, physical plant, and fiscal support—count for little without results—desired outcomes produced. Outcomes are specified by goals and objectives, and are normally derived from an institution's mission. Effective production of results presupposes knowing what these result *should be*. Planning should identify specific outcomes that can be expected to occur, either from routine institutional processes or, should the organization take a new tack, from innovative, strategically oriented activities. "It is not sufficient, for example, simply to state that the institution has an opportunity to attract students by establishing new majors. The specific outcomes that may result from pursuing this opportunity must be anticipated" (Horner, 1979, p. 18). Effective management of organizational processes also presupposes knowing to what degree desired outcomes are being achieved. This is where outcome assessment comes in.

Assessment as it is now being implemented in colleges and universities across the country can be an expensive process in staff and student time and energy, not to mention other costs such as for materials and computer time. In most cases these assessment activities can probably be justified only if they lead to significant improvements in an institution's outcomes.

Most of this handbook deals with the formulation of mission statements, goals, and objectives—planning processes that ordinarily precede assessment and evaluation of results. In Chapters Six and Eight goals and objectives are connected in very specific ways with the processes of assessment and evaluation.

This section attempts to describe more explicitly the respective roles of mission statements, goals, and objectives, especially the assessment and evaluation of goal achievement, in the process of institutional improvement. The principles described here apply to all sectors of academe and to activities within both an institution and its various subunits: the education and training of undergraduate and graduate students; faculty research, scholarship, and creative expression; an academic department, a dean's office, a buildings and grounds department; a college as a whole, a program, an individual member of the staff, or a student.

Chapter One described a cyclical representation of management in a college or university (Figure 1). In this model the results of the Study and Quality Control phase were fed into the Planning phase where, in an attempt to improve outcomes, modifications were made in current institutional procedures. Figures 3 and 4 earlier in this chapter elaborated on this simple cyclical model, bringing in other factors and processes, and demonstrating a higher, more realistic level of complexity for both the institution and its departments.

This section will take a closer look at the specific contributions that can be made to institutional and programmatic improvement by outcome and process assessment and evaluation. Undergraduate general education will be used as an example. Figure 5 outlines one conception of the overall performance improvement cycle and shows how various aspects of an institution or program fit together.

Figure 5 portrays selected aspects of the process and specifically relates the mission, goals, and objectives to assessment and evaluation used to improve organizational outcomes. The institution's (or program's) mission gives rise to **input goals and objectives** that specify the kinds of students the institution or program intends to serve. **Outcome goals and objectives** describe the end results whose achievement will be sought with these students, in this example, specific student characteristics upon graduation. **Process goals and objectives** describe the activities or means that will be used to achieve the desired outcomes.

There are in Figure 5 three major influences on the design of the **intended process: students, intended outcomes** for these students, and **education theory.** To be successful in achieving student outcomes an institution or program should have detailed knowledge of its students. It should know their characteristics at entry and, through outcome assessment, should continuously track their development in response to the **actual educational processes** the institution develops. **Input assessment and evaluation** of student characteristic on entry can provide information about important qualities such as their level of knowledge about the world and themselves; misconceptions concerning important phenomena (Helm and Novak, 1983); reading, writing, speaking, and listening skill; thinking and problem-solving skill (Segal, Chipman, and Glaser, 1985); quantitative ability; learning style (Claxton and Murrell, 1987); attitudes and values toward the college experience; and academic and career goals.

These student input characteristics, together with the intended outcomes desired by the faculty, provide the basis for selecting where possible from education theory the assistance required to guide the design of effective educational processes. Education theory can also provide guidance to determine, for example, the knowledge, skills, and attitudes necessary for the faculty and other professional staff members to participate in and effectively control the educational process.

As suggested by Figure 5, the effects on colleges and universities of unclear goals, or processes that are only tenuously linked to educational theory, can be substantial. The result may be actual outcomes that are only to a limited extent affected by institutional processes widely assumed to cause them. For example, unclear goals may mean:

> . . . that students are only minimally affected by their educational experience because the experience itself is not cohesive. This would appear to be the case particularly in those institutions that have no or minimal core requirements. Here *the educational process is not in control of the institution. . . .* If we desire tighter coupling or control of the student experience, then there has to be closer organizational control through more extensive requirements and greater articulation of programs. (Hall, 1981, pp. 46–47, emphasis is added)

More carefully and explicitly stated outcome goals and objectives can, among their other benefits, suggest "requirements" that are significant and whose purpose is clear to everyone, and aid in designing effective articulation among an institution's activities and programs. Staying close to modern knowledge of how student development occurs can produce organizational processes that should generally have the good effects desired, daily life of the institution? A question of quality and performance that is related to the comparison of intended and actual outcomes is one of value added. Are the intended and actual outcomes at levels that indicate that significant growth is occurring in students beyond their level upon entry into the institution? How does one know?

The Performance Improvement Cycle

Figure 5 illustrates a performance improvement cycle where both actual outcomes and the institutional processes thought to produce them are continuously monitored. These actual results, determined by outcome assessment, are in each case compared with what was intended. If actual outcomes are judged inadequate, processes may be modified to yield a more satisfactory level of outcomes. For example, process assessment and evaluation can reveal a need for new faculty instructional skills, a need that might be addressed through a faculty development program. Improved faculty moral, newer equipment, better facilities, additional secretarial support for the faculty, and many other needs may be revealed. Thus, a cycle of performance improvement is established, which, if well designed and systematically and continuously used, can through operational planning help control the institutional processes and thus improve the results.

How closely does the institution's actual process conform to accepted expert professional practice, presumably the intended process? To what extent is current theory being actualized in the daily life of the institution? A question of quality and performance that is related to the comparison of intended and actual outcomes is one of value added to students by the institution or program.

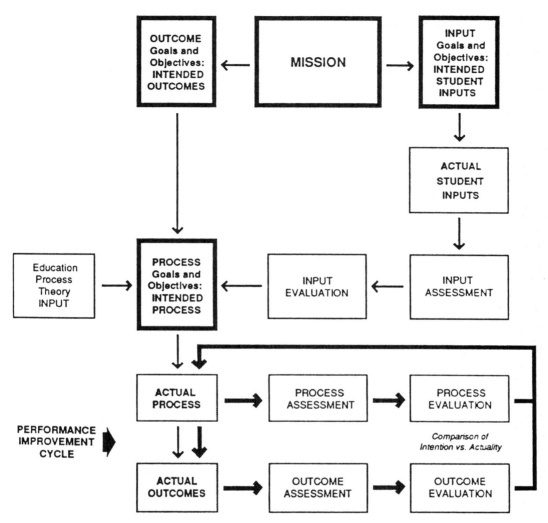

FIGURE 5 A performance improvement cycle: Using assessment and evaluation to improve outcome goal achievement for institution or program. Undergraduate or graduate education is used as an example. Selected organizational features and relationships are shown. Dark arrows indicate major performance improvement processes. Intended results are in heavy boxes; actual results are shaded.

Are the intended and actual outcomes at levels that indicate that significant growth is occurring in students beyond their level upon entry into the institution? How does one know? **Value-added assessment** is assessment that attempts to determine if this institutional or programmatic effect is present.

> To understand the actual effects of a given instructional process, however, only one type of comparison must be accomplished: that between student profiles at the beginning of the process and at its conclusion. More importantly, only the comparison between before and after will provide the kind of information needed to intervene in and improve the instructional process. (Ewell, 1984, p. 20, emphasis original)

The level of intended outcomes should be influenced not only by professional judgment of what students should be like upon graduation, but by an input assessment of the actual knowledge, skills, attitudes, values, and other important characteristics of the students when they enter the institution. This entry level should be regularly compared with actual outcome achievement in an attempt to determine the value added to its students by the institution. Baird (1988), Northeast Missouri State University (1984), and Terenzini (in press) discuss the value-added concept.

Endnotes

1. The literature on assessment in higher education uses both the singular "outcome" assessment and the plural "outcomes" assessment interchangeably and inconsistently, sometimes in the same publication. In this handbook the singular form is used throughout to maintain a consistent parallelism to the professional use of input assessment and process assessment. Neither *of* these terms is used in the plural.

Trends in Evaluation

ERNEST R. HOUSE

When I began a career in evaluation more than 20 years ago, I tossed all the papers I could find about the topic into a small cardboard box in the corner of my office and read them in one month. Since that time, program evaluation has been transformed from a small, sideline activity conducted by part-time academics into a professionalized minor industry, replete with its own journals, awards, conventions, organizations, and standards. Evaluation even has its own entry in the *Dictionary of Modern Thought* (Bullock, Stallybrass, & Trombley, 1988). During this time, both the structural basis and conceptual underpinnings of the field have changed dramatically. Structurally, evaluation has become more integrated into organizational operations, and conceptually, evaluation has moved from monolithic to pluralist notions, to multiple methods, criteria, and interests.

Evaluation is usually defined as the determination of the worth or value of something, in this case of educational programs, policies, and personnel, judged according to appropriate criteria, with those criteria explicated and justified. At its best, the evaluation of educational and social programs aspires to be an institution for democratizing public decisions by making programs and policies more open to public scrutiny and deliberation. As such, it should serve the interest not only of the sponsor but of the larger society and of diverse groups within society. Of course, evaluation has not always lived up to its own noble aspirations.

Structural Changes

The strongest stimulus to development was Lyndon Johnson's Great Society legislation, which, although not capable of changing American society as a whole, certainly transformed educational research. At Senator Robert Kennedy's insistence, the Elementary and Secondary Education Act of 1965 mandated evaluation of programs for the disadvantaged, and this mandate spread to all social programs and beyond (McLaughlin, 1975). Before 1965, evaluation meant testing or curriculum evaluation, and a handful of measurement people struggling to come to grips with the import of the new curricula. After 1965, the field resembled the early California gold camps, with large numbers of individuals from many disciplines straggling in to offer their ideas about how evaluation should be done. In addition to measurement and content specialists, psychologists, sociologists, administrators, and even a few philosophers came in large numbers. Although initially dominated by psychology's view of research, a new brew of people, ideas, and problems were simmering.

The field became multidisciplinary, with separate traditions and multiple histories of development. Educational evaluators usually start their historical accounts with Ralph Tyler, psychologists with David Campbell, and sociologists with Edward Suchman. Previous experience with testing and curriculum development gave educational evaluators a head start, and they have been among the most influential theorists in the melded evaluation field. This is an unusual accomplishment for researchers in education, who rarely are accorded equal status with social scientists.

From this strange melange, several major schools of evaluation emerged: Illinois, with its long experience in measurement and curriculum development; Northwestern, with its strong experimental design; Western Michigan, with its focus on decision-making; UCLA, with the federal research and development center; and Stanford, with a cross-disciplinary effort. Projects multiplied, evaluation models proliferated, and new organizations came into being. The evaluation field lived in intellectual and entrepreneurial ferment for more than a decade—until the cuts in social programs. The Reagan years brought fewer opportunities for evaluation, at least on an external, contractual basis, and the field of evaluation entered a more sober, sedate existence, quite distinct from the gold rush days.

During the quiet decade of the eighties, other transformations became apparent as well. Evaluation had become too important to be left to the evaluations, and large bureaucracies developed their own evaluation offices. Not only large school districts and state departments of education, but also organizations such as the F.B.I., the Food and Drug Administration, and the General Accounting Office hired internal evaluation staffs. These internal units posed novel questions of credibility and procedure, for much evaluation theory had been constructed on the basis of contractual relationships between external evaluators and the organization. To whom are the internal evaluators responsible? How public should their work be? What scientific controls are suitable? A new set of issues emerged as the structural base of the field shifted.

In addition, the new school reforms initiated by state legislatures during the Reagan years brought a renewed emphasis on standardized achievement testing for purposes of centralized accountability. Increasingly, tests were employed more as instruments of discipline than of diagnosis. William Bennett's Wall Chart became a report card for the nation's schools without benefit of research design. Interpretation of test results become overtly political, with ideology supplying the putative causes for educational decline or resurgence. The curriculum itself began reflecting what the tests emphasized. Educational evaluators, who thought they had moved beyond the test score as the sole criterion of success, were faced with even more testing than before.

Conceptual Changes

Between 1965 and 1990, the methodology, philosophy, and politics of evaluation changed substantially, partly in response to the structural transformations. Evaluation moved from monolithic to pluralist conceptions, to multiple methods, measures, criteria, perspectives, audiences, and even multiple interests. Methodologically, evaluation moved from a primary emphasis on quantitative methods, in which the standardized achievement test employed in a randomized experimental control group design was most highly regarded, to a more permissive attitude in which qualitative research methods become acceptable. Mixed data collection methods are now routinely advocated in a spirit of methodological ecumenicalism. Having achieved legitimacy within the evaluation community, qualitative evaluators have begun to quarrel among themselves.

Philosophically, evaluators ceased to believe their discipline was value-free and realized their practice entailed promoting the values and interests of some groups over others, though they were by no means clear on what to do about this discovery. They struggled with the seemingly conflicting demands of being scientific on the one hand and being useful on the other. Politically, evaluators moved from a position in which they saw themselves as technical experts opposed to the evils of politics to a position in which they admitted evaluation itself was an activity with political effects. These conceptual changes were stimulated by the rapidly evolving social context, as the United States itself changed character.

Following World War II, the United States achieved a preeminence in world affairs that had rarely been matched in history. In what Hodgson (1976) called the "ideology of the liberal consensus," Americans believed that their system of free enterprise had a revolutionary potential for social justice, that the economy could produce enough for everyone so that conflict between social classes, indeed social classes themselves, could be eliminated, and that social problems could be solved like industrial problems. The problem would be identified, solutions would be generated by government (enlightened by science), resources would be applied, and the problem would be solved. The key to this revolutionary system was ever-increasing economic productivity, which could provide enough for all.

In early formulations, evaluation was assigned the task of discovering which programs worked best, such as Elementary Secondary Education Act (ESEA), Head Start, and Follow Through. Most evaluators thought that social science would point to the clear causes of social problems and to interventions for overcoming them, that these interventions would be implemented and evaluated in ways that provided unambiguous answers, that these findings would be greeted enthusiastically by managers and policy makers, and that the problems would be solved. They were to be disappointed on all counts (Cook & Shadish, 1986).

The methodology for best accomplishing this task was deemed to be the experiment, lauded in seminal works: "This chapter is committed to the experiment: as the only means for settling disputes regarding educational practice, as the only way of verifying educational improvements. . . . (Campell & Stanley, 1963, p. 2). This rationale for strong designs was carried forward in federal policy for many years, leading to what Scriven (1983) has called the doctrines of managerialism and positivism. That is, studies were conducted for the benefit of managers of programs, and evaluators acted as value-neutral scientists who relied on the accepted methods of the social sciences to protect against bias. Evaluations were primarily experimental, quasi-experimental, or survey in methodology, utilizing quantitative outcome measures to meet the demand for surrogate measures for economic growth.

Mixed Methods and the Unraveling of Consensus

Evaluators soon encountered many problems in these large-scale quantitative studies that were unexpected and not easily surmountable. Programs varied greatly from one site to another, so that a program such as Follow Through that performed well on one site did not do well on another. Statistical models, such as analysis of covariance, overadjusted or underadjusted. Participants squabbled among themselves about the purposes of the different programs. Tests suitable for measuring the outcomes of one program did not seem appropriate for another. Additionally, most of the reform programs did not have powerful effects. The evaluations proved far more equivocal in providing definitive answers than anticipated. All in all, discovering solutions to social problems was considerably more difficult than originally envisioned.

Furthermore, the social consensus began unraveling. Martin Luther King, Jr., who began his civil rights crusade as a devout affirmation of the American dream, ended his life in disillusionment and assassination in 1968. Dissident groups marched in the streets, not only for civil rights and against the Vietnam War, but also for a number of other causes. These causes included feminism, black power, gay liberation, and ecology. The national economy staggered, with median family income reaching a peak in 1973, decreasing 6% by 1984, and becoming more unequal in distribution (Levy, 1987). Something was wrong, even with the economic pie. What had begun as an era of social consensus dissolved into an age of conflict and diversity.

This unraveling of the social consensus was reflected in evaluation methodology. If diverse groups wanted different things, then collecting the views of people in and around the programs themselves seemed to make sense. Qualitative methodology useful for obtaining the views of participants came into vogue. Qualitative methods had long been employed in anthropology and sociology, but had been judged to be too subjective for use in program evaluation. Led by evaluations like Robert Stake an Barry MacDonald, qualitative methodology developed a following, a practice, and eventually research rationales. At the same time, many evaluators remained fully committed to quantitative methods as the methods of choice, and the battles between quantitative and qualitative advocates were hard fought in the seventies (Boruch & Riecken, 1975; Eisner, 1979). Gradually, after considerable dispute, a rapprochement was achieved in which most theorists advocated mixed methods (Cronbach, 1982).

Even so, it is still the case that the quantitative or qualitative distinction is a major mark of identity for evaluators. In a multidimensional scaling exercise contrasting 14 evaluation theorists, Williams (1989) found that the major theoretical issue on which they were differentiated was qualitative versus quantitative methodology. The second dimension was accountability versus policy orientation. This dimension was distinguished by whether evaluation should be used to judge programs and personnel for the purposes of holding them accountable, or whether it should be used in a less judgmental way to inform. The third dimension was client participation versus nonparticipation, that is, the degree and manner in which clients should be involved in the evaluation.

The methodology debate, now 20 years old, eventually spread to issues other than legitimacy and to the areas of educational research. Recent debate concerns whether quantitative and qualitative methods are commensurable. Some theorists see quantitative and qualitative methods as representing fundamentally different ways of viewing the world whereas others see the different methods as being essentially compatible (Guba & Lincoln, 1982; Smith, 1983). Most evaluators accept the view that quantitative and qualitative methods are complementary, if not fully commensurable, though no one has shown exactly how disparate methods can be melded together. A related issue is what standards are appropriate for qualitative studies and whether standards can be general ones or must be derived from parent disciplines (Howe & Eisenhart, in press).

Underlying these disputes is the conflict over the nature of causation itself. Cronbach (1982) has challenged the standard conception, arguing that social phenomena are far less predictable than the standard formulation would imply and that traditional notions of internal and external validity must be redefined in such a way that people using evaluation findings should make their own judgments as to the utility of the information. In his view, external validity is partially dependent on the users' judgments in context, and is more important than internal validity. These ideas have yet to be assimilated and are certain to provoke extensive debate.

Utilization of Findings

Another area of interest during the past 10 years has been utilization of evaluation findings. The idea that program managers would readily accept the findings of evaluations and adjust the findings of evaluations and adjust or terminate their programs accordingly was not supported by the course of events. Debate has ranged as to what extent findings are ever used, with Weiss (1988) contending that instrumental uses, that is, revisions of programs as a direct result of the evaluation, rarely occur. She contends that enlightenment, in which results are incorporated gradually into the users overall frame of reference, is the matter in which findings are used, if at all.

In contrast, Patton (1988) argues strongly for the viability of instrumental use, contending that findings will be used if properly presented. Some of these differences may reside in the level of government at which attention is focused. Changes seem to come irregularly at the federal level, in line with political and ideological forces, whereas change in local school districts seems to be more instrumental (Smith, 1989). An issue on which evaluators do agree is that if evaluations are to be useful, they must provide better descriptions of the programs and their context.

An emerging idea is that of misuse of findings. The original debate was about use and nonuse of evaluation results. However, results from poorly conceived studies have frequently been given wide publicity, and findings from good studies have been improperly used. Alkin (1990) has introduced a taxonomy of misuse of evaluation results in which use and misuse lie on opposite ends of a scale with nonuse in the center. The fact that so much standardized achievement testing is reported to the public in general and interpretation left to the media or government officials makes misuse particularly salient.

In fact, the professional standards for evaluation, developed by a committee led by Daniel Stufflebeam, devoted considerable space to issues of misuse, but the context in which evaluation results are presented does not lend itself to the employment of such standards, even though they are widely accepted in the evaluation community (Joint Communittee, 1981). How misuse can be curtailed or circumvented is by no means clear.

The Role of Values

The increasing social conflict of the past two decades throws the problem of values into prominence. Where do the values come from in an evaluation? The act of public evaluation requires that some criteria of merit be established and that these criteria be justified. Typically, the stated program goals have served as the source of criteria, with the evaluator assessing whether the problem has met its goals. Furthermore, by taking the program manager as the client for the evaluation, the evaluator could act on what was important to the manager.

However, several theorists challenged this acceptance of managerial goals as the essence of evaluation. Scriven in particular worked out the logic of evaluation in general terms, contending that the question Is x good (bad, indifferent)? and its variants (How good is x? Is x better than y?) are the prototypical evaluative questions, and the answering these questions requires identifying and validating standards of merit for x and discovering x's performance on dimensions that are merit-related (Scriven, 1980). According to this reasoning, the program goals themselves must be assessed. For example, a responsible evaluator would not accept General Motor's contention that the best car is the one that earns the highest profit as the criterion for evaluating cars.

This general logic still leaves open the question of where the particular criteria of merit come from. One can say in general that criteria are derived from what is appropriate for things of this kind. For example, one would not say that an educational program which warped personality and retarded intellectual growth was a good educational program, regardless of whether the developers wanted this effect. Given a particular entity in a particular context, criteria of merit which are not arbitrary can be justified. The fruit of this reasoning is that evaluative judgments are not arbitrary any more than is a descriptive statement thay an elephant is large compared to her animals, but small compared to an office building.

Of course, the social world is not simple. For complex entities like educational programs, there are multiple and often conflicting criteria of merit. There is immediate retention versus long-term recall, knowledge of facts versus critical thinking, more history versus more math. Furthermore, people do not always want the same things from public programs. Their values, and in fact their interests, differ. A program good for one group may not be good for another. Yet for the practicing evaluator, there is no choice but to make a choice of criteria of merit.

Many choose the traditional measures of educational achievement, believing that those best reflect overall interests. Others contend that parents, students, administrators, teachers, and citizens should be enlisted in defining what is important for the evaluation, by soliciting opinions from them, by attending to them as audiences, or even by engaging them in the conduct of the study itself. Multiple criteria, multiple perspectives, multiple audiences, multiple interests—pluralist conceptions, reflecting the change from consensus to pluralism that has occurred in the larger society.

Of course, having multiple criteria does not solve the problem of how to combine these multiplicities into overall judgments. How does one put together the results of different methodologies, for example? How does one combine several perspectives? How does one adjudicate conflicting group interests? On these issues there is a little agreement. Some evaluators believe that they themselves should make these judgments, others that they should only present the findings and have the various audiences make their own judgments. Still others propose ways of resolving conflicting interests by invoking techniques like cost-effectiveness analysis (Levin, 1983), by appealing to procedures like negotiated agreements, or by employing explicit theories of justice (House, 1980).

The Role of Politics

Over the years evaluation has come to been seen as political. That is, it is affected by political forces and in turn has political effects. Whose interests are served and how interests are represented in an evaluation are critical concerns. In the early days, it was assumed that the interests of all parties were properly reflected in the traditional outcome measures. This assumption came to be questioned, and it was recognized that different groups might have different interests and might be differentially affected by both the program and its evaluation. The term *stakeholders* (those who had taken a stake in the program under review) became commonly used, and representing stakeholder views in the evaluation became an accepted practice.

The stakeholder concept is based on the prevailing pluralist-elitist-equilibrium theory of democracy, which disclaims any normative judgments and which holds that the current system of competing parties and pressure groups performs the democratic function of equilibrating the diverse and shifting political demands (MacPherson, 1987). It is believed that describing what others value is the stance best suited to the political context in which evaluators operate, because decision-making depends on the values held by relevant policymakers and stakeholders. Presumably, these parties will use the findings to make informed decisions. Neither the government nor the evaluator is supposed to intervene to support any particular interests but rather only to provide information which is value-neutral and interest-neutral. The interest of various groups somehow dissolve into the values of decision makers and stakeholders.

The stakeholder approach has defined limitations, however. For example, in two highly visible, stakeholder evaluations funded by the federal government, that of Cities in Schools and Jesse Jackson's PUSH/Excel program, the evaluations worked against the interest of the program participants and the inner city students they were supposed to serve, thus calling into question the justice of these evaluations (House, 1988; Stake, 1986). The results of the PUSH/Excel evaluation were used not only to discredit the program, but also to question Jesse Jackson's ability to manage large enterprises during the ensuing presidential campaigns. In actual fact, stakeholders do not have equal power to influence and use the evaluation, nor equal protection from the evaluation.

The problem of multiple interests and how they should be represented in the evaluation takes one into the realm of social justice. Although the reality of multiple stakeholders who have legitimate and sometimes conflicting interests is recognized, how these interests should be adjudicated remains unresolved. The practice of describing various interests in a neutral fashion seems inadequate, and the fact that much evaluation activity has now moved inside the large organizations and is subject to bureaucratic authority adds new pressures. The critical political question remains: Whose interest does the evaluation serve?

Summary

Evaluation originally developed as a strategy to find grand solutions to social problems but this proved to be a disappointing and chastening venture. The initial ideological consensus was that solutions to educational problems could be discovered by suing the proper methodology, which usually meant quantitative outcome measures employed in experimental, quasi-experimental, or survey designs. Group interests were assumed to be represented in the traditional measures of educational attainment and achievement. It was also assumed that program managers and policymakers would enthusiastically accept the results of evaluations for the purposes of program revision and termination. None of these presumptions proved to be correct.

As the larger social consensus fragmented, evaluators turned to qualitative methods to record the views of participants and clients, that is, the stakeholders. Gradually, evaluators recognized that there were many interests to be served in an evaluation and that some of these interests might conflict with one another. The result was pluralist conceptions of evaluation in which multiple methods, measures, criteria, perspectives, audiences, and interests were recognized. Conceptually, evaluation moved from monolithic to pluralistic conceptions, reflecting the change from consensus to pluralism that had emerged in the larger society. How to synthesize, resolve, and adjudicate all these multiple multiples remains a formidable question for both evaluators and the larger society. Evaluation, which was invented to solve social problems, was ultimately afflicted with the problems it was meant to solve.

References

Alkin, M. C. *(1990). Debates on evaluation.* Beverly Hills: SAGE Publishing.

Boruch, R. F., and Riecken, W. H. (Eds.). (1975). *Experimental testing of public policy.* Boulder, CO: Westview Press.

Bullock, A., Stallybrass, O., and Trombley, S. (1988).*The Harper dictionary of modern thought*(rev. ed.). New York: Harper and Row.

Campell, D. T., and Stanley, J. C. (1963). *Experimental and quasi-experimental designs for research.* Chicago: Rand McNally.

Cook, T. D., and Shadish, W. R., Jr. (1986). Program evaluation: The worldly science*American Review of Psychology,* 37, 193–232.

Cronbach, L. J. (1982). *Designing evaluations of educational and social programs.*San Francisco: Jossey-Bass.

Eisner, E. W. (1979). *The educational imagination.* New York: Macmillan.

Guba, E. G. and Lincoln, U.S. (1982).*Effective evaluation.* San Francisco: Jossey-Bass.

Hodgson, G. (1976). *America in our time.* New York: Vintage.

House, E. R. (1980). *Evaluating with validity.* Beverly Hills: SAGE Publishing.

House, E. R. (1988). Jesse Jackson and the politics of charisma: The rise and fall of the PUSH/Excel Program. Boulder, CO: Westview Press.

Howe, K., and Eisenhart, M. (in press). Standards in qualitative research: A prologomenon.*Educational Researcher.*

Joint Committee on Standards for Educational Evaluation. (1981). *Standards for evaluations of educational programs, projects, and materials.* New York: McGraw Hill.

Levin, H. M. (1983). *Cost-Effectiveness: A primer.* Beverly Hills: SAGE Publications

Levy, F. (1987).*Dollars and dreams: The changing American income distribution.*New York: Russell Sage Foundation.

Macpherson, C. B. (1987). *The rise and fall of economic justice.* Oxford: Oxford University Press.

McLaughlin, M. W. (1965). *Evaluation and reform: The elementary and secondary act of 1965 title 1.* Cambridge, MA: Ballinger.

Patton, M. Q. (1988). The evaluator's responsibility for utilization. *Evaluation Practice, 9(2),* 5–24.

Scriven, M. S. (1980). *The logic of evaluation.* Inverness, CA: Edgepress.

Scriven, M. S. (1983). Evaluation ideologies. In G. F. Madaus, M. Scriven, & D. L. Stufflebeam (Eds.), Evaluation models:View points on education and human services evaluation (pp. 229–260). Boston, MA: Kluwer-Nijhoff.

Smith, J. K. (1983). Quantitative versus interpretive: The problem of conducting social inquiry. In E. R. House *(Ed.), Philosophy of evaluation* (pp. 27–51). San Francisco: Jossey-Bass.

Smith, N. L. (1989). The Weiss-Patton debate: Illumination of the fundamental concerns. *Evaluation Practice,* 10(1), 5–13.

Stake, R. E. (1978). The case study method in social inquiry. *Educational Researcher, 7:* 5–7.

Stake, R. E. (1986). Quiet ingre form: Social science and social action in an urban youth program. Urbana, IL: University of Illinois Press.

Weiss, C. H. (1988). Evaluation for decisions: Is anybody there? Does anybody care? *Evaluation Practice, 9(1),* 5–19.

Williams, J. E. (1989). A numerical taxonomy of evaluation theory and practice (Mimeo). Los Angeles: University of California, Graduate School of Education.

Note

Thanks to Steve Lapan and Ken Howe for comments on earlier drafts.

Assessing Assessment:
An In-depth Status Report
on the Higher Education
Assessment Movement in 1990

REID JOHNSON, JOSEPH PRUS, CHARLES J. ANDERSEN
AND ELAINE EL-KHAWAS

Introduction

For the nearly twenty years since pioneering colleges took their first concerted steps toward systematically evaluating the quality of their academic programs, the higher education assessment movement has been growing in breadth and impact to the status of a national and even international phenomenon. During that period, the assessment of institutional effectiveness has increasingly influenced not only college students, faculty, administrations, and curricula, but has also affected—and been affected by—accreditation agency standards and state executive and legislative education policies as well. And all indications point to assessment's continued growth as a major factor shaping the future of higher education.

Tracing the development of the assessment movement is difficult since, except in the cases of a few institutions, detailed information on its early period is lacking. But patterns of progress since the mid-1980's have been better documented, primarily through surveys by the American Council on Education (ACE) and the Education Commission of the States (ECS). We know, for example, that close to forty of the fifty states now actively promote higher education assessment—mostly through legislative or regulatory mandates—as compared to only three or four in 1985 (Finney, 1990); and that 82% of all colleges report having assessment activities underway today, up from 55% just two years ago (El Khawas, 1990 and 1988).

Results like these have been invaluable in outlining the general profile of the assessment movement, but what of the all important operational details? How many colleges and universities are actually implementing comprehensive assessment programs, as required by most mandates? What indicators of quality are they measuring? What assessment methods are they using? How are assessment programs organized? And what sorts of higher educators are leading campus efforts? What are the key pitfalls in assessment, and perhaps more to the heart of the matter, how are faculty and administrations dealing with such problems? In other words, specifically whom is doing specifically what in higher education assessment, and how is it going?

Now, for the first time, these and many other "nuts and bolts" questions have been posed to a stratified sample of 455 colleges and universities representative of over 2600 two- and four-year postsecondary institutions in the United States. With nearly an 80% usable response rate (357 schools: see the Technical Notes in Appendix B), this ACE-Winthrop survey constitutes the most thorough study of higher education assessment practices accomplished to date.*

Prior to this report, anyone in need of a reasonably detailed overview of what was happening in the assessment movement faced a daunting quest. Although valuable information abounds in the literature, it is too widely dispersed and varied in quality to be easily located, digested, and/or utilized. There is no higher education assessment journal, only one national newsletter, and no "handbook" compendium of relevant models, methods and materials. (Helpful efforts in this direction have been made by the American Association for Higher Education's Assessment Forum, the federal Fund for the Improvement of Post Secondary Education's Assessment Program Book, and the Assessment Resource Center at the University of Tennessee-Knoxville, but much remains to be done.)

A few assessment information clearinghouses have sprung up, but they are overextended, understaffed, and generally unable to provide integrated pictures of assessment efforts across models, institutions and topics. More in-depth knowledge of particular assessment approaches can be obtained via reports or workshops from individual institutions with more advanced assessment programs, but finding comparative frames of reference is time consuming and difficult.

As another option, one might attend one or more assessment conferences where a broader mosaic of experiences from across the higher education spectrum are available. But while all attendees will find some of what they need to know, and a few will find much of what they need to know, most will leave the conference with their appetites for assessment information more whetted than satisfied.

This study is an attempt to help narrow this higher education assessment "information gap." As compared to other sources, this study was designed to provide more information on the inner workings of assessment programs, yet on a much broader scale. The survey included both forced choice and open-ended items (see survey Questionnaire in Appendix A) divided into three sections covering overall program status, program personnel and organization, and program evaluation, respectively. Institutions with assessment programs in place were also asked detailed questions regarding the methods and strategies they are using, and the perceived strengths and weaknesses of their efforts thus far.

It is intended that the present summary, as well as more in-depth treatments to follow, will constitute a useful frame of reference against which institutional assessment efforts—models, methods, options or issue can be compared. By doing so, we hope the present results will facilitate the development of more date-based, better quality higher education assessment programs in the future, which is our primary goal for this study.

Assessment Program Status

According to our results, 30% of American colleges and universities report they are operating comprehensive student assessment programs (hereafter called CSAPs) as a primary indicator of institutional effectiveness. This much lower figure than those from the ACE Campus Trends and ECS surveys mentioned earlier may be explained by two major differences between this study and those. First, this survey specifically requested information on comprehensive assessment programs; i.e., efforts to measure undergraduate students' progress toward one to five categories of

* Note: Additional support for this study was provided by South Carolina Commission on Higher Education and American Association for Higher Education grants to Winthrop College.

higher education objectives, usually in the arts and sciences. Institutions which would have responded affirmatively to other surveys on the basis of, for example, fledgling efforts or very limited assessment activities or primarily graduate-level measures, would likely respond in the negative here, thus lowering the percentage. A second important distinction of these results is that they address institutional-level assessment efforts rather than those at the state or program level, both of which would be expected to produce higher percentage responses. The percentage of states with at least one institutional assessment effort or the percentage of institutions with at least one program assessment effort (e.g., even a single survey, basic skills test, credentialing exam, etc.) would obviously be much higher than the percentage of only those institutions implementing more comprehensive assessment programs. This study, therefore, rather than conflicting with previous results, is more complementary and elaborative, providing a better estimate of the numbers of broad institutional assessment programs that most assessment experts and mandates have been urging.

The Overall Picture

There was remarkable consistency in general assessment activity across the institutions surveyed, with the type or category of institutions having little bearing on the likelihood of a campus CSAP. (See Technical Notes for institutional category distinctions.) As is indicated in Table 1, approximately equal percentages of baccalaureate institutions, comprehensive colleges, and universities reported having a comprehensive program to measure student progress toward the institution's educational and related student development goals. A slightly higher percentage (32%) of public colleges and universities than independents (28%) appear to have such programs in place.

Most institutions without an assessment program show a clear trend toward developing one. Twenty-seven percent (27%) of institutions who reported having no CSAP at the time of this survey have established specific timelines for program initiation and another 57% stated that assessment planning was underway although no implementation date had been set. This means that only 16% of institutions without a current program (approximately 11% of all institutions) report no current plans for comprehensive assessment.

This pattern of development from 1984, when less than 10% of all institutions surveyed reported having CSAPs, to 1990, when 89% report operational programs or plans for CSAPs, shows dramatic progress in the national trend to assess institutional effectiveness. These results are also in accord with the earlier mentioned ACE Campus Trends and ECS reports on the higher education movement's current status.

When and Why Were Assessment Programs Begun?*

Of those campuses reporting CSAPs, 64% were begun within the past six years. While this time frame coincides with the spread of state government and regional accreditation assessment mandates, and such external pressures are commonly cited as a primary force behind higher education assessment, the reasons for CSAP initiation cited by institutions in our sample are considerably broader and more varied. (See Table 2.)

Among the top nine reasons given for establishing a CSAP, a decision by campus administration, was cited most frequently (73%). Accreditation standards at 46% and state mandates (including legislative and executive policies) at 39% were cited by less than half of the sample. Other intrainstitutional factors were also clearly prominent, with faculty initiatives (41%), following

---

* Note: Form this point on, percentage responses and operational details refer to the 30% of institutions surveyed who report having CSAPs already in place as of 1990. (A few percentage totals may not equal exactly 100% due to rounding.)

"national trends" (39%), and following other institutions' examples (20%) making up four of the top five reasons cited for beginning assessment programs. In the widely discussed matter of external versus internal incentives for assessment, internal factors appear to be as important, if not more important, than external pressures. The typical pattern portrayed in this study is that of institutional leaders becoming cognizant of assessment efforts on other campuses across the country and rallying the faculty to initiate their own local program, whether they are under an assessment mandate or not.

What Is Being Assessed . . . And How?

The advice of experts in higher education assessment has strongly emphasized the need for program models and methods tailored to the unique needs and characteristics of each institution. Yet, common institutional program objectives would suggest that common assessment components might be included in the efforts of most colleges and universities. To explore this question we divided institutional objectives into five categories (see Table 3), and asked institutions in the sample to indicate which components were included in their CSAP.

Additionally, one of the most important objectives of this study was to find out what measurement methods were being relied on for student assessment. Are "off the shelf" commercial tests and surveys dominating the CSAP scene? How willing are faculty to devote the time and effort needed to develop "local" instruments? Have more competency-based "performance measures" made significant inroads? To what extent are available student records being used? In other words, we were very interested in learning just how institutions are measuring what they're measuring. (See Table 4.)

The student learning and development objectives most frequently cited as a component of campus assessment programs was basic college-readiness skills. This component—defined as measuring student progress in such entry-level areas as reading, writing, and mathematics—was listed by 94% of institutions with assessment programs. Among these institutions, commercial tests were the most frequently cited method for assessing basic college readiness, with 82% reporting their use. Locally developed tests were utilized by approximately half of respondents who evaluate college readiness in their program, followed in frequency by available archival records (27%), performance-based methods (16%), and student self-reporting (10%). The frequencies with which all individual methods were reported suggest that multiple methods of assessing this area are being used by many institutions.

The second most frequently reported assessment program component was career preparation/ alumni follow-up, which was cited by 76% of schools with CSAPs. Self-report was clearly the "method of choice" for assessing career development and following-up with alumni, with no other method being used by over 20% of the sample.

The assessment of general education/liberal studies was reported as a component of the assessment programs of 67% of responding institutions. Commercial tests were again the most frequently cited measurement method, with about four in ten institutions reporting their use. Performance-based methods were second in frequency of use at 24%, followed by locally developed tests (15% of institutions), student self-reporting (14%) and available archival records (14%).

Approximately two-thirds of college and universities stated that major fields were being assessed in their CSAPs. Locally-developed tests and performance-based methods were more likely to be included in assessing major specialty areas than in any other program component, with 39% and 38%, respectively, of all institutions reporting their use. Commercial tests, used by 27% of the sample, were the next most frequently reported method of assessing majors followed by available archival records (17%), and student self-reporting (12%). Again, these data suggest that multiple methods are being widely used to assess major fields in institutions, but it is not known to what extent multiple measures are typical within individual major departments.

The last assessment component reported by a majority of respondents (65%) was the assessment of students' personal growth and development. This area was defined as "measuring values, attitudes, social development and/or other nonacademic changes attributable to the college experience." Commercial instruments were the most frequently reported method of assessment in this area (reported by 29% of institutions), followed closely by the student self-reporting at 24%.

Taken as a whole, it is clear that a wide range of institutional objectives measured by a variety of methods are typical of the CSAPs in this study. And while traditional strategies like commercial tests, surveys, and student records are prominent, more innovative options such as locally developed instruments, performance appraisal, and qualitative student reports are also playing important roles.

Assessment Program Organization and Personnel

CSAP Structure

The organizational structure of any program, including a CSAP, is an important determinant of its long term stability and success. Furthermore, the administrative division to which a CSAP is assigned makes a strong statement about how assessment's role in higher education is actually perceived on that campus.

At this point assessment is apparently being seen as a primarily educational endeavor, with a clear majority of surveyed institutions (59%) giving an academic officer (i.e., vice president or dean of academic affairs) executive responsibility for their CSAP. Thirteen percent have put CSAPs in student affairs, 7% fall under institutional research, and 5% have added assessment leadership to the chief executive officer's duties. The remaining 17% have assigned their CSAPs elsewhere (14%) or are undecided/made no response (3%). (See Table 5).

Many key decisions and actions which ultimately determine assessment's success in enhancing the quality of institutional programs are also made by the individual(s) on the front lines charged with the day-to-day operations of CSAPs. We now briefly review who these "assessment coordinators" are—regardless of specific title—and how their efforts are being organized.

As Table 6 shows, a majority of all institutions (62%) have put administrators in charge of ongoing program direction, as well as executive oversight duties, for their assessment efforts. Overall, only 20% have faculty member(s) coordinating CSAPs, 10% put operational responsibilities in the hands of a faculty committee, and 6% say "others" coordinate their CSAP, presumably referring to staff in student affairs and/or institutional research.

A large minority of institutions with CSAPs (40%) have created an on-campus assessment coordinating office. The majority of those institutions report that such offices perform the following services: Consultation with faculty (83%), CSAP coordination (81%), hands-on assessment implementation (79%), liaison with students (65%), planning (65%), research and development (58%), and technical assistance (53%). Budgeting (46%) and assessment program evaluation (38%) were also frequently cited assessment office functions.

In addition to such student assessment coordinating centers, 85% of institutions with CSAPs report other assessment support structures, including faculty councils/committees (69%) and/or administrative councils/committees (40%). Only 8% of all institutions report using assessment consultants, and only 3% of institutions with CSAPs directly involve student councils/committees in their operational structure.

Faculty Roles in Assessment

Most experts strongly advocate high faculty involvement in CSAPs to prevent higher education assessment from becoming—in appearance or in fact—merely an administrative function or an exercise in external accountability. Thus, we made a point in this study to examine the roles being played by faculty members in CSAPs. (See Table 7.) Thus far, faculty appear most prominently in the planning and designing of CSAPs, with 45% of institutions reporting faculty as "heavily involved" and another 50% cited slight to moderate faculty involvement in that program phase. In terms of directing or coordinating CSAPs, most institutions see that as an administrative role, with only 19% reporting heavy faculty involvement and 68% slight to moderate. Faculty participation increases again in CSAP operation and implementation, with 34% heavily involved and another 53% at least somewhat involved; but faculty play less of a role in CSAP program evaluation with only 21% heavily involved, and 9% of institutions reporting no faculty role at all. While it is clear that at least some faculty input is common in almost all phases of CSAP activities, it does appear that the higher the level of assessment decision-making (i.e., direction and evaluation), the lower the level of faculty involvement.

Finally, in another example of conventional higher education wisdom apparently not being taken to heart in most CSAPs, only 10% of the institutions sampled reported being members of an assessment consortium.

Assessment Leaders: A Profile

Higher educators who have reviewed the assessment literature or attended conferences or institutional workshops have observed an extraordinary diversity in the backgrounds of leading experts in the higher education assessment movement, and this seems to be true at both the national and institutional level. Yet the present survey is the first known effort to systematically study the assessment related backgrounds of a vital group of such leaders; i.e., those responsible for campus CSAPs.

Since CSAPs are relatively new programs, with no traditionally dominant disciplinary qualifications associated with leadership positions, we asked respondents to identify the individual leader "most involved with your campus assessment program." We then posed questions regarding that leader's academic discipline, degree level, position title, provenance, and assessment related training and experience. In fact, we asked for the same information on the two most involved CSAP leaders to better encompass situations where assessment responsibilities are split or layered among more than one individual.

The expected diversity is, in fact, evident in reported CSAP leaders' backgrounds (see Table 8), with at least one percent of the sample utilizing at least one coordinator from each of six broad discipline categories. Overall, institutional assessment leaders are most likely to come from three disciplinary backgrounds: education (29%), social and behavioral sciences (25%), and arts and humanities (21%). The secondary CSAP leader profile is very similar, with only one other area (physical sciences/engineering/math at 7% for Leader #1 and 12% for Leader #2) accounting for 5% or more of the total.

There is considerable agreement among respondents that CSAP leaders are doctoral-level personnel (59% for Leader #1, 57% for #2), with only 2-year institutions using significant members of master's degree people, and less than 1% reporting CSAPs headed by bachelor's-level individuals. There is even more unanimity that assessment leaders for CSAPs are chosen from within the institution (86% for both Leaders #1 and #2) as opposed to bringing someone in from another college or other outside source.

Surprisingly, when we inquired regarding the specific training and experience of CSAP leaders, only 16% reported having taken a degree program with an emphasis on assessment, and 4% reported no prior training or experience with assessment whatsoever. By far the most common training experience reported by CSAP leaders was attending workshops or seminars (73%), with a degree in education or higher education (47%), and experience in assessment at the disciplinary program level (40%) or institutional level (20%), also being often reported as primary higher education assessment qualifications. A large number of institutions (45%) also cited other kinds of relevant experiences as important.

Assessment Program Evaluation

Evaluating the effectiveness and efficiency of CSAPs should be a high priority as the higher education assessment movement progresses toward maturity. But, with the exception of the "first and second waves" of pioneer institutions in the 70's and early 80's, most colleges and universities are at much too early a stage of development to draw valid conclusions regarding the outcomes of their CSAPs. Thus, since product evaluation was unlikely to produce very meaningful results, this study focuses on information regarding the process of assessment; what did respondents think was going right, what was going wrong, and what were they doing about both?

Current Assessment Challenges and Steps Toward Resolution

Institutions in the survey were provided a list of eleven potential challenges or problems related to implementation of a successful student assessment program and were asked to rate each on a five point scale from "no problem" to "very severe problem." They then were asked to identify the two most severe challenges. Respondents were also asked to list the two "most helpful" decisions they made in establishing their assessment program. Decisions identified as being "most helpful" were categorized to facilitate analysis, interpretation, and reporting. Problem rating totals are shown in Table 9.

Considering all degrees of challenges together for the moment, a majority of all institutions identified the following as a least some problem: the availability of valid assessment methods and student motivation/participation (both 79%) tied for the most frequent cited problem, with coordination of all aspects of the CSAP (77%) and financial support for the CSAP (75%) closely following. Other widely reported problem areas were faculty motivation/participation (70%), using CSAP results for institutional program enhancement (69%), and analyzing CSAP results (67%). No other problem was cited by over half of the sample.

When severity of problems is taken into account a slightly reordered pattern emerges. The number of problem areas rated as severe or very severe drops off dramatically and is headed by inadequate financial support (20%), availability of valid assessment methods (19%), student motivation/participation (14%), CSAP coordination (13%), and both faculty motivation/participation and using CSAP results for program improvement (at 11%). A similar hierarchy was formed from responses to an open-ended question asking which two challenges were most severe. (See Table 10.) Significantly, over one-third of the sample did not identify any of the problem areas as "most severe."

It is also of note that four widely assumed higher education assessment challenges were not seen a significant problems by our sample. In fact, at least half of the respondents reported them as "no problem" at all. These include administrative support (68%), misuse of results by the media or public (58%) or by regulating or accrediting agencies (55%), and undue influence on CSAPs by outside agencies (50%).

Thus, the survey found little, if any, support for the concern of some in higher education that assessment programs and their results are a vehicle for undue influence from outside agencies or an invitation for misuse of results by media, government, or other outside parties. Two percent (2%) or less of responding institutions cited any of these problems as "severe," although many colleges and universities may be at such early stages of the assessment process that potential problems regarding results and their interpretation and dissemination have not yet manifested themselves.

In terms of how CSAP leaders are trying to resolve these and other assessment challenges, we asked an open-ended question regarding what decision or actions taken by respondents they considered most helpful in setting up their programs. While a disappointing—or perhaps revealing —number of respondents (29%) gave no response, the following "best decisions" were cited by a significant percentage: getting faculty involved (23%), integrating CSAPs with institutional planning (19%), careful analysis and feedback of results (15%), a determined commitment to and prompt implementation of the CSAP (14%), increased allocation of resources (12%), and local development of assessment methods (11%). Somewhat surprisingly, only 5% listed making local as opposed to externally mandated decisions concerning the program as one of their best moves.

Nearly one in four institutions cited a decision "most helpful" to assessment implementation that could not be classified into one of the major categories cited above. These decisions included such ideas as having ample time to plan and implement assessment, seeking student support, maintaining flexibility in each discipline's assessment program, obtaining assistance from consultants; and staffing an office specifically for assessment. The variety of decisions/suggestions received in response to this survey suggests a substantial degree of creative problem-solving at work in higher education assessment, as well as a need for approaches that are geared to the unique problems and characteristics of individual institutions.

Perceived Benefits and Liabilities of Assessment

With due caution regarding the previously noted fact that most CSAPs are in such a relatively early stage of development that respondents may be in a poor position to make retrospective judgments regarding their programs' ultimate worth, we next solicited open-ended comments on what the main beneficial and detrimental effects of assessment had been to date. Responses were then classified into the categories listed in Tables 11 and 12, which contain the percentages of institutions citing particular positive or negative effects.

Again, a significant number (26%) indicated that it was too soon to respond, but 30% felt academic program planning had been enhanced, 29% saw assessment feedback improving students' efforts, and 3–10% said their CSAPs had increased their administration's cooperation and involvement in programs, upgraded standards, and improved faculty cooperation and morale.

Regarding possible detrimental effects of CSAPs (Table 12) no single problem was cited by more than 9% of the respondents, a truly encouraging finding. Between 4-9% of respondents said assessment had produced or exacerbated the following problems: extra work for faculty and administration, increased drain on resources, "turf" problems, and declines in morale. Of particular note is the fact that 53% of the sample institutions listed nothing in the "main detrimental effects" blanks, and 9% wrote in "no detrimental effects." With 62% of surveyed institutions citing no detrimental effects and only 26% reporting no present indications of beneficial effects, it seems safe to say that our sample sees CSAPs as "more worth than they're trouble."

Current Unmet Needs and Assessment Program Evaluation

The last open-ended survey item asked respondents to list their three greatest unmet needs in implementing successful CSAPs and utilizing the results for educational program enhancement. Against aggregating first, second, and third for all institutions, the most frequently cited needs were: more resources (42%), better analysis and utilization of CSAP results (33%), better assessment methods (28%), greater faculty involvement (28%), better CSAP planning and goal setting (28%), and "other" types of needs (15%). Relatively few respondents said that greater administrative interest (11%) or greater student interest (8%) were significant unmet needs, and 19% did not respond to this item.

Finally—and again noting the interim nature of such judgments—we asked how respondents would rate the quality of their current CSAP. Only 9% said excellent, 49% said good or very good,

27% said only fair to poor, and 16% had no basis to judge or gave no response. Considering the scope of the challenges posed by higher education assessment under the best of circumstances—much less the difficult economic times many institutions have faced in the past few years—for over half of our respondents to rate their CSAP programs as good to excellent is taken as a very optimistic indicator of assessment's future development as a positive force in the improvement of higher education.

Summary and Conclusions

Summary

This first in-depth study of the higher education assessment movement's status, on a representative stratified sample of campuses across the country, portrays a vibrant, growing phenomenon already having significant effects on academic programs. While other national studies have reported as many as 82% of colleges and universities having some assessment activities underway, our criteria for comprehensive student assessment program (CSAP)—which are much closer, not incidentally, to the assessment recommendations of most experts as well as state and accreditation mandates produced a much lower prevalence of 30%. Still, we found that the number of schools either currently operating a CSAP or planning to do so in the near future stands at an impressive 89%.

The impetus for assessment is seen by institutional representatives as being as much internally as externally based, if not more so. Despite the existence of higher education assessment mandates in close to forty states (and in 60% of the public institutions in our sample), a considerably higher percentage of institutions view their college or university administration as the major force behind assessment. Internal administrative decisions followed by accreditation standards, state mandates, and faculty initiatives, were the most frequently reported reasons for having begun a CSAP.

The large majority of institutions with comprehensive assessment programs are addressing a broad range of student learning and development areas including entry-level basic skills, general education, major fields, alumni follow-up /career development, and personal growth and development. Multiple methods of assessment, most often including commercial and locally developed instruments, also are reported to be in place at most schools. A multi-method approach is apparently more likely to be utilized for assessing basic college readiness (i.e., reading, writing, quantitative skills) and major fields of study than other assessment components. More innovative methods are also utilized by a significant minority of CSAPs.

The importance of assessment is attested to by the fact that 40% of colleges and universities have established a coordinating center (i.e. an "assessment office,") specifically designed to address this area. Most of these centers, as well as assessment programs in general, are run on a day-to-day basis by an administrator who usually reports to the chief academic office or vice-president for academic affairs. Faculty groups such as academic councils are the most likely assessment support unit related to the CSAP on most campuses. Nearly 70% of our respondents reported faculty as "moderately" or "strongly" involved in assessment planning and implementation, with considerably less faculty involvement reported for important program supervision and evaluation functions. Most also reported no student involvement in CSAP development whatsoever. Thus, there is an opportunity and, if the advice of many assessment experts is followed, a substantial need for more faculty and student participation in CSAP operations on most campuses.

The perception of many observers and participants of the higher education assessment movement is that assessment leaders tend to come from remarkably diverse backgrounds. This hypothesis was supported by the data from the present study. Leaders of campus assessment efforts come from a wide variety of disciplines, although degrees in education, social sciences, and humanities are most common. Another perception, that a little experience and a few workshops or conferences can lead to one becoming viewed as an assessment "expert," was also borne out by our data.

Although most assessment leaders possess terminal degrees, their credentials seldom include either formal education related to assessment or measurement, or significant prior experience in assessment. More than likely, such leaders have received their primary or sole training through conferences and workshops. This fact serves to emphasize the critical role of events such as the American Association for Higher Education's annual conference on assessment in higher education, state and regional meetings, and on-campus workshops, as important means of sharing much needed expertise.

At this point in time, institutional representatives are considerably more likely to cite beneficial effects than detriments of assessment, with 62% reporting no detrimental effects at all or saying it was too soon to cite any liabilities. The enhancement of academic planning and of student efforts and feedback appear to be the most clearly recognized benefits of comprehensive assessment programs. The most frequently mentioned detriment, although cited by less than 10% of the sample, is the extra work for faculty and administrators that assessment programs tend to demand.

The implementation of a successful CSAP presents many challenges for institutions and for administrators and faculty charged with being "assessment leaders." Those problems which appear to be most severe in the minds of the institutional representatives completing our survey are student motivation/participation, financial support, faculty motivation/participation, availability of valid assessment methods, and use of results for program enhancement. Yet, these problems do not appear to be considered major impediments to the assessment efforts of most institutions. Additionally, problems related to "outside interference" or misuse of assessment results by outside agencies appear to be more apparent than real, at least thus far (a finding we'd like to see replicated in future surveys).

Despite the earlier mentioned relatively attenuated on faculty roles in CSAPs, strong faculty involvement in assessment was the most frequently cited helpful decision in establishing a comprehensive assessment program. Additionally, the variety of other successful resolutions and decisions given by institutions support the strong need for opportunity to share ideas and creative solutions to the complex issues raised by higher education assessment activities.

Opportunities for sharing resources may also need to be pursued more rigorously by institutions in the future. (The need for more resources was the most frequently cited unmet need in our survey.) One way in which resources can be shared among institutions is through assessment networks, but thus far only 10% of colleges and universities report belonging to such a consortium. Analysis and feedback of results, better assessment instruments, greater faculty involvement, and better planning and goal setting are a few of the other unmet needs which institutions face as they strive to implement effective CSAPs.

A Developmental Pattern of Assessment Programs?

While this study includes a wide variety of CSAP origins, organizations, operations, and issues, present response trends and case-study reports from veteran assessment institutions seem to form enough of an empirical pattern to derive a typical nine-step CSAP development cycle:

1. An institution's administration—with or without external assessment mandate pressure and/or meaningful faculty input—commits to the establishment of a CSAP as a primary indicator of the institution's effectiveness.

2. A relatively latent "behind the scenes" period of information gathering, goal setting, planning, consensus-building, program design, resource-seeking, and trial-and error exploration of assessment models ensues.

3. Then a concerted CSAP efforts begins, supplementing existing data-gathering activities with "pilot" assessments in selected programs across the campus.

4. Gradually the process effects of CSAP implementation are evidenced. Students, faculty, administrators, outside mandaters and others begin to be influenced by assessment activities (e.g., defining program objectives, finding and/or developing measures, piloting assessment strategies, analyzing preliminary evaluative feedback, preliminary reporting, etc.)

5. Assessment refinement eventually matches program objectives with effective measures at a manageable cost sufficiently to implement an institution-wide CSAP.

6. Finally product analysis of the CSAP begins to yield a definitive database on academic program quality, and the strengths and weaknesses in the curriculum, instruction, policies, and resources which are responsible for that level of quality.

7. Reactions to those results come from program faculty, institutional administrators, assessment mandaters, and others.

8. Changes in educational programs and/or policies and/or CSAPs are made to enhance the institution's effectiveness.

9. Those changes are, in turn, assessed, . . . and the higher education assessment cycle continues.

According to the results of this study, the majority of U.S. colleges and universities (59%) are at Step 1 or 2, just feeling their way into the assessment movement. Another 30% are somewhere between steps 3 and 5, making a serious effort towards implementing a CSAP, but still wrestling with significant methodological, logistical, motivational and financial issues. A much smaller percentage—mostly those pioneering schools to whom those that follow owe such a debt of gratitude—are at Step 6 and beyond. And somewhere around 10% of American institutions either haven't gotten the word, are still trying to find a way around assessment, or are still at a preplanning stage of CSAP implementation.

Some Unanswered Questions on the Future of the Higher Education Assessment Movement

As we've stressed throughout this report, it is premature to be making confident long-term predictions. But in the short-term—i.e., the next few years—the expansion of current CSAPs and assessment mandates, and continued new institutional commitments to CSAPs, seem assured. Still, we must be cautious, since even for most institutions with state and/or regional accreditation mandates the first rounds of assessment reports, self-studies, and team visits have just recently gotten underway. Until the assessment—>report—>feedback loop has been closed, nothing is certain.

Many important process questions remain to be answered if assessment growth is to be sustained. For example, will increased roles for faculty and students be achieved? Will administrator resolve remain firm? Can the resources needed for quality assessment be found? Are assessment process benefits sufficient to sustain motivation? Are the necessary CSAP quality control safeguards in place to assure useful assessment results?

Soon more pressing assessment product questions will take center stage, and many of the answers will come from outside the institutions. How will state and accrediting mandaters react to positive CSAP results? . . . to negative CSAP results? What will states or accreditors do if certain schools or programs refuse to implement CSAPs? . . . or do so in a perfunctory or clearly invalid manner? Will good programs and proficient faculty be rewarded? Will struggling but needed programs and overworked but underachieving faculty receive increased resources and support? Will unnecessary, inefficient, and unproductive programs suffer any meaningful sanctions? . . . and what of poor faculty and unsuccessful administrators? What will happen to students who—because of CSAPs—show they haven't been learning what we've always thought they were learning? Will CSAPs produce higher achievement but at the expense of student retention? . . . or student body diversity? . . . or faculty research productivity? . . . or academic creativity? . . . or what?! CSAPs' future will, at the very least, be interesting.

Even broader issues and questions, which are beyond the scope of this survey, are perhaps equally likely to determine the longer term future of assessment in higher education as we move toward the 21st century. How substantial an effect, for example, will the current general economic downturn have on resources allocated to higher education? Will education in general and higher education in particular continue to be highly valued by state decision-makers and private funding sources? Will the trend toward an increased emphasis on the quality of education and teaching versus research continue to grow and be supported by higher education institutions? In other words, can the educational and economic climate necessary to sustain this movement toward increased effectiveness be expected to last long enough to achieve its goals?

Not one of these questions can be answered definitively at this time, nor should we expect to have sufficiently valid outcomes results from most institutions' CSAPs to draw informed conclusions for many years. Thus, as of 1990, the jury on the higher education assessment movement's long term future is still very much out.

Some Contingent Predictions

In our view, the next two to five years will be crucial to the assessment movement, and thereby to a large extent, to the future course of higher education in this country. Assessment clearly has the potential to be a major factor in upgrading quality, but there are many important conditions yet to be met. If CSAPs are implemented widely, efficiently, and validly . . . and IF the results are utilized wisely for program improvement . . . and IF state agencies, accreditors, the media and the public deal fairly with assessment processes and products . . . THEN we are convinced that CSAPs will become such valued fixtures on college campuses that educators and students alike will wonder how we ever got along without them as long as we did.

On the other hand, the higher education assessment movement certainly has potential for abuse. IF administrators don't involve faculty and students in the forefront of CSAPs, little meaningful progress should be expected. IF assessors aren't highly selective and careful with their CSAP methods and procedures, accurate results will be few and far between. IF institutions and funding sources aren't supportive of quality CSAP requirements, a costly and demoralizing triumph of form over substance may well ensue. IF assessment mandaters don't demand valid CSAPs, and substantially reward good programs and sanction bad ones . . . or IF administrators, the government, and/or the media turn our movement into a corruption of assessment (such has been the case with much of primary and secondary education's group test-based "assessment" programs) . . . THEN assessment runs the risk of becoming an academic and political debacle, with an anti-CSAP "baby-with-the-bathwater" counter-assessment movement not far behind.

Given the high degree of assessment planning and implementation occurring in our nation's colleges and universities, future surveys on assessment in higher education will likely find new perspectives, methods, processes, issues, and concerns. Given the high quality of educators we have working in assessment, new solutions to even the toughest questions will likely be forthcoming as well. This is entirely fitting, since assessment is, after all, a dynamic process of systematic self-examination intended to stimulate improvement.

We are dedicated to doing our part in support of conscientious higher educators and CSAP assessors everywhere to see that assessment fulfills its promise, and hope this report and the other results of our study to follow are significant contributions toward that end.

PART II

The primary Audiences in Assessment and Program Evaluation

Introduction

Program evaluation and assessment involve more than technical activities of deciding the methods or instruments to gather information, collecting and analyzing the data, and writing a report. From decisions about who will be involved and which questions to ask through interpretation of results, assessment is a highly political activity. Therefore, assessors need to identify and understand the perspectives various audiences bring to the process. This knowledge can assist in involving audiences and ensuring the ultimate success of the program, i.e., effective use of the information.

The various audiences in higher education bring unique perspectives from their academic disciplines, professional orientations, and current responsibilities. For example, the variation found among academic disciplines regarding the modes of inquiry and the types of data used is reflected in the different approaches to assessment among faculty members. Faculty with a background in the natural sciences may have different ideas about measurement and methodology than those in the social sciences or humanities. Due to their different roles and responsibilities within higher education, the audiences of state legislators, institutional administrators, faculty, and students are likely to embrace different purposes for assessment. Since the purpose of an assessment shapes the assessment program, differences produce diverse ideas about what should be measured, and how and by whom the information should be used.

Because the purpose of an assessment is central to all subsequent activity, the discussion below of the key assessment audiences is tied to the two basic alternatives for the purpose of assessment in higher education: accountability and improvement. In general, "accountability assessment" is conducted to inform judgment about value or worth by some higher authority such as accrediting and governmental bodies. "Improvement assessment" is conducted by faculty and administrators to inform decisions which may change and enhance teaching and learning.

Although most assessment programs include some aspects of both improvement and accountability, the primary audiences will determine the balance. The primary audiences, except for students, are addressed in the selected readings. The most relevant literature regarding the student and assessment activity is closely related to the teaching and learning literature, which is covered in other ASHE readers.

External audiences: Accrediting agencies. Accrediting agencies and state and national policy makers are generally concerned about broad issues. Their questions may concern the extent to which the public is receiving an adequate return for its funding, or the ability of the institution to produce the student outcomes represented in its institutional and program literature. All six regional accrediting associations now require outcome assessment; in some regions these requirements are more prescriptive than in others.

Millard provides a history of the role of accrediting agencies in assessing and enhancing quality in higher education. He also raises some current issues in the accrediting process; he offers suggestions about definitions and indices of quality and about the nature of the standards used to judge quality. Wolff extends the discussion of assessment and accreditation by exploring the relationship between regional accreditation activity and institutional assessment programs. To assure that accreditation achieves its goal of improving quality in higher education, he argues that accrediting agencies should adopt a more comprehensive definition of quality than student outcomes and a broader model of assessment than the goal-oriented approach. Such an approach would provide an institution with greater flexibility in designing and conducting assessment; these changes are likely to enhance ownership, utility, and eventual change and improvement. Examples of institutional effectiveness criteria and assessment procedures are provided in documents from two regional accrediting organizations, the **Southern Association of Colleges and Schools** and the **North Central Association of Colleges and Schools.**

The selections relating to accrediting agencies include two editorials about possible intrusion into the accreditation process by the national government. **Dumke** presents several steps that can be taken to strengthen the accreditation process and improve public confidence in the voluntary accreditation activity so that the responsibility is not assumed by state and national governments. **Atwell** discusses the general implications of a specific case of the U. S. Department of Education withholding approval of a regional association and making it contingent upon revision of its affirmative action plans.

External audiences: State and national policy makers. The federal role is rapidly evolving; the successor of the Council on Postsecondary Accreditation (COPA), recently discontinued, has yet to be determined. Major national initiatives in recent years include the federal "Student Right to Know" legislation (mandating reports of student retention and graduation rates), the "Ability to Benefit" legislation (requiring students without high school diplomas to pass a standardized test for federal student aid), and the National Education Goals to develop performance based assessment for graduating seniors (see ECS article in additional core readings cited below).

In contrast to the national government, many states took a more proactive role in assessment in the mid-1980s, focusing specifically on outcomes and accountability. This role in quality issues may have been a natural extension of a structure of program review that already existed in many states. An analysis of six dimensions that distinguish among state level program reviews is provided by **Walhaus**. He cites the strengths and weaknesses of each alternative and provides various models for the relationships between program review for institutions and for state-level agencies.

Ewell addresses state policies that are most likely to promote institutional ownership and change versus mere compliance. The discussion focuses on the issues of how state policies can be and have been used to affect teaching and learning. He pursues several questions about state policies that link resource allocation by the state with the teaching practice and curriculum, primarily the responsibility of the faculty.

Internal audiences: Institutional policymakers. In some states, the state institutional review process, addressed in the selection by Walhaus, is linked with campus academic review programs. Campus review programs typically are conducted periodically, e.g, every five years, by departmental or program units. **Conrad and Wilson** discuss alternatives regarding the models used and the purposes of academic program reviews, which may be for administrative decisions or for improvement.

While external audiences focus on outcomes, internal audiences who are responsible for the implementation of changes are likely to rely on more than outcome information to perform their responsibilities. They will need information about the educational processes and encounters upon which the outcomes depend. They ask improvement questions: Are the learning experiences congruent with and supportive of the intended outcomes? Are the type and level of resources congruent with and supportive of the intended educational experiences? If not, what changes in the resources or educational encounters are needed?

Tensions between state and institutional assessment initiatives are dependent, in large part, on the state model. The effects on internal audiences at a community college with a state-based, standardized testing model of outcome assessment measure is reported by McCabe, an administrator at the institution.

Internal audiences: Faculty. The increasing emphasis on assessment for improvement rather than for and sense of ownership of the primary audiences, particularly faculty. In an assessment program conducted for improvement purposes, the faculty must be centrally involved in the program if change is to take place. Faculty are, affer all, the key players in academic change at an institution. Understanding the perspectives faculty bring to the assessment activity is essential in conducting assessments.

Schneider notes the importance of faculty becoming collectively engaged in all aspects of an assessment program if improvement in learning is to take place. She addresses common fears and doubts of the faculty based on concerns that assessment will diminish their autonomy and that it will not adequately reflect what they teach.

Additional Core Readings

Banta, Trudy W. "Toward a Plan for Using National Assessment to Ensure Continuous Improvement of Higher Education." *The Journal of General Education* 42(1) (1993), pp. 33–58.

Education Commission of the States. "Assessing College Outcomes: What State Leaders Need to Know." *Report No. PA91–03.* Denver, Colorado: Education Commission of the States, 1991.

Ewell, Peter T. *Assessment, Accountability and Improvement.* Washington, D.C.: American Association for Higher Education, 1987.

Ewell, Peter T. "Institutional Characteristics and Faculty/Administrator Perceptions of Outcomes: An Exploratory Analysis." *Research in Higher Education* 30(2) (1989), pp. 113–136.

Ewell, Peter T. *Assessment and the "New Accountability": A Challenge for Higher Education's Leadership.* Denver, Colorado: Education Commission of the States, 1990.

Assessment and Accreditation: A Shotgun Marriage?

RALPH A. WOLFF

One of the effects of the explosive growth of the assessment movement has been to force all six of higher education's regional accrediting associations to revise their procedures and place greater emphasis on assessment as a form of institutional accountability. Undoubtedly, the increasing involvement of accrediting associations in assessment will affect institutions and the assessment movement alike. The question is: How can accreditation and assessment work together most effectively for educational reform?

While there are similarities of approach among the regional commissions, there are significant differences, too. Among the regionals, the Southern Association of Colleges and Schools (SACS) took the lead in 1985-86 by adopting a major new standard on institutional effectiveness as part of an effort to more consciously link outcomes assessment to the accreditation process. This was followed by a SACS initiative, supported by a FIPSE grant, to hold statewide conferences on assessment and publish a resource manual to assist institutions in meeting the SACS mandate. Shortly thereafter, the Senior College Commission of the Western Association of Schools and Colleges (WASC) adopted a new standard on institutional effectiveness; it has followed up with workshops and development of support materials on assessment. WASC has adopted much of the Southern Association's language but applied it in significantly different ways.

In 1989, the North Central Association followed with a new policy on assessment, requiring that all institutions assess student achievement as part of the self-study process. This past year, Middle States Association has been developing a guidebook for institutions called *A Framework for Outcomes Assessment*. Both the Northwest and new England associations have accrediting standards calling for outcomes assessment, but they have been less active in developing assessment initiatives. The Northwest Association does incorporate discussion of outcomes assessment in its self-study workshops and the New England Association is currently engaged in a process leading to the revision of its accrediting standards; the revision is likely to place greater emphasis on the role of assessment. In general, however, in the regional associations as with other accrediting associations, there is often a wide gap between the stated expectations of accreditors and implementation by institutions and accrediting teams.

As accrediting agencies move into this area, and as our approaches are still being defined, it is important that we take the time of step back and ask: Are we heading in the right direction? Has accreditation adopted an appropriate stance toward assessment and the assessment movement? What, exactly, do we want assessment to accomplish? And what are the pitfalls of assessment we need to avoid, the mistakes of earlier assessment from which we can learn?

I am increasingly concerned that a framework for the *accreditation* response to assessment has not yet been well developed. In expressing my concern I want to be clear that I am not approaching this topic from a dualistic point of view, i.e. that there is a right way and a wrong way for accrediting agencies to engage assessment issues; rather, there are many ways. I wish to present my own thoughts, reflections, and some approaches that I think should be incorporated into accreditation, using lenses borrowed in part from other fields such as intellectual and personal development, evaluation and decision-making theories, and from the literature on innovation.

I. The Context: Challenges to Accreditation

Regional accreditation is a product of the American genius. Nearly a century old, it is a creature of the higher education community itself, serving as a nongovernmental, voluntary process of peer review. Accreditation has two main purposes—assuring basic institutional accountability and improving institutional quality and effectiveness. This causes accrediting commissions to serve in opposing roles, sometimes as judge and sometimes as colleague. F. Scott Fitzgerald once wrote that "the test of a first-rate intelligence is the ability to hold two opposed ideas in mind at the same time and still retain the ability to function." The fact that accreditation, with its dual and sometimes opposing missions, has been able to function so well is testimony, as Fitzgerald might say, to the intelligence of its design and its ability to respond to social and institutional needs over time.

The accountability function of accreditation has historically taken the form of minimum standards for new institutions seeking accreditation or for institutions in serious academic or financial difficulty. For more established institutions, accountability has meant engaging seriously in a periodic process of comprehensive self-reflection and self-improvement, called a self study. This has proven to be an extraordinarily effective *process* of evaluation leading to institutional improvement. Moreover, by placing the responsibility for improvement directly into the hands of the institution, the diversity of institutions can be respected and each institution can focus on those issues most relevant to its own circumstances.

The flexibility represented by this process has proved to be accreditation's greatest strength; in recent years, however, it also has become its greatest weakness. A series of challenges to accreditation has converged over the past fifteen years to cause significant changes in the way accreditation has been perceived and in its credibility and effectiveness among various constituencies. This, in turn, has shaped the character of our regional commissions and the way we are responding to assessment issues.

The first of these challenges has been the perceived failure of accreditation to respond effectively to nontraditional education, particularly off-campus programs operating outside the state of the home campus. During the 1970s and 1980s state licensing agencies deplored the inability of regional commissions to develop effective collective systems of review and oversight of such programs. In response, a number of states enacted legislation designed specifically to regulate offcampus programs, particularly those operating from outside the state or the accrediting region. However one may view the response of accrediting commissions to this issue, the situation impaired the credibility of accreditation and opened the door to increasing state involvement in higher education issues.

A second challenge came in the '80s from a series of national reports on the baccalaureate. The reports critiqued the state of undergraduate education within our institutions and called for a series of reforms. Conspicuously absent was any significant mention of the role accrediting agencies have played or could play in improving the quality of the baccalaureate experience. Accrediting commissions were stung by this absence, since each of the regional associations can identify numerous cases of real success in curricular or institutional reform as a result of the accreditation process. Accreditation has been the victim of its own invisibility: Accreditation reports are confidential, and accrediting associations have avoided "going public" with their successes stories as well as with their problem institutions.

A third challenge came in the late '80s with the call from state legislatures, the National Governors Association, and federal policy makers for increased institutional accountability. This challenge has been grounded in the concern that higher education no longer deserves increasing public investment unless institutions are held accountable for the educational performance of graduates. Accreditation reports and decisions do not appear to be based upon the type of assessments that would satisfy the state officials who make funding or other policy decisions.

Most recently, the United States Department of Education established new criteria for the recognition of accrediting bodies, calling for a focus on "educational effectiveness." Regional commissions are now expected systematically to obtain and consider information on educational effectiveness as part of the accreditation process, and to determine whether institutions or programs "document the educational achievement of their students." In this way, state and federal policy makers are drawing accreditation more heavily into the process of holding institutions accountable for effective performance through the assessment of graduates. The adoption of such a regulation by the Department of Education is in itself a major step for it imposes on accrediting associations a substantive requirement that must be incorporated into accrediting standards and processes.

Within this historical and political context, we need to consider the fit between assessment and accreditation and the ways in which assessment and accreditation may be mutually supportive. The American system of peer review and accreditation is unique and needs to survive, yet its influence and prestige have taken some severe blows in the past decade of educational reform. Absent from national reports and not involved in policy talk at state or national levels, the accrediting community must figure out how it can use its expertise in American education to influence educational improvement in meaningful ways. In other words, accreditation needs to be more visible, more vocal, and create a more widespread, public identify for itself as a force for quality.

II. Accreditation and Assessment

Assessment has a key role to play in this process. Assessment can keep accreditation vital, just as accreditation can keep assessment on the map for the long term, after its novelty wears off. It would seem to be a marriage made in heaven. After all "educational improvement" and "accountability" are the twin purposes of both assessment and accreditation, and an emphasis on process and the asking of good questions about educational performance and standards is common to the best practice of both. Both assessment and accreditation can help campuses to advance important but difficult agendas like quality general education or diversity. Both have the potential to focus an institution's attention—at a time when such attention is sorely needed—on the quality of the entire undergraduate experience.

So it is appropriate and understandable that accrediting agencies have attempted to assert their influence with institutions, and have begun to increase emphasis on assessment in the accreditation process. At the same time, it is clear that the pressure for accreditation to move into the assessment arena has largely come from outside the accreditation community. It is important that these external pressures not control the form or content of the approach taken by each accrediting agency in implementing assessment. Now that accreditation is linked to assessment, it is inevitable that all institutions will be asked to engage in assessment activities in the format called for by the institution's regional accrediting association. Just as mandatory testing can cause "teaching to the test," so too will the adoption of accreditation standards cause institutions to "assess to the accreditation standards."

This is not to suggest that these new accreditation initiatives or "assessing to the standard" will necessarily be bad, any more than "teaching to the test" is necessarily bad, if the test in fact encourages the kind of learning we value. But it does highlight the need for accreditors to recognize the implications of their actions: By entering the assessment field, accrediting associations will acquire a new level of influence, if not power, in their relationship to institutions and will play a significant role in determining how assessment is understood and implemented on the vast majority of American college campuses.

As the regional accrediting associations proceed, I am concerned that their approach may resemble not so much voluntary peer review as supervision by a state agency. The danger exists that accrediting associations may direct institutions to embrace assessment in ways that are out of keeping with established accreditation practice. For example, accreditors may promote models borrowed from state mandates, yet many state-mandated assessment initiatives are rooted in skepticism about the value and worth of higher education. Accountability in this setting is a deficit mode, putting the onus on institutions to prove their worth. Such a notion is alien to accreditation and should not form the basis on which accreditation embraces assessment. Assessment for this kind of accountability is also a major source of faculty defensiveness and resistance, yet accreditation depends on faculty cooperation and candor.

III. Toward a "Culture of Evidence"

What, then, should be the basis on which accrediting associations embrace and promote assessment? What is the overriding point? In my view, all the initiatives undertaken by the various regional accrediting associations should have one goal in common: the creation of what we in the Western region are calling a "culture of evidence," that is, a culture within which the institution welcomes critical questions about institutional performance and uses data in responding to such questions. Accrediting agencies need better evidence to support the assertions of quality found in institutional self studies; and institutions need better evidence to inform decision making, budget setting, and improvement efforts. All institutions have considerable amounts of data already that are not adequately disseminated or used within the institution or as part of an accreditation self-study-process. Beyond that, additional relevant information needs to be identified and gathered, particularly with regard to—but not limited to—undergraduate learning outcomes.

Currently, many institutions fail to meet the standards of evidentiary support that we as teachers would require in a freshman essay. Many self studies are submitted with a shockingly low awareness of what is actually happening on the campus and in the educational programs sponsored by the institution. A "culture of evidence" would reflect attentiveness in institutional decision making to questions, particularly questions about educational purposes, and to indicators that lead to the development of information about issues of importance to stakeholders within the institution. Our goal for every institution in the Western region is an inquiring spirit, an attitude that welcomes critical questions about institutional functioning at all levels, and searches out evidence-based answers. In this process, raising the right questions and collecting relevant evidence are as important as the answers.

Assessment is a tool that produces evidence, and an accrediting association should expect all its institutions to use assessment techniques to build a "culture of evidence." At the same time, however, the association should respect the autonomy of each institution and should encourage it to determine for itself the form and scope of assessment efforts. In this spirit, special priority should not be directed to any particular facet of assessment such as testing, value-added approaches, or comprehensive institutional goal-setting. There should be no intention to use assessment punitively, or to compare institutions to one another. The spirit of assessment for all accrediting associations should be to connect better evidence to the accrediting process so that the twin purposes of accreditation—accountability and improvement—can be fulfilled more effectively.

IV. Good Practice: Principles and Caveats

Although the language may look the same, it often means different things in the various regions with different associations moving into the assessment arena in very different ways. Experimentation and diversity of approaches is healthy, as we can all learn from each other's experiences. But institutions within each region cannot shop around for the regional format they like best. Thus, I think it is timely to discuss what principles should underlie *all* accreditation approaches to assessment—and where I detect some dangers.

A. What Do We Mean By "Assessment," Anyway?

One of the first problems we encounter in dealing with assessment is that the term spans many definitions, some narrow, others broad. Adherents of the current assessment movement themselves appear to use "assessment" in a variety of ways, ranging from a definition that includes all testing and evaluation activity to one restricted to information about student learning. Still others use the terms "assessment" and "evaluation" interchangeably.

One stream within the assessment movement places a priority on identifying student achievement as the goal of assessment. There is a growing body of literature, technical instruments, and qualitative approaches that are yielding valuable information about what students learn. Clearly, this is a critically important dimension of assessment. Indeed, in some regions this is the primary emphasis. For example, Middle States has defined assessment as "congruence between an institution's mission, goals, and objectives, and the outcomes of its programs and activities . . . assembled and analyzed *in order to improve teaching and learning*" (emphasis added). But that puts a rather narrow focus on assessment. The North Central Association policy similarly emphasizes student achievement, stating: "An institution should consider a broad range of traditional outcomes, but it must have and describe a program by which it documents student achievement."

Of course student achievement is critical, but when related to the function of accreditation, assessment must extend beyond student achievement. I believe a preferable approach is to adopt consciously a broad definition of assessment, one that includes but reaches beyond a focus on student learning and achievement to encompass the collection and analysis of evidence of effectiveness for *all* parts of an institution. Thus evidence for the quality of student learning is a major concern, for example in general education, the major, or professional training; but so, too, is evidence of the institution's success in such areas as the co-curricular program or establishment of a multicultural and ethnically diverse campus community. Assessment techniques can and should be used to inform discussion and decision making regarding the whole range of major policy issues within an institution.

To illustrate the importance of assessment that extends beyond student achievement, let me cite one of the most important issues facing higher education today—diversity. In Hawaii already, and in California in the next ten to fifteen years, there will no longer be a majority racial group within the state's population. This has enormous implications for every aspect of higher education's functioning. Assessment can and should play a central role in addressing diversity issues; it can be instrumental in improving the quality of student experience on campus, not only for majority students but also for racial and ethnic minorities and nontraditional or returning adult students.

In order to assess how it should respond to the implications of California's changing demographics, Stanford University undertook a two-year self evaluation around diversity issues, culminating in a report entitled *Building a Multiracial, Multicultural University Community*. Central to the findings of this report were the data, qualitative and quantitative, collected as part of this study. There were structured and informal interviews with students and staff members of different minority and ethnic backgrounds. Courses relating to diversity themes were reviewed and minority faculty and graduate student distribution throughout the institution was analyzed, as were completion rates, and a host of other variables. In my opinion, this was an exemplary model of institutional assessment, yet it did not directly address issues of student learning or achievement, at least not in the narrow sense. To the extent we truly believe that assessment is just a means, and not the end itself, we must promote within institutions the use of assessment techniques to address *any* **issue** of importance.

Accrediting commissions need to be careful about whether they are limiting the construction of assessment efforts by the ways in which they explicitly or implicitly define the term. I would argue that assessment techniques of various types can play an important role in providing evidence about the effectiveness of *all* aspects of institutional functioning. Accrediting associations should not be linked with only one strand of a very wide spectrum of approaches, and institutional attention should not be limited to only one assessment focus.

B. The Utility—and Tyranny—of Goals

In their book, *Assessing Institutional Effectiveness,* Peter Ewell and Robert Lisensky state, "Any textbook on evaluation methods will emphasize the proposition that assessment begins with goals." Much of this very useful book like others on the subject, deals with how to work with goals: defining them, refining them, gathering evidence of their achievement, and so on. Goals are commonly assumed to be the indispensable starting point for any assessment effort, the *sine qua non* from which all else follows: choice of method, collection and interpretation of data, the use of information for change and improvement. While many institutions or programs find defining goals the most difficult part of the whole assessment process, they also frequently find it the most productive part. A conversation about goals shifts attention from inputs to educational outcomes, flushes out unspoken assumptions, and contributes to clarity and focus as few other activities can.

The primary approach adopted by the regional commissions, has been to link assessment to the specification and accomplishment of institutional goals. The Southern Association, for example, states in its standard on institutional effectiveness that a program of planning and evaluation consists of "the establishment of a clearly defined purpose," followed by the "formulation of educational goals consistent with the institution's purpose." This is followed by the statement that "the institution *must* define its expected educational results and describe how the achievement of these results will be ascertained." Similarly, The Middle States Association has embraced a goal-oriented model of assessment; the March 20,1990, draft of *A Framework for Outcomes Assessment* defines outcomes assessment as a process which looks for "congruence between an institution's stated *mission, goals and objectives* and the outcomes of its programs and activities" (emphasis added).

As useful as the goal-oriented model of assessment may be, I would argue that it is just *one* way to approach assessment; in many cases it is not the best way, and it certainly should not be prescribed as the only way. Such an approach is essentially hierarchical, linear, deductive: It first establishes a broad principle a goal—and then moves toward stating the goal in sufficiently specific terms to assess its accomplishment. In some institutions, particularly relatively small and homogeneous ones such as liberal arts or church-affiliated colleges, it may be possible to achieve consensus on goals with a reasonable expenditure of time and effort, in which case organizing assessment activities around goals may be entirely appropriate. But for many institutions, particularly larger, more complex ones, focusing energy on goal specification can be an enormously labor intensive and unproductive process. If work gets bogged down at the outset in this way, the entire assessment effort may be at risk. Or the goal-setting exercise may become a meaningless, empty activity. As one campus representative put it to WASC recently, "An institution's development of 'an explicit set of goals' is often solely prompted by external requests. . . . The institution needs to come up with something and as a result ends up with goals to which no one is committed."

One problem with a linear, goal-centered approach is that it is commonly viewed as the only model of reality. We are learning from new theories of intellectual development that there are other equally valid models of human and organizational functioning, other ways of knowing, that also can be applied to assessment. For example, goal-free models can be used or models built on inductive approaches to assessment that generate data around questions of importance. From such questions specific data can be collected and analyzed, and insights drawn about institutional goals. In other words, the derivation of institutional goals become the last rather than the first step in the process. Such analysis can then serve as the basis for further assessment activity.

So there are other ways to skin the assessment cat. One important place for an institution to begin is with "critical questions" about which there is shared concern. Assessment efforts should address those questions negotiated among the institution's stakeholders as most important to answer. They should not be based primarily on an accrediting association's separate agenda. Otherwise the stakeholders' ownership of not only the process of assessment but also of its results can be quickly lost. For example, as part of a review of the general education program, assessment efforts can be designed to address those issues of greatest concern to faculty. Thus an institution might initially choose not to use a testing technique to identify comprehensive general education outcomes, but rather focus on specific questions, e.g.: What general education courses are actually being taken by the students? How effectively do students write or think? How do students perceive and value cultural or ethnic differences?

Even for those institutions wishing to work with goals, it is not necessary to first reach consensus on *all* educational goals. It may be possible to move ahead on some of the least controversial (such as writing or critical thinking skills), and assessment efforts can begin there. Alternatively, various communities—students, faculty, alums, employers—can be surveyed to determine what they think the goals of the institution are or ought to be, and the resulting goals can be acknowledged as merely tentative working statements. The campus can go directly to collecting samples of student work, course syllabi, and the like, and on the basis of these documents, working "backward," infer inductively what the *defacto* goals of the institution seem to be.

We should be open to these alternatives not least of all because it is far from clear that a goal-oriented model corresponds to common practice anyway. In current theories of institutional decision making, the goal-oriented model is called the Rational Choice Model. It assumes that an institution develops a set of goals and collects data about alternative choices, then analyzes the data and chooses the alternative most beneficial to the accomplishment of institutional goals. Baldridge and Deal, in their book *The Dynamics of Organizational Change in Education*, state that in the 1970s the rational choice model was posed as the best theory to describe institutional behavior. Research showed, however, that institutions simply don't function this way. In a section labeled "From Rational Systems to Organized Anarchies," the authors explain that "earlier theories . . . assumed a fairly tight connection between goals, structures, activities and outcomes. People were seen as rational actors whose behavior would and should be guided by what was best for the collective welfare. But one by one, these assumptions have been called into question . . . [I]t soon became apparent that people and organizations are not very rational." Certainly my own experience suggests that educational institutions, like other organizations, generally do not regard goals as their first priority or use them as the reference point for decision making.

Similarly, evaluation theory raises important questions about whether a goal-oriented approach is the most effective. In the evaluation field some people posit four generations of evaluation theories: the first, measurement, relies heavily on statistical analyses; the second, description, focuses on the extent to which stated goals have been accomplished; the third, judgment, calls for a judgment about the quality or worth of an institution (such as is done in making an initial accreditation decision or imposing a sanction on an institution); and the fourth is built on negotiation between stakeholders and evaluators. While accrediting agencies use the second, third, and fourth generations of evaluation most frequently, goal-oriented assessment would seem to limit us to the second generation. But assessment efforts are significantly enhanced by those other dimensions of evaluation.

The point here is that accrediting bodies should be cautious about placing such strong emphasis on goal-oriented approaches to assessment. Volumes have been written on goals and their importance, but the fact of the matter, is that institutional behavior has not been consistent with this literature, and now the literature is beginning to catch up with institutional realities. Other assessment models exist or can be developed, and they may well be superior to such an approach, at least in some circumstances.

C. The Perils of "Comprehensive" Assessment

Accrediting agencies frequently link assessment with "institutional effectiveness." Implicit in this language is the expectation that there will be an effort to assess the effectiveness of the institution as a whole. As stated in the SACS *Resource Manual* on Institutional Effectiveness, "depending upon the size and purpose of the institution, the goal statements may reflect institution-wide aspirations." Folger and Harris in their book *Assessment in Accreditation* state that "the second phase in the evaluation of a purpose statement is to determine whether it covers all significant parts of an institution." Several of the national reports on the baccalaureate suggested in a similar vein that institutions identify expected learning outcomes of the entire college experience and periodically assess for the accomplishment of these goals. State mandates, too, regularly call upon institutions to develop "comprehensive" assessment plans.

Just what types of assessments are intended by such a focus on *institutional* effectiveness, beyond the aggregation of a series of program and co-curricular reviews? I am not sure how an institution would go about this kind of assessment. Moreover, comprehensive assessments of this sort are beyond the technical expertise or financial resources of nearly all institutions. Institutions must start with small pilot projects, learn from them, and build increasing confidence in the role and value of assessment. They should resist external pressure to compromise on the integrity or utility of their assessment process.

The accrediting community must be careful that its policy statements on assessment do not mandate broad, comprehensive assessments, at least initially. Instead, numerous smaller efforts within the institution should be encouraged, taking into account what data and activities are already in place. There is simply no point in asking institutions to undertake assessments for which they lack the resources, experience, and sophistication; I know of institutions that attempted to undertake comprehensive assessments at great cost but with limited value because the infrastructure simply was not present in the institution to support or make use of such efforts. Clearly, such an approach can do more harm than good.

D. Accrediting Commissions Have to Hold Up Their End, Too

If accrediting commissions are going to require assessment from their institutions, they also have an obligation to provide training in assessment, both to institutions undertaking self study and to the members of their visiting teams. At the same time, accrediting commissions should not require more of institutions than they themselves are able to evaluate. These twin principles would seem self-evident, yet accreditation policy statements and resource manuals on assessment frequently set expectations that are beyond not only the capacities of most institutions but of the accrediting process itself.

Few evaluators—or administrators or faculty members for that matter—are trained in assessment, and of those who are, many hold strong opinions about what constitutes proper assessment. Without clear guidance from the accrediting commission about the principles that underlie its approach to assessment, single evaluators are liable to misinterpret the intentions behind assessment requirements and can wield exaggerated influence over an institution's assessment efforts. In order for accreditation initiatives on assessment to be effective, *all* evaluators will need to be properly informed regarding an accrediting association's interpretation of the role and value of assessment data. Similarly, in the conduct of evaluation visits, *all* evaluators should be alert to the use of data to support institutional assertions of quality and effectiveness.

In training as in other areas of assessment, the accrediting associations are groping along at about the same pace as institutions. This, too, is an occasion for collegial cooperation, for consistent attention and incremental development; here, too, we need to start small and build together from a base of common experience.

E. Multiple Realities, Limited Vision

By nearly all definitions, assessment, whether of curricular or co-curricular outcomes, should be far more than the collection of objective clinical data. It may include numbers, but with or without emphasis on quantitative data, there is need for sensitivity to the multiple realities that coexist within our institutions. Our understanding of those multiple realities has been greatly aided by the work of the last two decades on learning styles and intellectual, personal, and moral development, much of it pioneered by gender and ethnic studies. That understanding should be reflected in our assessments, as well.

By "sensitivity to multiple realities" I mean much more than remembering to assess interdisciplinary women's studies courses as well as "mainstream" western civ courses, or coding data so it can be broken out by race, gender, and socio-economic status. I would argue that the multiple constituencies on any campus hold multiple perspectives on the "reality" of that campus's academic and co-curricular life. The range of those perceptions, perspectives, and realities is already extraordinarily wide and growing wider as faculties and student bodies become more diverse. To capture those multiple realities, to learn anything meaningful about a campus, we have to start with the assumption that a single answer to anything just isn't adequate. We need multiple answers, and beyond that, multiple methods that evoke different kinds of answers.

But we need to go even further. We need to recognize that the very act of establishing what we want to assess, the very questions we seek to answer, are in themselves value-laden. They, too, represent not "reality" but *one* reality among many on campus. Embedded in the assessment questions that get asked are a particular hierarchical position, a particular set of values held, for example, by those who sit on the curriculum and courses committee or run academic affairs. Faculty and administrators, particularly white males, need to acknowledge the internalized hierarchy and values encoded in the questions they raise and the outcomes they look for or regard as significant. They need to understand that in the process of collecting such data, they may *not* be raising the kinds of questions or collecting data that meaningfully reflect the values or experiences of their students, particularly the minority and non-traditional students who comprise an increasing proportion of the student body.

At both Stanford and Berkeley, for example, it turns out that efforts to achieve a diverse student body are viewed quite differently by the administrators who lead such efforts and the minority students who supposedly benefit. Surveys have shown that those engaged in recruiting and supporting minority students view their efforts quite positively, even heroically; the "beneficiaries," however, often find themselves isolated and alienated on campus, suffering deeply from the racism they find permeating the curriculum and their interactions with faculty. In the curriculum, they miss serious treatment of minority topics or concerns, while their interactions with faculty are characterized by demeaning and stigmatizing behaviors. At both campuses, minority and majority members of the campus community alike have been shocked to discover the intensity of feeling and the extent of the divergence in perspective. Who can say, in such circumstances, what the "reality" of campus life "really" is?

It follows that assessments should involve multiple methods and multiple judgments of performance; and information should be provided on multiple dimensions of performance and experience. Similarly, all assessment results—whether cognitive, affective, or behavioral—should be collected and presented in a manner that reflects the diversity of the student population and the authenticity of individual student experiences. This principle requires the collecting of information that reflects appropriate differences as well as similarities in student experience, based on such attributes as race/ethnicity, gender, or socio-economic background. It also encourages attention to the diverse ways in which students may learn and develop, based on their own learning styles, past experience, or psychological types. Over all, *"averages"* are to be discouraged as the sole means of reporting assessment results. Aggregate scores are simply less useful in guiding improvement efforts than results broken down by appropriate student subpopulations to show variety in patterns of development and learning.

But beyond all that, on an even more fundamental level, from planning for assessment procedures in both academic and co-curricular areas through collection of data to meaning-making and use of the information, the work must be done by as inclusive and diverse a group as possible—not just because it's politic, but because it's essential.

V. Conclusion

How do we get from where we are now to a "culture of evidence?" What strategies can accrediting agencies and those interested in the growth of the assessment movement employ to foster broader adoption of assessment techniques? The key thing, I believe, is to remember that implementing assessment is a process, not an act. For that process to proceed productively, appropriate communication and support is required, along with opportunities for institutions to adopt assessment to their own campus culture at a pace that they can at least in part control.

Ultimately, I would argue, both accreditation and the assessment movement will be better served by broader and more flexible approaches to assessment. Neither accrediting agencies nor institutions should simply fall in behind a goal-oriented model, when in fact interests on both sides may be better served by a developmental, incremental model that understands assessment above all as a set of central questions about under graduate education from which speculative answers, rationales, information gathering, analysis, conversation, and ultimately, yes, even goals may follow. Neither the integrity of the accreditation process nor educational excellence is served when institutions are pressured into assessment programs more comprehensive than their expertise and infrastructure can support; accreditation and assessment *are* advanced when institutions start small, work collaboratively, and build carefully on a foundation of consent and real utility.

Assessment as it's been commonly understood over the last five years is challenging enough: it demands a major shift of attention within institutions from inputs and resources to evidence of what is actually happening, what educational *results* are occurring. And now, in a sense, I am throwing out yet another challenge on top of that first one: to make assessment less formulaic, *more* flexible, more institution-specific. I'm suggesting that we let go of recipes and give up our adherence to the letter of mandates in order to better serve their spirit.

Experimentation requires courage. The changes that I am suggesting, like any change, can be threatening, and there are legitimate concerns we need to address along the way. But I'm assuming that the risk will be worth it in the end. I'm reminded of James Baldwin, who writes in the book *Nobody Knows My Name* that "any real change implies the breakup of the world as one has always known it, the loss of all that gave one identity, the end of safety. And at such a moment . . . one clings to. . . what one possessed or dreamed one possessed. Yet it is only when man is able, without bitterness or self-pity, to surrender a dream he has long cherished, or a privilege he has long possessed, that he is set free—that he has set himself free—for higher dreams, for greater privileges."

Assessment can provide the lever for this kind of change: for a major shift of attention within institutions to evidence of what is actually happening; and for the educational improvement that will hopefully ensue. Such a change will affect us all, accrediting commissions and institutions alike. As accrediting associations act, there will be state and federal agencies watching, and institutions, and the public, each with different concerns. I believe the accrediting community is capable of meeting this challenge. The marriage of accreditation and assessment isn't really a shotgun marriage, and it hasn't yet proven to be one made in heaven, either. Let's work for a satisfying partnership.

A Handbook of Accreditation

NORTH CENTRAL ASSOCIATION OF COLLEGES AND SCHOOLS

I. The Commission on Institutions of Higher Education

Voluntary accreditation as carried out by the various accrediting bodies is a process uniquely American. Accreditation is sought voluntarily by institutions and is conferred by non-governmental bodies. Voluntary accreditation has two fundamental purposes: quality assurance and institutional and program improvement. There are two types of educational accreditation: institutional accreditation and specialized accreditation.

Institutional Accreditation

Institutional accreditation evaluates an entire institution and accredits it as a whole. An institutional accrediting body evaluates more than the formal educational activities of an institution; it assesses as well such characteristics as governance and administration, financial stability, admissions and student personnel services, institutional resources, and relationships with outside communities. The widely different purposes and scopes of educational institutions demand that the criteria by which an institutional accrediting body makes its judgments be broad enough to encompass, if not encourage, innovation yet clear enough to assure acceptable quality.

Several agencies provide institutional accreditation. Within the Council on Postsecondary Accreditation (COPA), a national umbrella organization for accrediting associations, six regional (Middle States, New England, North Central, Northwest, Southern, and Western) and six other accrediting associations are recognized as institutional accrediting associations. Some, such as the Association of Theological Schools and the American Association of Bible Colleges, provide institutional accreditation for institutions with particular religious purposes. Others, such as the Association of Independent Colleges and Schools and the National Association of Trade and Technical Schools, accredit primarily institutions that are for-profit. The National Home Study Council accredits institutions that provide correspondence programs. While independent of one another, the six regional associations cooperate extensively and recognize one another's accreditation.

A number of the institutions affiliated with the Commission on Institutions of Higher Education of the North Central Association of Colleges and Schools are accredited by more than one institutional accrediting association. The Commission requires that these institutions describe themselves in identical terms to both associations in regard to purpose, governance, programs, degrees, diplomas, certificate, personnel, finances, and constituents. The commission also requires that it be apprised of any changes in status made by the other accrediting agency.

Specialized Accreditation

Specific programs within an educational institution can also seek accreditation. This specialized (or program) accreditation evaluates particular units, schools, or programs within an institution and is often associated with national professional associations, such as those for engineering, medicine, or law, or with specific disciplines, such as business, education, psychology, or social work. There are more than forty such specialized bodies recognized by COPA. Institutional accreditation is separate from the accreditation given or withheld by professional associations, although the Commission does take cognizance of the standards set by professional bodies.

The North Central Association

On March 29 and 30, 1895, thirty-six school, college, and university administrators from seven Midwestern states met at Northwestern University in response to an invitation signed by the presidents of the University of Chicago, the University of Michigan, Northwestern University, and University of Wisconsin, and by the principals of Grand Rapids High School, Michigan Military Academy, and the Michigan Normal School. They had been called to "organize, if deemed expedient, an association of colleges and schools of the North-Central States." The constitution of the association these educators formed stated that the North Central Association's object would be "the establishment of close relations between the colleges and secondary schools" of the region. In February 1991, a specially appointed Committee that includes representatives of both Commissions began preparations for the celebration of the Association Centennial in 1995.

Within a short time, the desire to improve articulation between secondary schools and colleges led to extensive examination of the quality of education at both levels; and that led to the accreditation of secondary schools and, later, colleges and universities.

Two histories of the Association—Calvin O. Davis' *A History of the North Central Association* (1945) and Louis G. Geiger's *Voluntary Accreditation: A History of the North Central Association 1945–1970* (1970)—trace this evolution and chronicle the decisions and actions the Association has taken to provide educational leadership to the region and the country.

Today, the Association serves colleges and schools in nineteen states—Arizona, Arkansas, Colorado, Illinois, Indiana, Iowa, Kansas, Michigan, Minnesota, Missouri, Nebraska, New Mexico, North Dakota, Ohio, Oklahoma, South Dakota, West Virginia, Wisconsin, and Wyoming—and the American Dependents' Schools operated overseas for the children of American military and civilian personnel. Its day-to-day operations are conducted by its two Commissions: the [postsecondary] **Commission on Schools,** located in Tempe, Arizona, which accredits institutions below the post secondary degree-granting level; and the **Commission on Institutions of Higher Education,** in Chicago, Illinois, which accredits institutions of higher education.

A Brief History of the Commission

Since it began accrediting higher education institutions in 1913, what is now known as the Commission on Institutions of Higher Education of the North Central Association of Colleges and Schools has tried both to reflect and to encourage progress in higher education. At first, higher education institutions were measured against a set of standards. Some were quite explicit ("the college, if a corporate institution, shall possess a productive endowment of not less than $200,000"; "the college should limit the number of students in a recitation or laboratory class to thirty"); others were broader ("the college should be provided with adequate books in the library and laboratory equipment to develop and fully illustrate each course taught"). During the first decades of the century, such quantitative and prescriptive standards helped to bring some order to higher education.

But as early as 1921 President Henry Pratt Judson of the University of Chicago warned against the danger of excessive rigidity in the standards; and by the end of the twenties, critics charged that the standards had become roadblocks to legitimate experimentation and constructive change. The North Central Association's colleges commission responded to these concerns by undertaking an exhaustive study of its accreditation process.

This reconsideration ended in a fundamental shift in the emphasis of the accreditation process that led the Commission to the principles that still guide it today. The concept process of standardization was abandoned. Henceforth, the Association declared in 1924, an institution would be judged "on the basis of the total pattern it presents. . . . It is accepted as a principle of procedure that superiority in some characteristics may be regarded as compensating, to some extent, for deficiencies in other respects . . . an institution will be judged in terms of the purpose it seeks to serve." Under this new approach, strengths were to be weighed against weaknesses to evaluate the "total pattern" of the institution. Before, it was assumed that all institutions had the same fundamental purposes; now, the increasing diversity of institutions was to be recognized. Each institution was to be judged in the light of its own self-declared purposes—as long as these were appropriate to a higher education institution. "Standards" were replaced by "criteria"; "inspectors" became "examiners"; and the basis for accreditation decisions became a comparison of data concerning an institution against a set of "norms" derived from data accumulated from many institutions. The "pattern" of data from the institution being evaluated was compared to a "pattern map" based on these norms, and the institution was accredited if the two patterns seemed to match.

The normative technique was used until after World War II. It became apparent that the notion of standardization—the pressure to conform—was inherent in the very idea of norms. The idea of a norm assumes similarity; institutions could not be measured against a norm unless they were basically alike. Moreover, using normative data to make evaluation decisions also conflicted with the principle that an institution was to be judged in terms of its own purposes. Further, in 1957 the Commission began a program of periodically reaffirming the accreditation of member institutions. As a consequence, a new emphasis was placed on institutional renewal and improvement.

In response to these developments, the Commission produced its *Guide for the Evaluation of Institutions of Higher Education* (1958). The *Guide* moved beyond the idea of norms and the pattern map to direct the attention of both institutions and Commission examiners to seven basic questions that were considered indicative of the areas that needed to be assessed in order to determine the quality of an educational institution (e.g., "What is the educational task of the institution?"; "Are the necessary resources available for carrying out the task . . .?" "Is student life on campus relevant to the institution's task?"). The focus of evaluation became more qualitative, less quantitative; and, as a result, the professional judgment of the Commission's examiners became proportionately more important in the evaluation decision. The *Guide* was in use in various editions until the early seventies, and the areas it addressed are still present in the Commission's current Criteria.

In the sixties and seventies, the Commission's membership increased both in size and variety. Community colleges, vocational-technical institutes, and specialized institutions assumed an increasing importance in American education; and the configurations of resources and organization appropriate to them were not always comparable to those traditionally found in four-year colleges and universities. The Commission joined the other regional postsecondary accrediting commissions in responding to these changes by adopting a set of "conditions for eligibility" in the early seventies; in effect, these conditions limited and described the kinds of postsecondary institutions the regional associations would accredit. Since the mid-seventies, when its *Handbook on Accreditation* first appeared, the Commission has increasingly emphasized the self-study process as both a procedure for gathering data for accreditation decisions and a means to institutional improvement.

In 1981, the Commission adopted the **Criteria for Accreditation and Criteria for Candidacy for Accreditation,** which incorporate and supersede all previous statements and serve as the basis for the accreditation process as it is currently conducted by the Commission. In 1987, the Commission reformulated its **General Institutional Requirements,** which define the essential characteristics of all its affiliated institutions (see Chapter II).

Committed to continual review of the effectiveness of its work, the Commission in 1991-92 has undertaken a significant reexamination of its policies, procedures, requirements, criteria, and mission through a Committee on Critical Issues. Among the Committee's concerns are issues of consistency and fairness, the universe of institutions served, promotion of quality higher education, and greater public awareness and understanding of the role and function of accreditation. The Commission will share its findings and recommendations with member institutions for thorough review and discussion at various points in the process. Proposed changes will then be circulated to all member institutions before the Commission takes final action. The project is expected to be completed in mid-1993.

The Mission of the Commission

The mission of the Commission, as adopted on January 21, 1980, reads as follows:

The Commission on Institutions of Higher Education, a component of the North Central Association of Colleges and Schools, is an organization of those member institutions of the Association accredited by the Commission. These institutions are joined together for two fundamental purposes

1.   **to establish and apply criteria for the accreditation of postsecondary education;**

2.   **to assist affiliated institutions in the improvement of their educational programs and related activities.**

In addition to the member institutions, institutions judged by the Commission capable of achieving accreditation in a reasonable time may be affiliated with the Commission in nonmembership categories.

The Commission limits its scope of activities to postsecondary institutions located in the North Central region and having certain organizational, operational, and educational characteristics as set forth for various types of institutions by the Commission.

The primary means utilized to achieve the purposes of the Commission is the accreditation process. Beginning with the institutional self-study and self-evaluation as a device both for institutional improvement and for assembling the information needed for external evaluation, the accreditation process subjects an institution to an external evaluation by persons from peer institutions. At the successful conclusion of the evaluation the Commission accepts the institution as a member of the Association and certifies that the institution meets the Criteria for Accreditation set forth by the Commission.

In addition to conducting the accreditation process, the Commission in furtherance of its fundamental purposes

1.   regularly monitors institutions affiliated with it, both to ascertain that they continue to achieve their avowed purposes and to become aware of ways in which the Commission can assist them in improving their effectiveness;

2.   maintains a continuing relationship with other groups concerned with accreditation and education improvement, especially the schools;

3.   subjects its criteria and procedures for accreditation to continuing study to be sure they represent the best theory and practice of institutional accreditation and are responsive to the educational need of society;

4.   provides reasonable and appropriate public information about the institutions affiliated with the Commission;

5. provides assistance to affiliated but unaccredited institutions to assist them in fulfilling the requirements of accreditation;

6. studies, and assists others to study, current issues in postsecondary education bearing on the maintenance and improvement of educational institutions;

7. prepares and disseminates publications, provides counsel, and conducts meetings directed at the improvement of postsecondary education;

8. promotes the self-regulation of institutions by requiring or recommending good practices for the conduct of institutional activities.

The Commission fulfills these purposes by formulating criteria appropriate to the task, assisting institutions engaged in self-study, requiring periodic evaluation visits by peers, monitoring institutional developments between evaluation visits, and publishing materials and conducting programs bearing on institutional evaluation and improvement. Through its processes the Commission aims at strengthening its affiliated institutions; through its evaluation and monitoring the Commission seeks to assure the public of the acceptable nature of accredited institutions.

The Commission Offices and Services

A full-time staff in the Commission's Chicago office responds to inquiries and provides assistance to institutions, evaluation teams, other agencies, and the public.

The Commission and its staff provide a number of services for institutions. Each institution affiliated with the Commission is assigned to a member of the Commission's professional staff. This staff member serves as the institution's resource person and liaison with the Commission office. The relationship is particularly important when an institution is engaged in self-study for evaluation for initial or continued candidacy or accreditation. (Because of the importance of this working relationship, the Commission will remove liaison activities with an institution from a member of the professional staff when it appears that a conflict of interest might be present. The Commission policy, available on request, outlines some potential areas of conflict of interest.)

Institutional representatives are invited to visit the Commission's office in Chicago and meet with their staff liaison; Commission staff visit institutions on request. Institutions preparing for an evaluation of any kind are encouraged to communicate with their staff liaison. Although not all institutional changes require Commission action, it is essential that an institution contact the staff whenever it considers a change that might affect its status with the Commission (see Chapter IV.) To assist in communication, the Commission maintains a WATS line, an 800 toll-free line, and a fax machine.

Through its publications, the Commission provides information about its work. *A Handbook of Accreditation, A Guide to Self-Study for Commission Evaluation,* and *A Manual for the Evaluation Visit,* the principle publications of the Commission, should be consulted for essential information about Commission policies and procedures. The *Briefing* newsletter, published three times each year, is especially helpful for information on current developments. The *NCA Quarterly is* another useful resource, with each of the Association's two Commissions responsible for two issues a year—one issue providing that commission's formal list of affiliated institutions, the other serving as a journal of articles relevant to that Commission's work.

The Commission also conducts an extensive program on self-study, evaluation, and institutional improvement for institutional representatives and Consultant-Evaluators as a part of the Annual Meeting of the North Central Association held in early spring in Chicago. One outcome of this program is the annual publication, *A Collection of Papers on Self-Study and Institutional Improvement,* which provides useful information from the perspective of persons who have recently been involved in self-study, experienced evaluators, and others involved in higher education.

The Commission receives a wide variety of communications from the general public. The office responds directly to such matters as they relate to affiliation; many inquiries are referred to other appropriate associations and agencies. The Commission's brochure, *Accreditation of Postsecondary Institutions: An Overview,* is particularly helpful in explaining the work of the Commission to the general public.

Relations with Governmental Agencies

To determine eligibility for the United States government assistance under certain legislation, the U.S. Department of Education consults the lists of postsecondary institutions affiliated with nationally recognized accrediting agencies that the government views as reliable authorities on the quality of educational institutions and programs. Since the Commission on Institutions of Higher Education is among these governmentally-recognized authorities, affiliation with the Commission helps an institution become eligible for various federal funds. The most recent review of the Commission by the USDE was conducted in 1987. The Commission is scheduled for review for continued recognition in 1991–92.

The Commission also maintains communications and discussions with officers of state coordinating and governing boards to clarify the functions and concerns of the Commission with respect to its affiliated institutions affected by these types of boards.

The Council on Postsecondary Accreditation

The Council on Postsecondary Accreditation (COPA) is a national nongovernmental organization that works to facilitate the role of accrediting bodies in promoting and ensuring the quality and diversity of American postsecondary education. The accrediting bodies, while established and supported by their memberships, are intended to serve the broader interests of society as well. To promote these ends, COPA periodically reviews the activities of the accrediting bodies it recognizes and provides other services directed at the improvement of accreditation.

The Commission has been recognized by COPA since COPA's founding in 1975. The Commission's recognition was continued in 1991 following its periodic review.

II. Affiliation with the Commission

Forms of Affiliation

Postsecondary educational institutions may be affiliated with the Commission on Institutions of Higher Education, and through it with the Association, in either of two ways. One is as a **candidate** institution; the other is as an **accredited** institution. Both affiliations are voluntary and are initiated by an institution.

Since candidacy is not a prerequisite to accreditation, an institution applying for initial affiliation with the Commission may apply for either status. The staff member assigned to work with the institution will explain the options available as the institution begins its self-study. New or developing institutions will usually choose to seek candidacy; older, more established institutions sometimes choose to seek accreditation, The choice of which form of affiliation to pursue will be based on the institution's assessment of whether it meets the Criteria for Candidacy or the Criteria for Accreditation.

Unaffiliated institutions initiate the affiliation process by formally contacting the Executive Director of the Commission. The Commission office provides the institution with a copy of *A Handbook of Accreditation* and a **Preliminary Information Form** (PIF) (see Appendix B) that is designed to assist the institution in preparing the materials needed to demonstrate that it meets the General Institutional Requirements. The institution then submits its PIF documentation to the Commission for review by the staff. To support the PIF, the institution must submit the institutional catalog, faculty and student handbooks, certification of legal authorization to operate, and the report of the most recent external financial audit. A fee of $1,000 must accompany the PIF materials. Following the staff review, the institution receives a copy of the staff analysis. If any questions have been raised about one or more of the General Institutional Requirements, these are indicated on the analysis. When the review indicates probable compliance with all of the General Requirements, the institution is invited to begin its preparation for a comprehensive evaluation and is assigned to a Commission staff member. At that time the institution pays an additional fee of $500. The institution should contact the Commission staff member before beginning the self-study process. A complete Self-Study Report—not a completed Preliminary Information Form—is the formal application for affiliation with the Commission.

Candidacy Status

Candidacy is a preaccreditation status and, unlike accredited status, does not carry with it membership in the Association. Candidacy indicates that an institution meets the Commission's General Institutional Requirements (GIRs) and Criteria for Candidacy and is progressing toward accreditation; it does not automatically assure eventual accreditation. Candidacy gives an institution the opportunity to establish a formal, publicly-recognized relationship with the Association. It is the recommended approach to seeking accreditation for most non-affiliated institutions.

An institution achieves candidacy status after the Commission has determined through the process outlined in Chapter IV that it meets the GIRs and the Criteria for Candidacy.

- An institution being evaluated for candidacy must have students actively pursuing its programs at the time of the team visit.

- An institution continues its candidacy for a fixed period of time until it either fulfills the Criteria for Accreditation or has its affiliation with the Commission terminated. The maximum length of candidacy is six years. Extensions of candidacy beyond the sixth year are granted only rarely and require special Commission action.

- An institutional holding candidacy may request, after consultation with Commission staff, that it be evaluated for accreditation—rather than continued candidacy—whenever it believes that it can demonstrate that it meets the Criteria for Accreditation.

- An institution denied candidacy upon initial application must wait one year before reapplying. This period of time may be shortened by action of the Commission.

Accreditation Status

Accreditation indicates both to other institutions and to the public that an institution meets the Commission's General Institutional Requirements and Criteria for Accreditation. It also indicates the institution's commitment to the purposes and goals of the Association.

An institution becomes accredited, and thus a member, after the Commission has determined through the evaluation process outlined in Chapter IV that it meets the GIRs and the Criteria for Accreditation.

- An institution being evaluated for accreditation must have students actively pursuing its programs at the time of the team visit.

- An institution must have graduated at least one class of students before Commission action is taken. If the institution has graduated its first class not more than one year before the Commission's evaluation, the effective date of the accreditation will be the date of graduation of that first class.

- An institution continues its membership and accreditation as long as it continues to meet the GIRs, the Criteria for Accreditation, and the other obligations of membership.

- An institution denied accreditation upon initial application must wait two years before reapplying. This period of time may be shortened by action of the Commission.

Resignation from Affiliation

Affiliation with the Association and the Commission is voluntary, and an institution may resign its affiliation at any time. Resignation from affiliation terminates the institution's candidacy on accreditation; it must be initiated by action of the legally designated governing body of the institution. Resignation does not release the institution from past and current financial obligations with the commission. An institution wishing to reaffiliate must follow the same procedures as an institution never affiliated with the Commission.

General Institutional Requirements

Every postsecondary educational institution affiliated with the Commission must demonstrate that it satisfies each of the following **General Institutional Requirements**. Taken together, they define the kind of institution that the Commission considers a part of its educational universe.

The General Institutional Requirements

An institution affiliated with the Commission by either accreditation or candidacy has to meet the following requirements:

1. Mission and Authorization

a. **The institution has formally adopted and made public its statement of mission.**

The term "statement of mission" refers to a general statement of the goals the institution wishes to pursue, such as might be found in the statutes establishing a public institution or in the incorporation statement of an independent institution. More precise goals ("purposes") against which the institution can measure its accomplishments are the subject of Criterion One.

b. **The statement of mission is appropriate to an institution of higher education.**

This Requirement specifies that affiliated institutions have a statement of mission appropriate to an institution of higher education. In choosing the words "higher education," the Commission attempts to differentiate between those institutions with missions to supplement secondary education and training (such institutions typically seek accreditation from the Commission on Schools) and those institutions with missions to provide degree programs of rigor and discipline sufficient to warrant the name higher education. Institutions of higher education, however, share some goals and purposes with all postsecondary institutions. Therefore, Criterion One uses the term "postsecondary educational institution" to incorporate the full scope of institutional goals and purposes.

---

c. **The institution confers certification, diplomas or degrees.**

d. **The institution has legal authority to confer its certificates, diplomas and degrees.**

e. **The institution meets all legal requirements to operate wherever it conducts activities.**

This Requirement is of particular legal importance to institutions offering courses and/or programs in several locations. It is the institution's responsibility to document that it has necessary authorizations.

2. Educational Programs

a. **The educational programs are compatible with the institution's mission.**

b. **The principal educational programs are based on recognized fields of study at the postsecondary level.**

The Commission permits—and expects—reasonable experimentation in developing and defining new fields of study, but its scope is limited to institutions doing this in the context of fields already recognized in higher education. Judging the recognition of a field of study is made by considering a number of indicators. For example, considerations might include whether the field is taught in several different institutions; whether there is literature distributed to others through journals and monographs and widely available in libraries; whether the field has given rise to a licensed profession or vocation; and whether there are professional organizations among persons in the field. An institution offering work only in fields not yet fully formed and recognized lies outside the Commission's ability to evaluate and certify.

c. **At least one of the undergraduate programs is two or more academic years in length (or the equivalent). If no undergraduate programs are offered, at least one of the graduate programs is one or more academic years in length.**

While the Commission regards offering short courses as appropriate, its scope is limited to institutions that do this in a context established by the presence of more extended programs. "Academic year" denotes the amount of instructional and study time required, using the typical academic year as the standard.

d. **General education at the postsecondary level is an essential element of undergraduate degree programs and a prerequisite to graduate degree programs.**

The Commission's understanding of the term "general education" is expressed in its 1983 Statement on General Education:

> General education is "general" in clearly identifiable ways: it is not directly related to a student's formal technical, vocational or professional preparation; it is a part of every student's course of study, regardless of his or her area of emphasis; and it is intended to impart common knowledge, intellectual concepts, and attitudes that every educated person should possess.

Since general education is regarded as primarily an undergraduate component, the Commission has explicitly provided that graduate programs appropriate speak through their admissions requirements to the need for general education.

Institutions should include in their discussion of this Requirement a statement regarding an overall philosophy of general education, the ways in which it relates to specific majors and specialized areas, and an indication of its critical role in the total educational program.

e. **General education and/or a program of related instruction at the postsecondary level is an essential element of undergraduate certificate and diploma two or more academic years in length.**

Undergraduate certificate and diploma programs that extend as long as degree programs should provide for more than immediate vocational interests. Because of the strong vocational component in such programs, general education or related instruction or a combination of general education and related instruction may be used to provide this broadening. "Related instruction" is drawn from the usage in vocational-technical education: instruction broadening a curriculum beyond purely vocational purposes, but closely associated with those purposes, and sometimes incorporated into vocational courses. Such instruction commonly provides for the development of knowledge and skills in language, mathematics, and human relations. Institutions should include in their discussions of this Requirement a statement regarding the purposes that related education is expected to serve and the way in which related education is an essential part of the overall educational program.

f. **The certificate, diploma or degree awarded upon successful completion of an educational program is appropriate to the demonstrated attainment of the graduate.**

The integrity of each institution's credential is a necessary condition to sustain public confidence in higher education. While specific degree requirements vary among institutions, there are general understandings of the meanings of several degrees, and institutions are expected to follow these understandings in naming degrees.

3. Institutional Organization

a. **There is a governing board, legally responsible for the institution, which establishes and regularly reviews basic policies that govern the institution and protect its integrity.**

The hallmark of the governing board is that it bears the legal responsibility for the institution. This Requirement mandates both Board establishment and regular Board review of basic policies. By "integrity" the Commission means coherence between word and deed. Although a governing board may have some members who are employees of the institution, substantial overlap may jeopardize the integrity of the institution.

b. **The governing board includes individuals who represent the public interest.** (Note: In rare situations the Commission may approve alternative means by which the interest of the public are appropriately represented when unusual circumstances prohibit public representatives on the board.)

The activities of educational institutions have long-term effects on society. Consequently, the Commission requires that there be opportunity for appropriate expression of the public interest in the policy and decision making activities of the institution. That opportunity is most reasonably assured if there are governing board members whose connections to the institution do not raise the possibility that institutional decisions and actions will affect them personally and who recognize an obligation to represent the public interest in their governing board service. With increasing frequency the Commission expects to find a substantial portion of the Board representing the public interest.

c. **An executive officer is designated by the governing board to administer the institution.**

The Executive Officer is the Commission's usual point of contact with the institution.

d. **A faculty comprising persons qualified by education and experience is significantly involved in the development and review of the educational programs.**

"Faculty" refers to a body, not to individuals, and this clearly identified group of qualified persons must participate in the oversight of the educational programs. The composition of the faculty is the institution's responsibility; in most institutions teachers compose the largest component of the faculty. The requirement specifies "significant involvement" which need not include final approval authority. Both the development of new educational programs and the review of existing educational programs fall within the work of the faculty.

e. **Admissions policies are consistent with the institution's mission and appropriate to the educational programs.**

f. **Admissions practices conform to the admissions policies.**

Requirements 3.e. and 3.f. reflect the Commission's concern about the ethics of an institution's student recruitment practices. Admissions practices are especially important as institutions venture into new programs or contractual agreements.

• • •

1. **The institution has clear and publicly stated purposes, consistent with its mission and appropriate to a postsecondary educational institution.**

Each of the other Criteria is related to this fundamental one that embodies the Commission's philosophy of judging an institution on the basis of its own purposes and their appropriateness to a postsecondary educational institution. As it is used here, "purposes" refers to the multiple and specific ends the institution wishes to achieve in order to carry out its more general "mission." Most institutions have broad, general statements of mission that are relatively brief. Statements of purposes,—of long- and short-range institutional goals, of programmatic objectives—are more specific and detailed. "Consistent" means that the relationship between the stated mission and stated purposes must clear. For example, an institution's mission might be, in part, "to meet the educational needs" of its community; a related might be "to provide vocational and technical training through continuing education to adults."

Determining whether these purposes are "clearly and publicly stated" involves judgment of more than where and how they are published and found; it also involves determining whether there seems to be among its various constituents and members a common understanding of the purposes of the institution.

2. **The institution has effectively organized adequate human, financial and physical resources into educational and other programs to accomplish its purposes.**

This Criterion focuses on whether an institution has the necessary resources appropriately organized into its educational and other programs so that it can be expected to accomplish its purposes. Judging that an institution meets this Criterion requires comprehensive information—about governing boards, administrators, faculty, staff, students and the community; about the institution's financial condition; about its facilities—and careful evaluation of how the institution's resources are deployed and administered to make accomplishment of its purposes feasible.

3. **The institution is accomplishing its purposes.**

This Criterion requires a critical appraisal of the entire institution, an evaluation of its current record in achieving its own purposes. The Commission dictates no single methodology for accomplishing this appraisal, but does expect that an institution will assess its successes and failures systematically and objectively, both as a basis for accreditation judgment and as a prerequisite to self-improvement.

To make explicit its position on the rigorous assessment of institutional efforts, and to ensure that every accredited institution includes documentation of its students academic achievement as a part of the evidence that it meets this criterion, the Commission adopted the following statement in October 1989:

To assure that member institutions take the initiative necessary to comply with the specific requirement on the documentation of student academic achievement at the undergraduate and graduate levels, the Commission has established the following schedule that requires all affiliated institutions to be reviewed for compliance by June 1995. This schedule was reported to all affiliated institutions and evaluators through a series of special mailings and through articles in the Commission's *Briefing* newsletter.

- **Institutions scheduled for evaluation in 1991–92**

  — The statement was implemented in the 1991–92 evaluation cycle. Evaluation teams conducting comprehensive visits include a review of the progress made by institutions in responding to Commission's initiative.

  — Some 1991–92 Commission-mandated focused visits will also review the institution's progress in this area. Staff determined these visits in consultation

---

Commission Statement on Assessment and Student Academic Achievement

The Commission affirms that the evaluation/accreditation process offers both a means of providing public assurance of an institution's effectiveness and a stimulus to institutional improvement. The Commission's criteria require an institution to demonstrate the clarity and appropriateness of its purposes as a postsecondary educational institution; to show that it has adequate human, financial, and physical resources effectively organized for the accomplishment of those purposes; and to provide assurance that it can continue to be an effective institution. A variety of assessment approaches in its evaluation processes strengthens the institution's ability to document its effectiveness.

The Commission reaffirms its position that assessment is an important element in an institution's overall evaluation processes. The Commission does not prescribe a specific approach to assessment. That determination should be made by the institution in terms of is own purposes, resources, and commitments. Assessment is not an end in itself, but a means of gathering information that can be used in number of areas. An assessment program, to be effective, should provide information that assists the institution in making useful decisions about the improvement of the institution and in developing plans for that improvment. An institution is expected to describe in its self-study the ways that it evaluates its effectiveness and how those results are used to plan for institutional improvement.

The Commission wants to make clear that all institutions are expected to assess the achievement of their students. With this statement we make explicit the Commission's position that student achievement is a critical component in assessing overall institutional effectiveness. Our expectation is that an institution has and is able to describe a program by which it documents student academic achievement.

with the institutions. If the focused visit was **not** expanded, the institution was placed in one of the categories listed below.

- **Institutions scheduled for evaluation in 1992–95**

  — All comprehensive evaluations scheduled in these cycles will include a review of institutional progress in developing and implementing a program to document student academic achievement.

  — All Commission-mandated focused visits will be expanded to include evaluation of the institution's progress in responding to the Commission's initiative.

- **Institutions scheduled for evaluation after Spring 1995**

  — Affiliated institutions not scheduled for any evaluation (comprehensive or focused) until the beginning of the 1995–96 cycle (September 1995) must submit a report documenting an institutional plan or program sometime before June 30, 1995. With each Annual Report from 1993 through spring 1995, the Commission will provide a special reminder letter to an institution that has not yet filed that report. (See Chapter V for further information about these reports.)

  On receipt of the reports, staff together with appropriate Consultant-Evaluators will evaluate the documents and determine whether further information or monitoring is needed. The determination will reflect the passage of the time; that is, the closer to 1995, the greater the expectation of more specificity and evidence of implementation.

  In the summer of 1995, the staff and appropriate Consultant-Evaluators will review the list of institutions that have not submitted a plan or program. They will develop recommendations for Commission action for each institution, with most recommendations requiring the scheduling of a focused visit

4. **The institution can continue to accomplish its purposes.**

If accreditation is to serve both educators and the public, it is necessary to make predictions about the strength and stability of educational institutions.

While accreditation cannot guarantee that an institution will always remain strong, it represents the best judgment at the time of the evaluation about the institution's prospects for the future.

Judgments about an institution's future must be based, in part, on the success of its past and present. How well it has developed its resources to their present condition, how stable its faculty and administration have been, how strong it is at the moment are all indicators of the future. But the Commission also seeks information about the institution's plans and outstanding commitments: about whether it has a good sense of its effectiveness, whether it is capable of addressing its inadequacies, whether it has realistically assessed the conditions that will impinge upon it in the future, whether it has the financial and other resources necessary to respond to unforeseen circumstances, whether it has leadership wise and farsighted enough to anticipate future opportunities and difficulties and respond to them in constructive and creative ways. The Commission also considers how effectively the institution used the self study process to enhance its plans for improvement.

The Criteria for Candidacy

To be granted candidacy by the Commission on Institutions of Higher Education, an institution must demonstrate that it fulfills the General Institutional Requirements and the **Criteria for Candidacy for Accreditation.**

The Criteria for Candidacy for Accreditation

A candidate for accreditation:

1. has clear and publicly stated purposes, consistent with its mission and appropriate to a postsecondary educational institution;

2. has effectively organized adequate human, financial and physical resources into educational and other programs so that it is accomplishing is immediate purposes;

3. is following realistic plans to acquire and organize any additional resources needed to accomplish its stated purposes;

4. has the potential to achieve accreditation within the candidacy period.

The Criteria for Candidacy are closely related to the Criteria for Accreditation since they are meant to provide candidate institutions with foundation for logical development toward accreditation. The Criteria for Candidacy differ from those for accreditation, reflecting the fact that a candidate institution has not yet developed to the point where it meets the Criteria for Accreditation and is, therefore, accreditable.

The following is a brief commentary on the Criteria for Candidacy.

1. **The institution has clear and publicly stated purposes, consistent with its mission and appropriate to a postsecondary educational institution.**

   This Criterion is identical to Criterion One for Accreditation, since every institution affiliated with the Commission must have at least such purposes.

2. **The institution has effectively organized adequate human, financial and physical resources into educational and other programs so that it is accomplishing its immediate purposes.**

   This Criterion differs from the second Criterion for Accreditation in that it speaks of a candidate's accomplishing its **immediate** purposes. The difference is meant to acknowledge that a candidate is not yet fully developed to the point at which it has the ability to accomplish *all* of its purposes. However, the wording of this Criterion—unlike that of Criterion Two for Accreditation—requires that the candidate not only have organized the resources to accomplish these immediate purposes, but that it be accomplishing them. . . .

3. **The institution is following realistic plans to acquire and organize any additional resources needed to accomplish all of its stated purposes.**

   This Criterion directs attention to the institution's plans for development over the candidacy period. It requires that the candidate demonstrate that it has conducted a Self-Study and that it has planned or implemented reliable mechanisms by which it can assess and address institutional strengths and weaknesses on an ongoing basis, including an institution-wide program for the systematic documentation of its students' academic achievement. The Criterion expects that information from assessment, now and in the future, will be linked to systematic planning (for students, faculty, staff, curriculum, finance, physical plant, development, etc.), and that sufficient to accomplish *all* of its stated purposes within the candidacy period.

4. **The institution has the potential to achieve accreditation within the candidacy period.**

    In making this judgment, the candidate's present condition, its plans and its timetable for developing to the point where it meets the Criteria for Accreditation must be examined. Candidacy is of limited duration, and the Commission seeks to determine through this Criterion that the candidate's current plans are likely to allow it to achieve accreditation within this limited period.

Obligations of Affiliation

All institutions affiliated with the Commission voluntarily agree to meet institutional obligations of affiliation, including undergoing periodic review and making reports as requested by the Commission. Failure to fulfill these obligations could result in loss of affiliation.

Payment of dues and fees is also an obligation of affiliation. The Commission bills affiliated institutions for annual dues that are payable on receipt of the billing and are not refundable under any circumstances. The Commission reserves the right to withdraw the affiliation of an institution that, after due notice, fails to meet its financial obligations.

The Periodic Review Cycle

Candidacy is continued by evaluations scheduled at least every two years during the candidacy period. These **biennail visits** are conducted to determine that the institution continues to meet the Criteria for candidacy and also to assist the institution as it moves toward fulfilling the criteria for Accreditation.

Every accredited institution must have its status reaffirmed not later than five years after it has been initially granted, and not later than ten years following each subsequent reaffirmation. The time for the next comprehensive evaluation for continued accreditation is explicitly stated in the Commission's accreditation action; however, the time of that evaluation may be changed and may occur sooner if the institution introduces or plans changes that substantially alter its mission, functions, or character (see Chapter VI).

Criteria for Accreditation: Commission on Colleges

SOUTHERN ASSOCIATION OF COLLEGES AND SCHOOLS

Principles and Philosophy of Accreditation

The Commission on Colleges of the Southern Association of Colleges and Schools is the recognized accrediting body in the 11 U.S. Southern states (Alabama, Florida, Georgia, Kentucky, Louisiana, Mississippi, North Carolina, South Carolina, Tennessee, Texas and Virginia) and in Latin America for those postsecondary institutions that award associate, bachelor's, master's and doctor's degrees. The Commission on Colleges is a representative body elected by the College Delegate Assembly and charged with carrying out the accreditation process. Accreditation is principally concerned with the improvement of educational quality throughout the region and the assurance to the public that regional institutions meet established standards.

The task of accreditation is related to the traditional public philosophy of the United States— that a free people can and ought to govern themselves and that they best do so through a representative, flexible and responsive system. Accordingly, the purposes of accreditation can best be accomplished through a voluntary association of educational institutions.

The Commission on Colleges holds to the principle that regional accrediting should not be identified with either a state or a national framework. Furthermore, there are many issues to be shared at the regional level that might not be handled as effectively in a state or national association. This does not in any way limit cooperation and exchange of ideas with other regional and professional accrediting associations which are largely parallel in aims and functions. The several regional associations in combination form an effective national system for the assurance and improvement of quality in higher education.

Regional accrediting agencies accredit the total institution. However, the accreditation of professional schools, divisions, departments or programs within complex institutions is also provided by other accrediting organizations. It is the responsibility of the Commission on Colleges to evaluate the work of specialized schools, divisions, departments or programs, whether or not they are accredited by the appropriate professional agencies. It is the prerogative of the Commission to accept or reject the evaluations of such professional accrediting agencies.

The Commission on Colleges supports the right of an institution to pursue its established educational purpose; the right of faculty members to teach, investigate and publish freely; and the right of students to have opportunities for learning. However, the exercise of these rights must not interfere with the overriding obligation of the institution to offer its students a sound education leading to a recognized certificate or degree. Thus, criteria and procedures for accreditation have

133

been developed which are used in evaluating an institution's educational effectiveness, defined in the broadest sense to include not only instructional effectiveness, but also effectiveness in research and public service where these are significant components of an institution's purpose.

Initially and periodically, each member institution is required to conduct a self-study, which is subsequently evaluated at the institution by a committee of peer educators. This requirement helps ensure that an institution meets minimum standards of quality and that it evaluates the extent to which its educational goals are met. The successful fulfillment of this requirement results in initial accreditation or reaffirmation of accreditation.

The self-study program, begun by the Commission on Colleges in 1957, has proven successful in subsequent years. Once each decade, colleges and universities holding membership in the Southern Association of Colleges and Schools have conducted comprehensive self-examinations from which were formulated recommendations for future improvements. The studies have been broadly participatory. On each campus, faculty, administrative officers, staff, students and trustees have engaged in a close examination of the institution. At the culmination of the study, a visiting committee of peers from other institutions has assessed the educational strength of the institution in reaffirming accreditation. The program is a regional tradition which has strengthened higher education in the South.

The criteria for institutional membership are designed to allow for new demands on postsecondary institutions. The self-study program evaluates an institution not only to ensure that it meets minimum standards of quality, but also to ensure the effective fulfillment of its educational purposes.

The Commission on Colleges is particularly concerned with follow-up procedures and requires progress reports resulting from the self-study and the committee visits. The Commission on Colleges reserves the right, with due notification to the institutions involved, to make special studies of and visits to member institutions when circumstances warrant.

Accreditation is specific to an institution, is based on conditions existing at the time of the most recent evaluation, and is not automatically transferable. Any time an institution changes the nature of its affiliation or its ownership, a substantive change review is required. (See Commission document "General Substantive Change Policy for Accredited Institutions.")

The philosophy of accreditation of the Commission on Colleges precludes denial of membership to an institution of higher education on any ground other than failure to meet the requirements as outlined in the latest approved edition of the *Criteria for Accreditation*. In accordance with the procedures described in the Commission policy entitled "Appeals Procedures of the College Delegate Assembly," when an institution is denied candidacy or membership, or has grounds for appeal of official sanctions in the accreditation process, the chief executive officer of the institution may submit to the Executive Director a request for a hearing to appeal the decision. The Executive Director shall then arrange for a hearing according to established appeals procedures.

Institutional Commitment and Responsibilities in the Accreditation Process

The effectiveness of self-regulatory accreditation depends upon an institution's acceptance of certain specific responsibilities, including institutional involvement in, and commitment to, the accreditation, process. *Institutions are required to conduct self-studies at intervals specified by the Commission and, at the conclusion of the self-study,* accept an honest and forthright peer assessment of institutional strengths and weaknesses. *The Commission requires that the self-study assess every aspect of the operation of the institution; involve personnel from all segments of the institution, includingfaculty, staff, students, governing board and administration; and provide a comprehensive analysis of the institution, identifying strengths and weaknesses.* An adequate institutional follow-up plan to the self-study **is required.**

Additionally, an institution must be committed to participation in the activities and decisions of the Commission on Colleges. This commitment includes a willingness to contribute to the decision-making processes of the Commission and a willingness to adhere to all policies and procedures, including those for reporting changes and expansion within the institution. All existing or planned activities must be reported according to the policies, procedures and guidelines of the Commission on Colleges and must be in compliance with the *Cntena. Only* if member institutions accept seriously the responsibilities of membership will the validity and the vitality of the accreditation process be ensured.

An institution of higher education is committed to the search for truth and its dissemination. Integrity in the pursuit of truth is expected to govern the total environment of an institution. Each member institution is responsible for insuring integrity in all of its operations in dealing with all of its constituencies, in its relations with other member institutions, and in its accreditation activities with the Commission on Colleges. Each institution **agrees** to provide the Commission access to all parts of its operations, and complete and accurate information about the institution's affairs, including reports of other accrediting, licensing and auditing agencies.

Each institution seeking candidacy, membership or reaffirmation with the Commission on Colleges must document its compliance with the Conditions of Eligibility as outlined in Section 1.4.

Application of the *Criteria*

The Commission on Colleges recognizes that there are diverse ways of responding to the changing demands and new opportunities in postsecondary education. The *Criteria for Accreditation* applies to all institutional programs and services wherever they are located or however they are delivered. It is designed to guide institutions through all stages of membership from initial application through initial accreditation or reaffirmation of accreditation as a result of the institutional self-study program The *Criteria for Accreditation is* intended to assist an institution in achieving overall effectiveness in all areas of its growth and to ensure the quality of its educational programs.

Although recognizing the diverse nature of its membership, the Commission on Colleges shall uniformly apply the *Criteria* to all applicant, candidate and member institutions regardless of the type of institution. Whether the financial or organizational structure is for profit, not-for-profit, private, or public, the same standards, neither less stringent nor more rigorous, will be applied. The Commission grants or reaffirms accreditation only to those institutions which comply with the *Criteria for Accreditation.*

An institution must refrain from making a substantive change, defined as a change modifying the nature or scope of an institution or its programs, except in accordance with the Commission's policy "General Substantive Change Policy for Accredited Institutions." If an institution fails to follow the procedures outlined in the above policy, the institution's total accreditation will be placed in jeopardy.

The Commission on Colleges takes no position on collective bargaining agreements, neither encouraging nor discouraging them. When an institution's purposes, policies or procedures are modified by collective bargaining agreements, such modifications do not affect the application of the *Criteria,* the self-study evaluation or reporting processes. The total institution is the focus of accreditation; therefore, the nature and impact of any collective bargaining agreements will be included in accreditation processes when appropriate. When accreditation-related recommendations or suggestions are sent to an institution, they are intended to strengthen the total institution, not to serve to influence collective bargaining negotiations.

It is necessary and appropriate that peer evaluators representing the Commission apply professional judgment when assessing overall institutional effectiveness and compliance with the *Criteria;* however, final interpretation of the *Criteria* rests with the Commission.

Separately Accredited Units

The accreditation of an institution includes all its units, wherever located. A unit of an institution may be separately accredited if a significant portion of responsibility and decision-making authority for its educational activities lies within the unit and not in the other units of the institution or system.

It is the responsibility of the Commission on Colleges to determine, following consultation with the chief executive officer of the institution, whether the institution will be considered for accreditation as a whole or whether its units will be considered for separate accreditation, and how the evaluation will be conducted. A unit of an institution or system is eligible for separate accreditation if it is apparent from evidence that it has achieved a significant degree of autonomy and possesses the attributes which will enable it to comply with the requirements of the *Criteria for Accreditation. A* unit i9 required to apply for separate accreditation or to maintain separate membership if, in the judgment of the Commission, the unit has achieved this level of autonomy.

If an institution decides to seek separately accredited status for one of its units, it **must** notify the Executive Director of the Commission on Colleges of its intent and follow procedures established by the Commission. In all cases, the Commission on Colleges reserves the right to determine the accreditation status of separate units of an institution.

Institutional Purpose

Because the College Delegate Assembly is composed of representatives of diverse institutions, the stated purposes of member institutions may vary. An institution must have a purpose appropriate to collegiate education as well as to its own specific educational role. The statement of purpose **must** address all components of an institution's purpose, including research and public service, where these are significant institutional responsibilities. This purpose must represent the official posture and practice of the institution. Appropriate publications **must** accurately reflect the current statement of purpose.

The formulation of a statement of purpose is a major educational decision. It should involve the efforts of the faculty, administration and governing board and must be approved by the governing board. An institution should study periodically its statement of purpose, taking into account internal changes as well as the changing responsibilities of the institution to its constituencies. The institution **must** demonstrate that its planning and evaluation processes, educational programs, educational support services, financial and physical resources and administrative processes are adequate and appropriate to the institution's stated purpose and role.

Institutional Effectiveness

The quality of education provided by member institutions is the primary consideration in the decision to confer or reaffirm accreditation. The evaluation of educational quality is a difficult task requiring careful analysis and professional judgment. Traditionally, accreditation has focused attention almost exclusively upon institutional resources and processes. It has usually been assumed that, if an institution has certain resources and uses certain processes, effective education will occur. A comprehensive approach to accreditation, however, must take into account not only the resources and processes of education, such as faculty and student qualifications, physical plant, fiscal resources and other elements addressed in the *Criteria*, but also the evaluation of the results of education and plans for the improvement of the institution's programs.

The level of institutional quality depends not only on an institution's educational processes and resources, but also on the institution's successful use of those processes and resources to achieve established goals. An institution must engage in continuous study, analysis and appraisal of its purposes, policies, procedures and programs. An institution **has an obligation** to all constituents to evaluate effectiveness and to use the results in a broad-based, continuous planning and evaluation process.

Planning and Evaluation

To focus attention on the effectiveness of the educational program, the institution must establish adequate procedures for planning and evaluation. The institution **must** define its expected educational results and describe how the achievement of these results will be ascertained. Although no specific format for this planning and evaluation process is prescribed, an effective process should involve broad-based participation by faculty, staff, students and administration. *Furthermore, it must include the following:*

1. the establishment of a clearly defined purpose appropriate to collegiate education,

2. the formulation of educational goals consistent with the institution's purpose,

3. the development of procedures for evaluating the extent to which these educational goals are being achieved, and

4. the use of the results of these evaluations to improve institutional programs, services and operations.

In addition to establishing procedures for evaluating the extent to which their educational goals are being achieved, institutions should ascertain periodically the change in the academic achievement of their students. Procedures used to evaluate instructional programs may include: peer evaluation of educational programs; structured interviews with students and graduates; changes in students' values as measured by standard instruments or self-reported behavior patterns; pre- and post-testing of students; surveys of recent graduates; surveys of employers of graduates; student scores on standardized examinations or locally constructed examinations; performance of graduates in graduate school; performance of graduates of professional programs on licensure examinations; or, the placement of graduates of occupational programs in positions related to their fields of preparation.

Institutions with research or public service missions must develop and implement appropriate procedures for evaluating their effectiveness in these areas.

The appropriateness of any evaluation procedure depends upon the nature of the institution and the institution's goals for instruction, research and public service. The Commission on Colleges prescribes no set of procedures for use by an institution and recognizes that an effective program to evaluate institutional effectiveness will usually require the use of a variety of procedures.

Institutional Research

Because institutional research can provide significant information on all phases of a college or university program, it **is an essential** element in planning and evaluating the institution's success in carrying out its purpose. The nature of the institutional research function depends on the size and complexity of the institution and may vary from a part-time operation to an office staffed by several persons. Institutions should assign administrative responsibility for carrying out institutional research. Institutional research should be allocated adequate resources, and those responsible for it should be given access to all relevant information. Institutions must regularly evaluate their institutional research function.

Educational Program

The principal focus of the total institution must be the education of students. All aspects of the educational program must be clearly related to the purpose of the institution. Although an institution may use a variety of educational delivery systems at various locations, the institution **must** demonstrate the comparable quality of its educational programs for all students. The student enrollment and the financial resources of an institution must be sufficient to support an effective educational program. The institution must provide competent faculty, adequate library and appropriate computer resources, instructional materials/equipment and physical facilities to support its educational program. The institution also should demonstrate efficient and effective use of these resources.

Many institutions have developed technology-based and other kinds of innovative delivery systems to provide educational programs and services for their constituents both on and off campus. The Commission on Colleges recognizes and encourages innovative activities, but an institution **must** formulate clear and explicit goals for these activities and demonstrate that they are consistent with its stated purpose. Further, an institution must demonstrate how it will achieve these goals and how it will ensure overall effectiveness and quality consistent with the *Criteria*.

An institution ***must*** *make available to students and the public accurate and current catalogs or other comparable publications setting forth its purpose and objectives, entrance requirements and procedures, rules and regulations for conduct, programs and courses, degree completion requirements, full-time faculty and degrees held, costs and other items relative to attending the institution or withdrawing from it.*

Undergraduate Program
4.1.1 Undergraduate Admission

The admission policies of an institution must be clearly stated, published and made available to all constituencies, including potential students. Each institution must regularly evaluate its admission policies. It is the responsibility of the institution to ascertain that its recruiting activities and materials accurately and truthfully portray the institution.

The admission policies **must** be related to the educational purposes of the institution. They **must** establish such qualitative and quantitative requirements so as to admit students who demonstrate reasonable potential for success. In the absence of such requirements, an institution **must** offer appropriate developmental or remedial support to assist students in overcoming deficiencies in their preparation for collegiate study. Diagnostic testing can be an important element of a developmental or remedial program.

The general institutional admission policies are normally established by the governing board on recommendation of the administration. The board, for example, **is responsible** for deciding the size and character of the student body. Implementation of specific admission policies, however, is **the responsibility** of the administration and faculty of the institution. The unit responsible for administering the policies must be clearly identified. In those institutions where various subdivisions maintain separate admission requirements, there must be provision for institution-wide coordination of all admission policies and procedures.

To be admitted to degree programs, students must show evidence of high school graduation or other successful experiences which demonstrate their ability to make satisfactory progress at a particular institution. Each institution **must** assess the appropriateness of experiences offered in lieu of a high school diploma and must justify any deviations.

An institution must clearly define and publish its policy on the admission of transfer students. The following **must** be included: the requirement of official transcripts of all postsecondary credits previously earned; qualitative and quantitative limitations determining the acceptability of transfer work; criteria regarding the granting of advanced standing, whether by credit earned at another institution, by advanced placement examinations, or through experiential learning; and conditions governing admission in good standing, admission on probation and provisional admission.

The institution **must** inform transfer students of the amount of credit which will transfer, preferably prior to their enrollment, but at the latest, prior to the end of the first academic term in which they are enrolled.

Institutions which award credit based on advanced placement or other examinations; training provided by non-collegiate institutions, such as armed forces and service schools; professional certification; or experiential learning **must** meet the following conditions governing the awarding of this credit:

1. The amount of credit awarded is clearly stated and, is in accordance with commonly accepted good practice in higher education.

2. Credit is awarded only in areas which fall within the regular curricular offerings of the institution, and must be appropriately related to the student's current educational goals.

3. Decisions regarding the awarding of credit and the determination of such credit are made by qualified faculty members at the institution or according to procedures and standards approved by qualified faculty. Faculty members ensure that assessment procedures are appropriate for the credit awarded.

4. Institutions using documentation and interviews in lieu of examinations demonstrate that these methods provide assurances of academic comparability to credit earned by traditional means.

5. Portfolio-based credit for prior experiential learning is awardedfor no more than 25 percent of the credit hours applied toward a degree. In exceptional individual cases, however, the nature and content of the prior learning experience may be such that additional credit may be appropriately awarded. The institution **must** justify each such case. In awarding credit for prior experiential learning, the institution: (a) awards credit only for documentedlearning which ties the prior experience to the theories and data of the relevant academic field; (b) awards credit only to matriculated students; identifies such credit on the student's transcript as credit for prior experiential learning, and is prepared, upon request from another institution, to document how such learning was evaluated and the basis on which such credit was awarded; (c) takes steps to ensure that credit for prior experiential learning does not duplicate credit already awarded or remaining courses planned for the student's academic program; (d) adopts, describes in appropriate institutional publications, implements and regularly reviews policies and procedures for awarding credit for experiential learning; and (e) clearly describes, and establishes the validity of, the evaluation process and criteria for awarding credit for prior experiential learning.

Coursework transferred in, or accepted, for credit toward a degree **must** be completed at an institution accredited as degree-granting by a postsecondary regional accrediting commission at the time the coursework was completed. Exceptions to this requirement are allowed, such as: (a) transfer credit from foreign institutions not accredited by a regional postsecondary accrediting commission; (b) transfer of coursework completed at an institution accredited by an accrediting body recognized by the Council on Postsecondary Accreditation; (c) acceptance for credit of education accomplished in a non collegiate setting which has been evaluated and recommended for credit by an organization generally recognized as an authority by the higher education community, such as the American Council on Education. Such education would include military schools: (d) conversion of credit earned in a non-degree program—at the institution or another institution— to credit toward a degree; or (e) transfer to "block" credit from non-degree-granting institutions accredited by accrediting body recognized by the Council on Postsecondary Accreditation. When "block" credit is awarded in such cases, the institution **must** demonstrate that any such "blocks" have been reviewed on a course-by-course basis to ensure that the above requirements have been satisfied. The above exceptions **must** be adequately justified by the institution.

Justification for exceptions **must** include adequate documentation that the credit awarded represents: postsecondary coursework relevant to the degree, with comparable and appropriate course content and level of instruction resulting in student competencies at least comparable to those of students in the institution 's own degree programs; and coursework taught by faculty who are qualified to teach at the appropriate degree level. In assessing and documenting comparable learning and qualified faculty, institutions may appropriately use recognized guides which aid in the evaluation for credit. Such guides include those published by the American Councd on Education, the American Association of Collegiate Registrars and Admissions Officers, and the National Association of Foreign Student Affairs.

There **must** be clearly defined policies regarding the academic dismissal, suspension and readmission of students. The re-admission of students dismissed or suspended for academic reasons **must** be consistent with the academic policies of the institution.

The procedures established for implementation of the institutional admission policies **must** be followed in the admission of all students. The institution **must** provide evidence that it selects students whose interests and capabilities are consistent with the admission policies. An institution's admission and retention policies should not be compromised in order to maintain adequate enrollment. An institution must publish both the general criteria for admission and any special admission criteria for individual programs.

4.1.2 Undergraduate Completion Requirements

In each degree program, there **must** be an identifiable pattern of courses leading to the degree. An institution **must** state *and publish* the requirements for each degree it awards. The statement of requirements must specify: the total credits to be earned; the number and distribution of general education credits to be completed; the *number of* credits to be earned in the major or area of concentration; the *number of electives to be completed;* and *other requirements which students* **must** *meet* in order to receive a degree.

Undergraduate degree programs **must** contain a basic core of general education courses. A minimum of 15 semester hours for associate programs and a minimum of 30 semester hours for baccalaureate programs **are required** for degree completion. The core **must** include a least one course from each of the following areas: the humanities/fine arts, the social/behavioral sciences, and the natural sciences/mathematics. Within this core, or in addition to it, the institution must provide components designed to ensure competence in reading, writing, oral communication and fundamental mathematical skills. Because the computer is an important means of both communication and computation, institutions should provide means by which students may acquire basic competencies in the use of computers.

An institution **must** clearly define what is meant by a major or an area of concentration and **must** state the number of credits required for each. An adequate number of hours with appropriate prerequisites **must** be required in courses above the elementary level. *Provision must be made for one or more electives chosen from disciplines outside the student's area of specialization.*

For degree completion, at least 25 percent of credit semester hours, or the equivalent quarter hours, must be earned through instruction offered by the institution granting the degree.

4.1.3 Undergraduate Curriculum

The curricular offerings of an institution **must** be clearly and accurately described in published materials. Curricula **must** be directly related and appropriate to the purposes and goals of the institution and the diploma, certificate or degree awarded, to the ability and preparation of the students admitted, and to the financial and instructional resources of the institution.

The institution must have a clearly defined process by which the curriculum is established, reviewed and evaluated. This process must recognize the various roles of the faculty, the administration and the governing board.

In each curricular area in which a major in a degree program is offered, the institution **must** assign responsibility for course or program oversight and coordination, as well as for curriculum development and review, to persons academically qualified in the field. At least one full-time faculty member with appropriate credentials, as defined in Section 4.4.2, **must** have primary *teaching* assignment in each such curricular area.

The governing board must be responsible for approving the number and types of degrees; the number and nature of departments, divisions, schools or colleges through which the curriculum is administered; and the extent to which the institution should offer undergraduate work and *off-campus* programs.

The administration and faculty **must** be responsible for the development of proposed academic programs to be recommended to the governing board. They are **also responsible** for implementing and monitoring the general curriculum policy and the academic programs approved by the board. There should be an institution-wide process to coordinate programmatic and curricular changes.

Efforts should be made to avoid the unwarranted proliferation of course offerings and degree programs. The development of new educational programs should be considered only after the institution has completed a needs assessment and identified resources to support the programs. The decision to proceed should be made only after a careful review by appropriate faculty and administrative bodies, approval by the governing board, and any necessary review and approval by state agencies.

Curricula intended to provide basic preparation for students who will subsequently transfer to another institution **must** be designed to consider the institutions to which these students transfer. Articulation agreements for upper division study should be developed and periodically evaluated to ensure an equitable and efficient transfer of students. "Inverted," "two plus two" and similar programs must include an adequate amount of advanced coursework in the subject field.

4.1.4 Undergraduate Instruction

Instructional techniques and policies **must** be in accord with the purposes of the institution, as well as appropriate to the specific goals of an individual course. Instruction **must** be evaluated regularly and evidence collected to demonstrate that efforts are being made to improve instruction.

Students and faculty must have a clear understanding of the goals and requirements of each course, the nature of the course content, and the methods of evaluation to be employed. Methods of instruction **must** help fulfill the goals of each course and be appropriate to the capabilities of the students. Experimentation with methods to improve instruction must be adequately supported and critically evaluated.

The institution should develop a variety of means for evaluating student performance. The evaluation of students must reflect concern for quality and properly discern levels of student performance.

The institution should evaluate the effectiveness of its instructional program by a variety of techniques which may include: the use of standardized tests and comprehensive examinations, the assessment of the performance of graduates in advanced programs or employment, and the sampling of the opinions of former students.

Courses offered in non-traditional formats, e.g., concentrated or abbreviated time periods, **must** be designed to ensure an opportunity for reflection and analysis of the subject matter. The institution must demonstrate that students completing these programs or courses have acquired comparable levels of knowledge and competencies as would be required in more traditional formats.

Effective instruction depends largely upon the maintenance of an environment conducive to study and learning. For this reason, an institution of higher education must provide for its students a learning environment in which scholarly and creative achievement is encouraged.

In certain professional, vocational and technical programs (for example, the allied health areas), appropriate clinical and other affiliations with outside agencies may be necessary. In all such cases, learning experiences for which credit is awarded **must** be under the ultimate control and supervision of the educational institution.

For programs designed to prepare students for a specialized profession or occupation, the institution must demonstrate that an effective relationship exists between curricular content and current practices in the field of specialization.

Graduate Program

4.2.1 Initiation and Expansion of Graduate Programs

An undergraduate institution planning to initiate its first graduate program, a graduate institution planning to initiate a program at a degree level higher than that already approved, or a graduate institution planning to initiate a program at the same level but substantially different from degree programs already approved, must inform the Executive Director of the Commission on Colleges in advance of the admission of students.

(See the Commission document, "General Substantive Change Policy for Accredited Institutions. ") The institution also must be able to document that any necessary approval from state or other agencies has been secured.

Before an institution moves from a baccalaureate to a graduate status or attempts to expand in number its graduate programs at the same level, an institution **must** be able to demonstrate that systematic and timely plans have been developed to assess needs, market and other environmental factors, resource requirements and financial implications for the institution. (See Commission document "General Substantive Change Policy for Accredited Institutions.")

A graduate program **must** have curricula and resources substantially beyond those provided for an undergraduate program. Research, scholarly activity and/or advanced professional training **are essential** ingredients of graduate studies and **must** be properly supported by adequate resources. An institution **must** provide for its graduate programs a competent and productive faculty, the library, computer and laboratory facilities adequate to support them, and an adequate administrative organization.

The Dangers of U.S. Intervention in Accreditation

ROBERT H. ATWELL

This week an Education Department panel will decide whether to recommend continued recognition of the Commission on Higher Education of the Middle States Association of Colleges and Schools. The recommendation, and Education Secretary Lamar Alexander's subsequent decision, could have a significant impact on colleges' efforts to achieve student and faculty diversity, as well as on our system of voluntary accreditation and the degree to which institutions are regulated by the federal government.

Because only students in institutions certified by recognized accrediting agencies can receive federal student aid, the most immediate effect of denying recognition to Middle States would be to bar students at over 500 colleges in five states, the District of Columbia, Puerto Rice, and the Virgin Islands from receiving federal aid. The Department of Education then would have to find another way to certify those institutions.

Middle States, one of six major regional organizations that accredit colleges and universities, came up for renewed recognition last fall. The department's National Advisory Committee on Accreditation and Institutional Eligibility initially voted to support the Middle States petition, but a day later voted by a narrow margin to delay recognition after several members attacked the criteria that the agency uses in evaluating diversity at institutions.

This past April, Secretary Alexander sent the petition back to the committee for reconsideration. Echoing the committee's concerns, he cited two controversial cases: that of Bernard M. Baruch College of the City University of New York, whose reaccreditation was withheld by Middle States until the institution submitted a plan to increase the number of minority faculty members and retain more minority students; and that of Westminster Theological Seminary, which had resisted Middle States' request that it include women on its governing board. He also questioned whether Middle States was attempting to impose quotas.

Some background is necessary to understand the broad issues raised by the Middle States case.

Accreditation is not only voluntary, it is participatory. Institutions themselves control the operations of the accrediting bodies. They, not the accrediting agencies' small professional staffs, set the policies and standards. Accreditation is carried out not by a faceless bureaucracy, but by faculty members and administrators who make up the various visiting teams and commissions. Those reviewers must ascertain whether an institution is meeting the accrediting body's criteria as well as the educational goals that it has set for itself.

Having served on numerous accrediting teams, I can testify that the system is anything but coercive. The process provides extensive chances for discussion, exchanges of information and, if necessary, appeals.

Voluntary accreditation by institutions' peers is one of the unique aspects of American higher education. In most other countries, the function of assuring quality and integrity is undertaken by the national government. Congress has always been clear that it does not want the federal government assuming any direct regulation of colleges and universities. Rather, the federal interest in accreditation is tied almost exclusively to student aid. Although the Department of Education establishes the criteria that accrediting bodies must meet to gain recognition, it is explicitly prohibited by law from controlling, managing, or regulating these organizations' policies or procedures.

Given this background, the actions by the advisory committee and Secretary Alexander in the Middle States case are without precedent. Even more, they represent a potentially illegal and dangerous Federal intrusion into the accreditation process. If the Secretary believes that more federal control over accreditation is warranted, he should follow the normal rule-making process, including public notice, hearings, and a comment period, so that he can hear a broad range of views. And, where important legal questions are involved, he should solicit formal opinions from legal officials.

The *ad hoc*, case-based approach taken by Mr. Alexander poses several dangers. It may prejudice any future policy-making procedures. It may politicize the department's recognition process and render it arbitrary and unpredictable. It also risks enmeshing the Secretary in the internal politics of institutions and accrediting bodies. And it opens the recognition process to manipulation by individuals or groups seeking their own personal, political, or ideological ends.

The latter certainly has been true in this instance. After Mr. Alexander announced that he was delaying recognition of Middle States, several conservative political columnists hailed him for striking a blow against "political correctness" and its attendant evils: affirmative action, quotas, multiculturalism, declining standards. Similarly, the National Association of Scholars urged its members to write the Secretary and oppose continued recognition of Middle States, warning that otherwise "'PC' may well be elevated to a national policy implemented via accreditation."

Despite the politicization of the issue, the particular concerns raised by Secretary Alexander deserve considered response:

- *Do the Middle States diversity standards threaten academic freedom and institutional integrity?*

I have seen no evidence that Middle States' accrediting activities have in any way compromised these principles. The diversity standards—like similar ones adopted by other accrediting agencies—were not the work of an isolated staff, but were developed and approved by the collegiate members of the association, acting through their elected committees. The members of Middle States had—and still have—ample opportunity to reject or revise these standards, if they wish.

As many as 300 institutions have gone through—or now are going through—Middle States' accreditation process since the current standards were adopted, without controversy. In the case of Westminster Theological Seminary, discussions about adequate representation of women in its governance process began in 1984, long before Middle States adopted its current diversity standards. A settlement recently was reached that apparently satisfies both parties.

In addition, Middle States' actions in the Baruch College case were based on the institution's own goals, identified in its self-study. The process may be painful, but its effectiveness is attested to by the fact that, in the end, Baruch and Middle States also reached a mutually agreeable settlement.

It seems to me that *ex post facto* departmental intervention in the accreditation process poses a far greater danger to academic freedom and institutional integrity than any actions by Middle States.

- *Is Middle States assuming federal responsibilities by fashioning remedies under civil-rights laws?*

There is a big difference between legal and voluntary remedies. Compliance with civil-rights laws does not require institutions to wait until the marshal is at the door before they act to eliminate discrimination or call on outside bodies to determine whether they are achieving their goals. If non-discrimination goals are part of a college or university's basic mission, it is appropriate for an accrediting body to judge the institution's effectiveness in meeting them.

- *Will the application of Middle States' standards force some institutions to change their educational missions, thus imposing an undesirable uniformity?*

Such a fear is totally unfounded. The regional accrediting bodies are made up of widely varying colleges and universities, which are quite vigorous in defending and maintaining their distinct identities and missions.

However, diversity *among* institutions does not satisfy the need for diversity *within* institutions. As our nation has progressed beyond the era of legal segregation, and as the composition of our population has changed dramatically, many people in higher education and in other sectors have come to understand the critical importance of recognizing and cultivating the diversity that exists among the various cultures that compose the United States. Applying this concept to higher education requires a comprehensive approach that encompasses the makeup of the faculty, student body, and staff; the curriculum offered by the institution; and the climate on the campus itself.

- *Will applying diversity standards undermine the reliability of accreditation in indicating the adequacy of an institution's training and education?*

On the contrary, diversity is essential to quality. An institution cannot adequately educate its students if it does not familiarize them with the people, cultures, and ideas that they will live with in the 21st century. In fact, the importance of preparing all our citizens to function effectively in a highly competitive international economy is a basic premise of President Bush's "America 2000" plan for reforming our educational system.

Every person affected by the institutions of a democratic society—and those include its colleges and universities—deserves the opportunity to share in imagining, building, and running them. Creating such opportunity for individuals and groups that previously have been excluded or underrepresented provides them with a critical entree to participation in our democracy—and is essential to its preservation.

- *Will use of diversity standards lead to race-based quotas?*

Such standards, in one form or another, have been used for some time, and no evidence exists that any accrediting body has attempted to impose quotas on any institution. Again, the focus of the process is on the institution's own goals, which may not be quantified at all. And if the institution itself has adopted numerical goals, it would seem reasonable for the accrediting body to check on its progress toward achieving them.

Since April, in its actions and its arguments, Middle States has demonstrated that its standards are not inflexible or unfair. In fact, it recently adopted guidelines for applying its equity and diversity criteria that emphasize the paramount importance of assessing these principles in relation to the unique mission, goals, objectives, legal responsibilities, and values" of the institution.

Middle States has demonstrated its willingness to meet its critics' concerns. I hope that the recent agreement between President Bush and Congress on the civil-rights bill now will provide a model for resolving this case. Secretary Alexander and the advisory committee should emulate the spirit of compromise displayed by the President. They can extricate themselves from this potentially divisive and destructive situation by renewing the recognition of Middle States.

Accrediting: The Weak Link in Education Reform

Glenn Dumke

If colleges and voluntary bodies balk at evaluating institutional quality, government regulationis likely to follow.

If the enthusiasm for reform in education is to bear permanent fruit, attention must be paid to the accreditation process, which is not doing everything it should be doing. Because education bureaucrats, like nature, abhor a vacuum, if accreditation does not rise to its responsibility, the government will move in. Actually, it has already begun to do so. The federal government, faced with allocating large amounts of money to qualified institutions, is reluctant to depend on the voluntary accrediting process as a basis for its decisions.

The Secretary of Education is frankly supportive of voluntary professional accreditation. Yet the Education Department's Division of Accreditation and Eligibility, because it does not trust voluntary accreditation as a basis for government grants, clings to its role of publishing annual lists of institutions that qualify for government largess. State governments, too, are becoming increasingly involved, and several states have already established bureaus or commissions to monitor "educational quality" at public colleges and universities.

Even where such commissions do not exist—as in California, for example—the legislature, through its budget process, is exerting similar controls. "Budget language" in California jargon means footnoted statements in state-university budgets saying, in effect, "You can have these dollars, but you must spend them in a certain way." This is curriculum control with a vengeance.

Government control of education is moving ever closer. If it becomes a fact, sooner or later the United States will emulate most other countries and establish a Ministry of Education, which will end forever the self-regulation that has characterized American education for years.

One of the paradoxes of the situation is that college and university presidents, staunchly defending "local autonomy" against the inroads of the accreditation process and keeping that process weak in so doing, are by the very act inviting government takeover. As resentful as they are of tightened accreditation standards, their resentment will be as nothing compared with their feelings when licensing replaces accreditation, federal standards replace the voluntary ones now in existence, and state commissions move in to control the curriculum.

If accreditation is to recover the confidence it once enjoyed, it must do something about degree requirements. There was a time in this country when a bachelor's degree denoted certain abilities, including some competence in written and spoken English, some understanding of the cultural amenities, a knowledge of history, and some basic skills in mathematics and science. Today, however, an employer interviewing a job applicant with a bachelor's degree might very well confront a person unable to write and spell effectively, awkward in oral expression, with little or no knowledge of history or the American business system, and no competence in mathematics beyond simple arithmetic or, with luck, basic algebra, but who has college credits in courses such as leadership, minority studies, stage production, and the politics of revolution. A few years ago, when there was enthusiasm for the idea of students' structuring their own curriculum, the situation was even worse.

It is high time that educators recognize that, much as they hate to admit it, they, too, have a product: graduates. And although the analogy may be distasteful, their product often fails to meet the demands of the market. As a result, just as American automobile buyers became dissatisfied with American product and turned to Germany and Japan and Sweden for better results, so now employers are starting their own training programs to produce a product in which they have confidence.

Of course, employers are not the only factor to be considered. A liberal-arts education has often been defined as having as its main purpose the enabling of men and women to live better and fuller lives. And perhaps a curriculum limited to ethnic studies, literary criticism, and film-making might produce that result for certain people. But that is not the only obligation an educational system has in today's complex world. The educational system is the means—as it always has been—for the society that created it to develop and prosper. To prepare the individual to survive economically in that society is surely another obligation, even though it is not the only one. Higher education is short-changing the society that depends upon higher education's product when accreditors fail to separate the sheep from the goats.

Another step toward strengthening the accreditation process would be to redefine it. Now, in the six regional accrediting associations an institution is deemed accredited if it lives up to its own "statement of mission and purpose." This presents a serious problem, because many weaker institutions have mission statements so loose as to be worthless. Obviously the institution's wishes in the matter should be respected, but the appropriateness of such statements, their basic reasonableness and effectiveness, should be adjudged, and the accrediting agency should have the authority to make such judgments.

In addition, the scope of accreditation should be enlarged so that its evaluations are not limited to establishing minimum standards. The educational system does not cringe from grading its clients, and there is no reason that educators engaged in accreditation should not rigorously grade their client institutions, to bring them up to speed if they are clearly lagging behind in any respect. It is patently unfair to good and sound institutions for a college existing on the margin of acceptability to be able to advertise itself as "fully accredited." It is one thing to have a different mission and purpose; it is quite another to be unable to produce educated graduates. Accreditation agencies should have the freedom and power to assure that "accredited" means what it says.

To further strengthen accreditation, it is necessary that it be financed differently. Currently, regional associations depend on institutional dues for their support and, as a result, find it difficult to be tough in enforcing the rules. As long as their policies do not offend the majority of dues-paying members, they can afford occasionally to be rigorous with a lone campus, but when their policies threaten the interests and comfort of the majority, then their own boards, composed of representatives of those very institutions, object and change the approach. The most obvious alternative to this system would be to have state governments finance the accrediting process as they do the public institutions themselves—but that brings us back to the specter of government intrusion and political influence.

Probably the best solution would be to have a foundation, governed by a board of leading and disinterested citizens, manage the financing and assessments of the accrediting agency, and in so doing perhaps develop multiple new sources of revenue. Such third-party control of financing would have the advantage of making it possible to report to and appeal to the public if events begin moving in the wrong direction. Until the financing problem is finally solved, the question of rigor in accrediting procedures will continue to confront us.

Finally, the Council on Postsecondary Accreditation, which represents both regional and specialized accrediting agencies, should boldly assume its role as the accrediting agency for accrediting agencies, and hold its members to standards that have some meaning. This is not to say thatCOPA is doing a bad job; in fact, considering the constraints under which it operates, it is doing quite well. Those constraints—the absence of any set of agreed-upon achievement levels for the bachelor's degree, the fact that accreditation is subservient to an institution's own view of itself, the limiting of the agency to establishment of minimum standards, the agency's dependence for financing on the subjects of its scrutiny—must be removed.

A Ministry of Education for the United States? Certainly, if those constraints are not removed, and if current practices continue without major changes. Certainly not, if accreditation becomes what it started out to be, a true evaluation of institutional quality, and if COPA assumes its proper—albeit difficult—role of accreditor of accreditors.

Resolving the issues will not be easy, but worthwhile solutions to difficult problems never are.

Accreditation

RICHARD M. MILLARD

Accreditation does not determine institutional or program quality. Educational quality is a characteristic of institutions or programs, not of accrediting associations. The primary responsibility for institutional and program integrity and quality assurance rests with the individual programs, institutions, or governance systems in higher education. The commitment to educationally sound objectives and effective means of attaining them lies with faculties, administrators, trustees, students, and alumni of programs, institutions, or systems. While accreditation cannot create quality, it has or it should have a crucial role in determining whether an institution or program has accepted and is carrying out its commitment to quality. It also provides incentives to encourage enhancement of quality.

Accreditation is the primary communal self-regulatory means of academic and educational quality assessment and enhancement. As a condition, it is a status granted to an educational institution or program that has been found by its peers, including professional and public representatives, to meet stated criteria bearing on educational quality and accomplishment. As a process, it has two fundamental purposes: to attest to the quality of an institution or program and to assist in improving that quality. As an activity, accreditation is the members of academic and professional communities working together to develop and validate standards, to assess the adequacy of their own operations, and to offer peer judgment and guidance to assure students and the general public of the integrity and quality of education.

Accreditation attests that an institution or program has clearly defined and educationally appropriate objectives, that it maintains conditions under which it is reasonable to expect that they will be achieved, that it appears to be accomplishing them, and that it can be expected to continue to do so. Accreditation is accomplished through accrediting associations that consist of institutions, programs, professional groups and their representatives, and representatives of the public. The strengths and the weaknesses of accreditation reflect its status as the academic conscience of the education community.

The accreditation process has four major components: The institution or program develops an adequate statement of institutional or program mission, goals, and objectives. The institution or program conducts an effective analytic self-study focused on the way and the extent to which it achieves its objectives. A selected group of peers carries out an on-site visit to evaluate the adequacy and accuracy of the self-study and the institution's effectiveness in meeting its objectives. Finally, an independent accrediting commission reviews the self-study and the report of the site visitors and decides, in view of its standards, whether the institution or program is worthy of accreditation.

Types of Accreditation

There are two types of accreditation and accrediting associations—institutional and specialized or programmatic. Institutional accreditation is carried out by institutional accrediting associations, which are national or regional in scope and which include the institutions that have achieved and maintain accreditation. Institutional accreditation focuses on the institution as a whole. Thus, it gives attention not only to the educational program but to such areas as effective management, student personnel services, financial and physical resources, administrative strength, and consumer protection. In addition to nine regional commissions, four national institutional accrediting associations accredit specialized types of separate institutions, three of which include primarily proprietary schools: the Association of Independent Colleges and Schools (for business schools), the National Association of Trade and Technical Schools, the National Home Study Council (for correspondence schools), and the American Association of Bible Colleges.

Specialized accreditation is carried out by accrediting associations within specific professional, occupational, or disciplinary areas that usually are closely related not only to the educational programs but to the professional associations in these areas. Specialized accrediting associations accredit programs or schools in complex institutions that prepare professionals, technicians, or members of special occupations. Most specialized associations require that the programs evaluated be part of an institutionally accredited college or university. Through their relations with professional associations, they are able to provide not only assurance that the program is educationally sound but that it is relevant to current practice in the appropriate professional field.

Not all disciplines in postsecondary and higher education have specialized or programmatic accrediting bodies. Most disciplines within the arts and sciences are considered integral parts of the institutional core and fall within the purview of institutional accreditation. On the whole, programmatic accreditation is developed in and applies to areas that prepare persons for particular occupational or professional fields and in which there is a recognized first professional degree. These tend to be fields where issues of public welfare, health, safety, and need for assurance of professional competence are matters of academic, professional, and public concern.

Interassociation Activities

Until mid century, accrediting associations, whether institutional or specialized, tended to operate independently. There was little or no systematic communication among them, and there was no oversight of their activities. As early as the 1920s, some institutions had become concerned about the number and impact of specialized accrediting bodies. However, a coordinating agency was not established until 1949—at the urging of college presidents—by seven of the institutionally based higher education organizations. The National Commission of Accrediting (NCA) was established in an attempt to reduce the number of specialized agencies (twenty-three at the time) and incorporate their activities under the regional associations, although the Western association was just being formed, and it had not started accrediting. NCA did not attain either objective. However, it did establish a review and recognition process that most of the specialized accrediting associations voluntarily subscribed to and applied for. NCA was funded directly by institutions and gained its influence from the commitment of some institutions to invite only NCA-recognized associations on to campus. It helped to establish a bond among the specialized associations and to increase their awareness of one another.

In the same year, the regional commissions established a very different kind of group, the National Committee of Regional Accrediting Agencies (NCRAA), to facilitate cooperation and the development of common or complementary policies among those associations. In 1969, the NCRAA became the Federation of Regional Accrediting Commissions of Higher Education (FRACHE). While federation policy setting required five of the six regional commissions to concur, it opened a continuing forum for testing new ideas, dealing with common concerns, and exchanging information. It had minimal involvement with the NCA or the specialized accrediting associations.

With the increasing prominence of accreditation and with the federal government's use after 1952 of accreditation as a condition of eligibility for federal funds, the need for developing a single coordinating and recognizing body for accrediting associations became insistently clear. The first steps toward a merger between NCA and FRACHE took place in 1971, and after much negotiating the merger occurred in 1975. The Council on Postsecondary Accreditation (COPA) was the result. COPA has evolved to become an integral part of the self-regulating structure that characterizes accreditation. A voluntary organization of accrediting associations and national postsecondary organizations, it has three primary objectives: to recognize accrediting associations that accredit institutions and programs of postsecondary education on the basis of demonstrated need and specified standards relating to accrediting policies and practices; to provide national leadership and understanding for accreditation by cultivating broad understanding of accreditation, serving as a spokesman for accreditation at the national level, and interacting with educational institutions, government agencies, foundations, and other interested groups on matters of accreditation; and to provide services to accrediting associations, postsecondary educational institutions, and the public by assisting in improving the general accrediting process, improving the policies and practices of recognized accrediting associations, facilitating coordination among accrediting associations, and encouraging, sponsoring, and conducting research relating to the understanding and improvement of accreditation.

Accreditation: Origins and Development

Beginnings of Regional Associations. The regional accrediting associations began in the last decades of the nineteenth century. During this period, higher education represented a disparate composite of institutions. The leading institutions faced three related problems. The first was admissions from secondary schools that varied considerably in character and quality. The second was transfer from institution to institution, particularly from colleges that maintained their own preparatory programs and did not clearly distinguish between preparatory and college-level courses. The third was admission to the newly emerging graduate schools of students from a variety of undergraduate colleges across the country. As a result, the major institutions in various sections of the country formed associations to increase articulation of secondary schools, to deal with problems of transfer and cooperation, and to develop lists of schools whose students could be admitted for graduate study.

The New England Association of Colleges and Secondary Schools began in 1885 as the result of requests from principals and headmasters of academies to President Eliot of Harvard to bring together college leadership and secondary school personnel. The Middle States Association of Colleges and Schools was organized in 1887, followed by the North Central Association of Colleges and Secondary Schools and the Association of Colleges and Secondary Schools of the Southern Association in 1895. The Northwest Association of Schools and Colleges was established in 1917, and the Western College Association was founded in 1924.

None of the regional associations began accreditation of higher education immediately. The first to do so was North Central, which published its first list of accredited institutions in 1913. North Central was followed in 1917 by the Southern Association and in 1919 by the Middle States. Northwest began accrediting in 1923. The Western Association did not begin accrediting until 1948. The New England Association, the first to be organized, utilized criteria for admission from an early date but did not undertake periodic review of institutions until 1952.

Beginnings of Specialized Accreditation. Specialized accreditation antedates regional and institutional accreditation. Specialized accreditation reflects the interest of professional and occupational associations and fields in the adequacy of educational preparation for practice in fields where concern for public health, safety, and welfare and public and professional expectations of professional competence are high. The associations are also concerned with defining or delimiting their professional fields and ensuring that educational requirements are related to current requirements for professional practice.

The American Medical Association, established in 1847, developed a committee on medical education. However, not until it was reorganized around 1900 did this organization turn its attention to strengthening medical education and ensuring that it had a sound scientific base. It published its first differentiated list of medical schools, based on the percentage of licensure examination failures, in 1905. In 1907, the 160 existing schools were classified as approved, on probation, or unapproved. Eighty-two schools appeared on the approved list. With help from the Carnegie Foundation, Abraham Flexner and N. P. Colwell visited all existing medical schools. The result was the Flexner report of 1910, which revolutionized medical education. By 1915, the number of medical schools had dropped to 95 (a 40 percent reduction), and medical education was established on a strong scientific base.

Three other professional associations came into existence and began accrediting activities at about the same time. The American Osteopathic Association was established in 1897 and began accrediting in 1901. The Association of American Law Schools and the Society of American Foresters both began in 1900. By the beginning of World War II, there were at least sixteen other specialized associations that accredited colleges and universities. Today, the Council on Postsecondary Accreditation recognized thirty-seven specialized accrediting bodies.

Other Early Accreditation Activities. Beginning in 1882, the American Association of University Women inspected and listed institutions that, according to its standards, produced graduates meriting membership in the association. It continued this listing until 1963.

Of considerably more impact was the listing published by the Association of American Universities (AAU). As early as 1904, the University of Berlin had used AAU membership as a basis for admitting graduating students. The German universities requested the AAU to prepare a somewhat longer list of certified institutions. Beginning in 1914, the AAU did so. At the outset, the list was based on records of transfer and graduate students at AAU institutions. However, from 1923 onward, inspection visits to institutions were the basis for inclusion in the list. This practice continued until 1948. Soon after, the Western Association and the New England Association began accrediting in the full sense.

One early attempt that might have given quality assessment in this country a very different history if it had succeeded was carried out by the United States Bureau of Education. In cooperation with the AAU, Kendric Babcock, a bureau specialist, prepared a list that used achievement of advanced degrees to rate undergraduate colleges. President Taft had the list withdrawn, and President Wilson vetoed the idea on the grounds that the federal government had no business assessing higher education institutions. This was the list that the AAU sent to Germany. If Presidents Taft and Wilson had not decided against it, quality assessment in higher education might well have become a function of the federal government.

Evolving Nature of Standards. Interestingly, some of the early standards used by accrediting associations and groups, such as the Bureau of Education and the AAU, were essentially results- or outcome-oriented. For example, AAU institutions used records of transfer and graduate student success. These were essentially student outcome measures. On the whole, however, the earliest standards used by accrediting associations can be described as definitional-prescriptive; that is, they were quantitatively reportable institutional characteristics that defined what a "good" institution was. In most areas, these characteristics were input factors, and the implicit norm was what the "best" institutions did, how the "best" institutions were organized, and what the "best" institutions offered. In a sense, these characteristics were an extension of the elitism that led the faculty of Yale University in 1828 to close the curriculum for all time against intrusions by such deviations from true education as the natural sciences and modern foreign languages. Although the Land Grant Act and Eliot's adoption at Harvard of the elective system based on the German model have intervened, the assumption that quality can be defined by characteristics, including curriculum, drawn from the elite institutions has persisted.

The major break in the definitional-prescriptive approach, led by the North Central Association, came in the 1930s. In 1929, North Central appointed a committee on the revision of standards. The committee report was completed in 1934 and published in 1936 (Zook and Haggerty, 1936). North Central adopted and implemented the report in part. The Middle States Association was the first to implement the report in full. Essentially, the report proposed that an institution should be judged not on the basis of a series of fixed characteristics but in terms of the purposes that it seeks to serve and of the total pattern that it presents as an institution of higher education. This approach might be described as a mission-objective model, with the standards developed as conditions of effective fulfillment of mission. With this model, the concept of accreditation changed from a process primarily of assessment to a process of assessment that provided institutions with external stimulation for continued improvement. Accreditation thereby acquired a dual function: quality assessment and quality enhancement. With this development, the analytic self-study gained new importance, as did the role of the visiting team as a group of peer consultants. Over a relatively short period of time, the mission-objective model was adopted by all the regional associations, and it gained considerable ground with the specialized associations as well. However, the tension between the mission-objective and the definitional-prescriptive models has tended to persist.

A third approach, which tends to characterize many of the specialized accrediting associations, can be described as the program-professional model. It modifies the mission-objective approach in that the mission or objective is not the institution's overall mission or total pattern but rather the institution's mission or objectives in education for a particular professional field, modified by conditions and expectations of practitioners within the field itself. Thus, this model is designed to assure that the program is both educationally sound and relevant to current practice in the field. It offers a unique opportunity for consideration of outcome factors, but that opportunity has not always been recognized or used by the agencies in question. Moreover, the program-professional model can create tensions within an institution between programs, between programs and the institution as a whole, or between institutions and professional associations. This potential led to the effort, which emerged in the 1930s, of some presidents and presidential associations to curb both the proliferation and the independence of specialized accrediting associations. Formation of the National Commission on Accrediting was part of this effort. The same concern motivates the recent charge of the Carnegie Foundation for the Advancement of Teaching (1982) that specialized accreditation constitutes a threat to institutional autonomy and independence. However, this charge tends to overlook the fact that, in developing professional programs, an institution accepts responsibilities for preparation of competent professionals and stakes its integrity on doing so effectively.

The G.I. Bill and Federal Concerns. In 1944, the Congress passed the Serviceman's Opportunity Act, generally known as the G.I. Bill, and thereby brought the federal government into higher education in a major way. As originally passed, the bill had no provision for distinguishing legitimate institutions from unscrupulous ones. The result was a series of scandals. The Congress turned to the self-regulatory structure of the academic community for help in correcting the situation. To be eligible to receive federal funds, institutions would have to meet certain conditions. One condition was that an agency recognized by the Commissioner of Education as a reliable authority on the quality of education or training offered had to accredit the institution. There were alternate ways of establishing eligibility, such as the three-letter rule and direct program approval by the Veterans Administration. However, the three-letter rule required acceptance of transfer credits by three accredited institutions, and the Veterans Administration was encouraged to use accreditation, when it applied, in place of its own review. The commissioner was directed to prepare a list of recognized accrediting agencies. In addition to accreditation, an institution had also to be authorized or licensed to operate in its state. These provisions have been repeated with little or no modification in all subsequent major higher education legislation, including the landmark Higher Education Act of 1965. While making accreditation a condition of eligibility for federal funds did not technically change the voluntary nature of accreditation, it clearly created a major incentive for institutions desiring federal funds to seek accreditation.

Increasing Role of Regional Accreditation. After the AAU list of approved institutions was withdrawn in 1948, institutional accreditation was left to the regional accrediting associations. With accreditation as a condition of eligibility for federal funds, the pressure increased on the regionals to expand their scope. They had accredited primarily nonprofit baccalaureate institutions. They adapted slowly and with some reluctance to the rapidly growing community college movement, but they resisted consideration of proprietary institutions and vocational and technical institutes. The issue of proprietary schools reached a head with a suit in 1969 by Marjorie Webster Junior College, a proprietary junior college in Washington, D.C., against the Middle States Commission on Higher Education, which had refused to consider it because of its proprietary status. While the final decision was in favor of Middle States, it was something of a Pyrrhic victory. Soon after, not only Middle States but other regional associations changed their rules and began to accredit proprietary schools, partially as a result of the negative publicity that ensued but more fundamentally as a result of growing recognition of the North Central principle that the form of governance, while relevant, is not a determinant of quality.

The occupations-vocational issue took a somewhat different form. The primary pressure to extend accreditation to occupational and technical schools came from the political community, where it was rather clearly related to the issue of eligibility for federal funds. The lead was taken by governors and state legislators, who over a period of four or five years passed a series of resolutions at national and regional meetings requesting the regionals to extend accreditation in these areas. The various regionals responded in different ways. Three developed separate commissions, while three expanded the scope of their existing commissions. Somewhat ironically, by the time the Congress authorized the Commissioner of Education in 1972 to recognize the right of state vocational agencies to attest to the quality of vocational education programs for eligibility for federal funds, all six regionals had provided for accreditation of occupational and vocational schools.

Emergence of National Institutional Accrediting Bodies. Unlike the regional associations, the national institutional accrediting bodies are primarily concerned with particular types of postsecondary institutions. The National Home Study Council began in 1926. The American Association of Bible Colleges was established in 1947, the Association of Independent Colleges and Schools in 1952, and the National Association of Trade and Technical Schools in 1965. All four operate in areas that the regionals were reluctant to occupy in the 1940s and 1950s. With the possible exception of the National Association of Trade and Technical Schools, these organizations were not developed primarily to provide federal conditions of eligibility for their schools. However, there is little question that passage of the Servicemen's Opportunity Act in 1952 greatly enhanced their position. Regardless of the conditions that gave rise to them or that enhanced their development, they serve a large and important sector of the postsecondary education community.

Expansion of Specialized Accreditation. While the number of specialized accrediting agencies probably has not increased as much as it would have without the National Commission on Accrediting (NCA), the number has increased considerably since 1949. By 1957, NCA recognized twenty-one specialized agencies, all older than NCA itself. By 1965, the number had increased to twenty-nine. In 1983, the Council on Postsecondary Accreditation recognized thirty-seven, a decrease of two since 1975. However, one of this number is the Committee on Allied Health Education and Accreditation, which includes twenty-four collaborating organizations in allied health areas and sixteen joint review committees that review different specialized allied health programs. Thus, the actual number of programs accredited has increased from thirty-three in 1965 to sixty-seven in 1982.

This increase in the numbers of specialized agencies and programs accredited clearly reflects the development of specialty fields, an unavoidable phenomenon as knowledge advances and as new specialties and professional areas emerge. Most of the increase has been in technical areas—the majority in allied health. If proliferation simply means increase in numbers, then clearly there has been proliferation. However, if proliferation means duplication and unwarranted increase, the answer may be quite different. The problem is not one of checking unwanted growth but one of dealing with desirable growth—with the need for educated and trained individuals and with the demands that preparing these individuals place on institutions.

Accreditation in the Period of Expansion. The 1960s and 1970s saw the most rapid expansion of enrollments in higher education in the history of this country. This expansion was the result not only of the post-World War II baby boom but of national policy launched under the Great Society and continued in subsequent administrations. This policy placed the emphasis on education as the door to social mobility.

The period of expansion severely strained the accrediting associations. The number of reviews increased tremendously. By expanding their use of volunteers, the associations were able to meet the challenge. However, the great increase in the number of institutions made it inevitable that some programs, particularly at the graduate level, were not monitored as carefully as they might have been.

To complicate the picture, federal assistance to higher education saw a rapid growth during this period, particularly student assistance in the form of grants and guaranteed student loans. While most institutions handled federal funds with integrity, a few did not. Those cases were blown out of proportion, with charges of fraud, abuse, and error, and the accrediting agencies were blamed for not policing their institutions more effectively. Critics forget that, while accrediting associations can and do attest to the general fiscal integrity of institutions at the time of accreditation, they cannot continuously police specific institutional activities, nor is it their function to enforce specific federal regulations. As a result, the tensions between the federal government and accrediting associations began to increase.

The most serious threat to the credibility of higher education and accreditation came from the student unrest of the late 1960s and the early 1970s. While the unrest had its roots in social and international conditions that lay outside the academy, it seriously undermined public confidence in higher education. To many it appeared that something was seriously awry not only in the methods of higher education but in its objectives, structure, and basic assumptions as well.

At the same time, recognition was growing that traditional higher education is by no means the whole of post-high school education. In 1972, Congress took the initiative by declaring in amendments to the Higher Education Act of 1965 that the universe of that measure was postsecondary education, with higher education a subclass within it. On both federal and state levels, this redefinition had the effect of extending concerns and benefits to all legitimate educational opportunities beyond high school. Another development involved the increasing emphasis among governments and the public on protection of students as educational consumers. A number of states developed authorization or licensure laws, and accrediting associations began to appreciate their consumer protection role. Finally, the concept of accountability became far more central, not only in government circles but in the academic community itself. The concept extended both to fiscal integrity and management and to academic results.

As the period of expansion drew to a close in the mid and late seventies, higher education institutions became progressively more involved with off-campus programs. These programs were not limited to the vicinity or even the state of the parent institution; they extended across state, regional, and even national boundaries. Many were programs on military bases. Both off-campus programs in general and military programs in particular pose a series of problems for accrediting associations: reviewing off-campus operations in relation to the institution as a whole, the same criteria are relevant to off-campus sites, finally, the cost of sending visiting teams to a dozen or more sites around the world. With support from the Kellogg Foundation, the Council on Postsecondary Accreditation undertook a major study of accreditation of nontraditional and off–campus education in 1978. One result of the study was establishment of the principle that an institution's integrity is as closely involved with its off-campus operations as it is with its home campus operations and that the same criteria should be applied to off-campus operations and to home campus operations.

Accreditation and Retrenchment. The period of expansion has been succeeded by what can only be described as a period of retrenchment: The number of eighteen- to twenty-four-year-olds has decreased, and the general trend in enrollment is downward. Some institutions will not survive. Others will have a difficult time in maintaining sufficient enrollment. The fiscal stringencies produced by the recent recession and, for public institutions, the decrease in and resulting competition for state funds pose additional problems. Finally, the issue of accountability has become even more acute, heightened as it has been by the need for a clear rationale for the use of the limited funds available. All these factors have tremendously increased the competition among institutions for students and funds. Under such circumstances, the temptation is great for some institutions to try to meet the competition by lowering standards and by adding off-campus programs designed more for market appeal than to provide quality educational services. This creates additional problems not only for institutional accrediting bodies but for specialized accrediting bodies as well.

This period of retrenchment already has led to some closures and mergers. The accrediting community is particularly concerned that students in these circumstances be protected. The retrenchment has also led to further erosion of public confidence in higher education and in the ability of accrediting associations to assess quality and encourage its enhancement when survival is at stake. For these and other reasons, the issue of quality has been identified as one of the most critical issues for higher education in this decade. It is an issue that extends considerably beyond the institutions and the accrediting associations. It has in effect become everybody's business.

As already noted, the accrediting associations have been dealing with quality assessment and quality enhancement for some seventy years. Their approach to these issues has evolved over time. The accrediting associations are constantly reviewing and validating their standards and procedures and adapting to changing conditions. Theoretically, their standards and procedures should be as adaptable to retrenchment as they are to expansion. However, it is critical at this point for the premises and concepts involved to be clearly understood by the academic community and by the various publics that the associations serve.

Quality, Educational Integrity, and Accreditation

The debate about the nature and definition of quality is about as old as the human species itself. It is neither possible nor desirable to recount the history of that debate here, since our concern is with the monitoring of educational quality. However, there is a basic definitional problem caused in part by mixing different but related terms. These terms include *definition, standard, criterion,* and *index.* A definition is a statement of the precise meaning or significance of a word or term—in this case *quality,* particularly as it characterizes education or the educational process. In contrast, a *standard* is a norm or acknowledged measure of the status or condition characterized by quality. A single standard can designate one aspect of the condition and serve as one basis for judgment of approximation to that condition, although a number of standards may be necessary to judge whether the condition in fact is met. *Criterion* and *standard* are often used interchangeably. When both terms are used, *criterion* usually implies a further specification of the standard or a test or rule for assessing whether the standard has been achieved, while an *index is* a sign or indicator that some condition prevails. In far too many discussions about accreditation, standards, criteria, and even indexes are confused with definitions. As a result, the parties to discussion are talking about means of determining the status or partial characteristics of the status, not about the condition itself. To define quality in terms of faculty characteristics, or resources available, or even outcomes is to create such confusion. To judge that accreditation is irrelevant to quality because it relies on input factors is to assume a partial definition in terms of a particular set of criteria or indexes; thus, this judgment may miss the point altogether. Some of the research that concludes rather quickly that there is little correlation between accrediting standards and educational quality may in fact be using an alternate set of indexes to define quality.

If the standards must be relevant to and in some sense derived from the definition of quality, a far more fundamental problem lies in the definition itself. If a definition is to be more than an arbitrary stipulation, part of its relevance or significance lies in what can be done with it and in how it relates to or orders its universe of application.

Definitionsof Quality. At least four definitions of quality have been applied in the educational sphere. It is important to look briefly at each definition to assess its relevance to standard setting and to determine how it orders the educational universe. The first definition of quality is that quality is in fact undefinable. It is an ineffable characteristic of something—in this case education—that is recognized intuitively, and something either has it or does not. This is a rather widely held view, even within the academic community. However, it is not very useful.

The second definition approaches quality from the standpoint of social consensus. It usually is refined so that quality becomes what is agreed on by knowledgeable people. It sounds democratic, perhaps because it places quality in the eye of the beholders, but it does not advance us very far beyond the first definition. Even if we limit the consensus to knowledgeable people, such people disagree, and the definition itself gives no basis for deciding among the judgments of knowledge-able groups. The current reliance on statistical surveys to determine what the components of quality should be makes the definition of quality a popularity vote.

The third definition uses a single paradigm to signify quality. This is essentially the Platonic view. If such a paradigm could be used, it would clearly order its universe. Individual objects—in this case, individual educational institutions or programs—would embody the paradigm to vary-ing degrees. Standards in the area could either be derived from it, or they would be norms for assessing approximation to it. The difficulty lies in identifying or discovering the paradigm. In the Platonic universe, quality was to be discovered through dialogue that moved people ever closer to the universal or the ideal. In practice, the third definition has tended to take the form of a single model of what connotes the ideal college or university. Usually, this model has been someone's idea of the best college or the better colleges. Thus, the third definition is closely related to the definitional-prescriptive concept of standards, and it has all the elitism, rigidity, and qualitative criteria that that involves. Where this definition is applied, the result is likely to be homogeniza-tion—leading institutions, copies of leading institutions, copies of copies of leading institutions—and disregard for the excellence in institutions or programs of radically differing types.

The fourth definition accepts the idea of a paradigm, but it defines quality contextually, thus placing the paradigm withiin the activity itself. Quality is thus defined as achievement in kind. The quality of a knife lies in its ability to cut what it is supposed to cut. Quality is clearly related to objective—an objective appropriate to the entity or the process in question. In relation to an educational institution or program, quality is a function of the effectiveness with which the institution or program uses resources to achieve appropriate educational objectives. Thus an institution's or program's norm is implicit within it, and its quality is determined by how well its various components cohere in achieving its educational objective or objectives. Students, faculty, resources, location or locations, and results are integral to the quality of the operation, and the key to integration of all these elements in quality is mission or objective and its educational appropri-ateness. Thus one can expect quality equally in a complex university, a single-purpose institution, a community college, a selective liberal arts college, an occupational or technical institute, and a center for adult and continuing education.

At first glance, the fourth definition may seem to imply that the standards for assuring quality must be unique to each institution or program. That is not so. As the conditions for assessing effective use of resources for the achievement of educationally appropriate objectives, standards are generalizable. In fact they must be generalizable, given our definition of standard. However, the application of these standards, must be adaptable to many different conditions and situations. What the standards address basically are the components or factors involved in achieving operationally effective educational synthesis in the light of objectives.

Quality in the Educational Context. If we accept achievement in kind as the basic concept of quality and effective use of resources to achieve appropriate educational objectives as its specification in education, we make quality not only contextual but judgmentally determinable and comparable given the context. Further, this concept of quality is applicable to educational activities, students, programs, larger units such as colleges or schools within institutions, institutions as a whole, and even systems.

Obviously students are the focus of and reason for educational activities. But the quality of a student's educational activity has to be determined contextually, and that context includes what students bring with them, their educational objectives, how they use the opportunities or resources available, how their objectives cohere with the program or institutional objectives, what takes place as a result, and the extent to which the objectives are realized. In this framework, value added, outcomes, results, and the processes for attaining them all become relevant to the quality of education participated in and achieved. The results are both unique to individual students and comparable among groups of students who have similar objectives.

This does not assume that students' objectives are fixed at the beginning of their educational experience. Part of a student's objective may be to discover what his or her objectives are even whether he or she has any. But, as students' objectives become more focused in the process, so do the conditions for achieving them as well as the results or outcomes to be expected. This is not an argument for grading on value-added factors only, for part of the educational process for the individual involves recognizing levels of achievement essential to attainment of objectives. This conception of quality of education as achievement in kind as that achievement relates to the individual student recognizes four things: first, as objectives change, the determination of the quality of the student's educational experiences also change; second, the quality of the student's education is not a function of institutional type or social role stereotypes; third, the quality of the student's experience can vary considerably among students in the same institution or program; fourth, what the institution or program provides are conditions that may be more or less conducive to assurance of that quality.

Obviously, facilitation of students' achievement of their educational objectives is critical on a program level. However, other factors also enter the picture. A program, particularly on a professional, preprofessional, or occupational level, presupposes that students have focused their objectives on that program area. Accordingly, the objectives of the program and their adaptability to student objectives and background become crucial. Clearly defined program objectives are essential, as is spelling out the conditions needed for achieving them and communicating these to students. The objectives include the competencies to be attained and the rationale for attaining them, whether by traditional or by nontraditional means. In occupational and professional or preprofessional areas, where specialized accreditation becomes relevant, determining that these competencies are adequate for practice in the field must involve not only the program faculty and the institution but professionals or practitioners in the field as well. If the objectives are clear, then three questions arise: Are the resources adequate to achieve those objectives? Are the resources used in a way that is conducive to achieving the objectives? Have students who completed the program achieved the objectives? Quite clearly, the types of resources required—facilities, equipment, faculty and faculty qualifications, learning resources, and even research activity—vary with program objectives. Outcomes are most relevant to program objectives, and with such objectives desired outcomes can best be defined in terms of experiential competencies. While the quality of programs within an institution can vary, the institution's integrity and quality are at stake in the effectiveness with which its programs fulfill their specific objectives. This is particularly important when we consider the role of specialized or professional accrediting associations and their relation to the issue of institutional integrity.

On the institutional level, program quality and institutional quality can be one and the same when the institution is relatively small and essentially single-purpose in character. At more complex institutions, particularly in systems involving multiple programs and services that have various objectives, the key to total institutional quality lies in the effectiveness with which these objectives are reflected and advanced within the institutional goal or mission. An institution has characteristics as a whole that the programs individually may or may not have. At the institutional level, the administrative structures, the adequacy of student support services, the effectiveness of management and resource allocation, and a series of other factors that facilitate or hinder accomplishment of objectives and mission become considerably more crucial. Regardless of the type of institution, a clear determination of mission is essential to assessing whether resources are being used effectively to achieve appropriate educational objectives. But any type of institution is subject to such analysis in light of its unique characteristics. At the institutional level, the balance of programs and program objectives in the light of mission is essential. This includes both on– and off–campus programs, programs of traditional and nontraditional character, and even provisions for alternatives in achieving specific objectives. There frequently will be tensions between programs and between programs and institutional mission. At the institutional level, hard decisions involving the overall quality of the institution must be made. Unless these decisions are to be made on noneducational, political grounds—in which case quality control becomes questionable—they need to be made in the light of mission and the resources available to accomplish the objectives. An academically strong institution with a weak law school may confront a difficult choice—in order to maintain quality, it must either modify its mission and drop the law school or direct scarce resources toward increased efforts to ensure that the law school meets its objectives.

Focus of Applicability for Accreditation. The concept of quality as achievement in kind is central to the theory and process of accreditation, both institutional and specialized. It is the basis of accreditation's assessment both of quality and of enhancement of quality. As noted earlier, accreditation attests that an institution or program has clearly defined and appropriate objectives, that it maintains conditions under which achievement of these objectives can reasonably be expected, that it appears in fact to be accomplishing these objectives, and that it can reasonably be expected to continue to do so. Thus accreditation recognizes that educational processes are not ends in themselves but means to the end of preparing citizens to cope with life and perform a variety of functions in a complex society.

Recognition of the variety of objectives raises another crucial question in the accrediting context. One part of the definition of educational quality calls for appropriate educational objectives. How do we determine that educational objectives are appropriate? Some critics have argued that basing quality judgments on objectives means that all the objectives that an institution has are equally relevant; thus if the institution or program has preparing thieves as an objective, the only question is how successful it is in doing so. Here the answer depends on social relevance and acceptability as they relate to types of human activity. Clearly, certain socially destructive types of activity are not appropriate educational objectives. Within the acceptable types of activity, what is appropriate educationally is determined by a combination of peer-group and public assessment. The peer-group concept is thus crucial to the self-regulatory character of quality determination, where it guards against idiosyncratic definitions of appropriateness.

Indexes of Quality. Clearly, assessment of educational quality as effective use of resources to achieve appropriate educational objectives has major implications for the nature of standards and for the responsibilities of accrediting associations. It means that some existing indexes of quality either lose their relevance or need to be placed in wider contexts. Reputation, resources, process, and outcomes are some of the ways in which quality has been judged in the past.

Reputation has been used as a basis for ranking institutions and programs. It is a component, although not the only component, in the recent ranking of graduate departments developed by the National Academy of Sciences (1982). Indeed, reputation tended to be the critical factor in earlier studies of this sort. While reputation may be of some value as an index of particularly good or bad programs and may even have some relevance to comparative rankings of outstanding programs, it has little to do with the current quality of the programs in question. Reputation involves a time lag, and actual performance tends to change more rapidly than reputation. Reputation can be based on one aspect of a program—for example, research publications—that has little relevance to effectiveness of the program or institution in enabling students to reach their objectives. Clearly, it relates to the general visibility of an institution or program, so that quality programs that are geographically limited or isolated can go unnoticed. For many institutions and types of institutions, the reputational sphere has only peripheral relevance for the quality actually present.

Resources are relevant to quality. However, resources alone are no assurance of quality. What is important is how the resources are used to achieve appropriate educational objectives. An institution can be well endowed and have large and dependable sources of income yet be far from realizing its educational potential. In contrast, an institution with limited resources and clear objectives can through efficiency and dedication use its resources far more effectively in achieving its objectives. While a large but underutilized library may be a point of pride, it is hardly a guarantee of quality education. A highly qualified faculty who devote only minimal time to the teaching-learning function are no guarantee of quality education. Without adequate resources to accomplish its objectives, an institution cannot achieve quality, but the presence of these resources alone does not guarantee that quality education is taking place.

Accreditation has often been criticized as too concerned with processes and input factors and not sufficiently concerned with results. In some cases, this criticism has been valid. Consideration of process without concern for results clearly provides little if any basis for evaluating the process itself. Results are critically important to assessment of quality. Outcomes, both intended and unintended, are what education is all about. In emphasizing objectives and missions, most accrediting associations are increasing the emphasis on outcomes. However, insofar as the outcomes are outcomes of process, the process and the results are clearly germane to each other. Considered in isolation, outcomes are as limited as process.

Nature of Standards. The conception of quality as it relates to process and results has major implications for the nature of the standards that accrediting associations use. Clearly, it means that definitional-prescriptive standards have outgrown their usefulness and that they have little to do with determining educational quality. To the extent that they persist, they do a disservice to institutions, students, and the public. Fixed characteristics do not take into account differences in function and changing processes to achieve sound educational objectives.

Standards must relate to accomplishment of educational objectives, goals, and missions. Their functions are to formulate the factors conducive to and indicative of goal accomplishment. In this sense, they translate indexes of goal accomplishment into characteristics statements relevant to mission accomplishment. In this sense, for example, a standard should be not *Three quarters of the faculty must have a Ph.D.* but rather *Faculty qualifications are commensurate with accomplishing the educational objective.* A standard should not be *The library contains 150,000 volumes* but rather *Library resources are adequate for the types of programs offered and the research expectations of faculty, and they are effectively utilized by students and faculty.* A standard should not be *Students will attend so many laboratory sessions a semester* but rather *Students will demonstrate competencies in specified areas.* Where called for, comparative judgments are possible, but the basis for comparison is the institution's or program's success in achieving appropriate educational objectives.

Relevance to Institutions and Specialized AccreditingAssociations. There is a difference, not in theory but in application and development, between the standards of institutional accrediting bodies and the standards of specialized accrediting bodies. An institutional accrediting body is primarily concerned with the characteristics of the institution as a whole, including the way in which its various objectives complement one another in the total institutional mission. The institution must direct its self-study to its total operation and programs. Institutional accreditation does not involve specific review of every program but rather the total context of institutional offerings. Specialized accreditation is concerned with a more limited set of programs or school objectives. On the one hand, these objectives include the institution's commitment to the area in question. On the other hand, they also include the characteristics of the field and the expectations of practitioners and the public for that field. This means that part of what is being assessed in assessments of program effectiveness and integrity is the correlation between institutional objectives and professional objectives. To some extent, this limits the institutional options, but it also ensures, or it should ensure, the integrity of the institution in relation to professional or preprofessional preparation. Finally, the nature of standards as statements of characteristics relevant to accomplishment of objective or mission constitutes a firm basis for cooperation among accrediting associations, both institutional and specialized, in working with institutions to conduct complementary or combined self-studies and evaluations. The full potential for such cooperation has yet to be realized, but important steps in this direction are under way.

Effective Use of Accreditation. Given the evolving history of accreditation and the present concern for the quality of postsecondary education at both the national and local levels, the effective use of accreditation as a self-regulatory means of quality assessment and enhancement by the academic and professional communities has great importance for the future health and welfare of postsecondary education and of the students and public that it serves. Quality in postsecondary education is not something mysterious and the processes for determining whether it exists are neither arcane or unmanageable.

Assurance of institutional and program quality and the credibility both of institutions and programs and of their accrediting activities can be strengthened. To do so will require rapid movement in at least five directions. The first involves the institutions themselves and their participation in and use of the accrediting process. Each institution needs to recognize more fully than many now do that accreditation is directly related to its own self-assessment, planning, and institutional research activities. This applies both to institutional and specialized accreditation. In both cases, the accreditation process is based on assessing the extent to which the institution uses its resources to achieve its mission and its particular appropriate objectives. Thus if accreditation is to fulfill its function and if the institution is to benefit fully from it, the institution must internalize the process and relate it effectively to its own self-analysis, planning, and institutional research activities and cycles.

The second direction involves sustained review by the accrediting associations of their standards and criteria. Any criteria that still reflect the definitional-prescriptive mode must be modified. The primary concern of an accrediting association, whether institutional or specialized, should be the appropriateness of institutional or program objectives and the effectiveness with which these objectives are being realized. Thus each accrediting association should constantly review the validity and reliability or effectiveness of its standards in the light of the conception of educational quality.

The third direction involves increasing the cooperation among accrediting associations in their interactions with one another and with institutions. Efforts in this area should include developing data bases to reduce requests for the same or similar information from different associations. It also includes working with institutions on request to provide joint or sequential reviews and site visits and even common self-studies where applicable.

The fourth direction, both for institutions and for accrediting associations, is clear recognition that the primary function of accreditation is not punitive, but supportive of quality maintenance and enhancement. This recognition does not relieve accrediting associations of making negative judgments when they are called for. It does make the major thrust of accreditation the support and reinforcement of the quality of an institution as a whole and of its fulfillment of its particular educational objectives.

The fifth direction is for accrediting associations to expand their educational activities for peer review and site visitors so that these persons clearly understand the character and purposes of the accreditation process. Some associations with well-developed standards related to the concept of quality have used site visitors who operated on considerably different assumptions.

The five directions just outlined are illustrative, not exhaustive. Accreditation has come a long way from its activities in the first year of this century. The issue of quality always will be with us. If we are to strengthen quality in a period of fiscal stringency, variable enrollment, increased competition, and demands for increased accountability, accreditation must continue to evolve.

Reference

Carnegie Foundation for the Advancement of Teaching. *The Control of the Campus.* Washington, D.C.: Carnegie Foundation for the Advancement of Teaching, 1982.

Kaplan, W. A. *Accrediting Agencies' Legal Responsibilities in Pursuit of the Public Interest.* Washington, D.C.: The Council on Postsecondary Accreditation, 1982.

National Academy of Sciences. *An Assessment of Research Doctorate Programs in the United States: Biological Sciences.* Washington, D.C.: National Academy Press, 1982.

Zook, G. F., and Haggerty, M. E. (Eds.). *The Evaluation of Higher Institutions. Vol. 1. Principles of Accrediting Higher Institutions.* Chicago: University of Chicago Press, 1936.

State Policy on Assessment: The Linkage to Learning

PETER T. EWELL

Introduction

The rhetoric of assessment in higher education, regardless of its source, has always been the improvement of teaching and learning. For those concerned with assessment within the academy, this motive is a given. Absent a visible connection to teaching and learning, faculty argue, there is little point to the exercise. For the most part, state policy makers agree. Rather than narrow "accountability," they see in assessment a way to redirect higher education's attention toward critical societal challenges for the future. Above all, they see in assessment a means to induce faculty at colleges and universities to *take active responsibility* for student learning, an obligation which many feel, over the years, has been badly neglected.

How to actually use state policy to achieve these ends, however, remains elusive. Partly this is because the entities to be linked, "state policy" and the "improvement of teaching and learning," are themselves ill specified. Partly it is because the causal chain between what a legislature enacts and what a classroom teacher does is dauntingly complex. We intend this seminar to explore both murky areas in a manner that both can promote future dialogue and that can provide some immediate guidance to those at the state level who will provide the immediate policy environment within which we all must function. What follows are brief discussions of three related policy areas. Within each is a series of questions that we are asking all participants to address, and that we hope will provide a framework for our deliberations. Like those posed in assessment itself, we do not expect those questions (or their answers) to be definitive; they have done their job if only our thinking is clarified.

Assessment and the Curriculum

Assessment and undergraduate curricular reform are intimately related, for the language of assessment itself implies a curricular agenda. "Assessment" first requires some explicit standards of performance; curricula that contain none cannot be assessed. More importantly, "assessment" implies an instructional design that is both coherent and interconnected. Even posing assessment as a required activity will inevitably raise important curricular issues. As a result, both institutional and state proponents of assessment are apt particularly to emphasize its role in promoting curricular change; indeed, curricular change in itself is often seen as convincing evidence that the process

165

is "working." To inform assessment's impact on the curriculum, we believe, three distinct policy questions must be addressed:

1. *How can assessment focus attention on what we expect college graduates in a democratic society to know and be able to do?*

   Though frequently seen as a prerequisite for assessment, the development of more explicit goals for teachinghas proven to be one of its most ubiquitous actual products. And policy makers repeatedly claim that clear goals are badly needed. Part of the problem here is that most institutions cannot as yet provide answers to the question that policy makers most want to know: what is the outcome of the curriculum *as a whole?* This question is important, because policy makers do not see undergraduate education as an end in itself—a "public service" to be provided—but rather as a critical investment in the future. But many issues spring from this simple demand.

   First, what ought curricular goals *look like*. Is it meaningful, for example to formulate this question for an entire state, such as New Jersey has done with its "General Intellectual Skills" (GIS) examination (which covers such areas as "gathering, analyzing, and presenting information"), or as several states have done with respect to basic skills? If so, should goals be couched as minimum standards that all students should demonstrably meet, as "central tendencies" for college graduates as a body, or as aspirational challenges to guide future development? This is a central policy dilemma in many states: "mandating adequacy" through minimum standards can potentially narrow curriculum and leave more selective institutions unaffected, as has happened for the most part in Florida;" challenging excellence" through higher standards on the other hand, can raise issues of equity that often entail substantial political costs.

   A second issue is which goals, if any, should be held *in common. Is* it appropriate for state policy to articulate for all institutions the actual kinds of knowledge and skills required as, for example, is suggested by Virginia's "Curriculum for the 21st Century?" Or ought state policy to be confined to requiring institutions to address goals in common areas—for example general education, student satisfaction, or major field achievement? Those states, such as Colorado, which have followed the latter course have found remarkable overlap in the actual content of institutional goal statements, once developed, though each was developed "independently." Rather than mandating uniform goal statements, this finding suggests a strategy of allowing them to emerge gradually.

   A final issue concerns who should be *invol ved* in the goal-setting process. Structuring a statewide dialogue about desirable outcomes, for most states, remains largely unknown territory. One alternative is to attack theproblem by involving business and industry leaders directly with academics in the goa l-setting process, as was practiced by the College Outcomes Evaluation Program (COEP) in New Jersey. Another, as in Colorado, is to require institutions to provide evidence that their own assessment activities include efforts to determine the needs and perceptions of the various "communities" that they are intended to serve.

2. *What assessment information is useful for mahng sure that the curriculum provides the necessary skills and content?*

   In order to be useful for guiding improvement, information derived from assessment must meets everal conditions, First, it must address multiple dimensions of student capacity and performance; capacities such as "critical thinking," for example, are notoriously resistant to useful general measures. Secondly, it must be provided in a form that is sufficiently *disaggregated* to guide intervention; overall summaries of institutional performance will often mask substantial and important variations across departments and programs, or among different types of students. Finally, it must address instructional *processes* as well as obtained outcomes; if institutions know nothing about the actual delivery of instruction in the classroom, or about the choices that students are making about what classes to take, it is next to impossible to know what to "fix" if outcomes deficiencies are detected. As a result, the most useful assessment information for guiding curriculum renewal is often the most difficult to meaningfully aggregate and summarize.

And as in the case of goals, much turns on what is considered "the necessary skills and content." If the resolution to this question is collective, uniform performance information such as that provided by basic skills examinations in Florida or New Jersey may provide an appropriate answer; both are being used in the teaching of mathematics where important changes and improvements in performance have in fact occurred. But if the resolution to this question is local, "accountability" may rest largely upon a demonstration that obtained information has been effectively used to address curricular issues. In the latter case, state policies that encourage and recognize information *use* rather than information *reporting* may be most needed.

3. *How can assessment support departments and disciplines in assuming collective responsibility for the outcomes of college curricula?*

A critical condition for curricular reform is for faculty in diverse departments and disciplines to recognize their responsibility for undergraduate education as a whole. Current organizational and reward structures in most colleges and universities are strongly at odds with this condition. One virtue of assessment is that it raises the question of collective responsibility in concrete ways that are difficult to ignore.

The most visible place where issues of "joint product" arise is in the assessment of general education, and it is no coincidence that assessment in this arena has proven the most difficult for institutions to actually implement. A major policy dilemma here is illustrated by the common decision to require institutions to report on the assessment of "general education" as a separate enterprise, when arguably the kinds of outcomes claimed for "general education" are coincident with the college experience as a whole. But by not calling explicit attention to general education, state assessment policies risk encouraging an institutional response that may ignore collective products altogether.

Additional "collective responsibilities" cut across institutional boundaries. In many state university systems, as many as a third of the baccalaureate degrees granted in a given year are "joint products" of university and community college instruction. Yet curricular articulation between two-year and four-year institutions remains a significant challenge. Here a primary contribution of assessment policy can be to formulate the question of "articulation" on different grounds. Instead of matching individual courses content-for-content, the policy question becomes, "what particular areas of knowledge and skill are required of students as a prerequisite for upper-division work?" One accomplishment of CLAST in Florida has been to address this question in rudimentary form. More sophisticated examples include attempts to define core transfer competencies among community colleges in Texas and Washington.

Assessment and Teaching

If linkages between state policy and college curriculum are indirect, those between policy and teaching practice are looser still. Yet a significant development in the practice of assessment in the last few years has been an increased emphasis on improved pedagogy. In contrast to large-scale culminating examinations, assessment practitioners are increasingly urging faculty to "embed" assessment in regular coursework and to undertake a systematic program of "classroom research" to determine what teaching strategies are working and how students are actually experiencing the classroom.

Emerging campus experience suggests that techniques such as these are significantly more likely to yield faculty engagement and positive change; but they at first appear to be far from the influence of state policy. Narrowing this distance, we believe, requires attention to three distinct policy questions:

1. *How can assessment help to inform the teaching and learning process within the classroom?*

   Assessment processes such as "classroom research" are notoriously difficult to mandate. Like the familiar "course evaluationn processes required at many institutions, success depends upon the perceived utility of the process to individual instructors. *Requiring* course evaluation, research has shown, has in itself had remarkably little impact on classroom behavior. As with the curriculum, therefore, the greatest impact of state policy in this area may be symbolic: it signals clearly that faculty must *take responsibility* for student learning rather than, as many believe, simply providing an arena for it to happen.

   State assessment policies may nevertheless profoundly influence classroom behavior in at least two ways. First, they may help to determine who is actually *in* a particular college classroom. Coupling basic skills assessment with initial student placement and advisement, as is done in Tennessee and New Jersey, seems reliably to increase a student's chances of success, though it may also increase the amount of time needed to attain a degree. But mandatory placement can also raise significant equity questions—particularly if test bias becomes an issue, or if it is difficult to show a significant relationship between test performance and later performance in the curriculum.

   State assessment policy can also focus greater institutional attention upon *classroom process.* Are students engaging in "active learning" or "group study," as advocated by such sources as the recently-issued Wingspread "Seven Principles of Good Practice in Undergraduate Education"? Are they engaged in learning on their own, in parallel with classroom instruction? Are they choosing courses in a manner that allows them to avoid key learning experiences, such as library research, interaction with a computer, or a sustained piece of writing or analysis? Some state assessment approaches (most recently, the "Q-7" quality indicators project of the Minnesota State University System) are now attempting to address such questions.

2. *How can assessment be used in designing state policies that support good college teaching?*

   Addressing this question suggests an important policy linkage between assessment and faculty development. Early experiments in statewide collegiate skills assessment such as the New Jersey GIS Examination, suggest that students may systematically lack contextual knowledge (a solid grasp of physical geography, for example) that their instructors may take for granted in instructional delivery. Students may also profoundly misunderstand what is really being sought in a typical intellectual task (in the GIS, for instance, the term "essay" had to be explicitly defined before meaningful responses were obtained). Both kinds of insights can be particularly helpful in structuring faculty development.

Considerable experience has also shown that *designing* assessment procedures can itself be a significant faculty development activity. Most college and university teaching faculty have had little or no explicit training in how to write good examination questions or how to explicitly recognize and foster specific aspects of student growth and development. To the extent that state policies encourage this kind of faculty engagement, they are also pursuing faculty development.

3. *How can assessment be lined to the institutional reward structure to support good teaching?*

A major intent of state policy on assessment is deceptively simple: to shift a greater proportion of scarce institutional attention toward undergraduate education. Permanent shifts of attention, however, are generally accomplished only in the context of an underlying shift in incentives. So long as faculty perceive their own reward structures to be predominantly research-based and discipline-oriented, there is little possibility of widespread attention to good teaching.

But altering faculty reward structures on the basis of an activity as controversial as assessment poses critical policy changes. First, in examining the incentive structure surrounding teaching, it is important to distinguish *individual payoffs* from *collective investments*. Coupling the results of assessment to individual faculty rewards—either in the promotion and tenure system or in the form of additional dollar incentives for "exemplary" performance—risks incurring faculty behaviors, such as "teaching to the test," that are directly counterproductive to improved teaching. More importantly, coupling assessment with individual rewards may foster collective responsibility for curricular outcomes. A second issue concerns the degree to which "assessment" is seen as an *additional, fundable, faculty responsibility*, distinct from instruction itself. Not paying for the incurred costs of assessment, on the one hand, risks sending the signal that the activity is seen as of low priority. Negotiating a full-cost "rate scale" for faculty participation in assessment, as many collective bargaining units now advocate, risks stifling the kind of creativity needed for a meaningful program.

Both issues highlight the importance of taking a broad, systemic view of the reward structure for teaching. At bottom, institutional experience shows that faculty will become involved in assessment primarily because they feel that it enables them to do a better job as teachers, and because they can, in fact, take collective pride in doing so. To the extent that resources are involved, the key may be to clearly channel resources toward addressing concrete instructional problems that faculty identify, rather than to provide individual dollar rewards.

Assessment and Resource Needs

In contrast to curriculum and teaching practice, resource allocation has always been a premier domain of state higher education policy. As a result, when thinking about ways to harness assessment as a policy tool for improvement, legislators and state board members can be quick to seek concrete linkages to allocation. Varieties of "performance funding"—often proposed, but to date actually implemented only in Tennessee—generally lead the list of proposed innovations. But the realities of linking assessment results directly to resource issues can in practice prove complex. At minimum, we believe, the following questions must be addressed:

1. *How can assessment be related to the determination of resource needs?*

    To address this question coherently, "resource needs" must first be distinguished for *institutions* and for the system *as a whole*. In the latter, assessment results are potentially powerful tools for making an effective case about overall need. In both Florida and New Jersey, for example, lower-than-expected basic skills results have bolstered the case for greater investment in remedial and basic skills instruction, particularly among community colleges. But demonstrating need on, the basis of visible shortfalls in performance can prove a risky long-term strategy, particularly if the reasons for shortfall are persistent and systemic. Indeed, higher education leaders have been historically sensitive about sharing "bad news" explicitly with state policy makers, even if it can potentially be used to make a case for increased investment.

    At the institutional level, the use of assessment information to make the case for need encounters a similar dilemma. But here, state policy can in principle be more consistent. Funding preference can be given, for example, to institutional special budget requests that make visible and effective use of locally-collected assessment information as has been the case, for example, in New Jersey's "Governor's Challenge Grant" or in the Colorado "Centers of Excellence" program. The key to success in such programs is that they foster a healthy competition among institutions while at the same time linking new investments clearly to desired state purposes.

2. *How can assessment help to inform the allocation of resources?*

    The nature of the link between assessment and resource allocation is probably the most important single assessment policy question at the state level. If there is no link, assessment cannot in the long run be taken seriously by faculty and institutional administrators. But if the link is inconsistent, unclear, or even too directive, the chances of meaningful impact on teaching and learning can be equally reduced.

    Most states, for better or worse, have chosen *not* to link assessment results directly to resources. Where such linkages are present, they tend to be both indirect and tied to the process rather than the results of assessment. (Both Virginia and New Jersey, for example, have invested heavily in marginal allocations to support assessment at the institutional level, as did Florida when CLAST was implemented several years ago.) When pressed, however, state leaders say they hope to make more visible use of assessment results through such processes as program review and improvement, faculty development, and additional marginal incentive grant programs.

    Effectively linking assessment results to institutional resource allocation involves resolution of at least three major policy dilemmas. First, should the philosophy of allocation be driven by *rewarding performance* or by *addressing need?* The classic model of "performance funding" ties positive assessment results to increased allocation. Because it appears to provide incentives for improvement, performance funding has inherent appeal to legislators and state boards. In practice, however, it may direct investment away from where it is most needed, and may cause institutions to give undue attention to narrow conceptions of performance. Directing resources toward detected problems, on the other hand, can tend to obscure real excellence and innovation. Both situations can be exacerbated when, as in Colorado, resource consequences are negative in the form of a budget penalty.

A second dilemma involves the *level of resources* at issue. For good reasons, most states continue to allocate resources to institutions on the basis of imputed cost—either through formula or through incremental adjustments to base. What is generally at stake, therefore, are "marginal" investments of from 2% to 10% of available resources, allocated by a special process. But the higher the stakes, the greater the dilemma. If little is seen to be at stake, as in states like Missouri or Illinois, institutions may pay little attention. If much is at stake, as in Tennessee, Colorado, or Virginia, the incentive may be to take few risks, to report only good news, and to see assessment primarily as an administrator's responsibility. In Tennessee, for example, one unintended consequence of performance funding is an institutional perception that assessment is "too important to be left to the faculty."

A final dilemma concerns the actual *mechanism to be used* to allocate funds. On the one hand, equity demands the consistent application of clear criteria, lest institutions rightly charge that assessment-based resource allocations are made capriciously. But, as in Tennessee, this may drive policy inexorably toward narrow quantitative criteria that can be "unambiguously" applied. The result may be a system little different in function from a traditional enrollment-driven formula. The increasing use of "peer institutions" in a wide range of state budgetary mechanisms represents one attempt to get around this problem. Lack of clarity in the allocation process, on the other hand, can render it sufficiently political that the real ends of improvement become obscure.

3. *How can assessment be used to examine and increase the "return on investment" of public resources in higher education?*

An undoubted stimulus for assessment is a growing demand for evidence of "return on investment." Legislators and state board members are increasingly impatient with claims that the complexity of higher education renders infeasible any attempt to gather evidence of its effectiveness. As a result, many have been quick to press for assessment "solutions" that attempt to provide such evidence promptly and simply. Many in the academy, in turn, have been quick to condemn such motives as inconsistent with the real goal of assessment: improving teaching and learning.

Before immediately characterizing these motives as antithetical, it is important to recognize the reality of the forces that lie behind them. One is a real decline in *public credibility* for higher education as an enterprise; as costs have grown so has the public's conviction that colleges and universities are not as focused on their own and society's needs as they once were. At the same time, political champions of higher education increasingly believe that they need *better evidence to "sell" needed increases* to their doubting colleagues. More and more, they speak of such evidence inc orporate language, calling for the equivalent of "shareholders' reports" or "annual earnings statements." Ironically, when pressed, their motives resemble those of the academy: they want assessment processes that are real, engaging, complex, and that have the potential to actually have an impact on undergraduate classrooms. But they must also meet the demands of a constituency that wants to keep things straightforward, and that is growing impatient about what is seen as unresponsiveness.

Significant gaps between the language and timeframes of the academic and political worlds raise additional policy issues. If "improvement" is indeed a long-term enterprise, what can the public be told in the *short run*? Once it is known that "assessment" is occurring, as in New Jersey, public pressures for early disclosure become enormous. Should preliminary results be disclosed, no matter how uncertain? Or, as in South Dakota, should institutions be allowed to protect the confidentiality of their individual results for a limited period while remedial actions are taken? Or should the emphasis of reporting be placed upon communicating institutional *actions taken* in response to assessment, as in Virginia or Colorado? And if so, is it necessary to report results as well as remedies, if only to demonstrate that a credible process is in fact in place? Finally, who are the *primary constituencies* for reporting? Should they be legislators and public officials primarily, who can at least minimally be expected to know the policy contexts within which assessment information belongs, or should reporting be extended to prospective students and employers of graduates, as has been posed in California, and as is currently called for in new "track record disclosure" rules for federally-supported occupational and technical programs?

At bottom, of course, evidence of "return on investment" is provided by improvement itself. State policies which can in fact foster improvement in the long run, will at the same time achieve "accountability" as a by-product.

Process Issues in State-Level Program Reviews

ROBERT A. WALLHAUS

Differences in state-level program review processes can be explained in terms of six key design decisions and the implementation environment.

There are several determinations that must be made in designing any program review process. These decisions, which will characterize the program review process and ultimately determine its acceptance and effectiveness, include:

1. Determining the purposes and objectives of program review,

2. Determining and defining the scope and focus of the program review,

3. Determining the schedule and timing of program reviews,

4. Determining criteria to be used in program assessment and how to support the application of such criteria,

5. Determining who will be involved in program review and their roles and responsibilities,

6. Determining what decisions will be made as a result of program review.

The major differences among program review processes utilized in different states are related to how these issues are resolved. In each case there are various alternatives; each alternative will offer certain advantages and disadvantages depending largely upon factors related to the environment in which they are to implemented (for example, the statutory authorities of the state postsecondary education agency in relation to various campuses and sectors of higher education). Craven (1980) analyses the full scope of issues that arise in designing program evaluations, and, in a section entitled "Conducting an Evaluation" (pp. 444–449), he proposes a series of questions that must be answered in designing and implementing an effective evaluation. Barak and Berdahl (1978) study the different approaches to program review that are utilized by different state agencies across the country, and Engdahl and Barak (1980) report the results of a survey and analysis of program reviews carried out in the thirteen western states that are included in the Western Interstate Commission for Higher Education (WICHE) compact.

This chapter identifies the possible choices in each of the six areas just identified and analyzes the pros and cons associated with these alternatives. Particular attention in this analysis is given to the relationship between state- and institutional-level program reviews.

Determining the Purposes of Program Review

The definition of purposes is logically the first step in developing a program review process, and yet it is a step that is frequently never clarified. Often this lack of clarity reflects an unwillingness to face the reality that a well-conceived examination will result in conclusions—some good, but some bad, at least from certain perspectives. On the other hand, leaving purposes and objectives undefined can result in distrust and, in the extreme, manipulation of the process and its outcomes.

Table 1 displays a range of purposes and objectives for program review. Although no single program review could serve all of these purposes, most program reviews are designed to serve multiple objectives. Certain purposes and objectives are relevant to the responsibilities of state agencies, while others are more closely tied to decisions that are made by governing boards, campuses, or academic units within an institution. Table 1 classifies these purposes and objectives according to whether they are primarily related to institutional, as opposed to state-level, decisions and responsibilities to show areas of overlap and potential conflict. However, considerable variations along this continuum occur according to such factors as state agency statutory authorities, type of institution (for example, public or private), academic environment (selective versus "open door"), and governance structures (local versus statewide board of control). Chance (1980) analyzes the purposes of program review that are appropriate to state-level agencies and discusses how these can be complementary to purposes at the institutional level. Those purposes and objectives outlined in Table 1 with state-level implications are discussed briefly here.

Statewide Educational Policies and Plans. It is impossible to examine statewide educational policies, long-range plans or programmatic priorities on the basis of independent reviews of individual programs. At the same time one must recognize that individual programs are the building blocks that, taken collectively and properly integrated, serve to define a statewide master plan. Thus, an assessment across the board of the strengths and weaknesses of existing programs and the future plans and priorities for program development become the basis for accomplishing the purpose of program review. Such reviews are usually initiated by the coordinating or governing board for higher education in the state, but should include all sectors of higher education in the design, collection of data, interpretation of results, and formulation of policy and plans. Often it is desirable to facilitate statewide planning purposes by focusing on an academic discipline or group of related disciplines (for example, all programs for education in the health professions) or selected functions, such as research or continuing education. It is particularly important to establish criteria and to seek information that extend beyond the individual programs in the academic area being studied. For example, national trends in student demand and projected statewide and national employment opportunities should be considered.

Statewide Program Mix. Program duplication, or the need for additional programs, cannot be considered from the perspective of isolated individual program by program reviews. But, the capability of existing programs to handle projected student interests and job market demands, the possibility of expanding existing programs without impairing their quality, and the appropriate distribution of programs geographically, by sector, and by institutional mission—serving a local, regional, or in-service clientele, for example, are certainly factors to consider in determining the proper programmatic mix from a statewide perspective. These insights can be partially derived from individual program reviews.

Educational and Economic Justification. The greatest potential for conflict between state agencies and institutions arises when the purpose of program review centers on the determination of educational and economic priorities. First, this question is usually relevant to state agencies responsible for planning and budgeting and is certainly relevant to budget decisions of campus level administrations, as well as each level of academic unit within the campus. In other words, there is considerable overlap in responsibilities with regard to this purpose of program review, and questions of turf will surely be raised. Second, this is a double-edged purpose. When programmaticdeficiencies are found, the deficiency can be corrected, which usually requires additional resources—a good outcome for the campus directly involved, or the program can be eliminated. Given these risks and uncertainties, some people would rather avoid the assessment altogether.

Although state agencies have responsibilities and interests in such areas as establishing quality standards, preparing for entry into professions, improving communications with constituents, and the other purposes for program review identified in Table 1, the driving force for these purposes runs more in the direction of institutional responsibilities. Nevertheless, in designing a state-level program review, one should recognize that the purposes of program review are not unidimensional. These purposes overlap, and if properly conceived, can be mutually supportive.

Table 1
Purposes and Objectives of Program Review

	Tends to be more closely tied to state-level responsibilities	Tends to be more closely tied to institutional responsibilties
A. Determination of statewide educational policies, long-range plans, and programmatic priorities that is, support development of statewide master plans)	X	
B. Elimination of unnecessary program duplication, or, conversely, identifiation of needs for new programs	X	
C. Determination of educational and economic priorities in terms of:		
consistency with role and mission	X	
need for improvement or expansion and additional resources necessary to accomplish (linkage to budget decisions)	X	
decisions to decrease or terminate (linkage to resource reallocation decisions)	X	
D. Determination of relationship to established standards of quality, or preparation for entry into professions, and so on (linkage to accreditation, continuation of operating authority or licensing authority)	X	
E. Improving communications with constituents; assuring information provided to students and prospective students, parents, alumni, governmental agencies, and others is consistent with actual practice	X	
F. Determination of quality controls and policies (for example, admission policy, graduation requirements)		X
G. Determination of curricular modifications, advisement procedures, institutional plans and priorities relative to instructional, research, and service objectives		X
H. Personnel and organizational decisions—faculty promotion and tenure, academic leadership, organizational structures, and philosophies		X

Determining and Defining the Scope and Focus of the Program Review Process

The general thrust of program review, that is, an assessment of strengths and weaknesses, is equally applicable to nonacademic areas as it is to research, public service, and instruction. Theoretically, a program review process could be designed to encompass academic as well as support areas. However, differences in objectives and definitions of productivity between instructional programs and support programs are considerable and would preclude the possibility of a single grand design for program review. Program reviews cannot ignore the nonacademic areas, which typically account for approximately 40 percent of total institutional expenditures. Approximately 40 percent of total institutional expenditures. However, the key issues for administrative and support functions center on operational efficiencies and management and personnel concerns, and it is very difficult to define an appropriate state-level role in this context. For this reason, most state agencies have focused their program review efforts on academic programs.

However, difficulties also arise in defining the scope and focus of program reviews in the academic areas. On the one hand, there is a close relationship between the research, instruction, and public service that is carried out in a given discipline. On the other hand, there are considerable differences in objectives and clientele served by research, public service, and instructional programs. A program review designed to examine statewide planning and policy issues related to research (that is, purpose A in Table 1) would focus on such questions as the appropriate mix of state support relative to external funds, the extent to which research enterprise and resources in colleges and universities are congruent with the problem-solving priorities of the state's industry and social agencies, and the delineation of institutional research missions. But a different set of issues would be raised at the institutional level, including questions concerning the critical mass of resources, such as faculty interests and expertise, that is necessary to advance knowledge at the leading edge of the discipline or compete effectively in the arena of national research priorities. Consequently, it is difficult to build upon institutional level reviews of research and public service programs to accomplish state-level purposes. Thus, most state-level studies related to research and public service have been conceptualized as a unique effort to examine a particular policy issue.

A key question in designing state-level review processes for instructional programs is whether the focus should be on degree programs, or on disciplines or organizational units, such as academic departments or colleges. Student objectives, as well as those related to societal concerns and occupational opportunities, are closely aligned with degree programs. This perspective is consequently more compatible with state-level interests in program review as defined in Table 1. It is virtually impossible, however, to separate certain fundamental programmatic characteristics by degree program. For example, it is unrealistic to delineate particular faculty activities by degree level. Furthermore, purposes related to determination of admissions policy and graduation requirements, curriculum, and personnel and organizational decisions that are of primary interest to the campus and academic units are more closely aligned with a discipline structure. (See items F, G, and H in Table 1.) Consequently, the discipline or organizational unit perspective is most compatible with institutional objectives related to program review. This definitional incompatibility between state-level and institutional-level perspectives becomes particularly pronounced in the area of greatest overlap in purpose—namely, with regard to establishing educational and economic priorities (purpose C in Table 1). The usual compromise is to review concurrently all degree programs within a given discipline. This permits various purposes to be served simultaneously and alleviates data development problems.

Some states have chosen to focus their program review activities on a particular level of instruction; for example, they may review all doctoral programs within a specific time. This decision is undoubtedly driven by a preconception of where the major problems lie with program quality, unnecessary duplication, or ineffective use of resources. Structurally, this definition of the scope and focus of program review creates many of the definitional difficulties already identified, such as the problem of determining the resources, activities, and objectives that are neatly aligned with doctoral offerings, as opposed to other degrees within a given discipline. In addition, because the implied thrust is to deal with certain preconceived problems, this definition of scope is likely to meet considerable resistance.

Determining the Schedule and Timing of Program Reviews

The question of when program reviews should be carried out is, of course, closely tied to the question of the focus and scope of program review discussed in the preceding section. Aside from the obvious advantages of attenuating the faculty and staff effort that is involved in program review, there are other good reasons to structure program review as a systematic, continuous process as opposed to a one-shot, grand-scale effort to be carried out over one or two years. Momentum is hard to achieve, given the complexity of most program reviews. In addition, there are many questions and concerns with regard to purpose, criteria, and procedure, and these must be addressed. Considerable time and commitment is required to implement a process for program review, and it makes little sense to periodically dismantle and then reconstruct the process again at a later time.

Table 2 identifies several alternatives for scheduling program reviews and briefly comments on the advantages and disadvantages of each. Obviously, various combinations of these alternatives could be employed. For example, all programs could be scheduled initially for cyclical review, say over a five year period (Alternative A). But during the second cycle only those programs falling outside certain trigger parameters based on key indicators would be reexamined (Alternative C). Perhaps during a third cycle all programs would again be scheduled for review.

A state agency cannot examine in depth all programs in the state over any reasonable time period. Therefore, some form of "management by exception" approach is needed, particularly for the large number of community college programs in those states with extensive community college systems. Although various alternatives in Table 2 are designed to screen out a more limited number of programs for special attention, an approach based on successive iterations of great depth and detail may have considerable utility at the level of the state system or the central campus administration. For example, Illinois public universities review instructional programs on a cyclical basis. A synopsis of one to two pages, which focuses on the conclusions and recommendations resulting from the annual program reviews is transmitted to the Illinois Board of Higher Education, rather than sending the entire set of review materials and voluminous data collected during the course of the review. The Board of Higher Education staff examines these conclusions and recommendations in conjunction with basic program data on such topics as enrollment trends and cost study analyses; in the case of certain programs, the board identifies concerns or questions that they feel should be pursued further. Perhaps 90 percent of the program review synopses are accepted with no further examination deemed necessary. The general nature of the questions and concerns that are of interest to the board have been previously communicated to the universities, along with suggested data that would be responsive to these questions. Based on their in-depth review the universities submit additional information in response to the board staff's requests. Several, successively more detailed iterations, may be pursued prior to the formulation of staff recommendations that are ultimately presented to the Board of Higher Education. Thus, program review schedules can be designed around the concept of selective examination, both in terms of the number of programs reviewed as well as in terms of the depth of review that is deemed appropriate. Groves (1979) presents an historical account of how this process of state-level program review evolved in Illinois, how various difficulties were overcome, and the reasons for the number of false starts that occurred over a decade as the state-level review process was being designed and negotiated.

Table 2
Alternatives for Scheduling Program Reviews

	Advantages	Disadvantages
A. All programs reviewed on a cyclical basis (for example once every five years)	Assures all programs are periodically examined Easier to organize and manage; allows units to systematically prepare for reviews; Smooths workload at campus and state levels	Potential for redundant or wasted effort (that is, the process is carried out whether it is warranged or not)
B. Schedules meshed with external requirements (for example, accreditation reviews)	Eliminates redundancy, which is inevitable if this is not done	Internal purposes may be driven by external requirements and hence not realized to fullest possible extent
C. Selection based on key indicators (for example, enrollment or resource trends)	Serves to focus review efforts in areas where program modifications may be necessary	Raises concerns relative to the unreliabillity of the indicators, which may not be sufficiently sensitive or applicable to avoid triggering "unwarranted" reviews Does not ensure that all programs will be examined even over long periods of time Usually carries negative connotations; indicators point to problems
D. Crisis selection (for example, reviews based on student complaints or concerns raised by state agency or other institutions relative to unnecessary program duplication)	Focus of program review is on problem areas and needed modifications	Reviews driven largely by negative factors, most of which may be external to program Crisis management, the problem may be too large to address positively if uncovered too late
E. Seleciton based on policy or planning rationale related to certain categories of programs (by instructional level or by discipline, for example)	Facilitates comparative analyses, particularly from a state perspective Serves to more clearly delineate purposes of review	Driven largely by needs external to institutions (purpose more closely aligned with state-level interest—see Table 1). Institutional purposes may be submerged or institutional scheduling disrupted

In summary, the scheduling of program reviews involves a consideration of a number of tradeoffs: (1) frequency of program reviews versus work-load requirements, (2) flexibility to respond to various purposes and external audiences versus the need to systematically organize and effectively manage the program review, and (3) rigor and depth of review versus demands on the faculty and staff at all levels.

Determining Criteria to be Used in Program Assessment and How to Support the Application of Such Criteria

Purpose, criteria, and data can be thought of as tumbling dominoes: Without well-defined purposes for program review, it is impossible to specify, communicate, or gain acceptance of the criteria that will be utilized as the basis for evaluation. And, without criteria it is impossible to define what data should be assembled, since the purpose of collecting information during a program review is to enable judgments to be made along specified dimensions.

Unfortunately, the dominoes often fall backward during the design of many program reviews. First, an attempt is made to determine what data are available. Then, there may be some consideration of what these data might mean. Finally, an attempt is made to tie this usually faulty interpretation to decisions related to the future development of the program. As a result of this approach, the program review design does not fully capitalize on the opportunities to have a valid impact on decision-making processes. Hence, no decisions result and program review is an expensive but ineffective exercise. Or, even worse, decisions are misled because the criteria utilized are inappropriate or the information examined leads to misinterpretations.

There are no set rules for establishing criteria for program reviews, but there are many trade-offs and issues that need to be considered. Table 3 addresses the extremes of those issues. The truth lies somewhere between these end points and must be determined through careful study, conceptualization, and negotiation. Barak and Berdahl (1978) identify program review criteria that are utilized in different states.

Determining Who Will be Involved in the Program Review and Their Roles and Responsibilities

In designing an effective program review, some crucial questions that must be answered are who is to be involved and what will be the roles and responsibilities of these individuals? These questions are extremely difficult to answer because a number of organizational objectives are in potential

Table 3
Considerations in Developing Criteria as a Basis for Program Evaluation

On the One Hand	On the Other Hand
Criteria need to be defined with as much specificity as possible (for example, a quantitative minimum number of enrollments or awards granted) if they are to be understood and applied.	Criteria for program evaluation must be establishe with flexibility because of the significant differences in mission, programmatic objectives, clientele served by the program, and so on.
Criteria need to be pragmatic—if quantitative data cannot be obtained relative to a criterion it should be discarded because it cannot be evaluated objectively.	Criteria need to be established to reflect the character and objectives of the program even though it will be difficult or impossible to evaluate them quantitatively. Considerable room for judgement, and subjectivity is appropriate.
Criteria ultimately will need to be determined by administrative fiat, or the review process will never get underway.	Criteria should result from consensus among all who are involved in or affected by the program review results or, at minimum, should be established by the individuals most directly associated with the program—the program faculty.
Criteria can be established in one broad conceptualization and applied to all institutions or programs. To do otherwise will preclude any comparative analyses, will create strawmen, and will consume more energy than is warranted.	Criteria must be tailored, otherwise serious misinterpretations will resust and will mislead any decisions based on the program review conclusions.

conflict and sensitive balances must be achieved. That is, accomplishing certain objectives related to roles and responsibilities may well compromise others. This can be demonstrated by outlining some of the characteristics that would ideally be built into the organizational structure of program review.

Expertise. The objective is to involve in the process to the furthest extent possible those individuals with the greatest expertise and insights relative to the program or discipline being reviewed. Since program reviews address an array of different questions, they will frequently need to draw upon insights, expertise, and perspectives from a number of different quarters. This is one reason that the organizational structure for program review is often complex and seemingly involves a cast of thousands. Although these organizational configurations can be burdensome, this is usually a smaller price to pay than that of reaching invalid or unacceptable conclusions because the best available expertise and understanding was not utilized at the appropriate points in the review. (A more in-depth discussion of this topic is presented by House in his chapter.)

Credibility. Generally, the individuals who have greatest expertise for assessing programmatic strengths and weaknesses—the faculty—are also the individuals whose self-interests are closely tied to the conclusions of the program review. State agency staffs understand these realities and, as a result, are constantly on the alert for a whitewash. Uncertainty about motives may lead the faculty to believe that all external parties are seeking evidence that would support program discontinuance. On the other hand, state agency staffs may view any data or conclusions developed by those directly responsible for the program with considerable skepticism; because of this, they may reject relevant information or fail to act on the basis of sound conclusions. So a conflict in objectives—involving expertise while maintaining trust and credibility—is always present. Too many program reviews have not resolved these conflicts and are consequently counterproductive. The chapters by Hoyt and by House discuss the ramifications of this issue.

Checks and Balances. A program review process is often organized around a complex mosaic of interlocking committees to establish checks and balances that simultaneously strengthen credibility and provide channels for consultation and information flow. Many campuses have established hierarchical committee structures involving the program faculty as well as faculty in other disciplines that have a reputation for academic leadership and understanding. From a state perspective, a program review would be well advised to understand these checks and balances, insist that they are workable and, hence, credible, and then build upon them. Even though some colleges and universities give considerable attention to establishing appropriate organizational structures to support a program review process, these efforts often fail because the responsibilities and reporting relationships of each group or committee are not clearly defined. Again, this lack of definition is often a subtle way of circumventing conflicts and tensions. In the end, however, this strategy will lead to even greater distrust.

External Consultants. External consultants offer an opportunity to replicate much of the expertise that is available through the program's faculty and, at the same time, external consultants are further detached from the ramifications of the recommendations that result from program review. Consequently, external consultants are likely to call the shots as they see them. But external consultants can add substantial costs to the program review process. Furthermore, the question of who commissions the consultants is a sensitive issue. For example, if a state agency selects or pays the consultants, they may well be viewed as "hired guns." If the program faculty selects the consultants, the review will be viewed as another "inside job." There are, of course, options between these extremes. For example, consultants can be commissioned by one party with the advice or consent of other parties. Such compromises can result in satisfactory choices from the perspective of all involved. An in depth discussion of the pros and cons associated with the use of consultants in program review is presented by Petrie in Chapter Two.

Positive Incentives. Although it is not easy, creating positive incentives in a program review can be accomplished through such means as:

- Assurance of due process; the program review process does not always lead to positive conclusions from everyone's perspective, so it is important that all perspectives are heard and carefully considered.

- Building in the potential for tangible payoffs; a clean bill of health may be viewed as a nice result (given all the bad things that could have occurred), but a commitment to capitalize on what has been learned from a review, even though this may involve considerable expense, can be far more meaningful.

- Linkage to other decision-making processes; a program review can easily become a process unto itself, with no realizable outlets. In such instances there is little reason to take reviews seriously.

Determining What Decisions Will be Made as a Result of Program Review

Sometimes the conclusions and recommendations resulting from program reviews are transmitted to state agencies without the endorsement of the governing board or top level administrative officials. This is often true at other administrative levels within the institution. When this occurs surely something is amiss. The program review is seen as a half-hearted response to some externally imposed mandate, the results are not deemed to be valid, or key decision makers are ignoring the recommendations—perhaps because they feel that they are unsound, or perhaps because they do not believe they are in a strong enough position to implement them. Underlying all these possibilities frequently is a failure to conceptualize how program review results are to be linked effectively to other established decision-making processes of the academic unit, the institution, or the state agency, in particular, decisions related to budgets, personnel, curriculum, and future programmatic directions.

These decisions are closely aligned with many of the purposes of program review outlined in Table 1. The difficulties that are often encountered in implementing program review recommendations are a result of never having clarified or achieved a consensus on the purposes of the program at the outset. A related explanation for the problem that many institutions and state agencies face in implementing the recommendations of program review is that two different casts of characters are involved in the review process and the formal decision-making structures for budget, planning, personnel, and curriculum. For example, academic units, institutions, and state agencies have well established protocols for their budget processes. It is very difficult for an independently conceptualized and managed program review process to be superimposed upon these established budget protocols.

Program review, a relative newcomer in most institutions and state agencies, is likely to be staffed as an add-on, rather than integrated into the more established functions and organizational structures. Program review processes will be successful to the extent that they are conceptualized and staffed within the established organizational structures at all levels of higher education.

References

Barak, R. J., and Berdahl, R. O. *State Level Academic Program Review in Higher Education.* Denver, Colo.: Education Commission of the States, 1978.

Chance, W. "State Level Program Review." In *Postsecondary Educahon Program Review.* Boulder, Colo.: Western Interstate Commission for Higher Education, 1980.

Craven, E. "Evaluating Program Performance." In P. Jedamus and M. W. Peterson (Eds.), Improving Academic Management: A Handbook of Planning and Institutional Research .San Francisco Jossey-Bass, 1980.

Engdahl, L., and Barak, R. "Study of Academic Program Review." In *Postsecondary Education Program Review*. Boulder, Colo.: Western Interstate Commission for Higher Education, 1980.

Groves, R. T. "Program Review in a Multi-Level State Governance System: The Case of Illinois." *Planning for Higher Education*, 1979, 8 (1),1–9.

Academic Program Reviews: Institutional Approaches, Expectations, and Controversies

Clifton F. Conrad and Richard F. Wilson

Major Issues in Program Review

Six issues concern the individuals in colleges and universities who are involved in academic program review: (1) accommodating multiple purposes; (2) selecting an evaluation model; (3) assessing quality; (4) using external reviewers; (5) increasing use of evaluations; and (6) assessing the impact of evaluations. (The selection of these six issues was based on two considerations—the significance of the issue and the extent to which a review of the literature might aid in illuminating its dimensions.) This chapter defines and clarifies these issues and presents alternative perspectives regarding their resolution. Those engaged in program review need to address these issues regularly.

Accommodating Multiple Purposes

Because a number of reasons usually exist for establishing a program of review, institutions have developed a fairly lengthy list of purposes to guide their review efforts. The following list represents those adopted by many institutions:

- to assess program quality, productivity, need, and demand
- to improve the quality of academic offerings
- to ensure wise use of resources
- to determine the program's effectiveness and to consider possible modifications
- to facilitate academic planning and budgeting
- to satisfy state-level review requirements

The advantage of designing an evaluation system that incorporates all of these purposes is that it will appeal to several constituencies. Such support is often needed in the early stages of implementation, but it can become self-defeating. It is possible, however, to design an evaluation system in which information is collected and judgments made that respond to widely different expectations.

Serious questions can be raised about two accommodations of purposes. The first involves institutional efforts to combine program improvement and resource reallocation as major purposes of the review. The second concerns an institution's attempts to use a single review process to satisfy both its own review agenda and that of a state-level coordinating or governing board.

Combining Program Improvement with Resource Reallocation

Although many institutions conducting program reviews emphasize either the improvement of program quality or resource reallocation (including program discontinuance), a growing number of institutions combine both emphases into a single process. At first glance, the two purposes would seem compatible. Each requires an assessment of current quality to identify where strengths exist and where improvement is warranted. Most people also would agree that quality assessment is an important first step in deciding how to reallocate resources. The problem, however, is that it is difficult, if not impossible, for those responsible for the review process to achieve both objectives at once. "Quality assessment should not be ignored in a retrenchment process, but the two distinct motivations of improvement and reduction in resources will generally involve somewhat different processes and may produce quite different results" (George 1982, p. 45). Several distinct difficulties in merging these two purposes merit consideration.

A major problem in attempting to achieve both purposes in a single review system is that the underlying assumptions and ultimate objectives may not be easily reconciled, if at all. When an institution wishes to assess the quality of its programs and to improve programs where weaknesses appear, the emphasis of the evaluation will be on how to assess current performance, on what progress has been made over time, and on what institutional strategies might facilitate further improvement. At the University of North Carolina—Asheville, for example, program improvement, not resource allocation, was the principal incentive behind recent program reviews. After studying a range of data, nine department chairs rated the institution's programs on the basis of nine criteria. Future resources of the institution were earmarked for programs with low rankings to promote program improvement (Cochran and Hengstler 1984).

On the other hand, the approach to evaluation is likely to depart from this strategy if an institution concludes it must reduce the number of program offerings or reallocate resources away from low-priority or low-demand programs. In this case, evaluators must judge relative worth and value and often must act quickly in the face of immediate budget pressures. In this situation, quality is only one of several factors that gets considered.

In distinguishing between the two types of evaluations, it is useful to consider the "industrial" and "biological" models of evaluation (Pace 1972). The industrial model focuses on quantitative measures used to judge efficiency and productivity, and the biological model searches for ways to enrich experiences and to assess broader and more enduring program effects on students and society (Pace 1972). It is not stretching this analysis too far to suggest that most resource reallocation processes are frequently industrial in orientation, while program improvement processes are more biological. Others have questioned the compatibility of the two purposes, pointing out the great difference between a unit thinking it is being evaluated to identify areas needing additional strength and units thinking such an assessment serves to identify areas where quality is low and support should be diminished or even eliminated (Arns and Poland 1980).

The discussion of the review activities of the Select Committee on Academic Program Priorities at SUNY—Albany supports this view: "The Select Committee . . . felt a certain frustration that the budget recommendations had created a climate that led to the implementation of its negative recommendations but not its positive ones" (Volkwein 1984, p. 393).

Yet another problem in merging these two purposes is a temporal one: The careful assessment of quality and the development of recommendations for improvement require considerable time. Most institutions are unable to conduct more than six or eight program reviews each year. Such a protracted schedule does not mesh well with resource reallocation reviews, which usually transpire within relatively short periods in response to anticipated budget problems. The latter reviews use extant information on quality but usually lack sufficient time to conduct detailed analysis of the quality of every program offered. Hence, a timing factor militates against efforts to combine the two types of reviews.

Accommodating Institutional and State-Level Purposes

A second accommodation of purposes concerns how institutional review processes relate to the expectations for review of state higher education agencies. State agencies' authority and activity in program review have increased dramatically in the last few years, and the proper role of state boards in institutional review processes continues to be debated.

A key issue in this debate is whether institutional and state-level interests converge or are sufficiently complementary so that a single review process can achieve the aims of both. Some believe that state-level interests can indeed mesh with those of institutions (Hines 1980). In Hines's view, the predominant institutional interest lies in assessing merit, while state agencies are most interested in statewide needs or plans. Although the primary objective of review differs for the two groups, the secondary objectives overlap considerably; that is, states have more than passing interest in merit, and institutions frequently want to know how programs could be more responsive to statewide needs.

An analysis of the relationship between program review for institutions and for state-level agencies identified eight purposes for undertaking program reviews and discussed how review responsibility varies by purpose (Wallhaus 1982) (see table 5, pp. 44–5). In this view, responsibility for review is vested in the state agency when the review serves to develop a statewide plan or overall programmatic priorities. Conversely, reviews focusing on curricular and personnel matters are the province of institutions. Between these two extremes exist a number of purposes where the assignment of responsibility is not so straight-forward. It is these purposes that institutions and state agencies frequently try to accomplish cooperatively through a single review process.

These cooperative efforts have been labeled "shared reviews" (Floyd 1983). Responsibilities in shared reviews are defined variously. Frequently, the institution conducts the review and endeavors to attend to matters of interest to both the institution and the state. On the surface, this plan would seem to be reasonable and efficient. The issue, again, is whether a single review process can have more than one driving purpose.

In the last few years, a number of states have adopted shared responsibilities for reviews. Illinois, Idaho, New Mexico, California, Oregon, and Ohio have adopted review processes in which the state agency, rather than conducting reviews itself, simply ensures that each institution is doing so (Barak 1982). In a comparable arrangement within the University of Wisconsin system, each institution is required to have a review process and must report its findings to the system office (Craven 1980b). Only in unusual circumstances, such as when enrollments are low or when unnecessary duplication seems to exist, does the system office conduct a review of its own.

In shared reviews, then, institutions attempt to accommodate institutional and state-level purposes by developing an evaluation process that satisfies both institutional and state board requirements. In theory, the institution designs an evaluation system to meet its own needs and, by making minor adjustments in, say, data collection or reporting lines, is able to satisfy state-level needs as well. Moreover, this strategy minimizes duplication of review activities.

Despite these positive features, the shared review approach has drawn criticism. While combining reviews appears to be a solid idea, theoretical and practical reasons militate against the success of such an approach (Barak 1982, p. 84). For example, whereas institutions frequently establish the need for a program on the basis of students' or faculty members' perspectives, state agencies usually look at program need from a societal or manpower perspective. Another example

Table 5
Purposes and Objectives of Program Review

	Tends to be more closely tied to state-level responsibilities	Tends to be more closely tied to institutional responsibilities
• Determination of statewide educational policies, long-range plans and programmatic priorities (that is, support development of statewide master plans)	X	
• Elimination of unnecessary program duplication or, conversely, identification of needs for newprograms	X	
• Determination of educational and economic priorities in terms of:		
1. consistency with role and mission	X	
2. need for improvement or expansion and additional resources necessary to accomplish (link to budget decisions)	X	
3. decisions to decrease or terminate (link to resource reallocation decisions)	X	
• Determination of relationship to established standards of quality, or preparation for entry into professions, and so on (link to accreditation, continuation of operating authority, or licensing authority)	X	
• Improvement of communications with constituents; assurance that information provided to students, prospective students, parents, alumni, governmental agencies, and others is consistent with actual practice	X	
• Determination of quality controls and policies (for example, admission policy, graduation requirements)		X
• Determination of curricular modifications, advisement procedures, institutional plans, and priorities relative to instructional, research, and service objectives		X
• Personnel and organizational decisions—faculty promotion and tenure, academic leadership, organizational structures, and philosophies		X

of potential conflict centers on efficiency. Institutions tend to assess efficiency by comparing similar departments on campus or by collecting data from peer departments. State agencies tend to look at efficiency from a statewide perspective, for example, how costs in a discipline vary among institutions in the state. Thus, separate reviews by institutions and state agencies may be the best solution (Barak 1982, pp. 84–88).

Under certain conditions, combined reviews may not be productive (Wilson 1984). If the system office or state-level board prescribes the review process in too much detail, local initiatives aimed at establishing an effective system may be stifled. Where the state agency insists upon close adherence to a prescribed format, it may be more useful for separate reviews to be conducted, one by the institution for its own use, another by the state agency.

Selecting an Evaluation Model

The key issue for evaluators is which model—goal-based, responsive, decision-making, and connoisseurship—should guide program reviews in higher education, and the decision is an important one:

> Where an administrator has a choice with regard to the type of evaluation to be conducted . . . that individual should be fully aware of the fundamentally different assumptions and outcomes that obtain when a particular type of strategy is selected (Gardner 1977, p. 572).

Goal-Based Model

The goal-based model focuses principally on assessing the extent to which a program's formal objectives are being achieved. As part of this effort, considerable attention is given to specifying program objectives, establishing standards of performance, identifying data to assess performance, and evaluating whether objectives have been achieved.

A goal-based approach to evaluation offers a number of positive features. First, the importance placed on objectives focuses attention on what those responsible for a program hope to accomplish. These goal statements become more than general statements of intent; they are specified as precisely as possible because of their significance to the subsequent assessment of performance. Second, a goal-based system can be used to make periodic checks of progress (formative evaluation) as well as to make consummate judgments of program worth (summative evaluation). Third, the approach encourages systematic attention not only to whether program goals have been reached but also to those features contributing to success or failure. For example, if the desired goal is to increase student retention and if certain actions are taken to achieve this goal, the goal-based design would require both an assessment of whether retention had improved and an understanding of the effect on retention of the actions themselves.

To be sure, the goal-based model has some limitations. The specification of goals can become an obsession resulting in lengthy lists covering every conceivable desire, significant as well as trivial, for a program. "Some people believe that when every objective is related to every other, the program is properly managed" (House 1982, p. 10). But "a major criticism of evaluation as congruence between performance and objectives is that a focusing on measurable products rather than processes occurs. This may permit the overlooking of important side effects" (Feasley 1980, p. 9). In essence, this criticism berates the propensity of evaluators to focus on whether goals have been accomplished while ignoring other, unintended contributions that goal statements have not captured.

On a related matter, the goal-based system has been criticized because of the inflexible way in which a priori goals drive the process (Guba and Lincoln 1981). Evaluators have a tendency to accept the goal statements and to pursue data relating to those goals in a very determined way. If, in mid-evaluation, it becomes apparent that some of the goal statements no longer apply or that those responsible for the program should change directions, the goal-based evaluator might not perceive the necessary changes or, more significantly, might not be inclined to suggest that plans be changed, even if the need is apparent. Thus, the goal-based model sometimes engenders a singleminded pursuit of information relating to goal statements while ignoring everything else.

Perhaps the major defect of the goal-based approach lies in its assumption that ways can be found to measure performance in relation to all goals. This observation is especially significant for those institutions of higher education in which goals, such as those of program quality or centrality, frequently are elusive. Attempts to "force" a goal-based model in a particular setting may result in redefining the goals in ways that can be measured (for example, number of publications equals research quality), thus trivializing what is being done.

Use of the goal-based model, therefore, offers the two advantages of a systematic attention to how a program has performed in relation to its intent and of a concern for the factors contributing to its success or failure. The model's chief limitations are the propensity to reduce everything to a goal statement, the insensitivity to outcomes that are unrelated to goal statements, and the assumption that valid measures can be found for all goals.

Responsive Model

The driving objective of the responsive model is to collect information to illuminate the concerns and issues of those who have a stake in an evaluation. Programs goals are not central. In essence, a responsive evaluation investigates what various constituents believe a program is accomplishing and their concerns about the program.

The strength of this model is that it can help those responsible for a program to understand both its actual achievements and where action is needed to reconcile results with plans. For this reason, a responsive approach can be especially helpful during the early and middle stages of program implementation.

One major criticism of the responsive model is that it is "unscientific and lacks an emphasis on formal measurement (Gardner 1977). Critics suggest that the role of the evaluator is not to observe a program from afar and to make judgments based on the analysis of "objective" data but to become immersed in the program to the point of rendering an accurate description and interpretation of its accomplishments. Such immersion, however, may well sacrifice objectivity, and it certainly increases the time commitment to a review.

One particular type of responsive evaluation—the case study—has some definite shortcomings: the fact that the evaluator assumes enormous responsibility in trying to portray a program accurately; the difficulty for the evaluator to protect against bias; the requirement for a large number of subjective judgments (House 1982).

Decision-Making Model

The main purpose of the decision-making model is to conduct evaluations responsive to the informational needs of decision makers. The strength of this model derives from the explicit connection between evaluation and decision making, a link that focuses the evaluation and increases the likelihood that results will be used.

"The principal criticism of the decision-oriented approach is that the evaluator accepts the decision context and values/criteria that have been defined by the decision makers" (Feasley 1980, p. 10). This criticism implies that the evaluator is aligned with the decision makers and may find it difficult to remain objective. The evaluator collects data according to the questions defined by decision makers and accepts the values implicit in their questions. If those responsible for the program do not share such values or consider the questions unimportant, the evaluation will not be credible.

Another problem is that this model assumes rational decision making (Gardner 1977). The task of the evaluator is to identify the questions of interest, collect pertinent information, present findings, and wait for the results to be used. The evaluation therefore becomes a critical ingredient in decision making. This approach is likely to overemphasize the importance of evaluative information and to fail to recognize that evaluations provide only one source of data for decision makers. Further, to assume that all decision alternatives can be accurately anticipated and that sufficient data can be collected in relation to these alternatives is to place unrealistic expectations on an evaluation.

Decision makers are frequently biased in their acquisition and processing of information (O'Reilly 1981, pp. 55–57), and this bias occurs in the search for information, in the preference for information that is easy to secure and supports preconceived ideas, in the transmission of information that distorts reality if it optimizes certain outcomes, in the selective use of available information, and in the preference for vivid examples, even if they are misleading.

A final criticism of this model relates to an evaluator's ability to identify decision makers. It is not easy to identify decision makers in many complex organizations (Guba and Lincoln 1981). Decisions are frequently made at several organizational levels, by various individuals. Most actions involve more than one decision maker and a number of key decision points. It is almost impossible to identify all of these individuals and to collect all of the data necessary to inform them.

Connoisseurship Model

The central tenet of the connoisseurship model is that an expert (a connoisseur) can use his experience and expertise to judge a problem. In essence, the human being is the measurement instrument.

The use of outside reviewers in higher education is a good example of the connoisseurship model. The strength of this model is that those who are most knowledgeable about a subject are asked to make the assessment. The connoisseurship model has high credibility because those within a discipline or profession are judged by peers who have a sound basis for understanding what is—or is not—being accomplished.

One problem is that the connoisseurship model frequently lacks evaluative guidelines, so that a premium is placed on the evaluator's judgment; it is hard to know whether the evaluator's perceptions are accurate (Guba and Lincoln 1981). Many institutions attempt to sidestep this problem by inviting more than one expert to participate in a review, a strategy introducing valuable "triangulation." At the same time, however, this strategy can yield as many different assessments as there are evaluators.

Another problem with this approach lies in the difficulty of generalizing across programs (Feasley 1980, p. 8). In rating different programs, no two experts will have the same value structure or will weigh criteria equally. One evaluator may rate a program weak because of difficulties in its graduate instructional program; another may overlook the graduate program entirely if the record of faculty research is strong.

The connoisseurship model is popular in higher education because most faculty members believe that only those within a discipline can adequately evaluate accomplishment. Certainly, a disciplinary background can greatly enhance an evaluation. At the same time, certain problems are inherent—the ability to generalize procedures across programs, the subjectivity of perceptions, and the emphasis placed on the person chosen to conduct the evaluation.

Assessing Quality

For those engaged in program review, the assessment of quality has generated more confusion and debate than any other issue. Pressure always has existed to define "quality" and to determine which types of information should be collected, but more recently, interest has burgeoned because of the emphasis on program review for reallocation and retrenchment. The problem is that no one has yet found a way to measure quality directly. The issue for evaluators is how to define this concept and how to determine what types of information (indicators) should be used to guide data collection.

The literature (cf. Astin 1980; Conrad and Blackburn *In press* b) and institutional documents identify four perspectives on how to define quality: a reputational view, a resources view, an outcomes view, and a value-added view. The particular view held affects the kind of information used to assess quality. The issue is which of these views of quality is most accurate and helpful (see Table 6).

Reputational View

This view of quality is derived from the connoisseurship model of evaluation and assumes that experts in the field make the best judgments on the criterion. In essence, the reputational view reflects a belief that the optimum way to assess quality is to seek a consensus of informed opinion. The typical indicator is some type of reputational survey. The past two decades have seen a number of surveys of this type (Carter 1966; Jones, Lindzey, and Coggeshall 1982; Roose and Anderson 1970).

The main strength of this view lies in the fact that the raters are those who supposedly know best what quality is. It also has an intuitive appeal to ratings, reflecting what most people believe is true (Webster 1981).

Reputational rankings are criticized, however, because, while the raters may have insight into the scholarly productivity and reputation of a department, they are not likely to know much about the instructional program. Surely a program assessment must include more than research and scholarship (Conrad and Blackburn 1985). The lack of national visibility for many programs suggests that even reputational rankings based on faculty members' scholarly productivity are not likely to be meaningful below the top 15 or 20 programs in the country (Webster 1981). Other problems are apparent—"reputational lag" (the ranking of programs based on their quality several years old) and "halo effects" (ranking a program high because the institution is held in high regard). These and other limitations are discussed extensively in the literature (Conrad and Blackburn 1985; Dolan 1976; Lawrence and Green 1980; Webster 1981).

Despite these limitations, such ratings have received support:

> In our view controversy over reputational studies should not deter researchers from conducting such studies in the future. If reputational studies are designed to respond to the criticisms . . . we are persuaded that they can make an important contribution to the evaluation of quality in higher education (Conrad and Blackburn 1985, p. 23).

Table 6
Views of Quality and Representative Indicators

Reputational View	Outcomes View
• Peer judgments of the quality of program, students, faculty, or resources	• Fauclty scholarly productivity
	• Faculty awards and honors
	• Faculty research support
Resources View	• Faculty teaching performances
• Student selectivity	• Student achievement following graduation
• Student demand	• Student placement
• Faculty prestige	• Student achievement
• Faculty training	• Alumni satisfaction
• Faculty teaching loads	
• Budget affluence	**Value-added view**
• Library holdings	• Change in students' cognitive abilities
• Equipment adequacy	• Student personal development
• Size of endowment	• Student career development
	• Social benefits

Resources View

This particular view of quality emphasizes the human, financial, and physical resources that go into a program. According to this view, high quality exists where these resources—bright students, excellent faculty, adequate budgets, strong research support, strong libraries, and adequate facilities—are plentiful. The extent to which these resources are available to a particular program has been measured in various ways—for example, student test scores, proportion of the faculty with a doctorate, grant support, and number of volumes in the library. The advantages of using such measures of resources are that relevant data are readily available at most institutions, that the measures reflect what exists today, not what the situation was a decade ago, and that comparisons can be made across all colleges and universities, not just a few highly ranked institutions (Webster 1981).

Notwithstanding these benefits, the resources view suffers some serious limitations. Little evidence supports the view that more resources equate with increased student learning (Astin 1980). Further, and more important, the resources approach places a false ceiling on the amount of quality that can exist in higher education by asserting that "such resources as bright students and prestigious faculty are finite" (Astin 1980, p. 4).

Outcomes View

Another way to define and assess quality is to emphasize results—what the investment of resources produces. Here, attention is focused on the quality of the product. Typical indicators associated with this view are faculty productivity, students' accomplishments following graduation, employers' satisfaction with program graduates, and institutional contributions to the solution of local, state, or national problems. Specific outcome measures include the number of faculty publications in scholarly journals, the number of graduates admitted to leading graduate or professional schools, employer surveys, percentage of graduates finding employment soon after graduation, and lifetime earnings of graduates.

Collecting information on outcomes boasts a number of advantages. Chief among them is the emphasis on what is happening to those who are or have been part of a program; the focus of attention shifts from the resources invested to the results. Like the resource measures, many of the outcomes measures hold relevance for all institutions; all institutions, for example, are interested in the accomplishments of their alumni (Webster 1981).

Perhaps the most significant problem with the outcomes view is the difficulty of delineating the special institutional contribution to results. "Most output measures depend more on the quality of students admitted to the institution than on the functioning of the institution or the quality of its program" (Astin 1980, p. 3). Another disadvantage is that outcomes measures frequently limit themselves to the past. The period between graduation and inclusion in *Who's Who in America* obstructs the drawing of precise conclusions about the current quality of a program (Webster 1981).

Value-Added View

This view of quality focuses attention on program impact. "The basic argument underlying the value-added approach is that true quality resides in the institution's ability to affect its students favorably, to make a positive difference in their intellectual and personal development" (Astin 1980, pp. 3-4). Consonant with this view, evaluation should attempt to identify what a program contributes to students' learning. One typical indicator is what students learn while enrolled, which is sometimes measured by administering an achievement test at the time of enrollment and at graduation.

The chief advantage of this view is that one takes into account the quality of students at entry. This approach is especially attractive to institutions seeking to respond to "the twin doctrines of entitlement and equal education opportunity" (Lawrence and Green 1980, p. 54). Thus, institutions are judged by how much they help students, by how much they "add" to students' knowledge and personal development.

Like the other views of quality, the value-added approach has limitations. First, it is expensive, both in time and money. Investigating a program's contribution requires extensive recordkeeping for a large number of students. Another problem is the difficulty of reaching consensus on what students should learn and on measuring such quantities, even if they are defined (Lawrence and Green 1980, p. 40). For example, significant measurement problems are associated with assessing how much a student has improved in critical thinking skills. Finally, it is no easy matter to determine what one program's contribution is to a student's learning or development. The effects of other variables, such as maturation, travel experiences, and summer employment are difficult to control.

Using External Reviewers

This review of current evaluation processes indicates that most institutions have incorporated the judgments of external reviewers into their program reviews. Most often, these reviewers are faculty members within the same discipline but at another institution or within the institution but outside the program under review. The issue faced by those designing an evaluation system is to decide which of these two types of reviewers to use. Knowledge of the possible strengths and limitations of each should prove helpful in making the choice.

Reviewers From Other Institutions

The use of peers from other institutions to help in institutional reviews is rapidly becoming the norm rather than the exception. The program review process at California State University at Long Beach illustrates the use of outside reviewers. That institution's review process consists of four phases: (1) a self-study prepared by those in the program under review; (2) a review by a subcommittee of faculty from other programs on campus; (3) an external review by disciplinary experts; and (4) a "response report" prepared by those in the program (Office of the Associate Vice President n.d.). The external review serves to provide a comparative perspective, which is balanced with the program's own view and that of colleagues on campus.

Like other approaches to assessing program quality, the use of external peers has its strengths and weaknesses. Characteristics of the problems are the following observations on experiences with outside reviewers at the University of Nebraska—Lincoln: The selection of a review team was frequently controversial; the review teams suffered because of lack of knowledge about the local context; too little time was available for the reviews; the review teams tended to focus on insignificant issues; the review teams often were asked to address problems they could not resolve; the review teams were provided with more information than they could comprehend; and the review teams tended to solve all problems by recommending additional resources (Seagren and Bean, 1981, pp. 20–24).

In a more positive vein, the use of external peers provides a perspective that is frequently helpful. In most program reviews, it is considered crucial to have some kind of disciplinary perspective on the quality of what is being done and to seek advice on future directions. In addition, reports from external peers are usually perceived as objective and therefore can stimulate change that might not otherwise be possible.

Reviewers From the Same Institution

A number of institutions choose to use on-campus (but outside the discipline) colleagues to help evaluate programs. At California State University at Long Beach, for example, faculty from within the institution conduct an internal review of a program to provide an assessment based on institutional (as opposed to disciplinary) standards of performance and quality (Office of the Associate Vice President n.d., Appendix B, p. 14). This strategy offers the advantages of familiarity with the local context and norms and a stake in the results. The recommendations will affect not only those evaluated but also the evaluators—they must live with what they recommend. On the other hand, such reviewers may frequently be unfamiliar with the discipline under study or, conversely, tend to allow previous familiarity with a program or its personnel to bias results.

Despite these criticisms, many believe that reviewers outside a particular discipline can recognize quality as long as enough information is available and enough opportunities exist to interact with program personnel. An interesting test of this idea examined results of faculty ratings of students' oral examinations (DiBiaso et al. 1981). A graduate school representative from outside the student's discipline was appointed to each of the review committees. A comparison of the ratings of the internal and external reviewers revealed

> no evidence of a significant difference between how graduate school representatives rate examinations conducted inside their own colleges compared to their ratings of examinations outside their own colleges. These results suggest that members have some common perceptions about the quality of doctoral examinations, regardless of discipline (DiBiaso et al. 1981, p. 10).

Thus, the issue is not whether to use reviewers in higher education, but whether to use on-campus colleagues or disciplinary peers.

Increasing Use of Evaluations

One of the most perplexing issues facing evaluators is how to increase the likelihood that others will employ the results of their efforts. Considerable time and attention is being given to evaluation these days, yet a frequent criticism is that the results of such efforts really have no effect on decisions. The perception is that evaluations are undertaken not because the results are expected to be used but because someone simply feels they "ought to be done." This criticism is so prevalent that it must be taken seriously.

To the uninitiated, it would seem that the issue of use should not even arise. Is not the basis of an evaluation the need for information to make a decision or to become more knowledgeable about a program or activity? If so, then every evaluation should be used. Nevertheless, utilization is a problem.

The results of program evaluations are not used for four general reason: (1) organizational inertia; (2) the state of evaluation practice, for example, the inability to define valid measures of important criteria; (3) the uncertainty about the need for some evaluations; and (4) the multiple sources of information competing for the attention of decision makers (Anderson and Ball 1978).

The conflicting information needs of people at different levels of an organization make it difficult to conduct a useful evaluation (Patton 1985, p. 13). Highly detailed discussion of a specific case is seldom of much use at higher organizational levels; aggregate comparisons are of little use at the unit level. One important reason for lack of use of an evaluation is the inadequate personal involvement and commitment of key people. The personal factor is more crucial than structural, organizational, or methodological variables (Patton 1981, pp. 15–16).

Use of evaluation is also hindered because institutions compartmentalize the function of evaluation. Typically, the responsibility for program review is assigned to a staff office or to a specific individual. The delegation of responsibility for program review by the executive officers of an institution relieves them of the responsibility for such activities and places distance between those conducting the reviews and those in a position to use the results.

Utilization is also impeded because the decisions frequently involve social, political, and financial considerations outside the task of evaluation. It should not be too disturbing to evaluators to know that occasionally these other considerations will outweigh the findings of an evaluation report (Dressel 1976; O'Reilly 1981).

Given that these problems exist, the issue of how to increase the likelihood that results will be used warrants special attention. This matter has engendered a number of views. Anderson and Ball (1978), for instance, recommend encouraging communication between those evaluated, those evaluating, and those responsible for the process; varying the modes for disseminating results according to audiences; identifying users early and finding ways to make sure that their questions are being addressed; finding ways to include those responsible for the evaluation in its planning; reporting results in a timely way; and maximizing such virtues as brevity, timeliness, and responsiveness. Others suggest that utilization should become an immediate rather than a post-report concern, that reports relate to the concerns of decision makers, that credibility and rapport be maintained, and that all participants in the evaluation communicate among themselves (Brown and Braskamp 1980). "Evaluation is undertaken in a social and political environment in which various groups have vested interests in the evaluation process. . . If an evaluation is to be used by these groups in their deliberations, discussions, and policy making, the evaluation system must be designed to maximize communication between the audiences" (Braskamp 1982, p. 58).

A critical element in utilization relates to the approach of the evaluator (Alkin 1980). In particular, rapport established with program staff can enhance use of results. Use is not related to any particular evaluation model; the most important consideration is to adapt the strategy to the program and to the questions being asked.

One of the most important ways to increase utilization is for decision makers and information users to be clearly identified (Patton 1978). Decision makers cannot be treated as "abstract audiences" (p. 284). Decision makers should not delegate responsibility for an evaluation but should assume an active role in its implementation:

> There has been considerable discussion in the literature and among evaluators about how to make managers, clinicians, board members, and others better consumers of evaluations. . . . This effort is misplaced. For evaluations to be useful and to be used, the managers have to accept responsibility for owning and defining the evaluation function (Clifford and Sherman 1983, p. 32).

One way to increase use is to ensure that evaluators focus their efforts on three issues: (1) who the decision makers will be; (2) what information is needed; and (3) when the information is needed (Feasley 1980, p. 43). Perhaps the most important issue is to identify the evaluative question (Patton 1978).

A study of the characteristics of decision makers identifies six managerial characteristics relating to the issue of utilization:

1. Decision makers work at an unrelenting pace;

2. their daily routines are characterized by brevity, variety, and fragmentation;

3. they prefer active rather than passive use of time;

4. they prefer verbal as opposed to written communication;

5. they serve as active communication links;

6. they blend rights as well as duties so that personal objectives can be realized (Mintzberg 1973, chap. 3).

This list suggests that evaluations are more likely to be used if they relate to decision makers' concerns, are communicated clearly and concisely, and are presented both verbally and in written form.

In wrestling with the question of utilization, institutions have adopted several strategies to try to ensure that results of evaluations will somehow link to other decision-making processes. Ohio State University has developed the concept of a loosely coupled system, which means that all "parties to a review," including the college dean, the university's chief academic officers, the graduate dean, and those in the program, are consulted throughout the review process. At the conclusion of the review, a "memorandum of understanding is developed in which the parties agree on actions to be taken. These agreements are monitored and updated each year (Arns and Poland 1980).

At the University of North Carolina at Asheville, six aspects of the program review process contribute to its usefulness:

1. clarity of purpose

2. involvement of decision makers in all stages of the process

3. maximization of communication

4. understanding of the political nature of the environment

5. recognition of the subjectivity of evaluation

6. competence of the institutional research staff and confidence in the data collected (Cochran and Hengstler 1984, p. 184).

At the State University of New York at Albany, evaluations are an integral part of a planning process. The evaluations consist of both annual monitoring of programs and five-year in-depth reviews This arrangement is useful because:

1. *it capitalizes on an annual, synoptic view all major university activities;*

2. *it is a goal-driven activity;*

3. *it is merged with resource allocation, thereby linking budgeting with evaluation*

4. *evaluation (both ongoing and annual monitoring as well as selected in-depth reviews) provides feedback for planning and resource allocation;*

5. *it more clearly integrates evaluation with existing decision-making structures and processes (Hartmark 1982, p. 16).*

Thus, a review of the literature on utilization reveals consensus on the objective of utilization but little agreement on how it is best accomplished, and suggestions vary from encouraging decision makers to participate more actively in evaluation to accounting for the managerial characteristics of decision makers to conducting evaluations in a manner responsive to those characteristics.

Assessing Impact

If results are used, another issue emerges—the impact of those results. The basic concern is whether the consequences of implementing an evaluation are positive or negative. First, however, one must distinguish between the outcomes and the effects of a review—a subtle but important distinction. Decisions to eliminate a program, to increase admissions requirements, to change department heads, or to establish consortia are outcomes, not effects, of program reviews. As defined here, "effect" refers to the consequences of actions taken. Concern about the effects therefore requires attention to the long-term effects of decisions, for example, whether the program is stronger, more efficient, or higher quality. Some believe the effects of program review are salutory; others are less optimistic. The question is which view is more correct.

How does one make such assessments? Efforts should focus on the question, "Does the system function better as a result of the evaluation effort?" (Cronbach 1977, p. 2). Explicit in this question is the principle that an evaluation must be beneficial.

The following kinds of consequences should be noted:

> The ideal held forth in the literature is one of major impact on concrete decisions. The image that emerged in our interviews is that there are few major, direction-changing, decisions in most programming . . . (Patton 1978, p. 32).

Most conceptions are too narrow (Alkin 1980). Consequences cannot be examined solely on the basis of immediate impact; longer-term implications must also be considered. Evaluations have unintended results that go beyond the formally stated recommendations. Further, the evaluation process often generates benefits beyond those chronicled in a report. Thus, the assessment of impact must be done in a naturalistic way, as in conducting case studies and recording participant observations. Finally, one should not confuse lack of implementation with lack of impact. An evaluation report frequently provides valuable information even though no specific recommendations are implemented (Alkin 1980, pp. 21–22).

The assessment of impact must not be limited to immediate and direct influences; indirect, catalytic, and inclusive results also demand attention (Braskamp and Brown 1980, p. viii). This approach requires special skill in analyzing multiple causes of specific actions as well as a willingness to view utilization broadly. Thus, those assessing impact must heed results that may be latent as well as immediate, incremental as well as radical, subtle as well as obvious. This view of impact is consistent with the admonition that "most change in education is incremental rather than radical, and advertising of this fact would improve the climate for evaluation" (Dressel 1976, p. 5).

Just as the advice on how to assess impact is far from uniform, so too is the evidence on impact far from definitive. Most campuses have critics who believe that the costs of program review outweigh the results. Several criticisms have been cited frequently:

- Time and effort are wasted because more data are collected than can be productively used.

- Viewed as inherently threatening and negative, the review process creates unwarranted anxiety.

- Leaders' credibility is diminished because the information requested is not used, or its use is not made visible enough.

- Distrust is created because the uses of the information are not conceived and articulated clearly enough from the outset, confidentiality of the report is not clarified, or the various roles in the process are not adequately determined.

- Inaccurate information causes unwarranted embarrassment or pride.

- Attention and time are diverted from the institution's teaching, research, and service functions.

- Resentment arises because the process is not designed to be useful at the program level as well as at higher organizational or system levels.

- The review leads to raised expectations for resources that are unavailable, which causes disappointment (Seeley 1981, p. 56).

On the other hand, program review—"if implemented properly and combined with other retrenchment strategies—can be a major tool for effectively reducing expenditures while maintaining essential program quality" (Barak 1981, p. 219). A study of program reviews in research universities found, not surprisingly, that the benefits were greatest at the program level and least at the institutional level (Poulton 1978). Table 7 displays the nature of the effects at three organizational levels.

The results of graduate program reviews at the University of California indicated several conclusions: (1) the institutions conducting reviews did not save money and, in fact, lost money (if the cost of the review process itself is taken into account); (2) reviews did not uncover previously unknown information; (3) reviews did stimulate change in some situations; (4) the reviews did tend to clarify impressions and develop a fair portrayal of programs; and (5) many of the reviews' recommendations were implemented (Smith 1979, pp. 2–3). Overall, the study concluded that the institution benefited from the reviews. A similar assessment at the University of Iowa took place in 1977, when an ad hoc committee of the faculty senate was appointed to evaluate the program review process on campus (Barak 1982). Through interviews with participants, the committee found that the reviews required a substantial commitment of time and effort but that many positive benefits accrued to the institution. The self-study process was found to benefit the units and to lead

Table 7
Typical Effects of Program Reviews

Organizational Level	Relative Utility	Nature of Changes
Department/Program	Greatest Utility (primarily from single reviews)	• Increased introspection • Revised objectives for teaching and research • Better organized qualitative and quantitative information • Clarified unit/program goals, strengths, and deficiencies • Improved unit procedures • Improved contact among unit members • Improved rationale for resources • Potentially increased frustrations
School/College	Moderate Utility	• Improved information on unit trends and priorities, strengths, and weaknesses • Better indications of unit quality and responsiveness • Adjusted college policies and procedures • Adjusted resource decisions (occasional) • Adjusted organizational structures (occasional)
University Administration	Least Utility (requires accumulation of reviews)	• Revised institutional policies and procedures policies and procedures • Major organizational changes (rare) • Major budgetary commitments or cuts (rare)

to improvements. The reviews also provided systematic information useful in keeping faculty and administrators knowledgeable about programs.

A survey of the program review authority and practices of 37 state-level higher education agencies, paying special attention to results in terms of resources, found:

> Despite the concern about resource savings, only one respondent supplied a dollar figure for resources saved. In fact, 95 percent of the 20 respondents who have discontinued programs do not know the amount of resources saved or reallocated and only 35 percent of those same 20 respondents believe that resources have been saved, even though they could not supply a dollar figure (Skubal 1979, p. 231).

On the basis of these results, one of three possible scenarios is taking place: (1) savings accrued at the institutional level, rather than at the state level; (2) it was impossible to attach a dollar amount to the savings; and (3) the review activity was purely cosmetic—programs being eliminated involved no resources (Skubal 1979). As far as the state boards were concerned, program discontinuance had not had a substantial impact on resources (p. 232).

A study of the effects of program reviews conducted by state-level higher education agencies gave careful attention to the effects of the Louisiana Board of Regents' program reviews involving Louisiana State University-Baton Rouge (LSU) and Northeast Louisiana University (Mingle 1978). At LSU, no cost savings were realized, but the belief persisted that the reviews facilitated cooperation among programs, provided a basis for judging programs' worth and for reallocating resources, stimulated personnel changes, and enhanced quality standards. By contrast, the reviews at Northeast were viewed as biased and as having fostered a "sense of declining prestige and fear for the future" (p. 64).

Reviews conducted by the Florida Board of Regents used outside consultants to review selected programs in the nine universities of the system (Hill, Lutterbie, and Stafford 1979). The consultants' task was to review a particular program at all of the institutions and to make recommendations on "program quality, duplication of programs, financial support, and the need for any additional programs or a shifting of programs in the discipline under review" (p. 3). These reviews provided better documentation of the need for new programs, resulted in a small number of programs' being eliminated, and controlled program growth. Further, the reviews led to the establishment of several cooperative programs among institutions within the system and between those institutions, and private colleges and universities in the state. For example, an engineering consortium was established, and contracts between the state and several private colleges and universities were developed. Further, the reviews helped the board identify underfunded areas and provided some systematic information that could serve as part of a recently initiated planning exercise (pp. 5–8).

While several problems with the review process were noted in Florida, the overall assessment was quite positive. The consultants' reports were believed to have aided greatly in identifying the strengths and weaknesses of programs in the system and in stimulating plans to strengthen some programs and to address important issues in others. "Some of the impact [of the reviews was] felt immediately by the universities, but the larger impact [was] more subtle as the intricate process of change in a multicampus system [was] initiated, developed, and brought to conclusion" (p. 9).

Although some evidence suggests that program reviews are helpful, the basis for this conclusion is weak, because only a few studies have examined effects systematically. Some evidence also suggests that such reviews do not achieve desired results. The stubborn fact is that not much is known about the effects of program review.

The Assessment Movement: What Next? Who Cares?

Robert H. McCabe

How has assessment reached the present high level of interest? What is going on in assessment? Where is the thrust coming from, and why?

The Florida Experience

Let me turn to my own state, Florida, as an example of the extreme side of the state-based, standardized test-oriented approach to assessment. I am going to be very critical, but I want to say up front that the project has had some positive impact. There is no doubt that the Florida higher education institutions are more concerned about student information skills, and there is more effort in placement and remediation. However, on the whole, it is my opinion that the Florida approach is not the right one. It should be modified in Florida and not copied in other states.

Let's begin with the first part of the Florida program, a state-wide, standardized test for placement. Legislators are comfortable with this requirement because it allows them to say: "Okay, now we have uniform data. We know whether students are really academically deficient or not." Without doubt, mistrust is part of the appeal of the statewide placement testing as it provides a standard which won't allow institutions to "cheat." Cheat, that is, with regard how they are funded and how they report enrollment. This approach has two major disadvantages. First of all, each of our institutions has a different curriculum—and we certainly want to keep it that way. The use of a placement test should be tied to the curriculum and its special features. For example, at my institution, our approach to placement (which we were doing before the state mandated it) was to determine placement only after we examined the relationship between performance on the test and performance in college general education courses. That is, we based placement on what we knew about student performance in our curriculum. Second, once students were placed, the faculty could adjust placement based on classroom performance. For example, in writing courses, on the first day of class students wrote an essay, and on that basis faculty could move them to a more appropriate class.

The point is that placement testing is more likely to benefit students when it is designed and administered by the institution. It should be tied to the curriculum; its primary purpose should not be reporting to the state, but improving the growth and development of students. The college has the advantage of using faculty judgment and classroom performance for classroom placement, and can follow up on the programs of placement and remediation to determine if they have the intended effect.

The next piece in the Florida program is the rising–junior test: the College Level Academic Skills Test (CLAST), required of all students in public institutions (or in independent institutions receiving state aid) for entrance to upper level coursework or the award of an associate in arts degree. This is the most controversial component of the testing program. The CLAST experience shows the concerns that all of us should have about standardized rising–junior examinations. One concern is that it drives curriculum. In the case of this examination, which was designed by faculty from across the state, there are five subdisciplines in the mathematics test. Therefore, the colleges have had to redesign the curriculum in order to align with that particular set of mathematics competencies. It appears that many of those competencies are not needed by many of the students, but their curriculums by necessity include a sequence of courses to learn these competencies. A similar problem occurs in the area of composition. In my institution, half of our 45,000 credit students have a native language other than English. You can imagine the task of getting these students through the composition section of CLAST—particularly as it is timed, and it may be on a topic with which they have no familiarity. It makes it very tempting (and I heard this proposed on one of our campuses) to turn the English curriculum into a program to teach students how to produce a credible essay within extreme time constraints—simply test preparation. And this flies in the face of what most faculty tell me they should be teaching. They tell me that they teach students to organize ideas, to outline, to revise, and to use dictionaries. The need to help students pass CLAST drives us toward a curriculum that the faculty do not support. This is certainly not in the best interests of students. Further, the increase of English and mathematics enrollment is squeezing students out of sophomore level courses in the humanities, sciences, and social sciences. CLAST is beginning to dominate curriculum.

Most important is the unquestioned use of CLAST as an independent criterion of student success. Is a statewide standardized test a valid predictor of students' ability to succeed? The fact is, there are large numbers of students who did not pass CLAST and proceeded to the upper division (when that was permitted), and are performing well at the junior and senior year. Studies suggest that the best forecaster of success is a combination of grades and a standardized test, the next best is grades, and the least effective is a standardized test by itself.

CLAST is having a particularly devastating impact on minorities. The number proceeding to upper division is in sharp decline, and our data suggest that many of those could be successful. So why not consider grades along with test scores? One must ask, in a country where there is a severe problem with the small number of minorities advancing through each level of education, why would a program be utilized that is cutting out many of those who could succeed from proceeding through baccalaureate programs. It simply doesn't make any sense.

Unfortunately, public relations plays an important part in statewide test programs. It has impact on the public image of the institutions, and can result in decisions based on that rather than what is good for students. I know of two institutions in Florida that are screening students before they take the CLAST. So, in fact, only those students whom they are convinced will pass take the test. The result when the newspaper article comes out and ranks institutions by results, those two institutions look good. But is that good for students? How about the student who has a good, though not sure, shot at passing? That student ought to have the opportunity to take the test. The question shouldn't be "what's going to give us the best public image," but "what is in the best interest of the student?" A year ago the legislature passed a rule which permitted students to take the CLAST at any time. That made sense as students who had the competencies at admission or early in their student careers, could be exempted for the CLAST curriculum sequence and permitted to enroll in a richer curriculum. One of my colleagues argued against this. "Wait a minute," he said, "if we do that, the pass percentages on CLAST for my institution aren't going to look as good." And frankly, when institutions are ranked in the newspaper four times a year on the basis of scores, it is hard not to think that way. It is a serious problem.

And so I hope we can make some changes in the Florida program, not do away with it, but make changes that will make it more beneficial to students. We need to keep in view two things that distinguish American higher education from other systems. One is institutional and curricular diversity, which is threatened by the imposition of a standardized test; and the other is giving second and third chances to students, which is threatened by making judgments about students on the basis of a single criterion—a standardized test.

Finally, we come to an issue that underlies all the others—the continuing thrust toward centralization. Everything I read about management indicates the importance of making decisions as close to the action as possible, and involving people in decisions that impact them. What Florida is doing in assessment runs contrary to good management practice. The program does not tie to the curriculum. It is not designed to give feedback to students, and it bypasses faculty. Basing decisions on a single statewide measure sets aside all of the expert judgment that faculty have exercised over the years in the classroom. And I think in some cases it can force students into poor practices. Florida has taken leadership in utilization of statewide assessment, and much has been learned—positive and negative. Now we need to utilize our experience and take responsibility to design an assessment program that helps students learn and grow. At the same time, we must recognize that the public has every reason to expect us to do more and to show the results of our efforts.

Institutional Assessment Initiatives

I would like to turn now to the other aspect of what is happening in assessment—institutional initiatives. They have great potential. Much of the impetus here comes from institutions looking at themselves, their programs, and results, and asking, "Do we really know what we're trying to achieve?", and "Have we got any way of determining whether we are being successful?"

There may have been a time when one of the roles of universities and colleges was to screen out students who were not prepared for immediate success. Full responsibility was on the student. We all know the stories of the dean addressing freshmen at orientation and saying, "Those of you who don't find the library by the end of the first football game won't be here by Thanksgiving." Underlying this attitude was an assumption that entering students had been well-prepared and should be able to take care of themselves. I think that approach is history, for all but a few institutions. When we look at the students who are entering colleges today, and consider the needs of the society for increased numbers of people who have strong information (academic) skills, it is clear that institutions must take greater responsibility for student success. The job is no longer to screen out, but to help more students, including the underprepared, to quality academic performance. Placement and program guidance are now important concerns, so there is good reason to develop assessment programs. Not only does the public have a right to know how well we are doing, it is vital to students that we know more about them. The idea that students either get it or get out just isn't appropriate in the face of massive underpreparation and growing diversity. This nation needs to develop all of its talent, and the fact that an individual is not well-prepared academically at one point in life does not mean that he or she has no talent or potential. Assessment can help us tap that talent and potential.

For assessment to help it must involve faculty. When we assess the effectiveness of the curriculum, the faculty must participate in determining those desired program outcomes. There must be overall purpose and unity to the curriculum. The major hurdle is for faculty to understand that the courses they teach are not entirely independent. That is going to be very difficult to achieve, but it is essential if assessment is going to make any difference in improving student programs. The key is to understand that the focus is on the student and what the courses can contribute to his or her development. Moreover, I would argue that we have some obligation to assess teaching itself. Colleges have the reverse of the problem in K-12, where the concern is that the faculty do not have adequate mastery of their subject matter. In higher education faculty are well grounded in their disciplines, but they don't really know a great deal about teaching or learning. This is particularly striking when considered in light of the significant body of knowledge about teaching and learning that has accumulated in the past thirty years—knowledge that is not a part of the vocabulary of our faculty. Most come to college teaching with a love for their subject matter, and a love for the kind of work they did in graduate school. But teaching is something they learn on the job or not at all. A medical analogy is suggested. If I needed heart surgery, I would look for a doctor who knew more about the heart than anybody else in the world. But if that person had never had a scalpel in hand, I'm not sure I'd want to be operated on. And to a great extent, this is the situation with faculty. They have wonderful knowledge about their special field, but little knowledge of "the operation"— teaching and learning. College teaching is one of the few professions where we don't stand on the shoulders of those who went before, learning from them, so each generation improves. That really needs to change, especially as institutions and faculty take greater responsibility for student performance. It is time to come to grips with what is expected in faculty performance, and to think about that in light of what assessment can tell us about student learning. We need to help faculty become better teachers, and we need to help them assess how well they succeed.

Related to this is shifting concern to our output instead of input. What do colleges brag about? The SAT scores of incoming students—how many students came with this or that level of ability. Most have little to say about how students grew or what they can do as a result of our programs. I was at a meeting of state leaders in Florida. They were discussing a suggestion that our goal should be to improve the quality of higher education in Florida. I stated my belief that this was an inappropriate goal. Why? Because it would be very easy to improve the quality of higher education by simply reducing the number of students admitted by screening out the less well-prepared. Presto! The equality of higher education would be enhanced. But the goal must be for education to be more successful in meeting the needs of society. If you put it that way, you come up with a very different kind of solution. Improving quality involves expanding the number of students gaining academic achievement. To realize this goal, colleges should assess the effect of educational programs on students and develop methods to get that information back to students in ways that help them know how they are doing, what they can do better, and what their next step needs to be. The same information needs to be available to each teaching faculty member as a basis for improving teaching.

This, it seems to me, is what Pat Cross has been talking about—classroom research. I am very impressed with the potential at the level of assessment she advocates—assessment that gets down to what each faculty member does with students—the place where the real learning takes place.

Summary

Where are we and what has happened with assessment? I have commented about state initiatives and about institutional initiatives, and some of the issues that arise in the tension between those initiatives. Should assessment be the responsibility of the state or each institution? Is it to make determinations about individual students or to evaluate the institution? Is it for both? Should it be standard across institutions, or diverse? How should the results be utilized?

Where do we go from here? There is little doubt that this assessment movement is going to grow. There is no doubt that the interest of legislators and the public is increasing. And I am encouraged by the growth of interest that I see within institutions, particularly geared to student learning and student growth. Hopefully that is where the most energetic assessment efforts will occur. Assessment should be an ongoing vehicle for self-awareness and change.

The assessment movement is growing in tandem with the teaching/learning movement. In fact, it could be considered an element of it. There is tremendous interest in improving teaching and doing more to improve student learning. Assessment is essential to that, whether it be classroom research or program assessment. The most promising assessment programs now in progress deal with the impact of teaching on student learning and feedback to students and faculty. Lee Shulman's work comes to mind, as does the program at Alverno College. What I am suggesting is that the future of assessment will be in improving student development through more effective teaching and learning. In the 1960s community colleges operated on the basis that students had a "right to fail." We should not operate on the basis of their having a "right to succeed," and assessment can contribute to that success.

Involving Faculty Members in Assessment

Carol Schneider

Discourse

Daniel Resnick and Marc Goulden have argued recently that there is a close connection between periods of rapid expansion and innovation in American higher education and renewed attention to assessment. We saw such a connection in the first part of this century, when rapid curricular and institutional development gave way—in the late 1920s and 1930s—to comprehensive examinations. Comprehensives were seen as a way to redress both the loss of coherence and the erosion of standards in college and university education. American higher education has entered an analogous period of consolidation and review in the 1980s following the unprecedented expansion, both in scope and student numbers, of postsecondary education. The current interest in assessment serves both as index and strategy for our current self-examination.

The Consequences of Assessment

As many commentators have pointed out, however, the current assessment movement is beset by contradictory impulses. One impulse is a laudable concern for the substance and quality of student learning. As programs have become more fragmented, and as students have become more diverse in background and preparation, many proponents of assessment see the study of learning outcomes and "value added" as a way to focus attention on both fundamental educational goals and on the quality of learning in relation to those goals. AAC's own 1985 and 1988 reports on the baccalaureate degree and on general education each reflect this view of assessment. From this perspective, assessment is seen as diagnostic, providing a way to help focus students, faculty members, and institutional resources on common goals and on areas where additional effort is needed.

At the national level, in some state legislatures, and even on many campuses, however, assessment is demanded as evidence of higher education's willingness to be "accountable" to the constituencies it serves. The consequences of this accountability can be both unclear and intimidating. The outcomes of institutional and program assessment may have budgetary implications; they may have program implications. Does one penalize a program whose assessments show problems? Or endow it with extra resources? When a system is involved, how will its different elements fare comparatively once the assessment findings are compiled? The potential consequences of accountability can make institutions reluctant rather than eager to provide documentation about the quality of real learning on their campuses.

A further danger of this focus on assessment as a means of public accountability is that it can make data-based portraits of outcomes ends in themselves. This prospect has troubling implications both for the choice of assessment instruments and for questions about who will be actively involved in implementing and interpreting the assessment. In terms of assessment instruments, assessors often face trade-offs concerning interinstitutional comparability versus local usability. When a program, department, or colleg develops assessment approaches and instruments that are highly responsive to its priorities and traditions, it generally yields ease of comparability with other institutions. Bobby Fong's article on external examiners and Clifford Adelman's report on an approach to assessing student learning in biology each reflect this difficulty. Conversely, as Ted Marchese's report on "The Uses of Assessment" makes clear, when a college concerned with showing how it compares to others selects available normed tests for its assessments, it often finds itself with a result that is hard to connect usefully to its programs and faculty priorities. Moreover, as both Fong and Stephen Ehrmann suggest, an institution—simply by choosing a standardized test for its assessments—may generate faculty incredulity that the findings measure anything either significant or important.

The Consequences of Bypassing Faculty

A related and even more basic concern is that assessment focused on the production of public portraits may become the primary responsibility of an office of research specialists producing reports that have no effect on the classroom. The assessment experts report findings, and some of the results may lead to the development of new program interventions: more tutoring in math, an expansion of the writing program, better student placements. The danger is that it is entirely possible to mount such assessment programs in ways that bypass almost completely the typical faculty member in the typical classroom. Yet to bypass faculty members is to bypass those interactions around teaching, learning, and classroom-level assessment that are fundamental to strengthening the quality of student learning and achievement.

The reality compounding this danger, unfortunately, is that many faculty members are very ready to be bypassed by the assessment movement. When I first began attending conference sessions on assessment five or six years ago, I observed that they typically attracted assessment specialists and academic administrators. The rare faculty member or two joining such a group was the exception who proved the rule. As either topic or process, assessment—especially assessment that leads to the possibility of formed comparisons—does not interest faculty members. In fact, many faculty members believe fervently, as one asserted to me, "The things I value in my teaching cannot be quantified with scores and numbers."

Although assessment has since become far more visible on the educational agenda, little or nothing has happened to alter such longstanding faculty attitudes. Faculty responses to the furor over assessing learning outcomes range from neutrality to active hostility. Some see assessment as make-work. One faculty member at a selective liberal arts college told me, "We work closely with our students. They go to Yale, Harvard, Columbia, and other top institutions for graduate school. We faculty members are very busy and we just don't see a need to spend our limited time finding new ways of asking questions about what they are learning. Others, in similar institutions, tie the whole assessment movement to William Bennett's administration in the U.S. Department of Education, and wait impatiently for the day that both Bennett and the assessment initiative will retire from view.

In other settings, where assessment is not a voluntary activity, faculty members are often similarly skeptical. Some departments are apprehensive about pending assessment initiatives, seeing their students' academic weaknesses as symptoms of longstanding and perhaps systemic problems that they cannot hope to redress in a single course. Other faculty members echo the skepticism of those who think that gathering numbers can never address the most important questions about teaching and learning.

Yet if the resources now being devoted to assessment of student learning are to make any difference at all in the quality of either student learning or educational programs, assessment initiatives must centrally involve faculty members. Faculty members need to be involved in the formulation of the important questions to be asked through assessment, in decisions about the strategies to be used in asking questions, and above all in the interpretation of the findings. Despite faculty apprehensions, there is no inherent need for assessment strategies to be cripplingly reductionist—excluding nuances and differences among students' patterns of development. Indeed, as the articles in this issue imply, assessment need not be primarily quantifiable. It can and should bring into play the qualities of judgment and interpretation that faculty possess in abundance.

The critical factor is that faculty need to become *collectively engaged* in the assessment of both programs and learning. Such engagement requires a shift in emphasis from technical decisions—about which instruments to use—to strategic questions about how to generate the widest possible institutional learning from the interpretation of the findings. If the ultimate objective of assessment is to find ways of strengthening students' learning, then it defeats the purpose to delegate assessment to an office—or even to a committee of faculty members—whose deliberations and activities only peripherally involve the majority of their colleagues.

Assessment can and should be an opportunity for faculty members responsible for departments and programs to come together to revisit the purposes of these programs and consider ways of learning from evidence that can be gathered and collectively interpreted at central points in those programs. In such a process, faculty members may well be interested in the results of standardized tests. But they might find it even more valuable to collect portfolios of students' analytic work during the course of a program and to assess the quality of that work over time. Clifford Adelman's article in this issue on a proposed strategy for assessing learning in biology describes a matrix of outcomes and evidence that could be used for gathering and assessing such portfolios. Faculty members working together can develop other effective approaches.

Reviewing such portfolios allows faculty members to see and evaluate both the kinds of challenges their programs are placing before students and students' development in meeting those challenges. Over time, such a review is likely to lead to something now absent on most college campuses: searching discussion of the kinds of challenges that should be put before students and of the differences between entry-level, intermediate, and genuinely advanced work in a program.

The articles in this issue and the several programs described in Praxis—describe approaches to assessment that can centrally involve faculty members. Ted Marchese's introduction to our Praxis section provides important suggestions about ways to link assessment to questions that faculty—and other members of the community—want to pursue. Stephen Ehrmann takes on the knotty and challenging question of how we assess the open-ended and unique uses that students ought to be making of their college experience. He stresses the importance of course assignments to assessment that is likely to influence learning, and he suggests ways that technology can improve both the quality of our assignments to students and our ability to learn—and help students learn—from their performance on those assignments. He points out, moreover, that students' unique uses of the curriculum can become a basis for program evaluation as well as for individual assessment and that technology can help us achieve that elusive synthesis.

Many of the campus attempts to assess learning outcomes have focused on general education. But for most students, and indeed for faculty members, the major is the most important element of the education experience. Bobby Fong and Clifford Adelman each address national projects to find ways of identifying and assessing the most important outcomes for learning in the major.

Finally, George Klemp's Perspective brings us full circle from assessment back to questions of goals. Our current assessment efforts are highly focused, as both Fong and Adelman indirectly illustrate, on content and cognitive process outcomes of undergraduate learning. But as Klemp's comments on assessment findings from the world of work suggest, there may be other outcomes from liberal learning that are also important and make a critical difference to the quality of a graduate's life beyond campus. Klemp introduces another dimension to the assessment question. We need to know not just how well we are doing with our educational priorities but whether the priorities themselves capture the full range of our students' learning needs.

Notes

1. Daniel P. Resnick and Marc Goulden, "Assessment, Curriculum, and Expansion: A Historical Perspective,"in Student Outcomes Assessment: What Institutions Stand to Gain, ed. Diane F.Halpern, New Directions for Education series, no. 59 (San Francisco: Jossey-Bass, 1987), 77–88. The Halpern volume is a helpful introduction to the whole topic of outcomes-based assessment. It contains informative reports on campus struggles to find assessment strategies appropriate to curricular objectives.

2. Select Committee on the Project on Redefining the Meaning and Purpose of Baccalaureate Degrees, *Integrity in the College Curriculum* (Washington, D.C.: Association of American Colleges, 1985); Task Force on General Education, *A New Vitality in General Education* (Washington, D.C.: Association of American Colleges, 1988).

PART III
PLANNING ASSESSMENTS
AND EVALUATIONS

Introduction

Early tasks in the assessment process include involving and gaining support of various audiences and clarifying the purpose. Is the activity to be conducted primarily for accountability, for improvement, or for some combination of both? Communicating to various audiences about the purposes and goals of the assessment is also an essential early step. Clarifying purpose may include issuing policy statements about what the purpose is not, what the program is not intended to do, and how the results will not be used, for example, stating that results will not be used to make important decisions about individual faculty or students.

Programs undertaken without adequate planning often result in a compliance mode of "if we have to do assessment, let's do it and get it over with." Premature assessment activity can lead to wasted valuable resources for useless or misleading information as well as possible loss of credibility of the assessment by various audiences. Sound planning will clarify what questions will drive the assessment program, how and from whom the information will be gathered, how the information will and will not be used, the feasibility of the program, how the ethical issues will be addressed in the planning, and other critical issues identified in the literature below.

Planning in advance. The planning process is critical and should be given adequate time; authors suggest spending at least a year to develop an institutional assessment plan. Authors in this section note the importance of advance planning to avoid false starts, wasted resources, unusable information and alienated faculty and students. **Thomas** emphasizes the importance of early planning and addresses a wide range of issues associated with six assessment phases: clarifying the assessment object, designing the assessment, collecting and analyzing data, communicating the findings, using the findings, and evaluating the assessment.

The selection by **Sell** expands, on some of these planning issues. Suggestions address the tensions between an organization that offers stability and an assessment that suggests change. Sell is critical of assessment activities in higher education that have informed judgments of quality about students, faculty, programs and institutions, but are not designed to provide information that can be used for improvement.

The guidance offered by the authors in this section was supported in an evaluation study of pilot assessment projects by **Worthley and Riggs**. They identified eight major environmental and methodological factors as critical to effective assessment programs. The factors included measurement quality issues, audience, administrative support, faculty involvement, assessment expertise, faculty workload, multicultural issues, and multiple measures. Some of these areas are explored further in the other articles.

Involving audiences in appropriate roles. The literature notes the need for early, active involvement of individuals from a broad range of audiences who will be affected by and/or responsible for the results. This advice recognizes the political nature of assessment as well as the practical issue of utilization of results. Since faculty and staff are ultimately the key players in using the information to make changes and improvements in their areas of responsibility, they must be the primary participants in the assessment activity. Assuring that assessments result in academic benefits is also supported in the selection by **Mentkowski,** who notes the key role of both faculty and students in the academic functioning of an institution.

The literature selections provide many guidelines about how to plan and conduct an assessment. An example of how that advice worked at one institution is provided by **Wright,** who documents the first eighteen months of a university assessment project. The faculty author gained a greater understanding of assessment and its potential to support renewal and growth. The activity encouraged new thinking and dialogue among faculty about what it is they do to foster specific student abilities—the foundation for change and improvement.

Choosing models and designs. In Part I, Gardiner provided a "mission-input-process-outcome" assessment model, an overall model of the relationships among the mission of the institution and its resources and processes, and its intended student outcomes. This overall model provides a basis for many diverse assessment programs. A program could focus only on outcomes, although much of the literature notes that such information alone is not very helpful in providing direction for change. A program could focus on the input-outcome relationship, a value-added model. A program could focus on the process-outcome relationship, an improvement model designed to provide information for needed change in the process to improve the outcomes. Judgments about quality using only such factors as average SAT scores of incoming freshmen are based on input or resource factors models. The model used in an assessment program provides critical guidance in the assessment planning and activity. The literature selections in this section provide a basis for thinking about possible assessment models.

The selections also reveal diverse models that have been implemented on campuses. This variety reflects diversity among the campus contexts in institutional mission, type of entering students, academic fields of campus assessment leaders, available resources, institutional reward system, and external and internal pressures for assessment. The assessment programs differ in several dimensions: purpose (accountability vs. improvement), locus of responsibility (centralized vs. decentralized), focus (resources vs. process vs. outcomes), level (individual vs. program vs. institution vs. system), tasks (measurement only vs. evaluation), and data type (quantitative vs. qualitative). The dimensions provide a useful basis for the study of the various examples in the field; a typical program is likely to lie someplace between the extremes rather than at either end. For example, the data type may be chiefly quantitative with some qualitative data, or the locus of responsibility may be centralized for the assessment of a general skill but decentralized for a specialized skill.

Models used in the field of evaluation were introduced earlier in Part I; **Stufflebeam and Webster** expand on these models and provide a basis for thinking about the relationships among the purpose of assessment, key audiences, questions to be asked, and ways to gather the information. Various assessment models used by institutions can be identified within Stufflebeam and Webster's framework, e.g., value-added model that responds to consumer-oriented questions, assessment for feedback that informs decisions about development, self-reports of alumni that provide satisfaction information, connoisseur-based program reviews with outside experts, and accreditation reviews.

The value-added model that was so much in the forefront of discussion in the early years of assessment is the focus of a selection by Warren (1984). In addition to the weaknesses of the model, Warren addresses assessment options to take advantage of existing information. Ewell (1991a) discusses the evolution of value-added as a model to that of a metaphor as found in Astin's Input–Environment–Output model. He also provides information about the strengths and weaknesses of other assessment models such as the longitudinal design (using complex analyses from cohort student data that include process as well as input and outcomes), the holistic student development model (incorporating cognitive and non-cognitive elements), the curriculum-embedded assessment (exploiting existing points of contacts with students), and the classroom research model (using assessment in the classroom as a part of teaching).

The history of assessment in community colleges has been different from that in most other colleges; community colleges have long been required to report transfer rates and success rates on licensing examinations. The history and the unique mission of community colleges are reflected in the designs of assessment for those institutions. A model from the **League for Innovation in the Community Colleges** provides an overall perspective of a mission-based approach to assessment.

Selecting a focus. To answer the question of what should be assessed, some assessment programs begin with the selection of outcomes of greatest importance to the mission and goals from a list of intended outcomes compiled by a representative campus committee or department faculty. Other assessment programs identify the current burning issues on the campus or in the department. The burning question may be a "why" question attempting to identify what inputs or processes are related to particular outcomes, for example, why the retention rates in the sciences are higher for men than women. Regardless of how the focus of an assessment is chosen, no issue or area should be selected because it is easy to measure or because other institutions are focusing on the topic. Both approaches sometimes result from inadequate consideration of possible outcomes at the outset. To address this need, the first selections included in this section describe several different outcome taxonomies.

Jacobi, Astin and Ayala present four educational outcome taxonomies developed by Lenning, Bowen, and Astin, and by Alverno College. Contrasting and comparing these different taxonomies provide valuable insights about the relationship between the contents of the taxonomy and the specific purpose or specific institution for which it was developed. The taxonomies also provide institutions with a comprehensive set of outcomes from which to compile a unique set that reflects the mission of the institution and serves as the basis for an assessment program.

Alexander and Stark extend the discussion of the above classifications of outcomes. On the basis of their analysis of gaps in the existing classifications, they developed a nine-cell matrix framework representing the areas of college student growth and development (social, personal and academic) and the form of the demonstrated change (cognitive, motivational, and behavioral).

Gagne provides a classification of outcomes from the field of psychology. He identifies five categories of human learning and performance: declarative knowledge, procedural knowledge, cognitive strategies, motor skills, and attitudes. **Baird** contributes a comprehensive framework that goes beyond outcomes and also includes inputs and processes for a total of twenty areas that could serve as a basis for an assessment program. He also provides a summary of the current literature regarding what is known and unknown about each of those areas as possible direction for future assessment.

The remaining selections in this section address the assessment of a specific student outcome or institutional focus. **Richardson, Matthews and Finney** provide a comprehensive guide for assessing campus environments to promote the participation, retention, and graduation of diverse students. Nettles underscores the need for such assessment of the institutional climate to forward institutional goals regarding minorities in higher education. Other assessment foci addressed in the selections include the major (**Fong, and Applebaum**), critical thinking (**Carpenter and Doig**), cognitive learning (**Warren**, 1988), student nonacademic development (**Kuh**), nonacademic units (**Brown**), and professional education (**McGaghie**). See other selections for additional information on general education (Banta, and Wiggins in Part IV) and coursework patterns (Ratcliff in Part IV).

Addressing ethical and human issues. Applications of the ethical issues of research and evaluation to the new assessment activity are seldom found in the literature. The selections addressing the ethical and human issues are from related fields. Important ethical issues for assessment include professional conflict of interest, professional competency, potential for abuse due to authority differential, potential for harm to individuals because of negative results, student consent documentation, coercion of students, data collection/instrument bias, privacy and confidentiality, potential for bias on the part of those making judgments of value or those who define the right-and need-to-know audiences, responsibility for reporting limitations of data, responsibility for use of findings, and responsibility for evaluating assessment side-effects.

The selection by **Erwin** includes some of these ethical issues. A selection of excerpts from standards by **the Joint Committee on Standards for Educational Evaluation** is also included. The complete document consists of thirty standards and principles of sound practices of evaluation of all educational programs, projects, and materials. Of the four groups of standards (utility, feasibility, accuracy, and propriety) only propriety, which addresses ethical and human issues, is included in this selection.

Experts in testing and measurement have established standards directed at both test users and test publishers. Standards from the **Joint Committee on Testing Practices** are included in the selections to provide guidance for those responsible for selecting or designing the methods for collecting information. While guidance from specialists is needed for instrument development, those who receive the guidance must accept responsibility for appropriate test administration and use.

Estimating costs and benefits. The feasibility of undertaking an assessment should be estimated as part of the initial planning. Open consideration of the needed resources can help to establish credibility of an assessment effort with constituent groups. Programs may suffer credibility if they are viewed as too ambitious or spend more time or money than is available; they may also lack credibility if they are perceived as being narrow or inadequate. Both situations can lead to the conclusion that the assessment is not being taken seriously at the institution.

To assure that an assessment plan includes realistic and cost effective predictions about necessary resources, an examination of the costs in relation to the actual and potential benefits needs to be made. Ewell (1991b) provides a framework for considering costs and benefits and also includes examples of programs to illustrate the benefits, direct costs, and externalities of each.

Additional Core Readings

Braskamp, L. A. "So, What's the Use?" *In Achieving Assessment Goals Using Evaluation Techniques, New Directions for Higher Education No. 67* edited by P. J. Gray. San Francisco: Jossey-Bass, 1989, pp. 43–50.

Ewell, Peter T. "Establishing a Campus-Based Assessment Program." In *Student Outcomes Assessment: What Institutions Stand to Gain, New Directions for Higher Education No. 59* edited by D. F. Halpern. San Francisco: Jossey-Bass, 1987, pp. 9–24.

Ewell, Peter T. "Implementing Assessment: Some Organization Issues." In *Implementing Outcomes Assessment: Promise and Perils, New Directions for Institutional Research No. 59* edited by T.W. Banta. San Francisco: Jossey-Bass, 1988, pp.15–28.

Greenberg, K. L. "Assessing Writing: Theory and Practice." In *Assessing Students' Learning, New Directions for Teaching and Learning No. 34* edited by J. McMillan. San Francisco: Jossey-Bass, Summer 1988, pp. 47–59.

Pace, C. R. "Perspectives and Problems in Student Outcomes Research." In *Assessing Educational Outcomes, New Directions for Institutional Research No. 47* edited by Peter T. Ewell. San Francisco, Jossey-Bass, 1985, pp. 7–18.

Pettit, J. "Listening to Your Alumni: One Way to Assess Academic Outcomes." *AIR Professional File* 41 (Summer 1991), pp. 1-10.

Rudolph, L. and Poje, D. J. "Higher Education Assessment: Don't Overlook Ethical Practices." In *Assessment Update* 3 (4) (July/August 1991), pp. 4–5 edited by Trudy W. Banta.

An Organizational Perspective for the Effective Practice of Assessment

G. ROGER SELL

Although the current emphasis on assessment in higher education is the appraisal of student outcomes (Adelman, 1986, Ewell, 1985), colleges and universities engage in a wide variety of assessment activities. These activities focus not only on students but also on faculty, programs, and the institutions themselves. The treatment of assessment in this chapter reflects an organizational perspective that includes, but goes beyond, student assessment.

There is not a single organizational approach to the study of higher education institutions as organizations but rather several theoretical frameworks, such as bureaucratic (Blau, 1973), collegial (Millett, 1962,1978), political (Baldridge, 1971), and organized anarchy (Cohen and March, 1974). While each of these approaches emphasizes particular features of and assumptions about colleges and universities, the essence of an organizational perspective is that it brings attention to collective concerns. These concerns include but are not limited to the acquisition of resources to maintain and develop the institution, the allocation of authority and the structure of decision-making processes, the design and performance of work, and the outcomes and impacts associated with an institution.

An organizational perspective on assessment can have a number of benefits. It can help reveal relationships among assessment activities and the use of scarce resources for them. It can help locate and diagnose competing purposes that assessment serves. It can help identify constraints as well as opportunities for assessment in the service of institutions. And it can help formulate actions to remove barriers and provide support for effective assessment practices.

This chapter begins with a broad description and critique of assessment activities in colleges and universities. The ideals of assessment are then discussed along with organizational realities that temper and restrain them. The chapter concludes with some suggested strategies for practicing assessment in such a way that its perils are reduced and its contributions are enhanced.

The Scope of Assessment in Higher Education Institutions

With the primary attention of assessment activities in higher education now focused on student outcomes, those who are calling for more and better assessment have emphasized approaches such as:

- Standardized tests of student knowledge, general as well as specialized
- Follow-up studies of graduates and their careers
- Student attrition and retention studies

- Surveys and interviews of students to discuss their perceptions of the quality of their educational experiences, the climate of their institutions, and gains from their educational experiences.

One might conclude from listening to and reading the claims of critics that colleges and universities are neglecting their assessment responsibilities—that little is done in the way of assessment in higher education. From an organizational perspective, however, higher education institutions have been and continue to be actively involved in a wide range of assessment activities. Often these activities are overlooked when assessment is limited to the appraisal of student outcomes using specific measures or techniques.

Most colleges and universities are already doing extensive work in assessment if we define the term *assessment* as a process for informing decisions and judgments through (1) framing questions; (2) designing or selecting instruments and procedures for collecting data; (3) collecting, analyzing, and interpreting data; and (4) reporting and using information that is derived from qualitative as well as quantitative data. Some might object to this broad definition (Hartle, 1986). However, in conversations as well as in the literature, the term *assessment* is often used interchangeably with terms such as *testing, evaluation,* and *appraisal.* While clarity and precision in the use of terminology is surely desirable, the purpose here is not to settle long-standing arguments about the proper domains of research, evaluation, assessment, and related concepts (for a discussion of these terms, see Shalock and Sell, 1971). Readers who are more comfortable with substituting *evaluation* or *appraisal* for the term *assessment* should do so.

The various assessment activities of higher education institutions can be grouped generally into four broad categories. These include student assessment, faculty assessment, program assessment, and institutional assessment.

Student Assessment. While the recent attention given to assessment has focused on measuring institution wide student outcomes, the most frequent and often overlooked form of student assessment occurs in courses and academic departments (McMillan, 1988). Student assessment at the course and department levels frequently serves the primary purpose of awarding grades and credits. However, institutions also conduct student testing for selection and placement before students enroll in courses and sometimes after they matriculate. In addition, some colleges and departments use senior exams, internships, and major projects as capstone experiences for assessing student performance.

Faculty Assessment. Most institutions have at least annual reviews of faculty performance, some for merit salary increases, and virtually all institutions have periodic reviews of faculty for tenure and promotion decisions (Centra, 1979). Some institutions have implemented assessment procedures for the posttenure evaluation of faculty (Bennett and Chater, 1984; Licata, 1986). Faculty are also nominated and judged for distinguished teaching, research, and/or service awards (Beidler, 1986). Each of these activities is an example of some form of assessment as that concept is developed here.

Program Assessment. In addition to accreditation reviews of academic programs, many institutions have established procedures for internal reviews and self-studies of academic programs (Arns and Poland, 1980; Conrad and Wilson, 1985). Some institutional procedures and responses are linked to state-level program reviews (Barak, 1982; Ohio Board of Regents, 1979). Academic programs are also at times rated or ranked by external reviewers and peers at other institutions (Lawrence and Green, 1980).

Institutional Assessment. Each of the regional accrediting associations conducts periodic reviews of higher education institutions in their area. Self-studies and external visitors are usually part of these reviews. In addition, institutions respond to federal and/or state compliance reviews for affirmative action, auditing and data reporting, health and safety, and so forth. Colleges and universities have also initiated assessments associated with strategic planning and the annual budgeting process (Barak, 1986; Micek, 1980; Shirley and Volkwein, 1978).

A Critique of Assessment Practices

The claim of critics that most colleges and universities are ignoring or neglecting their assessment activities is simply off target. It is not that institutions fail to engage in assessment; rather, institutions may lack systematic and reflective examinations of the purposes that assessment serves and the compatibility of practices with realizing the selected purposes. It would appear that the large portion of assessment activities in universities and colleges is directed more at summary descriptions and periodic judgments about quality than at specific diagnoses for the improvement of performance. Examples of this counterclaim are provided for each of the major groupings of assessment activities.

Student Assessment. Even when we change our instructional objectives, materials, or procedures, it is not uncommon that we use the same tests or other performance measures of student achievement. Student assessment can be conducted on the basis of expediency, habit, or external pressure rather than for ensuring that what we try to assess is worthy of assessment, is related to our instruction and objectives, and is a trustworthy indicator of student learning and development. Student assessment more frequently serves the purpose of awarding credits and grades (Milton, Pollio, and Eison, 1986) than the purpose of providing students with feedback that can improve their learning or providing instructors with feedback that can improve their teaching and courses (Loacker, 1988). One consequence of an overemphasis on grading is that students tend to view academic work through the "grade point average perspective" (Becker, Geer, and Hughes, 1968).

Student assessment and learning can and should be integrally related. Learning, in the broad sense, is both a process and an outcome, resulting in some qualitative change in knowledge, skills, attitudes, and/or values. Feedback resulting from both informal and formal means of student assessment can aid the learning process if that feedback is specific, timely, and on target with clear performance expectations. A test score or grade without such diagnostic feedback or explanation lacks completeness for the learner. Furthermore, frequent opportunities to perform and practice with informed and diagnostic feedback are usually necessary for novice learners to become more expert. The formative use of student assessment can help learners to become more proficient in their own self-assessments and in learning how to learn, as well as in acquiring substantive knowledge and skills (Study Group, 1984).

Similarly, faculty can improve their instructional performance through student assessment. The construction and use of student assessment measures is one of the most critical, yet underemphasized, instructional responsibilities of faculty. No matter what we say our expectations are for student performance, the instruments, procedures, and interpretations we use in student assessment constitute the operational objectives of our instruction. Significant gains can occur in the quality of our instruction when we make changes in our student assessment practices that are consistent with the learning outcomes we wish our students to attain and when we modify our instruction based on what we learn from student assessment. Student performance on carefully selected and developed assessment measures can provide important indicators of instructional practices that are relatively weak or strong. Along with other information, assessment results can help locate particular aspects of instruction that can be improved. In these respects, the quality of student assessment is closely associated with the quality of instruction that students actually experience (Loacker, 1988).

Faculty Assessment. Our disposition toward counting things and quantifying performance is often reflected in decisions about faculty involving promotion, tenure, and merit salary increases (Tuckman, 1976). Examples of the propensity to quantify performance include such measures as the number of published articles in particular refereed journals (indicator of research productivity), student ratings of instructors using Likert-type scales (indicator of teaching productivity), and the number of professional association and university committees served on (indicator of service productivity). The problem is not with these quantitative measures themselves. The problem is that quantitative evidence of faculty performance is susceptible to use independent of the objectives, substance, context, or other circumstances surrounding the tasks that faculty actually perform (Scriven, 1987). Furthermore, an overemphasis on quantifying performance can result in "bottomline" calculations or comparisons that overlook the responsibilities, effort, and outcomes representing individual faculty members' contributions to their academic units.

With regard to formative feedback, faculty have reported generally receiving little (Davey and Sell, 1984, 1985). Prior to fourth-year or sixth-year reviews, new faculty may not have received any detailed and diagnostic feedback from colleagues or the department chairperson. Faculty claims that they are not sure of the basis on which their performance is judged or how their performance could be improved can sometimes be traced to omissions of sound personnel practices (Miller, 1987). Tenured faculty, especially full professors, sometimes do not seek or receive feedback that could improve their teaching, research, or service performance.

In most institutions, the front-line responsibilities for faculty assessment fall on the shoulders of department chairpersons, with faculty committees or the faculty at large contributing recommendations on which the chairpersons are expected to act. The role of the department chairperson in the assessment of faculty is reflected in two main responsibilities. One is to work with faculty in the assessment of colleagues (or prospective colleagues) and of their own performance. Another is to make judgments about the worth and merit of individual faculty for personnel decisions. A complicating factor is that chairpersons tend to walk a thin line between being a faculty colleague and being an administrator (Tucker, 1981).

The responsibilities of department chairpersons imply technical and interpersonal expertise, as well as legal savvy, associated with faculty assessment. Seldom are department chairpersons formally prepared or mentored for their complex roles in faculty development and evaluation. Acquiring knowledge and skills related to chairperson responsibilities for faculty assessment usually occurs on the job and through trial and error. Bennett (1983) illustrates some of these dilemmas and ambiguities faced by academic unit administrators.

Program Assessment. Program reviews may serve a wide range of purposes. When conducted for the purpose of external accreditation or recognition, they tend to be directed toward providing evidence of how well instruction, research, and/or service activities are performed, usually based on perceptions of quality (Conrad and Wilson, 1985). In this sense, not only is feedback for improvement underemphasized but also program weaknesses may be camouflaged or rationalized because of the sanctions they could bring.

External program reviews, similar to student and faculty assessments, often emphasize the quantitative aspects of performance. Examples of such quantitative measures of programs include: the number and high school background of students served; the standardized test scores of students who apply and are admitted; class size; the number of credit hours and grade point averages of students who take particular courses or who are majors in particular programs; the number or percent of undergraduates who are accepted to graduate school or who pass a certifying exam; the publication, citation, and grant record of faculty; the size and currency of physical facilities, equipment, and materials; and so forth. While important judgments about quality are embedded within these kinds of quantitative data, the underlying qualitative factors often must be unraveled and systematically examined in detail to reach a more profound understanding of program quality. Given these kinds of data normally collected and examined during program reviews, we should not be surprised that external program reviews lead to recommendations such as downsizing or eliminating programs, implementing or elevating selective admissions policies, expanding library holdings, updating physical facilities, and conducting more focused or larger research projects. Attention to the detailed and in-depth diagnosis of what and how programs could improve can be easily overlooked in assessments associated with program reviews.

When institutions establish their own form of internal program review, these reviews may be tied to budget decisions or designed to emphasize the improvement purpose of assessment. Using a combination of department and institution wide representatives who concentrate on understanding how a program works and why, internal program reviews can, with proper arrangements, lead to action plans for improving academic performance (Arns and Poland, 1980). Furthermore, internal program reviews can help prepare for external reviews and provide information beyond the quantitative and comparative features of programs.

Institutional Assessment. Many of the comments about external program reviews can also be applied to institutional accreditation reviews, which are usually conducted by one of the regional accrediting associations. The process usually includes an institutional self-study, documentation of evidence responding to several prescribed issues, an on-site visit by a team of external reviewers, and a written report by the review team (North Central Association of Colleges and Schools, 1984). Since there is a relatively long time between institutional accreditation reviews and since such reviews for a complex institution are so vast, they may be perceived more as a formal procedure than as an instrumental undertaking that can result in significant changes for improvement. The recent emphasis of accrediting associations on evidence of student outcomes as part of institutional self-studies has the potential to change some institutional assessment practices, but this development is in an early stage, and its role in using assessment to improve performance is yet to be demonstrated.

The most common form of institutionwide assessment occurs through data bases that are regularly collected and updated. Colleges and universities have a long history of collecting institutional data that can serve a number of useful purposes. Examples of these purposes include recruiting, selecting, and placing students; making judgments about students, faculty, and program performance; forecasting and controlling income and expenditures; scheduling and servicing classroom facilities; and so forth.

However, potential users of institutional data bases may not know they exist, may not have access to them, or may not know how to access them. In some cases, institutions may not be collecting data that would be useful. In other cases, existing institutional data bases may have structural or technical defects, such as the lack of relational properties for linking or comparing two sets of data or the lack of conceptually sound and discrete data categories with explicit definitions of data elements.

Then, too, data that could be useful for institutional assessment are often mindlessly (that is, in a mechanical or routine manner) collected, stored, retrieved, analyzed, and reported. Sometimes mindlessness extends to the use of institutional data because of the form in which they are reported, the lack of contextual information, inadequate preparation of those who use the data, and so forth. For the most part, institutional data are reported and used in a summary fashion—that is, in gross detail and from one time period to the next. Relatively little attention is given to the diagnostic value of institutional data—that is, their use as indicators of what could be improved and what could be looked at in greater detail. Data-rich institutions can still be information poor because (1) the proper data are not available to the relevant users in a timely or convenient fashion, (2) data are viewed as power and access to them is strictly limited, (3) capabilities are lacking for organizing and translating data into useful information for particular audiences, uses, and circumstances, or any combination of these.

When we consider the breadth of student, faculty, program, and institutional assessment activities that colleges and universities undertake, with concomitant commitments of human and financial resources, there appear to be serious shortcomings in realizing the promises of assessment for improvement and development. An institution that effectively practices assessment for both improvement and accountability (including demands originating from sources outside the institution as well as decisions involving resource allocation, personnel decisions, certification, and so forth within the institution) is an ideal that few have realized. After a description of this ideal, some of the organizational realities that confront the practice of assessment are addressed, followed by a discussion of some strategies that could enhance the benefits of assessment.

A Model of the Ideal Self-Assessing Institution

Wildavsky (1972) has given considerable thought to the characteristics of institutions that have strong commitments to assessment. Although Wildavsky did not concentrate on any particular type of organization, the model he describes could be applied to colleges and universities. The ideal college or university, slightly adapted from Wildavsky's description, would have the following characteristics that cut across student, faculty, program, and institutional assessment:

1. Activities would be continuously monitored so as to determine whether goals were being met or even whether those goals should continue to prevail.

2. When assessment suggests that a change in goals or in the means to achieve them is desirable, these proposals would be taken seriously by those in the institution who could effect changes.

3. Organizational members would not have undue vested interests in the continuation of current activities; they would steadily pursue new alternatives to better serve the latest desired outcomes.

4. In some meaningful way, the entire institution would be infused with the assessment ethic, both for accountability and for improvement.

5. Assessments would result in the alteration or abolition of activities when the analyses indicate that changes are desirable.

6. All knowledge would be contingent, because improvement is always possible and change for the better is always in view though not necessarily yet attained.

7. Assumptions would be continuously challenged and reinforced by an attitude of scientific doubt rather than dogmatic commitment.

8. New truth would be sought rather than the defense of old norms and errors, and testing hypotheses would be essential to the main work of the institution.

9. The costs and benefits of alternative strategies (approaches, programs, policies) would be analyzed as precisely as available knowledge permits.

10. Assessments would be open, truthful, and explicit; conclusions would be publicly stated, showing how they were determined and giving others the opportunity to refute them; everything would be aboveboard, nothing would be hidden.

These characteristics of the self-assessing organization would seem on the surface to be entirely compatible with and reinforcing of the nature of academic pursuits in higher education institutions. However, does this model of the ideal assessing organization square with the needs of institutions and their individual members? Assuming that assessment is desirable, to what extent can we reasonably expect that colleges and universities will fully practice it? Which organizational characteristics might account for varying degrees of success with assessment, and how might these characteristics be changed?

Organizational Realities

As Wildavsky (1972) points out, the concepts of organization and assessment may be contradictory notions. At the institutional and academic unit levels, organization provides a structure that, among other things, offers stability for its members, generates and supports long-term commitments to the academic enterprise, and relates existing activities and programs to clientele and sponsors external to the university. Assessment, on the other hand, is an intervention that suggests change or at least the potential for change, that promotes skepticism and criticism, and that seeks to establish (and question) relationships among needs, objectives, and actions.

At the level of the individual faculty member and administrator, the potential conflict between assessment and individual needs is also apparent. The change threshold for individuals is limited. If assessment is forever challenging cherished beliefs and seeking to promote changes on a continuing basis, faculty and administrators could experience disabling stress and anxiety, finding it difficult to get their bearings and being in a quandary about what they should be doing. Continuing assessment activities could lead to severe individual hesitation or random behavior designed to cover as many bases as possible. Widespread confusion among faculty and administrators would produce unacceptable inefficiencies and adversely affect a necessary degree of cohesiveness and stability in academic units and central administration.

Beyond these general considerations, other more specific conditions are encountered in the assessment activities of higher education institutions. Attention is given here to six such organizational conditions that are viewed as restraining or tempering the practice of assessment.

Required Effort and Expertise. If faculty and administrators were fully involved in all aspects of assessment, there would be little time available for other responsibilities related to teaching, research, service, student advising, administration, and external relations. Needs for assessment must be balanced somehow with other institutional responsibilities.

Then, too, not everyone is equally qualified to perform all aspects of assessment. Effective assessment requires a mix of conceptual, technical, and interpersonal skills for which individual faculty and administrators may not be adequately prepared or experienced. Yet my assertion is that, to make formative and summative assessment most useful, faculty and administrators should be involved as practitioners of assessment and not just as passive recipients of assessment information.

Some of the organizational issues related to required effort and expertise for assessment include: To what extent will faculty and administrators be involved in assessment? Are assessment responsibilities considered as part of, or in addition to, ongoing tasks? How will faculty and administrators be supported and rewarded in their continuing professional development of assessment capabilities? If other people besides faculty and administrators will be involved with assessment, what will they be expected to do, with what authority, and in which realms (student, faculty, program, institution) of assessment activities? How will the responsibilities for assessment be divided among faculty administrators and staff, and to what extent will assessment be decentralized?

Costs and Benefits. Resources used for assessment are part of institutional costs, and incremental assessment activities add to institutional costs. On the other hand, existing or new assessment practices can produce benefits not only for satisfying accountability requirements but also for meeting the continuing development needs of students, faculty, programs, and the institution itself.

There is little evidence in the literature that trade-offs between the costs and benefits of various kinds of assessment have been systematically examined (Halpern, 1987). For example, do institutions have a reasonable fix on the cost of student assessment that occurs as a regular part of testing and grading within courses? Have institutions examined what benefits are associated with current assessment practices? Do institutions have any baseline for comparing either the benefits or costs of assessment alternatives?

Ewell and Jones (1986) sidestep these issues in favor of exploring incremental or marginal costs associated with adding new assessment activities, primarily student assessment instruments (tests and surveys) administered at the institutionwide level. They consider the direct costs of instruments constructed locally or purchased from an outside vendor, of administration of the instruments, of instrument scoring and data analysis, and of coordination of the assessment effort. Taking four different types of institutions (private liberal arts college, major public university, comprehensive regional university, and community college), Ewell and Jones construct four sets of institutional cost estimates based on student samples within each kind of institution. Their cost estimates show a range of approximately $29,000 to $130,000 for an annual student assessment program limited to quantifiable indicators within relatively constricted measures of student development. Assuming for the moment the accuracy of these cost estimates, we can see that student assessment (not to mention other aspects of faculty, program, or institutional assessment) can add significantly to institutional costs. These incremental requirements for assessment compete with other institutional priorities for attention and, for most institutions, do so without reference to other ongoing assessment costs or the current and potential benefits from these investments.

In addition to direct and indirect costs for assessment, there are likely to be opportunity costs since attention to assessment could reduce or eliminate effort devoted to other productive activities. Perhaps equally or even more significant, there are additional costs of changes linked to the assessment process and its results. As with other initiatives, a university or college will be limited in the resources it can allocate for assessment and the changes associated with it.

The main point here is that the various costs of assessment should be carefully considered in relation to the actual and potential benefits. Assessment can have both positive and negative effects as well as intended, unintended, and unanticipated outcomes (see Conrad and Wilson, 1985, for a discussion of the possible differences between outcomes and effects). Just as not all change is for the better, not all assessment is for the better. A thorough and continuing examination of the costs and benefits of assessment (current and proposed practices) would seem to be an organizational imperative.

External Support. If the survival and vitality of institutions is dependent, in large part, on the supply of resources (financial, human, and so forth) from their environments (Pfeffer and Salancik, 1978) and if a college or university is not strongly committed to particular programs, clientele, and sponsors (one of the qualities of the self-assessing organization), it may be unreasonable to expect that assessments will lead to the building of external support (although assessment may be required as a condition for funding or accreditation). Furthermore, if one requirement of an organization is to adapt to its environment, it may also be unreasonable to expect that administrators and faculty will select priorities and programs that are based primarily on internal assessments and their justification. Faculty and administrators, for reasons of both self-interest and institutional interest, may interpret and use assessment results with a view toward receiving external support and achieving some relatively high degree of success. The ideals of a higher education institution as a self-assessing organization become suspect, however, if faculty and administrators (1) seek out problems that are easy to solve and changes that are easy to make because they do not require radical departures from the past, (2) hold back assessment information until the time is propitious for its release, or (3) seize an opportunity whether or not the assessments are completed or justified. All of these conditions limit the potential of assessment in colleges and universities.

Internal Politics. Assessments may be wielded as a weapon in institutional wars—that is, they may be used by one party against another or for one cause, policy, or program against another. When this happens, assessment becomes much less than an ideal organizational characteristic as described by Wildavsky (1972). The assessment enterprise depends on a common recognition and respect that the activity is being carried out in order to secure better programs and practices, whatever these may be, and not to support a predetermined position or decision.

Equilibrium and Stress. As with other organizations, higher education institutions require some balance between efforts that provide stability and those that induce changes. If those involved in assessments try to do too much—that is, undertake initiatives that lead to sustained and widespread organizational changes—they risk failure in maintaining a "vote of confidence." If they try to do too little, they risk abandoning their own beliefs and losing the support of their most dedicated followers. The strains of maintaining a balance between change and stability are not easy for those dedicated to assessment. Likewise, the dissemination of assessment information can cause negative side effects that create instability in the organization. If assessment information shows how badly off an institution, program, faculty, or student body is compared to what it ought to be, this can create (or accelerate) paranoia, distrust, or general dissatisfaction detrimental to the college or university and its constituencies.

Rewards and Disincentives. In the ideal situation, the assessment ethic would be infused throughout the institution and would be equitably rewarded. Other considerations (such as required effort, financial implications, external image, internal politics, and stability) can often prevail, however, over assessment initiatives and their results. Furthermore, if assessments are accepted when they lead to a reduction in required resources and rejected when they require increases in expenditures, individuals and organizational units are likely to withhold information or selectively offer information to protect themselves. As Wildavsky (1972) aptly summarizes, "it's the same the whole world over: The analytically virtuous are not necessarily rewarded nor are the wicked (who do not evaluate) punished" (p. 515).

Making Assessment Effective

In view of the organizational realities of most colleges and universities, it is possible to practice effective assessment within some reasonable constraints and expectations. Some actions that administrators and faculty could take are discussed next.

Involve Individuals and Offices with Recognized Authority, Leadership, and Expertise. Wildavsky (1972) observes: "If evaluation is not done at all, if it is done but not used, if used but twisted out of shape, the place to look first is not the technical apparatus but the organization "itself" (p. 518). Two important features of college and university organization that are necessary for a viable assessment enterprise are recognized authority and leadership with expertise. Authority is legitimated power (French and Raven, 1968). One approach to attaining such, authority for the assessment function is to institutionalize it in some manner. While the ideal institutionalization of assessment is to diffuse and embed it in activities throughout a college or university, a more common approach is to establish one (centralized) or several (decentralized) units or offices within the institution to spearhead this function. The institutionalization of assessment requires resource commitments that involve a dependable flow of resources beyond one-shot studies. Adequate financial resources for assessment activities, with their associated accountability, might be allocated to established units, such as offices of institutional research, planning, evaluation, or program review; new offices or units charged with the specific mission of assessment or some subset of assessment activities; or external assessors or firms who conduct specific studies for the institution and report to a designated office, committee, or administrator. Whichever arrangements are made for the institutionalization of assessment, the works of Clark (1987) and others have underscored the importance of "organizational culture," especially faculty norms and values, in establishing and maintaining institutional support. The faculty role in staffing and governing the assessment function, wherever it is located, is a critical consideration for its legitimization. A blend of administrative, collegial, and individual authority (Bess, 1988) will probably be necessary for the effective performance of assessment activities in colleges and universities.

The leadership requirement for assessment has at least three dimensions. First, leadership is needed in the form of advocacy for assessment. Without strong and influential advocates for assessment, adequate resources and other forms of authority are not likely to be available. Second, leadership is required in the practice of assessment. If we assume that proper assessment requires both expertise and dedicated effort, relating assessment activities to the most important concerns of faculty, academic units, and central offices is a significant leadership task. Arrangements for the support and reward of those engaged in assessment is also associated with this leadership task. Third, leadership is needed in the allocation and use of computer technology for assessment. Two particular kinds of expertise for technology-related assessment activities are becoming more evident. These are the design and development of academic information systems that conveniently link data to the tasks that faculty and administrators perform and the translation of data into information and knowledge that is useful for particular audiences and purposes. The potential of assessment activities to support organizational inquiry is closely linked to the effective use of computer technology (Fincher, 1985; Rohrbaugh and McCartt, 1986).

Undertake Affordable Assessments That Demonstrate Effects. If one of the deficiencies of ineffective organizations is that they do not learn well from their experiences, an effective organization seeks to inquire into its experiences and to organize related information so that knowledge can be gained from these informations (Mandelbaum, 1979). The most important part of this process is to select organizational questions that are worthy of pursuit and that are susceptible to some form of disciplined inquiry within available resources. In other words, assessment activities must be affordable while addressing questions and issues of significance to the quality and effectiveness of the institution. Cameron (1987) provides a conceptual framework for examining literature on the quality and effectiveness of higher education institutions.

Assessments and their results should also be more than a set of good ideas without a notion of how they can be implemented. The proof of a good idea is that it works when tried, realizing that implementation may require a number of trials, errors, and their associated learnings. The implementation of new assessment practices, as well as changes resulting from assessment activities, may depend on the ability of those who produce the changes to make others (including those outside the institution and clients) pay for the associated costs. If the change makers are themselves forced to bear the financial brunt of their actions, they are likely to become conservative and try to stabilize their environment (Wildavsky 1972). This all suggests that some slack resources may be required within the institution for assessment practices to be effective.

In addition, the selection, design, and use of assessments should be informed by the diagnosis of costs and benefits of associated with current and alternative courses of action. An examination of the cost-effectiveness or cost-benefit of assessment alternatives should include the immediate resources and effects attributed to particular practices as well as the longer-term ones.

Maintain Discretion, Diversity, and Flexibility. Assessments that become public and reveal findings or promote changes that are perceived as detrimental to institutional constituencies are likely to be rejected by them. In addition, assessment information should be always treated with sensitivity and discretion.

Just as diversity of programs can enable institutions to be more responsive to a range of problems and clientele, a similar case could be built for the diversity of assessment practices. Placing all of the assessment eggs in one methodological basket—such as standardized instruments or informal ways of assessing student outcomes—is not a sound strategy for any institution. Neither is it sound practice for an institution to emphasize only one dimension of assessment (for example, the cognitive development of students in quantitative reasoning or the lecture performance of faculty in multimethod courses) to the exclusion of other dimensions that are necessary to understand and enrich the meaning of particular findings. Again, some reasonable balance should be sought between being spread too thinly across assessment methods and topics and concentrating attention on only one area. Teaching and learning and the environments that influence them are complex phenomena that require suitably matched approaches to assessment. Being wed to only one approach or area of assessment not only limits the realms of understanding but also constrains the ability of the institution to shift its assessment strategy.

Form Internal Coalitions to Cooperative Endeavors. Institutional assessment activities, in the broad view, are political in the sense of policy or program advocacy. "Without a steady source of political support . . . assessment will suffer the fate of abandoned children" (Wildavsky, 1972, p. 515). In addition, effective assessment is simply not possible without adequate data that can be turned into useful and timely information. To secure data from various sources, assessment activities require cooperation. The incentives (or potential gains) for cooperation must outweigh the disincentives (or potential losses).

Building support for assessment and related concerns in the institution usually requires some internal selling and, frequently, the formation of coalitions or special-interest groups. However, "political muscle" within colleges and universities must be exercised cautiously and within the rules for exercising power (more precisely, authority or legitimated power) with respect to particular decisions and decision-making processes. University policies, faculty rules, governance structures, and administrative procedures each play a part in shaping the arena in which decisions related to assessment are made and implemented. In addition, as noted earlier, the culture of colleges and universities often characterized by faculty autonomy, academic freedom, discipline affiliations and specializations, and decentralization of authority—plays a powerful role in shaping decisions and decision-making processes (Clark, 1987).

Attend to Institutional Characteristics and Readiness to Change in Assessment Design and Implementation. Assessments of student outcomes, general education curricula, or faculty performance can occur without regard to the particular characteristics of a college or university or its readiness to support assessment initiatives. However, unless key organizational factors are anticipated and accommodated or changed in assessment activities, it is highly unlikely that existing assessment practices will be altered or made more effective. Examples of organizational features of colleges and universities that should be examined for their changeability in relationship to assessment activities and findings include: institutional mission, priorities, and diversity of programs; course schedules and offerings; instructional formats and approaches; academic calendars; space and equipment restrictions; budgeting processes and financial resources available; faculty assignments and workloads; student selection, enrollment, and graduation requirements; collective bargaining agreements (if applicable); and so forth.

Assessment can be adapted to particular organizational characteristics as well as serve as an organizational change agent. Both individual and organizational changes are potentially involved in implementing assessment practices. The success of assessment may depend on readiness to change—that is, readiness to accept certain assessment practices or to implement recommendations growing out of assessment findings. When individual faculty members or administrators are the focus, readiness for change can involve a combination of attitudes, values, beliefs, skills, and knowledge about assessment and its uses. When organizational units and the total organization are the focus, readiness for change can involve a combination of structures, rewards, norms, resources, and policies that bear on assessment (Abedor and Sachs, 1978).

Those involved in deliberation about undertaking new assessment initiatives could profitably address the following issues: Is the institution (faculty, students, administrators, support staff, trustees) prepared to undertake new assessment practices with reasonable expectations for success? What can be done to prepare individuals and organizational units for a proposed change in assessment? How can assessment practices accommodate needs for individual and organizational stability while providing evidence for changes that can lead to improvements?

Build Community That Values Assessment. One of the most fundamental steps for colleges and universities wishing to upgrade their assessment practices is to ascertain whether prevalent values in the institution support the notion of assessment and, if not, what can be done to develop support. Two shared values, in particular, are directly related to the effective practice of assessment.

One value is an orientation toward experimentation and reasonable risk taking. Experiments are necessary for testing hypotheses and relating goals and objectives to results in the context of limited resources. In this sense, a college or university is a natural laboratory for experimentation and for assessment aimed at the improvement of performance.

Cooperation and collaboration comprise a second shared value essential to an effective assessment program. If the primary orientation of faculty and administrators is that organizational members (and units) are competing for a fixed pie of limited resources and if information about individuals and units is a powerful source to be protected, then collaboration within and across groups is likely to be limited. If, however, the primary orientation is that the pie of organizational resources can expand and that the performance of individuals and units is interdependent, then there is a much more positive environment for cooperation in assessment activities. Astin (1985) discusses these and other issues related to values that underlie concepts of quality in higher education.

The sense of trust among individuals and groups underlies cooperative acts beneficial to assessment activities. The credibility and equitability of assessment activities can, in turn, build trust that promotes cooperation and an experimental attitude. However, more assessment information alone will not necessarily lead to greater agreement or collaboration if the institution is wracked by fundamental differences in values. Assessment need not create agreement, but it may presuppose agreement (Wildavsky, 1972).

Conclusion

I do not wish to play down the importance of student outcomes assessment. It is terribly important, is often not adequately attended to, and should be vigorously and thoughtfully pursued on each college and university campus. Beginning with work initiated almost two decades ago at the Western Interstate Commission for Higher Education (Lawrence, Weathersby, and Patterson, 1970) and extended through current work at the National Center for Higher Education Management Systems (NCHEMS) under the leadership of Peter Ewell and Dennis Jones, I have been both an observer and participant in the formative stages of the assessment movement. For example, the NCHEMS student outcomes structure was applied in my work on adult and continuing education with the late John Putnam at the National Center for Education Statistics (Putnam and Sell, 1983). I have also been fortunate for nearly the past ten years to be located at an institution that has provided "hands-on" experiences with student assessment as a teacher, researcher, consultant, and administrator for an office of instructional development and evaluation. All of these experiences have enhanced, not reduced, my sense of the importance of student outcomes assessment.

What I have tried to emphasize in this chapter is the organizational context and forces within colleges and universities that inhibit as well as nurture assessment in its many forms. I have tried to say that student outcomes assessment is never separate from other institutional issues, is affected and used by other kinds of assessment activities, and should be carefully examined for its avowed purposes, actual uses, and consequences. Throughout this chapter I have pleaded a case for balance—of the purposes that assessment serves, of methodological approaches and foci for assessment, of effort given to assessment and other critical activities, and of response to external concerns while continuing to develop and improve individual and organizational performance.

I wish to conclude on an upbeat note. The outlook for the future of higher education and for the contribution of assessment to that future has never been brighter. With the possible exception of the late 1960s and early 1970s, higher education is more visible and more widely discussed today than in any preceding period. All kinds of audiences and stakeholders have high expectations for colleges and universities and the models and benefits that they provide for other segments of society.

I believe that most institutions are becoming highly sophisticated in dealing with a variety of assessment issues. Many of these assessment issues will continue into the next decade, but some new challenges and opportunities will also present themselves. If we are able to balance and meet the competing needs for our attention and to use assessment for enhancing the worth of individuals as well as our institutions, we will be on our way toward building strong colleges and universities for the twenty-first century.

References

Abedor, A. J., and Sachs, S. G. "The Relationship Between Faculty Development, Organizational Development, and Instructional Development: Readiness for Instructional Innovation in Higher Education. In R. K. Bass and D. B. Lumsden (eds.) *Instructional Development: The State of the Art.* Columbus, Ohio: Collegiate Publishing, 1978.

Adelman, C. *Assessment in Higher Education.* Washington, D.C.: Office of Educational Research and Improvement, U.S. Department of Education, 1986.

Arns, R. G., and Poland, W. "Changing the University Through Program Review." *Journal of Higher Education,* 1980, 51(3), 268–285.

Astin, A. W. *Achieving Educational Excellence: A Critical Assessment of Priorities and Practices in Higher Education.* San Francisco: Jossey-Bass, 1985.

Baldridge, J. V. *Power and Conflict in the University.* New York: Wiley, 1971.

Barak, R. J. *Program Review in Higher Education: Within and Without.* Boulder, Colo: National Center for Higher Education Management Systems, 1982.

Barak, R. J. "The Role of Program Review in Strategic Planning." *Association for Institutional Research Professional File,* 1986, 26, 4–7.

Becker, H.S., Geer, B., and Hughes, E. C. *Making the Grade: The Academic Side of College Life.* New York: Wiley, 1968. Beidler, P. G. (ed.). *Distinguished Teachers on Effective Teaching: Observation on Teaching by College Professors Recognized by the Council for Advancement and Support of Education.* New Direction for Teaching and Learning, no. 28. San Francisco: Jossey-Bass, 1986.

Bennett, J. B. *Managing the Academic Department: Cases and Notes.* New York: American Council on Education, 1983.

Bennett, J. B., and Chater, S. S. "Evaluating the Performance of Tenured Faculty Members." *Educational Record,* 1984, 65, 38–41.

Bess, J. L. *Collegiality and Bureaucracy in the Modern University.* New York: Teachers College, Columbia University, 1988.

Blau, P. M. *The Organization of Academic Work.* New York: Wiley, 1973.

Cameron, K. S. "Improving Academic Quality and Effectiveness." In M. W. Peterson (ed.), *Key Resources on Higher Education Governance, Management, and Leadership: A Guide to the Literature.* San Francisco: Jossey-Bass, 1987.

Centra, J. A. *Determining Faculty Effectiveness: Assessing Teaching, Research, and Service for Personnel Decisions and Improvement.* San Francisco: Jossey-Bass, 1979.

Clark, B. R. *The Academic Life: Small Worlds, Different Worlds.* Princeton, N.J.: Princeton University Press, 1987.

Cohen, M. D., and March, J. G. *Leadership and Ambiguity;* New York: McGraw-Hill, 1974.

Conrad, C. F., and Wilson, R. F. *Academic Program Review: Institutional Approaches, Expectations, and Controversies.* ASHE-ERIC Higher Education Report, no. 5. Washington, D.C.: Association for the Study of Higher Education, 1985.

Davey, K. B., and Sell, G. R. "The Role Evaluation Could Play in Improving and Developing Instructional Excellence in a Doctoral-Granting University." Paper presented at the joint meeting of the Evaluation Research Society and Evaluation Network, San Francisco, October 11, 1984.

Davey, K. B., and Sell, G. R. "Instructional Evaluation for Development/Improvement: Fact or Fiction Based on a Case Study of Faculty Practices?" Paper presented at the annual meeting of the American Educational Research Association, Chicago, April 1, 1985.

Ewell, P. T. (ed.). *Assessing Educational Outcomes*. New Directions for Institutional Research, no. 47. San Francisco: Jossey-Bass, 1985.

Ewell, P. T., and Jones, D. P. "The Costs of Assessment." In C. Adelman (ed.), *Assessment in Higher Education*. Washington, D.C.: Office of Educational Research and Improvement, U.S. Department of Education, 1986.

Fincher, C. "The Art and Science of Institutional Research." In M. W. Peterson and M. Corcoran (eds.), *Institutional Research in Transition*. New Directions for Institutional Research, no. 46. San Francisco: Jossey-Bass, 1985.

French, R. P., and Raven, B. "The Bases of Social Power." In D. Cartwright and A. Zander (eds.), *Group Dynamics: Research and Theory*. (3rd ed.) New York: Harper & Row, 1968.

Halpern, D. F. (ed.). *Student Outcomes Assessment: What Institutions Stand to Gain*. New Directions for Higher Education, no. 59. San Francisco: Jossey-Bass, 1987.

Hartle, T. W. "The Growing Interest in Measuring the Educational Achievement of College Students." In C. Adelman (ed.), *Assessment in Higher Education*. Washington, D.C.: Office of Educational Research and Improvement, U.S. Department of Education, 1986.

Lawrence, B., Weathersby, G., and Patterson, V. W. *Outputs of Higher Education: Their Identification, Measurement, and Evaluation*. Boulder, Colo.: Western Interstate Commission for Higher Education, 1970.

Lawrence, J. K., and Green, K. C. *A Question of Quality: The Higher Education Ratings Game*. AAHE-ERIC Higher Education Report, no. 5, Washington, D.C.: American Association for Higher Education, 1980.

Licata, C. M. *Post-tenure Faculty Evaluation: Threat or Opportunity*. ASHE-ERIC Higher Education Report, no. 1. Washington, D.C.: Association for the Study of Higher Education, 1986.

Loacker, G. "Faculty as a Force to Improve Instruction Through Assessment." In H. McMillan (ed.), *Assessing Students' Learning*. New Directions for Teaching and Learning, no. 34. San Francisco: Jossey-Bass, 1988.

McMillan, J. H. (ed.), *Assessing Students' Learning*. New Directions for Teaching and Learning. no. 34. San Francisco: Jossey-Bass, 1988.

Mandelbaum, S. J. "The Intelligence of Universities." *Journal of Higher Education*, 1979, 50 (6), 697–725.

Micek, S. S. (ed.). *Integrating Academic Planning and Budgeting in a Rapidly Changing Environment*. Boulder, Colo.: National Center for Higher Education Management Systems, 1980.

Miller, R. I. *Evaluating Faculty for Promotion and Tenure*. San Francisco: Jossey-Bass, 1987.

Millett, J. D. *The Academic Community*. New York: McGraw-Hill, 1962.

Millett, J. D. *New Structures of Campus Power: Success and Failures of Emerging Forms of Institutional Governance*. San Francisco: Jossey-Bass, 1978.

Milton, O., Pollio, H. R., and Eison, J. A. *Making Sense of College Grades: Why the Grading System Does Not Work and What Can Be Done About It.* San Francisco: Jossey-Bass, 1986.

North Central Association of Colleges and Schools. *A Handbook of Accreditation.* Chicago: Commission on Institutions of Higher Education, North Central Association of Colleges and Schools, 1984.

Ohio Board of Regents. *Developing a Process Model for Institutional and State-Level Review and Evaluation of Academic Programs.* Columbus: Ohio Board of Regents, 1979.

Pfeffer, J., and Salancik, G. R. *The External Control of Organizations: A Resource-Dependence Perspective.* New York: Harper & Row, 1978.

Putnam, J. F., and Sell, G. R. *Adult Learning Activities: A Handbook of Terminology for Classifying and Describing the Learning Activities of Adults.* Washington, D.C.: National Center for Education Statistics, 1983.

Rohrbaugh, J., and McCartt, A. T. (eds.). *Applying Decision Support Systems in Higher Education.* New Directions for Institutional Research, no. 49. San Francisco: Jossey-Bass, 1986.

Schalock, H. D., and Sell, G. R. "A Framework for the Analysis and Empirical Investigation of Educational RDD&E." In H. D. Schalock and G. R. Sell (eds.), *The Oregon Studies in Educational Research, Development, Diffusion, and Evaluation (RDD & E): Conceptual Frameworks.* Monmouth, Ore.: Teaching Research, A Division of the Oregon State System of Higher Education, 1971.

Scriven, M. "Validity in Personnel Evaluation." Journal of Personnel Evaluation in Education, 1987, 1 (1), 9–23.

Shirley, R. C., and Volkwein, J. F. "Establishing Academic Program Priorities." *Journal of Higher Education,* 1978, 49 (5), 472–489.

Study Group on the Conditions of Excellence in American Higher Education. *Involvement in Learning: Realizing the Potential of American Higher Education.* Washington, D.C.: National Institute of Education, 1984.

Tucker, A. *Chairing the Academic Department: Leadership Among Peers.* Washington, D.C.: American Council on Education, 1981.

Tuckman, H. P. *Publication, Teaching, and the Academic Reward Structure.* Lexington, Mass.: Health, 1976.

Wildavsky, A. "The Self-Evaluating Organization." *Public Administration Review,* 1972, 32 (5), 509–520.

Consideration of the Resources Needed in an Assessment Program

ALICE M. THOMAS

The traditional meaning of assessment focused on gathering information about an individual, usually through multiple tests and procedures, for purposes of placement or guidance (Hartle, 1985). In current usage, it applies to the process of gathering information to indicate the extent to which an institution is achieving what it purports to do, that for which it is accountable. It answers the question: Are students growing in the intended dimensions as expressed in the institution's mission, and reflected in the course work and other learning experiences? This discussion uses the following definition.

Assessment: The use of various methods to gather both quantitative and qualitative information at the level of program, institution, and/or system, to describe and to make judgments about the inputs (resources), the processes (educational encounters), and outcomes of an undergraduate education for purposes of improvement and/or accountability (individual student assessment used only for diagnostic purposes is omitted from the definition) [modification of definition used by Boyer & Ewell, 1988].

Background

A national survey of state assessment activities indicated that states with assessment programs greatly underestimated the costs of such programs, especially staff time (Boyer, Ewell, Finney & Mingle, 1987). Some programs undertaken with insufficient resources of time, budget, or staff have suffered serious consequences: prematurely discontinued programs due to inadequate funds; longterm negative attitudes of faculty as a result of insufficient program planning time; and uncooperative students because of unreasonable time demands or inappropriate intrusion into their lives.

Assessment is not only a technical endeavor, but also an intensely human enterprise with social, educational, and highly political components. In addition to the obvious resources needed for an assessment, e.g., personnel and instruments, considerations should also be given to the less tangible, but no less critical sources of support for the social and political aspects of assessment. As indicated below, these less visible necessary resources and aids eventually evolve into time and money expenditures.

Resources by Phase of Assessment

Six general phases of an assessment will be used as a framework for this discussion about resources and aids that are needed to support an assessment.

Phase I: Clarifying the Assessment Object and Context

Phase II: Designing the Assessment

Phase III: Collecting and Analyzing the data

Phase IV: Communicating the Findings

Phase V: Using the Findings

Phase VI: Evaluating the Assessment

Regardless of the model, all assessment programs will progress through each of the phases, although the various programs will differ in the way the tasks of each phase are completed, e.g., persons responsible, time spent, and methods used. Nor will all components of an assessment program within an institution progress simultaneously through the phases.

Although little prescriptive advice is provided in this discussion, the wide variety of issues addressed should facilitate and enhance discussion and planning. Decisions about the resources and aids needed to support an assessment should reflect the context and complex milieu of each institution.

Phase I—Clarifying the Assessment Object and Context

The tasks for this phase include clarifying the purpose of the assessment, and describing the component of institution/program to be assessed and its context.

- **Statement of Purpose.** Early clarification and communication of the purposes of an assessment are critical aspects of a successful program. The basic alternative purposes of assessment are accountability or improvement, or some combination (Terenzini, 1989). Accountability assessment is conducted to inform some judgment about value or worth to be made by some higher authority such as external constituencies; improvement assessment is conducted to inform decisions for the purpose of change and the enhancement of teaching and learning towards institutional self-improvement. The question of purpose must be answered early and clearly, since the purpose affects all subsequent decisions about what and how to assess. An unclear purpose may result in the gathering of "interesting" or easily collected data that have little relevance to the purpose.

  Audience concerns and uncertainty about the use of data can seriously affect the credibility and functioning of an assessment program. A statement of purpose is enhanced if it also identifies what the purpose *is not*, and how the results *will not* be used. Such a policy statement might explicitly state that the program is not intended to be used as a basis for eliminating programs, making decisions about individual faculty, or determining graduation status of a student (Ewell, 1988a; Dennison & Bunda, 1989).

- **Audience Involvement.** Primarily in recognition of the political nature of assessment, audience involvement is one of the most frequently mentioned necessary resources in the assessment literature. Such involvement includes early, active participation of credible individuals from a broad range of audiences who will be affected by and/or responsible for the results.

The support and participation by individuals who have high credibility and serve as opinion leaders of the groups they represent can be critical. Selection of a representative group to be actively involved in the assessment might also include such factors as academic field, gender, length of service, and ethnicity. Too many perspectives in the design, however, can result in an overly ambitious, and unwieldy assessment. The critical nature of the involvement of some of the essential audiences warrants a brief clarification.

— *Faculty*. Faculty resistance can be, and has been, the demise of assessment programs (Astin & Ayala, 1987; Hillman, 1987; Miller, 1988). Understandably, faculty have many potential fears and concerns: a fear that they will be negatively evaluated, conviction that classroom outcomes are inherently unmeasurable by anyone but faculty, a threat of loss of individual prerogative and faculty autonomy, and a view that it is busywork. Early participation in the decision making by faculty opinion leaders can mitigate these fears, establish a sense of ownership, provide sound program guidance, and promote the eventual use of information for change and improvement.

   Faculty are also potential resources for tasks in later phases that require special expertise, e.g., research design, testing and measurement, and interpretation of information. Incentives should be provided for faculty to prevent the assessment responsibility from becoming another add-on in an already heavy schedule. Some institutions have used a combination of released time and compensation for faculty with major assessment responsibilities.

— *Students*. Student involvement and the consideration of their viewpoints in assessment decision making are important for several reasons. From an ethical standpoint, student involvement seems warranted since they will be most affected by the outcomes, and are also likely to invest considerable time in the assessment process. On a practical basis, involvement encourages students to cooperate in the gathering of information, and to provide valid measurements of their performance (Erwin, 1991).

— *Administrators*. Visible commitment to an assessment program by the institution's president and other key administrators has been noted as essential. The appropriate role of the higher level administrators in the assessment process, however is not active involvement in committee work or formulation of recommendations based on the results. A more consonant role is limited to providing the general assessment parameters and necessary support, e.g., providing a rationale for the program in the institutional context, setting the initial direction and limitations, and offering moral and financial support for the program and implementation of recommendations (Miller, 1986; Rossman & El-Khawas, 1987).

   Since important student learning clearly occurs outside as well as inside the classroom, persons who have responsibility in such areas should be included in the planning. For example, involvement of student life personnel seems critical if improvement is expected from an assessment addressing an area of their responsibility, e.g., student development of leadership skills.

— *Other Personnel*. The appropriate role for personnel who might serve as a facilitator/director of an assessment program will vary considerably among institutions and will depend on several factors including the preferred assessment model and the locus of needed expertise. One option is a highly centralized model in which the assessment activities are integrated into a permanent, funded office. This model clearly promotes efficiency, and can also serve as a symbol of institutional commitment to assessment. Some view the institutional or educational researcher, who has an established office and access to high level administrators, as an individual who might play a critical role in assessment (Ewell, 1988a; Nichols, 1989).

Although more efficient, a central office is viewed by some as being too distant from the actual teaching and learning activity. Ewell (1989) issued warnings about a highly centralized model becoming a "free-standing assessment bureaucracy with few links to the faculty or to real academic decision making" (p. 12). Sell (1989) suggested that "if assessment is to serve its ultimate purpose—improvement and development of individuals and organizations—the primary actors for both conducting assessments and using the results from them should be the folks in the trenches" (the faculty and administrators responsible for programs) (p. 119). This position is also supported by other higher education leaders such as Cross and Angelo (1988) who emphasized that assessment in the classroom by faculty has greater utility than programs conducted as the institutional or state level.

A combination of these approaches is used at some institutions where faculty conduct assessment in the classroom of such areas as cognitive skills, and a central office engages in the assessment of areas that are a campus-wide responsibility such as moral development. These varying patterns result in a researcher serving as the central coordinator or director of assessment at some institutions, while a similar person may serve chiefly as a technical consultant on other campuses.

At many institutions, a major responsibility for assessment has been assigned to researchers whose past responsibilities were chiefly in support of administrative and management decisions (Ewell, 1987). These decisions often used quantifiable, single source data such as student/faculty ratio, and cost/credit hour. In contrast to such efficiency questions, assessment focuses on effectiveness, and the complex functions of teaching and learning. Such behavioral and psychological research in the cognitive and affective domains requires a different set of knowledge, skills, and methodologies than necessary for these researchers in the past. An institution may incur expenses for personnel training needed for these important skills.

A strong potential for conflict of interest may exist for some individuals who might benefit from the assessment model selected through advancement or building of a large support structure. The assessment model chosen may be beneficial to an individual who has had a role in the decision making, but it may not be the best program for the institutions. Questions about the motives or competence of such key persons can adversely affect the quality of the data, and eventual acceptance and use of the findings. The best answer for each institution regarding who should be assigned the various tasks, and whether a centralized or decentralized model should be used depends on contextual factors at the institution.

- **Political Climate.** Another important aid in the design of a successful program is a strong, positive political climate. Incentives to participate, rather than directives or mandates, are viewed as critical for a positive climate, whether the incentives come from institutions to faculty or from state legislatures to institutions (Miller, 1988; Sell, 1989).

The campus climate for assessment can be strongly affected by the level of understanding about the topic. To enhance the understanding of the various audiences about assessment, many institutions have found it helpful to send a campus team to assessment conferences. Many conferences are offered by educational organizations and institutions experienced in assessment; the most valuable will not promote a specific assessment model.

Phase II Designing the Assessment

Tasks for This phase include identifying the questions to be answered, developing an overall assessment plan including the approach to be used and the tactics for gathering information, developing a management plan for use of the resources, and deciding whether to conduct assessment.

- **Mission/Goals Statement.** Because the design of an assessment program follows from the goals and intended outcomes of the institution, updating and clarifying the mission statement is necessary. Failure to give adequate attention to this clarification task may result in assessment programs that are unrelated to the institution.

   The planning time required for updating the mission statement should allow for an iterative revision and review process involving several groups, e.g., a committee, the faculty, higher level administrators, and trustees. Gardiner (1989) provided information about how to clarify institutional goals.

   Although it is initially important to consider all educational goals as *possible* foci of an assessment program, some time will be needed to prioritize among all possible dimensions, and to select a manageable number to be included in the initial assessment program. The scope of the selected goals could include different educational areas of the institution, thus avoiding a narrow focus that might provide a limited view of the institution's overall learning activities. Focusing solely on academic programs from the very beginning, for example, can create resistance to assessment from faculty.

- **Assessment Framework.** Before deciding on an assessment plan, an institution should examine assessment frameworks and models used on other campuses for possible adaptation. Several existing frameworks provide guidance in answering the questions of purpose, who will be assessed, and what will be assessed (Astin, 1991; Terenzini, 1989; Thomas, 1988). Pratt & Reichard (1983) offered techniques for identifying goals and for moving from goals to specified outcomes and potential measures. Institutions need to spend time to "adapt" rather than "adopt" assessment plans from other campuses, i.e., adapting to their own context including its unique goals, political climate, and human material resources. Spending a year to examine programs at other campuses, and to plan their own is time well invested (Terenzini, 1989).

- **Assessment Tools and Instruments.** Information about available assessment tools and instruments can be found in this publication. The appropriate use of such instruments carries many implications for personnel resources. Fincher (1988) warned that "there are very few 'ready-made' methods of assessment available to the college with little or no measurement, assessment, or evaluation expertise in its administrative staff and faculty" (p. 7).

Assessment is a complex task, often using multiple measures, multiple methods, and collection of both quantitative and qualitative information. The possible inadequacy of methodology expertise on a campus to address the complex teaching/learning activity can have implications for the needed resources and the quality of the program. For example, a lack of familiarity with qualitative research on the part of those planning the assessment can lead to using only the methods that are familiar, i.e., those providing quantitative data.

Intrusion and disruption by assessment into the teaching and learning activities can be minimized if the assessment procedures are incorporated into the normal operations and policy of the institution. Such an approach is also likely to obtain more valid data from students, to user fewer resources, and to assure that the assessment is given appropriate, continued attention.

The determination of what already is known about the impact of the institution on students is one of the first steps of many of the successful assessment programs. An institution generally has a significant amount of diverse, useful data on the campus. The information often is widely dispersed among offices, and will need to be inventoried and integrated for analysis.

- **Funding.** During the planning phase, institutions should make some realistic prediction of the resources that might be necessary for assessment on their campus. Such a projection can allow the institution to judge the overall feasibility of assessment, compare the costs and benefits of alternative assessment plans, and make needed improvements in the design for more efficient use of resources.

While the factors affecting costs vary greatly among institutions, the types of expenses incurred at one institution might be helpful in projecting categories of likely expenses at another. Since the cost of an assessment is closely linked to the goals and design of the assessment program, few have attempted to generalize about the probable total cost to an institution. Bowen (1985) suggested that institutions use 1–3% of their educational budgets for such activity. Ewell (1988b) examined the costs of assessment activities at several institutions and reported that they were well within the 1–2% of budget guidelines for evaluation of public programs.

An assessment will add to the institutional costs, both in the resources allocated to the assessment itself and to the changes suggested by the assessment. In addition, Terenzini (1989) suggested considering the opportunity costs, i.e., the resources devoted to assessment that are not available for other uses. Lewis (1988) provided a cost-benefit paradigm for gathering facts about the costs and benefits of various assessment plans.

- **A Plan for the Protection of Human Subjects and Other Audiences.** Designing an assessment that protects the rights of humans who are involved in the assessment and who might be adversely affected by it is essential from an ethical, professional, and legal standpoint. Federal guidelines, professional codes of ethics, and concern for the welfare of others dictate that human subjects be treated with respect, assured confidentiality and/or anonymity, and protected from participation under coercive conditions.

Each campus is likely to have its own existing set of ethical guidelines for human subject research that cover such data gathering issues, as well as the questions of who is entitled ethically and legally to be informed. Examples of guidelines can also be obtained from several professional associations: the American Psychological Association (1982), and the American Sociological Association (1971). Kimmel (1988) provided a comprehensive and practical discussion of the ethical issues, problems, and potential dilemmas, and the appropriate designs for avoiding particular problems.

Phase III Collecting and Analyzing the Data

The tasks for this phase include collecting and preparing the data and information, and analyzing and interpreting the results.

- **Personnel.** Personnel with special expertise in the areas of research, evaluation, testing, and measurement are required for the activities in this phase involving data collection. In contrast to the need for specialists to collect the data, the use of a broadly based team is advocated by many assessment experts for the subsequent data analysis and interpretation (Dennison & Bunda, 1989; Marchese, 1988; Terenzini, 1989). Such a team approach can provide the necessary special insights and understandings, and encourage support and use of the results; including faculty in this activity is imperative.

- **Equipment and Space.** Planning for resources should include any unusual demands on equipment and space that may be made by some data collection methods, e.g., standardized testing that requires group administration, or portfolio assessment that may consume considerable departmental space for storing the student portfolios.

- **Student Cooperation.** Some institutions have expended considerable resources on assessment instruments only to find that the students do not cooperate. Although the most effective way to motivate students and to gain their cooperation will differ among institutions, resources for some type of incentive may be needed. The reward system has been used with limited success; some contrasting approaches seem to approach violation of the rights of human subjects through use of coercive methods. Students have generally been more responsive to appeals if they can see they will directly benefit, e.g., instances in which they are given feedback about their progress or areas of strengths and weaknesses. Such feedback is not without cost; it requires considerable staff time and effort if adequately conducted (Erwin, 1991). Institutions may gain greater student cooperation if statements are added to the college catalog about the institution's commitment to excellence and assessment, and the expectation that students will participate during their college career as part of their enrollment commitment.

Phase IV Communicating the Findings

The tasks in this phase of an assessment relate to making judgments about worth, writing the report, and releasing the information.

- **Report Production Staff and Equipment.** The success of the next phase, the utilization of the information, is dependent upon receiving understandable and concise information in a timely manner requiring adequate staff and equipment. To assure fair and complete written reports, some have suggested using a mixed group of generalists and specialists with specific areas of expertise and special skills (Dennison & Bunda, 1989; Marchese, 1988). Including multiple perspectives from various knowledgeable groups addresses the need to provide balanced reporting of strengths and weakness, and to safeguard against distortion by personal feelings of biases.

A mixed group of writers can also provide valuable guidance in the targeting of reports, i.e., targeting to specific audiences. The reports may vary in length, amount of technical information, data or release, emphasis of particular topics, and medium of dissemination (Nichols, 1989). Participating groups should review early drafts of reports to correct errors of fact, or to clarify potential misinterpretations. Involving various group representatives in the design and distribution of communications targeted for their respective groups can create a sense of ownership, and encourage use of the results. Kinnick (1985) and Nichols provided information about report writing techniques that can enhance understanding, and promote the use of the information.

- **Distribution Plans.** As Braskamp (1989) argued, "Assessment is everybody's business; however, one person's assessment business does not necessarily have to be everybody else's assessment business" (p. 48). At the core of this issue is the question of who are the right-to-know audiences.

A diversity of ethical stances surrounding the issue of disclosure is likely to exist among the various disciplines and professions represented on and off the campus. Some may adhere strictly to "full and frank" disclosure regardless of consequences, while others may embrace ethical standards that include greater consideration for the welfare of individuals and their programs (Kinnick, 1985). Regardless of the decision, dissemination plans about who will receive what information, and when they will obtain it, should be agreed upon early in the assessment for use in this phase.

Phase V Using the Findings

The tasks for this phase include using the findings in applying results, making judgments about quality, making decisions about improvement, and making and reporting recommendations.

Utilization of results was noted by Ewell (1989) as the "primary emerging challenge for the assessment movement" (p. 20). Few institutions have had assessment programs long enough to provide guidance for this stage. Several factors discussed in earlier phases will affect utilization; an agreed-upon purpose; a political climate supportive of change; early involvement of relevant audiences; an assessment framework appropriate for the institution; valid, reliable and credible data; and understandable, concise, and timely presentation of information (Sell, 1989). Other resources discussed below are also be important to utilization.

- Standards. The use of some standard, whether spoken or unspoken, is inherent in making any judgment of quality. Each of the many assessment audiences, e.g., students, parents, faculty, administrators, trustees, legislators, and boards of higher education, will have different standards resulting in multiple, diverse value judgments about quality.

The issue of the standards to be applied in the assessment can be addressed by answering several questions. Will multiple standards be used? Will they be absolute standards (e.g., 85% of the students should be able to achieve at a particular level), or will they be relative standards (e.g., senior results should be significantly higher than freshman results, than results in 1980, or than results of comparable institutions)? If the assessment information is to have credibility, the criteria for making the judgments of quality must be clarified.

- **Monitors of Information Use.** Individuals and groups of people may be seriously affected by assessment. Care and responsibility must be taken for the use of findings; that may require additional resources such as personnel for appropriate precautionary measures. This obligation is particularly important in higher education assessment, since use is often out of the direct control of those conducting the assessment and the potential for misuse is so great. Inappropriate interpretations and conclusions may result when assessment data are reported beyond the campus to audiences who may lack adequate knowledge or expertise for interpretation.

  Taking responsibility for the use of information includes continuing to educate audiences about the limitations of the assessment process and information, adhering to the use of information agreed upon at the outset of the assessment process, focusing audiences' attention on the ethics of use and the avoidance of unnecessary social and psychological harm, being aware of the audiences' uses of the information, and providing any necessary clarification and rebuttals of misinterpretations.

- **Administrative Structure Link.** Because of the size, complexity, and loose coupling at some educational institutions, the use of assessment information may be a fragile link in an assessment program. As an aid to utilization, some have advocated that the institution's planning and budgeting program be closely tied to the assessment process in a visible, ongoing manner (Dennison & Bunda, 1989; Ewell, 1989).

- **Incentives for Use of Information.** The purpose of assessment is not to complete the exercise itself, or to report that an assessment was done; assessment provides a basis for decision-making and possible action. Although requiring additional resources, follow-through on the assessment results can be encouraged by helping the audiences learn how to use the information; providing necessary follow-up support, encouragement, and possibly incentives to take the information seriously; and requiring evidence of the use of the information in accountability plans (Ewell, 1989).

Phase VI Evaluating the Assessment

The task of this phase is the investigation of the outcomes of the assessment and the quality of the conduct of the assessment program. Because assessment is most profitably viewed as an ongoing process, evaluation of that process is particularly important for monitoring resource use, and for guiding subsequent follow-through and assessment activity. An evaluation can provide information about the impacts of the current assessment efforts, e.g., the side effects and outcomes of the assessment—both positive and negative. Given the complexity and political nature of higher education, the potential adverse effects of assessment should be monitored, e.g., effect on faculty morale, minority student access to higher education, and unfavorable cost/benefit ratio. In addition to the outcomes of the assessment, an examination of the process of the assessment may be useful. To guide evaluation of an assessment, Thomas (1990) provided some important principles or standards by which assessment should be conducted.

Comments

Whether through formal or informal analyses, the feasibility of undertaking the assessment should be estimated, and should include consideration of the somewhat hidden but necessary resources and aids discussed above. Careful, open consideration of the needed resources can help establish credibility of an assessment effort with constituent groups. Institutions with experience in assessment have warned against trying to do too much in too little time (Marchese, 1987). Programs may suffer from a lack of credibility if they are viewed as being too ambitious, or spending more time or money than available. Many successful assessment programs began small and developed gradually (Terenzini, 1989). Beginning with a pilot program provides an opportunity to assuage concerns about unclear motives, identify unanticipated consequences before making major commitments, and allow time for refinements in the process.

In contrast to setting overly ambitious goals, excessive or single-minded concern about necessary resources may lead to a program that is not comprehensive enough, one that provides easily collected but less worthwhile information, or in other ways stifles the development of a creative program. Such narrow or inadequate programs may lack credibility, and lead to the conclusion that the institution is not serious about assessment. If viewed as only an academic exercise, the program is unlikely to obtain the necessary cooperation and acceptance.

This discussion identified some of the complexities and interrelatedness of the various resources and aids associated with an assessment program. Although a multi-faceted and an intensely human endeavor, a properly conducted assessment can be an extremely valuable tool for an institution of higher education in its effort to improve, and to achieve academic excellence.

References

American Psychological Association. (1985). *Standards for educational and psychological testing*. Washington, D.C.: Author.

American Sociological Association. (1971). *Code of ethics*. Washington, D.C.: Author.

Astin, A. W. (1991). *Assessment for excellence*. New York: American Council on Education and Macmillan Publishing Company.

Astin, A. W., & Ayala, F. (1987). A consortial approach to assessment. *Educational Records, 68*(3), 47–51.

Bowen, H. R. (1985). *The Reform of undergraduate education: Estimated costs*. Invited paper presented at a Wingspread Conference, Racine, WI.

Boyer, C. M. & Ewell, P. T. (1988, March). *State-based approaches to assessment in undergraduate education: A glossary and selected references*. Denver, CO: Educational Commission of States.

Boyer, C. M., Ewell, P. T., Finley, J. E., & Mingle, J. R. (1987). Assessment and outcomes measurement: A view from the states. *AAHE Bulletin, 39*(7), 8–12.

Braskamp, L. A. (1989). So, what's the use? In P. J. Gray (Ed.), Achieving assessment goals using evaluation techniques. *New Directions for Higher Education, 17*(3), 43–50.

Cross, K. P. & Angelo, T. A. (1988). *Classroom assessment techniques*. Ann Arbor, MI: National Center for Research to Improve Teaching.

Dennison, G. M. & Bunda, M. A. (1989). Assessment and academic judgments in higher education. In P. J. Gray (Ed.), Achieving Assessment goals using evaluation techniques. *New Directions for Higher Education, 17*(3), 51–70.

Erwin, T. D. (1991). *Assessing student learning and development.* San Francisco: Jossey-Bass.

Ewell, P.T. (1987, June). Assessment, accountability and improvement aging the contradiction. Paper presented at the second national conference on assessment of the American Association for Higher Education, Denver, Co.

Ewell, P. T. (1988a). Implementing assessment: Some organization issues. In T. W. Banta (ed.), Implementing outcomes assessment: Promise and Perils. New Directions for institutional Research, 15(3), 15–28.

Ewell, P.T. (1988b). Benefits and costs of assessment in higher education: A framework for policy choice and *comparison.* (ED306 809). Alexandria, Virginia: ERIC Document Reproduction Services.

Ewell, P. T. (1989). "Hearts and minds": Some reflections on the ideologies of assessment. *Three presentations: From the fourth national conference on assessment in higher education,* June 21–24,1989, Atlanta. Washington, D.C.: The AAHE Assessment Forum.

Fincher, C. L. (1988, Feb.) Assessing educational outcomes: Are we doing good, can we do better? *Institute of Higher Education Newsletter,* University of Georgia, Athens, GA, pp. 3–7.

Gardiner, L. F. (1989). *Planning for assessment: Mission statements, goals, and objectives.* Trenton, NJ: New Jersey State Department of Education.

Hartle, T. W. (1985). The growing interest in measuring the educational achievement of college students. In C. Adelman (ed.), *Assessment in higher education.* Washington, D.C.: The American Association for Higher Education.

Hillman, M. (1987, March 4). *Comments.* In a joint legislative hearing of the Minnesota House and Senate Higher Education Policy Committees. St. Paul, MN.

Kinnick, M. K. (1985). Increasing the use of student outcomes information. In P. T. Ewell (ed.), Assessing educational outcomes. *New Directions for Institutional Research, 47,* 93–109.

Kimmel, A. J. (1988). *Ethics and values in applied social research.* Newbury Park, CA: Sage Publications.

Lewis, D. R. (1988). Costs and benefits of assessment: A paradigm. In T. W. Banta (Ed .), Implementing outcomes assessment: Promise and perils. *New Directions for Institutional Research, 15(3),* 69–80.

Marchese, T. J. (1987, May). Assessment, accreditation, and institutional effectiveness: Implications for our profession. *General sessions presentations of the 27th annual forum.* Tallahassee, FL: The Association for Institutional Research.

Marchese, T. J. (1988). The uses of assessment. *Liberal Education, 74(3),* 23–36.

Miller, R. I. (1986). Evaluating institutional quality: Some ways and some problems. *International Journal of Institutional Management in Higher Education, 10(3),* 241–251.

Miller, R. I. (1988). Using change strategies to implement assessment programs. In T. W. Banta (Ed.), Implementing outcomes assessment: Promise and perils. New Directions for institutional Research, 15(3), 5–14.

Nichols, J. O. (1989). *Institutional effectiveness and outcomes assessment implementation on campus: A practitioner's handbook.* New York, NY: Agathon Press.

Pratt, L. K. & Reichard, D. R. (1983). Assessing institutional goals. In N. P. Uhl (ed.), Using research for strategic planning. *New Directions for Institutional Research, (37),* 53–66.

Rossman, J. E. & El-Khawas, E. (1987). *Thinking about assessment: Perspectives for presidents and chief academic officers.* Washington, D.C.: American Council on Education and the American Association for Higher Education.

Sell, G. R. (1989). Making assessment work: A synthesis and future directions. In P. J. Gray (ed.), Achieving assessment goals using evaluation techniques. *New Directions for Higher Education,* 17(3), 109–120.

Terenzini, P. T. (1989). Measuring the value of college: Prospects and problems. In C. Fincher (ed.) *Assessing institutional effectiveness: Issues, methods, and management* (pp. 338). Athens, GA: Institute of Higher Education at the University of Georgia.

Thomas, A. M. (1988, May). *Using an evaluation model to guide development of a quality assessment program.* Paper presented at the Annual Forum of The Association for Institutional Research, Phoenix, AZ.

Thomas, A. M. (1990, Oct.) *Differences in importance of standards among phases of a quality assessment program.* Paper presented at the Annual Meeting of the American Evaluation Association, Washington, D.C.

Lessons from Pilot Projects

Joanna S. Worthley and Matt L. Riggs

The goal of the evaluation study was to identify features across the fifteen pilot projects which were consistently associated with effective assessment programs. Effectiveness was defined by a number of outcomes, including project longevity, impact on curriculum, cooperative attitudes toward assessment, and visibility of assessment efforts. At the outset, we identified 24 *environmental* and *methodological* factors expected to influence project success. Among those, eight variables emerged as the strongest predictors of both direct and indirect outcomes of the project initiatives. In brief, the eight are:

- **Measurement issues:** Measurement adequacy, especially reliability and validity

- **Audience:** Intended breadth of project dissemination

- **Administrative support:** Helpful administrative practice/policy

- **Faculty involvement:** Faculty "ownership"/investment

- **Assessment expertise:** Project directors' assessment background/experience

- **Faculty workload:** Perceived "burden" of assessment activities

- **Multicultural issues:** Attention to diversity in measurement content/ strategies

- **Multiple measures:** Extent of "cross-checking" through use of multimeasures in a single domain

Our study showed that in the pilot projects overall, careful attention to these eight factors was consistently associated with several measures of effectiveness. The identification of a "common list" confirms our expectation that characteristics of successful projects could be defined across curricular boundaries, and provides a baseline prescription for implementing assessment. Thus, for the "big picture" the projects' curricular diversity is an advantage—it allows us to say that specific features of assessment initiatives are critical to outcomes—whatever the discipline.

Nonetheless, the projects' diversity shouldn't be ignored; their differences may be a source of information. The assessments we surveyed differed on several dimensions, including *setting, focus,* and *strategies*. For example, among the project *settings* were a theatre department, a gerontology program, and an economics department; project focus included the assessment of an experimental theatre ensemble curriculum, a cross-campus description of curricular goals and content for CSU-based gerontology programs, and the creation of a "local" manual for computer-assisted teaching in economics; and assessment *strategies* involved evaluations conducted by hired consultants, evaluations based on a systemwide survey of gerontology initiatives, and student evaluations of the laboratory component of introductory economics courses. In addition, the projects differed on *level* of assessment—from the level of development of individual measurement strategies, through program-, campus-, and course-level assessments.

As we've noted, differences on these dimensions do not prevent general inferences based on project outcomes overall; in fact, they provide essential guidelines for "big picture" planning, certainly for planning at the campus or system level. However, these same differences are likely to assume more importance for planning individual projects. Given the range of these projects, faculty just embarking on assessment will surely be interested to know whether the specific factors we've identified take on differential importance for different kinds of assessment attempts.

To provide some help with this, we looked for ways to group the projects on the basis of shared features. On most dimensions (i.e., setting, strategy, focus, and level), subgroups can be discerned. For example, on the *strategy* dimension, we can identify projects using similar measurement techniques (e.g., "homegrown" v. "off-the-shelf" measurement), or, within *focus*, locate projects which have assessed comparable programs. In fact, the dimensions above form a continuum of shared features. Beginning with setting, we find little basis for grouping the projects, but as we move across focus, strategy and level, the number of shared features increases. What would seem most useful for assessment planning, then, is to look at the projects by *level*, in part because *level* strongly influences *strategy and focus*, but, more importantly, because grouped by level, the projects appear similar in "magnitude" and audience.

Arranged by *level*, the projects form four groups: (1) measurement-level; (2) program-level; (3) campus-level; and (4) course-level evaluations of student outcomes. Within each level we describe projects *by focus* and *strategy*, then present the predictor variables from which inferences for the project *type* may be drawn. What we focus on in this second analysis is the order of the eight predictor variables which showed the strongest association with project success in our original analysis. The order for each project type was established through a reanalysis of the original data with the projects now grouped by level.

Project Type

Measurement-Level Assessment Strategies

Project	Focus and Strategy
Theatre Program Outcomes	Sought to document formative and summative achievement through development of a mastery test in theatre knowledge, plus evaluation of theatre ensemble teaching method.
Evaluation of Teacher	Designed an "assessment course" to test subject mastery.
Credential Candidates Competency in English Language Arts	
Exit Assessment for Majors in Mathematics/Biology/Economics	Three "sister" CSUs designed major "comp" exams in collaboration with faculty from relevant departments. The assessment includes an innovative plan to administer exams using faculty from cooperating departments as "outside" consultants.

Rank Order of Variables

- Multiple measures
- Measurement issues
- Faculty involvement
- Multicultural issues
- Audience
- Assessment expertise
- Faculty workload
- Administrative support

The rank order of predictor variables for measurement-level projects is consistent with their focus: Each of these projects developed a comprehensive measure of end-point outcomes where none existed before; not surprisingly, measurement issues appear at the top of the list. Bear in mind that in most cases, each of the eight indicators contributes importantly to project success; what the *relative* importance of these variables can tell us is which types of projects will put particular pressures on specific resources for assessment activities. For example, in the list above, faculty workload and administrative support assume the least importance with respect to the other predictors; this was not the case for the projects overall, where both indicators ranked higher on the list. In the measurement level group, we can speculate that faculty workload is a somewhat less important indicator because comprehensive exams are typically developed by faculty in their own major departments, where certification of majors is an expected (not added) part of workload. Similarly, administrative support is relatively less important at this level, probably because "comps" are part of the normal departmental agenda and require more measurement expertise than administrative backing.

Program-Level Assessment Strategies

Project	Focus and Strategy
Assessment of Systemwide Gerontology Programs	Measuring effects of curricular variety and program type/organization on student outcomes, particularly for post-graduates.
Portfolio Assessment in Liberal Studies	Design and implementation of a portfolio assessment system for outcomes in an interdisciplinary liberal studies program to make assessment activities an integral part of the curriculum.
Nursing School Program Outcomes	Evaluating competency test ourcomes, worlplace competency, and the relation of program performance indicators (e.g., GPA) to job performance.
Review of General Education	Program evaluation in an Interdisciplinary General Education program.
Program Review in 5 Areas	Exit and post-grad assessment of majors' performance and student/employer perceptions of program effectiveness in 5 areas: anthropology, political science and sociology.
Evaluation of a Liberal Studies Program	Multimeasure assessment of student outcomes in a liberal studies program.

Rank Order of Variables

- Faculty involvement
- Administrative support
- Faculty workload
- Audience
- Assessment expertise
- Measurement issues
- Multicultural issues
- Multiple measures

Here, where the reach of the projects is greater, faculty, audience, and administrative features take on greater importance. Most of the projects in this category include both current students and alumni in their assessments, most are intended to survey large numbers of students, and several are designed to continue data collection well beyond the year term of the pilot projects. Moreover, the directors of these projects expect to share information fairly widely, both with analogous CSU programs and, in some cases, with non-academic constituencies, particularly potential employers for the discipline area. Consistent with this wider scope, administrative backing is more closely tied to project outcomes. No longer "in house," the program-level projects need both the resources and the legitimacy that administrative sponsorship can provide. Project scope is also one likely reason that faculty workload appears high on the list; project directors' self-report indicates that assessments beyond the course or department level are likely to be conducted as "overload" activities. A second reason for the significance of workload in this group of projects may be that faculty with measurement skills are likely to be recruited to the "ambitious" projects, with little guarantee that their discipline-based quantitative skills (e.g., in the physical or behavioral sciences) applied to assessment will count toward promotion and tenure.

Once more, the indicators which are ranked lower in terms of project outcomes for this group aren't unimportant; their link to outcomes is established. What seems to be true for this set of projects is that directors who have undertaken program assessments already have some assessment expertise, so the measurement aspects are perceived to be "under control."

Campus-Level Assessment Strategies

Project	Focus and Strategy
Assessment of Undergraduate Writing Competence	Analysis of student outcomes on upper division (UD) writing exam assesses student performance as a function of enrollment in UD writing course and language proficiency.
Assessment of Undergraduate Reading Competence	Analysis of students' reading strategies/skills related to differential course assignments and library skills/use.

Rank Order of Variables

- Measurement issues
- Assessment expertise
- Multicultural issues
- Faculty workload
- Audience
- Administrative support
- Multiple measures
- Faculty involvement

The pilot projects in the group we defined as campus-level operate in a particular niche: These are projects which assess an aspect of the shared curriculum in the CSU. One example in this category is the assessment of campus strategies for certifying students' writing proficiency at the level required for graduation. The focus of such projects is both sweeping and narrow: Upper division writing competence is required of everyone, so the samples are very large, but the assessment itself looks at a limited but critical sample of student performance. The indicators most closely associated with outcomes for this type of project, measurement issues, assessment expertise, and multicultural issues, make sense: This is an assessment initiative with high visibility, with important implications for large groups of students, and one in which multicultural issues play a crucial role through the relationship of such culturally related aspects of performance as proficiency in first and second languages. Of course, measurement issues (especially reliability and validity) are key factors at every level of assessment; what probably accounts for their primacy in the campus-level initiatives reported here is the level of methodological sophistication demanded by the goals of this project type, which include: (1) the assessment of undergraduate competence in a basic skill area, (2) the statistical comparison of proficiency levels by group-based characteristics such as course experience, primary language, transfer status, etc., and (3) the statistical demonstration of relationships between competency in basic skill areas and performance outcomes on a variety of other academic measures.

Course-Level Assessment Strategies

Project	*Focus and Strategy*
Western Civilization Course Review	Assessment of pre- and post-course knowledge and attitudes in a Western civilization class.
Student Outcomes in Remedial Writing	Assessment of an Intensive Learning Experience (ILE) writing course sequence.

Rank Order of Variables

- Multiple measures
- Administrative support
- Faculty involvement
- Faculty workload
- Multicultural issues
- Audience
- Measurement issues
- Assessment expertise

Course level assessments in our study have focused on the measurement of post-course changes in attitudes and performance for limited student samples. This project type shares several problems related to short-term assessment, including: (1) time limitations, (2) limited control over non-course influences which may produce changes attributed to in-course experience, and (3) problems with conclusions resulting from the gap between attitude/perception change and *behavioral* change. It's no surprise then that the indicator most related to project outcomes is multiple measures: One way to increase confidence in pre/post-test results is to collect performance evidence using more than one method. An example of this strategy from this group is the multiple measurement of outcomes in the writing project: Student gains were indexed through portfolio evaluations, a questionnaire aimed at affective and cognitive variables associated with growth in writing, and a statistical comparison of "pass" rates for students in different course sequences. In light of the relatively lower ranking of administrative support in measurement-level projects, its higher ranking here seems anomalous, since several features of these project types overlap. A likely explanation is that the significance of this variable for the two projects in this group is project–specific rather than a general phenomenon. On the other hand, the other top indicators, faculty involvement and faculty workload, could be anticipated for course-level assessment. There are at least three features of course-level assessments that make special demands on faculty. First, by definition these assessments are undertaken by individual faculty, who may be adopting the pre/post-design to replace post-only testing. Pre/post-testing suggests an expanded commitment to assessment; tracking changes in student outcomes over time means increased demands on individual faculty's resources. Second, course-level initiatives differ from grade-driven testing in content areas in that the former develop explicit mechanisms to compare outcomes as a function of course content and approach; that is, they establish the link between assessments and course modifications to improve teaching. Finally, in our study, course level assessments piloted the inclusion of affective as well as cognitive variables in looking at student outcomes. While there is considerable interest in the assessment of affective variables, e.g., commitment to life-long learning, altruism, and social consequences (Virginia Commonwealth University, 1988), affective outcomes are difficult to capture, and require specific faculty expertise for adequate measurement.

Summary and Conclusions

Our efforts to define the baseline characteristics of successful assessment projects in the CSU provide two crucial lessons for future assessment initiatives. First, the results of our study suggest that attention to eight factors: measurement, audience, administrative support, faculty involvement, assessment experience, faculty workload, multicultural issues, and multiple measures is critical to effective assessment practice. Moreover, our reanalysis of the key indicators shows that in each project group, the ordering of predictor variables changes, suggesting that a project's level influences the *relative* contribution of these factors to project outcomes. Grouping the assessments allows planners to locate their project type among the levels we've identified, and to use the *order* of the critical variables presented as guidelines in project development. Thus a second lesson for future assessments emerges from the projects' diversity: At least within systems comparable to the CSU, settings (e.g., department or program affiliation) have less impact on assessment effectiveness than focus (e.g., curriculum or program revision), strategy (e.g., "local" versus "off-the-shelf" measures), or level (e.g., measurement construction or departmental self-study). In particular, establishing the level of proposed projects can help anticipate the differential impact of the factors we've identified as critical to project success. Attention to these baseline characteristics, and to their relative importance for specific project types, should prove helpful in future assessment initiatives in the CSU.

References

Virginia Commonwealth University (1988). *Values.* Unpublished report of the VCU Ad Hoc Value Committee, Office of Vice President for Academic Affairs.

Creating a Context Where Institutional Assessment Yields Educational Improvement

Marcia Mentkowski

A multitude of settings and a variety of definitions characterize assessment today. Educators and administrators from a wide range of large and small, public and private, institutions are struggling with the process of assessing student performance, program validity, and institutional effectiveness (American Council on Education 1990; El-Khawas 1989; Ewell 1984, 1987, 1988; Heywood 1989; Hutchings and Marchese 1990). Whether we are veterans or novices in this complex, almost chaotic world of discussion about and experience with assessment, we do have much in common.

First, we all want assessment to make a difference. Those of us who are just beginning the discussion in our institutions are wary of jumping onto a bandwagon without a clear view of the pitfalls (Banta 1988; Terenzini 1989). (Some may even feel tempted at times to obstruct or denature assessment for fear it will have a negative impact. Such an attitude is not opposition to assessment; it is a passionate dedication to seeing that assessment makes the right kind of difference.) Indeed, institutions first joining the issue may have the most intense concern with impact and results: they may be the most under the gun to come up with results that people want to use.

Similar issues arise for those of us who are heavily involved in doing assessment (Hutchings 1988). Each of us is trying to figure out how to refine the ways assessment works in our classroom, our department, our institution, or our state. The more we succeed, the more others want in on the action. We become more and more concerned not only with whether and how to do assessment, but with ensuring that our efforts matter (Loacker 1988). And some of us now know the questions, issues, and problems involved in making results matter. We now have something in place and are free to refine assessment, even to create new ways of doing it. But that also puts us in the position, like it or not, of helping to set the tone for the national dialogue about how to make assessment a keystone in educational reform. Assessment will rise or fall as educators like us grapple frankly with the issue of how to improve programs, not just to make institutions accountable.

Second, we share some common educational values that center on expanding human knowledge and educating diverse students for a changing and challenging world. Many of us spend a major part of our lives working to add to or restructure the knowledge in our disciplines and to transform that knowledge into an effective, vital force in individual and public life. Our pilgrims' progress toward assessment represents an unparalleled research opportunity: to discover how adults learn, and in particular how they learn the perspectives and values, the information and skills, the trained habits of mind, that characterize our respective fields.

Many of us also struggle daily to educate students who will make it in college and in society only if what we do makes a difference. Our dream of effective assessment will not be realized until assessment benefits the learning of each and every student who comes to us. Obviously, the major benefits for students lie in direct assessment of individual student learning (Hutchings 1990; Loacker et al. 1986). But program and institutional assessment will also benefit each and every student—if we build meaning into these broader processes, so that the results matter to educators and administrators who are in a position to use the information to improve teaching and learning.

Qualities of Institutional Assessment

Amid our diverse definitions and practices of assessment nationwide, I have seen a developing consensus about several essential qualities that distinguish assessment as an emerging practice in higher education from measurement practices in other kinds of institutions. Some of these qualities are ones that professionals in measurement (Messick 1988; Tittle 1989), evaluation (Gray 1989; Guba & Lincoln 1989; Patton 1986), educational research (Astin 1985,1991; Light et al. 1990), and institutional research (Ewell 1985) would recognize as universally desirable; others emerge from the particular goals of the educational enterprise.

1. *Assessment is a means, not an end.* Whether we are conducting an external evaluation of programs at the institutional level or assessing the individual student in the classroom, we are not merely gathering data for its own sake, or measuring just anything because an instrument happens to be available. Our efforts are defined by our values and goals, by what we intend to *do* with the information. Basically, in an educational environment, that intention is always two-fold.

2. *Assessment is a means not only to establish accountability but also to achieve educational benefits.* Educators use assessment both to "prove" and to "improve." The state or the trustees may seek evidence of effectiveness for certification, accreditation, or even funding purposes. Educators also assess in order to increase their knowledge of the learning process and to improve its main outcome—student learning.

We may begin educational assessment in order to demonstrate something, but we will remain committed to it only if it results in tangible, day-to-day benefits—not only examining whether we are doing what we intend to do but also suggesting specific efforts and experiments to do it better.

3. *Assessment purposes, goals, and methods emerge from the setting.* An assessment instrument or process that measures something other than what we are trying to do or why we are doing it is at best pointless, at worst damaging. Educators involved in a program are the best source of definition for their values, rationales, and objectives, for some of the tough questions that need to be asked, and for what kinds of information will make a positive difference.

Even the best external models and materials must be painstakingly adapted to the institution, program, and classroom in which they are being used. This also holds true over time: as courses programs and institutions evolve, so will their specific objectives and the challenges they face. Purposes goals and methods for assessing their performance must evolve accordingly. Effective assessment considers the immediate context as an essential source of the *what, why,* and *how* of assessing.

4. *Assessment encourages multiplicity.* Successful assessment information especially in such a complex, rapidly changing environment as higher education may yield *comparability* of insights and interpretations about diverse programs. Yet each educational institution has a particular mission and serves a unique population; each program and department, each course, and each educator plays a distinct role in meeting that mission and serving that population.

Educators need to shape varied approaches to assessment, responding to their own questions and situations before they can reach interdepartmental or interinstitutional understandings of what why and how to assess. Likewise different schools and departments will use assessment data to do different things; for a full return on our investment in assessment we need to encourage and develop such multiple strategies.

5. *Assessment encourages coherence.* Assessment is a means toward connected purposeful education. It calls for reexamining the explicit and implicit links between educational goals and student outcomes. It focuses a critical eye on relationships among teaching, learning, and any means that mirror or evaluate the consequences. Assessment encourages coherence when student learning outcomes are mapped in relation to institutional mission values and educational assumptions.

   Effective assessment ultimately demands that its many forms across the institution be connected—if only to make assessment practical and possible. It joins mechanisms that are already delivering useful information with new strategies and reaches out to reconnect itself with all the elements of an effective curriculum and its administrative functions. This may call for discipline-based as well as interdisciplinary approaches and methods. Thus, assessment draws on multiple modes of inquiry.

   Assessment generates even broader connections to all institutions concerned about educational effectiveness. Assessment information stimulates coherence within the institution: students question how to improve; faculty rethink their teaching; departments refine their goals. The results from this process provide a base for communicating with legislators and employers. Ultimately each of society's institutions in kinship with higher education ask "How are we linked to higher learning? How do we achieve a connected, supportive interdependence with postsecondary education?"

6. *Feedback is the essence of assessment.* How, and whether, assessment information is communicated critically affects its value. Different audiences—the state trustees, the registrar, the corporate faculty, the individual instructor, the student, the prospective employer or graduate school—want different kinds of information for their different purposes. But all need timely feedback from the assessment process, data that have been turned into usable information by being made relevant to their concerns. And in educational assessment, two key audiences are educators and students. Unless the data generated by assessment returns to the educational process to improve program and student performance, they will die upon dissemination.

From observing and participating in the nationwide assessment scene for a couple of decades now, this is what I see as an emerging consensus about some essential distinctive qualities of educational assessment. Against that backdrop, I offer the following guidelines for creating a context where educational assessment programs at any level will yield the optimum in educational benefits.

Six Guidelines for Constructing an Assessment Context

1. Make a Long-Term Commitment to a Dynamic Plan

A *long-term commitment* provides stability, allowing us to develop one thing at a time to stay in the present and to keep the future in its place. One of the most frustrating aspects of doing assessment is starting up, working to develop one part of a complex plan, and having someone constantly pressuring you to work on another part of the plan, whether you are ready or not.

By 1973, for example, at Alverno, the faculty had created both a new curriculum and a process for assessing each student's abilities sequentially as she moved through it (Alverno College Faculty [1976]1985, [1979]1985). But as early as 1974, we began receiving a good deal of outside pressure to do program evaluation. By that time, faculty were ready for validating faculty-designed instruments, testing educational assumptions, researching ability definitions, and evaluating alumnae outcomes. Not until 1976, however, when faculty had their new program well in place and we had our first graduates could we turn our attention to evaluating our program systematically or researching its basic educational assumptions. Having a long-term commitment enabled us to stick to the task at hand, refining our assessment of individual student abilities, before we took up the larger, logically subsequent question of validating the broad outcomes of college.

Once we began program assessment and establishing validity, we used a longitudinal design, working with two complete entering classes. For example, one component assessed student performance on outside measures three times during their college years (Mentkowski & Doherty 1983, [1983]1984, 1984; Mentkowski & Loacker 1985). We fed each round of data immediately back into the curriculum. But no sooner had we started than we began to get outside pressure to study our alumnae.

Now, any research and evaluation effort should do followup studies of alumni. But at the time, when we had only a few alumnae from Alverno's new curriculum, it would not have made sense. We held off in fact until 1980, by which time we had researched outstanding professionals (who were not our graduates) for ability models. And by then we had a much clearer view of which overall outcomes of college we wanted to study in our alumnae's lives and careers; we just realized our first full set of longitudinal data in 1988. A long-term commitment helped us keep our eye on what we *could* do and our reasons for doing assessment.

A long-term commitment also creates an atmosphere of purpose and support for using assessment data. Most of us will use information, even though it is at first sketchy and incomplete, if we know there is more coming and that the quality will get better. For example, one group of faculty is currently redesigning one of our in-place, cross-college instruments that we know is not working as well as it might. But because there was a long-term commitment, those who depended on the instrument for individual student feedback as well as those who depended on it for aggregate data were willing to make adjustments until this faculty group had the time—and the insight from other assessment results—to refine it. We were able to deal with what was there, until we had time to make it better (Rogers 1988). An institution, department, or faculty members in the classroom cannot deal with every aspect of assessment at once. But they can resist outside pressures to do something else first, if they have a long-range commitment to what they intend to do.

A *dynamic plan* handles pressure inside the institution as well. It provides an atmosphere of changes, time for redesign, and the constant opportunity to build in elements one might not have thought of at the beginning; the experiences of James Madison University, Kean College of New Jersey, and Kings College bear this out (Farmer 1988; Office of the Vice President for Academic Affairs 1985; Presidential Task Force on Student Learning and Development 1986).

Assessment plans change many times as they are being implemented. A dynamic plan specifically includes the kind of time we need not only to implement but also to revise, rethink, and refine assessment designs. In a dynamic plan, we can at any moment spend time and effort where we really need it, trying out some aspect and making it work on a day-to-day basis, so we can see some results that matter in improved curriculum and student performance.

A dynamic plan is the best response to well-meaning observations from outside about what one should be doing. I learned early on that with a long-range commitment to a dynamic plan, you can satisfy your most stalwart critics. One question we were often asked was, Why not computerize your student information system? We were able to say, "That sounds like a good idea. In fact, we plan to have a completely computerized system including all the relevant information students generate on in-class assessments, so we can see which outcomes of college are realized across the board in classes. That will probably be in 2001. In the meanwhile, we will be working to figure out what kind of information we really want to collect, what we will do with the information once we get it, and how we will use it. In fact, two of our major departments are trying out some ideas like that this semester, to give us a preview of what such a system might look like."

A dynamic plan also influences assessment development. As instructors assess student performance in their courses, discussion and planning for departmental assessment become all but inevitable. Departments planning to collect aggregate data on the outcomes of their major programs are on to a surefire way to inspire better institutional assessment. That puts assessment designers in a better position to create the connections between individual student assessment in the classroom and departmental and curricular evaluation processes. The overlaps in design and multiple uses for assessment data, often from the same instruments, become apparent. Some assessments can be used to give individual feedback to students, enable an instructor to probe the effects of a new teaching strategy, and also form the backbone of a longer-term research and evaluation effort. A dynamic plan encourages such grass-roots development of assessment.

In my early work with assessment, I often made the mistake of being reactive, responding to outside pressure instead of being proactive and communicating the dynamic nature of what we were doing. I have learned that the most convincing argument for what you are doing is actually doing it.

2. Rely on Faculty Questions for Direction

It is a cardinal rule of program evaluation that unless data responds to questions important to those who will *act* as a result of the Wormation it is not good data (Weiss 1983). Students are best helped by information from tests if they can use it to improve. Faculty are best helped by assessment results—to improve instruction or advise students more effectively—when assessment is derived from their questions as educators.

Finding out what educators' questions are has proven to be a remarkably simple process, one that also shows faculty how easily they can become involved in assessment. It presents assessment designers with the issues and realities of their own institution's context. At Alverno, we draw our student-assessment and program-evaluation-research designs from faculty questions. In fact, we have gathered complex arrays of inquiry to guide a year or more of work from a faculty workshop at a year-end institute. Since 1985, the AAHE Research Forum at the ACHE annual conference has engaged nationwide samplings of educators in a similarly compact, productive exercise (Mentkowski & Chickering 1987). In a 1989 preconference session, 42 conference presenters spent three hours generating a host of questions on six conference topics expected to help improve teaching, learning, and assessment. The next day, 129 educators produced additional sets of questions on the six topics, including "assessment of student learning" and "assessment of institutional effectiveness" (AAHE Research Forum 1989; Mentkowski & Banta 1989). The annual AAHE Research Agenda (available from this author) is created from this broad array of educator questions and disseminated to other higher education associations.

Educators know what they need to know to improve education: data gathered in response to educators' questions will more likely be used. Through questions, faculty establish both the meaning of assessment and the uses to which its results will be put. This helps guarantee that assessment's results are linked intimately to its purposes, to create a feedback loop that faculty can rely on. In addition, assessment generated from faculty questions gains credibility among students. Because it is linked to their most important concerns about teaching and learning, faculty reinforce student participation and belief in assessment.

3. Create Interactive Processes

Once an assessment plan is in place, faculty involvement continues to establish its meaning and use. Educators begin to establish which instruments are valid and relevant and which interpretations of results are credible for what purposes. Faculty involvement in deciding which instruments to use, and in designing and developing instruments that measure outcomes they see as essential, is becoming important in assessment practice. Just because an instrument is psychometrically valid does not necessarily mean it will yield results that are credible and useful to a particular educator or group of educators. Credibility emerges only through an interactive process, in which faculty construct assessment and so maintain their involvement.

Such interactive processes create a context where people can respond to each other, connect with each other's interests, work out emerging concerns, and begin to construct a conceptual base for assessment (Mentkowski 1990). They begin to take collaborative responsibility for assessment. For example, the New Jersey Department of Higher Education (College Outcomes Evaluation Program 1987) involved educators across the state in designing assessment. Julia Rogers and her colleagues at the University of Montevallo (Rogers et al. 1988) and Michael McGuire (1988) at the college of Lake County involved faculty at their respective institutions in reviewing a standardized measure of college outcomes against institutional goals to determine whether results would have credibility at their institutions. Would student data from this instrument be meaningful to faculty? Would it help them improve teaching and learning? Faculty at both institutions already had identified goals and detailed views on which information could be used effectively, and how. Soliciting and being guided by those goals and views averted major difficulties and created a system for communicating credible, usable results.

Two task forces—community college and baccalaureate—representing Washington State institutions of higher education engaged in a similar exercise. Along with administering three standardized measures to students in the consortium, more than 100 of their faculty completed some of the same materials and critiqued them for how they reflected institutional goals and whether the information would be useful (Council of Presidents and State Board for Community College Education 1989). Such critique, in advance as well as after use of standardized measures (Banta et al. 1987), can lead to improved assessment techniques.

A similar kind of faculty involvement occurred in a 24-institution consortium organized on assessment design (Alverno College/FIPSE Assessment Project 1987; Schulte et al. 1989). After designing their own instruments for measuring abilities important at their campus, faculty collaborated in a critique of their work across two Alverno workshops. Among other approaches, they reviewed initial designs against criteria and studied student performance examples to extend the evaluation (Alverno College Office of Research and Evaluation/Assessment Committee, in press). The result was a set of improved instruments. Similarly, faculty at the University of Wisconsin Medical School at Madison developed ability criteria and refined them over time through progressive tryouts (Stone & Meyer 1989).

At Alverno our interview studies of the abilities of outstanding professionals in nursing and management were designed and conducted by Office of Research and Evaluation staff (DeBack & Mentkowski 1986; Mentkowski et al. 1982). But faculty from both departments were involved in deciding which professionals to interview, choosing and creating instruments, coding the interviews, and interpreting and writing up the results. The next task, comparing the professionals' abilities with those taught in college, proceeded apace, since the study had been crafted to yield results meaningful to educators in both departments. Another interview study extended the method across a range of departments (Schall et al. 1984). Our new computer studies department used a similar interview strategy to test whether their curriculum was advancing or trailing this newly emerging field, and how the abilities of new graduates were actually being played out in a range of postcollege settings (Kennedy 1988). Our faculty and others ("Student Potential Assessed at Rhode Island College" 1989) used modified versions of the interview (Council for Adult and Experiential Learning and McBer & Company 1987) to help determine the abilities of prospective students with weak academic credentials. Taken together, these examples expand the role and benefit of faculty investment in assessment.

Interactivity also enhances student involvement in program assessment. Alverno students whom we asked to volunteer were willing when given extensive rationales for the project and regular reports of individual and group results. By giving them individual feedback on their development in learning styles and then showing how their participation could help lead to greater degree credibility, for example, we were able to sustain participation in a longitudinal study (Mentkowski & Strait 1983).

In our followup study of alumnae five years after college, providing individual and group feedback has been the key to sustaining participation. Preliminary data from a group with 85 percent participation, given to another group to show what graduates were doing five years after graduation, increased the second group's participation (Reisetter & Sandoval 1987).

When faculty, students, and alumnae actively participate in assessment, results are more credible for all of them—and for additional audiences such as trustees, nationwide colleagues, and government agencies.

4. Define Criteria and Comparisons Publicly

To make meaning out of data, people generally try to make some kind of comparison. The notion of "good" student performance, for example, almost inevitably elicits the question, "good compared to what?" Unless we deal with that question, assessment information can lack credibility. Establishing credibility of the criteria—of the comparisons they imply—is one of the most difficult tasks in assessment. If assessment judgments are to be useful for improving performance, the criteria must be *publicly* defined and reflect a *consensus* on the "good" being sought at the level of action and change. This is as true for general education or a major department as for the institution as a whole.

Faculty involvement in defining criteria and making them public is critical. Educators defining general education goals may work across disciplines and from their experience with past student performance to reach consensus on goals, standards, and criteria. They create a community of judgment for deciding what is "good" and work to help each other and their students understand the "why" behind their expert judgment, the "how" of improving.

Faculty in a major department are also the key link between assessment and improvement. As they make clear what the goals and criteria are and where they come from, they simultaneously point out specific avenues for curricular design. Aided by analyses of student performance on course exams, portfolios, or capstone measures, they continue to illuminate criteria for good performance, relying in part on expertise, on years of deciphering and judging student work. In part, faculty are often relying on fairly clear-cut criteria developed by a discipline for text analysis in literary criticism, for example, or the scientific method in lab experiments. On a psychology department comprehensive exam, students may be meeting criteria established not only by their professors but by all the psychology departments in the state. But in each case—general education or the major—faculty motivation to use information from assessment to improve depends on whether they have implicitly or explicitly defined the criteria explaining what is "good" and why. And these criteria can inform comparisons within and across departments.

Defining standards at the institutional level provides a similar challenge. It is often made more difficult by the temptation to select external measures created outside the department or university, without a faculty review process. Bypassing the faculty may appear justified when curriculum goals and criteria are only implicit and there is outside pressure for immediate results. But insisting that goals and criteria from general education and the major stay up front stimulates faculty investment in this process and can lead to their involvement in clarifying goals.

Some years ago, such external tests often had automatic credibility because they were standardized, now their results often have little credibility with faculty if curriculum goals cannot be clearly linked to what a test measures and its implied comparisons (Council of Presidents and State Board for Community College Education 1989). Standardized tests seldom can publish their assumed criteria or identify enough of the characteristics of norm groups to enable credible comparisons. Many of the most familiar standardized tests were not designed as college-outcomes measures. Nor is it fair to assume that an instrument designer or company creating measures for cross-institutional use could answer for a single institution's faculty what is good, at what level their students should perform, or what the criteria should be.

A faculty, for example, may have decided and set forth in its mission statement that their students should develop "critical thinking." External measures may seem to offer an "objective" or "outside" reading and be readily available. What can such a test really tell this faculty? With a recognition measure, an item-by-item readout may help a faculty analyze patterns for clues to how students perform on items related to department goals.

An objective test, standardized to the current levels of student performance across the country at other colleges, cannot tell the faculty at what level they want their students to perform. Nor can its purveyors offer many clues as to the relationship between scores on the test and the components of critical thinking defined in a department's goals: the latter remains a faculty task—possible only if item-by-item scores are part of the package. Production measures can open up a more in-depth analysis of performance on broad abilities. For example, Perry's patterns of intellectual development in the college years may help a faculty draw relationship between sophistication in intellectual development and students' performance on class or capstone seminar papers and projects (Knefelkamp & Widick 1982; Mentkowski, Moeser & Strait 1983; Perry 1970).

The faculty might find a college in one state that seems similar in size or entrance standards or governance or even programs and compare scores or patterns with that school. But what would they do with the findings then? In fact, such comparison scores may have little educational improvement meaning for either institution, particularly if one cannot easily factor in specific information on students' preparation for college, retention rates, or cultural background.

Faculty are far more likely to be motivated by data from measures they have had a hand in designing, that take into account their own criteria for student performance, drawn from their institutional goals. And they are likely to find far more meaning and use in a range of comparisons. In fact, ACE's 1990 Campus Trends data reports that 66 percent of the respondents design their own instruments (American Council on Education 1990).

Using faculty-designed measures as one basis for comparison, a number of others will likely arise. Many faculty are acutely aware of employers' dissatisfaction with graduates' communication and thinking abilities. Undergraduate professional school students take teacher tests or nursing state boards. Many major departments take readings of student performance on graduate school entrance exams and consequent admissions. Alumni satisfaction, salary, and job surveys are common. While these comparisons may yield success indicators, they are less likely to yield information on the "how" of improving. Extending the range of comparison yields that benefit.

Student's performance data could be compared to criteria drawn from institutional mission statements and department goals. But student performance could also be compared to beginning, developing, and advanced descriptions of student potential; to the judgments of colleagues from other colleges; and to disciplinary or professional standards; and/or the abilities of outstanding alumni and other professionals. In the 1970s, for example, seven colleges agreed to use a number of instruments as part of a study of college outcomes from critical thinking to self-definition and maturity. With the help of a FIPSE grant, students at each college completed McBer & Company's "Cognitive Competence Assessment Battery" at the beginning and end of college. The investigators could have simply compared each college's freshman-senior score gains against the average of the other six, assuming that a high score is the "good" all seven institutions sought. Instead, they analyzed the several mission statements and when they reported their data added whether the college had in fact selected that outcome as one they intended to develop, and then achieved it (Winter et al. 1981). This approach helped set the context for using the data once delivered, because it had been related directly to whether and how closely each institution's goals were being met. Instead of wondering, "Do we look good?" "Do we look bad?" each faculty could ask some serious questions: "How do we want our students to change?" "Are we satisfied?" and "What could we do better?"

In the Appalachian College Assessment Consortium, assessment questions are likewise drawn from the goals of the general education program at each college (Carey 1987). In one component of their approach, selected faculty members are each directly involved in conducting interviews with three seniors not from the faculty member's discipline. These faculty interviewers pool their information about college outcomes, along with reflections about what worked and did not during the interviews. Such a strategy that involves faculty in the data collection as well as the interpretation provides a unique opportunity for cross-institution comparison within the framework of each college's distinct mission.

Similarly, learning and personal growth outcomes of students can be compared against those descriptions of human growth and potential that emerge from the psychological literature (e.g., cognitive-developmental patterns of growth or arrays of critical thinking skills) (Chickering & Associates 1981; Gardner 1983; Mentkowski 1988; Sternberg 1985). Each of these more external pictures of what students ought to achieve given what is expected in work and personal life can stimulate comparisons that faculty and students consider credible. Trustees, higher education boards, and legislative groups are drawn toward comparisons that ask: Are we educating students toward abilities that project what society will need years from now?

The Association of American Colleges created opportunities for faculty from fifty-one departments in eighteen institutions to collaborate on designing senior-level assessments. Then faculty served as "external examiners" for the culminating work of seniors who were not their own. The comparison led to a new appreciation by departments of an outside view of student achievement. Contrary to their expectations, students greeted with enthusiasm the chance to present their work to a broader range of expert judgments (Fong 1988; Resnick & Schneider in press).

A dozen learned societies responsible for arts and sciences fields are involved with the Association of American Colleges in rethinking their majors, and are designating content knowledge and intellectual abilities that should be developed by students through the major. As this work develops, these descriptions could form another backdrop against which a department can view its own goals for its undergraduate majors (Carol G. Schneider, personal communication, 22 February 1990).

Another comparison that can be helpful is between abilities selected by faculty and those demonstrated by outstanding members of the discipline's professional groups. For example, the explicit descriptions of the effective professional drawn from performance studies (Boyatzis 1982; Mentkowski et al. 1982) can stimulate a professional school faculty to view the expected abilities of their graduates against the actual performance of partitioners they respect (Evarts 1982); a curriculum can be reviewed with an eye toward how well it prepares students to take on professional roles, abilities, and skills. These professional abilities can be further compared against a department's own effective alumni.

The point is that there is a wide array of meaningful and challenging comparisons that educators and their constituencies can make with their assessment data. And making such comparisons clear and public draws faculty more and more into involvement with assessment while enabling them to learn more and more from it.

5. Translate Results into Relevant, "Live" Information

The last two guidelines get down to the nitty-gritty of communicating assessment data so that it results in decisions and action plans for improvement. Assessment information, effectively transmitted, should raise even more questions than it provides answers; our challenge is to turn data into the kinds of "live" information that inspires student or faculty insights and questions that foster change. Whether or not people use information to improve depends on how they get the message. That the medium is the message is as true of assessment data as it is of any other information. Understanding data and interpreting it is a prerequisite for using it.

In the classroom, individual performance data needs to be made understandable and personal to each student; program assessment data often need to be communicated across a wide range of disciplines and even institutions. How do we engage people in the data we are reporting, and how do we provide avenues for them to enter the work of improvement? First, we must speak in plain English. As a developmental psychologist, I tended to throw numbers and charts at faculty, whether they were from the fine arts or the sciences. After one such presentation, a music instructor commented that it was a fine performance but asked, "What did it all mean?" Second, we must address our listeners' common concerns. As one colleague said to me, "You'll need to do more than use beautiful colors and well-executed graphics to draw fine arts faculty into analyzing charts. Maybe you should step back and ask yourself what *all* of our faculty have in common." Of course, what they have in common is students—and that is why assessment data need to evoke understanding of the individual student's performance and perspective. Faculty are eager to learn the educational beliefs, goals, and motivations of students, as well as to see their personal growth, abilities, and learning. After all, understanding students is how educators become better at what they do.

I also learned that most of us have to hear one student voice first. Aggregate data does not relate directly to our experience of students as individuals: we are motivated to help students improve by listening to them one at a time. I finally hit upon the technique of presenting students' testimony and photographs, in a slide-accompanied audiotape. This is something that works; it starts faculty talking, and before you know it, they are asking, "Is this how we want our students to turn out? What in our curriculum might be causing this?" Criteria for good performance get clarified; further inquiries and experiments are born. After an early slidetape, that same music instructor asked whether we also had any *quantitative* patterns that further illustrated students' learning. Once he had heard one student, he began to ask about patterns.

Aggregate data can be valuable if we make the link between it and individual data. Without that connection, and without visible intra- and interindividual patterns, aggregate data seldom makes sense (Collins & Horn, in press; Willett 1988). This flies in the face of the way we are used to seeing data presented—group results, a synthesis of interview topics and patterns, a set of numbers with group averages highlighted.

Experience has also taught me that department or institutionwide assessment programs, no matter how well conceived, are no substitute for the ongoing assessment of individual students in classes and the clues to educational improvement that such data provide. Institutional assessment is a way to step back from a whole curriculum, but it does not do the job that individual educators must do to give ongoing, personal feedback to their students.

6. Create Feedback—Usable Knowledge About Performance— that Stimulates Improvement

Communicating "live" information enables faculty and students to understand assessment data, to make meaning out of it for themselves, and to focus on change. Another element also enables the move from data to decisions: feedback—usable knowledge about performance. Working with both student and program assessment, we have found that the most critical element in using data to improve is feedback that encourages students and faculty to create change. Whether it is presented to a student or to an institution, feedback needs *to focus on strengths as well as weaknesses* (Loacker et al. 1986). In fact, in the beginning of an assessment process, whether individual or institutional, it is essential to begin with strengths, to present confirming information. It is clear that strength-first feedback to a student that clarifies the positive aspects of a performance builds the confidence that allows her to examine more closely what parts missed the mark.

I used a similar strategy in one of the first presentations I made to our faculty on program evaluation data drawn from in-depth interviews of ten students who had just graduated from our new curriculum. I did not attempt to compare one student with another, or to compare this group to earlier graduates. Instead, I prepared a synthesis of some of the constructions these students made about their educational experience, sketching them in broad terms and then illustrating with quotes from the students. This was very confirming for faculty: They had evidence that *some* students were internalizing *some* of the broad educational principles undergirding lifelong learning on which the curriculum was built. Soon afterward they wanted to know, "Do all students make meaning like this?" No, not all; but by that time they were open to hearing about those who did not.

Second, to elicit implications for change, feedback works best when it comes from *more than one data source*, from multiple measures and standards. Data often goes unused when faculty's numerous, urgent questions have been reduced to a single measure, or worse, to one issue. Such data most often elicit dichotomies from listeners. Recall the student who says, "Well, maybe I didn't show I could do it on *that* test, but I did it in class the rest of the semester." Recall the college that says, "Well, maybe our students didn't show change *here, but* after all, this measure is fallible."

One measure we used, an attitude survey, showed that students had upward, positive attitudes toward the curriculum for the first two years of college, followed by a negative drop toward the end of the junior year. At the end of the senior year, attitudes returned to their previous positive levels. The faculty worried about this junior-year decline until we examined data from concurrent student interviews, which suggested students were necessarily experiencing conflicts in the transition to their senior year. Using one measure only, however, faculty had no idea what to do with the data. Feedback should focus *on patterns* to encourage the broadest possible thinking about meaning and implications. When we are interested in complexities, we are less likely to see only problem areas. We look for ways to improve and then think about other data we might need.

In one case, when we were presenting data on several learning outcomes at once, we used learning-style measures, samples from student interviews and samples from interviews with alumnae. This enabled faculty to think about the data broadly, rather than focusing only on negative information. And there did seem to be negatives: Some measures showed up-and-down movement over time (similar to that in the attitude survey), while others showed down-then-up. By no means all showed the steady upward climb we associate with "growth." Another pattern appears to underlie the patterns—a new model of growth. That is, when individuals experience new situations, they recycle through earlier forms of thinking and use less sophisticated methods of coping; development is thus more a spiral than a steady upward curve, or a stepwise series of stages (Mentkowski 1988).

This finding flies in the face of much of the psychological literature, which often seems to describe development as linear progress toward maturity. But it has won immediate acceptance from faculty at Alverno and from faculty visitors from other colleges, who quickly see that it confirms a puzzling part of their own experience. We have all been in the situation of assuming that students would come to a new class with all the learning from previous courses at their fingertips, then blaming other faculty or high school teachers when that did not occur. Once this "spiral" picture of learning was explicit, faculty could stop blaming one another and instead could concentrate on learning how to bring students quickly up to speed in new learning situations, to use the kinds of thinking they are capable of. This cemented new bonds among faculty rather than tearing down morale, although many individual results had looked "negative" at first. By focusing on patterns from many sources of data, we were able to create constructive, significant change.

Feedback should *be developmental;* it should *encourage productive change.* Often, this means that the information generated from assessment should include both the clues and tools that clearly suggest next steps.

Departments at the University of Tennessee at Knoxville have also used assessment data to review and subsequently revise departmental goals. The act of engaging in assessment built faculty confidence to make changes. Most important, faculty began "paying more attention to student experience that will increase their ability to *apply* what they are learning in class—providing opportunities for term projects, field trips, and in-class problem solving" (Banta & Schneider 1988, 79).

In one analysis of longitudinal interviews, Alverno students clearly attributed their ability to gradually take responsibility for their own learning to two components of the assessment-forlearning process: feedback on their performance and the opportunity to self-assess (Mentkowski 1988). A faculty committee quickly moved to review key instruments: Did *each* feedback strategy encourage independence? Did self-assessment opportunities gradually elicit *autonomous* evaluations?

Interview studies of professional competence were designed primarily to hold Alverno faculty's ability definitions to the standards of outstanding professional performance. But these studies also generated many descriptions of complex problem situations and the behaviors that led to their resolution. This library of examples keeps classroom case studies up to date, explicit, and engaging. Here, information from assessment helped refine department goals and assessment criteria while providing concrete examples for creating instruction.

Finally, feedback that can be used to improve performance develops self-confidence—and mutual confidence—in students and faculty. One of the major outcomes of an assessment program that encourages change is that individuals become more independent in their own learning and more able to cooperate effectively. Students and alumnae report that the experience of feedback enables them to undertake active, self-sustained learning during college and afterward. Faculty report that having "live" results and feedback from assessment likewise enables them to take risks. When you know you will be getting feedback on new programs, they say, you are more willing to try things out. No longer is there an all-or-nothing atmosphere or sink-or-swim pressure. Instead, students and faculty are alike buoyed by an attitude of support, encouraged to initiate, and given feedback to reflect on and time to experiment and improve.

Conclusions and Next Questions

Six guidelines help construct a context where program and institutional assessment of student learning outcomes result in improvement. The emphasis is on creating a culture where assessment can become an institutionalized component of a university, college, or department's educational enterprise.

First, *making a long-term commitment to a dynamic plan* with both short- and long-term goals can help an institution respond to expectations for immediate results. This creates space to gradually build processes and systems that meet our more ideal purposes, and time to consider newer approaches to assessment design. Second, *relying on faculty questions for direction* helps identify key issues and specific teaching and learning areas most in need of insight and intervention. Generally, some very simple strategies can tap a wide range of faculty perspectives. Third, *creating interactive processes* sets the stage for gathering the right kinds of information, involving the central players, and holding the kinds of dynamic discussions for interpreting results and debating implications. A culture of assessment is a product of student and faculty investment.

I am persuaded that one of the more challenging tasks in assessment of student learning outcomes is to generate credible assessment information. This leads to the fourth guideline: *Define criteria and comparisons publicly*. What student outcomes are "good"? Are they "good" compared to "what"? The challenge comes in achieving a consensus on the "good" at the level of action and change. Once again, involving faculty and staff directly responsible for using the information to improve student learning is critical.

The kinds of credible comparisons available to answer the "good compared to what" questions are few. That is another part of the challenge. Examples that have some track record include comparison of student learning outcomes to criteria drawn from: (a) institutional mission statements or department goals; (b) developmental pictures of student growth during college; (c) judgments of interdisciplinary colleagues or those from another campus; (d) disciplinary or professional standards as these become available; and/or (e) abilities of outstanding alumni and other professionals. It takes a good deal of effort to identify and then deliver on sets of comparisons that will engage a faculty or staff in interpreting the data and implementing implied changes.

Guidelines 5 and 6 argue for *translating results into relevant, "live" information* and *creating feedback—usable knowledge about performanc—that stimulates improvement*. Assisting each audience to build interpretations from information that addresses common concerns, crosses disciplinary boundaries. meets disciplinary criteria, and stimulates improvement is a tall order. But the benefits yield a gradual confidence-building atmosphere where many students, faculty, staff, and administrators are willing to tackle the tough problems a department or institution faces.

Institutional assessment described here reflects an emerging national consensus around several distinctive qualities: these respond to an institution's ideals and purposes as well as the expectations and hopes of its beneficiaries and external audiences. Two of these qualities are: *Assessment is a means, not an end. Assessment is a means not only to establish accountability but also to achieve educational benefits*. Thus assessment-as-improvement is framed and shaped within an institution or department's mission, goals, educational assumptions, and purposes, as well as all the other elements that characterize that particular setting.

As such, assessment-in-context has three other qualities: *Assessment purposes, goals, and methods emerge from the setting. Assessment encourages multiplicity. Assessment encourages coherence*. Thus assessment processes include sets of dynamic methods for examining student learning outcomes that emerge from a particular context. Assessment processes are not relegated to particular office or committee or subsumed under an educational speciality such as measurement, evaluation, or institutional or educational research. Rather, assessment methods emerge from the same, overarching sources as do the teaching and learning processes that shape curriculum and consequent student learning experiences. Does this mean that future assessment methods might be drawn equally from the arts and humanities as from the natural and behavioral sciences? Does this mean that each member of an institution or department will come to see some part of his or her role as assessment?

The complexities of creating assessment-in-context lead to a multiplicity of methods and uses. This diversity creates an apparent paradox with another of its qualities, that assessment encourages coherence. Can assessment processes with many methods and uses simultaneously serve as mechanisms for curricular coherence and connection across departments? Can institution-specific results that benefit students in a single setting also provide effectiveness evidence to higher education's external constituencies?

Solutions to these contradictions may well depend on another of assessment's qualities: *Feedback is the essence of assessment*. Returns may well depend on how results are communicated to each of the many audiences who will directly benefit from the information, and to whom an institution is responsible. Over the long run, will students begin to ask for specific feedback on how to improve after they complete course assessments? Will legislators, state boards, and accrediting agencies begin to ask equally for processes and products, stories and statistics?

Doing assessment often means taking on the paradigms and paradoxes of an emerging field. I believe assessment is new partly because it cannot easily be subsumed under prior categories of inquiry. Assessment seems to require, for example, measurements' long-term validation strategies along with the immediate usefulness of evaluation techniques. It calls for designs to improve a particular setting that can also yield more externally drawn, generalizable insights. Results that meet a faculty's standards and needs may not necessarily speak to all of society's expectations for "improved" undergraduate education. Yet the costs of assessment demand economical data sets that satisfy diverse purposes and users.

Clearly, a consensus around assessment's qualities can benefit from everyone's ongoing experience. Are the difficulties of assessment a reflection of a rough road in a new field? This might mean thinking smarter, but along similar lines. Or are current assessment methods in conflict with our educational values? This might mean reconstructing how we conceptualize assessment, and that task brings us to an examination of our educational assumptions and values.

Summary: Assessment as Values in Action

These six guidelines and the qualities of assessment we come together around say a great deal about our shared educational values. How we design and do assessment reflects—in fact, it embodies and ultimately advances—our educational philosophy. If assessment is to have integrity, the values that underlie it at the classroom, institutional, statewide, and national levels need to be more explicit, so we can question their consistency. If assessment is a means to an end, the values that define that end must be in harmony with the highest values of higher education. Assessment must call us to the best in ourselves, just as we call for the best in each of our students.

References

Alverno College Faculty. *Liberal Learning at Alverno College,* Milwaukee: Alverno Productions, 1976, revised 1985.

Alverno College Faculty. *Assessment at Alverno College.* Milwaukee: Alverno Productions, 1979, revised 1985.

Alverno College/FIPSE Assessment Project, "Faculty Consortium for Assessment Design." Judeen Schulte, Project Director, 1987.

Alverno College Office of Research and Evaluation/Assessment Committee. *Putting the Validahon Process to Work: A Series of Strategies for Establishing the Validity of Faculty-Designed Performance Assessment Instruments.* Milwaukee: Alverno Productions, Forthcoming.

American Association for Higher Education Research Forum. "Improving the Odds for Student Achievement: A Research Agenda." In *Improving the Odds for Student Achievement: A Research Agenda.* Co-chairs Arthur W. Chickering, K. Patricia Cross, Catherine Marienau, and Marcia Mentkowski, Washington, D.C., 1989.

American Council on Education. *Campus Trends, 1990,* Washington, D.C.: Author, 1990.

Astin, Alexander W. *Achieving Educational Excellence: A Critical Assessment of Priorities and Practices in Higher Education.* San Francisco: Jossey-Bass, 1985.

Astin, Alexander W. Assessment for Excellence: The Philosophy and Practice of Assessment and Evaluation *in Higher Education.* New York: Macmillan, 1991.

Banta, Trudy W., ed. "Implementing Outcomes Assessment: Promise and Perils." In *New Directions for Institutional Research,* no. 59, 95–98. San Francisco: Jossey-Bass, 1988.

Banta, Trudy W.; Lambert, E. Warren; Pike, Gary; Schmidhammer, James; and Schneider, Janet. "Estimated Student Score Gain on the ACT COMP Exam: Valid Tool for Institutional Assessment?" *Research in Higher Education: Journal of the Associationfor Institutional Research,* 27, no. 3 (1987):195–217.

Banta, Trudy W., and Schneider, Janet A. "Using Faculty-Developed Exit Examinations to Evaluate Academic Programs." *Journal of Higher Education* 59, no. 1(1988):69–83.

Carey, Karen. Appalachian College Assessment Program: Assessing General Education; Interview Questions *for Seniors.* Lexington: University of Kentucky, College of Education, Educational Policy Studies and Evaluation, 1987.

Chickering, Arthur W., & Associates. *The Modern American College.* San Francisco: Jossey-Bass, 1981.

College Outcomes Evaluation Program. New Jersey Department of Higher Education, *Final Report of the Student Learning Outcomes Subcommittee.* Trenton, N.J.: Author, 1987.

Collins, Linda M., and Horn, John L. *Best Methods for the Analysis of Change?* Washington, D.C.: American Psychological Association Press. Forthcoming.

Council for Adult and Experiential Learning, and McBer and Company. *Student Potential Interview.* Columbia, M.D.: Author, 1987.

Council of Presidents and State Board for Community College Education. *The Validity and Usefulness of Three National Standardized Testsfor Measuring the Communicahon, Computation, and Critical Thinking Skills of Washington State College Sophomores: General Report.* Bellingham: Western Washington University Office of Publications, 1989.

DeBack, Vivien, and Mentkowski, Marcia. "Does the Baccalaureate Make a Difference: Differentiating Nurse Performance by Education and Experience." *Journal of Nursing Education* 25, no. 7 (1987):275–85.

El-Khawas, Elaine. "How Are Assessment Results Being Used?" *Assessment Update 1,* no. 4 (Winter 1989):1–2.

Evarts, H. F. "The Competency Program of the American Management Associations." New York: Institute for Management Competency, American Management Associations, 1982.

Ewell, Peter T. The Self-Regarding Institution: Information for Excellence. Boulder, Colo.: National Center for Higher Education Management Systems, 1984.

Ewell, Peter T. "Assessing Educational Outcomes," *New Directions for Institutional Research,* no. 47, San Francisco: Jossey-Bass, 1985.

Ewell, Peter T. "Assessment: Where Are We?" *Change 19,* no. 1(1987): 2–28.

Ewell, Peter T. "Outcomes, Assessment, and Academic Improvement: In Search of Usable Knowledge," *Higher Education Handbook of Theory and Research* 4, ed. J. C. Smart, 53-108. New York: Agathon, 1988.

Farmer, Donald W. *Enhancing Student Learning: Emphasizing Essential Competencies in Academic Programs.* Wilkes-Barre, P A : Kings College, 1988.

Fong, Bobby. "Old Wineskins: The ACC External Examiner Project," *Liberal Education* 74, no. 3 (1988): 12–16.

Gardner, Howard. *Frames of Mind: The Theory of Multiple Intelligence.* New York: Basic Books, 1983.

Gray, Peter J., ed. "Achieving Assessment Goals Using Evaluation Techniques," *New Directions for Higher Education,* no. 67. San Francisco: Jossey-Bass, 1989.

Guba, Egon G., and Lincoln, Yvonna S. *Fourth Generation Evaluation.* Newburg Park, Calif.: Sage, 1989.

Heywood, John. *Assessment in Higher Education,* 2d ed. New York: John Wiley & Sons, 1989.

Hutchings, Pat. "Six Stories: Implementing Successful Assessment." Paper presented at the Second National Conference on Assessment in Higher Education, Denver, June 1988.

Hutchings, Pat. "Assessment and the Way We Work," Closing Plenary Address at the Fifth National Conference on Assessment. Washington, D.C.: American Association for Higher Education and the AAHE Assessment Forum, 1990.

Hutchings, Pat, and Marchese, Ted. "Watching Assessment: Questions, Stories, Prospects." *Change* 22, no. 5 (1990):12–38.

Kennedy, Margaret. "Abilities that Define Computer Studies," Presentation to Alverno Faculty, May 1988 Institute. Milwaukee: Alverno Productions, 1988. Videotape.

Knefelkamp, L. Lee, and Widick, Carole. "The Measure of Intellectual Development." College Park: Center for Applications of Developmental Instruction. University of Maryland, 1982.

Light, Richard; Singer, Judith D.; and Willet, John B. *By Design: Planning Research on Higher Education.* Cambridge, Mass.: Harvard University Press, 1990.

Loacker, Georgine. "Faculty as a Force to Improve Instruction Through Assessment." In *Assessing Students' Learning: New Directions for Teaching and Learning,* no. 34, ed. J. McMillan, 19–32. San Francisco: Jossey-Bass, 1988.

Loacker, Georgine; Cromwell, Lucy, and O'Brien, Kathleen. "Assessment in Higher Education: To Serve the Learner." In *Assessment in Higher Education: Issues and Contexts,* ed. C. Adelman, Washington, D.C.: U.S. Department of Education, 1986, Report No. OR 86–301, 47–62.

McGuire, Michael. "A Content Validity Study of the ACT-COMP for use in the Assessment of Undergraduate Learning." Paper presented at the annual meeting of the American Educational Research Association, New Orleans, April 1988.

Mentkowski, Marcia. "Paths to Integrity: Educating for Personal Growth and Professional Performance." In *Executive Integrity: The Search for High Human Values in Organizational Life,* Suresh Srivasta & Associates, 89–121. San Francisco: Jossey-Bass, 1988.

Mentkowski, Marcia. "Higher Education Assessment: Connecting to Its Conceptual Base." (Cassette Recording No. APA-90-164.) In K. A. Weaver (Chair). Facing the Challenge of Student, Program, and *Institutional Assessment.* Symposium conducted at the Meeting of the American Psychological Association, Boston. Washington, D.C.: American Psychological Association, 1990.

Mentkowski, Marcia, and Banta, Trudy W. "Collaborating in Setting Directions for Assessment Research," *Assessment Update 1,* no. 4 (Winter 1989):3.

Mentkowski, Marcia, and Chickering, Arthur W. "Linking Educators and Researchers in Setting a Research Agenda for Undergraduate Educators," *The Review of Higher Education* 11, no. 2 (Winter 1987):137–60.

Mentkowski, Marcia, and Doherty, Austin. *Careering after College: Establishing the Validity of Abilities Learned in College for Later Careering and Professional Performance* (Final Report to the National Institute of Education). Milwaukee: Alverno Productions, 1983. ERIC Document Reproduction Service ED 239 556/ED 239 566.

Mentkowski, Marcia, and Doherty, Austin. *Careering after College: Establishing the Validity of Abilities Learned in College for Later Careering and Professional Performance* (Final Report to the National Institute of Education: Overview and Summary). Milwaukee: Alverno Productions, 1983, revised 1984. ERIC Document Reproduction Service ED 239 556.

Mentkowski, Marcia, and Doherty, Austin. "Abilities that Last a Lifetime: Outcomes of the Alverno Experience." *AAHE Bulletin* 36, no. 6 (1984):5–6 and 11–14.

Mentkowski, Marcia, and Loacker, Georgine. "Assessing and Validating the Outcomes of College." In *Assessing Educational Outcomes, New Directions for Institutional Research*, no. 47, ed. P. Ewell, 4764. San Francisco: Jossey-Bass, 1985.

Mentkowski, Marcia; Moeser, Mary; and Strait, Michael J. *Using the Perry Scheme of Intellectual and Ethical Development as a College Outcomes Measure: A Process and Criteria for Judging Student Performance, Vols. 1 and 2.* Milwaukee: Alverno Productions, 1983.

Mentkowski, Marcia; O'Brien, Kathleen; McEachern, William; and Fowler, Deborah. *Developing a Professional Competence Model for Management Education* (Final Report to the National Institute of Education: Research Report No. 10). Milwaukee: Alverno Productions, 1982. ERIC Document Reproduction Service ED 239 566.

Mentkowski, Marcia, and Strait, Michael J. *A Longitudinal Study of Student Change in Cognitive Development, Learning Styles, and Generic Abilities in an Outcome-centered Liberal Arts Curriculum.* (Final Report to the National Institute of Education: Resear ch Report No. 6). Milwaukee: Alverno Productions, 1983. ERIC Document Reproduction Service ED 239 562.

Messick, Samuel. "The Once and Future Issues of Validity: Assessing the Meaning and Consequence of Measurement.n In *Test Validity*, ed. Howard Wainer and Henry I. Braun, 33–48. Hillside, N.J.: Erlbaum, 1988.

Office of the Vice President for Academic Affairs. *Initiatives for Excellence and Accountability: A Five Year Plan.* Harrisonburg, V.A.: James Madison University, 1985.

Patton, Michael Quinn. *Utilization-Focused Evaluation*, rev. ed. Newbury Park, Calif.: Sage, 1986.

Perry, William, Jr. *Forms of Intellectual and Ethical Development in the College Years: A Scheme.* New York: Holt, Rinehart and Winston, 1970.

Presidential Task Force on Student Learning and Development. *A Proposal for Program Assessment at Kean College of New Jersey* (Final Report). Union: Kean College of New Jersey, 1986.

Reisetter, Judy, and Sandoval, Pamela. "Flexible Procedures for Efficiently Maximizing Participation in a Longitudinal Study." Paper presented at the annual meeting of the Midwest Educational Research Association. Milwaukee: Alverno Productions, October 1987.

Resnick, Daniel, and Scheider, Carol G. *Assessment and Learning.* Washington, D.C.: Association of American Colleges. Forthcoming.

Rogers, Glen. "Validating College Outcomes with Institutionally Developed Instruments: Issues in Maximizing Contextual Validity." Paper presented at the annual meeting of the American Educational Research Association, New Orleans. Milwaukee: Alverno Productions, 1988.

Rogers, Julia S.; Bullard, Jerri H.; Ernest, Patricia S.; Bolland, Kathleen A.; and McClean, James E. "Evaluating General Education Outcomes Instruments: Relating Test Goals to Institutional Goals." Paper presented at the annual meeting of the American Educational Research Association, New Orleans, April 1988.

Schall, Celestine; Guinn, Katherine; Qualich, Ruth; Kramp, Mary K.; Schmitz, JoAnn; and Stewart, Kyle. Competence and Careers: A Study Relating Competences Acquired in College to Career Options for *the Liberal Arts Graduate*. Milwaukee: Alverno Productions, 1984.

Schneider, Carol. Telephone conversation with author 22 February 1990.

Schulte, Judeen; Benson, Sterling O.; Scarboro, Allen, and Turcotte, Judith. *Keeping It Local: Report from a Twelve-Campus Faculty Consortium on General Education Assessment*. Presentation at the Fourth National Conference on Assessment in Higher Education sponsored by the American Association for Higher Education. Atlanta, June 1989.

Sternberg, Robert J. *Beyond IQ*. Cambridge: Cambridge University Press, 1985.

Stone, Howard L. and Meyer, Thomas C. *Developing an Ability-Based Assessment Program in the Continuum of Medical Education*. Madison: University of Wisconsin Medical School, 1989.

Student Potential Assessed at Rhode Island College. *Assessment Update 1*, no. 2 (1989):10.

Terenzini, Patrick T. "Assessment with Open Eyes: Pitfalls in Studying Student Outcomes," *Journal of Higher Education* 60, no. 6 (1989):643–64.

Tittle, Carol K. "Validity: Whose Construction Is It in the Teaching and Learning Context?" *Educational Measurement: Issues and Practice 8*, no. 1(1989):5–13, 34.

Weiss, Carol H. "The Stakeholder Approach to Evaluation: Origins and Promise." In *StakeholderBased Evaluation: New Directions for Program Evaluation 17*, ed. A. S. Bryk, 13–14. San Francisco: Jossey-Bass, 1983.

Willett, John B. "Questions and Answers in the Measurement of Change." In *Review of Research in Education*, 15, ed. E. Rothkopf, 345–422. Washington, D.C.: American Educational Research Association, 1988.

Winter, David G.; McClelland, David C.; and Steward, Abigail J. *A New Case for the Liberal Arts: Assessing Institutional Goals and Student Development*. San Francisco: Jossey-Bass, 1981.

---

*These guidelines have been tested against the insights and experience of college and university faculty, administrators, and assessment specialists from a range of institutions who attended the institutional assessment track of the Alverno College Assessment Workshop in 1987,1988,1989, and 1990; and a 24-institution consortium organized on assessment design (Alverno College/FIPSE Assessment Project 1987).

"But How Do We Know It'll Work?"

Barbara D. Wright

In May of 1988, the University of Connecticut received a grant from the Fund for the Improvement of Postsecondary Education (FIPSE) for a three-year project to assess its new general-education curriculum. For the next eighteen months I served as project director, until my departure for AAHE. The funding not only allowed us to carry out the project; it also profoundly changed my thinking about assessment.

At the outset, we conceived of our job as data collection and analysis, and the project's still working hard on that. But by the time I left, before any data had been collected, I'd come to believe that the greater value of the whole effort lies in the *conversations* about general education that it provoked. That sea change in my understanding of assessment is what this little memoir is all about.

The story begins on a balmy spring day in 1986, when the University of Connecticut's faculty senate voted to accept a new general-education curriculum to be required of all entering students beginning in September 1988. As a collective sigh of relief passed through the meeting room—even those who were unhappy with the curriculum had reached a point of exhaustion—a brave skeptic rose and asked, "But how do we know it'll work?" He then moved the creation of an *ad hoc* committee charged to evaluate the curriculum, plot its effects, and eventually make recommendations. The motion passed.

Recommendations for what? For improvement of the curriculum? For its abolition? That was never entirely spelled out. And so assessment was launched at UConn into the mists of ambiguity. At least our fate was in our own hands; in contrast to assessment projects elsewhere, which were initiated by a legislature, governing board, or by administrators, assessment at UConn began and has remained entirely a faculty affair. That's not to say the project has been spared political overtones. But it's been family politics. And more often the target of political maneuvering has been the curriculum itself rather than its assessment.

The "evaluation committee" (which in its innocence didn't even learn the "A" word for what it was trying to do until more than a year later) decided early on that its first task was to define specific student outcomes for each of the six cognitive areas of the curriculum. Subcommittees produced "goal statements," which were widely circulated and went through several revisions. Through 1987–1988, the committee reviewed the literature on assessment, consulted with testing companies, talked strategies for assessing the curriculum, looked for outside money, and made complete, periodic reports to the Senate. No one much noticed.

What was this curriculum on which the committee lavished so much attention? Like many other schools, UConn adopted a structured menu. It consists of six cognitive areas: foreign language, literature and the arts, Western/non-Western civilization, philosophy and ethics, social science, and science and technology; and it includes writing, quantifying, and computing requirements. Students fulfill their general-education requirements by choosing courses in each of these categories.

But for a lot of UConn faculty, the "new" curriculum was actually a disappointing case of deja vu: a slightly modified version of the requirements that had been in effect in the College of Liberal Arts and Sciences (CLAS) since 1979. So the recycled curriculum brought with it the baggage of unresolved conflicts and dubious compromises. Moreover, courses from the old CLAS curriculum were to be grandfathered into the "new" curriculum with no review, meaning that the majority of offerings in each category would not be scrutinized for alignment with Senate guidelines or our committee's student goals.

There were plenty of other problems, too, problems hardly unique to UConn. There was general lack of "ownership" of the general-education curriculum, except to the extent that liberal arts departments saw it as a path to additional faculty and resources. Even as they jockeyed for students, the departments disdained a mere "service" role. UConn's new ambition to become a "top-twenty" research university seemed in direct conflict with the demands of general education, which implies a commitment to undergraduates. The "poor relation" status of general education was reinforced by a lack of financial or even moral support from academic affairs—or so it seemed to faculty.

Into this sea of competing agendas and general dispirit sailed the FIPSE project, full of optimism and energy and fueled by a bit of money. A $150,000 grant was fairly big news on the Storrs campus, given the committee's obscurity up to then. Despite warnings that long hours and hard work would be involved, the project succeeded in recruiting a cadre of highly respected faculty with reputations for solid research and fine teaching. In return for their efforts, we offered them an intellectually interesting task, an opportunity for professional development, and a modest stipend.

The faculty were organized into six teams, corresponding to the categories of the curriculum, and set to work reviewing course syllabi, exams, and available instruments; and devising a strategy to assess their area of the curriculum. If the team decided to fashion its own instruments, they would be developed that spring and field-tested during 1989-1990.

Faculty embarked on the project with seriousness, good will, and curiosity—as well as outspoken skepticism that the job could be done at all. The latter didn't bother me; I wasn't entirely convinced about the value of assessment, either.

In the composition of the six teams, the project aimed for a mix of specialists and generalists, within-field and out, enthusiasts and the unconvinced, simply because this sort of "balance" seemed sensible. We also tried to appoint as team chairs people who did not come from the dominant department in a given area. This policy of mixing viewpoints and sharing power turned out to be even more important than we thought at the outset. As the project progressed, we discovered how essential it was in the assessment process to question old assumptions and habits of thought (especially disciplinary isolation and chauvinism). The most heterogeneous teams proved the most flexible, produced the most creative instruments, and seemed most exhilarated by the intellectual exchange with newfound colleagues.

The process was an eye-opener, startling even, for many faculty participants. First, they learned they were to look at courses in their category in relation to a set of "student goals" that they barely knew existed. Second, they were supposed to look for "commonalities" *across* the courses within a given category—a daunting task for people who had seldom thought beyond the unit of the individual course. It was news enough to realize that there were even supposed to *be* these connections, never mind finding and describing them, then building an assessment instrument around them.

Problems arose with the goals, with the ways we would examine for them, and with the results that faculty anticipated. Getting clear about the specific content of the goals was only the first problem; then the teams had to reach some consensus that the goals were generally acceptable and figure out how "appreciation" and "understanding" could be *demonstrated*. Finally, there was the temptation to bolt when it turned out one ha‚dn't really been teaching these things at all. And there remained those principled souls, primarily in the humanities, who objected to the very idea of goals because, they believed, goals would inevitably trivialize the complex and ineffable things we taught.

The discrepancy between the new goals for general education and departmental practice could be pretty stark. The natural scientists, for example, realized they taught a lot of facts but much less about general principles of scientific thought and nearly nothing about the impact of science on society. The foreign language goals placed a strong emphasis on oral communication and cultural sensitivity—a reflection of the interests of faculty in the school of business, for example—while language faculty preferred to train students to read and analyze literature.

Then there was the issue of instruments. What format (i.e., multiple-choice, true/false, openended, essay) should be used? What signal would a particular format send to students about our educational values? And what about content? Should the instrument include generic intellectual skills, or discipline-based knowledge, or both? In what proportions? The commercially available instruments turned out to be either too generic for us (for example, the ACT COMP or the Academic Profile), or too discipline-specific (the GRE). By making up our own instruments, we hoped to get something tailored to our specific curriculum. But faculty design of the instruments also led to one additional and significant benefit over outside purchase: the work involved everyone far more deeply in discussion of the curriculum itself.

Faculty began to talk about the fact that the aims of a general-education course were perhaps different from, say, an introductory course for a prospective major. Or that what mattered for general education was perhaps less the facts regurgitated on the final exam than what students would still have with them five or ten years down the road, indeed for the rest of their lives—the will and intellectual discipline, for example, to grapple with ethical problems. The assessment project forced such questions about the curriculum to the surface; for those faculty who taught general courses, the activity became a kind of examination of conscience.

Many faculty on the project became nervous about the Pandora's box we appeared to be opening. A frequent line of argument, as instruments were being developed, was: I know this is in the goals, but do we have to include it? ("it" being any number of difficult things: critical thinking, cultural sensitivity, and so on). My answer was always yes, it's in the goals, so let's look for the evidence. The next objection was: But we don't teach this. But that, it became more and more apparent to us all, was precisely the point of the project: to figure out what we *should* be teaching, and then do it. The unspoken fear of course, is that if "we don't teach this," students will do poorly and the department will look bad. An assessment project needs policies for the *use* of results, to protect individuals and departments and leave them free to identify problems without fear of punishment.

It's often noted that the campuses where assessment has been most powerful and effective—places like Alverno and King's College—tend to be smaller and have a clearly defined teaching mission. Common wisdom has it that research universities, on the other hand, offer distinctly uncongenial environments for assessment. Certainly many things at a comprehensive university do work that way: the low status of undergraduate teaching, the lack of monetary or even symbolic rewards for engagement with problems of student learning, the orphan status of general education. And there's the ease with which sophisticated researchers can fault any instrument or research design. A large, decentralized campus and poor communication don't help.

Fortunately, the UConn committee had no idea when it started that assessment was supposed to be difficult or impossible on such a campus. On the contrary, we found that some characteristics of our university worked for assessment. It was possible, in a place as large as UConn, to find many individuals with strong research interests *and* a genuine concern for teaching and learning, people who hungered for a project that legitimized their concern for students. The project provided things that they missed on campus, like reinforcement of the value of teaching and the pleasure of making friends with people from other corners of the campus. There was the uniqueness of being on a committee that talked about education for a change, instead of about the failings of the academic calendar or the number of parking spaces devoured by the new sports pavilion.

A year and a half into the project, a significant number of faculty participants still express skepticism about the value of assessment and its ability to measure general-education outcomes. I can accept that; skepticism, after all, is the nature of the academic beast. But if that is their "text" on this issue, there is also a "subtext": by the quality of their effort, these faculty have demonstrated a very real commitment to students' education and a hope that their efforts can improve it.

There are other issues that the UConn project evoked, issues by no means unique to the Storrs campus. One of them is the relationship between assessment and change. I heard people on the campus say they didn't want to do assessment because inevitably it *would* used as a lever to change the curriculum: assessment would "drive the curriculum," and faculty would be pressured to "teach to the test." I also heard assessment used as an excuse for why we *couldn't* change the curriculum: with an assessment project in progress, changing the "treatment" in the middle of the experiment would destroy the validity of the instruments and render any longitudinal data meaningless.

The common denominator here seems to be that people resist change. But what *should* be the relationship between assessment and change?

In my view, there is nothing wrong with assessment "driving the curriculum," if we are driven toward worthwhile goals that we agree we ought to be achieving anyway. The trick is to make sure that all important goals are built in, and a range of assessment methods are used, so that stated goals are not achieved at the cost of more important and complex but unstated ones. Second, it seems to me that under no circumstances may assessment be allowed to become reified, a purpose unto itself with no connection to the larger campus environment. A campus (unlike a scientific laboratory) must change in response to new pressures and needs. For example, there have been calls on the Storrs campus to add a new "diversity" requirement to the gen-ed curriculum, and there have been objections to this modification—among them that it'll ruin the assessment project. But assessment should serve the campus, not control it; to use assessment in any other way becomes perverse.

The problem here is accepting contingency . . . the contingency of a particular curriculum, or set of goals, or a particular instrument or method. All these things, to me, are working hypotheses, not ultimate definitions of "truth." In Lee Knefelkamp's phrase, we're dealing here with the difference between "the truth" and "truthfulness." We know very well, in the rest of our professional lives, that we'll never approach "the truth," but still we strive mightily to be "truthful" in our research and teaching. It's easy to turn the imperfections of a curriculum or a set of goals into an excuse for not even trying to assess. Nevertheless, we *can* work with them, just as inquiry in any discipline proceeds largely from hypotheses and theories, not proven laws. If we can accept this in our own research, why not in assessment?

There's an even bigger "change" question now lurking in the wings, one raised by the project's FIPSE program officer. After a visit to campus, she wondered whether our work in assessment would be a mere "blip on the screen" or lead to real change in the "campus culture." My God, I thought in a panic, as I read her letter, is *that* what we're supposed to do? *Change the campus culture?* Our ambitions had been far more modest. But on second thought, this is not a bad way to look at assessment.

"Changing the campus culture" suggests that assessment is ultimately not data collection or reports to authorities but an attitude: one that includes listening to students, examining our own teaching, and rededicating ourselves as a campus to improvement of undergraduate education. Obviously, assessment can't do this single-handedly, but it can help: it puts the right questions on the table. In Storrs, there are people who have been putting serious work into assessment for more than three years now. About seventy-five faculty members have worked on the project, either as team members or as reviewers of instruments, and hundreds more have heard of our work. Maybe someday we *will* look back and say we helped transform the campus culture.

Eighteen months into the project, the six teams are on track and on schedule. There are instruments for five out of six areas of the curriculum, with the last set nearing completion. Most of the instruments have already been pilot-tested on incoming and exiting students. The project is finding out not only how well students perform in these exercises but also what they think of the assessment process. Often, in writing or in conversation, the students turn from the assessment to reflect on the education they've received so far—and that's all to the good.

At this point in the project, the questions we began with—"Is the curriculum working? Is it better than what we had before?"—seem a little naive. We have different questions now: Are students able to gather, evaluate, and synthesize information? Do they have the literacy and numeracy skills they should? Can they recognize the rationale behind a philosophical position, even when they don't personally hold it? Are they capable of aesthetic response to a painting or a poem or a piece of music? Do they see connections among the courses they take in general education, or between their general education and their major field of study? And what, exactly, do the faculty do in their courses to foster these abilities, these habits of mind and spirit?

These are the sorts of questions that occupy the project now. They can't possibly be answered in relation to the old curriculum because we never even *asked* them of the old curriculum. "Does it work?" was a good and necessary starting point, but we had to go beyond it.

I truly didn't know what we were getting into three years ago; the power of assessment's questions, their bedrock fundamentalness, has dawned on me only gradually. For me and others, the project became a journey of personal and intellectual exploration at the misty fringes of what we know about education—intensely personal, unsettling, difficult. Not all of us feel comfortable with this sort of thing, and it's sometimes tempting to just turn and run. Indeed, the project seems to have pushed at least one faculty member I know closer to early retirement.

I sympathize, but this discomfort is not unique to assessment and it shouldn't bog us down. Almost ten years ago, the eminent feminist scholar Peggy McIntosh published an article called "Warning: The New Scholarship on Women May Be Hazardous to Your Ego." She noticed that even the most well-intentioned faculty often reacted defensively to the suggestion that, say, a reading list of all white, all-male authors was "unbalanced"; after all, these academics had put years of effort into producing the best scholarship and teaching they could—and now women's studies was telling them that their work, because it overlooked half the human race, was fundamentally flawed. Once she said it, of course, the problem was utterly obvious. And yet somehow, they'd never noticed. It was the perfect moment for denial and retreat.

Assessment is a little like that. We've invested vast amounts of time and effort in our teaching—happily or grudgingly as the case may be—and then assessment comes along and asks us a set of truly fundamental questions about teaching that we've never even bothered to deal with. Suddenly a raking light is cast over the work of an entire career. It's devastating, or can be. But realizations like that aren't the end of the world, any more than they were in women's studies. After the initial shock, there are wonderful opportunities for new thinking, experimentation, renewal, growth. If we want our students to grow, surely we owe it to them to keep on growing ourselves.

At the risk of turning this little essay into a homily, it strikes me that ultimately, perhaps, for both faculty and students, assessment is the embodiment of humility, honesty, and democracy in academe. If we want students to admit candidly the limits of their own knowledge and work to expand them, we must find the courage to do likewise. If we expect students to engage the ideas of others, we must show that same respect and seriousness. If we want students to learn from us, we must be willing, in a spirit of equity, to learn from them and from their assessments of us.

The question "How do we know it'll work?" can be asked not only of a curriculum but of assessment itself. The answer is that we don't know whether it'll work. That depends, as Pat

Hutchings and Ted Marchese are wont to say, not on assessment itself but on the people who carry it out. I agree with that; I would only add my own corollary: "Given the right people, it may very well work—in ways utterly different from what you expected when you started."

Assessment Through the Major

Mark I. Applebaum

For many years the informal assessment of the quality of programs in higher education has been concentrated at the level of the major, department, or school. For instance, the subjectively ranked quality of graduate education in the non-professional schools (e.g., the Rouse-Andersen ratings, 1970) is always reported by department or major. The quality of graduate professional schools has frequently been judged (particularly by groups such as boards of governors, State legislatures, and senior administrative officials), at least in part, by passing rates on disciplinary credentialling examinations such as State Bar Examinations and Medical Board Examinations. Similarly, the quality of undergraduate professional programs such as those in nursing and education are assessed, in part, by passing rates on certifications such as state licensing tests in nursing and the National Teachers Examination.

The use of the department or major as the unit of assessment has several distinct advantages over an institution-wide assessment scheme which attempts to assess the quality of undergraduate education *in toto*. These advantages include:

(1) the size of the assessment project itself, with a small number of well conceived and designed assessments phased in each year;

(2) the greater possibility of a proper fit between the form of the assessment and specific features of the instructional program; and

(3) the close connection between the assessment unit and the instructional unit.

Let us briefly examine each of these advantages.

Two concerns dominate the planning of assessment programs in higher education: the quality of the assessment itself and its acceptability to both the faculty of the institution and the eventual consumers of the information it yields. By basing the assessment at the level of the department (or major) it is possible to phase in the assessment process in stages. The selection of the first participating programs should be based on a combination of factors including the perceived quality of the department or major, the potential acceptance of the assessments by the faculty involved, the experience of the field with such assessments, and the technical competence of involved faculty to launch such an assessment. By selecting the initial participants so that the first experiences with this type of assessment are as positive as possible, the overall acceptance of such assessments by the faculty in general may be enhanced.

The second, and perhaps most important, advantage of basing the assessment program at the major or department level is that of optimizing the fit between the content and form of the assessment and the particular goals and sensibilities of the instructional unit. There is no reason to assume that every department has the same instructional objectives. Some may emphasize the knowledge base of the field, while others may emphasize the role of theory; some may emphasize performance and production, and still others may emphasize the role of empirical research. Some departments may build their curriculum around a narrow set of required courses and prerequisites while others may offer a curriculum with few requirements and many electives. Some departments may structure their programs around formal lecture/discussion courses while others may provide a substantial amount of field experience, research experience, individualized reading courses, or other alternatives to formal classroom instruction. Such differences clearly exist between disciplines within an institution as well as within disciplines across institutions.

For example, psychology departments vary widely in the role of field and clinical experiences within the curriculum, in the number and types of laboratory experiences available, as well as in their orientation towards clinical, cognitive, and biological issues. And if the course-taking patterns of majors are influenced by particular faculty (e.g. a leading authority on Chinese history), then a department's expectations for student learning will take on a different configuration than the "core" of most history curricula. By basing the assessment program within the major or department, such differences in approach and expectations can more easily be recognized and the assessment designed accordingly.

Basing the assessment at the departmental level also has the advantage of linking the assessment unit and the instructional unit. This linkage is clearly advantageous should the evidence produced by the assessment indicate that the instructional program is operating at less than an optimal level. Since the content and form of the assessment would have been established by the instructional unit itself, there could be little convincing argument that the problem is with the assessment rather than with the instructional program. Further, the involvement of faculty in the design and implementation of the assessment *per se* should provide some motivation towards rethinking and reevaluating instructional objectives.

Issues in Designing the Assessment

Should the decision be made to base the assessment within the individual department or major, a number of issues must be considered in the early phase of design. These include the purpose of the assessment, content and coverage, form and format, sampling and motivation of respondents, timing of the assessment, and the technical characteristics of the assessment instrument and methods, including a consideration of the "norms" to be applied. While each of these issues will be explored separately, one must recognize that they are not independent and that decisions made in one forum will have implications for the others.

The Assessment Team and Its Charge

It is essential that each of these issues be considered by that group of individuals charged with the responsibility of designing implementing and reporting the results of the assessment. This group of individuals must be a carefully selected team, collectively knowledgeable about the instructional goals of the unit, current directions in the field, and technical knowledge of the principles of evaluation. While most members of this group should be faculty in the department being assessed, it would be wise to include at least one senior faculty member from outside the department but in a related area, one individual experienced with the administrative sensitivities of the institution, one person experienced in the assessment field if no such individual is available from the target department, and at least one advanced undergraduate in that discipline. The advantage of creating a fairly broadly based assessment team is that while the disciplinary concerns of the area being assessed are represented by those faculty in the department, the presence of individuals outside of the unit (including a student) prevent the assessment from being excessively parochial or self-serving.

It is also essential that this panel be clearly charged by those with the overall administrative responsibility for the assessment as to its purpose, scope, financial limitations, and the expectations the administration may have for the assessment process. Included in the charge must be a specification of how the results of the assessment are to be reported and to whom.

It may well be the case that several forms of an assessment report will be necessary—one for the student participant in which her or his individual performance is reported (with relative strengths and weaknesses noted); one for the faculty in which detailed analyses of the strengths and weaknesses of the curriculum are noted along with suggestions for changes; and one for the senior level administrator which accurately and succinctly summarizes the findings of the assessment and recommendations for improvements in the curriculum. In this latter report it is important that the assessment procedure itself be described in some detail so that the process can be evaluated by those receiving the results. Indeed, the senior-level administrator responsible for the several assessments should ask for interim reports detailing the assessment plan prior to its implementation to ensure prior agreement on its adequacy.

All too often assessment projects are seen by faculty as time-wasting exercises with no real consequences other than to fill filing cabinets in the administration building. Thus, in addition to charging the assessment team with regard to the purpose of the assessment, the appropriate academic administrator should give clear indications of how the assessment results are to be used.

Purposes of the Assessment

The first issue that must be clearly specified and understood by all parties involved in the design and execution of the assessment is the purpose for which it is being conducted. The first of these purposes is to *audit the content* of the curriculum and to assure that all aspects of the discipline that ought to be offered are offered, and that a suitable proportion of students who graduate in that "discipline" have been exposed to that content. A second purpose of the assessment may be to provide some *measure of the efficacy* of the undergraduate instructional unit (be it a single department or an interdepartmental "committee"). An evaluation at this level would necessarily involve the assessment of not only what is taught, but also how well it is taught, retained and internalized by the "typical" or "representative" student in that discipline. A third purpose for which an assessment might be designed is the *certification* of the individual student, i.e., to measure the degree to which each student in the field has mastered the objectives of the curriculum and to provide some qualitative or quantitative index of the degree and level of that mastery. Such an index might be employed to determine minimal competence for graduation (or honors).

It is essential for those ultimately responsible for the conduct of the assessment to understand that these purposes are quite different (although related); that for each purpose a different form of assessment with rather different considerations (both technical and pragmatic) would be necessary; and that the results of one form of assessment cannot be utilized directly for one of the other purposes.

Content and Coverage of the Assessment

If the content of the assessment does not correspond to the agreed upon goals set by the faculty, the results of the assessment surely will be dismissed as irrelevant to the instructional program. In the following discussion it is assumed that the assessment will focus on the knowledge obtained as a result of instruction in the discipline and that the mechanism will be some form of "testing," be it multiple choice, essay, or some other format. Should it be decided that some alternative format, such as a "senior essay," experimental project, position paper, or examination by an external visiting committee be adopted, then other considerations of content and coverage would need to be applied. But assuming that the test mode would be the most prevalent format, the following issues should be considered carefully.

First, the scope of coverage. It might be decided that the assessment should be based upon the entire field as it is conceived by the mainstream of the profession. This scope of coverage is perhaps the most commonly used and represents the type of knowledge testing employed throughout the educational community when it elects to use commercially developed tests at any level. For example, each of the Graduate Record Examination Subject Area tests consists of a set of items determined by a panel of disciplinary experts to represent a field broadly conceived, but without regard to the course offerings in any particular department or institution. The utility of this approach has been discussed by McCallum (1983) in the context of the evaluation of a psychology program, but its limitations have been sufficiently recognized (see, e.g., Burton, 1982) so that ETS has now developed an alternative: the Major Field Assessment Tests (MFATs).[1]

A limited number of professional associations (e.g., the American Chemical Society) have developed examinations to assess the knowledge base of the field as defined by the professional association. This latter form of assessment device has often been developed in conjunction with the association defining a model curriculum in the field or responding to traditional divisions of knowledge within a field (e.g., organic chemistry, physical chemistry, etc.). The advantage of such an approach is that it assesses the instructional program in the context of the field and tends to ensure that the local curriculum has not become either dated or extremely idiosyncratic. Further, this approach allows the possibility of the use of norms (see below) which can be based on more extensive samples than any locally developed test. The major disadvantage of such an approach is that it cannot be sensitive to the locally established goals of the instructional program and can easily ignore major thrusts of the curriculum being assessed. Also, this approach tends to under-evaluate small programs which simply cannot provide coverage of all aspects of the field.

A second approach to the scope of coverage issue is to use the full array of course offerings in the department being assessed to define the content domain of the assessment and to then sample items from that domain (see below) thereby producing a "comprehensive" examination as defined by the courses in the department. Banta and Schneider (1986) discuss the development of such comprehensive examinations as part of an institution-wide effort at the University of Tennessee.

Finally, one might decide to take a more "minimal competency" approach to assessment at the departmental level by defining a smaller set of courses (perhaps the core courses or areas required of all majors) as the domain of coverage. Under this approach one might expect to find a narrower but deeper form of testing. In a limited number of cases, course-based tests such as those developed by the American Chemical Society (see above) could be employed as long as the tests reasonably correspond to the content of the selected courses. Should one decide to take the "minimal competency" approach, it is critical that the defined minimum be rich enough so as not to trivialize the assessment program. Minimal breadth does not mean minimal depth.

The problem of the scope of coverage becomes more complicated in the case of interdepartmental B.A. programs such as Area Studies, Criminal Justice, Comparative Literature, and so forth. In these cases, special attention needs to be directed to the assessment of the curriculum offered by a set of faculty members specifically designated as the core faculty, as well as the assessment of those areas of coverage provided by the other faculties allied with the core curriculum.

In those disciplines in which "outside of classroom" activities such as field placements and internships are considered to be essential features of the curriculum, special attention should be given to the manner in which the results of these activities are to be built into the assessment. An example of the assessment of one such activity can be found in Morris and Haas (1984).

Determination of Content

A starting point for determining of the content of the assessment instrument would be an explicit statement of objectives by the instructional program faculty. This process is difficult and time consuming, but of great importance and benefit. (It well may be the first time that some faculties have collectively discussed the objectives of their total educational program.) From the resulting grid of curricular objectives, a subset must be selected depending upon the decision that has been made with regard to scope. From this point the actual development of items can be undertaken by (a) writing items *de novo* that match the curricular objectives selected, (b) selecting items from existing examinations or other item pools available within the unit, (c) selecting a commercially available test that has a high content overlap with the curricular objectives selected (say an 80 percent overlap), or (d) creating a hybrid instrument. This last approach is one in which a set of items from tests with known properties (such as norms) is imbedded within a batch of locally developed items. This use of reference items, as they are technically known, allows a partial comparison of the results of a local assessment with those of other assessments utilizing the same reference items. Once problems of copyright are solved, the use of a hybrid instrument mitigates a number of the technical problems cited in this essay.

No matter which of these approaches is preferred, the selection of particular items (or tests) should be informed by a content representativeness study. The basic idea underlying this type of study is the formation of a grid which has as its columns the specified objectives of the instructional program and as its rows the items under consideration, be they an item pool or the items on an established test. The task in such a study is to then determine the match between each item and the stated objectives. This grid also may be used to discard items which do not measure any of the department's curricular objectives and to generate new items to measure objectives for which no items yet exist. The same approach can be taken with essay and other performance assessments, though the task is more difficult. Generally, the more restricted the possibilities of student response (as is the case with test items requiring choice or completion) the greater the precision of a content representativeness study.

Examples of this approach can be seen in a recent series of studies sponsored by the Office of Research of the U.S. Department of Education. These studies evaluated some of the leading content area examinations in selected fields against surveys of faculty and professional consensus on the objectives of undergraduate learning in the major, and offer a useful starting point for considering commercially available instruments for assessment.[2] In addition, some test publishers have sponsored content representativeness studies of their tests which may also be of use. For instance, Oltman (1982) and DeVore and McPeek (1985) offer content assessments of several of the GRE Area Examinations (specifically biology, literature, political science, chemistry, education, and computer science). These content assessments, however, are stated in rather general terms (e.g. the categories of content representativeness for the Computer Science Area Examination are Software, Systems and Methodology, Computer Organization and Logic, Theory, Computational Mathematics, and Special Topics) and are not substitutes for a detailed examination of the individual instruments by a local faculty. On the other hand, the methodology described in both of the papers is valuable and should be considered by the assessment team.

Form and Format of the Assessment Instrument

Having decided on content, one next needs to consider the administrative form and test format of the examination itself. There are a number of alternatives. Concerning administrative form, one could elect a single sitting examination (traditionally a three-to-four-hour exam—a period thought to be near the limit of good student performance) in which all of the agreed upon content is examined. Alternatively, one could assess subsets of the agreed upon content in shorter sessions spread over a longer period of time. A third alternative is one in which a single session is scheduled, but in which a multiphasic battery of tests is employed. Under this plan a potentially different set of sub-tests is administered to each student based upon the specific courses the examinee has taken.

A variant of this third scheme might prove useful if it is determined that the domain of coverage is too great to allow a single test to be administered to all examinees. Under this variant, random subsets of the total item pool are gathered together to form several weakly-parallel forms of the test, and each is administered to a different subset of examinees (see Millman's discussion of matrix sampling above). While this system of testing is generally not accepted for purposes of individual assessment (i.e. certification) it has proven useful in a number of program assessment applications, most notably in the recent rounds of the National Assessment of Educational Progress (Beaton, 1987). This system has the additional advantage of maintaining test security in multiple administrations of the assessment.

A second and more serious decision concerns test format. There are many formats, each with its own distinctive advantages and disadvantages. The decision on test format will undoubtedly have many consequences ranging from the number of students who can be tested to the cost of the assessment process. The most common format for assessment of this type is the multiple choice format. The primary advantages of the multiple choice format are its familiarity, the precision and ease of scoring either by hand or machine, and the ease of establishing the psychometric properties of such tests. The net result of these advantages is that the assessment can be quickly, accurately, and inexpensively administered once the test has been constructed, and consequently a large number of students can be included in the assessment. One further advantage of the multiple choice format is that most (but certainly not all) commercially available assessment devices, such as the public release forms of the GRE subject area tests, are written in this format. (The public release forms of the GRE change fairly often and, if employed as part of an assessment program, it is desirable to use the most recently released form if for no other reason than to minimize the chances that students will have seen the items as part of their preparation for taking the GRE.)

There are a number of serious disadvantages to the multiple choice format. The most serious of these disadvantages deals with the level (in terms of cognitive demands) at which multiple choice items tend to operate. Bloom's *Taxonomy of Educational Objectives* lists knowledge (recall and recognition), comprehension, application, analysis, synthesis, and evaluation as the goals of the educational process in increasing order of cognitive demand. Analyses of multiple choice items have repeatedly shown that this form of test item rarely, if ever, operates beyond the level of simple recall and recognition. The problem with multiple choice items seems to be inherent in the item type itself, for when attempts have been made to rewrite items to require a higher level of cognitive functioning (in Bloom's sense) experienced item writers were unable to produce substantial numbers of items which operated beyond the recall/recognition level (Levine, McGuire, and Natress, 1970). As Lyle Jones has noted, "There is evidence that the form of the multiple choice item is intractable with respect to measuring higher cognitive skills" (Jones, 1987).

Clearly, the degree to which multiple choice format examinations pull for "recall and recognition" level skills is somewhat a function of the area being tested. In some areas (e.g., chemistry, physics, and the various specialties in engineering) it has been well demonstrated that multiple choice items that demand higher level cognitive skills, such as analysis and synthesis, *can* be constructed. (This is not to imply, however, that commercially available tests in these areas tap these higher order skills.)[3]

The concern that commercially available multiple choice format examinations do not tap a proper level of cognitive functioning is clearly expressed by Peterson and Hayward (1987) in their "A Review of Measures of Summative Learning In Undergraduate Biology." After reviewing fourteen instruments purported to examine general biology, they remark:

> We are alarmed and perplexed that there appear to be no standardized tests available in the U.S. that attempt to determine the degree to which graduates are able to function as scientists, or more specifically as biologists. That is, existing tests do not measure whether an individual can identify a problem, ask a research question, develop hypotheses, test them, or draw a conclusion and report the results. . . . The evaluation of learning pertaining to the *process* of scientific inquiry may be severely limited as long as we rely on multiple-choice tests as the principal method of measuring achievement.

The second disadvantage of the multiple choice item for the type of assessment envisioned is actually an interaction of the problem of the "cognitive demand" level of multiple choice items with a fear that testing drives instruction and the curriculum. This concern is perhaps best summarized in the following brief statement from the Committee on Research in Mathematics, Science, and Technology of the National Research Council (1987, p.20):

> Most present classroom methods of testing what students know emphasize the recall of facts—as does most teaching. If tests are not to trivialize instruction further, new approaches to assessing student achievement must be developed that aim at conceptual understanding, the ability to reason and think with scientific or mathematical subject matter, and competence in the key processes that characterize science or mathematics.

Should the assessment instrument consist mainly of items that demand only recall and recognition and should the assessment have any pragmatic impact, the net result might be to dilute—rather than to improve—instruction. A somewhat more optimistic view of the potential for multiple choice items and the conditions under which this optimism might be realized can, however, be found in Frederiksen (1984), Frederiksen and Ward (1978), and Ward (1986). Their work indicates that items (both multiple choice and brief answer formats) can be developed that tap scientific creativity and problem-solving abilities. The dominant format of experimental items developed by Frederiksen and Ward involves the presentation of a situation with tabular data such as the relationship between birth weights and I.Q. scores or the capacity, patient turnover and death rates in a hospital in 18th century London, and asks the student first to generate a series of hypotheses to account for the major relationships among the data and then to indicate the most likely hypothesis. This format combines features of a free-response question with those of a restricted-choice question.

Other formats traditionally used in classroom assessment are obviously available. These include open-ended and free-response questions which require the examinee to generate a correct answer as opposed to simply recognizing one; essay questions which further require the examinee to analyze, synthesize, and organize a body of knowledge as opposed to a single fact or issue; or even a production task which might be designed to assess the student's ability to apply a body of knowledge to a well-structured problem or (perhaps even more importantly) to an ill-structured problem.

While each of these approaches allows the assessment of higher level cognitive domains, they are not without some limitations. These limitations include the substantially higher cost of administering and evaluating the assessment, the greater subjectivity attendant upon their scoring and interpretation, and the lack of familiarity that most academics have with the technical demands of such forms of assessment (despite the fact that they frequently use them in the classroom). Nonetheless, if the goal of the instructional program is to achieve excellence in the use of these higher order skills within the context of the discipline, the designers of the assessment must carefully consider the format of the instrument and its implications in light of that goal.

Other Forms of Assessment

The system of examination commonly employed in the British university and polytechnic system merits some attention at this point. This system, discussed at some length by Lawton (1986), Sawyer (1976), Tannenbaum (1986), and Williams (1979) among others, combines an extensive written senior comprehensive examination (a series of extended essays) with the use of an examination board that includes at least one external examiner. While the basic purpose of the system is to award degree levels, it also achieves certain of the goals of assessment envisioned in this volume including assessment of students on higher order cognitive levels. Additionally, the presence of the external examiner allows for at least a partial assessment of the overall program of instruction across institutions. As noted by the Committee of Vice Chancellors and Provosts (1986):

The purposes of the external examiner system are to ensure, first and most important, that degrees awarded in similar subjects are comparable in standard in different universities in the United Kingdom, though their content does of course vary; and, secondly, that the assessment system is fair and is fairly operated in the classification of students.

Experiences of American universities and colleges with the external examiner system are detailed in Fong (1987). There is a fundamental difference between the two systems. The British external examiner is essentially an auditor and mediator, functioning at the second level of review. In the few cases of external examining in the U.S. (e.g. in Swarthmore's honors program), the external examiner functions at the first level, writing and grading senior examinations, and possessing the sole authority to recommend honors. For this system to work in relation to local curricula and local faculty expectations for student learning, there must be a high degree of explicit prior consensus between the external and internal faculty on performance objectives.

The designers of large scale assessments should not restrict themselves to a single mode of examination. There is no reason, save cost and complexity, that the assessment cannot be multimethod in design (i.e. that a number of techniques be incorporated into an overall assessment package). Thus, the assessment designer can utilize one or more comprehensive, multiple choice instruments in order to provide information about the knowledge base acquisition of students, and can also include one or more senior essays, problem solving simulations, oral examinations, and the like in order to assess more fully the higher order skills and proficiencies of a sample of undergraduate majors. A mix of these various formats and contents could be selected to represent the relative importance of each component in the curriculum. A multi-method formulation of an assessment would also allow the relative strengths and weaknesses of the program to be assessed in terms of cognitive skills as well as the specific content of the curriculum.

Sampling and Program Evaluation

When selecting the sample of students to be included in the assessment, it is important to recall the purpose of the assessment. If the goal of the assessment program is to measure the efficacy of the instructional program (as opposed to certifying the individual student), then while students are the means by which information on program effectiveness is obtained, they are not the ultimate focus of the assessment. Nonetheless, it is necessary that a procedure be developed such that once a comprehensive program is fully implemented (i.e., functioning in all majors), each and every undergraduate at an institution is *eligible* for assessment in at least one major. It is not necessary that a single strategy for sampling be adopted on an institution-wide basis, but rather, the sampling approach should reflect the nature of the particular unit of the assessment. The simplest method of obtaining the sample is simply to include all students in a given major in the assessment of that major, as would be necessary if student certification were the goal of the assessment. This approach may work in those programs that are small enough to allow such an inclusion rule, but in a majority of cases it will be necessary to use a sample.

The first step in selecting a sample is the formal specification of an inclusion rule (i.e. who is eligible to be included within a specific assessment package). The listing of all eligible students is technically called the sampling frame. Among the considerations necessary to specify the sampling frame are: Should the assessment be limited to senior majors only? Should part time students be included? Should double majors be included in the assessment if the area being assessed is their second major? Should "concentrators" (i.e. students whose formal degree programs include less than a full major in the area being assessed) be included? Should "special" (i.e. non-degree students) be included? The answer to these and related issues will depend upon the mission statement of the particular program and the goal of the assessment program. Whatever the answers might be, it is important that they be formally specified prior to the onset of any sampling plan and that the rules be consistent from unit to unit.

The second step in selecting a sample is to specify the sampling method to be followed. There are four essentially different types of samples which may be drawn—a random sample, a stratified (or quota) sample, a representative sample, and a volunteer sample. Each of the samples differ in terms of the validity of the conclusions which may be drawn from the ensuing assessment and in the difficulty of obtaining the sample. A random sample (the basic sample of most statistical theory) is a sample in which each and every unit (individual) in the sampling frame has the same probability of being included in the sample actually drawn. In order to draw a random sample, one must first have a complete listing of all eligible students (determined by the considerations discussed above) and then a random process that allows a sample of a predetermined size to be drawn from the sampling frame. Having obtained the listing of the sample, each individual so selected must then be individually contacted and persuaded to participate in the assessment.

The advantage of the random sample is its validity. Since each and every individual has the same probability of being selected, there is no long-range possibility of the sample being biased as long as all selected individuals participate in the assessment. If a random sample is actually obtained, all of the extensive power of statistical and psychometric theory can be brought to bear on the analysis of the resulting data, and the conclusions drawn can be framed in proper probabilistic terms.

There are, however, several difficulties in using the random sample that should not be overlooked. The first of these is that the sample is unbiased only in the long range sense. It is perfectly possible that a truly random sample will not "look right"—that is, it may lack face validity. In drawing a random sample, certain groups of individuals may be under-represented or not represented at all (e.g. if there are relatively few minority students in a particular major, it may be that that minority group will not be included at all in the assessment sample). The second problem with the random sample is that students are included in the sample without regard to their willingness to participate in the assessment. Depending on who participates in any or all of the assessment, results may be invalid. The significance of this limitation will depend upon the ability of the assessment team either to persuade the selected individuals to participate or the degree to which participation is required (e.g. is a condition of graduation) or is made a desirable activity (e.g. by offering significant payment for participation). While these problems are indeed real, the advantages of the random sample make it a worthy model for which to strive.

As an alternative to a simple random sample, one may select the sample using a stratification procedure. In this process, subgroups of interest (e.g. minorities, double majors, etc.) are first identified, followed by the drawing of a random sample of students within each of those identified groups. Under this sampling plan, it is not necessary that students be drawn from their respective groups in proportion to the group size in the total population. A "back weighting scheme" can be used to adjust the impact of each subgroup's responses in the final outcome result in proportion to the size of that group in the population. In this way, the special groups may be over-represented in the actual assessment, but then included in the final results in an appropriate manner. This approach may be particuelarly effective if the performance of one or more of the identified subgroupings is of particular interest at the time the assessment is conducted.

Two methods of sample recruitment which are probably best avoided in conducting an assessment are those which lead to the "representative sample" and the volunteer sample. A representative sample is one which is artificially constructed to match the demographic characteristics of the population as a whole but without the random selection found in a stratified sample. The volunteer sample is one in which the participants are exclusively those who have volunteered to serve in the assessment. Both of these sample types suffer from the possibility of biasing the results before the fact. The first is problematic because students who meet certain characteristics are intentionally "sought out" in order to build the representative sample. Volunteer samples are generally unacceptable because they are very likely to be composed of more able and serious students.

Norms

No single issue in the development of an assessment package is likely to prove more difficult and require more careful thought than that of establishing an appropriate set of norms (i.e., a scale against which to judge the results of the assessment). The selection of a norming approach will depend upon virtually all of the factors considered heretofore.

Two general approaches to the establishment of a norm can be taken: "criterion referencing" and norm referencing. Under a criterion-referenced system, the standard against which performance is judged is the minimal acceptable performance within an objective. Thus, if an instrument has been developed to assess a certain number of goals or objectives within a specific curriculum or major, the criterion-referenced approach would require the further step of specifying the minimum number of items within each objective which must be passed by the typical student in order to exhibit mastery of the objective. Results of assessments based upon a criterion-referenced system are then generally reported in terms of the percentage of test takers who have exhibited mastery in each of the objectives. The use of the criterion-referenced system depends on the development of an instrument which has been organized around specific objectives or domains as well as an agreement upon what constitutes mastery of a domain. This consensus is particularly critical when the format of assessment consists of free response questions, essays, or production tasks, and (as previously noted) when external examiners are involved.

The fact that a criterion-referenced system can be purely local (i.e., requires no information on how students outside the specific major in the particular institution being assessed perform) provides at once a great strength and a great weakness. On the positive side is the fact that one can use a locally developed instrument without having to concern oneself with the lack of national data; nor (if one is using a commercially available instrument) does one have to worry about the comparability of the local sample to the "norm" sample, as would be the case, for instance, if a random sample of majors took the GRE Area Examination where the "norm" group would consist largely of majors seeking admission to graduate school. Other strengths of a criterion-referenced system are that it provides detailed information by objective and immediately suggests domains in which excellence exists or in which improvement is needed. The major weakness of the system is that if it is created in a purely local context, there is no assurance that the results are not artificially inflated (or deflated) by the inclusion of only very easy (or difficult) items or items that are not specific to the curriculum under review.

The alternative (and more customary approach) is that of norm referencing. Essentially, this approach involves collection of data on a wide range of students at many institutions, with the results of the individual institutional assessment being judged in terms of the standing of its students in relation to the performance of the norming group. The norm-referenced approach is most desirable when one wishes to be able to make *comparative* statements. While norm-referenced tests (e.g. the SAT, ACT, or GRE) are used more than other forms, they are not necessarily the most desirable (the desirability of an instrument being judged in terms of the use to which it is to be put).

The underlying validity of a norm-referenced test, for the purposes discussed in this essay, depends upon the content of the instrument, its technical characteristics, and the adequacy of the norming sample. Since the local institution will have little if anything to do with the establishment of the norm sample for a commercially available test, it is of particular importance that those responsible for the selection of the instrument pay as close attention to the norm sample as to the content of the test itself. It is essential that the norm sample provide an appropriate basis of comparison.

There is no reason before the fact to prefer one form of "norming" over another, and there are certainly cases where the distinction between the two forms of norming are not as clear cut as presented here. The basic validity of the criterion-referenced approach rests with the assessment instrument and the definition of the mastery criterion, that of the norm-referenced approach with the assessment instrument and the norming sample. The decision one takes will depend on the purpose of the assessment together with a consideration of these elements.

When components of the assessment are not in traditional testing formats and do not produce numerical indices (e.g. juried performance, exhibitions, or summative papers) norm scales are generally not available, although one could establish a criterion-referenced system. Although the lack of a norming system for this type of assessment may make the reporting of the outcomes of the assessment difficult, that should not discourage the use of alternative approaches to assessment.

Timing of the Assessment

Another issue of practical concern is timing. If the goal of the assessment is to evaluate the overall impact of the instructional program, then it will be necessary that the assessment be conducted after the student has completed all or nearly all of the course work in the major (including a senior thesis, etc. if that is part of the curriculum). This generally means during the last semester of the student's residency (generally the second semester of the senior year), a time well known to be rather difficult to obtain student cooperation.

Detailed planning of the exact calendar time of the assessment may be more important. Factors such as conflict with examinations, major campus events, universal testing schedules (such as the GREs), and vacation periods must be considered carefully in order to assure maximum participation. Further considerations such as holding the assessment during regular class hours, in the evening, or over a weekend period must be made. Each of these factors can have a great impact upon participation rates and student performance. In general, it is wise to schedule programs of this nature in such a way as to minimize conflicts with other scheduled activities even if it means a brief interruption of the normal academic calendar. If a multiple assessment method approach is taken, schedules can be created that offer alternative times to students selected to participate.

Student Participation

Any assessment effort which is based in part or in whole upon student responses will depend, in the final analysis, upon the magnitude and quality of student participation. There are a number of options, ranging from cash payments in the case of "one shot" assessment projects (treating participation as if it were an *ad hoc* campus job), to requiring a passing grade on the assessment for graduation (provided, of course, that the instrument is appropriate for assessment at the level of the individual student). Carrots may produce a full examination room, but do not guarantee maximum effort.

Given the need to have full participation from the sample as well as the need for students to give a good faith performance, this issue cannot be stressed strongly enough. After all the work that is necessary to plan and execute a first-rate assessment, it would be tragic to have the effort prove futile because of a lack of student participation, or a half-hearted effort on the part of students.

Alternatives to Student-Based Assessment: The Audit

All of the approaches discussed have involved assessment through student responses. That is, they have assumed that the proper approach to assessment is through measuring what the student has gained as a result of the instructional program. They assess the results of the sequence of exposure (curricular experience), acquisition (learning), and retention (of specifics and general "rules") as they exist in the students selected for the assessment at the time of the assessment.

It is not absolutely necessary, however, that an assessment be based on student responses in the after-the-fact manner implicit in the assessment schemes previously discussed. It is possible (although not without some limitations) to base an assessment upon a thorough cataloguing of the materials to which the student-has been exposed and some indexing of the student's performance with that material at the time of exposure as well as other non-obtrusive means.

This assessment scheme would begin with the systematic collection of course syllabi, course lecture notes (if available), course quizzes and examinations, and details of course projects. In order to utilize the information contained in these documents in an optimal manner, it would be first necessary to have a detailed grid of curricular objectives prepared. The information available in the collected documents would then be set in the curricular grid on a course-by-course basis, thereby providing detailed information concerning the exposure of students to each objective. Information could also be obtained from these documents concerning student performance on each objective, as well as the stress placed on each objective in terms of its occurrence on quizzes, examinations, or projects. With such an assessment for each course offered in the curriculum, a composite could then be built from information available on student utilization of each course. With This procedure, a detailed picture of the manner in which curricular objectives are distributed could be constructed.

While it is unlikely that this approach to assessment would be seen as totally adequate (particularly from the perspective of accountability), it has its virtues. Foremost among these is that it allows a fairly accurate assessment of the degree to which putative curricular objectives are actually realized in the existing instructional program. Further, if student-based assessments identify areas of deficiency in learning, this analysis can be utilized in order to determine if the objective was actually presented or if it was presented only in a course not commonly taken by students in the major.

A variation on this approach was suggested by an anonymous reviewer of this essay. Essentially, the system involves the collection of materials which "define" the major (i.e., a statement of overall requirements, course syllabi, course quizzes, examinations and paper topics, assigned reading lists, and any general capstone documents such as senior theses). These materials are then reviewed by a panel of external examiners who are charged with assessing the major program based upon the submitted documentation. The utility of this approach depends in large measure, on the charge given to the examiners, the questions asked of them, and the manner in which their responses are treated. The point, however, is that innovative alternatives to student-based systems for assessment are possible.

Special Problems in Certification

When considering the various purposes of assessment, special attention must be given to problems associated with the "certification of individuals" goal of assessment. If this approach is selected, special precautions will need to be taken—particularly with regard to the technical characteristics of the assessment instrument, the determination of a cut score (if a "pass" level is to be established), and to appropriate before-the-fact communication to students that such a certification test will be required as part of the requirements for graduation. Among the additional technical requirements for an instrument used for the certification of individual students is a much higher reliability index for the instrument than is generally required for other purposes of assessment.

The problem of establishing a valid cutscore is an even more difficult issue—particularly given the legal problems that one may face if, such a test or instrument is part of the criterion for graduation (or possibly for the awarding of honors, etc.). While the courts generally have not intruded in issues of the grade-setting behavior of individual instructors, it is not clear what their approach might be to institutionally set, single instrument policies. (Note that this is a different situation from the one in which a minimum grade point average criterion is used, for that criterion can be reached by performance in many individual courses.) Indeed, the use of an assessment instrument for the purpose of individual certification invites a host of legal issues. One might wish to consult Baldus and Cole (1980) for a sampling of the statistical and psychometric issues involved in the potentially discriminatory aspects of such an approach.

Finally, there is the bothersome issue of the need for prior notification of students. It is a general policy of many academic institutions that new requirements may not be instituted until they have been published and are known to an entering class (i.e., students already enrolled are generally "grandfathered" out of new requirements). Were this policy followed in the case of an assessment instrument employed for the purpose of certification, the instrument could not routinely be used (except on a volunteer basis) for up to five years after its inception, a delay that might not be acceptable.

Summary

While we have seen that there are many advantages to basing an assessment of the academic outcomes of higher education in the discipline, there are many thorny issues which any assessment planner (and administrator responsible for the assessment effort) must consider. These issues may be roughly divided into two broad classes—one which deals with the purposes for which the assessment is being conducted and the second which has more to do with technical issues involved with the design and conduct of an assessment. Both sets of issues are critical, but until the basic issues of purpose are clearly stated and agreed upon by all parties to the assessment effort (i.e. administration, faculty, and student) there is little hope that the technical issues can be resolved in such a way that the assessment will have the benefits envisioned.

Notes

1. Scheduled to be available in the Fall of 1988, the Major Field Assessment Tests (MFATs) are constructed from "no longer used" item pools of the GRE Subject Area tests together with new items to keep the tests current. The two-hour exams are specifically designed for use in program evaluations, though they will be reliable at the level of the individual student. The tests will be normed on a scale different from those used on the GREs in order to preclude misinterpretation. Results will be reported by both gross and sub-test scores, as well as through profiles of specific strengths and weaknesses.

2. Five contracts were awarded in 1986 for 18-month studies to develop model indicators of student learning in the disciplines. The five winning fields were Biology, Chemistry, Computer Science, Mechanical Engineering, and Physics. Each contractor evaluated existing assessment instruments (both U.S. and foreign) and methods against consensus models of learning goals, and developed frameworks for disciplinary faculty to assess learning more accurately in light of the discrepancies. Final reports were submitted in the Spring of 1988. For further information, contact: Office of Research, Division of Higher Education, 555 New Jersey Ave., N.W., Washington, D.C. 20208.

3. The OERI-sponsored project in Physics referred to above, however, demonstrated that the GRE Area Test in Physics demands both manipulation and application of variables.

References

Baldus, D.C. and Cole, J.W. *Statistical Proof of Discrimination*. Colorado Springs: Shepard's/McGraw Hill, 1980.

Banta, T.W. and Schneider, J.A. *Using Locally Developed Comprehensive Exams for Majors to Assess and Improve Academic Program Quality*. Knoxville, TN: Learning Research Center, Univ. of Tennessee, 1986.

Beaton, A. The NAEP 1983-84 *Technical Report* (NAEP Report No. 15-TR-20). Princeton, NJ: Educational Testing Service, 1987.

Burton, N. *Trends in the Performance and Participation of Potential Graduate School Applicants.* 1987 Princeton, NJ: Educational Testing Service, 1982. GREB #82–5.

Committee on Research in Mathematics, Science, and Technology Education, National Research Council. *Interdisciplinary Research in Mathematics, Science, and Technology Education.* Washington, D.C.: National Academy Press, 1987.

Committee of Vice Chancellors and Provosts. *The External Examiner System for First Degree and Taught Master's Courses.* London: Author, 1986.

DeVore, R. and McPeek, M. *Report of the Content of Three GRE Advanced Tests.* (GREB #78-4R). Princeton, N.J.: Educational Testing Service, 1985.

Dressel, P.L. *Handbook of Academic Evaluation.* San Francisco: Jossey-Bass, 1976.

Fong, B. *The External Examiner Approach to Assessment.* Washington, D.C.: Association of American Colleges, 1987.

Frederiksen, N. "The Real Test Bias: Influences of Testing on Teaching and Learning," *American Psychologist,* vol. 39 (1984), pp. 193–202.

Frederiksen, N. and Ward, W.G. "Measures for the Study of Creativity in Science Problem-Solving," *Applied Psychological Measurement,* vol. 2 (1978), pp. 1–24.

Jones, L.V. *Educational Assessment as a Promising Area of Psychometric Research.* Paper delivered at the annual meeting of the American Psychological Association, New York, N.Y., September, 1987.

Lawton, R. "The Role of the External Examiner," *Journal of Geography in Higher Education,* vol. 10 (1986), pp. 41–51.

Levine, H., McGuire, C. and Natress, L. "Content Restructuring of Multiple Choice Items." *Journal of Educational Measurement,* vol. 7 (1970), pp. 63–74.

McCallum, L.W. "Use of a Senior Comprehensive Exam in Evaluation of the Psychology Major," *Teaching of Psychology,* vol. 10 (1983), pp. 67–69.

Morris, S.B. and Haas, L.J. "Evaluating Undergraduate Field Placements: an Empirical Approach," *Teaching of Psychology,* vol. 11 (1984), pp. 166–168.

Oltman, P.K. *Content Representativeness of the Graduate Record Examinations Advanced Tests in Chemistry, Commuter Science, and Education* (GREB #81–12P). Princeton, NJ: Educational Testing Service, 1982.

Peterson, G.W. and Hayward, P.C. *A Review of Measures of Summative Learning In Undergraduate Biology.* Contract report (Contract 400-88-0057) to the Office of Research, U.S. Department of Education. Tallahassee: Florida State University, 1987.

Roose, K.D. and Anderson, C.J. *A Rating of Graduate Programs.* Washington, D.C.: American Council on Education, 1970.

Sawyer, T.M. "External Examiners: Separating Teaching from Grading," *Engineering Education,* vol. 66 (1976), pp. 344–346.

Tannenbaum, A.G. "Teaching Political Science in Britain: The Final Examination System," *Teaching Political Science,* vol. 13 (1986) pp. 168–173.

Ward, W.C. "Measurement Research That Will Change Test Design for the Future," in Educational Testing Service, *The Redesign of Testing for the 21st Century.* Princeton, NJ: Author, 1986.

Williams, W.F. "The Role of the External Examiner in First Degrees," *Studies in Higher Education,* vol. 4 (1979), pp. 161–168.

In Their Own Words:
What Students Learn
Outside the Classroom

George D. Kuh

I've learned a lot about a lot of things . . . I care more about how I interact with other people. That is, I care about helping people learn and sharing my ideas with others. I definitely feel more confident in conveying what I have to say. I can express myself better. . . . An important part of what I've done [is] the classes and seeing how things connect and seeing how things work in an in-depth way. (Earlham College senior).

Assessments of student learning in college usually focus on academic aspects of the undergraduate experience—the classroom, laboratory, studio, and library. Transcripts and test scores, however, reflect only a fraction of how students change (Light, 1992). Wilson (1966), for example, estimated that more than 70% of what students learn during college results from out-of-class experiences. According to Moffatt (1989):

> For about 40% of students, the do-it-yourself side of college [what took place outside the classroom] was the most significant educational experience. And for all but 10%, extracurricular learning had been at least half of what had contributed to their maturation so far in college (p. 58).

Other scholars also have linked many of the benefits of attending college to out-of-class activities and experiences (Astin, 1977; Bowen, 1977; Boyer, 1987; Chickering, 1969; Feldman & Newcomb, 1969; Pace, 1979, 1990; Pascarella & Terenzini, 1991; Thomas & Chickering, 1984). These benefits include, among other things, gains in confidence, self-esteem, and altruistic values (Astin & Kent, 1983; Pascarella, Ethington, & Smart, 1988). Out-of-class experiences that contribute to these and other aspects of student learning and personal development include conversations with faculty after class and collaboration in research and teaching projects, living in a residence hall, working on or off campus, participating in institutional governance, involvement in clubs and organizations, and voluntarism.

For the most part, the research methods used to assess the impact of college have been quantitative and positivistic (Pascarella & Terenzini, 1991). Such methods require that researchers determine both the questions to be asked and the response categories. Attinasi (1992) argued that "progress in understanding college student outcomes . . . has been retarded by our failure to adequately take into consideration the meanings that the phenomenon of going to college holds for students" (p. 68). This view holds that it is impossible to understand the human experience *without* taking into account the complicated, mutually shaping events, actions, and motivations of the individual or group under study. According to Bogdan and Biklen (1982), "people act, not on the basis of predetermined responses to predefined objects, but rather as interpreting, defining, symbolic animals whose behavior can only be understood by having the researcher enter into the defining process" (p. 38). Attinasi (1992) recommended use of "phenomenological interviews" whereby the inquirer gains access to the meanings individuals attach to their own experience using a semistructured interview guide.

There is a tradition of using qualitative research methods (e.g., phenomenological interviews) to discover what happens to students during college (Freedman, 1967; Madison, 1969; White, 1966). Several such inquiries culminated in popular, wide-used theories of college student development (i.e., Chickering, 1969; Kohlberg, 1984; Perry, 1970). However, the bulk of qualitative research about college students was conducted 25 years ago with traditional-age (18–22) students enrolled full time who lived on campus. Today, only about one sixth of undergraduate students fit that description (Levine, 1989). As Pascarella and Terenzini (1991) concluded, "specifying the effects of college for the vast numbers of non-traditional students . . . may be the single most important area of research on college impacts in the next decade" (p. 632). Through the use of interviews, we may be able to discover those aspects of college considered important by students whose frames of reference were not taken into account when many of the current research instruments and models of college impact were developed.

Purpose

The purpose of this study was to discover, by asking undergraduates to reflect on their college years, the impact of out-of-class experiences on their learning and personal development. Three research questions guided the study: (a) What did students learn from their experiences outside the classroom? (b) In what ways have they changed since starting college? and (c) Do the outcomes considered by students to be important differ by type of institution attended and student background characteristics?

Although seniors from multiple institutions participated, this study did not seek to obtain generalizable results. Rather, the purpose was to generate an accurate and trustworthy picture of the perceptions and experiences of learning and personal development of undergraduates as told by the students themselves. As we shall see, most students found it difficult to bifurcate their college experience into two separate categories of learning; that is, one linked to experiences outside the classroom and the other a function of the formal curriculum.

Conceptual Framework

According to Pascarella and Terenzini (1991), studies of what happens to students during college follow one of two general approaches: developmental and college impact.

Developmental Approaches

The vast majority of theory-driven research on change during the college years is developmental (Kuh & Stage, 1992). Inquiries grounded in this perspective emphasize discrete periods or stages of development that are presumed to emerge in an orderly and hierarchical manner. Developmental models are heavily influenced by psychological theory; therefore, intrapersonal dynamics are considered to be more important to development than the environment. Some developmental theories focus on the *content* of the changes in cognitive, affective, and behavioral domains (e.g., psychosocial, typological) that occur during college while others describe the *processes* (cognitive-structural, person-environment interaction) by which these changes take place (Kuh & Stage, 1992; Pascarella & Terenzini, 1991; Rodgers, 1989).

An example of the latter is Baxter Magolda's (1992) study of cocurricular influences on intellectual development. Using the Epistemological Reflection model, Baxter Magolda found that students' ways of knowing, or epistemologies, influenced their interpretations of the importance of out-of-class experiences. For example, when asked to talk about important aspects of the collegiate experience, absolute knowers (i.e., students who assume knowledge is certain) tended to talk about how they had to "adjust" to college life (e.g., take more responsibility for their own affairs); transitional knowers described the importance of peers to learning how to function effectively in the college environment; and independent knowers talked of how they "discovered their own voices" (Baxter Magolda, 1992, p. 211) through dealing with people different from themselves.

College Impact Approaches

The study reported in this paper uses the college impact approach to discover outcomes that college students associated with out-of-class experiences. To account for learning and personal development, college impact models emphasize interactions between students and the institution's environments (broadly conceived). For example, in Pascarella's (1985) model, outcomes (learning and cognitive development) are a function of reciprocal influences among the structural and organizational characteristics of the institution (e.g., enrollment, control, selectivity, affluence), student background characteristics (e.g., sex, aspirations, aptitude, ethnicity), the perceptual and behavioral environments created by interactions with peers and institutional agents (e.g., faculty seem friendly and helpful, peers are competitive), and the "quality" of effort (i.e., time and energy) students invest in educationally purposeful activities.

Various outcome taxonomies have been developed to account for changes that occur during college (Astin, 1973; Bowen, 1977; Lenning, 1976; Micek, Service, & Lee, 1975). These taxonomies typically encompass two types of outcomes, affective and cognitive, which can be assessed using either psychological instruments or observations and reports of behavior, or both. (Astin, 1977; Kuh, Krehbiel, & MacKay, 1988; Pascarella & Terenzini, 1991). An example of an affective outcome is enhanced aesthetic awareness, which could be assessed psychometrically, such as with the estheticism scale of the *Omnibus Personality Inventory* (Heist & Yonge, 1968). A behavioral measure of aesthetic awareness could be observations or self-report information about frequency of participation in cultural events.

The most comprehensive synthesis of college outcomes is Pascarella and Terenzini's (1991) review of 2,600 studies. They divided affective and cognitive outcomes into nine domains: knowledge and subject matter competence, cognitive skills and intellectual growth, psychosocial changes, attitudes and values, moral development, educational attainment, career choice and development, economic benefits, and quality of life after college. Pascarella and Terenzini found that, in general, college attendance typically was associated with "net" and "long-term effects" for each of the domains. Net effects are changes due to attending college, as contrasted with changes resulting from maturation or experiences other than college. Long-term effects refer to whether the changes that occur during college persist after college.

Research conducted using the college impact approach reflects aggregated group effects. Although not every student changes on every domain, on average, college attendance is associated with modest gains in verbal and quantitative skills, substantial gains in knowledge (particularly in the major), and increased cognitive complexity; greater social maturation, personal competence, and freedom from irrational prejudice; increases in appreciation for the aesthetic qualities of life; clarification of religious views; substantial gains in personal autonomy and nonauthoritarianism; and modest decreases in political naivete and dogmatism. Also, college students become more introspective and more aware of their own interests, values, and aspirations. The crystallization of these diverse aspects of personality functioning into a sense of identity is one of the most important outcomes of college (Bowen, 1977; Chickering, 1969; Feldman & Newcomb, 1969; Pascarella & Terenzini, 1991). Equally important, the college experience leaves a "residue" (Bowen, 1977) manifested as an openness to new information and ideas, a facility for meeting and dealing with a wide variety of persons, and a practical sense of competence and confidence that enables a college-educated person to successfully cope with novel situations and problems.

Methods

To determine the impact of out-of-class experiences on student learning and personal development, seniors were interviewed from 12 institutions in different regions of the continental United States.

Participants

Participants were students classified as seniors at the following institutions: Berea College, Earlham College, Grinnell College, Iowa State University, Miami University of Ohio, Mount Holyoke College, Stanford University, The Evergreen State College, University of California, Davis, University of Louisville, Wichita State University, and Xavier University of Louisiana. These institutions were selected because they were known to provide rich out-of-class learning and personal development opportunities for their students (Kuh et al., 1991). Each institution was visited twice by a team of two to four investigators; the interviews with students on which this study is based were conducted during the second visits to these colleges.[1]

The institutional contact (typically someone designated by the chief student affairs officer) was asked to identify 10 to 12 seniors who, as a group, reflected a range of involvement in various aspects of the undergraduate experience. For example, we asked that no more than half the students selected for interviews be a highly visible student leader (e.g., editor of the student newspaper, varsity athlete, president of a social organization); the remainder, then, would likely be more typical of undergraduates at that institution in their level of campus involvement. We also requested that several students from historically underrepresented racial and ethnic groups be invited to participate. For the two metropolitan colleges, Louisville and Wichita State, a proportionate number of older, part-time, and commuting students were represented.

Problems related to scheduling and other vagaries (e.g., some students did not show up at the appointed hour) resulted in fewer than 10 students being interviewed at some institutions (i.e., Iowa State = 7; Xavier = 7; UC Davis = 9). Because members of the research team were employed at two of the institutions, they were able to conduct some interviews beyond the target number of 10. As a result, 28 students from Stanford University and 18 students from Wichita State University are included among the respondents.

In all, 149 seniors were interviewed: 69 men, 80 women; 101 whites, 30 African Americans, 6 Hispanics, 6 Asian Americans, and 6 international students; 129 students of traditional age (18–23) and 20 older than 23 years of age. Even though the numbers of students from most of the institutions are relatively small, as a group the participants reflect the diversity that characterizes undergraduate students enrolled in institutions of higher education in the United States.

Data Collection

A semistructured interview protocol was developed for this study and was field-tested during the first campus visit during the fall of 1988. The protocol subsequently was reduced to four general probes designed to elicit the most important things that the respondent learned during college—about oneself, others, interpersonal relations, cultural differences, academics, and so on—rather than the interviewer suggesting specific categories of outcomes. The four probes were: (a) Why did you choose to attend this college and in what ways has it been what you expected? (b) What are the most significant experiences you had here? (c) What are the major highlights of your time here? Low points? High points? Surprises? Disappointments? and (d) How are you different now than when you started college?

Interviews were conducted between January and June of 1989. Prior to the interviews, students received a letter from the investigators outlining the purpose of the study. By informing them in advance about the topics to be covered, some students were able to give the topics considerable thought before the interview.

Interviews were conducted by eight people. Seven of the interviewers were members of the College Experiences Study (CES) research team; by the time these interviews were conducted (during the second visit to the institutions), all the CES project staff had acquired extensive interviewing experience. The eighth interviewer, a graduate student in higher education, concluded 16 of the 28 interviews with Stanford students as part of an internship.[2]

No systematic effort was made to match interviewers and respondents on gender, race, and ethnicity. The interviews occurred in private rooms in campus buildings (e.g., administration buildings, libraries, student unions) that were reserved for this purpose. Interviews ranged in time from 35 minutes to 1 and one-half hours; the modal length was about 1 hour. All interviews were tape-recorded and transcribed verbatim.

Data Analysis

Transcribing interviews required 16 months (April, 1990 through July, 1991). Four people participated in the analysis of interview transcripts. Three were doctoral students in higher education with some training in qualitative research methods. They did not conduct any of the interviews. The fourth person (the author) conducted 21 of the interviews.[3]

To accomplish the purpose of the study, a two-stage, multimethod data analysis procedure was used. The first stage was inductive and the second deductive. As Reichardt and Cook (1979) argued:

> There is no need to choose a research method on the basis of a traditional paradigmatic stance. Nor is there any reason to pick between the two polar opposite paradigms. . . . There is every reason (at least in logic) to use them together to satisfy the demands of . . . research in the most efficacious manner possible. (p. 27)

The inductive stage began by examining what respondents said were—for them—important benefits of attending college that they associated with out-of-class experiences. The interview transcripts were analyzed using a five-phase iterative procedure. First, each transcript was reviewed by one of the doctoral students who assigned an identification number to the transcript including the institution, a student identification number, and the student's age, sex, and ethnicity. This initial reading of the transcripts yielded a set of eight categories reflecting outcomes mentioned by the participants (Miles & Huberman, 1984). Second, another reader analyzed several dozen transcripts and, based on her suggestions, the initial set of outcome themes was revised and expanded to 10 categories. Third, a transcript was selected which was read by all four readers to determine how well these themes accommodated the student-reported outcomes contained in this transcript. This revised set of themes was then discussed at some length by the four readers. The product of these discussions was a taxonomy comprised of 13 outcome categories. Fourth, four additional transcripts were selected; each reader read a copy of all four. The experience of coding these transcripts was discussed, and several minor revisions were made to the taxonomy including the addition of the miscellaneous "other" category. Finally, all 149 transcripts were read and coded by the author, which included assigning outcome category numbers in the margin of the transcript next to relevant passages. Thus, a single "human instrument" was responsible for analyzing and interpreting all the data, thereby avoiding potential interrater reliability problems.

The second stage of data analysis was deductive. As Miles and Huberman (1984) suggested, one can more quickly analyze massive amounts of data in the form of words by transforming categories of information into numbers; in addition, numbers can protect against investigator bias, thus ensuring intellectual honesty. Following Miles and Huberman, after the transcripts were coded, quantitative data analysis procedures were used to identify patterns in the data that had empirical and conceptual integrity, not to test hypotheses about out-of-class experiences and student learning.

Measures of central tendency were computed for each outcome category. A factor analysis was performed to determine whether the outcome categories (excluding the miscellaneous "other" category) could be reduced to a more wieldy number of outcome domains. Using the factor solution, t-tests and analysis of variance (ANOVA) were used to determine if the outcomes mentioned by students differed by certain student background characteristics (age, sex, ethnicity) and institutional size (large = 5,000 or more undergraduates, which included Iowa State, Louisville, Miami, Stanford, UC Davis, and Wichita State; small = fewer than 5,000 undergraduates, which included Berea, Earlham, Evergreen State, Grinnell, Mount Holyoke, and Xavier); control (public = Evergreen State, Iowa State, Louisville, Miami, UC Davis, Wichita State; private = Berea, Earlham, Grinnell, Mount Holyoke, Stanford, Xavier), and mission (liberal arts = Berea, Earlham, Evergreen State, Grinnell, Mount Holyoke, Xavier; metropolitan = Louisville, Wichita State; comprehensive = Iowa State, Miami, Stanford, UC Davis). . . .

Discussion

This section is divided into four parts: (a) the contribution of the study to the literature, (b) reflections on using interview data to assess college outcomes, (c) limitations of the study, and (d) thoughts on using quantitative data analysis procedures with qualitative data.

Contribution of the Study

The outcome categories that emerged from the inductive analysis of senior interview transcripts were, for the most part, similar to those developed by others to define and categorize college outcomes (e.g., Bowen, 1977; Ewell, 1984; Feldman & Newcomb, 1969; Lenning, 1976; Micek, Service, & Lee, 1975). For example, compared with the categories used by Pascarella and Terenzini (1991), the only outcomes *not* mentioned by seniors were those that cannot be determined until after graduation—educational attainment, economic benefits, and quality of life after college.

Given the focus of the study—learning and personal development associated with out-of-class experiences—it was not surprising that some outcomes, such as academic skills, were mentioned less frequently than other outcomes, such as autonomy and confidence. At the same time, it is disappointing that knowledge application was not mentioned by more than a quarter of the respondents. Collegiate environments offer innumerable opportunities to use information obtained from many courses of study (e.g., political science, psychology, sociology) in dealing with the problems and challenges of daily life. To encourage more knowledge application, faculty could structure assignments that require students to illustrate how they are using class material in other areas of their lives. Institutional agents whose primary work is with students outside the classroom (e.g., student affairs staff, academic advisors) could promote more knowledge application by asking students on a regular basis to apply what they are learning in class to life outside the classroom. Simple illustrations of how this might work are the residence hall director who routinely invites students during casual conversation to share the three or four most important things they learned that week, or the student government advisor who challenges student leaders to apply material from their political science, psychology, and communications classes to their student government role.

One outcome frequently mentioned by participants as important was learning about and gaining experience with people from different racial, ethnic, and cultural backgrounds (Altruism and Estheticism). Earlier studies of attitudinal changes during college usually found increased tolerance for racial and ethnic differences (e.g., Clark, Heist, McConnell, Trow, & Yonge, 1972; Hyman & Wright, 1979; Winter, McClelland, & Stewart, 1981), an affective psychological outcome (Astin, 1973). This study suggests that experiences outside the classroom are an important venue where students not only develop an appreciation for people from backgrounds different from their own (the affective psychological outcome), but also cultivate skills that enable them to relate personally to such students (an affective behavioral outcome).

College impact models emphasize the influence of institutional and student characteristics on learning and personal development (Pascarella, 1985; Pascarella & Terenzini, 1991; Tinto, 1987; Weidman, 1989). Institutional control, size, and mission were associated with differences in Cognitive Complexity, Knowledge and Academic Skills, and Altruism and Estheticism. However, in this study sex was the only student characteristic associated with a difference in reported outcomes (Cognitive Complexity). That other student background characteristics were not systematically associated with differences in outcomes may be explained by the nature of the institutions. These institutions shared a number of properties, including cultural assumptions that every student can succeed and that every student is expected to participate fully in the life of the institution (Kuh et al., 1991). These colleges and universities have created something akin to a level playing field, an institutional context wherein student characteristics become neutral factors in terms of their learning and personal development (Kuh & Vesper, 1992).

Pascarella and Terenzini (1991) found that within-college differences (i.e., what a student does in college) were greater than between-college differences (i.e., type of institution attended). Few studies compared the effects of attending *specific* institutions on college impact, such as assessments of gains of students attending Indiana University, Ball State University, and Hanover College. Therefore, whether *individual* institutions have distinctive impacts on their students is not known because any differences in student outcomes that may be associated with salience and character of institutional mission become obfuscated by aggregating data from a number of institutions. For example, do students at colleges such as Berea, Earlham, and Grinnell, where the institutional mission emphasizes service to others, report patterns of outcomes that differ from those of their counterparts at other college and universities that do not emphasize service in their missions? Of course, institutions with salient service-oriented missions attract many students with humanitarian interests. Therefore, efforts to examine the relationship between institutional mission and student outcomes must attempt to estimate the relative contributions of the institutional environment and students' pre-college predilections to changes compatible with those valued by the institution's mission and philosophy. The contextual properties of these 12 colleges and universities differed in myriad, subtle ways that may influence student learning (Kuh et al., 1991), a point to which we shall return in the "Limitations" section.

Using Interviews to Assess Outcomes

The words of seniors describing the role of out-of-class experiences to their learning and development during college are compelling evidence of the value of using interviews to assess the impact of college on students. At the same time, using unstructured interviews to better understand what happens to students is not without potential pitfalls.

The quality of the information obtained from interviews is a function of the respondent's capacity to reflect on and discuss the topics under investigation and the interviewer's skill in creating the conditions which encourage the respondent to talk freely. Many seniors interviewed for this study spoke with clarity and precision about how they benefited from out-of-class experiences. Others, when asked to reflect on changes associated with experiences outside the classroom, invariably used illustrations from both in-class and out-of-class experiences. In other instances, students described a seamlessness between learning in and out of the classroom, suggesting that the boundaries between academics and student life beyond the classroom—often perceived by faculty and administrators to be real—were blurred so as to be indistinguishable to students. Still others were not very articulate in talking about how or whether they had changed during college. The best example is a Rhodes Scholar who, during the course of a 75-minute interview, was asked three times to describe how he had changed. Each time, however, he took the conversation in other directions. In all likelihood, this student—who had achieved national honors and a spate of institutional recognitions—benefited more from the undergraduate experience than his interview transcript revealed.

Finally, another plausible explanation for variation in the richness of interviews is the nature of a student's experiences in college. Some respondents may not have learned or changed very much as a result of experiences outside the classroom. Recall that seniors at small colleges with liberal arts missions were more likely to report changes in Cognitive Complexity, Knowledge and Academic Skills, and Altruism and Estheticism. Small classes and dorms place a greater obligation on students to actively participate; therefore, students at small colleges may have more opportunities to engage in activities—both in and out of the classroom—that require reflection and application of knowledge and skills (Barker, 1968; Chickering, 1969); thus, they have more practice in expressing themselves orally. At the same time, it may be that students who choose to attend small colleges are predisposed to such behavior and that these apparent differences in outcomes are a function of college recruitment, and not college impact (Pascarella & Terenzini, 1991).

Limitations

This study has several limitations. The first, and perhaps most important, is the nature of the institutions from which participants were selected. These colleges and universities were known to provide high quality out-of-class learning opportunities. Thus, it is possible that the range and degree of changes reported by students in this study may be richer than those of students at other institutions. Indeed, comparative analyses of *College Student Experience Questionnaire* (Pace, 1987) data indicated that students from these 12 institutions were more involved in their education (i.e., expended greater effort in their studies and educationally purposeful out-of-class activities) and benefitted more than their counterparts at other institutions (Kuh et al., 1991; Kuh & Vesper, 1992). Thus, the special qualities of these colleges and universities should be considered when determining the transferability of these findings.

Although these institutions are similar in that they provide rich out-of-class learning environments, they differed—as mentioned earlier—in other ways that influence student learning. More information about the contextual conditions of these colleges would provide a framework within which to interpret students' experiences and explain, perhaps, why what appear to be similar experiences and outcomes differ qualitatively. One example must suffice.

All of the quotations from students at The Evergreen State University mention their program of study. This may seem out of place in a paper focused on out-of-class experiences, unless one is familiar with the Evergreen ethos. At this college, many students have difficulty distinguishing between in-class and out-of-class learning. During our first visit to this campus, before we began interviewing for this study, we discovered that students viewed the terms, "in class" and "out of class" as irrelevant. At Evergreen, learning and personal development is a 24-hour-a-day activity, an expectation reinforced by an academic program that is markedly different from the traditional curriculum in which students select majors and take four or five courses a semester. Evergreen students ("junior learners" in the vernacular of that campus) match up with faculty ("senior learners") and form groups of 20 to 40 or so to study some topic in depth from an interdisciplinary perspective for a few months to, on occasion, a year. For many students, these groups, called "Programs," constitute one's primary academic *and* affinity groups. That is, the Program *is* the college experience, and to ask students to compartmentalize their learning experiences contradicts the mission of the institution and makes no sense to students. Hence, an understanding of the contextual conditions of these institutions would allow additional interpretations of these data.

Another limitation is the nature of the data—student reports of what happened to them since coming to college. Self-report data have been found to be moderately correlated ($r = .25$ to $r = .65$) with objective measures of knowledge acquisition (Pascarella & Terenzini, 1991). Nonetheless, memories are selective, and it is possible that students failed to mention certain changes. Recall could have been prompted by the use of a structured protocol based on an existing taxonomy of outcomes, such as Lenning (1976) or Micek, Service, and Lee (1975): This approach was rejected because it was incompatible with the phenomenological interview method. However, if respondents could have reviewed a verbatim transcript, or summary of their comments, they might have added other changes (Kvale, 1983). Therefore, the data reported in this paper almost certainly underestimate the benefits students derive from attending college in general and from out-of-class experiences in particular.

Finally, multiple investigators were needed to interview students at a dozen institutions in different regions of the country. Although all research team members were skilled in interviewing techniques, some were more successful than others in getting students to talk about the impact of out-of-class experiences on their learning and personal development.

A Note on Using Quantitative Data Analysis Procedures With Qualitative Data

The appropriateness of mixing quantitative and qualitative methods is the subject of continuing debate (Howe, 1988; Jick, 1979; Smith & Heshusius, 1986). The issues are complicated and cannot be resolved here; rather, the purpose here is to illustrate an important tradeoff associated with being "shamelessly eclectic" (Rossman & Wilson, 1991) in mixing methods: efficiency versus investigator influence. As mentioned earlier, employing quantitative procedures allows the researcher to more quickly identify patterns in large amounts of information (Miles & Huberman, 1984). However, using quantitative data analysis procedures limits the investigator's capacity to understand the nature, meaning, and impact of the information, the natural by-product of joining personal interpretations as one analyzes the data inductively (Peshkin, 1988).

This study took a middle road in that many weeks were devoted to the inductive analysis of more than 12 dozen interviews prior to employing quantitative techniques to distill patterns in the data. These procedures (e.g., factor analysis, ANOVA) allowed the researcher to classify the information in ways (e.g., by institutional type) that would have required substantially more time using the inductive approach exclusively.

Conclusions

This study provides a contemporary view of the changes students attributed to out-of-class experiences. Based on their "voices," four conclusions about student learning and personal development associated with out-of-class experiences are warranted.

First, consistent with earlier studies (e.g., Wilson, 1966), experiences beyond the classroom made substantial contributions to student learning and personal development. All students reported personally meaningful changes in one or more areas considered to be important outcomes of college (e.g., interpersonal and practical competence, critical thinking). The relationships among these outcomes were complex, suggesting cumulative and mutually shaping effects of knowledge, and enhanced capacity for critical thinking, personal reflection, competence, and self-direction. With all the attention given to outcomes assessment (Ewell, 1991), it is disappointing that the contributions of out-of-class experiences to learning and personal development have received so little attention, particularly given that students attach so much importance to such experiences.

Second, knowledge acquisition and academic skills were more frequently associated with classroom, laboratory, and studio activities than with out-of-class experiences. When talking about how they had changed during college many students mentioned skill areas such as writing and knowledge about specific subjects. The quotations illustrating this outcome domain suggest that students view the classroom as the primary source of these changes. At the same time, although students attributed gains in knowledge to classroom assignments and experiences, life outside the classroom provided ample opportunities to test the value and worth of these ideas and skills.

Third, student background characteristics were, for the most part, unrelated to the learning and personal development outcomes they considered important. The kinds and degree of changes reported by seniors in this study were similar, regardless of age and ethnicity. It is reassuring to know that the benefits associated with attending college reported by "new majority students" (i.e., students of color and those who are over the age of 23, attend college part time, live off campus, have families, or work more than 20 hours a week; Ehrlich, 1991) did not differ from those of traditional age and white students. The lone difference associated with sex regarding application of knowledge is a reminder that collegiate climates for learning often are less empowering for women than for men. If women are taken seriously in and out of the classroom by faculty and administrators, perhaps they will be encouraged to the same extent as their male counterparts to apply what they are learning.

Finally, the type of institution attended was related to differences in the frequency with which certain outcomes were mentioned. For example, students at the smaller colleges with a liberal arts mission more frequently reported changes in intellectual and aesthetic areas. To what degree pre-college characteristics of students contribute to these differences cannot be determined from this study. However, others have argued that a salient, consistently articulated mission focuses student effort (Chickering, 1969; Keeton, 1971). To the extent that this is the case of these colleges, the results of this study affirm Bowen's (1977) conclusion that large size does not necessarily offer educational advantages.

There is more to discover about the contributions of out-of-class experiences to student learning and personal development. For example, studies that attempt to link various out-of-class experiences (e.g., voluntarism, student government, on-campus job) with specific outcomes would be useful to institutional decisionmakers responsible for weighing the merits of allocating resources to such activities. Because many of the benefits of college attendance seem to persist well beyond graduation, it would be instructive to examine the relationships between involvement in out-of-class activities and the long-term effects of college. The words of a senior from The Evergreen State College convey a thought consistent with this last point:

> My educational experience here, it's been more like preparing for my journey. [College] has been a journey within itself, but it's more a preparation for my real journey.

Notes

1. The research reported in this paper was funded in part by grants from The Lilly Endowment, Inc., the National Association of Student Personnel Administrators, and the Education Division of the Marriott Corporation. However, any endorsement by these agencies of the findings presented here should not be inferred.

2. I gratefully acknowledge the splendid work of collaborators on the College Experiences Study. Without them, the information on which this paper is based could not have been gathered: Rosalind Andreas, Herman Blake, James Lyons, Lee Krehbiel, Kathleen MacKay, John Schuh, Carney Strange, and Elizabeth Whitt. Also Jeff McCollough, while he was a graduate student at Indiana University, did an internship at Stanford (his alma mater), part of which included interviewing Stanford students.

3. The contributions of Caitlin Anderson, James Arnold, and John Downey, all doctoral students in higher education at Indiana University, were essential to completing this project. They played key roles in developing the outcomes taxonomy distilled from the interview transcripts and made many helpful comments on an earlier draft of this paper. Special thanks also are due to Nick Vesper of Indiana University who cheerfully, skillfully, and in a most timely fashion, performed the computer analysis of outcomes data. Finally, I wish to acknowledge the helpful comments of John Centra and Elizabeth Whitt on an earlier version of this paper and the suggestions of the anonymous reviewers and John Rury.

References

Astin, A. W. (1973). Measurement and determinants of the outputs of higher education. In L. Solmon and P. Taubman (Eds.), *Does college matter? Some evidence on the impacts of higher education.* New York: Academic Press.

Astin, A. W. (1977). *Four critical years: Effects of college on beliefs, attitudes, and knowledge.* San Francisco: Jossey-Bass.

Astin, H. S., & Kent, L. (1983). Gender roles in transition: Research and policy implications for higher education. *Journal of Higher Education, 54,* 309–324.

Attinasi, L. C., Jr. (1992). Rethinking the study of college outcomes. *Journal of College Student Development, 33,* 61–70.

Barker, R. (1968). *Ecological psychology: Concepts for studying the environment of human behavior.* Stanford, CA: Stanford University Press.

Baxter Magolda, M. B. (1992). Cocurricular influences on college students' intellectual development. *Journal of College Student Development, 33,* 203–213.

Bogdan, R. C., & Biklen, S. K. (1982). *Qualitative research for education: An introduction to theory and methods.* Boston: Allyn and Bacon.

Bowen, H. R. (1977). *Investment in learning.* San Francisco: Jossey-Bass.

Boyer, E. (1987). *College: The undergraduate experience in America.* New York: Harper & Row.

Chickering, A. W. (1969). *Education and identity.* San Francisco: Jossey-Bass.

Clark, B. R., Heist, P., McConnell, T. R., Trow, M. A., & Yonge, G. (1972). *Students and colleges: Interaction and change.* Berkeley: University of California, Center for Research and Development in Higher Education.

Ehrlich, T. (1991). *Our university in the state: Educating the new majority.* Bloomington: Indiana University.

Ewell, P. T. (1984). *The self-regarding institution: Information for excellence.* Boulder, CO: National Center for Higher Education Management Systems.

Ewell, P. T. (1991). Assessment and public accountability: Back to the future. *Change, 23*(6), 12–17.

Feldman, K. A., & Newcomb, T. M. (1969). *The impact of college on students.* San Francisco: Jossey-Bass.

Freedman, M. B. (1967). *The college experience.* San Francisco: Jossey-Bass.

Heist, P., & Yonge, G. (1968). *Omnibus Personality Inventory manual (Form F).* New York: Psychological Corporation.

Hyman, H., & Wright, C. (1979). *Education's lasting influence on values.* Chicago: University of Chicago Press.

Howe, K. R. (1988). Against the quantitative-qualitative incompatibility thesis or dogmas die hard. *Educational Researcher, 17*(8), 10–16.

Jick, T. D. (1979). Mixing qualitative and quantitative methods: Triangulation in action. *Administrative Science Quarterly, 24,* 602–611.

Keeton, M. (1971). *Models and mavericks.* New York: McGraw-Hill.

Kohlberg, L. (1984). *Essays on moral development: Vol. 2. The psychology of moral development: The nature and validity of moral stages.* New York: Harper & Row.

Kuh, G. D., Krehbiel, L., & MacKay, K. A. (1988). *Personal development and the college student experience: A review of the literature.* Trenton, NJ: New Jersey Department of Higher Education, College Outcomes Evaluation Program.

Kuh, G. D., Schuh, J. S., Whitt, E. J., Andreas, R. E., Lyons, J. W., Strange, C. C., Krehbiel, L. E., & MacKay, K. A. (1991). *Involving colleges: Successful approaches to fostering student learning and personal development outside the classroom.* San Francisco: Jossey-Bass.

Kuh, G. D., & Stage, F. K. (1992). Student development theory and research. In B. R. Clark & G. Neave (Eds.), *Encyclopedia of higher education* (pp. 1719–1730). Oxford and New York: Praeger.

Kuh, G. D., & Vesper, N. (1992, April). *A comparison of student learning at "involving" and "other" metropolitan universities.* Paper presented at the Annual Meeting of the American Educational Research Association, San Francisco.

Kvale, S. (1983). The qualitative research interview: A phenomenological and hermeneutical mode of understanding. *Journal of Phenomenological Psychology, 14,* 171–196.

Lenning, O. T. (Ed.). (1976). *Improving educational outcomes.* San Francisco: Jossey-Bass.

Levine, A. & Associates. (1989). *Shaping higher education's future: Demographic realities and opportunities, 1990–2000.* San Francisco: Jossey-Bass.

Light, R. J. (1992). *The Harvard assessment seminars: Explorations with students and faculty about teaching, learning, and student life* (Second report). Cambridge, MA: Harvard University Graduate School of Education and Kennedy School of Government.

Madison, P. (1969). *Personality development in college.* Reading, MA: Addison-Wesley.

Micek, S. S., Service, A. L., & Lee, Y. S. (1975). *Outcome measures and procedures manual.* Boulder, CO: National Center for Higher Education Management Systems, Western Interstate Commission on Higher Education.

Miles, M. B., & Huberman, A. M. (1984). *Qualitative data analysis: A sourcebook of new methods.* Beverly Hills, CA: Sage.

Moffatt, M. (1988). *Coming of age in New Jersey: College and American culture.* New Brunswick, NJ: Rutgers University Press.

Pace, C. R. (1979). *Measuring outcomes of college: Fifty years of findings and recommendations for the future.* San Francisco: Jossey-Bass.

Pace, C. R. (1987). *CSEQ: Test manual and norms: College Student Experiences Questionnaire.* Los Angeles: The Center for the Study of Evaluation, Graduate School of Education, University of California, Los Angeles.

Pace, C. R. (1990). *The undergraduates: A report of their activities and progress in college in the 1980s.* Los Angeles: University of California at Los Angeles, Center for the Study of Evaluation.

Pascarella, E. T. (1985). College environmental influences on learning and cognitive development: A critical review and synthesis. In J. Smart (Ed.), *Higher education: Handbook of theory and research (Vol. 1).* New York: Agathon.

Pascarella, E. T., Ethington, C. A., & Smart, J. C. (1988). The influence of college on humanitarian/civic involvement values. *Journal of Higher Education, 59,* 412–437.

Pascarella, E. T., & Terenzini, P. T. (1991). *How college affects students: Findings and insights from twenty years of research.* San Francisco: Jossey-Bass.

Perry, W. G., Jr. (1970). *Forms of intellectual and ethical development in the college years. A scheme.* New York: Holt, Rinehart, & Winston.

Peshkin, A. (1988). In search of subjectivity—one's own. *Educational Record, 17*(7), 17–22.

Reichardt, C. S., & Cook, T. D. (1979). Beyond qualitative versus quantitative methods. In C. Reichardt & T. Cook (Eds.), *Qualitative and Quantitative methods in evaluation* (pp. 7–32). Beverly Hills: Sage.

Rodgers, R. F. (1989). Student development. In U. Delworth & G. Hanson (Eds.), *Student services: A handbook for the profession* (pp. 117–164). San Francisco: Jossey-Bass.

Rossman, G. B., & Wilson, B. L. (April, 1991). *Numbers and words revisited: Being "shamelessly eclectic."* Paper presented at the Annual Meeting of the American Educational Research Association, Chicago.

Saufley, R. W., Cowan, K. O., & Blake, J. H. (1983). The struggles of minority students at predominantly white institutions. In J. Cones III, J. Noonan, & D. Janha (Eds.), *Teaching minority students: New directions for teaching and learning, No. 16* (pp. 3–15). San Francisco: Jossey-Bass.

Shrader, W. (1969). *College ruined our daughter: Letters to parents concerning the baffling world of the college student.* New York: Harper & Row.

Smith, J. K., & Heshusius, L. (1986). Closing down the conversation: The end of the quantitative-qualitative debates among educational inquirers. *Educational Researcher, 15*(1), 4–12.

Thomas, R., & Chickering, A. W. (1984). *Education and Identity* revisited. *Journal of College Student Personnel, 25,* 392–399.

Tinto, V. (1987). *Leaving college: Rethinking the causes and cures of student attrition.* Chicago: University of Chicago Press.

Weidman, J. (1989). Undergraduate socialization: A conceptual approach. In J. Smart (Ed.), *Higher education: Handbook of theory and research (Vol. 5).* New York: Agathon.

White, R. W. (1966). *Lives in progress* (2nd ed.). New York: Holt, Rinehart, & Winston.

Wilson, E. K. (1966). The entering student: Attributes and agents of change. In T. Newcomb & E. Wilson (Eds.), *College peer groups* (pp. 71–106). Chicago, Aldine.

Winter, D., McClelland, D., & Stewart, A. (1981). *A new case for the liberal arts: Assessing institutional goals and student development.* San Francisco: Jossey-Bass.

Assessing Institutional Effectiveness in Community Colleges

EDITED BY DON DOUCETTE AND BILLIE HUGHES

An Approach to Assessing Institutional Effectiveness

Purpose

This monograph outlines an approach for assessing institutional effectiveness that can be both usefully and fairly applied to community colleges and identifies resources to assist practitioners in conducting such an assessment.

The fundamental perspective is that assessing the effectiveness of any institution should be based upon a systematic evaluation of how effective it is in performing its explicitly stated missions. Assessment of the institutional effectiveness of a community college, then, is a systematic evaluation of how well such an institution performs not only the missions it has in common with other community colleges but also the missions peculiar to the needs of its local constituents and community.

This monograph provides a rationale and a process for assessing the effectiveness of community colleges in performing their missions that reflects their specific character and circumstances. An underlying premise is that community colleges are not well-served by assessment processes designed for four-year colleges and universities that ignore the substantial differences between types of institutions. Thus, while this monograph is, in part, a reaction to difficulties that community colleges have historically had in responding to requests to document the effectiveness of their efforts using inappropriate measures and models, it also responds to the opportunity that community colleges now have to determine the criteria by which their various publics will evaluate them.

Perspective

Issues involved in assessing institutional effectiveness are not new. They have long been addressed by private and public institutions of higher education, as well as institutions and agencies outside of education. For the most part, answers to questions regarding effectiveness were informal: informal in the manner in which they were used, informal in the processes by which the answers were derived, and informal in the way answers were communicated to others. Students, faculty, and community members who came in contact with a college or university usually discussed their impressions with family, friends, and relatives; word-of-mouth reputations and casual assessments were either the downfall or the foundation for the survival of institutions. Granted, some institu-

303

tions were mismanaged or poorly financed and thus failed, but it is arguable that the fates of many institutions were determined by relatively informal institutional effectiveness assessment measures. Frequently, the only formal measure was undertaken by regional accrediting agencies, which traditionally focused on process rather than outcome measures.

However, assessment of institutional effectiveness has become more rational, more public, more systematic, and more consistently based upon data and other objective measures. Recently, the focus of such assessments has been on student outcomes, which is a significant departure from process measures historically used by all regional educational accrediting agencies. The shift to an emphasis on outcome measures, in addition to the continued use of appropriate process measures, is a positive direction for community colleges because such a focus allows accountability and effectiveness to be assessed according to criteria that can be established, in part, by faculty, administrators, and other college constituents.

While most would agree that institutions should assess their effectiveness, less agreement exists as to what should be assessed and what constitutes acceptable and appropriate measures. Peter Ewell, senior associate, National Center for Higher Education Management Systems, places this problem in its simplest terms: assessing institutional effectiveness is a "comparison of results achieved to goals intended." For community colleges, this directive translates into assessing an institution's effectiveness in terms of its performance of its stated missions—which presumably represent the explicit and consensual goals of the college. Of course, this also means that institutions lacking a clear sense of purpose will have a difficult time determining their effectiveness.

For community colleges, the issues related to effectiveness are often quite different from those of four-year colleges or universities. Although much of higher education is currently being criticized, open-door, two-year colleges are especially prone to criticism from those who use traditional, but sometimes inappropriate, standards for evaluating institutional effectiveness. Fundamental differences between the missions of community colleges and universities have been ignored too often and have resulted in community colleges being judged by university expectations. For example, providing access to all constituents in a service area, not just a select group seeking degrees, is a primary concern of nearly all community colleges. Thus, while the number of degrees conferred in a given time period may be a critical measure of effective performance for a four-year institution, more appropriate measures for a community college are likely to be the number of students who successfully transfer, the number of students who find satisfying employment, or the number of students who master basic literacy skills.

The issue of effectiveness is complicated because community colleges are to a large degree reflections of the localities they serve. Because no two communities are identical, no two community colleges have exactly the same missions, even though most have their primary missions in common. Therefore, the measures used by each community college to assess its effectiveness can legitimately be designed to reflect each college's specific purpose, as determined by the consensus of its key constituents.

Community colleges now have an historic opportunity to overcome attempts to assess their effectiveness with inappropriate measures. Outcomes-based assessment allows community colleges to demonstrate their effectiveness by developing and implementing criteria appropriate for evaluating their performance of their separate missions. This monograph is a specific response to the opportunity.

Organization and Audience

This document is organized around the premise that community colleges should implement programs to assess their effectiveness in performing their various missions using outcomes-based measures for each mission. It presumes that community colleges take seriously their stated missions and that they possess or can develop the expertise required to monitor objective measures or indicators for each mission.

The remainder of this chapter considers the examination of institutional mission statements, and the following chapters contain pertinent reviews of the four key missions of most community colleges—transfer, career education, basic skills and developmental education, and continuing education and community service. Then, the access mission, a superordinate mission for most community colleges, is considered as it relates to assessing institutional effectiveness. Each of these five chapters introduces the mission in the context of assessment issues, describes the principal clients served by each mission, and details the major programs offered by most community colleges for these clients. Finally, each chapter concludes with a series of questions and corresponding data sources that could form the basis for an assessment of an institution's performance of the mission.

The chapters on mission are intended for two different audiences. First, the descriptions provide a context in which internal audiences can view their own college's efforts, with specific guidance for implementing an institutional effectiveness assessment program available in the questions and data sources sections. Equally important, interested external audiences, including members of boards of trustees, legislators, state officials, and business and community leaders, may use the outlines of the major missions, clients served, and programs offered by most community colleges as an overview of the issues involved in assessing the effectiveness of these unique and often misunderstood institutions.

Following this focused discussion of community college missions are chapters that address general issues involved in implementing institutional effectiveness programs and responding to calls to demonstrate accountability, as well as appendices that identify key methods and resources to support assessment programs.

Caveats

A few caveats are in order. Appropriate missions for community colleges have been debated almost as long as the institutions have been in existence. The four principal missions described in this document are intended to represent the major categories of programs and services provided to community college clients. While the terms used to describe these missions and the activities included in each are subject to discussion and suggestions for alternative groupings, together these incorporate the great majority of community college efforts. Similarly, the broad range of programs and services described in the mission category termed "access" could just as easily be described as the "student development" or "student success" mission. However, the term "access mission" was chosen because it best describes an intended outcome of this range of activities and reflects the most distinctive characteristic of community colleges.

Finally, while the approach recommended is a mission-by-mission examination, it is understood that the final result must be a holistic assessment of an institution's effectiveness in meeting its own expectations and those of its publics. Analysis by mission category is intended to assist community colleges to develop appropriate criteria and to implement realistic measures for each of their major functions. However, the boundaries of most missions are blurred, and programs and clients overlap among them. An overall institutional assessment combines the results of examining effectiveness in performing individual missions; such a broad assessment may even take into account the fact that some missions may be higher institutional priorities than others.

Mission Statements

Because this monograph is organized to support a mission-by-mission examination of a community college's effectiveness, institutions without an explicit and up-to-date mission statement probably cannot employ this approach. Admittedly, mission statements have too often been treated as glowingly vague statements of the motherhood-and-apple-pie intentions of a college or university, generally confined to catalog copy filler or filed with institutional charters and by-laws. However, mission statements can be vital documents that reflect a college's explicit and focused purposes, which are examined and updated regularly by a consensual process involving all of its major constituents.

The assessment approach described in this monograph requires such a mission statement. In some cases, a college may find it helpful to begin an assessment of its institutional effectiveness with the development or re-examination of its mission statement. The process for doing either has much in common with strategic planning and results in a straightforward statement of the priority activities of an institution. The following describes the steps of such a process.

1. *Review Current Institutional Activities and Mission.* The development of a new mission statement or the review of an existing one begins with a comprehensive listing of all current institutional activities and a comparison of the list with the current mission statement. Many institutions add functions over time that may not be reflected in their mission statements. Any planned future activities should be added to the list, which should then be organized into major groups of activities with a summary statement or category title heading each subsection.

2. *Determine Future Directions.* A mission statement sets direction for an institution. Therefore, strategic planning processes, such as environmental scanning, values clarification, and resource allocation studies, can be used to assist in developing a vision of the desired future of the college that should be reflected in its mission statement. Such forward-looking thinking should result in additional intended activities to incorporate into the master list of activities.

3. *Review Lists and Categories.* Once developed, the lists and categories of activities should be reviewed by a broadly representative group to insure that all activities in which the college is or is proposing to become involved are included. Such a review can take place at various levels; for instance, initial review might be limited to a manageable number of key college staff that represent all college functional areas, as well as selected representatives of special interests and college constituents.

4. *Insure Involvement in Determining Priorities.* Collegewide involvement, starting with the firm and enthusiastic endorsement of the president and other college leaders, is essential to creating a statement that both reflects and inspires the college's goals and values. The process of determining the priority activities to be reflected in the mission statement can take place in stages. For instance, an initial review by a smaller group could eliminate the least feasible of the activities, but the process should move towards inclusion of the broad college community. This critical step of determining college priorities can be accomplished using a variety of methods, including formal surveys, task forces or committees focusing on certain areas or representing specific interests, or even a convocation or convention of the entire college.

5. *Write a Draft Statement.* A draft mission statement should then be written to reflect the consensus reached in the previous steps about the college's priority activities. Most mission statements are usually one or two pages in length, with an introduction expressing the college's principal commitments followed by a priority list of the major activities or functions. In addition, some colleges also publish other related materials with a mission statement, including a brief history of the college, pertinent descriptive information, statements of institutional values, outlines of functional organizations, a description of student characteristics, lists of intended student outcomes, and vision statements describing ideal operating environments and institutional responses.

6. *Seek Consensus.* Once drafted, a mission statement needs to be reviewed as broadly as feasible by all important college constituents with the intention to develop a broad-based consensus. All comments, editorial suggestions, and requests for additions and deletions need to be considered—even if ultimately rejected as unrepresentative of the college community—in developing subsequent drafts of the statement for review and revision.

7. *Adopt the Statement Formally.* After careful review and editing to reflect the greatest possible consensus of the college community, the board of trustees should formally act to accept the mission statement as official policy of the college.

8. *Disseminate.* After formal adoption, a mission statement should be disseminated to all college constituents in appropriate ways. Key publications, such as the college catalog, master plan, and annual report, should include it as an appropriate expression of the college's intentions and purpose. It should guide major decision making and important college processes, especially strategic planning and resource allocation.

9. *Review and Update.* Finally, once adopted, a college's mission statement should be reviewed and updated regularly, especially to reflect major changes in college emphases or developments in the external environment to which the college intends to respond. At a minimum, a college should conduct a formal process to review and update its mission statement every three to five years.

While this brief section is not a complete discussion of the development and review of community college mission statements, a college must explicitly articulate its purposes as a prerequisite to any serious attempt to determine how effectively it is achieving them.

Issues in Assessing Institutional Effectiveness

The move toward formal, outcomes-based programs for assessing institutional effectiveness is a relatively new development for institutions of higher education. Demands that community colleges implement assessment programs raise a host of issues, particularly as this approach is quite different in focus from assessments previously required by accrediting bodies or government agencies. This chapter attempts to address many of these issues; the discussion is organized in the question and answer format.

Questions and Answers

Should community colleges respond to requests for documentation for institutional effectiveness? Community colleges have an obligation to respond in a positive manner to reasonable requests for measures of institutional effectiveness. Examples of these include 1) measures to be used internally for improvement of programs and services, 2) measures to be used by government agencies for regulatory functions, 3) measures to be used by the public and students in making decisions as consumers, and 4) measures to be used by regional accrediting agencies. Accrediting agencies traditionally emphasize process and include faculty credentials, facilities, library collections, financial resources, and operating efficiency but are now increasingly requesting outcome measures.

On occasion, institutions will be faced with unreasonable requests for information, or for inappropriate information. In these cases, rather than refusing to comply, institutions should suggest alternative information that is both reasonable and accurate.

Is assessment the same as evaluation?
The term assessment is often mistakenly used interchangeably with evaluation and measurement. Assessment is essentially the process of gathering data or measures and assembling them in some understandable form. Once gathered, judgments or evaluations may be made on the basis of the evidence. Measurement is only part of the process of assessment, and evaluation implies judgments based upon the collated measures.

Can community colleges be evaluated by a single measure?
The complexity of the community college requires multiple measures of effectiveness. No single measure can describe an institution's effectiveness; measures viewed in isolation may result in a very inaccurate and potentially damaging perception of institutional effectiveness. For example, degrees awarded is one reasonable indicator of institutional effectiveness at four-year colleges and universities. However, in community colleges, where a majority of students are not pursuing degrees or certificates, it is certainly not a sole criterion. This measure, by itself, gives the perception that, by comparison, community colleges are not as effective as four-year colleges. This ignores how many students are meeting their individual goals, such as upgrading job skills or preparing for transfer to other institutions. Such a measure also fails to reflect the impact the college has on its community and the economy. Thus, single measures are measures out-of-context and misrepresent the effectiveness of the institution as a whole.

Are there general criteria that should be applied when selecting measures?
The measures selected as indicators of institutional effectiveness must be practical and relevant to the mission of the college. Institutions need to resist the temptation to use measures simply because they are easily obtained. The fact that the outcomes of certain college programs and services are difficult to measure does not diminish their importance. Colleges should continue to seek means to demonstrate effectiveness in performing their clearly identified missions.

The measures selected should have a reasonable chance of contributing to the improvement of institutional effectiveness. Many possible measures can be identified, but institutions will not have the resources to collect all of them. Those selected, by either external agencies or college personnel, should be those most relevant to the institution and its community, as well as those that can lead to improvements in teaching, learning, and the delivery of services to students.

Will access to the community college be affected by an emphasis on institutional effectiveness?
A danger of the move toward outcomes assessment and accountability is that colleges could inadvertently lose sight of some of their important missions in the quest to demonstrate institutional effectiveness. One of the easiest ways to raise success rates of students would be to limit acceptance of high-risk students into the college. This, however, would directly contradict access to nontraditional students, which is a priority goal of most community colleges. The Report of the Commission on the Future of Community Colleges (1988) urges that caution be exercised to insure that outcomes assessment and accountability do not become synonymous with a new elitism. For this reason, consideration of the access mission, along with the four core educational missions of most community colleges, is critical to the overall assessment of institutional effectiveness.

How much data is enough to demonstrate institutional effectiveness?
This is a difficult question to answer. The college's primary role is to provide services to constituents. Programs for measuring institutional effectiveness should not become ends in themselves, but rather should become an ongoing process for institutional improvement. Two criteria can be applied to this determination:

1. The effort and expense involved in collecting and disseminating measures of institutional effectiveness should not be greater than the benefits to be received as a result of the measurement. Each measure to be used should be considered against this

criterion. Of course, this can be a difficult judgment to make, and such discretion can be limited by mandates from external bodies.

2. Information collected should facilitate decision-making and be relevant to decisions the institution is prepared to make. Collecting information only because it would be "nice to know" should be avoided. In this regard, institutions and external agencies should require specific plans for the utilization of each measure prior to requesting its collection.

Who should be involved in identifying the measures used to assess institutional effectiveness? The focus should be on overall institutional effectiveness, not the success of individual departments or divisions; therefore, to the extent possible, a wide range of staff from throughout the institution should be involved. The commitment must begin with the chief executive officer. Staff and faculty must see that the institutional commitment is real in that top administrators sincerely value these activities as important to the institution. The institution needs to internalize the importance of demonstrating institutional effectiveness and accept it as a legitimate, self-imposed institutional function—not as a onetime examination, but rather as an ongoing, valuable institutional enterprise.

Determining the specific measures to be used should be a joint function. Faculty and staff often feel that others in the institution do not fully understand their programs and cannot effectively establish the appropriate criteria for evaluating them. Results that indicate a need for change will be best accepted if faculty and staff are involved in selecting the measures, participate in the data collection, and help interpret the results. Thus, the active participation of the faculty and staff is essential to the success of any assessment of institutional effectiveness. If planning, data collection, and the use of results are mandated from above, the process is bound to fail.

Institutional researchers play a key role in assisting faculty and staff in identifying the measures and in collecting relevant data. In the ideal situation, however, the final responsibility for identifying appropriate measures and using the results rests with the faculty and staff who provide the programs and services.

Who are the major audiences for data assessing institutional outcomes?
Different aspects of institutional effectiveness data will be of interest to various concerned parties, including college administrators, faculty and staff; board members; legislators and staff in state coordinating or governing boards; regional, state and professional accrediting organizations; foundations and other funding agencies; and the general public.

Internal audiences, including administrators, faculty, and staff require the results of outcome assessment to guide program improvements. Members of boards of trustees have similar informational needs to insure that programs are designed and implemented as effectively as possible. External audiences, especially legislators and state officials, will use assessment results in making policy decisions.

Another key audience is current and potential students and, when appropriate, their parents. The results of outcomes assessments for each mission should be made available to these constituents as consumers and sponsors of college programs. Of course, this audience tends to be particularly interested in information regarding the specific programs in which they are considering enrolling. Those intending to prepare for transfer to a four-year college or university want to know the success rates of previous students with similar intentions, and those exploring career programs are interested specifically in the placement rates and initial salaries earned by graduates of the program. Community colleges have a special obligation to provide complete and accurate information to this audience.

Recipients of program graduates also have a keen interest in the results of outcome assessments. In particular, employers and others in local business, industry, and labor will want to know the level of preparation they can expect of those who complete career programs, various courses, or continuing education training. Transfer institutions want to know both the level of preparation they can expect of entering students and their rates of success completing baccalaureate degree programs.

Finally, members of the community at large are an important constituency for outcomes information. Their interest will be the most broad-based, though assessment results can be critical in maintaining their continuing support for the college.

How should assessment data be used?

The purpose for determining measures of effectiveness should be prescriptive, not punitive. This will reduce resistance to collecting and using assessment results. If participants in the assessment process understand that the purpose is to improve, rather than to penalize individuals or programs, the chance that the results will be accepted and used appropriately is much greater.

Assessment results should certainly not be used as part of faculty evaluation, nor as a barrier for the advancement of students to higher levels of learning. The determination of institutional effectiveness should never become a process that mitigates against faculty and student involvement. Neither should outcomes be used to rank college programs, groups of students, or institutions against one another. As convenient as it might be to compare the number of transfer students accepted from one community college to that from another, this in itself, may say more about the nature of the students entering the colleges than the effectiveness of the colleges' respective programs.

To have meaning, promote involvement, and sustain long-term value, the information-gathering process must ultimately result in aggregate benefits, not punishments, to the students, faculty, and administration of any institution.

What precautions should be taken in reporting measures of effectiveness?

Overall, colleges need to exercise particular care in reporting measures of institutional effectiveness to external agencies. The equivalent of Murphy's Law for institutional researchers is that if data can be misunderstood, it will be. The corollary is that if data can be misused, it will be (even if inadvertently).

Some measures are potentially harmful to groups of students if not handled sensitively. For example, cumulative grade point averages of transfer students are not generally comparable across institutions. Further, minority students as a group traditionally have fared poorly on standardized assessment instruments when compared to nonminority students. If results not favorable to subgroups of students are widely reported and subject to misinterpretation, they may lead to reinforcing of stereotypes and be counterproductive to improving institutional effectiveness.

Even when individuals are well-intentioned, misinterpretation and misuse can occur. Educating agency personnel on interpretations, uses, and limitations of the data is a critical part of the dissemination process. Agencies requesting the information have an obligation to use it responsibly. Likewise, colleges have an obligation to provide data in a manner that allows agencies to use it responsibly.

Who should pay the costs of assessing institutional effectiveness?

The costs of collecting and disseminating measures of institutional effectiveness should not be greater than the benefits to be received as a result of the measurement. The costs of conducting programs for measuring institutional effectiveness should not necessarily fall on the college. If the benefit is primarily to the institution, as a form of self-assessment leading to improvement of services, the cost should be borne primarily by the college. However, if the request originates from a state board, accrediting body or other external agency and is primarily for regulatory purposes, those agencies should consider funding those assessments.

In some cases an external agency may fund measures of institutional effectiveness that are, in the opinion of college personnel, inappropriate. The institution should not automatically gather the measures just because it can receive funds to do so. The criteria of usefulness and appropriateness should be applied in determining whether to accept such funding. If the measures are deemed inappropriate, the college might propose other measures that are more suitable.

In Conclusion

A combination of systematically gathered and reported data along with reasonably stated goals and processes to achieve the goals can provide invaluable help for community colleges to demonstrate their accomplishments to themselves and their constituencies. They will be able to deflect criticisms based upon measures or comparisons that are not compatible with the missions of community colleges. The straightforward approach recommended in this monograph can contribute to better understanding by significant college constituencies of the complex and appropriate role that community colleges play in the overall educational system. The approach should also result in the gathering and reporting of information that is educationally meaningful and useful to students, faculty, and administrators.

If properly planned and implemented, with appropriate faculty and staff involvement at all levels, ongoing institutional effectiveness assessment can be an integral part of a comprehensive program of institutional improvement. Using effectiveness data in a formative way to improve programs may ultimately prove to be the most important use of outcome measures. The same data can be used to respond to various external demands to demonstrate institutional effectiveness.

Appendix B

Using Standardized Assessment Instruments

A principal concern in higher education assessment is that the tests and the results they yield be used properly. Proper test use involves a range of concerns, both technical and practical. This appendix identifies and comments on major elements that an institution should consider in selecting and using a test to assess institutional outcomes to help create a more effective institution.

To be reiterated is that testing is *only* one method of assessing effectiveness. Successful assessment includes other methods such as interviews, surveys, and case studies. Further, the adoption and use of tests require careful planning, administration, and interpretation. The following points are guidelines for organizing a testing program.

Quality of Data

Providing sufficient lead time

A major cause of failure in assessment endeavors is trying to complete all of the steps in a two to four-week period of time. To lay an adequate foundation for success, an institution should expect to spend at least four to six months prior to the administration of any instrument. In numerous instances, individuals have made quick decisions and subsequently have achieved no meaningful results from testing. In fact, attempting to move the process along too quickly and without appropriate collaboration often endangers the assessment effort.

Selecting an adequate sample

A question commonly asked is "What constitutes an adequate sample?" Unfortunately, no simple formula exists for determining a sample. When test data are not representative of the student population because a biased sample was chosen or resulted, or because only data from volunteers were collected, the value and meaning of the group data are highly questionable. Institutions that do not require testing of the full group of students must select their sample carefully or run a significant risk of obtaining data of limited quality. One should consult a good text on this topic (e.g., *Sampling in Education and Social Sciences* by Richard M. Jaeger) and perhaps contact a representative from a testing company for advice.

Generally speaking, the greater the number of students tested, the more accurate the results will be. In terms of raw numbers, institutions should test at least 100 students for each type of test used. Further, a determination should be made if the students to be tested will be randomly selected or whether other variables will be used in selecting students (e.g., freshmen, freshmen with majors declared in business, sophomores who have transferred and/or earned all of their credits at a single institution, all students in classes being held at a specific time, all students in specific classes, etc.). Appropriate sampling is important if the results are to be of maximum value to the institution.

Student participation and effort

One of the critical problems in assessment is securing appropriate and effective participation of students. If students do not take the assessment effort seriously and do not put forth their best effort, the data, at least for those students, are of little or no value. Solving both of these problems is not easy and no quick or universal solutions are available. Getting and keeping student cooperation is serious and difficult work but essential for successful assessment.

Student committees can help identify the best ways to insure student participation. Some possibilities include: 1) requiring participation in order to enroll, register for classes, or graduate; 2) offering a chance in a drawing for a VCR or CD player; 3) giving away coupons for pizza, tee shirts acclaiming their participation, or tickets for cultural/sporting events; 4) appealing to their altruism and getting them to participate because it will help their school do a better job.

Persuading students to take the test seriously and do their best is not as easily addressed. Unless a minimum score is required to move to another education level, there is no compelling incentive to do well. An exam that is challenging can increase motivation. Also, a faculty that enthusiastically supports the assessment efforts can influence student performance. Support of student leaders and organizations is also helpful.

Spot checking student exam performance and test scores is useful in assessing how seriously the students took the exam. A brief questionnaire may be distributed to students to determine whether they took the test seriously and did their best. Moreover, student exit interviews can be helpful in this matter. Institutions must be sensitive to the motivation issue in all assessment efforts that require student participation.

Interpreting Results

Avoiding misuses of data

Interpret test results carefully and avoid misuse of data. Standardized tests are typically constructed very carefully. They can provide reliable and valid information if used correctly. Guidance on the correct use(s) of standardized tests is readily available from testing companies. If an institution follows this advice, it will generally avoid misuse of the results.

A program assessment model will not necessarily allow institutions to make decisions about individuals. For example, flexible sampling models can be very useful for program assessment but do not necessarily provide individual assessment data. On the other hand, if testing is implemented to obtain valid individual results, these results will be viable for program evaluation.

Scores based on subtests may be desirable for program evaluation. However, subscores should be used with great caution unless they are shown to be reasonably reliable. In other words, there should be sufficient numbers of items within each subscore area to provide stable information (e.g., a minimum of approximately 20–25 items for any subscore area). Nevertheless, subscores should be considered primarily as indicators of areas for further evaluation.

Value added

There is great interest in using test results to establish the "value added" by an educational program. This is usually approached using residual scores, which are the difference between pre- and post-test results. While appealing in concept, institutions using such approaches should be aware of the effects of reliability on the quality of the judgment possible. (For example, the statistical phenomenon "regression toward the mean" is important in value added approaches. Simply stated, regression toward the mean is the tendency for those with lower scores to get higher scores on retesting and those with higher scores to get lower scores. Controlling for differences in ability levels through a more sophisticated statistical technique, e.g., analysis of co-variance, may be required.

In addition, norm-referenced scores assume that movement anywhere on the scale is equal. This assumption may mask real gains within a test-retest situation. For example, students who increase their basic arithmetic ability will appear in a norm-referenced comparison the same as students who improve their performance in basic algebra, if both are covered on the same test.

Limitations of standardized tests

While standardized tests have many benefits—objectivity, high reliability, demonstrable validity, low cost, ease of administration, efficient and effective coverage of large amounts of material in a limited time period—they are not a panacea and should not be the sole means of assessment. Other kinds of assessments—essay tests, survey results, performance data—should be used along with or instead of objective instruments when they can improve the quality of the assessment. Critical decisions about individuals or programs should not be made on the basis of test results alone.

Selecting Testing Instruments

Matching tests to goals

Instruments are selected based on institutional goals. These goals need to be stated in a measurable way. If they are not, restating them is a worthwhile exercise. Even if they are stated in a measurable way, they may need fine tuning before selection of testing instruments.

Involving faculty

A committee approach for instrument selection is often effective. The committee can contact the various testing companies for details about their instruments and then match the test objectives with their institutional goals. The number of commercial tests available (see Appendix A) is relatively small, so this review of standardized options can be completed in a reasonable period of time. Publishers provide considerable detail on each test. Some companies even make review copies of actual tests available if stringent security precautions are met. There is some overlap among the tests offered by the various companies, so selection may be made not only based on objectives covered, but also on services provided.

If, after a review of commercial tests, no tests are found to be appropriate, an institution should develop its own instruments. Usually, however, commercial tests can meet at least some of the local assessment needs, so institutions can direct their efforts to supplementing what is available.

Normative and comparative data

Most test scores are "norm" referenced; that is, the scores derive meaning in comparison to the scores of others. How fast a runner can run the 100-yard dash is usually interpreted against how fast others run the same distance. Many different comparisons are possible. Typical comparisons include:

1) comparison with others at the same institution,

2) comparison with those at other institutions, and

3) performance of the same individuals over time.

Norms are difficult to obtain and maintain and, if available for an outcome measure, should be reviewed carefully for appropriateness.

Criterion-referenced

Unlike norm-referenced scores, criterion-referenced scores have meaning in and of themselves. For example, one either meets or fails to meet the criteria for a life saver's certificate. While comparative data can be generated to support use of criterion-referenced scores, it is not necessary for the criterion-referenced data to have meaning. What is important in the use of criterion-referenced data is that the data deal with information of importance and utility to the institution.

Validity

Perhaps the most critical aspect of test use is that a test be valid for the intended use. For example, is it designed to measure the institution's goals? An instrument can be highly valid for one purpose and be totally invalid for another. Validity can be conceived of in several different modes. All are important but for most outcomes assessment purposes, content and construct validity are most critical.

A test is content valid when it covers adequately the content to be measured. In the case of outcomes measures, the test or instrument should cover what an institution is teaching and seeking to accomplish through its educational program.

Construct validity refers to the extent to which a test measures the theoretical construct it is intended to measure. Construct validity is typically demonstrated through an accumulation of research results, such as factor analysis, studies of scores of students who have experienced what is being tested versus those who have not, and correlations with practical criteria and with other tests of the same construct.

Reliability

Reliability is the consistency or accuracy of the measure. Can the results be counted on to be the same over repeated measures? Or, must one expect a great deal of variation in scores obtained from the same individuals at different times? A number of factors determine the reliability of a test—

length, internal consistency, relationship of item performance to scores—and the level of reliability required varies with the use to which the scores will be put.

Scores used to make nonreversible decisions about individuals (e.g., admission to a nursing program) must be much more reliable than scores used to suggest areas of interest, for example. Similarly, scores that are reliable for a group may not be, and may not need to be, reliable for individuals.

No test is perfectly reliable. All involve measurement error. This error comes from a number of sources—some internal to the test and some external. It is important in using test results for assessment purposes that users recognize the imperfection of any measure. When comparisons are made, results should be discussed in terms of either ranges or probabilities of the score distributions overlapping.

Conclusion

The success or failure of using standardized instruments in assessing institutional effectiveness depends upon a variety of factors. If these factors are considered carefully, the chances of achieving success are increased greatly. However, there is no magic formula that can be applied universally. An approach that provides adequate lead time and involves as many faculty, administrators, and students as possible in the whole process (planning, implementation, and evaluation) will be well on the way to attaining good results.

The Blind Alley of Value Added

Jonathan Warren

Quality is a hot issue in higher education today. The public wants it, legislators demand it, students seek it out. Those of us in education have come to see that the decisions our constituencies make hinge on our ability to assess quality and convey its meanings to others.

But how do you assess quality in higher education? Most educators would respond instinctively with today's reigning gospel: value added. That is, you have to look at more than a reputational rating (derived from opinion surveys), more than certain "inputs" of education (Ph.D. degrees, books in the library), and more than certain "outcomes" (percent who go on to graduate school or landing up in *Who's Who*). Instead, you have to look at the changes that occur in students as the result of their college experience, to the "value added" from their time spent in the classrooms and programs of an institution. You look to the characteristics of students at the start of the experience, measure those same characteristics at the end, then adduce from the changes the impact of education. High impact means high quality.

In the abstract, the logic of value added gives it great appeal. In practice, I'll argue, it seldom leads anywhere. Its results are too often trivial, difficult to make sense of, and peripheral to most instructional purposes. An undue focus on value added may mean that today's opportunity to improve quality will slip away from us. We have to get on with alternative ways of demonstrating that what we do for students is to good effect.

Value Added's Appeal

Before enumerating the difficulties with the value added approach, let me record its virtues—theoretical as they may be.

- the concept properly focuses our attention on students (not just on institutions), asking us to know them as they enter and as they leave and to determine what effect we had to their benefit.

- the concept values growth in student capabilities, and helps us avoid outdated practices of instruction that have little or no impact.

- the concept is applicable whether the unit of analysis is a course, a program, or an entire college experience .

- the concept fits the democraticization of higher education, allowing us to see quality in all its settings, not just with the brightest students in the wealthiest colleges.

Again, these advantages seem attractive. The problem lies in translating the concept into practice. When one does so, the results are rarely useful.

Trivial Pursuits

The triviality of many value-added assessments stems from their assumption that students at the beginning of a course (or any other educational experience) do not yet have the knowledge or capabilities the course is intended to teach. Of course they don't, and therefore no elaborate scheme of pre-test and post-test is usually needed to infer that a change has occurred.

Consider an upper-division course in electromagnetic theory, for example. At the end of that course, when the professor finds, through normal examinations, that students as a group have a good understanding of the concepts of the course and can apply the necessary mathematical tools to problems involving those concepts, he or she does not need a pre-course test to infer that most of the observed student learning was a consequence of the course. No doubt students varied in what they knew about electromagnetic theory when they entered the course, just as they differed at the end; but when students as a group end with the desired capabilities, the effectiveness of the course is self-evident. Pre-course information "proving" that students were less competent in the subject at the course's start would be trivial.

But, value added's proponents will argue, the example is too limited. It doesn't account for the student who may have been underprepared for the course's demands, who didn't have the needed prerequisites, or who already knew the course material and enrolled to relax and fatten a GPA. That's why you need pre-course performance data against which to assess post-course outcomes— the value-added approach.

I'd agree that any course might enroll a student who was underprepared or overprepared, but so what? It still would hold that for most students in most courses the level of performance at the end of a course was a good representation of learning attributable to the course. The problem of misenrollment, to the extent that it exists, should be handled through normal mechanisms of prerequisites and academic advisement.

Suppose the example shifts to a course in freshman English or American government, two common courses in which students vary widely in ability, prior knowledge, and interest. To the extent these courses duplicate learning acquired in high school, performances at the end may merely reflect what students knew at entry. My sense is that freshman placement, imperfect as it is, accommodates at least the significant variability in prior learning among entering students, and that most freshman courses are not often either far over the heads of their students or already mastered by them. If that is so, performance at the end of a course still stands as an acceptable indicator of the effects of the course.

The Problem of Meaning

Introducing the qualification that a course suit the characteristics of the students who take it seems to require an assessment of student capabilities at the beginning of a course, the first part of the value-added formula. Indeed it may—but not in the sense that value added requires.

What should we know about students at the start of a course? Basically, we'd like to know whether the student is educationally ready; pre-course assessment would look to the student's mastery of prerequisite knowledge. But prerequisite knowledge is not the knowledge or capability expected at the course's end. So a useful pretest does not measure the same capabilities the course is intended to produce. If the same test is used in a pre-test/post-test mode, you begin the course without the useful information you need. If different tests are used, changed scores lack meaning.

Other pre-course information, such as a student's prior experience or reasons for taking the course, can aid in interpreting end-of-course accomplishments. But such information does not refer to the capabilities acquired during the course and is not commensurable with them. This is the reason value added as a concept breaks down when you try to apply it in a way that makes sense.

Up to now, all of my examples have entailed courses. But it is similarly difficult to use the concept when comparing institutions. Unselective institutions that produce excellent educational results with poorly prepared students cannot usefully be compared with selective institutions that bring their well-prepared entrants to levels of accomplishment rarely reached by the graduates of unselective institutions. The educational achievements of the two kinds of students cannot be compared as if they were distances each student had moved. The content, objectives, and activities of upper-division courses in selective institutions are often qualitatively different from any encountered in unselective institutions. Value added, implying a specified commodity, is conceptually inadequate for comparing the educational achievements of the two types of institutions.

A few educational objectives are broad enough and common to so many academic settings that changes in performance on a single dimension can usefully be examined and compared. Writing ability, for example, can be assessed at the beginning and end of an educational program and the changes compared. Other intellectual capabilities, such as analytic reasoning or critical thinking, can be treated similarly.

Still, value added raises problems of meaning. Differences between levels of performance separated in time are not easily interpreted even when they are easily calculated, as is the case with changes in writing ability. An observed difference may or may not be attributable to the educational program. Often you reasonably can infer that it is, as we did earlier with the example of the course in electromagnetics. Other times, it is difficult.

With a class of poorly prepared students, a large change in performance may be due almost entirely to the fact that they started so far back. Conversely a small change may be the best that can be expected in view of their poor preparation. With well-prepared students, a large change in performance may be due almost entirely to their ability to learn regardless of the quality of their education. A small change may be due to their already high level of performance at entry, leaving little room for growth.

All these interpretive ambiguities, of course, can be reduced through additional information about the students, the instruction, and what has happened with other students in other courses. But that same supplementary information would serve just as well to reduce interpretive uncertainties about end-of-course information alone. Any observation of student learning raises interpretive problems; with value added, in which the attempt is to assess *growth* over *time*, problems of meaning become that much more severe.

Peripheral Applications

The requirement that before-and-after observations of educational accomplishment must be taken on a common scale of measurement raises another problem: the nature of the method thwarts its application to most of the learning objectives faculty members set for their courses.

The knowledge, the understanding, the abilities to manipulate the concepts of a course, or whatever other kinds of learning objectives faculty members set for their students cannot be usefully measured at the start of a course. A test at the start will simply demonstrate that students have not yet acquired that kind of learning. On the other hand, the broad kinds of learning that can be assessed along a dimension that remains reasonably interpretable from the beginning to the end of a course or program—such as writing ability or analytic reasoning—are usually peripheral objectives of particular courses or programs, when attention is given to them at all.

The same problem exists at the institutional level; we simply do not have ways to measure the concrete effects of cumulative instruction over time. Economists attempt to counter this problem, and give meaning to value added, by converting educational achievement into dollar equivalents. The idea is to place a monetary value on the learning representative of the beginning and end of a course of study, then take the "growth" associated with that study, and mark it off in dollars. It's an interesting approach. Most faculty members, however, teach for a range of outcomes that few of us would concede can be assessed adequately in monetary terms. Again, what is measured is peripheral.

One could go on about the practical problems of implementing a value-added scheme in a college: it can be a costly, intrusive, cumbersome thing to do; it can wear people out with tests. In fairness, too, the concept has provoked some valuable lines of research and intriguing project work. My overall sense is that, for practical purposes, value added isn't a workable concept and we have to get on with alternative ways at looking at the effect of what we do.

What Can Work?

I have no sweeping alternative to value added to recommend to a college. But every college already has several kinds of information available to it that permit inferences about student learning. These almost always are underused. Let me mention a few.

To begin with a simple example, the number of degrees awarded in various fields of study can be an indicator of the nature of an institution's educational product. The ratio of degrees in business and engineering to degrees in arts and letters, and its trend from year to year, says something understandable about student learning patterns at the institution. How do graduation rates compare with intentions to major at entrance, or with declarations of major? Readily available statistics such as these often do not get the careful reflection they deserve.

One hears about "laxity" in college curricula, that loose breadth requirements have quietly scuttled general education. Why not look more carefully at student transcripts? They may show, for example, that students have been using their program options to load up in courses in their major at the expense of courses that would broaden their intellectual horizons. Even within a major, do student course choices show the development of sound concentrations? Are they taking the recommended supporting work in allied disciplines?

Transcripts can help you chart students' shifting preferences as they move through college. They can help you know something about the scope, depth, complexity, and variety of learning students have acquired at any point in their program. More importantly, do the varied patterns of learning make educational sense? When you know those patterns, you have a detailed though imperfect picture of the institution's educational product (better, let me add, than anything you'll learn from studying GPAs or GRE scores).

The shortcoming in a study of courses completed is the absence of information on what students have actually learned. While that can never be known completely, various approximations to it are possible, one of which is the pattern of courses completed. If, for any particular pattern, all the examination questions and assignment of major papers in all the courses that enter that pattern were listed, they would represent the academic accomplishments to be expected of the students completing that pattern. Students don't learn everything they are presented in a course, but the list of requirements on exams and major papers is an approximation. It can be brought closer to actuality by adding information about the *level* of performance on each examination question—by representative students, poor students, and unusually good students—and by asking faculty members to verify the accuracy with which exam questions and paper assignments reflect the important issues in the course.

That level of detail for complete undergraduate programs may be more than anyone would want or be able to use. For limited groups of courses—four to ten courses in a major, preprofessional program, or in a general education sequence, for example—detailed information may be just the ticket for getting a handle on what students actually are learning. It would tell you much more than you could otherwise know about the significance of your educational product. No pre-enrollment, normative, or comparative information need complement it. The assertion is simply that Program X as typically completed by a known number of students produces the described learning.

An analysis of what students can reasonably be expected to have learned in a program answers important questions about quality and outcomes, albeit not every last question. We still couldn't claim to know whether the accomplishments of our college's students as a group was ordinary, poor, or unusually good (among other things, we'd need cross-institutional data for that). Even so, a great gain would have been realized, especially given how little we know at present about the learning associated with any college program.

The process I've described illustrates the kind of information about educational accomplishment that can be developed largely from already existing resources. Realistically, it cannot he applied across an entire curriculum; the process would be overwhelming. Over a period of time, however, it would be very worthwhile to observe and document the educational effects of a select number of heavily subscribed course patterns. One result would be that a college could speak more concretely about student accomplishment. Another would be that the process itself would almost certainly bring to light necessary course and curricular revisions.

In short, moving beyond the blind alleys of value added, a college can look to its own records for ways to keep the education it offers fresh while providing documented evidence of its success.

Cognitive Measures in Assessing Learning

Jonathan Warren

Cognitive measures play a limited but crucial role in educational assessment. They are defined here as procedures for observing and recording students' intellectual accomplishments. The information they provide should inform students about what they have and have not learned, faculty members about the successes and failures of their instruction, and department heads and deans about the suitability of the curriculum in bringing students to the desired academic capabilities. The first of these functions requires information about individual students; the other two, information about collective learning.

The Cognitive Complexity of Learning

In the past several decades, cognitive science has grown dramatically as a discipline and as a context in which to examine and perhaps restructure education. One point on which cognitive scientists agree is that knowledge and cognitive skills, or methods of using and manipulating knowledge, are both necessary components of successful intellectual activity (Gardiner, 1985; Simon, 1980). A second point of agreement is that cognitive or intellectual activities are numerous and diverse: "Even if the processes by which individuals reason or classify may be similar the world over, the actual products and *the ways they are thought about* may be so different as to make illuminating generalizations elusive" (Gardiner, 1985, p. 357; emphasis added). The failure of educators to settle on common goals for the teaching of thinking is understandable (Nickerson, Perkins, and Smith, 1985).

Although there can be only slippery generalizations about the most useful cognitive processes or domains of learning in the undergraduate years, attempts to grasp such generalizations are frequent. A common response to recent criticism of higher education's fragmented curricula has been to construct new "core" curricula that incorporate general intellectual goals—problem solving, historical consciousness, global awareness, analytical reasoning, and other broad rubrics that have not often served as explicit goals of instruction. As those goals are introduced into existing courses and curricula, methods for evaluating their impacts on student learning are needed; yet their variety, in both content and processes, creates problems in assessing how well students reach them.

The Gap in Information About Learning

The assessment of students' learning has remained strangely out of step with the growing complexity of that learning. Only the rare institution, such as Alverno College, has any record of the substance of what its students have learned (Alverno College Faculty, 1985). Typically, the only record related to learning is the list of courses students took and the grades they received. Grades indicate students comparative levels of accomplishment of unspecified kinds of learning, relative to the unknown achievement of anonymous groups of other students. No adequate evaluation can be made, nor record kept, of the success of an educational enterprise without information about the substantive learning of its students—their knowledge of content and their facility with advanced cognitive processes.

The simple convenience of grades and test scores gives them great appeal; their cost, in terms of loss of meaning when widely diverse kinds of performance are forced onto a single scale, tends to be ignored. Grades represent a mix of different kinds of knowledge, cognitive skills, personal qualities or work habits, and faculty emphases. Nevertheless, these components are all presumed equivalent when a student's performance is placed on a one-dimensional scale of achievement. Standardized tests have the same one-dimensional quality, purposely built into them for high reliability. However widely an achievement test's items sample the domain of a field, the resulting score is based on the assumption that the items contribute to a single, uniform dimension of knowledge or ability. For some purposes, such as for indicating which applicants are best prepared for admission to an educational program, that assumption is acceptable; a general picture of academic preparation can be conveyed without providing details. In contrast, when the information's purpose is to provide a record of what students have accomplished in a program, and when that record is used by faculty, administrators, and external constituencies, the details of the learning and their variations become important. Grades may be acceptable as general indicators of relative academic success, but for evaluating the specific success of a particular educational program, more informative indicators are needed. We take pride in students who achieve academic honors, but we can seldom say in any detail what these students accomplished that other students did not. If a group of foreign professors visiting an American university were to ask about the accomplishments of, say, its history graduates, the only information they could be given would be impressionistic. The local faculty members could describe what they hoped their students would accomplish and the usual degree of student success, but they would have nothing to document or demonstrate those accomplishments. If pressed, or if embarrassed by their inability to show any evidence of what their students had learned, the faculty might bring out syllabi, textbooks, or sample examinations, but these would only indicate expectations for learning; nothing would describe what typical students in those courses had actually learned or what the more capable students had learned beyond what was typical. Some of the host faculty members might then describe their grade distributions, pointing out that almost 50 percent of the history majors got B's or better in their history courses, 50 percent C's, and only 1 or 2 percent D's and F's. Yet some of the host history faculty might find those figures embarrassing, thinking that more than half the history majors should have history grade point averages above C. Others might take pride in the same information, seeing as evidence of the department's rigor that not even half the students averaged better than C. In fact, however, grade distributions have no known reference points and no one substantive interpretation; they say nothing about the quality of learning, in terms of either content or cognitive skills.

The seriousness of the gap in information about what students learn is illustrated in a recent article on engineering education (Kerr and Pipes, 1987). The authors argue that undergraduate engineering education has declined over the past thirty years because engineering curricula have shifted their emphases from the poorly defined problems typical of engineering practice (which often require intuitive rather than analytical approaches) to the analytical methods of theoretical science. Graduating engineers, they claim, are less able to handle typical engineering problems than former graduates were. Their evidence comes from comparisons of college catalogues and textbooks, from which only limited inferences can be drawn about what engineering students learn. Whether current engineering graduates are actually less able to solve poorly defined problems than former graduates were can be known only from the percentages of engineering students today and in previous years who have worked successfully with various kinds of problems. To be complete, that information should describe variations in student achievement in terms of cognitive processes required to solve the problems, as well as in terms of content; neither kind of information appears in catalogues or textbooks.

Monitoring trends in the content, strengths, and weaknesses of the educational product is part of using assessment to demonstrate accountability to external constituencies, but information on the substance of what students have learned also has other uses. The special strengths of similar programs, or of courses that differ in their emphases, can be identified. Several courses' combined effects on student learning can be disentangled from their individual effects. The effects of different kinds of educational preparation for a program can be separated from the effects of the program itself. Differences between what ordinary students learn and what the best students learn can suggest modifications of instruction to accommodate students who have distinct purposes or abilities. Indicators that lack information on what was learned cannot adequately serve purposes such as these.

Sources of Information on Learning

In the following discussion, the phrase *indicators of learning* refers to the collective learning of groups of students, which is assumed to be reportable beyond the boundaries of those groups. A professor who observes that a student's oral or written report shows particularly keen understanding of a complex issue, and who reports that to the student, is engaging in the gathering and reporting of information about student learning. Similar observations of other students, if cumulated into a summary statement of the students' collective performance, would contribute to an indicator of learning, as the term is used here.

Course Examinations. The periodic examinations faculty members give their classes—quizzes, midterms, and finals—overwhelm all other sources of information on learning, in terms of time and effort given them. Those examinations have strengths most other indicators lack. First, they are directly related to the material studied. Even when wide agreement exists about the content of an undergraduate field, as in chemistry, every department has its own strengths and areas of emphasis, which are often not adequately represented in exams prepared outside the courses in which the material is taught. Second, the frequency of exams in each course makes them more comprehensive of the material covered than any so-called comprehensive exam given only at the end of an academic year. Third, they permit timely feedback about where students have succeeded and where further effort is needed. Fourth, they perform the same function for the faculty, providing information on students' difficulties soon enough for instructors to help. Fifth, they avoid the pressures of comprehensive exams, which some students find intimidating. Sixth, exams in a course usually elicit students best efforts, but that is not always true with end-of-year exams given for the benefit of the institution. Finally, course exams require no additional time outside regular course activities from either faculty or students.

Course exams do have weaknesses, particularly if the information is to be used outside a particular course. First, as noted above, course exams rarely leave any record of what students have learned. Second, they provide no reference group against which collective learning (whether substantive or not) in a particular course or program can be compared. Much of the meaning of test results is lost in the absence of suitable reference groups. If a large proportion of students in a course get every question on an exam right, no one can be sure whether the test was too easy and the course undemanding, or whether the students were particularly capable and had learned the material unusually well. Faculty members can and do compare performances of current and past classes, but they rarely know what similar students in similar courses at other institutions have accomplished. Their expectations rnay be unnecessarily low or unrealistically high. Moreover, even the information that does let faculty make sense of their students' test results is often left unrecorded. Finally, course exams are often justifiably criticized for testing only what is tested easily, but often not well. The higher cognitive skills essential to academic success are sometimes difficult to observe. This is a universal problem in the assessment of learning, however, and whether it applies more severely to course exams than to other forms of assessment is questionable. If the exercise of higher cognitive skills depends on their substantive content, then faculty members are in a better position than external testing agencies to assess them. Many faculty members make good tests. Improving their test-making skills, when necessary, is not difficult.

Informal, Course-Based Observations. Apart from the formal assignments and examinations that faculty members give students, and the papers, reports, and test results that students give to their professors, there is a variety of less formal kinds of communication between faculty and students. The approach that faculty members take to a topic, the questions they raise and pursue, the kinds of assignments they give, and the attitudes they convey—through these and more subtle cues—tell perceptive students not only which issues are important but also the reasons for their importance. The questions students ask, the comments they make, and even their body language are all cues to learning that faculty members pick up (Rice, 1987). These observations are usually unsystematic, intuitive, and unrecorded, yet their results often influence grades; and grades, with all their limitations, are the most important record of learning now used.

Except in large classes, faculty members rarely have difficulty knowing which students are understanding the material, picking up the fine points, and incorporating them into an integrated understanding of a course. Faculty also know which students do the assignments, study the material regularly but mechanically, miss subtle connections among a course's concepts and issues, and leave with an acceptable grade but with only a superficial grasp of what a course was about.

The informal, intuitive sources of information that faculty members in small classes use for evaluating their students can be made more systematic and used in large as well as small classes. Faculty members can often translate the informal indicators of learning that they use intuitively into one- to five-minute written exercises, given to students at the beginning or the end of class. The results can be examined quickly for indications of where the class collectively lags in understanding or completely misses the point. At the end of the term, those collective results, briefly recorded, can constitute a detailed and virtually continual documentation of the development of understanding among the students in the course and of the variations in their collective accomplishment.

Locally Developed Comprehensive Examinations. Comprehensive exams developed by an institution for its own use are one alternative to course exams for documenting what students have learned. They may be given at the end of each academic year, at the end of the sophomore and senior years, or on completion of a program. They may be written or oral; composed of multiple choice questions, essay questions, quantitative problems, or mixes of these; or focused on learning in the students' major fields or on general education. They may be observed and graded by local faculty, or by experts from other institutions or from outside higher education (Fong, 1987; O'Neill, 1983).

Whether comprehensive exams are developed within or outside an institution, persons other than those who taught the students usually assess them. This procedure can remove the "conflict of interest" held to exist when the instructor sets the standards, instructs the students, and evaluates their performance. It may also improve learning by allowing students and faculty to be collaborators rather than adversaries in learning. Yet the adversarial relationship is fostered more by the assignment of grades than by the examination process itself. When exams are used only as sources of information, for students and for faculty, about the substance and level of learning that has occurred, then the adversarial nature of the relationship is diminished.

Comprehensives may introduce students to perspectives on course material that differ from those of their instructors. That result, although it is unfair to students if it is used to evaluate them individually, can be valuable to the institution if it indicates portions of the curricula that have been unintentionally slighted. Developed at the students' own institution, comprehensives can be kept relevant to local curriculum and simultaneously separate assessment from teaching.

Removing assessment from individual courses has another potential advantage: Comprehensive exams may be designed to indicate how well students have integrated the learning from several courses or incorporated experiences from outside courses. Comprehensive exams provide an opportunity for documenting the synergistic effects courses are hoped to have.

Whether local or external, comprehensives have inherent weaknesses. They cannot realistically cover the entire scope of student learning, even when given each academic year. Coming at the end of a year, their results cannot be used as guides to study or instruction. They are costly in terms of student and faculty time. Finally, if they have any effect on students' academic standing, the resulting pressure on students is liable to bias the results, but if they do not affect grades, some students will not take them seriously.

One of the strengths claimed for comprehensives is that they indicate what students have really learned, rather than what they have learned just long enough to pass an exam, but that may be another weakness. Some of what students have learned a few months before the comprehensive will have been forgotten by the time the exam is given but could quickly be relearned should the need arise. Thus, comprehensives may not show some prior learning, but that does not mean the learning has been lost.

Other weaknesses, although not inherent, require careful circumvention. The material covered in comprehensives, in addition to being "uncomprehensive," may be uneven and haphazard, largely because so much material must be covered in so little time. Further, the learning that students demonstrate is rarely recorded, whether the exams are oral or written. Particularly if exams are oral, their scope, relevance, and validity may all be questionable.

An irony in the use of comprehensive exams is that their results typically take the form of a single grade. Assessment results that leave no record of the substance of learning, putting the record they do leave in a form suitable only for one-dimensional learning, are hardly comprehensive.

Externally Developed Comprehensive Examinations. Comprehensive exams developed outside an institution differ from locally developed comprehensives. The most important differences are the external exams' systematic coverage of the most common areas of a field and their provision of an independent reference group for interpreting results. Externally developed exams are usually multiple-choice tests devised by commercial testing agencies or state agencies. Comprehensive oral exams are occasionally conducted by persons from outside an institution, but they are more similar to locally developed than to external comprehensives, since they follow locally developed guidelines.

Multiple-choice exams tend to be technically well constructed, with high reliability in the form of internal consistency—that is, high interitem agreement but that reliability makes these tests less valid as indicators of accomplishment across complex areas of learning. Even in well-specified fields like organic chemistry or mechanical engineering, competence does not consist of any uniform body of knowledge, understanding, and intellectual capabilities, which every competent person in the field can be assumed to possess. Nevertheless, such assumptions underlie tests that have high internal consistency. The variety and the complexity of learning in any field, even among graduates in highly structured fields, are too great to be accommodated by a test that assumes a single dimension of competence.

The provision of a reference group, which gives institutions a yardstick against which the performance of their own students can be measured, is also an illusory benefit. The characteristics of the students and institutions that constitute the reference group are seldom even known, and this lack of information makes comparisons questionable.

Commercially developed tests of such general academic skills as critical thinking and problem solving have become more popular with growing attention to general education. They are similar to commercial tests of achievement in subject-matter fields. Faculty members, however, are less sure of what constitutes something like critical thinking or problem solving than of what makes up the content of their own fields, and they look for expert help; but lack of agreement among the experts, as well as the interdependence between knowledge and cognitive processes, raise doubts about the superiority of external-tests of general skills over locally developed tests.

Promising Prospects

Several related trends are apparent. The most obvious is the growing expectation of legislatures, governing boards, and academic administrators for information on students' academic accomplishments to be made available. At present, few constraints are placed on the forms that such information should take. The virtual absence, however, of any information on the substance of student learning (except at the occasional institution like Alverno College) is unlikely to be ignored for long.

Several years ago, colleges and universities responded to the pressure for assessment of students' learning by looking to external test developers. The trend among institutions now seems to favor relying more on their own ability to assess the learning they want their own students to demonstrate. Greater interest in short-essay tests and free-response problems, rather than in multiple-choice tests, is accompanying that shift to local resources. As faculty members shift their purposes in examining students' performance from assigning grades to investigating the substantive and cognitive effects of instruction, they will begin to engage in the kind of instructional research Cross (1986) has urged them to adopt.

Retreat from external test development accompanies a tendency among neighboring institutions to pool assessment efforts. Collaboration can lead to better specification of instructional objectives and more accurate assessment. Faculty members teaching courses with overlapping goals can include a few common questions on their retrospective exams, and have accessible, identifiable reference groups to compare performance among students.

Institutions concerned with students' collective learning need not test every student on the same material. A department can organize the core of its program—the key kinds of understanding, capabilities, and appreciations required into 120 ten-minute exercises (a daunting 20-hour test). To make such time requirements more manageable, three of the exercises can be incorporated into the final exams of each of 40 upper-division courses in several fields. If some redundancy is built into the exercises and if the upper-division courses are chosen carefully, the results can indicate students' accomplishments accurately and comprehensively (including variations within the same field of study and across different fields). Collaboration of several neighboring institutions can extend the usefulness of results while distributing the costs of test development.

There should be continual interplay among the processes of clarifying instructional purposes, devising assessment exercises to reflect them, observing results, improving instruction to meet revised purposes, sharpening purposes and assessment exercises, and so on. Alverno College's elaborate but decentralized assessment program clearly demonstrates that interplay (Alverno College Faculty, 1985). With such a process, neither teaching nor learning remains stagnant, and changes and accomplishments are documented.

Potential Perils

Separating assessment from instruction has advantages as well as risks. Students may see an assessment program that is not directly related to their courses as an unnecessary burden, and faculty members may find little value in the program's results. If so, the program will be abandoned as a sterile process, and more promising attempts to assess what students have learned will have trouble getting accepted.

Few major changes in curricula or academic procedures occur without the involvement of faculty committees, yet that form of faculty involvement is often not enough; the committee perspective is too general. Committees tend to draft new statements of educational goals and then work from them toward the selection or construction of assessment devices. These goal statements, with their related assessment procedures, tend to be so broad that they have little direct bearing on courses that are currently taught. Such a procedure implies that what has already been taught and assessed is not in itself an appropriate guide to what should be done, and faculty members are reluctant to embrace the results of assessments conducted in this way.

A more productive approach is to examine what faculty members already assess, how they do it, and how closely the results reflect their expectations for student learning. That process will probably suggest clarification and restatement of purposes. It may also indicate purposes that are inadequately assessed or suggest improved or expanded assessment procedures, but the recommendations will have grown from and respected faculty members' previous efforts.

The introduction of a wholly new, externally devised assessment process is rarely necessary and is often self-defeating. An assessment program that builds on what already exists not only can provide better information than a new one on the quality of education but also can be linked more readily to the improvement of teaching and learning.

References

Alverno College Faculty. *Assessment at Alverno College.* (Rev. ed.) Milwaukee, Wisc.: Alverno Productions, 1985.

Cross, K. P. "A Proposal to Improve Teaching." *AAHE Bulletin,* 1986, 39 (1), 9–14.

Fong, B. "The External Examiner Approach to Assessment." Paper commissioned by the American Association for Higher Education at the second National Conference on Assessment in Higher Education, Denver, June 14–17, 1987.

Gardner, H. *The Mind's New Science: A History of the Cognitive Revolution.* New York: Basic Books, 1985

Kerr, A. D., and Pipes, R. B. "Why We Need Hands-On Engineering Education." *Technology Review,* 1987, 90 (7), 34–42.

Nickerson, R. S., Perkins, D. N., and Smith, E. E. *The Teaching of Thinking.* Hillsdale, N.J.: Erlbaum, 1985.

O'Neill, J. P. "Examinations and Quality Control." In J. R. Warren (ed.), *Meeting the New Demand for Standards.* New Directions for Higher Education, no. 43. San Francisco: Jossey-Bass, 1983.

Rice, E. "Education as a Human and Humane Affair." *Liberal Education,* 1987, 73 (3),14–21.

Simon, H. A. "Problem Solving and Education." In D. T. Tuma and F. Reif (eds.), *Problem Solving and Education: Issues in Teaching and Research.* Hillsdale, N.J.: Erlbaum, 1980.

An Analysis of Alternative Approaches to Evaluation

DANIEL L. STUFFLEBEAM AND WILLIAM J. WEBSTER

The field of educational evaluation has developed dramatically over the past 10 years. Following a period of relative inactivity in the 1950's, educational evaluation efforts experienced a period of revitalization in the mid 1960's. This revitalization was influenced by articles by Cronbach (1963), Scriven (1967), Stake (1967), and Stufflebeam (1966). The field's development was further stimulated by the evaluation requirements of the "great society" programs that were launched in 1965; by the nationwide accountability movement that began in the early 1970s; and, most importantly, by the mounting responsibilities and resources that society assigned to educators.

Developments of particular interest are the diverse ways in which educational evaluation has been conceptualized. This paper is an attempt to characterize and assess the different theoretical approaches to evaluation.

The study of alternative approaches is important for both the operation and the scientific advancement of evaluation. Operationally, a critical review of alternatives can help evaluators to consider and assess optional frameworks which they can use to plan and conduct their studies. Scientifically, such a review can help evaluation researchers to identify issues, assumptions, and hypotheses that should be assessed. However, a main value in studying alternative approaches is not to enshrine any of them: on the contrary, the purpose is to discover their strengths and weaknesses and to obtain direction for devising better approaches.

Thirteen types of studies that have been conducted in the name of educational evaluation are identified and assessed in this paper. These 13 types are each unique and comprise most efforts to evaluate education. Whereas some of these types are used legitimately to assess worth, others are used illegitimately to create a false impression of an object's worth.

In analyzing the 13 types of studies, prior assessments regarding the state of the art of educational evaluation were consulted. Stake's (Note 1) analysis of nine evaluation approaches provided a useful application of advance organizers (the types of variables used to determine information requirements) for ascertaining different types of evaluation studies. Hastings' (Note 2) review of the growth of educational evaluation theory and practice helped to place the field in an historical perspective. Finally, Guba's (Note 3) presentation and assessment of six major philosophies in educational evaluation was provocative. Although we did not always agree with the conclusions forwarded in each of these papers, all of the prior assessments helped sharpen the issues addressed.

331

Alternative Conceptualizations of Educational Evaluation

In developing a characterization and assessment of different evaluation approaches, careful consideration was given to different kinds of activities conducted in the name of educational evaluation. These activities were classified according to their degree of conformity to a particular definition of educational evaluation. According to that definition, *an educational evaluation study is one that is designed and conducted to assist some audience to judge and improve the worth of some educational object.* This definition should be widely acceptable because it agrees with definitions of evaluation that appear in most dictionaries. However, it will become apparent that many studies done in the name of educational evaluation either do not conform to this definition or directly oppose it.

The proposed definition of an evaluation study was used to classify studies into three main approaches. The first approach includes politically oriented evaluations, which promote a positive or negative view of an object, irrespective of its actual worth. The second approach includes evaluations that are oriented to answer specified questions whose answers may or may not assess an object's worth. The third approach involves studies that are designed primarily to assess and/or improve the worth of some object.

Of the 13 types of studies identified, two pertain to the political approach, five to the questions-oriented approach, and six to the values-oriented approach.

Each type is further analyzed in terms of seven descriptors: (1) advance organizers, that is, the main cues that evaluators use to set up a study; (2) the main purpose served; (3) the sources of questions that are addressed; (4) the questions that are characteristic of each study type; (5) the methods that typically are used; (6) the persons who pioneered in conceptualizing each study type; and (7) other persons who have extended development and use of each study type. Using these descriptors, comments on each of the 13 types of studies are presented.

Politically Oriented Studies (or Pseudo-Evaluations)

Politically Controlled Study

The first type of study is labeled the politically controlled study. Its advance organizers are implicit or explicit threats faced by the client for an evaluation. The client's purpose in commissioning a politically controlled study is to secure assistance in acquiring, maintaining, or increasing the client's sphere of influence, power, or money. The questions addressed are those of interest to the client and special groups that share the client's interest. The main questions of interest to the client are: What information would be advantageous in a potential conflict situation? and, What data might be used advantageously in a confrontation? Typical methods of conducting the politically controlled study include covert investigations, simulation studies, and private information files. Generally, the client wants information obtained to be as technically adequate as possible, but the client also wants guarantees that he or she can control the dissemination of the information. Because the information might be released selectively to create a distorted picture of an object's worth, this type of study must be labeled a "pseudo-evaluation study."

It should be noted that persons have not been nominated to receive credit as pioneers or developers of the politically controlled study, although real cases do exist.

To avoid the inference that the politically controlled type of study is imaginary, consider the following example. A superintendent of one of the nation's largest school districts once confided that he possessed an extensive notebook of detailed information about each of the school buildings in his district. The information included student achievement, teacher qualifications, racial mix of teachers and students, average per-pupil expenditure, socioeconomic characteristics of the student body, average length of tenure in the system for teachers in the school, and so forth. The aforementioned data revealed a highly segregated district. When asked why all the entries in the notebook were in pencil, the superintendent replied it was absolutely essential that he be kept informed about the current situation in each school; but, he said it was also imperative that the community at large, the board, and special interest groups in the community, in particular, not have access to the information. For, any of these groups might use the information to harm the district and to threaten his tenure there. Hence, one special assistant kept the document up-to-date: only one copy existed, and the superintendent kept that locked in his desk. The point of this example is not to make a negative judgment about the superintendent's behavior in this case. The point is that the superintendent's ongoing covert investigation and selective release of information was decidedly not a case of true evaluation, for it did not include full and open disclosure. Instead, this instance may appropriately be termed a pseudo-evaluation.

Public Relations-inspired Studies

The public-relations type of study is a similar case of politically oriented or pseudo-evaluation. In the public-relations type of study, the advance organizer is the propagandist's information needs. The purpose of the study is to help the client or propagandist create a positive public image for a school district, program, or process. The questions that guide such a study are derived from the public-relations specialists' and administrators' conceptions of which questions would be most popular with their constituents. In general, the public-relations study seeks information that would be most helpful in securing public support.

Typical methods used in public-relations studies are surveys, experiments, and the use of "expert" consultants. A pervasive characteristic of the public-relations evaluator's use of dubious methods is a biased attempt to nurture a good picture of the object of the evaluation .

A recent contact with an urban school district illustrates the second type of study. A superintendent requested a community survey for his district. The superintendent said, straightforwardly, he wanted a survey that would yield a positive report on the performance of the school district. He said such a positive report was desperately needed at the time so that community confidence in the school district could be restored. The superintendent did not get the survey and positive report, and it soon became clear why he thought one was needed. Several weeks after making the request, he was summarily fired.

Before addressing the next group of study types, perhaps a few additional comments should be made concerning politically oriented studies. Perhaps it is confusing to understand why any time at all has been taken to discuss the first two study types, since they certainly are not recommended in efforts to evaluate education. These studies have been considered because they are a prominent part of the educational evaluation scene. Sometimes evaluators and their clients are co-conspirators in performing the first two types of studies. On other occasions, evaluators, believing they are doing an objective assessment, discover that their client has other intentions. When the time is right, the client is able to subvert the study in favor of producing the desired biased picture. It is imperative that evaluators be more alert than they often are to these kinds of potential conflicts; otherwise, they will be unwitting accomplices in efforts to mislead through evaluation.

Questions-oriented Studies

Questions-oriented studies are so labeled because they start with a particular question and then move to the methodology appropriate for answering that question. Only subsequently do they consider whether the questions and methodology are appropriate for developing and supporting value claims. These studies can be called "quasi-evaluation studies," because sometimes they happen to provide evidence that can be used to assess the worth of an object, while, in other cases, their focus is too narrow or is only tangential to questions of worth. Quasi-evaluation studies have legitimate uses apart from their relationship to evaluation: hence, the main caution is that these types of studies not be equated with evaluation.

Objectives-based Studies

The objectives-based study is the first questions-oriented study to be considered. In this type of study, some statement of objectives provides the advance organizer. The objectives may be mandated by the client, formulated by the evaluator, or specified by the teachers. The usual purpose of an objectives-based study is to determine whether the objectives have been achieved. Program developers, sponsors, and managers are typical audiences for such a study. The clients of objectives-based studies usually want to know which students have achieved which educational objectives.

The methods used in objectives-based studies essentially involve the collection and analysis of performance data relative to specified objectives. Ralph Tyler is generally acknowledged to be the pioneer in the objectives-based type of study, although Percy Bridgman and E. L. Thorndike probably should be credited along with Tyler.[1] Many people have furthered the work of Tyler by developing variations of his objectives-based evaluation model. A few of them are Bloom (1956), Hammond (1972), Metfessel & Michael (1967), Popham (1969), and Provus (1971). Undoubtedly, the objectives-based type of study has been the most prevalent type used in the name of educational evaluation. It is one that has good commonsense appeal; educators have had a great amount of experience with it; and it makes use of technologies of behavioral objectives and standardized testing. Common criticisms are that such studies lead to terminal information that is of little use in improving a program, and that this information often is far too narrow in scope to constitute a sound basis for judging the worth of a program.

Accountability Studies

The accountability study became prominent in the early 1970's. Its emergence seems to have been connected with widespread disenchantment with the persistent stream of evaluation reports that indicated that massive state and federal investments in programs to improve education were not showing significant results. One proposed solution posited that accountability systems could be initiated to ensure both that educators would carry out their responsibilities to improve education and that evaluators would do a thorough job of identifying the effects of improvement programs.

The advance organizer for the accountability study is the set of responsibilities that personnel in institutions have for implementing educational programs. The purpose of the study, as already noted, is to provide constituents with an accurate accounting of results and to ensure that the results are primarily positive.

The questions that are addressed in accountability studies come from the constituents of programs such as taxpayers, parent groups, school boards, and local, state, and national funding agencies. The main question that the groups want answered concerns whether the involved personnel and organizations charged with responsibility for educating students and for improving education are achieving all they should be achieving, given the investments of resources to support their work. Methods used in accountability studies include mandated testing programs, performance contracting, and procedures for auditing the design, process, and results of evaluation studies.

The person who is generally acknowledged as the pioneer in the area of educational accountability is Lessinger (1970). Some of the people who have extended Lessinger's work are Stenner and Webster (Note 4), in their development of a handbook for conducting auditing activities, and Kearney, in providing leadership to the State Department of Education in Michigan in developing the first statewide educational accountability system.

The main advantages of accountability studies are that they are popular among constituent groups and are aimed at improving the quality of education. A main disadvantage is that they produce a good deal of political unrest and acrimony among professional educators and between them and their constituents. Another disadvantage is that political forces tend to force the implementation of accountability efforts before the needed technology can be developed and field tested.

Experimental Research Studies

The experimental research type of study is quite prominent in educational evaluation. It is labeled as a questions-oriented or quasi-evaluation strategy because it starts with questions and methodology that may or may not be related to assessing worth. The experimental research type of study calls to mind Kaplan's (1964) famous warning against the so-called "law of the instrument," whereby a given method is equated to a field of inquiry. In such a case, the field of inquiry is restricted to the questions that are answerable by the given method. Fisher (1951) specifically warned against equating his experimental methods with science.

The advance organizers in experimental studies are problem statements, hypotheses, and investigatory questions. The usual purpose of the experimental research study is to determine causal relationships between specified independent and dependent variables such as a given instructional method and student standardized test performance. It is particularly noteworthy that the sources of questions, investigated in the experimental research study, are researchers and the developers of educational programs, and not usually the constituents, practitioners, or financial sponsors.

The frequent question in the experimental study is: What are the effects of a given intervention on specified outcome variables? Typical methods used are experimental and quasi-experimental designs. Pioneers in using experimentation to study education are: Campbell and Stanley (1963), Cronbach and Snow (1969), and Lindquist (1953). Other persons who have developed the methodology of experimentation substantially for use in education are Glass and Maguire (1968), Suchman (1967), and Wiley and Bock (1967).

The main advantage of experimental studies in evaluation work is that they provide strong methods for establishing relatively unequivocal causal relationships between treatment and student achievement variables. The problems, however, are that the strategy is usually not workable in field settings and provides a much narrower range of information than is needed to evaluate educational programs. In addition, experimental studies tend to provide terminal information that is not useful for guiding the developmental process.

Testing Programs

Since the 1930's, American education has been inundated with standardized testing programs. Probably every school district in the United States has some type of standardized testing program, and, formerly, many educators have tended to equate the results of a standardized testing program with the information needed to evaluate the quality of a school district, a school, a program, and, in some cases, even a teacher.

Advance organizers for the testing study include areas of the school curriculum, tests that are available from publishing companies, and specified norm groups. The main purpose of testing programs is to compare the test performance of individual students and groups of students to that of selected norm groups.

The sources of questions that are addressed by the testing programs are usually test publishers and test selection committees; the typical question addressed by tests concerns whether the test performance of individual students is at or above the average performance of local, state, and national norm groups. The main process involved in using testing programs is to select, administer, score, and report standardized test results.

One of the major pioneers in this area was Lindquist (1951), who was instrumental in developing the Iowa Testing Program, the American College Testing Program, the National Merit Scholarship Testing Program, and the General Educational Development Testing Program, as well as the Measurement Research Center at the University of Iowa. Many people have contributed substantially to the development of educational testing in America, including Ebel (1965), Flanagan (1939), Lord & Novick (1968), and Thorndike (1971).

The main advantages of standardized testing programs are that they are efficient in producing valid and reliable information on student performance in many areas of the school curriculum and that they are a familiar strategy at every level of the school program in virtually all districts in the United States. The main limitations are: they provide data only about student performance, they reinforce students' multiple-choice test-taking behavior rather than their writing and speaking behavior, and in many cases, they are perhaps a better indicator of the socioeconomic levels of the students in a given school or school district than they are of the quality of teaching and learning in that district. It has also been argued effectively by Stake (1971) that standardized tests are poor approximations of what teachers actually teach.

Management Information Systems

The management information system is the final type of questions-oriented study. It is like the politically controlled studies, except that it supplies managers with the information they need to conduct their programs, as opposed to supplying them with the information they need to win a political advantage. The management information type of study is also like the decision-oriented study, which will be discussed later, except that the decision-oriented study provides information needed both to develop and defend the worth of a program, which goes beyond providing information that managers need to implement their management responsibilities.

The advance organizers in most management information systems include program objectives, specified activities, and projected program milestones or events. The purpose of a management information system, as already implied, is to continuously supply the information managers need to plan, direct, and control their programs.

The source of questions addressed is the management personnel. The main question they typically want answered is: Are program activities being implemented according to schedule, according to budget, and with the expected results?

Methods commonly used in management information systems are system analysis, Program Evaluation and Review Technique (PERT), Critical Path Method, Program Planning and Budgeting System (PPBS), Management by Objectives, computer-based information systems, and cost analysis.

Cook (1966) introduced the use of PERT in education. And Kaufman (1969) has written widely about the use of management information systems in education.

A major advantage of the use of management information systems is in giving managers information they can use to plan, monitor, and control complex operations. A major difficulty with the application of this industry-oriented type of system to education is that the products of education are not amenable to a narrow, precise definition as is the case with a profit and loss statement of a corporation. Also, the information gathered in management information systems typically lacks the scope required to assess the worth of a program.

Values-oriented Studies

Accreditation/Certification Studies

Most educational institutions have periodically been the subjects of an accreditation study, and most professional educators, at one time or another, have had to meet certification requirements for a given educational position. Such studies of institutions and personnel are in the realm of true evaluation efforts, since institutions and personnel are studied to prove whether they are fit to serve designated functions in society.

The advance organizers used in the accreditation/certification study usually are guidelines that have been adopted by some accrediting or certifying body. As previously suggested, the purpose of the study is to determine whether institutions, programs, or personnel should be approved to perform specified functions.

The source of questions for accreditation or certification studies is the accrediting or certifying agency. Basically, the question they address is: Are institutions, programs, and personnel meeting minimum standards, and how can their performance be improved?

Typical methods used in the accreditation/certification study are self-study and self-reporting by the individual or institution. In the case of institutions, panels of experts are assigned to visit the institution, verify a self-report, and gather additional information. The basis for the self-studies and the visits by expert panels are usually guidelines that have been specified by the accrediting agency.

Accreditation of education was pioneered by the College Entrance Examination Board around 1901. Since then, the accreditation function has been implemented and expanded, especially by the Cooperative Study of Secondary School Standards dating from around 1933. Subsequently, the accreditation approach has been developed, expanded, and administered by the North Central Association of Secondary Schools and Colleges, along with their associated regional accrediting agencies across the United States, and by many other accrediting and certifying bodies.

The main advantage of the accreditation or certification study is that it aids lay persons in making informed judgments about the quality of educational institutions and the qualifications of educational personnel. The main difficulties are that the guidelines of accrediting and certifying bodies typically emphasize the intrinsic and not the outcome criteria of education. Also, the self-study and visitation processes used in accreditation offer many opportunities for corruption and inept performance.

Policy Studies

The policy study is the second type of true evaluation. It is recognized as a true evaluation approach because it sets out to identify and assess, for society or some segment of society, the merits of competing policies.

The advance organizer for the policy study is a given policy issue, for example: What is the best way to meet federal guidelines for equal education opportunity? The purpose of the policy study is usually to identify and assess the potential costs and benefits of competing policies for a given institution or for society.

Legislators, policy boards, and special interest groups often posit the questions that are addressed by policy studies. A main question they pose is: Which of two or more competing policies will maximize the achievement of valued outcomes at a reasonable cost?

Methods used in policy studies include the Delphi Technique (described by Anderson, Ball, Murphy, & Assiociates, 1973), experimental and quasi-experimental design, (as in New Jersey's negative income tax experiment [Kershaw, Note 51]), scenarios, forecasting, and judicial proceedings.

Joseph Rice (discussed in Anderson, et al., 1973) can be mentioned as the pioneer in this area, as he conducted massive studies around 1900 to help education decide on the merits of continued concentration on spelling. Other persons who have contributed substantially to the methodology for conducting policy studies in education are Coleman, Campbell, Hobson, McPartland, Mood, Weinfeld, and York, (1966), Jencks, Smith, Adand, Bane, Cohen, Gintis, Heynes, and Michelson (1972), Clark (1965), Owens (Note 6), and Wolf (1973).

The main advantage of policy studies is that they are essential in guiding institutions and society. The main problems are that policy studies, over and again, are corrupted or subverted by the political environment in which they must be conducted and reported.

Decision-oriented Studies

The decision-oriented study emphasizes that evaluation should be used proactively to help improve a program as well as retroactively to judge its worth. As mentioned previously, the decision-oriented study should be distinguished from management information systems and from politically controlled studies because of the emphasis in decision-oriented studies on questions of worth.

Decision situations provide the advance organizer for decision-oriented studies. Basically, the purpose of the studies is to provide a knowledge and value base for making and defending decisions.

The source of questions addressed by the decision-oriented studies is involved decision makers, which include administrators, parents, students, teachers, school boards, taxpayers, and all others who make decisions about funding, conducting, and using the results of education. The main questions addressed are: How should a given enterprise be planned? How should a given plan be carried out? How should a program be revised? Answers to these questions are based on the underlying standard of good education, which is that educational enterprises should foster human growth and development at a reasonable cost.

Many methods may be used in a decision-oriented study. These include surveys, needs assessments, case studies, advocate teams, observations, and quasi-experimental and experimental designs.

Cronbach (1963) first introduced educators to the idea that evaluation should be reoriented from its objectives-based history to a concern for helping educators make better decisions about how to educate. Later, Stufflebeam (1966, 1967) introduced a conceptualization of evaluation that was based on the idea that evaluation should help educators make and defend decisions that are in the best interest of meeting students' needs. Many other persons have since contributed to the development of a decision-oriented concept of evaluation. Included among them are Alkin (1969), Reinhard (1972), Taylor (1974), Ashburn (Note 7), Guba (Note 8), Merriman (Note 9), Ott (Note 10), Walker (Note 11), and Webster (Note 12).

A main advantage of the decision-oriented strategy is that it encourages educators to use evaluation continuously and systematically in their efforts to plan and implement programs that meet educational needs. It also presents a rationale for helping educators to be accountable for decisions they have made in the course of implementing a program.

A main limitation is that the collaboration required between an evaluator and decision-maker introduces opportunities for biasing the evaluation results. External meta evaluation has been introduced to offset such opportunities for bias.

Consumer-oriented Studies

In the consumer-oriented approach, the evaluator is the "enlightened surrogate consumer." Advance organizers are societal values and needs. The purpose of a consumer study is to judge the relative merits of alternative educational goods and services and, thereby, to help taxpayers and practitioners to make wise choices in their purchase of educational goods and services.

Questions for the consumer-oriented study are derived from society, from constituents of educational institutions, and especially from the evaluator's frame of reference. The general question addressed is: Which of several alternative consumable education objects is the best buy, given their costs, the needs of the consumer group, and the values of society at large? Methods include checklists, needs assessments, goal-free evaluation, experimental and quasi-experimental designs, modus operandi analysis, and cost analysis (Scriven 1974). Also a popular method is for an external independent consumer advocate to conduct and report findings on studies of publicly supported educational programs.

Scriven (1967) pioneered the consumer-oriented approach in education, and there are strong parallels between his work and the concurrent work of Ralph Nader in the general field of consumerism. Glass (Note 13) has been an avid supporter and developer of Scriven's work.

One of the main advantages of this approach is that it is a hard-hitting, independent assessment intended to protect educators and the consumers of education from shoddy educational products and services. The approach has high credibility with consumer groups.

The main disadvantage of this approach is that it can be so independent from practitioners that it may not assist them to do a better job of serving consumers. Also, the consumer-oriented study requires a highly credible and competent expert plus sufficient resources to allow the expert to conduct a thorough study. Often this approach is too costly to be carried out well and produces faulty, unrealistic data.

Client-centered Studies

In direct contrast to the consumer-oriented study is the client-centered study. The client-centered study takes the local autonomy view and helps people who are involved in a program to evaluate it and use the evaluation to improve it.

The advance organizers are concerns and issues in the program itself. The purpose of the study is to help people in a local setting understand the operations of their program, the ways the operations are valued by the people affected by them, and the ways they are valued by people who are expert in the program area.

Community and practitioner groups in the local environment plus external educational experts are the sources of questions that are addressed by the client-centered study. In general, the groups usually want to know about the history and status of a program and the ways in which it is judged by involved persons and experts in the program area.

Typical methods used in the client-centered study are the case study, adversary reports, sociodrama, and what Stake (1970) has called "responsive evaluation."

Stake (1967) is the pioneer of the client-centered type of study, and his approach has been developed by McDonald (1975) in England, Rippey (1973), and, most recently, Guba (1978).

The main strength of this approach is that it is an action-research approach, in which people implementing programs are helped to conduct their own evaluation. It's main weakness is its lack of external credibility and its susceptibility to bias on the part of people in the local setting since they, in effect, have great control over the evaluation study.

Connoisseur-based Studies

The connoisseur-based study is the most recent entry among the 13 study types. This study assumes that certain experts in a given field are capable of in-depth analysis and evaluation that could not be done in other ways. Just as a national survey of wine drinkers would undoubtedly produce information concerning overall wine preferences among the group, it would not provide the detailed judgments of the qualities of different wines that might be derived from a single connoisseur who has devoted a professional lifetime to the study and grading of wines.

The advance organizer for the connoisseur-based study is the evaluator's special expertise and sensitivities. The purpose of the study is to describe critically, appraise, and illuminate the particular merits of a given object.

The source of questions addressed by the connoisseur-based evaluation is the expert evaluators; that is, the critics and authorities who have undertaken the evaluation. The major question they can be expected to ask is: What merits and demerits distinguish the particular object from others of the same general kind?

The methodology of connoisseurship includes the critics' systematic use of their perceptual sensitivities, past experiences, and refined insights. The evaluator's judgment is then conveyed to help the audience appreciate and understand all of the nuances of the object under study.

Eisner (Note 14) has pioneered this strategy in education. Guba (1978) and Sanders and Hershiser (Note 15) have further explored and developed its use in educational evaluation.

The main advantage of the connoisseur-based study is that it exploits the particular expertise and finely developed insights of persons who have devoted much time and effort to the study of a precise area. They can provide an array of detailed information that the audience can then use to form a more insightful analysis than otherwise might be possible. The disadvantage of this approach is that it is dependent on the expertise and qualifications of the particular expert doing the evaluation, leaving much room for subjectivity, bias, and corruption.

Conclusion

This completes our review of the 13 types of studies used to evaluate education. As stated at the beginning of this article, a critical analysis of these study types has important implications for both the practitioner of evaluation and the theoretician who is concerned with devising better concepts and methods.

A main point for the practitioner is that evaluators may encounter considerable difficulties if their perceptions of the study being undertaken differ from those of their clients and audiences. Typically, clients want a politically advantageous study performed, while the evaluators want to conduct questions-oriented studies, since these allow the evaluator to exploit the methodology in which they were trained. Moreover, the audiences usually want values-oriented studies that will help them determine the relative merits of competing educational goods and services. If evaluators are ignorant of the likely conflict in purpose, the evaluation is probably doomed to failure from the start. The moral is, at the onset of the study, evaluators must be keenly sensitive to their own agendas for an evaluation study as well as those that are held by client and audience. Further, the evaluator should advise involved parties of possible conflicts in the purposes for doing the study and should negotiate a common understanding at the start. Presented alternatives could be legitimately either a quasi-evaluation study directed at assessing particular questions or a true evaluation-type study directed at searching for all evidence that could help the client and audience assess the worth of the object: It is not believed, however, that politically inspired and controlled studies serve appropriate purposes in the evaluation of education. Granted, they may be necessary in administration and public relations, but they should not be confused with, or substituted for, evaluation. Finally, it is imperative to remember that no one type of study consistently is the best in evaluating education.

A main point to be gleaned from the review of these 13 types of studies, for the benefit of the theoretician, is that they have both strengths and weaknesses. In general, the weaknesses of the politically oriented studies are that they are prone to manipulation by unscrupulous persons, and may help such people mislead an audience into developing a particular opinion of a program's worth that is unfounded and perhaps untrue. The main problem with the questions-oriented studies is that they often address questions that are more narrow in scope than the questions needing to be addressed in a true assessment of worth. However, it is also noteworthy that these types of studies are frequently superior to true evaluation studies in the efficiency of methodology and technical adequacy of information employed. Finally, the values-oriented studies undertake an overly ambitious task. For it is virtually impossible to assess the true worth of any object. Such an achievement would require omniscience, infallibility, and a singularly unquestioned value base. Nevertheless, the continuing attempt to consider questions of worth certainly is essential for the advancement of education.

In conclusion, there is clearly a need for continuing efforts to develop and implement better approaches to evaluation. Theoreticians should diagnose strengths and weaknesses of existing approaches, and they should do so in more depth than we have been able to demonstrate here. They should use these diagnoses to evolve better, more defensible approaches; they should work with practitioners to operationalize and test the new approaches; and, of course, both groups should collaborate in developing still better approaches. Such an ongoing process of critical review and revision is essential if the field of educational evaluation is not to stagnate, but instead is to provide vital support for advancing education.

A summary of our analysis appears in Tables I, II, and III.

References

Alkin, M.C. Evaluation theory development. *Evaluation Comment*, 1969, 2, 2–7.

Anderson, Scarvia B., Ball, Samuel, Murphy, Richard T., and Associates. *Encyclopedia of educational evaluation*. San Francisco, Calif.: Jossey-Bass, 1973, 142.

Bloom, B.S., Englehart, M.D., Furst, E. J., Hill, W. H., & Krathwohl, D. R. *Taxonomy of educational objectives: Handbook I: Cognitive domain*. New York: David McKay, 1956.

Campbell, D.T., and Stanley, J.C. Experimental and quasi-experimental designs for research on teaching. In N. L. Gage (Ed.), *Handbook of research on training*. Chicago: Rand McNally, 1963.

Clark, K. *Dark ghetto*. New York: Harper & Row, 1965.

Coleman, J.S., Campbell, E.Q., Hobson, C J., McPartland, J., Mood, A. M., Weinfeld, F. D., & York, R. L. *Equality of educational opportunity*. Washington, D.C.: U.S. Department of Health, Education, and Welfare, Office of Education, 1966.

Cook, D.L. Program evaluation and review techniques, applications in education. *U.S. Office of Education Cooperative Monograph, 17*, (OE-12024), 1966.

Cronbach, L.J. Course improvement through evaluation. *Teachers College Record*, 1963, 64, 672–683.

Cronbach, L.J., and Snow, R. E. *Individual differences in learning ability as a function of instructional variables*. Stanford, Calif.: Stanford University Press, 1969.

Ebel, R.L. *Measuring educational achievement*. Englewood Cliffs, N.J.: Prentice-Hall, 1965.

Fisher, R.A. *The Design of experiments* (6th ed.) New York: Hafner, 1951.

Flanagan, J. C. General considerations in the selection of test items and a short method of estimating the product-moment coefficient from data at the tails of the distribution. *Journal of Educational Psychology*, 1939, 30, 674–680.

Glass, G.V., and Maquire, T. O. *Analysis of time-series quasi-experiments*. (U.S. Office of Education Report No. 6-8329) . Boulder, Col.: Laboratory of Educational Research, University of Colorado, 1968.

Guba, E.G. Toward a methodology of naturalistic inquiry in educational evaluation. *CSE Monograph Series in Evaluation*, Los Angeles, Calif.: Center for the Study of Evaluation, 1978.

Hammond, R. L. *Evaluation at the local level*. (Mimeograph) Tucson, Ariz.: EPIC Evaluation Center, 1972.

Jencks, C., Smith, M., Adand, H., Bane, M.J., Cohen, D., Gintis, H., Heynes, B., and Michelson, S. *Inequality: A reassessment of the effect of family and schooling in America*. New York: Basic Books, 1972.

Kaplan, A. *The conduct of inquiry*. San Francisco, Calif.: Chandler, 1964.

Kaufman, R.A. Toward educational system planning: Alice in Educationland. *Audiovisual Instructor*, 1969, *14*, (May), 47–48.

Lessinger, L.M. *Every kid a winner: Accountability in education*. New York: Simon and Schuster, 1970

Lindquist, E.F. (Ed.). *Educational measurement*. Washington, D.C.: American Council on Education, 1951.

Lindquist, E.F. *Design and analysis of experiments in psychology and education*. Boston: Houghton-Mifflin, 1953.

Lord, F.M., and Novick, M.R. *Statistical theories of mental test scores*. Reading, Mass.: Addison-Wesley, 1968.

McDonald, B. Evaluation and the control of education. In D. Tawney (Ed.), *Evaluation: The state of the art*. London: Schools Council, 1975.

Metfessel, N.S., and Michael, W.B. A paradigm involving multiple criterion measures for the evaluation of the effectiveness of school programs. *Educational and Psychological Measurement*, 1967, *27*, 931–943.

Popham, W.J. Objectives and instruction. In R. Stake (Ed.), *Instructional objectives. AERA Monograph Series on Curriculum Evaluation* (Vol. 3). Chicago: Rand McNally, 1969.

Provus, M.N. Discrepancy evaluation. Berkeley, Calif.: McCutcheon, 1971.

Reinhard, D.L. *Methodology development for input evaluations using advocate and design teams*. Ph.D. dissertation. The Ohio State University, 1972.

Rippey, R.M. (Ed.). *Studies in transactional evaluation*. Berkeley, Calif.: McCutcheon, 1973.

Scriven, M.S. The methodology of evaluation. In R. E. Stake (Ed.), *Curriculum evaluation. AERA Monograph Series on Curriculum Evaluation* (Vol. 1). Chicago: Rand McNally, 1967.

Scriven, M. Evaluation perspectives and procedures. In W. James Popham (Ed.) *Evaluation in Education: Current Applications*. Berkeley, Calif.: McCutcheon, 1974.

Stake, R.E. The countenance of educational evaluation. *Teachers College Record*, 1967, *68*, 523–540.

Stake, R. E. Objectives, priorities, and other judgment data. *Review of Educational Research*, 1970, *40*, 181–212.

Stake, R.E. *Measuring what learners learn*. (mimeograph). Urbana, Ill.: Center for Instructional Research and Curriculum Evaluation, 1971.

Stufflebeam, D.L. A depth study of the evaluation requirement. *Theory into Practice*, 1966, 5 (June), 121–134.

Stufflebeam, D.L. The use of and abuse of evaluation in Title III. *Theory into Practice*, 1967, 6 (June), 126–133.

Suchman, E.A. *Evaluative research.* New York: Russell Sage Foundation, 1967.

Taylor, J.P. *An administrator's perspective of evaluation.* Kalamazoo, Mich.: Western Michigan University, 1974. (Occasional Paper #2).

Thorndike, R.L. *Educational measurement* (2nd ed.). Washington, D.C.: American Council on Education, 1971.

Wiley, D.E. and Block, R.D. Quasi-experimentation in educational settings: Comment. *The School Review*, Winter, 1967, 353–366.

Wolf, R.L. How teachers feel toward evaluation. In E. R. House (Ed.), *School evaluation: The politics and process.* Berkeley, Calif.: McCutcheon, 1973.

Notes

1. Stake, R.E. *Nine approaches to educational evaluation.* Unpublished chart. Urbana, Ill.: Center for Instructional Research and Curriculum Evaluation, 1974.

2. Hastings, T. *A portrayal of the changing evaluation scene.* Keynote speech at the annual meeting of the Evaluation Network, St. Louis, Mo., 1976.

3. Guba, E.G. *Alternative perspectives on educational evaluation.* Keynote speech at the annual meeting of the Evaluation Network, St. Louis, Mo., 1976.

4. Stenner, A.J., and Webster, W.J. (Eds.). Technical auditing procedures. *Educational Product Audit Handbook,* 38–103, Arlington, Va.: Institute for the Development of Educational Auditing, 1971.

5. Kershaw, D.N. The New Jersey negative income tax experiment: A summary of the design, operations andresults of the first large-scale social science experiment. *Dartmouth/OECD Seminar on Social Research and Public Policies,* 1974.

6. Owens, T. *Application of adversary proceedings to educational evaluation and decision making.* Paper presented at the annual meeting of the American Educational Research Association, New York, 1971.

7. Ashburn, A.G. *Directing education research training toward needs of large school districts.* (mimeo) Texas A & M University, Office of Educational Administration, Prairie View, Texas: 1972.

8. Guba, E.G. *A study of Title III activities: Report on Evaluation.* (mimeo) Bloomington, Ind.: National Institute for the Study of Educational Change, Indiana University, 1966.

9. Merriman, H.O. *Evaluation of planned educational change at the local education agency level.* (mimeo) Columbus, Ohio: The Ohio State University Evaluation Center, 1968.

10. Ott, J.M. *A decision process and classification system for use in planning educational change.* (mimeo) Columbus, Ohio: The Ohio State University Evaluation Center, 1967.

11. Walker, J. *Influence of alternative structural, organizational, and managerial options on the role of evaluation.* Paper presented at the annual meeting of the American Educational Research Association, Chicago, 1974.

12. Webster, W. *The organization and functions of research and evaluation in large urban school districts.* Paper presented "Webster, W.J." at the annual meeting of the American Educational Research Association, Washington, D.C., March, 1975.

13. Glass, G. V. *Design of evaluation studies.* Paper presented at the Council for Exceptional Children Special Conference on Early Childhood Education, New Orleans, La., 1969.

14. Eisner, E. W. *The perceptive eye: Toward the reformation of educational evaluation.* Paper presented at the annual meeting of the American Educational Research Association, Washington, D.C., March, 1975.

15. Sanders, J. R. and Hershiser, M. A. *A proposal to study the attributes of a classroom that determine its pervasive quality.* Kalamazoo, Mich.: The Evaluation Center, Western Michigan University, 1976.

[1]Presentation by Robert W. Travers in a seminar at the Western Michigan University Evaluation Center, Kalamazoo, MI, October 24, 1977.

Table 1
An Analysis of Political Orientation Study Types
(Pseudo Evaluation)

Approaches	Political Orientation (Pseudo Evaluation)	
Definitions	Studies that promote a positive or negative view of an object irrespective of its worth	
Study Types	Politically Controlled Studies	Public Relations Inspired Studies
Advance Organizers	Implicit or explicit threats	Propagandist's information needs
Purpose	To acquire, maintain, or increase a sphere of influence, power, or money	To create a positive public image for an object
Source of Questions	Special interest groups	Public relations specialists and administrators
Main Questions	What information would be best to report or withhold in a projected confrontation?	What information would be most helpful in securing public support?
Typical Methods	Covert investigations and simulation studies	Biased use of surveys, experiments, and "expert" consultants

Table II
An Analysis of Questions Orientation Study Types (Quasi-Evaluation)

Approaches

Questions Orientation (Quasi-Evaluation)

Definitions

Studies that address specified questions whose answers may or may not assess an object's worth

Study Types	Objectives-based Studies	Accountability Studies	Experimental Research Studies	Testing Programs	Management Information Systems
Advance Organizers	Objectives	Personnel/institutional responsibilities	Problem statements, hypotheses, and questions	Areas of the curriculum, published tests, and specified norm groups	Program objectives, activities, and events
Purpose	To relate outcomes to objectives	To provide constituents with an accurate accounting of results	To determine the causal relationship between specified independent and dependent variables	To compare the test performance of individual students and groups of students to select norms	To supply continuously the information needed to fund, direct, and control programs
Source of Questions	Program developers and managers	Constituents	Researchers and developers	Test publishers and test selection committees	Management personnel
Main Questions	Which students achieved which objectives?	Are those persons and organizations charged with responsibility achieving all they should achieve?	What are the effects of a given intervention on specified outcome variables?	Is the test performance of individual students at or above the average performance of the norm group?	Are program activities being implemented on schedule, at a reasonable cost, and with expected results?
Typical Methods	Analysis of performance data relative to specified objectives	Auditing procedures and mandated testing programs	Experimental and quasi-experimental design	Selecting, administering, scoring, and reporting standardized tests	System analysis PERT, CPM, PPBS, computer-based information systems, and cost analysis
Pioneers	Tyler	Lessinger	Lindquist, Campbell and Stanley, and Cronbach	Lindquist	Cook, Kerr
Developers	Bloom, Hammond, Metfessel and Michael, Popham, and Provus	Stenner and Webster, Kearney	Suchman, Wiley, Glass	Flanagan, Lord and Novick, Hyronymous, Thorndike, and many more	Kaufman

Table III
An Analysis of Values Orientation Study Types (True Evaluation)

Approaches		Values Orientation (True Evaluation)				
Definitions		Studies that are designed primarily to asses object's worth				
Study Types	Accreditation/ Certification Studies	Policy Studies	Decision-oriented Studies	Consumer-oriented Studies	Client-centered Studies	Connoisseur-based Studies
Advance Organizers	Accreditation/ certification guidelines	Policy issues	Decision situations	Societal values and needs	Localized concerns and issues	Evaluators' expertise and sensitivities
Purpose	To determine whether institutions, programs and personnel should be approved to perform specified functions	To identify and assess the potential costs and benefits of competing policies for a given institution or society	To provide a knowledge and value base for making and defending decisions	To judge the relative merits of alternative educational goods and services	To foster understanding of activities and how they are valued in a given setting and from a variety of perspectives	To critically describe, appraise and illuminate an object
Source of Questions	Accrediting/ certifying agencies	Legislators, policy boards and special interest groups	Decision makers (administrators, parents, students, teachers) their constituents, and evaluators	Society at large, consumers, and the evaluator	Community and practitioner groups in local environments and educational experts	Critics and authorities
Main Questions	Are intstitutions programs and persennel meeting minimum standards; and how they can be improved?	Which of two or more competing policies will maximize the achievement of valued outcomes at a reasonable cost?	How should a given enterprise be planned, executed, and recycled in order to foster human growth and development at a reasonable cost?	Which of several alternative consumable objects is the best buy, given their costs the needs of the consumers and the values of society at large?	What is the history and status of a program and how is it judged by those who are involved with it and those who have expertise in program?	What merits and demerits distinguish an object from others of the same general kind?

TABLE III (continued)

Typical Methods	Self study and visits by expert panels to assess performance in relation to specified guidelines	Delphi, experimental and quasi-experimental design, scenarios, forecasting, and judicial proceedings	Surveys, needs assessments, case studies, advocate teams, observation, and quasi-experimental and experimental design	Checklists, needs assessment, goal-free evaluation, experimental and quasi-experimental designs, modus operandi analysis, and cost analysis	Case study, adversary reports, socio-drama, responsive evaluation	Systematic use of retinal perceptual sensitivities and various ways of conveying meaning and feelings
Pioneers	College Entrance Examination Board (1901)	Rice	Cronbach, Stufflebeam	Scriven	Stake	Eisner
Developers	Cooperative study of secondary school standards (1933)	Coleman, Jenks, Clarke, Owens, Wolf	Alkin, Ashburn, Brickell, Estes, Guba, Merriman, Ott, Reinhard	Glass	MacDonald, Rippey, and Guba	Guba, Sanders

A Map of Postsecondary Assessment

LEONARD L. BAIRD

Although most discussions of "postsecondary assessment" focus on students' knowledge and skills, these cannot be fully understood without assessing the ways they are influenced by other aspects of postsecondary education. These aspects are described in a "map" consisting of 20 points which depicts the flow of students through institutions and experiences from precollege to adulthood. Consideration of the map identifies areas where better assessments and models are needed, particularly the areas of adult learners, graduate and professional education, and the characteristics and plans of college seniors.

Perhaps the best way to begin an evaluation of the status of postsecondary assessment is with a bagful of clichés such as the following: Postsecondary education is a multibillion-dollar enterprise in the United States, involving millions of people, including some of the best minds in our society. It has profound effects on the future of our economy, and, more important, on the nature of our civilization. In addition to its scope, postsecondary education is very complex and diverse. *Students* range from the barely literate to those with perfect scores on the SAT, from 12-year-olds to retirees, from Eskimos to inner-city dwellers, and from those attending classes simply to learn about a hobby to those pursuing advanced academic or professional degrees. *Colleges* vary in many ways: in size, from institutions such as Deep Springs College with 20 students to those such as Ohio State University which, with 55,000 students (46,000 full-time), qualifies as a small city; in selectivity, from open-door colleges that accept everyone with a high school diploma or a GED certificate to colleges such as Cal Tech, where 99% of the students are from the top 10th of their high school classes; in curricula, from St. John's, which offers one course of study, to the University of Michigan, with over 200 possible majors; and in student life, from those where all students are commuters to those where all live on campus. Thus, what a college "is" can vary enormously, as can the college experiences for students.

Given these clichés about the size, importance, and diversity of postsecondary education, how can we make sense out of it? How can we assess such an immense and complicated social institution?

I think that we can only address those questions by carefully examining *what* we want to know and whether we have the conceptual tools to understand what we are concerned about, by identifying the *information* we would need to tell us what we want to know, and by determining the extent to which it is possible and practical to obtain this information.

By far the most important consideration among these is *what* we want to know about postsecondary education. I have several perspectives on this question. I have recently been helping my son choose a college and will soon go through the same exercise with my daughter. As a parent, I have a number of questions that I expect are shared by other parents. Some are obvious: What are the costs, what are my son or daughter's chances of admission, what is the curriculum like, what are the requirements for degrees, and what programs or facilities are available for my son or daughter's special interests? Most of these questions can be answered by the catalog or guidebooks. Others become more difficult to answer from available information but often can be, such as: What are the chances a student will drop out, will get A's, or will go on to graduate or professional school? Finally, there are questions that may be very hard to answer: What is the daily experience like? What is the intellectual climate? Are students more concerned with football or Freud? Parties or Plato? Is there a sense of community among students? What happens to students like my son or daughter after going to this college? How go they grow intellectually? Do they become mature individuals? How are their ethical and social values affected? Will my son or daughter be a better person? How will he or she look back on the college years?

Besides my role as a parent, I am also a citizen-taxpayer. I have concerns about the uses of my tax dollars in my state and nationally. I am concerned about the costs, of course, but am even more concerned about the purposes or goals these dollars are put to. Are the colleges in my state meeting the current and future needs of my state and community in terms of the training they provide students? Is there provision for both excellence and equity? Nationally, I want to know the same sort of things, with some other concerns, particularly, whether first-class education is available for students with many different kinds of talents; whether able students from families of limited means are attending and graduating from colleges; whether research funds are going for the most recent trends or "hot topics" or are concentrating on fundamental issues; whether going to college makes a difference for individuals in terms of both their careers and the quality of their contribution to society; and whether colleges make a difference to the economy and the culture.

Finally, as an academic and a researcher, I have additional concerns: What are the implications of the rise in student careerism and concern for wealth for colleges and for students? What is the extent of "underpreparedness" among new students? What are the consequences of those facts for colleges? What is the meaning of that elusive idea *quality* in postsecondary education? What do students know at the end of college? Is "involvement" the way to reach excellence? What conditions promote research among faculty? How much emphasis is placed on faculty publications? What is the relationship of faculty publication activity to teaching excellence?

These various questions cover the gamut from the naive to the sophisticated, from the practical to the speculative, and from the simply factual to the very interpretive. But each of them has been the object of some attempt at systematic study. That is, there have been research efforts to develop the assessment instruments needed to address these questions, and various studies have used the instruments in attempts to answer the questions. These efforts have varied in sophistication and success, but the point remains that we have a considerable arsenal of instruments and information that bear on the major issues in postsecondary education. However, as I've suggested, these attempts at assessment have met with different degrees of success. Which brings me to our second and third major concern, the availability of conceptual models to help us understand the issues in question and the identification of the information we would need to address these questions. The last concern is whether it would be feasible to obtain this information on a wide scale.

Rather than discussing these other concerns at this point, let me propose a scheme—a map, if you will—of major processes in postsecondary education that puts the various questions for which we want answers into focus, and which then allows us to consider the availability of models, the identification of variables, the measurement of those variables, and the feasibility of obtaining those measures on a large-scale basis.

The map is shown in Figure 1. Let me define each area, and make a few comments about current issues in the area, whether they deal with conceptual models, definition of variables, measurement, or feasibility. Then I will discuss the areas that I believe would be most fruitful for further work, the importance of conceptual or theoretical models, and finally, how the entire process might be considered.

Figure 1
A Map of Postsecondary Assessment

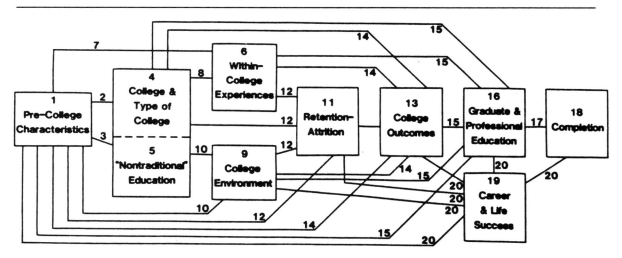

Also, let me note that this map is not meant to be a causal diagram or a totally complete description of how all the variables in postsecondary education affect one another. Rather, it is a device—a map—of how various important parts of postsecondary education are interrelated and flow into each other.

I should also point out that the map includes a great deal of information beyond what is frequently considered "postsecondary assessment" today. That is, what many people think of when they read the words *postsecondary assessment* is measurement of what students know and what their academic skills are when they apply to or enter college, their knowledge and skills in the middle, and their knowledge and skills when they leave. These things are important, of course, and involve many conceptual and technical problems. However, they are only *part* of the story. I think it should also be strongly emphasized that *we cannot fully understand why students know what they do or do much about it until we have understood the other parts of the "map."*

The first point on the map is precollege characteristics. These include the level of academic preparation, educational and career goals, attitudes and views about postsecondary education, motivation, social class, age, sex, ethnicity, and so on. These variables are important because they are the starting point for everything else. There are measures for virtually every characteristic. The task here is deciding which variables are most pertinent to our purposes and choosing the measure that best assesses the variable. (See, for example, the discussion of academic preparation in such sources as the American College Testing Program, 1976; the role of a range of personal factors in college admission in Willingham and Breland, 1982; and the role of social class and cultural sophistication in preparation for the subtleties of college life in Feldman and Newcomb, 1969.)

Point Number 2 on the map is the high–school–college transition, which is concerned with how students choose to attend college, the influence on college attendance of finances, access, gender, social class, ability, ethnicity, and so on. This area has been the subject of a great deal of research. I think the task here is choosing among various explanatory models and philosophical interpretations (e.g., see Manski and Wise, 1983: Zemsky and Oedel, 1983: Lowery et al., 1982).

In contrast, Point 3, adult entrance into postsecondary education, is not nearly as well understood but is put into this map because it is becoming an increasingly important social fact (Peterson, 1979: Cross, 1981: Cross and McCartan, 1985). I will discuss this area in more detail later.

The fourth area, colleges and college characteristics, concerns our understanding and assessment of the important distinctions among colleges, as well as their influences on the flow of students to different postsecondary options. We know that research universities differ in many ways from denominational colleges. We also know that the students who attend community colleges have a different aggregate profile from those who attend selective liberal arts colleges. The challenge here is to interpret the significance of these differences. (The series of volumes on different types of colleges prepared for the Carnegie Commission on Higher Education, although slightly dated, provide many facts and insights into the significance of these differences. Some examples are Astin and Lee's 1972 portrait of the largest group of institutions, small private colleges with limited resources; Dunham's 1969 profile of state colleges and regional universities; and Greeley's 1969 description of Catholic colleges. Other, more recent portraits include Cohen and Brawer's 1982 account of the community college and Fleming's 1984 portrait of black colleges.) However, perhaps a more important concern is the nature of various "nontraditional" forms of post-secondary education and the flow of people into them (Point 5 on the map). It has been estimated that the majority of postsecondary educational instruction is conducted in such nontraditional settings as corporations, organizations, governmental agencies, and community groups. It is very difficult to assess this tremendous diversity of educational experiences, but it is probably true that many of them represent high-level instruction and learning, however brief they may be. I think it is critically important that we understand the scope of these activities, assess the quality of the instruction, and see how the *educational* outcomes of such experiences can translate into the *credential* requirements of traditional forms of postsecondary education (e.g., see Keeton, 1980; Knapp, 1981; Scott, 1985).

The sixth point on the map involves the assessment of the types of within-college experiences. That is, we know that some of the most important effects upon students during their college years are produced by choice of major, residence grouping, and so on. The point here is whether we have the proper characterizations of the collegiate experience. For example, there is convincing evidence that living on campus or commuting can have substantial effects on students' collegiate careers. However, do we have any ideas to explain why living on campus or commuting have effects that go beyond common sense (e.g., see Chickering, 1974; Pascarella, 1985a)? Perhaps the most important of the choices students make within college is the choice of major, because that choice bears directly upon students' educational experiences and careers (Holland, 1985).

The seventh point in the model is the influence of precollegiate characteristics upon within-college experiences. The importance of this point is underlined by the fact that fewer and fewer students with high test scores are choosing to major in primary or secondary education, leading some, such as the Carnegie Foundation, to speculate that we may not have enough capable schoolteachers in the future. There is a considerable literature that shows that students choose majors based on their backgrounds, abilities, interests, and their perceptions of the job market (Holland, 1985). The evidence on other choices is less substantial, but it is clear that students choose experiences consistent with their characteristics, and that understanding this process offers one of the main fulcrums by which policy can affect students (See Weidman, 1984, for some evidence). For example, scholarships for students considering a career in schoolteaching may lead them to follow through on that choice.

The next point on the map (8) is the influence of college characteristics on these choices of within-college experiences. An example is the evidence that students tend to drop out even more than expected from their characteristics when they attend two-year colleges and less than expected when they attend residential liberal-arts colleges, largely because the within-college experiences differ. Here, however, the conceptual problem may be that we lack general theoretical models of how colleges affect students choices. (However, see Pascarella's, 1985b, general causal model.)

Point 9 on the map is the college environment, which is the subjective nature of the college experience. Some of the major dimensions of the environment, identified by a variety of methods, are the sense of community, the degree of academic rigor, and the level of formality (Baird 1980; Baird 1988; Moos, 1979). In the last several years much more attention has been devoted to the environment, particularly to how it leads to "involvement."

Point 10 is the influence of types of college and student characteristics on the environment. An old debate concerning the environment is whether it is aggregate student characteristics that make the environment or whether the environment is created by something external to the students, that is, for example, whether it is the presence of many able students that creates a sense of academic rigor or whether it is the standards and demands of the college that do so (e g., see Feldman, 1971). There are a variety of methods to assess the environment, but there is little agreement on the best way to understand the environment (Baird, 1988; Baird and Hartnett, 1980).

The next point on the map (11) is simply the facts on retention and attrition. There have been numerous attempts to define and codify the possible meanings of retention and attrition. These can vary greatly (Patrick Terenzini, a major researcher in this area, said that he can give over fifty different responses to the question "What is the dropout rate?"—all of which are factually accurate.) However, there is some consensus on definitions, and it has been possible to chart the extent of retention across types of colleges, for students with different characteristics, and over time (Tinto, 1982; Noel, 1985)

A related area, Point 12 on the map, is the prediction or understanding of the retention/ attrition process. This is one area where there are testable conceptual new assessments of theoretically important variables. I will expand on this point later.

The next point on the map (13) concerns college outcomes, which are the subject of a great deal of current discussion. About ten years ago, NCHEMS had an extensive project to define and measure these outcomes, producing, among other documents, *A Structure for the Outcomes of Postsecondary Education* (Lenning, 1976). That structure listed ten categories of characteristics, such as "competence and skills," and over fifty somewhat more specific areas, such as "intellectual skills," which, of course, have many subelements. The point is that there are many possible outcomes of higher education, including virtually every human characteristic. Clearly, the task here is *what* to focus on, that is, deciding what is *most important* to consider. A very reasonable approach is that of Bowen (1977), who attempted to describe a consensus about what the *goals* of postsecondary education are, and to relate the assessment of outcomes to these goals. Clearly, the choice of outcomes depends on one's values and interpretations of the purpose of postsecondary education. The appropriateness and technical quality of possible assessments depends on the choice of outcomes. The situation is complicated by the fact that many observers argue that the pluralism of postsecondary education requires each institution to have its own set of goals and outcomes. Here, perhaps more than in any other area, the issue is the logic of the choice we make in choosing which outcomes to study. (For general discussions of outcomes, see Lenning, 1976, and Ewell, 1985.)

The next point on the map (14), college effects, concerns the general influence of colleges and their programs on student outcomes. As the discussion of the last point would suggest, consideration of the variety of outcomes produces a complicated picture. However, virtually all of the research on college effects deals with change or gains in a relatively small group of outcomes: career choices, educational aspirations, and academic achievement tests. The emphasis here should be on the words *change* and *gains*. Essentially, college effects research is concerned with the *differential* impact of colleges, that is, why one college has a more positive influence than another. For example, once you control for the ability and background of students, does Harvard have any better effects on students than Mississippi State? (Note that this is a different—and more sophisticated— question from the more simple-minded question of the "value-added" or "talent-development" approaches, which focus on single colleges.) The point is to attempt to attribute change in growth in student characteristics to the college characteristics or environment, controlling for the students' initial status. This creates many problems, since students' final status is highly determined by initial status. The assessments in this area are subject to a wide variety of logical and psychometric considerations. These include the usual concerns with reliability and validity in their multiple meanings. But they also involve considerations of the sensitivity of the measures to real change, as well as the meaning of the measures at the beginning and end of postsecondary education (for example, a career choice of professor or physician may be a vague aspiration for a freshman, but may be based on a much more realistic self-evaluation for a senior). This area is fraught with problems of logic, measurement, statistical design and evidence (see Pascarella, 1985b, for a trenchant discussion of these points). In sum, there is great sophistication in this area, and a high level of understanding, but the evidence to date shows few consistent or powerful college effects. This may be due to the lack of the most appropriate measures, or to the relatively small impact of any new educational experience on students who have had twelve years of study.

The next point on the map (15), the transition to graduate or professional education, has not been well studied, largely because of the logistical problems of conducting longitudinal studies of college graduates. (There are some exceptions, such as Baird, 1976; Ethington and Smart, 1986.) However, many of the same variables that influence the high-school-college transition also influence the transition to graduate or professional school, such as previous academic performance and the requirements of one's career field. It is difficult to summarize all of these variables, and the theories of career choice and educational aspirations are often not helpful. For example, in recent years, large numbers of the students who have chosen to pursue MBA degrees have little intrinsic interest in business and are simply reacting to their perceptions of the job market (more on this later). In sum, identification of and assessment of the important variables in this area seems to be complicated and incomplete, especially for the large numbers of older students continuing their education. For example, what do the Graduate Record Examination scores of a thirty-five-year-old applicant, who has been away from institutionalized education for fourteen years, mean?

The next point on the map (16), the assessment of the types, characteristics, and environments of graduate and professional education, has seldom been studied systematically. Although a great deal has been written about the professions and the process of professionalization, there have been few empirical studies comparing advanced education across disciplines, and even fewer studying differences within a discipline, for example, how the environments for learning differ across medical schools. In addition, the existing work has focused almost entirely on the more prestigious professional schools, such as law and medicine, or on doctoral study at the elite graduate departments in traditional letters-and-science fields (e.g., Baird, 1974; Clark, Hartnett, and Baird, 1976; Katz and Hartnett, 1976). Very little has been done in the less prestigious professional fields or at the master's level, which is where the largest share of the enrollment is. However, the existing research suggests that professional and academic disciplines differ widely among each other and within the disciplines. I think this is a very promising area for the development of models and measures.

The next point on the map (17) concerns attrition and retention in advanced studies. (Lines linking this to earlier variables are not shown, to simplify the diagram.) Partly because of the difficulties in tracking students in often highly individualized programs, there is little research in this area. For example, is an ABD a dropout? Is a student who has spent ten years in studies without obtaining a doctorate making normal progress? If not, as many as half of the graduate students in some disciplines are not making normal progress. Despite the logistical problems involved, this area is very important to understand, and it is one that would profit from even the simplest of studies.

The next point on the map (18), completion status, is an area where it is very difficult to know what we want to understand. For example, we might like to know how much the recipients of various degrees have learned. Although a few professions, such as law, have external examinations required for final admittance to the profession, for most disciplines in graduate and professional education it is unclear what we would look for, although there have occasionally been reviews of dissertations by external evaluators. Although much has been written about academic socialization and professionalization, there are no clear criteria by which these might be assessed. This area seems to lack both models and measures.

The next point on the map (19), career of life success, is considered by some to be the most important area of all (Lenning et al., 1975). However, as I have written elsewhere (Baird, 1985), the assessment of "success" is quite problematical. For example, the clearest kinds of criteria of "success" apply only to a few, such as publications and citations among Ph.D. recipients who work in academe. Most careers involve complex and multiple indicators of success. Even such seemingly objective criteria as annual salary are very problematical. And such complex careers as medicine can have a bewildering number of possible criteria, many of which are negatively related. (For example, the most thorough attempt to define success in the physician's role resulted in some eighty measures, many of which were negatively related—Price et al., 1973). The final point on the map (20) is the *prediction* of career and life success, an area that has been the subject of considerable debate, involving many political and philosophical questions, which I will not go into here. I will just note that, despite my comments on success *within* certain areas and its problematical nature, at a very gross level it is possible to roughly assess *general* "success" in terms of educational and occupational attainment. The sociological literature is full of models attempting to account for these variables in American life (Baird, 1985).

So, having described the "map," where does it leave us? I think there are several implications from our consideration of the map. One is the content, one is the use of models, and one is our interpretation. On content, I would like to suggest that there are several areas in which we need to improve our understanding and our assessments. One area concerns the increasing numbers of adults who enter postsecondary education for the first time or who are returning to pursue further education. It is unclear what methods are appropriate to assess their readiness for college or graduate education. Although older applicants as a group score lower on admissions tests, they often do much better than predicted in their classes, so some other variables are operating. But what are they? One possibility derives from various conceptions of the growth of intelligence, which suggest that its meaning and form change over the life span (Schaie and Parr, 1981; Berg and Sternberg, 1985). What are the appropriate ways of assessing and matching instruction and colleges to these changing abilities? In general, although there are many small studies of adult learners in higher education, we would greatly benefit by some large-scale studies of their characteristics, motivations, learning styles, and achievement.

A second large gap is information about graduate and professional education. Although we know about the total enrollment and the numbers of degrees awarded in different disciplines, we could profit from much more information. Although there are a handful of studies of the factors influencing attendance in graduate and professional school, attrition in graduate school, and the graduate or professional school experience, there is a crying need for more information in this area. As I noted before, most of what is known is based on elite professional and graduate schools and misses the experiences of the great majority of advanced students.

Yet another gap in our information concerns the attainments, plans, aspirations, and views of college seniors. Here, I am not concerned with assessing outcomes in the ways that most researchers of outcomes are concerned with. I am talking about the kinds of information collected by the ACE/UCLA Cooperative Institutional Research Program (CIRP) in its freshman surveys. This survey includes data on students' career choices, educational plans, financial indebtedness, attitudes toward education, views on social issues, reports on their academic performance and experiences, and so on. If this same kind of information were routinely obtained for seniors, it could allow us to chart trends in such areas as student career choices, academic performance, views of the purposes of college education, plans for further study, academic and social experiences in college, and students' satisfaction with their college. We could also compare these data for students in different kinds of colleges and in different majors, and for different groups of students, such as minority and majority students and women and men. And if these data were accumulated over a number of years, as the CIRP data have been, we could trace a number of variables that are important in postsecondary education. One example is tracing grades received in college to examine grade inflation, that is, to see whether an A average is more or less common from year to year. Another example is charting changes in student indebtedness. In addition, if it were possible to link the responses from the CIRP freshman survey to those from the senior survey, it would be possible to conduct studies of how students change during the course of college, and how various experiences influence these changes. There are some methodological problems in this area, such as dropouts and correctly controlling for initial status or characteristics, but I think the value of the information gained makes dealing with such problems worth the effort.

The information collected would be at least as useful to colleges as the CIRP freshmen data, since students could be asked about their reactions to their college's programs and services. In these times, when colleges are being called upon to demonstrate that their graduates have gained from their programs, and to show that students are satisfied with the quality of their education, this kind of data would seem to offer a great deal of value to colleges responding to such calls.

In addition to proposing a senior survey, I would like to recommend that data from the American College Testing (ACT) Program and the Educational Testing Service—the two major testing programs for the high–school–college transition—be analyzed to yield data that would meet some of our national concerns. They could routinely provide profiles for students with different characteristics. For example, by routinely breaking down results by ethnic group, they could provide considerable data about American minority students who are bound for college. Note here that I am not calling for comparisons of test scores so much as for descriptions of the goals, interests, high school accomplishments, and plans of students from various groups. I'm sure the reader can think of other possible uses for these vast databases. However, the main point is to capitalize on these sources in useful and imaginative ways.

An example of a possible analysis using ACT data would exploit the vocational interest test that they have administered for several years. Specifically, we could compare the measured vocational interests of students who currently say they are going to major in business and other fields with the interests of students who said they were going to major in those fields in the national data of some years ago. This would suggest whether students are making choices less *consistent* with their interests, perhaps due to their perceptions of which fields are marketable. Many other questions could be addressed using these data. Since the data of the national testing programs have already been collected and processed and are based upon immensely large samples, they would seem to be a resource—and a very inexpensive one—that could be used to address many questions.

Note that to this point, I have said nothing about the technical side of assessment, that is, new psychometric approaches, the possibilities of computerized assessments, sampling procedures, statistical models, and so on. Nor have I attempted to review specific measures and their strengths and weaknesses, although there are many intriguing recent developments, such as various measures of students' personal and moral maturity and Robert Sternberg's attempts to assess cognitive capabilities based on recent models of how the mind functions. Although useful, I don't think the advances we have made in postsecondary assessment are due to such technical improvements. Rather I have concentrated on the major questions that I think we want to answer because I believe true progress in postsecondary assessment comes from developing an understanding of the areas we are concerned with, and from the construction of *testable models*. That is, I believe we have the technical tools to develop assessments of most of what we are interested in studying.

The task is to develop concepts and models. Let me give an example. There have been hundreds of studies of attrition in higher education for at least fifty years. For many years, these studies were entirely empirical, searching for some measures that would lead to better prediction of student attrition and retention. Study was piled upon study with no advances in our understanding or prediction of attrition. Then, in 1970, Spady proposed a model of attrition-retention, which was adapted by Tinto in 1975. Instead of a shotgun approach, these researchers proposed that students enter college with varying degrees of "goal commitment" (the value they place on graduating) and "institutional commitment" (the value they place on the particular institution they are attending), as well as of their academic preparation and backgrounds. Interacting with the academic and social systems of their college, students have various experiences which affect the extent to which they are integrated into the social and academic life of the college. The level of academic and social integration then affects their goal and institutional commitment during the course of college. When students are integrated and have a high level of goal and institutional commitment, they stay in college; when they are not well integrated and their goal and institutional commitment is low, they leave. Thus, the model stipulates how different student characteristics and college experiences *interact* to affect the decision to stay or drop out.

This model has been tested in a wide variety of studies. Not every prediction from the model has been supported consistently, but it has increased our understanding of the *processes* involved in attrition, and it has led to the search for better assessments of the variables in the model. The search for better assessments in the model has led, in turn, to a reconsideration of other ideas. For example, "academic integration" has many possible elements which revolve around how a student begins to feel part of the academic life of a college. One obvious element is interaction with faculty outside of class. However, there are several possible kinds of faculty-student interaction. Some analyses (Pascarella and Terenzini, 1978) suggest that the most important kinds of interaction are those that focus on academic advising and discussions of campus issues—not discussions of personal problems, general issues, and so on. Thus, the attrition-retention model has led both to attempts to produce better assessment of the variables in question and to a more thorough understanding of the nature of students' college experiences. The Spady-Tinto model is an example of a model that has been developed and tested.

Another area that I believe will be extremely fruitful in the future is one where a model seems to be developing: the assessment of the meaning of *involvement*. Although Astin (1985) has some ideas he labels a "theory of involvement," there still needs to be a tighter set of concepts and clear specification of how and why the elements in the theory affect each other. However, there has been at least one important attempt to assess the extent and significance of student "involvement." This is Pace's (1984) College Experiences Questionnaire, which is designed to estimate a student's quality of effort in various areas of college life. Analyses using this instrument have indicated that effort in certain areas promotes progress toward goals in those areas. Almost certainly, there will be other attempts to define the meaning and assess the components of involvement that will increase our understanding of the interaction of student and college. The area of involvement seems to be an example of what may be gained from a model in the making.

Finally, I would like to turn to our *interpretation* of assessment information and how it can increase our understanding of postsecondary education. In this case, various kinds of information about *how* postsecondary education is changing in response to social changes can lead to ideas about the *nature* of those changes, which then lead to further considerations of postsecondary education. For example, as I've mentioned, numerous observers have pointed to indications that students have become increasingly careerist in their choices and orientations over the last twenty years (Katchadourian and Boli, 1985). This has happened almost simultaneously with the increase in educational opportunity. These facts, combined with evidence that the economic return on education has declined, have led to reconsiderations of the meaning of postsecondary education in American society (Collins, 1979). In a phrase, this has led to the idea that postsecondary education has changed from *opportunities* to *ultimatums*.

Let me briefly outline this argument.[1] Before and after World War II, a college education was an opportunity for people who wished to move up in American society. That is, admission to college was a privilege, and the completion of college was almost a guarantee of a well-paying and satisfying career. It was not always important *what* one's degree was in, as much as it was that one

Assessment and Program Evaluation

had a college degree. Naturally, individuals and public policymakers looked to increased educational opportunity as a way to increase the life and career opportunities of many segments of our society. There were movements for open admissions, large-scale financial aid, and majors designed to meet the needs of students. And these policies seemed to work. Many more students attended college, many more graduated, and it seemed that the egalitarian goals of the policies had been successful. There were opportunities for most, if not all. However, what seemed to happen was that the meaning of a college degree began to change. Instead of a rarity, it became relatively common. It was no longer an entrée into a wide variety of careers. Since there were so many college graduates, employers began to look for graduates with degrees in just the fields they were interested in, and since a degree was not necessarily a guarantee of talent, they began to pay more attention to *where* graduates had obtained their degrees. Thus, one of the unexpected consequences of the success of the egalitarian reforms in postsecondary education was to make prestige and specific training *more* important rather than less. However, an even more important point is that a degree, once seen as almost always leading to success, was now seen simply as another requirement to get into the game, that is, an ultimatum. One solution to getting more out of one's degree was to choose fields that promised success, for example, business and engineering, which has resulted in the careerist tendencies we have seen among students. Another was to go to a more prestigious college, which has been reflected in the desires for status that the Carnegie studies have noted. A third was to up the ante and obtain more degrees, which has been reflected in the rise in graduate and professional school enrollments.

I do not wish to argue whether this conception is correct. I am putting it forward as an example of the use of *general* models, which allow us to make sense of the overall changes in the postsecondary system. This is also an example of what one might call a metamodel, that is, one that steps above the level of specific domains and attempts to put the entire process of postsecondary education into an understandable picture. It suggests that some other measures might be needed, such as students' views of the economic payoffs of various majors, schools, and degrees, as well as the extent to which their perceptions of reality affect their choices. But most of all, it helps our perceptions of what is really happening in higher education, and what our "facts" signify.

I have covered a wide variety of topics in this article, attempting to focus on what we want to know, and on the gaps in our knowledge. I have emphasized formulating the right questions and the use of models because I believe that the "state of the art" in assessment in postsecondary education today is not due to technical advances, but to increases in our understanding. What is important is not so much the quality of our methods as the quality of our ideas.

Acknowledgments. Work on this paper was supported by the Center for Educational Statistics, U.S. Office of Education. An earlier version was printed in the proceedings of a conference, "Postsecondary Assessment: Report of a Planning Conference." None of the opinions or positions advanced in this article should be taken as representing the opinions or positions of the U.S Department of Education or any of its officials, past or present.

Notes

1. This argument was suggested by my University of Kentucky colleague, Richard Angelo.

References

American College Testing Program. (1976). *Assessing Students on the Way to College.* Iowa City: American College Testing Program.

Astin, A. W. (1985). *Achieving Educational Excellence.* San Francisco Jossey-Bass.

Astin, A., and Lee, C. B. T. (1972). *The Invisible Colleges*. New York: McGraw-Hill.

Baird, L. L. (1969). Big school, small school: A critical examination of the hypothesis. *Journal of Educational Psychology* 60:253–260.

Baird, L. L. (1974). *Careers and Curricula*. Princeton, N.J.: Educational Testing Service.

Baird, L. L. (1976). Who goes to graduate school and how they get there. In J. Katz and R. T. Hartnett (eds.) *Scholars in the Making*. Cambridge, Mass.: Ballinger.

Baird, L. L. (1980). Importance of surveying student and faculty views. In L. L Baird, R. T. Hartnett, et al., *Understanding Student and Faculty Life*. San Francisco: Jossey-Bass.

Baird, L. L. (1985). Do grades and tests predict adult accomplishment? *Research in Higher Education* 23: 1–85.

Baird, L. L. (1988). The college environment revisited. In J. C. Smart (ed.), *Higher Education: Handbook of Theory and Research*, Vol. IV. New York: Agathon Press.

Baird, L. L., and Hartnett, R. T. (1980). Directory of lending instruments for assessing campus environments. In L. L. Baird and R. T. Hartnett, *Understanding Student and Faculty Life*. San Francisco: Jossey-Bass.

Berg, C. A., and Sternberg R. J. (1985). A triarchic theory of intellectual development in adulthood. *Developmental Review* 5:334–370.

Bowen, H. R. (1977). *Investment in Learning*. San Francisco: Jossey-Bass.

Chickering, A. (1974). *Commuting versus Resident Students*. San Francisco: Jossey-Bass.

Clark, M. J., Hartnett, R. T., and Baird, L. L. (1976). *Assessing Dimensions of Quality in Doctoral Education: Summary of a Multidimensional Approach*. Washington, D.C.: Council of Graduate Schools.

Cohen, A. M., and Brawer, F. B. (1982). *The American Community College*. San Francisco: Jossey-Bass.

Collins, R. (1979). *The Credential Society: An Historical Sociology of Education and Stratification*. New York: Academic Press.

Cross, K. P. (1981). *Adults as Learners*. San Francisco: Jossey-Bass

Cross, K. P., and McCartan, A. (1985). *Adult Learning: State Policies and Institutional Practices*. Washington, D.C.: Association for the Study of Higher Education.

Dunham, E. A. (1969). *Colleges of the Forgotten Americans: A Profile of State Colleges and Universities*. New York: McGraw-Hill.

Ethington, C. A., and Smart, J. C. (1986). Persistence to graduate education. *Research in Higher Education* 24: 287–303.

Ewell, P. T. (ed.) (1985). *Assessing Educational Outcomes*. San Francisco: Jossey-Bass.

Feldman, K. A. (1971). Measuring college environments: Some uses of path analysis. *American Educational Research Journal* 8:51–70.

Feldman, K. A., and Newcomb, T. M. (1969). *The Impact of College on Students*. San Francisco: Jossey-Bass.

Fleming, J. (1984). *Blacks in College*. San Francisco: Jossey-Bass.

Greeley, A. M. (1969). *From Back Water to Main Stream: A Profile of Catholic Higher Education.* New York: McGraw-Hill.

Holland, J. L. (1985). *Making Vocational Choices: A Theory of Vocational Personalities, and Work Environments* (2nd ed.). Englewood Cliffs, NJ: Prentice-Hall.

Katchadourian, H. A., and Boli, J. (1985). *Careerism and Intellectualism among College Students.* San Francisco: Jossey-Bass.

Katz, J., and Hartnett, R. T. (eds.). (1976). *Scholars in the Making.* Cambridge, Mass.: Ballinger.

Keeton, M. T. (ed.). (1980). *Defining and Assessing Quality in Experiential Learning* New Directions in Experiential Learning, No. 9. San Francisco: Jossey-Bass.

Knapp, J. E. (ed.). (1981). *Financing and Implementing Prior Learning Assessment.* New Direction for Experiential Learning, No. 14. San Francisco: Jossey-Bass.

Lenning. O. T. (ed.). (1976). *Improving Educational Outcomes.* San Francisco: Jossey-Bass.

Lenning. O T., et al. (1975). *The Many Faces of College Success and Their Non-Intellective Correlates.* Iowa City: American College Testing Program.

Lowery, W. R., et al. (1982). *College Admissions Counseling.* San Francisco: Jossey-Bass.

Manski, C. F., and Wise, D. A. (1983). *College Choice in America.* Cambridge, Mass.: Harvard University Press.

Moos, R. (1979). *Evaluating Educational Environments.* San Francisco: Jossey-Bass.

Noel, L. (ed.). (1985). *Improving Student Retention.* San Francisco: Jossey-Bass.

Pace, C. R. (1984). *Measuring the Quality of College Student Experiences.* Los Angeles: Higher Education Research Institute, UCLA.

Pascarella, E. T. (1985a). The influence of on-campus living versus commuting to college on intellectual and interpersonal self-concept. *Journal of College Student Personnel* 26:292–297.

Pascarella, E. T. (1985b). College environmental influences on learning and cognitive development: A critical review and synthesis. In J. C. Smart (ed.), *Higher Education: Handbook of Theory and Research,* Vol. 1. New York: Agathon Press.

Pascarella, E., and Terenzini, P. (1978). Student-faculty informal relationships and freshman-year educational outcomes. *Journal of Educational Research,* 71:183–189.

Peterson, R. E., et al. (1979). *Lifelong Learning in America.* San Francisco: Jossey-Bass.

Price, P. B., et al. (1973). *Measures and Predictors of Physician Performance: Two Decades of Intermittently Sustained Research* (Department of H.E.W. Grant No. PM00017 Report). Salt Lake City: University of Utah.

Schaie, K. W., and Parr, J. (1981). Intelligence. In A. W. Chickering et al., *The Modern American College.* San Francisco: Jossey-Bass.

Scott, J. A. (1985). Integration of non-traditional programs into the mainstream of academic life. *Innovative Higher Education* 9:81–91.

Spady, W. (1970). Dropouts from higher education: An interdisciplinary review and synthesis. *Interchange* 1:6–85.

Tinto, V. (1975). Dropout from higher education: An interdisciplinary review and synthesis. *Interchange* 1:6–85

Tinto, V. (1975). Limits of theory and practice in student attririon. *Journal of Higher Education* 53: 587–600.

Willingham, W. W., and Breland, H. M. (1982). *Personal Qualities and College Admissions.* New York: College Entrance Examination Board.

Zemsky, Robert, and Oedel, Penny. (1983). *The Structure of College.* York: College Entrance Examination Board. Willingham, W. W., and Breland, H. M. (1982). *Personal Qualities and College Admissions.* New York: College Entrance Examination Board.

To Capture the Ineffable: New Forms of Assessment in Higher Education

Peter T. Ewell

New Models of Student Development

In 1985, the rhetoric of the national assessment movement in higher education centered almost completely on measuring discrete cognitive outcomes. This, after all, was what was missing in most practice-oriented investigations of student experience in college, and was the arena in which new instrumentation was most in demand. Five years of evolution, however, has brought assessment practice to the brink of rediscovering two elements of traditional wisdom embodied in decades of scholarly research on collegiate learning and development: Outcomes cannot be understood independently of the processes that preceded them, and student learning and development is a complex, multifaceted phenomenon unusually resistant to single-factor explanations (Ewell, 1988a; Pascarella, 1985). The result for emerging assessment practice has been twofold. First, both individual and group-level efforts are increasingly being based on truly longitudinal rather than one-shot or test-retest research designs. Second, the outcomes to be assessed are increasingly being modeled holistically, as complex combinations of cognitive and noncognitive attributes. Neither trend, it must be stressed, is currently typical, as most institutional efforts are in an initial stage dominated by the short-term need to respond to state accountability mandates. But both are strongly present in a growing body of more mature institutional initiatives, begun some 4 to 5 years ago.

Longitudinal Designs: The New Face of Value-Added

Considerable stimulus for the operational use of true longitudinal research designs derived in part from ongoing debates about the merits and interpretation of gain scores. Popular and much-discussed early models of assessment based on the concept of value-added (Astin, 1977) emphasized the repeated administration of comparable instruments in a test-retest design as the optimal core of an assessment strategy aimed at isolating real institutional impacts (Jacobi, Astin, & Ayala, 1987; McClain & Krueger, 1985). At the same time, test designers at ACT were designing the COMP largely around a test-retest design, and the state of Tennessee had made the decision to incorporate the concept as a key component of statewide performance evaluation. But objections to the value-added concept were legion. One such objection was philosophic—that the term's implied identification of student learning with an industrial production process was inappropriately mechanistic. Others were more practical; for example, little of importance could be learned from pretesting students on material to which they had not yet been exposed (Pace, 1979; Warren, 1984). But some of the most important objections to value-added were technical—that the use of difference scores themselves (particularly if based on estimated gain) entailed multiplicative sources of error and could lead to critical misinterpretations regarding actual patterns of development (Baird, 1988; G. Hanson, 1988; McMillan, 1988; Pascarella, 1987).

Defenders of value-added as a useful metaphor for institutional quality quickly realized the need to distance the concept from a particular measurement technique (Astin & Ewell, 1985). Resulting reformulations of the basic notion in the form of "talent development" (Astin, 1985) not only proved more acceptable philosophically but also entailed a quite different methodological core for assessment. Within a single longitudinal database, information on student input characteristics, environmental experiences, and learning outcomes might be combined to support complex multivariate studies of talent development in different settings (Astin, 1990). This reformulation of the basic value-added concept, however, had major implications for both institutional assessment practice and the analytic paradigm used to make sense of its results.

In terms of practice, this new conceptual foundation for institutional assessment was already being piloted in the field. Indeed, by 1989 several institutions were embarking on complex, multifaceted longitudinal studies of student impact as a cornerstone for institutional assessment. One much-imitated study involving 320 students was begun at Stanford in 1977 (Katchadourian & Boli, 1985). Through a combination of quantitative questionnaire-based techniques and qualitative interviewing techniques, students in the sample were followed up each year of their college careers, with results providing a rich array of insights into both differential patterns of development and the ways in which the college environment was perceived and experienced. Similar studies under way at the University of Arizona (Dinham, 1988) and the University of Virginia (Kellams, 1989), both undertaken largely in response to state mandates on assessment, also are attempting to integrate survey questionnaire and face-to-face annual interviews. Advances in computer technology, moreover, allow considerably more background and experience information about students in the study population to be compiled from existing student records data. Early results of these studies, partly because of their richness and immediacy, have proven particularly easy to communicate to a campus community (University of Virginia, 1990).

Longitudinal research designs of this kind have considerable research potential in their own right and enjoy growing popularity as a foundation for institutional assessment. But they have many problems. One is the sheer level of resources involved, particularly if face-to-face interviewing is used and if sample sizes are large enough to sustain reasonable generalizations. Costs for the 4-year University of Virginia panel study, for example, are substantial, and resource limitations have confined the University of Arizona project to perilously small sample sizes. Another challenge is panel attrition and the resulting representativeness of a survivor population; in this respect, it is no coincidence that the institutions most interested in pursuing such studies have graduation rates that are well above average. Most challenging, however, are potential experimenter effects induced by the repeated interview design itself. Despite these difficulties, ongoing longitudinal studies of varying complexity, founded on an explicit database, will probably become the design of choice for most institutional practitioners.

More subtly, reformulation of the value-added concept and its embodiment in longitudinal research designs has profound implications for the analytic paradigm for assessment. Although test-retest designs clearly reflect the methodological imprint of controlled experiments drawn from cognitive psychology, making sense of longitudinal databases requires an analytic model based on multivariate statistical control more akin to the disciplines of sociology and econometrics. Statistical techniques pioneered by Astin (1977) that use the residuals obtained from regressing outcomes variables on a range of input controls as the primary criterion variable for environmental effect studies have thus become accepted practice in recent attempts to document curricular impact (Pike & Philippi, 1989; Ratcliffe & Associates, 1990). This approach, of course, reflects a methodological tradition already established in the scholarly literature of college student development (e.g., Pascarella, 1985), but its effective practice requires a level of statistical sophistication in assessment practitioners that is not often attained. One result, and clearly a trend for the future, is a growing demand for formal practitioner training in assessment emphasizing statistical analysis (Astin, 1990).

Holistic and Hierarchical Learning Models: The New Face of Student Development

A second emerging conceptual rediscovery in assessment practice is the value of a holistic model of student development. This, too, arose partly in reaction to proposed test-retest methodologies. Not only did the production process analogy embedded in value-added imply linear development, but it also suggested that developmental attributes could be examined one at a time. As a result, although many early assessment efforts were appropriately founded on multiple methods, they made little attempt to incorporate separate investigations of discrete student attributes into an integrated developmental pattern. More recent and sophisticated assessment approaches reject this notion and, like the reformulation of value-added, the resulting change has implications for both practice and analysis.

By 1985, the practical application of an integrated model of student learning and development to ongoing institutional assessment had already been demonstrated at a handful of institutions, most effectively, perhaps, at Alverno College (Mentkowski & Loacker, 1985). Beginning in the early 1970s, Alverno faculty not only pioneered the practice of individual performance assessment in higher education, but they also made integrated developmental abilities the primary foundation of their instructional program. Indeed, the two were intimately related—a linkage often lost on those who later attempted to imitate Alverno's approach to assessment without having previously thought through what was meant by developmental abilities and how they might be taught. Alverno's curriculum is currently founded on eight well-defined abilities—communication, analysis, problem solving, valuing, social interaction, taking environmental responsibility,involvement in the contemporary world, and aesthetic response—each of which is a complex combination of cognitive, affective, and behavioral traits (Alverno College Faculty, 1976; Ewens, 1979). As they progress through the curriculum, students are successively certified at each of six levels within each ability through a performance assessment process involving both self-assessment and feedback from multiple trained assessors (Alverno College Faculty, 1979). At the same time, the individual assessment process is periodically validated externally through a group-level evaluation process that employs a range of external cognitive and affective instruments and an ongoing longitudinal follow-up design (Mentkowski & Doherty, 1984). At the heart of Alverno's assessment concept is the proposition that integrated abilities are not simply additive trait combinations, observable in isolation, but are undifferentiable learned performance capabilities that can neither be defined nor observed in the absence of actual performance settings (Mentkowski & Rogers, 1988).

As in the case of longitudinal research designs, the conceptual foundations for integrated developmental approaches were already well established in the literature of student development. On the basis of extensive student interviewing over time, Perry's (1970) model of staged development combining traditional cognitive and noncognitive traits had substantial impact on student development practice (e.g., Mentkowski, Moeser, & Straight, 1981). These and other holistic developmental conceptions, such as Chickering's "vectors of identity" (Chickering, 1969) and Kohlberg's "scale of moral development" (Kohlberg, 1981), were actively used in assessment at Alverno and are being increasingly discussed in the assessment approaches of other institutions. By 1985, all had also been embodied in more tractable formats for use in large-scale assessment through paper-and-pencil techniques (Erwin, 1983; Erwin & Delworth, 1980; Rest, 1986, 1987).

Currently, the effects of these concepts are visible in assessment practice in at least two ways. One is a growing breakdown in the classic cognitive/noncognitive distinction underlying much early institutional assessment work. To some extent this is due to increased recognition on the part of faculty—who ground and direct most current institutional assessment efforts—that much of the impact of college is not strictly cognitive. At the same time, many faculty now recognize that such distinctions can leave important things out. Intellectual "habits of mind" such as intellectual integrity, openness to different points of view, and intellectual curiosity and commitment to continued learning are thus emerging as salient assessable general curricular objectives within a growing number of proposed institutional assessment plans (e.g., College of William and Mary, 1989; Conrad, Jamison, Kroc, MacCorquodale, & Summers, 1987). Similarly, the most recent overall treatments of assessment practice (e.g., Erwin, in press) feature developmental objectives as equivalent in status to classic knowledge and skills objectives in the design of assessment programs, and intentionally blur classic divisions between cognitive and affective outcomes.

A second impact of holistic developmental conceptions is to highlight the importance of individual differences in the assessment process (Knefelkamp, 1989). Particularly important here have been gender differences in both outcomes and perceptions of the collegiate experience (e.g., Light. 1990), and outcomes differences based on learning style and personality type. Assessment practitioners now recognize that conclusions based only on the high levels of aggregation typically used in sample-based institutional assessment can be extremely vulnerable to misinterpretation if such differences are not taken into account. As a result, most now emphasize substantial disaggregation of obtained results (Astin, in press; Erwin, in press).

Three Implications for Practice

Beyond their conceptual impacts, emerging developmental models have more specific methodological consequences for assessment practice. First, the need to identify "environmental" or "treatment" effects in complex longitudinal research designs has led to considerably greater attention to documenting student behavior. Because most of the data required are already available in computerized student record systems, the greatest recent progress has been the ability to efficiently extract such information in a format suitable for supporting studies of longitudinal student development (Ewell, Parker, & Jones, 1988). Using such techniques, for example, institutions have been able to determine the overall effectiveness of remediation efforts (Adelman, Ewell, & Grable, 1989) or the relative effects of different general education core course sequences. Methodologically more sophisticated course-taking pattern studies have established not only the general existence of "behavioral curricula" within typical distribution-based requirements (Boyer & Algren, 1987; Zemsky, 1989), but also the relationships of specific course clusters to selected outcomes measures (Pike & Philippi, 1989; Ratcliffe & Associates, 1990). Unfortunately, no such ready data source as registrar's records currently exists for documenting other forms of student experience, particularly in the co-curriculum, and most practitioners continue to rely on survey self-reports of such activities for inclusion in longitudinal databases.

A second implication for practice is the need to more fully ascertain student motivations and goals—particularly among nontraditional students. Community college populations, for example, may attend college-level classes for many reasons other than to earn a degree or transfer to a 4-year institution. Among the reasons are job or skills upgrades, retraining, or simple personal interest. Yet students with quite different goals may inhabit the same classrooms and enroll for the same programs as students with more traditional objectives. As a result, emerging assessment practices focused on nontraditional college populations increasingly stress early goal assessment of incoming students (e.g., Walleri & Japely, 1986). In more sophisticated applications, results of goal assessments are used to develop student typologies based on clusters of related characteristics (Aquino, 1989; Sheldon, 1981). In others, changes in student goals are tracked over time or compared to later self-reports of goal fulfillment. In the ultimate extension of this logic, goal assessment can be extended to the individual course or curriculum as an ingredient of "classroom research" (Stark, Shaw, & Lowther, 1989). Given anticipated increases in student diversity, whatever the mechanism used, periodic goal assessments of this kind will remain important in making sense of longitudinal student behavior.

A third ingredient, partially related to goals, is the student's own investment in the learning process. Part of this investment is time on task, an often cited factor in learning research (Astin, 1985; Pascarella, 1985). As a result, items tapping student out-of-class time spent studying and preparing for class are sometimes now included in regularly administered student assessment questionnaires or course evaluations (e.g., Krueger & Heisserer, 1987). A parallel but more intensive technique is the use of time diaries (Astin, 1979) for selected bodies of students—an ingredient in several current longitudinal interview studies (e.g., Angelo, 1988). Its most extensive variant is the concept of "quality of student effort" embodied in the now widely administered College Student Experiences Questionnaire (CSEQ), which contains 14 involvement scales that tap levels of student use of or participation in a range of campus resources, services, and activities (Pace, 1984). Quality of effort as assessed by the CSEQ has been related to persistence and performance across a range of college settings (Pace, 1990), and the instrument is increasingly in demand as a key ingredient in institutional assessment.

Overall, recent evolution in assessment's core model of student learning toward continuous and holistic development raises important issues regarding future practice. One implication is the level of investment required to do good work. The increased sophistication required for longitudinal data collection and analysis not only demands technical sophistication, but also requires an administration with a long attention span. Political support may not persist as long as students do, and there may be little long-term constituency for activities such as assessment that seem to take so long to show results (Ewell. 1990). More disturbingly, unless assessment is made integral to teaching practice, faculty also may lose interest. Indeed, a real danger inherent in assessment approaches founded largely on integrated developmental concepts in the absence of real curricular transformation is that faculty may come to see assessment as the province of specialists. Fortunately, for different reasons, a strong countervailing trend is moving assessment practice more extensively into the classroom and curriculum. But the threat of bureaucratic isolation—already partly induced by the fact that assessment is, for most institutions, seen initially as an external reporting requirement—can potentially be exacerbated by increasing methodological sophistication. In most institutions, faculty ownership and involvement in assessment remains strong, and there is an appropriate balance between technical evolution and grass-roots applicability. Recently characterized as "happy amateurs" (Hutchings & Marchese, 1990), assessment practitioners retain their faculty roots as they refine their methods. As a result, the slow evolution of a relatively simple technique will probably be the dominant pattern for the future.

A "Naturalistic" Mode of Inquiry

When assessment first emerged as a major topic of college and university discussion, it was clearly seen as a new activity, quite different from anything already in place. This was, in part, in response to accountability demands that appeared to require a distinctly identifiable bureaucratic process. Also, it was due to the language of academic reform that in the same period appeared to require technically proven, externally credible measurement devices. Whatever the stimulus, initial concern with assessment at most institutions tended to focus on creating a visible capability, located perhaps in a professionally staffed and adequately funded assessment center and founded upon periodic large-scale data-gathering efforts. The most prominent prototype, of course, was mass testing (often on a designated "assessment day") using a specially designed, nationally normed standardized assessment instrument.

Currently, this methodological center of gravity appears to be shifting. Imitating the history of more general program evaluation efforts in the 1970s, the primary mode of inquiry for assessment has become increasingly naturalistic, relying less heavily on distinct special-purpose instruments and data-collection opportunities and conforming instead to the existing rhythms of college and university life. Partly, the reasons are similar to those that drove practitioners of program evaluation to a more naturalistic approach (Shapiro, 1986). Complex research designs involving carefully selected samples and special-purpose instruments often broke down under the practical demands of field settings. In many cases, moreover, student motivation problems proved intractable, particularly where testing was implemented quickly or its purposes were not made plain. More significantly, it was often difficult for assessment practitioners to gain political support among faculty for an activity that seemed an add-on to existing classroom instruction, requiring additional resources and having only a small chance of local benefit. Indeed, experiences were sufficiently similar for members of the evaluation community to quite rightly, and somewhat smugly, point them out (e.g., Davis, 1989).

At the same time, it was becoming clear that, as in program evaluation, some of the greatest benefits of assessment occurred in its early stages, when faculty were forced to actively wrestle with questions of curriculum-wide instructional goals and how they might be recognized. Also, such benefits occurred particularly in situations where faculty, by choice or circumstance, designed their own assessments (Banta & Moffett, 1987). For most institutions, this initially took place in the major field. But by 1988, significant numbers of institutions had also begun to experiment with locally designed techniques in general education (e.g., Hutchings 1987; Paskow, 1988). Although in many cases methodologically problematic, these approaches had the major virtue of engagement, and if, as many claimed, the primary goal of assessment was to get faculty to think more critically about what they were doing, increased engagement was well worth a sacrifice in measurement precision. In general, this shift toward more naturalistic methods is visible in two main arenas. First, there is a strong trend toward exploiting existing points of contact with students rather than developing large numbers of new special-purpose data-collection methods. Second, reflecting the fact that most existing points of contact lie within the curriculum itself, there is an emerging trend toward curriculum-embedded techniques and classroom research conducted independently by individual faculty members.

Using What You Have: Curriculum-Embedded Assessment

Exploiting existing data-collection opportunities as occasions for assessment began with recognition that much that might be called "assessment" was already taking place on most college campuses (Ewell, 1983). Community colleges, for example, are increasingly building on initial orientation and placement testing as settings for collecting additional information on student goals, perceptions, and anticipated difficulties (Adelman et al., 1989; Vorhees & Hart, 1989). Common data-collection opportunities are less frequent at later points in most college curricula, but they are not unknown and, if available, they can be used in alternative ways. Upper level writing requirement examinations at Bethany College (West Virginia), for example, are now used to examine not only individual writing proficiency, but are also used at the group level to tap student perceptions of the campus environment (Ewell & Lisensky, 1988). Where formal opportunities involving all students do not exist, individual curricular requirements may already be structured in such a way that many students pass through a particular course at about the same time. Assessment guidelines at Kean College, for example, suggest that departments might use "key courses" of this kind as occasions for broader inquiry (Kean College of New Jersey, 1986). Existing student surveys often present an additional opportunity. Inventories of such instruments undertaken as a first step in assessment generally identify dozens of such instruments of uncertain quality, administered on a one-shot basis; a first step in many emerging institutional assessment plans, therefore, is to consolidate such efforts into a few carefully designed comprehensive survey instruments. Similarly, some institutions now include items on self-reported gain or quality of effort on the course evaluation forms traditionally used to rate faculty (Ewell & Lisensky, 1988).

A more important naturalistic line of development involves incorporating assessment techniques directly into the classroom or curriculum. Because of the enormous diversity of such efforts, it is useful to classify them along two descriptive dimensions. One is *domain*, as most institutions make a clear distinction between assessment in the major field—which is generally the responsibility of each individual department—and assessment processes intended to determine the broader outcomes of general education. Initial experiments with curriculum-embedded techniques first took place in the major field, where clear course progressions often existed and where faculty were better able to identify appropriate opportunities. Only recently have such techniques begun to emerge in general education, usually after extensive consideration of or a disappointing experience with standardized general education instruments.

A second distinction addresses the *level of intervention* involved. In its most active form, curriculum-embedded assessment may involve explicitly designed performances, exercises, or examinations that are carefully crafted to provide group-level as well as individual-level information and intended to be inserted into classroom or field settings. Primary examples here include integrated performance assessments as pioneered by Alverno, as well as more traditional devices such as senior seminars and comprehensive examinations. In its least obtrusive form, curriculum-embedded assessment may include systematically collecting existing student products, generated as a natural result of the curriculum as currently taught, for later evaluation as evidence of overall curricular goal attainment. Most salient examples here involve extensions of the portfolio approach traditionally used for evaluating writing or performance in the fine arts. Between these two extremes lies a continually expanding range of practice.

Curriculum-embedded assessment in the major field. Within the major field, curriculum-embedded assessment takes a variety of forms. Perhaps the most popular alternative, though highly obtrusive, is a faculty-designed examination. Traditional comprehensive examinations that must be passed in order to graduate, and that require students to demonstrate both broad disciplinary knowledge and its application to typical problems or settings, are enjoying a significant revival on many college campuses. Like their standardized counterparts, however, such examinations have severe limitations in producing group-level assessment information. Carefully designed multidimensional rating schemes are required to render these examinations useful in providing program-level information (Erwin, in press), and multiple readers may be needed to ensure adequate reliability. Faculty-designed major field examinations intended from the outset to produce group-level results about the attainment of curricular goals are also visible in growing numbers. Among the best current examples are a range of major field examinations at the University of Tennessee, Knoxville, and James Madison University, developed in response to state mandate. Here, examination items typically are first designed by faculty themselves, with substantial assistance from campus assessment professionals (Banta & Schneider, 1988). For the most part these examinations are based on multiple-choice items, though more recently, faculty are being encouraged to include performance-based items or tasks. An extensive literature of practice has grown up around the construction of such instruments (e.g., Appelbaum, 1988; Erwin, in press; Pike, 1989b). Not surprisingly, the bulk of this advice follows the logic of standard instrument development methods, beginning with a clear specification of objectives, the costs and benefits of different testing modalities and formats, establishment of item and obtained score validity and reliability, and interpretation of results. Instruments constructed in this fashion, with domains carefully matched to local curricular coverage, have proven powerful departmental tools for curricular review and improvement (Boyer 1989; Farmer, 1988). But because performances are not generally of consequence for individual students, such examinations can also suffer from the high nonparticipation rates and uncertain student motivation experienced by their standardized counterparts.

An alternative to stand-alone examinations is to embed assessment exercises in an existing capstone experience (e.g., a senior seminar, project, internship, or field placement). Less obtrusive, this approach is also less likely to provide complete coverage of any particular curricular goal domain. Existing individual student evaluation procedures in some disciplines are particularly amenable to curriculum evaluation purposes and can be modified with relatively little difficulty. At Glassboro State College in music, for example, consistent numeric rating schemes are incorporated into existing auditions and performances, and tapes of the performances are archived for comparison over time (Keith, 1989). In other professional or practice disciplines, a senior project or common experience is either already present in the curriculum or can appropriately be created. Examples include marketing at Kings College (Farmer, 1988), where seniors take a capstone course that involves team development and presentation of a complete marketing plan, or social work at Kean College of New Jersey (Boyer, 1989), where departmental assessment is grounded partly on ratings of student journals kept during field practice placements.

The success of such ventures in producing usable group-level assessment information depends heavily on three factors. First, the capstone exercise must truly be comprehensive (i.e., effective performance must depend on knowledge and skills learned throughout the curriculum); the more limited the domain of the performance (e.g., a senior thesis on a specialized topic), the less useful it is for evaluation. Second, judgment of the performance must involve multiple raters who can achieve reasonable consensus about what they see; typical senior capstone courses taught by single faculty members without cross-grading or external validation do not achieve this standard. Finally, rating scales must contain a sufficient number of dimensions that group-level diagnostic information can be obtained by aggregating obtained ratings on a single dimension across individuals; capstone experiences, senior seminars, or projects in which only a single summative grade is awarded do not meet this criterion. As in the case of faculty-designed major field examinations, substantial advice on practices that embody such principles is now available (Alverno College Faculty, 1979; Erwin, in press), and institutional use of this approach will undoubtedly accelerate.

The least obtrusive approaches to major field assessment rely entirely on a review of existing products. Appelbaum (1987), for example, suggests an "audit" procedure consisting of intensive reviews of course syllabi and required exercises, together with sample student products at different stages to roughly determine curricular goal achievement. Somewhat similar are portfolio techniques that collect systematic examples of student work over time for later collective review. An emerging vehicle for such exercises is program review. For example, in its most recent history review, the University of Virginia requested visiting scholars serving as external reviewers not only to inspect the undergraduate curriculum but also to read and comment on a selection of student theses (Moomaw, 1989).

Curriculum-embedded assessment in general education. Parallel assessment approaches in general education also span the continuum of active to unobtrusive. Although faculty-designed general examinations are rare, occasional well-grounded attempts to provide local, tailored alternatives to available standardized instruments such as the ACT COMP, CAAP, and Academic Profile have emerged (e.g., at James Madison University; Erwin, in press). These examinations have the substantial advantage of being carefully configured to fit local curricular requirements, but they are expensive to produce and validate and are equally subject to problems of student motivation. An interesting variant is the "sophomore-junior project" at Kings College: Before entry into the major, students are required to complete a transition exercise that emphasizes the use of general skills in the context of the discipline they are about to enter (Farmer, 1988).

A more common approach is course-embedded assessment, in which specifically designed questions addressing cross-curricular abilities are included in the final examinations of existing general education courses (Warren, 1988). Faculty read and grade examinations in the usual way, but the answers to the specially constructed items are also read collectively and rated against curricular goals using defined scoring criteria. This approach effectively obviates the student motivation problem often encountered by more obtrusive assessment techniques. In six core general education courses at Kean College of New Jersey, for example, faculty worked with ETS to develop special essay questions designed to tap carefully specified analytic abilities; responses are scored by teams of faculty readers using ETS core scoring methods (O'Day & Kelly, 1987). At Kings College (Farmer, 1988), "pretest" and "posttest" essays are used in interdisciplinary core course sequences, both to assess skills development within each course and to determine the degree to which analytical skills learned in one context can be effectively transferred to another (e.g., one such question asks students to apply previously learned economic concepts of profit, capital, interest, loans, principal, and assets to the physical arena of energy, currently being covered by an interdisciplinary science course).

Major challenges to widespread use of this technique are domain specificity and the degree of faculty agreement required. Most institutional definitions of general education goals, in themselves, provide an insufficient basis for developing the kinds of specific scoring guides required— partly because they are designed to politically accommodate courses drawn from many disciplines and departments and partly because they are rarely stated in outcomes terms. At the same time, unless courses offered for general education credit are designed and taught consistently, faculty will see the inclusion of general purpose questions in their own examinations as intrusive. Promising though it is, therefore, this approach has yet to be applied successfully outside curricula that lack a common core.

Less obtrusive approaches, as in the major field, rely heavily on secondary analysis of naturally occurring student products. The most popular emerging technique is the portfolio, in which representative samples of student work are compiled across courses and assembled for secondary reading according to defined criteria (Hutchings, 1990). This is a well-known technique in the evaluation of writing, and, not unnaturally, it has been most fruitfully applied in writing. A carefully executed recent experiment with sample portfolios at the College of William and Mary illustrates both the pitfalls and potential of this approach as a prime ingredient of general education assessment (College of William and Mary, 1988). An initial sample of 50 students was selected for the project, and their current courses were determined. Faculty were asked to duplicate selected students' work for combination into portfolios, which were then read by multiple readers using defined rating criteria. Reviewers believed that writing and critical thinking capability could be meaningfully assessed; however, they felt that additional general abilities could not be assessed because they were insufficiently delineated and, more important, because the class assignments associated with most of the instances of student work collected did not actually require the relevant skill.

Other general education portfolio review projects have foundered on sheer volume and confusion of purpose. Because portfolios undoubtedly have benefits for individual students when used to anchor feedback and self-assessment (Elbow & Belanoff, 1986), many institutions initially propose to apply the portfolio technique universally to achieve both group-level and individual assessment purposes. This is rarely successful, as maximum individual benefit requires the portfolios to be compiled and held by the students themselves, whereas collective review is a time-intensive exercise that can only be effectively accomplished on a sample basis. These drawbacks will probably temper the current heavy interest in portfolio evaluation techniques. As a result, future applications of portfolio methods in general education will probably be confined, appropriately, to the evaluation of student writing and critical argument.

A promising alternative to longitudinal portfolios, related to curricular audit techniques, is to systematically sample and analyze median performance. Essentially, this technique involves sampling the classroom products of the median earned-grade performer in each class and evaluating the results collectively as a work sample of a composite average performer. Although this technique, by definition, reveals nothing about the distribution of performance, it does allow central performance patterns to be readily identified across a range of general education dimensions. Because the maximum number of work samples collected is equivalent to the number of course sections offered, moreover, the process is fairly manageable logistically. It is interesting to note that median performance samples of this kind have occasionally been collected over time by individual faculty members who teach the same course year after year to determine trends in ability and as a hedge against unconscious shifts in personal grading standards (H. Friedman, personal communication, June 1988).

Fusing Assessment and Teaching Practice: Classroom Research

Simple techniques such as median performance sampling also emphasize the ultimate possibility for naturalistic practice—the use of assessment by individual faculty members in their own classrooms as an integral part of teaching. Dubbed "classroom research," such techniques enjoy increasing popularity as an approach to assessment because of their extreme flexibility and because their coverage and employment remain within the control of individual faculty members. In contrast to more formal assessment approaches that rely on an external proactive research strategy to effect instructional change, proponents of classroom research maintain that widespread innovative activities across hundreds of classrooms, though diverse and uncoordinated, will eventually induce a set of far more fundamental (and effective) changes in instructional practice (Cross, 1990).

In essence, classroom research consists of a diverse body of techniques intended to be flexibly used by individual faculty members to (a) directly assess student learning of class content and taught developmental skills, (b) assess and provide feedback to students about the ways they learn and their own self-consciousness as learners, and (c) obtain immediate feedback about how delivered instruction is being received (e.g., which concepts are being understood and which are not) in order to immediately adjust what is taught and how. Emphasis is placed on straightforward techniques that provide immediate information on student perceptions or levels of comprehension. Cross and Angelo (1988), for example, classify and fully describe such techniques in three general areas—assessing academic skills and intellectual development, assessing students' self-awareness as learners and self-assessments of learning skills, and assessing student reactions to teachers and teaching methods or materials. Among the latter, perhaps the most widely cited and employed is the "one-minute paper" that students are requested to complete after every class, documenting the most important thing they learned and the most important unanswered questions remaining (e.g., Light, 1990). More sophisticated techniques include "focused dialectical notes," in which students actively create a critical dialogue around statements encountered in assigned reading in order to practice critical thinking skills, and "one-sentence summaries," in which students are asked to concisely reorganize the essence of a particular concept in a single grammatical sentence. Such techniques have been extensively field tested, particularly in community college settings, and have proven powerful tools for focusing faculty attention on what constitutes good teaching.

Classroom research of this kind enjoys strong advantages as a general approach to assessment. Because its unit of analysis is the individual classroom, results can be applied directly in an arena in which faculty are directly invested and over which they, in fact, have control. More significantly, classroom research appropriately refocuses analytical attention on the *process* of instruction, in contrast to merely documenting outcomes. This shift is critical and is visible in a growing variety of assessment settings. Widely cited findings from the Harvard Assessment Seminar on the value of group study or the characteristics of highly respected courses (Light, 1990) provide a salient example of this critical redirection. At the same time, recent studies on the physical attributes of effective teaching practice (e.g., Chickering & Gamson, 1987; Gamson & Poulsen, 1989) are beginning to directly influence institutional assessment design, particularly in their demands for better information about classroom process and out-of-class student behavior (e.g., Minnesota State University System, 1989; Winona State University, 1990). Both developments, partly stimulated by the classroom research movement, promise a return of assessment's attention to neglected process and environmental concerns.

Emerging Issues of Naturalistic Assessment

Taken together, recent shifts in assessment technique toward a more naturalistic approach raise important practical issues. One is a concern about technical quality. At its extreme, the impetus toward more naturalistic designs can be seen as sanctioning a methodological philosophy of "anything goes"—an opinion that measurement advocates in assessment are quick to point out (Adelman, 1986, 1988). If formal assessment practices result in the same kinds of impressionistic evidence about educational effects as does traditional wisdom, the entire impetus of assessment's development since 1985 may be in jeopardy (Ewell, 1989). At minimum, if appropriate technical rigor is to be maintained, a major faculty development effort is required, guided by clear standards and principles of good practice (e.g., Light, Singer, & Willett, 1990).

Another emerging dilemma is the appropriateness of data aggregation across successively more inclusive units of analysis. By definition, naturalistic studies produce greater volumes of information in less compatible forms than do more intrusive and standardized measurement techniques. Already, in states that have mandated assessment while allowing considerable diversity in institutional data-gathering practices, there is growing concern about how to summarize and communicate results. Institutional leaders recognize and voice similar concerns. An emerging demand may be for layered instead of cumulative assessment designs, in which the results of assessment studies undertaken at different levels of analysis are neither aggregated nor directly compared because fundamentally different questions are being investigated in each. Despite these issues, current trends toward naturalistic inquiry in higher education assessment are unlikely to be reversed. The challenge for the future is to develop more rigorous measurement metrics and concepts better suited to such designs without doing violence to their intent or authenticity.

Emerging Issues and Future Directions

As assessment in higher education continues to evolve, its practitioners cannot avoid some fundamental questions of meta-methodology. Most now recognize that the movement's early promise, rooted in a simple linkage between measurement technology and academic reform, will be hard to fulfill without seriously rethinking some basic assumptions of measurement theory. Most are also vexed by the question of use, and in practice are finding the application of obtained results to decision making a difficult business. Like everything else in assessment, these questions are not new. Indeed, they are a limited replay of recent rethinking in the educational measurement and evaluation communities.

The majority of these questions can be treated through the recent conceptual development of the term *validity* (Messick, 1975, 1988a) traced by the testing and measurement community. Initially conceived of as a narrowly technical property of the measurement device, validity is now proposed as a unitary but "faceted" concept that embraces, at minimum, the intent and design of the instrument, the nature of the results obtained, the interpretation of these results, and the uses to which the findings are put. Conceptual discussions among assessment practitioners are currently centering on validity in these terms for at least two reasons. First, as the enterprise becomes increasingly localized through the use of faculty-designed instruments and naturalistic techniques, there is an urgent need for credible local validation procedures (Mentkowski & Doherty, 1980), both to ensure sound intervention and to engender external confidence. Second, as policymakers increasingly consider assessment results in making high-stakes decisions, there is an urgent need to ensure that the instruments and techniques used are sound enough to support these applications (e.g., Banta, 1988). Central concerns in these discussions can be effectively summarized in terms of three major questions embedded in the concept of validity that each attempt at assessment must pose and answer.

What's the Construct?

The growing use of performance measures in higher education assessment raises important questions about both the nature of the phenomenon being investigated and the epistemology underlying the investigation. Most assessment practitioners now agree that the kinds of cognitive properties claimed as collegiate outcomes are complex, and far more so than those addressed by traditional educational measurement practice. But do they require, as some now claim, completely rethinking the model of inquiry? Critics of current measurement practice point out that traditional assessment technology is wedded to a model of discrete trait estimation founded on the use of large numbers of independent compensatory items (e.g., Rogers, 1988). Although this approach may suffice for estimating basic skills or cognitive content, they claim, it is ill-suited for investigating complex, integrated abilities. The choice of demonstrated performance as the primary mode of inquiry, moreover, is not simply a question of face validity or authenticity but involves a radically different concept of the trait itself. Is the intent to estimate how much of a defined something an individual *has*, or to determine, in particular, what that individual can and cannot *do*? In the first case, the individual becomes one among many instances of the trait; in the second, the trait is inseparable from the individual.

The answer to this question matters for future assessment practice in at least three ways. First, if complex abilities are integrated and developmental, obtained trait estimates may mean different things for the same individual at different points in time. Measurement theorists increasingly recognize this proposition as they experiment with the kinds of hierarchically staged developmental models embodied in item response theory, with "inference networks" in which evidence from a wide variety of sources can be used to iteratively obtain probability estimates about an individual's current characteristics, and with more sophisticated "tectonic plate," "latent class," and "componential" models of test theory founded upon examining the response patterns typical of different states and stages rather than upon estimating overall proficiency (Mislevy, 1990). Advocates of performance assessment, moreover, argue that quite different kinds of tasks are appropriate at different points in a developmental sequence and that a repeated measures design tells little about the actual development of a complex ability.

Second, if complex abilities are not abstractly present but are properties of a given individual, obtained response patterns may legitimately differ from individual to individual regardless of any underlying proficiency. Not only does this raise questions about interpreting individual assessment results for purposes of feedback, it poses major challenges to the common use of analyses based on central tendency for grounding valid group-level inferences. The use of IRT-based techniques in test development, for example, allows much more sophisticated theory-based conclusions about group functioning to be drawn from a particular item response pattern but also demands identification of those (sometimes significant in number) for whom the theory-based response pattern does not hold (Mislevy, 1990). At the same time, in group-level work on student affective development using questionnaires and interviews, G. Hanson (1988) cautions against the unexamined use of central tendency methods and instead argues for response interpretations based primarily on the identification of "themes and patterns" in the data.

A final implication involves the nature and treatment of measurement error. Classical theory based on discrete trait estimation conceives of measurement error as an obtained deviation from a hypothetical true result, occurring because of imperfections in instruments, administration procedures, scoring procedures. and testing conditions. In the use of multiple-judgment rating scales,for example, interrater reliability calculations are needed to establish the range of judgmental variation that typically occurs around repeated observations of a presumed trait or ability across individuals. Evaluators of writing (and increasingly other advocates of complex performance assessment) disagree, maintaining that the different judgments of independent, professional raters may legitimately diverge and that such differences should not be lightly averaged to approximate a single hypothesized "true score" (White, 1990).

All three implications converge on a single admonition for future assessment practice: the need to be much more precise up front about the nature of the ability being investigated and how it might be recognized at different stages of development. If assessment is to prosper, currently predominant "menu-driven" practices of method selection will need to be replaced by choices based on an explicit theory of instruction.

What's the Context?

The emerging naturalistic paradigm for assessment allows for a vast range of possibilities for practice, but at the same time raises fundamental questions about the confidence that can be placed in obtained results. Lacking validation, critics maintain, admittedly innovative local practices are no more sound a basis for making inferences and decisions than the course grades and accumulated credit hours that they were intended to supplant. The resulting dilemma leads assessment practitioners to two current concerns—the nature of contextual validity and the contents of appropriate validation procedures for locally developed techniques.

The notion of contextual validity (Mentkowski & Rogers, 1988; Rogers, 1988) parallels that of authenticity recently called for in K–12 assessment (e.g., Wiggins, 1989), and the procedures it requires have much in common with established guidelines for naturalistic evaluation practice (Lincoln & Guba, 1986). In essence, its proponents argue, contextual validation requires establishing appropriate congruence among three elements: (a) the elicited performance itself and particularly its depth and complexity, (b) the typical contexts in which performances requiring the ability actually occur, and (c) the ways in which obtained results will be used to provide feedback or to make decisions. Validation in this sense becomes less a process of statistical confidence building than one of iterative negotiation among a variety of stakeholders in an attempt to establish common ground. As described, the proposed process resembles that which naturally occurs in the development of many assessments. Design of the GIS in New Jersey, for example, extended over a 2-year period and involved extensive consultation with faculty drawn from different disciplines and types of institutions as well as members of the business and professional communities (COEP Council, 1990). Throughout the pilot process, contextual validation was constantly sought in the form of faculty comments on the depth and appropriateness of the tasks required given what students were typically asked to produce in college classrooms.

But far too many local assessment decisions are currently made without such a process. As a result, they are vulnerable to charges of inappropriateness or inapplicability only after the results are in. To address this situation, proposals for local validation of faculty-designed instruments and assessment procedures are beginning to emerge in greater numbers (e.g., Erwin, in press; Mentkowski & Rogers, 1988). Their intent is not to supplant existing technical components of a validation—such as interjudge agreement, comparisons between obtained results and those produced by other similar instruments and techniques, and demonstrable linkages to the curriculum or other environmental effects. But they typically add to the validation process such components as practitioner judgments about the appropriateness of posed problems and limits regarding how obtained results should be used or not used. In the future, much will depend on the ability and willingness of faculty to rigorously apply such processes to their own instruments and procedures. Absent them, obtained results will be neither used inside the institution nor believed outside it.

What's the Use?

Probably the most often voiced current concern about assessment is the inappropriate use of its results. For the most part, moreover, concerns about use turn on the presumed technical limits of a given instrument or approach in providing information of sufficient quality to ground a reasonable decision. This is particularly the case where the decision in question involves high stakes (e.g., preventing a student from graduating, terminating a program, or denying significant levels of funding to an institution). Where high-stakes decisions are based on instruments with wide error ranges, this situation is extreme. Tennessee's performance funding program, for example, has been criticized for allowing the allocation of many thousands of dollars to ride on what may in essence be a random process, because current allocational decision points lie well within the standard error range of the procedure used (Banta, 1988). Similar concerns arise where an instrument designed for one high-stakes purpose is used for another. Comparative aggregate pass rates on Florida's CLAST examination, for example, occasionally have been used to evaluate institutional performance without taking into account either differences in test-taker characteristics across institutions or the technical capability of the CLAST instrument, designed to assess individuals, to support inferences about curricular impact (Ewell, 1990). Both situations, although rare so far in higher education assessment, raise additional validity issues with which testing and measurement professionals are familiar. Messick, for example, argues cogently for a comprehensive definition of validity that prominently includes considering the consequences of use (Messick, 1975, 1 988a). Instruments and techniques are not "valid" in this construction, but rather interpretations and uses. Each time the use context changes, the question of validity must be raised and addressed anew.

Growing recognition of this insight, in conclusion, brings the assessment movement in higher education face to face with its initial roots and values. Conceived as an integral part of an explicit reform agenda, assessment first arose as a technology in use. The promise of outcomes measurement appeared bright because its powerfully perceived technical merits seemed deployable in the service of improved undergraduate teaching and learning. Lurking within a technical approach to reform, however, was always a danger of reification: Assessment might easily become an end in itself, the exclusive province of an isolated professional measurement cadre little concerned with how its results were applied. That this has not occurred is due to the unwillingness of both faculty and public policymakers to let go of assessment's initially motivating question—how to better understand and improve collegiate learning. Evolution of a predominant method toward naturalistic inquiry, ultimately rooted in the individual classroom, signals not only methodological maturation but also a determination to keep that question vital. Equally important for the long run, it may help keep measurement honest.

References

Adelman, C. (1985). *The standardized test scores of college graduates, 1964–82.* Washington, DC: U.S. Government Printing Office.

Adelman, C. (1986). To imagine an adverb: Concluding notes to adversaries and enthusiasts. In *Assessment in American higher education: Issues and contexts* (pp. 73–82). Washington, DC: U.S. Government Printing Office.

Adelman, C. (1988). Metaphors and other guidances in higher education assessment. In C. Adelman (Ed.), *Performance and judgment: Essays on principles and practice in the assessment of college student learning* (pp. 279–293). Washington, DC: U.S. Government Printing Office.

Adelman, C. (1989). Indicators and their discontents. In C. Adelman (Ed.), *Signs and traces: Model indicators of student learning in the disciplines* (pp. 1–10). Washington, DC: U.S. Government Printing Office.

Adelman, S. I., Ewell, P. T., and Grable, J. R. (1989). LONESTAR: Texas's voluntary tracking and developmental education evaluation system. In T. H. Bers (Ed.), *Using student tracking systems effectively* (New Directions for Community Colleges No. 66, pp. 75–82). San Francisco: Jossey-Bass.

Alverno College Faculty. (1976). *Liberal learning at Alverno College.* Milwaukee, WI: Alverno Productions.

Alverno College Faculty. (1979). *Assessments at Alverno College.* Milwaukee, WI: Alverno Publications.

American College Testing Program. (1988). *Collegiate assessment of academic proficiency (CAAP): Guidelines.* Iowa City: ACT.

Angelo, T. A. (1988). *Assessing what matters: How participation in work, athletics and extracurriculars relates to the academic success and personal satisfaction of Harvard undergraduates*(A First Report on the Harvard Assessment Seminar's 1987–88 Interview Study). Cambridge, MA: Harvard Graduate School of Education.

Appelbaum, M. I. (1987). Assessment through the major. In C. Adelman (Ed.), *Performance and judgment: Essays on principles and practice in the assessment of college student learning*(pp. 117–138). Washington, DC: U.S. Government Printing Office.

Aquino, F. J. (1989, April). *A five year longitudinal study of community college student behaviors: Toward a definition of student success and student failure.* Paper presented at the Association for Institutional Research Annual Forum, Baltimore.

Association of American Colleges. (1985). *Integrity in the college curriculum: A report to the academic community.* Washington, DC: Association for American Colleges.

Astin, A. W. (1977). *Four critical years: Effects of college on beliefs, values and knowledge.* San Francisco: Jossey-Bass.

Astin, A. W. (1979). Student-oriented management: A proposal for change. In *Evaluating educational quality: A conference summary* (pp. 3–18). Washington, DC: Council on Postsecondary Accreditation.

Astin, A. W. (1985). *Achieving educational excellence: A critical assessment of priorities and practices in higher education.* San Francisco: Jossey-Bass.

Astin, A. W. (1990, June). *Proposed assessment curriculum.* Paper presented at the Fifth National Conference on Assessment, Washington. DC.

Astin, A. W. (in press). *Assessment for excellence.* New York: Macmillan.

Astin. A. W., and Ewell, P. T. (1985). The value-added debate . . . continued. *AAHEBulletin*, 37(8), 11–13.

Baird, L. L. (1988). Value added: Using student gains as yardsticks of learning. In C. Adelman (Ed.), *Performance and judgment: Essays on principles and practice in the assessment of college student learning* (pp. 205–216). Washington, DC: U.S. Government Printing Office.

Banta, T. W. (1985). Use of outcomes information at the University of Tennessee, Knoxville. In P. T. Ewell (Ed.), *Assessing educational outcomes*(New Directions for Institutional Research No. 47, pp. 19–32). San Francisco: Jossey-Bass.

Banta, T. W. (1986). *Performance funding in higher education: A critical analysis of Tennessee's experience.* Boulder, CO: National Center for Higher Education Management Systems.

Banta, T. W. (1988). Assessment as an instrument of state funding policy. In T. W. Banta (Ed.), *Implementing outcomes assessment: Promise and perils*(New Directions in Institutional Research No. 59, pp. 81–94). San Francisco: Jossey-Bass.

Banta, T. W., Lambert, E. W., Pike, G. R., Schmidhammer, J. L., and Schneider, J. A. (1987). Estimated score gain on the ACT COMP exam: Valid tool for institutional assessment?*Research in Higher Education, 27,* 195–217.

Banta, T. W., and Moffett, M. S. (1987). Performance funding in Tennessee: Stimulus for program improvement. In D. F. Halpern (Ed.), *Student outcomes assessment: What institutions stand to gain* (New Directions in Higher Education No. 59. pp. 35–44). San Francisco: Jossey-Bass.

Banta, T. W., and Pike, G. R. (1989). Methods for comparing outcomes assessment instruments. *Research in Higher Education, 30,* 455–470.

Banta, T. W., and Schneider, J. A. (1988). Using faculty-developed exit examinations to evaluate academic programs. *Journal of Higher Education, 59,* 69–83.

Bennett, W. J. (1984). *To reclaim a legacy: A report on the humanities in higher education.* Washington, DC: National Endowment for the Humanities.

Berdahl, R. O., & Studds, S. M. (1989). *The tension of excellence and equity: The Florida enhancement programs.* College Park, MD: National Center for Postsecondary Governance and Finance, University of Maryland.

Blood, M. R. (1987). *Outcome Measurement Project, Phase III Report, May 1987.* St. Louis: American Assembly of Collegiate Schools of Business.

Bowen, H. R. (1977). *Investment in learning: The individual and social value of American higher education.* San Francisco: Jossey-Bass.

Boyer, C. M. (1989). *Improving student learning: The Outcomes Assessment Program at Kean College of New Jersey.* Union, NJ: Kean College of New Jersey.

Boyer, C., and Algren, A. (1987). Assessing undergraduates' patterns of credit distribution: Amount and specialization. *Journal of Higher Education, 58,* 430–442.

Boyer, C. M., Ewell, P. T., Finney, J. E., and Mingle, J. R. (1987). Assessment and outcomes measurement: A view from the states. *AAHE Bulletin, 39*(7), 8–12.

Campione, J. C., and Armbruster, B. B. (1985). Acquiring information from texts: An analysis of four approaches. In J. W. Segal, S. F. Chipman, & R. Glaser (Eds.), *Thinking and learning skills* (Vol. VI, pp. 317–362). Hillsdale, NJ: Erlbaum.

Cheney, L. W. (1989). *50 Hours: A core curriculum for college students.* Washington, DC: National Endowment for the Humanities.

Chickering, A. W. (1969). *Education and identity.* San Francisco: Jossey-Bass.

Chickering, A. W., and Gamson, Z. F. (1987). Seven principles for good practice in undergraduate education. *AAHE Bulletin, 39*(7), 3–7.

The College Board. (1987). *Computerized placement texts: An exciting and innovative placement tool.* New York: The College Entrance Examination Board.

College Outcomes Evaluation Program Council, New Jersey Department of Higher Education. (1990). *Report to the Board of Higher Education on the first administration of the General Intellectual Skills (GIS) Assessment.* Trenton: Department of Higher Education, State of New Jersey.

College Outcomes Evaluation Program, State of New Jersey Department of Higher Education. (1987). *Report to the New Jersey Board of Higher Education from the Advisory Committee to the College Outcomes Evaluation Program.* Trenton: Department of Higher Education, State of New Jersey.

College of William and Mary, Office of the Associate Provost. (1988). *Portfolio assessment: A pilot project*. Williamsburg, VA: Author.

College of William and Mary, Office of the Associate Provost. (1989). *Assessment of undergraduate liberal education: A report to the State Council of Higher Education for Virginia*. Williamsburg, VA: Author.

Conlin, G. (1987, April). *Core scoring: A method of evaluating written free responses*. Paper presented at the annual meeting of the American Educational Research Association, Washington, DC.

Conrad, C. F., Jamison, A., Kroc, R., MacCorquodal, P., and Summers, G. (1987). *Plan for assessing undergraduate education at the University of Arizona* (Report of the Task Force on Assessment of the Quality and Outcomes of Undergraduate Education). Tucson: The University of Arizona.

Council of Presidents and State Board for Community College Education. (1989). *The validity and usefulness of three nationally standardized tests for Washington college sophomores: General report*. Bellingham, WA: Western Washington University Office of Publications.

Cross, K. P. (1990, June). *Collaborative classroom assessment*. Paper presented at the Fifth National Conference on Assessment in Higher Education, Washington, DC.

Cross, K. P., and Angelo, T. A. (1988). *Classroom assessment techniques: A handbook for faculty*. Ann Arbor: National Center for Research to Improve Postsecondary Teaching and Learning, University of Michigan.

Darling-Hammond, L. (1988). Assessment and incentives: The medium is the message. In *Three presentations: From the Third National Conference on Assessment in Higher Education*. Washington, DC: American Association of Higher Education Assessment Forum.

Davis, B. G. (1989). Demystifying assessment: Learning from the field of evaluation. In P. J. Gray (Ed.), *Achieving assessment goals using evaluation techniques*. (New Directions for Higher Education No. 67, pp. 5–20). San Francisco: Jossey-Bass.

Dinham, S. M. (1988). *Summary of assessment activities at the University of Arizona* (Report No. 4). Tucson: Center for Research on Undergraduate Education, University of Arizona.

Edgerton, R. (1987). An assessment of assessment. In *Assessing the outcomes of higher education, Proceedings of the 1986 ETS Invitational Conference* (pp. 93–110). Princeton, NJ: Educational Testing Service.

Education Commission of the States. (1986). *Transforming the state role in undergraduate education: Time for a different view*. Denver: Author.

Educational Testing Service. (1989a). *New Jersey College Outcomes Evaluation Program: A report on the development of the General Intellectual Skills Assessment*. Princeton, NJ: Author.

Educational Testing Service. (1989b). *The new academic profile: Assessing the outcomes of general education*. Princeton. NJ: Author.

Elbow, P., and Belanoff, P. (1986, October). Portfolios as a substitute for proficiency examinations. *College Composition and Communication*.

El-Khawas, E. (1987). *1987 campus trends survey*. Washington, DC: American Council on Education.

El-Khawas, E. (1989). *1989 campus trends survey*. Washington, DC: American Council on Education.

Erwin, T. D. (1983). The Scale of Intellectual Development: Measuring Perry's scheme. *Journal of College Student Personnel, 24*, 6–12.

Erwin, T. D. (in press). *Assessing student learning and development in college*. San Francisco: Jossey-Bass.

Erwin, T. D., and Delworth, U. (1980). An instrument to measure Chickering's vector of identity. *National Association of Student Personnel Administrators Journal, 17*, 19–24.

Ewell, P. T. (1983). *Information on student outcomes: How to get it and how to use it*. Boulder, CO: National Center for Higher Education Management Systems.

Ewell, P. T. (1984). *The self-regarding institution: Information for excellence*. Boulder. CO: National Center for Higher Education Management Systems.

Ewell, P. T. (1986). Performance funding and institutional response: Lessons from the Tennessee experience. In T. W. Banta (Ed.), *Performance funding in higher education: A critical analysis of Tennessee's experience* (pp. 105–120). Boulder, CO: National Center for Higher Education Management Systems.

Ewell, P. T. (1987). Establishing a campus-based assessment program: A framework for choice. In D. Halpern (Ed.), *Student outcomes assessment: A tool for improving teaching and learning* (New Directions for Higher Education No. 59, pp. 9–24). San Francisco: Jossey-Bass.

Ewell. P. T. (1988a). Outcomes, assessment, and academic improvement: In search of usable knowledge. In J. C. Smart (Ed.), *Higher education: Handbook of theory and research* (Vol. IV, pp. 53–108). New York: Agathon Press.

Ewell, P. T. (1988b). Implementing assessment: Some organizational issues. In T. W. Banta (Ed.), *Implementing outcomes assessment: Promise and perils* (New Directions for Institutional Research No. 59, pp. 15–28). San Francisco: Jossey-Bass.

Ewell, P. T. (1989). Hearts and minds: Some reflections on the ideologies of assessment. In *Three presentations from the Fourth National Conference on Assessment in Higher Education* (pp. 1–26). Washington, DC: American Association of Higher Education.

Ewell, P. T. (1990). *Assessment and the "new accountability": A challenge for higher education's leadership*. Denver: Education Commission of the States.

Ewell, P. T., and Boyer, C. M. (1988). Acting out state-mandated assessment: Evidence from five states. *Change, 20*, 40–47.

Ewell, P. T., Finney, J. E., and Lenth, C. (1990). Filling in the mosaic: The emerging pattern of state-based assessment. *AAHE Bulletin, 42*, 3–7.

Ewell, P. T., and Lisensky, R. P. (1988). *Assessing institutional effectiveness: Redirecting the self-study process*. Washington, DC: Consortium for the Advancement of Private Higher Education.

Ewell, P. T., Parker, R., and Jones, D. P. (1988). *Establishing a longitudinal student tracking system: An implementation handbook*. Boulder, CO: National Center for Higher Education Management Systems.

Ewens, T. (1979). Transforming a liberal arts curriculum: Alverno College. In G. Grant & Associates (Eds.), *On competence: A critical analysis of competence-based reforms in higher education* (pp. 259–298). San Francisco: Jossey-Bass.

Farmer, D. W. (1988). *Enhancing student learning: Emphasizing essential student competencies in academic programs*. Wilkes-Barre, PA: Kings College.

Folger, J., and Berdahl, R. O. (1987). *Patterns in evaluating state higher education systems: Making a virtue out of necessity*. College Park: National Center for Postsecondary Governance and Finance, University of Maryland.

Fong, B. (1987). *The external examiner approach to assessment.* Washington DC: American Association for Higher Education.

Forrest, A. W. (1982). *Increasing student competence and persistence: The best case for general education.* Iowa City: American College Testing Program.

Forrest, A. W., and Steele, J. M. (1978). *College Outcomes Measures Project.* Iowa City: American College Testing Program.

The Gallup Organization. (1989). *A survey of college seniors' knowledge of history and literature, conducted for the National Endowment for the Humanities.* Princeton, NJ: Author.

Gamson, Z. F., and Associates. (1984). *Liberating education.* San Francisco: Jossey-Bass.

Gamson, Z. F., and Poulsen, S. J. (1989). Inventories of good practice: The next step for the seven principles for good practice in undergraduate education. *AAHE Bulletin, 42,* 7–8.

Grant, G., and Kohli, W. (1979). Contributing to learning by assessing student performance. In G. Grant & Associates (Eds.), *On competence: A critical analysis of competence-based reforms in higher education* (pp. 138–159). San Francisco: Jossey-Bass.

Grant, G., and Riesman, D. (1978). *The perpetual dream: Reform and experiment in the American college.* Chicago: University of Chicago Press.

Guba, E. G., and Lincoln, Y. S. (1981). *Effective evaluation: Improving the usefulness of evaluation results through responsive and naturalistic approaches.* San Francisco: Jossey-Bass.

Hanson, D. C. (1990). Federal disclosure regulations: The "worst case" scenario for outcomes assessment. *AAHE Bulletin, 42,* 9–10.

Hanson, G. R. (1982). Critical issues in the assessment of student development. In G. R. Hanson (Ed.), *Measuring student development* (New Directions for Student Services No. 20). San Francisco: Jossey-Bass.

Hanson, G. R. (1988). Critical issues in the assessment of value added in education. In T. W. Banta (Ed.). *Implementing outcomes assessment: Promise and perils* (New Directions for Institutional Research No. 59. pp. 53–68). San Francisco: Jossey-Bass.

Heffernan, J. M., Hutchings. P., & Marchese, T. J. (1988). *Standardized tests and the purposes of assessment.* Washington, DC: American Association of Higher Education.

Hirsch, E. D. (1987). *Cultural literacy: What every American needs to know.* New York: Houghton Mifflin.

Hirsch, E. D. (1989). *Cultural literacy: Form A, standardized edition.* Chicago: Riverside.

Hutchings, P. (1987). *Six stories: Implementing successful assessment* (Paper prepared for the Second National Conference on Assessment in Higher Education). Washington, DC: American Association for Higher Education Assessment Forum.

Hutchings. P. (1990). Learning over time: Portfolio assessment. *AAHE Bulletin, 42,* 6–8.

Hutchings, P., and Marchese, T. W. (1990). Watching assessment: Questions, stories, prospects. *Change, 22*(5), 12–38.

Hyman, R., Jamison, A., Woodard, D., and von Destinon, M. (1988). *Student outcomes assessment survey, 1987–88.* Washington, DC: National Association of Student Personnel Administrators.

Jacobi, M. Astin, A. W., and Ayala, F. (1987). *College student outcomes assessment: A talent development perspective* (ASHE-ERIC Higher Education Report No. 7). Washington, DC: ERIC Clearinghouse on Higher Education, The George Washington University.

Katchadourian, H. A., and Boli, J. (1985). *Careerism and intellectualism among college students.* San Francisco: Jossey-Bass.

Kean College of New Jersey. (1986). *A proposal for program assessment at Kean College of New Jersey: Final report of the Presidential Task Force on Student Learning and Development.* Union, NJ: Author.

Kean, T. H. (1987, September/October). Time to deliver before we forget the promises we made. *Change,* pp. 10–11.

Keith, N. (1989). *Report on student learning and development assessment at Glassboro State College* (Prepared for the College Outcomes Evaluation Program, State of New Jersey Department of Higher Education). Glassboro, NJ: Learning Assessment Center, Glassboro State College.

Kellams, S. (1989). *University of Virginia longitudinal study of undergraduate education: Interview program methods and results.* Charlottesville: Student Assessment Program, Office of the Provost of the University, University of Virginia.

Knefelkamp, L. L. (1989). Assessment as transformation. In *Three presentations from the Fourth National Conference on Assessment in Higher Education, June 1989, Atlanta.* Washington, DC: American Association for Higher Education Assessment Forum.

Kohlberg, L. (1981). *The meaning and measure of moral development.* Worcester, MA: Clark University Press.

Krueger, D. W., and Heisserer, M. L. (1987). Assessment and involvement: Investments to enhance learning. In D. F. Halpern (Ed.), *Student outcomes assessment: What institutions stand to gain* (New Directions in Higher Education No. 59, pp. 45–56). San Francisco: Jossey-Bass.

League for Innovation. (1988). *Computerized adaptive testing: The state of the art in assessment at three community colleges.* Laguna Hills, CA: Author.

Lenning, O. T., Munday, L., & Maxey, J. (1969). Student educational growth during the first two years of college. *College and University,* 44, 145–153.

Levy, R. A. (1986). Development of performance funding criteria by the Tennessee Higher Education Commission: A chronology and evaluation. In T. W. Banta (Ed.), *Performance funding in higher education: A critical analysis of Tennessee's experience* (pp. 13–26). Boulder, CO: National Center for Higher Education Management Systems.

Light, R. J. (1990). *The Harvard assessment seminars: Explorations with students and faculty about teaching, learning, and student life* (First Report, 1990). Cambridge, MA: Harvard Graduate School of Education and Kennedy School of Government.

Light, R. J., Singer, J. D., and Willett, J. B. (1990). *By design: Planning research on higher education.* Cambridge, MA: Harvard University Press.

Lincoln, Y. S., and Guba, E. G. (1986). But is it rigorous? Trustworthiness and authenticity in naturalistic evaluation. In D. D. Williams (Ed.), *Naturalistic evaluation* (New Directions for Program Evaluation No. 30, pp. 73–84). San Francisco: Jossey-Bass.

McCabe, R. H. (1983). *A status report on the comprehensive educational reform of Miami-Dade Community College.* Miami, FL: Office of the President, Miami-Dade Community College.

McClain, C. W. (1984). *In pursuit of degrees with integrity: A value-added approach to undergraduate assessment.* Washington, DC: American Association of State Colleges and Universities.

McClain, C. J., and Krueger, D. W. (1985). Using outcomes assessment: A case study in institutional change. In P. T. Ewell (Ed.), *Assessing educational outcomes* (New Directions for Institutional Research No. 47, pp. 33–46). San Francisco: Jossey-Bass.

McMillan, J. H. (1988). Beyond value-added education. *Journal of Higher Education, 59,* 564–579.

Mentkowski, M., and Doherty, A. (1980). *Validating assessment techniques in an outcome-centered liberal arts curriculum: Insights from the evaluation and revision process.* Milwaukee, WI: Office of Research and Evaluation, Alverno College.

Mentkowski, M., and Doherty, A. (1984). *Careering after college: Establishing the validity of abilities learned in college for later careering and performance.* Milwaukee, WI: Alverno Publications.

Mentkowski, M., and Loacker, G. (1985). Assessing and validating the outcomes of college. In P. T. Ewell (Ed.), *Assessing educational outcomes* (New Directions for Institutional Research No. 47, pp. 47–64). San Francisco: Jossey-Bass.

Mentkowski, M., Moeser. M.. and Straight, M. J. (1981). *Using the Perry scheme of intellectual and ethical development as a college outcome measure: A process and criteria for assessing student performance.* Milwaukee, WI: Office of Research and Evaluation, Alverno College.

Mentkowski, M., and Rogers, G. P. (1988). *Establishing the validity of measures of college student outcomes.* Milwaukee, WI: Office of Research and Evaluation, Alverno College.

Messick, S. (1975). The standard problem: Meaning and values in measurement and evaluation. *American Psychologist. 30,* 955–966.

Messick, S. (1988a). The once and future issue of validity: Assessing the meaning and consequence of measurement. In H. Wainer & H. I. Braun (Eds.), *Test validity* (pp. 33–48). Hillside, NJ: Erlbaum.

Messick, S. (1988b). *Meaning and values in test validation: The science and ethics of assessment.* Princeton, NJ: Educational Testing Service.

Minnesota State University System. (1989). *A proposed quality indicators process.* St. Paul: Author.

Mislevy, R. J. (1990). Foundations of a new test theory. In N. Frederiksen, R. J. Mislevy, & I. Bejar (Eds.), *Test theory for a new generation of tests* (pp. 3–40). Hillsdale, NJ: Erlbaum.

Moomaw, W. E. (1989). *First annual report on the Student Learning Assessment Program at the University of Virginia.* Charlottesville: Student Assessment Program, Office of the Provost of the University, University of Virginia.

National Evaluation Systems. (1987). *Texas Academic Skills Program (TASP).* Amherst, MA: National Evaluation Systems, Inc.

National Governors' Association. (1986). *Time for results: The governors' 1991 report on education.* Washington, DC: National Governors' Association.

National Institute of Education, Study Group on the Conditions of Excellence in American Higher Education. (1984). *Involvement in learning: Realizing the potential of American higher education.* Washington, DC: U.S. Government Printing Office.

Nichols, J. O. (1990). *The role of institutional research in implementing institutional effectiveness or outcomes assessment* (AIR Professional File No. 37). Tallahassee, FL: Association of Institutional Research.

O'Day, D., and Kelly, M. (1987). *Kean College General Education Program: Report on assessment activities, 1986–87.* Union, NJ: General Education Program, Kean College of New Jersey.

Osterlind, S. J. (1988). *College Basic Academic Subjects Examination: Guide to test content.* Columbia: Center for Educational Assessment, University of Missouri—Columbia.

Pace, C. R. (1979). *Measuring the outcomes of college: Fifty years of findings and recommendations for the future.* San Francisco: Jossey-Bass.

Pace, C. R. (1984). *Measuring the quality of college student experiences.* Los Angeles: Higher Education Research Institute, University of California, Los Angeles .

Pace, C. R. (1990). *The undergraduates: A report of their activities and progress in college in the 1980s.* Los Angeles: Center for the Study of Evaluation, University of California, Los Angeles.

Pascarella, E. T. (1985). College environmental influences on learning and cognitive development: A critical review and synthesis. In J. C. Smart (Ed.), *Higher education: Handbook of theory and research* (Vol. 1, pp. 1–61). New York: Agathon Press.

Pascarella, E. T. (1987). Are value-added assessments valuable? In *Assessing the Outcomes of higher education, Proceedings of the 1986 ETS Invitational Conference* (pp. 71–92). Princeton, NJ: Educational Testing Service.

Paskow, J. (Ed.). (1988). *Assessment programs and projects: A directory.* Washington. DC: American Association for Higher Education Assessment Forum.

Paulson, C. P. (1990). *State initiatives in assessment and outcome measurement: Tools for teaching and learning in the 1990's.* Denver: Education Commission of the States.

Perry, W. G. (1970). *Forms of intellectual and ethical development in the college years.* New York: Holt, Rinehart and Winston.

Pike, G. R. (1989a). Background, college experiences, and the ACT-COMP exam: Using construct validity to evaluate assessment instruments. *Review of Higher Education, 13,* 91–117.

Pike, G. R. (1989b). Assessment measures. *Assessment Update,* 1(2), 8–9.

Pike, G. R. (1989c). Assessment measures. *Assessment Update,* 1(1), 10–12.

Pike, G. R., & Phillipi, R. H. (1989). Generalizability of the differential coursework methodology: Relationships between self-reported coursework and performance on the ACT-COMP exam. *Research in Higher Education, 30,* 245–260.

Postsecondary Education Planning Commission. (1988). *College level academic skills test review: Prepared in response to specific appropriation 537A of the 1987 General Appropriations Act.* Tallahassee: Postsecondary Education Planning Commission, State of Florida.

Ratcliffe, J. L., and Associates. (1990). *Determining the effect of different coursework patterns on the general learned abilities of college students* (Working Paper OR 90-524). Research Institute for Studies in Education at Iowa State University and Center for the Study of Higher Education at The Pennsylvania State University.

Resnick, D., and Goulden, M. (1987). Assessment, curriculum and expansion in American higher education: A historical perspective. In D. Halpern (Ed.), *Student assessment: A tool for improving teaching and learning* (New Directions for Higher Education No. 59, pp. 77–88). San Francisco: Jossey-Bass.

Rest, J. R. (1986). *Moral development: Advances in research and theory.* New York: Praeger.

Rest, J. R. (1987). *Guide for the Defining Issues Test.* Minneapolis: Center for the Study of Ethical Development, University of Minnesota.

Richardson, R. C., Fisk, E. C., & Okun, M. A. (1983). *Literacy in the open-access college.* San Francisco: Jossey-Bass.

Rogers, G. P. (1988). *Validating college outcomes with institutionally developed instruments: Issues in maximizing contextual validity.* Milwaukee, WI: Office of Research and Evaluation, Alverno College.

Shapiro, J. Z. (1986). Evaluation research and educational decisionmaking. In J. C. Smart (Ed.), *Higher education: Handbook of theory and research* (Vol. 11, pp. 163–206). New York: Agathon.

Sheldon, M. S. (1981). *Statewide longitudinal study: 1978–81 final report.* Los Angeles: Los Angeles Pierce College.

Shulman, L. S. (1987a). Assessment for teaching: An initiative for the profession. *Phi Delta Kappan, 69*(1), 38–44.

Shulman, L. S. (1987b). Assessing content and process: Challenges for the new assessments. In *Three presentations from the Second National Conference on Assessment in Higher Education* (pp. 1–14). Washington. DC: American Association for Higher Education.

Southern Regional Education Board. (1985). *Access to quality undergraduate education: A report to the Southern Regional Education Board by its Commission for Educational Quality.* Atlanta: Southern Regional Education Board.

Stark, J. S., Shaw, K. M., & Lowther, M. A. (1989). *Student goals for college and courses: A missing link in assessing and improving academic achievement* (1989 ASHE-ERIC Report 6). Washington, DC: ERIC Clearinghouse on Higher Education, George Washington University.

Steele, J. M. (1988, May). *Using measures of student outcomes and growth to improve college programs.* Paper presented at the National Forum of the Association for Institutional Research.

Stone, H. L., & Meyer, T. C. (1989). *Developing an ability-based assessment program in the continuum of medical education.* Madison: Medical School University of Wisconsin.

Terenzini, P. T. (1989). Assessment with open eyes: Pitfalls in studying student outcomes. *Journal of Higher Education, 60,* 644–664.

Thorndike, R. M. (1990). The Washington State assessment experience. *Assessment Update, 2*(2), 7–9.

Thrash, P. A. (1988). Educational "outcomes" in the accrediting process. *Academy, 74,* 16–18.

U.S. Department of Education. (1987). Notice of proposed rulemaking, secretary's procedures and criteria for recognition of accrediting agencies, 34 CFR Parts 602 and 603. *Federal Register, 52.* 33906–33913.

U.S. Department of Education, National Commission on Excellence in Education. (1983). *A nation at risk: The imperative for educational reform* (Report to the nation and the secretary of education). Washington, DC: U.S. Government Printing Office.

University of Virginia, Office of the Provost. (1990). *Undergraduate learning at the University of Virginia: A first report to the UVA community.* Charlottesville: Student Assessment Program, Office of the Provost of the University, University of Virginia.

Vorhees, R. A., & Hart, S. (1989). A tracking scheme for basic skills intake assessment. In T. H. Bers (Ed.), *Using student tracking systems effectively* (New Directions in Community Colleges No. 66, pp. 31–38). San Francisco: Jossey-Bass.

Walleri, R. D., and Japely, S. M. (1986, May). *Student intent, persistence, and outcomes.* Paper presented at the 26th annual forum of the Association for Institutional Research, Orlando, FL.

Warren, J. (1984). The blind alley of value added. *AAHE Bulletin, 37*(1), 10–13

Warren, J. (1988). Cognitive measures in assessing learning. In T. W. Banta (Ed.), *Implementing outcomes assessment: Promise and perils* (New Directions for Institutional Research No. 59, pp. 29–40). San Francisco: Jossey-Bass.

White, E. M. (1990, June). *Language and reality in writing assessment.* Paper presented at the Fifth National Conference on Assessment in Higher Education AAHE Assessment Forum, Washington, DC.

Wiggins, G. (1989). A true test: Toward more authentic and equitable assessment *Phi Delta Kappan, 70,* 703–713.

Winona State University. (1990). *Draft indicators for improving undergraduate instructional quality.* Winona. MN: Office of the President. Winona State University.

Wolff, R. A (1990, June). *Assessment and accreditation. A shotgun marriage?* Paper presented at the Fifth National Conference on Assessment in Higher Education, AAHE Assessment Forum, Washington, DC.

Zemsky, R. (1989). *Structure and coherence: Measuring the undergraduate curriculum.* Philadelphia: Institute for Research on Higher Education, University of Pennsylvania.

Focusing on Student Academic Outcomes

JOANNE M. ALEXANDER AND JOAN S. STARK

Approaches to Outcomes and Outcome Assessment

A number of researchers have attempted to classify outcomes and specify approaches for assessing outcomes. In this section, approaches by Ewell, Astin, Lenning et al., and Bowen are discussed.

Ewell (1983) discusses three approaches that have been used to measure student outcomes: academic investigation perspective, student-personnel perspective, and management perspective. Actually these approaches are based on the purpose of the investigators and thus use different perspectives on outcomes, have different goals for using outcomes, and involve different data requirements.

Academic investigation (research) is the oldest and most commonly used reason for measuring student outcomes. The college experience is investigated in a typical research fashion: theories about student growth are developed, tested, and refined as a result of data collection. From this perspective, most of the research on student outcomes has been done by psychologists and sociologists. Frequently psychologists have focused on the impact of college on personal and cognitive development and sociologists have concentrated on such issues as the impact of college on social mobility and socialization of students into the professional fields. In this perspective the goal to explain (and ultimately to predict) human behavior and the data collected must have high empirical quality and be objective. While some of the relationships discovered in this research have been used by institutional policy makers, it should be noted that divisional utility is not the goal; the purpose is to successfully account for a given outcome.

The student personnel approach uses student outcomes as a means for evaluating students for admission to programs and placement on completion of the program. The data are also used for counselling students in career selection and for evaluating the effectiveness of programs for meeting student needs. In this perspective the goal of outcome measurement is to gain assessment information about individual students. Data is considered useful if it provides information for student placement or if it is diagnostic of student problems. The theoretical constraints of data collection are not crucial when using this approach.

The management perspective for measuring outcomes is a still different approach to outcome assessment. From this perspective the focus is on the use of outcome assessment as a method to improve administrative decisions, particularly those involving program planning and budgeting. The goal of outcome assessment in this perspective is to improve the quality of resource-allocation decisions. To meet this goal, data must be empirically valid, reliable, and perceived by the decision makers as relevant to the decision.

Ewell's classification of approaches to student outcomes is useful because it calls attention to varied uses of outcomes and the ways in which different goals influence the collection of student outcome information.

In addition to classifying approaches to outcome assessment based on proposed uses, researchers have attempted to classify types of educational outcomes. Astin (1974) developed a taxonomy of student outcomes involving three dimensions: type of outcome, type of data, and time. The types of outcome are split into two domains: cognitive and affective. The cognitive domain includes outcomes such as basic skills, general intelligence, and higher-order cognitive processes. The affective domain includes outcomes often described as attitudes, values, and self-concept.

The data dimension is also split into two domains: behavioral and psychological. This dimension distinguishes between outcome data that are covert and those that are observable. The behavioral domain refers to observable activities of the individual. The psychological domain refers to the internal states or traits of the individual. While the actual outcomes may be the same, the ways in which the information is gathered to represent them are different.

The primary two dimensions of Astin's approach are shown in Table 1. This typology has been widely accepted as method for classifying outcomes. In Astin's typology the third dimension, time, stresses the importance of including both the long- and short-term outcomes of college. Some examples of applying the time dimension to the outcome cells are provided in Table 2.

In addition to the typology, Astin (1974) provided some insights into the assessment of educational outcomes. To him the fundamental purpose of assessment is to produce information that is useful for decision making. Thus measurement should begin with a value statement—an idea about what future state would be desirable or important.

Lenning and Associates (1983) at the National Center for Higher Education Management Systems (NCHEMS) developed an extensive framework for identifying the universe of major "outputs" and outcomes of postsecondary institutions. In developing this taxonomy, the authors sought to develop an exhaustive list of outcomes to assist in the assessment of managerial effective-

Table 1
A Typology of Student Outcomes

Data	Outcome	
	Affective	Cognitive
Psychological	Self-concept	Knowledge
	Values	Critical Thinking Ability
	Attitudes	Basic Skills
	Beliefs	Special Aptitudes
	Drive for Achievement	Academic Achievement
	Satisfaction with College	
Behavioral	Personal Habits	Career Development
	Avocations	Level of Educational Attainment
	Mental Health	Vocational Achievements
	Citizenship	Level of Responsibility
	Interpersonal Relations	Income
		Awards or Special Recognition

Source: Alexander W. Astin, R. J. Panos, and J. A. Creager, *National Norms for Entering College Freshmen-Fall 1966* (Washington, D.C.: American Council on Education, 1967): p. 16.

Table 2
Outcomes Over Time

Outcome	Data Indicator	Short-Term Indicator	Long-Term
Affective	Behavioral	Choice of major field of study	Current Occupation
Affective	Psychological	Satisfaction with college	Job Satisfaction
Cognitive	Behavioral	Persistence	Job Stability
Cognitive	Psychological	LSAT score	Score on law boards

Source: Astin, 1974, p. 33

ness. As a result of the management perspective, Lenning et al. did not focus exclusively on student outcomes but rather included them in two of the several categories: human characteristics outcomes and knowledge, technology, and art forms outcomes. Viewed in Astin's terms, the human characteristics outcomes include primarily affective and personality characteristics, as well as skill outcomes. The knowledge, technology, and art form category includes the typically cognitive outcomes: both specialized and general knowledge and scholarship. Additional outcome categories in this framework include (1) economic (e.g. economic security, standard of living), (2) resource and service provision (e.g., teaching, facility provisions), and (3) other maintenance and change (e. g., traditions, organizational operation). A listing of the complete NCHEMS taxonomy is included in Appendix A. Clearly this framework includes both long- and short-range student outcomes as well as outcomes at the program and institutional level.

Bowen (1974) took a slightly different approach from the two previous researchers when discussing outcomes. Instruction is related to the outcome of learning and changes in human traits. Research and scholarship relates to the outcomes of preservation, discovery, and interpretation of knowledge, artistic and social criticism, philosophical reflection, and advancement of the fine arts. Public service results in societal outcomes such as improved health, solutions to social problems and agricultural productivity (p. 2–3).

Of these three services, Bowen believes that instruction is the primary goal of higher education and bringing about desired changes in students in central to this mission. Bowen's approach could be viewed, therefore, as primarily academic in nature. He focused on investigating the changes that occur among students without emphasizing the use of these measures in either placement or decision making.

In a later work, Bowen (1977) broadened his view of student learning and offered a more elaborate catalogue of accepted goals. This catalogue of goals serves also as a typology of student outcomes derived from three widely accepted goals of instruction. These three general goals are: educating the whole person, addressing the individuality of students, and maintaining accessibility. The first goal, educating the whole person, refers to the idea that education should cultivate both the intellectual and affective dispositions of persons, thereby enhancing intellectual, moral, and emotional growth. The second goal, addressing individuality, requires that the uniqueness of individuals be taken into account in the educational process. Accessibility refers to the notion that education should be readily available to a broad range of persons.

According to Bowen, the catalogue of goals derived from these general goals constitutes both a model for the educational system and the criteria by which the system can be judged. While Bowen recognized that his goal typology has utopian qualities, he posits that it provides a useful model that can be used to shape and guide institutional functioning.

In Bowen's scheme specific educational goals are divided into two groups: goals for individual students and goals for society. The five categories of goals for individual students include: cognitive learning, emotional and moral development, practical competence, direct satisfactions from college education, and avoidance of negative outcomes. In a further subdivision, cognitive learning includes ten specific areas of learning. They are:

1. Verbal skills: Ability to read, speak, and write clearly and correctly.

2. Quantitative skills: Understanding of mathematical and statistical concepts.

3. Substantive knowledge: Acquaintance with Western culture and traditions and familiarity with other cultures. Knowledge of contemporary philosophy, art, literature, natural science, and social issues. Understanding of facts, principles and vocabulary within at least one selected field.

4. Rationality: Ability to think logically, and analytically, and to see facts clearly and objectively.

5. Intellectual tolerance: Openness to new ideas, curiosity, and ability to deal with ambiguity and complexity.

6. Esthetic sensibility: Knowledge of and interest in literature, the arts and natural beauty.

7. Creativeness: Ability to think imaginatively and originally.

8. Intellectual integrity: Respect for and understanding of the contingent nature of truth.

9. Wisdom: Ability to balance perspective, judgment and prudence.

10. Lifelong learning: Sustained interest in learning. (Bowen, 1977, pp. 35–36)

Bowen's remaining four categories of student goals are focused primarily on affective and long term student outcomes.

Bowen also suggested seven principles that should be used in the identification of outcomes and thus in outcome assessment at particular colleges. The first principle is that inputs should not be confused with outputs. Bowen claims that high institutional expenditures (an input) do not guarantee equivalently high outcomes; the differences between inputs and outputs has too often been ignored. The only valid outcome measurement is of the development and changes that occur in students as a result of their college experience.

The second principle suggests that assessment should be linked to all educational goals, not just to those developments easily measured or related to economic success. Bowen offers his catalogue of goals as a starting point on which to build an assessment plan.

The third principle states simply that educational outcomes should relate to the person as a whole; and the fourth principle posits that outcome assessment should include the study of alumni as well as current students. The fifth principle suggests that outcome assessment should measure changes that occur as a result of the college experience.

The sixth principle states that an evaluation scheme must be practical: not too time-consuming or expensive. The assessment should focus on major goals of the institution and need not be based on the entire population of students. However, results must be reported in a form that the general public can read and understand.

The final principle asserts that assessment should be controlled from within the institution rather than being imposed by external agencies. Assessment programs should be designed for each institution, keeping the special missions and philosophies of the institutions in mind.

Ewell (1983) mentions additional outcome dimensions that should be considered. These include whether (1) the effects are short- or long-term, (2) the student is aware or unaware of the outcome, (3) the effect is direct or indirect (i.e., how closely the outcome is connected to the educational program), and (4) the outcome is intended or unintended. These dimensions represent important differences between outcomes that should be considered in outcome research and assessment.

In more recent work than that reviewed earlier, Astin (1979) identifies three core measures of student outcomes that should be included in a student outcome data base. First, students' successful completion of a program of study should be included. More specifically, information is needed to determine whether students' accomplishments are consistent with their original goals. Second, a measure of cognitive development must be included and more than grade point average and class standing are needed. Preferably, repeated measurement will be used so that change can be assessed by comparing performance at two points in time. Third, measures of student satisfaction should include satisfaction with the quality of the curriculum, teaching, student services, facilities, and other aspects of the college.

Beyond these essential measures, the student data should include information gathered on entry, during the educational process, and at exit or another designated point of time. Student characteristics should be recorded when they first enroll, information on what happens to the student while enrolled at the college must be available, and measures of the degree of attainment of desired or behavioral objective at exit must also be assessable. This approach, developed by Astin, is known as the "value-added" approach. It asserts that outcome measures alone tell us very little about institutional effectiveness or impact. By controlling for entry characteristics, however, a more accurate picture of outcomes will emerge. In the absence of such data, outcome measures may be grossly misinterpreted when used for assessing institutional effectiveness because most outcomes are highly dependent on the characteristics of students at entry.

NCRIPTAL's Delimited Outcome Framework

As discussed earlier, NCRIPTAL's mission includes both conducting basic research on the effects of various aspects of the teaching and learning environment on student outcomes and providing leadership and assistance to institutions in their own assessment and evaluation efforts. Thus, in the terms of Ewell's "perspectives," we must engage in a dual approach, combining the academic-investigative spirit of basic research and a management perspective that can help institutions construct their own assessment processes and uses of the information.

Fulfilling this dual mission with available resources requires delimitation of the arena in which our work will be conducted and a selection of outcome measures and assessment principles that seem most closely related to practical concerns in improving teaching and learning. Existing typologies, such as that proposed by Astin (see Tables 1 and 2), the list of principles by Bowen, and the important distinctions mentioned by Ewell, as well as the work of many other scholars, have been helpful in formulating our plans. In Table 3 we have summarized some of these propositions, attempting to group them as accurately as possible under the "technical parameter" headings discussed earlier, namely, "type of outcome to be measured," "level of measurement," and "form of measurement." This grouping forms the basis for our discussion of outcome measures to be used in NCRIPTAL's work. It bears repeating that only these three parameters of type, level, and form are discussed because we have already focused our work on a specific purpose (improvement of teaching and learning) and assume that results will be used for decisions consonant with that purpose. Furthermore, our efforts are based on the assumption that the administrative locus of assessment activities and evaluative decisions about this information all rest within the college or university.

Table 3
Propositions and Caveats about Type, Level, and Form of Outcome Measurement

	Bowen	Ewell	Astin
Type of Outcome Measures	Assess all outcomes, even those difficult to measure.	Distinguish intended and unintended outcomes.	
	Relate outcomes to whole person.	Distinguish outcomes of which student is aware and unaware.	
	Focus on changes attributable to college.	Distinguish outcomes closely linked to educational program.	
	Focus on major institutional goals.		
Level of Outcome Measures	Study alumni as well as current students.	Distinguish short- and long-term outcome measures.	Record whether students completed program and whether accomplishments were consistent with their goals.
Form of Outcome Measures	Separate inputs and outputs.		Measure at various points in time; include information at entry, during program, and on exit.
	Use practical and feasible means.		Use measures of cognitive development beyond grade point average.
			Include measures of student satisfaction.

Type of Outcome Measures

However desirable it might be for researchers and institutions to follow Bowen's suggestion to assess all possible outcomes and relate outcomes to the development of the whole person, such a global program would readily encounter problems of feasibility and lack of consensus. Nonetheless, our discussion of outcome measures begins with the whole-person approach in an effort to determine which subsets of this universe are of greatest importance.

During such discussions we found many benefits, but some pitfalls, in Astin's encompassing four-fold typology of student outcomes (see Table 1). Specifically, although Astin acknowledged interactions between affective and cognitive outcomes, his typology used these concepts as two different primary dimensions. Consequently, the typology made little provision for attention to cognitive-personal outcomes or affective-academic outcomes. Yet, many cognitive psychologists and personality theorists believe that, particularly for students who enter college with undeveloped motivation or low self-efficacy, affective outcomes may be related to academic as well as to personal and social growth. As a result of these and related discussions, we drew a slightly different type of typology framework which notes three "arenas" of student growth in college and

Table 4
A Whole-Person Approach to College Student Outcomes

Form of Demonstrated Change	Arenas of Growth and Development		
	Social	Personal	Academic
Cognitive			
Motivational			
Behavioral			

three forms through which changes in these arenas may be observed. The resulting nine-cell framework, which we stress was derived a priori from our accumulated experience, is shown in Table 4.

The *arena* dimension refers to the various aspects of life in which the outcome is important. The three arenas are personal, social, and academic. The personal domain includes outcomes like personal worth, feelings about oneself, satisfaction with personal accomplishments, ability to make decisions, and using one's skills appropriately. The social arena outcomes include ability to function in interpersonal relationships, citizenship, social responsibility, social awareness, and contributions to society. The academic arena includes academic achievement, self-efficacy, motivation, critical-thinking abilities, problem-solving skills, and goal exploration behaviors.

The form dimension also has three categories: cognitive, motivational, and behavioral. This dimension specifies the form in which the outcome is demonstrated. Cognitive outcomes are internal outcomes. Typically they occur within individuals' mental processes and their existence is inferred, usually through testing. Motivational outcomes consist largely of the feelings that individuals have about themselves, their capabilities, and the world around them. These outcomes are generally self-reported, though some social-psychological methods exist that tap these attitudes more discretely. Behavioral outcomes may be reported by the individual or directly observed.

As mentioned earlier, NCRIPTAL's research program will focus on the academic arena shown in Table 4. In selecting this subset of the universe of college outcome measures for attention, we risk posing for others the same difficulty that Astin's typology posed for us. We acknowledge that the

Table 5
NCRIPTAL's Outcome Framework

Forms of Measurement	Academic Arena
Cognitive	Achievement (facts, principles, ideas, skills) Critical-thinking skills Problem-solving skills
Motivational	Satisfaction with college Involvement/effort Motivation Self-efficacy
Behavioral	Career and life goal exploration Exploration of diversity Persistence Relationships with faculty

personal and social arenas cannot be separated from the academic arena; one's personal and social development affects one's academic development and the reverse is also true. Nonetheless, by constructing a framework that includes three cells, academic-cognitive, academic-motivational, and academic-behavioral, we are able to encompass a broad set of outcomes of primary concern to colleges and the public as well as to incorporate recent theories of cognitive development. Table 5 shows a more detailed view of the academic arena and the types of outcomes that seem to fit into each of the three major cells.

At first glance, some observers will believe we have violated Bowen's principle of separating inputs and outputs by classifying as outcomes some of those items listed in the academic-motivational cell. Traditionally, motivation, self-efficacy, involvement, and effort have been viewed as fixed attributes students bring to the educational process. Our view that these characteristics are subject to change (in an intended or unintended direction) as a result of the educational process is, in part, what caused us to modify previously existing outcome typologies. Although little attention has been given to these ideas, most colleges would agree, for example, that improved motivation is an outcome to be sought. While the original motivation a student brings to college is an input, a new motivational level based on educational experiences becomes an outcome the student takes to the next stage of learning.

An additional previously neglected aspect of the iterative outcomes conception relates to Ewell's distinction between student awareness or lack of awareness of changes. Although we have not included it in the list at this time, if students are to take increased responsibility for their learning, awareness itself may be an outcome to be sought.

Level of Outcome Measures

As already mentioned, both practicality and technical difficulties have caused us to set aside Bowen's suggestion that alumni be studied in addition to current students. Instead, NCRIPTAL's agenda will focus on outcome measures that can be related directly to classroom and program educational experiences. In general, our unit of analysis will be the individual student and groups of students sharing a common educational experience in a course or program. Whenever possible, outcome measures for special populations of students (e.g., minorities, women, adult students) will be examined in relation to similar data for traditional students.

Astin's point about whether students' eventual accomplishments are constant with their goals will be a special focus of one of our research programs. In fact, goals of students at college entry are subject to change in both intended and unintended directions. Since there would likely be disagreement about what constitutes positive change, we have included an academic-behavioral outcome called "career and life goal development." The implication is that the student should gain in ability to explore, consider, and make decisions about eventual goals.

Form of Outcome Measures

For many institutions, there may be an inherent conflict between observing Bowen's caveat about feasibility of measurement and adopting Astin's value-added approach, which statistically controls for student entry characteristics when observing changes in student outcomes over time. This is particularly true if measures of cognitive development, such as reasoning skills and critical thinking, are used to supplement more traditional measures of academic achievement. In developing new measures and in assisting institutions with the use of already developed measures, NCRIPTAL will attempt to help simplify the appropriate use of outcome measures.

The next section of this paper describes some of the academic measures already in use by colleges and alerts the reader to some new measures that NCRIPTAL staff hope to make available for future use.

Learning Outcomes and Their Effects

ROBERT M. GAGNÉ

Abstract: The outcomes of learning are persistent states that make possible a variety of human performances. While learning results are specific to the task undertaken, learning investigators have sought to identify broader categories of learning outcomes in order to foresee to what extent their findings can be generalized. Five varieties of learning outcomes have been distinguished and appear to be widely accepted. The categories are (a) intellectual skills (procedural knowledge), (b) verbal information (declarative knowledge), (c) cognitive strategies (executive control process), (d) motor skills, and (e) attitudes. Each of these categories may be seen to encompass a broad variety of human activities. It is held that results indicating the effects on learning of most principal independent variables can be generalized within these categories but not between them. This article identifies additional effects of each type of learning outcome and discusses the current state of knowledge about them.

The question of understanding how human beings learn has been a central theme of psychological research since the time of the English associationist philosophers Hobbes, Locke, and Mill, and experimental work of Ebbinghaus (1913) in 1885. From that time until the present day, learning has been understood as a change of state of the human being that is remembered and that makes possible a corresponding change in the individual's behavior in a given type of situation. This change of state must, of course, be distinguished from others that may be effected by innate forces, by maturation, or by other physiological influences. Instead, learning is brought about by one or more experiences that are either the same as or that somehow present the situation in which the newly acquired behavior is exhibited.

Psychologists who have studied the phenomenon of learning have sometimes confined their observations to human learning. Such learning was studied by the followers of the Ebbinghaus tradition and was usually referred to as *verbal learning*. Verbal learning was studied by such investigators as Robinson (1932), McGeoch (1932), Melton (1963), Postman (1961), and Underwood (1957), among others. Many students of learning, however, did not hesitate to study the behavior of animals as well as humans nor to relate the phenomena observed across the species gap. Pioneers in this tradition include Thorndike (1898), Guthrie (1935), Tolman (1932), and Hull (1943). Other differences in fundamental approaches to the study of human learning arose from points of view noted by Bower and Hilgard (1981) as empiricism versus rationalism, contiguity versus reinforcement, and gradual increments versus all-or-none spurts. These issues persist down to the present day and cannot be said to have been resolved in the sense of having attained a consensus of scientists.

Perhaps, though, the most distinctive differences among studies of learning, as reported to us by various investigators, are differences in the *behavior-in-situation* that identifies the new learning. This is often referred to as the *learning task*, a phrase that implies that its specification includes both the external situation and the behavior that interacts with it. This tendency to identify learning with the situation is reflected in texts having learning as a subject, such as Hulse, Deese, and Egeth (1975), or Hill (1981). When Melton (1964) assembled chapters in *Categories of Human Learning*, they dealt with such familiar situations as the classically conditioned eye blink, operant conditioning of pigeons, rote learning of verbal associates, incidental learning of word pairs, and perceptual-motor skills learning. Even when theories of learning are addressed directly, as by Bower and Hilgard (1981), we find the theoretical ideas tied to situations such as dogs salivating to the sight of food, pigeons pecking at circular spots, rats running to food boxes, or people learning paired associates.

The advent of the cognitive psychology of learning, as represented in books done by Klatzky (1980), Bransford (1979), and Anderson (1980), among others, has broadened the situations employed for the study of learning. Thus, we now have insightful studies of the learning of elementary arithmetic (Resnick & Ford, 1981), of constructing geometric proofs (Greeno, 1978b), of story comprehension (Stein & Trabasso, 1982), and of the prediction of rainfall (Stevens & Collins, 1982). Most surely, it is a welcome change to find investigators of human learning choosing schoolroom situations for learning or at least situations that have what might be called "face validity" with tasks encountered by students. The greater diversity of such situations, as contrasted with the narrowly defined learning of paired associates on a memory drum, is a welcome change. If there are cautions to be noted, they may be expressed in the hope that these new school-learning tasks will not themselves become frozen into narrow channels of study, so that we end up with the "psychology of arithmetic learning," the "psychology of reading learning," the "psychology of geometry learning," and the like. I do not think this will necessarily happen. Nevertheless, in our enthusiasm for a newly found freedom from a set of traditional learning tasks, we should, I think, keep firmly in mind that a psychology of learning seeks generalizations that are not tied to particular learning situations. The history of paired-associate learning should help us remember this lesson. For many years, studies of paired associates sought to discover *general* principles about the learning of associations. As understanding increased, however, such studies came to be seen as dealing with a very particular kind of learning task called "paired-associate learning." Many, perhaps most, of the results obtained apply only to that specific learning task.

Should the study of learning continue to be situation bound? Of course, the conceptions of Skinner (1969) offer a way out. Those who view learning as a matter of arranging contingencies of reinforcement can demonstrate how that principle applies to virtually every situation. The case for application of reinforcement techniques as a way of arranging situations for learning is entirely convincing; it is indeed difficult to find contrary evidence. Yet the tendency of learning investigators to seek more detailed specifications for learning situations, from mazes to geometry, implies that reinforcement contingencies are not enough. Greater specificity continues to be sought in the description of the interaction between learner and environment—in the *task*, in other words. Students of learning phenomena continue to find dimensions of the learning situation that do not contradict the operation of reinforcement but that must be described in greater detail.

How can we achieve a psychology of learning that is not tied to specific situations or tasks and that at the same time has the potential for generalization that we value as a scientific goal? My suggestion is that now is a good time to look closely and intensively at the question, what do people learn? This question must be examined as broadly as possible. By this I mean, we need to gain an idea of what all kinds of people learn—not only school children or laboratory subjects but masons, carpenters, astronauts, politicians, housewives, and word-processing operators. Most of the overt behavior people engage in during each day, of course, is what they have learned to do. As observers of behavior, we know what has been learned by perceiving what people can do. In other words, we know that learning has occurred when we observe its outcomes or effects.

How can we find principles of learning that can be generalized and that are not tied to specific subject matter? Actually, it seems to me that learning psychologists, particularly those in the information-processing tradition, are coming close to a satisfactory answer to this question. I trust they will continue to keep the appropriate goal in mind and will not be too seriously distracted by trendy issues suggested by neighboring disciplines. The question continues to be, how do people learn what they learn? That is not the same question, obviously, as how does a person become an expert? Certainly, expertness is learned, but many people learn many things without ever becoming experts.

Categories of Learning Outcomes

A number of years ago (Gagné, 1972), I proposed a set of categories of learning outcomes that seemed to me to possess certain desirable distinctive properties. While I do not intend here simply to cover the same ground, it is worthwhile to state what the characteristics of such categories should be:

1. Each category of learning outcomes should be distinguishable in terms of a formal definition of the class of human performance made possible by the learning.

2. Each category should include a broad variety of human activities that are independent (excluding the extremes) of intelligence, age, race, economic status, and so on. The possibility of special categories (e.g., music virtuosity, expert wine tasting) is acknowledged but is not relevant to the main point. In order not to be narrow, each category must apply to widely diverse set of human activities.

3. Each category should be seen to differ in the nature of information-processing demands for its learning. Specifically, each kind of outcome should require different (a) substantive type of relevant prior learning, (b) manner of encoding for long-term storage, and (c) requirements for retrieval and transfer to new situations.

4. It should be possible to generalize the principles concerning factors affecting the learning of each category to a variety of specific tasks *within* the category but not to learning tasks in other categories. Excluded here is the factor of reinforcement, assumed to apply to all categories.

With such characteristics in mind for the principles of learning that can be generalized, I identified five categories of learning outcomes: (a) intellectual skills, (b) verbal information, (c) cognitive strategies, (d) attitudes, and (e) motor skills. I will discuss each of these categories again from the viewpoint of contemporary learning psychology and from the standpoint of learning effects. Where possible, I will mention a few of the things I think we still need to discover about the effects of learning.

Intellectual Skills

As a category of learning outcome, intellectual skills have in recent times appeared to find their proper place in the scheme of things. Intellectual skills include concepts, rules, and procedures. Perhaps the best known synonym is *procedural knowledge* (Anderson, 1976, 1980). Some investigators prefer the computer-derived language of Newell and Simon (1972), who call this category *production systems.* Some would prefer to distinguish procedures, conceived as having a number of sequential steps, from rules, which may have only two or three. Since I view them as the same category, I have used the phrase "procedural rules" (Gagné, 1977) for the former.

Does procedural knowledge show itself as a learning outcome in a great diversity of human activity? Of course it does. Consider all the rules that govern the use of language both in speaking and writing. This complex set of rules applies to reading in the sense of the phonological and semantic processing of printed discourse. Intellectual skills are easiest to exemplify in the field of mathematics, where there are rules for computation, for interpretation of word problems, and for verifying mathematical solutions (Resnick & Ford, 1981). Procedural rules are involved in the application of scientific principles to real-world problems (Larkin, 1980). But beyond the various subjects of school learning, procedural rules govern a great many common activities of our daily lives—driving an automobile, using a lawnmower, making a telephone call, or shopping in a supermarket. Think of what kinds of knowledge are possessed by a technician in an nuclear power plant or by an aircraft mechanic. Obviously the knowledge most highly relevant to jobs like these, or to a whole host of other jobs, involves items of procedural knowledge, ranging from the simple to the highly complex. There should be little doubt, then, that intellectual skills of this sort occur in an enormous variety of essential human activities.

As described by Anderson (1980), the representation in memory of procedural knowledge is production systems. Each production has a *condition* and an *action*. For example, "IF the goal is to generate a plural of a noun and the noun ends in a hard consonant THEN generate the noun + s" (Anderson, 1980, p. 239). What is apparent about this representation is that it includes a number of concepts that have previously been learned, such as *noun, plural, end* (of word), *hard consonant, add* (a letter to a word), and *s* . Intellectual skills, then, must typically be composed of concepts. An individual who possesses such a rule is able to apply it to *any* noun ending in a hard consonant, even one that may be have been previously encountered (such a *nib*). The other characteristic of procedural knowledge is also made apparent by this example. A procedure involves a *sequence*—first an individual takes one action, then another, followed by another. In the case of this example, the steps might be described as follows: (a) identify the word as a noun; (b) identify an ending consonant; (c) identify the ending consonant as a hard sound; (d) recall *s;* (e) add *s* to the word; and (f) give the plural.

In summary, the possession of an intellectual skill (an item of procedural knowledge) is shown when a person is able to apply a sequence of concepts representing condition and action to a general class of situations.

What do we know, or need to know, about the learning effects of this kind of learning outcome? First, it would seem likely that very simple rules, involving only a small number of steps, are acquired abruptly. For instance, determining the sign of a product of two positive and negative numbers involves two fairly simple rules that would seem to be learned in an all-or-none fashion. What could possibly be gradual about such learning? It would appear, then, that there must be a phase of learning that ought to be identifiable as *initial acquisition*. If learning has occurred, the rule or procedure can be applied to any instance; if the application cannot be made, learning in this initial sense has not yet happened. But in a sense I am using it here, learning *cannot* have occurred partially. The evidence for these ideas is currently weak; yet they appear to be of some importance for the understanding of this kind of learning outcome.

There is more to this story, however, particularly when we consider procedures that are complicated and have many steps. Learning must somehow be devoted to acquiring the sequence of the procedure in such a way that it can be retrieved readily. Neves and Anderson (1981) discuss a possible way of processing for what they call *proceduralization*. Going beyond that stage, they point out that continued practice may lead to composition, which involves combining production systems, to speeding up the action of the procedure, and ultimately to *automatization*. These, then, are some of the additional possibilities for learning effects when we are dealing with this type of outcome called procedural knowledge. It is notable that these effects of practice do not involve a change in the nature of the outcome itself; being able to add two-digit numbers is still the same outcome. But the procedure may be accomplished by somewhat different process and more rapidly. It may come to demand a smaller amount of the attentional resource, as Shiffrin and Schneider (1977) suggest. Yet the essential outcome remains the same. The effects of learning, beyond the stage of initial acquisition, must be looked for in processing changes, not in changes in the nature of the outcome itself.

Verbal Information

A second category of learning outcome is what I have called *verbal information*. *Declarative knowledge* is probably a better name, implying that its presence is shown by the ability of a person to "declare" or "state" something. Yet I do not necessarily retreat from the supposition that such knowledge, when it is displayed, typically takes the form of verbal statements.

As a learning outcome, is declarative knowledge a widespread and diverse occurrence? It is curious that when attempting to address this question, it is necessary to take account of the fact that there are different kinds of packages for this information. There are "facts" that may be more or less isolated from other knowledge, such as the names of particular persons, the names of the months of the year, or the names of metric measures of length. Another kind of "package," however, is meaningfully connected prose or poetry that is learned and recalled in verbatim form. We recall the "Salute the Flag" and the words of the "Star Spangled Banner." Some of us may recall Hamlet's soliloquy and the "seven ages of man" and the words to Cole Porter's song, "You're the Top," in both the square and profane versions.

Still another kind of package for declarative knowledge is composed of organized, meaningful domains to be identified and recalled in a great variety of ways. We realize that the name for a common class of objectives, an era of history, or one of the nations of the world can call up for us a complex of interconnected knowledge. A number of different suggestions have been made by various theorists regarding the nature of organization attained by such knowledge in its stored form. One suggestion is that knowledge is organized as networks of units connected to properties (Collins & Loftus, 1975). Another is that concepts form a semantic space and are related to each other in terms of their attributes (Smith, Shoben, & Rips, 1974).

But of greater immediate relevance is the idea that knowledge is stored in networks of propositions. Each proposition is complete with its syntactic structure—at least a subject and predicate and probably a good deal more than that. Many investigators hold the view that the organization of each such network forms a *schema*. A schema is a representation of a situation or event. It may be viewed as a prototype that indicates the usual sequence of events to be expected. Events (such as those of a story) may be stored as a *script*, according to Schank and Abelson (1977), who also describe other forms of organized knowledge called *goals*, *plans*, and *themes*, from which scripts can be constructed. While it is not yet clear that the concept of schema has been well defined in a general sense, it surely represents a widely accepted way of describing organized knowledge.

What, then, is the nature of the learning outcome for this category of declarative knowledge? This question must be answered differently for the different "packages" in which such knowledge comes. On the one hand, the investigator seeks the exact reinstatement of a word, phrase, or sequence of words in sentence form. If an individual has learned the names of persons, objects, or foreign-language words, exact reproduction of these entities is expected. If someone has committed Lincoln's Gettysburg address to memory, that person is expected to be able to repeat the address word for word without paraphrase or omission. On the other hand, what will convince someone that a student "comprehends" or " understands" a chapter in a textbook such as that dealing with the history of disarmament in the 1920s? Obviously, no one expects such knowledge to be displayed by a verbatim recitation of the chapter's text, word by word. A recognition of the "main ideas" may be expected or perhaps a description of the learner's schema.

It should be possible now for me to propose a definition that runs as follows: the learning of verbal information (declarative knowledge) may be confirmed when the learner is able either to: (a) reinstate in speech or writing the word or sequence of words in the same order as presented; or (b) reconstruct an organized representation of a verbal passage, containing identifiable main and subordinate ideas arranged in a meaningful schema.

One of the most interesting facts about such knowledge, which we do not yet fully understand, is the following. Despite the fact that both of these packages are varieties of declarative knowledge, they are intuitively very different. Most teachers would strongly aver, for example, that being able to recite Lincoln's Gettysburg address is very different from displaying "understanding" of President Lincoln's message. It is conceivable that a learner might be able to recite the speech without being able to recount any of its meaning. Nevertheless, knowing the address in verbatim form may well contribute to a performance that intends to produce only a paraphrase of its main ideas. There are puzzles here about memory that have not yet been explained. It is clear that knowing the sequence of main ideas in a long passage of prose or poetry is helpful in remembering that passage in a verbatim sense. Is the reverse true? Is the retention of a passage in the sense of a schema influenced by certain partial features, words, or phrases that are remembered the their precise form? It may be helpful to think about this question in terms of "levels of processing" (Craik & Lockhart, 1972).

As for the question of learning effects, this also must deal with the distinction between verbatim reinstatement and the recounting of main ideas or themes. As we know from the work of Gates (1917) and other studies of more recent vintage, added practice in the form of recitation increases the quality of verbatim recall. Errors and hesitations are reduced, and the performance becomes more sure. But additional learning experience with passages of meaningful prose has quite a different effect. As learning proceeds, additional links with other concepts and other networks of concepts are formed. What is learned is elaborated (Anderson, 1980) or processed more deeply (Craik & Tulving, 1975). The schema as originally acquired becomes more elaborate as the empty slots in its outline are filled in. It seems clear, then, that the effects of continued learning of this second kind of package are very different from such effects on verbatim learning. In this case, there is a definite qualitative change in the performance of the learner. New elements, additional ideas, are added to the main themes with which the learning began.

Notable, too, are the differences in learning effects for declarative knowledge from those I previously described as applicable to procedural knowledge. For verbatim reinstatement, it is not at all evident that the learner goes through any phases comparable to what Neves and Anderson (1981) called composition, speed-up, or automaticity. While a familiar word may be more rapidly responded to than an unfamiliar one, it is not evident that the other criteria of automatism, such as the allocation of attentional resources, are applicable to verbatim recall of verbal material in quite the same manner as to an intellectual skill. Of course, when we consider the other package, the reconstruction of meaningful discourse, the effects are very different indeed. Rather than a condensation of procedural steps, as in what is called *composition*, we see the effect of greater and greater elaboration. These are some of the reasons for believing that procedural knowledge and declarative knowledge are highly distinctive kinds of learning outcomes.

Cognitive Strategies

Most cognitive learning theorists distinguish another type of cognitive skills besides the procedural knowledge previously mentioned. Most speak of these learned entities as *executive control processes* (Atkinson & Shiffrin, 1968) or more generally as *strategic knowledge* (Greeno, 1978a). In many studies of learning and of human problem solving, it has been repeatedly shown that learners bring to new tasks not only previously learned declarative knowledge and procedural knowledge but also some skills of when and how to use this knowledge. Cognitive strategies for recalling word pairs may consist of constructing images and sentences, and such techniques have been taught to both children and adults (Rohwer, 1970). Strategies for encoding and for cueing retrieval are suggested by research from many sources (Anderson, 1980; Brown, 1978). Strategies of problem solving have been the subject of a good deal of research (Wickelgren, 1974). Greeno (1978b) has written an excellent article on geometric problem solving.

Cognitive strategies vary considerably in the degree of specificity or generality they process. Some appear to be highly specific to the task being undertaken or to the problem being solved. A strategy of checking subtraction by converting numbers to multiples of ten is surely a useful strategy of limited generality. Strategies such as constructive search, limiting the problem space (Greeno, 1978a), and dividing the problem into parts have been suggested as having general applicability. The strategy called *means-end analysis* is very general in its applicability, according to Newell and Simon (1972). Correlated with the specificity of cognitive strategies may be their ease of learning and recall. Some strategies seem very easy to communicate to learners faced with a particular learning or problem-solving situation ("put the two words into a sentence" is an example). Usually, though, these are the strategies that are very specific to the task. More general strategies, such as "break the problem into its parts," although clear to the learner in relation to one task, may not be readily transferable to other novel problem-solving situations.

The definition I suggest for this kind of learning outcome is as follows. A cognitive strategy enables a learner to exercise some degree of control over the process involved in attending, perceiving, encoding, remembering, and thinking. Strategies enable learners to choose at appropriate times the intellectual skills and declarative knowledge they will bring to bear on learning, remembering, and problem solving, Differences in strategies are usually inferred from differences in efficient processing (as it occurs in learning, thinking, etc.). Evidence of strategies and their use comes from learner's reports, or protocols, of their own processing methods.

Despite the inferential nature of the evidence for one cognitive strategy or another, it is difficult to deny their existence or their role as executive processes that influence other forms of information processing. If we admit that cognitive strategies apply not just to problem solving but to all of the kinds of processing involved in cognition—perceiving, learning, remembering, thinking—then there must be many kinds of strategies for almost any conceivable kind of task. Greeno (1978a) has written about the ways strategies enter into problem solving, as has Newell (1980). Learning-to-learn strategies have recently been critically discussed by Langley and Simon (1981).

The effects of continued learning, or continued practice, on cognitive strategies are not well known. Presumably, though, they behave somewhat like intellectual skills. For one thing, cognitive strategies are often learned abruptly. When children are told to remember a set of pictures by putting them in categories, they do it right away and are not particularly better at it after five trials than after one. If a learner discovers a "working backwards" strategy for solving a Tower of Hanoi problem, he or she puts it into effect abruptly and continues to use it thereafter. Whether or not strategies exhibit practice changes, such as composition and automatization, has not been shown. It seems reasonable to suppose, though, that these executive skills may behave similarly to their more pedestrian cousins, the procedural skills, which have external rather than internal targets for their effects. The problem of how to make cognitive strategies generalizable to new learning and problem-solving situations is also a feature shared with procedural knowledge. The question of transfer of training for both these categories of intellectual skills continues to be a problem not yet well understood.

Motor Skills

We're all familiar with the motor skills we use in writing, using tools, skating, riding bicycles, and performing various athletic activities. These performances are based on the possession of learned skills. Should we bother to distinguish them from intellectual skills, or should we simply call them all *skills* and let it go at that? I think the distinction is an important one. Of course, all performances are in some sense "motor," or we would be unable to observe them at all. Stating something, pointing at something, or pushing a button are all motor responses. In fact, they are motor skills that we have learned in the early years of life and have practiced ever since. But if we are attempting to identify a category of learning outcome that reflects new learning, we must have in mind activities such as fly casting, top spinning, lariat twirling, or others that have not previously been done. A skill is identified as a *motor skill* when gradual improvements in the quality of its movement (smoothness, timing) can be attained only by repetition of that movement. That is to say, learning consists of practice of the movement itself, under conditions in which reinforcement occurs, resulting in gradual improvement in the skill (Singer, 1980).

Surely it is evident that procedural knowledge (intellectual skill) does not have these characteristics. Intellectual skills frequently seem to be acquired abruptly, and this is never the case with motor skills. Practice of intellectual skills means applying a general rule to varied examples. It is not apparent that the practice of motor skills can be described in such terms since it requires repetition of the particular muscular movements involved. Finally, there seems nothing comparable in the area of intellectual skills to the increase in smoothness and timing of movement that is observed in motor skills. I would emphasize, then, that although both deserve to be called skills, the intellectual type and the motor type should not on that account be considered a single category.

Fitts and Posner (1967) provided a description of three phases in learning of a motor skill. The earliest they called a *cognitive* phase, and this was devoted primarily to the learning of the procedure that underlies the skill, the *executive subroutine*. For example, in making a tennis serve, the movements required involve shifting body weight to one foot, tossing the ball in the air bringing the racquet up, and striking the ball with the racquet while aiming in a particular direction. All of these movements must be learned as a procedure during the early phase of skill learning, even though at that time the motor skill itself may be of minimal quality. A next phase, according to Fitts and Posner, is an *associative* phase, during which all the parts of the skill come to be fitted together. This phase, of course, establishes the smoothness and timing we recognize as characteristic of motor skill. A third phase they called *autonomous*, in which skill can be exercised without the need for much attention. Presumably, this is the same as what is meant by automatization.

Fitts and Posner, then, have provided us with a basic account of learning effects, so far as this category of learning outcome is concerned. Motor skills begin with the learning of the sequence of muscular movements, the executive subroutine. Continued practice, (successive repetitions of this same set of movements) brings about increased quality of skilled performance, observable as improved timing and smoothness. Continued practice, sometimes over long periods of time, results in automatization of the skill, evidenced by the ability to carry on the skill in the presence of potentially interfering activities.

If the effects of continued practice of motor skills are similar to those of intellectual skills, this similarity may be structurally true, or it may be a kind of coincidence. Is the improvement in smoothness and timing of a motor skill comparable to what is meant by composition and speed-up of procedural knowledge? As a general description, these terms sound right. Yet it is not easy to accept the idea that a well-practiced intellectual skill (such as mentally adding positive and negative numbers) exhibits a phase that can be characterized as smooth or well-timed. One other learning effect that should be mentioned for this category of motor skill is the fact that improvement in performance continues for very long periods of time (Fitts & Posner, 1967). Any particular level of performance at which the skill is treated as fully learned is presumably an arbitrary limit. However, this does not seem a proper way to describe the effects of long-continued practice of a intellectual skill. Whatever comparison is made, motor skills are different.

Attitudes

The fifth kind of learning outcome to be considered is an attitude. There can be little doubt about pervasiveness of efforts to establish and modify our attitudes. The medium that is most heavily devoted to such aims is television. The commercial messages of television are textbook examples of how attitudes are affected. Not only that, it seems likely that the remaining television fare, including soap operas, continues to produce and reinforce attitudes toward the various problems of everyday living. Whether these attitudes are beneficial in the long run is a matter of opinion, but their existence is surely apparent. Of course, there are other sources that attempt to modify our attitudes, and these include all other communication media with which we are surrounded. Even schools do a great deal to establish attitudes. Schools are fairly successful in establishing socially beneficial attitudes (such as fairness or thoughtfulness of others) in the primary grades but are apparently much less successful in getting across attitudes such as avoidance of smoking or harmful drugs in later years. At any rate, we can readily realize that many forces are at work in our society to determine our attitudes.

Attitudes are inferred internal states. We cannot observe them directly, but must make inferences from one or another kind of observable behavior. Furthermore, as many investigators have pointed out.(Rokeach, 1969; Triandis, 1971), the relation between reported attitudes and overt behavior is seldom found to be a close one. Attitudes are sometimes described as having both cognitive and emotional components. These ideas surely have an intuitive appeal, but they do little to provide a scientific explanation of attitudes. All we are able to say is that attitudes *influence* behavior. They do not determine human performance in the sense that both procedural and declarative knowledge do; they appear instead to modulate behavior. Thus, when performance itself is considered, the distinctive qualities of attitudes can readily be seen.

I find my definition of attitude to be remarkably similar to Allport's (1935), or at least it seems to be highly compatible with it. An attitude is an internal state that influences the choice of personal action. As an example, a positive attitude toward listening to classical music influences the behavior of an individual to choose such listening when a choice is provided. An attitude of rejection toward using a harmful drug influences the behavior of rejection when the individual is confronted with choices of this nature.

What about learning effects of this category of learning outcome? The contrast with other kinds of outcome is marked. Whereas we expect declarative knowledge, procedural knowledge, and cognitive strategies to be acquired in some circumstances when learners are told what we want them to learn, it appears extremely unlikely that attitudes are ever acquired this way. Communications that attempt to establish attitudes directly, whether by persuasive logic, emotional appeal, or otherwise, have consistently been found to be ineffective (McGuire, 1969). Whatever conditions must be arranged for the learning of attitudes, they must apparently be different from directly telling learners what we want them to learn.

Are there, then, distinctive conditions for attitude learning? This world appear to be the case, although it can't be said that the precise nature of these conditions is well understood. Some investigators see conflicts in beliefs or between beliefs and other information as origins of attitudes; others give emphasis to contingencies of reinforcement. I am impressed with the evidence found by Bandura (1969) and his associates, which assigns a critical function to the *human model*. It seems to me that at least one highly common way in which attitudes are acquired or changed is through the mediation of a human model. Bandura has described the typical procedure by which such learning occurs; it involves a statement or demonstration of the choice of personal action by the model, followed by learner observation of reinforcement to the model, which is called *vicarious reinforcement*. My view is that this is more than simply observational learning, although I have no doubt of the reality of such learning. However, I tend to think that for attitude learning, the human model is an essential component. What is encoded, I suggested, is a representation of the human model making the choice of action, which is compared with the planned behavior of the learner himself or herself.

Other differences in learning effects serve to distinguish attitudes from other learning outcomes. It is a common observation that particular attitudes may persist for many years and be highly resistant to change. Such persistence may take place regardless of the frequency with which the action choice takes place. Reinforcement of action choices seems to have its expected effect. However, we do not appear to know with any degree of assurance what happens to an attitude when it is "practiced," or when it is displayed in many different circumstances over a period of time. The way attitudes are represented in memory may turn out to be a matter of considerable complexity.

Why Five Kinds of Learning Outcomes?

Now I have described five kinds of learning outcomes, stated why they appear to be different from each other, and suggested some areas in which the effects of learning are still not well understood.

It seems to me that the recognition of distinctive characteristics for these five learning outcomes has gained increasingly wide acceptance among learning psychologists in recent years. The distinction of motor skills from verbal learning has a long history in psychology. Attitudes have usually been assumed to occupy a special place as learned entities. Developments in the psychology of information processing have lead to an emphasis on the distinction between verbal information and intellectual skills (or declarative and procedural knowledge). Investigation of artificial intelligence and human problem solving has given renewed evidence of the need to infer executive control processes, or cognitive strategies, in human thinking. Accordingly, it seems that students of learning and its processes have come to accept and to depend upon these five distinctions.

No particular reason exists to think of these five different learning outcomes as constituting a taxonomy or as having been derived for that reason. As I have tried to show, the five learning outcomes exist because they differ, first, as human performances; second, because the requirements for their learning are different despite the pervasiveness of such general conditions as contiguity and reinforcement; and third, because the effects of learning, and of continued learning, appear also to differ from each other.

There are good reasons why we should not be content with the idea that learning is learning is learning. Of course, learning has some common conditions for its occurrence that are quite general. Those of us who have tried to apply principles of learning in practical situations, whether in connection with school learning, military training, or adult professional development, have become keenly aware that greater detail in specification of learning conditions is required than is provided by general "laws of learning" (cf. Gagné, 1962, 1977). The contrasting viewpoint about types of learning is equally unacceptable. This is the view that we must discover and formulate principles of mathematics learning, science learning, automobile repair learning, and so on. We overlook truly important generalities, for example, when we refuse to look at the resemblances in learning outcomes between, say, arithmetic and reading, geometry and composition, or between the procedures of office management and the procedures of aircraft maintenance.

These five outcomes of learning represents a middle ground but not because a compromise has been sought. Instead, they are categories within which generalizations can legitimately be drawn, according to both reason and empirical evidence. They are also categories between which generalizations about learning are either impossible or very risky. Within these categories of declarative knowledge, procedural knowledge, cognitive strategies, motor skills, and attitudes, we have a continually increasing store of knowledge of when and how learning occurs. The effects of learning on these outcomes are better known for some than for others. For each of these categories, there are questions to be explored about the effects of continued or repeated learning experiences.

It appears to me that psychological research has been well served by these five categories. I believe they are widely accepted as distinctions and that the results of research are made more readily interpretable when the learning effects of these outcomes are made clear. To understand the learning differences and the memory-storage differences among these five outcomes is an intriguing challenge for cognitive theory.

References

Allport, G. W. (1935). Attitudes. In C. Murchison (Ed.), *Handbook of social psychology* (pp. 798–844). Worcester, MA: Clark University Press.

Anderson, J. R. (1976). *Language, memory, and thought.* Hillsdale, NJ: Erlbaum.

Anderson, J. R. (1980). *Cognitive psychology and its implications.* San Francisco: Freeman.

Atkinson, R. C., and Shiffrin, R. M. (1968). Human memory: A proposed system and its control processes. In K. W. Spense & J. T. Spense (Eds.), *The psychology of learning and motivation* (Vol. 2). New York: Academic Press.

Bandura, A. (1969). *Principles of behavior modification.* New York: Holt, Rinehart & Winston.

Bower, G. M., and Hilgard, E. J. (1981). *Theories of learning* (5th ed.). Englewood Cliffs, NJ: Prentice-Hall.

Bransford, J. D. (1979). *Human cognition.* Belmont, CA: Wadsworth.

Brown, A. L. (1978). Knowing when, where, and how to remember: A problem of metacognition. In R. Glaser (Ed.), *Advances in instructional psychology* (Vol. 1, pp. 77–157). Hillsdale, NJ: Erlbaum.

Collins, A. M., and Loftus, E. F. (1975). A spreading-activation theory of semantic memory. *Psychological Review, 82,* 407–428.

Craik, F. I. M., and Lockhart, R. S. (1972). Levels of processing: A framework for memory research. *Journal of Verbal Learning and Verbal Behavior, 11,* 671–684.

Craik, F. I. M. and Tulving, E. (1975. Depth of processing and the retention of words in episodic memory. *Journal of Experimental Psychology: General, 104,* 268–294.

Ebbinghaus, H. (1913). *Memory.* (H. A. Ruger & C. E. Bussenius, Trans.). New York: Teachers College.

Fitts, P. M., and Posner, M. I. (1967). *Human performance.* Belmont, CA: Brooks/Cole.

Gagné, R. M. (1962). Military training and principles of learning. *American Psychologist, 17,* 83–91.

Gagné, R. M. (1972). Domains of learning. *Interchange, 3,* 1-8.

Gagné R. M. (1977). *The conditions of learning* (3rd ed.). New York: Holt, Rinehart & Winston.

Gates, A. I. (1917). Recitation as a factor in memorizing. *Archives of Psychology, 40,* 1–104.

Greeno, J. G. (1978a). Natures of problem-solving abilities. In W. K. Estes (Ed.), *Handbook of learning and cognitive processes: Vol. 5. Human information processing* (pp. 239–270). Hillsdale, NJ: Erlbaum.

Greeno, J. G. (1978b). A study of problem solving. In R. Glaser (Ed.), *Advances in instructional psychology* (Vol. 1, pp. 13–75). Hillsdale, NJ: Erlbaum.

Guthrie, E. R. (1935). *The psychology of learning.* New York: Harper & Row.

Hill, W. F. (1981). *Principles of learning: A handbook of applications.* Palo Alto, CA: Mayfield.

Hull, C. L. (1943). *Principles of behavior.* New York: Appleton-Century-Crofts.

Hulse, S. H. Dees, J. and Egeth, H. (1975). *The psychology of learning* (5th ed.). New York: McGraw-Hill.

Klatzky, R. L. (1980) *Human memory: Structures and processes* (2nd ed.). San Francisco: Freeman.

Langley, P., and Simon, H. A. (1981). The central role of learning in cognition. In J. R. Anderson (Ed.), *Cognitive skills and their acquisition* (pp. 361–380). Hillsdale, NJ: Erlbaum.

Larkin, J. H. (1980). Teaching problem solving in physics: The psychological laboratory and the practical classroom. In D. T. Tuma & F. Reif (Eds.), *Problem solving and education: Issues in teaching and research* (pp. 111–125). Hillsdale, NJ: Erlbaum.

McGeoch, J. A. (1932). Forgetting the law of disuse. *Psychological Review. 39*, 352–370.

McGuire, W. J. (1969). The nature of attitudes and attitude change. In G. Lindzey & E. Aronson (Eds.), *Handbook of social psychology* (2nd ed., Vol. 3, pp. 136–314). Reading, MA: Addison-Wesley.

Melton, A. W. (1963). Implications of short-term memory for a general theory of memory. *Journal of Verbal Learning and Verbal Behavior. 2*, 1–21.

Melton, A. W. (Ed.). (1964). *Categories of human learning.* New York: Academic Press.

Neves, D. M., and Anderson, J. R. (1981). Knowledge compilation: mechanisms for the automatization of cognitive skills. In J. R. Anderson (Ed.), *Cognitive skills and their acquisition* (pp. 57–84). Hillsdale, NJ: Erlbaum.

Newell, A. (1980). One final word. In D. T. Tuma & F. Reif (Eds.), *Problem solving and education* (pp. 175–189). Hillsdale, NJ: Erlbaum.

Newell, A., and Simon, H. A. (1972). *Human problem solving.* Englewood Cliffs, NJ: Prentice-Hall.

Postman, L. (1961). The present status of interference theory. In C. N. Cofer (Ed.), *Verbal learning and verbal behavior* (pp. 152–179). New York: McGraw-Hill.

Resnick, L. B., & Ford, W. W. (1981). *The psychology of mathematics for instruction.* Hillsdale, NJ: Erlbaum.

Robinson, E. S. (1932). *Association theory today.* New York: Appleton-Century.

Rohwer, W. D., Jr. (1970). Images and pictures in children's learning. *Psychological Bulletin, 73*, 393–403.

Rokeach, M. (1969). *Beliefs, attitudes and values.* San Francisco: Jossey-Bass.

Schank, R., and Abelson, R. (1977). *Scripts, plans, goals and understanding.* Hillsdale, NJ: Erlbaum.

Shiffrin, R. M. & Schneider, W. (1977). Controlled and automatic human information processing: II. Perceptual learning, automatic attending, and general theory. *Psychological Review. 84*, 127–190.

Singer, R. N. (1980). *Motor learning and human performance* (3rd ed.). New York: Macmillan.

Skinner, B. F. (1969). *Contingencies of reinforcement: A theoretical analysis.* New York: Appleton-Century-Crofts.

Smith, E. E., Shoben, E. J., and Rips. L. J. (1974). Structure and process in semantic memory: A featural model for semantic decision. *Psychological Review, 81*, 214–241.

Stein, N. L., and Trabasso, T. (1982). What's in a story: An approach to comprehension and instruction. In R. Glaser (Ed.), *Advances in instructional psychology* (Vol. 2, pp. 213–267). Hillsdale, NJ: Erlbaum.

Stevens, A. L., and Collins, A. (1982). Multiple conceptual models of a complex system. In R. E. Snow, P. A. Federico, and W. E. Montague (Eds.), *Aptitude, learning, and instruction: Vol. 2 Cognitive process analyses of learning and problem solving* (pp. 177–197). Hillsdale, NJ: Erlbaum.

Thorndike, E. L. (1898). Animal intelligence: An experimental study of the associative processes in animals. *Psychological Review, Monograph Supplement, 2*, 8.

Tolman, E. C. (1932). *Purposive behavior in animals and men.* New York: Appleton-Century.

Triandis, H. C. (1971). *Attitude and attitude change.* New York: Wiley.

Underwood, B. J. (1957). Interference and forgetting. *Psychological Review. 64,* 49–60.

Wickelgren, W. A. (1974). *How to solve problems.* San Francisco: Freeman.

College Student Outcomes Assessment: A Talent Development Perspective

MARYANN JACOBI, ALEXANDER ASTIN, AND FRANK AYALA, JR.

Outcome Taxonomies

This monograph offers a broad definition of student outcomes as "the wide range of phenomena that can be influenced by the educational experience." While such a definition has the advantage of allowing practitioners to interpret talent development assessments in the manner that best fits their needs, it leaves a number of questions unanswered. For example, what behaviors, cognitions, and attitudes is the educational program designed to enhance? Can we observe outcomes of college while the college experience is still unfolding (that is, while students are still enrolled), or must we wait until many years after graduation? Should outcomes be limited to the effects of the formal educational program, or should we also examine the often serendipitous results of informal experiences? Is it appropriate to limit our assessments to the planned or expected effects of a program, or should we also examine possible unintended "side effects"?

The authors' definition should also be viewed in light of whether outcomes assessment is an exercise in *description* or in *explanation*. Research on outcomes can attempt to establish causal relationships between the college environment and observed student outcomes, or it can merely document students' performance at particular points in time. By focusing on outcomes that can be influenced by the educational programs, the authors' definition clearly reflects a concern with the impact of the college environment on students.

In implementing a talent development philosophy and assessment program, faculty, staff, and managers must carefully consider the outcomes of most importance to the mission and goals of the institution. Efforts to identify appropriate outcome measures can be aided by a variety of outcome taxonomies. Perhaps the most important contribution of such taxonomies to implementation of a talent development approach is to support institutional dialogue about the outcomes of most importance to a college or university. From this perspective, taxonomies provide a menu from which researchers and practitioners may select the items of greatest importance to measure and track.

This chapter describes four different outcome taxonomies, each of which has been widely used in institutional planning and research. Three of them (Lenning, Bowen, and Astin) were developed from relatively global or broad perspectives, providing a comprehensive set of potential outcomes. The fourth was developed by faculty, institutional researchers, and administrators in response to the goals and mission of a particular institution, Alverno College. Because these taxonomies differ in content, organization, and breadth, they are best viewed as complementary rather than competing schemas.

Lenning

Lenning and associates (1977, 1980) present a highly refined and detailed taxonomy of outcomes. In traditional taxonomic style, they offer several major headings, each of which includes various levels and types of outcomes. Major categories of outcomes include, first, *economic outcomes*, including students' access to resources, accumulation of resources, production, and so forth. Economic resource outcomes emphasize the contribution of higher education to an individual's future income, earning ability, and productivity. A second category Lenning proposes is *human characteristics outcomes*. This somewhat generalized phrase subsumes such outcomes as aspirations, competence and skills, morale, personality, physical/physiological characteristics, social activities, and social status and recognition. The third category, *knowledge, technology, and art form functions*, includes those outcomes most directly linked to substantive elements of college education, such as general and specialized knowledge, research and scholarship products, and art works. *Resource and service provision outcomes*, the fourth category, includes the provision of facilities, events, and services. The final category comprises *aesthetic and cultural activities* as well as the organization and operation of the institution.

Lenning's typology, which was derived from a content analysis of the literature on outcomes, is most distinctive for its comprehensive detail. (In fact, his typology is not restricted only to student outcomes, and the last two categories described in the preceding paragraph are focused on the organizational or community level of analysis.) Lenning's approach is most congruent with a management perspective, as the typology delineates a range of outcomes that can serve as evaluation criteria and guide decision makers in allocating resources (Ewell 1983).

The broad range of outcomes Lenning describes may suggest to researchers that an outcomes assessment should include an equally broad range of dependent variables. While this approach may be appropriate under certain circumstances, the most useful assessments will be based on outcomes that have been carefully selected for their relevance to institutional goals and policy questions.

Bowen

Like Lenning, Bowen (1980) offers a taxonomic system that is based on a review and content analysis of the literature on student outcomes and includes outcomes at levels of analysis other than the individual student. In contrast to Lenning, however, Bowen ties his typology to goals that many institutions hold for their students. In fact, he offers a catalog of goals rather than outcomes and then uses this catalog to organize his review of the literature on student outcomes. This organizational system may be directly translated into research objectives, as the selection of dependent variables is clearly linked to institutional goals.

Bowen's five main categories are *cognitive learning, emotional and moral development, practical competence, direct satisfactions from college,* and the *avoidance of negative outcomes.* The content of Bowen's schema differs from Lenning's in several ways. First, Bowen includes a more detailed list of outcomes of practical competence, while Lenning includes more outcomes involving human characteristics. Second, Bowen emphasizes the avoidance of negative outcomes, which can add an additional dimension to assessments of outcome (similar to side effects in medical research). Third, Bowen includes students' satisfaction with college as a major classification of outcomes.

Astin

Like Bowen's, Astin's taxonomy (1974, 1977) is driven by a consideration of the goals of higher education, which includes faculty development and community services as well as student outcomes. (This discussion, however, is limited to student outcomes.) Astin's taxonomy is more complex than Lenning's and Bowen's in the sense that it includes three dimensions: type of outcome, type of data, and time. Further, Astin provides a taxonomic system for *measures* of student outcomes, while Lenning and Bowen classify outcome *variables*.

The type of outcome is divided into cognitive and affective:

> *Cognitive measures have to do with behavior that requires the use of high-order mental processes, such as reasoning and logic. . . . Noncognitive, or affective, measures have to do with the student's attitudes, values, self-concept, aspirations, and social and interpersonal relationships* (Astin 1974, p. 30).

Type of data refers to the manner in which each outcome is actually measured. "Psychological" measures reflect the internal states of individuals, while "behavioral" measures refer to their observable activities.

Astin's third dimension is time. Some outcomes of college are observable after a brief period of time and may be measurable while the individual is still a student. Others may not be observable or measurable for many years. For example, students' knowledge of current research findings within their major field is a short-term outcome that can be measured after several semesters or classes. In contrast, students' ability to effectively apply this knowledge in their chosen careers is a long-term outcome that cannot be assessed until after the student has held a career position for some time.

Compared to Lenning and Bowen, Astin provides less detail about specific student outcomes. Because Astin argues, however, that a comprehensive outcomes assessment requires all eight types of data (2 x 2 x 2), his three-way matrix can provide a basis for evaluating available outcome data. For example, one might discover that some institutions collect data almost exclusively within one or two cells of the matrix and thereby obtain an incomplete picture of student outcomes. Other schools might have data available from all cells but might require more depth and detail within a single cell or better integration across cells.

Mentkowski and Doherty

One distinguishing aspect of Mentkowski and Doherty's taxonomic system (1983) is that it was collaboratively developed by faculty and administrators at Alverno College as an integral element of their efforts to implement an "outcome-centered liberal arts program." The other taxonomies described here were developed as part of scholarly research rather than as part of institutional management and decision making.

In response to increasing concerns about institutional accountability and changing needs of students, Alverno College decided to implement an outcome-centered liberal arts program in 1973. The faculty was asked to identify broad educational goals and to suggest how those goals could be defined, assessed, and validated. Students' progress toward the goals was measured at several points, both during and after college.

Faculty identified eight outcomes for assessment that reflected their views about the goals of the liberal arts program: *communications, analysis, problem solving, valuing, social interaction, taking responsibility for the environment, involvement in the contemporary world,* and *aesthetic response.* This broad taxonomy of outcomes became the basis for student assessments and evaluations of educational effectiveness.

Unlike the taxonomies previously presented, the Alverno taxonomy was developed in concert with a reconceptualization of the institution's goals. Lenning's, Bowen's, and Astin's taxonomies, in contrast, were derived from an analysis of the literature on student outcomes. The Alverno outcomes, however, cluster heavily in Lenning's "human characteristics" category. They appear to be somewhat more dispersed across Bowen's categories, covering "cognitive learning," "emotional and moral development," and "practical competence." Viewed from Astin's perspective, the Alverno model includes both affective and cognitive outcomes, both behavioral and psychological data, and assessments conducted at several points in time.

The advantage of the Alverno taxonomy is that it is highly congruent with the goals of the institution. Because the taxonomy was developed internally, key decision makers perceived it as valid and relevant. As a result, program evaluations and outcomes assessments derived from the taxonomy have become integral aspects of institutional management. One political disadvantage of this taxonomy is that it is restricted to those outcomes viewed as most important by the community. Consequently, research based solely on these eight categories may overlook outcomes that are potentially important from alternative perspectives.

The following discussion emphasizes cognitive outcomes of postsecondary education. Cognitive outcomes are typically perceived as the most important college outcomes and most related to primary goals of the institution. A broad range of constituents and decision makers within the institution share a concern with students' cognitive development as a result of their college education. Therefore, cognitive outcome assessments are most likely to gain acceptance from institutional leaders. A second reason for the emphasis on cognitive outcomes is that those who argue for greater "accountability" in higher education typically have cognitive outcomes in mind.

The assessment of cognitive outcomes of college is a challenging task. The following sections consider in depth both the technical and political problems such projects may encounter and offer guidelines to the solution of such problems.

Assessing the Departmental Major

Bobby Fong

Study in the major field is the centerpiece of the baccalaureate. While educators rightly stress the importance of liberal learning, general competencies, and cocurricular experiences in fully fostering student maturation, the focal point of the college experience remains study in depth, guided most commonly by concentration requirements within an academic department. Given the importance of study in the major, it is surprising how few approaches exist that are appropriate for assessing the cumulative learning that takes place. Any discussion of commercially designed and locally devised instruments, such as the discussion included in this chapter, must consider the purposes and uses of assessment. The very way learning is evaluated is intertwined with a department's conception of its curriculum and expectations for its students.

The usual means of evaluating student achievement in the major are the grades earned in required and elective courses. Unfortunately, writes Chandler (1986), "department major programs characteristically emphasize the number of courses required for a major but usually provide little or no rational for the major and no compelling statement of the goals of the major" (p. 5). Students must take a specified number of courses from a large list but are provided with no sense of the particular knowledge and skill that a graduate in the field should posses. Beyond ensuring the quality of individual courses, a department must concern itself with the shape of total learning in the discipline, which may be too dependent on the electives that make up the bulk of work done in the department. The sum of courses taken in a major by a student should add up to something coherent and comprehensive, but that too often is more a matter of hope than of design. For the individual student, few institutions have procedures to determine the degree to which the courses taken actually coalesce into an organized body of knowledge and competencies. For an entire graduating class, there may be no means of guaranteeing that majors share a common core of understanding.

Context of Assessments

Objectives, Purposes, and Effects. Methods for assessing cumulative learning have two potential objectives: to gauge individual student achievement, or to measure the performance of majors as a group with regard to common learning. In turn, the results may serve any of three related but distinguishable purposes: to select individuals for postbaccalaureate study or work; to certify basic disciplinary competence of individuals or groups, in order to meet accountability standards of external agencies; or to provide information for program review and improvement. Some assessment methods are particularly well suited to a given objective and purpose; others can serve more the one purpose. It is important to be clear about what is desired in a particular assessment effort and to use methods appropriate to it. Inappropriate methods give an incomplete or even false picture of the teaching and learning in a major program.

It follows that the selection of an assessment method is always embedded in a departmental philosophy of pedagogy and learning, whether enunciated in statements of purpose or implicit in ongoing practice. Selection is based primarily on a method's direct effects: the ways in which its results will be interpreted and used by students, external agencies, the institutional administration, and the department itself. Results may affect enrollment, licensure, funding, hiring, and curriculum requirements and offerings. But a method also has backwash effects in that what and how a department assesses will influence the context, mode, and climate of classroom instruction and learning. The use of a particular approach to evaluation represents a formal declaration by a department about the materials it believes important for students to know, abilities it expects students to demonstrate, and practices it wants to encourage among instructors. Also, what is omitted from an assessment has consequences. Frederiksen (1984) notes, "If educational tests fail to represent the spectrum of knowledge and skills that ought to be taught, they may introduce bias against teaching important skills that are not measured" (p. 193). Choosing or devising an approach to evaluate cumulative achievement in the major demands attention to the objectives, purposes, and effects of the approach.

Expectations and Faculty Culture. Assessing a major program engages a faculty in the process of forging agreement on what the major means. Politically, this is where attempts to assess the major flounder. An electives-based curriculum in the major can maximize the freedom of faculty to move between the specializations of scholarship and the demands of the classroom. One teaches from the results of one's research. It also, however, encourages the proliferation of courses that constitute narrower and narrower slices of a discipline. Depth of study is achieved at the expense of breadth, and since students have only a limited number of courses to take in the major, expertise is achieved at the expense of comprehensiveness. The situation is exacerbated by current development in fields where the notion of "canons," or a tradition of established authorities and readings, is being challenged. The appropriateness of a text depends on audience, culture, and pedagogical aim. The very presumption that there can be an identifiable core of necessary knowledge for a major becomes the point of dispute. I do not impugn the importance of research specialization or the critique of canons, for both represent the means to more sophisticated understanding of fields of knowledge. At the same time, if the major is to remain a viable basis of organizing knowledge for pedagogical purposes, then departmental faculty must engage in discussing the structure and function of that organization. The major is a pedagogical schema for the transmission of knowledge and skills. That is why a department requires a certain number of courses in the major, a critical mass of achievement. As a pedagogical schema, the major represents what the members of the department believe to be the necessary and sufficient attainments of a baccalaureate graduate in the discipline.

I make this point at length because without a determination to define the rationale and content of the major, assessment cannot proceed. Validity in assessment depends on the correspondence between what is tested and the body of knowledge and skills deemed important to be assessed. If faculty are not able to enunciate what they seek in a graduate in the major, they will not be in a good position to determine the appropriateness of an instrument, since they cannot specify what they seek to measure.

The goals of the major can be described in a number of ways—a designation of content, an enumeration of proficiencies, a declaration that the culminating work of a student can be certifiable by acknowledged experts—but whether it is to measure individual student learning or the learning of an entire cohort, assessment presumes that a department will enunciate the meaning of the major. The agreement may be local rather than national, a reflection of the particular priorities and expertise of the individual department, and it will likely change over time. But assessment to measure student achievement needs a clear declaration of what faculty expect students to achieve.

A disciplinary field is defined by a common vocabulary of discourse, common concerns, and a common body of knowledge and techniques. Like natives of culture, disciplinary faculty normally do not think about how they are distinguishable from the foreigners seeking to learn the folkways. As conveyers of the academic culture of the major, however, faculty need to give thought to exactly this matter, and departmental assessments of the major become occasions for such consideration. Chandler (1986) writes, "As I recall my own teaching career, I believe that some of the most valuable investment of my time was in the long hours that my colleagues and I spent designing questions and exercises for final examinations in the introductory course and for the comprehensive departmental examination...Working together on those examinations compelled us to review the purposes and goals of particular courses and consider the rationale of the overall structure of the departmental curriculum. Furthermore, those conversations were extremely valuable for young members of the department who were still making the transition from graduate student to full-time teacher" (pp. 6–7).

Assessment of the major thus entails far more than the choice of an appropriate method. It requires consideration of objective, purpose, and effects, and it is preceeded and continually sustained by recurrent faculty discussion of the rationale and content of the major. The major and its assessment are expressions of the culture of the discipline, represented and maintained by the faculty. These contexts must be kept in mind if the ensuing discussion of particular assessment: is to have any connection with the essential contribution of assessment: the yielding of imformation to support and improve teaching and learning.

Commercially Designed Examinations

Pros and Cons. Commercially available examinations have the advantage of being field-tested. They also permit the scores of individuals to be compared against national norms. The costs of these tests are high, typically above $30 per exam; but, being scored by machine, they do not make additional demands on faculty. Finally, the use of standardized examinations for licensure, certification, and admission to graduate study accords them authority among faculty, since the success or failure of majors on such instruments reflects directly on preparation received in the major program.

There are also a number of drawbacks to commercially available assessment devices. National examinations, by definition, do not respond to local emphases. A commercial test may not reflect what a particular department is trying to do. Then there is the matter of the multiple choice format. Objective tests are a superior means of sampling knowledge and comprehension, because the number of questions posed in a given time can be greater than might be possible in essay formats. At the same time, as Frederiksen (1984), Elton (1982), and Rowntree (1977) have argued, such a format is ill suited to the examination of such higher order skills as analysis, synthesis, and evaluation, for which students should respond to open-ended situations that call on a range of appropriate strategies. Moreover, the associated skill of being able to express oneself in expository prose is given short shrift.

Beyond content and format limitations, there is a difficulty in using the results of such examinations. Scores can be reported for individuals and groups, and certain exams can break performance down to subject subscores. Nevertheless, without item analyses, which cannot be made available without retiring the questions in that education of the test, it is difficult to use the information to improve program instruction. Furthermore, most commercially prepared achievement tests are not designed to compare a student's performance to an absolute standard of knowledge or skill, but to the performance of others. Such selection-reference tests are intended to maximize individual differences for purposes of comparison, in contrast to criterion-referenced tests, which seek to determine how much of a body of knowledge one knows, or how skillful one is, according to some preset standard. Harris (1986) cautions, "The selection test approach works well when the purpose is to spread individuals over a continuum. But it is awkward, to say the least, when the purpose is to certify a level of competence" (p. 16).

A final concern with the use of commercial instruments is the discontinuity between faculty control over instruction and faculty participation in assessment. If scoring is done by machine, and if results are only minimally useful as an aid to improving instruction, then the numbers generated by such tests may serve the purposes of external accountability or selection for postbaccalaureate activity without ever involving faculty in questions of curriculum and learning.

Current Instruments. Preprofessional majors such as nursing and education have licensure and certification processes that include commercially prepared examinations. The cutoff point for passing is set by state or professional bodies, and while faculty may have some influence on content and standards, the assessment instruments are beyond the control of any particular local department. The immediate object and purpose is to evaluate individuals for postbaccalaureate employment, but pass rates of graduating classes provide a measure of an institution's performance in teaching the necessary knowledge and skills. The effect has been to encourage standardized curricular offerings.

The situation is different for the liberal arts and the sciences, where a major does not presume a particular vocational outcome. Here, curricular offerings differ from institution to institution, and responsibility rests on local faculty to assess for learning, using instruments appropriate to departmental emphases. Some departments have chosen to require that all prospective graduates take the GRE area examinations in the appropriate disciplines. These tests, however, were designed to show students' command of curricula commonly offered to prepare undergraduates for graduate study. There is a problem with validity in the use of tests constructed to predict success in graduate study as measures of learning by all students in a major. The selection-referenced basis of the test may not be a good indicator of basic competence in the field. Moreover, since most liberal arts graduates do not go on to postbaccalaureate study in their disciplines, curricula designed to propagate graduate study may serve most majors badly.

Both the College-Level Examination Program (CLEP) subject examinations and the ACT Proficiency Examination Program (PEP) traditionally have been used to assess proficiency for the purpose of awarding college credit in lieu of the student's taking a course. Interest has developed, however, in using such exams for outcomes assessment after the student has taken the appropriate course (examples are projects discussed in "College-Level Examination Program at 20 . . ., 1987). While this may be a legitimate use of the tests to measure learning within a course, "they are not designed to reflect the comprehensive proficiency expected of a graduating senior in a major field" (Harris, 1986, p. 22). An alternative—to administer the entire battery of such tests in a given discipline—would be time-consuming and expensive.

New Developments. Between course-specific examinations and tests to select candidates for graduate study, there is a gap that may be filled by the proposed major field achievement tests of the Educational Testing Service (ETS). The GRE area examinations are being revised to become measures of cumulative learning in the major. They will be offered in one- and two-hour formats. The shorter form will yield aggregate information on the group of test takers at a particular administration; the longer one will give individual scores as well. Subscore breakdowns will be extensive enough to indicate strengths and weaknesses in particular subjects, so as to aid in program improvement. Comparative norms will be available, both nationally and by institutional groupings selected by individual departments as peer institutions. The tests will become available in September of this year.

In addition, two other ETS pilot projects may have long-term benefits for assessing the major. The Item-Banking Workshop will be a series of seminars to train faculty in writing test questions for end-of-course assessment in specific disciplines. The items will be edited and classified by test development staff and then pooled in a computer bank, from which tests can be constructed by faculty for local use. If a battery of subjects in a discipline can eventually be represented in the bank, faculty will be able to construct local comprehensives with items already reviewed by professional staff. The Benchmark Performance Technique is another ETS project, which will have faculty prepare end-of-course assessments in specific disciplines, using non-multiple-choice formats. Assessment of quality will involve the development of benchmark criteria for competence. An example of this approach would be the specimen essays in writing evaluations that embody standards of excellence, adequacy, and failure. Over the long term, development of benchmark performance standards should help faculty develop criteria for judging senior projects and other demonstrations of higher learning that exceed the limits of multiple-choice tests.

Locally Devised Approaches

Pros and Cons. Currently, no commercial instrument is wholly appropriate for assessing the cumulative learning of all students in the major, and results from available commercial tests should be supplemented by existing measures, such as grades, and by locally devised instruments. Characteristically, the most successful and enduring local approaches have tended to eschew the multiple-choice format in favor of processes whereby the student can demonstrate ability to structure the paths to a solution, not simply select an answer from a list of possibilities. There are wrong answers and interesting wrong answers. The path by which a student assays a problem can be as revealing of mastery of the discipline as the particular answer obtained. Moreover, the emphasis in using such approaches as seniors projects or comprehensives shifts from probing for gaps in learning (as in multiple-choice examinations) to providing a range of options from which students choose topics or questions that exhibit their interests and learning to best advantage. Primary attention is focused on what students do know and can do.

For this chapter, I will describe five assessment methods: theses and projects, orals, comprehensives, portfolios, and external examiners. These methods have been used singly and in various combinations at particular institutions, but a common characteristic of all five is the centrality of faculty in planning, administering, and evaluating them and their results. Controlled by local faculty, these methods remain sensitive to local educational missions and interests. Furthermore, faculty are involved in both instruction and assessment, rather than having these efforts separated by use of a method external to the duties of the department. Feedback regarding student performance tends to be more immediate, and students' successes as well as their failures are more readily owned by faculty, since performance has been tested by an instrument of the department's own devising.

However, involvement in assessment also represents an additional demand on instructors' time and energy. The determination to do assessment bespeaks a concern to demonstrate the quality of teaching and learning, but the temptation exists to avoid the requisite demand on faculty resources, which may already be stretched thin. Yet easing the faculty role in assessment means attenuating the usefulness of the process for understanding and aiding program improvement. If assessment is to be done well, faculty must be at the center of the effort.

One final problem with locally controlled efforts is that they may not give results that are readily comparable across institutions. There must be some provision for gaining perspective on how the standards and expectations of the department compare against those of peer institutions; otherwise, a department's own view of its educational effectiveness may remain skewed and provincial. At the same time, the difficulties of coming up with easily comparable results may not be altogether undesirable: institutions are justifiably leery of having student scores on an instrument reported without consideration for educational mission, student preparation and interests, and program emphases. An open-admissions state university may not post scores that are as high as those of selective, private liberal arts college, but it would be grossly unfair to assume that the disparity necessarily results from differences in instructional effectiveness.

Theses and Projects. In-depth study may culminate in the opportunity for independent study as a capstone experience. Green (1987), writing of Bradford College, reports that all majors must complete a senior project. "The student is asked to pose a significant question and, with the aid of a

418   Assessment and Program Evaluation

faculty advisor, work that question through too a solution and produce a final project in the form of a research paper, manuscript, portfolio, exhibit, or performance. This task demands that the student apply and demonstrate the skills and knowledge acquired over four years. It serves also as evidence of the student's passage to the stage of independent learner and producer."

Theses and projects have been widely required of candidates for honors degrees, and less frequently demanded of all majors in a department. The approach encourages the individual student to pursue his or her own interests and exhibit a personal synthesis of field. Since each project is unique, this approach succeeds less well at revealing common learning for all major or inspiring comparable products. Indeed, since a project is usually an investigation of narrow aspects of the discipline, the results may show little evidence even of the individual's comprehensive learning.

Another concern is whether independent work is a suitable task for students not able or committed to do honors-level work. The prospect that completing a thesis or project, drawn out over most of the senior year, may determine whether one graduates can be fearsome for less accomplished students and frustrating to their advisors. Reed College, which also requires senior theses and projects, administers junior qualifying examinations, consisting of a research paper, an essay exam, a group of problems, an oral, or another activity, which a student must pass before proceeding to the thesis.

A final concern has to do with evaluation. Unless a project is assessed by faculty other than the adviser, it remains a species of course work, not an exercises in mastery that can be recognized by authorities not previously involved in the activity; both Reed and Bradford require that projects and theses be evaluated by other faculty.

Orals. In addition to the thesis, Reed requires a two-hour oral examination by a board consisting of the project advisor, representatives from the same academic division, and at least one faculty member from outside the division. The exam includes a presentation of the thesis or project and an extended question-and-answer session that relates the work to the larger context of the examinee's studies. Departmental faculty are especially interested in students' ability to present their disciplines to people outside their fields.

King College in Tennessee uses visiting scholars and knowledgeable members of the community to administer half-hour oral interviews to honors candidates in the major. An ancillary benefit of such encounters have been the offer of jobs or fellowships for graduate study. A current Association of American Colleges (AAC) project, "Assessing Learning in Academic Majors Using External Faculty Examiners," includes participating institutions experimenting with oral examinations by having faculty interview groups of students. One possible strategy is to present each group with a problem or set of topics ahead of time and allow students to fashion a presentation, to be followed by questions. The assumption is that free-ranging discussion between students and faculty can be a valuable indicator of students' mastery of the discourse and methods of a field. In addition, students have some control over the direction of discussion and can use the situation to exhibit strength. Specific knowledge can only be sampled, of course, and the open-endedness of discussion may preclude any probing for comprehensive knowledge. For the same reason, it would be difficult to use orals alone to test for common learning across the group. There is also the problem that less voluble or slower-witted students may suffer in comparison to others. Nevertheless, the use of oral presentations, interviews, and examinations has proved a useful way to assess learning, particularly when these techniques are paired with projects or theses that provide initial points of focus.

Comprehensives. The particular need to assess for common learning, in addition to examining the individualized learning exhibited by projects, theses, and orals, suggests the use of comprehensive examinations. The posing of a common set of questions or problems to the entire class of prospective graduates in a major both establishes expectations of essential learning and probes to see if such learning has been achieved. At some time, offering some range of choice among the questions allows students to pursue lines of inquiry that reflect the emphases of their individual elective programs. The British university comprehensive examination system, where students from different colleges sit for a common set of disciplinary exams, has long been a means of maintaining program quality and comparability across departments.

There is also the backwash of such exams on programs and curricula. Historically, comprehensive examinations were designed to evaluate student learning; but, as Resnick and Goulden (1987) have noted, "they had the auxiliary effect of directing attention to the departmental curriculum, and the way the student ha[d] been prepared. Many institutions introduced reading lists, tutorials, senior seminars, and other restructurings of the undergraduate program that were designed to aid the student's performance" (p. 6).

Essential to the process, however, is the commitment of the departmental faculty. Advising a senior project or thesis is an extension of independent study arrangements, with which most faculty are comfortable. Administering oral examinations demands more scheduling and preparation, but the work of evaluating the performance is done during the oral. By contrast, written comprehensives demand that faculty meet each year to create the examination and, after the administration, to read and grade the papers. It is a substantial investment of time, and the process of agreeing to questions and norming marks can be stressful. There must be the conviction that the benefits to student learning (mainly in the preparation for comps) and to enhanced program coherence will repay the labor.

Portfolios. For students, the value of projects, theses, orals, and comprehensives lies primarily in their preparation and research. Judgments of such work usually come toward the end of matriculation, and unless a student fails and must repeat the work, the marks and comments rendered by reviewers simply certify the performance, rather than correcting and suggesting with an eye to further learning in the program. By contrast, the value of a portfolio approach, in which students are required over several years to assemble pieces of work attesting to their mastery, is that there can be mechanisms built in for continuous assessment, while students can still benefit from faculty suggestions.

At Alverno College, the Arts and Humanities division has an arrangement whereby the student, with the assistance of a departmental advisor, begins assembling a portfolio from the time he or she begins study in an area of concentration. Over two or three years, the student selects exemplary papers (including those where disciplinary knowledge and skills have been brought to bear on courses outside the field), speech notes, videotapes, and other records of performances that attest to achievement in the subject. At the end of the junior year, the student writes at analytical essay remarking on how the portfolio represents certain disciplinary emphases and approach, relation to other areas of study, and areas of weakness to be remedied. A panel of faculty, including one faculty member from outside the division, reviews the essay and portfolio and, in a one-hour oral interview, probes for further learning and makes recommendations for additional study in the field.

The great advantage of this arrangement is that the student can still benefit from faculty feedback. Rather than offering a summary judgment, this process allows for continuous assessment from the advisor and the panel. Furthermore, the products for assessment are actually those produced in the course of study, not specimens generated solely to exhibit summative learning. It should be possible to chart growth as well as achievement. Like senior projects and theses, however, portfolios shed more light on individual learning than on common learning across a group. The process also calls for a good deal of coordination and scheduling, and it relies heavily on the advisor-student relationship. The advisor becomes the principal tutor. (One positive effect may be to rejuvenate a task that in many institutions consists only of signing a schedule card once a term.)

External Examiners. This means of assessment is actually a component to be used in conjunction with one or more of the first four. O'Neill (1983) writes, "There is a conflict of interest in the way in which American colleges and universities certify instruction. . . . Faculty members not only teach but in effect guarantee, first, that their teaching meets established standards in both content and quality and, second, that students have learned what faculty have taught. There is no external mechanism to verify the integrity of the baccalaureate degree" (p. 71).

One answer is to invite faculty from other institutions and knowledgeable outsiders to serve as panelists or reviewers for projects, orals, comprehensives, or portfolios. External examiners offer a way to certify learning, without being open to the charge of conflict of interest, since they can assess student achievement without having departmental or institutional stakes in the outcome. This arrangement, of course, is an integral part of the British comprehensive system.

The best-known example of an ongoing American external-examiner arrangement is at Swarthmore College. There, the designation of honors depends solely on performance in the senior year on a series of comprehensive examinations and oral interviews prepared and graded by external faculty examiners. Students undertake a series of seminars beginning in the junior year, and the terminal examinations are on the seminar topics, not on an entire discipline. Nevertheless, the coverage afforded by the entire series of examinations is substantial.

The AAC project, already mentioned, is based on the Swarthmore model. It experiments with the use of written comprehensives, or other exercises, and oral examinations administered by outside examiners. Eighteen institutions have been clustered in groups of three, according to characteristics of region, institutional size, and similarity of academic program offerings. Each cluster has designated three majors that its institutions will examine in common. Beginning this year, fifteen students graduating in a given major will be examined by faculty in that discipline from the other two institutions of the cluster. Results will be provided to students, and visiting examiners will report to the department and to the institutional officers to help them assess how the objectives of the major are being met.

The use of visiting examiners represents a means of establishing external accountability. It may also lead to some comparability between departmental programs, if sister institutions that exchange examiners also agree to use the same comprehensive examinations or other exercises. The logistics of scheduling, costs for travel, and remuneration are causes for concern, however. In the British system, there now exists a tradition that serving as an examiner is a part of a tutor's normal duties and that remuneration is nominal. This is not the case in America. Still, Swarthmore and other institutions that have used external examiners (see Fong, 1987) find that faculty and industry professionals are willing to serve at rates far below their usual fees, because of the opportunity to learn about other programs and enhance their own companies and departments. It represents an extension of service to the profession and the community, and it reflects a desire to work with peers across institutional boundaries to facilitate the education of the next generation of professionals and academics.

Conclusion

Assessing a major is no simple matter of choosing or devising a method. Indeed, as the preceding discussion suggests, there is not one test or approach that is sufficient by itself to serve all the objectives and purposes of assessment. A strong case can be made for a multidimensional strategy, in which instruments are complementary, the combination depending on the priorities of local faculty to shape curricula to meet goals for students. Assessment cannot be justified as an end in itself; it will be a sterile exercise unless its results contribute to the support and improvement of teaching and learning.

References

Chandler, J. W. "The College Perspective on Assessment." Paper presented at an invitational conference sponsored by the Educational Testing Service, New York City, October 25, 1986.

"College-Level Examination Program at 20: Leading the Way in Higher Education Assessment." *The College Board News* 1987, 15 (3), 4.

Elton, L. "Assessment for Learning." In D. Bligh (ed.), *Professionalism and Flexibility in Learning.* Surrey, England: Society for Research in Higher Education, 1982.

Fong, B. "The External Examiner Approach to Assessment." Paper commissioned for the Second National Conference on Assessment in Higher Education, sponsored by the American Association for Higher Education, Denver, Colo., June 14–17, 1987.

Frederiksen, N. "The Real Test Bias: Influences of Testing on Teaching and Learning." *American Psychologist,* 1984, 39 (3), 193–202.

Green, J. "Assessment at Bradford College." Unpublished memorandum, Bradford College, 1987.

Harris, J. "Assessing Outcomes in Higher Education." In C. Adelman (ed.), *Assessment in American Higher Education.* Washington, D.C.: U.S. Department of Education, 1986.

O'Neill, J. P. "Examinations and Quality Control." In J. R. Warren (ed.), *Meeting the New Demands for Standards.* New Directions for Higher Education, no. 43. San Francisco: Jossey-Bass, 1983.

Resnick, D. P., and Goulden, M. "Assessment, Curriculum and Expansion in American Higher Education: A Historical Perspective." Paper presented at the Second National Conference on Assessment in Higher Education, sponsored by the American Association for Higher Education, Denver, Colo., June 14–17, 1987.

Rowntree, D. *Assessing Students: How Shall We Know Them?* London: Harper & Row, 1977.

Assessing Critical Thinking Across the Curriculum

C. BLAINE CARPENTER, JAMES C. DOIG

What professor would deny the importance of enhancing students' critical thinking? Recent national reports and publications identify critical thinking as an essential ingredient of higher education. However, while skill in critical thinking is a needed outcome, there has been relatively little discussion of how to test and evaluate a student's capability to think critically. In this chapter we will review assessment procedures that can be used in the classroom and on the institutional level to measure critical thinking. Our emphasis is on techniques that can be used across the curriculum.

Defining the Skill

The first issue of assessment is knowing what will be measured. It is important, then, to begin with an appropriate conception of critical thinking. There are many choices here, and selecting an appropriate one should not be arbitrary. A definition of critical thinking should be clear and sufficiently detailed to guide the assessment process. While we do not discuss the various conceptions, we urge that the assessment process begin with a consideration of possible conceptions. There are good sources to consider (Beyer, 1987; Ennis, 1987; McPeck, 1981; Meyers, 1986; Sternberg, 1985; and Young, 1980). Ennis (1987) for example, defines critical thinking broadly, including many different skills. Examples of such skills include judging the credibility of source, deduction, induction, identifying stated and unstated assumptions, and identifying fallacy labels like *name calling, straw person,* and *non sequitur.* The process of agreeing on a conception of critical thinking can be time consuming, especially if a common definition is used in different disciplines. The quality of the assessment, through, depends on this important step.

Choosing an Approach to Assess Critical Thinking

There are several points to keep in mind in selecting or developing an approach to assess critical thinking. First, it should clearly describe the process, skills, or strategies to be assessed. Such descriptions should be complete enough to give a detailed idea of the nature of each aspect of critical thinking to be assessed, the procedures to be followed in the assessment, and criteria to judge evidence of critical thinking. A successful approach will state how the thinking processes, skills, or strategies work together and will identify the form or type of thinking that is to be assessed. Approaches also should be selected or developed with regard to student motivation and the environments in which students live (Sternberg, 1984). For instance, the ethnic, religious, or cultural values and outlooks of students may require that instruction and exercises in critical thinking program be designed to develop students' awareness of their environments. Finally, the faculty should clarify its assumptions relative to the prerequisite knowledge and skills that students need prior to engaging in college-level critical thinking.

Generally speaking, approaches to the assessment of critical thinking will rely either on standardized examinations or on locally developed, performance-based instruments. Descriptions and critiques of a number of approaches to assessing critical thinking are found in Segal, Chipman, and Glaser (1985). A discussion of developing complete verbal descriptions of processes, skills, and strategies can be found in Beyer (1987). Meyers (1986) suggests that visual models are often more helpful than verbal descriptions. Visual models taking the form of diagrams can range from one that concretely represents a tree, composed of circles coinciding with concepts used in thinking operations, to one that abstractly represents the steps in problem solving.

To summarize, an informed choice of an approach to assessing critical thinking can be made only after faculty have reached the explicit determinations mentioned above; that is, by asking and answering these questions: What do we think critical thinking is? How do the critical thinking skills, processes, and strategies work together, and what aspects or combinations of them do we wish to assess? What are our students like? What are their motivations, and what are their environments? What are our assumptions relative to the knowledge and abilities that students need prior to engaging in college-level critical thinking?

Standardized Examinations. These are several standardized tests that may be appropriate for assessing critical thinking skills. These exams are not specifically geared to the distinctiveness of institutional programs, and because they measure general conceptions of critical thinking, they will not assess more specific, institutionally defined skills of individual students. These tests have good reliability; national norms are usually also available. Both Ennis (1985a, 1985b) and Beyer (1987) summarize existing standardized tests of critical thinking. Following are brief descriptions of some of these tests.

Cornell Critical Thinking Test, Level 2. This test was developed by Robert H. Ennis and Jason Millman and is available from Midwest Publications (P.O. Box 448, Pacific Grove, CA 93950). It contains 52 items for advanced or gifted high school students, college students, and other adults. There are also sections on induction, deduction, observation, credibility, defining, and assumption identification.

New Jersey Test of Reasoning Skills. This test was developed by Virginia Shipman and is available from IAPC, Test Division (Montclair State College, Upper Montclair, NJ 07043). The exam includes 50 items, untimed, for grades four through college. It contains items testing syllogistic reasoning, contradictions, causal relationships, assumption identification, induction, good reasons, and other topics.

Watson-Glaser Critical Thinking Appraisal (Forms A and B). This test was developed by Goodwin Watson and Edward Glaser and is available from the Psychological Corporation (c/o Harcourt Brace Jovanovich, 7500 Old Oak Blvd., Cleveland, OH 44130). It contains 80 items on two forms, timed or untimed, for grades nine through adult, as well as sections on inference, assumption identification, deduction, conclusion logically following beyond a reasonable doubt (interpretation), and argument evaluation.

Ennis-Weir Critical Thinking Essay Test. This test was developed by Robert H. Ennis and Eric Weir. Like the Cornell test, this is published by Midwest Publications. It is aimed at grades seven through college. Students are given forty minutes in which to write a letter in response to a "letter to the editor" that posits a particular position. Students critique the thinking exhibited in the letter. The test measures getting to the point, seeing reasons and assumptions, stating one's point, offering some good reasons, seeing other possibilities, and responding appropriately (for example, avoiding irrelevance, circularity, and overgeneralization).

The Academic Profile. This instrument comes from the Educational Testing Service (College and University Programs, Princeton, NJ 08541-0001). In 1987 ETS piloted a new assessment service for general education. The Academic Profile is intended to measure four academic skills (college-level reading, college-level writing, critical thinking, and using mathematical data) in three major discipline groups (humanities, social sciences, and natural sciences). The profile is available in long or short forms and reports a separate score for each skill and discipline group, with a total score. Thus, The Academic Profile provides a general assessment of critical thinking.

Locally Developed Instruments. For faculty whose goals require them to develop their own performance-based instruments, two types of assessment of critical thinking outcomes are most common: (1) paper-and-pencil items specifically intended to test skills, processes, or strategies, and (2) observation of student behavior. The former is used in regularly assigned classroom tests and is recommended for assessment of critical thinking as part of a course or program. However, regarding paper-and-pencil tests, a distinction should be made between assessment of newly introduced thinking skills or processes and those previously taught and assessed. In the case of newly introduced skills, all items designed for assessment are best grouped in a special section of the test. Further, to adequately assess such a skill, it is not enough to ask students to use the skill; they should also be required to define it, identify an example of its use, use it several times, and explain how to use it. An advantage of this approach is that different levels of proficiency can be assessed. The first level is attained by students who are able to define the skill correctly and identify an example of its use. The second level is reached by students who use the skill successfully, and the third level involves the ability to explain the skill. When a skill previously taught and assessed is being reassessed, the initial level of proficiency can be assumed (Beyer, 1987).

Since thinking skills are seldom used in isolation, one should be prepared to assess more complex thinking operations performed by students. Items similar to those on the SAT are a possibility. A situation students are to think about can be presented in a short paragraph, followed by a series of multiple-choice questions, each requiring the student to employ a different thinking skill (Beyer, 1987). Items in standardized examinations can serve as examples for locally developed tests of critical thinking.

Essay tests also can be developed by faculty. The criteria used to evaluate answers should be stated explicitly before students attempt an exam and should be focused on the thinking skills being assessed, not on the knowledge or writing skills demonstrated. Various types of essay questions can be developed. For example, data can be presented in different ways (written, orally, audiovisually), and students can respond to questions in a specified number of paragraphs. The answers can be graded for one or a combination of skills. Students can be asked to explain the use of some selected aspect or aspects of thinking, and the audience can range from an instructor to a less well informed student. Students can also be given essay assignments on regular subject-matter topics and asked to attach their completed essays brief explanations of the thinking processes involved in their writing (Beyer, 1987).

Meyers (1986) details the characteristics of writing assignments that are effective for teaching critical thinking. Two of these characteristics also appear to be useful in designing assessment instruments. First, essay assignments should follow a stepwise development of critical thinking skills. Since students learn by practicing the component abilities of critical thinking, assignments should begin by requiring the use of simple cognitive skills (observing or organizing) and then move gradually in subsequent assignments to more complex skills, such as synthesizing and evaluating. A second characteristic of effective writing assignments is their relation to real problems or issues and students' experiences. For example, instead of asking students to write on the United States constitutional guarantee for free speech, the assignment might be: "your roommate is organizing a campus protest against his or her government professor, who is teaching the theories of Karl Marx. What can you say to your roommate in terms of the constitutional guarantee of free speech, as it relates to his or her protest?" A more accurate picture of students' abilities will result when students are asked to struggle with problems that they actually encounter. In addition to discussions of the above characteristics, Meyers presented helpful descriptions of five types of writing assignments for critical thinking, two examples being brief summaries and problem-solving exercises.

An additional paper-and-pencil method of assessment involves determining certain general forms or types of critical thinking (for example, problem solving and decision making) that employ a variety of skills or strategies in an integrated fashion. Since it is the general form of thinking that is to be assessed, and not the individual skills (which can vary with the context), this is accomplished with performance criteria specific to the general form of thinking.

Besides the paper-and-pencil methods, assessment can be achieved through observation of student behavior. Here, the emphasis is on what students do as they go about developing answers. Costa (1984) has listed observable behaviors that indicate effective thinking. These include persisting in a thinking task and applying alternative methods until a goal is reached; deliberately planning how to execute a thinking task by clarifying goals, identifying givens, and carefully selecting methods and data; giving and requesting evidence and reasoning in support of assertions; and using and insisting on precise language. Beyer (1987) offers examples of forms for reporting observations.

Another possible approach for observing student behavior is based on the paired problem-solving techniques described by Whimbey (1977). Students work in pairs on thinking tasks, and while one student does the actual work of thinking and reports aloud what he or she is thinking, the other student keeps track of the process to ensure that no steps are skipped and no rules violated. A handbook by Whimbey and Lochhead (1982) incorporates this approach. Paired problem solving is utilized in the Integrated Science Laboratory at Alverno College (Loacker and others, 1984).

Some Institutional Examples

A number of institutions have made great strides recently in assessing critical thinking. In this section we describe six of them.

Northeast Missouri State University. This institution attempts to assess critical thinking as one aspect of the "intellectual value added" by classroom instruction. The key components of the assessment are nationally standardized tests administered to all students near the close of the liberal arts portion of their studies, and exams given during the semester prior to graduation. The tests given near the end of the student's liberal arts studies can be of two types. Since nearly all students have taken ACT tests prior to enrollment, half of each sophomore class is given an ACT retest to determine individual and cohort learning growth in four areas: English, mathematics, social science, and natural science. The other half of any sophomore class will have taken the ACT-COMP during the second semester of the freshman year and is retested with ACT-COMP toward the end of the sophomore year to determine individual and cohort learning growth in six liberal learning skill areas, one of which, problem solving, is related to critical thinking. Also, any of the items in the ACT-COMP require the use of thinking skills that some believe are part of critical thinking (analysis, application, and synthesis) (Smith, 1986, pp. 290–291).

University of Tennessee. This institution also administers the ACT-COMP, in this case to freshmen and seniors, to assess learning growth in the six areas, including problem solving. The ACT-COMP data on students' skills in solving problems, communicating, and clarifying values, in conjunction with performance on comprehensive exams in major fields, have led faculty to make changes in structure of courses, number of written assignments, and opportunities for students to apply their knowledge and skills through problem solving, term projects, field trips, and internships. Test results and faculty discussion of them have led to the development of more specific objectives for student learning and a better relation of course content to objectives (Banta and Fisher, 1986).

Alverno College. Critical thinking for Alverno is closely linked to the skill of analysis, although it also includes evaluating ideas, identifying problems, considering values, and finding creative approaches to problems. Analysis is also seen as varying with different kinds of knowledge. Hence, Alverno focuses attention on developing critical thinking skills within particular knowledge contexts (for example, the skills of the scientific method and literary analysis). Alverno and the other institutions yet to be described focus assessment on student learning in relation to precisely stated outcomes developed both for courses within programs and for programs as a whole. Further, assessment occurs within each course and becomes a means of determining how well each student is developing a critical thinking outcome. This type of assessment involves eliciting several samples of a student's critical thinking, judging those samples by publicly stated criteria, and providing feedback to the student about his or her performance.

Analysis is defined as the ability to examine the parts of a whole in order to gain better understanding of the parts and the whole. In each discipline, students learn about and analyze something unique to that discipline. An integrative approach has been developed that emphasizes the systematic "breaking open" of the ability, a sequential learning process that involves observing, inferring, making relationships, and integrating within a disciplinary context. Also emphasized is the translating of the "generic" ability into the concrete and specific terms of individual disciplines. Recognition of how different disciplines involve analysis is found by translating the basic analytical sequence into the language of each discipline. For example, one asks what it means to analyze, observe, infer, make relationships, and integrate the knowledge base in biology, history, literature, philosophy, and so on. These analytical abilities are also tied to the student's communication competence.

Alverno's assessment of an ability is initially broken into levels, ranging from what students should be able to do when entering college to what is expected of them by the time they graduate. In the case of analysis and the connected ability of communication, six levels are distinguished, with the first four general and required of all students and the last two specialized and appropriate to the student's major. These six levels are observing accurately, making justifiable inferences, relating parts or elements in patterns, integrating patterns into coherent systems, comparing and testing frameworks in a discipline, and integrating frameworks into a professional synthesis.

These levels identify standards by which student performance can be assessed and offer expectations for student development. The levels are not viewed as a rigid sequence of steps, but simply as a logical approach to assessing (and teaching) the analytical process.

Alverno College breaks each level into a more specific set of criteria. These criteria are developed with the various discipline faculties and then synthesized into generic criteria. For example, at level 4 ("Integrates patterns into coherent systems") they are described in this way:

- Out of an explicit framework, articulates and distinguishes between observations, inferences, and relationships in work under investigation

- Shows awareness of assumptions, implications, and limitations of any framework used

- Identifies principle(s) that organize(s) or account(s) for ways that elements relate in the work

- Articulates how above principle(s) provide(s) meaning in the work under investigation

- Shows awareness of how the affective and intuitive relate to the cognitive in one's own analyzing process and abilities.

The final element identified for each discipline and course is the performance that the student is expected to undertake; that is, an assignment is geared to a specific disciplinary task on a determined level, which includes specification of audience, purpose, and other circumstances aiding the student to write coherently about a given situation (Loacker and others, 1984).

Alverno College, through its emphasis across the curriculum on the generic ability of analysis, with assessment occurring on several levels, focuses the student's attention on one cognitive process at a time. For example, Alverno's level 4 appears similar to what others call synthesis (Bloom, 1956; Beyer, 1987). By implication, then analysis or critical thinking appears as the integration of a variety of cognitive skills.

King's College. At King's College, all students are required to take a critical thinking course. In this course, students are expected to develop and defend reasonable beliefs, to assess the beliefs of others, and to develop rational self-awareness (Hammerbacher, 1987). Initial instruction in this course if focused on aspects of thinking (for example, argumentation and rhetorical use of language), and subsequent assessment is focused on the use of these various aspects in a variety of knowledge contexts across the curriculum. Assessment measures for the critical thinking course are well defined: a pretest to assess entry-level competence; three tests of the student's knowledge of the content and processes appropriate to the course competencies; frequent quizzes and textbook exercises; two major writing assignments, one critical analysis and evaluation of an extended argument, and the other an argumentative essay on a controversial topic; and a posttest (usually the same as the pretest).

Unlike Alverno, King's College has not specified criteria for a variety of levels of competence in the use of critical thinking. Instead, a list of criteria has been developed, from which faculty select items appropriate to the particular degree of complexity of critical thinking to be assessed. Accordingly, the student:

- Demonstrates recall and understanding of the pivotal concepts of inductive and deductive reasoning

- Identifies an argument and distinguishes support from conclusion

- Identifies such problems as ambiguity, vagueness, and emotionally loaded language

- Identifies crucial fallacies in arguments

- Summarizes and reconstructs an argument contained in an extended prose passage

- Draws appropriate inferences from given data

- Recognizes the hidden assumptions and the implied premises and conclusions of an argument

- Distinguishes subarguments from the main argument in a prose passage

- Separates a problem into discrete units and sets forth evidence in separate, meaningful categories

- Uses the results of appropriate research (library, expert opinion, survey, poll, experiment) in the analysis, construction, and evaluation of arguments

- Identifies and explains the reasoning process applied to various disciplines and demonstrates that process by constructing a strong argument in one of those fields, preferably his or her own major

- Recognizes and performs the basic functions of deductive and inductive reasoning

- Chooses and defends an appropriate course of action from among a number of possible alternatives

- Relates an argument to broader issues and concerns

- Evaluates the acceptability of premises, their relevance to a conclusion, and the adequacy of their support of that conclusion.

The use of skills inherent in such cognitive processes as observing, clarifying, and evaluating is implicitly and, in some cases, explicitly expected of the students as they complete their assigned tasks. Thus, despite differences in terminology and procedure, it appears that both King's College and Alverno use assessment to develop similar abilities in their students.

Clayton State College. Like King's College, Clayton State has chosen to develop a course focused on teaching students the basics of critical thinking. This initial course focuses on instruction in the cognitive process skills—for example, observing, analyzing, and evaluating—and on students' use of combinations of these skills in a variety of knowledge contexts.

Assessment at Clayton State College is similar to that at Alverno College and King's College. Several examples of a student's critical thinking are judged according to publicly stated criteria, and feedback is provided to students. With this form of assessment as its goal, the college has defined critical thinking as information or knowledge gathering and reasoning characterized by careful and continual thought. The college also envisions the process of critical thinking in terms of continuum. One extreme is characterized by a contemplative approach, and the other by a highly structured approach. Although thinking may occur at any point along this imaginary "thinking continuum," the program involves the assessment of student performance at only two points. One point, thinking characterized by a highly structured and formulaic approach, is termed *problem solving decision making,* where the emphasis is on a product (that is, a solution or a decision). At the other extreme of the continuum is inquiry, a more contemplative, less structured approach that results in informed judgment. In any particular exercise of critical thinking, the student uses a combination of the cognitive process skills. The combination is determined by the purpose of the exercise, the material or subject matter of the exercise, and the appropriate form or type of critical thinking. Thus, Clayton State's assessments are different from those of Alverno and King's College in that emphasis is placed on assessment of the use of the cognitive process skills in two different types of applications, inquiry and problem solving/decision making.

For each of these two forms of critical thinking, criteria have been developed, and each form has four performance ratings. This arrangement enables an assessor to provide feedback to students on their levels of abilities. Clayton's criterion 1 for problem solving/decision making is shown in Exhibit 1; criterion 2 for inquiry is shown in Exhibit 2 (Clayton State College, 1985).

Exhibit 1. Criterion 1, Problem Solving/Decision Making, Clayton State College

Problem Identification
The student identifies the problem. This includes:
   a. Gathering information about the problem
   b. Identifying what needs to be solved and why
   c. Identifying constraints that must be addressed in a solution

Performance Ratings
   Excellent: The student's work comprehensively includes all key aspects of the criterion (a-c) that apply.
   Satisfactory: The student's work includes all key aspects of the criterion (a-c) that apply, but with some minor omissions and/or errors in the development of problem identification.
   Needs Improvement: The student's work includes all key aspects of the criterion (a-c) that apply, with some major omissions and/or errors in the development of problem identification. However, there is an indication that the student has general comprehension of what needs to be solved.

Unsatisfactory: The student's work omits one or more key aspects of the criterion (a-c) that apply. These omissions would make an accurate identification of the problem highly unlikely.

Exhibit 2. Criterion 2, Inquiry, Clayton State College

Information Identification
The student identifies relevant information about the work(s), object(s), and /or situation(s) under consideration. This involves:
a.   Identifying or recognizing significant and relevant information
b.   Distinguishing important and relevant from less important and irrelevant information
c.   Including information of appropriate depth and scope

Performance ratings
   Excellent: The student's work comprehensively includes all key aspects of the criterion (a-c) that apply.
   Satisfactory: The student's work includes all key aspects of the criterion (a-c) that apply, but with some minor omissions and/or errors in the development of information identification.
   Needs Improvement: The student's work includes all key aspects of the criterion (a-c) that apply, with some major omissions and/or errors in the development of information identification. However, there is an indication that the student has a general comprehension of the information needed for the inquiry.
   Unsatisfactory: The student's work omits one or more key aspects of the criterion (a-c) that apply. these omissions would make a comprehensive identification of relevant information unlikely.

As noted, initial instruction deals with the cognitive process skills and is provided by a separate course emphasizing the procedures to follow when using these skills. Beginning in the fall of 1988, every other course in the curriculum will build on the foundation provided by the critical thinking course through instruction in and assessment of either inquiry or problem solving/decision making, or both.
   Xavier University of Louisiana. At Xavier, two summer sessions are offered in critical thinking. One, called SOAR (Stress On Analysis Reasoning), is offered as preparation for students intending to major in the natural sciences. In this session, problem-solving skills are developed and practiced on exercises taken from such tests as the SAT and the ACT. Reading passages with accompanying questions are given to the student. The problem-solving steps are explained and then, in small groups, students work toward answering the questions. In subsequent science courses during the freshman and sophomore years, students continue the development of their problem-solving skills. At this level, students practice on these questions from such tests as the GRE and medical and dental school admission test. Small groups composed of both SOAR alumni and other students work to develop one set of answers to the problem-solving questions.
   An additional facet of Xavier's instruction in analytical reasoning in science is the reversal of the usual "lecture, then lab" format of science instruction. In each segment of a science course, students work first in the laboratory. Using the scientific method of discovery, students begin with a situation, recognize a problem, decide on a procedure for solving the problem, gather data, hypothesize, and test for verification.
   Xavier emphasizes both verbal and problem-solving skills, both in SOAR and in freshman and sophomore mathematics and science courses. There are weekly requirements for and testing of the student's growth in general and scientific vocabulary. Spokesmen for Xavier emphasize that problem-solving abilities are of little use if students cannot read scientific texts.
   In the second of the summer sessions, EXCEL, Xavier attempts to prepare students intending to major in the humanities and social sciences. Three hours are set aside in the morning for instruction

and exercises aiming at the development of four skills: the abilities to create and vary perspective (that is, look at a problem from all sides), recognize assumptions and constraints, formulate and test hypotheses, and recognize the value assumptions inherent in data. These morning periods concentrate on the use of these abilities in philosophy, history, English, argumentation/debate, and sociology. In the afternoon, another three-hour period continues the use of these skills, first in answering test questions measuring verbal and quantitative skills, and then in writing. The thinking skills developed in EXCEL have not yet been systematically reinforced in subsequent college courses.

Both of these summer sessions, described as resembling honors courses, enroll students accepted for college-level work. The positive results of these summer sessions have been increases in student retention rates and SAT scores. Surveys also indicate increased student understanding and appreciation of the skills learned in these seminars (Kleinhaus, Carmichael, and Beattie, personal communication, 1987).

Conclusion

The individual and institutional approaches described in this chapter all serve the goal of improving the critical thinking of students. However, all of them may not be relevant to a particular institution's or faculty member's purpose in teaching and assessing critical thinking. Some common features emerge, though, that can guide practice in this area. First, an assessment to determine students' abilities in critical thinking can be administered upon entrance into the course or program, as a baseline for teaching and assessment. Next, separate courses emphasizing cognitive process skills can be offered to provide initial instruction and systematic assessment of critical thinking. Then, later assessments can be administered to certify that students have maintained or improved their critical thinking abilities during their programs of study. A graduation assessment may also be appropriate. Finally, faculty development workshops to ensure campuswide understanding of an agreement on the institution's view of critical thinking are helpful as faculty integrate the assessment of critical thinking into courses across the curriculum.

References

Banta, T. W., and Fisher, H. S. "Assessing Outcomes: The Real Value-Added Is in the Process." *Proceedings from the Conference on Legislative Action and Assessment: Reason and Reality.* Fairfax, Va.: George Mason University, 1986.

Beyer, B. K. *Practical Strategies for the Teaching of Thinking.* Boston: Allyn & Bacon, 1987.

Bloom, B. S. (ed.). *Taxonomy of Educational Objectives: The Classification of Educational Goals.* Vol. 1. *Cognitive Domain.* New York: McKay, 1956.

Clayton State College. *Critical Thinking Outcome Council.* Morrow, Ga.: Clayton State College, 1985.

Costa, A. L. "Thinking: How Do We Know Students Are Getting Better at It?" Roeper Review, 1984, 6, 197–198.

Ennis, R. H. "Goals for a Critical Thinking Curriculum." In A. L. Costa (ed.), *Developing Minds: A Resource Book for Teaching Thinking.* Alexandria, Va.: Association for Supervision and Curriculum Development, 1985a.

Ennis, R. H. "Tests That Could Be Called Critical Thinking Tests." In A. L. Costa (ed.), *Developing Minds: A Resource Book for Teaching Thinking.* Alexandria, Va.: Association for Supervision and Curriculum Development, 1985b.

Ennis, R. H. "Critical Thinking Testing and Evaluation: Status, Issues, Needs." Paper presented at the 1986 annual meeting of the American Educational Research Association, San Francisco, April 1, 1986.

Ennis, R. H. "A Taxonomy of Critical Thinking Dispositions and Abilities." In J. B. Baron and R. J. Sternberg (eds.), *Teaching for Thinking*. New York: Freeman, 1987.

Hammerbacher, G. H. "Critical Thinking Assessment Criteria." Unpublished manuscript, King's College, 1987.

Loacker, G., Cromwell, L., Fey, J., and Rutherford, D. *Analysis and Communication at Alverno: An Approach to Critical Thinking*. Milwaukee, Wisc.: Alverno Productions, 1984.

McPeck, J. E. *Critical Thinking and Education*. Oxford, England: Martin Robertson, 1981.

Meyers, C. *Teaching Students to Think Critically: A Guide for Faculty in All Disciplines*. San Francisco: Jossey-Bass, 1986.

Segal, J. W., Chipman, S. F., and Glaser, R. (eds.), *Thinking and Learning Skills*. Vol. 1. *Relating Instruction to Research*. Hillsdale, N.J.: Erlbaum, 1985.

Smith, T. B. "The Uses of Assessment for Decision Making: A Primer about Northeast Missouri State University's Value-Added Program." *Proceedings from the Conference on Legislative Action and Assessment: Reason and Reality*. Fairfax, Va.: George Mason University, 1986.

Sternberg, R. J. "How Can We Teach Intelligence?" *Educational Leadership*, 1984, *48*, 38–48.

Sternberg, R. J. *Critical Thinking: Its Nature, Measurement, and Improvement*. In F. R. Link (ed.), *Essays of Intellect*. Alexandria, Va.: Association for Supervision and Curriculum Development, 1985.

Whimbey, A. "Teaching Sequential Thought: The Cognitive Skills Approach." *Phi Delta Kappan*, 1977, *59*, 255–259.

Whimbey, A., and Lochhead, J. *Problem Solving and Comprehension*. (3rd ed.) Philadelphia: The Franklin Press, 1982.

Young, R. E. (ed.). *Fostering Critical Thinking*. New Directions for Teaching and Learning, No. 3. San Francisco: Jossey-Bass, 1980.

Evaluating Competence for Professional Practice

William McGaghie

... Several definitions are needed here. A *profession*, according to *Webster's New Collegiate Dictionary,* is "a calling requiring specialized knowledge and often long and intensive academic preparation," and a *calling* is "a strong inner impulse toward a particular course of action, esp. when accompanied by conviction of divine influence." Pious overtones are evident here as well as in another definition of profession, "the act of taking the vows of a religious community." A profession, clearly, is not just a job or an artifact of chance. It is one's primary life's work, involving concrete knowledge and skill components joined with ineffable qualities of personal character, behavior, and spirit. The learning and practicing of a profession require large investments of one's time, effort, education, and ego.

Ideas about evaluating an individual's *competence for professional practice* are embodied in the AERA-APA-NCME *Standards for Educational and Psychological Testing* (1985, p. 63): "For licensure or certification [credentialing] the focus of test standards is on levels of *knowledge and skills* necessary to assure the public that a person is competent to practice" (emphasis added). Note that this statement does not include assessment of one's personal qualities, life-style, or private interests.

Assessment refers to the measuring instruments and procedures used to obtain data about an individual's competence for professional practice. *Evaluation* extends assessment by imposing policies (for example, education requirements) and standards (for example, a minimum passing score) on assessment methods. The policies and standards are expressions of prevailing values about basic requirements for competent professional practice.

These four terms—profession, competence for practice, assessment, and evaluation—coalesce to form the theme of this chapter. The theme can be expressed as two questions: How shall we go about assessing, evaluating, and credentialing the fitness of individuals for autonomous professional practice? How do we know that our motives and methods are right?

Three more thoughts need expression. First, competence evaluation always involves certification by a professional association or agency (for example, American Guild of Organists, 1988). However, professions under government regulation, such as veterinary medicine, also require licensure. Second, competence evaluation may or may not occur at the end of formal training. In medicine, most states grant a license for unsupervised practice during a physician's first of at least three years of postgraduate education, after Part III of the National Board Comprehensive Examinations is passed. Third, forms of professional credentialing vary widely. All it takes to become a university professor is an advanced degree, a good reputation, and a job offer. Sometimes, degree requirements are waived. This is very different from obtaining a military commission, becoming ordained, making the final cut for a National Basketball Association team, or getting a part in a Broadway play after an audition.

433

The title of professional may be obtained formally or informally, by competitive examination or competitive performance, for a lifelong career or for as long as one's body holds up (for example, ballerinas). Credentialing approaches are matched to the unique requirements of each profession. . . .

Central Ideas

Professional competence evaluation requires thoughtful attention to several key ideas. One idea concerns how professionals perform at the beginning of their careers and throughout the career continuum. A second idea concerns the nature of professional competence, including the skills, knowledge, and personal qualities that require evaluation and, by inference, those that can be ignored. The third idea is whether competence is a lasting trait or if judgment about one's competence are shaped by variables involving practice setting, time and other conditions. Finally, evaluators need to consider whether the competence of professional persons can be judged independently of their ability to achieve desired outcomes with clients, patients, or others who receive service.

Evaluation Continuum

The literature on professional competence evaluation tends to focus on evaluations for credentials that are made at the conclusion of professional school and the beginning of practice (Shimberg, 1983). This is shortsighted because evaluation and certification of an individual's competence for professional practice is rarely a "one-shot" event. Competence evaluation takes place throughout professional life, although with much variation in format and in what is at stake for an individual's career.

An illustration of a continuum of competence evaluation for one of the learned professions—medicine—is presented in Figure 10.1. This example shows that professional competence evaluation is sequential, beginning very early in a physician's career. It indicates that significant evaluations occur before and after the four years of undergraduate medical education. Evaluation addresses not only the outcomes that result from periods of formal education but also the screening and admission tests that grant access to more advanced medical training. Norcini and Shea (this volume) discuss the role of evaluation for recertification and relicensure, another location on the professional career continuum.

Stevens (1983) makes a similar case about the sequential character of competence evaluation in the legal profession. This is echoed throughout the chapter contributions to Hunt, Hinkle, and Maloney (1990). Evaluation of an individual's competence for professional practice is frequently a career-long enterprise.

Criterion Problem

What are the features of an individual's knowledge, skill, and personal qualities that need to be evaluated and approved before a credential is granted? What are the boundaries of professional practice that define limits for evaluation? Test developers wonder about the breadth and organization of content and skill domains from which content is sampled to prepare questions, checklist items, interview schedules, practical problems, and other materials (Millman and Greene, 1989).

This is the knotty and persistent criterion problem that for decades has vexed scholars of professional competence evaluation (Menges, 1975; Hunt, Hinkle, and Malony, 1990) and scholars in other fields, including personality measurement (Wiggins, 1973). The problem is vexing because, as noted in AERA-APA-NCME (1985, p. 64), "People who take licensure or certification tests . . . are seeking to be deemed qualified for a broad field, rather than for a specific job. This distinction has important implications for the content to be covered in licensing or certification tests." Wiggins

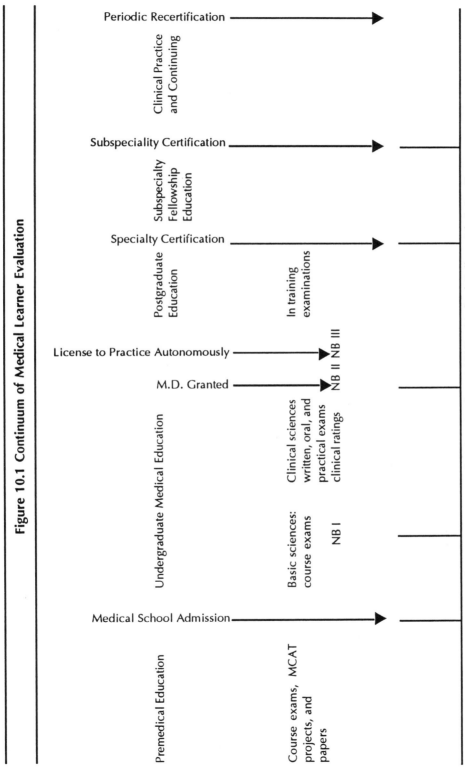

Figure 10.1 Continuum of Medical Learner Evaluation

Periodic Recertification

Clinical Practice and Continuing

Subspeciality Certification

Subspecialty Fellowship Education

Specialty Certification

Postgraduate Education

In training examinations

License to Practice Autonomously

M.D. Granted

NB II   NB III

Undergraduate Medical Education

Clinical sciences written, oral, and practical exams clinical ratings

Basic sciences: course exams

NB I

Medical School Admission

Premedical Education

Course exams, MCAT projects, and papers

Note: NB = National Board Comprehensive Part I, II, and III Examinations; MCAT = Medical College Admission Test,
Source: McGaghie, 1986, p. 131. Reprinted with permission.

(1973, p. 39) further clarifies the criterion problem: "The 'problem' resides in the considerable discrepancy that typically exists between our intuitive standards of what criteria of performance should entail and the measures that are currently employed for evaluating such criteria."

The criterion problem has theoretical and practical features. Theoretical matters surface whenever professional practice or education addresses problems that do not have straightforward, algorithmic, one-best-answer solutions. This is the realm of professional judgment, temperament, insight, and style, approaching what Wagner and Sternberg (1986) call "tacit knowledge." Tacit knowledge is neither visible nor tangible, cannot be evaluated using multiple-choice questions, yet is the touchstone of competent professional practice. Descriptive statements about knowledge and skill requirements for professional practice that fail to acknowledge its tacit, qualitative features are incomplete. Professionals are adaptive, can identify and frame issues that laypersons do not even recognize, understand problems in depth, and work fast. Eisner's (1991) approach to evaluation, which places much reliance on "connoisseurship," is probably the only way to evaluate the tacit knowledge of professionals.

In practice, of course, competence evaluations for most professions do not include assessments beyond probes of knowledge, and sometimes practical skill. This is because most of today's assessment technology is limited to measurement methods that only permit right or wrong answers to specific questions keyed to test blueprints covering professional knowledge. The domain of professional practice for an airline pilot, rabbi, or social worker encompasses much more than the knowledge base of each profession. However, until evaluation practices grow to embrace a broader conception of professional work, and assessment methods that have more than one-best-answer items, competence evaluations will remain a narrow scope.

Thorndike (1949), Wiggins (1973), and Menges (1975) separate immediate, intermediate, and ultimate criteria. Immediate criteria are bits of knowledge and skilled behavior needed to reach a short-run goal like passing a test, or achieving a high grade point average during the first year of professional school. Intermediate criteria go beyond acquired knowledge and skill to include one's ability to complete a required program of study, interact with clients tactfully, and preserve confidentiality. Ultimate criteria refer to value judgments about one's technical skill, professional manner, or character and life-style: being a good doctor, teacher, salesman, or funeral director. These are behaviors very distant in time and quality from those measured at the point of assessment for credential. To illustrate, one needs to pass a written test to become a licensed mortician. But Shakespeare reminds us that an undertaker's graveside manner is different from his or her fund of knowledge: "HAMLET: Hath this fellow no feeling of his business, that he sings at gravemaking? HORATIO: Custom hath made it in him a property of easiness" (*Hamlet*, act 5, scene 1, lines 65–67).

The criterion problem will not go away. It will persist because what professionals think and understand and how they act is far more complicated than what today's assessment technology can probe. Competence evaluations cover a small fraction of the real domain of practice for nearly all professions.

Trait Versus State Approaches

Is a professional's competence in practice a stable, enduring trait or a variable that changes with time, practice setting, client or patient characteristics, or phase of service or treatment? Is the attribution of competence to a professional person something permanent, or does it change due to location, service requirements, time available, and whether or not a crisis exists?

Research in several fields, including psychotherapy, medicine, and military combat, indicates that professional competence is not a general trait (Shaw and Dobson, 1988; Stillman and others, 1986; Shavelson, Mayberry, Li, and Webb, 1990). Instead, an individual's professional effectiveness is governed by the content of severity of clients' or patients' needs, the amount of professional preparation time, client or patient difficulty, and chance. In short, professional effectiveness is frequently case or situation specific, at least as assessed by current measurement technologies. Shavelson, Mayberry, Li, and Webb (1990, p. 129) state about military performance that "the major source of measurement error in job performance measurements is the heterogeneity of tasks that comprise the job."

Most evaluations of competence for professional practice assume that professional fitness is stable and does not change. A passing score on a test of acquired knowledge is an acceptable datum for establishing that a professional person is effective and safe, despite evidence that a much broader behavioral sample is required (Sternberg and Wagner, 1986). Valid evaluation of professional competence stems from performance assessment against a wide variety of practical problems and situations rather than just tests of what one knows (Engel, Wigton, LaDuca, and Blacklow, 1990).

Can Competence Be Evaluated Independently of Outcomes?

A key issue in professional personnel evaluation is whether individuals' competence can be evaluated separately from their effectiveness with clients, patients, or other recipients of service. Today's competence evaluations, chiefly tests of acquired knowledge, assume that there is a link between standardized test performance and behavior in practice. However, a metanalysis of thirty-five studies that assessed the link between performance in education settings and performance in professional practice did not find a strong correlation. Teaching, engineering, business, nursing, medicine, the military, and civil service were the professions covered in the metanalysis. The author of the report concluded that "the overall variance accounted for makes grades or tests nearly useless in predicting occupational effectiveness and satisfaction" (Samson, Graue, Weinstein, and Walberg, 1984, p. 320).

Several professions have adopted more lifelike evaluation approaches to tighten the link between behavior evaluated on competence tests and behavior needed to practice. In medicine, objective structured clinical examinations (Petrusa and others, 1991) and other practical examination formats (Barrows, Williams, and Moy, 1987) are growing in popularity due to their realism and congruence with what doctors actually do. Medical accreditation bodies are beginning to tighten standards to force education institutions to move testing in this direction (Langsley, 1991). An analogous technique in business is the assessment center (Gangler, Rosenthal, Thornton, and Bentson, 1987), chiefly used to evaluate middle and top managers. The military, of course, also has a long history of using assessment centers (Tziner and Dolan, 1982) and other practical examination formats for personnel evaluation (Shavelson, Mayberry, Li, and Webb, 1990; Webb, Shavelson, Kim, and Chen, 1989).

These examination formats are, of course, only approximations of the real world of patient care, managerial savvy, and combat effectiveness. In actual practice, professionals encounter such a wide variety of clients, settings, and unforeseen pressures that no approach to competence evaluation can completely capture professional work. For example, psychotherapy research has shown that due to variation among patients in terms of motivation and responsiveness to treatment, it would be unfair to judge therapists solely by patient improvement (Schaffer, 1983; Shaw and Dobson, 1988). A similar situation exists for treatment professionals who work with alcohol-dependent persons. Here, base rates for patient relapse are often 50 percent within one year (Marlatt, 1985). An individual therapist's competence can only be judged in this context, recognizing that for many patients backsliding is an inevitable phase in recovery.

Can competence be evaluated independently of outcomes? An honest answer is maybe, because today's evaluations for professional certification and licensure are distant approximations of actual practice. Results from competence assessments need to be interpreted and used with an understanding of the limits (not failure) of current assessment technologies.

Technical Problems

Research and writing about professional competence evaluation tends to dwell on technical problems in personnel evaluation because most authors are education evaluators or psychometricians. The current technical state of the art for the assessment and evaluation of professionals is embodied in the AERA-APA-NCME (1985) standards and their sequels (for example, Linn, 1989). Occasionally, such minimum standards for evaluation are amplified to suit the specific needs of a specific profession. For example, candidates for the Roman Catholic priesthood not only must submit to education evaluations that meet minimum technical standards, they must also "commit themselves to lives of service through the vows of obedience, poverty, and chastity" (Hall, 1990, p. 191).

Technical requirements for evaluations of professional competency typically focus on the twin concerns of reliability and validity. Historically, *test* reliability has been the minimum technical requirement for measures of professional fitness. This is because high test reliabilities are easy to achieve through item analysis and by increasing test length (Feldt and Brennan, 1989). Recent applications of generalizability theory extend classical approaches to reliability estimation for test scores (Shavelson, Mayberry, Li, and Webb, 1990; van der Vleuten and Swanson, 1990; Webb, Shavelson, Kim, and Chen, 1989). This approach permits estimation of the dependability of assessment results across various contextual factors, including occasions, test forms, and different administrators or observers. Generalizability theory is gaining popularity as the cutting edge among approaches to reliability estimation for education assessment (Shavelson and Webb, 1991).

Approaches to test validation are also undergoing transformation. It is now widely acknowledged that validity is an inherent property not of education measurements but rather of the way in which measurements are developed, used, and their results interpreted in specific contexts. Customary descriptions of content, criterion-related, and construct validity are now held insufficient (Messick, 1989). Newer and richer approaches to validation of education measurements attend to such factors as their consequences, fairness, transfer and generalizability, cognitive complexity, content quality, content coverage, meaningfulness, and cost efficiency (Linn, Baker, and Dunbar, 1991).

Measurement Methods in Competence Evaluation

Measures of professional competence, especially for the purpose of credentialing, have historically involved assessments of acquired knowledge and observations of professional behavior. More recent assessments include the use of open-ended problems and various types of simulations of professional practice.

Knowledge Assessment. Measures of professional knowledge acquisition have a long-established historical precedent. Paper-and-pencil knowledge assessments, using essay and multiple-choice formats, date to the early twentieth century (Levine, 1976). Oral examinations were used earlier. Such evaluations reflect an emphasis on educational efficiency and presumed objectivity that still exists in the 1990s. Measures of acquired knowledge are a well-established tradition in professional competence evaluation, especially in the health-related fields (Langsley, 1991).

The advantages of using knowledge measurements are straightforward. Then are relatively simple to create, can be administered and scored with great efficiency, and are suitable for use with large groups of candidates. However, knowledge measurements also have limits. They can only tap one's existing fund of knowledge, not how professional work is actually done in terms of focus or quality, or how knowledge is acquired or organized. Knowledge assessments enumerate sins of commission, that is, total number of questions correct and incorrect. They rarely probe for sins of omission, that is, "What would you do if . . . ?"

Observation of Professional Behavior. Direct and indirect observations of professional behavior are widely used as a part of competence evaluation plans in many professions. Direct observations are made under conditions of actual work performance, frequently with supervision. Examples include in-flight training, judgments about a young surgeon's skill at suturing, and evaluation by a jury of a vocalist's performance. Direct observations are often guided by a checklist or structured rating scale that specifies key evaluation criteria. Checklists yield nominal data about the evaluation criteria (for example, medical maneuver done or not done). Rating scales, by contrast, provide ordinal or interval data that express judges' views about the quality of professional performance (for example, high, average, or low skill at conducting a client interview). Careful attention to checklist or rating scale development and calibration is a key step in the use of direct observation as a facet of professional competence evaluation. Stiggins (1987) provides practical advice about the creation and use of these instruments.

A common pitfall in the use of direct observation for professional personnel evaluation is the lack of interrater agreement (Linn, Baker, and Dunbar, 1991; Liston, Yager, and Strauss, 1981; Shaw and Dobson, 1988). This happens when two or more evaluators observe the same professional activity yet disagree either about what was seen or about the quality of a professional performance. Since an independent gold standard or benchmark for evaluating professional competence frequently does not exist, evaluators rely on consensus among judges as the best available option. Problems arise when consensus is not achieved, even for such public skills as conducting a psychotherapeutic interview (Liston, Yager, and Strauss, 1981; Shaw and Dobson, 1988). Moreover, data from legal circles clearly show that the reliability of eyewitness testimony, of which direct observation of professional behavior is a special case, is highly suspect (Loftus and Schneider, 1987). Eyewitness testimony yields suspicious data unless the conditions of observation are managed tightly and evaluators are specifically prepared for the task.

Rater training is the single best way to boost the interrater reliability of professional performance observations. Research data support this generalization. Rater training under controlled laboratory conditions significantly increases judgment accuracy, in contrast with untrained controls (Thornton and Zorich, 1980). Field studies reinforce this conclusion. Rater training in the context of managerial evaluations in business settings (Pulakos, 1986) and in evaluations of the fitness of military personnel (Shavelson, Mayberry, Li, and Webb, 1990; Webb, Shavelson, Kim, and Chen, 1989) clearly demonstrates its utility in improving data quality.

Numerous anecdotal reports also address the importance of selecting, training, and regularly calibrating professional persons who judge consumer products, animals for work and show, world-class athletic competition, and beauty contests. Descriptive reports give detailed accounts about the training and experience needed to qualify as a U.S. Department of Agriculture meat inspector (Miller, 1958), or as a judge of farm and show horses (Daniels, 1987), men's Olympic competition (International Gymnastics Federation, 1989), or the Miss America Pageant (Goldman, 1990). These reports show that evaluations of hamburger, horseflesh, horizontal bar, and female chutzpah are not left to chance. This is in stark contrast with other fields such as clinical medicine where faculty who rate and judge medical students and residents are rarely prepared for the task (Herbers and others, 1989).

Indirect observations about professional behavior of trainees is another source of evaluation data. Indirect observations are notes for the record drawn from general impressions, comments about critical incidents, and global ratings about an individual's technical skill, character, or reliability that are made on occasions remote from the pressures of the practice setting. Examples include post hoc ratings of medical residents for submission to a specialty board and letters of recommendation for graduate study or employment. Indirect observations are subject to bias and distortion for many reasons, especially the fallible memories of evaluators who presumably render fair and honest judgments. Medical evaluators, in particular, have raised doubts about the utility of indirect observations for any meaningful purpose. Herbers and others (1989, p. 202) conclude from a rigorous education study that even under moderately controlled conditions, "Faculty internists vary markedly in their observations of a resident and document little." This circumstance has led physician Richard Friedman (1983) to call the act of interpreting deans' letters about medical students seeking residency training a "fantasyland," suggesting they are no more informative than a Ouija board.

New Assessment Formats. Several new approaches to the evaluation of competence among professional persons are growing in popularity. This is in response to widespread sentiment that current methods of competence evaluation—chiefly, tests of acquired knowledge—are far too narrow to capture the richness of professional practice. Linn, Baker, and Dunbar (1991) have discovered the need for more complex, performance-based assessments, with special reference to validation criteria. Two categories of these assessments are now being used as major parts of the credentialing schemes for several learned professions. The categories are open-ended problems and simulations.

Open-ended problems present candidates with cases or situations that are not defined completely. The initial task for each candidate is to frame and define the boundaries and elements of a problem. Later, the candidate must figure out a strategy to reduce the problem to a sequential series of tasks; rank the task series in order of priority; exercise judgment in developing and evaluating alternatives and proposing practical solutions; communicate effectively with clients, patients, or customers; and keep cool under pressure. The task of responding to such ill- or partially-defined problems is similar to what real professionals do everyday.

Despite their realism and face validity, open-ended problems give professional evaluators fits because they cannot accommodate the algorithmic, one-best-answer approach to scoring. Just as there is frequently no one best way to approach practical problems in professional life, evaluation problems need to leave room for a variety of scoring systems. This means that judges must act as "connoisseurs," to paraphrase Eisner (1991). The selection of training of judges for high-stakes evaluation take on added importance when their role as connoisseurs is acknowledged.

One professional association that has pioneered the large-scale use of open-ended problems and qualitative (yet very rigorous) judgment of candidate responses is the Canadian Institute of Chartered Accountants (1991), through use of its Uniform Final Examination (UFE) (McGaghie, 1991b). Validation research is under way to evaluate the inferences drawn from UFE data about the competence of accountants in practice.

Architecture is another profession that employs open-ended problems as a feature of its national certification program. The problems are embedded within the National Council of Architect Registration Boards site design subtest. Candidate responses to the evaluation problems, which call for creation of prototype architectural site design, are scored by panels of expert jurors. The jurors judge proposed site designs according to the presence or absence of various design features such as landscape contours and the spatial arrangement of a cluster of buildings. While the judgments are intuitive, research has shown that they are reliable. Work is now under way to computerize the scoring of the site design problems by capturing jurors' implicit judgment policies (Bejar, 1991).

The use of simulations of job performance has grown in popularity as a means of evaluating professional practice. Simulations are popular because they can mimic the problems and conditions that professionals encounter, from routine to crisis. Simulations vary in fidelity, from highly realistic devices used to train and evaluate commercial and military pilots to written patient management problems used in the health professions. Variation in the fidelity of simulations is linked to their utility for professional personnel evaluations. A growing body of data, chiefly from the health professions, indicates that low-fidelity written and computer-based simulations are inappropriate for competence evaluation (Jones, Gerrity, and Earp, 1990; Swanson, Norcini, and Grosso, 1987). Low-fidelity simulations remain a controversial issue and more validation research is needed about their utility for personnel evaluation.

High-fidelity simulations, by contrast, are being used with great success for competence evaluation in many professions. These are devices (for example, flight simulators), highly trained people (for example, standardized patients), and environments (for example, assessment centers for business and industry) that place competence evaluation candidates in extremely lifelike professional situations. Problems that vary in difficulty and urgency are presented to candidates, whose responses and nonresponses are recorded and judged. Descriptions of high-fidelity simulations used for personnel evaluation in several professions have been published. They include commercial aviation (Holahan, 1991), management (Thornton and Cleveland, 1990), and clinical medicine (Barrows, Williams, and Moy, 1987; van der Vleuten and Swanson, 1990).

One of the most ambitious uses of high-fidelity simulations for professional training and evaluation exists in the nuclear power industry. Power plant operators must be certified by industry and licensed by the U.S. Nuclear Regulatory Commission. In addition, the power plant simulators used for training and personnel evaluation must also be certified before use and recertified annually. The simulators are site specific. There is no presumption that training, certification, and licensure obtained for one power plant can be generalized to another nuclear power facility (American Nuclear Society, 1985).

Nuclear power plant simulators are required to have minimum capabilities. "The response of the simulator resulting from operator action, no operator action, improper operator action, automatic plant controls, and inherent operating characteristics shall be realistic to the extent that within the limits of the performance criteria the operator shall not observe a difference between the response of the simulator control room instrumentation and the reference plant" (American Nuclear Society, 1985, p. 2). The simulator performance criteria are complicated. They include steady-state operations, transient operations such as start-up and minor malfunctions and alarms, and major disasters. Given the potential consequences of real-life nuclear power plant malfunctions, it is reassuring that competence evaluations of plant operators and plant simulators are done with great rigor.

Unresolved Problems

Despite the advances that are being made using open-ended problems and performance simulations, professional competence evaluation faces a persistent set of unresolved problems. These problems are not unique to professional credentialing. They are noteworthy, however, because they define an agenda for thought and research in professional education.

Base rates or pretest probabilities of success should receive careful attention when professionals receive credentials to practice. Following admission to professional education, if attrition rate is very low (as in the case of U.S. medical schools), the use of *any* method of personnel evaluation may result in more wrong decisions about candidates than will no evaluation at all. The reason is that no method of personnel evaluation is flawless. The use of assessments that have imperfect reliabilities under circumstances where base rates of success are very high increases the odds that evaluators will make false-negative decisions about candidates.

Algina (1978) made this argument, cast in formal Bayesian terms, fifteen years ago. However, few programs of professional certification or licensure have taken his advance into account when making decisions about candidate credentialing.

Standard setting, which is most often expressed as a minimum passing score on an achievement test, is a problem that defies simple solutions. Many prominent education researchers have addressed this question, including Jaeger (1989) and Millman (1989). These authors conclude that while all approaches to setting education standards are arbitrary, they need not be capricious. Systematic and thoughtful approaches are superior to haphazard standard-setting methods. This is especially important when candidates undergo competence evaluation after one or more failures, increasing the likelihood of false-positive decisions (Millman, 1989).

Fitzpatrick (1989) presents a reminder that decisions about minimum passing standards on all evaluations are not made in a black box. There are, instead, many social and political factors that affect judgments about how well the minimally competent candidate should perform on professional assessments. Evaluators in all professional fields should take heed of social pressures when decisions about passing standards are made.

Rules of evidence are rarely established for the purpose of evaluating the competence of professional persons. Such rules would set inclusion and exclusion criteria about the admissibility of data when the fitness of candidates is judged. What are good data for the decision problem at hand? Are they numbers such as quantitative test scores or grade point averages? Conversely, are good data words in the form of qualitative expressions like a letter of recommendation?

Rules of evidence are commonly used in legal proceedings. One of a trial judge's chief responsibilities is to rule on the admissibility of evidence into the formal record. The purpose, of course, is to prevent information derived from bias, heresay, or privileged communication from affecting the jury's verdict (*Federal Rules of Evidence for United States Courts and Magistrates*, 1989). No such formal rules exist about the admissibility of evidence for professional competence evaluation.

Experts, even in the same profession, disagree about the utility of different types of evidence in reaching competence decisions about candidates. Data revered by some professionals are shunned by others. For example, some theologians, including John Westerhoff (McGaghie, 1991a), dismiss outright the objective, quantitative data used as primary evidence in the Readiness for Ministry Project of the Association of Theological Schools of the United States and Canada (Schuller, Strommen, and Brekke, 1980). This research project was undertaken to define the qualities needed for effective practice in the Christian ministry.

Westerhoff's logic is simple. Because the research data are secular, they have no meaning for the certification of professional ministries. Westerhoff says that numbers simply will not work here. On grounds of eschatology, real predictive validity cannot be quantified.

The issue of objectivity versus subjectivity stems directly from the rules-of-evidence question. Thoughtful persons readily acknowledge that assessment of many key features of professional competence must be subjective. They defy quantification. For example, regarding the education and certification of psychotherapists, Shaw and Dobson (1988, p.667) assert, "Although the definition of learning objectives is a necessary part of pedagogy, competency evaluations are often subjective, global, and dichotomous (that is, pass/fail)."

The real problem here is not recognition of the value of subjective data for professional competence evaluation. Instead, the problem concerns which subjective data to consider and how to fold such information into decision making in a fair and unbiased manner. Maybe this problem cannot be solved. There are, however, numerous opportunities for research, writing, and spirited argument on this topic for professional education in general and personnel evaluation in particular.

Summary

Earlier it was noted that four terms—profession, competence for practice, assessment, and evaluation—coalesce to form the theme of this chapter. The current portrait of evaluation of competence for professional practice has been painted deliberately with a broad brush. This is to argue that the psychometric details that usually dominate discussion about competence evaluation need to be understood in social, educational, and historical context. Glass (1978, p. 237) had it right when he wrote, "A common experience of wishful thinking is to base a grand scheme on a fundamental, unsolved problem." One hopes that fundamental, unsolved problems will receive more attention as the practical affairs of professional competence evaluation continue. . . .

Implications for Practice and Research

This chapter raises a number of implications about the practice of professional competence evaluation and about research on the subject. Some implications are obvious, others are subtle. What follows are short lists of suggestions that derive from this work.

Implications for Practice

First, organizations that accredit programs of professional education should insist that methods of learner evaluation closely match what professionals do in the practice setting. Several professions, including commercial aviation, nuclear power plant operators, and accountants in Canada, already use evaluation procedures that simulate professional practice. In medicine, the Liaison Committee on Medical Education of the American Medical Association revised its medical school accreditation standards in 1991. These standards now specify that "institutions must develop a system of assessment which assures that students have acquired and can demonstrate on direct observation the core clinical skills and behaviors needed in subsequent medical training" (Liaison Committee on Medical Education, 1991, p. 14). Policy statements like this need to be prepared and implemented by other professional accreditation bodies.

Second, those responsible for professional competence evaluation should give increased attention to assessments of individuals for the purpose of admission to professional school. This is especially the case for professions like medicine with low school attrition rates. Assessments made prior to professional school admission are an integral feature of competence evaluation to the extent that nearly everyone who is admitted eventually graduates and is credentialed to practice.

Third, more attention should be devoted to personal, qualitative variables that are crucial to professional practice: tact, reliability, honesty, confidentiality, humor, judgment, to name a few. Granted, these qualities are very difficult to judge systematically and without bias, thus fairly. There is, however, widespread agreement that professionals should be evaluated against such criteria, probably using the elements of Eisner's (1991) connoisseurship model. Bold steps should be taken in this direction.

Fourth, serious work should begin on the preparation of individuals to be evaluators of professional practice. The professional community can no longer presume that possession of an advanced degree warrants an individual's evaluation skill. This is especially true for medicine, where the evaluation situation is scandalous, and other health professions. At minimum, preparation would involve training faculty members to be raters of skilled performance and accurate interpreters of assessment data.

Fifth, an individual's professional competence should be reported and judged as a profile of skills, acquired knowledge, dispositions, and other achievements. Such a profile might look like a Minnesota Multiphasic Personality Inventory report, although the scales would be completely different. Competence evaluations must move beyond reports of cognitive test scores as the sole or primary source of assessment data. One's competence profile, perhaps maintained by a board or agency, could be updated and extended at planned career milestones.

Sixth, use of assessment centers should be expanded to professions beyond business, commercial aviation, and the military. Some progress has been made in using the assessment center approach for the comprehensive evaluation of competence in medicine (Vu and others, 1992). The method has also been proposed as a key feature of national certification system for elementary and secondary school teachers (National Board for Professional Teaching Standards, 1991). Other professions should weigh the benefits (and costs) of using the assessment center approach to competence evaluation.

Seventh, competence evaluation should become an integral feature of continuing education in the professions. There is no reason why continuing education programs should focus exclusively on instruction with almost no attention to assessment.

Implications for Research

First, a sustained program of validation research should begin to shed light on assessment methods used in profession competence evaluation. Rich and new suggestions about approaches to validation research made by Linn, Baker, and Dunbar (1991) and by Messick (1989) should be heeded. More studies using the multitrait-multimethod matrix (Forsythe, McGaghie, and Friedman, 1986) are needed to better understand the relative contributions of professional traits versus measurement methods when competence evaluations are done.

Second, one part of a validation research program should address the persistent criterion problem in professional competence evaluation. This line of research would aim to better define domains of professional practice and rules for sampling content that form the basis of competence assessments. Content inclusion and exclusion rules should be considered along with new ways to generalize an individual's performance across domains of practice. Attention to the criterion problem would also encourage studies on the linkage of the immediate criteria that are commonly measured to the more elusive intermediate and ultimate criteria that represent professional practice (Menges, 1975; Wiggins, 1973).

Third, longitudinal research is needed to better understand competence evaluations that are made at different stages on the professional career continuum. Such studies would involve variables assessed prior to and during professional school admission, throughout professional education, and at planned career intervals. By following cohorts of individuals in a variety of professions, research would clarify the cascaded inferences that are involved in attributing competence to professional people at different career stages.

Fourth, studies need to be done on approaches to scoring and judging responses to ill-defined professional problems, especially when the problems have more than one right answer. Bejar's (1991) work provides a point of departure in architecture, and the methods used by the Canadian Institute of Chartered Accountants (1991) to score its UFE provide a model from business. This research will probably lead advocates of objective scoring methods into partnership with colleagues who endorse Eisner's (1991) connoisseurship model of evaluation.

Fifth, on a broader scale, more research and writing should be encouraged on the sociology of professions. This scholarship is obscure to most educational evaluators and students of professional education. Sociological analyses in the manner of Abbott (1988), Berlant (1975), Derber, Schwartz, and Magrass (1990), Freidson (1970, 1986), and Moskos (1970) bear directly on the work and interests of professional educators. Topics such as the division of professional labor, power and authority relations, methods of credentialing, school accreditation, and the social context of professional education have been studied by sociologists. Educators can be enriched from a comprehension of this research.

Developing and Implementing a Process for the Review of Nonacademic Units

MARILYN K. BROWN

Review of academic departments is routine in most institutions of higher education. Few colleges and universities regularly review nonacademic units. A major research university has recently developed a process for the systematic review of nonacademic units. This paper outlines the steps taken in the development and implementation of the process: (1) a review of the literature on organizational effectiveness, (2) a survey of peer institutions, (3) the development of guidelines for the review of nonacademic units, and (4) the implementation of the process in several campus units.

"Evaluation" and "assessment" are certainly not uncommon words in the vocabulary of higher education. This familiarity with evaluation is in large part the result of the need of institutions of higher education to be accountable. Those colleges and universities that are state supported and accountable to the public through state officials, usually a board which oversees higher education in their state. Private institutions are no less accountable to their benefactors. All institutions have a responsibility to their students and their students' parents, if they're paying the bills. The federal government holds institutions accountable if they receive federal research grants or student-aid funds.

Most frequently the emphasis of accountability, and thus evaluation, is on the quality of the instructional program. How well are academic programs performing their functions of instruction, research, and service? Today many, if not most, institutions of higher education systematically assess their academic programs (Barak, 1982).

This is not the case with units that support the instructional enterprise, however. Academic-support units usually are not subjected to formal evaluation. Operations such as admissions, registration, computing, purchasing, personnel, resident life, and institutional research, to name a few—all so important to the accomplishment of a college's goals—are usually "left alone" unless someone in authority perceives a serious problem. Internal, and where appropriate, state auditors might review a nonacademic unit's operations to be certain the unit is conforming to institutional and/or state regulations and policies, but rarely does anyone formally assess the unit's performance in relation to its goals and the expectations of those the unit serves.

To correct this oversight, the University of Maryland at College Park (UMCP) is undertaking a formal systematic program of evaluation of nonacademic units. The impetus for such evaluation comes from a Campus Senate proposition adopted 17 years ago. Proposition XII of the "Proposals on Academic Reorganization to the College Park Senate of the University of Maryland" (August 1971) called for the development of recommendations for the regular review of academic and administrative units. In 1973, the Campus Senate approved "Procedures for the Review of the

Performance of the Academic Units and Their Administrators on the College Park Campus of the University of Maryland." Since then, these procedures have been refined and implemented. Indeed, the academic unit-review process is well established at UMCP.

The Senate never acted on the development of guidelines for the evaluation of nonacademic units. Determined "to increase the efficiency and effectiveness of campus administration," Chancellor John B. Slaughter, in his statement of "Goals, Objectives, and Initiatives," called for the development of "policies and procedures in each campus division for conducting periodic evaluations of all administrative units" (*Making a Difference: Goals, Objectives and Initiatives*, p. 5).

The effort to implement the systematic review of nonacademic units at UMCP began early in 1986 with the exploration of activities that might be under way in the area of evaluation at other major universities. A survey of public members of the Association of American Universities revealed that most universities conduct regular reviews of their academic units and many formally evaluate administrators. Only the University of Illinois at Urbana-Champaign has established a formal process for the evaluation of nonacademic units. The Illinois Board of Higher Education has mandated that such evaluation occur. A description of the process in place at the University of Illinois can be found in the Winter, 1987 edition of *New Directions for Institutional Research* (Wilson, 1987).

In spring 1986, UMCP's Chancellor appointed the Academic-Support Unit Review Guidelines Committee (henceforth referred to as the Committee) comprising representatives of the four vice chancellors, chaired by the Executive Assistant to the Chancellor, with staff support provided by the Director of Institutional Studies. The Committee was charged with developing a systematic process which would address the question of how effectively campus nonacademic units are operating, including an assessment of the extent to which they are contributing to the achievement of the goals, objectives, and initiatives established for the Campus.

The literature was reviewed to find a model for assessing the effectiveness of organizational subunits. While the literature is rich with ideas, theorists do not agree on what organizational effectiveness means or how to measure it (Cameron and Whetton, 1983). In fact many theorists themselves agree with John P. Campbell when he says that "*the* meaning of organizational effectiveness is not a truth that is buried somewhere waiting to be discovered if only our concept and data collection methods were good enough" (1977, p. 15). Goodman and Pennings (1977) elaborate on the "preliminary state" of the theoretical literature on organizational effectiveness. They point out that there is no agreed-upon definition of organizational effectiveness; there are differing views of the nature of organizations, which in one way or another determine the conceptual definition of effectiveness; knowledge about the construct validity of organizational effectiveness is lacking; the domain of effectiveness has not been specified; there has not been an examination of the effect of using different time periods in assessing organizational effectiveness; defining the role of constituencies has not been adequately addressed; and the structure of the determinants of organizational effectiveness have not been theoretically determined, nor is there agreement on how to distinguish between determinants and components of effectiveness.

Literature Review

The literature on organizational effectiveness is dominated by the discussion of two primary models: the goal model and the systems model. There are several variations of each of these, but elements of these two primary models appear in most other models or frameworks. It is appropriate, then, to begin with the discussion of these two models and proceed to the other models that have been developed more recently.

The Goal-Attainment Model

This model is based on Weber's concept of bureaucracy. It views organizations as rational and goal setting. Effectiveness is measured using a set of criteria which determine how well the goals are being achieved (Cameron, 1980; Campbell, 1977).

There are several definitions of goals that must be considered. Simon discusses goals in terms of the individual and defines goals as "value premises that can serve as inputs to decisions" (1964, p. 3). He couples his discussion of goals with a discussion of "motives" which he defines as the "causes . . . that lead individuals to select some goals rather than others as premises for their decisions" (ibid.)

Perrow (1961) discusses two categories of goals: official and operative. Official goals are those to be found in the organization's charter, mission statement, annual reports, and public statements. They are purposely vague and general. They ignore the many decisions that must be made concerning alternative ways of achieving these goals, the priority of multiple goals, and the many unofficial goals pursued by the organization.

Perrow uses "operative goals" to cover the aspects official goals ignore. Operative goals "designate the ends sought through the actual operating policies of organization" (ibid., p. 855). In a sense, operative goals are a means to achieving official goals. Operative goals also indicate the relative priority of diverse and conflicting ends such as employee morale, high productivity, or diversification.

The identification of goals, then, is not simple. If goals are multiple and not easily identified, measuring their achievement cannot be a simple task. Other criticisms of the goal-attainment model are raised by Georgiou (1973), who points out that the goal model doesn't reflect the interaction of the individual worker with the organization, and by Yuchtman and Seashore (1967), who note that this model does not consider the relationship of the organization with the environment.

Hannan and Freeman (1977) point out several difficulties with the goal model: (1) there are multiple and often conflicting goals in organizations; (2) goals are frequently unspecified; (3) goals may be defined only with respect to individuals and their interests within the organization.

The Systems Model

This model views organizations as open systems interacting with their environment. The systems-resource approach proposed by Yuchtman and Seashore (1967) defines effectiveness in terms of the organization's ability to bargain successfully in its environment for "scarce and valued resources." Such resources include capital, human energy, prestige, political influence, physical facilities, and technology. The value of such resources is derived from their utility to the organization as it engages in its activities. Acquisition is one of three major activities to be considered in bargaining for resources. The other activities are the utilization of resources (including allocation and processing), and their exportation as outputs which aid further input.

Scott (1977) criticizes the systems resource approach because (1) it focuses only on inputs, which may have damaging effects on outputs; and (2) it assumes the only valuable aspects of the organization are those which aid further input acquisition. Molnar and Rogers (1976) claim the system resource model is not appropriate in considering the effectiveness of public nonprofit organizations.

Georgopoulas and Tennenbaum also offers a systems view of organizational effectiveness. They define organizational effectiveness as "the extent to which an organization as a social system, given certain resources and means, fulfills its objectives without incapacitating its means and resources and without placing undue strain upon its members" (1957, p. 535). Criteria for effectiveness are: (1) organizational productivity, (2) organizational flexibility in adjusting to both internal change and changes in the environment, and (3) absence of strain or tension among organizational subgroups.

The Process Model

This model "relies on internal organizational processes as the defining characteristic of effectiveness" (Cameron, 1978, p. 605). It views organizations as a series of procedures, routines, functions, and structures. It assumes that goals are set and met as a result of the effectiveness of various management processes such planning, budgeting, and decision making (Cunningham, 1977).

Pfeffer (1977) discusses effectiveness as involving the study of several processes: (1) the process by which groups both within and outside the organization develop and articulate preferences; (2) the process by which the organization comes to perceive the various demands it confronts; and (3) the process by which actions and decisions are taken in this environment of frequently conflicting demands.

The model is criticized because of the difficulty of monitoring organizational processes (Dornbusch and Scott, 1975), the expense of gathering data on process (Scott, 1977), and the process' focus on means to the neglect of ends (Campbell, 1977).

The Multiple-Constituency Approach

This is one of the most recently proposed models of effectiveness. It is based on the premise that individuals involved with any given organization (constituencies) have different expectations. Effectiveness is defined as the degree to which each set of expectations is met (Connolly, Conlon, and Deutsch, 1980). Although Perrow doesn't explicitly describe a multiple constituency approach, he says that operative goals "are tied more directly to group interests" (1961, p. 856).

Scott (1977) also supports a multiple-constituency approach, although he doesn't give his model that name. In describing the different constituencies (rank-and-file participants, consumers or clients, regulators, stockholders) he says, "we may expect all of these groups to employ special criteria in assessing OE" (p. 70). Pfeffer also implies a multiple-constituency approach in his process model.

The literature doesn't present criticism of the multiple-constituency approach. However, one might critique the model on the grounds that value judgments must be made about which constituencies are to be considered in the evaluation of effectiveness. When conflicts arise among constituencies, who will set priorities and on what bases?

The Goodman and Pennings Framework of Organizational Effectiveness

Goodman and Pennings (1977) attempted to synthesize and extend the conceptualization of organizational effectiveness. They proposed a definition based on the concepts of goal, constraints, and referents:

> Organizations are effective to the degree that relevant constraints can be satisfied and organizational results made to approximate or exceed a set of referents for multiple goals. *Goals* are desired end states. *Constraints* are conditions that need to be satisfied. *Referents* are the standards against which outcomes are evaluated (p. 10).

This framework combines the goal approach of Cyert and March (1963) and the systems approach of Katz and Kahn (1966), "and follows Thompson's (1967) strategy of combining the open systems notion of complex organizations with the assumption that organizations represent a political arena where different groups try to promote their interests" (Goodman and Pennings, 1977, p. 148). The framework emphasizes subunits and their interrelationships with their total environment. This environment "consists of the individuals, groups and organizations that provide resources for organizational input and that are recipients of organizational output" (ibid., p. 154).

Seashore's Framework for an Integrated Model of Organizational Effectiveness

Seashore extends Goodman and Pennings' framework "to produce a framework that will aid coherent thought and judicious action by those who are compelled by their leadership roles or their research tasks to choose a definition of effectiveness that suites their unique purposes" (Seashore, 1977, p. 55). This framework merges the "contemporary theories" of the natural systems model, the goal model, and the decision-process model. It takes into account the perspectives arising from the interests of: (1) groups at all levels of the organization hierarchy, (2) individual members of the organization, (3) persons and organizations outside of the focal organization, and (4) the general societal or public interest. The model implies that influential constituents will make judgments about effectiveness and that "action implications will follow" (ibid., p. 66).

Development of a Framework for the Review of Academic-Support Units

After synthesizing the literature and establishing its own "Guiding Principles" (see Appendix), the Committee decided that reviews of nonacademic units should be conducted using a modified self-study approach. Self-study is a process familiar to members of the campus community. It is used in the accreditation review process and in the academic unit review process.

Utilization of a modified self-study concept requires the formation of a self-study committee to oversee the evaluation. This Committee should comprise representatives of the several constituencies with an interest in the unit. Constituencies to be represented would include the dominant coalition (senior administrators), unit managers, unit staff, campus users of the unit's services, external suppliers or users, and the unit head (usually a director). This committee, appointed by the senior administrator in charge of the unit, in consultation with the unit director, would oversee the self-study and prepare a report using the UMCP framework as a guide.

Upon completion of the self study, two or more external consultants would be brought to campus to perform an independent evaluation of the unit. Their report would be incorporated into the report of the self-study committee. The UMCP framework for the review of nonacademic units is based on the seven issues critical for a successful evaluation (Cameron and Whetton, 1983; Goodman and Pennings, 1980; Steers, 1975).

Purpose of Evaluation

Since significant resources in the form of both staff time and money will be invested in this evaluation process, it is important that the evaluations produce results that are useful to everyone involved, especially the senior administrator responsible for the unit and the director of the unit, but also the unit staff and other constituents as well. Therefore, the evaluation will be "utilization focused" (Patton, 1978). Utilization-focused evaluation is, by its nature, formative, as opposed to summative evaluation. The primary purpose of the assessment of academic-support units is to collect information that can be used to improve and further develop the unit.

It is also important to recognize that evaluation "is partly a political process" (Patton, 1978, p. 49). Decisionmakers use evaluation results to reduce uncertainty, through the generation of information for prediction and control. Unit heads could utilize the evaluation process to influence constituencies and use the results of the evaluation to garner additional resources.

The stated purpose of this evaluation process is to assess the effectiveness of the units. More to the point, however, is the purpose of the evaluation as viewed by the senior administrator as well as the unit head. The first step in a utilization-focused evaluation is to have the self-study committee discuss the evaluation with these administrators and determine particular issues and/or problems they would like to have explored in the course of the review of the unit (Patton, 1978). The evaluation cannot be useful if it doesn't provide the specific information these administrators need to make decisions and improve the operation of the unit. The primary purpose of the evaluation then is to meet the requirements of administrators for information concerning the effectiveness of their unit.

Another purpose of evaluation in any organization is to improve the quality of the organization. This is particularly important in an institution of higher education that is striving to achieve a high level of excellence. If a university is to achieve academic excellence, its leaders must also be concerned with the performance and quality of the institution's nonacademic units (Keller, 1984). It is equally important for senior administrators, as well as the university's constituencies, to know if the resources being expended on nonacademic support are being utilized as effectively and efficiently as possible.

Level of Analysis

The purpose of the evaluation process has determined that the academic-support unit is the level at which the evaluation will be conducted. Goodman and Pennings support assessment at this level: "It seems strategically advantageous to focus on subunits' characteristics, including their technological and human resources and the social structure and processes that they have developed" (1977, p. 150).

Constituents to be Included

The perspectives of all identifiable constituents of the unit should be considered in the evaluation. There are two ways of assuring that the perspectives of all constituents are considered in a review. First, a representative of the constituency can serve as a member of the self-study committee. Second, constituents can be surveyed.

The UMCP framework strongly recommends that senior administrators (an assistant vice president, perhaps), subunit supervisors, and staff of the unit be represented on the committee. The director of the unit should be included as well. Without these constituents the evaluation is not a self-study. Additionally, it is in the interest of the unit and the campus that the evaluation be perceived as a positive event and not a "witch hunt." It is normal for staff and supervisors of a unit to be apprehensive if their performance is being examined. Perhaps someone is "out to get them." These fears can be somewhat allayed by appointing one or more representatives of the supervisory and working staffs to the self-study committee. This is also a mechanism for providing the staff with insight into the perspectives of other constituents.

Users of the unit's services should also be represented. Some units have several distinct categories of users or "customers." For instance, the purchasing department in a university serves several kinds of academic departments. Some rarely buy anything more than office supplies and an occasional piece of office equipment. There are departments with large research components whose purchases comprise very sophisticated equipment required for conducting specific research projects and/or for instruction. Finally, there are users such as physical plant staff who buy large quantities of building materials and supplies, heavy equipment, and motor vehicles. Each of these types of customers has different requirements which translate into different goals for the purchasing department. Somehow all of these users' perspectives must be considered in the review. It would be advisable to include at least one of the large-volume purchasers on the self-study committee while utilizing the second method of recognizing constituent perspectives to consider the views of the less-frequent customers. In fact, a more complete picture of all customers' views would be obtained if all types of customers were surveyed (in addition to having large-volume users serve on the self-study committee).

Other constituencies whose perspectives are important in an evaluation are groups in the external environment who interact on a regular basis with the academic-support unit. These external constituents frequently are the source of constraints on the focal unit. Their rules and regulations, whether formal or implicit, can hamper the effectiveness of an operation. It is important to include representatives of these constituencies for two reasons: (1) to obtain their perspectives on the operative goals and processes of the unit, and (2) to make them aware of the extent to which their rules act as constraints and inhibit the effectiveness of the unit.

"External environment" in this context has two meanings. It includes departments outside of the focal unit, but inside the university. As an example, if the registration office were being evaluated it would be important to consider the perspective of the administrative computer center which provides the data-processing support for the registrations office. Individuals and/or organizations outside of the university are also part of the external environment. For some departments, such as purchasing, this includes suppliers and contractors with whom the university does business. While campus users of the purchasing department expect the department to provide prompt service and quality products at the lowest possible price, suppliers and contractors want to make the best "deal" and be paid promptly. Resolving these two possibly conflicting goals could be problematic, although enlightening, for the self-study committee.

It should be reiterated here that it is practical for representatives of only a few constituencies to sit on the self-study committee. The political decision concerning who the "most important" constituents are must be made by the senior administrator and the director. The self-study committee itself might later decide to add one or more constituents. Nonrepresented constituencies and/or all of the members of the constituencies that are represented can be surveyed using paper surveys, phone surveys, focus groups, personal interviews, or group forums to assure all perspectives are considered.

Domains of Activity to be Considered

The inclusion of the perspectives of all constituencies leads to the evaluation of activity in all of the domains in which the unit operates. Domains arise from the activities or primary tasks that are emphasized in the organization, from the competencies of the organization, and from the demands placed upon the organization by external forces (Cameron, 1981; Miles, 1980). (The Office of Institutional Studies, an academic-support unit, can serve to illustrate this point. The traditional responsibility of the institutional research office has been the collection and reporting of institutional data to federal and state agencies as well as to senior administrators. Analytical studies in support of decision making have also been the responsibility of this office. These activities represent two domains of activity. When federal regulations and court rulings required that an affirmative action plan be prepared, this office was seen by the administration as the office where the expertise resided for preparing such a document. The "competencies of the organization" as well as "external demands" thus created another domain of activity for the office.)

Cameron and Whetten point out that "no organization is maximally effective in all its domains" (1983, p. 271). Nevertheless, the self-study committee must examine the effectiveness of the unit in all of the areas in which the unit operates. Senior administrators, however, must not expect an equal level of performance in all domains. The evaluation might be useful in assisting the unit director and senior administrator to set priorities concerning domains of activity so the highest levels of performance can be achieved in those areas deemed most important to the campus at any given point in time.

As the self-study committee considers the domains in which the unit operates, it should consider the structure or organization of the unit. Are routine functions centralized and automated to the extent possible? Are functions requiring creativity decentralized to allow staff the freedom they need to perform effectively? Are job responsibilities distributed in the most efficient manner. Is the unit, within each domain, employing the appropriate technology, i.e., knowledge and machines? Is there evidence of creativity and innovation? Are new ideas and methods tested and adopted if they work? Is there evidence of a willingness on the part of staff as well as supervisors to adapt and change as the requirements of the environment change? Such attributes of unit performance must be considered in judging effectiveness (Hage, 1980).

One domain should exist in every unit and it deserves close scrutiny by the committee. This activity is the acquisition and utilization of resources for the purpose of obtaining additional resources. Does the unit attract, and utilize, bright, competent, dedicated employees? The reputation of a unit for having a high degree of competency brings respect and helps to attract additional able employees. The unit should also use the skills and competencies of its employees to get the most from its human energy. The acquisition and effective use of information can lead to innovation.

Another resource that isn't often recognized is the goodwill of the unit's users. Garnering goodwill can lead to improved effectiveness through cooperation and even to additional funding.

The committee should also consider whether the unit should be operating in all the domains that it does. In view of the limited resources with which units in higher education must operate, it's possible that the unit is continuing to engage in activities that are of limited value to the institution. Effectiveness in more important domains is likely to be improved if activity in one or more other domains is eliminated. A unit director might hesitate to make such a recommendation on his or her own initiative, but with the support of the self-study committee would find it more comfortable to take the step. It is also quite possible that the unit director never considered reducing services by limiting the unit's activities. Sometimes an outside perspective is required to see the obvious. The decision to deny a constituency an established service is not an easy one, but it is an appropriate recommendation resulting from this evaluation process.

Time Frame

The concept of self-study requires that the time frame considered in the evaluation is current. What's going on now and what results are being achieved? The committee might consider plans for change that are in the process of being implemented and comment on the expected results. The committee's report might also recommend changes that should be considered for the future.

Type of Data Utilized

There are two kinds of data that can be used in an evaluation—objective and subjective. Objective data are obtained from organizational records. Some examples appropriate to unit review are budget data, staff turnover rates, number of units processed (i.e., applications, student-aid requests, purchase orders, work requests), personal evaluations, absentee rate, to name some of the obvious. Subjective data are perceptual and are obtained from surveys or personal interviews. Cameron (1980) cautions that objective and subjective data are sometimes contradictory. Nevertheless, both kinds of data can contribute to the study of effectiveness.

Budget levels over time suggest whether a unit is being properly funded as its domains of activity expand or shrink and the number of units processed changes. Turnover rates can indicate the level of staff morale. (Caution should be exercised to also consider salary levels when looking at turnover. Poorly paid employees might be highly motivated but still require more money, so they leave.) Changes in units produced per employee can indicate the appropriateness of staffing levels. These are a few examples of ways in which organizational (objective) data can be used in the evaluation process.

Perceptual (subjective) data also play a role in evaluation. The importance of examining the perspectives of all the identifiable constituents of the unit has already been discussed. These are perceptual data. When considering subjective data, the committee must recognize that by their nature such data are biased. It is possible that lack of information or even dishonesty on the part of respondents can hinder the reliability of data. It should also be noted that the nature and time frame of the self-study does not permit the testing of survey instruments for reliability and validity. The instruments used will be designed by the committee or its designee and are likely to be used only once during the review process. (As the institutional process becomes established, it will be useful to develop specialized instruments or identify standard instruments that can be used routinely in every review. For instance, a survey to assess staff morale and attitudes that is applicable to all departments could be developed and tested. Use of such a survey, and any others that might be determined to be appropriate, would contribute to the consistency of the evaluations across departments.)

Referents

Referents are the standards against which the effectiveness of the academic-support unit will be judged. The UMCP framework will include the use of several referents. Since this evaluation process examines the perspectives or goals of the unit's several constituencies, use of the goal-centered approach is suitable. How well is the unit achieving the goals of the various constituents? As was the case in the discussion of domains, differential levels of goal achievement among constituents is to be expected. Again, the unit director and senior administrator must set priorities.

It is appropriate to compare the unit with similar units. Two sources of referents are applicable. First, if industry or government standards of performance are available for the type of activity conducted by the unit, they can be used to measure effectiveness. Such might be the case for personnel (number of job applicants processed per employee), purchasing (number of purchase orders filled per employee), or accounts payable (number of invoices processed per employee). Many units have no counterpart outside of higher education. Comparable data for these units (registration, admission, bursar, and student affairs units, to name a few) must be obtained from peer institutions. In selecting peers for comparison, care must be taken that only comparable institutions are selected. The admissions process at Harvard is probably quite different from the process at Penn State. Using Harvard's data as a measure of effectiveness at Penn State would be inappropriate. The instrument for collecting peer data must be very carefully designed to assure the clarity of the request. The director of the unit can offer the best advice on the development of such an instrument, whether the data are collected using a paper survey, by phone, or even in person.

Another form of comparative evaluation will occur when outside experts visit the campus and evaluate the unit. These experts will each have their own set of referents against which the unit will be judged.

Steps to Follow in Conducting an Academic-Support Unit Review

When an academic support unit is being reviewed, the following activities should occur:

1. Senior administrator and unit director form self-study committee and consider appropriate external reviewers.

2. Committee, senior administrator, and unit director discuss particular issues to be addressed in the review.

3. Committee prepares self-study plan and budget and submits it to the senior administrator.

4. Senior administrator approves plan and budget or makes suggestions for changes.

5. Committee conducts self-study addressing the following general issues and using the UMCP framework as a guide:

   a. Expectations of the various constituencies;

   b. Domains in which unit is operating;

   c. Structure, task differentiation and technology of the unit relevant to the expressed goals of the constituencies;

   d. Conformance with performance standards;

   e. Constraints imposed by the external environment (includes funding and staffing levels);

   f. Satisfaction of users with the unit's services;

   g. Qualifications/competencies and morale of the staff;

   h. General environment of the workplace;

   i. Recommendations.

6. Committee prepares self-study report.

7. Committee submits self-study to senior administrator and external reviewers.

8. External reviewers conduct on-site evaluation.

9. External reviewers submit evaluation report.

10. External review results are incorporated into the self-study report.

11. Director prepares response and plan to implement recommendations.

12. Senior administrator and unit director discuss report, director's response, and plans to implement report's recommendations.

13. Report and action plans are submitted to the chief executive officer.

Shortcomings of the Framework

Even though it drew from a variety of models of organizational effectiveness, the UMCP framework has several shortcomings.

1. There is no explicit evaluation of efficiency in the framework. Hannan and Freeman (1977) include efficiency in their definition of effectiveness since resource constraints exist within most organizations. Evaluators could calculate a cost-per-output ratio and compare it with similar ratios from other peer institutions. The problem that frequently confounds such a comparison is the likelihood that no units in higher education institutions are exactly alike. While different structures and/or technology should not prevent comparison of efficiency ratios, differing domains of activity

should. If one admissions office evaluates the transcripts of transfer applicants for applicability of credits toward a specific major and a comparison admissions office does not, their efficiency ratios are not comparable. Usually the self-study committee wouldn't be aware of such subtleties. Because such efficiency comparisons are problematic they have not been included in the framework.

2. Evaluations won't be identical in all units. The framework sets general guidelines, but self-study is subjective. Different committees will emphasize different areas for scrutiny. The senior administrator and unit director will suggest different issues for concentrated study. Some committees will have a stronger commitment to the process than others. There is probably no way to avoid such differences completely. The senior administrator has some control since he or she will approve the committee's plan. However, as long as the senior administrator and unit director receive the information they require from the evaluation, one need not be overly concerned with consistency as long as the basic framework is applied.

3. Unit evaluations over time aren't likely to be consistent for the same reasons evaluations among units might not be consistent. Ideally, in subsequent evaluations, the report from the prior evaluation would be considered and the committee would note if the recommendations had been implemented. It's possible that from one review to another constituencies and domains would change. Of necessity, the review would be somewhat different. Lack of consistency over time is not a serious problem.

4. Negativism concerning the evaluation can be a problem, especially for the first units to be reviewed. Unit directors as well as staff might be threatened by such close scrutiny of their unit. It is incumbent on senior administrators to allay such fears by describing the process beforehand and pointing out the positive aspects of the self-study. It was previously mentioned that involving the director and subunit managers and staff in the evaluation process will also serve to place the process in a more positive light.

5. The UMCP framework describes a multistage process which is expensive to implement. It is estimated that each self-study will take close to a year from planning to final report. A significant portion of the time of the unit director and the several staff who serve on the committee will be required for the self-study. It isn't likely that any additional people will be hired to assist with the normal workload. In addition, other university employees will be asked to serve on self-study committees as representatives of various constituencies. Employees will provide their services to the self-study committee by either slacking off on other responsibilities or, more likely, by spending more time on the job. Either way, the service exacts a price.

Other costs are also involved in the conduct of surveys and the preparation of committee working materials. The most significant financial outlay will be required to bring to campus experts for every evaluation. It is estimated that as many as ten reviews can occur in any given year on campus. The collective cost of conducting so many evaluations has not been estimated, but it is not insignificant.

Benefits of Review

Such an expensive process should provide some tangible benefits. What will the university gain from such a process? Probably the most obvious and desired benefit of unit evaluation is the diagnosis of problem areas and the resulting improvement in operations and decisions. Of equal importance, however, is the opportunity to discover and acknowledge excellence in an operation. In fact, evaluation is likely to be viewed more positively by those being assessed if this possible outcome of review is emphasized.

Brewer (1983) points out that another benefit of unit evaluation is complacency reduction. In the course of working with the self-study committee, unit personnel, and particularly the unit director, must clarify their own goals. Such introspection leads to clarity about what has to be done and the best way to do it. The unit-review process provides an opportunity for unit personnel to step back from the pressure of routine demands and think about what they're doing and how they're doing it.

The UMCP framework draws representatives of identifiable constituencies into the evaluation process. As the goals of the several constituencies are discussed, there is an opportunity for each constituent to recognize the goals of the others. Constituents will also be in a position of seeing the constraints they, and the others, place on the focal unit. A better understanding of all of the demands placed on a department coupled with the knowledge of budget and staff limitations should serve to make constituents less critical when their own expectations are not met.

Finally, the evaluation activity itself could enhance the image of the university. This outcome of assessment is also mentioned by Brewer (1983). Such activity is commonplace in industry, and introducing the practice should send a signal to those who provide funding, both public and private, that the university is committed to achieving the highest level of effectiveness and quality in its operations. By developing an evaluation system on its own initiative the university might forestall any effort on the part of state agencies to mandate such practices. While the process of assessing the effectiveness of academic-support units may be difficult, time consuming, and expensive, there are many benefits to be gained from such a practice.

Implementation of the Process

On February 11, 1987, Chancellor John B. Slaughter instructed the vice chancellors to establish a calendar and begin the review of academic-support units. As might be expected, the Guidelines have been implemented with varying levels of enthusiasm.

Three of four vice chancellors initiated reviews. The Vice Chancellor for Institutional Advancement intends to review his entire area simultaneously at a later date. In one vice chancellor's division, two units are conducting self-studies but have not included any constituents on the Self-Study Committee. Clearly, these units did not follow the prescribed Guidelines.

A second vice chancellor has just initiated his first review. The Self-Study Committee includes a wide range of unit's constituents and everyone on the committee appears to be dedicated to doing a thorough review. Although it has taken months to get this review started, the vice chancellor appears to have some commitment to the process. It should be noted that this vice chancellor did not share the Chancellor's Guidelines with the Self-Study Committee. The questions that are to be addressed in the course of the review were not made available. As a result, the Committee will address only those issues it believes are important.

The third vice chancellor is deeply committed to the process. One review in his division is already complete and two more are nearing completion. This division has a committee whose purpose is to oversee the review process across the division and help assure consistency in the process.

Since I've been involved in the reviews in the Administrative Affairs Division, I can speak a little more authoritatively about these reviews. The Guidelines were carefully followed in these reviews. In all three cases, the assistant vice chancellor responsible for the unit to be reviewed acted as Chair of the Self-Study Steering Committee. This assured a direct line of authority between the vice chancellor and the Committee. The vice chancellor requested time tables, letting it be known that he expected the plan to be followed. He discussed the composition of the Steering Committee with the assistant vice chancellor and the director of the Unit. He also indicated possible problem areas that he wanted the Committees to investigate.

The Steering Committees for all three reviews appointed "Internal" and "External" subcommittees comprised of Steering Committee members as well as other members of the campus community, usually staff of the department being reviewed. The Internal Subcommittee addressed issues related to the operation of the unit, i.e., unit organization, plans and resources, staff morale, and performance. The External Subcommittee evaluated the unit in relation to its external environment. This subcommittee analyzed user satisfaction and compared the unit with similar operations at peer institutions. The questions addressed by these subcommittees, and ultimately the Steering Committee, are presented in Attachment 1 to the Guidelines. (See Appendix. Most of these questions originated at the University of Illinois at Urbana-Champaign.) The report of the Steering Committees will ultimately result from the reports of these two subcommittees, along with the reports of the external evaluators.

Results of Reviews

What, in general, did the self-studies discover that wasn't already known? Not an awful lot, but then it's still early. The reviews aren't really complete. Directors of the units whose reviews were just about complete shared some of their thoughts about the process and its results.

The process itself takes a significant share of the unit's resources. There doesn't seem to be a good time to fit the review into the day-to-day workload. The directors didn't learn anything significant that they didn't already know. The results of the reviews confirmed and highlighted the problems they knew existed. The review teams did offer some solutions; however, only time will tell if the recommendations will be implemented. The important point is that dedicated people from many areas of the campus have invested a significant amount of time, thought, and effort in these reviews. It will be difficult for the administration to ignore their recommendations when it was the administration that instituted the process.

Role of Institutional Research

What role does the IR office play in this process? At College Park, the Director of Institutional Studies has been involved in developing the Guidelines and compiling and monitoring the campus schedule. The Director is also responsible for coordinating the process in the Academic Affairs Division, and will serve on every Self-Study Committee in that division.

More generally, review of the questions in Attachment 1 to the Guidelines will reveal several areas of involvement for IR. First, the IR office is called upon to provide the data basic to the review—items such as member of employees by EEO classification, length of employment, turnover rates, and budget levels, usually all for five years. Second, the IR office was asked to assist in collecting peer data. We also offered advice on the kinds of data it is reasonable to collect from peers.

The IR office at UMCP assisted in conducting user surveys, all of which so far have been paper surveys. Units required assistance in formulating questions, conducting the surveys, and analyzing results. The initiation of this review process at College Park has had a serious impact on the IR staff. During the next round of reviews we'll be able to draw on some of the instruments we've developed for use in other units. Ideally, we'll finalize a standard survey for employees of any unit to determine morale and attitudes toward the workplace. User surveys will also be adaptable to some extent. Like the campus, the Institutional Studies Office needs a little more experience with the process.

Conclusion

What has the campus learned about the process so far? Since only one review has actually been completed, the final paragraphs can't be written. We do know the Guidelines aren't being followed by all units. The Chancellor will have to reinforce their importance or decide that each Committee has freedom to develop its own study. The list of questions is too long and responses don't fit neatly into a report. Rather than require that the questions be answered, the Guidelines should suggest that the Committees investigate all of the areas suggested by the questions. Since a review requires a significant amount of the time of Self-Study Committee members, care should be taken to assure that faculty and staff aren't asked to serve on committees more than once every three or four years. On the other hand, service on a review committee is a learning experience and every effort should be made to include a wide variety of faculty and staff.

It's a little premature to make a judgment about the value of the process. It will be another year or so until the process can be evaluated. It will take even longer to see if recommendations are implemented. The ultimate test will be in the improvement of service to the campus community. If the quality of academic support improves, the time, effort, and resources expanded on the review process will be considered well spent.

Appendix A

Guiding Principles for the Review of Academic-Support Units

1. The process and guidelines developed for the review should serve all academic-support units and measure unit effectiveness. They should be generic in nature and set forth the basic issues to be addressed in the review.

2. The process should be perceived by the units reviewed as a positive and supportive one. It should provide them with an opportunity to step back and examine their operations objectively and comprehensively. Data collected should be kept to a minimum. It should also provide useful management information to unit heads and executives to whom the units report.

3. The process should be decentralized and focused in the vice chancellor's office. The committee anticipates that each vice chancellor will implement the process defined in this paper and follow the guidelines outlined. Each vice chancellor can supplement the guidelines with additional instructions, as appropriate. The vice chancellors will be expected to develop a calendar for the review of the units reporting to them. In addition, a report on division academic-support unit review activities will be submitted by each vice chancellor annually to the Chancellor.

4. Unit reviews should include a unit self-study based on the questions in the appendix, a survey of user perceptions of services provided, and a review by experts external to the Campus.

5. Each review process should begin with a clear statement of unit goals and objectives that have been approved by the unit's Vice Chancellor. Such a statement is essential to fair and effective reviews.

6. It should clearly be understood that a satisfactory review process will require resources. The committee believes, however, that a decentralized process can minimize cost.

7. Realistic expectations must be established for the process. It should be clear to units undergoing review that the new resources available to correct problems identified will be quite limited.

8. Interrelationships with other units should be analyzed in the review. Clearly when a user perspective is taken, effective relationships with other units are essential to reducing unit compartmentalization and needless effort on the part of user.

Attachment 1: Evaluation Questions for Academic-Support Unit Reviews

Section A: Unit Organization, Plans, and Resources

1. What are the goals and objectives of the unit as perceived by the unit head and the unit staff?

2. What priorities have been assigned to these objectives?

3. What is the organization of the unit, including line relationships? Is this structure adequate for the achievement of the current mission of the unit?

4. Are the internal structures of the unit appropriate to its objectives and work plan?

5. Does the unit have a procedure for evaluating its operation on a periodic basis? What's the nature of this procedure? How are the results of this procedure used?

6. Are the personnel and budgetary resources allocated to the unit adequate and commensurate with the mission assigned to it?

7. Do appropriate members of the staff participate in the formulation of budgets and decisions relating to expenditures of resources?

8. Is the space allocated to the unit adequate for its operations and appropriate to its role on campus?

9. Does the unit use the technologies that might be useful in improving its efficiency and overall performance?

Section B: Staffing

1. Are the personnel within the unit familiar with unit objectives and the importance of their work in achieving the stated objectives?

2. Is there effective communication among members of the staff?

3. To what extent is the quality of life for members of the unit addressed by the unit's manager and can improvements be made in this area?

4. What programs are available for staff training and development and how active is the unit in fostering participation in such programs?

5. Is the unit adequately responding to affirmative action and equal opportunity goals of the campus?

6. Do managers and staff maintain an adequate level of professional competence through participation in appropriate professional organizations, institutional training programs or other departmental activities?

Section C: Performance

1. Indicate the performance measures that have been established for the unit. What actions are taken when these measures indicate that a significant change in performance has occurred?

2. How does the unit evaluate the operational effectiveness and the quality of service to users?

3. Is the unit fulfilling its responsibilities with respect to external agencies?

4. Have significant findings of federal, state, and internal audits or management reviews been given satisfactory attention by the unit?

5. Have adequate internal controls been established for such activities as purchasing, equipment maintenance, and payroll procedures?

6. Are internal and external forms and reports reviewed on a regular basis to determine their need, relevance, and cost?

7. Are new methods, procedures, technologies, and equipment regularly studied in order to improve the effectiveness of operations?

8. What are the key problems facing the unit and what could be done to solve them?

9. Are internal and external support units providing adequate assistance to the unit?

10. How do external (i.e., UMCA, State) constraints impact on the performance of the unit?

Section D: Campus Role

1. Is the unit appropriately placed within the institution? Is it afforded appropriate status?

2. Is the administration sufficiently responsive to the needs of the unit?

3. What responsibilities of the unit must be closely coordinated with other units on Campus and how are these responsibilities allocated and coordinated?

Section E: User Satisfaction

1. What do users perceive the function and goals of the unit to be?

2. Are users asked regularly to appraise the effectiveness of the unit's operations and services? What are the results of these evaluations? Are users' recommendations considered for implementation?

3. Are user's expectations of the unit's performance in agreement with the unit's appraisal?

4. What changes and improvements have been suggested by users?

5. Is there a manual of instructions explaining how to use the unit's services? Have users been asked to evaluate the usefulness of the manual?

6. Are there training programs for users of the unit's services? Have users been asked to evaluate the usefulness of the training programs?

Section F: Other Relevant Background Data

1. Organizational Chart

2. Charge statement of the responsibilities of the unit

3. Current budget

4. Flow chart of major operations or systems

5. Financial reports including summary expenditure reports in relation to original and revised budget allocations

6. Workload data, measurements, and performance indicators used for major activities

7. Data on personnel actions for the past year; for example, data on turnover, new positions, merit raises, performance evaluations, promotions, and recruitments

8. Significant internal and external policies pertaining to the functional area

Section G: Function/Process Evaluation—
Role of Participants External to the Focal Unit

1. Do personnel who participate in the process under review, but who are not employed in the focal unit, perceive themselves to be part of the process? Are they aware of their role in the process? Are they aware of the goals of the process?

2. Is there effective communication between staff of the focal unit and outside participants in the process?

3. Are the responsibilities of process participants outside the focal unit clearly documented?

4. Are process participants outside of the focal unit aware of any external regulations which guide (control) the process?

5. Is feedback provided to process participants on their contributions toward the accomplishment of the goals of the process?

References

Barak, R. J. (1982). *Program review in higher education: within and without.* Boulder, CO: National Center for Higher Education Management System.

Brewer, G. D. (1983). Assessing outcomes and effects. In Cameron and Whetten, *Organizational Effectiveness: a comparison of multiple models.*

Cameron, K. S. (1978). Measuring organizational effectiveness in institutions of higher education. *Administrative Science Quarterly* 23:604–632.

Cameron, K. S. (1980). Critical questions in assessing organizational effectiveness. *Organizational Dynamics* 9(Autumn): 66–80.

Cameron, K. S. (1981). Domains of organizational effectiveness in colleges and universities. *Academy of Management Journal* 24:25–47.

Cameron, K. S., and Whetten, D. S. (1983). *Organizational Effectiveness: A Comparison of Multiple Models.* New York: Academic Press.

Campbell, J. P. (1983). On the nature of organizational effectiveness. In Goodman and Pennings, *New Perspectives on Organizational Effectiveness.*

Connolly, T., Conlon, E. J., and Deutsch, S. J. (1980). Organizational effectiveness: a multiple constituency approach. *Academy of Management Reviews* 5(2):21–217.

Cunningham, J. Barton (1977). Approaches to the evaluation of organizational effectiveness. *Academy of Management Review*, July, pp. 463–473.

Cyert, R. M., and March, J. G. (1963). *A Behavioral Theory of the Firm.* Englewood Cliffs, N.J.: Prentice-Hall.

Dornbusch, S. M., and Scott, W. R. (1975). *Evaluation and the Exercise of Authority.* San Francisco: Jossey-Bass.

Georgiou, P. (1973). The goal paradigm and notes toward a counter paradigm. *Administrative Science Quarterly* 18:291–310.

Georgopoulas, B. S., and Tennenbaum, A. S. (1957). A study of organizational effectiveness. *American Sociological Review* 22(5):257–278.

Goodman, P. S., and Pennings, J. M., et al., eds. (1977). *New Perspectives on Organizational Effectiveness.* San Francisco: Jossey-Bass.

Goodman, P. S., and Pennings, J. M. (1980). Critical issues in assessing organizational effectiveness. In N. E. Lawler, D. A. Nadler, and C. Cammann (eds.), *Organizational Assessment. Perspectives on the Measurement of Organizational Behavior and the Quality of Life.* New York: Wiley.

Hage, J. (1980). *Theories of Organization.* New York: Wiley.

Hannan, M. T., and Freeman, J. (1977). Obstacles to comparative studies. In Goodman, Pennings, et al., *New Perspectives on Organizational Effectiveness.*

Katz, D., and Kahn, R. L. (1966). *The Social Psychology of Organizations.* New York: Wiley.

Keller, George (1983). *Academic Strategy.* Baltimore: The Johns Hopkins University Press.

Making a difference: Goals, objectives, and initiatives (1984). The University of Maryland, College Park, Fall.

Miles, R. H. (1980). *Macro Organization Behavior.* Santa Monica, CA: Goodyear.

Molnar, J. J., and Rogers, D. L. (1976). Organizational effectiveness: an empirical comparison of the goal and system resource approaches. *The Sociological Quarterly* 17:401–413.

Patton, M. Q. (1978). *Utilization-Focused Evaluation.* Beverly Hills, CA: Sage Publications.

Perrow, Charles. (1961). The analysis of goals in complex organizations. *American Sociological Review* 26(December):854–866.

Pfeffer, Jeffrey (1977). Usefulness of the concept. In Goodman, Pennings, et al., *New Perspectives on Organizational Effectiveness.*

Scott, W. R. (1977). Effectiveness of organizational effectiveness studies. In Goodman, Pennings, et al., *New Perspectives on Organizational Effectiveness*. San Francisco: Jossey-Bass.

Seashore, S. E. (1977). An elastic and expandable viewpoint. In Goodman, Pennings, et al., *New Perspectives on Organizational Effectiveness*. San Francisco: Jossey-Bass.

Simon, H. A. (1964). On the concept of organizational goal. *Administrative Science Quarterly* 9:1–22.

Steers, R. M. (1967). Problems in the measurement of organizational effectiveness. *American Sociological Review* 32: 891-903.

Thompson, J. D. (1967). *Organizations in Action*. New York: McGraw-Hill

Wilson, Richard F. (1987). A perspective on evaluating administrative units in higher education. In J. F. Wergin and L. A. Braskamp (eds.), *Evaluating Administrative Services and Programs*. San Francisco: Jossey-Bass.

Yuchtman, E., and Seashore, S. E. (1967). A system resource approach to organizational effectiveness. *American Sociological Review* 32:891–903.

Propriety Standards

THE JOINT COMMITTEE ON STANDARDS FOR EDUCATIONAL EVALUATION

Organization of the Standards

In order to devise comprehensive standards, the Joint Committee identified four important attributes of an evaluation: *utility, feasibility, propriety,* and *accuracy.* The Committee is satisfied that standards which shape an evaluation so that it has these four characteristics are necessary and sufficient for sound evaluation in education.

Each standard in this book was developed to help define one of the four attributes. Several reviews of the standards revealed that a number of them applied to more than one attribute. Therefore, the Committee's grouping of the standards has been based on its judgment of each standard's main emphasis.

Utility, the first category, contains standards for guiding evaluation so that they will be informative, timely, and influential. These standards require evaluators to acquaint themselves with their audiences, ascertain the audiences' information needs, plan evaluations to respond to these needs, and report the relevant information clearly and when it is needed.

The standards included in this category are Audience Identification, Evaluator Credibility, Information Scope and Selection, Valuational Interpretation, Report Clarity, Report Dissemination, Report Timeliness, and Evaluation Impact.

Overall, the standards of Utility are concerned with whether an evaluation serves the practical information needs of a given audience.

Feasibility, the second category, contains standards which recognize that an educational evaluation usually must be conducted in a natural, as opposed to a laboratory, setting and that it consumes valuable resources. Thus, one concern is that the evaluation design be operable in the actual field setting in which it is to be applied, and another is that the evaluation not consume more materials and personnel time than necessary to achieve its purposes.

The three standards in this category are Practical Procedures, Political Viability, and Cost Effectiveness.

Overall, the Feasibility standards call for evaluations to be realistic, prudent, diplomatic, and frugal.

Propriety, the third category, contains standards which reflect in fact that educational evaluations affect many human beings in many ways. The standards in this group are intended to ensure that the rights of persons affected by an evaluation will be protected. Especially, the standards warn against unlawful, unscrupulous, unethical, and inept actions by those who produce evaluation results.

The eight standards dealing with Propriety are Formal Obligation, Conflict of Interest, Full and Frank Disclosure, Public's Right to Know, Rights of Human Subjects, Human Interactions, Balanced Reporting, and Fiscal Responsibility.

These standards require that those conducting evaluations learn about and adhere to laws concerning such matters as privacy, freedom of information, and the protection of human subjects. This group of standards charges those who conduct evaluations to respect the rights of others and to live up to the highest principles and ideals of their professional reference groups.

Taken as a group, the Propriety standards require that evaluations be conducted legally, ethically, and with due regard for the welfare of those involved in the evaluation, as well as those affected by the results.

Accuracy, the fourth category, includes those standards that determine whether an evaluation has produced sound information. The assessment of the object must be comprehensive, i.e., the evaluators should have considered as many of the object's identifiable features as practicable and should have gathered data on those particular features that were judged to be important for assessing the object's worth or merit. Moreover, the obtained information should be technically adequate; and the judgments rendered should be linked logically to the data.

The eleven standards placed in this category are Object Identification, Context Analysis, Defensible Information Sources, Described Purposes and Procedures, Valid Measurement, Reliable Measurement, Systematic Data Control, Analysis of Quantitative Information, Analysis of Qualitative Information, Justified Conclusions, and Objective Reporting.

This category includes those standards intended to ensure that an evaluation will reveal and convey accurate information about the features of the object being studied that determine its merit or worth. The overall rating of an evaluation against the eleven standards in this category gives a good idea of the evaluation's overall validity.

A review of the standards noted above suggests that some (e.g., Evaluation Impact and Valid Measurement) are relatively unique to evaluation, while others (e.g., Report Clarity, Conflict of Interest, and Human Interactions) are more general professional standards. This mix reflects the Joint Committee's belief that standards should be selected if they address persistent and important problems in evaluation, whether or not they are unique to evaluation. . . .

Propriety Standards
Summary of the Standards

C Propriety Standards

The Propriety Standards are intended to ensure that the evaluation will be conducted legally, ethically, and with due regard for the welfare of those involved in the evaluation, as well as those affected by its results. These standards are:

C1 Formal Obligation

Obligations of the formal parties to an evaluation (what is to be done, how, by whom, when) should be agreed to in writing, so that these parties are obligated to adhere to all conditions of the agreement or formally to renegotiate it.

C2 Conflict of Interest

Conflict of interest, frequently unavoidable, should be dealt with openly and honestly, so that it does not compromise the evaluation processes and results.

C3 Full and Frank Disclosure

Oral and written evaluation reports should be open, direct, and honest in their disclosure of pertinent findings, including the limitations of the evaluation.

C4 Public's Right to Know

The formal parties to an evaluation should respect and assure the public's right to know, within the limits of other related principles and statutes, such as those dealing with public safety and the right to privacy.

C5 Rights of Human Subjects

Evaluations should be designed and conducted, so that the rights and welfare of the human subjects are respected and protected.

C6 Human Interactions

Evaluators should respect human dignity and worth in their interactions with other persons associated with an evaluation.

C7 Balanced Reporting

The evaluation should be complete and fair in its presentation of strengths and weaknesses of the object under investigation, so that strengths can be built upon and problem areas addressed.

C8 Fiscal Responsibility

The evaluator's allocation and expenditure of resources should reflect sound accountability and procedures and otherwise be prudent and ethically responsible.

C1 Formal Obligation

Standard

Obligations of the formal parties to an evaluation (what is to be done, how, by whom, when) should be agreed to in writing, so that these parties are obligated to adhere to all conditions of the agreement or formally to renegotiate it.

Overview

A written agreement is a mutual understanding of specified expectations and responsibilities of both client and evaluator. Having entered into such an agreement, both parties have a legal and ethical obligation to carry it out in a forthright manner or to renegotiate it. Neither party is obligated to honor decisions made unilaterally by the other.

Guidelines of federal, state, and local agencies for external evaluations often require that evaluator and client enter into formal contract. But even when a formal contract is not mandated—commonly the case with internal evaluations—the parties to the evaluation should develop at least a brief memorandum of agreement spelling out what is to be done, by whom, how, and when.

School districts may deal systematically with evaluation contract issues by having their boards adopt policies pertaining to such matters as: responsibilities of district personnel for conducting and participating in evaluations; approval of evaluation plans; protection of human subjects; data collection, storage and retrieval; editing and disseminating results; use of external evaluators; and financing the evaluation effort.

Both client and evaluator usually begin their relationship in an atmosphere of mutual respect and confidence. This is the best atmosphere in which to negotiate a contract (or to establish general policies) to guide the behavior of both. The process of developing a written agreement provides evaluator and client the opportunity to review and summarize the total evaluation plan and to clarify their respective rights and responsibilities in the enterprise. A formal agreement can reduce and help resolve many of the day-to-day misunderstandings between evaluator and client, and, if serious misunderstandings occur, it can help resolve them. As an appendix to the final evaluation report, the evaluation contract or memorandum of agreement can promote understanding of the agreements that guided the evaluation.

Guidelines

A. Include in the agreement (allowing for appropriate adjustments in emergent designs):

1. objectives of the evaluation;

2. questions to be investigated;

3. data collection procedures, including data and data sources, sample size and selection, instruments and other data-gathering techniques, and any site-visiting plan;

4. data analysis procedures, including descriptive and comparative, statistical and nonstatistical;

5. reporting plan, including a consideration of report format and delivery (number and types of reports, length, audiences, and methods of presentation), anonymity of subjects/respondents, prerelease review of reports, rebuttal by those being evaluated, and editorial and final release authority over completed reports;

6. methods for controlling and assessing bias in data collection, analysis, and reporting;

7. services, personnel information, and materials provided by clients, including access to data;

8. timeline for work of both clients and evaluators;

9. contract amendment and termination procedures; and

10. budget for the work, including amounts to be paid upon completion of certain tasks or on specified dates.

B. Establish, within reasonable limits, what would constitute a breach of the agreement by either party and what consequent actions may be taken.

C. Ensure that the agreement conforms to federal and state statutes and local regulations applying to such contractual arrangements.

D. Have an outside party—an attorney, if possible—review the agreement for clarity and soundness.

E. Negotiate amendments as the work proceeds if changing circumstances make alterations in work scope, cost, or timetable necessary or desirable.

F. Collaborate with educational administrators in drafting policies for board approval covering the conduct of the evaluation.

Pitfalls

A. Allowing the original proposal to constitute the full written agreement.

B. Failing to consult with those who will be directly affected by the contract but who are not signatories—school principals and teachers, for example—before the agreement is signed (see A1, Audience Identification, A2, Evaluator Credibility, and B2, Political Viability).

C. Expecting performance by parties not under the control of the signatories without consulting these parties.

D. Acting unilaterally in any matter where it has been agreed that evaluator/client collaboration would be required for decisions.

E. Changing the design, scope, or cost of the study without officially amending the agreement.

Caveats

A. Do not adhere so rigidly to the contract that changes dictated by common sense are not made or are unduly delayed.
B. Do not develop contracts that are so detailed that they stifle the creativity of the evaluation team or require an undue amount of time and resources in their development.

Illustrative Case

A state education association, concerned about the ways in which school districts were holding teachers accountable for professional performance, decided to undertake a thorough appraisal of those procedures. Accordingly, an evaluation organization was commissioned for the task.

The state education association and the evaluators assumed that a formal agreement would be necessary before the study commenced. However, what should be included in the agreement was never fully addressed. Early discussions between the evaluators and the association authorities centered on procedures to be pursued in conducting the study, rather than on specific agreements about who would do what, for what reasons, and at what times. When the formal agreement was completed, both parties felt confident that the important issues had been covered.

Following a comprehensive investigation of accountability procedures used by school districts, the evaluators presented the report, as agreed, to education association authorities. The findings indicated that the school districts had employed inadequate and unreliable teacher-appraisal instruments, and that association officials had contributed to the general failure of the accountability strategies by encouraging teachers not to cooperate with school districts' initiatives to hold teachers professionally accountable.

As agreed contractually, the report was disseminated to specified audiences by the education association authorities according to a prearranged time schedule. The evaluators soon discovered that those sections which were critical of the teachers' association had been removed from the report. Moreover, the evaluators were at a serious disadvantage in seeking redress because the matter of final editorial authority had not been included in the formal agreement. At this point, the evaluators' options were limited to submitting to the action of the association or publicly condemning the behavior of the association officials.

Analysis of the Case

During preliminary discussions with the state education association authorities, the evaluators should have taken careful note of points for inclusion in the formal agreement, including possible difficulties arising from the controversial nature of the subject. Mutual agreement should have been reached, so that all crucial issues had been fully and fairly settled in the contract. When near completion, the contract should have been scrutinized by both parties and consideration given to the possibility of review by legal experts.

Under such an agreement, if the education association authorities had tried to persuade the evaluators to modify the report before it was disseminated, they could have refused to do so. No doubt, they would have concluded that the integrity of the report would be damaged by the requested modifications. The evaluators' final editorial authority, by this contract, would have assured the right to contest the issues.

C2 Conflict of Interest

Standard

Conflict of interest, frequently unavoidable, should be dealt with openly and honestly, so that it does not compromise the evaluation processes and results.

Overview

Conflict of interest exists in an evaluation when the evaluators' private interests might be affected by their evaluative actions. For example:

1. The evaluators might be able to advance their particular philosophical, theoretical, or political point of view by reporting particular findings.

2. They might benefit or lose financially, long-term or short-term, depending on what evaluation results they report, especially if the evaluators are connected financially to the object of the evaluation or to one of its competitors.

3. The evaluators' jobs and/or ability to get future evaluation contracts might be influenced by their reporting of either positive or negative findings.

4. The evaluators' personal or political ties to their client might be strengthened or weakened by reporting results that reflect positively or negatively on the client.

5. The evaluators' agency might stand to gain or lose, especially if they trained the personnel or developed the materials involved in the object of the evaluation.

The breadth of the above examples indicates that many evaluations contain the potential for conflict of interest; thus, the problem is frequently not a matter of how to avoid conflict of interest but of how to deal with it. It is a prevalent concern in internal evaluations where close friendships and personal working relationships are commonplace and may influence the outcomes of the evaluations. It is also a frequent problem in external evaluations, since clients have much freedom to choose external evaluators and external evaluators must win evaluation contracts in order to stay in business. Conflicts of interest can bias evaluations by corrupting their processes, findings, and interpretations.

Guidelines

A. In initial discussions with clients, identify and clearly describe possible sources of conflict of interest.
B. Seek advice from persons who have different perspectives on the evaluation in order to stay open to evaluation alternatives and philosophies and thus plan and conduct a less-biased evaluation.
C. Release evaluation procedures, data, and reports publicly, so they can be judged by other independent evaluators.
D. Agree in writing on procedures to protect against problems associated with conflict of interest in methodology or reporting (see C1, Formal Obligation).
E. Whenever possible, obtain the evaluation contract from the funding agency directly, rather than through the funded project.
F. Assess what advantages (monetary, social, moral, political) various parties may gain or lose as a result of the evaluation and be prepared to resist pressures they might exert.

G. Make internal evaluators directly responsible to agency heads, thus limiting the influence which other agency staff might have on the evaluators.

Pitfalls

A. Believing that calling the attention of officials of the client agency to a real or potential conflict of interest within the agency or its constituency will be sufficient to correct the problem (public disclosure or corrective action cannot always be expected, since it may reflect adversely on the officials or the agency)
B. Assuming that merely following a set of well-established "objective" procedures will eliminate all conflicts of interest
C. Assuming that independent, nationally known experts are unbiased and free from conflict of interest problems

Caveat

A. Take care not to exclude persons who are uniquely qualified to be involved in the evaluation solely because of the fear of conflict of interest allegations.

Illustrative Case

A school district curriculum director had worked with the system's reading specialists and teachers to develop a curriculum guide and materials for a three-stage individualized reading program in grades 1–4.

The director commissioned outside evaluators to evaluate the first stage, with the idea that if their work was satisfactory they would be engaged for the second and third stage evaluations—with considerably larger contracts. The evaluators soon realized that the curriculum director had been the major architect of the new curriculum guide and accompanying materials, that he believed strongly in their value, and that he would play a key role in awarding contracts for evaluations of the second and third stages of the program.

Rather than involving the reading specialists and school staffs directly in developing criteria for evaluating the guide and materials, the evaluators created a design that emphasized the strongest aspects of the guide and minimized its weakness. In addition, the evaluators added a person to their team who had previously served as a consultant to the curriculum director in the development of the guide and materials.

The evaluation report was highly favorable. However, when it was released, a substantial number of teachers complained to the superintendent of schools that major controversial elements of the curriculum guide as well as deficiencies in the materials had been glossed over during the evaluation, that the objectives of the teachers themselves had not been properly considered, and that one of the evaluators had been influential in writing the curriculum guide.

The superintendent concluded that the evaluators had been too eager to win future contracts, had compromised their objectivity, and had destroyed their credibility. He directed that they not be engaged further.

Analysis of the Case

At the beginning the evaluators should have assessed and dealt openly with their own potential conflict of interest, that of their client, and those of other involved parties. If they were not successful in instituting procedures that would keep the evaluation reasonably free from being influenced to serve vested interests, they should have declined to proceed with the evaluation. Certainly they should not have designed and staffed the evaluation so that a positive report was virtually assured.

They might have involved the reading specialists, the curriculum director, and the teachers in developing criteria for assessing the curriculum guide and accompanying materials. They then could have developed a design by which to describe and assess the guide and materials; and they could have collected and reported judgments of the materials from a wide spectrum of participants in the reading program.

C3 Full and Frank Disclosure

Standard

Oral and written evaluation reports should be open, direct, and honest in their disclosure of pertinent findings, including the limitations of the evaluation.

Overview

Full and frank disclosure means telling what one thinks and believes, as candidly as possible, based on one's best informed judgment. It requires that all acts, public pronouncements, and written reports of the evaluation adhere strictly to a code of directness, openness, and completeness.

Full and frank disclosure in reporting is essential if the evaluation is to be defensible. Its absence will severely threaten the evaluation's credibility. Audiences for the evaluation are entitled to reports that present clearly and frankly the evaluator's judgments and recommendations, and the information that was used to formulate them. Such reporting at the developmental stages may contribute substantially to bringing about needed program changes.

Guidelines

A. Report completely, orally and in writing, with full disclosure of pertinent findings and without omissions or other alterations based solely on the evaluator's opinions.
B. Show clearly the basis for the perceived relationship between the objectives of the evaluation, the data collected, and the findings (see D10, Justified Conclusions).
C. Present relevant points of view of both supporters and critics of the program being evaluated (see A3, Information Scope and Selection).
D. Report key factors which might significantly detract from or add to the evaluation's validity, whether discovered before or during the evaluation, and discuss frankly their implications for the findings and recommendations (see D2, Context Analysis).
E. Report judgments and recommendations that represent broad, balanced, and informed perspectives.

Pitfall

A. Issuing reports which have been altered to reflect the self-interest of the evaluator, the client, or the program staff.

Caveats

A. Do not confuse full and frank disclosure with premature disclosure of information in a condition that may lead to misinterpretation and misunderstanding.

B. Do not make so much of the limitations that the report will fail to gain the credibility it deserves.
C. Do not concentrate so heavily on being candid that the rights of persons involved in the evaluation are violated (see C1, Formal Obligation and C5, Rights of Human Subjects).
D. Do not design evaluations and construct and release reports without considering pertinent social and political factors (see D2, Context Analysis).

Illustrative Case

A staff evaluator was asked to develop an evaluation report covering the first year's operation of the USOE-funded early childhood education project in a native American community. While examining the data the evaluator discovered that parental involvement, crucial to carrying out certain features of the program in the home setting, had been seriously compromised because a small minority of parents opposed some of the program's basic assumptions and tenets. Consequently, not all of the program's first-year objectives had been met, and it was dubious whether the second year's activities could be mounted as originally planned.

The evaluator, concerned that the funding might not be renewed if the dissension were reported, omitted discussion of its negative effects. The evaluator rationalized his behavior to himself by arguing that, after all, the project would be evaluated in a full, summative report at the end of the second year; that there was no point in "throwing out the baby with the bath"; that project personnel were well-intentioned and deserved the opportunity to show what they could do; and that premature close-down of the project would unnecessarily disrupt the incomes and lives of the staff.

Full and frank disclosure presentation of the evaluation data, in all aspects, was thus compromised. The audiences, including project staff, were lulled into believing that all was well. Corrective actions could not be taken, and needed improvements were delayed. Further, the concerns and issues of the dissident parents were not addressed, so that it became likely that the disruptions would be repeated again during the second year. All in all, the probability was greatly increased that the project would fail, that possibly useful practices would be discarded, that potential adoptions in other settings would be aborted, and that the federal investment would be wasted.

Analysis of the Case

The evaluator should have reported all the findings openly and honestly. He should have realized that the judgment he made to suppress certain information was not his to make; indeed, that it bordered on the unethical even though his motives may have been good. He might have offered to work with both the project staff and the dissident parents in characterizing their differences more sharply and to collect information pertinent to those differences that would facilitate appropriate adjustments and refinements.

C4 Public's Right to Know

Standard

The formal parties to an evaluation should respect and assure the public's right to know, within the limits of other related principles and statutes, such as those dealing with public safety and the right to privacy.

Overview

A "right-to-know" audience is one that is entitled ethically and legally to be informed about the intents, operations, and outcomes of an evaluation. The principle that defines a right-to-know audience is that those persons who will be affected by the evaluation should be informed about how and why it was done and about its results, except where the disclosure of such information would endanger public safety or abridge individual freedoms.

If persons or groups who will be affected by the evaluation cannot get information about it, they cannot detect flaws in its procedures or data, nor can they make constructive use of its findings. As a consequence, these persons may unwittingly become the victims of unwarranted conclusions and actions, or may perform their functions less well than they might have had they been informed of the evaluation findings. Evaluations should be expected to withstand the critical examination of those whose lives they may affect and to provide them with useful information.

The evaluator's ability to identify and properly serve right-to-know audiences greatly influences the fairness and utility of the evaluation. In turn, the evaluator's ability to release information is often partially controlled by the client. Therefore, both the evaluator and client bear responsibility for meeting this standard.

Guidelines

A. Advocate the public's right to know. Encourage clients to provide constituents—pupils, parents, teachers, administrators, other employees, board members, and citizens—information that is appropriate and timely, and that helps them to be enlightened contributors, consumers, critics, and observers.
B. Become knowledgeable about the statutes bearing on the public's right to know, and how these statutes relate to (and are tempered by) other statutes on privacy rights, civil and human rights, health, safety, etc.
C. Reach a formal agreement with the client during the planning stages of the evaluation covering the client's and evaluator's roles in assuring compliance with right-to-know requirements, including: identification of audiences for interim and final reports; authority to edit reports; documentation of intents, procedures and outcomes; and when, how, and to whom information about the evaluation will be released (see C1, Formal Obligation).

Pitfalls

A. Determining right-to-know audiences on the basis of convenience or economy, rather than ethical and legal considerations.
B. Failing to be involved in the control and release of information about, or resulting from, the evaluation.
C. Agreeing to allow the client to select and release parts of the evaluation report without consulting the evaluator (see C1, Formal Obligation).
D. Giving the client unilateral authority to edit, censor, or in any other way change the evaluation report before its release (see C1, Formal Obligation).
E. Releasing information or endorsing the client's release of information to selected members of the right-to-know audience, while withholding the information from other members of this audience.
F. Releasing partial information that has been selected to serve the client's personal needs, beliefs, or professional biases.

Caveats

A. Do not violate any individual's right to privacy (see C5, Rights of Human Subjects).
B. Be considerate of the client's right, responsibilities, and needs (see C6, Human Interactions).

Illustrative Case

For almost two years, the residents of a school district had been clamoring against the injustices of the district's desegregation strategies. The most prominent minority group insisted that integration plans were a farce, while the majority group was equally vehement that there was a reverse discrimination favoring the minority children. The board of education decided to have the situation evaluated so that problems might be placed openly in their proper perspective. Moreover, it was hoped that as a result of an evaluation, decisions could be made which would alleviate the tense situation.

The evaluators selected were not knowledgeable about the laws governing the public's right to know. They had never been challenged over information disclosure and did not consider this aspect of an evaluation to be important.

In the formal agreement with the school board, the evaluators did not concern themselves with the matter of information dissemination to the public. Interested parties, the agreement stated, would be "informed of outcomes of the evaluation in due course and at the discretion of the Board." Although the evaluators soon became aware that negative feelings were running high between the minority and majority groups in relation to desegregation issues, they concentrated on the school situation and almost totally ignored parents and the public at all stages of the evaluation.

A report was eventually submitted to the board. After some changes had been made in deference to the board's requests (for example, elimination of the mention of questionable decisions about busing), the evaluators presented their findings at a public meeting. A large crowd attended, demanding to know why they had not been consulted about the planning of the evaluation, why they had not been involved, why intermediate reports had not been released, and why the final report failed to address questions about the propriety of board decisions on busing. The evaluators and board were accused of violating laws covering public disclosure of information and their credibility and integrity were questioned.

Analysis of the Case

The evaluators, whether or not they sensed the intensity of public interest over the desegregation issue, should have made sure that the formal agreement with the school board complied with federal and state laws relating to disclosure of public information. With the board's concurrence, the evaluators might have formed an advisory group—consisting of representatives of the school and community—and consulted them about what questions should be addressed in the evaluation.

During the course of the evaluation, intermediate reports might have been issued relating to completed aspects of the evaluation which could be pursued as entities—one dealing with a history of busing and the other with curricular offerings at the various schools within the district. Representatives of both the minority and majority groups could have been invited to respond to these reports as well as to other important findings during the course of the evaluation.

The final report should have been presented to the open, public meeting without being altered, even though many of the recommendations might have been unpalatable to either group, and to the board. If the public had been kept openly, honestly, and objectively informed at all stages of the evaluation, the report likely would have been accepted by more people and its credibility would not have been so susceptible to attack.

C5 Rights of Human Subjects

Standard

Evaluations should be designed and conducted so that the rights and welfare of the human subjects are respected and protected.

Overview

Rights of human subjects in an evaluation include those rights which apply specifically to their being part of the evaluation and those generic rights which apply to many other situations. Some such rights are based in law, and some in accepted ethical practice, common sense, and courtesy. Legal provisions bearing on rights of human subjects include those dealing with consent (of subject, parents, or guardians) for participation, privilege of withdrawal, privacy of certain thoughts and information, confidentiality of some information, and health and safety protections. Ethical and common sense considerations include the right to determine one's physical and emotional preparedness for treatment, to place limits on time spans of involvement, and generally to avoid physically harmful or uncomfortable experiences.

Evaluators, for both moral and pragmatic reasons, should be knowledgeable about and adhere to both the legal and other human rights requirements of their evaluations. Those who are not informed about the rights of human subjects may unwittingly ignore of abuse them and harm the participants in the evaluation. If evaluators violate legal and ethical rights, knowingly or not, they will be subject to legal prosecution and/or professional sanctions. Regardless of whether the violations are conscious or the evaluators are punished, the injured participants may become opponents of educational evaluation generally. In addition, some audiences may discount conclusions and recommendations if they learn that these were derived from information obtained illegally or unethically.

Guidelines

A. Be aware that the rights of human beings are either explicit or implied in many moral, ethical, and legal codes (e.g., amendments to the Constitution).
B. Be knowledgeable about due process and civil rights laws.
C. Before initiating an evaluation, determine which ethical and legal principles apply to it.
D. Do not deprive students of instructional methods that are normally available to them and that are known to be beneficial. For instance, students should not be assigned (randomly or otherwise) to a control group in which instruction previously available from public resources (such as the services of certified teachers or use of library materials) is purposely withheld to assess the effect of such deprivation.
E. Develop formal written agreements that explain the procedures that will be followed by the client and the evaluator to ensure that the rights of human subjects will be protected.
F. Immediately inform individuals and/or parents or guardians when it is intended that they are to become subjects.
G. Inform subjects and/or parents or guardians of their rights in the evaluation (e.g., that they can withdraw from the evaluation at any time without penalty or prejudice).
H. When permission of parents or guardians is needed in an evaluation (e.g., to test children) the evaluator should thoroughly inform the parents of the implications of the evaluation and should obtain a signed form from them giving permission to test the children. It is not enough to assume permission simply because parents or guardians do not specifically object to their children being tested.
I. Obtain appropriate written permission from relevant authorities (e.g., the subjects themselves, their parents or guardians, or relevant administrative authorities) for access to individual records.
J. When anonymity is guaranteed to those individuals who supply information for use in the evaluation, set up a procedure to guarantee that this anonymity will be protected (e.g., mark individual data records with identifying numbers rather than names, appoint an independent

escrow agent to keep the only list that links the numbers to the names, and arrange for the destruction of the list when it is no longer required).
K. In reporting the evaluation findings, sufficiently disguise the identities of individuals so that they cannot be identified from contextual clues.
L. Guard against the possibility that other parties will use the collected data for purposes different from those agreed to by the persons who provided the data.

Pitfalls

A. Promising confidentiality when it cannot be guarantee
B. Guaranteeing that information will be used only to serve the stated purposes, when the courts may legally order that the information be released to serve other purposes
C. Failing to communicate clearly how the information which persons are willing to provide will be used and the extent to which it can be kept confidential
D. Jeopardizing the self-esteem and reputations of participants by publishing a report that questions their professional ability or their personal ethics without giving them an opportunity to present their perspective

Caveats

A. Do not choose methods that theoretically are the best for obtaining unequivocal information if they have a significant potential for violating the rights of human subjects.
B. Beyond obtaining informed consent, weigh human costs against benefits, and consider not doing the evaluation if the benefits do not justify the costs.
C. Accord program administrators the right to remain silent on personal matters, but require them to give access to information about program effectiveness even if they consider it personally threatening.
D. Respect the right of those who carry out the program, such as teachers or tutors, legitimately to avoid supplying information about their effectiveness if they were not involved in planning the program and/or if they had no control over how it was implemented.
E. Do not allow one's inability to guarantee that no person's rights will be violated to prevent the implementation of needed evaluations. While it may or may not be possible to eliminate all violations of human rights, reasonable precautions should be put into effect.

Illustrative Case

A board of education decided to examine which of three different approaches to education ("traditional," "fundamental," and "experimental") worked best with which kinds of students. The district hired an evaluator who recommended that a stratified random sampling plan be used to assign students to schools representing the different approaches. Stratification variables included measures of students' personality, achievement, and socioeconomic characteristics. Included in the data collected from students was such sensitive information as how much money their parents earned per year.

Although there was a clear directive in the evaluation agreement to obtain prior approval from the district superintendent or her designated representative before any measures were administered to students, the evaluator decided to bypass this restriction in some instances in order to complete data collection in time to meet other contractual agreements. The evaluator carried out part of the testing program under the guise of field testing "draft" instruments.

Shortly after the data were collected, a principal at one school requested a particular student's scores on one of the experimental personality measures used for the evaluation, so that he could better understand why the student was frequently in trouble. The evaluator was happy to comply with this request, as doing so might improve worsening relations between the evaluator and the district staff.

The evaluator decided to discuss that student's data in the final report to illustrate specific findings. In doing so, she provided enough information to reveal the student's identity to anyone casually acquainted with the student. The parents of the student sued the school district for rights violations.

Analysis of the Case

All data collection instruments should have been considered and approved prior to their use. Time to carry out this process should have been anticipated by the evaluator in setting up the schedule of activities. If delays developed, the evaluator could have impressed upon the superintendent the impact of ignoring or circumventing those rights to expedite completion of the evaluation.

The principal's request for information about a particular student should have been denied because of restrictions regarding the confidentiality of such data. The restrictions also should have guided the evaluator's judgments regarding how to discuss particular cases, teachers, and schools in the final evaluation report.

C6 Human Interactions

Standard

Evaluators should respect human dignity and worth in their interactions with other persons associated with an evaluation.

Overview

Human interaction in the context of this standard pertains to evaluators' interpersonal transactions which affect the feelings and self-respect of those who participate in an evaluation. Most evaluations have the potential for reflecting either positively or negatively on individuals or groups and their work. The point of this standard is that evaluators must guard against the potentially harmful effects of their human interactions.

Evaluators who do not understand and respect the feelings of participants in an evaluation may needlessly sadden or harm these persons, or provoke in them hostility towards the evaluation. Such offense to people violates the moral imperative that human beings' essential dignity must be respected, and it inhibits human creativity. In addition, it is impractical, because participants who have been offended may be moved to do things that seriously jeopardize the evaluation. Evaluators should make a balanced effort to show respect for participants in an evaluation and should develop sound evaluative conclusions and recommendations.

Guidelines

A. Make every effort to understand the cultural and social values of the participants, particularly if their values are pluralistic or different from the evaluators' values (see A4, Valuational Interpretation).
B. Take time to learn from the participants their particular concerns about the evaluation (see A1, Audience Identification, A3, Information Scope and Selection, and B2, Political Viability).
C. Maintain good communication about the evaluation with participants through established channels.

D. Become familiar with the organization where the evaluation is to be done, and plan the evaluation activities for minimum disruption of the organization's staff procedures, routines, and work schedules (see D2, Context Analysis).

Pitfalls

A. Behaving attentively and respectfully toward those in positions of authority while largely ignoring their subordinates
B. Assigning greater or lesser importance to some persons because of their age, sex, or race
C. Violating legal requirements or protocol in contacting and addressing participants
D. Reporting findings as personal evaluations of, or attacks on, people involved in the program being evaluated
E. Discussing one's attitudes about the personal attributes—such as intelligence, physical attractiveness, taste, and social skills—of persons whose work is being evaluated

Caveats

A. Consider not collecting information which might embarrass participants, if this information is not essential, if it might be collected in an equally useful form that would protect the identity of the participants, and if not collecting it might, in the long run, be more beneficial to the evaluation or the program being evaluated.
B. Do not go to such lengths to avoid embarrassing people or hurting their feelings that the validity and utility of the evaluation are sacrificed and the findings are not reported honestly, or that incompetence or unethical behavior by program participants is covered up.

Illustrative Case

A university's curriculum department undertook an evaluation to determine the impact of a history course on the achievement of poverty-level secondary school students. By arrangement with the curriculum department and its team of evaluators, a local school district agreed to participate in the evaluation.

The evaluators developed an operational definition of a poverty-level student, identified all the students in the eleventh grade in the participating district who met this definition, then randomly assigned half of these students to be taught by the history course.

All the poverty-level students who had been identified were convened at the beginning and at the end of the evaluation for testing. On each occasion, they were told that they would be tested to help the evaluators determine the effectiveness of the school district's programs for serving the needs of disadvantaged students.

In addition to the testing, the evaluation design included extensive classroom observation and pupil interviews. To ensure that the teachers would not make unusual preparations for the observations, the evaluators visited classrooms unannounced and conducted their observations without any advance agreements with either the teachers or their school principals. Similarly, the evaluators went unannounced to the homes of students to interview them about their school experiences.

When the final report was published, criticisms of the evaluators' insensitivities towards participants began to arrive at the school district's central office. The critics charged, for example, that the evaluators had:

1. disconcerted teachers by extensive classroom observation;

2. made thinly veiled criticisms to some teachers about their implementation of the history course; and

3. caused acute embarrassment to poverty-level pupils by separating them from other pupils, publicly labeling them as disadvantaged, and intruding on their homes unannounced.

In the light of these persistent criticisms, the school administration and the board tended to place less confidence than they might have in the evaluators and thus in the report. Later, they discounted the report altogether when they learned that the teachers and students who allegedly had been demeaned had not cooperated with the evaluators. As a consequence of these problems, the relationship between the university and the school district was weakened.

Analysis of the Case

The evaluators should have realized that their evaluation would have to be handled carefully—particularly with respect to poverty-level students. They might have selected students randomly from the total student population and assured that no students were labeled or identified publicly with respect to income level or other sensitive characteristics. The test results then could have been analyzed and reported so as to assess the program's comparative effects on poverty-level and nonpoverty-level students without embarrassing any student. In any case, the students' names and test scores should not have been revealed. The interviews with students probably should have been conducted privately in the students' schools; if there was a compelling reason to use their homes, these interviews should have been arranged carefully with the full knowledge and consent of the students, parents, and school officials.

Teachers and school principals should have been involved in the planning of various aspects of the evaluation, especially concerning the classroom observations. Conferences involving teachers, principals, and the evaluators could have been held periodically to report progress and to deal with problems, fears, threats, and insecurities. If some teachers had expressed embarrassment at over-ambitious observing and probing by the evaluators, an alternative strategy could have been agreed upon.

Given these procedures, strong recommendations for use of the history course for poverty-level students might have gained general support among teachers when the report was disseminated, and beneficial change could have occurred.

C7 Balanced Reporting

Standard

The evaluation should be complete and fair in its presentation of strengths and weaknesses of the object under investigation, so that strengths can be built upon and problem areas addressed.

Overview

Balancing an evaluation does not mean generating equal numbers of strengths and weaknesses. It means being complete and fair in assessing and reporting both negative and positive aspects of the object being evaluated.

Even if the primary purpose of an evaluation is to determine the weaknesses of an object, it is essential to identify strengths as well. One reason for this is that strengths can sometimes be used to correct weaknesses. Another is that actions taken to correct weaknesses may inadvertently diminish some unidentified strengths.

Guidelines

A. Report findings which indicate either strengths or weaknesses, whether intended or unintended, and identify where each is substantiated.
B. List key characteristics of the object and, using one or more perspectives, classify each as a strength, weakness, or neutral feature (see C1, Formal Obligation).
C. Within limits of time and resources, before submitting the final report, solicit critical comments from the knowledgeable parties representing diverse perspectives about the balance of strengths and weaknesses.
D. When some kinds of relevant data are inaccessible because of time or cost constraints, report these omissions, estimating their effect on the overall judgment of the object if they were either strongly positive or negative.

Pitfalls

A. Manipulating the balance of strengths and weaknesses to please partisan interest groups or allowing these groups to delete from the report weaknesses which might prove embarrassing
B. Manipulating the balance of strengths and weaknesses to further or protect the evaluator's personal interests or biases
C. Reporting a value judgment as either a strength or weakness without considering alternative perspectives which might change that conclusion

Caveat

A. Do not report highly tentative feelings for the purpose of achieving balance; if the body of defensible findings reveals an imbalance of strengths and weaknesses, that should be reflected in the report.

Illustrative Case

An external evaluation group was hired to evaluate a two-week workshop which trained teachers to teach in teams. The trainers' materials and the teachers' materials developed for the workshop were the objects of the evaluation. The evaluation group was asked to find the weaknesses in the materials and to suggest improvements. Following the workshop, the evaluators interviewed the trainers and the teachers to discover deficiencies in the materials and collect suggestions for changes.

The report listed the weaknesses and recommended changes to correct them. Later, when the developers of the materials tried to use the report to guide revisions, they discovered that making the recommended changes would destroy characteristics they considered to be primary strengths of the materials. However, the report offered no data on whether the trainers and teachers shared that view or how these characteristics related to the identified weaknesses. Lacking that balance, the report could not be used as a blueprint for revising the materials.

Analysis of the Case

The evaluators could have asked the trainers and the teachers to identify both strengths and weaknesses in the materials, and to rate sections of the materials on their effectiveness or usability.

Furthermore, the evaluators could have gathered empirical data on how the materials were, in fact, used during the workshop and on whether teachers learned what the materials were designed to teach them.

The final report could have analyzed the relative strengths and weaknesses reported by those who used the materials, substantiated by data on the actual effects of the materials in producing skillful teachers with favorable attitudes toward team teaching. The materials then could have been revised accordingly.

C8 Fiscal Responsibility

Standard

The evaluator's allocation and expenditure of resources should reflect sound accountability procedures and otherwise be prudent and ethically responsible.

Overview

Evaluators are fiscally accountable when funds are used for the purposes and procedures stated in the evaluation agreement, expenditures are in compliance with pertinent state and federal statutes and associated rules and regulations, and financial transactions are verified by standard accounting and auditing procedures.

There is always the possibility that evaluators will misuse the funds for which they are responsible; in addition, certain groups or individuals, attempting to discredit an evaluation, find funding a tempting area to exploit. Therefore, it is important that evaluators exercise extreme care in their use and accounting of funds.

Guidelines

A. Maintain accurate records of sources of funding and expenditures in a clear and understandable format.
B. Maintain adequate personnel records with respect to job allocations and time spent on the job.
C. Be efficient without compromising the quality of the evaluation.
D. Specify major costs for the evaluation in agreements with the clients, including personnel, consultants, travel, supplies, postage, telephone, data processing, conferences and meetings, public information, printing, meta evaluation, and overhead (see C1, Formal Obligation).
E. Use contract bidding or comparison shopping for the purchase of resources and services.
F. Include an expenditure summary as part of the public report to enhance public confidence in the evaluation. If private evaluators prefer not to do this, they should, at a minimum, have such data available upon request.

Pitfalls

A. Commencing a study without a carefully planned budget
B. Changing the evaluation activity plan without making necessary budgetary adjustments
C. Being unaware of laws applicable to the expenditure of funds
D. Becoming encumbered with unethical ties of any nature related to the appropriation or use of funds

Caveats

A. Ensure that the budget is sufficiently flexible or renegotiable that reallocations can be made in the interests of successfully completing the evaluation or directly benefiting the program being evaluated.
B. Discuss openly and frankly with clients unexpected occurrences which threaten the financial viability of the evaluation. For example, salaries of project personnel may increase steeply because of an unexpected award in collective bargaining. Make an effort to achieve an equitable financial resolution that will not adversely affect the evaluation.

Illustrative Case

A university research group submitted a proposal to a federal agency for a regional evaluation of the effectiveness of representative community members as teacher aides. The evaluation was approved by an initial review panel. When the prospective funding agency reviewed the proposal for final approval, it was noted that the evaluation would take place in areas with predominantly white schools. The director of the funding agency insisted that the number of schools in the evaluation be increased by 50%, so that schools with large numbers of minority students would be included. Because of the federal agency's shortage of funds, it was not possible to increase the budget, and the investigators accepted the expanded plan without a budgeting increase.

When the investigators began the evaluation, they soon realized that including the additional schools required considerably more travel funds than were in the budget. It was also necessary to increase salaries to provide qualified staff members of minority background in order to have a research team that could relate to all the schools involved. The evaluators made no attempt to obtain additional funding from the supporting agency or elsewhere and did not receive permission to transfer funds between categories. In order to make the necessary savings, they replaced the professional classroom observers that were part of the planned evaluation team with unpaid undergraduate students. Further, they cut back markedly on the evaluation instruments that were to be used to measure student performance.

At the end of the first year of the project, the evaluators submitted a fiscal report that was superficially reviewed by the university fiscal officer and transmitted to the funding agency. The agency noted that funds had not been expended in accordance with the approved contract and immediately suspended support for the evaluation. The suspension continued for six months while new budget categories and an increased budget were negotiated. During this period, however, two of the five senior members of the evaluation team who were fully supported by the evaluation obtained employment elsewhere. The evaluation suffered considerably in rigor and definitiveness because of the staff turnover and activity delays.

Analysis of the Case

The evaluators should have anticipated the evaluation design elements that would become problematical during the evaluation and provided for them in the basic contract. Having failed to do this, however, the evaluators should have taken the matter up with the client as soon as it became apparent. At that time, the evaluators might have negotiated an appropriate change in the agreement. On the other hand, if the client would not agree to the change, the evaluators could have made the problem and their efforts a matter of record and proceeded with the original evaluation design to the best of their ability or could have withdrawn from the project.

Code of Fair Testing
Practices in Education

JOINT COMMITTEE ON TESTING PRACTICES

A. Developing and Selecting Appropriate Tests

Test developers should provide the information that test users need to select appropriate tests.

Test users should select tests that meet the purpose for which they are to be used and that are appropriate for the intended test-taking populations.

Test developers should:

1. Define what each test measures and what the test should be used for. Describe the population(s) for which the test is appropriate.

2. Accurately represent the characteristics, usefulness, and limitations of tests for their intended purposes.

3. Explain relevant measurement concepts as necessary for clarity at the level of detail that is appropriate for the intended audience(s).

4. Describe the process of test development. Explain how the content and skills to be tested were selected.

5. Provide evidence that the test meets its intended purpose(s).

6. Provide either representative samples or complete copies of test questions, directions, answer sheets, manuals, and score reports to qualified users.

Test users should:

1. First define the purpose for testing and the population to be tested. Then, select a test for that purpose and that population based on a thorough review of the available information.

2. Investigate potentially useful sources of information, in addition to test scores, to corroborate the information provided by tests.

3. Read the materials provided by test developers and avoid using tests for which unclear or incomplete information is provided.

4. Become familiar with how and when the test was developed and tried out.

5. Read independent evaluations of a test and of possible alternative measures. Look for evidence required to support the claims of test developers.

7. Indicate the nature of the evidence obtained concerning the appropriateness of each test for groups of different racial, ethnic, or linguistic backgrounds who are likely to be tested.

8. Identify and publish any specialized skills needed to administer each test and to interpret scores correctly.

6. Examine specimen sets, disclosed tests or samples of questions, directions, answer sheets, manuals, and score reports before selecting a test.

7. Ascertain whether the test content and norm group(s) or comparison group(s) are appropriate for the intended test takers.

8. Select and use only those tests for which the skills needed to administer the test and interpret scores correctly are available.

B. Interpreting Scores

Test developers should help users interpret scores correctly.

Test users should interpret scores correctly.

Test developers should:

9. Provide timely and easily understood score reports that describe test performance clearly and accurately. Also explain the meaning and limitations of reported scores.

10. Describe the population(s) represented by any norms or comparison group(s), the dates the data were gathered, and the process used to select the samples of test takers.

11. Warn users to avoid specific, reasonably anticipated misuses of test scores.

12. Provide information that will help users follow reasonable procedures for setting passing scores when it is appropriate to use such scores with the test.

13. Provide information that will help users gather evidence to show that the test is meeting its intended purpose.

Test users should:

9. Obtain information about the scale used for reporting scores, the characteristics of any norms or comparison group(s), and the limitations of the scores.

10. Interpret scores taking into account any major differences between the norms or comparison groups and the actual test takers. Also take into account any differences in test administration practices or familiarity with the specific questions in the test.

11. Avoid using tests for purposes not specifically recommended by the test developer unless evidence is obtained to support the intended use.

12. Explain how any passing scores were set and gather evidence to support the appropriateness of the scores.

13. Obtain evidence to help show that the test is meeting its intended purpose(s).

C. Striving for Fairness

Test developers should strive to make tests that are as fair as possible for test takers of different races, gender, ethnic backgrounds, or handicapping conditions.

Test users should select tests that have been developed in ways that attempt to make them as fair as possible for test takers of different races, gender, ethnic backgrounds, or handicapping conditions.

Test developers should:

14. Review and revise test questions and related materials to avoid potentially insensitive content or language.

15. Investigate the performance of test takers of different races, gender, and ethnic backgrounds when samples of sufficient size are available. Enact procedures that help to ensure that differences in performance are related primarily to the skills under assessment rather than to irrelevant factors.

16. When feasible, make appropriately modified forms of tests or administration procedures available for test takers with handicapping conditions. Warn test users of potential problems in using standard norms with modified tests or administration procedures that result in noncomparable scores.

Test users should:

14. Evaluate the procedures used by test developers to avoid potentially insensitive content or language.

15. Review the performance of test takers of different races, gender, and ethnic backgrounds when samples of sufficient size are available. Evaluate the extent to which performance differences may have been caused by inappropriate characteristics of the test.

16. When necessary and feasible, use appropriately modified forms of tests or administration procedures for test takers with handicapping conditions. Interpret standard norms with care in the light of the modifications that were made.

D. Informing Test Takers

Under some circumstances, test developers have direct communication with test takers. Under other circumstances, test users communicate directly with test takers. Whichever group communicates directly with test takers should provide the information described below.

Test developers or test users should:

17. When a test is optional, provide test takers or their parents/guardians with information to help them judge whether the test should be taken, or if an available alternative to the test should be used.

18. Provide test takers the information they need to be familiar with the coverage of the test, the types of question formats, the directions, and appropriate test-taking strategies. Strive to make such information equally available to all test takers.

Under some circumstances, test developers have direct control of tests and test scores. Under other circumstances, test users have such control. Whichever group has direct control of tests and test scores should take the steps described below.

Test developers or test users should:

19. Provide test takers or their parents/guardians with information about rights test takers may have to obtain copies of tests and completed answer sheets, retake tests, have tests rescored, and cancel scores.

20. Tell test takers or their parents/guardians how long scores will be kept on file and indicate to whom and under what circumstances test scores will or will not be released.

21. Describe the procedures that test takers or their parents/guardians may use to register complaints and have problems resolved.

Improving State and Campus Environments for Quality and Diversity: A Self-Assessment

RICHARD C. RICHARDSON JR.,
DEWAYNE A. MATTHEWS AND JONI E. FINNEY

I. Introduction

Purpose and Organization

This guide was written to provide policy leaders with information needed to develop or revise action plans aimed at improving learning environments for an increasingly diverse student clientele. The self-assessment is organized into three sections. The first section introduces the self-assessment, defines key terms, discusses the conceptual framework that organizes the questions and provides suggestions for using information from the assessment. The second section includes four sets of questions that state and campus officials can use to collect and organize information about the impact of state policies and practices on campus efforts to improve quality and diversity. In the third section, 12 sets of questions are provided to help campus leaders collect and organize information about the impact of campus policies and practices on the learning environment as it is experienced by faculty and students.

Because state policies provide the overall framework for issues related to achieving campus diversity, the most useful planning information comes from an assessment of *both* state and campus environments. However, the last two sections of the guide can be used independently of the other. It is suggested that campuses collect data from state policy officials as part of any evaluation of the campus environment. Similarly, the campus perspective is critical to any useful evaluation of state policy and planning.

The term *"diversity"* in the self-assessment refers to differences among students that affect chances for success in an academic program or institution. Examples of diversity that influence the way a student experiences a learning environment include:

1. African-American, Latino or Native American students enrolled in historically Anglo colleges and universities.

2. First-generation college students of any race or ethnicity.

3. Students whose previous academic preparation is a poor match for campus expectations. Such students are also referred to in this document as *underprepared*.

4. Women enrolled in historically male programs or institutions.

5. Older adults attempting to earn degrees while concurrently managing employment and family responsibilities.

6. Students with developmental or physical handicaps.

These categories are not mutually exclusive. Students are at risk to the extent that they differ from the clientele a campus typically serves.

"Quality" refers to the degree to which an institution's aspirations and its performance are one and the same. To assess quality, the campus must have a vision of what it wishes to become as well as a set of standards against which performance can be measured. In advancing suggestions for using the self-assessment, the following four assumptions are made:

1. The campus has a vision of what it hopes to become.

2. Strategic planning is used to translate the vision into measurable objectives and to pursue continuing improvements in quality.

3. Current objectives include an emphasis on responding to student diversity while maintaining or improving the quality of undergraduate education.

4. The campus maintains high expectations for student performance (quality should not be improved by lowering standards; diversity is not incompatible with high standards of student performance).

The absence of any of these four conditions will limit the value of the self-assessment as a tool for improving quality.

"Underrepresented" as used in the self-assessment refers to any dimension of student diversity (as discussed on the previous page) that is less well represented on the campus than in the population from which the campus draws its student body. As a prerequisite to using the self-assessment, each state or campus should identify the student categories defined as underrepresented.

"Minority" has been used sparingly in the self-assessment because, in a growing number of cities and in some states, it is no longer clear to whom the term refers or what it means. In the self-assessment, the term refers to any student who attends a campus where a majority of the participants are of a different race or ethnicity.

Refer to Appendix A for a listing of additional publications and resources for using the self-assessment.

How Colleges and Universities Adapt to Student Diversity

Selective institutions may seek great student diversity as part of a goal to enroll a student body reflective of the populations they serve. Open-door institutions may become more diverse because of changing demographics in their service area. All campuses may be encouraged or required to accommodate students previously unserved or underserved as a result of federal, state or governing board inducements or mandates. Regardless of the dimensions of student diversity, the more students differ from the clientele a campus has traditionally served, the less likely they are to graduate.

Research documents the process through which successful campuses adapt to serve a more diverse student body without relinquishing a commitment to rigorous academic standards. In a two-year study of the public, baccalaureate-granting colleges and universities, 10 states identified state and campus practices that explained why some colleges and universities got better results than others. While most historically white colleges and universities experienced declines in African-American participation and graduation rates during the 1980s, about 20% were able to improve both enrollment and graduation equity during this period. Institutions that improved diversity reported higher levels of administrative commitment, greater use of strategic planning, careful attention to institutional climate for underrepresented populations and greater emphasis on staff diversity. They also reported more extensive and systematic use of strategies to reduce barriers to participation, to help students achieve high expectations and to make learning environments more responsive to student diversity.[1]

Colleges and universities adapt to student diversity through three stages of activity. In the first, *barriers to participation are reduced.* Campuses improve participation rates through flexible admission practices, appropriate financial aid packages, transition programs and outreach to the public schools. Reducing barriers results in students who are different from the populations a campus has traditionally served. If campus climate and the learning environment remain unchanged, a more diverse student population will experience higher levels of attrition than more traditional counterparts.

In the second state, *colleges and universities improve student retention by improving the campus climate and providing learning assistance to students who lack adequate preparation* to cope with the demands of the teaching and learning practices on campus. They also recruit a diverse faculty and administration, thereby providing advocates and role models for the new student populations. Strategies that help new students adjust to prevailing campus practices improve retention rates. They do not have a similar impact on graduation rates unless a campus is willing to change its teaching and learning practices in addition to changing students.

In the third stage, *faculty become involved in helping more diversely prepared students achieve academic success* in all majors. Improvements in undergraduate education benefit all students, but have their most significant impact on underrepresented populations who tend disproportionately to have the least comprehensive preparations. Strategies for improving achievement include student assessment programs, learning assistance opportunities and a commitment to student success through improved teaching.

Leadership is essential for campuses to adapt successfully to diversity. Achieving both quality and diversity requires a systematic combination of reducing barriers to participation, helping underprepared students achieve, and improving teaching and learning throughout all academic programs. All three stages must be addressed for diverse students to achieve at rates comparable to traditional students. The key strategies for each stage must be sustained in a design that emphasizes coordination and continuity. Leaders guide their colleges and universities through the process by exhibiting commitment, recruiting a more diverse faculty and administration, and emphasizing assessment and strategic planning.

State leaders are responsible for shaping the policy environment to support campus efforts to improve opportunities for a diverse student body. Public campuses face conflicting demands and scarce resources. They make the most progress toward improving quality and diversity when they receive direction and support from state policy leaders in the form of clear priorities, capacity-building programs, strategic plans and consistent policies.

The full range of state policies, administrative actions and campus strategies are summarized in the chart according to the stages they affect and the outcomes they most directly influence. The map suggested by the chart organizes the questions appearing in Sections II and III of the self-assessment.

Achieving Quality and Diversity: A Model for State and Institutional Change

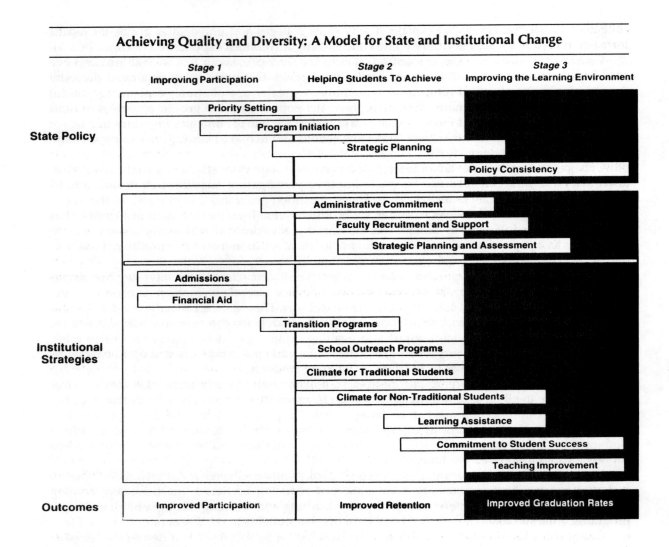

Suggestions for Using the Self-Assessment

Setting Standards and Assessing

The concept of assessment assumes the existence of standards against which current performance can be compared. Standards for colleges and universities should be developed in each state which reflect its traditions, values and population demographics. Such standards also should respect institutional differences in mission, selectivity and service-area demographics.

While each state should develop its unique set of standards, the self-assessment for quality and diversity proposes that *proportional participation rates and comparable graduation rates be included in the standards of every state.*[2]

Statewide underrepresentation of any group among college students or graduates points to a variance between aspirations and performance of any state committed to equal educational opportunity. States should strive to have underrepresented populations participating in higher education and proportionately represented in the system overall.

Campus objectives should contribute to the attainment of statewide diversity goals. If it has not already done so, the statewide coordinating or government board working with individual colleges and universities should adopt five-to-eight-year goals for diversity. These should be formally agreed to by the governor and the appropriate legislative leaders.

Campus assessment processes should take into account representation in and graduation from specific programs as well as overall participation and graduation rates. The institutional standard proposed in this document is completion of or graduation from an academic program. In assessing individual program performance, both quality and diversity should be considered. Program rigor is established by faculty members on each campus with attainment estimated by rates of student admission and transfer rates to baccalaureate programs, course grades, student performance on licensing exams, employer surveys, success rates of students who continue their education and other indicators suggested by accrediting associations and state evaluation programs. Low graduation rates and poor performance by graduates represent variances between state and campus aspirations and system performance.

Standards for state and campus practice are implicit in the questions that appear in the self-assessment guides in Sections II and III. Not all questions are relevant for all colleges and universities. Taken as a group, however, the questions provide a systematic and comprehensive view of policies and practices that contribute to improved quality and diversity. While states and campuses undoubtedly will tailor their uses for the self-assessment, campus and state assessment sections should incorporate the three-step process outlined below.

Step 1: Share information (obtained by answering questions in the self-assessment) about current practices or policies and the extent to which these practices or policies are embedded in the campus or state culture.

Step 2: Test the answers (perceptions) with a broader and appropriate campus or state constituency (other faculty, staff and students, or other state leaders) and determine the gap between current practice/policy and campus or state aspirations for building strategies for action.

Step 3: Use the data to inform campus or state planning processes.

Organizing the Assessment Process

Developing an Information Base. State leaders should answer the questions in Section II, "Assessing the State Policy Environment." A statewide task group should be convened to develop an information base (Step 1) from the answers to these questions. The group should include, as a minimum, representatives from (1) the statewide coordinating or governing boards and appropriate staff, (2) the campuses, (3) the legislature, and (4) the governor's office.

Campuses should answer questions in both Section II and Section III, "Assessing Campus Environments." Campuses may want to develop their information base (Step 1) by appointing a small steering committee to organize the self-assessment process, interpret the responses of the self-assessment and serve as the liaison to the appropriate institutional planning units.

Section II is designed for use by state officials in evaluating the policy environment they provide. It also is designed to be used by campus officials in encouraging a dialogue between campus and state leaders about the influences of state policy on institutional quality and diversity. Representatives of campuses participating in the self-assessment, along with representatives of the legislature, governor's office and coordinating or governing board, should form a study team and complete this section. [Note: Campuses may wish to complete the self-assessment without the involvement of state leaders. It is designed to be used either way.]

One approach at the campus level might involve appointing five task groups with responsibility for answering sections of "Assessing Campus Environments" as noted below. Knowledgeable faculty and staff leaders should develop concise answers to each of the questions as a vehicle for discussion about current practice and consensus about future directions.

Task Group 1: Assessing the State Policy Environment

Task Group 2: Administrative Commitment, Faculty Recruitment and Support, and Strategic Planning and Assessment

Task Group 3: Admissions, Financial Aid, Transition Programs and School Outreach Programs

Task Group 4: Campus Climate for Traditional and Non-Traditional Students

Task Group 5: Learning Assistance, Commitment to Student Success and Teaching Improvement

In addition to the people who have the information necessary to answer questions in each section, it also may be useful to involve representatives from key constituencies whose cooperation is essential to making the changes required to improve quality and diversity.

Validation and Assessment (for the state and campus self-assessment process). Step 2 includes validating the answers developed in Step 1 and determining the gap between what exists and what is needed. This provides state or campus leaders with a sense of how much consensus exists to support needed change. As a byproduct of this step, participants should enhance their level of understanding about current practice or policy significantly.

One way of validating answers and assessing consensus is to place the answers from the task groups in a survey format (see sample in Appendix B). Task group members then can be asked to answer two questions about each practice:

1. Does the answer accurately reflect campus (or state) practice/policy?

2. Does the practice/policy reflect what the campus (or state) should be doing in light of its goals?

Some alternatives to use of the survey format include department review, open forums and focus groups. However the validation and consensus-assessing process is organized, the results should provide state and campus planners with information about the gaps between current and needed practice as perceived by each of the constituencies whose cooperation is required to improve the campus or state environment.

Using the Data (for state and campus planning). Step 3 of the assessment process has been designed to inform both state and campus planning processes. It is most likely to achieve this objective if there is a timetable for developing responses that allows for completion of Step 2 in a sequence that coincides with the state or campus planning cycle.

A summary of responses to task group answers, collected through the survey format, can provide campus and state planners with information appropriate for targeting special education efforts, especially to develop a better state- and campus-wide consensus about goals for quality and diversity (Step 3). Each state and campus should invent its own process for planning and quality improvement. Information from the self-assessment should fit any process that incorporates a concern for quality and diversity. States and campuses should consider the improvement of undergraduate education and responding to student diversity as interrelated objectives within a single planning effort rather than as objectives to be pursued through separate planning efforts.

Space has been provided in Sections II and III for additional questions tailored to the unique circumstances of the user.

Sources of Additional Information

Appendix A lists publications that expand the discussion of the state role in creating a favorable climate for minority participation and achievement. Other recent publications that provide extensive discussions of campus concepts and interventions are included, too. Also listed are key ECS and Winthrop University staff to contact for technical assistance or advice.

Notes

1. An analysis of the survey results appears in Richardson, R. C. Jr. *Promoting Fair College Outcomes: Learning From the Experiences of the Past Decade*, Denver, CO: Education Commission of the States, 1991. The 10 states were California, Florida, Illinois, Massachusetts, New Jersey, New Mexico, Ohio, South Carolina, Tennessee and Texas.

2. Participation rates can be calculated for the state and for each institution by comparing a group's representation among college students with the same group's representation in the population from which the students were selected. States and institutions may find it useful to make the same comparison using a group's representation among recent high school graduates as a base. Graduation rates can be calculated by comparing a group's representation among a graduating class with the same group's representation among the students that produced the graduating class.

   The success of an institution in retaining students is usually measured by cohort survival. While retention is not an end in itself, students cannot graduate unless they are retained. Cohort survival studies should be interpreted with caution in assessing achievement among students whose differences influence academic readiness. Racial and ethnic minorities are disproportionately underprepared and significantly more likely to follow nontraditional patterns of college attendance. For these students, ratio data may be more useful than cohort survival in assessing state or institutional progress toward comparable graduation rates.

Reporting and Using Assessment Information

T. D. ERWIN

Ethics of Assessment

. . . In reporting assessment information, institutions must always observe ethical standards, such as those contained in the *Standards for Evaluation of Educational Programs, Projects, and Materials,* as outlined by a Joint Committee on Standards for Educational Evaluation (1981), representing twelve evaluation organizations. It covers four areas of evaluation: utility, feasibility, propriety, and accuracy. Another useful source is a statement of standards for test developers and users by a joint committee representing the American Psychological Association, the American Educational Research Association, and the National Council on Measurement in Education (Committee to Develop Standards for Educational and Psychological Testing, 1985). Anderson and Bell (1978), Guba (1975), and Riecken and Boruch (1974) have also written about potential ethical problems in evaluation. As these writers indicate, three major elements of ethics are particularly important in higher education: accuracy, quality, and confidentiality.

Departments and institutions have an obligation to report *accurately* the results of assessment (Guba, 1975). In reports to an institution's audiences, both the strengths and weaknesses of the program under review should be noted. As Wolf (1987) points out, it is often tempting to suppress "unflattering results." Departments are often reluctant to admit problems to upper-level administrators, and administrators are often reticent about releasing negative findings outside their institutions. The media report can help perform this task successfully. In addition, it is often helpful to describe the action that has been taken to rectify a weakness, since external audiences tend to view efforts for improvement or for "moving forward" in a positive light. Accuracy also dictates that evaluation results should not be made to appear more negative than the data support (Guba, 1975). On rare occasions, institutions have reported such results in order to gain extra funding or to elicit support from the outside to effect a major institutional change. Clearly, such reporting is unethical.

Departments and institutions also have an obligation to use "sound experimentation and evaluation" procedures (Anderson and Ball, 1978; Riecken and Boruch, 1974). Were methods with known biases used? Did an adequate number of students participate? Was an appropriate analytical model used? Were the limitations of the results admitted? Were the objectives assessed as stated? Validity of the assessment methods will always be a paramount issue. Gender bias and racial or ethnic biases should be considered in the selection and design of methods, especially in general education.

In some cases, sources may be unaware of proper assessment procedures. In other cases, major problems at the institution are skirted because of a fear of results. Most of these problems can be prevented if a wide array of participants is involved in the efforts. It is also helpful to include outside consultants to review procedures and techniques and to contribute other ideas.

Finally, departments and institutions have an obligation to keep student data confidential and to report individual information back to the student. Unless permission is secured beforehand, students are protected by the Buckley Amendment (the Family Education Rights and Privacy Act of 1974) from public release of identifiable assessment data. Some institutions collect data anonymously; however, this practice weakens assessment studies because such data cannot be linked to other available information about a particular student. For example, it is useful to compare test scores with courses completed, but such comparisons cannot be made unless individual test takers can be identified.

When assessment data are reported back to students after scoring, they learn from the assessment experience itself. Moreover, the assessment program is strengthened, since students who feel a part of assessment and who receive feedback are likely to take assessment more seriously.

One major problem with individual assessment reporting is that it requires considerable time and financial resources. Assessment information can be reported back through courses or through the advising programs. Longwood College in Virginia trains undergraduates to report information to their peers. Often, individual written score reports can be transmitted along with information about designated campus locations where further explanation can be obtained.

Institutions should make clear at the outset that students are required to participate in assessment activities. Statements about students' responsibilities should be included in the institution's catalogue and announced at convenient times—for instance, at orientation sessions for new students. To avoid confusion, an institution might have entering students read or sign a statement acknowledging that assessment is required. An example of such a statement is given in Chapter Two.

Issues of ethics also extend to faculty, who may feel that assessment can intrude into their academic freedom. On the one hand, faculty have a responsibility to teach what is stated in institutional and program objectives. For instance, if the "scientific method" is included as an objective under a general studies natural science distribution requirement, the instructors in all such courses (that is, general studies courses in geology, biology, physics, chemistry, and astronomy) will be expected to teach the scientific method. On the other hand, the objectives of any program should be determined by the faculty and student affairs staff, not by state officials. To avoid the imposition of statewide course requirements, such as those mandated for kindergarten through twelfth-grade levels, faculty will undoubtedly be motivated to state their own educational objectives and methods.

Conclusion

This chapter has explained the importance of the source, the channel or mode, the message communicated, and the audience for the assessment information, or *who* says *what* and *how* to *whom*. These four perspectives are important because the mere collection and interpretation of results does not guarantee that any *action* will be taken. Successful assessment efforts culminate in the use of the information for decision making. The final section of the chapter, addressing the ethical considerations of assessment reporting and uses, is meant to emphasize the importance of data accuracy, quality, and confidentiality.

Assessing Progress in Minority Access and Achievement in American Higher Education

MICHAEL T. NETTLES

Introduction

Assessment has become an essential component of America's educational policy development and of internal planning within schools, colleges and universities. Because President Bush and the 50 state governors have, for the first time in history, set national goals, measuring progress has been elevated to a higher status than ever before. In the present public policy environment, assessment is viewed as the primary means of ensuring that national and state goals are achieved. Periodic assessment is also a way to ensure that public and private schools, as well as colleges and universities, are held accountable for student achievement, which is the centerpiece of national goals. Similarly, individual school, college and university officials are finding assessment necessary for measuring progress toward achieving their own institutional goals and for informing various audiences about their status and progress.

Increasing minority participation and achievement in the nation's colleges and universities are issues of national and state, as well as institutional importance. There has been too little progress in enrolling and employing minorities in higher education, and the progress made has been too gradual. For example, despite representing over 12% of the U.S. population, African Americans were only 9.2% of the college enrollment in 1980 and 8.7% in 1989. Despite more than a 50% increase in the Latino population, Latino college students made up only 4% of college enrollments in 1980, increasing to 5.2% in 1989. African American faculty constituted only 4.5% of the nation's college and university faculty and Latinos only 2%. In addition, African Americans represented only 3.8% of the doctoral degree recipients and Latinos 2.7% of earned doctorates in 1989.

Imaginative strategic planning and new ideas and efforts are needed to make more progress. This paper examines ways that assessment and evaluation can be used to increase awareness and enhance plans and strategies for improving minority participation and achievement in higher education. Assessment and evaluation are important for clarifying issues, identifying models of success and reasons for failure, examining the impact of existing policies and strategies and providing the rationale for establishing new policies and strategies.

Assessment and Minority Students

Perhaps the most common notion of educational assessment is measurement of student aptitude or cognitive development and achievement, but assessment can and should involve much more. Student testing is important, but what is needed is more complete diagnoses that measure academic progress and performance as well as opinions, attitudes and behaviors and the impact that policies and programs have upon student and institutional achievement. Measures of cognitive development typically provide a report that reveals enormous gaps between minority and majority students. Trend analyses usually reveal little, if any, progress being made to eliminate the gaps.

Equally important are:

- Evaluations of the progress of college and university efforts to increase minority representation through affirmative action and other types of interventions

- Evaluations of minority students' social involvement and academic performance

- Measurements of their attitudes, behaviors and personal development

- Measurement of changes that colleges and universities officials make to improve environments to accommodate the needs of minorities

- Evaluations of the strengths of policies and programs and other interventions to help improve the plight of minorities attending college

- Evaluations of integration of people of various backgrounds into forming a mainstream of campus life and community

The purpose of assessment in this context then is to generate the data and information needed for setting goals, monitoring and reporting progress toward achieving goals and identifying the processes that lead to positive outcomes. With regard to minorities in American higher education, this means:

- Setting goals and measuring progress toward increasing minority students' preparation for entering and performing in college

- Improving the practices used by colleges and universities to identify and admit minority students and to predict and monitor their success in college

- Identifying the financial and other supports that minority students need to enroll, persist and progress through college

- Identifying the characteristics and factors about colleges and universities that contribute to enrolling and retaining more minority students through graduation

- Improving the academic performance (as reflected by grades and test scores) of minority students who enroll

- Improving the quality of the experience minority students have while they are enrolled in college

- Ensuring that minority students who enroll and persist through graduation are adequately prepared for their post-baccalaureate careers and educational experiences

- Increasing the supply of graduate-trained minority students

- Increasing minority representation and achievement on college and university faculty and administrations

With regard to assessments of programs and policies, the most common practice is to evaluate the impact of such initiatives as admissions policies and programs, financial aid and scholarship programs, summer enrichment programs, tutorial and retention programs, programs designed to increase student involvement and achievement in education and other special interventions affecting student access, retention, performance and graduation. . . .

Student Experiences and Institutional Practices

Student attitudes and experiences and institutional programs, practices and policies constitute what often has been called institutional climate. Like student background characteristics, institutional climate contributes to both student and institutional outcomes. It accounts for much of the persistence, progress and academic achievement of college students.

The published goal statements of many higher education institutions include their aspiration to improve the quality of all students' college experiences. Institutions that adopt such goals are compelled to compensate for student deficits that may result from disadvantaged backgrounds with the same vigor they address academic deficiency of entering students. Periodic assessments of student experiences help institutions measure progress toward achieving campus environments where satisfaction and normal social and academic functioning are not racially distinguishable. Assessing these non-cognitive dimensions of college is best conducted by measuring the attitudes, opinions and behaviors of students. This also helps to identify social factors beyond student background and academic preparation (institutional factors) that impede or promote student progress and achievement.

Some student indicators that are important in assessing the quality of life on campus include students' habits; participation in honors and other programs that provide privileges, prestige and status; satisfaction with faculty, administrators and the academic integration or relationships with faculty inside and outside of classrooms; social integration or involvement in campus social life; feelings about the existence of racial discrimination on campus; and feelings of equity and inclusion in all aspects of campus life.

The important generic institutional factors of campus environment include ethnic composition of the student body, faculty and administrators (Smith, 1988 and 1990).

Surveys or questionnaires are most often used to ascertain opinions, attitudes and behaviors. Other "unobtrusive" approaches, while typically unscientific, also can be valuable. These approaches might include observations of student behaviors in popular campus meeting places such as residence halls, cafeterias, student unions, sporting and intramural events as well as participation in clubs, organizations and volunteer activities. Such observations provide valuable insight into the quality of students' campus life and how it works for different ethnic groups. Other indicators include topics and tone of published articles in student newspapers and other campus publications and negative campus incidents or interactions involving people of different ethnic backgrounds. Such indicators help to shape perceptions of the public, many of whom are involved in developing college or university policies.

Such casual observations should not be generalized, however, without supporting evidence collected through more scientific methods. Assessments also should include adequate representation of each minority group, as well as of majority students. Surveys or observations of students belonging only to one ethnic group tend to disguise differences among groups (e.g., Mexican Americans, Puerto Ricans, African Americans). Studies that exclude majority students do not show how minority students' experiences compare. Comparisons are needed to monitor progress toward achieving equality among minority and majority groups.

Because student experiences, like student backgrounds vary, over time, and hopefully improve because of institutional actions and interventions, it is important to repeat studies of campus environments periodically in order to monitor trends. Pre- and post-assessments also may be useful for showing change in the quality of each class' experience over time, e.g., from freshman to senior year, as well as for comparing various classes, e.g., the class of 1985 and the class of 1992.

A literature review of the last 20 years of undergraduate student experiences and performance found only a small amount of research addressed the problems and issues of any minority group's experiences in the nation's colleges and universities. However, the amount of research on African Americans and Latinos exceeded that devoted to Asians and American Indians. The review also found that, as with personal and academic background characteristics and preparation, minority students of various ethnic groups differed from one another with respect to their experiences and performance in college. But the experiences of non-Asian minorities tended to be inferior to those of their majority students attending the same institutions. Findings of the research literature indicated that "the climate for minorities on campus is more alienating than involving. On more and more campuses, racism and racial hostility are no longer thinly disguised. Sadly, on many campuses racism is a fact of life" (Smith, 1990).

Student and faculty behaviors and perceptions can be powerful in fostering diversity and narrowing the gap between minority and majority student performance. Regardless of ethnicity, students who experience favorable and frequent interaction with faculty have strong commitment to their institution and high motivation to achieve academic success have more satisfying and healthy college experiences (Mow and Nettles, 1990). These factors, however, have been found to be more important in predicting outcomes, e.g., graduation and grades, of minority students than of majority students (Tracey and Sedlacek, 1987). Positive self-concept has also been found to be related to student performance and outcomes (Astin, 1982; Pascarella, Smart, Ethington, and Nettles, 1987), but prior research and assessments have not been designed to discern whether the positive self-concept—the chicken—precedes the positive outcomes—the egg—or vice-versa.

Additional behavioral differences between majority and minority students should be measured when assessing the educational experience and process. Such factors as differing rates of stopping-out and returning to college, transfer rates from both four-year and two-year institutions to other four-year institutions, and patterns of selection and distribution of minority students among the various major fields have consistently been found to be related to the relative quality of experiences students have in college, to the quality of their college environment and to institutional and student outcomes. . . .

Conclusion

The fact that assessment has moved to the forefront of higher education suggests that the process of setting goals and identifying areas in need of intervention can become much more refined. As colleges and universities gain greater appreciation of the need and value of assessment, they must be prepared and willing to take action to improve practices and outcomes.

In some cases, especially in the short term, assessment could reduce opportunities and access and lead to lower performance and outcomes for minority groups than might be expected, particularly blacks and Hispanics. This is evident in the admissions processes of undergraduate and graduate schools and academic programs such as teacher education where standardized test scores may be used to screen and select students (Simon, 1990). It is also evident in states with new assessment and testing policies, such as Florida. A higher proportion of minority than majority test-takers fail to meet the cut-scores required to move to junior class status in the curriculum (McTarnaghan, 1990).

At the same time, however, that these policies and practices restrict and/or alter opportunities, they reveal valuable information about the academic development needs of minority students that would otherwise go undetected and probably untreated. The fact that minority students, on average, receive lower scores on standardized admissions tests than majority students reflects in part the relatively low quality of schooling provided for minority children. Recognizing this relationship helps parents and policy makers understand that by improving the schools that minority children attend they are also likely to improve such outcomes as test performance, entry and success in colleges and, in turn, the overall quality of colleges and universities and their academic programs and courses.

The tension between greater access and college and university quality persists, but has never been more important to higher education than today. Assessments help to quantify and character-ize performance deficits. For example, one objective of national education goal #4—being first in the world in math and science by the year 2000—is to increase the number of minority students who enter and successfully complete math and science education curricula. This will require each U.S. college and university to identify the extent of underrepresentation in these fields and the obstacles to greater minority participation so they can develop strategies for more favorable outcomes. Assessments of student qualifications, aspirations, attitudes and behaviors; institutional and departmental admissions policies, racial composition of the faculty and administration; and institutional affirmative action initiatives should be examined in planning to increase minority representation and achievement.

The focus of contemporary assessments on college and university campuses is much broader than measuring student admissions qualifications. Measures of the characteristics, strengths and weaknesses of the general population and sub-groups of students, the attitudes and behaviors of students and faculty, observations of everyday student and faculty behaviors and measures of alumni attitudes and achievement are all important aspects of college and university assessment strategies. How colleges and universities use the results and findings to establish policies and programs to improve minority outcomes is an important factor to monitor, and assessment pro-vides a vehicle for doing so.

Benefits and Costs of Assessment in Higher Education: A Framework for Choicemaking

PETER T. EWELL

Some Caveats on Estimating the Costs and Benefits of Assessment

In attempting a comprehensive review of the costs and benefits of institutional assessment programs, a number of initial observations and caveats are in order. Each places important limits on what can meaningfully be accomplished.

First, comprehensive programmatic assessment efforts of substantial duration are quite new. Fewer than a dozen institutions have operated such programs for a sufficient length of time for their consequences to become clear. The vast majority only initiated assessment activity within the last two or three years and are still in a planning, shakedown, or implementation mode. Consequently, their cost and payoff structures are different from those typical of fully established programs. Despite similarities in coverage and function, moreover, institutional assessment programs differ markedly in administrative organization. This means that they may also differ significantly in the way they account for invested resources—particularly those having to do with reassigned personnel.

Second, because establishment of an explicit assessment function often involves a reassignment of existing activities, actually counting invested resources can be difficult. What is of interest is less the total cost of "assessment activity" than the net marginal investment in new assessment mechanisms established, plus the resource implications of reassigning old functions such as placement testing and student surveys. Moreover, because such existing functions are often scattered and inefficient, establishing a centralized coordinating mechanism can sometimes yield significant economies (Ewell and Lisensky 1988). As a result, past attempts to estimate the cost of institutional assessment programs have concentrated on establishing the *marginal* costs of such programs, rather than the total investment required (for example Ewell and Jones 1986, Lewis and Wasescha 1987).

Third, while the claimed benefits of institutional assessment are many, consistent valuation of these benefits is difficult. This situation is shared by most analyses of higher education's benefits: not only are dollar equivalents hard to come by, but estimates of benefit will vary considerably across different individuals with differing value structures and preferences (Bowen 1980). As a result, there have been few definitive studies of concrete rate-of-return for investments in instruc-

505

tional processes in colleges and universities beyond such relatively well-defined technical areas such as computer-assisted instruction. This situation considerably limits the applicability to assessment activities of formal "cost/benefit" techniques that compare the dollar values of investments with the dollar values of obtained results (Levin 1983).

Given this condition, past studies of the impact of particular educational innovations or reforms have generally concentrated on one of two alternatives. *Cost/effectiveness* analyses examine invested costs in the light of some identifiable common output or criterion measure for the activity in question. But with the exception of degree program completion, few common criterion measures exist for the outputs of higher education. Indeed, it is the very absence of such measures which in part inspires the call for outcomes assessment in the first place. The second alternative is to compare costs with "utilities"—identifiable benefits which may vary in value across beneficiaries depending upon their individual goals and preferences. Here the primary intent of analysis is to determine which alternatives provide which kinds of benefits to which beneficiaries at what cost. While such analyses do not provide unambiguous "cost/effectiveness ratios" upon which to decide what to do, they can nevertheless provide considerable guidance for policy. At the very least, they provide a coherent framework for thinking systematically about various available alternatives.

Fourth, like benefits, costs may also be subject to inconsistencies in valuation. In addition to identifiable fiscal and physical resources, the establishment of a new and controversial program may cost "political capital" or may cause considerable organizational friction over and above its observable cost. Focusing institutional and faculty attention narrowly on the implementation of assessment may preclude other opportunities or may inhibit instructional innovation or risk-taking. Like educational benefits, these effects are sufficiently ambiguous that converting them into estimated dollar equivalents may lose information. Beyond the issue of how much is invested there is that of who pays. Valuation of costs may vary significantly depending upon what particular parties-at-interest actually have at stake in the process.

Finally, the nature of assessment as a "management information" activity means that it is a special kind of investment—one not easily subject to the traditional rubrics of cost/benefit or cost/effectiveness analysis. Like all activities related to management, operating an assessment program involves the investment of real resources. These entail direct and observable costs to the institution. Benefits of information, however, are generally highly indirect. Literature on the "economics of information," for example, is founded on management's use of information to make effective choices among posed alternatives—each of which itself has an associated stream of costs and benefits (for example, Huber 1980, Day 1978). If additional information can increase the probability of choosing a "profitable" alternative, investment in obtaining this information is justified up to the point where the margin of incremental "profit" disappears. But decisionmakers in higher education are rarely presented with such choices. Far more common is a situation where information—obtained at an invested cost—indicates that a particular deficiency is present and suggests some lines of attack toward addressing it. To address the deficiency, however, requires the investment of yet another increment of resources. Absent this second increment (or absent its being effective), prior investment in information may pay no dividends whatever. This is one reason why proponents of educational assessment and evaluation pay so much attention to explicit mechanisms for connecting evaluation information to concrete decision processes, and to the use of information. Without effective use, the "benefit" side of the analysis approaches zero.

Taken together, these caveats suggest treating the costs and benefits of institutional assessment activities in the following ways:

- **Costs are appropriately treated as programmatic costs**—that is, the costs associated with a formal, established, identifiable activity with sufficient organizational and budgetary identity that resources can be consistently accounted.

- Costs are appropriately treated as marginal costs—that is the difference in investment between establishing an assessment program of given content and structure over existing information-gathering and utilization costs previously being incurred by the institution.

- Costs are appropriately treated as the costs of assessment itself, not the costs associated with actually addressing identified deficiencies; moreover, the costs of assessment are a part of any wider rate-of-return calculation for the costs and benefits of any instructional improvement efforts in undergraduate education.

- Some "costs," such as loss of access and reduction of risk-taking, are more appropriately treated as externalities than as direct dollar costs; while it is in principle possible to obtain rough dollar equivalents for these negative effects, analysis is more meaningful if they are considered explicitly.

- A few claimed benefits of assessment, while difficult to render consistently in dollar terms, are sufficiently comparable across situations to in principle support a cost/effectiveness estimate; where obtained results are comparable, for example in claimed increases in student persistence and graduation rates, cost/effectiveness calculations are appropriate.

- Most benefits of assessment are appropriately treated as "utilities" to particular constituents in the process, each of which may, (a) value obtained outcomes differently, and (b) pay different shares in the total investment.

These properties define the limits for the discussion that follows. . . .

Applying the Framework to Some Policy Choices

As emphasized throughout the prior discussion, derivation of a single cost/benefit estimate for all assessment programs is both impossible and inappropriate. Difficulties in consistently specifying costs and benefits in dollar terms, differences among proposed "assessment" programs in different institutional settings, and differences in the ways key participants value similar outcomes conspire against such a simple answer. What is possible is to use identifiable costs, benefits, and externalities to help sort through proposed policy alternatives. Two pairs of such alternatives are briefly discussed in this section—one for institutions and one for states—using the proposed framework as a guide.

Two Institutional Policy Alternatives

Assessment Using Available Instruments

One popular early option for institutions electing to embark on assessment is to found the program on existing standardized tests and surveys, most of which are commercially available. This approach has major virtues of proven technique and available normative data to inform comparisons, though it also has many drawbacks. The best known current example of this approach is Northeast Missouri State University (McClain and Krueger 1985); Tennessee's statewide "performance funding" program involves establishment of institutional programs with similar characteristics (Banta 1986). Among the institutions currently embarking upon assessment in response to state mandate, somewhere between one third and one half initially adopt such an approach. Its basic features include, a) administration to selected samples of students commercially available general education examinations such as the ACT-COMP, ACT-CAAP, or the ETS Academic Profile, b) administration to graduating seniors the GRE or ETS Major Field examination that corresponds to their major or administration of a relevant professional licensing or professional school admissions test and, c) administration to samples of current students, graduating seniors, and/or recent alumni an available survey such as the ACT Evaluation Survey Service (ESS), the NCHEMS/College Board Student Outcomes Information Service (SOIS), or the UCLA College Student Experiences Questionnaire (CSEQ).

Figure 2 presents major areas of benefit and cost for this alternative. Using the categories of benefit, cost, and externality previously discussed for each party-at-interest, the figure roughly indicates the presence and intensity of each. Particularly notable are the following:

- **Benefits.** Benefits of this alternative are due primarily to the perceived external credibility provided by the use of standardized instruments. Partly this is because instruments available through "third party" testing agencies such as the Educational Testing Service (ETS) and the American College Testing Program (ACT) are removed from direct institutional interest and can therefore be presumed to be more "objective." Partly it is due to the ability of standardized tests and surveys to provide a basis for evaluating comparative performance. For individual students, primary benefits are therefore in the area of better "consumer information" for college choice; Northeast Missouri, for example, was able to attract an increasingly more talented entering student body partly on the basis of the credibility provided by its assessment program. For faculty and institutions/programs, benefits are more mixed. Changes in curriculum and "targeted teaching" have been widely reported in Florida institutions as a result of "rising junior" examinations, but these responses are seen as both positive and negative depending upon the observer's value position. Clearly, however, the credibility of such a program can strongly benefit an institution in the acquisition of resources. Institutions such as Northeast Missouri that have adopted this approach can point to an impressive record of addition-to-base funding from state authorities.

- **Costs.** Direct dollar costs for a testing program of this kind have been estimated in the range of $7/student (Ewell and Jones 1985). This estimate assumes the use of "average cost" standardized instruments and testing samples of students rather than entire populations. In most cases, these costs have been covered through available institutional contingency funds (or, as in the case of Tennessee, are drawn from revenues "earned" through favorable test performance). In some cases, student fees are levied (in South Dakota institutions, for example, $15/student in 1989–90).

- **Externalities.** Primary externalities of this approach fall on individual students because in most cases standardized testing involves the sacrifice of out-of-class time and results in information which is of limited utility in enhancing individual student learning. Indeed, many obtained scores are not individually valid as the instruments are designed to produce group scores. At the same time, if scores are valid and used, students may lose access to particular courses or their progress impaired because of their performance. In such cases as well, there will likely be allegations of test bias if minority groups experience substantial adverse impact. These two effects, however, will occur only if the testing program functions as a "gateway" for students; the majority do not do so, and the major cost to students is in the form of time and effort that might have been invested elsewhere. For faculty and programs, externalities are minimal as this approach rarely involves additional effort. Perceived violations of "academic freedom" can be considerable—particularly if class time is used for test administration and if results are applied in an attempt to change class coverage or instructional practice. In addition, there will often be charges that available standardized tests do not adequately reflect what is actually taught. Both of these objections will likely be stronger in the major field than in general education, and are least strong with respect to surveys (Banta 1985). For the most part, however, faculty externalities will be minimal compared to administrative overhead costs. This approach, for instance, virtually requires establishment or enhancement of a testing/assessment office with responsibility for test coordination, scheduling, and reporting. For even a small institution, this function may require at least an additional one-half FTE administrative position.

This pattern of benefits, costs, and externalities assumes an "ideal type" program based solely on available instrumentation—an alternative which very few institutions actually adopt. More common is a "mixed" approach where standardized assessment instruments are used in some major departments and not others, according to the wishes and needs of their respective faculties. Where this occurs, many externalities can be avoided—particularly those associated with perceived violations of academic freedom and student-experienced burdens of testing. In general

Figure 2
Benefits, Costs, and Externalities of Institutional Assessment: Institutional Programs
Case 1: Available Standardized Tests and Surveys

Parties-at-Interest		Benefits		Direct Costs		Externalities
Individual Students	o	- Increase in knowledge/ skill	–	- Testing Fees	– –	- Burdens of additional testing
	o	- Increases in graduation/ persistence			–	- Loss of access/choice of classes/programs
	o	- Increased credibility of degree			–	- Loss of access due to biases and inequities
	++	- Better information for college choice				
Faculty	+/–	- Targeted teaching			o	- Burdens of designing and administering instruments
	o	- Better ability to design examinations			–	- Perceived violations of "academic freedom"
Institutions/ Programs	+/–	- Improved curriculum structure and sequence	–	- Full program cost, if unsupported	–	- Narrowed curriculum/ "teaching to the test"
	o	- Improved planning/ resource allocation			o	- Opportunity costs of faculty time
	o	- Increased faculty time committed to teaching			–	- Increased administrative "overhead"
	++	- Enhanced ability to acquire resources				
External Constituents	o	- Enhanced employee skills • general • job-related				
	o	- Better employee attitudes toward work				
General Public	+	- Assurance that tax dollars are well spent	–	- Additional tax dollars to support total or partial cost of program		
	o	- Increases in general welfare				

education, use of standardized instruments is often seen as an institutional "path of least resistance" for developing a credible program in response to state mandate. In these cases, faculty are rarely directly involved in the decision to proceed and the primary benefits, costs, and externalities of the program are experienced primarily among administrators. Line faculty may know little about the program and about how it operates.

Locally-Designed "Curriculum-Embedded" Assessment

An increasing number of institutions developing assessment programs are choosing to design their own instruments and to as fully as possible integrate assessment techniques with established points at which performance information is already collected. In the cognitive arena, this implies designing "curriculum-embedded" or "course-embedded" assessment techniques in which representative examples of student performance in regular coursework or examinations are collected and evaluated. In some cases, specially-designed examination questions are prepared for administration as part of the final examinations of regular classes; answers are used to both assign course grades and are scored for consistency with wider curricular objectives. In other cases, representative "portfolios" of existing student work are regularly collected and analyzed in a similar fashion. In both cases, a major benefit is that student motivation is unaffected: students know that their work will count for course grade credit, so are more inclined to do their best. Non-cognitive data-gathering is similarly integrated into regular data collection mechanisms and procedures. Existing questionnaires, such as those typically administered to current students by Student Affairs offices to determine their satisfaction with provided services, or those typically administered to graduates by Alumni Offices to determine current status and activities are often extended to include a range of non-cognitive developmental items (Ewell and Lisensky 1988). Another example of using existing opportunities is to extend the coverage of end-of-course questionnaires already administered to students for purposes of faculty evaluation.

Figure 3 presents primary areas of benefit, cost, and externality associated with this approach. The categories used are those of the previous section, and again an "ideal type" assessment program is assumed.

- **Benefits.** Direct benefits of this alternative accrue primarily to faculty and students. Experimental validation work at Alverno College, for example, has repeatedly substantiated the efficacy of faculty-designed assessment techniques in helping to produce gains that can be documented externally—often through subsequent administration of standardized measures or performance in the workplace (see Mentkowski and Doherty 1984). Other institutions have documented increased pass-rates on professional licensure examinations as a partial result of increased local assessment. For individual faculty members, particular benefits have been in the area of improved "test-making" skills. At Kean College in New Jersey, for example, a key secondary effect of "course-embedded" assessment in general education has been faculty-reported improvements in constructing their own examinations; similar effects are reported at the University of Tennessee, Knoxville, but are largely confined to those departments where faculty actually designed examination questions (Banta 1986). Closely related are faculty-reported benefits related to curriculum structure. In cases where faculty must design their own assessment processes, they must first refine their curricular objectives; often this process in itself can lead to improved curricular coherence and course structure. In contrast, this approach generally shows little of the short-term external payoff associated with the test-based alternative. Most faculty-designed instruments are initially not seen as credible by outside authorities.

Figure 3
Benefits, Costs, and Externalities of Institutional Assessment: Institutional Programs
Case 2: Locally-Designed "Curriculum-Embedded" Assessment

Parties-at-Interest		Benefits		Direct Costs		Externalities
Individual Students	+	- Increase in knowledge/ skill	o	- Testing Fees	o	- Burdens of additional testing
	+	- Increases in graduation/ persistence			–/o	- Loss of access/choice of classes/programs
	o	- Increased credibility of degree			o	- Loss of access due to biases and inequities
	o	- Better information for college choice				
Faculty	+	- Targeted teaching			– –	- Burdens of designing and administering instruments
	++	- Better ability to design examinations			–	- Perceived violations of "academic freedom"
Institutions/ Programs	++	- Improved curriculum structure and sequence	–	- Full program cost, if unsupported	o	- Narrowed curriculum/ "teaching to the test"
	+	- Improved planning/ resource allocation			– –	- Opportunity costs of faculty time
	+	- Increased faculty time committed to teaching			–	- Increased administrative "overhead"
	o	- Enhanced ability to acquire resources				
External Constituents	+	- Enhanced employee skills • general • job-related				
	+	- Better employee attitudes toward work				
General Public	o	- Assurance that tax dollars are well spent	o/–	- Additional tax dollars to support total or partial cost of program		
	+	- Increases in general welfare				

- **Costs.** Direct dollar costs of programs of this kind are uncertain because most costs are already embedded in institutional operations. The majority must be counted in the reallocation of faculty time. At an institution like Alverno, for example, it is difficult to determine what assessment "costs" because all faculty are doing it as a natural and regular part of teaching. Clearly, however, direct charges for students will be minimal. Equally clearly, incremental costs for designing and coordinating a new activity will have to be borne by the institution—either through reassignment of faculty time and/or through the employment of coordinating personnel and testing-measurement specialists to assist the faculty. Because such activities are arguably a part of teaching, moreover, they are less likely to be supported through increased revenue provided by the state. Indeed the recent trend among state initiatives is in the opposite direction: to require institutional assessment, but not to provide additional funding to institutions to pay for it (Ewell, Finney, and Lenth 1990).

- **Externalities.** Externalities associated with this approach are also largely concentrated among faculty and at the institution/program level. Just as direct dollar costs under this approach are difficult to estimate, the total amount of faculty time invested can prove considerable—particularly in the initiative's early stages. Not only is the investment considerable, but it is also likely to be unevenly distributed; most institutions rely heavily on the efforts of a few committed faculty members to serve as a core group during the program's initial years. Usually, such faculty serve as members of a multi-functional (and often overworked) "assessment task force" or are drawn from the faculty of initial "pilot" departments undergoing assessment on an experimental basis. In the long term, "burnout" among this group can be considerable. For other faculty, devoting the needed time to develop meaningful local assessment processes may mean taking faculty time away from other things. Because both the coverage and technology of assessment are determined by faculty themselves, this approach may avoid some of the political opposition encountered by approaches based on standardized testing that are held to violate faculty autonomy. But the integrated approach does compel faculty to agree on common teaching objectives, and this in itself may not be easy. At the same time, administrative overhead costs for assessment may equal those associated with a test-based approach because so many diverse activities must be coordinated.

Again, the above discussion assumes adoption of an "ideal type" program in which all assessment is developed locally. Most actual institutional programs will mix features of this approach with the use of existing standardized instruments and surveys. For the most part, the decision of which features to adopt is based upon local needs and expedients. Occasionally, however, institutions will consciously elect to adopt a mixed approach in order to maximize the different kinds of benefits associated with each approach. They may, for example, use local assessment for most departmental evaluation, but occasionally administer standardized instruments to small samples of students in order to help "validate" their local processes (for example, Mentkowski and Doherty, 1984). Similarly, they may employ consultants from national testing or assessment organizations not only to help faculty design better instruments, but also to help "certify" that local procedures are credible and sound.

Two State Policy Alternatives

Statewide Testing of Basic Skills

One leading set of state-level policy alternatives with respect to assessment centers on the perceived need to detect and remediate students entering higher education deficient in such basic skills as reading, writing, and computation. Statewide programs of this kind are currently in place in New Jersey, Tennessee, and Texas, and are being actively discussed in several other states. Basic features of such programs include, (a) use of a single standardized basic skills examination by all institutions in the state, (b) prohibitions against the use of results to deny admission to institutions, (c) use of results to place students assessed as deficient into appropriate remediation programs, and (d) exit testing of students using the same instrument on completion of remediation.

Figure 4 presents major areas of benefit and cost for such a program. Again using categories of benefit, cost, and externality discussed in the previous section for each party-at-interest, the figure roughly indicates the presence and intensity of each. Particularly notable are the following:

- **Benefits.** Program benefits will occur particularly for individual students in the form of documentable increases in knowledge and skills at the basic level and in increased chances of graduation. But both benefits, it is important to note, will *only* occur if remediation and associated placement are also successful—they are not direct results

Figure 4
Benefits, Costs, and Externalities of Institutional Assessment: State Programs
Case 3: Statewide Testing of Basic Skills

Parties-at-Interest		Benefits		Direct Costs		Externalities
Individual Students	++	- Increase in knowledge/ skill	+/–	- Testing Fees	–	- Burdens of additional testing
	++	- Increases in graduation/ persistence			–	- Loss of access/choice of classes/programs
	o	- Increased credibility of degree			–	- Loss of access due to biases and inequities
	o	- Better information for college choice				
Faculty	+	- Targeted teaching			o	- Burdens of designing and administering instruments
	o	- Better ability to design examinations			– –	- Perceived violations of "academic freedom"
Institutions/ Programs	o	- Improved curriculum structure and sequence	–	- Full program cost, if unsupported	– –	- Narrowed curriculum/ "teaching to the test"
	o	- Improved planning/ resource allocation			o	- Opportunity costs of faculty time
	o	- Increased faculty time committed to teaching			–	- Increased administrative "overhead"
	o	- Enhanced ability to acquire resources				
External Constituents	+	- Enhanced employee skills				
	o	• general				
		• job-related				
	o	- Better employee attitudes toward work				
General Public	+	- Assurance that tax dollars are well spent	–	- Additional tax dollars to support total or partial cost of program		
	o	- Increases in general welfare				

of the assessment program *per se*. Some benefits should also result for faculty, who are better enabled to teach at the appropriate level rather than being required to constantly remediate in the classroom. Moreover, external constituents and the general public will receive secondary benefits in the form of greater assurances about the skill levels of college students and greater accountability.

- **Costs.** Overall dollar costs for a testing program of this kind can be estimated from past experience in New Jersey and emerging experience in Texas. Both incurred initial test development costs in excess of one million dollars. Operating costs are about $9–11/student tested, or about $4/enrolled FTE student. How such costs should be paid is another matter. Both states currently fund the program out of general revenue. This entails a direct cost to taxpayers as well as an opportunity cost to institutions that might have received this funding for alternative purposes. Alternatively, direct costs could be passed on to students in the form of fees. In this case, there is a further choice between spreading the fee across all enrolled students as part of a tuition payment, or applying it only to those tested as they are tested. The latter alternative would have the advantage of clarity, but would be particularly burdensome for those assessed as deficient and forced to leave the institution.

- **Externalities.** A program of this kind will probably entail a range of negative externalities. For individual students, all three potential side-effects would be present. Certainly, total test-taking time would increase; evidence from New Jersey and emerging evidence from Texas suggest, for example, that institutions now administer both the statewide Basic Skills test and their own local placement examinations. Moreover, many students will be denied their initial choice of classes or programs because of deficient performance; in New Jersey, more than a third of test takers are assessed as deficient in one or more basic skills each year. If deficiencies are detected, directed placement may significantly increase the amount of time it may take a student to obtain a degree. Major negative impacts, however, would likely be initially incurred in the form of faculty opposition and "teaching to the test."

This overall pattern might be significantly changed if particular features of the proposed program were subject to modification. For example, changing the requirement that a single, statewide instrument be used would markedly reduce faculty opposition and teaching to the test. Negative impacts would remain in these areas, but would likely be not so strong. Allowing institutions to use their own instruments, moreover, would also reduce the burden of testing for individual students. It would not, however, provide as much payoff in accountability to the general public as would a program based upon common testing.

Changing the requirement that students be tested on exiting from remediation would also shift the payoff pattern for the program as a whole. Because of a demonstrable association between directed placement and persistence, individual benefits would not be so strong as in the base program, and the benefits associated with assuring external constituents and the public that college students possess basic skills would evaporate. At the same time, externalities such as teaching to the test and perceived violations of academic freedom would be all but eliminated.

Requiring Institutions to Undertake Local Assessment

As noted earlier, the center of gravity for most state-based assessment efforts has been to require institutions to design and implement their own local assessment programs (Ewell, Finney and Lenth 1990). Current assessment efforts in Virginia, Colorado, Missouri, South Dakota, New York, Arizona, Kansas, and many other states are consistent with this pattern. While many variations in what is required are apparent across the many states where such plans are in place, their general payoff pattern is presented in Figure 5. Once again, standard categories of benefit, cost, and externality are used. Notable features are as follows:

- **Benefits.** Most of the documentable benefits of this alternative are centered in the curriculum—particularly in improvements in curricular structure and sequence. Benefits to individual students are certainly present, but documentable increases in knowledge and skill will be difficult to claim. Some external benefits will also be present, but the primary focus on internal evaluation and improvement will also imply that obtained information is less directly useful to external constituents. All these benefits, of course, will depend heavily upon what the institution in fact proposes to do. Absent information on graduate placement, for example, benefits associated with consumer choice will largely disappear. Effective "packaging" of information intended largely for internal management, however, can also serve to demonstrate accountability to the public (Ewell 1990).

Figure 5
Benefits, Costs, and Externalities of Institutional Assessment: State Programs
Case 4: Requiring Institutions to Design and Implement Local Assessment Plans

Parties-at-Interest		Benefits		Direct Costs		Externalities
Individual Students	o	- Increase in knowledge/ skill	–/o	- Testing Fees	–	- Burdens of additional testing
	+	- Increases in graduation/ persistence			o	- Loss of access/choice of classes/programs
	+	- Increased credibility of degree			o	- Loss of access due to biases and inequities
	+	- Better information for college choice				
Faculty	o	- Targeted teaching			– –	- Burdens of designing and administering instruments
	+	- Better ability to design examinations			–	- Perceived violations of "academic freedom"
Institutions/ Programs	++	- Improved curriculum structure and sequence	–	- Full program cost, if unsupported	o	- Narrowed curriculum/ "teaching to the test"
	+	- Improved planning/ resource allocation			–	- Opportunity costs of faculty time
	+	- Increased faculty time committed to teaching			–	- Increased administrative "overhead"
	+	- Enhanced ability to acquire resources				
External Constituents	+	- Enhanced employee skills • general • job-related				
	o/+	- Better employee attitudes toward work				
General Public	o/+	- Assurance that tax dollars are well spent	–	- Additional tax dollars to support total or partial cost of program		
	+	- Increases in general welfare				

- **Costs.** Overall costs for programs of this design are in the standard estimated range of $7–12/FTE student. Once again, however, the question of who should bear these costs has a number of answers. Student fee alternatives, as practiced in South Dakota, seem comparatively inequitable because individual students do not generally receive proportionate direct benefit. Requiring institutions to fully absorb these costs as part of their existing budget, as practiced in most states, may require substantial reallocation and associated opportunity costs. Where such programs are substantially supported by additional dollars, as for example in Virginia and New Jersey, an additional burden is placed on the taxpayer, who may or may not receive commensurate payoff in the form of accountability and improvements in general welfare. In practice, many states share such costs between institutions and taxpayers—appropriating limited additional funds to support local assessment, or using existing categorical grant or non-base incentive funds to support a range of institutional efforts.

- **Externalities.** The most important negative consequences associated with this alternative occur for faculty and for institutions. For faculty, a major consequence is a considerable investment of time in the design of assessment instruments and in scoring and interpreting the results of local examinations. Although each institution is free to choose its own approach, many faculty will also feel threatened in the initial stages of the program. Both these consequences may change depending upon the kinds of assessment instruments used: faculty-designed instruments will increase faculty burden and reduce opposition; commercial standardized tests (even if chosen by faculty themselves) will increase the perceived threat but will substantially reduce direct faculty burden. For the institution, moreover, substantial costs may be incurred in establishing an additional administrative function.

This pattern can also be substantially altered by changing one or more features of program design. For institutions, the payoff structure shifts markedly depending upon the percentage of direct costs that is covered by additional resources. If the full cost of the program must be absorbed, most institutions will see such a program as a "break-even" proposition at best; most will therefore initially resist its adoption as state policy. For faculty, opposition and burden are directly affected by the kinds of approaches proposed—particularly the degree to which they rest upon standardized testing and the level of choice that faculty are allowed in choosing appropriate assessment instruments and techniques. Emerging experience seems clear on the point that some degree of faculty opposition will be experienced no matter what kind of program is proposed. It is also clear, however, that the greater the degree of faculty involvement, the more likely curricular benefits will be.

For individual students, however, few features of the program's design will cause a shift in preference: most benefits are indirect, and because assessment results are not used to determine the fates of individual students, important externalities are absent. The major exception here is cost, as given uncertain individual payoffs, it will be difficult to argue that individual students should bear a substantial cost burden for this activity.

PART IV

Conducting Assessment and Program Evaluation Studies: Technical Aspects

Introduction

In sound assessment and evaluation programs, the critical planning addressed in the earlier chapters takes place before the actual conduct of assessment and evaluation. The decisions and tasks addressed in this section focus on planning for the more technical aspects of assessment and evaluation, e.g., collecting and analyzing the information.

Unfortunately, some assessments and program evaluations are undertaken with the mistaken perception that they are primarily technical activities. This can have serious consequences. Instruments may be selected without consideration of the purpose or audience, leaving institutions with expenses and data but little usable information. The misperception can also lead to the assumption that the areas of expertise needed for the planning and other major program responsibilities match those of the current chief campus information providers. They may include researchers who do not have the necessary background in gathering qualitative data, measuring student cognitive growth, or negotiating with diverse audiences about the design of the program, the questions to be asked and the use of information.

The literature below includes several suggestions to enhance the quality of information collected and the interpretation of the information. The use of multiple methods, both qualitative and quantitative information, and broad based teams for interpretation are emphasized.

While some assessment authors have addressed these and other technical aspects in their literature, much of the useful literature comes from the long standing frameworks and tools of evaluation and research. The literature below provides a general introduction to the topics for novices in assessment and program evaluation. To acquire adequate skills for the conduct of assessment and evaluation, students will need to pursue the rich literature and curricula that exist for a diversity of specific areas, e.g., general research and evaluation design, and qualitative and quantitative methods (instrumentation, design, and analysis). Guidelines involving the collection and analysis of information are not needed specifically for assessment and evaluation. These tasks and issues are addressed in various professional literature and professional standards, e.g., the *Standards for Educational and Psychological Testing*.

Selecting designs. Overall frameworks for thinking about assessment were included in Part II. More direction for the program design is provided in these selections. **Terenzini** (1989) develops a taxonomy of design approaches in a matrix that addresses the specific questions of "why", "what", and "who" of assessment relating to the purpose, the object, and the level. He also discusses methodological problems associated with design, measurement, and statistical analyses. **Hanson** identifies some issues related to measurement of change and value-added assessment, and extends the discussion to include appropriate and inappropriate analysis techniques. Discussions about special design concerns and issues are provided in other selections. Those beginning assessment are often encouraged to compile an inventory of existing assessment activity and information. **Underwood** describes such an effort that, in addition to providing such information, served other purposes such as identification of those who are likely to be receptive to assessment, and visibility for the assessment efforts on the campus. **Ratcliff** presents a design model that analyzes student coursework patterns in order to inform the process of curriculum reform. **Wiggins** provides several principles to guide the design of an assessment program that is appropriate for the liberal arts, one that reflects the values, media, and goals of such study. Efforts by faculty in the assessment of general education are described by Banta (1991, March/April).

Choosing methods of gathering data. Earlier decisions about the focus of the assessment will provide direction for selecting the best methods to gather information about the dimension selected. For example, the measurement of mathematical skills might support using a quantitative pencil and paper instrument; measurement of a student attitude about the value of the study of mathematics would suggest using a qualitative technique such as a focus group.

While the collected information should be valid and credible to assure that it is both usable and used by audiences, the demand for these qualities sometimes creates a tension given the diverse audiences in assessment. What is a credible type of measurement or information to one group may not be so to another. State legislators may favor using commercial instruments providing data that they perceive can be used to compare institutions, while faculty may prefer institutionally designed instruments that reflect more accurately what is taught at their own institution.

Prus and Johnson provide an extensive analysis of the advantages and disadvantages of twelve assessment information collection options that include qualitative as well as quantitative methods. They also offer suggestions for addressing the weaknesses of each method.

Guidance in deciding between commercially available and locally developed instruments is provided by Ory. The two types of instruments are compared on several factors: purpose of assessment, match with goals and content, cost, availability of norms, institutional acceptance, quality, and student motivation to respond. These factors can be used to evaluate the match between the object of an assessment, that is, what is being measured, and the measurement options.

Ewell explores one of the major trends in the practice of collecting assessment data, decreased reliance on commercial instruments. He also discusses possible future directions for those instruments. The experiences of several institutions with specific methodologies to assess general education outcomes are reviewed by Banta (1991).

Additional selections address specific methods. Unobtrusive measures such as physical traces, observation, and archives and records are explored by Terenzini (1987).

Assuring quality information and interpretation. To assure reliability and validity of the information, guidance from those with appropriate backgrounds is critical in the selection of the method used to gather the information, and the actual gathering of the information. In interpreting the information, a broadly based team can provide the scope of insights and understandings that is necessary for valid interpretation in the context in which the information was gathered.

In the recent past, institutional data-gathering tasks often focused on efficiency concerns, leading to information that was easily quantifiable and often appropriately gathered using a single information source. Such information includes cost per graduate and student-faculty ratios. To enhance the quality of the information in the assessment of the complex activities of teaching and learning, different and richer data provided by multiple measures and different analyses are required.

Much relevant work relating to these technical tasks is found in quantitative and qualitative research and evaluation literature. Selections provided here are those that address assessment specifically; they represent only a sample of the valuable information available.

Millman addresses the issues of validity and reliability in a comprehensive article designed to help administrators, faculty and others understand the psychometric and design considerations involved in different types of student assessment. The discussion focuses chiefly on quantitative data and provides guidance for gathering evidence of reliability and validity in assessments for the purpose of placement, certification, program and course evaluation, and evaluation of institutions.

Lincoln and Guba offer a paradigm for considering the rigor of naturalistic inquiry. They provide criteria for two rigor facets of naturalistic studies: trustworthiness and authenticity. While the criteria for authenticity are still evolving, those for trustworthiness have parallels in traditional inquiry criteria: credibility (internal validity), transferability (external validity), dependability (reliability), and confirmability (objectivity).

Stark provides guidance for appropriate interpretation and conclusions based on the type of outcome model used. The three methodological levels outlined include description, change, and attribution. Each level has its concomitant limitations affecting the questions that can be asked and the conclusions that can be drawn. An expanded discussion of two methodological problems mentioned earlier by Terenzini and again by Stark, unit of analysis and change scores, is provided by **Pascarella** and **Terenzini**.

Additional Core Readings

Banta, T. W. and Pike G. R. "Methods for Comparing Outcomes Assessment Instruments." *Research in Higher Education* 30(5) (1989), pp. 455–469.

Boli, J., Katchadourian, H. and Mahoney, S. "Analyzing Academic Records for Informed Administration: The Stanford Curriculum Study." *Journal of Higher Education* 59(1) (1988), pp. 54–68.

Forrest, A. *Time Will Tell: Portfolio-Assisted Assessment of General Education.* Washington, D.C.: American Association of Higher Education, The AAHE Assessment Forum, 1990.

Lenning, O. T. "Use of Noncognitive Measures in Assessment." In *Implementing Outcomes Assessment: Promise and Perils, New Directions for Institutional Research No. 59* edited by Trudy w. Banta. San Francisco: Jossey-Bass, 1988, pp. 41–52.

Linn, R. L. and Slinde, J. A. "The Determination of the Significance of Change Between Pre-and Post-Testing Periods." *Review of Educational Research* 47(1) (1977), pp. 121–150.

Pike, Gary. "Lies, Damn Lies, and Statistics Revisited." *Research in Higher Education* 33(1) (1992), pp. 71–84.

Messick, S. "Meaning and Values in Test Validation: The Science and Ethics of Assessment." *Educational Researcher* 18(2) (March 1989), pp. 5–11.

Assessment with Open Eyes:
Pitfalls in Studying Student Outcomes

Patrick T. Terenzini

There can be little doubt that "assessment" is here to stay. At least seven national reports have appeared in the last five years, all critical of higher education in America and all giving a central role to "assessment"—the measurement of the educational impact of an institution on its students. At least eleven states have adopted formal assessment requirements [10], as many more are moving in that direction, and regional accrediting associations are writing student outcomes assessment activities into their reaccreditation requirements.

The fact that the origins of the push toward assessment are external to most campuses is significant. Surveys indicate that while "over 50 percent of college administrators support assessing general education . . . only 15 percent report doing anything about it. In the more complex area of 'value-added' assessment, some 65 percent support the concept but less than 10 percent are fielding value-added programs" [10, p. 25]. The clear implication of these findings is that for many colleges and universities, assessment is a relatively new undertaking: they are either just beginning to explore and implement assessment programs, or they have not yet even begun.

In fact, through such activities as course examinations, senior comprehensive examinations, periodic program evaluations, or some types of student, alumni and employer surveys, many campuses have been engaged in "assessment," by one definition or another, for some time. These efforts, however, are typically undertaken by individuals or by individual offices or committees and are not coordinated in any way. Nor are they part of any comprehensive, institutional plan for ongoing, systematic self-study and improvement. Much of the discussion which follows will be useful to such discrete, individual assessment activities (for example, a department's evaluation of its courses or programs), but because the major thrust of state boards or agencies and regional accrediting bodies is for systematic, campus-wide assessment activities, this article focuses on potential problems in the development of institution-wide assessment programs.

Moreover, as Astin [1] has pointed out, we have for years tended to think of undergraduate program "quality" as synonymous with "resources invested." The "best" colleges and universities are frequently thought to be those with high-ability and high-achieving students, more books in their library, more faculty with terminal degrees, lower student-faculty ratios, larger endowments and so on. Although a reasonable argument can be made that undergraduate program quality and resources invested are not independent, the increased emphasis on assessment has radically altered the nature of discussions of undergraduate program quality. Increasingly, claims to quality must be based not on resources or processes, but on outcomes. The benefits to institutions and students of this reformulation of the issues are substantial. Because they are detailed elsewhere, however [for example, 9, 23], the major ones will be only suggested here.

523

Perhaps most importantly, assessment requires a redirection of institutional attention from resources to education. Now that the costs of a college education are identifiable and measurable, important people (for example, legislators, parents, students) now want to know what the return is on their investments. What *does* one get out of a college education? The question forces a fundamental introspection on the part of both individual faculty members and institutions. Assessment requires reconsideration of the essential purposes and expected academic and nonacademic outcomes of a college education. It also requires a clarity of institutional and programmatic purpose as well as a specificity of practice often absent on many campuses or hidden in the generalities of recruiting materials. What *should* students get out of attending college? What should they get out of attending *this* college? In addition, assessment requires that we try to understand whether the things we do and believe to be educational in fact produce the intended outcomes.

These are all substantial benefits. Many campuses, however, fail to recognize them, instead viewing assessment as merely one more external reporting obligation, as something to be done as quickly and as painlessly as possible. When assessment is seen in this light, significant opportunities to enhance educational programs are likely to be lost.

But though advice on how assessment programs should be designed and implemented is easy to come by, the pitfalls of assessment are more obscure, typically treated only cursorily (if at all) in the literature. This article calls attention to some of those pitfalls and suggests, however briefly, how at least some of them might be avoided. The article is not intended to discourage institutions from developing assessment programs. On the contrary. Its purpose is twofold: first, to identify some of the serious conceptual, measurement, organizational, and political problems likely to be encountered in the process of designing and implementing an assessment program; and second, by identifying some of the pitfalls, to help people who are involved in assessment to "do" it well. To accomplish these purposes, the article focuses on three major areas: (1) definitional issues, (2) organizational and implementational issues, and (3) methodological issues.

Definitional Issues

One of the most significant and imposing obstacles to the advancement of the assessment agenda at the national level is the absence of any consensus on precisely what "assessment" means. Some have used the term to mean testing individual student achievement levels in various academic areas. To others it means a review of the general education program and an evaluation of whether students are receiving a "liberal education." To still others it means a series of surveys of current students, alumni, or even employers, undertaken for program evaluation and planning purposes. And to still others, it means nothing less than institution-wide self-study, applicable to teaching, research, service, and administrative and management functions. Lack of clarity about exactly what this term means on a campus constitutes a significant threat to the success of any assessment effort.

In thinking about what "assessment" can mean, it is useful to keep three questions in mind, for the answers will have a powerful influence on the kind of assessment in which a campus becomes involved, as well as on the issues and problems it will face. The first question is: "What is the *purpose* of the assessment?" *Why* is the assessment program being designed? Although something of an oversimplification, the answers to this question generally fall into one (or both) of two categories: assessment for the enhancement of teaching and learning or assessment for purposes of accountability to some organizationally higher authority, whether internal or external to an institution. The answers to this question parallel the purposes of formative and summative evaluations: the first is intended to guide program modification and improvement, while the second is undertaken to inform some final judgment about worth or value.

The second question is: "What is to be the *level* of assessment?" *Who* is to be assessed? Will the assessment focus on individual students, where the information gathered on each student is inherently interesting? Or will it focus on groups, where individual information is aggregated to summarize some characteristic of the group (for example, average performance on some measure)? In this instance, "group" refers to any of a wide variety of student aggregations, such as at the course, program, department, college/school, campus, or system level; or to students grouped by sex, race/ethnicity, class year, major, place of residence, or whatever.

The third question is: "*What* is to be assessed?" On which of a variety of possible educational outcomes will assessment efforts be focused? Several "outcomes" taxonomies are available [for example, 5, 6, 16, 17]. A simple yet useful general typology has been given by Ewell [9, 11], who suggests four basic dimensions of outcomes: (1) knowledge (both breadth and depth) outcomes; (2) skills outcomes (including basic, higher-order, and career-related skills); (3) attitudes and values outcomes (frequently overlooked); and (4) behavioral outcomes (what students do, both during and after college). If these three questions are juxtaposed in a three-dimensional matrix such as figure 1, one can begin to see how varying approaches to assessment can be categorized.

Some would assert that assessment in its purest form has the improvement of learning and teaching as its primary purpose and that it focuses on individual students. In this approach, most notably practiced at Alverno College, but also at King's College in Pennsylvania and Clayton State College in Georgia, analysis of individual student performance is an integral part of the teaching and learning process. Students receive regular feedback on their knowledge and skill development, and teachers use the same information to shape their teaching strategies, activities and styles, as well as to guide individual student learning.

Some other standard assessment practices also fall in this category. For example, placement examinations and other diagnostic measures are clearly teaching- and learning-focused at the individual level. They are intended to determine a student's learning readiness and to permit assignment of the student to the most beneficial learning sequence (for example, developmental studies or honors programs).

Individual assessment results may, of course, be aggregated to evaluate program effectiveness where the evaluation is intended to be formative, facilitating program modifications and increased effectiveness. (The multiple, often overlapping uses of assessment data are indicated by the broken lines and arrows between the cells in figure 1.) For example, assessments of general education program outcomes might fall in this category, unless of course the major purpose of such an assessment is for accountability purposes (that is, summative).

Moving to the right-hand column of figure 1, one can note that assessment programs with a clear accountability orientation can be of two varieties. At the individual level, assessment serves a gatekeeping function, sifting and sorting the qualified from the unqualified. This category includes such practices as admissions testing (for example, ACT, SAT, and others) and "rising junior" examinations employed in Florida, Georgia, and elsewhere. Other varieties of the accountability-oriented conception of assessment include comprehensive examinations in the student's academic major field (a practice enjoying a revival) and certification examinations in professional fields (for example, nursing).

These latter sorts of examinations may, of course, also serve accountability assessment purposes at the group level. Assessment programs comprising this group-accountability cell focus on group mean scores rather than on individual scores. The principal interest is in program enhancement, in determining the level of effectiveness or quality at which a program, department, school or entire campus is functioning. Assessment activities in this cell include academic program reviews, analysis of student attrition rates and reasons, alumni follow-up studies, and various forms of "value-added" assessment. The focus or purpose is primarily evaluative and administrative, and the information so obtained may be used for accounting to external bodies, although it may also be highly useful for internal program improvement and planning and for enhancing teaching and learning.

Each institution must decide for itself, consistent with its mission, what the character of its assessment program is to be on each of these three dimensions (and for subsets within these major

Figure 1
A Taxonomy of Approaches to Assessment

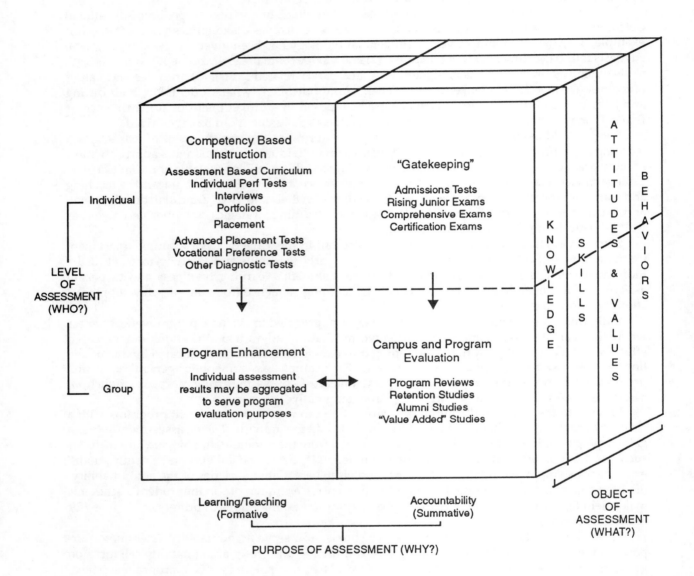

categories). The point, here, is the importance of being clear on a more-or-less campus-wide basis about why assessment is being undertaken, who is to be assessed, and what educational outcomes are to be assessed. Time spent in committee work and in other forms of public discussion of these three questions will be time extremely well spent. An inadequate conceptual foundation for an assessment program will produce confusion, anxiety, and more heat than light.

Organizational and Implementational Issues

Assuming some reasonable level of agreement is reached on the purposes and objects of assessment, it is important to keep always in mind that institutional change is embedded in any conception of assessment. Depending upon where the changes occur and how they are managed, they can produce higher levels of individual and organizational performance and pride in accomplishment, or they can produce internal insurrection. Several significant organizational and implementational hazards must be addressed at the outset.

Mobilizing Support

A vital and difficult task involves enlisting the support of concerned parties. The active and visible support of senior executive officers (particularly the president and chief academic officer) is absolutely necessary but, unfortunately, not sufficient. Faculty support is also needed, and without it prospects for a successful assessment program are dim. According to Ewell, faculty objections are likely to come from either or both of two sources: first, the fear of being negatively evaluated, and second, a philosophical opposition based on the belief that the outcomes of college are inherently unmeasurable and that the evidence from such studies is "misleading, oversimplifying, or inaccurate" [9, p. 73].

If sufficient attention has been given to public discussions and review of the program's purposes and objects, much will already have been done to allay the fears of faculty members and others. Assessment even when required by an external body should be, and be seen by all, as a developmental, not punitive, undertaking. It should be a vehicle for individual and institutional improvement, not as a search for documentation on which to evaluate individual faculty members, or to cut budgets or retrench programs. Indeed, in some institutions (for example, in Tennessee and at Northeast Missouri State University), it is used not as a basis for withdrawing departmental support but for increasing it, whether to reward good work or to help a unit improve. Some basic level of trust must be established, and good faith participation in assessment activities should not be discouraged.

Ewell [12] recommends being publicly clear about what an assessment program is not intended to do. This would include a clear and public specification of what data are to be collected, by whom, for what purposes, the conditions under which the data will be made available, and to whom they will be available. Northeast Missouri State University [19], one of the assessment pioneers, recommends against using assessment data to support negative decisions, and Rossmann and El-Khawas [23] caution against mixing assessment procedures with faculty evaluation procedures. These latter authors also recommend sensitivity to the timing of the initiation of assessment efforts. If a financial crisis, retrenchment, or major reorganization is imminent (or underway), individual and unit anxiety levels may already be high enough without introducing a potentially threatening program [23].

Yanikoski [29] has suggested thinking and speaking in terms of *"progress* assessment," rather than "outcomes assessment." The switch can be important symbolically as well as conceptually. "Assessing outcomes" implies a certain finality: that a summative evaluation and judgment are to be made, that the "bottom line" is about to be drawn. "Assessing progress," by contrast, implies an ongoing, formative process, which, in turn, suggests that time remains to make any necessary improvements. The whole tone of "progress assessment" is more positive, less threatening.

Faculty reservations about the measurability of outcomes must also be addressed, and several approaches are possible. One powerful way to allay faculty concerns about evaluation and the measurability of student progress is to include faculty in the design and implementation of the process and especially in the interpretation of results and development of recommendations. Respected faculty opinion leaders should be involved, and faculty members with technical specialties in research design, measurement, and other important areas should be recruited as consultants. Faculty members on most campuses constitute a significant, but untapped, source of technical and political support for an assessment effort.

Another way to ease concerns about the measurability of student progress is to ensure that multiple measures are incorporated into one's assessment program. The concept of triangulation in astronomy, surveying and map reading, and of successive approximations in probability theory, are familiar to most faculty members. Multitrait, multimethod matrices can be highly useful, arraying in the rows those content and skill areas to be assessed and across the columns the assessment techniques and approaches that might be used to assess each trait. One can then judge the extent to which each assessment area will be covered by multiple measures. Adoption of multiple measures is likely to have a face validity that will appeal to faculty members as well as increase the confidence that can be placed in interpretations of the data. The psychometric importance of using multiple measures is discussed further below.

Whatever approach is taken, however, everyone involved must recognize that judgments of program and institutional quality are made all the time by many different people. The issue is not really whether "assessments" should be made, but rather what is to be the nature, sources, and quality of the evidence on which those judgments are based.

Finally, assessment programs that start small, perhaps on a pilot basis, are more likely to draw support than elaborate plans. Most successful programs began small and grew incrementally [12]. The assessment efforts at Alverno College and Northeast Missouri State University have been underway for a decade and a half. It should be clear to all concerned, however, that any "pilot" project is not a test of whether the campus will proceed with assessment, but of how to do so in the most efficient and effective manner.

An inventory of current data collection activities (including the use of standardized measures, program review results, surveys, and standard institutional research studies) can be a politically and practically useful beginning. All academic and administrative offices should be surveyed to identify the information already on hand about students and about the effectiveness of their unit's activities. Such an inventory is likely to reveal far greater involvement in "assessment" than might at first have been believed.

In sum, one cannot overstate the importance of laying a strong political foundation. Without it, the assessment structure cannot stand. Faculty members, department heads, and deans are keen observers of their administrative superiors and readily discern which attitudes and behaviors are rewarded and which are not. For any assessment program to succeed, there simply must be some payoff for faculty members, whether in the form of additional funding to correct identified program deficiencies, rewards for a job well-done (say, some extra travel money), or other incentives to engage in assessment and enhance the quality of teaching and learning in a department.

Coordination

Assessment requires the involvement of a wide variety of people and offices, crossing not only academic departmental lines, but vice-presidential areas as well. Alternative approaches to the campus-wide coordination problem include assignment of coordinating responsibility to a currently existing office already significantly engaged in assessment and controlling many of the necessary resources (for example, the office of institutional research), creation of a new office, or assignment to a committee with representatives from the major affected organizational areas [12]. Each of these approaches has its assets and liabilities, of course, and though space precludes a detailed discussion of each, the reporting line(s) for the office or group should be given careful attention. Whatever approach is adopted, what will be the likely effects on traditional areas of responsibility and lines of authority? On informal power networks? On traditional distinctions between academic and student affairs? Ways will have to be found to coordinate activities in such a way that lines of authority and responsibility are clear, existing functions and activities are not duplicated, and support is received from each area [12]. As noted earlier, experience indicates that the support of the institutions' top executives, particularly the president and chief academic officer, must be active and visible, especially in the early stages of the program's development.

Costs

How much should an institution invest in its assessment program? The answer, of course, will depend upon the purposes and the extensiveness of the assessment program and its activities. Ewell and Jones have argued that the real question is one of marginal costs: "How much *more* money beyond that already committed to outcomes-related information gathering do we have to spend to put in place an assessment program that is appropriate to our needs?" [13, p. 34]. These costs are incurred in four areas: (1) instruments, (2) administration, (3) analysis, and (4) coordination [13]. Rossmann and El-Khawas [23] also note start-up costs, which can include consultant services, conference attendance and visits to other campuses, on-campus workshops, and faculty and staff time for organizing and perhaps instrument development.

According to Rossman and El-Khawas [23, p. 20], campuses with ongoing assessment programs spend $10–15 per enrolled student. Ewell and Jones [13], after making a series of assumptions about the nature of the assessment program likely to be mounted by institutions of varying types and sizes, estimate incremental costs ranging from $40,000 (for a small, private, liberal arts college) to $130,000 (for a major public research university). These latter estimates do not include personnel costs associated with faculty involvement in assessment.

Finally, opportunity costs must also be considered. Institutional resources (including time) invested in assessment are not available for investment elsewhere. Moreover, Governor Kean [15] of New Jersey has advised institutions not to ask for additional funds to cover assessment costs. According to Kean, legislators are unlikely to respond favorably to requests for money to determine whether past and current appropriations are being effectively utilized. If that is true, reallocation of currently appropriated funds will probably be necessary, although a variety of other sources are available, including grants from public agencies, private foundations, individuals, or even student fees to cover testing directly beneficial to students [23].

In considering the costs of assessment, however, the costs of not assessing educational outcomes must also be placed in the balance. Important opportunities may be missed, including, for example, the chance to clarify institutional goals, to review and revise (or reconfirm the value of) existing curricular purposes and structures, and to examine the successes and failures of current policies and practices. The costs of rejecting or deferring assessment may be substantial, if difficult to calculate.

Methodological Issues

The third major category of potential assessment pitfalls is methodological. Some of these problems are specific to particular approaches to assessment, whereas others are merely common and frequent violations of the canons of good research. Within this general area, potential problems fall into three subcategories: (1) design limitations, (2) measurement difficulties, and (3) statistical hazards.

Design Problems

From the outset it is important to keep in mind that research design is a series of compromises. Designs that increase the power of a study in one area come almost invariably at the expense of some other aspect of the study. Whenever something is gained, something else is given away. The key to useful and psychometrically sound inquiry is to know what is being gained and what is being given away [see 25].

The dominant theme in the chorus of demands for "accountability" through assessment is the need to demonstrate that college and university attendance makes a difference, that students leave colleges and universities with knowledge, skills, attitudes, and values they did not have when they arrived. An impressive number of studies [for example, 6, 20] demonstrate the fact that students change in a variety of ways between their freshman and senior years. The problem lies in specifying the *origins* of those changes. Students may change during the college years in response to many influences, including their own precollege characteristics and their noncollege experiences, not to mention normal maturation. Thus, collegiate impact is only one of the possible sources of freshman-to-senior year change. Collegiate experiences may be a significant source of change, but knowing with any degree of certainty whether and to what extent college has an effect is a very complicated matter.

A common approach to the assessment of change in students is the use of a successive cross-sections design, typically involving cross-sectional samples of current freshmen and senior students. The freshmen (the control group) are compared with the seniors (the treatment group) on some measure of the variable(s) on which change is being studied. Observed differences are then taken as an indication of the effects of the college on students. Such designs have a number of limitations, however, including the need to assume that current seniors, at the time they matriculated, were similar in important respects to current freshmen—a questionable proposition. Such designs also leave selective dropout during the college years uncontrolled. Not all students who begin college will finish it, and students who complete a college program, compared with those who do not, are likely to have higher aptitude and achievement records and greater commitment to college. Given such self-selection during the college years, freshman and senior group score means would probably be different even if the two classes had been identical at the time they entered college. Any changes over the period in admissions standards or recruiting strategies might also have produced initially nonequivalent groups in the two classes.

Pascarella [21] suggests several ways to reduce the nonequivalent-groups problem inherent in this design. One possibility is to control for age and entering academic aptitude through statistics, matching, or both. Use of samples of freshman and senior students of the same age is another option. Both are preferable, if imperfect, alternatives to the typical, unadjusted, successive cross-sections design.

Longitudinal designs are a frequently recommended alternative. One might measure the characteristics of an entering freshman class in a variety of areas and then, after a period of time (for example, two or four years) study the group again and compare students with themselves at the time they entered college, controlling for entering characteristics. At least some of the same people are being studied at the two different times, but the tendency of subjects to drop out of a study over time can be a significant problem with longitudinal research, particularly research that covers an extended period of time (for example, four years). As the response rates drop, study generalizability is threatened.

Ideally, one would follow over the same period of time a control group of high-school graduates who do not attend college (but who are presumably personally and academically equivalent to one's freshmen) and who could be compared after some period of time with the freshman group who have presumably benefited from college attendance. Although the equivalency of groups might be questioned even under this sampling plan, the design has obvious advantages over a successive cross-sections design. Obtaining a sample of students who do not attend college may be difficult, however, it may be reasonable for institutions serving a largely local or regional population (for example, community and commuting colleges). Institutions that draw students from a national base will probably find this alternative impractical.

The price paid for adopting a longitudinal design comes in several forms. Because of the unavoidable subject mortality problem, longitudinal designs also require larger samples. Increased sample sizes mean higher direct and indirect costs for personnel and materials as well as more complex data management requirements. Finally, longitudinal studies take longer to complete, and all too often the need for information is (or is thought to be) immediate.

Another group assessment pitfall arises in developing a sampling plan. Have clearly in mind the kind of subgroup analyses that are planned, for as the number of groups grows, or if one or more subgroups come from a small population (for example, minority students), simple random sampling may be inappropriate. Experience indicates, for example, that successful assessment programs provide unit-specific information. It is easy for deans or department heads to disregard assessment information when it comes from students or alumni of other schools or departments. The implication of this advice, however, often overlooked until it is too late, is that a census, not a sample, of students must be taken. Otherwise, group sizes may be too small to have face validity, political believability, or statistical stability. Costs and workload will, of course, go up accordingly.

Measurement Problems

However one defines "assessment," it will involve some form of measurement, and sooner or later one must deal with the problems and hazards of instrument selection. The common dilemma is whether to "buy, build, or borrow." Should one adopt a commercially available measure (for example ACT's COMP or Collegiate Assessment of Academic Proficiency [CAAP], or ETS's Academic Profile)? Or should one devise an instrument locally, or perhaps use a measure developed for similar purposes on some other campus? As noted previously, research is a series of compromises. Nationally available measures have several advantages, the first of which is that they have been developed by experts. Second, they have been field-tested, and their psychometric properties are known. Third, national scores or norms are usually available so one can compare one's students with those of other campuses of similar size, type, and purpose. Finally, use of commercial instruments can save substantial amounts of time and expense that would be required for local instrument development.

Such advantages come at a cost, however. In order to be usable in a variety of settings and for a variety of purposes, commercial measures are necessarily general and lack the specificity needed to focus in any detail on local conditions. Standardized achievement measures also focus unavoidably on a limited number of learning objectives. Do the substantive knowledge and skills measured by those instruments coincide with those that faculty want students to learn? Centra calls attention to the "faulty assumption . . . that commercial, standardized tests will adequately measure the student learning objectives of a typical general education program. But in fact it is unlikely that any of the tests measure more than half of what most faculty members believe should be part of general education" [7, p. 2].

Moreover, the format of any given measure constrains the range of what it can assess. For example, many standardized tests employ a multiple-choice structure that, no matter how clearly items may be written, limits the range of aspects of an educational outcome that can be examined [2]. One must remember that standardized, machine-scored tests were developed (and are popular) because they are comparatively easy to use, not because they are the best way to measure something. Centra [7] recommends, if commercial instruments are adopted, that they be supplemented with local measures.

As suggested earlier, the validity of assessments can be increased through the use of multiple measures. The allegory of the blind men seeking to describe the elephant has an important lesson to offer. Psychometricians know that each type of measurement has its characteristic sources of error [24], and reliance on one measure (or type of measure) is likely to produce data systematically biased by that measure's characteristic source(s) of error. In adopting multiple measures, one samples their strengths and their weaknesses, and as the number of different measures increases, so does the likelihood that any given measure's weakness(es) will be counterbalanced by the strength(s) of another.

One source of error characteristic of many of the assessment measures currently in use (commercially or locally developed) is their reactivity. Respondents to tests and surveys know they are being studied and that knowledge may influence their responses in varying and unknown ways. Such intrusive methods influence and shape, as well as measure. Unobtrusive measures— ones that do not require a conscious response from the subject, can be highly useful as well as efficient. For example, if one wishes to know whether students are receiving a general education, one alternative to the intrusive testing of students is an analysis of their transcripts. How many credits does the typical undergraduate take in various disciplinary areas? When are those credits earned (for example lower- or upper-division years)? How do these course-taking patterns vary across major fields? Transcript analysis is a reasonable basis for inference about the breadth and depth of students' formal learning [27], and numerous other unobtrusive measures are available to creative researchers [26].

Even if one successfully avoids these measurement pitfalls, however, additional hazards lie ahead as one begins the analysis of the data those assessment devices produce. The certainty implied by statistical testing can mask problems that may lead to the serious misinterpretation of results.

Statistical Problems

As noted previously, assessment (particularly the accountability strain) has embedded in it the expectation that change will occur, that the institution's contribution to student learning can be made apparent and even measured with some precision. Unfortunately, we rely almost without exception on average changes (for example, a comparison of a group mean at Time 1 with the same group's mean at Time 2). Group change, however, often masks individual change. Any observed freshman-to-senior year group change is related to the number of students who change and to the amount of change each student experiences. It may be useful to give attention to the frequency, direction, and magnitude of individual changes [see 14, pp. 52–69].

Moreover, change is often construed as "value-added," a frequently-heard phrase that can be highly misleading and damaging if not understood. Warren [27] and Pascarella [21] offer thoughtful and detailed discussions of this concept, but certain aspects of it require attention here. "Value-added" is both a metaphor and a research design. As a metaphor, it is a vivid and useful term focusing our attention on institutional effects rather than resources. Unfortunately, it can sometimes be too vivid, leading people inside and outside the academy to expect more of our assessment programs than can possibly be delivered. The reason for this lies not only in the metaphor's implication that "change" occurs, but also that it is positive change or growth. Can "value" be "added" without positive change? Legislators and others are likely to say "No." And therein lies the perniciousness of the metaphor, for it is important to distinguish "change" from collegiate "impact." As Pascarella notes: "In some areas of development . . . the impact of college (or other educational experiences) may be to prevent or retard decline rather than to induce major positive changes. Consequently, approaches to value-added assessment which focus only on pre- to post-changes may be overlooking important college effects" [21, p. 78]. For example, Wolfle [28] found that mathematics performance among a national sample of high-school graduates declined over the seven years following graduation. The data suggest, however, that the effects of college attendance may be to maintain precollege mathematics performance levels, whereas math achievement declines among those who do not go to college.

Similarly, it will be well to remember that one variable (for example, some aspect of the college experience) can influence another variable (for example, some outcome measure) in both direct and indirect ways. For example, evidence indicates that whereas participation in a pre-matriculation orientation program has no direct influence on freshman persistence into the sophomore year, attendance at an orientation session does positively influence students' level of social integration, which, in turn, is positively related to sophomore year enrollment [22]. Thus, any "value-added" approach that fails to take into account the indirect, as well as the direct, effects of college is likely to underestimate the full range of the collegiate influence [20].

One must also remember that college effects may not manifest themselves right away. For example, it is probably unreasonable to expect significant student progress over a one- or two-year period in acquiring the intellectual and personal knowledge, skills, attitudes, and values presumed to characterize a liberal education. Faculty, administrators, students, parents, and legislators must not expect (nor be led to expect) more of assessment programs than can reasonably be delivered. The benefits college is supposed to impart are not acquired overnight, and the programs intended to assess these benefits take time to design, implement, and fine-tune.

The "value-added" metaphor also promotes an analytical design that is correspondingly simple but potentially more dangerous. Common sense suggests that if one wishes to know whether something changes over time, one should measure it at Time 1 and again at Time 2. The difference between the pre- and post-test scores, the "change" score, presumably reflects the effects of some process. To many, this change score reflects the institutional "value-added." In this instance, however, common sense may harm more than help. Indeed, change scores have some positively alarming characteristics.

For example, simple difference scores are highly unreliable, and they can be shown to be negatively correlated with pretest scores [4, 18]. Second, it can also be shown that the higher the correlation between pre- and post-test measures, the lower the reliability of the gain score [18]. Such unreliability makes detection of reliable associations with other variables (for example, aspects of the institutional experience thought to produce a portion of the change) more difficult.

Third, simple difference scores are also subject to ceiling effects: students with high pre-test scores have little room for improvement and thus are likely to show smaller gains than students with lower initial scores. Similarly, gain scores are subject to regression effects, the tendency—due strictly to measurement error—for initially high (or low) scores to move ("regress") toward the group mean upon subsequent retesting.

One or more of the reasons probably lies behind the results reported by Banta, Lambert, Pike, Schmidhammer, and Schneider [3]. Many institutions are unable or unwilling to wait the usual two-to-four years needed for a longitudinal study following a cohort of entering freshmen through to the completion of a degree program. For that reason, and using the correlation between students' senior year "College Outcomes Measures Project" (COMP) scores and their freshman year ACT Assessment Composite scores, the American College Testing Program (ACT) has constructed concordance tables which permit institutions to estimate the COMP score gain, or value-added, that might have been recorded if the students had taken the COMP test in both freshman and senior years. [3].

In a series of tests on these estimated gain scores, Banta, et al. [3] made a number of striking (if not to say bizarre) findings. They found, for example, that the estimated gains for University of Tennessee-Knoxville students were underestimated by as much as 60 percent. Moreover, a large number of seniors had no ACT Assessment Composite score from which to estimate a gain score, and the students without assessment scores tended to be older, black, and from lower socioeconomic families, raising serious questions about the generalizability of any study based on estimated gain scores. Finally, the correlations between estimated gain scores and certain demographic and institutional variables were the opposite of what was expected. For example, the greatest gain scores tended to be those of students who had high school averages lower than 3.0, did not receive a scholarship, whose fathers did not graduate from college, who did not participate in honors mathematics sections, and who did not take more than two mathematics courses [3, p. 15]. In all likelihood, these startling findings are due to the unreliability of gain scores, as well as to ceiling and regression effects.

Such results raise serious questions about the reliability and validity of any estimated gain score, not just those produced using the ACT's COMP and assessment instructions. Indeed, Banta and her colleagues are quick to praise COMP as a "valuable tool for stimulating faculty discussion about the general education curriculum, and modes of instructions.... What is called into question is the usefulness, the validity, of employing *estimated* student score gain on the COMP for the purpose of making precise judgments about program quality that can serve as the basis for decisions about the allocation of resources in higher education" [3, p. 19]. And though one might infer from this that the use of actual gain scores may be a way of circumventing the problems Banta and her colleagues identified, the same problems afflict actual gain scores as well.

Thus, in considering the use of the "value-added" metaphor in a specific measurement setting, one would be well advised to follow the suggestion of Cronbach and Furby, who advised "investigators who ask questions regarding gain scores . . . [to] . . . frame their questions in other ways" [8, p. 80]. Centra recommends "a criterion-referenced approach in which the level and content of student learning is compared to standards and objectives established by the faculty and staff of a college" [7, p. 8]. A variant on that approach is to examine the trend over time in the proportion of students who score above a faculty-determined threshold of "acceptable" performance on any given measure. Linn and Slinde [18] and Pascarella [21] suggest a number of other alternatives, although space precludes their review here. The point is that there are conceptually understandable and methodologically preferable alternatives to the use of simple difference scores.

Finally, whether one is dealing with design, measurement, or analytical issues, it will be well to remember that campus-based assessment programs are intended to gather information for instructional, programmatic and institutional improvement, not for journal publication. Methodological standards for research publishable in scholarly and professional journals can probably be relaxed in the interests of institutional utility and advancement. The most appropriate test of the suitability of a design, measure, or analytical procedure is probably that of reasonableness [21]: Was the study conducted with reasonable fidelity to the canons of sound research? Given the constraints on the research methods used and the data produced, is it reasonable to infer that college has had an effect on student change? Although the methodological issues reviewed here cannot and should not be ignored, neither should one's concern about them stifle action.

Conclusion

The assessment of student outcomes has much to offer colleges and universities. In linking stated institutional and programmatic goals to the measurement of progress toward their achievement, assessment represents a significant refocusing of institutional efforts on the purposes and effectiveness of undergraduate education. Assessment requires consideration of three questions: (1) What should a student get out of college?, (2) What should a student get out of attending this college?, and (3) What does a student get from attending this college? Addressing these questions in a systematic, periodic assessment program is likely to foster increased clarity about the purposes of an undergraduate program (one can also engage in assessment at the graduate level), increased consensus on those goals, and a better understanding of the consequences of educational policies and programs. In many respects, assessment is really only something higher education should have been doing all along.

The assessment of student outcomes, however, is not something that can be done quickly or casually. Several conceptual, administrative, political, and methodological issues may prove troublesome in developing a successful and beneficial assessment program. At the same time, and with a little preparation and care, those pitfalls can be rather easily avoided. This article has sought to help in those preparations by increasing the likelihood that when a campus starts down the path to assessment, it will do so with open eyes.

References

1. Astin, A. W. *Achieving Educational Excellence*. San Francisco: Jossey-Bass, 1985.

2. Baird, L. L. "Diverse and Subtle Arts: Assessing the Generic Academic Outcomes of Higher Education." Paper presented to the Association for the Study of Higher Education, Baltimore, MD, 1987.

3. Banta, T. W., et al. "Estimated Student Score Gain on the ACT COMP Exam: Valid Tool for Institutional Assessment?" *Research in Higher Education*, 27 (1987), 195–217.

4. Bereiter, C. "Some Persisting Dilemmas in the Measurement of Change." In *Problems in Measuring Change*, edited by C. W. Harris, pp. 3–20. Madison: University of Wisconsin Press, 1963.

5. Bloom, B. S., et al. *Taxonomy of Educational Objectives: Handbook 1, Cognitive Domain*. New York: McKay, 1956.

6. Bowen, H. R. *Investment in Learning: The Individual and Social Value of American Higher Education*. San Francisco: Jossey-Bass, 1977.

7. Centra, J. A. "Assessing the Content Areas of General Education." Paper presented to the Association for the Study of Higher Education, Baltimore, MD, 1987.

8. Cronbach, I. J., and I. Furby, "How We Should Measure 'Change,' or Should We?" *Psychological Bulletin*, 74 (1970), 68–80.

9. Ewell, P. T. *The Self-Regarding Institution: Information for Excellence*. Boulder, Colo.: National Center for Higher Education Management Systems, 1984.

10. _____. "Assessment: Where Are We?" *Change*, 19 (January/February 1987). 23–28.

11. _____. "Establishing a Campus-based Assessment Program." In *Student Outcomes Assessment: What Institutions Stand to Gain*, edited by D. F. Halpern, pp. 9–24. New Directions for Higher Education, No. 59. San Francisco: Jossey-Bass, 1987.

12. _____. "Implementing Assessment: Some Organizational Issues." In *Implementing Outcomes Assessment: Promise and Perils*, edited by T. W. Banta and H. S. Fisher. New Directions for Institutional Research, No. 59. San Francisco: Jossey-Bass, 1988.

13. Ewell, P. T. and D. Jones, "The Costs of Assessment." In *Assessment in American Higher Education: Issues and Contexts*, edited by C. Adelman, pp. 33–46. Washington, D.C.: U.S. Office of Education, Office of Educational Research and Improvement, 1986. (U.S. Government Printing Office, Document No. OR 86–301).

14. Feldman, K. A., and T. M. Newcomb. *The Impact of College on Students*. San Francisco: Jossey-Bass, 1969.

15. Kean, T. H. "Time to Deliver Before We Forget the Promises We Made," *Change,* 19 (September/October 1987), 10–11.

16. Krathwohl, D. R., B. S. Bloom, and B. B. Masia. *Taxonomy of Educational Objectives: The Classification of Educational Goals, Handbook II: Affective Domain.* New York: McKay, 1964.

17. Lenning, O. T. *The Outcomes Structure: An Overview and Procedure for Applying It in Postsecondary Education Institutions.* Boulder, Colo.: National Center for Higher Education Management Systems, 1979.

18. Linn, R. I., and J. A. Slinde. "The Determination of the Significance of Change Between Pre- and Post-testing Periods." *Review of Educational Research,* 47 (Winter 1977), 121–50.

19. Northeast Missouri State University. *In Pursuit of Degrees with Integrity: A Value-Added Approach to Undergraduate Assessment.* Washington, D.C.: American Association of State College and Universities, 1984.

20. Pace, C. R. *Measuring the Outcomes of College: Fifty Years of Findings and Recommendations for the Future.* San Francisco: Jossey-Bass, 1979.

21. Pascarella, E. T. "Are Value-Added Analyses Valuable?" In *Assessing the Outcomes of Higher Education,* pp. 71–91. Proceedings of the 1986 ETS Invitational Conference, Princeton, N.J.: Educational Testing Service. 1987.

22. Pascarella, F. T., P. T. Terenzini, and I. M. Wolfle. "Orientation to College and Freshman Year Persistence/Withdrawal Decisions." *Journal of Higher Education,* 57 (March–April 1986). 155–75.

23. Rossmann, J. E., and E. El-Khawas. *Thinking About Assessment: Perspectives for Presidents and Chief Academic Officers.* Washington, D.C.: American Council on Education, 1987.

24. Sechrest, I., and M. Phillips. "Unobtrusive Measures: An Overview." In *Unobtrusive Measurement Today,* edited by I. Sechrest, pp. 1–17. New Directions for Methodology of Behavioral Science, No. 1. San Francisco: Jossey-Bass, 1969.

25. Terenzini, P. I. "An Evaluation of Three Basic Designs for studying Attrition." *Journal of College Student Personnel,* 21 (May 1980) 257–63.

26. _____. "The Case for Unobtrusive Measures." In *Assessing the Outcomes of Higher Education,* pp. 47–61. Proceedings of the 1986 ETS Invitational Conference, Princeton, N.J.: Educational Testing Service, 1987.

27. Warren, J. "The Blind Alley of Value Added." *AAHF Bulletin.* 27 (September 1984). 10–13.

28. Wolfle, I. M. "Effects of Higher Education on Ability for Blacks and Whites." *Research in Higher Education.* 19 (1982). 3–10.

29. Yanikoski, R. A . Comments made as part of a panel discussion on "Measuring the Value of College" at the annual meeting of the Illinois Association for Institutional Research, Champaign, IL, November 1987.

Methodological and Analytical Issues in Assessing the Influence of College

Ernest T. Pascarella and Patrick T. Terenzini

The Unit of Analysis

An important question in investigations of the influence of college on student development is the appropriate unit of analysis. This is most apparent when one is analyzing multi-institutional samples where data are collected at the individual level but where it is also possible to obtain average scores at the institutional or other level of aggregation (for example, the Cooperative Institutional Research Program data, the National Longitudinal Study of the High School Class of 1972, High School and Beyond). It is also possible, however, that one needs to consider the appropriate unit of analysis even when the data come from single-institution samples. What, for example, are the effects of classroom climate or residential unit composition on student learning (for example, Pascarella & Terenzini, 1982; D. Smith, 1977; Terenzini & Pascarella, 1984)?

The unit of analysis issue has been a complex and somewhat controversial one in research on the influence of college. It is often the case that scholars interested in essentially the same question have in various studies used institutions, departments, or individuals as the unit of analysis. Consider, for example, studies of the influence of different college characteristics on student learning (for example, Astin, 1968c; Ayres, 1983; Ayres & Bennett, 1983; Centra & Kock, 1971; Hartnett & Centra, 1977). Variation in the unit of analysis has perhaps contributed to the lack of consistent findings in several areas of inquiry (for example, Pascarella, 1985a). As suggested in a sophisticated and cogent discussion by Burstein (1980a), the issue is not so much that one unit of aggregation is more appropriate than another. Rather, the issue needs to be understood in light of the fact that different units of aggregation or analysis are asking different questions of the data. When the institution is the unit of analysis, for example, one is essentially asking what the average influence of certain college characteristics (student body selectivity, average faculty salary, and so on) is on average student development. Thus, one is primarily concerned with average effects among or between institutions. When individuals are the unit of analysis, however, the question is typically whether differences in individual students' collegiate experiences (for instance, academic major, extracurricular involvement, interaction with faculty) lead to differences in specified outcomes. Here the focus is on the effects of different experiences or exposures among or between individual students, even if the data are multi-institutional in form.

By focusing on one question, both institutional and individual levels of aggregation tend to ignore other questions. Aggregating at the level of the institution tends to mask possibly substantial variations between individual students' experiences within the same institution (Cronbach, 1976).

537

Assuming, for example, that an aggregate or global measure of the college environment accurately portrays a homogeneous stimulus experienced by all students in the institution ignores substantial evidence of influential subenvironments in an institution, subenvironments that are more proximal to the student's daily experience (for example, Baird, 1974; Berdie, 1967; Lacy, 1978; Newcomb & Wilson, 1966; Pascarella, 1976; Phelan, 1979; Weidman, 1979). Conversely, using individuals as the unit of analysis tends to ignore the dependencies (or correlations) of individual subject experiences within institutions; that is, the shared educational experience among individual students within the same college leads to the nonindependence of individual behaviors within the college (Burstein, 1980a). Thus, for example, institutional enrollment (size) may facilitate certain types of student-faculty relationships in a small liberal arts college that are quite different from the nature of the student-faculty relationships typically found in large research universities. These types of relationships may differentiate small and large institutions even when individual differences in student characteristics are taken into account. Moreover, as suggested by Burstein (1980a), standard statistical estimation techniques such as ordinary least-squares regression analysis can yield flawed or biased estimates in the presence of within-group dependencies.

Because of the dilemmas inherent in choosing one level of aggregation or unit of analysis over another, a number of scholars have suggested the appropriateness of using multilevels of analysis guided by appropriate theory (for example, Astin, 1970b; Burstein, 1980a, 1980b; Cooley, Bond & Mao, 1981; Cronbach, 1976; Cronbach & Webb, 1975; Terenzini & Pascarella, 1984; Rogosa, 1978). In such analyses, both between-student and between-aggregation effects could be estimated when one has multi-institutional (or even multimajor, multiclassroom, or multiresidential arrangement) data. (The appropriate level of aggregation, of course, depends on the substantive question being asked.) Routine use of a multilevel approach such as this might be one way to permit a more valid and informative comparison of results across studies. It would also permit one to compare differences in the aggregate effects of college (or some other unit of aggregation) with the effects of individual student characteristics and experiences. As suggested by Burstein (1980a), variables can have different meanings at different levels of analysis. Studies that choose colleges as the unit of analysis are asking different questions than studies that use the individual as the unit of analysis; consequently, we should expect different results.

Contextual Analysis

One way of combining aggregate and individual levels of analysis simultaneously is through a procedure known as contextual analysis. Contextual analysis is essentially the study of the influence of group- or aggregate-level variables on individual-level outcomes (Erbring & Young, 1980, Firebaugh, 1978, 1980; Lazarsfeld & Menzel, 1961). In this procedure the individual is the true unit of analysis, but instead of focusing only on the developmental effects of individual college experiences, one also attempts to estimate the effect of being a member of a particular group or aggregation (for example, college academic major, residential unit, classroom).

In its simplest form, contextual analysis can be defined by the following regression equation:

$$Y_{ij} = a + b_1 X_{ij} + b_2 \overline{X}_j + \text{error},$$

where Y_{ij} might represent the academic achievement (for instance, Graduate Record Examination Scores) of the ith student in college j, X_{ij} might be a measure of academic aptitude for the same student, and X_j would be the average (mean) value of student academic aptitude in college j. In short, X_{ij} might be thought of as a measure of student input or background, while X_j could be considered an estimate of college context or environment. The error or random disturbance term represents errors of measurement plus all causes of Y_{ij} (achievement) unspecified by the equation, such as student motivation and efficiency of study habits (Hanushek, Jackson, & Kain, 1974). The coefficients a (constant) and b_1 and b_2 (regression coefficients) can be estimated by ordinary least-squares regression procedures. A contextual or environmental effect is said to occur in this equation if the aggregate measure of student body aptitude has a significant regression coefficient with individual GRE achievement net of individual aptitude. If the coefficient for the contextual effect is positive, it would suggest that attending a college with a student body composed of "bright" students tends positively to influence a student's standardized academic achievement above and beyond his or her own academic aptitude.

One might posit the causal mechanism underlying the above example as due to the tendency for college faculty to gear the cognitive and conceptual level of instruction to the academic capacities of the students being taught or to the generally "higher" intellectual level of student discourse inside or outside the classroom. Hypothetically, then, students in more selective colleges might benefit from instruction (or an overall environment) geared to higher-level cognitive processes such as analysis, synthesis, and evaluation (Bloom, 1956), the results of which are manifest in higher GRE scores. In positing such a causal mechanism, however, we are again confronted by the disconcerting likelihood that selection (input) and aggregation (environmental) effects are substantially correlated. As such, it is extremely difficult, if not impossible, to accurately estimate and separate the effects of the latter from those of the former (Cronbach, Rogosa, Floden, & Price, 1977; Werts & Linn, 1971). In the above specification of the model, the unique effects of context or environment (as indicated by b_2) are likely to be quite conservative. Thus, a significant regression coefficient for average student body aptitude is reasonably convincing evidence of a unique contextual or environmental influence (Burstein, 1980a).

Frog-Pond Effects

Another approach to the combining of individual and aggregate level data is the "frog-pond" or relative deprivation effect as suggested by the work of Davis (1966), Alexander and Eckland (1975b), and Bassis (1977). This approach suggests that in order to understand individual behavior, one needs to be cognizant not only of individual attributes but also of how individual attributes position one in relationship to an important reference or peer group. In the above example of aptitude and achievement, the regression equation might be specified as follows:

$$Y_{ij} = a + b_1 X_{ij} + b_2 (\overline{X}_j - X_{ij}) + error$$

In this specification, hypothetical GRE achievement for an individual student (Y_{ij}) is posited as a function of individual academic aptitude (X_{ij}) and the difference between individual aptitude and the average college aptitude ($\overline{X}_j - X_{ij}$). A significant regression coefficient would indicate that a student's academic ability relative to the student average at the college attended has an influence on GRE achievement above and beyond individual aptitude alone. The sign of the regression coefficient would indicate whether the effect is generally beneficial to students below (+) or above (−) the college average.

As demonstrated by Burstein (1980a, 1980b), a regression equation including individual, contextual, and frog-pond effects is not estimable by standard means because the variables representing the three effects have a linear dependency. (The coefficients in an equation with any combination of two of the three effects represented, however, can be estimated.) Burstein (1980a) has suggested a way to deal with this problem. Specifically, he suggests that the investigator obtain more direct measures of the contextual or frog-pond effects. This means giving considerable thought to the specific and underlying causal mechanisms at work. For example, research conducted by Terenzini and Pascarella (1984) found that net of individual levels of institutional commitment, freshman-year persistence was independently and positively influenced by the average level of institutional commitment in the student's residence unit (contextual).

It is also possible that the student's level of institutional commitment relative to that of his or her residential unit peers (frog pond) would add significantly to an understanding of individual persistence or withdrawal behavior (an influence not estimated by Terenzini & Pascarella, 1982). That this effect operates through the influence of social involvement or integration is suggested by the theoretical work of Tinto (1975, 1982, 1987). Thus, instead of entering an unestimable frog-pond term operationalizing the student's standing relative to the average institutional commitment of the residence unit, one could substitute relative standing on level of social involvement. The equation then might be specified as follows:

$$P_{ij} = a + b_1 (IC_{ij}) + b_2 (\overline{IC}_j) + b_3 (\overline{SI}_j - SI_{ij}),$$

where

P_{ij} = an individual student's persistence or withdrawal behavior,

IC_{ij} = an individual student's level of institutional commitment,

$\overline{IC}_j$ = average level of institutional commitment in a particular student's residence unit,

$(\overline{SI}_j - SI_{ij})$ = an individual student's level of social integration relative to the average in his or her residence unit.

Burstein's (1980a) argument for focusing on direct measures of aggregate and/or frog-pond effects underscores a major conceptual problem in multilevel analysis. This problem, which has been forcefully articulated by analysts such as Hauser (1970, 1974) and Firebaugh (1978), is that contextual or frog-pond effects estimated atheoretically are often mechanistic and distally related to the underlying social-psychological processes they were designed to represent (Burstein, 1980a). For example, contextual or frog-pond effects estimated at the institutional level may have little relevance to and therefore little impact on individual cognitive development during college. Greater understanding may come from estimating contextual and relative standing effects at levels of aggregation that are not only theoretically justifiable but also more proximal and directly related to student learning (for example, classrooms, peer groups, roommates). In short, the most informative multilevel analyses are likely to be those "based on theories in which the source and form of group effects are measured directly" (Burstein, 1980a, p. 207).

It may be, of course, that aggregate effects at almost any level are simply too psychologically remote (or too globally measured) to have important direct effects on student development. Instead, the major aggregate-level influences on student development in college may be indirect, transmitted through their shaping of the individual student's interaction with important agents of socialization on campus, such as peers and faculty.

Change Scores

A substantial amount of the more recent research on the influence of college has a developmental focus and attempts to estimate how exposure to different collegiate experiences or environments leads to differential change on some trait over time. For example, do students who reside on campus tend to change more in critical thinking than students who commute to campus? One way in which this type of question has traditionally been approached is to compare pre- to postdifferences (such as freshman-to-senior scores) on an appropriate measure between groups of interest. If, for example, students residing on campus tend to change more in critical thinking than do those commuting to campus, one might conclude that the residential experience increases the impact of college, at least on critical thinking.

This is an intuitively appealing approach. There are, however, two problems with the use of change scores: reliability and the fact that the magnitude of the change or gain is typically correlated with the initial score (Linn, 1986). Reliability is an issue because change scores incorporate the unreliability of both the pre- and post test measures (Thorndike & Hagen, 1977). This can be a major problem when difference scores are used to make decisions about individuals, but it may not be a major issue when group comparisons are being made (Cronbach, 1970; Linn, 1986). The second problem with change scores, their correlation with the initial score, however, can confound attempts to attribute differential change to exposure to a particular group or educational experience. If one simply compared changes in critical thinking between residents and commuters, it would be extremely difficult, if not impossible, to determine whether the differential changes were due to differences in actual residence status or simply to differences in initial critical thinking status between the two groups.

Comparing simple change or gain scores cannot correct for the lack of random assignment to different groups or collegiate experiences. A better (though not totally adequate) approach would be to employ change or gain in critical thinking as a dependent measure in a regression model that includes both a measure of group membership (for example, 1 = residents, 0 = commuters) and initial level of critical thinking. This would indicate whether or not residence arrangement is significantly associated with critical thinking gains when the influence of initial critical thinking status is partialed out. It is of interest to note, however, that one need not use change scores to obtain essentially the same information. Exactly the same results in terms of the statistical significance of residence status would be obtained if senior-year critical thinking were regressed on a model containing both residence status and initial freshman-year critical thinking (Linn, 1986; Linn & Slinde, 1977). Similarly, in the fictitious example we have been using throughout this appendix, essentially the same *net associations* for *SIZE* and *IWF* would be obtained in either of the following regression equations:

$$IO_2 - IO_1 = IO_1 + SIZE + IWF + \text{error}$$

$$IO_2 = IO_1 + SIZE + IWF + \text{error}$$

In what has come to be regarded as a classic paper, Cronbach and Furby (1970, p. 80) have suggested that "investigators who ask questions regarding gain scores would ordinarily be better advised to frame their questions in other ways." In fact, as suggested above, questions about gain or change can typically be reformulated without sacrificing information. Regression analyses that treat the pretest (precollege) scores no differently from other independent variables in the model and use the posttest (senior-year) scores as the dependent variable provide essentially the same information while avoiding many of the problems associated with change scores (Linn & Slinde, 1977).

This is not to suggest that change should not be studied. Recent work by Bryk and Raudenbush (1987) and Willett (1988), as reviewed by Light, Singer, and Willett (1990), has suggested that the study of change becomes more valid and less ambiguous when it is measured over more than two time points. Light, Singer, and Willett (1990, p. 147) argue that assessing change over three, four, or even more time points permits one to trace the "shape of each student's growth trajectory" rather than just the difference between the beginning and end points. The use of multiple estimates of student status over time is a promising new methodological approach to the assessment of change or growth.

Conditional Versus General Effects

The analytical procedures we have discussed in the preceding sections have all assumed that the net effects of each independent variable on the dependent variable are general. That is, the effect is the same for all students irrespective of their status on other independent variables (Kerlinger & Pedhazur, 1973). Thus, in our fictitious example we are assuming that the net direct effect of IWF on IO_2 is the same regardless of the student's level on IO_1 or the size of the institution attended this assumption certainly has the appeal of parsimony (that is, other things being equal, the simplest explanation is often the optimal one). On the other hand, it can be argued that assuming only general effects in one's analytical approach ignores individual differences among students attending the same institution or exposed to the same educational or institutional experience. These individual differences among students may interact with different institutional, instructional, curricular, or other educational experiences to produce "conditional" rather than general effects. In a conditional effect, the magnitude of the influence of certain educational experiences on the dependent measure may vary for students with different individual characteristics. Thus, for example, the magnitude of the direct effect of IWF on IO_2 may vary, depending upon the student's precollege level of intellectual orientation (IO_1) or on other individual traits such as gender or race.

It is also possible that there may be patterns of conditional relationships or interactions that involve different levels of aggregation (Bryk & Thum, 1989; Raudenbush & Bryk, 1988). In a contextual analysis, for example, individual aptitude may influence achievement differently depending upon the aggregate level of institutional, departmental, or residence unit aptitude. Similarly, there may be interactions among college experience variables that do not directly involve individual differences among student precollege characteristics. The influence of informal contact with faculty on intellectual orientation, for example, may vary in magnitude in institutions of different size enrollment. Conditional effects of the various types described above may be masked by analyses that consider general effects only. Under certain circumstances this may lead the researcher to conclude that the effects of specific educational experiences are trivial or nonsignificant when, in fact, they may have statistically significant and nontrivial influences for certain subgroups in the sample. Thus, a narrow focus on aggregate means or tendencies as an index of college impact may mask important changes in individuals or student subgroups. (See Clark, Heist, McConnell, Trow, & Yonge [1972] or Feldman & Newcomb [1969, pp. 53–58] for a more extensive discussion of this point.)

The concept of conditional effects determined by the interaction of individual differences among students with different methods of teaching of the presentation of course content has a respected tradition in instructional research. Here it is typically referred to as aptitude (or trait) x treatment interaction (Berliner & Cahell, 1973; Cronbach & Snow, 1977). Underlying its application in instructional research is the more general perspective, stemming from the psychology of individual differences, that not all individuals will benefit equally from the same educational experience. Applications of the investigation of conditional effects with postsecondary samples are provided by Romine, Davis, and Gehman (1970) for college environments and achievement; by Holland (1963) for career choice and academic achievement; by Pfeifer (1976) for race and grades; by Andrews (1981), Born, Gledhill, and Davis (1972), Buenz and Merrill (1968) Domino (1968), Daniels and Stevens (1976), Gay (1986), Horak and Horak (1982), Parent, Forward, Canter, and Mohling (1975), Pascarella (1978), Peterson (1979), Ross and Rakow (1981), and Stinard and Dolphin (1981) for different instructional approaches; by Cosgrove (1986) for the effects of programmatic interventions; by Bean (1985), Pascarella and Terenzini (1979a), and Terenzini, Pascarella, Theophilides, and Lorang (1985) in research on student persistence and withdrawal behavior in college; and by Chapman and Pascarella (1983) on students' levels of social and academic integration in college.

The computational procedure for estimating conditional effects involves the addition of a cross-product term to a general effects equation. Thus, if one is interested in the interaction of IO_1 and IWF, the required regression would be the following:

$$IO_2 = IO_1 + SIZE + IWF + (IO_1 \times IWF) + error$$

Because the cross-product of $IO_1 \times IWF$ is composed of variables already in the equation, its introduction produces a high level of multicolinearity or intercorrelation among the independent variables. Since this can lead to biased and unstable regression coefficients, the estimation of conditional effects is usually conducted via a hierarchical regression approach (Overall & Spiegel, 1969). In this approach, the general effects IO_1, $SIZE$, and IWF (sometimes called main effects) would be entered in the first step. This would be followed by the addition of the cross-product or interaction term in the second step. If the cross-product of $IO_1 \times IWF$ is not associated with a significant increase in R^2, one can then eliminate the cross-product term from the equation and interpret the equation in terms of its general effects results. If, however, the cross-product is associated with a significant increase in R^2, it suggests the presence of a significant conditional effect (that is, the magnitude of the influence of IWF on IO_2 varies with the student's precollege status on IO_1).

This being the case, the results yielded by the general effects equation would be misleading. Rather, one would interpret the nature of the $IO_1 \times IWF$ interaction to determine variations in the effects (unstandardized regression coefficient) of IWF on IO_2 at different levels of IO_1. Cohen and Cohen (1975) provide a simple computational formula for interpreting the nature of a conditional effect when the two interacting variables are continuous in nature. This formula can also be applied when one variable is categorical (for example, treatment versus control) and one is a continuous covariate (for example, aptitude). In the latter case an additional analysis can be conducted to determine the range of the continuous variable (aptitude) for which significant differences in the dependent variable exist between treatment and control groups (Johnson & Fay, 1950; Serlin & Levin, 1980).

A final point needs to be made about the estimation of conditional effects. The presence of replicable aptitude x treatment interaction effects has not been particularly common in experimental instructional research. Thus, in correlational data where one needs to rely on less effective statistical controls, the presence of conditional effects can often be artifacts idiosyncratic to the particular sample being analyzed. Considerable caution is therefore recommended in substantively interpreting conditional effects in correlational data. The most trustworthy are those suggested by theory and replicable across independent samples.

Final Note

At about the time this volume went into production, two potentially important books on the methodology of research and assessment in higher education were published. The first, by Light, Singer, and Willett (1990), uses case studies of actual investigations in postsecondary settings to introduce and explicate in greater detail many of the issues in research methodology touched upon in this appendix. The second, by Astin (1990), is a detailed treatment of many of the important conceptual, methodological, and analytical issues involved in assessing the impact of college and the impact of different experiences in college. Of particular relevance to the present discussion is Astin's own technical appendix on the statistical analysis of longitudinal data. Therein, he deals with many of the statistical and analytical issues we have just discussed, though from a somewhat different perspective. He also demonstrates how elements of regression analysis and causal modeling are combined to assess college effects within his input-environment-output model. Both books provide important conceptual, methodological, and analytical tools for scholars interested in the impact of college on students.

The Truth May Make You Free, But the Test May Keep You Imprisoned: Toward Assessment Worthy of the Liberal Arts

Grant Wiggins

I confess that I have been kicking myself for getting involved with this topic. The more I looked at the title I obligated myself to, the more nervous I became. For one thing, I do not know as much as I should about current efforts to assess higher education. For another, I do not think anybody in his or her right mind can address this topic intelligently in so little time. And third, I think that the problem specified in the title of my talk is an insoluble one. It confronts us with one of many inescapable dilemmas about the liberal arts: the freedom of thought to go where it will versus the apparent need for uniformity in the testing process. In other words, we are not going to "solve" the assessment problem in the liberal arts, now or later. We are going to negotiate it—painfully; we are going to have to deal with some frequent, uneasy compromises.

So what I intend to do is a bit more modest than perhaps it first seemed. My aim is not so much to lay out a complete vision, but to give you my sense of the subtle but profound shifts that would be required if we were going to be serious about assessing for a liberal arts education. Second, I am going to propose to you a set of principles that we might call upon when liberal education is jeopardized—as it always will be—by an overly utilitarian or vocational view of teaching and learning. I think of these principles as mere first cuts, but perhaps they can hold you in good stead on a rainy day. Third, I will offer what I hope are some provocative and useful illustrations of alternative forms of assessment that befit the liberal arts. Many of the examples happen to come from the K-12 arena but nonetheless apply to your situations as well. I would encourage you, therefore, to resist a common nasty, little habit. If I should make reference to a fifth grade teacher's example, try not to be snooty about it. It is harder than you think to resist the feeling, and harder still to develop the almost anthropological mindset that enables one to find insight into one's own teaching from very different places in the system.

Let us begin thinking about dilemmas in education by returning to the first known assessor in the liberal arts. I am thinking, of course, of Socrates, the Socrates of the dialogues of Plato, where we regularly see those who either appear to be or profess to be competent put to the "test" of question, answer, and—especially—sustained and engaged conversation. (The dialogues themselves, of course, are filled with dilemmas. Many of them are left unresolved: a reminder of how these arts are meant to lead to questions, not answers—the little burrs that get under your saddle.) Socrates the assessor: he is certainly a strange one. He does not seem to have nice answer keys or scoring rubrics by his side. Yet I think that there is something to learn from thinking about assessment from a Socratic point of view.

I would like to view these issues through my favorite piece of literature, the dialogue called "Meno." Some of you no doubt know it. Meno, a brash young fellow, comes up to Socrates. The first line of the dialogue is, "Tell me, Socrates, how do we become virtuous.?" In other words, he is asking how morality develops: through upbringing? moral education? by nature? Socrates responds in a very annoying and typically Socratic way. He says, "Well, I cannot answer that question. I do not even know what virtue is." Meno is clearly astonished to think that this could be possible, that a *bona fide*, certified sage does not know what everybody knows, namely, what it means to be good. But of course, after Meno makes the foolish mistake of venturing to tell Socrates what virtue is, Socrates proceeds to undress him two or three times.

Finally, in exasperation, Meno says a terribly revealing thing that goes to the heart of the distinction between conventional assessment done well and an assessment for the liberal arts. Meno says, "Well now, my dear Socrates, you are just what I have always heard before I met you. Always puzzled yourself and puzzling everyone else. And you seem to me to be a regular wizard. You bewitch me. You drown me in puzzles. Really and truly my soul is numb. My mouth is numb. And what to answer you I do not know." And here is the important part. "Yet I have a thousand times made long speeches about virtue before many a large audience. And good speeches, too, as I thought. But I have not a word to say at all as to what it is."

Meno's comment (and indeed the progress of the whole dialogue) ironically reveals what so differentiates conventional academic mastery from excellence befitting the liberal artist. Meno is reduced to speechlessness, he thinks, because of the sophistry of Socrates's questions and analyses; the thoughtful reader knows, however, that Meno does not know what he is talking about. And yet Meno is a conventionally successful student. How do we know? Throughout the dialogue Meno is constantly dropping references—the ancient equivalent of footnotes—to all the famous people who say this and that about virtue, which he, of course, agrees with. And it is no doubt the case that Meno could be a successful speaker—effective, convincing. The point of the dialogue, of course, is that such rhetorical skill using borrowed ideas is not understanding; competent presentations are not sufficient. That is not what a liberal education is about.

What Socrates wants us to see—what Plato wants us to see by the way in which the dialogue is written—is that the conventional view of education is actually quite dangerous. If one gets better and better at what one does, one is less and less likely to question what one knows. Meno has been a dutiful student. (We are also meant to know that his name is a pun: It is very close in Greek to the word for memory: menon - mnemon.) Meno is an effective memorizer, able to make effective speeches with references to famous people. Isn't that what too much of our assessment is already about? Don't we too often fail to assess whether the student can do anything more than borrow quotes, facts, and figures?

But we also know from history that the real Meno was a nasty fellow: clever, ruthless. We are meant to know that. Because there is ultimately a lesson to be learned about "control" over knowledge and the ends to which "mastery" is put. Liberal education can never coexist happily with other, more "practical" views of education because a liberal education is about rooting out thoughtlessness—moral as well as intellectual thoughtlessness.

There is, alas, such a thing as "thoughtless mastery" (as I have elsewhere termed it) and our syllabi and assessments tend unwittingly to reinforce it. Many of our students are quite good at this thoughtless mastery; you all know it. You know those looks in class, those mouth-half-open looks, the eyes slightly glazed; when people are fairly attentive but the brain does not seem to be quite engaged; when, alas, their eyes only focus to check scores on other people's papers, and to press you for extra points here and there.

Paradoxically, many professions *require* unthinking mastery—and run the risk of an amoral technical approach to life. I think we forget this. I do not want the pilot who flew me to Washington to be questioning his knowledge or his existence. Nor do I want my brain surgeon to be thinking about what virtue is. One of my passions is baseball, and I was recently reading George Will's new book called *Men At Work* on the craft of playing and managing major-league baseball. There is an odd but insightful phrase in it about this kind of thoughtless mastery that rings quite true. The good hitters talk about not thinking too much—that it is very dangerous to do so. Rather, what has to take over the hitter is something called "muscle memory"—a wonderful phrase for the kind of unthinking skill that we admire in athletes.

There is no reason, however, for colleges and universities to assume that their job is to promote unthinking mastery of others' ideas (while also abetting the other forms of thoughtlessness that too easily follow). Colleges are derelict, I think, in giving up the only sanctioned time when we have *a moral obligation to disturb students intellectually.* It is too easy nowadays, I think, to come to college and leave one's prejudices and deeper habits of mind and assumptions unexamined—and be left with the impression that assessment is merely another form of jumping through hoops or licensure in a technical trade.

Certainly we *say* we would like to see more "real" thinkers, and we bemoan doltish behavior in our students. I think we protest too much. Our testing and grading habits give us away. If you do not believe me, look how often students give us back precisely what we said or they read. On the other hand, you should not think that I mean rigor does not matter. That is part of the dilemma . The great mistake that has been made in school reform by many so-called progressives, and by much of the alternative schools movement, is to assume that to be liberated is to be liberated from discipline. That is a mistake, and it is one reason why alternative school people end up shooting themselves in the foot: because they produce a lot of free spirits who are not always very capable. If I had to choose, I might go with the alternative schools, but it is a bad choice and it shows that we have not negotiated the dilemma in K-12.

So we have to think about rigor. We have to think about alternative assessment as more than just engaging students better, which it invariably does (you know this if you have done simulations, case studies, portfolios, or dramatic presentations with your students). We need more than engaging activities. We need truly standard-setting and standard-revealing assessments. Or as psychologist Lauren Resnick puts it: What we assess is what we value. We get what we assess, and if we don't assess it, we won't get it. True about rigor, but also true about the intellectual virtues.

Some of you know, if you have read some of the things that I have written on alternative assessment, that one of my definitions of authentic assessment is that it is "composed of tasks that we value." It is not a proxy. It is not an efficient system to shake out a grade. Efficiency and merely technical validity as the aims of assessment will *undermine* liberal education. Rather, the test should reveal something not only about the student but about the tasks and virtues at the heart of the subject—its standards. But it is damn hard to design tasks to meet those criteria. It is very easy to score for efficiency and to look at what is easy to score rather than what is essential.

Let me cite three other dilemmas before giving you some principles and examples of how we might think about assessment that would do justice to the liberal arts. The first dilemma, confronting you more often as a teacher the higher up you get in the system, is whether to stress students' mastery of the ideas of others or mastery over their own emerging ideas. In fact, we do believe that it is important for students first to control subject matter and acquire skill within the discipline before they get "creative." Or to paraphrase Thomas Kuhn, one must have complete control over the existing "paradigm" if dramatic new paradigms or original thoughts are to occur.

Whatever Kuhn's merits as a historian and philosopher of science, I think he is dead wrong about education. I think it is terribly important that would-be liberal artists immerse themselves, from the word go, in questioning the paradigm *as* they learn it: They should study it, poke it, prod it, and not wait until they have mastered it—because you can have a *long* wait. And many of your bright and able minds are likely to drop out mentally or physically because they cannot wait that long. Conversely, the ones that stick around may be more dutiful than thoughtful.

Inevitably, if we first demand control over the subject matter in its entirety, we run a moral as well as an intellectual risk. We run the risk of letting the student believe that Authority and authoritative answers matter more than inquiry. We may well end up convincing students that "Knowledge" is somehow something other than the result of personal inquiries built upon questions like theirs. And in fact, many students do believe that: There is "Knowledge" over there and there are "questions" over here and never the twain shall meet

A second way to put the dilemma is more classic: useful versus useless knowledge. There is an important sense in which the liberal arts *are* useless, summed up in that little comment supposedly made by Euclid 2,000 years ago when someone complained that geometry was not good for very much. He said, well, give him three drachmas if he has to get some usefulness out of studying it. But there is a more important truth in this desire. It is not at all clear that this unending inquisitiveness and poking over, under, and around knowledge is useful. Indeed, I can tell you from working with adolescents for so many years (prone to outbursts of honesty and not feeling the need to appear like eager apprentices), that many of them regard it as profoundly useless. On the other hand, we must ourselves keep clear the distinction between "useful" (or "relevant") and "meaningful." Students are *not* entitled to usefulness in a liberal education, but they *are* entitled to a meaningful encounter with essential ideas. We often disappoint—either by pursuing ideas that are *too* relevant but transitory; or by being insensitive to their need for provocations, not packages of predigested "knowledge," to chew on.

Third, we have to recognize that the urge to shun the liberal arts may have a great deal to do with the essential urge to feel competent. People go to school, it seems to me, indirectly to feel good about themselves. They want to develop competence because they want to develop confidence—or is it the reverse? The trouble with a liberal education is that it does not satisfy that need at all. It is unpleasant. It is disturbing. Many people drop out mentally and become hypercompetent because they cannot deal with the ambiguity and uncertainty that is the hallmark of the liberal arts.

Well, then, suppose I am right about this. Suppose we are in danger of treating assessment in higher education—as we are now increasingly in danger of treating assessment in lower education—as certification that a student possesses sanctioned knowledge. Where would we look for effective alternative strategies? How can we highlight the liberal arts side of the dilemma? What principles might guide us in designing assessments for the liberal artist in training?

Let me offer you 10 tentative principles.

Principle #1. The heart of the liberal enterprise is not a mastery of orthodoxy but learning to justify one's opinions. Because the modern university has its roots in the Middle Ages and in religious training, it is built upon an irresolvable tension between orthodoxy and the promotion of inquiry. We tend to forget that. To this day, it seems to me, we still lean pretty heavily on the orthodoxy side: Up until the graduate experience, students have first to demonstrate their control over other people's knowledge. Yet we would be wise to begin our reforms from the perspective of the ultimate educational experience with which we are all familiar: the dissertation and oral in defense of a thesis. We should think of all assessment as designed primarily to give students an opportunity to *justify* opinions that are being developed as they explore subject matter.

This implies that one of the most important things that we can do in assessment is to examine the students' response to our follow-up questions and probes of their ideas. It implies, for instance, in assigning a paper and evaluating it, that the student should have to formulate a response, to which we then respond as part of the formal assessment process, not as a voluntary exercise after the test is over or the paper done.

Taken to the limit, I would argue that one of the most important things that we can do with students is to assess them on their ability to punch holes in our own presentations. They have a right to demand from us justification of our point of view. That is what the liberal spirit is about. It sends a moral message that we are both, student and teacher, subservient to rational principle.

Principle #2. The second principle is that we really need to think of the student as an apprentice to the liberal arts. And like all apprentices, students should be required to recognize and produce quality work. They should not get out of our clutches until they have produced some genuinely high quality work. Now, what do I mean by that? Well, it is really a subtle shift in thinking. We all expect quality as teachers, but I do not believe that we demand it.

For instance—and here is one of those sixth grade examples—there is a teacher in Louisville who in one of her first assignments to her social studies students demands that every student read a book and do a book report. Not a particularly interesting task, but what is fascinating is what she demands. She demands that the paper be perfect. She demands that the students not turn it in until it is. She demands that they seek out anyone and everyone who will help them make it perfect.

Well, needless to say, the kids freak out. Especially the bad ones who are convinced that they cannot produce quality work. To make a long story short, they do. Oh, we could quibble with the idea of a perfect paper, but the kids understand full well what is meant. They really do. It is quite something to see. They understand that they have to ratchet up the seriousness with which they work. That they cannot wait to find out the quality of the work they produced. That they have to produce the quality work *first*. Making a point that many of you know is now critical to the alternative assessment conception: Assessment and self-assessment must be intertwined if we are serious about empowering people. To demand quality is also to structure assessment so that the student does not merely have the opportunity to rehearse, revise, rethink, but is actually required and expected to do so.

One of my favorite assignments when I taught at Brown was to ask students for their final paper to rewrite their first paper, based on all they had since learned or thought. A number of the upperclassmen told me that it was the most important event in their four years at Brown. They were astonished to see how their thinking had changed. They were astonished to discover how sloppy that early work seemed to them in retrospect. In short, they were learning about quality.

Further, they were learning about thinking, that thinking does not stand still and should not. Demanding quality, in other words—and this is part of the shift in thinking that is required—means we begin to focus our assessment on what Aristotle called the intellectual virtues. Does the student display craftsmanship, perseverance, tolerance of ambiguity, empathy when everyone else is critical, a critical stance when everyone else is empathetic? Can the student, without prodding, rethink and revise a paper or point of view? A liberal arts education is ultimately about those intellectual virtues. When all of the knowledge has faded away, when all of the cramming has been forgotten, if those intellectual dispositions do not remain, we have failed.

Now, some people get very squeamish about assessing things like perseverance, style, craftsmanship, love of precision. I do not. If we value it, we should assess it. That does not mean that we are arbitrary. That does not mean that we are subjective. Yes, we have to worry about validity and reliability. In fact, what I think it means to assess habits of mind is not to directly score them at all. But rather to devise tasks that *require* the habits we value.

My metaphor for this is "Outward Bound." Assessment should be like intellectual Outward Bound. It should reveal to the student what we value as traits in them by the virtues required to accomplish the task at hand. It should not be possible to do an end-run around those habits; students who can get A's by missing class and cramming are telling you something about the failings of your assessment system.

Sometimes it is as subtle a shift as sending the message day in and day out that quality matters and you are held accountable for quality. One of my favorite little tricks in that regard comes from Uri Treisman at Berkeley and his work with minority mathematics students. He demands that every piece of work the students hand in be initialed by another student; students get a grade both for their own paper and for the paper on which they sign off. This sends a message loud and clear that quality matters, that you are personally responsible for quality, and that it is in your interest to find out about quality *before* hearing from the authority. Quality control is about avoiding poor performance before it happens.

Principle #3. This leads directly to principle #3, a point familiar to many of you who have been at this kind of work, but one that cannot be made often enough. A liberal arts assessment system has to be based on known, clear, public, non-arbitrary standards and criteria. There is no conceivable way for the student to be empowered and to become a masterful liberal artist if the criteria and standards are not known in advance. The student is kept fundamentally off balance, intellectually and morally, if the professor has a secret test and secret scoring criteria.

Consider the performance world, as opposed to the academic world, and how much easier it is for performers to be successful because of this very basic fact. The test is known from day one. The music, the script, the rules of debate, the rules of the game are known: Genuine mastery in the performance arena means internalizing public criteria and standards until they become one's own. Unfortunately, in education, especially in higher education, there is a vestige of our medieval past, when tests were a bit of mystery and novices had to divine things. I was disappointed to learn when I was a teaching assistant at Harvard that most undergraduates are still not allowed to see their blue books. And then somebody told me that at Oxford and Cambridge they burn them.

I think this is an unfortunate and deadly tradition. It is also a legacy of tests used as gatekeepers, not as equitable vehicles designed for displaying all that a student knows. Most people in this room, I suspect, would say it is the *student's* responsibility to figure things out, to respond to the test as the test demands, and to produce quality work on *our* terms. I am not convinced of that. Why isn't the university required to meet students halfway and give them a chance to reveal their strengths and play from their strengths? It would be as simple as giving people the option of alternative forms of doing the same assignment.

But I think it runs much deeper. We are still using testing as a sorting and categorizing system. And elitism should not be confused with meritocracy. Our most common habit in scoring and grading, namely scoring on a curve, is unjustifiable in my view. Its sole purpose is to exaggerate difference rather than reveal strength. It makes our life easier and it relieves us of justifying the grades and scores that we give. It is needlessly debilitating—as opposed to a challenge that we can rise to when we know, understand, and appreciate the criteria

Of course, many of you know the solution. Scoring rubrics, model papers, videotaped model performances, anything that can give students an insight into, allow them to enter the field and acquire its standards, by seeing exemplary performance *before* they do their work. I do not know why in the world we keep such matters a secret. It is cuckoo—and dysfunctional.

Principle #4. It follows that what a liberal education is about—and what assessment must be about—is learning the standards of rational inquiry and knowledge production. And this implies that self-assessment is a critical and early part of assessment. Now, many of you know about Alverno's use of self-assessment and it has been borrowed by many of us. I just want to give you one of my favorite Alverno examples because I think it illustrates so well different ways of thinking about this.

One of Alverno's goals for students is competency in oral communication. Early on, a student must give a videotaped talk and so one's first hunch is, oh, well, you are going to assess the talk. No. After the student gives the first talk and it is videotaped, the student is assessed on the accuracy of the self-assessment of the videotaped talk. That is a fundamental shift in point of view. If we want people to gain control of important habits of mind and standards, then they have to know first of all how to view those things accurately and apply criteria to their own work, and not always depend upon another person to do that.

It is also a basic lesson in habit development. You have to know what you are *supposed* to be doing before you can do it. And that knowledge is crucial in making you stick with it and believing that it is possible. Otherwise I do not think any of us would quit smoking or lose weight. It suggests as a practical corollary that no major piece of work should get turned in without some self-criticism attached to it. And that self-criticism should be assessed for *its* accuracy.

Principle #5. Most education, it seems to me, treats the student as a would-be "learned spectator" rather than a would-be "intellectual performer." The student must metaphorically sit in the bleachers while others, mostly professors and writers of textbooks, perform. This arrangement takes us back to the idea that competency involves just remembering and applying what others say. It has dangerous consequences because it induces intellectual passivity. In an education for a would-be performer the student would experience the same "tests" that face the expert in the field—having to find and clarify problems, conduct research, justify one's opinion in some public setting—all while using (other people's) knowledge in the service of one's own opinion.

Let me give you a couple of my favorite examples of this. One of the finest classes that I have ever observed at any level was at a high school in Portland, Maine, where a veteran teacher offered a Russian history course. The entire syllabus consisted of a series of chronological biographies. It was, however, the *student's* job to become each person, in turn, in two senses: through a 10-minute talk, and then a simulation. After four or five students had presented their talks (and been assessed by other students on their talks), they had a Steve Allen "Meeting of the Minds" press conference which was chaired by the teacher; the "journalists" were the other students. Each party scored the other for its performance.

Now, I do not know about you, but I have sat through a lot of dreary reports. These were not dreary. In fact, they were as interesting and informative as any reports I had ever heard. I went up to the teacher and said, golly, how did you get them to do that? He said, well, it was very simple. There were only two criteria by which they were going to be judged and they were (a) whether the talk was accurate, and (b) whether it was interesting. This was real performing and using knowledge.

Principle #6. This one follows from #5. A liberal artist, if he or she has "made it," is somebody who has a style. Somebody whose intellectual "voice" is natural and clearly theirs. Read the turgid prose that we receive and you know that we are failing to develop style, voice, and point of view. (Read our own writing in journals. . . .) Students are convinced we want the party line, and that the quality and insight possible in compelling prose is not necessary. It is an option.

There would be a simple way to get at this. After writing a lengthy research paper with all the requisite footnotes and bibliographical information, the student could be asked to turn the paper into a one-page piece to be delivered, in an engaging and insightful way, to an audience of laypersons. But it is not just an aesthetic issue, this business of style. It is a question of one's inner voice. One's intuition. The seed of a new idea that is easily crushed if it is not allowed to be heard. All of these are related to the idea of conscience, and, of course, it is no coincidence that Socrates talked about his little voice.

It is easy for students in American universities to lose that little voice. But that little voice is not just a "personal" voice irrelevant to "academic" accomplishment. It is the voice of common sense. It is the voice that can turn around and question the importance of what one has just spent two months working on. It is the little voice that says, ahh, come on, is this really that important? Or it is the little voice that says, you know, there is probably another way to look at this. It is the little voice that says, I have a feeling that there is something behind what the professor is saying, but I do not know enough to really pursue it so I will not. It is the little voice that most of us do not hear in our students unless we ask for it. An assessment should ask for it.

Such assessing need not be difficult. I saw an English teacher do it. In using peer editing, he told his students that they should reject and turn back any paper that was boring or slap-dash—and mark the exact spot in the paper where they began to lose interest. Nothing sends a message faster to students about writing and its purpose and quality. Nothing sends a message quicker that technical compliance with criteria is not always of primary importance.

There is another point to be made about voice and style. The thing that is so ghastly about academic prose is that one really does sense that it is not meant for an audience. And, of course, sometimes it is not. It seems to me that if we are serious about empowering students. We must get them to worry about audience in a deeper way. We must demand that their work be *effective*. We must demand that it actually reach the audience and accomplish its intended purpose. There is nothing more foolish, in my view, than saying, "Write a persuasive essay" without the students having to persuade anybody of anything. So let us set up situations in which the student has to persuade readers, or at least get judged by an audience on more than just accuracy. Even Socrates knew, in the clash of Reason and Rhetoric, that teaching had to be not merely truthful but effective.

Principle #7. Too often in assessment we worry about whether students have learned what we taught. This is sensible, of course. But let me take an unorthodox position. Such a view of assessment, taken to extremes, is incompatible with the liberal arts. One important purpose of those "arts that would make us free" is to enable us to criticize sanctioned ideas, not merely re-tell what was taught.

A less confrontational way to make the point is to remind ourselves that it is the astute questioner, not the technically correct answerer, who symbolizes the liberal artist. The philosopher Gadamer (with an explicit homage to our friend Socrates) argued that it is the dominant opinion that threatens thinking, not ignorance. Ensuring that students have the capacity to keep questions alive in the face of peer pressure, conventional wisdom, and the habit of their own convictions is what the liberal arts must always be about.

Admittedly, *some* knowledge is required to ask good questions and pursue the answers we receive. But if we are honest about this we will admit that the kind of exhaustive expertise we typically expect in students is overkill. After all, children are wonderful and persistent questioners: recall the wisdom of H.C. Andersen's "The Emperor's New Clothes." Indeed, academics are invariably prone to making the mistake Gilbert Ryle called the Cartesian fallacy: assuming that "knowing that" must *always* precede and serve as a condition for "knowing how." No person who creates knowledge or uses knowledge to put bread on the table would ever be guilty of this fallacy. All apprentices or would-be performers learn on the job, yet as teachers we tend to over-teach or "front load" knowledge. So a good pedagogical rule of thumb would be: teach the minimum necessary to get the students asking questions that will lead to your more subtle goals.

We would do well, then, to think of our task as introducing the student to cycles of question-answer-question and not just question-answer—with one aim of a course being to make the student rather than the professor the ultimate initiator of the cycle. To postpone developing students' ability to ask important questions in the name of "mastery" is to jeopardize their intellect. Good judgment and aggressive thinking will atrophy if they must be endlessly postponed while professors profess. In any event, the most important "performance" in the liberal arts is to initiate and sustain good question asking.

A very mundane point about testing can be made out of this esoteric argument. We rarely assess students on their ability to ask good questions. Indeed, we rarely teach them a repertoire of question-asking strategies for investigating essential ideas and issues. It should become obvious to students through the demands of the course and our assessment strategies that question asking is central. Too often, however, our assessments send the message that mastery of the "given" is the exclusive aim, and that question asking is not a masterable skill but a spontaneous urge.

Principle #8. This principle follows from #7. The aim of the liberal arts is to explore limits—the boundaries of ideas, theories, and systems. To paint the starkest picture of the difference between a "liberal" and a "non-liberal" view of the disciplines, therefore, we might see our task as teaching and assessing the ability to gauge the strengths and weaknesses of every major notion we teach—be it a theorem in math, a hypothesis in science, or literary theory in English. We need to know whether students can see the strengths and weaknesses of "paradigms." This would include the limits of a theory not only within a subject but across disciplines, as when we apply the rules of physical science to the human sciences.

There is no novelty in this idea. I am invoking a notion about the liberal arts developed 30 and more years ago by Joseph Schwab at Chicago. He termed such a view of education the art of "eclectic," and I encourage you to return to his essays for numerous suggestions on how to help students explore the merits of sanctioned truths.

I fear that we no longer know how to teach science as a liberal art in this sense. When we make science merely abstruse and technical, we make it increasingly unlikely that non-scientists will profit from studying science enough to support intelligent science policy as adults. And we encourage science students to become too technical and insufficiently critical. I really think that the first years of study in college (and certainly throughout secondary school) have less to do with "mastering" science and more to do with orthodox algorithms—learning metaphysics instead of physics, sanctioned truths vs. the unstable results yielded by methods and questions that *transcend* the current results.

I know this weakness in our science students firsthand from my high school teaching days. My students did not understand, for example, that error is inherent in science and not merely the fault of immature students or poor equipment. (Many believe that when the "big boys and girls" do their measuring, the results are exact). Nor did many of them realize that words like *gravity* or *atom* do not correspond to visible "things" to be seen directly.

The point can be made another way. We still do a poor job of teaching and assessing the student's grasp of the history of important ideas. I know of no other method by which inappropriately sacred truths can be more effectively demystified. What questions was Newton, then Einstein, trying to answer? What did the first drafts of a history text look like, and why were they revised? To ask questions like these is to open up a new and exciting world for students. To be smug about our knowledge and to distance ourselves from "crude" and outdated theory is to ensure that we repeat the mistakes of our smug and parochial elders.

Consider the history of geometry, the very idea of which strikes many people as an oxymoron. Many college students are utterly unaware of the problems that forced Euclid to develop an awkward parallel postulate (which was instantly decried by his colleagues). So much for self-evident truths, that glib line found in superficial views of Greek mathematics! Further, most students are unaware that non-Euclidean geometries can be proven to be as logically sound as Euclid's; they have no idea how that result transformed epistemology for all fields of study.

The consequence of our failure to reveal to students the history of important ideas is twofold. For one, students easily end up assuming that axioms, laws, postulates, theories, and systems are immutable, even though common sense and history say otherwise. The second result follows from the first and does lasting harm to intellectual courage in all but our feistiest students. Students never grasp that "knowledge" is the product of "thinking"—thinking that was as lively, unfinished, and sometimes as inchoate as their own. One major reason for the intellectual poverty in this country is that most students either become convinced they are incapable of being intellectual, or they are uninterested in it if it involves only arcane expertise in a narrowly framed subject.

Some practical implications for assessment? First, we should require students to keep notebooks of reflections on coursework, their increasing knowledge, and important changes of mind about that knowledge. Second, we should assess this work as part of the grade. I did so for many years and found it to be the most important and revealing aspect of the students' work. I also learned a lot about how their thinking evolved in a way that improved the courses I taught. Third, even the most technical training should ask students to do critical research into the origins of the ideas being learned so that students can gain greater perspective on their work. If we fail to do this, whether out of habit or rationalization that there is no time for such reflective work, we risk producing a batch of thoughtless students.

Principle #9. Number 9 extends the moral implications of #8. When we encourage narrow, unchecked expertise, we may unwittingly induce students to be dishonest about their ignorance.

I am not even talking about the more heinous crime of cheating, something we know is all too common. Rather, I am talking about the moral obligation of the liberal artist to emulate Socrates's trademark: his cheerful admission of ignorance. Alas, our students rarely admit their ignorance. One of our primary tasks should be to elicit the admission and not penalize it. But the student's willingness to take such a risk depends upon our doing so. It is then, as the "Meno" reminds us, that mutual inquiry and dialogue become possible because we are placed on equal moral footing as thinkers. More pointedly, our inclination to "profess" is always in danger of closing off the doors through which our students can enter the liberal conversation without excessive self-deprecation. So many of our students preface a wonderful idea by saying, "I know this sounds stupid, but. . . ."

Let our assessments, therefore, routinely encourage students to distinguish between what they do and do not know with conviction. Let us design scoring systems for papers that heavily penalize mere slickness and feigned control over a complex subject, and greatly reward honest admissions of ignorance or confusion. Or, let us go the next step and ask students to write a second paper in which they criticize the first one.

Principle #10. The 10th and last principle extends the point. Intellectual honesty is just one aspect of self-knowledge and the absence of self-deception. One of my favorite notions was put forward by Leo Slizard in talking about how to assess doctoral candidates. He argued that students should be assessed on how precisely and well they knew their strengths and limitations—and that it was a mistake to err greatly in *either* direction.

I am not arguing for professors to become counselors. I am arguing for them to improve students' ability to self-assess, and to make sure that accurate self-assessment is more than a pleasant exercise. It is an essential tool for ensuring that students have neither excessive nor insufficient pride in their world, either of which closes off further intellectual challenges and rewards.

The inherent danger of scholarship is not so much error as blind spots in our knowledge—hidden by the increasingly narrowed focus of our work and the isolation that can then breed worse: arrogance. Excessive pride leads us not only to ignore or paper over our doubts but more subtly to be deceived about the uniqueness and worth of our ideas—we forget that it was a conversation in the coffee shop or reading an article that sparked the idea. A few collaborative assessment tasks, with some reflection on the role of each contributor, would provide useful perspective for everyone.

It follows that we should assess class discussions more than we do. We again fail to assess what we value when we make it possible for students to learn everything from only listening to us and doing the reading. I and many others have developed some good material for assessment (and self-assessment) of class discussions, and I encourage you to develop some methods of your own.

Which of course brings us back to Socrates. What the casual reader of Plato always fails to grasp—including some overly analytic philosophers, I might add—is that the dialogues invariably are about character, not "theories" of virtue, knowledge, or piety. The twists and turns of dialogue, the sparring with Sophists or young know-it-alls—ultimately all this is meant to show that character flaws, not cognitive defects, impede the quest for knowledge. It is one's *attitude* toward knowledge that ultimately determines whether one will be a liberal artist or merely proficient.

As Socrates repeatedly reminds us, we must love wisdom so much that we question our knowledge, even our pet ideas if need be. By extension, the more we gain confidence in our ideas, the more we must become vigilant about finding knowledge in unexpected places—and let others who seem incapable of it teach us something, as our students often do.

It is not a canon—of ideas or books—that defines the liberal arts, but a set of very hard-won virtues. Like all sophisticated dispositions, these liberal habits are typically only revealed when they are challenged. It is only when peer pressure is greatest, be it in the classroom with students or at conferences with our peers, that we learn who has the power to keep questions alive. The liberal arts, properly speaking, do not make you free; they *keep* you free. Wisdom—Socrates knew—reveals itself when persistent inquiry is threatened: externally by custom and "oh, *everyone* knows . . ."; and internally by the tendency to rationalize our own habits, beliefs, and fears.

How much do students really love to learn, to persist, to passionately attack a problem or task? How willing are they, like the great Indian potters of New Mexico, to watch many of their halfbaked ideas explode, and start anew? How willing are they to go beyond being merely dutiful, perfunctory, or longwinded? Let us assess such things, just as the good coach does when he or she benches the talented player who "dogs" it.

We are then quite properly assessing not skill but intellectual character. It is to our detriment and the detriment of the liberal arts if we feel squeamish about saying and doing so. Let us "test" students in the same way that the mountain "tests" the climber—through challenges designed to evoke whether the proper virtues are present. And if not present, the quality of the resultant work should seem so inadequate to the *student* that little need be said in the way of "feedback."

Let our assessments be built upon the distinction between wisdom and knowledge, then. Too subjective? Unfair? Not to those who have the master's eyes, ears, and sense of smell—tact, in the old and unfortunately lost sense of that word. For these traits are as tangible as any fact, and more important to the student's welfare in the long run. It is not the student's errors that matter but the student's response to error; it is not "thoroughness" in a novice's work that reveals understanding but awareness of the dilemmas, compromises, and uncertainties under the arguments one is willing to stand on.

If our testing encourages smug or thoughtless mastery—and it does—we undermine the liberal arts. If our assessment systems induce timidity, cockiness, or crass calculations about grades and the relevance of today's assignment, we undermine the liberal arts. If our assessments value correctness more than insight and honesty, we undermine the liberal arts. If our assessments value ease of scoring more than revealing to students the errors or tasks that matter most, we undermine the liberal arts. Let us ensure, above all else, that our tests do just what Socrates's tests were meant to do: help us—and our students—to distinguish the genuine from the sham authority, the sophists from the wise. Then we will have assessments that are worthy of our aims.

Taking Inventory:
Identifying Assessment Activities

DAVID G. UNDERWOOD

Those embarking on development of an assessment program are encouraged to identify assessment activities already being undertaken. Although this is excellent advice, it is not as simple as it sounds, particularly on larger campuses, and the method of identifying current assessment initiatives is usually not addressed. This paper presents a method whereby a simple survey was used to help educate the campus about outcomes assessment while identifying assessment activities already being undertaken. The results of the survey are discussed, although the focus is on the process, content, and application of the survey.

Institutions confronted with initiating a comprehensive assessment program are often overwhelmed by such a seemingly monumental task. Advice found in the literature on outcomes assessment while well intentioned, may be incomplete or inapplicable due to the uniqueness of each institution's operation, student makeup, and mission. A commonly recommended starting point, applicable to most institutions, is to identify assessment activities that are already taking place on the campus and to build on those activities (Astin, 1987; Ewell, 1987; Ewell, 1988; Ewell and Lisensky, 1988; Jacobi, Astin, and Ayala, 1987; Nichols, 1989). Although this advice is obviously sound, it is not as simple as it appears and few of the authors give a clear indication of how such activities should be identified, although Ewell (1983, 1988) is probably the most comprehensive and practical.

Ewell and Lisensky (1988, p. 54) suggest the use of a "formal information inventory" as a simple method of determining what outcomes data are already in existence and include examples of inventories that have been previously used. Inventories such as these are useful but require some prior knowledge of existing information. Rather than downplay the utility of such an inventory, a useful approach would be to conduct a survey such as the one advocated in this paper and to use the information obtained from the survey to complete a formal inventory.

Purpose

The purpose of this paper is to describe the procedure used to identify assessment activities on a campus of over 14,000 students while educating segments of the campus about outcomes assessment and identifying those campus units interested in participating in a pilot assessment project.

Methodology

The first step in this project was to develop an institutional statement regarding outcomes assessment. Preliminary efforts to develop an institutional statement included reviewing the university mission statement, discussing objectives with the outcomes assessment task force, reviewing the last accreditation self-study report, and holding discussions with various campus leaders. It was important that the institutional statement on outcomes assessment reflect the philosophy of the coordinator of outcomes assessment and at the same time meet with the approval of an outcomes assessment task force that had been previously appointed by the academic vice-president. The statement, which was accepted and approved, specified two purposes for instituting outcomes assessment on our campus:

1. To improve student learning and performance

2. To improve programs, program planning, and program development

The statement of purpose was written into a one-page document that acknowledged the imperfect nature of outcomes data, introduced the new coordinator of outcomes assessment, and outlined the approach that would be taken in establishing a coordinated program of outcomes assessment. The idea of imperfect data was introduced at this point to avoid what Ewell (1988, p. 20) calls the "perfect data fallacy." The resulting one-page document was then used as a cover page to introduce the instrument.

The survey was designed to be brief, to educate the respondent, and to collect useful information for the outcomes assessment coordinator. The educational aspect of the instrument was particularly important since most people tend to focus only on testing when the term *assessment* is mentioned. To enhance the educational purpose, a list of assessment activities was provided along with an option to add additional activities to the list (see Table 1).

No attempt was made to further define the activities, although many of them were very similar. The purpose of this item was to identify activities other than testing that are part of assessment, and to determine which activities, including testing, are currently being undertaken.

Table 1 List of Assessment Activities

If information from any three of the following assessment activities could be provided to you for the purpose of improving programs or services for which you are responsible, which activities would you choose? (Please choose only three.)

a. Student Satisfaction Study	n. Job Placement Study
b. Student Attitude Study	o. Employer Satisfaction Study
c. Student Perception Study	p. Alumni Activity Study
d. Student Need Study	q. Transfer Tracking Study
e. Faculty Need Study	r. Program Accreditation Study
f. Faculty Perception Study	s. Diagnostic Placement Testing
g. Faculty Satisfaction Study	t. General Education Testing
h. Student Evaluation of Teaching	u. Major Field Testing
i. Service Evaluation Study	v. Program Admission Testing
j. Program Evaluation Study	w. Prelicensing Testing
k. Withdrawing Student Study	x. Certification Testing
l. Program Attrition Study	y. Minimum Competency Testing
m. "High-Risk" Student Study	z. Other (Please Specify)

Once the instrument was developed, the coordinator scheduled time on the agenda of the Outcomes Assessment Task Force, the Deans Council, made up of the deans from all colleges, and the Deans Advisory Council, made up of all the associate deans. A short presentation about outcomes assessment was made at each of these meetings and the instrument was distributed for discussion. This process, although time consuming and often frustrating, was used to educate, to add to the visibility of the coordinator position, and to elicit cooperation and a feeling of joint ownership in the instrument and the outcomes assessment program. Only after these various groups reviewed the instrument and presented their comments was the instrument considered ready for use.

After examining a current organization chart of the university, all vice-presidents, deans, department heads, directors, provosts, and other professional administrators were selected to receive the questionnaire. The population, rather than a sample, was queried because the size was manageable and it would increase visibility and enhance participation. Administrators were chosen in the belief that they would have more knowledge of activities taking place within the units for which they were responsible.

A cover letter was developed and signed by the academic vice-president, the chief executive officer, giving the project the high level of visibility suggested by several authors (Ewell, 1988; Nichols, 1989; Rossman and El-Khawas, 1987). The cover letter was designed to be educational inasmuch as it talked about the task force and the new position of coordinator, and it asked that the statement on outcomes assessment be carefully read and the survey completed. The names of the vice-presidents and deans were used in a mail merge, personalizing the letters. Labels were generated for the other respondents and attached to the top of the institutional statement page to identify the individual from whom a response was desired.

Although the instruments were individually labeled with the name and address of the person from whom a response was desired, packets consisting of the cover letter, the statement on outcomes assessment, and the instrument were mailed directly to the appropriate vice-presidents, deans, directors, provosts, and department heads. These top-level administrators were given responsibility for delivering the packets of information to the designated individuals, collecting the completed forms, and returning them to the coordinator of outcomes assessment. This method was used in an effort to increase the response rate and to reemphasize the high level of involvement in the process.

Results

The instruments were sent to the entire population of administrators, both academic and nonacademic, on the campus. The population consisted of 102 individuals who were identified as being responsible for, or having knowledge of, any assessment activities within a department or area. A total of 93 responses were received for a response rate of 91%. The titles of those responding to the survey are listed in Table 2.

Those falling into the category of "other" had titles of assistant director, coordinator, specialist, or assistant provost.

Responses were received from all colleges within the university as well as numerous administrative units. Table 3 provides details of the various groups within the university from which returns were received.

The category of administration contained respondents from areas such as admissions, registrar, financial aid, placement, and career services.

Table 2 Titles of Respondents

Title	N
Dean	6
Director	22
Department Head	49
Provost	3
Other	13
Total	93

Table 3 Respondents by Group

College	N
Arts and Sciences	27
Agriculture and Home Economics	11
Business Administration	7
Education	7
Engineering	5
Human and Community Services	12
Graduate School	1
Administration	23
Total	93

Item 4 of the survey asked the respondents to choose three types of assessment activities that provide the type of information they could use to improve their programs or services. A list of the activities chosen and the number choosing each appears in Table 4.

In addition to the above choices, there were 11 that fell into the category of "other." Responses classified as "other" are detailed in Table 5.

There are several interesting findings related to Tables 4 and 5. First, one of the three most frequently selected types of information is the student evaluation of teaching. This is of particular interest inasmuch as the focus appears to be more on evaluating teaching than evaluating learning. This is almost the reverse of the normal focus of outcomes assessment activities where the student is measured rather than the professor.

Second, there is a great deal of consistency in the top four choices of information, with each of those being chosen by between 21 and 29 of the respondents. The indication is that an outcomes assessment program would provide information meaningful to the majority of those responding by focusing on a student satisfaction study, student need study, student evaluation of teaching, and job placement study.

Third, only five respondents chose general education testing and only one chose value-added testing, although these are two of the most often-cited foci of an outcomes assessment program. On this campus it would appear that the emphasis, from the viewpoint of these administrative respondents, should be on student needs, student satisfaction, student feedback to instructors, and job placement information.

Table 4 Choices of Activity Information

Choice	N
Student Satisfaction Study	29
Student Need Study	26
Student Evaluation of Teaching	22
Job Placement Study	21
Program Evaluation Study	17
Faculty Need Study	16
Employer Satisfaction Study	15
Alumni Activity Study	15
Withdrawing Student Study	12
Student Perception Study	11
Student Attitude Study	10
Program Attrition Study	10
Faculty Satisfaction Study	8
"High-Risk" Student Study	8
Major Field Testing	7
Service Evaluation Study	7
Other (Please Specify)	7
Transfer Tracking Study	5
General Education Testing	5
Program Accreditation Study	4
Minimum Competency Testing	3
Program Admission Testing	2
Certification Testing	1
Prelicensing Testing	1
Total	271

Table 5 Choices Categorized as "Other"

Choice	N
Standardized Student Opinion Survey	1
Employer Satisfaction Survey	1
Student Satisfaction Survey	1
Tracking Study Comparing Goals vs. Outcomes	1
Faculty Evaluation of Teaching	1
Alumni Satisfaction Study	1
Value-Added Testing (Faculty Developed Subject Test-Rising Junior)	1
Credit Articulation Study	1
Impact of Minority Student Study	1
Standardized Test for MultiSectioned Courses	1
Review of Clientele Needs	1
Total	11

Question 5 of the survey required the respondents to rank order their preferences for assessment instruments. The results of the ranking are detailed in Table 6.

There are two interesting aspects of these results. First, questionnaires and interviews are by far the most preferred means of collecting assessment information, according to the administrators on this campus. Second, only 4 individuals chose standardized tests as their first choice in providing feedback that could be used to improve programs or services despite their widespread use.

Question 6 of the survey required respondents to list current assessment activities, indicate how often each activity is being conducted, identify the appropriate person to provide additional information, and provide the phone number of the contact person. The information regarding the types of activities being undertaken is grouped according to the classification used in question 4 (see Table 1) and summarized in Table 7. The numbers in parentheses indicate the number of individuals or departments performing that type of assessment activity.

Two hundred sixty-five activities were identified with sixty-four of those defying classification in the categories listed. It was not unexpected to find student evaluation of teaching and program evaluation study as the most frequently listed activities due to the ubiquitous nature of these activities. However, the number of activities listed (265 in all) and the amount of duplication was much greater than anticipated. For example, rather than a university-sponsored alumni activity study, 20 alumni activity studies are being conducted by various departments and individuals across campus.

In question 7 of the survey the respondents were asked to rank order the frequency of use of the types of instruments actually being used to collect assessment information in activities they listed as having been conducted in question 6. The results are compiled and presented in Table 8.

The instrument being used most frequently to collect information is the questionnaire. Again, the standardized test was used least frequently as a data collection instrument. It is worth noting that the interview was rated first in terms of preference by 37 of those responding, but it was ranked as being used first most frequently by only 8 respondents.

In question 8, one of the more critical questions from a practical viewpoint, respondents were asked whether they would be willing to participate in a pilot outcomes assessment project. The results are listed in Table 9.

It was gratifying to find that 56% of the responses were in the affirmative, indicating a willingness to become involved in a pilot project. It is particularly important on our campus since voluntary participation in pilot projects is considered the desired way to move forward with an outcomes assessment program.

The last question asked if the respondent would like additional information about outcomes assessment. This question was included to provide another opportunity to make contact and discuss the positive benefits of an outcomes assessment program. The results are displayed in Table 10.

As one charged with implementing and coordinating an outcomes assessment program, I was gratified to note that 84% of the respondents indicated an interest in obtaining more information about outcomes assessment.

Implications

The survey identified 265 assessment activities that were currently being conducted or had been conducted recently. In addition, 49 campus units expressed a willingness to participate in a pilot project in outcomes assessment. The survey also identified student satisfaction studies, student needs studies, and student evaluation of teaching as the three types of studies that could most effectively be used to make improvements to the programs or services of the respondents.

Table 6 Rank Order of Preference for Assessment Tools

	First	Second	Third	Fourth	Total
Questionnaire	42	26	18	4	90
Interview	37	31	8	13	77
Faculty-Developed Tests	9	13	34	24	80
Standardized Tests	4	19	21	30	74
Other	2	1	1	4	8

Table 7 Types and Number of Assessment Activities Currently Being Conducted

a. Student Satisfaction Study	(2)	n. Job Placement Study	(9)
b. Student Attitude Study	(3)	o. Employer Satisfaction Study	(4)
c. Student Perception Study	(5)	p. Alumni Activity Study	(20)
d. Student Need Study	(6)	q. Transfer Tracking Study	(4)
e. Faculty Need Study	(3)	r. Program Accreditation Study	(10)
f. Faculty Perception Study	(2)	s. Diagnostic Placement Testing	(7)
g. Faculty Satisfaction Study	(1)	t. General Education Testing	(1)
h. Student Evaluation of Teaching	(48)	u. Major Field Testing	(6)
i. Service Evaluation Study	(1)	v. Program Admission Testing	(2)
j. Program Evaluation Study	(38)	w. Prelicensing Testing	(2)
k. Withdrawing Student Study	(5)	x. Certification Testing	(8)
l. Program Attrition Study	(2)	y. Minimum Competency Testing	(10)
m. "High-Risk" Student Study	(3)	z. Other	(64)

Table 8 Rank Order of Frequency of Use of Assessment Tools

	First	Second	Third	Fourth	Total
Questionnaire	48	10	4	0	62
Interview	8	20	7	3	38
Faculty-Developed Tests	6	7	6	4	23
Standardized Tests	3	4	5	4	16
Other	3	6	2	1	12

Table 9 Interest in Participating in a Pilot Project

Choice	N
Not Now	8
Perhaps Later	30
Interested in Participating	49
Total	87

Table 10 Interest in More Information

Choice	N
Not Now	3
Perhaps Later	11
Would Like More Information	75
Total	89

Two major areas of concern surfaced in the results. As was pointed out earlier, there is a discrepancy between the types of information desired on this campus and the types of information normally considered as part of outcomes assessment. Specifically, the respondents gave their lowest rankings to all of the cognitive measures listed. The same problem holds true for the assessment activities that were identified as being conducted or having been conducted recently; there were very few cognitive assessment activities listed. The implications of this finding should not be understated. The finding indicates that while noncognitive areas seem to be well covered, some method must be devised to account for the cognitive assessment necessary for a comprehensive assessment program. Those who responded must be encouraged to continue their efforts and to expand those efforts to provide indication of cognitive outcomes as well. Since cognitive outcomes are much more difficult, are more expensive, and attempts to measure them meet with more resistance, the task is no minor undertaking.

Although this finding indicates a weakness in the existing assessment efforts, it was not unexpected. Most institutions, particularly the larger research-oriented institutions, operate on the assumption that the cognitive development of students who successfully complete programs is a given. The cognitive aspect of assessment is accounted for by the normal end-of-course testing and the granting of degrees for successful completion of prescribed courses. It is expected that anyone attempting to begin a comprehensive assessment program under similar conditions would have similar feelings.

The second major area of concern involves the amount of duplication of effort taking place across campus. It seems wasteful to have 20 departments or individuals performing alumni activity studies when one well-designed study at the university level should provide information to all those constituencies. One of the initial efforts will be to coordinate the activities taking place and to attempt to avoid duplication of effort.

On a more positive note, the survey and the methods used provided visibility for the outcomes assessment initiatives and increased the awareness of administrators and others across campus about the outcomes assessment movement. As a direct result, numerous invitations have been extended to the coordinator to make presentations about outcomes assessment. Most of these presentations have been followed by invitations to meet more informally to determine the best course of action within a department or administrative office. The most recent invitation came from the College of Arts and Sciences, the largest college on our campus, to make a presentation to all arts and science faculty during a professional development day. These presentations and informal meetings provide an opportunity to discuss the necessity of adding a cognitive dimension to the assessment activities already being undertaken.

Although the study produced quantitative results relevant to this institution, the real value of the approach lies in the educational aspect of the instrument, the construction of an institutional statement regarding outcomes assessment, the high level of visibility given the project, and the involvement of high-level administrators in the data collection process. The results also provide a direction for the next step in beginning our assessment program. The spontaneous requests for presentations and additional information provide an open door and a point of continuing contact with these administrators. And, when an approach is made to those individuals who responded to the survey, it is possible to know in advance those who are likely to be receptive to assessment initiatives.

References

Astin, A. W. (1987). Assessment, value-added, and educational excellence. In D. F. Halpern (ed.), Student outcomes assessment: What institutions stand to gain. *New Directions for Higher Education*, number 50. San Francisco: Jossey-Bass.

Ewell, P. T. (1983). *Information on Student Outcomes: How to Get It and How to Use It*. Boulder, CO: National Center for Higher Education Management Systems. Eric Document Reproduction Service No. ED 246 827.

Ewell, P. T. (1987). Establishing a campus-based assessment program. In D. F. Halpern (ed.), Student outcomes assessment: What institutions stand to gain. *New Directions for Higher Education*, number 50. San Francisco: Jossey-Bass.

Ewell, P. T. (1988). Implementing assessment: Some organizational issues. In T. W. Banta (ed.), Implementing outcomes assessment promise and perils. *New Directions for Institutional Research*, number 59. San Francisco: Jossey-Bass.

Ewell, P. T., and Lisensky, R. P. (1988). *Assessing Institutional Effectiveness: Redirecting the Self-Study Process*. Washington, DC: Consortium for the Advancement of Private Higher Education.

Jacobi, M., Astin, A. W., and Ayala, F., Jr. (1987). *College Student Outcomes Assessment: A Talent Development Perspective*. ASHE-ERIC Higher Education Report No. 7. Washington, DC.

Nichols, J. O. (1989). *Institutional Effectiveness and Outcomes Assessment Implementation on Campus: A Practitioner's Handbook*. New York: Agathon Press.

Rossman, J. E., and El-Khawas, E. (1987). Thinking about assessment: Perspectives for presidents and chief academic officers. Preliminary edition of a monograph to be published by the American Council on Education.

What We Can Learn from Coursework Patterns About Improving the Undergraduate Curriculum

James L. Ratcliff

Most faculty and administrators are committed to improving the quality of undergraduate education. To make improvements, it is necessary to know what students learn in order to decide what ideally they should learn. Assessment plans and programs can monitor institutional performance relative to student learning. Over the past decade, colleges and universities have made substantial efforts to establish student outcomes assessment programs and to revise and reform the undergraduate curriculum. Unfortunately, these two endeavors have not concretely and substantively informed one another.

The 1980s were a decade of examination of the state and quality of education programs. National reports urged faculty and academic leaders to improve baccalaureate programs. The Study Group on the Conditions of Excellence in American Higher Education (1984), formed under the U.S. Department of Education, urged colleges to provide students clear academic direction, standards, and values. It urged researchers to use college student assessment information and to explore the use of student transcripts as resources in understanding more about which subjects students study in college and what they learn. The practical applications, procedures, and techniques of student and curriculum assessment described in the present volume are a direct outcome of those recommendations. Beginning in 1985, we developed specific procedures to determine the gains in student learning that were directly associated with enrollment in different patterns of undergraduate coursework.

In February 1985, the Association of American Colleges (AAC) issued the report *Integrity in the College Curriculum: A Report to the Academic Community* (Committee on Redefining the Meaning and Purpose of Baccalaureate Degrees, 1985), which concluded that undergraduate education was in a state of crisis and disarray. The report attacked the "marketplace"-oriented curriculum based solely on student choice, asking "Is the curriculum an invitation to philosophic and intellectual growth or a quick exposure to the skills of a particular vocation?" (p. 2). The report called on colleges and universities to live up to their stated goals for general education and liberal learning by providing a coherent curriculum. For AAC, a coherent curriculum at least entails inquiry, literacy, understanding of numerical data, historical consciousness, science, values, art, international and multicultural experiences, and study of some discipline in depth (Eaton, 1991). AAC reasserted the belief that an undergraduate education should produce learning outcomes common to all students irrespective of their major or minor fields of specialization.

At least three studies have tried to determine what improvements in the college curriculum have been accomplished since 1985. Zemsky (1989) examined thirty-five thousand student transcripts from thirty colleges and universities to determine the shape and substance of the undergraduate curriculum that the students had encountered. Zemsky found that the curriculum continued to lack structure and coherence, that students' enrollment in science and mathematics was quite limited, and that the humanities lacked sequential, developmental patterns of learning. Lynne V. Cheney (1989) analyzed humanities enrollments in colleges and universities to determine if there had been a fundamental change in baccalaureate programs between 1983 and 1989. She found little, if any, change in undergraduate degree requirements. She lamented,

> It is possible to graduate now, as it was five years ago, from *more* than 80 percent of our institutions of higher education without taking a course in American history. In 1988–89, it is possible to earn a bachelor's degree from:
>
> - 37 percent of the nation's colleges and universities without taking any course in history;
>
> - 45 percent without taking a course in American or English literature;
>
> - 62 percent without taking a course in philosophy;
>
> - 77 percent without studying a foreign language [Cheney, 1989, p. 5].

Not only was their little evidence of increased structure and rigor to the curriculum during this time period, there was also evidence that the curriculum was not having much impact on student learning. Astin (1991), in a national study of student transcripts, general education requirements, and student test scores and self-reports found no relationship between any general education curriculum structure and improvement in student learning.

There were strident calls in these national reports and studies to improve undergraduate education, and colleges and universities did not remain idle. During the past decade, more than 90 percent of colleges and universities have engaged in some kind of revision or reform of their undergraduate curriculum (Gaff, 1989). The American Council on Education repeatedly reported in *Campus Trends* (El-Khawas, 1988, 1990) that most colleges and universities were engaged in curriculum reform. These efforts led Eaton (1991, pp. 61, 63) to raise some rather uncomfortable questions about this flurry of activity:

> From a negative point of view, one can point to little in the way of completed curricular modifications or, more important, changes in student performance that . . . emerged . . . as the 1980's ended. Worse, one might view the decade . . . as an essentially unimportant ten-year saga during which the higher-education community continued an apparently endless and unproductive dialogue with itself on academic issues as opposed to engaging in construction action. . . .
>
> . . . Did institutional descriptions of academic reform fail to focus on those intended to benefit but, instead, confused expectations of student performance with descriptions of faculty involvement?

There has not been a meaningful and substantive connection between undergraduate curriculum content and improved student learning. The increased national attention given to improved student performance and stronger academic direction, standards, and values demands that we make more substantive links between what students study in college and gains in their learning. This volume offers a model for linking general education curriculum and student outcomes assessment. Before I describe this unique model, and before the contributors to this volume show how it can be used to answer tough questions of academic policy and curriculum reform, we first must examine why faculty and administrators are focusing more attention on the assessment of student outcomes.

Impetus for Assessment

A variety of both external and internal factors are compelling institutions not only to consider assessment but also to formalize plans and take specific actions to measure the educational impact of an institution on its students. One group of external factors involves state initiatives. Dissatisfaction with student learning has led an increasing number of states to expect colleges and universities to implement student assessment programs. Earlier state policies toward assessment took a decentralized approach, allowing institutions to develop their own systems of assessment. However, state policy makers are becoming increasingly dissatisfied with assessment programs that do not improve student learning. The result has been new state proposals for common student outcomes testing (Ewell, 1991). Some states have already adopted formal assessment requirements and many other states are moving in this direction. Every student in Florida who is preparing to receive an associate's degree from a two-year institution or who plans to become a junior in a four-year institution is required by the state to take the College Level Academic Skills Test. Since 1979 Tennessee has based part of its public college and university funding on student assessment results. Colleges and universities in Tennessee test seniors in general education and in their chosen majors, survey alumni, and use the results of assessment activities to guide improvements at the institutions (Banta and others, 1990).

Another set of external factors is composed of accreditation organizations. Most of the six regional accreditation associations have begun to incorporate outcomes assessment as a criterion for institutional approval. The North Central Association of Colleges and Universities has conducted regional seminars on assessment and prepared a workbook to aid in the evaluation of institutional effectiveness and student achievement. In addition, accreditation bodies that approve programs in the disciplines are beginning to include outcomes assessment in their criteria for approval.

Due to these external factors, institutions often have developed and implemented assessment programs to provide accountability. However, there are also internal factors that have encouraged institutions to undertake assessment activities for the sake of academic improvement. The information gathered from assessments can help reform the curriculum, strengthen academic programs and student services, and, consequently increase student satisfaction and enhance student recruitment and longterm retention. Using the information from assessment activities, faculty can give specific attention to the need for self-improvement in teaching and evaluating students in their own individual courses. The model described in this volume is focused on assessment for the purpose of academic improvement.

Development of the Coursework Cluster Analysis Model

Assessments describe and document the nature and extent of learning that has occurred. They cannot tell us, however, which courses most consistently produce gains in learning for specific groups of students over time at particular institutions. Such information would be extremely useful. Knowledge about the degree to which different courses contribute to different learning outcomes would provide a college or university with an empirical basis for curriculum review. Knowledge of such links between coursework and learning would complement faculty wisdom, student evaluation, and other means of appraising the extent to which particular sets and sequences of courses have their intended effects. Such information could also be used to improve the academic advising and guidance that students receive in making course selections (Ratcliff and others, 1990a, 1990b, 1990c, 1990d).

Over the past four years, my colleagues and I have developed a model for linking assessments of the general learning of undergraduates with their coursework (Ratcliff, 1987, 1988, 1989; Ratcliff and others, 1990a, 1990b, 1990c, 1990d, Ratcliff and Jones, 1990, 1991; Jones and Ratcliff, 1990a, 1990b, 1991). This research has proceeded under the rubric of the Differential Coursework Patterns Project, and the model for linking coursework to student assessment has been referred to as the Coursework Cluster Analysis Model (CCAM). Its development and testing was supported, first, by the Office of Educational Research and Improvement of the U.S. Department of Education. Subsequent qualitative validity studies of the Graduate Record Examination (GRE) item types, trend analyses of coursework patterns, and studies of the applicability of the model to curriculum reform, assessment program development, and academic advising have been supported by the Exxon Education Foundation. The CCAM has been tested at six institutions: Stanford and Georgia State universities, and Clayton State, Evergreen State, Mills, and Ithaca colleges. In addition, the CCAM has been applied to student reports of enrollment patterns and American College Test-Comprehensive (ACT-COMP) scores at the University of Tennessee, Knoxville (Pike and Phillippi, 1989). Research on the uses and limitations of the CCAM is continuing as part of the National Longitudinal Study of Student Learning at the National Center on Postsecondary Teaching, Learning, and Assessment.

In the most typical applications, assessment instruments are administered to graduating seniors. Since 1986, we have examined over seventy-two thousand courses appearing on the transcripts of approximately sixteen hundred graduating seniors. Each group of seniors came from a cross section of majors. They also reflected the full range of academic ability, as indicated by their Scholastic Aptitude Test (SAT) scores, for the general population of students at each institution. The results of posttests were compared with the results of corresponding pretests of the same students. Well-known standardized instruments were used: the SAT, GRE, ACT, and ACT-COMP, as well as the Kolb Learning Styles Inventory. Locally constructed measures of student-perceived course difficulty also were used. A great strength of the CCAM and an asset that seems to enhance its acceptability to faculty are that the model is not dependent on instruments supplied by external vendors. It can use a variety of locally developed instruments, tailored to particular needs and extensively employing local judgment. A college, for instance, might administer its own essay examinations to freshmen and seniors, and its own faculty might grade them holistically; so long as the final evaluation, or its subparts, can be translated into a numerical scale, this instrument would be entirely adequate for the purpose of the CCAM.

A common stumbling block in the development of an assessment program is that of determining what form of test or assessment information to use. Curriculum reviewers, reformers, and researchers quickly acknowledge that there is no clear conception of what constitutes general learning. Such recognition emerges regardless of whether it is the college curriculum or the various tests and assessment devices that are being examined. A college that attempts to reach consensus among its constituents either on general education goals or on the "best" measure of general learned abilities will foster heated discussion. The quest for consensus on what should be the common intellectual experience of undergraduates may end in irresolution or, worse, abandonment of the assessment initiative. Instead of searching for the ideal measure of general learning in a college, those charged with assessment can better direct their energies toward the selection of a constellation of assessment means and measures that appear to be appropriate criteria for describing one or more dimensions of the general learning goals of the college.

The CCAM provides a basis for determining the relative extent to which each measure explains general student learning within a given college environment. If we have nine different assessment measures, for example, we can determine what proportion of the variation in student scores is explained by each measure. This information leads to a decision point for the academic leader or faculty committee charged with the development and oversight of the assessment program. If a measure of general learning does not explain much of the variation in student scores, one option is to conclude that the measure is inappropriate to the students and the education program or that particular college or university. In short, the CCAM can assist in the discard of that particular form of evaluation as superfluous and unnecessary. An alternative conclusion is that the institution is not devoting sufficient attention to the type of learning measured. Here, an examination of the assessment instrument relative to the curriculum is called for. Again, the CCAM can point to those courses and classes that were associated with gains in student learning on the measure in question.

Steps in the Coursework Cluster Analysis Model

The CCAM is grounded conceptually to the finding that student learning varies more greatly within institutions than between them. The selection, testing, and adoption of a specific methodology for the analysis of coursework patterns were based also on repeated empirical investigation of the relationship between different patterns of coursework and variation in student learning. In this chapter, I describe the general methodology of the CCAM. The rationale and procedures of cluster analysis are described with reference to its application to the investigation of coursework patterns. Since cluster analysis currently is not widely employed in educational research, I begin this section by contrasting cluster analysis with other statistical methods of potential value in the assessment of student learning.

Previous assessment and transcript analysis studies have used the general linear model and regression analysis (Astin, 1970a, 1970b; Benbow and Stanley, 1983; Pallas and Alexander, 1983; Prather and Smith, 1976a, 1976b). The rationale for the use of regression is based on practical and theoretical justifications. Regression analysis allows maximum design flexibility and is statistically robust. Transcript analyses involve large amounts of data. For example, Prather and Smith (1976b) examined 8,735 student transcripts that collectively contained 189,013 individual course grades. Regression analysis provides an effective technique for presenting the diverse nature of the data while maintaining a consistent analysis rationale. However, the general linear model does not provide a direct means of assessing the additive and temporary aspects of course patterns, that is, course combinations and sequences. Moreover, use of linear regression alone would conceptualize the problem as that of finding the one best fit between students and learning experiences. It would not account for the appropriateness and benefits of different learning experiences for different groups of students.

The term *coursework* is used here to refer to the categorization of the courses in which students enrolled according to the multiple assessment criteria of their general education and liberal learning. It is the systematic and unique way in which a college or university labels and arranges its courses (for example, Honors 101, French 340); that scheme or arrangement of classes is already known in a disaggregate form on student transcripts. Identification is the allocation of individual courses to be established in categories on the basis of specific criteria (for example, Biology 205 is classified by many universities as a sophomore-level class in the Department of Biology).

Discriminant analysis is used in the CCAM to test the validity of the groupings and to identify those assessment criteria that tell us most about collegiate learning experiences. Discriminant analysis is a process used to differentiate between groups formed on an a priori basis (see Biglan, 1973, for an example). Discriminant analysis does not discover groups; rather, it identifies a set of characteristics that can significantly differentiate between the groups. The process allows the analyst to allocate new cases to one of the a priori groups with the least amount of error. In contrast, *cluster analysis* recovers groups representing particular patterns from diverse populations (Lorr, 1983; Romesburg, 1984). In the CCAM, cluster analysis is used to classify courses according to student achievement criteria, while discriminant analysis is used to test and provide secondary validation of the cluster groupings and to identify those criteria that significantly differentiate one cluster of coursework from another.

Cluster analysis is sometimes confused with factor analysis. Factor analysis is different from cluster analysis in that the analyst's attention is on the similarity of the variables (attributes). The aim is to identify a small number of dimensions (factors) that can account for individual differences on the various measures or attributes. Thus, the aim of factor analysis is to reduce or consolidate the number of attributes of a variable set, whereas the purpose of a cluster analysis is simply to classify or taxonomize data into groups on the basis of a set of attributes. Cluster analysis refers to a wide variety of techniques used to classify entities into homogeneous subgroups on the basis of their similarities.

The end products of cluster analysis are clusters or pattern sets. Since the exact number and nature of the course patterns is not known in advance, the clustering process is actually technically preclassificatory. In other words, cluster analysis techniques are used to construct a classification scheme for unclassified data sets. In this way, cluster analysis empirically arranges the courses of a college curriculum using student decision-making behavior (as represented on transcripts) as the primary source of information. The courses are classified in a hierarchical dendrogram or tree. The relationship between courses is determined by their similarity on the criteria used in the classification. In this way, the similarity between courses is determined empirically, rather than by arbitrary concepts (for example, life sciences) or levels (for example, freshmen-level survey). This conceptual-empirical approach was selected due to the lack of agreement in the higher education literature on a common research paradigm, model, or philosophy for the organization of coursework (Bergquist, Gould, and Greenberg, 1981; Biglan, 1973; Fuhrman and Grasha, 1983; Gaff, 1983; Rudolph, 1977; Sloan, 1971; Veysey, 1973).

Cluster analysis conforms to the conceptual restrictions placed on the CCAM to assess the effect of coursework patterns on student learning. Cluster analysis provides a statistical procedure for examining coursework using multiple criteria. It can classify different sets of coursework according to different net effects of learning associated with them. It can accommodate both quantitative and qualitative attributes of varying dimensions. Thus, the criterion selected need not be test scores; nominal ordinal interval, and ratio data have been successfully used as attributes in cluster analysis (Romesburg, 1984) . Cluster analysis uses these attributes to arrive at patterns of coursework independently of any institutionally prescribed a priori distinctions. Therefore, it can test the combinations, sequences, and progressions of courses within the undergraduate curriculum. It leads to the discovery of clusters (or patterns) of coursework in student transcripts, based on the multiple measures of student assessment employed. Since the purpose of the CCAM is to group coursework homogeneously relative to student learning criteria (Lorr, 1983; Romesburg, 1984), cluster analysis serves as the primary methodology for the analytical model.

Overview of the CCAM Steps. There are several steps to using the CCAM. First, student residual scores are derived. A residual score is the difference between the student's actual score on the outcomes assessment measure and the score predicted by the entrance measure used. Next, student transcripts are examined. Courses reported on them are clustered into patterns based on the residual scores of the students who enrolled in them. The resulting coursework patterns are then grouped or classified according to any of a wide variety of student or institutional factors. Patterns can be classified according to factors such as the entering ability level of the student, the type of coursework selected (general education, prerequisites), the campus at which the student enrolled, or the residence facilities housing the students. Adult versus traditional college-age students, commuter versus residential students, and part-time versus full-time students' coursework can be compared. Within systems of higher education with course comparability, transfer schemes, and articulation agreements, the model can be used to determine if coursework associated with students from branch campuses or with transfer students is associated with the same types of improvement in learning as found for students native to the campus.

A Closer Look at the CCAM Steps. The CCAM research design uses official student transcripts and assessment instrument scores as data sources for a sample of graduating senior students. To describe the model and to illustrate how CCAM is executed, I here use the nine item-type categories of the General Test of the GRE as examples of multiple measures of general learned abilities of college seniors. Standardized and nonstandardized, locally developed and commercially available assessment instruments and measures can be used with CCAM. In the following example, SAT scores are used as controls for the academic abilities of these students when they first entered college. The student transcripts are used as the unobtrusive record of the sequence of courses in which these seniors enrolled.

The first objective of the CCAM is to determine the extent of student improvement in general learned abilities over the time of their baccalaureate program. To achieve this objective, the residual score of each GRE item type for each student is calculated first; the residual score is the difference between the student's actual score and the score predicted by the student's corresponding SAT score. It is derived by regressing the outcomes measure (in this case, GRE item types) on the entrance measures (in this case, SAT scores). Thus, for each student outcomes measure there is a student residual score for each person in the sample group.

The second objective is to determine patterns of coursework on the student transcripts that are associated with the student score residuals. Cluster analysis gives us these patterns, using student residual scores (GRE item-type residuals) as attributes of the courses in which students enrolled. To achieve this second objective, we create a data matrix where all of the courses to be analyzed are in the columns and all of the assessment measures or criteria are in the rows. Each cell in this matrix is then filled with the appropriate mean course residual score. For example, let us assume that we have student assessment data on writing ability and understanding of scientific knowledge, and a writing sample that has been holistically scored. For the course Introduction to Political Systems, we calculate the mean of residual scores for all students enrolling in it for each of these measures. We do this for Introduction to Political Science and every other course on the students' transcripts that we select to analyze.

Now, with several rows of assessment data, a column for each course analyzed, and a course mean residual score in every cell of the data matrix, we are ready to determine how similarly students who enrolled in different courses performed. The course mean residual score is the metric value that we are going to use to make the comparisons of coursework. To determine how courses are similar to one another in this way, we use the correlation coefficient (Pearson's r) as the indicator of similarity.

Our task is to see how the performance of students in the course Introduction to Political Systems is similar to the performance of students in other courses, However, students take more than one course, so courses taken by a particular group of students will cluster together. That is because the course mean residuals for each assessment measure should look about the same for all of the courses taken by this group of students.

So, if we correlate the writing sample score of Introduction to Political Systems with the sociology course Mass Behavior, then the correlation will be high if students for both courses showed comparable improvement on that measure. What we are doing, then, is creating a second matrix to record our correlation coefficient. In this matrix, all of the rows are the courses analyzed, and all of the columns are a duplicate listing of all of the courses. Each cell contains the coefficient representing the extent to which each course is related to all other courses on all the assessment criteria. Obviously, the greater the assessment criteria, the more precision in establishing the relationship. Construction of these two data matrices, the raw data matrix and the course resemblance matrix, may seem like a lot of work. Fortunately, use of a computer with popular statistical programs, such as SPSS and SAS, makes the task easy. We do not even see these matrices as they are calculated at lightning speed as we move along performing the CCAM cluster analysis.

Once the resemblance matrix indicating the proportional relationship of courses is established, a clustering method is selected and executed to arrange a tree or dendrogram of courses related by the student score gains. Next, we conduct a discriminant analysis on the resulting clusters of coursework. The discriminant analysis tells us the extent to which the courses have been correctly classified according to the assessment criteria, which of the assessment criteria were correlated with particular discriminant functions, and which coursework clusters were associated with the improvement of student learning according to which assessment criteria. From the discriminant analysis, an association can be inferred between coursework patterns (clusters) and the assessment criteria (student score residuals on the multiple measures of learning). The cluster analysis procedure groups courses frequently chosen by students according to the strength of their associated effect on the student score gains.

The CCAM classifies the most frequently enrolled courses according to their associated effect on student improvement in learning. The procedure classifies courses according to a ratio index of similarity to other courses. This procedure is designed to examine those courses in which most students enroll. Thus, the analysis is limited to only a fraction of all of the courses in a college curriculum. For example, in the historical data base used in model building and testing, a 5 percent sample of student transcripts enabled an examination of only 5 percent of the courses appearing on those transcripts (the percentage of courses enrolling five or more students from the sample group). However, the courses examined in that 5 percent corresponded closely to those courses identified as meeting the college's distributional degree requirements in general education. The quantitative procedures and techniques are described in greater detail in Ratcliff, Jones, and Hoffman (1992).

The linking of coursework to assessment results is critical given the diversity of the undergraduate curriculum today. Most colleges and universities have an expansive curriculum representing the explosion of knowledge, diversity of students, and modes of inquiry that characterize higher education in the twentieth century. Given this observation about the undergraduate curriculum, we find that up to 20 percent of the courses are not to be found on the transcripts of the preceding or following year's graduating seniors. The reason for this is that annual course schedules do not represent all of the courses found in the college catalogue. Certain courses are given on a one-time experimental basis, and some are canceled due to lack of enrollment. Typically, the undergraduate student chooses thirty-five to forty-five courses to fulfill the baccalaureate degree requirements from a list of twenty-five hundred to five thousand courses at a large research university or from eight hundred to fifteen hundred courses at a liberal arts college. Therefore, what students learn and how much they learn at a given institution varies from year to year based on variations in course offerings and student course selections. This variation in student learning within a single institution often is greater than the variation in student learning across institutions.

Findings from Research Based on the Coursework Cluster Analysis Model

Students who take different coursework learn different content, cognitive skills, values, and attitudes. Student learning varies greatly in complex institutions of higher education because of their broad arrays of curriculum offerings. Critical to the success of general and liberal education for students in these institutions is some means for recognizing curriculum diversity and its effects. Thus, the more complex the curriculum offerings the greater is the challenge to determine the relationship between coursework taken and learning achieved.

Based on measures of general learning and the transcripts of graduating seniors, the coursework taken by students who showed large gains in these measures can be identified. In our research, we found that different patterns and sequences of coursework produced different types of gains in learning. For example, course sequences in a wide range of disciplines such as business, biology, and philosophy were associated with gains in student learning in analytical reasoning. Student improvement in mathematics was associated with coursework in economics, business, music, physical therapy, mathematics, and quantitative methods in management. Student gains in reading comprehension were associated with coursework in marketing, accounting, management, music, and history. These findings and relationships are described and illustrated more fully in Jones (this volume (Chapter Three), where the CCAM is used to test the viability of a core curriculum to engender improvement in students' learned abilities.

Consistently, we have found that students who take different coursework learn different things and develop different abilities. There are two lessons from this research. First, the courses that students take in college have a bearing on what they learn. Second, the structure of general education in the institutions that we examined did not produce a profound effect on the types of learning that we examined. While the current general requirements of American colleges and universities may show little effect on the development of general learned abilities of students (Astin, 1991) the specific coursework taken by those students does have an effect (Ratcliff and Jones, 1990, 1991). We believe that improvements in student learned abilities can be achieved by revising undergraduate curriculum experiences to emulate the coursework clusters, patterns, and sequences taken by those students who show large gains in student learning. Here lies the potential power of assessment to guide and monitor the reform of undergraduate education.

What the Coursework Cluster Analysis Model Can Do

The CCAM provides a way for faculty and administrators to make more substantive links between what students study in college and what they learn. It suggests that an ideal coursework pattern is one in which what is to be learned is well matched to the background, preparation, and interests of the learners. The more diverse the student population, the greater is the need for alternative coursework patterns to fulfill the general education requirements.

The model and method of analysis defined in this volume permit a college or university to achieve several tasks of curriculum reform: determine which assessment measures best describe the kinds of learning that take place among students at the institution, determine which parts of the curriculum are currently not monitored or described by the present assessment methods and measures, determine which patterns of coursework are associated with which kinds of learning and with which groups of students, determine the extent to which transfer students benefit from the same or different general education coursework as that taken by students who began their baccalaureate program at the same institution, determine the extent to which a core curriculum or a distributional requirement produces the greatest gains in learning among different groups of undergraduates at the same institution, and determine which course sequences contribute to general education and liberal learning and which do not. The CCAM has limitations as well. It is designed for assessment of general education and liberal learning, not learning within the major; those institutions that have a distribution plan of general education in which students have a fairly wide range of curriculum choices to fulfill the requirements for their baccalaureate; the identification of coursework *associated* with improvement in student learning in general education and liberal learning. It does not tell us that coursework *caused* the learning. Subsequent research and analysis are required to determine which factors contributed to that learning.

Advantages to Assessing Coursework Pattern

The CCAM provides a number of advantages and benefits in the assessment of general education. First, the model can use multiple measures of assessment, thereby allowing for a broader picture of student learning than any one measure can paint. It provides institutions with information regarding the extent of variation in student assessment results that is explained by any one of the measures used. This information can be helpful in a number of ways. Faculty and administrators need not decide on an ideal set of assessment measures. The extent to which such measures may overlap in describing student learning can be identified. The mix of assessment measures appropriate to the goals of the institution and the characteristics of the student population can be continuously monitored. When students show small amounts of growth on an indicator of student learning, the college or university can either develop strategies for improving student learning in the area identified or else discard the measure as inappropriate to the institution and its students.

Efforts to assess general education and liberal learning can become quickly bogged down in discussions over which measures, indicators, or examinations to use. Faculty feel pressured to commit to a set of measures that may not accurately reflect their visions of the goals of general education. By using multiple measures and by leaving the process of choosing measures open to continuous revision and updating, the college or university can proceed to develop a rational, cogent, and informative assessment plan. Eaton (1991, p. 66) has written about tensions that emerge over the discussion of the desired outcomes of general education and the desirability of such a contingency approach: "These tensions emerge when we are either unwilling or unable to commit some defensible approach to general education for fear that our commitment will be found lacking in some way. Waiting around for the ideal general education scenario, however, serves little purpose and harms students even more than a general education effort that possesses some flaws."

If a general education innovation holds promise to enhance student learning in some way, then there should be a means to ascertain whether or not that improvement has occurred. Linked analysis of assessment and enrollment data holds the promise of identifying when and, more important, under what circumstances the general education curriculum has been improved. The CCAM provides useful information to the college or university about the mix of assessment measures that reflects what the students learn and what the institution intends to teach them.

The model can provide concrete useful information about the curriculum to guide reform efforts. It is a tool ideally suited to institutions of higher education with distributional general education requirement and a wide array of programs, electives, and majors. From a catalogue of hundreds or thousands of courses, the CCAM can identify the courses taken by students who showed the greatest improvement in learning. For example, if one of the assessment measures that a college selects is a test of analytical reasoning, then the CCAM can identify those groups of courses taken by students who showed significant improvement in that area of general learning.

The finding that different courses engender different types of learning is actually a corollary to a larger, more important research finding affirmed in our research but best described by Pascarella and Terenzini (1991). They describe and analyze twenty years of research indicating that *differences in student learning are far greater within institutions than between them*. Given this finding, it stands to reason that students taking different coursework and having different extracurricular experiences should show differences in subject matter learned, in the type and extent of their general cognitive development, and in their values and attitudes toward learning.

This finding that variation in student learning is greater within institutions than between them also means that one intellectual shoe does not fit all freshmen feet. The efficacy of a single set of courses, a core, in fostering the intellectual development of college students can be easily examined using assessment results. Likewise, the efficacy of specific combinations and sequences of coursework can be scrutinized relative to the long-term learning gains of students. The specific learning preparation, interests, and outcomes of different groups of students can be examined, whether they are low ability, high ability, transfer students, or students from specific curricula or majors.

The student population can be subdivided by ability, by gender, race, or ethnicity, or by major. Then the CCAM can identify if the coursework associated with gains in learning among the total group is the same as that for the subgroups. Curriculum planners and curriculum committees can readily use this information. Courses in the general education sequence that are not associated with gains in student learning can be revised, enhanced, or dropped. Courses outside the general education requirements that contribute to gains in student learning can be included in the general education curriculum.

The model can also produce information that leads to better academic advising, since it links the coursework that students take with their improvement in learning. Students can choose from lists of courses taken by others with similar backgrounds and abilities—others who showed gains in performance and learning. This procedure takes advising beyond the mere listing of formal degree requirements. As more data are amassed, increasingly greater precision is generated in the linking of coursework and student learning. The CCAM may even be amenable to the development of a microcomputer-based advising system utilizing a relational data base of prior students' course-taking patterns and assessment results. Such a computer-based advising system would yield an array of effective coursework tailored to the abilities and interests of individual students and within the parameters of institutional degree requirements. In subsequent chapters, we explore and exemplify how the linking of curriculum information (transcripts, catalogue studies, course syllabi, and examinations) with student outcomes assessment data can guide undergraduate curriculum reform.

References

Astin, A. W. "The Methodology of Research on College Impact, Part 2." *Sociology of Education*, 1970a, *43*, 223–254.

Astin, A. W. "The Methodology of Research on College Impact, Part 2." *Sociology of Education*, 1970b, *43*, 437–450.

Astin, A. W. *Assessment for Excellence: The Philosophy and Practice of Assessment and Evaluation in Higher Education*. New York: Macmillan, 1991.

Banta, T., and others. *Bibliography of Assessment Instruments*. Knoxville, Tenn.: Center for Assessment Research and Development, University of Tennessee, 1990.

Benbow, C. P., and Stanley, J. C. "Differential Course-Taking Hypothesis Revisited." *American Educational Research Journal*, 1983, *20* (4), 469–573.

Bergquist, W. H., Gould, R. A., and Greenberg, E. M. *Designing Undergraduate Education: A Systematic Guide*. San Francisco: Jossey-Bass, 1981.

Biglan, A. "The Characteristics of Subject Matter in Different Academic Areas." *Journal of Applied Psychology*, 1973, *57* (3),195–203.

Cheney, L V. *50 Hours: A Core Curriculum for College Students*. Washington, D.C.: National Endowment for the Humanities, 1989.

Committee on Redefining the Meaning and Purpose of Baccalaureate Degrees Association of American Colleges. *Integrity in the College Curriculum: A Report to the Academic Community*. Washington, D.C.: Association of American Colleges, 1985.

Eaton, J. S. *The Unfinished Agenda: Higher Education and the 1980s*. New York: Macmillan 1991 .

El-Khawas, E. *Campus Trends, 1988*. Higher Education Panel Reports, No. 77. Washington, D.C.: American Council on Education, 1988.

El-Khawas, E. *Campus Trends, 1990*. Higher Education Panel Reports, No. 80. Washington, D.C.: American Council on Education, 1990.

Ewell, P. "Assessment and Public Accountability: Back to the Future." *Change*, 1991, *23*, 12–17.

Fuhrman, B., and Grasha, A. *A Practical Handbook for College Teachers*. Boston: Little, Brown, 1983.

Gaff, J. G. *General Education Today: A Critical Analysis of Controversies, Practices, and Reforms.* San Francisco: Jossey-Bass, 1983.

Gaff, J. G. "General Education at the Decade's End: The Need for a Second Wave of Reform. *Change,* 1989, 21, 11–19.

Jones, E. A., and Ratcliff, J. L. "Effective Coursework Patterns and Faculty Perceptions of the Development of General Learned Abilities." Paper presented at the annual meeting of the Association for the Study of Higher Education, Portland, Oregon, November 1990a.

Jones, E. A., and Ratcliff, J. L. "Is a Core Curriculum Best for Everybody? The Effect of Different Patterns of Coursework on the General Education of High and Low Ability Students." Paper presented at the annual meeting of the American Educational Research Association, Boston, April 1990b.

Jones, E. A., and Ratcliff, J. L. "Which General Education Curriculum Is Better: Core Curriculum or the Distributional Requirement?" *Journal of General Education,* 1991, 40, 69–101.

Lorr, M. *Cluster Analysis for Social Scientists: Techniques for Analyzing and Simplifying Complex Blocks of Data.* San Francisco: Jossey-Bass, 1983

Pallas, A. M., and Alexander, K. L. "Sex Differences in Quantitative SAT Performance: New Evidence on the Differential Coursework Hypothesis." *American Educational Research Journal,* 1983, 20 (2), 165–182.

Pascarella, E. T., and Terenzini, P. T. *How College Affects Students: Findings and Insights from Twenty Years of Research.* San Francisco: Jossey-Bass, 1991.

Pike, G. R., and Phillippi, R. H. "Generalizability of the Differential Coursework Methodology: Relationships Between Self-Reported Coursework and Performance on the ACT-COMP Exam." *Research in Higher Education,* 1989, 30 (3), 245–260.

Prather, J. E., and Smith, G. *Faculty Grading Patterns.* Atlanta: Office of Institutional Planning, Georgia State University, 1976a.

Prather, J. E., and Smith, G. *Undergraduate Grades by Course in Relation to Student Ability Levels, Programs of Study, and Longitudinal Trends.* Atlanta: Office of Institutional Planning Georgia State University, 1976b.

Ratcliff, J. L. *The Effect of Differential Coursework Patterns on General Learned Abilities of College Students: Application of the Model to a Historical Database of Student Transcripts.* Report on Task No. 3 for the U.S. Department of Education, Office of Educational Research and Improvement, Contract No. OERI-R-86-0016. Ames: Iowa State University, 1987.

Ratcliff, J. L. "The Development of a Cluster Analytic Model for Determining the Associated Effects of Coursework Patterns on Student Learning." Paper presented at the annual meeting of the American Educational Research Association, New Orleans, April 1988.

Ratcliff, J. L. "Determining the Effects of Different Coursework Patterns on the General Student Learning at Four Colleges and Universities." Paper presented at the annual meeting of the American Educational Research Association, San Francisco, March 1989.

Ratcliff, J. L., and Jones, E. A. "General Learning at a Women's College." Paper presented at the annual meeting of the Association for the Study of Higher Education, Portland, Oregon, November 1990.

Ratcliff, J. L., and Jones, E. A. "Are Common Course Numbering and a Core Curriculum Valid Indicators in the Articulation of General Education Credits Among Transfer Students?" Paper presented at the annual meeting of the American Educational Research Association, Chicago, April 1991.

Ratcliff, J. L., Jones, E. A., and Hoffman, S. *Handbook on Linking Assessment and General Education.* University Park: National Center for Postsecondary Teaching, Learning, and Assessment, Pennsylvania State University, 1992.

Ratcliff, J . L., and others. *Development and Testing of a Cluster-Analytic Model for Identifying Coursework Patterns Associated with General Learned Abilities of College Students: Final Report on Stanford University Samples Nos. 1–2.* Prepared for the U.S. Department of Education, Office of Educational Research and Improvement, Contract No. OERI-R-86 0016. Ames: Iowa State University, 1990a.

Ratcliff, J . L., and others. *Development and Testing of a Cluster-Analytic Model for Identifying Coursework Patterns Associated with General Learned Abilities of College Students: Final Report on Ithaca College Samples Nos. 1–2.* Prepared for the U.S. Department of Education, Office of Educational Research and Improvement, Contract No. OERI-R-86 0016. Ames: Iowa State University, 1990b.

Ratcliff, J . L., and others. *Development and Testing of a Cluster-Analytic Model for Identifying Coursework Patterns Associated with General Learned Abilities of college students: Final Report on Ithaca College Sample No. 3.* Prepared for the Exxon Education Foundation. University Park: Center for the Study of Higher Education, Pennsylvania State University, 1990c.

Ratcliff, J . L., and others. *Development and Testing of a Cluster-Analytic Model for Identifying Coursework Patterns Associated with General Learned Abilities of college students: Final Report on Ithaca College Sample Nos. 1-2.* Prepared for the U.S. Department of Education, Office of Educational Research and Improvement, Contract No. OERI-R-86-0016. University Park: Center for the Study of Higher Education, Pennsylvania State University, 1990d.

Romesburg, H. C. *Cluster Analysis for Researchers.* Belmont, Calif.: Lifelong Learning, 1984.

Rudolph, F. *Curriculum: A History of the American Undergraduate Course of Study Since 1636.* San Francisco: Jossey-Bass, 1977.

Sloan, D. "Harmony, Chaos, and Consensus: The American College Curriculum." *Teachers College Record* 1971, 73, 221–251.

Study Group on the Conditions of Excellence in American Higher Education. National Institute of Education. *Involvement in Learning: Realizing the Potential of American Higher Education.* Washington, D.C.: Government Printing Office, 1984.

Veysey, L. "Stability and Experiment in the American Undergraduate Curriculum." In C. Kaysen (ed.), *Content and Context: Essays on College Education.* New York: McGraw-Hill, 1973.

Zemsky, R. *Structure and Coherence: Measuring the Undergraduate Curriculum.* Washington, D.C.: Association of American Colleges, 1989.

Faculty-Developed Approaches to Assessing General Education Outcomes

Trudy W. Banta

Faculty contemplating an outcomes assessment initiative frequently ask, "What should we do first? Where should we begin? An appropriate response is "Start with the questions that are most important to the campus community. What are the student outcomes about which you would most like to have evidence of progress?"

The answer to the last question will certainly differ from one campus to another and from time to time at a given institution. But, at any particular time, interest in student learning as a result of experiences in the general education program, or the transfer curriculum at community colleges, will be of paramount concern at many institutions across the country. If a new design for general education is contemplated, under development, or in an early stage of implementation, faculty interest in evaluating its effectiveness may be sufficiently high to make general education a logical focus for early assessment efforts.

As faculty begin to consider ways to assess the impact of the program of liberal studies that lays the foundation for upper-division work, they may be tempted to move directly to the task of selecting or developing measuring instruments. They cannot proceed very far along this path, however, without direction from a statement of expected student outcomes. That is, what do the faculty hope students will know and be able to do as a result of their experience in the general education program.

Achieving broad consensus for this statement of expected outcomes may be the single most important benefit of the entire assessment enterprise. Until very recently, such statements were rare in higher education. Most goals for general education (and curricula in the disciplines, for that matter) are stated in terms of the concepts faculty will teach rather than the understanding and skills students will develop. Specifying the ends (goals or intended outcomes) to justify the means (assessment methods) may require wearying debate and intellectual struggle, but when faculty can finally agree on the ends, they can implement the program with a much stronger sense of shared purpose.

If assessment is to fulfill its promise for suggesting directions for improvement, it must be based on clear statements of goals for students, but its success also depends on the existence of a formal process for monitoring the curriculum, to ensure that the goals are being implemented. Faculty must provide oversight—periodic review of course syllabi, student assignments, and classroom tests—to guarantee that students have access to the experiences they need in order to develop the knowledge and skills inherent in the faculty vision of the competent student. If assessment procedures indicate that students are failing to achieve a certain goal, the monitoring process will assist in determining the source of the problem and the means for correcting it.

In stimulating faculty consideration and discussion of general education outcomes for students, of the supporting curriculum and instructional methods, of the quality of student learning, and of means for improving all the foregoing, the use of some standardized exams may be productive. However, large-scale studies conducted in New Jersey, Washington, and Tennessee and involving some of the best-known commercial tests available for assessment of general education outcomes have indicated that, at best, these exams test only a small fraction of the knowledge and skills specified in most college statements of goals for general education. At worst, students scores on some of the exams are so heavily dependent on verbal and quantitative aptitude that the tests offer little or no additional information beyond that derived from tests of entering ability, such as the ACT or the SAT. For these reasons, the remainder of this essay describes faculty-developed approaches to assessing general education outcomes. While the work on these measures is still in its infancy, and claims to technical adequacy are not yet well founded, the measures do, by definition, assess what faculty consider important, and they engage faculty in the healthy discussion and exploration of effectiveness that are characteristic of good assessment programs. In this presentation, examples are given of each of the critical components of the assessment process—goal setting, monitoring implementation, and gathering evidence of effectiveness.

Setting Goals

Faculty at Alverno College in Milwaukee and King's College in Pennsylvania are recognized as pioneers in basing programs of liberal education on statements of specific objectives for learners. At King's, for instance, faculty have been working for more than a decade on an approach designed to strengthen in each King's graduate eight transferable skills of liberal learning: critical thinking, creative thinking and problem-solving strategies, writing, oral communication, quantitative analysis, computer literacy, library and information technologies, and values awareness.

In the mid 1980s, the state higher education coordinating agencies in Virginia and New Jersey issued mandates for assessment that included explicit references to the need for goal setting. At James Madison University in Virginia, faculty adopted a comprehensive approach to student development during college that included goals for cognitive, moral, and psychosocial growth. In New Jersey, all public institutions were required to submit to the State Board of Higher Education by June 1989 faculty-developed statements of goals for general education that would serve as the basis for assessment plans. These documents were reviewed by external consultants, and each institution subsequently received a detailed written assessment of the perceived strengths and weaknesses of its goals statement.

Monitoring Implementation

Aubrey Forrest, in a series of national workshops sponsored by ACT during the mid 1980s, emphasized the need for conducting a curriculum audit—a careful ongoing monitoring by faculty of the courses designed to promote student achievement of an institution's goals for general education. Forrest collected materials from a variety of institutions that illustrated how faculty can construct course syllabi and exam questions to ensure that the general education program presented by faculty actually develops stated outcomes in students.

At Alverno College, every faculty member is continually conscious of the various levels of each of eight generic abilities that students must develop, and every course is designed to promote learning of one or more of the abilities. Students participate in faculty-designed performance-based assessments in each course, as well as at key points outside courses.

At Longwood College in Virginia, a transcript has been developed to record student involvement in college activities that contribute to the accomplishment of 14 faculty-developed goals for knowledge and skills. Students also complete an "Involvement Survey" that helps them note their progress toward the 14 goals and detect areas of development they may be neglecting.

Assessment Strategies

Faculty at King's College employ course-embedded assessment in order to give systematic feedback to students about their academic progress toward the development of the eight transferable skills of liberal learning that guide the King's approach to general education. All core-curriculum courses use pre- and post assessments that are common throughout all sections of the course and are designed by faculty teams. The post assessment is an integral part of the final grade for each course, and thus student motivation to do well is ensured. Each student has a "competence-growth plan," containing a record of his or her progress toward achieving the eight generic skills. As students complete their assessment experiences in designated courses, progress is noted in their individual plans. The activities associated with implementing this course-embedded assessment model serve to evaluate the outcomes-oriented curriculum designed by the King's faculty.

At Kean College in New Jersey, faculty have developed essay items to evaluate knowledge of content and critical thinking skills in five areas. These items are incorporated into course exams, and students' responses are read twice—once by the course instructor for purposes of assigning a grade, and again by a faculty committee looking at response patterns across students and across courses for purposes of evaluating the effectiveness of the general education curriculum. The Kean faculty also gather evaluative data from faculty and student surveys designed to elicit perceptions about the curriculum.

As Richard Larson notes in this issue, portfolios are growing in popularity as assessment tools that can be used in a wide variety of settings. Materials that might be collected in a portfolio include course assignments, research papers, materials from group projects, artistic productions, self-reflective essays, correspondence, and taped presentations. Student performances can be recorded on audio-tapes or videotapes. Potential materials for the cassette-recorded portfolio are speeches, musical performances, foreign-language pronunciation, group interaction skills, and demonstrations of laboratory techniques or psychomotor skills.

In 1986, the University of Kentucky established a consortium of 14 private liberal arts colleges in central Appalachia for the purpose of planning cooperative approaches to the assessment of general education. Senior interviews, considered the most valuable of a four-component program, took place in groups of three students, with a faculty member guiding a two-hour discussion. Students were given a chance to demonstrate generic skills through responses to such questions as "What is an educated person? What is the role of the artist in a culture? What were two or three of your most important college experiences?" Interviews on the 14 campuses were taped and then transcribed centrally and analyzed with a phenomenological/ethnographic approach.

Outcomes of Assessment

An encouraging outcome of the extensive activity that has taken place over the last decade in attempts to assess general education is that faculty are now engaged in more and better-informed discussions about the student experience in general education. This increase in conversation about student learning occurs even before faculty begin to collect evidence from students. Then, after the data begin to come in, faculty who are really invested in the project will see ways to improve the environment for learning. As a result of their involvement in general education assessment, faculty have learned that they must be more systematic in stating curriculum goals, in auditing the means of implementing the goals, and in collecting evidence that can be used to affirm or to suggest the need for modification of the original goals.

Jerry Gaff, perhaps the most persistent observer of developments in general education over the past two decades, has observed that assessment of general education outcomes has had a positive impact on the sense of identity and community within institutions that have approached assessment with seriousness of purpose. Involvement in assessment activities has also produced direction for faculty development and sparked faculty renewal. These changes, in turn, have been associated with improved student satisfaction and retention. Surely these are the most important outcomes that we could hope to associate with a successful assessment initiative.

Critical Issues in the Assessment of Value Added in Education

Gary R. Hanson

To examine how education outcomes are attained, educational researchers must understand the assumptions that form the foundation of value-added models. To design good research, we must be aware of inherent pitfalls. Most of these problems are related to conceptual issues, psychometric questions, or research designs. A careful analysis of these three areas show the importance of strategies that can explain how and why education adds value as students progress through college.

Underlying Assumptions in the Assessment of Value Added

The distinction between assessing student outcomes and assessing the value added by particular educational interventions seems clear. The focus of student outcomes assessment is on the "what" of education, and the focus of value added is on the "how." The assessment of value added forces a focus on the process of how educational goals are attained. Pascarella (1986) has defined the process of studying change and its antecedent as the "net effects" issue: "What kinds of students change in what kinds of ways when exposed to what kinds of educational experiences?" If we adopt this definition, we can assume the following assumption: (1) that meaningful characteristics of students can be measured; (2) that both the nature and the magnitude of change in these characteristics can be assessed; and (3) that such change can be attributed to specific educational interventions. Assessing value added is a process that occurs over time; assessing when and how students change, and linking such change to specific educational interventions, is a complex and difficult task that requires new strategies for conceptualizing issues, building new and different assessment instruments, and designing research with different purposes and outcomes than those found in many traditional methods of inquiry.

Conceptual Issues

To assess how students change during college, we must think about the nature of student growth and development. Conceptual models and theories of student behavior are most useful when they help us focus on which student characteristics we should measure, when they should be measured, and how they change over time, as well as on the level of assessment specificity (global versus conditional) and the anticipated consequences (direct or indirect effects) of educational interventions. Ideally, theory and practical experience should be used in the planning stages of any assessment project to ensure that these important questions are considered.

What Should Be Measured? Answers to this question come from three primary sources: national and state reports on the condition of higher education, existing research literature, and theories of learning and psychological development. A few brief examples of information from these sources will illustrate the kinds and scope of the student characteristics that seem important to measure.

The Association of American Colleges (1985) lists four categories of essential student abilities: inquiry; abstract, logical thinking; critical analysis; and reading, writing, and speaking with distinction. An understanding of science, history, politics, the arts, and foreign cultures were other important learning requirements cited in the report.

Literature reviews, such as those developed by Bok (1986), Bowen (1977), and Pace (1970), not only recommend what has been systematically studied in the past but also provide insight into student characteristics that show some potential for change. Pace (1979), for example, lists eighteen college objectives that students accomplished as a result of attending college.

Most theories of learning and psychological development focus narrowly on certain dimensions of student characteristics, but what these theories lack in breadth they make up in rich conceptual detail. Knefelkamp, Widick, and Parker (1978) and Rodgers (1980) provide an overview of several popular theories about the cognitive, psychosocial, and moral development of students, while Gilligan (1982) and Kitchener (1982) offer interesting new theories for constructing assessments.

When Should Students Be Assessed? Another crucial issue in conceptualizing value-added research is appropriate timing for data collection. Traditionally, value-added research has focused on the changes that occur between the freshman and senior years, but such a strategy may miss important changes that occur in the sophomore and junior years. If data were collected each year on student characteristic X, results (shown in Figure 1) might show that three students had changed in very different ways, while collecting data only for the freshman and senior years would show no change. In Figure 1, the mean for the three students is the same in the senior year as in the freshman year. A conclusion of no change would be very misleading however, since student A shows a substantial gain in X from the freshman to the sophomore year but then loses that gain during the junior and senior years. This pattern is not at all unusual in students who take mathematics early in their college careers. Student B shows a gradual year-to-year gain, and student C shows a high performance in the freshman year, maintaining for all four years. Students who already write well

---

Figure 1
Critical Issues in the Assessment of Value Added in Education

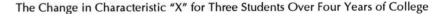

The Change in Characteristic "X" for Three Students Over Four Years of College

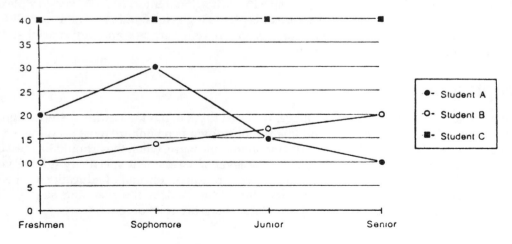

when they enter college may show this latter pattern. Hence, the timing of assessment is crucial. Theories of student learning and psychological development can help us know when to conduct assessment. Our knowledge about student learning patterns and other growth over the college years is equally important in the design of value-added assessment research.

How Do Student Characteristics Change Over Time? Knowing not only when student characteristics change but also how they change is crucial. The design of instruments and research strategies requires an understanding of whether the quality of a characteristic changes as students learn. Again, theories may help us understand the nature of such change. Perry (1970) postulates that the quality of cognitive development changes in some predictable ways as students move from simple to more complex thought processes. Likewise, theories that include the suggestion that students move through a series of stages in their development often note qualitatively different aspects at each stage (Chickering, 1969; Erikson, 1968; Kohlberg, 1972; Perry, 1970). Other theorists—for example, Gilligan (1982)—suggest that students show gender-based qualitative differences in development.

Are the Effects of College on Students Global or Specific? In the conceptualizing of value-added assessment, a decision must be made about the level at which assessment is conducted (Pascarella, 1986). Traditionally, we have assumed that the influence of college on students is the same for all students—that is, that college has a global effect. This assumption ignores individual differences among students who attend the same institution or participate in the same educational activities. Students with different backgrounds or learning styles or levels of motivation may experience the same educational programs in dramatically different ways. Thus, college may be seen to produce conditional rather than general effects. If a value-added assessment is based on the assumption of general effects, conditional effects may be overlooked. The danger of assuming general effects is that a given educational intervention may show no influence over a large group of students, while for a particular subgroup the intervention is highly successful. If this issue is not considered at the stage of conceptualizing a value-added assessment, the research design may be inappropriate, and statistical analyses may fail to detect a change that has occurred.

Does College Influence Students Directly or Indirectly? To determine whether a given educational experience adds value to what students already know, it may be necessary to examine direct as well as indirect effects of experience on students. Limiting exploration to direct effects may exclude important and powerful effects that influence students indirectly. Pascarella, Terenzini, and Wolfle (1986) have shown that students exposed to freshman orientation before enrollment may experience few direct influences on first-year persistence, but that indirect effects of the orientation program may be overlooked if only direct effects are analyzed.

Implications. An effective value-added assessment project must consider all these conceptual issues. Ideally an assessment model should specify what characteristics will be measured, how they are likely to change over time, and when assessment will be conducted. The model must also indicate whether educational interventions are likely to influence all students in the same manner or affect subgroups of students in different ways. Finally, the model should specify how interventions will influence students. Will an educational program influence students directly, or indirectly through some other program? If researchers consider these questions and design a model of what is expected, they can avoid serious errors in interpretation once the data are analyzed.

Psychometric Questions

The psychometric and statistical problems of assessing changes in student development and learning have plagued educational researchers for a long time. Since many of the major issues have been summarized by others (Bereiter, 1963; Cronbach and Furby, 1970; Harris, 1963; Linn, 1981; and Pascarella, 1987), only a brief overview will be provided in this section. These problems are twofold: First, the psychometric characteristics of tests make the assessment of change difficult or impossible; and, second, the advantages and disadvantages of various statistical techniques for analyzing change in student characteristics are often not well understood. Nevertheless, new psychometric and statistical procedures have been developed to avoid some of these problems. A brief presentation of their applications is included in the following discussion:

Psychometric Problems of Assessing Change. One of the most serious psychometric problems associated with assessing changes in student characteristics is that most available assessment instruments were designed to measure static traits, rather than developmental changes (Hanson, 1982; Mines, 1985). Assessment instruments that measure static traits typically have high degrees of stability; that is, highly similar scores are obtained by students over time. In addition, most measures of static traits assume that the underlying structure of the construct being measured does not change with time. Hence, these assessment instruments may not detect student characteristics that change.

One reason such assessment instruments do not work well when measuring change is a result of the inverse relationship between stability and change-score reliability estimates. Linn (1981) shows how the reliability of change scores varies with levels of correlation between pre- and postmeasures when a static instrument is used. To the extent that an assessment instrument is a static test and there is a high correlation across two points in time, there will be lower reliability of the change scores for individuals. A low change-score reliability means that the measures are not capable of providing enough precision to allow accurate statements about individual change, although some careful statements about group change may still be possible. Another aspect of this issue is that when change-score reliability improves, test stability declines. Thus, the underlying structure of the measures is called into question. It is difficult to have high change-score reliability without questioning whether a change in what is being measured has occurred.

Still another psychometric problem is that observed change is negatively correlated with initial testing status, and this relationship is a statistical artifact of measurement error (Bereiter, 1963). When the variance is approximately the same for the same measure taken at two different points in time, the correlation of the difference score with the first measure must be negative, by definition. Hence, in comparison of two groups over time, with existing first-time differences measured, the group that scores lower automatically shows greater change when measured the second time. This change has nothing to do with developmental growth or learning; again, it is an artifact of the measurement process.

Statistical Approaches to Analyzing Changes in Student Characteristics. Analyzing how students change, and attributing that change to educational interventions, has been studied and debated for years. Pascarella (1987) provides a comprehensive discussion of the advantages and disadvantages of most of the common statistical techniques. Only a brief overview will be presented here, with the recommendation that the interested reader review Pascarella for additional details.

Traditionally, the influence of an educational program on students has been studied by the assessments of the students at some time before the intervention and again at some point afterward. The difference in the two scores was used as a measure of students' growth or learning. The difference in scores did provide a simple interpretation of the magnitude of change, but the difference scores were notoriously unreliable and were negatively correlated with students' initial status on the measure. Statisticians and psychometricians have warned against using simple pretest-to-posttest gain scores for years (Lord, 1967; Linn, 1981; Banta and others, 1987), but their warnings seem to have had slight impact on applied research.

An early approach to avoiding the problems associated with simple gain scores was the use of residual gain scores. This statistical procedure requires student outcome measures to be regressed on the input measures, so that a "predicted" outcome measure can be computed. The predicted outcome is then subtracted from the observed outcome and used as a measure of change. This residual score can be correlated with measures of the educational intervention to obtain a "part" correlation, which represents the unique association of the intervention with the outcome measure from the time when the first score was obtained. This residual gain score has the advantage of not being correlated with initial status, but it has the disadvantage of displaying a score metric that is different from the original. This difference leads to problems in interpretation. Moreover, the use of residual gain is limited to two-wave data, but important changes may occur between the first and second measurements and may be overlooked. Another disadvantage of using the residual gain score to obtain the "part" correlation is the removal of any variance in the outcome measure that could be jointly attributable to the influence of both the input measure and the educational intervention. Hence, the residual score may overestimate the contribution of the input variable and underestimate that of the intervention. The bias introduced by this technique can be severe when there is a high correlation between the input measure and the intervention or a high correlation between the input and outcome measures.

Multiple correlation and regression analyses also have been used in the statistical analysis of change. Not only do these techniques provide a level of statistical control equal to that of residual scores and part or partial correlations, they also permit partition of the total variance of the dependent variables and an estimate of the relative influence of each independent variable on the dependent variable. The value of using a regression analysis is that it allows the researcher to estimate the net change in the outcome measure associated with unit changes in each of the independent variables. Nevertheless, the method does not help us understand how joint or common variance among independent variables may interact to influence outcome or dependent measures.

Causal analysis, sometimes referred to as path analysis, is a special application of regression analysis, which helps explain indirect as well as direct influences of independent variables on dependent variables. Its purpose is to determine the extent to which a preexisting model or set of interrelationships among variables is supported by actual data. Thus, models may be specified that include student background data, measures of educational intervention, and repeated measures of student growth and learning. Data are collected, and the pattern of relationships is tested to see if the data support the proposed model. While regression coefficients do not prove that causal relationships exist in the data, they may support the hypothesis that an observed relationship is causal. If the data do not support the model, then causal relationships can be disconfirmed (Pascarella, 1987; Wolfle, 1985). One advantage of causal analysis is that it forces the user to devise a model of the expected relationships among possible variables of interest. Not only must the independent and dependent variables be identified, the patterns of cause and effect among them must also be specified. Another advantage is that causal models allow researchers to examine direct as well as indirect effects—that is, some effects may not influence the dependent variables in a direct fashion but may influence one of the other variables in the model, which then may influence the dependent variable. To return to an example cited earlier (Pascarella, Terenzini, and Wolfle, 1986), an orientation program influenced the level of students' social integration into a college, and this effect in turn influenced student persistence. This is one case in which causal analysis will detect the effect, while simple regression analysis will overlook it.

Causal analysis is not without its problems, however, and the most difficult one is to develop a sound model. If important variables of influence are excluded, the result is a biased model, with potentially inflated path coefficients suggesting stronger relationships among variables in the model than may actually exist. A second issue, identified by Pascarella (1987) and others, is recursiveness: Most causal models assume a unidirectional causal flow and the absence of any feedback influence, but most educational interventions may be better described as interactive, with multiple opportunities for feedback to influence the direction of the causal relationship. For example, does interaction with a faculty member after class improve a student's performance in the class, or do students who perform well in the class seek out the instructor after class? Testing which of the two possible causal links is supported by the data may require the collection of longitudinal data. If the variables are assessed in a cross-sectional study, there may be no way to determine whether a unidirectional cause-and-effect relationship exists. This problem can be overcome by use of a two-stage regression analysis and development of a nonrecursive causal model, but meeting the assumptions of this more complicated model are difficult, according to Wolfle (1985). Nevertheless, several recent studies have used this methodology to study student change in college (Bean and Bradley, 1986; Bean and Kuh, 1984; Iverson, Pascarella, and Terenzini, 1984). Measurement error is a third disadvantage cited by Pascarella. Causal modeling assumes that there is no measurement error, but this is rarely the case. When measurement error exists, the regression or path coefficients are biased in unknown ways, although the use of maximum-likelihood estimation procedures provides less biased estimates than other procedures do (Joreskog and Sorbom, 1979).

Increasingly, researchers are calling for the use of multiwave data and more sophisticated models of student growth and development (Bryk and Weisberg, 1977; Bryk and Raudenbush, 1987; Strenio, Weisberg, and Bryk, 1983; Linn, 1981). The primary advantages of using growth curves based on multiple data points is that by plotting student changes, describing the nature of change, and noting the influence of educational interventions on subsequent measurement points, stronger statements can be made about the intervention's amount and type of influence.

One of the most promising statistical methods proposed for the study of change is the use of hierarchical linear models (Bryk and Raudenbush, 1987). This technique is based on regression analysis and can be used to study the structure of individual growth and the reliability of instruments for measuring status and change, assessing the correlates of status and change, and testing hypotheses about the effects of the background variables and educational interventions on individual growth. The use of this technique involves two stages of analysis. In the first stage, each individual's observed growth or development is considered as a function of an individual growth trajectory, plus random error. This growth trajectory is determined by use of a set of data points collected across time for each person. In the second stage, changes in the individual growth trajectory can be studied as functions of certain measurable characteristics of the individual's background (sex, age, ethnicity) and environment (participation in certain courses; extracurricular activities, or living arrangements).

The hierarchical linear model offers a number of statistical advantages over the use of other techniques. First, no assumptions are made about the nature of the growth curve. It need not be linear; it can be estimated on the basis of complex polynomial regression equations. Second, because the growth curve is estimated for each individual, this technique does not require the same data to be collected the same number of times for each individual. Thus, the problem of incomplete data, observed in longitudinal studies at various data-collection points, is simplified. Third, the variation in growth-curve models across individuals can be represented by a fixed between-subjects model, and changes in the growth parameters can be related to individuals' backgrounds or educational experiences. The between-subjects model can incorporate any number of background variables, and the between-subjects equation need not be identical for all growth parameters.

Hierarchical linear models provide flexibility in research design in that they allow a wide variety of between-subjects models and can be applied both to experimental and to quasi-experimental settings. This flexibility encourages researchers to expand the possible conceptualizations of research designs and eliminates the assumption that a given educational intervention adds a constant increment (or "value") to each individual (this assumption involves the issue of global versus conditional effects, mentioned earlier). Individuals may benefit to varying degrees, and this statistical technique will detect the magnitude and nature of changes. The primary disadvantage of the technique is that it requires sophisticated computer software programs that are not yet widely available.

Research Design

Because the assessment of value added in education assumes that students change over time, that the change can be measured, and that contributing influences on the quality and nature of change can be attributed to specific educational interventions, the design of research studies to support or refute evidence for such change is a most complicated affair. Careful consideration must be given to the selection of appropriate samples, the choice between a longitudinal or cross-sectional design, the determination of appropriate intervals between data-collection points, and the selection of units of analysis. In addition to the conceptual issues that make research design difficult in value-added assessment, issues specific to design also exist.

Isolating the Influence of Educational Interventions on Student Development. Potential influences on student growth and development can be categorized three ways: as intentional educational interventions, as unintentional educational interventions, and as growth or change that occurs without any kind of intervention (often called *maturation*). The first category includes all the planned courses, programs, and activities that we hope will influence students to change in beneficial ways. The second category includes the happy accidents that contribute to learning: We rarely have control over them, typically do not plan for them, but by putting students together on college campuses we may create them. We usually take credit for them, whether or not they were intentional, and call them "college effects." The third category includes experiences that are likely to happen to all individuals of a particular age and that are unrelated to the educational setting. Forming relationships with other people, learning to live independently, and maturing physically are developmental tasks that everyone experiences, regardless of attendance at college. The rate at which these tasks are fulfilled and the quality of the experience may differ, but the influence of maturation may be difficult to separate from the college experience. One of the most critical problems in value-added research design is to isolate the relative contribution of each type of influence on the growth and learning that students experience while attending college.

One approach to isolating relative effects is to use a control sample of students, who are followed over the same period of time but are not allowed to participate in the educational intervention under study. Control groups are often difficult to locate, however: Community standards, ethical concerns, and legal issues surrounding the restriction of certain educational practices make it difficult to use adequate control groups in a research design; random exposure of students to educational opportunities is almost never an option. Pascarella (1986) has suggested combined cross-sectional and longitudinal research designs, or the use of returning adult students to constitute comparison groups, as alternative designs that take maturation into consideration. The difference between longitudinal and cross-sectional results, adjusted for the effects of selective attrition, might be used as an estimate of normal maturation during college.

Isolating the effects of unintentional educational interventions is undoubtedly much more difficult, because these can rarely be discerned during data collection. Often, happy accidents come to light only when we try to explain some unusual finding. In monitoring the relative effects of multiple interventions, some degree of control is possible if we carefully document which students are participating in which of several possible educational activities (only some of which are the ones assessed intentionally). Students' involvement in extracurricular activities that lead to critical thinking, leadership skills, and social competence may well occur in a regular fashion outside the structured curriculum, and the preferred approach would be to identify the level of involvement and incorporate such variables as possible influences of growth and development into model building and research design. Obviously, the ethics of confidentiality and respect for individual rights would prohibit the monitoring of many unintentional educational interventions.

Choosing Appropriate Units of Analysis. Research designs used to study the effects of educational interventions on student growth and learning may use several units of analysis: the institution, classes or departments at a single institution, or the individual. For any given study, one unit of analysis may be more appropriate than another, but the use of different units of analysis forces a focus on different kinds of questions (Burstein, 1980; Pascarella, 1987). When the institution is the unit of analysis, the study results will answer questions about the average influence of the educational intervention on the average level of student development. Aggregating data at the institutional level tends to ignore possible variations among individual students' experiences within a single institution. When the individual is the unit of analysis, the focus is on whether differences in the individual's involvement in various educational activities lead to differences in specific outcomes; the data may be collected across multiple institutions, but the focus is still on the individual. Focusing on the individual, however, ignores other important questions, such as those that involve institutionwide influences on growth and learning. For example, the manner in which interaction with faculty facilitates student learning may be different at large and small institutions. A study that uses the individual as the unit of analysis and collects data across multiple institutions may miss this source of influence, even when controlling for differences in individual characteristics. Research studies that incorporate multiple levels of analysis (Burstein, 1980; Cronbach, 1976; Linn, 1981; Terenzini and Pascarella, 1984) avoid the problem of using only a single unit of analysis and thereby missing important influences on student development.

Choosing an Appropriate Number of Data-Collection Points. A design issue highly related to timing is the selection of an appropriate number of data-collection points. Both theory and experience help determine appropriate times to assess students. Timing is crucial to determining starting and ending points, but other factors often influence the number of possible data-collection points available in between. If the assessment is started either too early or late, or if it ends at the wrong time, the opportunity to observe and assess change in student characteristics is missed. Assessment that includes only two data-collection points may actually capture the total amount of change but will provide too few data-collection points to answer important questions about when change occurred in the total time interval. In addition, important information about the nature of the change, as it unfolds, is lost.

General Principles for Assessing Value-Added Education

The purpose of this chapter has been to identify some issues that are crucial to conducting research whose goal is to assess if and how students change and, more important, what factors contribute to such change. The following principles can be used as guidelines for implementing future studies.

Principle 1: Decide whether the purpose of the study is to assess student outcomes, or value added from educational interventions. Assessment of student outcomes is descriptive and determines only how students appear at the end of a certain period. To assess value added by educational intervention, one must focus on the process of how students change. Not only is the nature of change important to assess, but understanding the causes of change is also necessary to determine whether value has been added. The research designs and statistical analyses required to pursue value-added assessments are different from those used for assessment of student outcomes.

Principle 2: Build a model to represent variables of interest and their relation to outcomes. Since determination of value added is a process and not just an outcome, diagramming is essential. Knowing what to measure and when, anticipating types of changes that may occur, and including measures of the interventions likely to influence changes are prerequisites both of good design and of effective data collection and analysis. Causal modeling and hierarchical linear regression require specification of how growth is likely to occur. It is impossible to design and conduct good research without appropriate models of what is expected to happen.

Principle 3: Identify or build instruments that assess both status and change. The psychometric instruments available to higher education have done an excellent job of measuring a student's status at a single point in time, and they have been most useful in telling us how one student differed from another. To measure change, however, the assessment instrument must be capable of telling us how an individual student changes over time; the comparison with other students is less important. Such instruments not only must assess the magnitude of change but also must detect qualitative differences in underlying dimensions that are subject to change as a result of an educational intervention. New formats and scoring procedures are needed to summarize these kinds of assessment instruments.

Principle 4: Use theory and practical experience to identify critical data-collection points. After experiencing different kinds of educational interventions, students change at different times and at different rates. Completing an assessment before change has occurred is a waste of time and money, and collecting data long after the influence of an educational intervention has dissipated is likewise unproductive. Collecting data too infrequently may allow an accurate assessment of the magnitude of a change but may also prevent observation of the qualitative nature of the change. Hence, one of the most critical aspects of conducting good value-added assessment is knowing when and how many times to collect data. Some educational theories may provide ideas of how students change. These can guide research design. Likewise, faculty and staff knowledge that comes from day-to-day interaction with students also provides a good framework for collecting data at the optimum times.

Principle 5: Use statistical techniques appropriate to the analysis of change. In spite of admonitions to the contrary, researchers continue to use simple gain scores, collected at two different times, to measure the amount of change in student characteristics. These gain scores are often correlated with measures of educational intervention to determine the degree of influence. Inappropriate and incorrect interpretations nearly always result. Building good models (see Principle 1), and using causal analysis and hierarchical linear models to analyze the resulting data, will permit more sophisticated interpretation of a change and its correlates. Using poor or inappropriate data-analysis techniques can only obscure what we learn about how students change as a result of educational experiences.

References

Association of American Colleges. *Integrity in the College Curriculum: A Report to the Academic Community.* Washington, D.C.: Association of American Colleges, 1985.

Banta, T., Lambert, W., Pike, G., Schmidhammer, J., and Schneider, J. "Estimated Student Score Gain on the ACT COMP Exam: Valid Tool for Institutional Assessment?" Paper presented at the annual meeting of the American Educational Research Association, Washington, D.C., April 1987.

Bean, J., and Bradley, R. "Untangling the Satisfaction-Performance Relationship for College Students." *Journal of Higher Education,* 1986, *57, 57,* 393–412.

Bean, J., and Kuh, G. "The Reciprocity Between Student-Faculty Informal Contact and the Undergraduate Grade Point Average of University Students." Paper presented at the annual meeting of the Association for the Study of Higher Education, Chicago, 1984.

Bereiter, C. "Some Persisting Dilemmas in the Measurement of Change." In C. W. Harris (ed.), *Problems in the Measurement of Change.* Madison: University of Wisconsin Press, 1963.

Bok, D. *Higher Learning.* Cambridge, Mass.: Harvard University Press, 1986.

Bowen, H. R. *Investment in Learning: The Individual and Social Value of American Higher Education.* San Francisco: Jossey-Bass, 1977.

Bryk, A. S., and Raudenbush, S. W. "Application of Hierarchical Linear Models to Assessing Change." *Psychological Bulletin,* 1987, *101* (1).

Bryk, A. S., and Weisberg, H. I. "Use of Nonequivalent Control Group Design When Subjects are Growing." *Psychological Bulletin,* 1977, *84,* 950–962.

Burstein, L. "The Analysis of Multilevel Data in Educational Research and Evaluation." In D. Berlinger (ed.), *Review of Research in Education.* Vol. 8. Washington, D.C.: American Educational Research Association, 1980.

Chickering, A. *Education and Identity.* San Francisco, Jossey-Bass, 1969.

Cronbach, L. J. *Research on Classrooms and Schools: Formulation of Questions, Design, and Analysis.* Palo Alto, Calif.: Stanford Evaluation Consortium, Stanford University, 1976.

Cronbach, L. J., and Furby, L. "How We Should Measure Change—Or Should We?" *Psychological Bulletin,* 1970, *74,* 68–80.

Erikson, E. *Identity: Youth and Crisis.* New York: Norton, 1968.

Gilligan, C. *In a Different Voice.* Cambridge, Mass.: Harvard University Press, 1982.

Hanson, G. R. (ed.). *Measuring Student Development.* New Directions for Student Services, no. 20. San Francisco, Jossey-Bass, 1982.

Harris, C. *Problems in the Measurement of Change.* Madison: University of Wisconsin Press, 1963.

Iverson, B. Pascarella, E., and Terenzini, P. "Informal Faculty-Student Contact and Commuter College Freshmen." *Research in Higher Education,* 1984, *21,* 123–136.

Joreskog, K., and Sorbom, D. *Advances in Factor Analysis and Structural Equation Models.* Cambridge, Mass.: Abt Books, 1979.

Kitchener, K. "Human Development and the College Campus: Sequences and Tasks." In G. R. Hanson (ed.), *Measuring Student Development.* New Directions for Student Services, no. 20. San Francisco: Jossey-Bass, 1982.

Knefelkamp, L., Widick, C., and Parker, C. (eds.). *Applying New Developmental Findings.* New Directions for Student Services, no. 4. San Francisco: Jossey-Bass, 1978.

Kohlberg, L. "Stages of Moral Development." In C. M. Beck, B. S. Crittenden, and E. V. Sullivan (eds.), *Moral Education.* Toronto: University of Toronto Press, 1972.

Linn, R. L. "Measuring Pretest-Posttest Performance Changes." In R. Berk (ed.), *Educational Evaluation Methodology: The State of the Art.* Baltimore, Md.: Johns Hopkins University Press, 1981.

Lord, F. "A Paradox of the Interpretation of Group Comparisons." *Psychological Bulletin,* 1967, *68,* 304–305.

Mines, R. A. "Measurement Issues in Evaluating Student Development Programs." *Journal of College Student Personnel,* 1985, *26* (2), 101–106.

Pace, C. R. *Measuring Outcomes of College: Fifty Years of Findings and Recommendations for the Future.* San Francisco: Jossey-Bass, 1979.

Pascarella, E. T. "Are Value-Added Analyses Valuable?" Paper presented at the annual Educational Testing Service Invitational Conference, New York, October 25, 1986.

Pascarella, E. T. "Some Methodological and Analytic Issues in Assessing the Influence of College." Paper presented at join meeting of the American College Personnel Association and the National Association of Student Personnel Administrators, Chicago, 1987.

Pascarella, E., Terenzini, P., and Wolfle, L. "Orientation to College and Freshman Year Persistence/Withdrawal Decisions." *Journal of Higher Education*, 1986, *57*, 155–175.

Perry, W., Jr. *Forms of Intellectual and Ethical Development in the College Years: A Scheme.* New York: Holt, Rinehart & Winston, 1970.

Rodgers, R. "Theories Underlying Student Development." In D. G. Creamer (ed.), *Student Development in Higher Education.* Cincinnati, Ohio: American College Personnel Association (ACPA) Media, 1980.

Strenio, J. L. F., Weisberg, H. I., and Bryk, A. S. "Empirical Bayes Estimation of Individual Growth Curves Parameters and Their Relationship to Covariates." *Biometrics*, 1983, *39*, 71–86.

Terenzini, P., and Pascarella, E. "Freshman Attention and the Residential Context." *Review of Higher Education*, 1984, *7*, 11–124.

Wolfle, L. "Applications of Causal Models in Higher Education." In J. Smart (ed.), *Higher Education Handbook of Theory and Research.* New York: Agathon Press, 1985.

Suggestions for Deciding Between Commercially Available and Locally Developed Assessment Instruments

John C. Ory

In 1989, our office surveyed a sample of 33 large research universities to learn of their involvement in assessment activities (Ory and Parker, 1989). We used survey results to create a listing of instruments used at the different institutions to collect information on five dimensions of instructional quality: entry level characteristics of students, student activities, faculty/staff activities, institutional culture, and student outcomes. The listing reveals that commercially available *and* locally developed instruments were used for each of the five dimensions.

In 1990, the Campus Trends Survey (El-Khawas, 1991) conducted by the American Council on Education (ACE) revealed increasing usage of local instruments. Eleven percent more colleges and universities reported developing local instruments in 1990 (66%) than in 1989 (55%). El-Khawas suggests the increased use of local measures may be due to greater interest in collecting student portfolios and more use of assessment data for program evaluation purposes. Portfolios serve as a form of local instrumentation, and campus reviews or evaluations of academic programs have traditionally relied on locally generated information. The ACE survey showed that approximately one-third of the institutions reported collecting student portfolios while 85% reported using assessment results for program evaluation.

Whether one uses local instruments or commercially developed measures, how do individuals responsible for conducting assessment activities, choose between the two? There are several factors that need to be considered when making this decision:

- **Purpose of Assessment.** Why are the data being collected? Is the purpose to determine the achievement of departmental or college goals or learning outcomes? To compare the university student population to a national or regional population? To assess pre-enrollment and post-graduation differences in ability and knowledge? Or to diagnose areas of student deficiencies?

  The purpose for assessment and the use made of the assessment results should guide the type of data collected and the manner in which they are collected. The administration of a commercially available and nationally recognized biology exam to graduating seniors may be an appropriate way to assess how an institution's biology graduates compare or "measure up" to a national profile of biology students. But if the purpose of the testing was to determine how graduating biology students achieved departmental curriculum goals and objectives, the administration of a locally developed exam, tailored to the institution's curriculum, may be more appropriate.

- **Match Between Instrument and Local Programs.** What are the program/institutional goals, intended outcomes, difficulty levels, and areas of emphasis? Are these considerations appropriately addressed by any commercially available instrument? Can an existing instrument be modified to better match local needs?

For many assessment purposes, it is highly unlikely that a faculty committee will perceive much of a match between their curriculum and commercially available exams. For example, in my university's selection of new foreign language placement tests a faculty committee reviewed all available placement exams, including those written at other, similar universities. After long deliberation, the committee members decided to develop their own placement exam because none of the exams adequately matched our curriculum. A few telephone calls to institutions selling their placement exams revealed that similar committee decisions led to the creation of their local exams. Are all of these institutions teaching the foreign languages so differently?

- **Logistics.** There are several logistical considerations to address:

  — *Availability.* Does there exist an instrument that would fit the institution's need? Can an available instrument be easily modified to fit the need?

  — *Preparation Time.* Is there sufficient time (and resources) prior to the administration date to develop a local instrument?

  — *Expertise.* Does there exist the necessary expertise to develop a local instrument? Are the experts available?

  — *Cost.* What can the budget afford for purchasing or developing instruments? In addition to purchase and development costs, can you afford administration, scoring, and reporting costs? Are there sufficient funds to continue testing in subsequent years with the same instrument?

  — *Scoring.* Are scanning capabilities available on or off-campus? Can trained personnel be hired to score essays or evaluate orals?

  — *Testing Time.* How much testing time is required and available? How many administrations are needed? If testing in classes, will you have the cooperation of the faculty? For how long?

  — *Test Type.* What type of test is desired? Objective (multiple choice), subjective (essay), or performance?

  — *Ease of Administration.* Do the test administrators need to be specially trained? Do the respondents need special equipment (computers, pencils, calculators)?

  — *Availability of Norms.* Are the available norms appropriate for the population? Do you want to establish local norms or baseline data?

  — *Reporting Procedures.* How are the results reported? Individual student reports? University summaries? Departmental summaries?

- **Institutional Acceptance.** Will there be much difficulty in gaining acceptance of the chosen instrumentation by particular assessment audiences? Will faculty view locally developed instruments as more valid than commercial ones? Will state legislators prefer nationally administered exams over locally developed measures?

Does there exist a preference for or bias toward quantitative or qualitative data? Faculty in different academic disciplines often show preferences for different types of evaluative information. Faculty in the humanities may give more credence to exams requiring open-ended or written responses than to instruments with multiple-choice items. Fine and applied arts faculty may prefer performance measures rather than paper-and-pencil tests.

- **Quality.** While we would never want to administer an invalid or unreliable exam, just how important are the questions of validity and reliability? Do we need a "Cadillac" measure when a "Dodge" would suffice? Typically, commercially available tests will demonstrate much higher reliability coefficients and better item statistics than most classroom exams. Does this make classroom exams ineffective measures for evaluating student progress or assigning course grades? I do not believe so. But, how "good" do the statistics need to be to be useful for assessment purposes?

  I am not encouraging developing local instruments that lack quality and psychometric rigor. I am recommending that we avoid getting carried away, both in time and money, trying to develop local instruments that reflect "commercially" acceptable statistics. More than one campus expert has invested years trying to develop "THE" instrument at the expense of the bigger assessment issues of timing and usefulness. I have seen presentations of instrument development at professional meetings wherein the presenters explained years of developmental work, only to draw a blank to the question, "How is this going to be used at your institution"?

- **Student Motivation.** Will there be any difficulty in getting students to participate in the data collection? If so, what inducements can be offered to encourage response? Many campuses have experienced difficulty in having students take seriously the test administration without rewards for high performance or penalties for poor performance. Locally developed exams may be incorporated into the testing requirements of course. A writing assessment may be a graded component of the standard rhetoric course. Commercially available exams can sometimes be used to inform students of their comparison to students at a national level, thus providing useful information for individuals going on to graduate work.

Six Factor Comparison of the Instruments

Table 1 presents a comparison of locally developed and commercially available assessment instruments on the six factors mentioned above. The table could be considered a summary of trade-offs between the two types of instrumentation. In general, local measures may not have the psychometric rigor of commercially available instruments, but they can be developed with more flexibility and tailoring to local needs.

Checkpoints in the Decision Making Process

Described below are several checkpoints that need consideration when choosing between developing your own instrumentation or purchasing available measures.

Identify information needs. Assess "things" that are worth assessing.

Often when developing or selecting instruments, attitude surveys in particular, the temptation is to want to collect "everything-you-ever-wanted-to-know-about. . . ." Most first drafts of surveys are ten pages long, single spaced. Recently, our Chancellor established a

Table 1
Six Factor Comparison of Locally Developed and
Commercially Available Assessment Instruments

Factor	Locally Developed	Commercially Available
Purpose	Allows thorough diagnostic coverage of local goals and content	Allows for comparison to national norm group
Match	Tailored to local goals and content	Usually provides incomplete coverage of local goals and content
Logistics		
Availability	Takes time and resources to develop	Only the purchase price is necessary
Prep Time	Considerable amount of time for instrument development	Can be obtained in short amount of time
Expertise	Takes content and measurement expertise to develop instrument	Can be administered and used after reading manuals
Cost	Possibly expensive development costs	Purchasing/scoring/reporting expenses
Scoring	Immediate	Can be delayed if scored off-campus
Testing Time	Flexible	Fixed
Test Type	Built for local needs	Restricted to commercial availability
Ease in Administration	Flexible	Requires standardized administration
Norms	Allows for intra-institutional comparison only	Allows for national and inter-institutional comparisons
Reporting	Built for local needs	Restricted to commercial availability
Institutional Acceptance	• Local development can encourage local ownership and acceptance • Quality concerns may interfere with acceptance	• Professional quality and national use may enhance acceptance • Failure to completely cover local goals and content may inhibit acceptance
Quality	Lack of professional quality may affect results and influence institutional acceptance	Professional quality may compensate for incomplete coverage of local goals and content
Student Motivation	Local instrument may not "impress" or provide incentives for responding	Can provide incentives such as a national comparison or practice for a future administration

committee to develop a survey to be administered to all seniors prior to graduation. The committee included individuals from all parts of campus with various agendas for item selection. Before writing items that satisfied the various interests of the committee members, we needed to determine the Chancellor's purpose and intended use of the survey results. We could keep the instrument short and to the point only after we had a clear understanding of the need for the information.

When writing or selecting survey items one needs to consider at least two questions:

- What is the need for this information?
- What use can be made of this information?

Consider all costs in light of available resources.

The costs of test development or purchase need to be considered with respect to the types of resources available. The availability of faculty volunteers to develop local instruments may discourage the purchase of appropriate, but expensive, commercial exams. Or, an expensive telephone survey may not be prohibitive if it could be conducted as a class project in the survey lab.

Design a measurement that includes deadlines for information, available testing dates, method for reporting results, ways to access students, etc.

A well-developed measurement plan developed before deciding between local and commercial instruments may help guide the decision. Certain factors may encourage the use of one type of measure over the other. An early administration date mandated by some external agency may make impossible the time-consuming development of a local measure. Or, testing in multiple classes on different dates may suggest the use of multiple forms of the same test, an option that seldom exists with local instruments.

Do not reinvent the wheel. Gather information about available instrumentation by reviewing measurement literature, ("Buros Mental Measurements Yearbook, Tests in Print"), reviewing assessment literature ("Assessment Update"), or by contacting other universities involved in assessment activities.

Aside from the professional literature, stay in touch with other universities and make use of their assessment experiences. Each year hundreds of individuals responsible for institutional assessments share their experiences (and instruments) at the Assessment Forum sponsored by the American Association of Higher Education.

Get assessment stakeholders involved in the decision process.

Program evaluators learned many years ago that it is much more difficult for program personnel to discredit the evaluation results if they were first involved in the design of the evaluation. Determine who the critical shareholders are (administrators, legislators, parents) and get their input in the selection of the assessment instruments. Shareholders with relevant content can lend their expertise to the selection process.

Plan ways for using test results prior to developing or selecting an instrument.

Planning ahead of time how the test results will be used means knowing how the results are to be analyzed, summarized, and presented to the assessment audiences. Determining these three aspects early on should focus the development or selection process. For example, a common mistake in instrument development is to fail to collect all of the necessary demographic information about the respondents that would allow for separate analyses of sub-populations. "I wish we would have asked," is a statement often spoken after the data have been collected and are being analyzed.

Be reasonable in your expectations.

Our expectations of growth or change may exceed our ability to assess them. Often we are asked to assess advances in student achievement at the end of a one semester experimental course or program. Regardless of the quality of the experimental instruction, the tutorial components, or the computerized wizardry, student growth may not be measurable at the end of one semester or, even one year, irrespective of the instrument developed or selected. We must use our knowledge of teaching and learning research to temper our expectations for change.

Sometimes we also need to give an assessment program time to develop. One bad experience with a particular instrument may be an artifact of that particular administration. It may take one or two administrations of an instrument to yield desirable results.

Select or develop an instrument before one is selected or developed for you.

As difficult as it may be for an institution to decide upon the selection of an assessment instrument, it is even more difficult to live with an instrument mandated for use by an external agency, such as a state legislature or state board of education. Many state legislatures have jumped on the accountability bandwagon and are beginning to question the quality of higher education. A not so uncommon scenario has a state legislator hearing about an "interesting" test being given at one of the state institutions, soon without much discussion, a house bill is written mandating that the exam be given at all state schools. Obviously, what may be appropriate to administer at a small liberal arts college, may or may not be appropriate for the state land grant university. We need to be proactive in planning our assessment programs and avoid having to be reactive to someone else's plan.

References

Banta, T. W. (Ed.) (1989-90). *Assessment Update*, Vol. 1–2. San Francisco: Jossey-Bass.

Buros, O. K. (Ed.) (1974). *Tests in print: II.* Highland Park, NJ: Gryphon Press.

El-Khawas, E. (1991). Assessment on campus: Local instruments are strongly preferred. *Assessment Update*, Vol. 3, 4–5.

Mitchell, J. V. (Ed.) (1985). *The ninth mental measurement yearbook.* Lincoln, NE: University of Nebraska Press.

Ory, J. C. & Parker, S. (1989). A survey of assessment activities at large research universities. *Research in Higher Education*, 30, 373–383.

A Critical Review of Student Assessment Options

JOSEPH PRUS AND REID JOHNSON

Introduction

As higher educators plan and implement strategies to assess the quality of their programs, they will face no more important decision than choosing which method(s) to utilize for measuring each objective. Whether the goal is to assess an objective in basic skills, general education, the major, career preparation, or student personal growth and development, one overriding truism will apply: good methodological choices will produce results useful for program enhancement, and poor methodological choices will be detrimental to that process.

Complicating the method selection process—especially for those inexperienced in probability theory, program evaluation, and principles of psychoeducational measurement—are some additional facts of higher education assessment (HEA) life:

1. There will always be more than one way to measure any objective; i.e., there are always options.

2. No single method is good for measuring a wide variety of different student abilities; i.e., there's no "one true way."

3. We cannot rely on popularity, tradition, sales propaganda or primary/secondary education practices to separate the assessment "wheat from the chaff" for us in higher education, i.e., it isn't simply a matter of choosing the most attractive available option.

4. As in virtually all other domains of human assessment, there's a consistently inverse correlation between the quality of measurement methods and their expediency; i.e., the best methods usually take longer and cost more, in faculty time, student effort, money, etc.

5. The only way to be certain that a particular methodological option is good for your program is to pilot-test it on your students, in your curriculum, with your faculty; i.e., an "educated trial-and-error" approach.

What we're recommending in terms of method selection, therefore, is a two-step process. First, use the HEA literature, conferences, models and methods from other institutions, and consultations to tentatively identify a range of methods which appear to fit your needs and standards of quality. Second, "pilot-test" the best candidates on a limited trial basis with a representative

603

student sample at your institution. *Only proceed to full scale, implementation for those methods which are proven valid for your program(s).*

Validity—the key selection criterion for any HEA option—is made up of three equally vital attributes: *relevance* (the option measures your educational objective as *directly* as possible); *accuracy* (the option measures your educational objective as *precisely* as possible); and *utility* (the option provides formative and summative results with *clear implications* for educational program evaluation and improvement). If an assessment method doesn't measure what your program teaches, or doesn't measure it exactly, or doesn't suggest what the program's strengths and weaknesses are, then that assessment method *cannot* serve the institutional effectiveness goals of your program.

Although finding an ideal assessment method for each educational objective is probably unrealistic, we should strive for that goal in order to maximize the effectiveness and efficiency of our assessment efforts. Some characteristics of an "ideal method" would include:

1. Maximum relevance to the unique aspects of the "local" program curriculum (= internal validity);

2. Maximum generalizability to similar programs at colleges across the state, region and nation (= external validity);

3. Results useful for evaluating both program objectives and individual student progress;

4. Maximum incorporation into activities in the ongoing academic program;

5. Minimum latency between assessment and educationally useful results;

6. At a reasonable cost in terms of time, effort, and money.

It is also important to recognize that the validity of any student assessment method can be effectively evaluated only in relation to the educational objective that is intended to be measured. A method may be very relevant, accurate, and useful for assessing some objectives but be invalid for assessing others. Thus, a review of methodological assessment options needs to take into account the types of educational objectives for which each option might be suited. Objectives for student learning and development can be classified as

- student *knowledge,* or the quantity and quality of information acquired toward an educational objective;

- student *skills,* or the abilities acquired toward an educational objective;

- student *attitudes,* or the feelings, values, motives, and/or other affective orientations toward an educational objective;

- student *behavior,* or the actions or habitual patterns which express an educational objective; or

- some *combination* of two or more of these four types of student learning and development indicators.

Taking these and other educationally, statistically, and practically important factors into account, the most common methodological options for assessing student learning and development in higher education are briefly reviewed in the following section. The relative advantages and disadvantages of various types of tests, competency-based methods, self and third party reports, and other methods are outlined. Possible means by which to reduce the disadvantages associated with each method are also provided.

Tests

(Demand-response tasks utilizing standard stimulus items and pre-established criteria for "correctness/incorrectness" scoring.)

> 1. **Commercial Norm-Referenced, Standardized Exams** (Group administered, mostly or entirely multiple-choice, "objective" tests in one or more curricular areas. Scores are based on comparison with a reference or norm group.)

Advantages:

- Can be adopted and implemented quickly
- Reduce/eliminate faculty time demands in instrument development and grading (i.e., relatively low "frontloading" and "backloading" effort)
- Objective scoring
- Provide for exernality of measurement (i.e., external validity)
- Provide reference group(s) comparison often required by mandates
- May be beneficial or required in instances where state or national standards exist for the discipline or profession

Disadvantages:

- Limit what can be measured to relatively superficial knowledge/learning
- Eliminate the important process of learning and clarification of goals and objectives typically associated with local development and measurement instruments
- Unlikely to measure the specific goals and objectives of a program, department, or institution
- "Relative standing" results tend to be less meaningful than criterion-referenced results for program/student evaluation purposes
- Norm-referenced data is dependent on the institutions in comparison group(s) and methods of selecting students to be tested in those institutions. (Caution: unlike many norm-referenced tests such as those measuring intelligence, present norm-referenced tests in higher education do not utilize, for the most part, randomly selected or well stratified national samples.)
- Group administered multiple-choice tests always include a potentially high degree of error, largely uncorrectable by "guessing correction" formulae (which lowers validity)
- Summative data only (no formative evaluation)
- Results unlikely to have direct implications for program improvement or individual student progress
- Results highly susceptible to misinterpretation/misuse both within and outside the institution

Ways to Reduce Disadvantages

- Choose test carefully, and only after faculty have reviewed available instruments and determined a satisfactory degree of match between the test and the curriculum

- Request and review technical data, especially reliability and validity data and information on normative sample from test publishers

- Utilize on-campus measurement experts to review reports of test results and create more customized summary reports for the institution, faculty, etc.

- Whenever possible, choose tests that also provide criterion-referenced results

- Assure that such tests are only *one* aspect of a multi-method approach in which no firm conclusions based on norm-referenced data are reached without cross-validation from other sources

Bottom Lines

Relatively quick, easy, and inexpensive, but useful mostly where group-level performance and external comparisons of results are required. Not as useful for individual student or program evaluation.

2. **Locally Developed Exams** (Objective and/or subjective tests designed by faculty of the program being evaluated.)

Advantages

- Content and style can be geared to specific goals, objectives, and student characteristics of the institution, program, curriculum, etc.

- Specific criteria for performance can be established in relationship to curriculum

- Process of development can lead to clarification/crystallization of what is important in the process/content of student learning

- Local grading by faculty can provide immediate feedback related to material considered meaningful

- Greater faculty/institutional control over interpretation and use of results

- More direct implication of results for program improvements

Disadvantages

- Require considerable leadership/coordination, especially during the various phases of development

- Costly in terms of time and effort (more "frontload" effort for objective; more "backload" effort for subjective)

- Demands expertise in measurement to assure validity/reliability/utility

- May not provide for *externality* (degree of objectivity associated with review, comparisons, etc. external to the program or institution).

Ways to Reduce Disadvantages

- Enter into consortium with other programs, departments, or institutions with similar goals and objectives as a means of reducing costs associated with developing instruments. An element of externality is also added through this approach, especially if used for test grading as well as development

- Utilize on-campus measurement experts whenever possible for test construction and validation

- Contract with faculty "consultants" to provide development and grading

- Incorporate outside experts, community leaders, etc. into development and grading process

- Embed in program requirements for maximum relevance with minimum disruption (e.g., a "capstone" course)

- Validate results through consensus with other data

Bottom Lines

Most useful for individual student or program evaluation, with careful adherence to measurement principles. Must be supplemented for external validity.

3. **Oral Examination** (An evaluation of student knowledge levels through a face-to-face interrogative dialogue with program faculty.)

    (Oral exams generally have the same basic strengths and weaknesses of local tests, plus the following advantages and disadvantages:)

Advantages

- Allows measurement of student achievement in considerably greater depth and breadth through follow-up questions, probes, encouragement of detailed clarifications, etc. (= increased internal validity and formative evaluation of student abilities)

- Non-verbal (paralinguistic and visual) cues aid interpretation of student responses

- Dialogue format decreases miscommunications and misunderstandings, in both questions and answers

- Rapport-gaining techniques can reduce "test anxiety," helps focus and maintain maximum student attention and effort

- Dramatically increases "formative evaluation" of student learning; i.e., clues as to how and why they reached their answers

- Identifies and decreases error variance due to guessing

- Provides process evaluation of student thinking and speaking skills, along with knowledge content

Disadvantages

- Requires considerably more faculty time, since oral exams must be conducted one-to-one, or with very small groups of students at most

- Can be inhibiting on student responsiveness due to intimidation, face-to-face pressures, oral (versus written) mode, etc. (May have similar effects on some faculty!)

- Inconsistencies of administration and probing across students reduces standardization and generalizability of results (= potentially lower external validity)

Ways to Reduce Disadvantages

- Prearrange "standard" questions, most common follow-up probes, and how to deal with typical students' problem responses; "pilot" training simulations

- Take time to establish open, non-threatening atmosphere for testing

- Electronically record oral exams for more detailed evaluation later

Bottom Lines

Oral exams can provide excellent results, but usually only with significant—perhaps prohibitive—additional cost. Definitely worth utilizing in "Low N" programs, and for the highest priority objectives in any program.

Competency-Based Methods

(Measuring pre-operationalized abilities in most direct, real-world approach.

4. **Performance Appraisals** (Systematic measurement of overt demonstration of acquired skills.)

Advantages:

- Provide a more direct measure of what has been learned (presumably in the program)

- Go beyond paper-and-pencil tests and most other assessment methods in measuring *skills*

- Preferable to most other methods in measuring the *application* and *generalization* of learning to specific settings, situations, etc.

- Particularly relevant to the goals and objectives of professional training programs and disciplines with well defined skill development

Disadvantages:

- Ratings/grading typically more subjective than standardized tests

- Requires considerable time and effort (especially front-loading), thus being costly

- Sample of behavior observed or performance appraised may not be typical, especially because of the presence of observers

Ways to Reduce Disadvantages

- Develop specific, operational (measurable) criteria for observing and appraising performance

- Provide training for observers/appraisers

- Conduct pilot-testing in which rate of agreement (inter-rater reliability) between observers/appraisers is determined. Continue training and/or alter criteria until acceptable consistency of measurement is obtained

- Conduct observations/appraisals in the least obtrusive manner possible (e.g., use of one-way observational mirrors, videotaping, etc.)

- Observe/appraise behavior in multiple situations and settings

- Consider training and utilizing graduate students, upper level students, community volunteers, etc. as a means of reducing the cost and time demands on faculty

- Cross-validate results with other measures

Bottom Lines

Generally the most highly valued but costly form of student outcomes assessment—usually the *most* valid way to measure skill development.

5. **Simulation** (Primarily utilized to approximate the results of performance appraisal, but when—due to the target competency involved, logistical problems, or cost—direct demonstration of the student skill is impractical.)

Advantages

- Better means of evaluating depth and breadth of student skill development than tests or other nonperformance-based measures (= internal validity)

- Very flexible; some degree of simulation can be arranged for virtually any student target skill

- For many skills, can be group administered, thus providing an excellent combination of quality and economy

Disadvantages

- For difficult tasks, the higher the quality of simulation the greater the likelihood of the problems of performance appraisal; e.g., cost, subjectivity, etc. (see "Performance Appraisals")

- Usually requires considerable "frontloading" effort; i.e., planning and preparation

- More expensive than traditional testing options in the short run

Ways of Reducing Disadvantages

- Reducing problems is relatively easy, since degree of simulation can be matched for maximum validity practicable for each situation

- Can often be "standardized" through use of computer programs (= enhanced external validity)

Bottom Lines

An excellent means of increasing the external and internal validity of skills assessment at minimal long-term costs.

Self and Third Party Reports

(Asking individuals to share their perceptions of their own attitudes and/or behaviors or those of others.)

6. **Written Surveys and Questionnaires** (Including direct or mailed, signed or anonymous)

Advantages:

- Typically yield the perspective that students, alumni, the public, etc., have of the institution which may lead to changes especially beneficial to relationships with these groups

- Convey a sense of importance regarding the opinions of constituent groups

- Can cover a broad range of content areas within a brief period of time

- Results tend to be more easily understood by lay persons

- Can cover areas of learning and development which might be difficult or costly to assess more directly

- Can provide accessibility to individuals who otherwise would be difficult to include in assessment efforts (e.g., alumni, parents, employers)

Disadvantages

- Results tend to be highly dependent on wording of items, salience of survey or questionnaire, and organization of instrument. Thus, good surveys and questionnaires are more difficult to construct than they appear

- Frequently rely on volunteer samples which tend to be biased

- Mail surveys tend to yield low response rates

- Require careful organization in order to facilitate data analysis via computer for large samples

- Commercially prepared surveys tend not to be entirely relevant to an individual institution and its students

- Forced response choices may not allow respondents to express their true opinions

- Results reflect *perceptions* which individuals are willing to report and thus tend to consist of indirect data

- Locally developed instrument may not provide external references for results

Ways to Reduce Disadvantages:

- Use only carefully constructed instruments that have been reviewed by survey experts

- Include open-ended, respondent worded items along with forced-choice

- If random sampling surveying of the entire target population is not possible, obtain the maximum sample size possible and follow-up with nonrespondents (preferably in person or by phone)

- If commercially prepared surveys are used, add locally developed items of relevance to the institution

- If locally developed surveys are used, attempt to include at least some externally-reference items (e.g., from surveys for which national data are available)

- Word reports cautiously to reflect the fact that results represent perceptions and opinions respondents are willing to share publicly

- Use pilot or "try out" samples in local development of instruments and request formative feedback from respondents on content clarity, sensitivity, and format

- Cross-validate results through other sources of data

Bottom Line

A relatively inexpensive way to collect data on important evaluative topics from a large number of respondents. Must always be treated cautiously, however, since results only reflect what subjects are willing to report about their perception of their attitudes and/or behaviors

7. **Exit Interview and Other Interviews** (Evaluating student reports of their attitudes and/or behaviors in a face-to-face interrogative dialogue.)

Advantages

- Student interviews tend to have more of the attributes of surveys and questionnaires with the exception of requiring direct contact, which may limit accessibility to certain populations. Exit interviews also provide the following additional advantages:

- Allow for more individualized questions and follow-up probes based on the responses of interviewees

- Provide immediate feedback

- Include same observational and formative advantages as oral examinations
- Frequently yield benefits beyond data collection that come from opportunties to interact with students and other groups
- Can include a greater variety of items than is possible on surveys and questionnaires, including those that provide more direct measures of learning and development

Disadvantages

- Require direct contact, which may be difficult to arrange
- May be intimidating to interviewees, thus biasing results in the positive direction
- Results tend to be highly dependent on wording of items and the manner in which interviews are conducted
- Time consuming, especially if large numbers of persons are to be interviewed

Ways to Reduce Disadvantages

- Plan the interviews carefully with assistance from experts
- Provide training sessions for interviewers that include guidance in putting interviewees at ease and related interview skills
- Interview random samples of students when it is not feasible to interview all
- Conduct telephone interviews when face-to-face contact is not feasible
- Develop an interview format and questions with a set time limit in mind
- Conduct pilot-testing of interview and request interviewee formative feedback
- Interview small groups of individuals when individual interviewing is not possible or is too costly

Bottom Lines

Interviews provide opportunities to cover a broad range of content and to interact with respondents. Opportunities to follow-up on responses can be very valuable. Direct contact may be difficult to arrange, costly, and potentially threatening to respondents unless carefully planned.

8. **Third Party Reports** (Influences regarding student/alumni attitudes or observations on student/alumni behaviors, made by someone other than the student or assessor; e.g., parents, faculty, employers, etc.)

Advantages

Third-party reports tend to have attributes similar to student self-reports, plus the following additional advantages:

- Can provide unique *consumer* input, valuable in its own right (especially employers and parents). How is our college serving *their* purposes?

- Offer different perspectives, presumably less biased than either student or assessor

- Enable recognition and contact with important, often under-valued constituents. Relations may improve by just *asking* for their input

- Can increase both internal validity (through "convergent validity"/"triangulation" with other data) and external validity (by adding more "natural" perspective)

Disadvantages

Similar disadvantages to self-reports, plus . . .

- As with any indirect data, inference and reports risk high degree of error

- Third-parties can be less biased too, in directions more difficult to anticipate than self-reports

- Less investment by third-parties in assessment processes often means lower response rates, even lower than student/alumni rate

- Usually more logistical, time-and-motion problems (e.g., identifying sample, making contact, getting useful responses, etc.), therefore more costly than it looks

- If information about individuals is requested, confidentiality becomes an important and sometimes problematic issue that must be addressed carefully

Ways to Reduce Disadvantages

- Conduct face-to-face or phone interviews wherever possible, increasing validity through probing and forming evaluation during dialogue

- Very careful, explicit directions for types and perspectives of responses requested can reduce variability

- Attain informed consent in cases where information about individuals is being requested

- Coordinate contacts with other campus organs contacting the same groups, to reduce "harassment" syndrome and increase response rates

- Other self-report and interview "ways to reduce . . ." apply here as well

Bottom Lines

Third-party reports are valuable in that they access important data sources usually missed by other methods, but they can be problematic in cost of implementation and in gaining access to respondents. If personally identifiable information about individual students or alumni is requested, informed consent is needed.

Other Measures

9. **Behavioral Observations** (Measuring the frequency, duration, topology, etc. of student actions, usually in a natural setting with non-interactive methods.)

Advantages

- Best way to evaluate degree to which attitudes, values, etc. are really put into action (= most internal validity)

- Catching students being themselves is the most "natural" form of assessment (=best external validity)

- Least intrusive assessment option, since purpose is to avoid any interference with typical student activities

Disadvantages

- Always some risk of confounded results due to "observer effect;" i.e., subjects may behave atypically if they know they're being observed

- Depending on the target behavior, their may be socially or professionally sensitive issues to be dealt with (e.g., invasion of privacy on student political activities or living arrangements) or even legal considerations (e.g., substance abuse or campus crime)

- May encourage "Big Brother" perception of assessment and/or institution

- Inexperienced or inefficient observers can produce unreliable, invalid results

Ways to Reduce Disadvantages

- Avoid socially or ethically sensitive target behaviors, especially initially

- Include representative student inputs in process of determining "sensitivity" of potential target behaviors

- Utilize electronic "observers" (i.e., audio and video recorders) wherever possible, for highly accurate, reliable, permanent observation record (although this may increase assessment cost in the short run if equipment is not already available.)

- Strictly adhere to ethical guidelines for the protection of human research subjects

Bottom Lines

This is the best way to know what students actually do, how they *manifest* their motives, attitudes and values. Special care and planning are required for sensitive target behaviors, but it's usually worth it for highly valid, useful results.

10. **External Examiner** (Using an expert in the field from outside your program—usually from a similar program at another institution—to conduct, evaluate, and/or supplement the assessment of your students.)

Advantages

- Increases impartiality, third party objectivity (= external validity)

- Feedback useful for both student and program evaluation. With a knowledgeable and cooperative (or well-paid) examiner, provides an opportunity for valuable program consultation
- May serve to stimulate other collaborative efforts between departments/institutions

Disadvantages

- Always some risk of a misfit between examiner's expertise and/or expectations and program outcomes
- For individualized evaluations and/or large programs, can be very costly and time consuming

Ways to Reduce Disadvantages

- Share program philosophy and objectives—and agree on assessment criteria—beforehand
- Form reciprocal external examiner "consortia" among similar programs to minimize costs, swapping external evaluations back and forth
- Limit external examiner process to program areas where externality may be most helpful

Bottom Lines

Best used as a SUPPLEMENT to your own assessment methods to enhance external validity, but not as the primary assessment option. Other benefits can be accrued from the cross-fertilization that often results from using external examiners.

11. **Archival Records** (Biographical, academic, or other file data available from college or other agencies and institutions.)

Advantages:

- Tend to be readily available, thus requiring little additional effort
- Further utilize efforts that have already occurred
- Cost efficient
- Constitute unobtrusive measurement, not requiring additional time or effort from students or other groups
- Very useful for longitudinal studies

Disadvantages:

- Especially in large institutions, may require considerable effort and coordination to determine exactly what data are available campus-wide

- If individual records are included, may raise concerns regarding protection of rights and confidentiality

- Easy availability may discourage the development of other measures of learning and development

- May encourage attempts to "find ways to use data" rather than measurement related to specific goals and objectives

Ways to Reduce Disadvantages:

- Early-on in the development of an assessment program, conduct a comprehensive review of existing assessment and evaluation efforts and data typically being collected throughout the institution and its units (i.e, "campus data map")

- Be familiar with the Family Educational Rights and Privacy Act (Buckley Amendment) and avoid personally identifiable data collection without permission. Assure security/protection of records

- Only use archival records that are relevant to specific goals and objectives of learning and development

Bottom Lines

Relatively quick, easy, and cost-effective method. Usually limited data quality but integral to valuable longitudinal comparisons. Should be a standard component of all assessment programs.

12. **Portfolios** (Collections of multiple student work samples usually compiled over time.)

Advantages:

- Can be used to view learning and development longitudinally (e.g. samples of student writing over time can be collected), which is a most valid and useful perspective

- Multiple components of a curriculum can be measured (e.g., writing, critical thinking, research skills) at the same time

- Samples in a portfolio are more likely than test results to reflect student ability when pre-planning, input from others, and similar opportunities common to most work settings are available (which increases generalizability/external validity of results)

- The process of reviewing and grading portfolios provides an excellent opportunity for faculty exchange and development, discussion of curriculum goals and objectives, review of grading criteria, and program feedback

- Economical in terms of student time and effort, since no separate "assessment administration" time is required

- Greater faculty control over interpretation and use of results

- Results are more likely to be meaningful at all levels (i.e., the individual student, program, or institution) and can be used for diagnostic/prescriptive purposes as well

- Avoids or minimizes "test anxiety" and other "one shot" measurement problems

- Increases "power" of maximum performance measures over more artificial or restrictive "speed" measures on test or in-class sample

- Increases student participation (e.g., selection, revision, evaluation) in the assessment process

Disadvantages

- Costly in terms of evaluator time and effort

- Management of the collection and grading process, including the establishment of reliable and valid grading criteria, is likely to be challenging

- May not provide for *externality*

- If samples to be included have been previously submitted for course grades, faculty may be concerned that a hidden agenda of the process is to validate their grading

- Security concerns may arise as to whether submitted samples are the student's own work, or adhere to other measurement criteria

Ways to Reduce Disadvantages

- Consider having portfolios submitted as part of a course requirement, especially a "capstone course" at the end of a program

- Utilize portfolios from representative samples of students rather than having all students participate (this approach may save considerable time, effort, and expense but be problematic in other ways)

- Have more than one rater for each portfolio; establish inter-rater reliability through piloting designed to fine-tune rating criteria

- Provide training for raters

- Recognize that portfolios in which samples are selected by the students are likely to represent their *best* work

- Cross-validate portfolio products with more controlled student work samples (e.g., in-class tests and reports) for increased validity and security

Bottom Lines

Portfolios are a potentially valuable option adding important longitudinal and "qualitative" data, in a more natural way. Particular care must be taken to maintain validity. Especially good for multiple-objective assessment.

Summary of Bottom Lines

1. The most valid methods (for each student objective) produce the most useful results.

2. Invalid methods yield useless or misleading results (which may leave you worse off than when you started).

3. All assessment options have advantages and disadvantages. An effective comprehensive assessment program seeks to maximize strengths of methods while minimizing disadvantages.

4. It is crucial to use a multimethod/multisource approach to assessment in order to obtain maximum validity and to reduce potential error and/or bias associated with any one approach.

5. Always consider initial implementation of an assessment method as a "pilot test". Then seek to validate the method and results through comparisons with results from other methods or sources. In other words, be cautious in utilizing any one method and in interpreting results.

6. Search for "ideal" methods, but recognize that the ideal usually means methods that are the "best fit" between program needs, satisfactory validity, and affordability (in time, effort, and money).

7. Recognize that development of an assessment program is a *dynamic* process. Ongoing assessment of assessment methods themselves is an important part of that process.

The Case for Unobtrusive Measures

Patrick T. Terenzini

There can be little doubt that much of what we know from the social sciences has been developed from interview or questionnaire data. But what can we say about the fidelity of those portraits for the social and educational behaviors and phenomena they depict? Consider the following:

> ... research in intelligence testing show(s) that dependable gains in test-passing ability (can) be traced to experience with previous tests even where no knowledge of results (has) been provided. . . . Similar gains have been shown in personal adjustment scores (Webb et al., 1966, p. 19).

> Male interviewers obtain fewer responses than female, and fewest of all from males, while female interviewers obtain their highest responses from men, except for young women talking to young men (Benney, Riesman, & Starr, 1956, p. 143).

> Sequences of questions asked in very similar format produce stereotyped responses, such as a tendency to endorse the righthand or the lefthand response, or to alternate in some simple fashion. Furthermore, decreasing attention produces reliable biases from the order of item presentation (Webb et al., 1966, p. 20).

Thus, much of what we know may be biased in various and sometimes unknown ways. But if what one blind man learns about elephants is biased by the data-gathering procedures adopted, measurement and sampling theory suggest it is reasonable to expect that the evidence gathered by multiple blind men, when pooled, will give a better, if imperfect, approximation of an elephant. There is, after all, more than one way of knowing. The central thesis of this paper is that multiple research designs and measures of educational outcomes are more likely to yield reliable and valid assessments of educational outcomes than is the current reliance on interviews and questionnaires.

Consider the following:

The wear in the floor tiles in Chicago's Museum of Science and Industry.

The shrinking diameter of a circle of seated children.

Pupil dilation in the eyes of jade customers.

The bullfighter's beard.

Each of these conditions can, under certain circumstances, be taken as a measure of a phenomenon of interest to someone. Taken from Webb et al. (1966), each is an example of what has come to be called "unobtrusive measures," a general class of measurements presumed to reduce or eliminate the potential for reactive bias: responses uncharacteristic of the attitude or behavior outside the measurement situation and induced by the measurement act itself. The premise is that when interviews and questionnaires are used in social science research, the process of data collection intrudes itself into the consciousness of the subject and, as a consequence, alters the subject's responses. Unobtrusive measures, by their nature, avoid most, if not all, of the reactive bias associated with interview and questionnaire methodologies.

Webb et al. (1966) have described five categories of unobtrusive measures: physical traces (natural erosion or accretion processes, such as the wear on library book pages or the refuse left behind by an earlier civilization); continuous archival records (e.g., actuarial records, government records); intermittent archives (e.g., written documents, sales records); simple observations (e.g., of behaviors), and physical devices (e.g., cameras, video and audio tapes).

The measures listed above index some interesting illustrations of physical traces and simple observations. For example, the fact that the floor tiles around the hatching-chick exhibit require replacement approximately once every six weeks, compared to a replacement rate of several years for the tiles around other exhibits, can be taken as a reasonably clear reflection of the relative interest-value of the exhibit. So far as the shrinking diameter of the circle of children is concerned, if it were also known that the shrinkage was observed during a ghost-story-telling session, then the observation would have been recognized for what it is: an unobtrusive measure of the degree of fear induced in the children by the stories (and how much more reliable and valid than what the children might tell us if asked, "How scared were you?") As for the dilation of the pupils in customers' eyes, Chinese jade dealers have used it as an indicator of customer interest in various stones. And bullfighters' beards have been observed to be longer on days when the matador must enter the ring. There is no consensus whether the longer growth is attributable to higher anxiety or to whether he simply stands farther from the razor on those days. Probably both (Webb et al., 1966, pp. v and 2).

Much has been written on how the methods of the social sciences might be brought to bear on questions of outcomes assessment in higher education (e.g., Ewell, 1985, 1985; American College Testing Program, 1980; Astin, 1977). Less attention, however, has been given to the measurement problems inherent in these methods and to how those problems might be avoided or at least counterbalanced. Some critics consider the present reliance on interviews and questionnaires to be both unwise and unnecessary. Webb et al. (1963), for example:

> lament this overdependence upon a single, fallible method. Interviews and questionnaires intrude as a foreign element into the social setting they would describe, they create as well as measure attitudes, they elicit typical roles and responses, they are limited to those who are accessible and will cooperate, and the responses obtained are produced in part by dimensions of individual difference irrelevant to the topic at hand.
>
> *But the principal objection is that they are used alone* (p. 1; emphasis in the original).

Unobtrusive measures, such as those listed above, offer an important methodological counterweight to the unknown and unbalanced reactive bias in interview- and questionnaire-generated data sets, such as those upon which we now rely to assess the educational outcomes of college.

The remedy for these ailments, of course, lies not in the replacement of the research tools now in widespread use. This is no call to rally the Assessment Luddites. Rather, the intention is to encourage outcomes researchers to supplement standard approaches with methods and measures now largely unknown, unconsidered, or ignored. The purpose, here, is to make "The Case for Unobtrusive Measures," and that warrant can be argued on at least three grounds (one major, and two secondary): 1) measurement, 2) cost, and 3) prudence.

The Measurement Warrant

The strongest arguments for the use of unobtrusive measures can be made (appropriately enough) on measurement grounds. Recall that the principal objection of Webb et al. (1966) to the current reliance on interviews and questionnaires was that "they are used alone" (p. 1). The foundation of this objection is that:

> Every measurement procedure carries with it certain characteristic sources of error . . . it follows that they are in error in different ways and different degrees. The errors we refer to are constant *within* types of measures—the direction and size of the error are assumed to be fixed for a given set of measurement operations. However, the direction of errors is assumed to be random *across* procedures. For any given measurement task, the errors are additive: an error in one direction will tend to cancel out an error in the other direction (Sechrest and Phillips, 1979, p. 2).

Sechrest and Phillips go on to note problems occasioned by differences in the magnitudes of the errors involved and their effects on the precision of measurement, but the point is clear and the strongest argument for the use of multiple and *different* measures of the same trait or behavior— what Webb et al. (1966) and others (e.g., Campbell & Fiske, 1959) refer to as "multiple operationism." The intent is to employ multiple measures that "share in the theoretically relevant components (of the trait or behavior under study) but have different patterns of relevant components" (Webb et al., 1966, p. 3). When one samples measures, one also samples their strengths *and* their weaknesses. And as in sampling theory, the larger the sample size, the greater the reliability of estimation.

The utility of multiple measures in general, and unobtrusive measures in particular, is apparent in another way. Much of the research on student outcomes, particularly that focusing on institutional contributions to student growth, relies on various causal modelling techniques based on multiple regression. The multicolinearity among theoretically independent predictor variables, and the autocorrelations among the same measures used over time in longitudinal designs, present well-known, but frequently ignored, problems for the interpretation of path coefficients or regression weights. The problems of "bouncing betas" and the difficulty of replicating most studies in the social sciences are also well-known. Such interpretive difficulties notwithstanding, however, one researcher (cited in Kerlinger & Pedhazur, 1970, p. 446) has suggested that regression coefficients give us the laws of science, and many who employ regression analysis, or who read and rely on the results of such studies, may be similarly inclined to place more credence in the findings than is warranted.

The wisdom of multiple—and unobtrusive—measures is evident in still other ways. Research on the dynamics of attitude and value formation and change has both perceptual and behavioral dimensions. What correspondence exists between what a respondent professes to believe and how that person actually behaves? Reliance on questionnaires and interviews in such investigations requires an act of faith that the correspondence is high, when the fact of the matter may very well be otherwise. One can have significantly greater confidence in the reliability and validity of interview- or questionnaire-based claims about attitudes and beliefs if those claims are manifested behaviorally in natural settings. Used in this fashion, unobtrusive measures constitute a form of convergent validation and go a long way toward reducing the internal validity problems inherent in *ex post facto* research designs.

Unobtrusive measures have their own limitations, of course, for we rarely, if ever, know *their* characteristic sources of error. Thus, we cannot confidently estimate the extent to which use of an unobtrusive measure would be a useful and complementary addition to a series of measurement procedures or simply increase the error already present. And, like interview and questionnaire items, to the extent that unobtrusive measures rely on single observations, they are likely to be unreliable and, consequently, of limited validity (Sechrest & Phillips, 1979, p. 5–7). Despite more than a two-decade history, much research remains to be done on the measurement characteristics of unobtrusive measures.

Before all hope and confidence in the utility of unobtrusive measures is abandoned, however, it is useful, at least insofar as the assessment of educational outcomes is concerned, to differentiate "unobtrusive measures" as a set of scientific research tools from "unobtrusive measures" as a metaphor. In the first instance, it is quite possible to apply unobtrusive techniques and measures in a remarkable variety of experimental studies (see Bochner, 1979). As such, the rigor characteristics of true experiments can be brought to bear in naturalistic settings (like colleges and universities) and threats to internal validity are significantly reduced if not eliminated.

For example, if an institution wished to know the extent to which cultural and racial openness was a trait characteristic of the campus, one might design a study similar to that reported by Campbell, Kruskal and Wallace (1966). In that investigation, the tendency of White and Black college students to sit by themselves in racially homogeneous groups in classrooms (rather than mixing randomly) was studied as an indicator of racial attitudes.

While such formal unobtrusive research efforts are certainly possible, they are probably not likely to comprise a complete or adequate outcomes assessment program. "Unobtrusive measures" as a metaphor for non-reactive sources of information that *already exist* in various forms and locations across a campus are more likely to yield useful vehicles of assessment. Examples include such standard records as registrar's files, disciplinary records, Graduate Record Examination (GRE) scores, and alumni giving records. The category can also include less conventional measures, however, ranging from transcripts sent to other undergraduate institutions (student satisfaction), to case loads in the health services and psychological counseling service (amount of stress on campus), to library usage rates (students' intellectual curiosity). Unobtrusive measures may be based on observations as well as records. Such measures in colleges and universities might include assessment of a campus's intellectual climate as revealed on bulletin boards and in graffiti (see Ciardi, 1970, for a delightful discussion on this topic) and in conversations overheard in a student union snack bar. The point to be made is that unobtrusive measures—whether scientifically formal or causal—offer a source of information about the educational process and its outcomes that serves a legitimate and important measurement role by counterbalancing the systematic error characteristic of conventional measurement and research designs and by validating information gathered by means of those standard procedures.

The Cost Warrant

The costs of assessing educational outcomes are little understood. The proponents of the "benefits" portion of the cost-benefits equation have been dominant, and only recently has attention been turned to an estimation of the other side of the balance scale. How much in the way of resources is and should be invested in the production of outcomes information? The question applies to all information gathering, of course, whether outcomes or otherwise, but costs in other sectors are better understood and estimated than they are in outcomes assessment. The real issue, as Ewell and Jones (1986) put it is: "How much *more* money (beyond that already committed to outcomes-related information gathering) do we have to spend to put in place an assessment program that is appropriate to our needs?" (p. 34).

Based on a set of assumptions about the nature of the assessment programs likely to be mounted by institutions of varying types and sizes, Ewell and Jones (1986) estimate incremental costs ranging from $30,000 (in a small, private, liberal arts college) to $130,000 (in a major public research university). It is important to bear in mind that these are incremental, not total, cost estimates. It is revealing to notice Ewell and Jones' assumption of the use of conventional questionnaires, whether commercially available (e.g., the ACT's COMP) or locally developed (e.g., senior examinations in the major field disciplines).

No one has attempted to estimate the incremental costs of assembling information unobtrusively. Given the fact that much of this sort of data already exists, and given that much of it is electronically stored and retrievable, it seems reasonable to suggest that the costs of unobtrusive measurement and analysis are likely to be lower than those of more conventional measures and methods, perhaps significantly lower. There is, of course, considerable room for cost variability, but the initial proposition holds: analyzing data that are already available in one form and place or another is likely to be less costly and time-consuming than gathering data *de novo*.

The Prudence Warrant

Ewell (1984) has written that "the most vehement objections to the systematic assessment of institutional impact will come from faculty" (p. 72). These objections, says Ewell, are likely to derive from either or both of two sources: first, the fear of being negatively evaluated, and second, a philosophical opposition based on the belief that the outcomes of college are inherently unmeasurable and that the evidence from such studies is "misleading, oversimplifying, or inaccurate" (p. 73).

To counter faculty opposition, Ewell recommends that persons responsible for outcomes assessment "recognize publicly the inadequacy of any *single* outcome measure or indicator and . . . collect as many measures of program effectiveness as possible" (p. 73). The point is related to the argument for unobtrusive measures made earlier on measurement grounds and is likely to be recognized and given weight by faculty of all disciplines. The effect is likely to be a reduction in faculty resistance to educational assessment. Even if the measurements cannot be easily explained to non-social scientists, most faculty members will be familiar with the concept of "triangulation" in astronomy, as well as in map-reading and surveying. The use of multiple measures to portray some education outcome is likely to have a face validity that is appealing to faculty members. It seems reasonable to expect such an effect to influence positively both faculty participation in outcomes assessment programs and confidence in the conclusions derived from the evidence assembled.

Unobtrusive Measures in Higher Education

What are some unobtrusive measures in higher education and how might they enhance our understanding of various educational outcomes? Ewell (1984), following a review of various structures and taxonomies, has suggested that educational assessment should focus on three major areas: knowledge, skills, and values and attitudes, with a fourth category, students' relations with various groups in the lager society, representing the behavioral manifestations of the first three areas. Juxtaposition of these four dimensions against three of the general types of unobtrusive measures described earlier affords a useful framework for thinking about the sorts of institutional information that might be used to aid educational assessment. The matrix below is intended to be suggestive, to focus thinking on important assessment topics, and, thereby, to highlight the potential opportunities to employ unobtrusive measures.

	Types of Unobtrusive Measures		
Outcome Categories	Physical Traces	Achives & Records	Observations
Knowledge			
Skills			
Attitudes/Values			
Relations w/Society			

Space precludes discussion of possible measures that might occupy each of the cells in this matrix, and, as will be seen, the boundaries between the several categories of unobtrusive measures that are not always precise. Moreover, some of the cells are of greater interest than others, and some unobtrusive measures are more readily accessible than others. Two cells easily meet both of these criteria, namely, the "Knowledge-Archives" cell and the "Attitudes/Values-Observations" conjunction, and attention will be focused on them for illustrative purposes, beginning with the latter of the two cells.

The observational techniques of Campbell, Kruskal and Wallace (1966) for inferring racial attitudes and relations on a campus have been summarized. Variations on this approach might include a study of "aggregating" (Campbell, Kruskan and Wallace, 1966) in dining halls and cafeterias, in clusters of students studying in the library or gathering in other public areas, in institutional residence hall roommate patterns, and in other institutional settings.

Something of the importance students attach to the life of the mind might be inferred from several sources, including the number, size, and participation rates in formal student organizations and clubs that have some specific academic purpose (e.g., discipline-based clubs, literary and artistic publications, performing arts groups), as compared with organizations that have athletic, recreational, entertainment, social, or other purposes as their principle raison d'être. (Some of this information might be gleaned from records.)

Similarly, inferences about the relative emphasis given to the academic and social life of a campus might be made based on an examination of the content of campus concert, film, lecture, and speaker series, as well as attendance records. For residential campuses, the institution's role in students' lives—and its potential for influence—may be reflected in the extent to which students evacuate the campus for other locations on weekends. Ciardi (1970) has suggested that the content of graffiti reflect the intellectual tenor of a campus. One might add the content of bulletin boards to that reflection.

The number of students who are registered—and active—voters can be taken as a sign of students' interests in, sense of responsibility toward, and willingness to participate in the political life of a larger community. Or one might explore the level of social responsibility in a student body by designing an experiment around the frequency with which students returned library books that were presumably "lost." More simply, the proportion of the library's total overdue volumes that are signed out to students (or faculty) provides at least one index of the level of simple courtesy, if not social responsibility, on a campus. Vandalism, both in absolute magnitude and rate of change over time, offers another reflection of the quality of life and the attitudes and values prevalent on a campus. As suggested earlier, the rates over time at which the health service's physicians prescribe stress-related medicines, and variations in the case loads of the counseling center staff, might both be used to index the amount of potentially unhealthy—and perhaps educationally dysfunctional— stress in the campus environment. Hodgkinson and Thelin (1971) offer an impressive list of other possibilities. The variety is limited only by one's imagination and ingenuity.

Without question, the major impact of college on students' cognitive development is delivered through the curriculum, and any outcomes assessment program must deal in one fashion or another with the curriculum and with classroom-based learning. A variety of reactive measures have been developed to assess the nature and extent of students' cognitive growth (e.g., the ACT-COMP and Graduate Record Examinations subject tests), and these measures are typically used in "value-added" research designs of varying degrees of sophistication and validity.

Warren (1984) and Pascarella (1986) discuss some of the conceptual and methodological limitations of this approach to educational assessment, and those critiques need not be reiterated here. The point to be made is that something of the nature and extent of student learning can also be inferred from unobtrusive measures, from a data base that already exists and that has reasonable claims to reliability, namely, the registrar's file, which contains extensive information on the courses students have taken and the grades received.

Fincher (1984), recognizing the weaknesses and disadvantages of the grade-point average as a criterion of what has been learned, also marvels that "it works as well as it does" (p. 380). He writes:

> ... the freshman GPA will often display scalar features that are quite remarkable: a tenacious arithmetic mean, a standard deviation of about one-half letter grade, and a range of five or more standard deviation units. More remarkable, perhaps, the freshman GPA appears to be more immune to contamination than separate course grades are, and it is a relatively independent criteria despite being a faulty one. In addition, the freshman GPA is relevant to such educational decisions as the dean's list, student probation and dismissal, the maintenance of athletic eligibility, the continuance of scholarships, etc. If not a completely adequate criterion of academic performance, the freshman GPA still serves many educational purposes (p. 380).

Wilson (1983) reports that admissions measures are essentially as valid for predicting long-term GPA as freshman year GPA. Because of this property, Fincher suggests, cumulative GPA may yet be a useful measure in educational assessment and worthy of analysis. It might, for example, be used as the criterion in regression models and covariance and analyses in which pre-college academic aptitudes and achievements (and other potentially confounding variables) have been controlled in a study of the residual variance in long-term GPA attributable to student effort and to instruction and student learning. Similarly, if pre-college predictors of academic performance are found to have high multiple correlations with actual college achievement, reasonable suspicions might be raised about the overlap of high school and college coursework (Fincher, 1984).

The registrar's files offer other possibilities. For example, an examination of the distribution of courses taken by size and type of instruction (e.g., lecture, seminar, lab, independent study) might prove extremely revealing of the nature of the formal educational process experienced by students (e.g., graduating seniors). How many opportunities were there for students in small numbers to study with a faculty member? Such a review might focus on students' first two years. Do large lecture sections dominate students' early contacts with faculty and collegiate instruction? What is the relative balance of opportunities for active vs. passive student participation in their own learning? While recognizing that "small" is not necessarily "better," most faculty and administrators would probably be concerned if students' opportunities for small-group instruction were rare.

Examination of the relative proportional distributions of students majoring *and graduating* in particular disciplines will tell something of the nature of the educational program being delivered, and comparisons of such distributions, both one with the other and each over time, will detect shifting emphases in what students are interested in and what the institution is providing. Similarly, student retention rates, both within and across majors, may yield useful information. While such rates must be interpreted with considerable care, rates occupying one or the other tail in the distribution suggest something about students' views of the education afforded in those programs. Precisely what an extremely low retention rate means may be open to dispute, but at the very least it calls attention to the need for further investigation.

Transcript analysis affords a more detailed examination of curricula structures and student course-taking patterns and brings one still closer to the substance of students' formal education.

Using this technique, Blackburn et al. (1976) undertook a national study of changes in degree requirements between 1967 and 1974, exploring the amount, structure, and content of general education, and the structure and flexibility in selected major degree programs. They found, for example, that the typical baccalaureate degree recipient in 1974, compared to 1967, had taken about 22 per cent less coursework in general education.

Galambos et al. (1985), in a study of teacher education in the states comprising the Southern Regional Educational Board, used transcript analysis to compare the course-taking patterns of teacher education and arts and sciences degree graduates. They found that, on the average, teacher education graduates took proportionally fewer general education credits in all areas except the social sciences than did arts and sciences graduates. Their analyses also led them to conclude that "Given latitude, some students will ferret out the routes of least resistance to meet their general education requirements, and then pass the word on to others" (Galambos et al., 1985, p. 78). Such a finding on an individual campus is likely to be justifiable cause for a detailed—and important—review of general education courses and requirements.

The State University of New York at Albany used transcript analysis to test a belief prevalent among faculty and administrators that students were not gaining a "general education" because the only degree requirements were those of the major program; all other degree credits were electives. The analysis provided information of the average number and percentage of course credits taken by graduates of each academic department in each of some 20 content areas. Results indicated that, while students in certain major field areas were apparently avoiding certain content areas (e.g., natural and physical sciences, or foreign languages), the deviations from what most academicians might consider a "general education" were by no means so great as had been anticipated.

A variation on this approach is afforded by the following matrix (adapted from Blackburn et al., 1976, who also offer some useful classification rules):

	Per Cent of Courses Taken	
Type of Course	Breadth	Depth
Required		
Restricted		
Elective		
Full Elective		

Using this matrix, a computer-based analysis of the transcripts of all students, or of sub-groups of students (e.g., selected majors, transfers, freshmen), would afford several kinds of information. It would reveal something of the variety and depth of the course work to which students have been exposed during any given period of time in their college careers. In addition, it would suggest the relative control over students' course-taking exercised by the institution and the major department, and one might expect considerable variation across departments even within the same institution. Blackburn et al. (1976) offer a useful variant of the above matrix that differentiates general education requirements and courses from those of the major field. If still another variation were adopted to take into account *when* the course work was taken (i.e., a matrix that has the same breadth and depth columns, but has for its rows the time dimension of course-taking, say, lower and upper division), information would be gained on whether students are taking "breadth" courses prior to the selection of a major, or later in their college years, perhaps *after* the major program requirements have already been satisfied. The timing issue is important to the educational purposes of "general education" requirements. Do the requirements exist to ensure that students have a broad exposure to the various disciplines and on the basis of which they can make a more informed selection of a major program? Or are the requirements intended primarily to ensure that students are exposed to a broad intellectual experience at *some* point before they graduate?

Warren (1984) has suggested the analysis might be taken a step further. One might be inclined to believe, for example, that such course-taking pattern analyses do not provide a sufficiently detailed portrait of students' academic experience, for such analyses tell nothing of what students have learned. Warren suggests that a reasonable approximation of what has been learned might be obtained by reviewing examination questions and major paper assignments in courses that recur in the pattern of requirements for general education or for a specific major field—whether those courses are elective or required. As Warren (1984, p. 13) notes: "No pre-enrollment, normative, or comparative information need complement it. The assertion is simply that Program X as typically completed by a known number of students produces the described learning." A certain amount of faith is required, of course—faith that examinations and paper assignments reflect course content and that a passing grade reflects the occurrence of learning above some threshold of acceptability.

It should be evident by now that researchers in higher education have a wide variety of research designs and measures upon which to draw in their efforts to assess the outcomes of a college education. Thus far, however, the record indicates a virtually exclusive reliance on a subset of those designs and methods. The purpose of this paper has been to suggest ways in which conventional methods of assembling information on student growth might be supplemented in ways that illuminate rather than obscure. Webb et al. (1966, p. 34) put it succinctly:

> So long as we maintain, as social scientists, an approach to comparisons that considers compensating error and converging corroboration from individually contaminated (measures), there is no cause for concern. It is only when we naively place faith in a single measure that the massive problems of social science research vitiate the validity of our comparisons.

References

American College Testing Program. *College Outcomes Measurement Project* (COMP): *Summer Report of Research and Development 1976-80.* Iowa City, Iowa: American College Testing Program, 1980.

Astin, A. W. *Four Critical Years.* San Francisco: Jossey-Bass, 1977.

Benney, M., D. Riesman, and S. Star. "Age and Sex in the Interview." *American Journal of Sociology,* 1956, 62, 143–152.

Blackburn, R., E. Armstrong, C. Conrad, J. Didham, and I. McKune. *Changing Practices in Undergraduate Education.* Berkeley: Carnegie Council on Policy Studies in Higher Education, 1970.

Bochner, S. "Designing Unobtrusive Field Experiments in Social Psychology." In L. Sechrest (ed.), *Unobtrusive Measurement Today. New Directions for Methodology of Behavioral Science, No. 1.* San Francisco: Jossey-Bass, 1979.

Campbell, D. T., amd D. W. Fiske. "Convergent and Discriminant Validation by the Multitrait-Multimethod Matrix." *Psychological Bulletin,* 1959, 56, 81–105.

Campbell, D. T., W. H. Kruskal, and W. P. Wallace. "Seating Aggregation as an Index of Attitude." *Sociometry,* 1966, 29, 115.

Ciardi, J. "Graffiti." *Saturday Review, 53,* May 16, 1970, 10ff.

Ewell, P. *Information on Student Outcomes: How to Get It and How to Use It.* Boulder, CO: National Center for Higher Education Management Systems, 1983.

Ewell, P. *The Self-Regarding Institution: Information for Excellence.* Boulder, CO: National Center for Higher Education Management Systems, 1984.

Ewell, P. (ed.). *Assessing Educational Outcomes. New Directions for Institutional Research, No. 47.* San Francisco: Jossey-Bass, 1985.

Ewell, P., and D. Jones. "The Costs of Assessment." In C. Adelman (ed.). *Assessment in American Higher Education: Issues and Contexts.* Washington: U.S. Office of Education, Office of Educational Research and Improvement, 1986. (U.S. Government Printing Office, Document No. OR 86–301).

Fincher, C., "Educational Quality and Measured Outcomes." *Research in Higher Education,* 1984, *20,* 379–382.

Galambos, E. C., L. M. Cornett, and H. D. Spitler. *An Analysis of Transcripts of Teachers and Arts and Sciences Graduates.* Atlanta: Southern Regional Educational Board, 1985.

Hodgkinson, H., and J. Thelin. *Survey of the Applications and Uses of Unobtrusive Measures in Fields of Social Science.* Berkeley: University of California at Berkeley, Center for Research and Development in Higher Education.

Kerlinger, F. N., and E. J. Pedhazur. *Multiple Regression in Behavioral Research.* New York: Holt, Rinehart and Winston, 1973.

Pascarella, E. T. *Are Value-Added Analyses Valuable?* Paper presented to the Educational Testing Service Invitational Conference on "Assessing the Outcomes of Higher Education." New York, October 25, 1986.

Sechrest, L., and M. Phillips. "Unobtrusive Measures: An Overview." In L. Sechrest (ed.), *Unobtrusive Measurement Today. New Directions for Methodology of Behavioral Science, No. 1.* San Francisco: Jossey-Bass, 1979.

Warren, J. "The Blind Alley of Value Added." AAHE *Bulletin.* September 1984, 10–13.

Webb, E. J., D. I. Campbell, R. D. Schwartz, and L. Sechrest. *Unobtrusive Measures: Nonreactive Research in the Social Sciences.* Chicago: Rand McNally, 1966.

Wilson, K. M. *A Review of Research on the Prediction of Academic Performance after the Freshman Year.* College Board Report No. 83–2. New York: The College Board, 1983.

Contemporary Approaches to Assessing Student Achievement of General Education Outcomes

Trudy W. Banta

"With Great Difficulty"

"Specific Disciplines are the New Focus of Movement to Assess Colleges' Effectiveness" was the title chosen for the *Chronicle of Higher Education* article describing the fourth national conference on assessment held in Atlanta in June 1989. Denise Magner, the author of the article, stated: "As the move toward greater assessment of the educational accomplishments of colleges and universities enters its fifth year, educators say it is drifting from its initial focus on general course requirements to a wider interest in evaluating individual majors."[1]

I remember trying to resist Magner's thesis when she asked about my perceptions of what was happening at the conference. I believed that while the number of faculty interested in talking about assessment within their own disciplines certainly was growing, this did not necessarily mean that fewer colleges and universities were interested in assessing their general education programs. My experience in the last eighteen months in visiting campuses and talking with colleagues at national meetings has served to confirm that belief. Moreover, an inspection of the list of projects currently supported by the Fund for the Improvement of Postsecondary Education (FIPSE) reveals no less than a dozen ongoing studies of ways to improve the assessment of general education. Only one-third as many FIPSE projects are concerned with assessment in major fields.[2] On many campuses where a comprehensive approach to assessment is being considered, concern about measuring student achievement in general education is actually promoted by faculty discussion of methods for assessing student achievement in the major. As groups of faculty begin to talk about measuring student learning in the major, they find that they share with colleagues in other disciplines a concern about students' basic skills and knowledge as developed in a program of liberal studies. Then faculty in various disciplines will ask that some central action be taken to assess student achievement in general education as a means of freeing them to focus specifically on the knowledge and skills developed within the curriculum in the major.

Despite the relative ease with which faculty can agree that there are some domains of knowledge and basic skills in which all graduates should develop competence, specifying exactly what knowledge and which skills is much more difficult. According to Jerry Gaff, "Developing an education philosophy shared by all segments of the college community and finding the means to carry that philosophy out in practice is an aspiration realized only infrequently, with great difficulty, and after long struggle."[3]

In thinking about ways to assess the core of liberal studies, which provides the foundation for upper-division work at a four-year institution and the basis for a transfer program at a community college, faculty must think first about goals and the methods for implementing those goals, and only then about assessment. Many institutions have no written statements of goals. Among those that do, few have in place a formal audit process that provides for continuous faculty review of course syllabi and classroom tests to guarantee that the goals are being put into practice. And only in the last five years have substantial numbers of institutions begin to work on the assessment of student achievement of general education goals.

By 1989, however, more than 60 percent of the chief academic officers responding to the annual American Council on Education survey of 456 public and private colleges and universities reported that faculty on their campuses were assessing the outcomes of general education or making plans to do so.[4] If these faculties are simply looking at goals and measuring student outcomes without at the same time studying how the goals are being implemented, the long-term results may be disappointing. If, for example, it is determined through assessment procedures that students are not attaining a particular goal, in the absence of an audit process it may be impossible to determine why students are not achieving according to faculty expectations. Are the students failing to grasp certain concepts as they are being presented? Or does the explanation lie in the fact that the course intended to promote the mastery of the concepts no longer includes any reference to them? Only if faculty can obtain accurate, specific information about what needs to be changed can they effect improvements that will enhance student learning.

Beginning with Standardized Measures

In the wave of higher education assessment that began in the early 1980s, there was a rush to tap the inventory of extant standardized instruments to assess student achievement in general education. For instance, by that time both the College Level Examination Program (CLEP) tests in English composition, humanities, math, natural science, and social science/history and the Sequential Tests of Educational Progress (STEP) in English expression, reading, math, science, and social studies were established measures for assessing student attainment. Northeast Missouri State University (NEMU) secured its reputation as a "self-regarding institution"[5] on the basis of administering the ACT assessment test of academic aptitude to entering freshmen and again at the end of the sophomore year in an attempt to assess "value added" by the general education curriculum. NEMU also became one of the first institutions to use ACT's College Outcome Measures Program (COMP) exam, which was designed specifically to assess growth in general education outcome areas during the college years. By the end of the decade, the Academic Profile from ETS, ACT's Collegiate Assessment of Academic Proficiency (CAAP), and the College Basic Academic Subjects Exam (CBASE) published by Riverside had joined the COMP exam in this arena.

Initially, faculty were motivated by the knowledge that these standardized exams were readily available, presumably reliable and valid, and accompanied by norms that would permit comparison of the performance of their students with that of students at similar institutions across the country. However, thoughtful objections to the use of standardized exams were soon raised. First, these instruments may not test what a particular faculty is teaching—virtually no group of individuals at a single institution can cover the entire range of specialties in a given discipline. Since the format is usually multiple-choice, standardized exams also have been criticized because they assess primarily lower-order intellectuals skills. These tests may be standardized on unrepresentative norm groups: most of the new generation of exams developed specifically to assess general education outcomes provide user norms, and the users may not be at all typical of a given institution or its approach to general education. Moreover, little is known about the nature of the student samples these "user" institutions employ, or about the timing of the tests or the level of motivation with which students approach the testing experience. Standardized exams usually yield only a few subscores, thus making it difficult to decide exactly what piece of the curriculum or method of instruction ought to be investigated for flaws when scores are lower than expected. Finally, no standardized test score comes with an explanation of *why* it may be lower than anticipated. And the level of mystery about what should be done to improve low scores is intensified by the lack of detailed knowledge about the method faculty are using to deliver the knowledge and skills associated with an institution's goals for general education.

If there ever was a bloom on the rose called standardized testing, it faded rather quickly as the method of choice for assessing program effectiveness in higher education. As early as 1986, Russ Edgerton, president of the American Association for Higher Education (AAHE), warned that many of the standardized tests faculty were trying to use in assessing program outcomes had actually been designed to measure individual attainment; that is, how one student performs relative to others taking the test rather than what groups of students learn in college.[6]

Even the president of the Educational Testing Service, Greg Anrig, in "A Message for governors and State Legislators" in 1986, noted that "testing alone cannot evaluate institutions."[7] Anrig emphasized that higher education is concerned with far more than the minimum competencies that national exams might measure with a fair degree of accuracy. He urged faculty at each institution to identify the types of knowledge and skills they hoped to develop in graduates and to use this information to shape an assessment program encompassing "a wide range of data and measures."

In one of the largest studies to date of the use of standardized exams in general education assessment, Robert Thorndike found that the COMP exam and pilot versions of the Academic Profile and the CAAP were not appropriate measures of general education, as defined by faculty in the state of Washington. According to Thorndike, "None of the tests measured the separate academic skills (communication, computation, and critical thinking); rather, these tests primarily measured verbal and quantitative aptitude."[8] Further, test scores were not sensitive to specific aspects of the college experience, such as estimated time spent studying and credits earned.

These results have been confirmed by Gary Pike at the University of Tennessee, Knoxville, who compared the ACT-COMP exam with pilot versions of the Academic Profile and the CAAP in a series of controlled studies begun in 1987.[9] Each of these studies used the following sources of data: (1) A group of seven faculty members representing five colleges conducted content analyses of the three exams, matching the content of each with the university's formal statement of goals for general education; (2) all seniors (participation in general education testing is a graduation requirement, and seniors were randomly assigned to take one or the other of the tests being studied) were asked to rate the exam they took on the basis of its usefulness in measuring general education knowledge and skills and its appeal to their interest; (3) students volunteering to take *both* tests under investigation were interviewed individually to determine their reactions and preferences; and (4) several technical analyses of students' scores were conducted, including a study of scale intercorrelations and reliabilities, a principal components analysis, and an investigation of the sensitivity of each exam to the effects of education. Faculty concluded that neither the COMP nor the Academic Profile nor the CAAP measured student mastery of more than 30 percent of the knowledge and skills specified in the goals for general education at UTK. Fewer than half of the students tested considered any of the three exams a "good test" of what they had learned in their general education program. Significant correlations among the subscales on each test, coupled with the principal components analyses, provide strong evidence that the instruments are simply measures of intellectual ability. They appear to be insensitive to the effects of education and thus offer little or no additional information beyond that derived from tests of entering ability such as the ACT or SAT.

Results of a similar study at UTK comparing the COMP and the College BASE[10] provided only slightly more encouragement for the use of a standardized test in assessing general education outcomes. According to the judgment of the faculty evaluators, the College BASE covered 36 percent of the university's goals for general education. Factor analysis confirmed the existence of a factor structure corresponding to the subject scores offered by the CBASE developers. CBASE scores were not significantly correlated with student demographic characteristics, such as age, gender, and race, as was the case with the COMP, Academic Profile, and CAAP. Moreover, the CBASE was found to be slightly more sensitive to the effects of coursework than were the other tests. However, the CBASE does not cover adequately the attitudes and values dimensions of general education; it too is highly sensitive to entering ability. And since the CBASE is just beginning to be used broadly for general education assessment, the generalizability of its user norms is quite limited.

The process of bringing faculty together to discuss the goals for general education, the supporting curriculum and methods of instruction, the quality of student learning, and means of improving all of the foregoing constitutes the single greatest benefit to be derived from assessing outcomes. Since faculty may in fact come together for these discussions before selecting and again after administering a standardized exam, this kind of test could provide a useful starting point for assessment at any institution. Ohio University, Austin Peay State University in Tennessee, and Northeast Missouri State University, among others, still use the COMP exam to stimulate faculty discussion about their programs of general education.

However, faculty at many institutions are now moving ahead to develop their own measures of student achievement in general education. An indication of the national trend in this direction comes from the 1990 American Council on Education survey of chief academic officers: 66 percent reported that they are developing their own assessment instruments, an increase from just 45 percent in 1988.[11] Moreover, in 1989 Alexander Astin and associates at UCLA, following some disappointing personal experiences in trying to use standardized measures of cognitive skills, obtained an Exxon grant to initiate a multiyear study of alternative forms of assessment. The starting point for this research is faculty and student opinion about issues that might be considered within a collegiate general education program. A second component is a look at student change over four years in certain attitudes and behaviors after four years in college. Data are being collected from faculty and students at 50 colleges and universities with "distinctive approaches" to general education chosen from the 546 institutions that administered Astin's national survey of college freshmen in Fall 1985.[12]

The remainder of this article addresses the components of the planning-implementing-assessing model discussed above. Examples are drawn from contemporary practice to illustrate goal-setting, auditing to ensure implementation, and finally, assessment.

Beginning with Goals

The faculty at Alverno College in Milwaukee are recognized as pioneers in basing a program of liberal education on a set of specific objectives for learners. In the late 1960s the faculty began to question what knowledge and skills were needed for competent adult functioning and developed descriptions of eight abilities that characterized the kind of person Alverno faculty as educators seek to develop.[13] Since 1973, a student earning a degree at Alverno must have demonstrated satisfactory levels of competence in all the following broad abilities: communications, analysis, problem-solving, valuing, social interaction, responsibility toward the global environment, citizenship, and aesthetic responsiveness.[14]

In the early 1980s, the faculty at King's College in Pennsylvania began an intensive study of their approach to liberal learning and developed a list of eight "transferable skills of liberal learning," which they hoped to strengthen in each King's graduate: critical thinking, creative thinking and problem-solving strategies, writing, oral communication, quantitative analysis, computer literacy, library and information technologies, and values awareness.[15]

In the mid-1980s, the state higher education coordinating agencies in Virginia and New Jersey promulgated mandates for assessment that included explicit references to the need for goal-setting. At James Madison University in Virginia, faculty adopted a comprehensive approach to student development during college that included goals for cognitive, moral and psychosocial growth.[16] In New Jersey, all public institutions were required to submit to the State Board of Higher Education by June 1989 faculty-developed statements of goals for general education that would serve as the basis for assessment plans. These documents were reviewed by external consultants, and each institution subsequently received a detailed written assessment of the perceived strengths and weaknesses of its goals statement.

The recognition of differential institutional missions and programs implicit in the Virginia and New Jersey requirements that institutions prepare for assessment by developing their own goals statements stands in stark contrast to the assessment mandates in a few other states. In Tennessee and South Dakota, for example, the policies issued in 1979 and 1985, respectively, simply specified that standardized exams be used in assessment. In Tennessee, the issue of institutional goals for general education is ignored in the directive that every two- and four-year institution in the state must administer the COMP Objective Test to its graduates in order to assess general education outcomes.[17]

Recognizing that faculty might need assistance in constructing goals statements, the College Outcomes Evaluation Program (COEP) staff of the New Jersey Board of Higher Education commissioned a reference work on the topic. Lion Gardiner's *Planning for Assessment: Mission Statements, Goals, and Objectives* subsequently has been made available at no charge to all New Jersey institutions.[18] And at King's College, recognition that faculty need preparation for the task of redefining curricula led the chief academic officer to offer five years of faculty development experiences prior to the first discussions of new goals for general education.

Monitoring Implementation

In 1982, in his study of general education competence and persistence, Aubrey Forrest emphasized the need for the "curriculum audit," or a careful ongoing monitoring by faculty of the courses designed to promote student achievement of the institution's goals for general education.[19] In his reference work, *Good Practices in General Education*,[20] Forrest included materials collected from a variety of institutions that illustrate how faculty can construct course syllabi and exam questions to ensure that the general education program as presented by faculty actually develops stated outcomes in students.

The Alverno faculty has established comprehensive mechanisms for guaranteeing that its eight abilities are developed with the curriculum. Every faculty member is conscious of the various levels of each of the eight abilities that students must develop, and every course is designed to ensure learning of one or more of the abilities. In every course, as well as at key points outside courses, students participate in faculty-designed performance-based assessments, the outcomes of which become part of their permanent records. In addition, students learn to assess themselves.[21]

At King's College, faculty are expected "to be able to explain clearly to students the specific way the intended educational outcomes of the curriculum related to the College's definition of an educated person."[22] Moreover, continuous efforts are made to prepare faculty to implement changes in their own teaching related to the eight liberal learning goals of the college. Faculty have been trained for their roles in teaching writing across the curriculum, critical thinking, computer literacy, valuing, quantitative analysis, library and information technologies, oral communication, and problem-solving.

At James Madison University, a review process has been established to ensure that student activities outside the classroom play specified roles in promoting the cognitive, moral, and psychosocial goals of the institution. At another Virginia institution, Longwood College, a transcript has been developed to furnish a record of student involvement in college activities that contribute to the accomplishment of 14 goals for knowledge and skills. Students also complete an "Involvement Survey," which helps them note their progress toward the 14 goals and detect areas of development that they may be neglecting.[23]

Contemporary Assessment Strategies

Recognizing that use of standardized instruments to measure student achievement in general education will, at best, provide evaluative data bearing on only a portion of the curriculum, faculty at many institutions have taken assessment into their own hands. Since the beginning of the last decade, several institutional consortia, all supported by grants from the Fund for the Improvement of Postsecondary Education, have been formed for the purpose of inventing new assessment strategies.

Consortium Approaches

In 1986 the Association of American Colleges brought together representatives of 18 diverse institutions for the purpose of conducting an experiment with alternative approaches to assessing learning in liberal arts majors. The set of guiding principles adopted by this consortium are applicable to assessment in general education as well. Bobby Fong has summarized these principles as follows: (1) Assessment should use instruments that provide evaluative feedback that can be used to improve instruction and learning and to strengthen academic programs. (2) Assessment instruments should be sufficiently supple to take into account the diversity of educational missions across institutions. (3) Assessment should provide opportunities for students to demonstrate what they know, not merely where gaps exist in their knowledge. In addition to testing for common learning, assessment should give students ways to show that they have developed unique competence and knowledge. (4) Assessment instruments should allow students to work through a problem or issue so that they can receive credit for the process they use as well as the solution they reach.[24] The AAC consortium also acted on the belief that assessment should include participation by qualified outside parties to avoid the risk of being skewed toward local concerns and standards. Thus faculty from triads of similar institutions served as external examiners for each other's students.

In the early 1980s, the American Association of State Colleges and Universities developed a consortium of ten colleges for the purpose of evaluating the general education component of baccalaureate programs in those institutions. The Academic Program Evaluation Project (APEP) was based on the assumption that generic intellectual skills are measurable and can be used to evaluate student learning. The APEP took place on each campus according to a series of five stages that would soon become a familiar sequence in similar projects: defining generic skills; identifying performance indicators, criteria, and testing procedures; assessing student performance and program effectiveness; judging student and program performance; then making decisions and developing policies.[25]

In 1986 the University of Kentucky began a similar sequence of steps with a consortium of 14 private liberal arts colleges in central Appalachia. These institutions worked cooperatively to develop a plan for assessing the outcomes of their general education programs that eventually included four components: a freshman essay repeated in the senior year, the Academic Profile, the College Student Experiences Questionnaire, and senior interviews. The interviews, which were considered the most valuable of the four components, took place in groups composed of three students with a faculty member guiding a two-hour discussion. In the discussion, students were given a chance to demonstrate generic skills through responses to such questions as, What is an educated person? What is an effective citizen? What is the role of the artist in a culture? What is work? What were two or three of your most important college experiences? Interviewees on the 14 campuses were taped, then transcribed centrally and analyzed using a phenomenological/ethnographic approach.[26]

Building upon their own assumptions about assessment as learning, the Alverno College faculty in 1987 developed a consortium of 23 institutions for the purpose of demonstrating in a wide variety of institutional settings that faculty could design and implement assessment procedures to facilitate and measure student achievement of general education outcomes. The 68 college and university educators who met at Alverno for three annual summer workshops were asked to work on one of the expected general education outcomes that their institution had identified. In an extended process, they worked out specific components of that outcome within a course of program and identified indicators of student performance that would facilitate making judgments about student success in attaining the outcome. Finally, they designed methods of assessment. The educators then developed criteria for judging student performance, providing feedback to the learner, and evaluating the assessment procedure itself. Monographs describing more than 30 field-tested instruments for assessing liberal arts outcomes, as well as processes for validating such instruments, will be published by Alverno College in 1991.[27]

Institutional Approaches

The paradigm of assessment-as-learning pioneered by the faculty at Alverno College almost twenty years ago stands as a primary example of the way in which an assessment program can transform an institution. Alverno is known throughout the world for its ability-based curriculum. More recently, other institutions have effected fundamental changes in their approaches to general education via innovative approaches to assessment. Projects at King's College, Kean College, Lehman College, and the University of Connecticut provide examples.

Since the mid-1980s, faculty at King's College have been experimenting with course-embedded assessment, which is intended to be "diagnostic and supportive of student learning." The purpose of assessment at King's is to "provide systematic feedback to students on their academic progress toward meeting the expectations of faculty throughout all four years of undergraduate studies."[28] All core curriculum courses use pre- and postassessments that are common to all sections of the course and are designed by faculty teams. Postassessments are administered to students two weeks before the end of each course so that instructors will have ample time to provide feedback to students. The postassessment is an integral part of the final grade for each course, and thus student motivation to do their best work is ensured. Courses are designated for delivery of one or more of the eight transferable skills of liberal learning that guide the King's approach to general education. Each student has a Competence Growth Plan that provides a record of his or her progress toward achieving the eight skills. As students complete their assessment experiences in the designated courses, progress is noted in their individual plans. The activities associated with implementing this course-embedded assessment model serve to evaluate the outcome-oriented curriculum designed by the King's faculty.

At Kean College, faculty have developed essay items to evaluate knowledge of content and critical thinking skills in five areas: composition, emergence of the modern world, intellectual and cultural traditions, inquiry and research, and landmarks of world literature.[29] These items are incorporated in course exams, and students' responses are read twice—once by the course instructor for purposes of assigning a grade, then again by a faculty committee looking at response patterns across students and across courses for purposes of evaluating the effectiveness of the general curriculum. The Kean faculty also gather evaluative data from faculty and student surveys designed to elicit perceptions about the curriculum.

At Lehman College of the City University of New York, faculty undertook an evaluation of the general education curriculum in 1986. As at Kean, questionnaires were developed for faculty and for students to gauge their perceptions of the effectiveness of the curriculum. Other measures were obtained from student records, including persistence in college since the inauguration of a new general education curriculum, grade point averages, length of time needed to meet central college requirements, and the mix of courses taken. The Lehman faculty then developed procedures for testing student's abilities to read verbal tests, interpret quantitative data and present it graphically, evaluate data and arguments, and argue for points of view on complex issues. A significant part of this project was the training of faculty to score these assessments of cognitive abilities.[30]

In 1986 the University of Connecticut faculty adopted a plan scheduled to begin in September 1988 that would require all entering students to complete a structured menu of courses in six cognitive areas: foreign language, literature and the arts, Western/non-Western civilization, philosophy and ethics, social science, and science and technology. The program was also intended to develop students' skills in writing, quantifying, and computing. In 1988 some 50 faculty organized into six teams, corresponding to the categories of the curriculum, for the purpose of reviewing course syllabi, examinations, and available assessments. Multidisciplinary groups, each of which was chaired by an individual from a discipline other than the dominant one in the given area, developed a series of tasks for assessing student achievement that was pilot-tested during 1988–89. A wide variety of measures was constructed, including multiple-choice items as well as tasks such as identifying the rationale behind philosophical positions, and responding aesthetically to a painting, a poem, or a piece of music.[31] The University of Connecticut faculty also measured student response to the general education program in two ways: Students were asked to record their perceptions of their abilities in the six goal areas, and a series of focus groups was conducted to obtain qualitative information about the program.[32]

The development of tasks as prompts for constructed responses by students is an approach that has guided one state's approach to assessing the generic skills of sophomores in all of its public colleges and universities. The College Outcomes Evaluation Project (COEP) of the State Board of Higher Education in New Jersey engaged a representative group of faculty in constructing free-response tasks to measure students' skills in gathering, analyzing, and presenting academic information in the domains of social science, natural science, and humanities/fine arts. By subdividing the three major skills, a taxonomy of 48 skills was devised. The skill of analyzing, for instance, is composed in part of forming hypotheses and drawing conclusions. The tasks, which were pilot-tested as the General Intellectual Skills (GIS) Assessment during 1989–90, consists of series of problems or questions that proceed from less to more demanding as they draw a student toward a solution or answer. Core scoring is used to evaluate responses, with each task reading by four evaluators—two scoring skills and two scoring writing competence.[33]

Specific Techniques

Faculty are experimenting with a number of specific assessment techniques as they attempt to identify strengths and weaknesses of their general education programs. For instance, faculty at the State University of New York at Fredonia concluded that historical, scientific, cultural, and ethical understanding could be assessed using paper-and-pencil tasks. In the first task students were asked to list ten of the most important events in human history, then describe three consequences of one event's not having taken place. Responses were scored for chronological ordering, selection of important events, understanding of cross-cultural cause-and-effect relationships, and the presence of ethnocentrism and presentism. The second task asked students to consider an imaginary European exchange student's criticisms of American practices or problems. Responses were scored according to the same set of constructs, with the exception that sense of history was eliminated and the criteria of understanding of mainstream American values and questioning of stereotypes were added.[34]

Portfolios are growing in popularity as assessment tools that can be used in a wide variety of settings. Examples of materials that might be collected in a portfolio include course assignments, research papers, materials from group projects, artistic production, self-reflective essays, correspondence, and taped presentations. Student performances can be recorded using audio- or videotapes. Potential materials for the cassette-recorded portfolio are speeches, musical performances, visual arts productions, foreign-language pronunciation, group interaction skills, and demonstrations of laboratory techniques or psychomotor skills.

Pioneering work in portfolio assessment was conducted at Alverno college in 1970s. Today, faculty who have participated in one of Alverno's periodic workshops are undertaking their own experiments. For instance, at Millsaps College in Mississippi faculty are developing with FIPSE support a curriculum-embedded assessment procedure that will "measure and promote students' development as thinkers and writers by using writing done in course and assembled in individual portfolios."[35] Faculty assessors are developing criteria for assessing student writing that use analysis of content and the process of revision for clues that may signal cognitive growth.

While the concept of using portfolios is immediately appealing to many faculty, portfolio assessment is not easily implemented, as the FIPSE project director, David Lutzer, at Virginia's College of William and Mary, discovered. In the first year of their general education assessment project, the William and Mary faculty collected portfolios from instructors rather than students. They simply asked for some samples of what seniors were writing. The resulting portfolios were so lacking in uniformity that they proved nearly impossible to evaluate.[36] With a little more experience in this arena, Lehman College faculty devised specific criteria for portfolios, including number, length, and type of manuscripts to be submitted. Scoring of portfolios is also problematic, but Millsaps, Lehman, and others have reported that teaching instructors to use holistic scoring has constituted a valuable faculty development experience that proved to be somewhat unanticipated benefit of engaging in assessment activities.

Technology is also being employed to advance the state of the art of assessment. At Texas College of Osteopathic Medicine, Frank Papa and Jay Shores are using expert systems to assess the problem-solving skills of medical students and then to provide individualized instruction designed to improve these skills.[37] And at the University of Denver, Karen Kitchener and her colleagues are developing an interactive, computerized test of reflective judgment and teaching faculty how to use the resulting assessment information to adapt their instruction to the developmental characteristics of their students.[38] Both of these projects are supported by grants from FIPSE.

What Have We Learned from Assessment?

What have we learned from the extensive activity that has taken place over the last decade in attempting to assess general education? According to Jim Watt of the University of Connecticut, "during the first year, committees involving over 50 faculty members evaluated course content, and translated the goal statements into evaluation instruments. A very encouraging outcome of this process was the level of discussion of general education which the project generated within the faculty."[39] It is this focused discussion among faculty who are interested in improving student learning that has been one of the most salient positive features of assessment. And this benefit becomes evident immediately. It usually happens before faculty even begin to collect evidence from students. Then after the data begin to come in, faculty who are really invested in the process will see ways to improve the environment for learning, which is by far the most important outcome of assessment.

Faculty have learned that they must be more systematic in stating their goals for general education, in auditing the means of implementing the goals, and then in assessing outcomes in ways that provide evidence that can be used to confirm or to modify the original goals. This iterative process is not well understood, and certainly not widely practiced, in higher education; engagement in assessment may serve to increase understanding and thus improve practice. Faculty have also learned that assessment cannot be episodic—rather, it must be ongoing in an effort to provide for continuous improvement of the environment for student learning.

With regard to specific techniques, faculty have not found standardized tests to provide substantial assistance in suggesting modifications in courses or curricula that would improve general education. However, standardized exams may provide a starting point for the focused discussion that has been identified as a principal benefit of faculty involvement in assessment activities.

Recognizing the weaknesses inherent in standardized exams, faculty in consortia of institutions as well as individual colleges and universities have begun to experiment with a variety of homegrown assessment methodologies. Most of these could be characterized as qualitative in nature. Students are asking to construct their own responses orally and/or in writing, thus revealing much more about the extent of their knowledge and unique abilities than could ever be captured in responses to multiple-choice items. Extended interviews and collections of work in the form of portfolios are giving faculty opportunities to assess student learning comprehensively. Assessment activities that are embedded in courses are most likely to elicit students' best efforts. Finally, interactive computer technology is being developed that not only assesses current status but also can assist students to improve their skills and grasp of content.

While most of the recent development activities have produced measures of students' cognitive abilities and knowledge, faculty seeking ways to assess the effectiveness of general education programs have also sought some information about faculty and student perceptions of quality. Questionnaires and interviews have been employed for this purpose on a number of compuses. Student investment in activities, such as use of the library, that are assumed to promote learning has been noted through the use of instruments like the College Student Experiences Questionnaire. Student records have yielded information on persistence rates, college grades, and course-taking patterns that can also play a valuable role in assessing the effectiveness of the general education program.

Jerry Gaff has observed that assessment of general education outcomes has had a positive impact on the sense of identity and community within institutions that have approached assessment with seriousness of purpose. Involvement in assessment activities has also produced direction for faculty development and sparked faculty renewal. These changes have subsequently been associated with improved student satisfaction and retention.[40] These observations are borne out in the comments of some of the most committed practitioners.

In describing portfolio assessment at Lehman college, Dick Larson has said, "Our scoring constructs an *affirmative* statement about students' achievements, not a list of deficits. We also learn useful information about what faculty ask students to write, how they make assignments, and how they respond to students' writings."[41] According to Minda Rae Amiran, "[Students'] answers are immensely rich and educators at SUNY Fredonia are learning much about their students' socioethical understanding. The detailed descriptions of the eight constructs are also helping them refocus assignments and teaching methods in general education courses."[42] In summing up the impact of the changes in general education stimulated by the outcomes-oriented approach at King's College, Peter Ewell has written, "As evidenced by rising enrollments, and improved academic profile of entering students, and growing regional reputation. King's exemplifies an ancient piece of wisdom. The heart of academic institution is its curriculum. If the integrity of the curriculum is maintained and its effectiveness demonstrated, external benefits will naturally follow."[43]

Notes

1. Denise K. Magner. "Specific Disciplines Are the New Focus of Movement to Assess Colleges' Effectiveness," *Chronicle of Higher Education*, 5 July 1989, A26.

2. *Fund for the Improvement of Postsecondary Education Program Book* (Washington, D. C.: FIPSE, 1990).

3. Jerry G. Gaff. *General Education Today: A Critical Analysis of Controversies, Practices, and Reforms* (San Francisco: Jossey-Bass, 1983), xi.

4. Elaine El-Khawas. *Campus Trends, 1989.* Higher Education Panel Report No. 78 (Washington, D.C.: American Council on Education, July 1989), vii.

5. Peter T. Ewell, *The Self-Regarding Institution: Information for Excellence* (Boulder, Colo.: National Center for Higher Education Management Systems, 1984).

6. Russell Edgerton, "An Assessment of Assessment." Closing Plenary Session of the Educational Testing Service Annual Invitational Conference, New York, 25 October 1986.

7. Gregory R. Anrig "A Message for Governors and State Legislators: The Minimum Competency Approach Can Be Bad for the Health of Higher Education." (Princeton, N.J.: Educational Testing Service, 1986).

8. Robert M. Thorndike, "Assessment Measures," *Assessment Update* 1(3) (1989):8.

9. Gary R. Pike and Trudy W. Banta, *Using Construct Validity to Evaluate Assessment Instruments: A Comparison of the ACT-COMP Exam and the ETS Academic Profile.* American Educational Research Association, San Francisco, 28 March 1989; and Gary R. Pike, "A Comparison of the College Outcome Measures Program (COMP) and the collegiate Assessment of Academic Proficiency Exams," in *Performance Funding Report for the University of Tennessee, Knoxville 1988-1989* (Knoxville, Center for Assessment Research and Development, University of Tennessee, 1989), II-1–27.

10. Gary R. Pike, "Comparison of ACT COMP and College BASE," in *1989–90 Performance Funding Report for the University of Tennessee, Knoxville* (Knoxville: Center for Assessment Research and Development, University of Tennessee, 1990), 47–57.

11. Elaine El-Khawas, *Campus Trends, 1990,* Higher Education Panel Report Number 80 (Washington, D. C.: American Council on Education, July 1990), vii.

12. Alexander Astin et al., *A National Study of General Education Outcomes* (Los Angeles: Higher Education Research Institute, University of California, Los Angeles, 1989).

13. Alverno College Faculty, *Assessment at Alverno College* (Milwaukee: Alverno College, 1979).

14. Alverno College Faculty, *Liberal Learning at Alverno College* (Milwaukee: Alverno College, 1989).

15. D. W. Farmer, *Enhancing Student Learning: Emphasizing Essential Competencies in Academic Programs* (Wilkes-Barre, Pa.: King's College, 1988), 57.

16. T. Dary Erwin, "Virginia Assessment Requirements," paper presented at the Strategies for Assessing Outcomes Workshop, Knoxville. Tennessee. 5 November 1990.

17. *Performance Funding Standards for Public Colleges and Universities* (Nashville: Tennessee Higher Education Commission. 9 February 1990).

18. Lion F. Gardner. *Planning for Assessment: Mission Statements, Goals, and Objectives.* (Trenton: New Jersey Department of Higher Education. 1989.)

19. Aubrey Forrest, *Increasing Student Competence and Persistence: The Best Case for General Education* (Iowa City: ACT National Center for the Advancement of Educational Practice, 1982).

20. Aubrey Forrest, *Good Practices in General Education* (Iowa City: American College Testing Program, 1986).

21. Georgine Loacker, Lucy Cromwell, and Kathleen O'Brien, "Assessment in Higher Education: To Serve the Learner." In *Assessment in Higher Education*, ed. C. Adelman (Washington, D.C.: Office of Educational Research and Improvement. 1986).

22. Farmer. *Enhancing Student Learning*, 12.

23. Longwood College, *Longwood College Involvement Project* (Farmville, Va.: Longwood College, 1986).

24. Bobby Fong, "Old Wineskins: The AAC External Examiner Project." *Liberal Education* 74(3) (1988):12–16.

25. "Defining and Assessing Baccalaureate Skills: Ten Case Studies. A Report on the Academic Program Evaluation Project." American Association of State Colleges and Universities, Washington, D.C.: 1986.

26. Karen W. Carey and Charles F. Elton, *The Appalachian College Assessment Consortium* (Lexington: University of Kentucky, 1990).

27. Judeen Shulte, *Refocusing General Education Outcomes Through Assessment-as-Learning*, paper presented at the FIPSE Project Directors' Meeting, Washington, D.C., 27 October 1990.

28. Farmer. *Enhancing Student Learning*, 157.

29. Peter J. Gray, "Campus Profiles," *Assessment Update* 2(3) (1990):4–5.

30. Personal communication from Richard Larson, 15 October 1989.

31. Barbara D. Wright. "But How Do We Know It'll Work?" *AAHE Bulletin* 42(8) (1990):14–17.

32. James Watt, "Assessing General Education Outcomes: An Institution-Specific Approach," in *Fund for the Improvement of Postsecondary Education Program Book* (Washington D.C.: FIPSE, 1990), 60.

33. Personal communication from Robert J. Kloss, 23 April 1990.

34. Fredonia Designs Socioethical Assessment Measures," *Assessment Update* 1(4) (1989):4.

35. Austin Wilson, "Assessing Student Intellectual Growth Through Writing," in *Fund for the Improvement of Postsecondary Education Program Book* (Washington, D.C.: FIPSE, 1990), 103.

36. David Lutzer, "Assessing General Education," panel presentation at the FIPSE Project Directors' Meeting, Washington, D.C., 27 October 1990.

37. Frank Papa and Jay Shores, "Expert Systems-Based Clinical Tutorial Project," in *Fund for the Improvement of Postsecondary Education Program Book* (Washington D.C.: FIPSE, 1990), 160.

38. Karen Strohm Kitchener, "Assessing Reflective Thinking Within Curricular Contexts," in *Fund for the Improvement of Postsecondary Education Program Book* (Washington, D.C.: FIPSE, 1990), 67.

39. Watt, "Assessing General Education Outcomes," 60.

40. Jerry Gaff, "Assessing General Education," panel presentation at the FIPSE Project Directors' Meeting, Washington, D.C., 27 October 1990.

41. Larson, 15 October 1989.

42. Fredonia Designs Socioethical Assessment Measures," 4.

43. Peter T. Ewell, Foreword, in *Enhancing Student Learning: Emphasizing Essential Competencies in Academic Programs*, ed. D. W. Farmer (Wilkes-Barre, Pa.: King's College, 1988), viii.

To Capture the Ineffable: New Forms of Assessment in Higher Education

PETER T. EWELL

Defining Assessment Practice

. . . Interactions among these internal and external reform agendas yield a complex pattern of activities now undertaken in the name of assessment. Before 1984, the number of institutions possessing identifiable assessment programs was extremely small. Best current estimates, however, indicate that up to 70% of American colleges and universities are establishing such programs, most of them in the last 2 or 3 years (El-Khawas, 1989; Hyman, Jamison, Woodard, & von Destinen, 1988). At the same time, continuing developments in individualized testing, performance assessment, and program evaluation consistent with the academic reform tradition have generated additional activities also grouped under the terminological rubric of assessment.

Faced with such escalating diversity, some observers have claimed that the term *assessment* itself in current higher education usage is insufficiently discriminating to be of descriptive value (Edgerton, 1987). More common have been attempts to systematically classify diverse assessment activities in terms of their visible attributes, for example, by the methods and standards of evidence used, by their basic purposes or applications, or by the disciplinary traditions that provide their theoretical grounding.

A Basic Taxonomy

Perhaps the most useful such classification (Erwin, in press; Ewell, 1987; Terenzini, 1989) combines two quite different criteria (see Table 1). A first taxonomic dimension is basic purpose, founded

Table 1
A Taxonomy of Assessment Activities in Higher Education

Unit of analysis	Purpose of assessment	
	Improvement (formative)	Demonstration (summative)
Individual level	diagnosis/feedback	certification/"gatekeeping"
Group level	evaluation/self-study	accountability/quality assurance

Note: From "Assessment with Open Eyes" by P. T. Terenzini, 1989, *Journal of Higher Education, 60,* p. 648. Adapted by permission.

upon the classic distinction between formative and summative evaluation design. Here the primary object of analysis varies from information-based improvement to unambiguous demonstration of attainment against previously defined performance standards. A second dimension is based on primary unit of analysis. Performance information can be gathered and reported for individuals—the most commonly understood traditional notion of assessment—or it can be compiled across analytic aggregations of individuals, most commonly programs, curricula, institutions, and geographic or demographic groupings. (A third dimension, sometimes added, is the domain of assessment, which encompasses traditional college outcomes categories such as knowledge, skills, and attitudes/values [Ewell, 1984, Terenzini, 1989].) Cells within this matrix enable important distinctions among assessment activities to be drawn. At the same time, the classification allows location of the many existing assessment activities that occur routinely (though in uncoordinated fashion) on most college and university compuses. Finally, the taxonomy allows the current state of the art in higher education assessment, including those areas where most of the new approaches have emerged, to be described in an efficient manner.

Most obviously included in the *individual/improvement* cell, for example, is the diagnostic basic skills placement testing that frequently occurs on entry into college. Testing of this kind on a statewide basis is currently in place in Texas, Tennessee, and New Jersey, and is often accompanied by mandatory course placement and/or remediation. More commonly, institutions engage in placement testing on an individual basis, using a range of commercially available standardized instruments. Less commonly, noncognitive instruments (e.g., the Myers-Briggs type indicator or the Strong-Campbell personal interest inventory) are used for individual counseling or advising (G. Hanson, 1982). Rarely, however, are assessments of this kind conducted beyond the freshman year. The major *new* development within this cell is performance assessment designed to document individual mastery of complex, integrated abilities. The best current examples of this practice in higher education are at Alverno College (Alverno College Faculty, 1979), although the method is now being extended to a wide range of settings—particularly medical education (Stone & Meyer, 1989) and teacher education (Shulman, 1987a). At the same time, the practice has much in common with the way individual student work is routinely evaluated in the fine or performing arts through portfolio review or audition. Typically, this method involves placing individuals in actual or in carefully simulated performance settings that demand the simultaneous deployment of judgment and a range of integrated abilities. Individual performances are rated by multiple expert judges (termed *assessors*) who can both certify the ability at a given proficiency level and provide detailed feedback to the learner. Consistent with the curricular reform agenda, frequent and active feedback on performance is a hallmark of the method; indeed, a major objective is for students to become continuous "self-assessors" (Mentkowski & Doherty, 1984).

Established activities within the *individual/demonstration* cell of this taxonomy include credentialing and gatekeeping, both of which may entail substantial consequences for the individual student. The former is best exemplified by the vast range of professional certification or licensure examinations required for practice in professions such as medicine, accountancy, engineering, nursing, and, in many states, K-12 teaching. An additional variant embraces graduate or professional school admissions examinations (e.g., Medical College Admissions Test [MCAT], Law School Admissions Test [LSAT], or Pre-Professional Skills Test [PPST]) used to select or screen potential students. Gatekeeping examinations, in contrast, are intended to directly regulate student progress by requiring explicit demonstration of established proficiency as a condition for advancement. Florida's College Level Academic Skills Test (CLAST), for example, is a basic skills examination that all public college students must pass to achieve full standing as juniors. Similarly, upper-level writing requirements at institutions as diverse as the University of Arizona, the University of Northern Colorado, Wayne State University, Bethany College, and the California State University system consists of locally designed and administered essay examinations to certify writing proficiency; these are expected to be taken at the end of a student's sophomore year, but all must be passed before a degree is conferred. A more traditional gatekeeping practice, senior comprehensive examinations in the major field, was once a common feature of undergraduate liberal arts college curricula; currently, such end-of-program examinations are reemerging in response to external assessment mandates. Consistent with traditional practice, many senior comprehensives require more than one reader, whereas some use external examiners recruited from other institutions (Fong, 1987). Although the current assessment movement has yielded few new activities within this cell, performance-based assessment methods are finding their way into professional certification, most notably, at present, in the proposed assessment of teachers (Shulman, 1987b).

Activities within the *group/improvement* cell have probably seen the greatest development as a result of an explicit national assessment movement. Partly in response to emerging state mandates—most of which assign responsibility for designing and carrying out assessment activities to individual institutions—and partly in response to the internal imperatives of curricular reform, many institutions are now undertaking identifiable assessment efforts. Within these programs, many existing institutional data-collection activities are subsumed (Ewell, 1983). Generally lacking, however, are an explicit coordination function and information on the effectiveness of the curriculum as a whole, particularly in general education. Although details of emerging institutional assessment programs vary widely, most contain a number of common features. This is, in part, because many such programs have been modeled on a few widely quoted examples. The following are the most prominent: for public research universities, the University of Tennessee, Knoxville (Banta, 1985); for public state colleges, Northeast Missouri State University (McClain & Kruger, 1985) and Kean College of New Jersey (Boyer, 1989); for private institutions, Alverno College (Mentkowski & Loacker, 1985) and Kings College (Farmer, 1988); and for public community colleges, Miami-Dade Community College (McCabe, 1983). Another reason for this uniformity is that the majority of recently established programs have been developed in response to state guidelines, which strongly resemble one another.

Among the most common features of such programs are (a) an identified office or individual assigned explicit responsibility for coordinating the assessment function, for advising individual academic units in the design of assessment procedures, and for helping to interpret obtained results; (b) systematic basic skills testing in reading, writing, and computation; (c) evaluation of the effectiveness of general education through examining the development over time of such integrative skills as critical thinking and problem solving; (d) evaluation of the effectiveness of instruction in the student's major field; and (e) determination of current and former student satisfaction and behavior through periodic follow-up surveys (Ewell, 1987). Often, such programs involve recognition of existing information functions on campus, and responsibility is assigned to an established testing office or office of institutional research rather than to a free-standing assessment office (Nichols, 1990).

Finally, the *group/demonstration* cell of the matrix contains some of the most debated assessment proposals in higher education. Here, relevant practices and discussions are largely colored by the perceived experience of large-scale accountability testing in K-12 education (Darling-Hammond, 1988). For the most part, higher education has not experienced assessment activities of this kind in the past. Institutional accreditors, though their actions are summative, have only recently recognized learning outcomes as indicative of quality (Thrash, 1988; Wolff, 1990). Professional program accreditors are also moving in this direction, but none as yet requires administration of a particular outcomes instrument to demonstrate program effectiveness. Some state-based assessment mandates, consistent with the thrust of the National Governors' Association (NGA) report, to have come closer to this summative ideal; they include Tennessee's performance funding program, South Dakota's 3-year experiment with commonly administered institutional outcomes testing, and New Jersey's current statewide program to assess "general intellectual skills." In each of these cases, a primary motivation was to provide the public with comparative performance information as a form of accountability or consumer protection. Both motivations have been given additional impetus by recent actions of the federal government. Regulations promulgated in the fall of 1987 require all federally approved accreditation organizations to collect outcomes information as a part of the accreditation process (U.S. Department of Education, 1987); new "track record disclosure" regulations passed for 2-year occupational/technical programs and currently under consideration for 4-year programs also require institutions to provide potential students with such statistics as program completion and job placement rates (D. Hanson, 1990).

Some Implied Methodological Imperatives

Not only do these two taxonomic dimensions delineate distinct kinds of assessment activities, but they also help to highlight some profoundly different approaches to measurement. Within the primary purpose dimension, for example, demonstration requires, above all, measurement precision with respect to an obtained estimate of performance. The dominant required is for instruments and techniques that can, as fully as possible, *determine* whether or not a given performance standard has been achieved. Information-based improvement, in contrast, demands a different kind of optimization. Here, the dominant requirement is to chart a process of change and to determine what in the curriculum or environment is responsible for it. This fundamental difference underlies much recent debate regarding the appropriateness of so-called value-added assessment (e.g., Baird, 1988; G. Hanson, 1988; Pascarella, 1987; Terenzini, 1989). Beyond the technical properties of difference scores in this discussion lie profound differences in analytical requirements.

Similarly, shifting the unit of analysis may entail significant changes in measurement assumptions and opportunities. Traditional testing and measurement practice in higher education, reflecting the customary applications of tests, has been overwhelmingly concentrated on obtaining usable individual scores. Here, embodied in such instruments as collegiate or graduate admissions examinations and basic skills placement examinations, the dominant requirements of individual reliability and predictive value have largely determined what constitutes adequate practice. Estimating *group* properties and performance, however, allows the application of new techniques and poses additional conceptual challenges. First, of course, reliable group-level estimates can be established without assessing all individuals. But any sample-based strategy may raise profound questions not only about representativeness, but also about the political credibility of obtained results (Ewell, 1988b). Second, not all items in a given domain need be given to every individual. As a result, item spiraling techniques have become a common feature of emerging group-level assessment techniques. But using these techniques means accepting some critical assumptions about uniform item functioning across individuals and about the appropriate interpretation of composite scores compiled from the individual performances of different test takers on quite different tasks (Mislevy, 1990).

Methodological tensions such as these have been visible throughout the practice of higher education assessment. A well-known instance is the use of Graduate Record Examination (GRE) scores as an aggregate comparative indicator of higher education effectiveness (Adelman, 1985, 1989). Although a proven device for use in individual/summative decision making, the form and content of the GRE general examinations reflect little of the domains most observers see as important cross-disciplinary college outcomes. Using such scores effectively for group/improvement purposes, moreover, requires the release of item scores, but releasing items may severely compromise the examination's original purpose as a secure selective device.

More subtle methodology tensions are illustrated for institutions and states by the respective cases of Northeast Missouri State University and the statewide General Intellectual Skills assessment in New Jersey. At Northeast Missouri the original motivation for assessment was clearly demonstrative—to provide credible evidence that the institution was producing "degrees with integrity" (McClain, 1984). Within this context, the choice of nationally normed standardized instruments included the American College Testing Program (ACT) Assessment and GRE subject examinations as the major vehicle for assessment was not merely a matter of convenience; it was entirely consistent with the program's intent. Charges of inappropriateness since directed at these methods miss this primary purpose, assuming instead that the principal goal was formative. Similarly, an announced policy intent of New Jersey's new General Intellectual Skills examination was to provide a statewide accountability benchmark with regard to collegiate skills—and goal quite similar in essence to that of the National Assessment of Educational Progress (WAEP) in K–12 education (College Outcomes Evaluation Program [COEP] Council, 1990). The choice of a nontraditional, performance-based format for the examination, using extended intellectual tasks instead of multiple-choice items, was based as much on the need to build credibility for the instrument within the academic community as it was on the technical grounds of improved validity that an actual production measure might yield. Ironically, the resulting task-based instrument now in use may be far better suited to local diagnostic applications than to producing a stable, easily interpretable summative snapshot of collegiate abilities in New Jersey.

So long as assessment is undertaken for different purposes, such tensions will inevitably be present. As a consequence, any methodological comment and criticism must rest on a clear understanding of what a given assessment initiative is ultimately *for*, and how its results will be applied in decision making.

Three Emerging Trends in Higher Education Assessment

Even though the extent and diversity of assessment activities in higher education have rapidly expanded, and even though only a partial consensus has been achieved about the dimensions underlying these assessment activities, some clear patterns in the technical practice of such assessments have nonetheless emerged. Although far from settled, these patterns suggest an emerging consensus regarding "meta-methodology," regardless of purpose or unit of analysis. More important, the direction of these tendencies suggest an eventual outcome far different from the current practice of assessment in K–12 settings.

In brief, three major trends in assessment technology can be noted. The first is the development of new, special-purpose instruments to replace the available off-the-shelf testing technology used in most pioneering institutional assessment efforts. More significant, there is an emerging shift in the model of student development underlying assessment—from an additive 'production process' view of education to one that recognized complex, often nonlinear paths of development. Finally, there has been a clear trend toward more naturalistic approaches—on one hand, taking greater advantage of existing settings as vehicles for assessment, and, on the other hand, stressing actual task performance rather than indicative item performance as its primary vehicle. Each trend can be used both to succinctly summarize current practices and to briefly suggest the most probable future developments.

New Kinds of Tests

At the beginning of the assessment movement in 1985, numerous commercially available examinations already existed for purposes of individual placement, admissions, and certification. But little technology was available in higher education to compare with NAEP in K-12, capable of supporting more general evaluation. Ironically, by 1982, the Educational Testing Service (ETS) had allowed its Undergraduate Assessment Program (UAP), founded upon both general and discipline-based examinations, to lapse. Normed at the college senior level and intended to provide evidence of overall curricular effectiveness, these examinations were build on items derived from parallel GRE exams and were fairly widely used in the 1950s. Simultaneously, ETS abandoned work on a new general education assessment instrument intended primarily to provide group-level results.

With a resurgence of interest in group-level results, the response of the standardized testing community followed two lines of development. A first response was to reengineer existing placement and disciplinary knowledge examinations for newer purposes. Although this filled an immediate need, it did little to change existing test-making technology. A more far-reaching result was development by the major testing companies of a second generation of general purpose instruments that emphasized production of group-level results, particularly in general education.

Old Wine in New Bottles

Given an escalating interest in assessing group-level performance after 1985, an obvious first approximation was to use off-the-shelf technology. Thus, several pioneering institutional, curricular, and state-mandated assessment programs used the ACT Assessment—designed to generate individual scores for college admissions decision making—in a test-retest design (Lenning, Munday, & Maxey, 1969; McClain & Krueger, 1985). At the same time, available discipline-based tests such as the GRE field examinations and the College Level Examination Program (CLEP) area examinations were used to assess group-level knowledge outcomes, particularly in the student's major field. Obvious drawbacks to extending such examinations beyond their designed purposes, however, quickly emerged. Off-the-shelf examinations rarely covered the curricula domain actually taught by the institution, and the few obtained scores provided by the test makers were often ill-suited to formative use in guiding curriculum improvement (Banat & Pike, 1989; Heffernan, Hutchings, & Marchese, 1988). At the same time, because of self-selection, the norm bases of most of these examinations were of little value in judging the performance of representative college-going populations (Adelman, 1989).

To address many of these deficiencies, existing content-based examinations could fairly easily be reconfigured for the production of group-level results, using shorter forms and a recalculated norm base. By 1990, ETS had in place over a dozen new "major field achievements tests" of approximately an hour in length, drawing heavily on prior experience with equivalent GRE field examinations. At the same time, some professional fields moved to construct model content assessments of their own. For example, by 1987 the American Association of Collegiate Schools of Business (AACSB), working with ACT, had piloted several specially constructed examinations designed to assess the content of the basic business core (Blood, 1987). Other content-specified designs followed particular curricular prescriptions—for example, a cultural literacy examination (Hirsch, 1989), drawn from the controversial work of the same name (Hirsch, 1987), and the content-based Survey of College Seniors' Knowledge of History and Literature (The Gallup Organization, 1989) based on the "Fifty Hours" curriculum proposed by the national Endowment for the Humanities (Cheney, 1989).

The many new basic skills tests emerging during the same period also entailed few departures from traditional testing practice. Development of instruments to support the Texas Academic Skills Program (National Evaluation Systems, 1987) in 1987–1988, for example, followed a path similar to that of the New Jersey Collegiate Basic Skills Placement Test and Florida's College Level Academic Skills Test (CLAST) almost a decade before (Postsecondary Education Planning Commission, 1988), and resulted in comparable instruments. Similar commercial offerings such as ACT's ASSET are designed to be multipurpose and to be more compatible with other instruments in supporting longitudinal research but are otherwise familiar. For placement testing, however, new developments in computerized test administration offer considerable potential for the future. Here, computer-adaptive techniques that allow test takers to be given items whose difficulty levels are tailored to prior performance promise enormous savings in test-taking time. The latest "computerized placement tests" offered by ETS, for example, can be administered in approximately a third of the time required by conventional paper-and-pencil alternatives (The College Board, 1987). Field evidence also indicates that computerized test administration is more satisfying to students because it provides immediate scoring and feedback, avoids the frustrations associated with inappropriate difficulty levels, and reduces test anxiety (League for Innovation, 1988).

New Tests for General Education

Although such developments were promising, they did little to address the pressing need to gather group-level information about general education. This was a far more serious enterprise partly because, for many observers, such claimed results of general education as critical thinking or solving problems remained definitionally elusive. By 1989, however, four second-generation examinations were available for use in assessing general education outcomes (Pike, 1989b), only one of which was in place before 1985. They include the ACT College Outcomes Measures Project (COMP), the ETS Academic Profile, the ACT Collegiate Assessment of Academic Proficiencies (CAAP), and the College Basic Subjects Examination (College-BASE) developed by the University of Missouri. For most institutions, these four examinations remain the universe of standardized alternatives for assessing the effectiveness of general education. Although each is distinct in architecture, all four have characteristics in common.

The earliest of the four, the ACT COMP, was ground breaking in several respects when it was introduced in 1976 (Forrest & Steele, 1978). First, its domain is defined by a matrix of three process and three content areas, with each test item contributing to two or more subscores depending on its position in the matrix. Second, COMP's design emphasizes knowledge and skill *use*, with most items confronting test takers with a multifaceted problem-solving situation; in the long-form "composite examination," for example, students write and speak in response to questions, and stimulus material in presented across a range of media both visually and aurally. Content areas are primarily applications based rather than knowledge based (e.g., "functioning within social institutions" and "using the arts"). Third, the examination's design optimizes estimation of group-level results through a shorter testing form (the "objective test") that requires 2-1/2 hours of testing time rather than the 4-1/2 hours needed for the composite. Scores derived from the objective test are not individually reliable and must be used in aggregated form. Finally, COMP's approach emphasizes examining curricular impact through the use of test-retest difference scores; in cases where pretests are not available, the instrument's design allows estimation of imputed COMP scores from existing ACT Assessment scores. COMP's ready availability in the mid-1980s resulted in its substantial use as state assessment mandates began to emerge and no alternative standardized examinations were available. Current estimates suggest that at least 500 institutions have used the examination (Steele, 1988), and it remains a key common component of such approaches as Tennessee's widely publicized performance funding program (Levy, 1986).

Other more recently developed second-generation general education instruments share many features of COMP's basic design. Although a far more traditional examination, the ETS Academic Profile is equally founded on a matrix of domains (four skills and three content areas), and also uses a short form optimized around the need to estimate group scores (Educational Testing Service, 1989b). In its short form, however, required testing time has been cut to less than 50 minutes through the use of item spiraling and design based on item response theory (IRT). The latest version of the Academic Profile provides criterion-based performance information in the form of the percentage of test takers attaining each of three hierarchical proficiency levels within each skill area, in addition to traditional norm-referenced scores. This feature meets a growing assessment demand for information about curricular goal achievement.

College-BASE, in contrast, was designed from the outset around criterion-referenced reporting (Osterlind, 1988). Also founded on a matrix design (four skills and four content areas), its architecture is more complex. Content areas, for example, are organized into levels of increasing specificity, with two to six "enabling subskills" successively defining skills, aggregate skill clusters, and, finally, entire subject domains. Similarly, the four tested skills areas ("competencies") are not independent, but are organized hierarchically. The result is an examination that is unusually theory driven, though also theory bound if individuals do not fit the test's implied models of cognitive functioning. As is the case with the COMP and the Academic Profile, moreover, short and long forms are available for College-BASE, with an "institutional matrix" form allowing group-level results to be estimated in approximately an hour of testing time.

Easily the most traditional examination of the four, the ACT CAAP is the only one not founded on a matrix design (American College Testing Program, 1988). Instead, the CAAP is intended to fit comfortably in ACT's traditional array of instruments (e.g., the ACT Assessment and the ASSET) as a collegiate midpoint examination. A modular design consisting of fire self-contained, 40-minute multiple-choice tests (writing skills, mathematics, reading, critical thinking, and science reasoning) and a writing sample of equivalent length allows flexible administration in any combination. All score reporting for CAAP is on a norm-referenced basis, with pilot norming data being compiled through the end of 1990. Although the newest of the four, CAAP's design signals a return to more traditional purposes. Modular scores are individually reliable so that they can be used independently or can be combined to yield group results for institutional assessment. At the same time, the test's reversion to easily understandable, free-standing content domains reflects some of the difficulties encountered in meaningfully interpreting and applying the more analytic subscores produced by the COMP.

Standardized Testing: The Face of the Future?

Three features of these second-generation instruments appear to point strongly toward future test development: (a) further concentration on underlying integrative and analytical skills as proper domain of assessment, (b) increased focus on group performance with consequent use of item or form spiraling and ITR to produce shorter testing times, and (c) further experimentation with produced response as an alternative to classic multiple-choice items. All three trends are visible in perhaps the most innovative current instance of large-scale assessment in higher education: the New Jersey General Intellectual Skills (GIS) Assessment, first administrative in 1990 (CEOP Council, 1990).

The GIS is an integral part of a much larger state-based assessment effort, the college Outcomes Evaluation Program (COEP), initiated in 1986. After a year of statewide discussion, a task force charged with developing appropriate approaches to determine student cognitive development concluded that although assessable outcomes might differ in many areas from institution to institution, "students general intellectual skills are developed and refined at all of New Jersey's institutions of higher education . . . no matter which program or department students major in, or what degree or certificate they ultimately attain" (College Outcomes Evaluation Program, State of New Jersey Department of Higher Education, 1987, p.7). Intended to define and provide benchmark performance information on the development of such skills in college students across the state, initial requirements for the GIS were thus for an instrument that could be administered at several points in a typical college career and that could adequately encompass the complexity of college-level work.

With the assistance of ETS, a highly innovative large-scale assessment approach was designed. First, following ETS experience with the Academic Profile and other matrix-based examinations, faculty drawn from across the state developed a taxonomy consisting of three kinds of skills: gathering information, analyzing information, and presenting information. After pilot testing, an additional quantitative analysis skill was identified and added to the taxonomy (COEP Council, 1990). Each skill, though a general outcome of college, might be manifested in one of the three basic disciplinary groupings—the humanities, social sciences, and sciences—with scores for each skill combined across all three groupings.

More radically, the entire GIS examination would be performance based, engineered around extended 90-minute "tasks" with required performance components carefully designed to cover one or more cells of the skills/content matrix. Each student would complete only one task, and results would be combined to yield reliable group-level estimates. Pilot testing confirmed that at least seven tasks would be required to adequately cover the taxonomy's domain and that approximately 200 students per institution would suffice to produce usable group-level results. Task scoring would be accomplished by teams of faculty members using a "core scoring" technique recently developed at ETS (Conlin, 1987). According to this method, a minimally adequate core score is determined for each task element, with additional scores above and below this point assigned on the basis of specific response characteristics defined by a scoring guide.

Pilot tested twice in 1988–1989, the GIS was first administered on a statewide basis in the spring of 1990. Results of both the pilots and the operational program suggest that task-based technology is feasible for large-scale assessments and is significantly more likely than standard multiple-choice testing to be acceptable to faculty and students as representing college-level work (COEP Council, 1990). Statistical analyses using parallel forms of assessment based on tasks and standard multiple-choice items, moreover, clearly suggest that different skills are being tapped (Educational Testing Service, 1989a). Statistical properties of the scores obtained, however, are still being explored, as the combined effects of a spiraled matrix designed in which different parts of the domain are taken by different students, a new task-based testing technology based on judgmental core scoring, and an intact classroom sampling strategy at the institutional level render issues of statistical confidence exceedingly complex. Nevertheless, the GIS is a path-breaking effort, perhaps nothing less than the prototype for a "third generation" of standardized general purpose assessment instruments in higher education.

Generic Instruments: Enduring Issues, Uncertain Future

Fulfilling the strong promise of these new testing technologies, however, will demand resolution of a number of persisting questions. First, can common skills dimensions appropriate to higher education settings really be identified and estimated across disciplinary contexts?" One difficulty encountered by developers of the ETS Academic Profile in its pilot year, for example, involved extremely high intercorrelations among taxonomic skills scores—a phenomenon also reported by other general skills test developers (Pike, 1989c). In a major exploratory research effort in Washington that cross tested students on the ACT COMP, the ACT CAAP, and the Academic Profile, moreover, results strongly indicated that despite differing testing architecture and conceptual foundations, obtained results on the three examinations were very similar (council of Presidents and State Board for Community College Education, 1989; Thorndike, 1990). These results were sustained by large-sample studies at the University of Tennessee, Knoxville, in which students were cross tested on the COMP and the Academic Profile (Banta & Pike, 1989). At the same time, persistent reports of age/performance correlations on the ACT COMP suggest that some general skill elements may be a product of social maturation and that the COMP remains a better measure of individual differences than an indicator of program effects (Pike, 1989a). These finding echo earlier debates about whether or not such attributes as critical thinking are true generalizable abilities (e.g., Campione & Armbruster, 1985) and raise doubts about the ultimate utility of instruments that seek to assess them.

Second, if general abilities do exist, can they be connected to anything? Initial research and development findings on the ACT COMP reported detectable curricular impacts, but also noted more significant relationships with such general adult functioning indicators as employer ratings of employee performance (Forrest, 1982). More significantly, on the basis of a substantial multiyear sample of students, researchers at the University of Tennessee, Knoxville, were unable to identify interpretable linkages between student experiences and positive difference scores obtained on the

COMP using a freshman-senior test-retest design (Banta, Lambert, Pike, Schmidhammer, & Schneider, 1987), although later work at the University of Tennessee using a differential coursework pattern methodology did identify clusters of courses associated with greater than expected performance on some COMP dimensions (Pike & Phillipi, 1989). No similar studies have as yet been executed using CAAP, the Academic Profile, or College-BASE. At minimum, therefore, given the often limited correspondence between the domains typically assessed by general purpose instruments and what college faculty say they teach (Banta & Pike, 1989), the effectiveness of such instruments in guiding curricular improvements remains uncertain.

Overall, these two factors leave the future potential of commercial general-purpose assessment instruments in some doubt. Clearly, there is strong faculty affect against any kind of standardized testing as an appropriate vehicle for assessing collegiate outcomes, and using such instruments is likely to entail considerable political opposition. Emerging experience with the logistics of these examinations also suggest that problems of student motivation for an exercise involving few stakes for the learner, although possible to overcome, are substantial and often unpredictable. Experience indicates that once students sit down to take an examination, they either take it seriously or their response patterns are easily detectable. But in initial attempts to use such examinations without sufficient time for preparation, many institutions have experienced no-show rates in excess of 50%, largely obviating a valid sample. Although material inducements such as cash payments or gift certificates have some effect, more successful have been clear and repeated explanations of assessment's purpose, the promise of individual feedback on results, and making participation a curricular requirement (Erwin, in press). Nevertheless, concerns about motivation are real and are increasingly dominating discussions of test administration using standardized instruments.

On the other hand, ease of procurement means that such instruments are often as institution's first encounter with assessment. In this respect, their use can raise important process questions about curricular goals, and their results can stimulate a range of productive faculty discussions (e.g., Banta & Moffett, 1987). At the same time, the perceived unambiguity of obtained scores may be the only basis on which to found such statewide summative applications of testing as performance funding (Banta, 1988; Ewell, 1986). Finally, the promise of such performance-based approaches as the GIS in addressing state and system-level assessment needs in a manner parallel to the role of NAEP in K–12 education remains alluring. These implications yield a conclusion that new test technology will play a strong but controversial role in higher education assessment for the foreseeable future. . . .

But Is It Rigorous?
Trustworthiness and Authenticity in
Naturalistic Evaluation

Yvonna S. Lincoln and Egon G. Guba

Until very recently, program evaluation has been conducted almost exclusively under the assumptions of the conventional, scientific inquiry paradigm using (ideally) experimentally based methodologies and methods. Under such assumptions, a central concern for evaluation, which has been considered a variant of research and therefore subject to the same rules, has been how to maintain maximum rigor while departing from laboratory control to work in the "real" world.

The real-world conditions of social action programs have led to increasing of the rules of rigor, even to the extent of devising studies looser than quasi-experiments. Threats to rigor thus abound in sections explaining how, when, and under what conditions the evaluation was conducted so that the extent of departure from desired levels of rigor might be judged. Maintaining true experimental or even quasi-experimental designs, meeting the requirements of internal and external validity, devising valid and reliable instrumentation, probabilistically and representatively selecting subjects and assigning them randomly to treatments, and other requirements of sound procedure have often been impossible to meet in the world of schools and social action. Design problems aside, the ethics of treatment given and treatment withheld poses formidable problems in a litigious society (Lincoln and Guba, 1985b).

Given the sheer technical difficulties of trying to maintain rigor and given the proliferation of evaluation reports that conclude with that ubiquitous finding, "no significant differences," it is not surprising that the demand for new evaluation forms has increased. What is surprising—for all the disappointment with experimental designs—is the *continued* demand that new models must demonstrate the ability to meet the same impossible criteria! Evaluators and clients both have placed on new-paradigm evaluation (Guba and Lincoln, 1981; Lincoln and Guba, 1985a) the expectation that naturalistic evaluations must be rigorous in the conventional sense, despite the fact that the basic paradigm undergirding the evaluation approach has shifted.

Under traditional standards for rigor (which have remained largely unmet in past evaluations), clients and program funders ask whether naturalistic evaluations are not so subjective that they cannot be trusted. They ask what roles values and multiple realities can legitimately play in evaluations and whether a different team of evaluators might not arrive at entirely different conclusions and recommendations, operating perhaps from a different set of values. Thus, the rigor question continues to plague evaluators and clients alike, and much space and energy is again consumed in the evaluation report explaining how different and distinct paradigms call forth different evaluative questions, different issues, and entirely separate and distinct criteria for determining the reliability and authenticity—as opposed to the rigor—of findings and recommendations.

Rigor in the Conventional Sense

The criteria used to test rigor in the conventional, scientific paradigm are well know. They include exploring the truth value of the inquiry of evaluation (internal validity), its applicability (external validity or generalizability), its consistency (reliability or replicability), and its neutrality (objectivity). These four criteria, when fulfilled, obviate problems of confounding, atypicality, instability, and bias, respectively, and they do so, also respectively, by the techniques of controlling or randomizing possible sources of confounding, representative sampling, replication, and insulation of the investigator (Guba, 1981; Lincoln and Guba, 1985a). In fact, to use a graceful old English cliché, the criteria are honored more in the breach than in the observance; evaluation is but a special and particularly public instance of the impossibility of fulfilling such methodological requirements.

Rigor in the Naturalistic Sense: Trustworthiness and Authenticity

Ontological, epistemological, and methodological differences between the conventional and naturalistic paradigms have been explicated elsewhere (Guba and Lincoln, 1981; Lincoln and Guba, 1985a; Lincoln and Guba, 1986; Guba and Lincoln, in press). Only a brief reminder about the axioms that undergird naturalistic and responsive evaluations is given here.

The axiom concerned with the nature of reality asserts that there is no single reality on which inquiry may converge, but rather there are multiple realities that are socially constructed, and that, when known more fully, tend to produce diverging inquiry. These multiple and constructed realities cannot be studied in pieces (as variables, for example), but only holistically, since the pieces are interrelated in such a way as to influence all other pieces. Moreover, the pieces are themselves sharply influenced by the nature of the immediate context.

The axiom concerned with the nature of "truth" statements demands that inquirers abandon the assumption that enduring, context-free truth statements—generalizations—can and should be sought. Rather, it asserts that all human behavior is time- and context-bound; this boundedness suggests that inquiry is incapable of producing nomothetic knowledge but instead only idiographic "working hypotheses" that relate to a given and specific context. Applications may be possible in other contexts, but they require a detailed comparison of the receiving contexts with the "thick description" it is the naturalistic inquirer's obligation to provide for the sending context.

The axiom concerned with the explanation of action asserts, contrary to the conventional assumption of causality, that action is explainable only in terms of multiple interacting factors, events, and processes that give shape to it and are part of it. The best an inquirer can do, naturalists assert, is to establish plausible inferences about the patterns and webs of such shaping in any given evaluation. Naturalists utilize the field study in part because it is the only way in which phenomena can be studied holistically and *in situ* in those natural contexts that shape them and are shaped by them.

The axiom concerned with the nature of the inquirer-respondent relationship rejects the notion that an inquirer can maintain an objective distance from the phenomena (including human behavior) being studied, suggesting instead that the relationship is one of mutual and simultaneous influence. The interactive nature of the relationship is prized, since it is only because of this feature that inquirers and respondents may fruitfully learn together. The relationship between researcher and respondent, when properly established, is one of respectful negotiation, joint control, and reciprocal learning.

The axiom concerned with the role of values in inquiry asserts that far from being value-free, inquiry is value-bound in a number of ways. These include the values of the inquirer (especially evident in evaluation, for example, in the description and judgment of the merit or worth of an evaluand), the choice of inquiry paradigm (whether conventional or naturalistic, for example), the choice of a substantive theory to guide an inquiry (for example, different kinds of data will be collected and different interpretations made in an evaluation of new reading series, depending on whether the evaluator follows a skills or psycholinguistic reading theory), and contextual values (the values inhering in the context, and which, in evaluation, make a remarkable difference in how evaluation findings may be accepted and used). In addition, each of these four value sources will interact with all the others to produce value resonance or dissonance. To give one example, it would be equally absurd to evaluate a skills-oriented reading series naturalistically as it would to evaluate a psycholinguistic series conventionally because of the essential mismatch in assumptions underlying the reading theories and the inquiry paradigms.

It is at once clear, as Morgan (1983) has convincingly shown, that the criteria for judging an inquiry themselves stem from the underlying paradigm. Criteria developed from conventional axioms and rationally quite appropriate to conventional studies may be quite inappropriate and even irrelevant to naturalistic studies (and vice versa). When the naturalistic axioms just outlined were proposed, there followed a demand for developing rigorous criteria uniquely suited to the naturalistic approach. Two approaches for dealing with these issues have been followed.

Parallel Criteria of Trustworthiness. The first response (Guba, 1981; Lincoln and Guba, 1985a) was to devise criteria that parallel those of the conventional paradigm: internal validity, external validity, reliability, and objectivity. Given a dearth of knowledge about how to apply rigor in the naturalistic paradigm, using the conventional criteria as analogs or metaphoric counterparts was a possible and useful place to begin. Furthermore, developing such criteria built on the two-hundred-year experience of positivist social science.

These criteria are intended to respond to four basic questions (roughly, those concerned with truth value, applicability, consistency, and neutrality), and they can also be answered within naturalism's bounds, albeit in different terms. Thus, we have suggested credibility as an analog to internal validity, transferability as an analog to external validity, dependability as an analog to reliability, and confirmability as an analog to objectivity. We shall refer to these criteria as criteria of trustworthiness (itself a parallel to the term *rigor*).

Techniques appropriate either to increase the probability that these criteria can be met or to actually test the extent to which they have been met have been reasonably well explicated, most recently in Lincoln and Guba (1985a). They include:

For credibility:

- Prolonged engagement—lengthy and intensive contact with the phenomena (or respondents) in the field to assess possible sources of distortion and especially to identify saliencies in the situation

- Persistent observation—in-depth pursuit of those elements found to be especially salient through prolonged engagement

- Triangulation (cross-checking) of data—by use of different sources, methods, and at times, different investigators

- Peer debriefing—exposing oneself to a disinterested professional peer to "keep the inquirer honest," assist in developing working hypotheses, develop and test the emerging design, and obtain emotional catharsis

- Negative case analysis—the active search for negative instances relating to developing insights and adjusting the latter continuously until no further negative instances are found; assumes an assiduous search

- Member checks—the process of continuous, informal testing of information by soliciting reactions of respondents to the investigator's reconstruction of what he or she has been told or otherwise found out and to the constructions offered by other respondents or sources, and a terminal, formal testing of the final case report with a representative sample of stakeholders.

For transferability:

- Thick descriptive data—narrative developed about the context so that judgments about the degree of fit or similarity may be made by others who may wish to apply all or part of the findings elsewhere (although it is by no means clear how "thick" a thick description needs to be, as Hamilton, personal communication, 1984, has pointed out).

For dependability and confirmability:

- An external audit requiring both the establishment of an audit trail and the carrying out of an audit by a component external, disinterested auditor (the process is described in detail in Lincoln and Guba, 1985a). That part of the audit that examines the process results in a dependability judgment, while that part concerned with the product (data and reconstructions) results in a confirmability judgment.

While much remains to be learned about the feasibility and utility of these parallel criteria, there can be little doubt that they represent a substantial advance in thinking about the rigor issue. Nevertheless, there are some major difficulties with them that call out for their augmentation with new criteria rooted in naturalism rather than simply paralleling those rooted in positivism.

First, the parallel criteria cannot be thought of as a complete set because they deal only with issues that loom important from a positivist construction. The positivist paradigm ignores or fails to take into account precisely those problems that have most plagued evaluation practice since the mid 1960s: multiple value structures, social pluralism, conflict rather than consensus, accountability demands, and the like. Indeed, the conventional criteria refer only to methodology and ignore the influence of context. They are able to do so because by definition conventional inquiry is objective and value-free.

Second, intuitively one suspects that if the positivist paradigm did not exist, other criteria might nevertheless be generated directly from naturalistic assumptions. The philosophical and technical problem might be phrased thus: Given a relativist ontology and an interactive, value-bounded epistemology, what might be the nature of the criteria that ought to characterize a naturalistic inquiry? If we reserve the term *rigor* to refer to positivism's criteria and the term *reliability* to refer to naturalism's parallel criteria, we propose the term *authenticity* to refer to these new, embedded, intrinsic naturalistic criteria.

Unique Criteria of Authenticity. We must at once disclaim having solved this problem. What follows are simply some strong suggestions that appear to be worth following up at this time. One of us (Guba, 1981) referred to the earlier attempt to devise reliability criteria as "primitive"; the present attempt is perhaps even more aboriginal. Neither have we as yet been able to generate distinct techniques to test a given study for adherence to these criteria. The reader should therefore regard our discussion as speculative and, we hope, heuristic. We have been able to develop our idea of the first criterion, fairness, in more detail than the other four; its longer discussion ought not to be understood as meaning, however, that fairness is very much more important than the others.

Fairness. If inquiry is value-bound, and if evaluators confront a situation of value-pluralism, it must be the case that different constructions will emerge from persons and groups with differing value systems. The task of the evaluation team is to expose and explicate these several, possibly conflicting, constructions and value structures (and of course, the evaluators themselves operate from some value framework).

Given all these differing constructions, and the conflicts that will almost certainly be generated from them by virtue of their being rooted in value differences, what can an evaluator do to ensure that they are presented, clarified, and honored in a balanced, even-handed way, a way that the several parties would agree is balanced and even-handed? How do evaluators go about their tasks in such a way that can, while not guaranteeing balance (since nothing can), at least enhance the probability that balance will be well approximated?

If every evaluation or inquiry serves some social agenda (and it invariably does), how can one conduct an evaluation to avoid, at least probabilistically, the possibility that certain values will be diminished (and their holders exploited) while others will be enhanced (and their holders advantaged)? The problem is that of trying to avoid empowering at the expense of impoverishing; all stakeholders should be empowered in some fashion at the conclusion of an evaluation, and all ideologies should have an equal chance of expression in the process of negotiating recommendations.

Fairness may be defined as a balanced view that presents all constructions and the values that undergird them. Achieving fairness may be accomplished by means of a two-part process. The first step in the provision of fairness or justice is the ascertaining and presentation of different value and belief systems represented by conflict over issues. Determination of the actual belief system that undergirds a position on any given issue is not always an easy task, but exploration of values when clear conflict is evident should be part of the data-gathering and data-analysis processes (especially during, for instance, the content analysis of individual interviews).

The second step in achieving the fairness criterion is the negotiation of recommendations and subsequent action, carried out with stakeholding groups or their representatives at the conclusion of the data-gathering, analysis, and interpretation stage of evaluation effort. These three stages are in any event simultaneous and interactive within the naturalistic paradigm. Negotiation has as its basis constant collaboration in the evaluative effort by all stakeholders; this involvement is continuous, fully informed (in the consensual sense), and operates between true peers. The agenda for this negotiation (the logical and inescapable conclusion of a true collaborative evaluation process), having been determined and bounded by all stakeholding groups, must be deliberated and resolved according to rules of fairness. Among the rules that can be specified, the following seem to be absolute minimum.

1. Negotiations must have the following characteristics:

    a. It must be open, that is, carried out in full view of the parties of their representatives with no closed sessions, secret codicils, or the like permitted.

    b. It must be carried out by equally skilled bargainers. In the real world it will almost always be the case that one or another group of bargainers will be the more skillful, but at least each side must have access to bargainers of equal skill, whether they choose to use them or not. In some instances, the evaluator may have to act not only as mediator, but as educator of those less skilled bargaining parties, offering additional advice and counsel that enhances their understanding of broader issues in the process of negotiation. We are aware that this comes close to an advocacy role, but we have already presumed that one task of the evaluator is to empower previously impoverished bargainers; this role should probably not cease at the negotiation stage of the evaluation.

    c. It must be carried out from equal positions of power. The power must be equal not only in principle but also in practice; the power to sue a large corporation in principle is very different from the power to sue it in practice, given the great disparity of resources, risk, and other factors, including, of course, more skillful and resource-heavy bargainers.

   d. It must be carried out under circumstances that allow all sides to possess equally
       complete information. There is no such animal, of course, as "complete informa-
       tion," but each side should have the same information, together with assistance as
       needed to be able to come to an equal understanding of it. Low levels of under-
       standing are tantamount to lack of information.

   e. It must focus on all matters known to be relevant.

   f. It must be carried out in accordance with rules that were themselves the product
       of a negotiation.

2. Fairness requires the availability of appellate mechanisms should one or another
   party believe that the rules are not being observed by some. These mechanisms are
   another of the products of the pre-negotiation process.

3. Fairness requires fully informed consent with respect to any evaluation procedures
   (see Lincoln and Guba, 1985a, and Lincoln and Guba, 1985b). This consent is obtained
   not only prior to an evaluation effort but is continually renegotiated and reaffirmed
   (formally with consent forms and informally through the establishment and maintenance of trust and integrity between parties to the evaluation) as the design unfolds,
   new data are found, new constructions are made, and new contingencies are faced by
   all parties.

4. Finally, fairness requires the constant use of the member-check process, defined
   earlier, which includes calls for comments on fairness, and which is utilized both
   during and after the inquiry process itself (in the data collection-analysis-construc-
   tion stage and later when case studies are being developed). Vigilant and assiduous
   use of member-checking should build confidence in individuals and groups and
   should lead to a pervasive judgment about the extent to which fairness exists.

Fairness as a criterion of adequacy for naturalistic evaluation is less ambiguous than the
following four, and more is known about how to achieve it. It is not that this criterion is more easily
achieved, merely that it has received more attention from a number of scholars (House, 1976;
Lehne, 1978; Strike, 1982, see also Guba and Lincoln, 1985).

Ontological Authentication. If each person's reality is constructed and reconstructed as that
person gains experience, interacts with others, and deals with the consequences of various personal
actions and beliefs, an appropriate criterion to apply is that of improvement in the individual's (and
group's) conscious experiencing of the world. What have sometimes been termed *false consciousness*
(a neo-Marxian term) and *divided consciousness* are part and parcel of this concept. The aim of some
forms of disciplined inquiry, including evaluation (Lincoln and Guba, 1985b) ought to be to raise
consciousness, or to unite divided consciousness, likely via some dialectical process, so that a
person or persons (not to exclude the evaluator) can achieve a more sophisticated and enriched
construction. In some instances, this aim will entail the realization (the "making real") of contextual
shaping that has had the effect of political, cultural, or social impoverishment; in others, it will
simply mean the increased appreciation of some set of complexities previously not appreciated at
all, or appreciated only poorly.

Educative Authentication. It is not enough that the actors in some contexts achieve, individually,
more sophisticated or mature constructions, or those that are more ontologically authentic. It is also
essential that they come to appreciate (apprehend, discern, understand)—not necessarily like or
agree with—the constructions that are made by others and to understand how those constructions
are rooted in the different value systems of those others. In this process, it is not inconceivable that
accommodations, whether political, strategic, value-based, or even just pragmatic, can be forged.
But whether or not that happens is not at issue here; what the criterion of educative validity implies

is increased understanding of (including possibly a sharing, or sympathy with) the whats and whys of various expressed constructions. Each stakeholder in the situation should have the opportunity to become educated about others of different persuasions (values and constructions), and hence to appreciate how different opinions, judgments, and actions are evoked. And among those stakeholders will be the evaluator, not only in the sense that he or she will emerge with "findings," recommendations, and an agenda for negotiation that are professionally interesting and fair but also that he or she will develop a more sophisticated and complex construction (an emic-etic blending) of both personal and professional (disciplinary-substantive) kinds.

How one knows whether or not educative authenticity has been reached by stakeholders is unclear. Indeed, in large-scale, multisite evaluations, it may not be possible for all—or even for more than a few—stakeholders to achieve more sophisticated constructions. But the techniques for ensuring that stakeholders do so even in small-scale evaluations are as yet undeveloped. At a minimum, however, the evaluator's responsibility ought to extend to ensuring that those persons who have been identified during the course of the evaluation as gatekeepers to various constituencies and stakeholding audiences ought to have the opportunity to be "educated" in the variety of perspectives and value systems that exist in a given context.

By virtue of the gatekeeping roles that they already occupy, gatekeepers have influence and access to members of stakeholding audiences. As such, they can act to increase the sophistication of their respective constituencies. The evaluator ought at least to make certain that those from whom he or she originally sought entrance are offered the chance to enhance their own understandings of the groups they represent. Various avenues for reporting (slide shows, filmstrips, oral narratives, and the like) should be explored for their profitability in increasing the consciousness of stakeholders, but at a minimum the stakeholders' representatives and gatekeepers should be involved in the educative process.

Catalytic Authentication. Reaching new constructions, achieving understandings that are enriching, and achieving fairness are still not enough. Inquiry, and evaluations in particular, must also facilitate and stimulate action. This form of authentication is sometimes known as feedback-action validity. It is a criterion that might be applied to conventional inquiries and evaluations as well; although if it were virtually all positivist social action, inquiries and evaluations would fail on it. The call for getting "theory into action"; the preoccupation in recent decades with "dissemination" at the national level; the creation and maintenance of federal laboratories, centers, and dissemination networks; the non-utilization of evaluations; the notable inaction subsequent to evaluations that is virtually a national scandal—all indicate that catalytic authentication has been singularly lacking. The naturalistic posture that involves all stakeholders from the start, that honors their inputs, that provides them with decision-making power in guiding the evaluation, that attempts to empower the powerless and give voice to the speechless, and that results in a collaborative effort holds more promise for eliminating such hoary distinctions as basic versus applied and theory versus practice.

Tactical Authenticity. Stimulation to action via catalytic authentication is in itself no assurance that the action taken will be effective, that is, will result in a desired change (or any change at all). The evaluation of inquiry requires other attributes to serve this latter goal. Chief among these is the matter of whether the evaluation is empowering or impoverishing, and to whom. The first step toward empowerment is taken by providing all persons at risk or with something at stake in the evaluation with the opportunity to control it as well (to move toward creating collaborative negotiation). It provides practice in the use of that power through the negotiation of construction, which is joint emic-etic elaboration. It goes without saying that if respondents are seen simply as "subjects" who must be "manipulated," channeled through "treatments," or even deceived in the interest of some higher "good" or "objective" truth, an evaluation or inquiry cannot possibly have tactical authenticity. Such a posture could only be justified from the bedrock of a realist ontology and an "objective," value-free epistemology.

Summary

All five of these authenticity criteria clearly require more detailed explication. Strategies or techniques for meeting and ensuring them largely remain to be devised. Nevertheless, they represent an attempt to meet a number of criticisms and problems associated with evaluation in general and naturalistic evaluation in particular. First, they address issues that have pervaded evaluation for two decades. As attempts to meet these enduring problems, they appear to be as useful as anything that has heretofore been suggested (in any formal or public sense).

Second, they are responsive to the demand that naturalistic inquiry or evaluation not rely simply on parallel technical criteria for ensuring reliability. While the set of additional authenticity criteria might not be the complete set, it does represent what might grow from naturalistic inquiry were one to ignore (or pretend not to know about) criteria based on the conventional paradigm. In that sense, authenticity criteria are part of an inductive, grounded, and creative process that springs from immersion with naturalistic ontology, epistemology, and methodology (and the concomitant attempts to put those axioms and procedures into practice).

Third, and finally, the criteria are suggestive of the ways in which new criteria might be developed; that is, they are addressed largely to ethical and ideological problems, problems that increasingly concern those involved in social action and in the schooling process. In that sense, they are confluent with an increasing awareness of the ideology-boundedness of public life and the enculturation processes that serve to empower some social groups and classes and to impoverish others. Thus, while at first appearing to be radical, they are nevertheless becoming mainstream. An invitation to join the fray is most cheerfully extended to all comers.

References

Guba, E. G. "Criteria for Assessing the Trustworthiness of Naturalistic Inquiries." *Educational Communication and Technology Journal*, 1981, 29, 75–91.

Guba, E. G., and Lincoln, Y. S. "Do Inquiry Paradigms Imply Inquiry Methodologies?" In D. L. Fetterman (Ed.), *The Silent Scientific Revolution*. Beverly Hills, Calif.: Sage, in press.

Guba, E. G., and Lincoln, Y. S. *Effective Evaluation: Improving the Usefulness of Evaluation Results Through Responsive and Naturalistic Approaches*. San Francisco: Jossey-Bass, 1981.

Guba, E. G., and Lincoln, Y. S. "The Countenances of Fourth Generation Evaluation: Description, Judgment, and Negotiation." Paper presented at Evaluation Network annual meeting, Toronto, Canada, 1985.

House, E. R. "Justice in Evaluation." In G. V. Glass (Ed.), *Evaluation Studies Review Annual, no. 1*. Beverly Hills, Calif.: Sage, 1976.

Lehne, R. *The Quest for Justice: The Politics of School Finance Reform*. New York: Longman, 1978.

Lincoln, Y. S., and Guba, E. G. *Naturalistic Inquiry*. Beverly Hills, Calif.: Sage, 1985a.

Lincoln, Y. S., and Guba, E. G. "Ethics and Naturalistic Inquiry." Unpublished manuscript, University of Kansas, 1985b.

Morgan, G. *Beyond Method: Strategies for Social Research*. Beverly Hills, Calif.: Sage, 1983.

Strike, K. *Educational Policy and the Just Society*. Champaign: University of Illinois Press, 1982.

Designing a College Assessment

Jason Millman

This paper addresses nine questions that should be asked and at least nine decisions that should take place when designing, using, and evaluating college assessment instruments that measure student knowledge, skills, attitudes, and interests.[1] I do not identify all decisions (e.g., assignment of responsibility) here, but emphasize those most directly affecting the technical quality of the enterprise. Subsequent essays in this volume will cover the assessment of specific areas of knowledge, skills and attitudes and will provide examples of instruments and suggestions for their use. Still other essays will identify special issues and new approaches. But this paper will provide the terminology, concepts and framework in which to place the more specific ideas and exemplars offered later in this volume.

This paper discusses each decision, beginning with determining the purpose of the assessment. I place purpose first because the optimal design of an assessment follows the function it serves. In each of the subsequent sections, I introduce the key decision, discuss related concepts and issues, and indicate how the decision should be applied within each of four purposes of assessment: placement, certification, course/program evaluation, and institutional evaluation.

Purposes of a College Assessment

The usual purpose of a college assessment is to make an inference on the basis of students' performance.[2] The inference can be directed to three domains. The educator might want to say something about competence with respect to what is intended to be taught (the curricular domain), about the students' level on some more general ability or trait (the cognitive domain), or about expected performance or behavior in some other situation (a future criterion setting). When inferences are to the curricular domain, they might occur before, during or after instruction. These domains of inference are identified in Figure 1.

The other dimension portrayed in Figure 1 is the subject of the inference: an individual student or a group of students. It is in part because purposes differ both in the domain of inference and in focus on individual or group performance that the assessment effort proceeds differently in each case. The four purposes listed inside the rectangles are the ones emphasized in this essay.

Purpose 1: Placement

A placement decision occurs when a student is assigned to one of two or more educational categories. Examples of placement decisions include assignment to remedial programs, honors programs, or levels of instruction in such disciplines as foreign language or mathematics.

Figure 1
Purposes of College Assessment of Student Outcomes

Domain to Which Inferences Will be Made

Subject of the Inference	Curricular Domain			Cognitive Domain	Future Criterion Setting
	Before Instruction	During Instruction	After Instruction		
Individual	Placement	Diagnosis	Grading and Promotion	Certification	Vocational Counseling
Group		Course and Program Evaluation			
				Evaluation of the Institution	

Two placement situations are worth distinguishing. In a quota situation, the number or proportion of students who can be placed into, or selected for, one or more of the courses or programs is fixed. An honors program that is limited to 60 students is a quota situation. In a quota-free situation, any number of students can be assigned to any given course or program. For example, if it is the case that no student need be assigned to the remedial program if all demonstrate the requisite skills, then a quota-free situation is in effect. In practice a mixture of both situations is usually present.

Purpose 2: Certification

When an institution certifies a student, it stands behind the claim that the student has the competence implied by the certification award. An academic skills test required to proceed to the junior year and a graduation test are examples of assessment instruments for certification. Some certifications, for example, those enabling a student to obtain a temporary teaching license, are based on assessments more diverse than a single examination.

Assessing for certification has much in common with placement testing, since each involves pass-fail decisions about individuals. In contrast to a placement examination, in a certification assessment inferences are directed to a cognitive domain rather than to a single knowledge domain; the institution and the students have a greater stake in the decision; the institution has the obligation to give the students an opportunity to acquire the competencies being assessed; and the students typically have several opportunities to achieve certification.

Purpose 3: Course and Program Evaluation

When the purpose of assessment is to reach a judgment of merit about the course or program itself, not every student needs to be assessed in the same way or even assessed at all. The course or program, not the student (or the instructor)[3], is the principal focus.

Evaluating a course or program typically includes obtaining evidence of students' performance with respect to the curriculum. It can also include information about students' abilities and opinions, hence the rectangle in Figure 1 extends under the column, "cognitive domain," to suggest this broader range to which inferences will be directed. The dotted section of the rectangle indicates that course or program evaluation that takes place during instruction (presumably to improve instruction through mid-course corrections and refinements) will not be emphasized here, as that function is typically reserved for a single or small group of instructors concerned with a specific course.

Purpose 4: Evaluation of the Institution

Although a frequent reason for assessments is to meet state-mandated accountability requirements, a more immediate reason is to judge how the institution is doing with respect to student learning outcomes. While some may be used in placement and certification decisions concerning individuals, the instruments employed in producing data to assess institutional effectiveness include college and university admissions tests, rising junior examinations, college level skill examinations, general education outcome measures, student attitude and opinion surveys, and exit examinations. Performance on these examinations at two points in time is sometimes assessed to obtain a value-added indicator.

Like the certification function but unlike program evaluation, institutional assessment employs measures that reference primarily a cognitive domain. Like program evaluation but unlike certification, institutional evaluation focuses on groups of students rather than on individual students. The dotted portion of the rectangle in Figure 1 for institutional assessment indicates that discussion of long-term outcomes of higher education is excluded from this volume.

Can an assessment procedure designed for one purpose work for another? Sometimes it can, but rarely is one instrument or design optimum for several purposes. If too many students are tested, the assessment is no longer efficient. If the wrong skills or too narrow a set of skills are measured, the assessment is no longer valid. The educator who wishes one procedure to suffice for more than one purpose can expect to be frustrated since the responses at the decision points in the design of a college assessment differ for each purpose.

What Content Will be Included in the Instrument?

The content of an instrument consists simply of the questions asked, the statements posed, or the performances elicited. The content of the assessment instrument determines the information that it can generate. For this reason, the decision about what to include is extremely important.

Concepts and Issues

No consensus exists regarding the best way to taxonomize content. A useful distinction can be made between knowing, doing, and believing. The modal assessment methods, correspondingly, are conventional tests (recognition items), performance measures (observing a process and rating a product), and self-reported interest and attitude questions. Controversy most often arises over whether to spend the time and money to assess performance. Performance assessment is practically a requirement in some fields, performing and studio arts being clear cases. But in many other fields, a harder choice exists between measuring what a person knows versus what a person can do.[4]

Content is popularly divided into basic skills, subject matter, general education, and higher-level thinking skills. Because these categories overlap, and because general education is particularly vague, I find it more descriptive to place cognitive measures with respect to content on three different continua. One is lower- to higher-level thinking skills, where the former consists of measures of recall and the latter of measures of critical and analytical thinking, ability to apply principles, and the like. A second continuum is the degree to which students entering at the institution should be expected to know the content or to demonstrate the skill.[5] The third continuum is subject-matter specific to subject-matter general, where the former consists of content specific to a given discipline and the latter of content that crosses disciplines, such as reading comprehension ability.[6]

Keep in mind that the purpose of an assessment instrument is to make an inference based on students' performance. Another scheme for categorizing content is according to how closely the assessment content mirrors the knowledge, skill or trait being inferred. Most achievement tests are direct measures of the desired knowledge and would be classified as low-inference measures. Student enrollment data would be a high-inference measure of course effectiveness, since many factors determine enrollments. The Mosaic Comparisons Test, in which students are asked to identify differences in paired mosaic patterns, is an indirect, hence high-inference indicator of "suitability for certain careers in business."[7]

Other content-related questions that should be asked of a contemplated assessment include: How detailed should the definition of the domain of interest be?[8] How difficult should the knowledge questions be?[9] Should any aspect of that domain receive special emphasis? How broad should the assessment be? (E.g., Should untaught subject matter be included? Should measures of unintended outcomes be developed?) The reason to ask such questions is that if one is too narrow in coverage, what one learns from an assessment enterprise is limited.

Let us examine the form these content issues and questions take under each of the four purposes of assessment. That is, given a specific purpose for an assessment, what special considerations concerning content issues should be considered?

Purpose 1: Placement. Two views about the appropriate information for a placement decision dominate practice. One emphasizes previous courses taken and credits earned; the other emphasizes knowledge and skills that can be displayed. I favor the latter, and recommend that placement decisions be based on the tested level of knowledge and skills of the student, not on high inference proxy measures.

In the quota-free situation, the domain of content should be quite narrow and focus upon that body of knowledge and skills most apt to differentiate among students at the borderline between placement categories. It is sometimes helpful to consider the examination questions answered correctly by students who barely qualify for the more advanced course or program and incorrectly by students who do not qualify. Alternatively, one can consider those students who barely miss qualifying for the more advanced course or program and analyze their responses. In short, the placement examination in the quota-free situation should concentrate at that level of functioning near the borderline between categories.

In the quota situation, the function of assessment is to identify the highest "X" number of qualifying students, where X is a value determined before the assessment begins. If X is a small fraction of the students, then the questions or tasks should be somewhat difficult so that it will be possible to differentiate reliably among the able students. Similarly, if X is a large fraction of the students, then the questions or tasks should be somewhat easy.

Purpose 2: Certification. Regardless of what competencies are being certified, be they academic skills, thinking abilities, or knowing and being able to do what an educated person knows and can do, the competencies should be clearly defined. Students have a right to know what is required of them—not the specific examination questions, but the domain of coverage. Further, clear definition of the content will assist the institution in designing instruction to fulfill its obligation to provide students with the opportunity to acquire the competencies. And the competencies measured by the assessment instruments ought to be worth acquiring.

In determining the domain of coverage, faculty must be sensitive to the diversity of programs in their institution. Knowledge and skills required of all students seeking the same certification, regardless of their differing educational goals, should not be chosen lightly.

Purpose 3: Course and Program Evaluation. A broad range of content can, and probably should, be covered. For example, it is not necessary to limit the measurement of student achievement to a narrow interpretation of subject matter taught. Questions can be posed differently than presented in the textbook or class. Questions can probe whether students are able to transfer what they have learned to situations not covered in the course materials. Unanticipated outcomes or side effects should also be probed. What misconceptions emerge? What new attitudes have been developed? What effects have the course or program had on the students' general abilities? How, if at all, has the course or program changed students' feelings about themselves, about the institution, and about issues related to the subject matter?

The evaluation designers would do well to begin by asking a small group of students and interested others to share their perceptions of the course or program. These perceptions form the grounds for some of the items in the assessment instruments. College students are an excellent source of information about a course or program, as they are first-hand witnesses to the instruction, facilities and materials for an extended period of time. Nevertheless, a more thorough evaluation would include other sources of information than that obtained from tests, surveys, and academic products.[10]

Purpose 4: Evaluation of the Institution. One focus of the debate over the evaluation of the academic effectiveness of colleges and universities is on the content of assessment measures. Should they

> emphasize the acquisition of facts and the mastery of simple skills. . . . [or] how clearly students think about issues of social justice, how deeply they can appreciate a painting or a literary text, how much they have gained in intellectual curiosity, how far they have come in understanding their own capacities and limitations?[11]

The choice of content for the evaluation of the institution says much about the institution's view of its educational mission.

It is not enough to provide a general label for content. The domain must be clearly specified not only so valid measures can be constructed to reflect the desired outcomes, but to guide curricula and instruction. Students typically do not grow into renaissance people, lustful for learning and sparkling in curiosity, without assistance. Promoting growth requires a clear sense of direction.

It may be tempting to let a convenient, commercially available instrument or an examination now in use at the institution, such as a general education examination, serve as the principal instrument to evaluate the institution. But educators need to ask whether these devices both capture the richness of the educational outcomes desired for students and yield data that can inform the evolution of academic programs.

Will the Instruments Be Developed Locally or Obtained from Another Source?

College administrators and faculty have a choice of whether or not to construct their own assessment instruments. If the decision is to look elsewhere for an instrument, several options are available. One is to purchase an off-the-shelf instrument from a commercial publisher. A similar option is to secure permission to use an instrument developed by a state agency or another college. A third option is to engage the services of a test-development firm or consultant, either inside or outside the institution, to build an instrument to the institution's specifications. Still another option is to work with other institutions to build, jointly, the desired instrument.

Concepts and Issues

Availability, quality, cost, and sense of ownership are four factors that influence the decision whether to develop one's own instrument or obtain it from another source.

Availability means finding an existing instrument that matches the content coverage desired by the institution. Existing instruments are identified in several sources. A bibliography of assessment instruments appropriate for college assessments is available from the University of Tennessee.[12] A more extensive list of tests as well as test critiques are available both in hard copy and on-line computer from the Buros Institute.[13] The Test Corporation of America also offers lists of tests and test critiques.[14] There is even a bibliography of test bibliographies.[15] Even if the decision is to develop the instrument locally, evaluating existing instruments can broaden one's perspective of a domain and how to measure it. For a modest fee, most companies will send prospective users a specimen set that contains a copy of the test together with related material. Some tests are kept secure, however, thus denying educators an opportunity to compare the items on the test against the qualities the institution wants to measure before purchasing rights to the instrument.

A second consideration is quality. Criteria of quality include validity, freedom from bias, and reliability, all of which are discussed later in this essay. A match between the content of the instrument and the content desired is extremely important. Educators should not assume that because an instrument is published, it is of high quality. On the other hand, local educators often have neither the time nor the expertise to write, edit and try out an instrument to the degree commercial publishers do.

An important consideration is the relative cost of purchasing existing instruments versus developing one's own. Exceptions exist, but if the time of faculty/staff and other opportunity costs are factored in, using existing instruments is less expensive. Instrument development is a demanding, time-consuming activity. Noting the approach and items used in existing instruments, however, can make a local development effort more efficient.

Developing one's own instrument, while sometimes difficult, is nonetheless attractive, particularly if resistance to the assessment is anticipated. A sense of ownership and acceptance of the assessment is more likely for a home-grown than for an imported product. The process of creating an examination can have a greater effect on an institution than the examination itself.

Two other factors sometimes considered in this decision are credibility and availability of norms. Some publics consider externally constructed instruments more credible than locally developed ones. The credibility (but not the validity for the institution) rises if the instrument or the publisher is well know. Availability of results from comparison groups (i.e., norms) is considered by some to be a strong reason for purchasing an existing instrument. This advantage may be illusory because the norm groups are usually ill-defined, thus not interpretable, and because normative information is not particularly valuable for most assessment purposes.

If the instrument is to be used for placement or certification decisions, it must be related to instruction, and thus faculty involvement in the decision is important. For these assessment purposes, the decision to purchase a test or construct one's own should depend heavily on the availability of instruments that match the instruction. Fortunately, a number of examinations in basic skills and college subjects are available for purchase. On the other hand, they are also easier to construct locally than instruments that measure harder-to-define domains such as critical thinking, creativity, or aesthetic sensibility.

For course and program evaluation, locally produced instruments will likely be needed to attend to specific concerns about the course or program being evaluated. Such instruments might supplement one or more commercially available ones. For course, program or institutional evaluation, wide faculty and student participation in either constructing or selecting an instrument is important. Since any evaluation (especially an evaluation of the value of the college or university experience) benefits from multiple measurements, it may be that a combination of commercially available and locally developed instruments will work best.

How Will the Data Be Collected?

The general question is, Who will be administered what instruments or questions and how? The "who" and "what" part of the question leads to a consideration of sampling. The "how" part includes questions of student motivation and preparation and test administration.

Concepts and Issues

Sampling. One part of the sampling question is simply a concern about who should be included in the assessment. Sometimes the appropriate group of students is obvious; other times it is not so clear. Will part-time and transfer students be included? Should any subgroups of students be treated differently? The decision about who is to participate will determine the student population to which the results can be generalized. To increase the interpretability of the results, assessment specialists recommend that the rules for inclusion and exclusion be clear and objective.

Another aspect of the sampling question is how many students (in the specified population or group of students) should be included? One answer is to include all the students, perhaps because it is thought to be too much trouble to do otherwise or perhaps because results based on a sample are less credible in the eyes of some people. A different answer is to recognize that random or representative samples can be cost efficient and that an appropriate sample size is the number of students that will produce the degree of precision desired by the user. Random samples of 100 students can yield estimates with a margin of error of 10 percent or less. Quadruple the sample size and the margin of error is cut in half, so that if n=400, the margin of error is 5 percent or less. In reverse, reducing the sample to one-fourth its original size will only double the margin of error. If the margin of error is small to begin with, the loss in precision of estimates by reducing the sample size can be tolerated. The decision to sample only some students saves money at the expense of precision—although precision may be only marginally affected if the sample is large and representative.

An important (though often neglected) aspect of the sampling question is what instruments or questions should be sampled? It may not be necessary for everyone to be exposed to the same assessment device. For some purposes, some students can be administered part of the assessment instruments and other students a different part. This scheme is called "matrix sampling" because a matrix of students and assessment items are sampled. For example, a 120-item survey could be divided into four forms of 30 items each. One-fourth of the students in the sample might be asked to answer each of the forms. Matrix sampling has the advantage of covering the domains of inference more broadly than possible if every student responds to the same, more restricted set of questions. The decision to use matrix sampling increases the scope of the assessment at the expense of precision of any one estimate. In the above example, the scope is increased four-fold and the margin of error associated with any one item is doubled.

Student Motivation and Preparation. Identifying the students is one activity; convincing them to submit to an assessment is another. And motivating them to do their best is yet another. Success in these activities is important if the assessment is to be valid. Experience in the context of certification examinations has clearly demonstrated that adults perform markedly poorer when little is at stake than when an important decision depends upon their performance.

One educator in charge of a college assessment program said to me, "If I had to do it over, I'd have started with the students rather than with the faculty." The suggestion is not only to involve the faculty, but the students as well. Having students and faculty help design the assessment, construct or select the instruments, and even take the tests and surveys is one way to increase participation and motivation. Using tasks that make students think, that offer feedback, or that promise changes is another way. Harvard University had excellent participation from its students in a survey when they were given immediate feedback about their responses and, a short time later, comparative information about other students.[16] Another option is paying students when participation in the assessment is of no obvious benefit to them, but this strategy will likely work only for "one-shot" ad hoc evaluations.

Optimum performance on achievement and aptitude measures is clearly a goal of an assessment program. Valid assessment of student knowledge and skills requires not only motivated students, but students who are appropriately prepared for the assessment tasks. For most assessment applications, students should be informed ahead of time about the general areas being measured (not the specific test questions) and given practice with unusual question formats. If, after a little instruction and practice, students can greatly improve their performance on a particular assessment task, then assessing this enhanced performance is usually more meaningful than assessing their initial level of performance.

Instrument Administration and Security. Assessment will be used to make comparisons. Results will be compared to standards or to the performance of different groups or at different times. For these comparisons to be valid, standard administration practices have to be followed. If more time is given one group than another, if more help is offered one time than another, or if testing conditions on one occasion are noticeably different than on another, the comparative data are contaminated.

Test compromise (i.e., cheating) also invalidates assessment results. Especially in high-stake situations, students' methods of gaining illegitimate help on an assessment exercise are often quite sophisticated. At one extreme, some test sponsors never use a particular instrument more than once, believing that it is impossible to secure the questions. At the least, instruments intended for multiple administrations should be carefully inventoried and kept under surveillance. Physical separation of students at the assessment site and use of multiple assessment forms lessen the risk of test compromise.

Special populations, such as linguistic minorities and the physically handicapped, require special attention. There are published professional standards for testing such groups,[17] and the concluding essay to this volume offers additional guidance.

These data collection issues require different emphases under each of the previously described four purposes of assessment:

Purposes 1 and 2: Placement and Certification. In any given context, the identity of the students who should be administered a placement or certification examination will be obvious. No sampling of students is involved, since all students for whom a placement or certification decision is required should take the examination.

It is important that students do their best so that the decision will be based on knowledge of their true abilities. Motivation is important. These considerations suggest the advisability of distributing advance information about the content and importance of the examination. In particular, topics that can be quickly learned or reviewed should be brought to the attention of students.

Examination administration conditions should be constant, so that the cutscore (passing score) value has constant meaning across administration sites. Adaptive testing approaches (see Grandy's essay on "Computer-Based Testing," below) in which students are administered items close in difficulty to their own level of functioning, have no advantage in the typical quota-free, two-category placement setting or the typical pass/no pass certification situation. Especially since placement and certification decisions can be important to students, guarding against prior circulation of the examination and other instances of test compromise is warranted.

When the purpose of assessment is certification, students should have more than one opportunity to demonstrate competency. The individual stakes are too great for the decision to rest on a single administration of a single, less-than-perfect instrument. Providing students an opportunity to take the examination a year or even more before the deadline date is not unusual.

Purposes 3 and 4: Course Program, and Institutional Evaluation. In these applications, as previously noted, the performance of individual students is not being compared and the content or domain coverage is broad. Matrix sampling is optimum under these conditions. Allocating different assessment measures to different students permits the evaluator to learn much about the course or program while limiting the burden on any one student.

A possible exception occurs when results are to be disaggregated into units (i.e., courses or departments) having relatively few students. That is, if precise information is wanted about a course with a small enrollment (e.g., 35), essentially all students should participate. Matrix sampling will work well, however, in a department with 300 majors.

A special student sampling concern arises when the evaluation follows the value-added model. In the value-added approach to assessment, effectiveness is measured by the difference in performance of beginning and graduating students. The strongest design compares the results on a constant set of instruments administered to the same group of students when they entered and left the program or institution. Often, however, it is not feasible to assess the same students at two different points in time. A common but flawed approach is to compare unselected groups of beginning and graduating students. These groups are not comparable. Even in the absence of any program or institutional effect, graduating students could be expected to be more able on the average than entering students (a group including many who will drop out). Another common approach is to use ACT or SAT admissions test results to predict what graduating students would have scored on the assessment instrument as beginning students. This estimate is taken as the base from which the value added is computed. In my view, a better approach is to construct a sample of entering students who match the graduating group as closely as possible on indicators of ability or predictors of success, such as admission test scores, high school grades, college major, gender, race, and even initial grades in the college.

Because little is at stake for individual students in a course, program, or institutional evaluation, motivating them to participate and do well can be a particular problem, while providing practice opportunities and assuring test security are likely to be of relatively little concern. Efforts are clearly called for to raise the level of seriousness with which the assessment exercises are taken.

Following rather rigid, formal administration procedures is advisable if the results for different groups will be compared or if the assessment will be replicated in the future. If, however, the purpose of the assessment is open-ended, designed more to generate ideas than to confirm hypotheses, a more informal administration of the instruments is reasonable.

What Additional Instrument-Development Efforts Will Be Needed?

Three activities that are desirable in certain assessment contexts are selecting or constructing additional forms of the instrument, equating forms, and establishing passing scores. The associated questions are: Is more than one form of the instrument needed? If so, Should the forms be equated? and, if so, How? Is a cutscore required? and if so, How will it be set?

Concepts and Issues

Multiple Forms. Multiple forms of an assessment instrument are particularly desirable if any of three conditions exist. The first is when the instrument cannot be kept secure, a condition that exists when a great deal hinges on the outcome. The second is when the goal of the assessment is to measure change and the questions are such that previous exposure to the same items (rather than improvement in knowledge, skills or ability) will lead to improved performance. A third condition occurs when the content of an instrument is no longer current or is judged less representative of a domain due to changes in the curriculum.

Equating. Two instruments are equated if, on the average, it doesn't matter which one is administered. No two instruments can be exactly the same in difficulty, but it is possible to adjust scoring so that, on average, students will not receive higher or lower scores on one form compared to another. If performances (of the same or of different students) on two or more forms of an instrument are to be compared, they should be equated. Otherwise, these differences might be due to the instrument rather than to the underlying ability.[18]

Cutscores. Cutscores are needed if decisions about students depend upon their performance. An exception occurs if a decision is based on several factors and no minimal level of performance on the instrument is required. Many methods of setting a cutscore have been suggested.[19] The most favored are those methods that depend upon judgments by experts who are informed by data about student performance. Although the standard-setting process need not be arbitrary, it does require judgment.

Because no measure is infallible, errors will occur regardless of where the cutscore is placed or how it is established. Students who deserve to pass may be failed (false negatives) and students who deserve to fail may be passed (false positives). Educators in the position of having to make pass-no pass (or select-not select) decisions about students, and who believe that in their situation it is more important to avoid false negatives than false positives, will want a low cutscore so that anyone who fails clearly does not possess the required level proficiency. On the other hand, educators who believe that in their situation it is more important not to pass anyone who might not possess the required level of proficiency, will establish a high cutscore. Although errors of classification cannot be eliminated, they can be reduced with more valid and reliable instruments, and the ratio of false negative or false positive errors can be controlled by where the cutscore is placed.

It is almost always the case that differential passing rates will result for identifiable groups, such as black and white or male and female. The group with the lower passing rate is said to be adversely impacted by the test. The extent of the adverse impact of an examination depends heavily on the cutscore. No adverse impact would result if the cutscore is so low that everyone is placed in the more advanced course or program or meets the certification requirement, or if the cutscore is so high that no one passes. On the other hand, if the cutscore corresponds to a score midway between the averages of the two groups, adverse impact would likely be very high.

How do these three issues play out under each of the four purposes of assessment?

Purposes 1 and 2: Placement and Certification. The need for multiple forms typically differs for these two assessment purposes. Placement examinations are often given only once to any individual, and often the educator can maintain security of the instrument. This is especially true if the examinees have recently been admitted to the college. Thus, one form of the test may be sufficient and, since only one form is used, equating is not necessary. If the assessments result in placement in remedial courses for which post-tests are used, then obviously more than one form of the tests should be developed and equated.

More than one form of the assessment instrument is strongly suggested in the certification context. Since each student may be given more than one chance to pass the examination, multiple forms mean that the student can be administered different questions on each testing occasion, thus providing some assurance that the test measures the competency intended rather than the ability to learn the answers to one set of questions. Also, security is increased with multiple forms. These forms should be equated in difficulty so that a students' chances of achieving certification do not depend upon which form was administered. Equating test forms thereby ensures a common passing standard.

Cutscores are required for placement and certification purposes because decisions rest on the examination results. The location of the cutscore affects the adverse impact of the assessment, the passing percentage, and the relative mix of false positives and false negatives. Cutscores should therefore be set thoughtfully. Once set and used, instructors can be asked how many of their students, in their judgment, were incorrectly placed or certified. For example, if a much larger than usual number of students in an advanced course or program are so identified, then that would be evidence that the cutscore on the placement examination might be too low. Similarly, if many more students than usual are judged misplaced in a less advanced course or program, that would be evidence that the cutscore might be lowered.

The relative values placed on avoiding false negatives and false positives will help determine the cutscore. If one type of misclassification error is considered more serious than another, the cutscore should be raised or lowered accordingly. In the certification context, the institution has some stake in avoiding false positives, and students may have more than one opportunity to take the examination. For these reasons, the cutscore on a certification examination might be set a shade higher than otherwise.

One variation on the sharp cutscore approach, in which those who score above it are treated differently than those who score below it, is to establish an uncertainty band on either side of the cutscore. Falling in the uncertainty band could trigger the gathering of additional assessment data before a decision is made. In the placement situation, students who fall in that band can be given a choice of course or program.

Purpose 3 and 4: Course, Program and Institutional Evaluation. Test security is relatively less important for these assessment uses, so only one form of the assessment instruments is needed. Even if a value-added assessment is conducted, it is likely that a sufficient time period will elapse between assessments so that administering the same form of the instrument will be of little consequence. If only one form is employed, equating procedures are not applicable. Finally, cutscores are not required because no decisions about individuals are involved.

How Will Bias Be Detected and Minimized?

Instrument bias is a major concern of many groups in our society, and emotions and preconceptions are strongly rooted. Bias is a source of invalidity. It is important to be clear about what is meant by bias and how to identify and eliminate it from our assessments.

Concepts and Issues

In a rational discussion of bias, three distinctions are helpful to keep in mind. The first distinction is between instrument bias and adverse impact. One racial, gender, or other group may be adversely affected by the assessment. It may score appreciably lower, and thereby be denied opportunities given to those who score higher. Quite often black and Hispanic students score much lower on achievement and aptitude tests than do white students, and for some tasks, women score noticeably lower than men. As a result, these groups may receive fewer scholarships, be placed more often in remedial courses, and the like. Such impact, however, does not mean the instrument is biased. It could be that the adversely impacted groups truly do achieve less in the terms measured by the instrument. Years of educational deficit or other social differences between the groups may have taken its toll on the present knowledge and skills of its members. Because a thermometer records different temperatures in two rooms of a house does not mean the thermometer is biased.

The second distinction is between instrument bias and unfair use. An instrument may be a near-perfect measure of what it is supposed to measure, but nevertheless be used inappropriately. As Appelbaum notes in his essay on basic skills assessment in mathematics in this volume, using the SAT/Quantitative (a perfectly valid measure of learned abilities) to place students into remedial courses is inappropriate, in part, because it would be unfair to students whose general quantitative reasoning abilities are low, but who nevertheless had previously learned the specific content of such courses. Instrument bias is assessed by considering the evidence for the validity of the inferences or uses to which it is put, or by judging the bias of the items that compose the instrument.

Item bias versus instrument bias is the third distinction. Most of the techniques for judging bias are attempts to identify biased items. If the items are found to be unbiased, then the instrument as a whole is considered unbiased. Two broad categories of techniques for detecting item bias are in use.[20] The first category consists of methods by which appropriate groups of raters consider whether the content of the items reflect bias. In addition to judging whether all groups have equal familiarity or experience with the particular examples and language included in the items, the raters often are asked to identify items with stereotypical or offensive content. It is advisable to include among the raters representatives of black, Hispanic, female or any other group likely to be adversely impacted, particularly if the purpose of assessment is certification.

Statistical methods of detecting bias in items that have right and wrong answers is the other category of techniques for detecting item bias. In the methods in this category, the responses of students who are from different gender, racial or cultural groups and who are considered equal in ability are compared. In one method, for example, students receiving the same score on the entire examination are assumed to be equal in ability. If the members of one group consistently miss an item proportionately more often than the members of a second group having the same total examination score, the item is considered biased. For results to be reliable, statistical techniques of bias detection require 200 or more students in each of the groups being compared (if necessary, this number can be achieved by aggregating data from previous years, provided that the same instrument was used). When both categories of methods are applied to the same instrument, they often identify different items as biased. When the purpose of the assessment is certification, the use of statistical indicators of bias is feasible since relatively large numbers of students are involved in the assessment. But it is probably best to think of the statistical results as a supplement to, rather than a substitute for, the judgments of educators.

In the cases of course, program, and institutional evaluation, instrument bias is less of a concern because the evaluations have little immediate effect on students. Bias in the design and implementation of a course or program itself is more apt to be a concern, and data that address this concern might well be built into the evaluation plan.

It may be that the results of an evaluation of the institution will be used to judge the institution unfairly, which happens when the capabilities of entering students are not considered in judging student outcomes. It may also be that some educational segment of the institution will be adversely affected by the evaluation because the educational goals of that segment are not sufficiently represented in the student outcome measures being employed. This possibility underscores the desirability of having a broad representation of the institution serve on an assessment development committee.

How Will the Validity of the Assessment Instruments Be Determined?

The most important characteristic of a college assessment is the correctness—that is, validity—of the descriptions and decisions that emerge from it. Correspondingly important are decisions about how faculty will determine the validity of their assessment instruments and methods.[21]

Concepts and Issues

Technically, it is the inference from the instrument and not the instrument itself that is valid. For example, a test may measure basic skills very well. Thus, the inference about basic skills is valid; the inference about general education knowledge is not valid.

The first step in validation is to determine exactly what inferences are desired—what curricular domain, cognitive ability, or criterion behavior is targeted (see Figure 1). The remaining steps consist of gathering evidence that is credible to others and that addresses the accuracy of the inference. Establishing validity is like performing research. The hypothesis is that a given inference is correct, and the effort is to marshal evidence in support of or against that hypothesis.

The evidence that will be credible and relevant depends upon the inference. For example, when the inference is to a curricular domain, properly collected judgments from respected and knowledgeable individuals about the appropriateness of the assessment instrument's content can be persuasive. To take another example, if the results of a placement test are used to place individuals into one of two levels of Spanish, then the validity of the inferences would be supported by evidence that the individuals in the first course were appropriately challenged and those in the second course performed well.

Evidence that will be credible and relevant also depends upon the concerns that have been expressed about the assessment. For example, if the instrument is viewed by some to contain irrelevant content, or to have been administered inappropriately, or to favor one group over another, then information that addresses these concerns should be gathered. Test and item bias are sources of invalidity.

Under each of the four purposes of college assessments, different kinds of validity evidence are important:

Purpose 1: Placement. Two types of validity evidence are particularly relevant for placement examinations, namely, faculty judgments and student performance. Faculty knowledgeable about the subject can examine the congruence between the items on the examination and the skills and knowledge needed to perform in the more advanced course or program. They might be asked the specific question, Do the items measure the prerequisite knowledge and skills? Instructors in the course or program could be asked whether students in the more advanced course or program are sufficiently prepared or whether students in the less advanced course or program appropriately placed?

As for student performance, a high correlation between actual grades in the more advanced course and placement test scores would provide additional evidence for the validity of the placement decisions.

Purpose 2: Certification. Two types of evidence are particularly appropriate for competency examinations. One, content validity, would be revealed by the judgments of a heterogeneous set of faculty that the questions on the examination both match the abilities defined by the domain and are a representative sample of them. A clear definition of the domain is helpful in this task. For example, if a test claims to measure a learned ability such as "solving problems,"[22] then the judgment task is greatly assisted if the types of problems a person with the ability is expected to solve are identified in detail.

A second type of evidence is curricular or instructional validity, i.e. documentation that students had an opportunity to acquire the skills measured by the assessment instrument. Note that the issue is not whether the students actually have acquired the skills, but whether courses or materials were available from which the skills could have been acquired. The courts have held that at the high school level at least, curricular or instructional validity is required for tests used as a requirement for graduation.[23]

College educators should avoid the trap of claiming that specific competencies or knowledge are required for success after college. Success depends upon many factors; academic and related skills is but one configuration of factors. For that reason, finding a high correlation between performance on a certification instrument and future success is very unlikely.

Purpose 3: Course and Program Evaluation. In these applications, we want to know not only whether the assessment instruments are valid, but also whether the evaluation itself is valid. In the case of instruments, we can check whether our inferences about students' subject matter knowledge or attitudes and opinions are correct. A number of techniques have been developed to assist in these validation tasks (see end note 21). For example, if all the items on an assessment measure the same attitude, students who answer an item in a positive direction should be expected to answer the other items in the same direction.

Student response data, by themselves, are insufficient to answer the second question, How valid are the judgments of merit of the course or program? A sound evaluation of a course or program requires additional survey and analysis data that attend to such questions as the need, intrinsic value, relative value, use, costs (direct and opportunity) and future potential for the course or program.[24]

Purpose 4: Evaluation of the Institution. In this application, the validity questions are whether an instrument accurately measures the intended ability or attitude and whether a valid evaluation of the institution was conducted. The first asks if the assessment device measures what it purports to measure. Judgment of the congruence of the items to the definition of the domain helps. Techniques are available to assess whether the student responses to the instrument follow patterns that are expected if the inferences from the instrument were valid (see end note 21).

The second concern, evaluation validity, asks whether the instruments measure a reasonable range of student outcomes in which the institution should be interested. Judgments of a cross-section of faculty and others are useful in assessing the validity of the evaluation.

Often only a single instrument is administered during the evaluation. In such cases, the inferences from the instrument may be judged more or less valid, but the evaluation itself may be found to be seriously limited in its ability to determine how the institution is doing.

How Will the Reliability of the Assessment Instruments or Methods Be Determined?

Reliability refers to consistency. Valid inferences can be enhanced by reliable measurement. Results which fluctuate from instance to instance cannot be relied upon. Evaluating the reliability of assessment instruments is standard practice in the testing industry, and the task is just as important when assessment methods other than paper-and-pencil tests are at issue.

Concepts and Issues

Three kinds of reliability are of varying importance depending upon the purpose and design of the assessment.[25] The first is the precision of the results. How much fluctuation can be expected in the assessment results (individual scores, group means, measures of differences or change) if the assessment were redone either at a different time or with a different, but similar set of questions? The expected fluctuation is expressed by a statistic called the standard error of measurement.

The second kind of reliability refers to the consistency of decisions. What proportion of the decisions (e.g., passed the test, placed in a remedial program, etc.) would be the same if the assessment were redone, presumably with different, but equivalent instruments? The consistency is often expressed as a simple proportion. A decision consistency of .80 would be interpreted to mean that 80 percent of the students would achieve the same classification decision on the two assessments.

The third notion of reliability refers to the consistency of the raters. How well do the judges who grade or score the assessment agree? Rater or scorer reliability is particularly important when subjective measures of student performance are employed. Experience has shown that when essays or other educational products are graded or when performance is observed and rated, the score values assigned are likely to differ unless standards are agreed upon ahead of time by the evaluators. In assessing rater reliability, the scores should be assigned independently.

The validity of the findings of a college assessment are seriously threatened if its instruments are unreliable. Unreliability means that, depending upon which questions happen to be asked or which raters happen to be judging the student's performance, the scores, decisions, or ratings would be different.

Three facts about reliability are important to keep in mind. The first is that reliability is heavily dependent upon the length of the assessment instrument. If the assessment is found to have unsatisfactory reliability, the condition can be ameliorated by including additional questions similar to those on the instrument or by including additional, but equally trained judges.

Second, measurements about individual students are less reliable than measurements about groups of students. Longer assessments are required when the results affect and will be communicated to individual students than when group averages will be reported. For example, the Academic Profile referenced in end note 6 consists of three, one-hour forms. For individual assessment, the publisher recommends that the forms be combined and administered to each student. For group assessment, the publisher recommends a matrix sampling design in which the forms are randomly distributed within each group such that each student responds to only one form.

The third important fact about reliability is that assessments are less reliable when they are expressed as differences between two scores, such as occurs in the value-added approach to assessment. Reporting differences in a student's performance (two different instruments or the same instrument at two different times) requires longer assessments than reporting differences in group means.

As in the case of validity, the purpose of the assessment determines which kinds of evidence and procedures are particularly relevant. In this light, let us pass the plane of the reliability issue through our four purposes.

Purposes 1 and 2: Placement and Certification. The reliability of the examination should be high in part because the decisions are important and in part because the subject of the assessment is the individual student. Consistency of decisions is the type of reliability most appropriate for placement and certification examinations. The question is whether the same decision would be made if the student were administered another assessment like the first. Procedures for estimating decision reliability are referenced in end note 25. If this proportion is too low, the examination should be lengthened, particularly by adding items that discriminate at the cutscore. Alternatively, those students scoring near the cutscore could be administered additional questions to improve faculty confidence in its decision.

A lengthy assessment instrument is also suggested in the certification context since the institution has some stake in avoiding false positives. With multiple opportunities to take the assessment, a student who does not have the requisite level of competence is more apt to pass an unreliable assessment at least one of the times it is attempted than to pass a reliable assessment instrument.

Purposes 3 and 4: Course Program. and Institutional Evaluation. Because data for groups of students (rather than for individual students) are being reported, reliability is of less concern. It is true that if a matrix sampling plan is used, results could be different not only because of measurement error (e.g., using a different sample of items) but also because of sampling error (using a different sample of students). Nevertheless, assuming a representative sample of students responds to the evaluation instruments, scores computed by aggregating responses to several items will be sufficiently precise for most purposes, even with samples as few as 25 or 50. (Such aggregation, however, comes at the price of less detailed information.) Suppose, instead, one wished to report the results for a single item, such as what percentage of students would answer "yes" to question 13 if asked. As indicated previously, a random sample as small as 100 students, regardless of how many are in the course, program, or institution, is sufficient to answer such a question with a margin of error of 10 percent or less.

Value-added claims will be somewhat less reliable because they are based on the difference of two measures, but even so, representative samples of a few hundred are more than sufficient.

What Assessment Results Will Be Reported?

A major value of a college assessment is the information it generates. This information can be conveyed in different forms. How much detail is needed? How should the results be expressed? What comparisons are important?

Concepts and Issues

Diagnostic Information. The more scores that are reported, the more diagnostic the information. Fine-grained reporting can be helpful to the student and the institution. Knowing strengths and weaknesses, highs and lows, can be an aid in studying, planning a curriculum, and communicating the assessment findings. The ability to provide diagnostic information, however, comes at a cost. Information based on only part of an examination can be quite unreliable and misleading; complicated score reports can be misunderstood. Assessments need to be noticeably longer if the detailed results are to be reliable.

Reporting Formats and Metrics. Results can be expressed as number correct (raw scores), units of proficiency, or in some type of norms such as percentile ranks or standard scores. Raw scores and units of proficiency are most useful for well structured domains in which the institution wishes to focus on a comparison between the performance and some standard. Criterion referenced interpretations are those in which results have meaning in reference to a standard rather than in reference to how other students did. Examples are: the student can type 45 words per minute, can write an essay at Level 3 (where examples of Level 3 writing are shown), or can carry on a simple conversation in French.

In contrast, norm-referenced interpretations are those in which examination results are compared to those of a reference group, called a norm group. Commercially-published assessment instruments frequently have norm group data. It is important that the institution using these data be sure that the norm group is one to which it wants its students to be compared. Faculty should also be sure that the instrument is administered according to the procedures specified by the publisher. Unfortunately, many norm groups are poorly defined or consist of student volunteers with unknown characteristics, thus preventing intelligent interpretations of the results. As an alternative, the institution can establish its own norm group, for example, a current or previous class.

Comparative Analyses. Any information can be analyzed a great many different ways. Typically, any of several procedures and analyses are valid. In these days of computers, workers no longer have to limit themselves to one or a few analyses. For example, if one is uncertain whether or not to include certain students in a particular analysis, the data can be analyzed both ways.

Comparisons hold much interest. For example, comparisons of this year's data with data for previous years; comparisons among groups of students, programs, and institutions; and relationships between selected individual, departmental, and institutional variables and the assessment results may all be of interest. Adverse impact statistics are frequently sought. The general principle is that the data being compared should be contributed by groups that are as much alike as possible except on the dimension of interest. Thus, for example, if the data from two different years are being compared, the students in both groups should meet the same criteria for being included (e.g., only juniors, from the same department) and the instruments should be administered under the same conditions.

As indicated below, the purpose of the assessment will determine how important diagnostic information and norms are and what comparisons are of most interest. In any report, the scores of individuals identified by name should be revealed only with their informed consent or only to those with a legitimate professional interest in particular cases.[26]

Purpose 1: Placement. Because the purpose of the examination is to place students into appropriate courses or programs, the availability of diagnostic information and norms is of secondary importance. Nevertheless, many examinations of basic skills yield diagnostic information and are recommended for use in placement decisions. Of course, providing all students with a full profile of their strengths and weaknesses would be helpful, and offering some of that information might be possible. The content of a placement examination is not intended to sample all aspects of the subject matter, and those it does include are not weighted equally. The items are chosen for their discriminatory value, not because they are representative of items measuring a particular skill. The position taken here is that a single, fixed-length examination cannot be optimum for both the placement and diagnostic functions.

If the student retains the option of which course or program to select, and the placement examination functions primarily as a guidance tool, then the student should be provided sufficient information to make an informed decision. Such information might include a table showing, separately for groups of students having similar examination scores, the grade distribution for these students in each course under consideration. Needless to say, analyses of the background and subject matter preparation of those students who pass and those who fail the placement examination also would be of particular interest.

Purpose 2: Certification. In addition to reporting the student's score and the cutscore, it would be especially helpful to the failing student if diagnostic information were presented. One form of this diagnostic information that does not compromise the effectiveness of the examination as a certifying instrument is to indicate the number of items associated with each major category of the ability domain and the number of these items the student answered correctly. Norms have little value in this context.

The institution should assemble data on the pass rate for first-time examination takers and for all examination takers, regardless of the number of previous attempts. The second rate will be higher than the first. These pass rates should be shown separately by class year, gender, major racial and ethnic groups, and discipline or major.

Purpose 3: Course and Program Evaluation. The goal of the evaluation is to acquire a reasonably complete picture of the effects of a course or program. Reporting the results in as much detail as the audience is willing and able to comprehend is consistent with this goal. Disaggregated information is especially valuable for curriculum and instructional planning. Differences among subgroups of students, correlations within the data set and with other variables, and comparisons with previous years' data or with available norms can be informative. Comparisons among programs within an institution, unless carefully designed and executed, can be invidious and breed corruption if used selectively to reinforce previously set, politically-determined conclusions.

Purpose 4: Evaluation of the Institution. Detailed reporting should benefit the institution. Although the amount of detail can vary for different audiences, a broad assessment has the potential to provide diagnostic information for the institution. On which outcomes and for which groups were the results encouraging? Disappointing?

When norms are available, they, too, can be informative. Noninstitutional norms may be needed to communicate to interested publics how the institution is doing. A full description of any norm samples employed should be provided. When available, comparisons with outcome data from a previous class can be illuminating. Comparisons with other institutions can be misleading. Student performance depends partially on factors that the institution can do little to change, such as student intellectual aptitude.

A comprehensive evaluation of an institution offers numerous choices for analyses. The assessment data can be supplemented with the growing body of institutional information available in various national data banks. In fact, the institution may wish to store its assessment results in a data bank for secondary analyses by faculty and students.

Summary

This paper has focused principally on examinations and other instruments used in college assessments. It raised a number of critical questions—what to measure, how to measure it, how to know if the measurement is any good, and how to report the results—not for purposes of providing a textbook on measurement, rather to winnow out the concepts and issues that are particularly applicable in higher education settings. Toward that end, I have stressed the practical implications of these issues in each of four major purposes that govern higher education assessment programs: placement, certification, program evaluation and institutional evaluation. This presentation has been intentionally general, and has served to establish a framework for the subsequent essays in this volume that deal with specific areas, problems, and technologies of assessment.

Decisions informed by assessment results can affect the life and spirit of students, courses, and colleges themselves. If those decisions are to be beneficial, the results of assessments must be of a quality worthy of their importance. It is toward that end that this essay has sought to guide the reader through the questioning process.

Notes

1. The discussion in this chapter is limited to tests (including performance measures), surveys, and student-constructed academic products. Excluded are a myriad of other indicators of the value of a college program, including measures of cost, enrollment data, testimonials about the reputation of the institution, earnings of graduates, and so on.

2. Other compatible purposes include encouraging faculty to examine their curricula, meeting a State mandate, and sending a public message about what the institution values.

3. Although program evaluations or institutional assessments may not purport to evaluate faculty, they may be perceived to do just that. Fear that the assessment is a covert faculty evaluation mechanism can result in a low degree of faculty cooperation.

4. For an excellent introduction to performance assessment, together with practical guidelines, see Richard J. Stiggins, "Design and Development of Performance Assessments," *Educational Measurement: Issues and Practice*, vol. 6, no. 3 (1987), pp. 33–42.

5. The MAPS (Multiple Assessment Programs and Services) instrument contains subtests that vary along this continuum. For further information, write The College Board, 45 Columbus Ave., New York City, N.Y. 10023–6917.

6. The Academic Profile contains items measuring one of four general skills (college-level reading, college-level writing, critical thinking, and using mathematical data) within one of three broad subject areas (humanities, social sciences, natural sciences). For further information, see John Centra's essay in this volume.

7. *How MAPS Can Help You with Placement*. New York: The College Entrance Examination Board, 1980, p. 6.

8. College BASE (Basic Academic Subjects Examination) is a standardized, college assessment instrument that clearly specifies the content domain. The instrument describes content in terms of learning outcomes based on a 1983 statement by the College Board of the academic preparation needed for college. For further information, write the Center for Educational Assessment, University of Missouri, 403 S. Sixth Street, Columbia, Mo. 65211.

9. Recognizing the colleges want measures of the outcomes of instruction in the disciplines that would not be as difficult as the Graduate Record Examination Subject Area Tests, the Educational Testing Service and the Graduate Record Examinations Board have constructed a set of new examinations based on the GREs. The sponsors claim that these examinations are less difficult, appropriate for all seniors majoring in a field, more convenient to administer than the GRE Area Tests, and hence more appropriate for program or

institutional evaluation. For further information, write Major Field Achievement Tests, 23-P, Educational Testing Service, Princeton, N.J. 08541-0001.

10. Other sources include expert judgments about the merits of course materials (syllabus, assignments, class handouts, examinations, textbooks, etc.) enrollment and attrition figures, costs data, and facilities.

11. Derek C. Bok, *Higher Learning*. Cambridge: Harvard Univ. Press, 1986, p.59.

12. Write to the Assessment Resource Center, University of Tennessee, 2046 Terrace Ave., Knoxville, Tenn. 37996–504.

13. The Institution published the *Mental Measurements Yearbooks*, which include comprehensive descriptive information and critical reviews of commercially published tests. The Institute also offers an online computer database service through BRS Information Technologies, that provides monthly updates in between publication of the *Yearbooks*. The label for the database is MMYD. Further information and announcements may be obtained by writing the Buros Institute, University of Nebraska, 135 Bancroft Hall, Lincoln, Neb. 68688–0348.

14. Write to the Test Corporation of America, 330 W. 47th Street, Suite 205, Kansas City, Mo. 64112.

15. See Emily Fabiano and Nancy O'Brien, *Testing Information Sources for Educators*. ERIC TME Report 94. Princeton, N.J.: Educational Testing Service, 1987. Includes a listing of printed material and computer-based sources of test bibliographies, agencies providing test information, locations of major and regional test collections, and names and addresses of test publishers. Write to the ERIC Center, American Institutes for Research, 3333 K Street, N.W., Washington, D.C. 20007.

16. Richard Light, personal communication, Dec. 7, 1987.

17. American Educational Research Association, American Psychological Association, and the National Council on Measurement in Education. *Standards for Educational and Psychological Testing*. Washington, D.C.: American Psychological Assoc., 1985. See especially Sections 13 and 14.

18. A good introduction is G.L. Marco, "Equating Tests in an Era Of Test Disclosure." In B.F. Green (ed.), *New Directions for Testing and Measurement*, No. 11. San Francisco: Jossey-Bass, 1984, pp. 105–122. Further introduction and details can be found in W.B. Angoff, *Scales, Norms, and Equivalent Scores*. Princeton, N.J.: Educational Testing Services, 1984. The 1984 publication is a reprint of Angoff's classical, but very relevant treatment of the topic in 1971.

19. An elementary introduction can be found in S.A. Livingston and M.J. Zieky, *Passing Scores: A Manual for Setting Standards of Performance on Educational and Occupational Tests*. Princeton, N.J.: Educational Testing Service, 1982. Other key references on this topic include L.A. Shepard, "Standard Setting Issues and Methods," *Applied Psychological Measurement*, vol. 4 (1980), pp. 447–467, and R.A. Berk, "A Consumer's Guide to Setting Performance Standards on Criterion-Referenced Tests," *Review of Educational Research*, vol. 56 (1986), pp. 137–172. The latter reference identifies and rates 38 methods.

20. See R.A. Berk, (ed.), *Handbook of Methods for Detecting Test Bias*. Baltimore: Johns Hopkins Univ. Press, 1982.

21. A brief introduction to current thinking about test validity can be found in Section 1 (pp. 9–18) in the *Standards* (see end note 17), as well as in Howard Wainer and Henry Braun (eds.), *Test Validity*. Hillsdale, N.J.: Lawrence Erlbaum Assoc., 1988. A thorough treatment of the topic will appear in R.L. Linn's edited volume, *Educational Measurement* (3rd edition), which will be published by Macmillan in 1988.

22. A subscale of the College Outcome Measures Project (COMP) of the American College Testing Program. For more information, write to ACT COMP, P.O. Box 168, Iowa City, Iowa 52243.

23. See George F. Madaus, "Minimum Competency Testing for Certification: The Evolution and Evaluation of Test Validity." In G.F. Madaus (ed.), *The Courts, Validity, and Minimum Competency Testing*. Boston: Kluwer-Nijhoff Publishing, 1983, pp. 21–61.

24. See Jason Millman, "A Checklist Procedure." In N.L. Smith (ed.), *New Techniques for Evaluation*. Beverly Hills, Calif.: Sage Publications, 1981, Vol. 2, pp. 309–314 and 316–318.

25. A brief introduction to current thinking about test reliability can be found in Section 2 (pp. 19–23) of the *Standards* (see end note 17). A thorough treatment of the topic will appear in Linn's forthcoming 3rd edition of *Educational Measurement* (see end note 21). Traditional formulas for reliability and the standard error of measurement can be found in any elementary textbook on educational measurement. One notable review of methods for determining decision consistency is that of Roos E. Traub and Glenn L. Rowley, "Reliability of Test Scores and Decisions," *Applied Psychological Measurement*, vol. 4 (1980), pp. 517–545. A computationally simple procedure for estimating decision consistency with only one test administration is offered by Michael Subkoviak, "A Practitioner's Guide to Computation and Interpretation of Reliability Indices for Mastery Test," *Journal of Educational Measurement*, in press (1988).

26. See Section 16 (pp. 85–87) of the *Standards* (see end note 17).

Approaches to Assessing Educational Outcomes

Joan S. Stark

Based on public concern about what their students are learning, colleges and universities are experimenting actively with ways to measure student outcomes. The locus of outcome measurement recently has shifted from the classroom, where individual instructors traditionally have assessed student's work, to the academic programs, where groups of faculty try to assess students' competence and progress in more systematic and comprehensive ways. Increasingly, professional and accrediting associations require evidence that program assessment results are obtained and considered in curricular improvement. AUPHA is no exception, as evidenced by adoption of new program criteria for full undergraduate membership that include outcomes.

Assuring the public of student competence may be new to faculty in liberal arts programs, but it is familiar to those teaching in health fields and in other professions as diverse as accounting and social work. The need to protect the public interest long ago stimulated many professional program faculties to devise ways of documenting student achievement. Even so, it is timely to reexamine and to improve ways of measuring what students learn and to have faculty in professional fields demonstrate leadership in higher education by sharing broadly successful strategies with colleagues in various fields of study.

In the spirit of sharing across disciplinary boundaries, this article discusses why assessment of student learning is important, reviews some key models educators have used to discuss program and college goals and outcomes, and then focuses on technical issues that health administration educators might consider as they refine measurement strategies relevant to their particular educational responsibilities. Although the conceptual and technical issues are common to measurement of student growth in all fields, understanding and discussing their application in each specific field is crucial at a time when outcome measures are receiving extensive public attention.

Why Assess Student Progress and Competence?

Accountability to various constituents, including employers, students, and the public, is an important reason for assessing student progress and competence, but it is not the only one. There are at least five other reasons, as follows:

1. The time-honored reason for assessing student competence is to help students gauge their own progress. Periodically assessing competence as it develops helps students to know what skills and understandings they need to strengthen. When conducted in a supportive and timely way, assessment can enhance student motivation to learn.

2.   Assessment can help students understand *why* they are learning certain skills and concepts. In fact, an important outgrowth of assessment can be better understanding for students of their own professional development. For example, at successive levels of educational maturity, students should be able to define skills and knowledge they are developing, identify examples of where the skills and knowledge might be useful, demonstrate the ability to use the skills or knowledge, and, finally, demonstrate ability to make appropriate professional judgments of how, why, and when to use the skill or knowledge. When the results of assessment are used effectively for student guidance, secrecy about what is to be demonstrated or tested is inappropriate.

3.   Systematic assessment of student outcomes can help faculty members understand students' development. Lacking information about outcomes, faculty members may assume intellectual, technical, and interpersonal maturity that students have not yet acquired, or they may unwittingly attribute their own interests and backgrounds to students. Understanding the progress of patterns of student development can help faculty to construct more individual learning sequences.

4.   Faculty understanding of those intended student outcomes achieved and those not achieved is useful in evaluating and improving the academic program. Curricular changes frequently involve tinkering, that is, changing the time frame or organizational patterns of courses rather than the content taught or the teaching methods used. Even when reasoned substantive change occurs, it is often the case that one untested program replaces another with little solid evidence about the success of either. Examining student outcomes can help to pinpoint deficiencies in the academic program and focus change directly on alternative teaching and learning models to remedy the identified problems.

5.   Finally, assessing student outcomes can help faculty members keep programs responsive to changing needs in the profession. Academic programs can be strengthened and modernized by utilizing information from employers and graduates about capabilities that are particularly strong or weak at career entrance. For professional careers, the capabilities examined should include not only technical knowledge specific to a profession but broader competencies, such as communication, leadership, and interpersonal skills. Thus, program responsiveness that is based on assessment will broaden and deepen the academic program.

Models Used by Educators to Discuss and Measure Outcomes

Educators may choose from numerous and diverse models on which to pattern their plans for assessing outcomes. Some models are comprehensive, serving primarily to establish a conceptual base for thinking about college outcomes generally. Others, although generic, are sufficiently specific to be readily applied to a variety of academic programs. At one extreme, several models are theoretically based in developmental psychology; at the other extreme, some are devised pragmatically and based on demonstrated activities of graduates in occupational practice. To illustrate the extensive thinking that has been devoted to defining outcomes and goals and the wide diversity of models, I mention here several examples, starting with the broadest models and moving to those focused more closely on student outcomes for professional programs.

Probably the most inclusive model of college outcomes is a lengthy taxonomy of educational outcomes categorizing the many and varied contributions that colleges make to society [1]. Major categories here include economic development, production of technical and artistic knowledge, provision of resources and services to the community, and sponsorship of aesthetic and cultural activities. In this comprehensive view, the section of the taxonomy dealing with student learning outcomes is but a small part of the whole and is labeled "human characteristics." Although useful for institutional review of programs that emphasize research and service as well as teaching, this taxonomy is not immediately helpful in measuring student outcomes. Nevertheless, it has stimulated some useful student and alumni goal and self-reported outcome surveys.

An inclusive listing of college goals was constructed by Bowen [2], who divided them roughly into two categories, goals for society and goals for students. Goals for students are then further categorized as (1) cognitive learning, (2) emotional and moral development, (3) practical competence for life, (4) direct satisfaction, and (5) avoidance of negative outcomes. Theoretically, goals for students should be directly related to student outcomes. In reality, though, educators probably need to consider the effects of the students' own goals, too. Students may not exhibit the same interest in each of these categories as faculty would wish. Clearly, Bowen's broad goal categories would need considerable refinement to be useful at the academic program level.

Focusing more narrowly on the psychology of student development, a taxonomy of outcomes constructed by Astin and Panos [3] over twenty years ago remains popular today. This model has three dimensions, each of which is divided into two dichotomous categories. Thus, the model is often visualized as a cube, or a 2 x 2 x 2 table. The first dimension describes the type of outcome: the two types of outcomes are cognitive (intellectual, concerned with knowledge) and affective (emotional, attitudinal, value-related). The second dimension describes the kind of data typically collected to measure the outcome: behavioral (actually observed) or psychological (inferred from a nonbehavioral test). The third dimension describes the time frames for outcome measurement: short-term (close to the time of learning) or long-term (distant from the time of learning, such as during a career). Although this entire model is intuitively appealing, educators have explored the cell defining cognitive outcomes measured by psychological data in a short-term time frame most extensively. They have seldom been willing to undertake behavioral observations of either cognitive or affective outcomes in a long-term time frame after graduation.

A problem with the Astin and Panos model is that many academic specialists in colleges feel that their teaching role concerns primarily students' intellectual development. Instructors are wary of accepting responsibility for influencing or measuring student outcomes in the affective or attitudinal domain. Arguably, however, faculty members elicit attitudinal changes in their students whether or not they intend to do so. The attitudes (or motivations) toward learning that students develop during college courses affect (positively or negatively) their subsequent learning experiences. Interpreted this way, attitudes are important academic outcomes and are not totally afield of the faculty members' responsibility.

For the current assessment era, in which faculty are closely involved in measurement, a typology is needed that centers on students' academic growth but recognizes important academically related attitudinal outcomes. To these ends, we developed such a model at the National Center for Research to Improve Postsecondary Learning and Teaching [4]. The framework (See Figure 1) includes three outcome domains: cognitive, motivational, and behavioral. These domains can be measured in three time frames: a short time frame, such as a course; an intermediate time frame, such as a college program or major; and a long time frame, such as a career. Academic program faculty who are just beginning to think about measuring outcomes might start by refining their use of the most familiar outcome measures (short time frame cognitive classroom measures) with a plan to extend the assessment, based on their experience, to the intermediate time frame attitudinal measures, such as job-related attitudes of newly graduated professional workers. Finally, with adequate resources and cooperation from practicing professionals, professional fields with defined career patterns can extend assessment activities to more comprehensive behavioral measurement encompassing long time frames. Some illustrations of this 3 x 3 matrix for a few outcomes relevant to health administration programs are given in Figure 2.

Finally, I mention two outcome models of importance to educators in professional fields because they incorporate both educational and work competencies. The Alverno model [5] assumes that educators should not be content to measure cognitive outcomes on paper or observe incidental behavior when convenient. A serious effort must be made to provide situations in which assessors can observe the student using and linking cognitive, affective, and behavioral outcomes in practical life and work situations. Alverno is a women's liberal arts college that prepares its students for many fields of professional work, including nursing, social work, and teaching.

Figure 1
National Center for Research to Improve
Postsecondary Teaching and Learning's Outcome Framework

Form of Measurement	Academic Arena
Cognitive	Achievement (facts, principles, ideas, skills) Critical-thinking skills Problem-solving skills
Motivational	Satisfaction with college Involvement/effort Motivation Self-efficacy
Behavioral	Career and life goal exploration Exploration of diversity Persistence Relationships with faculty

Figure 2
Examples of Health Administration Outcomes
in a Framework of Varied Domains and Time Frames

Time Frames	Domains		
	Cognitive	Motivational	Behavioral
Short-term	Knowledge of health maintenance organizations	Confidence in one's ability as a learner and emerging professional	Discussing varied career paths with faculty
Intermediate-term	Accuracy in preparing written problems analyses on institutional financial margin	Membership in ACHE and ACHCA, implying professional commitment	Balancing ethical and economic considerations in making decisions
Long-term	Contributing new and unique ideas in professional papers	Volunteering support for health-related community endeavors	Serving as preceptor for young administrators

For this context, the college has defined eight essential competencies, has learned to involve both students and faculty in assessing them, and has actively shared their techniques with other educators. The eight competencies are communications, analysis, problem solving, valuing, social interaction, responsibility for environment, involvement in the contemporary world, and aesthetic response. The relevance of each of these domains to fields such as health administration is immediately clear. To select only three examples, the competent health administrator is concerned with medical waste disposal (responsibility for environment), is abreast of issues concerning catastrophic health insurance for the elderly (involvement in the contemporary world), and may be engaged in planning new facilities (aesthetic response).

With the help of faculty from a many professional fields, we have developed a career-linked model that stresses the ability to integrate and apply learning both within the professional component of education and between professional and general education [6, 7]. This model defines two categories of outcomes: (1) outcomes frequently considered primary goals of professional preparation in college (traditional professional competencies), and (2) outcomes encompassing goals of liberal education but phrased in terms especially relevant to students preparing for professional positions (liberal/professional education outcomes). The ten liberal/professional competencies are important and desired outcomes in many undergraduate professional fields, including health administration [8]. The generic outcomes and their brief definitions are given in Figure 3.

Although no specific assessment indicators have yet been devised, some are on the horizon. For example, a recent study has produced a self-report instrument in which nurses report not only the extent to which they use liberal/professional competencies at their work but also which educational and personal experiences led to these competencies [9]. Such an instrument can readily be adapted to other health-related fields.

New models are emerging regularly as many accreditors, several nationally funded projects, and individual colleges and programs experiment with defining and assessing student educational outcomes.

Refining Measurement Strategies

Even a brief examination of the different models designed to guide outcome measurement reveals a lack of agreement on how student outcomes or their measures are defined. Therefore, to facilitate discussions, I propose a definition specifically crafted to illustrate some important measurement issues. *An educational outcome may be any characteristic an educator or group of educators believes important for a student to demonstrate or possess.* Following from this definition, it is useful to view the measurement of such an outcome as involving three levels of increasing specificity: description, change, and attribution. Thus, an educational outcome can be measured at each of three levels as described and illustrated below. The illustrations have been selected to include liberal education outcomes essential to health administrators as well as outcomes more specific to health administration.

Figure 3
Outcomes Considered Important by Educators in Eight Undergraduate Professional Fields

	Ten Outcomes in Common with Liberal Education
Communication competence	The graduate can read, write, speak, and listen and use these processes effectively to acquire, develop, and convey ideas and information.
Comment	Reading, writing, speaking, and listening are skills essential to professional practice and to continued professional growth as well as to informed citizenry and continued personal growth.
Critical thinking	The graduate examines issues rationally, logically, and coherently.
Comment	Although critical thinking is a universally desired educational outcome, professionals particularly need a repertoire of thinking strategies that will enable them to acquire, evaluate, and synthesize information and knowledge. Since much professional practice is problematical, students need to develop analytical skills to make decisions in both familiar and unfamiliar circumstances.
Contextual competence	The graduate has an understanding of the societal context (environment) in which the profession is practiced.
Comment	The capability to adopt multiple perspectives allows the graduate to comprehend the complex interdependence between the profession and society. An enhanced understanding of the world and the ability to make judgments in light of historical, social, economic, scientific, and political realities is demanded of the professional as well as the citizen.
Aesthetic sensibility	The graduate will have an enhanced aesthetic awareness of arts and human behavior for both personal enrichment and application in enhancement of the profession.
Comment	Sensitivity to relationships among the arts, the natural environment and human concerns epitomizes aesthetic awareness. Through learning to approach life as an aesthetic experience and by viewing work as an act of aesthetic judgment, professionals can more effectively assess and understand the world and their roles within it.
Professional identity	The graduate acknowledges and is concerned for improving the knowledge, skills, and values of the profession.
Comment	Professional identity both parallels and supplements the liberal education goal of developing a sense of personal identity. The sense of personal worth and self-confidence that develops from experiencing success in professional practice, often including a contributing or altruistic relationship with clients, is an effective vehicle for gaining a sense of one's place in the world as an individual and citizen.
Professional ethics	The graduate understands and accepts the ethics of the profession as standards that guide professional behavior.
Comment	Liberally educated individuals are expected to have developed value systems and ethical standards that guide their behavior. Since in every field professionals face choice and responsibility in the process of making decisions with full understanding of their consequences, the study of ethics provides a context for development of professional ethics.

Adaptive competence	The graduate anticipates, adapts to, and promotes changes important to the profession's societal purpose and the professional's role.
Comment	A liberally educated person has an enhanced capacity to adapt to and anticipate changes in society. Since professional practice is not static, adaptability can be fostered by promoting the need to detect and respond to changes and make innovations in professional practice.
Leadership capacity	The graduate exhibits the capacity to contribute as a productive member of the profession and to assume leadership roles as appropriate in the profession and society.
Comment	All education carries with it the responsibility of developing leadership capacity. This is particularly true for professional education where the problem-decision-action cycle may have broad environmental, social, and individual ramifications. Not only does leadership imply both functional and status obligations, it requires the intelligent, humane application of knowledge and skills.
Scholarly concern for improvement	The graduate recognizes the needs to increase knowledge and advance the profession through systematic, cumulative research on problems of theory and practice.
Comment	The heart of the intellectual process is attention to a spirit of inquiry, critical analysis, or logical thinking. Although many critical analysis skills are developed as theory and practice are integrated, the professional curriculum can be specially designed to foster among graduates an obligation to participate in inquiry, research, and improvement of the profession.
Motivation for continued learning	The graduate continues to explore and expand personal, civic, and professional knowledge and skills throughout a lifetime.
Comment	A truly educated person will wish to continue learning throughout life. In professional education, substantial emphasis can be placed on fostering individual responsibility for continued professional growth.

Level I. Description

An educational outcome measurement is a description of a student characteristic accepted as consistent with an educational goal. The following are examples:

1. The student demonstrates acceptable communication skills by writing a short paper on an assigned general topic.

2. On a multiple choice examination, the student can recognize and define various planning and marketing techniques.

Level II. Change

An educational outcome measurement is a change in a student characteristic between two points in time. The following are examples:

1. The papers the student writes at the end of the term are clearer and better organized than those he or she wrote at the beginning of the term.

2. On a test using Lotus 1-2-3 as a spreadsheet for budget analysis, the graduating student performed better than on a placement test that assessed his or her familiarity with computer programs when he or she entered the program.

Level III. Attribution

An educational outcome measurement is a change in a student characteristic between two points in time, in an intended direction, that can be traced or reasonably attributed to an educational experience. The following are examples:

1. The student lacked knowledge of catastrophic health insurance or the elderly when entering a health administration program. By the end of the program he or she is able to discuss the advantages and disadvantages of this program to elderly people of various income levels.

2. Following appropriate instruction, the student can apply planning and marketing techniques to health care managerial problems in appropriate ways.

One reason why this three-level definition of educational measurement is useful is that it is not program-specific. Rather, it is general enough to be adaptable to any program or any local context and therefore allows for a generic discussion of the technical issues in measuring outcomes. A second reason the definition is useful is that it helps to avoid confusing student demonstration of outcomes with our success in teaching students to demonstrate the outcome. Finally, the definition is useful because the three levels clarify that exceedingly complex measurement strategies are needed to credit or blame an educational program for student outcomes. To illustrate, in the Level II examples above, it is possible that the student learned better writing skills or acquired facility with Lotus 1-2-3 by working at a job unrelated to his or her health administration studies or by studying independently. Because of the nature of the Level III examples, there is more reason to believe (but certainly not definitive evidence) that the learning may be due to the program of study. Even so, whether for purposes of accountability to external sponsors or program review and improvement, it is inappropriate to assume that academic programs have produced changes in students unless other potentially responsible change agents have been discounted. This caveat leads us to discussion of the technical issues.

Technical Issues in Outcome Measurement

Whether behavioral observations, paper and pencil tests of cognitive knowledge, or attitude surveys are used, measuring outcomes involves an increasingly complex and expansive set of methodological difficulties as one moves from Level I to Level III. The difficulty for Level III is greatest since in addition to its own relevant cautions and limitations, all of those applicable to Levels I and II apply as well. The technical issues at each level parallel the issues in experimental and quasi-experimental design [10]. I will mention them briefly, simply as a reminder for those who are serious about measuring program outcomes; they should review carefully this sophisticated methodological material familiar to faculty in many fields of pure and applied science and of social science.

Level I

When describing student characteristics (Level I) we are operating at a simple level of measurement. It can usually be determined easily that students demonstrate the characteristic. Further, it is possible to measure a demonstrated level of the attribute that allows students to be compared with a designated standard or with each other. But nothing can be claimed about whether the student acquired this characteristic during the educational program or whether the program caused the change. We pose several key, general questions below and illustrate them with specific questions directed at a selected behavioral outcome: caring, people-oriented behavior. We could just as easily have used another outcome, for example, the ability to analyze financial ratios for a specific health care institution.

1. Regarding *domain*: Is the student characteristic or demonstrated behavior relevant? Is the characteristic consistent with an established educational goal?

    Example: Is caring behavior a necessary or desirable outcome in educating health care administrators?

2. Regarding *validity*: Does the characteristic actually imply skill or knowledge that it appears to demonstrate, or could it be interpreted differently? Is the observation or measure used to identify and measure the characteristic for a group of students equally valid for individual students?

    Example: Is there a clear indication that the student really demonstrates concern for others? Alternatively, could the same behavior be exhibited for self-serving reasons, for example, to gain a good grade or impress a supervisor?

3. Regarding *reliability*: Do the students demonstrate the characteristic consistently at different times?

    Example: Does the student continue to exhibit caring behavior when he or she does not know he or she is being observed? When he or she is under stress?

4. Regarding *floor and ceiling effects*: Are there extensive differences among students who are most adept and least adept in demonstrating the characteristic?

    Example: Is it possible for an observer to identify students who *seldom or never* demonstrate the desired caring behavior? Are the characteristics that distinguish these students from those who do demonstrate caring behavior the ones that are used as measures of the outcome?

5. Regarding *absolute and normative references*: Is it desirable that students demonstrate the characteristic at a specified or absolute level of competence? Or is it sufficient that they demonstrate it to a greater degree than some comparison group?

    Example: Must health care administrators be more likely to demonstrate caring behavior than, say, construction engineers? How consistently must the behavior be demonstrated to be professionally acceptable?

Level II

When attempting to measure student change over time (Level II), all of the above concerns remain important although they now apply to observing the student characteristic at both points in time. In addition, we must be concerned with the following questions:

6. Regarding *testing effects*: Is it possible that the change we observe is due to the method of observation, such as learning from taking a test, rather than a true educational change?

    Example: Could it be that students have learned to demonstrate specific caring behaviors when being observed?

7. Regarding *systematic observer or instrument errors*: Is it possible that our instrument or observation indicates a change merely because the measurement varies at two points in time?

    Example: Do two different instructors or supervisors judge a student's behavior differently?

8. Regarding *group attrition*: When a group of students shows a change in a characteristic over time, is it due to a change in composition of the group caused by dropout or failure to record observations?

    Example: Did some students who initially valued self-interest more than concern for others drop out of the program? Does this attrition, rather than actual changes in student behavior, explain why the group mean score on a scale of caring behavior is higher at the end of a course?

9. Regarding *statistical regression and effects of input characteristics*: Has there been a control for the possibility that change differs among students who possessed the characteristic to different degrees when first measured? Avoiding measurement errors due to different initial levels of a measured characteristic usually requires more complex statistical treatment than simply subtracting test scores at two points in time.

    Example: If a student consistently demonstrates caring behavior before entering the program, will there be an opportunity for instructors to compare his or her improvement with that made by some other students? Some evaluators use multiple regression upon the initial measured characteristic and subsequent comparison of regression residual measures.

Level III

Despite the public's tendency to credit or blame educational programs for students successes and failures, it is most difficult of all to establish that a change in student characteristics actually can be so ascribed (Level III). Of course, the task is easiest when the student outcome being examined is unique to the program and unlikely to have been achieved in other ways. To illustrate, it is easier to show that a nursing student learned to give injections as a result of training than to show that her knowledge of literature was acquired in the classroom. When attributing impact to educational programs, we usually have limited confidence in our attributions. All of the cautions mentioned earlier must be observed, as well as the following:

10. Regarding *events and occurrences*: Is it likely that some event outside the educational program has caused students to change over time in the intended way?

    Example: Might a student begin to show greater concern for the aged because an elderly relative has recently become ill or handicapped?

11. Regarding *maturation*: Is it likely that students will have changed in the intended way just because they are older or more mature?

    Example: Over a four- or five-year period of education, students enrolled in all educational programs may become more concerned about the welfare of others simply as a result of maturing personal relationships. Although it is hoped that health administration students will show an increase in such concern, these changes in life perspective are not limited to those enrolled in certain college programs.

Ideally, in order to deal with the issues of history and maturation encountered at measurement Level III, we would have to eliminate alternative causes of change in student characteristics by examining control groups of students who experienced all the same world events but did not study in the educational program. Since education takes place in natural settings and involves human beings, it is not always feasible to use such controls. For educators who are serious about assessing their program outcomes, however, some creative possibilities bear examination. For example, health administration programs in two universities with similar student groups could choose a set of desired outcomes that both agree to measure. Since the two sets of students are unlikely to interact, certain skills and concepts can be taught in varying order or by different instructional methods. Because of this sequence difference, outcome measures taken at appropriate points in time allow one group to serve as a control group for another and the reverse.

To summarize, outcome assessment can be descriptive, describing students or changes in students. At a more refined level it can attempt to identify and verify the source of the student change. The methodological levels at which assessment is undertaken and the conclusions that are drawn should be carefully related to the process used.

Some Recommendations

As academic programs attempt to respond more fully to assessment demands, the following list may be useful to assure attention to important issues covered in the previous discussion.

1. Determine what is to be assessed, why it is to be assessed, and which level of outcome measurement is desired.

2. Determine in advance how the results will be used to improve the educational program. Do not collect data for which the use is unclear.

3. Determine the means and criteria of assessment and be sure they satisfy the technical cautions appropriate to the level of measurement. Think creatively; methods other than paper and pencil tests may produce important results. For example, a student who can score high on a test of group process theories may not apply these ideas when relating to groups in a managerial role. Think beyond your own college and university to find statistical control groups and to discount alternative explanations for outcomes.

4. Use multiple measures whenever possible. In what ways, for instance, could we know whether a graduate is likely to balance the health care needs of the community with the economic needs of his or her employing institution?

5. Interpret the results cautiously, particularly when attribution is sought. Can we be sure that students who behave ethically learned this behavior as a result of case study instruction in the health administration program?

6. Provide feedback to students and faculty, including appropriate limitations and qualifications. For example, students who have poor interpersonal skills need to know specific ways to improve them.

7. Use the feedback to improve the teaching and learning program as planned.

8. Be alert for unanticipated negative and positive effects of the assessment process.

Some unanticipated negative effects of assessment include student test anxiety, test fatigue, faculty emphasis on teaching for tests, inappropriate use of assessment measures for faculty evaluation, false pride from exaggerated claims or effects incorrectly attributed to the education program, and faculty concern over reduction in class time.

Some unanticipated positive effects of assessment include among students, an increased sense of responsibility for their own development and increased motivation; and among faculty, an increased sense of community and collaboration, clarification of teaching goals and strategies, and provision of feedback to students.

If the approaches to assessment, its purposes, and the technical measurement issues it involves are given thoughtful consideration by well-intentioned faculty members, the positive effects are likely to outweigh the negative.

References

1. Lenning, O.T., et al. *A Structure for the Outcomes of Postsecondary Education* Boulder, CO. National Center for Higher Education Management Systems, 1977.

2. Bowen, H.R. *Investment in Learning: The Individual and Social Value of American Higher Education.* San Francisco: Jossey-Bass, 1977.

3. Astin, A.W., and R. Panos. *The Educational and Vocational Development of College Students.* Washington, DC: American Council on Education, 1969.

4. Alexander, J.M., and J.S. Stark. *Focusing on Student Outcomes: A Working Paper.* Ann Arbor, MI: University of Michigan, National Center for Research to Improve Postsecondary Teaching and Learning, 1986.

5. Mentkowski, M., and A. Doherty. Abilities That Last a Lifetime. *AAHE Bulletin* 36 (6): 3–14, 1984.

6. Stark, J.S., and M.A. Lowther. *Strengthening the Ties That Bind: Integrating Undergraduate Liberal and Professional Study.* A Report of the Professional Preparation Network. Ann Arbor, MI: University of Michigan, 1988.

7. Stark, J.S., and M.A. Lowther. Exploring Common Ground in Liberal and Professional Education. In *Integrating Liberal Learning and Professional Education, New Directions for Teaching and Learning,* ed. Robert Armour and Barbara Fuhrmann. San Francisco: Jossey-Bass, 1989.

8. Association of University Programs in Health Administration. *Full Undergraduate Membership Criteria.* Arlington, VA: AUPHA, 1989.

9. Hagerty, B.M.K. Measuring Nurses' Use of Applied Liberal Education Competencies in Professional Nursing. Doctoral diss., University of Michigan, 1989.

10. Campbell, D.T. and J.C. Stanley. *Experimental and Quasi-Experimental Designs for Research.* Skokie, IL: Rand McNally, 1966.

PART V
Communicating and Using Results

Introduction

In some programs communicating results may be a formal process, while in others it may be informal. Formal communication of the results can be achieved through written reports, verbal reports, audio-visual or other aids. Regardless of the medium, it should be tailored to the intended audience regarding detail, length, and language. Using a mixed group of writers can assist in designing effective communications for various audiences.

Several ethical concerns relate to the communication of the assessment results. These include right-to-know audiences, opportunity for audiences to review and respond to information, and appropriate delivery of unwelcome news. The answer to who has a right to know and how much should be shared may elicit varied opinions reflecting the various disciplines and professions represented on and off the campus. While some may adhere strictly to full disclosure, others may embrace ethical standards in consideration for the welfare of individuals. Clearly, dissemination plans about who will receive what information and when they will obtain it should be agreed upon early in the assessment.

Because of the size and complexity of some educational institutions, assessment information may not be readily used. Factors that affect use of the information include a sense of ownership and involvement, perception of the validity of the indicators and measures, confidence in those gathering and interpreting the information, and clarity and timeliness of the information. These and other aspects of dissemination and utilization of the information are addressed in the selections.

Professional literature in program evaluation discusses many issues about communication of the results and the utility of the information, but the assessment literature gives short shrift to those matters. Communication seems particularly critical for evaluations conducted at institutional levels when the users of the information may be somewhat removed from the activity.

Ways to enhance use. Effective assessments attend to utilization issues in the initial planning. Decisions about critical elements precede dissemination and include the model selected, level of involvement, and credibility of information. **Jacobi, Astin and Ayala** provide a summary of factors that affect use and discuss tensions between them, for example, audience involvement versus timeliness.

Linking with faculty development and teaching. The purpose and design of the assessment determines, in large part, the extent to which the assessment program has an effect on the academic program. The authors of the selections in this section advocate an assessment model closely linked to the normal teaching and learning function. **Hutchings** asks that assessment be viewed and practiced as a way of teaching and working with students and colleagues for the improvement of student learning.

Use of information also underlies course-embedded assessment activity as described in the selection by **Angelo**. In classroom research, faculty continuously and systematically gather information about how students are learning in their classrooms to inform and improve instruction.

Linking with institutional planning and decision making. **Ewell** (1989) describes four ways that decision makers use information: to identify problems, to set a context for a decision, to induce action, and to promote or legitimize a decision. For each type, he presents strategies for the content and format of the disseminated information that address the need for linkages and use.

Barak and Breier discuss the interactions between program review and other campus information gathering and decision making activities including assessment, accreditation, and strategic planning. They view a college's strategic planning as encompassing the remaining activities of assessment, accreditation, and program review.

Ewell (1991) analyzes the parallels between assessment and Total Quality Management (TQM). He notes the convergence in activity between TQM and the best examples of assessment, models that are not commonly practiced. Assessment trends consistent with TQM include the rediscovery of the importance of the instructional process, the use of naturalistic inquiry, and the use of classroom research assessment.

Additional Core Readings

Arns, R. G. and Poland, W. "Changing the University Through Program Review." *Journal of Higher Education* 51(3) (1980), pp. 268–284.

Ewell, Peter T. "Putting It All Together: Four Questions for Practitioners." In *Enhancing Information Use in Decision Making, New Directions for Institutional Research No. 64* edited by Peter T. Ewell. San Francisco: Jossey-Bass, 1989, pp. 85–90.

Loacker, G. "Faculty as a Force to Improve Instruction through Assessment." In *Assessing Students' Learning, New Directions for Teaching and Learning No. 34* edited by J. McMillan. San Francisco: Jossey-Bass, 1988, pp. 19–32.

Shapiro, J. Z. "Evaluation Research and Educational Decision-Making: A Review of the Literature." In *Higher Education: Handbook of Theory and Research Volume 1* edited by John Smart. New York: Agathon Press, 1986, pp. 163–206.

Increasing the Usefulness of Outcomes Assessments

MARYANN JACOBI, ALEXANDER ASTIN, AND FRANK AYALA, JR.

A successful student outcomes project not only measures impact: It also *produces* impact. The successful project becomes a tool for administrators, trustees, faculty, students, and external reviewers to use in evaluation and decision making. Yet all too often, outcomes assessments fall short of this goal (Astin 1977; Baird 1976; Bowen 1980; Ewell 1983; Weiss 1988).

The difficulties of applying research findings to curriculum, policy, and program development are not unique to higher education. Utilization studies have repeatedly indicated that practitioners from a variety of disciplines and settings often neglect relevant research and evaluation data (Ciarlo 1981; Knorr 1977). In response to such observations, evaluation researchers have increasingly turned their attention to the use of assessment data in program and policy development (Weiss 1988). This section reviews some literature on use and discusses its application to student outcomes assessment.

Several aspects of the talent development perspective contribute to bridging the gap between researchers and practitioners. By rejecting an adversarial approach to evaluation in favor of an information approach, the talent development perspective reduces defensiveness and hostility to evaluation. By emphasizing longitudinal designs with pre- and posttesting, talent development assessments reduce the ambiguity of assessment findings; researchers and practitioners are more likely to agree on the interpretation of the results. Evaluation data are most likely to influence decision making when top administrators and researchers agree on the goals of the institution and the goals of the assessment and perceive information about outcomes as an important source of feedback about organizational effectiveness (Weiss and Bucuvalas 1977). The talent development approach addresses each of these issues and thereby provides a framework that researchers, faculty, administrators, students, and others can share.

Before discussing more specifically the factors that promote or hinder utilization of data about outcomes, we need to define utilization. How do we know whether the research findings have been used? If we think of utilization as a continuum rather than a dichotomy, then what level of utilization might we strive for or accept as sufficient?

For the most part, researchers in applied outcomes hope that their findings may be "directly translated into political measures and action strategies" (Knorr 1977). When this situation occurs, researchers will see their recommendations widely read, discussed, and adopted.

While this approach may represent an ideal model, data are often used in other ways:

- To focus attention on an issue or to generate activity related to the issue. For example, the recent evaluative reports on higher education have served a generative function by stimulating discussion and activity about the quality of postsecondary education.

- To delay, substitute for, or legitimate a policy decision. Administrators may stall action on an issue by requesting a research project to "collect additional information" or "make sure all the facts are in." Or the administrator may use data about outcomes to support a decision that has been made for other reasons.

Information about outcomes is sometimes most useful in establishing a context for decision making rather than in establishing the single correct decision (Ewell 1983). "Increased use of student-outcomes information often leads to changes in the way certain kinds of decisions are approached—in the kinds of alternatives considered, for example—rather than changes in the substance of decisions" (p. 48). "What is needed is information that supports negotiation rather than information calculated to point out the 'correct' decision" (Cronbach and Associates 1980, p. 4).

Research findings are only one of many things that practitioners typically consider in decision making and planning (Weiss 1988; Weiss and Bucuvalas 1977). In the assessment of institutional performance, data about outcomes are supplemented by a variety of information, including subjective impressions, informal interaction, anecdotes, committee reports and recommendations, reports by external funding and accreditation agencies, and institutional ratings and reputation. Further, while researchers may be convinced of the validity of their data relative to other evidence, the administrator may see no reason to elevate research findings above other sources of information. And while researchers often assume that decision making within the institution is a rational process, it is in fact subjective and unsystematic (cf. Weick 1979).

Facilitators of Useful Research

How then can researchers encourage campus leaders to apply data about outcomes in decision making? This section discusses a variety of factors that increase the likelihood that data about outcomes will be applied to curriculum, policy, or program development.

Involvement

The literature on use of outcomes and evaluation shows consensus on the importance of involving practitioners in research, from the initial conceptualization of research questions to the content and organization of the final report. "The greater the level of participation of potential users in the various phases of the project, the more likely users are to identify with the success of the project" (Siegel and Tucker 1985, p. 323).

Similarly, useful research emerges from an action research perspective that requires interpersonal and political as well as technical abilities (Buhl and Lindquist 1981). Action research is characterized by communication between researchers and key practitioners for the duration of a project on outcomes. In addition to research skills, the active researcher must develop facilitative skills and networking information diffusion skills and must learn about alternative administrative and faculty practices (Lindquist 1981).

In addition, reporting should be a continuous activity, not only the final activity (Guba and Lincoln 1981). The researcher and the target audiences must interact in producing judgments and recommendations.

A review of 20 case studies from the evaluations filed at the Office of Health Evaluation of the U.S. Department of Health, Education, and Welfare concludes that use strongly depends on personal and interpersonal factors (Patton et al. 1977). If research is to have an impact, somebody must care about it and must have the leadership activity, energy, and commitment to ensure that the research receives attention. Institutional researchers can facilitate this process by identifying key decision makers and by working collaboratively with them to provide relevant and credible information.

Involvement of practitioners provides both direct and indirect benefits. Among the former are assurance that practitioners are aware of the research project, that the research addresses issues of concern to them, that the methods used are credible, and that the results are presented in a format that facilitates use. Involvement of decision makers also provides indirect benefits by increasing participants' sense of investment in, or ownership of, the project. They will be less likely to neglect a report that incorporates their suggestions and concerns, and they will be more interested in seeing the project succeed as a consequence of contributing to its development. They will be more likely to trust the researcher and to perceive him or her as competent for having taken the time to consult with campus leaders and respond appropriately to their suggestions.

A number of activities can be used to increase decision makers' involvement in research (Lindquist 1981). For example, participants can be asked to listen to taped interviews and analyze them together. Before data analysis, decision makers can be exposed to the raw data or to preliminary tabulations and asked to indicate the types of analyses they would most like to see. Brainstorming sessions can be scheduled after data analysis to generate recommendations and discuss the implications of the findings.

The participants in the collaborative process should include not only the identified "client" (that is, the administrator or department that requested the research) but also all the potential audiences for the research, which would probably include a range of administrators, program personnel, faculty, and students (Dawson and D'Amico 1985; Deshler 1984; Guba and Lincoln 1981; Moran 1987).

The involvement of practitioners in the research process is a necessary, but not sufficient, element of useful research. For example, such involvement will not be fruitful if stakeholders in the assessment hold conflicting assumptions and values about the goals of the institution or of the assessment. Thus, before involving practitioners directly in the design of an outcomes assessment, the researcher may need to resolve conflict in value.

Values

The choice of outcomes to assess, the instruments used, sampling and analysis procedures, the selection of comparison groups, and the organization of the final report are all value–based to some extent. Utilization is enhanced when both practitioners and researchers accept the same underlying model or theory of student outcomes and agree on the importance of assessing specific outcomes among particular students in a certain manner.

Research based on models or theories different from those held by decision makers is likely to be perceived as inappropriately oriented and therefore irrelevant. "It is important to stress that while [outcomes] information ... should be as accurate as feasible, standards of accuracy are less important than are standards of relevance" (Ewell 1984, pp. 57–58).

The talent development approach provides opportunities for researchers and practitioners to clarify their implicit values and beliefs. Discussions among faculty, administrators, students, trustees, and legislators about educational and developmental priorities are a crucial element in designing assessments of outcomes. The resulting longitudinal assessment reflects institutional values by focusing on the outcomes of most importance to those involved in the assessment.

By involving practitioners in the design and analysis of research and by clarifying previously implicit values and assumptions, the researcher is attending to process issues. Process threats to utilization can be further reduced by acquiring support for the assessment from institutional leaders.

Support of Top Administration

The support of top administrators is often crucial to the use of research results. Chief executive officers should communicate to their managers and administrators the importance of the project to create a climate on campus that is receptive to the data (Forrest 1981). And utilization can be increased when administrators offer incentives to those willing to undertake "information-based qualitative improvements in programs and services" (Ewell 1984, p. 58). Administrative support has certain advantages:

> Any effort at dissemination [of research data] is unlikely to be successful unless the top administration clearly supports the project. Strong administrative backing serves at least two critical functions: it provides committee members with an incentive to move ahead with the project and to find policy-relevant recommendations in the data; and it maximizes the chances that recommendations will be put into action (Astin 1976, p. 65).

Technical Factors

The issues involving process are necessary but not sufficient in conducting useful research. Reviews of utilization demonstrate that the quality of the research is also positively associated with utilization (Forrest 1981; Guba and Lincoln 1981; Kinnick 1985). An issue that many researchers have ignored, however, is the interaction of technical and political factors, such that some research is subject to extensive methodological criticism while other research, sometimes of questionable quality, wins acceptance quite easily. Especially in academic settings, technical criticisms of research may mask other motives for disregarding the data.

Interviews with 200 decision makers in mental health administration found that quality of research was an important predictor of use (Weiss and Bucuvalas 1980). Respondents rated quality of research as the single most important factor in determining their own likelihood of using research in decision making but as only the second most important factor (behind "action orientation") in determining use by others. Thus, attributional patterns and social desirability may have influenced respondents' ratings.

The actual importance of the quality of research to its use is also questionable, as members of an organization often claim to support a rational model of decision making that may have little correspondence to their actual decision-making patterns (McClintock 1984; cf. Campbell 1984).

The perfect study of outcomes has not yet been conducted and never will be, and all outcomes research is therefore subject to methodological criticism. Probably the best way to avoid politically motivated criticism of methodology is to involve potential critics in the design of the project. Under this approach, debates about research methods occur before rather than after data collection and analysis, and target audiences are less likely to dismiss results emanating from a research design they had a part in shaping.

Because the methodological challenges in outcomes research have been reviewed previously, a comprehensive review of technical factors is not provided here. The literature about utilization of social science data raises a number of additional issues for consideration, however.

First, qualitative approaches can often be a useful supplement to quantitative methods. Qualitative data provide a behind-the-scenes look at statistical data that can render research reports more interesting and less intimidating to decision makers. For example, case studies are recommended for four purposes: to chronicle, to characterize, to teach, and to test (Guba and Lincoln 1981). This approach is often dangerous, however, because qualitative or anecdotal information may be incorrect or misrepresent the actual meaning of quantitative findings. A case study of a "useful" program evaluation describes the use of an "interactive methodology" that combined qualitative and quantitative data to inform administrative decision making (Moran 1987).

Second, qualitative data alone are generally insufficient to satisfy the concerns of target audiences. Data about outcomes are most likely to be applied to policy development when objective techniques are used (Forrest 1981). An important element is comparative data that allow decision makers to compare findings against some meaningful norm or standard. A finding that 12 percent of graduating seniors go on to graduate or professional school, for example, has more meaning when decision makers know that the figure is 24 percent for similiar schools or was 8 percent two years ago (cf. Kinnick 1985).

Third, because practitioners often have difficulty basing important decisions on a single study, survey, or test, convergent findings can lead to more confidence in the accuracy of data about outcomes. Some writers recommend that researchers adopt a strategy of multiple perspectives (Palola and Lehmann 1976). This approach has five components: multiple observers of students' learning, multiple methods of assessment, multiple standards for evaluating students' learning, multiple decision makers using data for a variety of policy issues, and multiple time periods for measuring change in students' learning. In this manner, decision makers' concerns about any one approach could be reduced by providing convergent or alternative measures. Further, the multiple perspectives approach maximizes opportunities to apply the research to various policy issues within the university. A "multimodel" for evaluation research is recommended, to include multiple perspectives, levels, methods, functions, impacts, reporting formats, and so on (Scriven 1983).

A number of researchers with experience in value-added assessment report on the benefits of multiple measures. "Together, different kinds of measures of the same outcome dimension undoubtedly provide a full picture of the dynamics of a particular educational experience" (Ewell 1983, p. 63; cf. Banta and Fisher 1987; McClain and Krueger 1985; Mentkowski and Loacker 1985).

Dissemination

The manner in which research findings are disseminated significantly influences the extent to which and the manner in which the findings are used in decision making. Ideally, dissemination is an ongoing process of communication between researchers and practitioners. It should be conceptualized as a mutual exchange between researchers and target audiences rather than as a flow of information in one direction (from researcher to decision maker) only. In this way, the final report becomes a product of the collaboration between researchers and administrators, and administrators are therefore more likely to perceive it as useful (Forrest 1981; Guba and Lincoln 1981).

Congruent with multiple perspectives, a variety of methods of dissemination can be employed, ranging from informal brainstorming sessions to formal, written reports. A number of researchers suggest that several different reports should be prepared, each one tailored to the specific concerns of target audiences (Ewell 1983; Forrest 1981).

When communication between researchers and administrators has been ongoing and open, the final report will contain no major surprises. Although many researchers believe their data may receive more attention if the findings are unexpected, counterintuitive finds are instead likely to be dismissed or ignored (cf. Guba and Lincoln 1981), which is not meant to suggest that only findings that confirm decision makers' beliefs or knowledge will gain recognition. Rather, unexpected results should be communicated to target audiences at an early stage to provide opportunities for decision makers to assimilate the new information and avoid defensive reactions.

Timing

The timing of reports is a crucial factor in use of results. One approach is to release reports when funding decisions are being made, as student outcomes may provide information about the effectiveness of existing programs, the need for additional services, or the need for program or curricular revisions (cf. Siegel and Tucker 1985). If the study is being sponsored by a campus committee or department, researchers must strive to deliver the final product on schedule. A possible exception is when other events occurring at the time would overshadow the release of the report on outcomes; under such conditions, the researcher might wait until the audience(s) would be more likely to pay attention to the findings (cf. Siegel and Tucker 1985).

Recommendations

Some disagreement emerges in the literature regarding the risks and benefits of providing recommendations for action based on research findings as opposed to simply presenting the data and allowing practitioners to develop their own recommendations. Not surprisingly, recommendations for incremental changes have met with less opposition from policy makers than recommendations for fundamental changes.

> In some instances recommendations that state goals (ends) are more effective than those that delineate specific courses of action. This provides direction to users while permitting them considerable latitude in selecting ways of achieving the goals of the recommendations. Also it is oftentimes easier to achieve a consensus around ends rather than means. Parties asked to make changes are usually more willing to do so if they retain some control over how these changes will be realized (Siegel and Tucker 1985, p. 316).

Further, researchers should make clear the connection between their recommendations and their data. To the extent that recommendations are perceived as politically based rather than data based, decision makers are less likely to use them.

Other researchers, however, have found that utilization was positively associated with reports that contained explicit recommendations for action—have, in fact, found a positive association between reports that challenge the status quo and utilization of research by decision makers (Weiss and Bucuvalas 1980).

Guba and Lincoln (1981) suggest one way to understand these different findings. Whereas Siegel and Tucker implicitly assume that researchers develop recommendations independently and then provide them to decision makers, Guba and Lincoln suggest that researchers develop recommendations in collaboration with decision makers. Under these circumstances, target audiences might more positively receive explicit recommendations for action or recommendations of a more fundamental nature.

Another approach to developing useful recommendations suggests that time constraints often force researchers to develop recommendations without a full consideration of the possible alternatives for action suggested by the data (Roberts-Gray, Buller, and Sparkman 1987). Rather than leave recommendations to the end of the research process, perhaps researchers should write recommendations during research design, using a "what if" approach.

> By thinking at the beginning about recommendations that may be made at the close of the evaluation, the evaluator helps ensure that evaluation results will contribute to program improvement. . . . The logic linking data with action is spelled out and easy to trace. . . . It can show where additional data are needed and identify areas where data thought to be needed would be useless in fact (Roberts-Gray, Buller, and Sparkman 1987, p. 681).

Report Format

The format of the report is another factor related to utilization. Several researchers recommend that reports be organized around issues rather than methods (DeLoria and Brookings 1984; Ewell 1983; Forrest 1981; Kinnick 1985). Reports should directly address practitioners' concerns—which may require writing several reports or memos, each focusing on a different issue. Reports should be brief, avoid research jargon, and use graphics to summarize and display major findings (Forrest 1981; Guba and Lincoln 1981).

A set of useful recommendations about writing research reports for decision makers suggests that the traditional "dissertation-style" approach may be inconvenient for decision makers because "the details needed to answer a single policy question may be scattered across several chapters" (DeLoria and Brookings 1984, p. 648). The time and effort required to locate and integrate relevant information may deter use of the report.

As an alternative to the traditional approach, researchers should prepare two reports—one scientific and one policy (DeLoria and Brookings 1984). The latter would be brief, organized around major policy questions, and in the language of the practitioner. Reports that get used in decision making have the following characteristics:

1. The questions addressed are clearly linked to real policy decisions.

2. At least some questions in each report consider the costs affecting policy.

3. Policy questions form the central organizing theme of the report.

4. The reports describe enough of the policy context to permit informed interpretation without outside sources.

5. Evaluation methodology is played down.

6. Reports begin with a brief summary of the essential findings.

7. Backup narrative for the executive summary is "chunked" into easily located, brief segments throughout the body of the report.

8. Only simple statistics are presented.

9. Where jargon is used, it is the jargon of the practitioners, not of the evaluators.

10. Concrete recommendations for action are based on specific findings (DeLoria and Brookings 1984, pp. 660–62).

Within higher education, researchers must walk a fine line between turning off their audience by being too technical and turning off their audience by being too simplistic. Especially when professors trained in research will be reading the reports, detailed information about sampling, design, and analysis may be desirable to establish the validity of the methods employed. This technical information, however, should be provided in an appendix or self-contained chapter, with the most important information repeated in other sections that are devoted to major questions of research and policy.

Structures and Settings

The ideal setting is one in which decision makers can jointly review and discuss the research data. Committees associated with the major campus issues provide opportunities for consideration of research findings and implementation of recommendations. Open forums could be held as well to encourage a broad range of students, faculty, and staff to discuss the findings. Or top administrators might sponsor a retreat for administrators to review the data and brainstorm about its implications for action.

Special events created specifically to consider the research on outcomes have the advantage of emphasizing administrative commitment to the project and of providing a setting in which the project is a primary (or exclusive) focus. On the other hand, when discussion of the findings is integrated into ongoing committees or task forces, the research on outcomes may come to be perceived as relevant to day-to-day decision making and an integral part of "management systems."

The importance of organizational factors can be summarized as follows:

> One way of increasing the likelihood that student outcomes information will be used by decision makers is to put the information in a form suited to some of their regular activities. For most decision makers, student outcomes information falls into the category of "nice to know" rather than "need to know." Outcomes information is much more likely to be recognized as relevant if it is not seen as distinct from the kinds of productivity information upon which most decision makers claim to base their findings (Ewell 1983, p. 48).

Barriers to Use

This section describes additional factors that hinder utilization.

Gap Between Researchers and Practitioners

While researchers traditionally strive for objectivity and neutrality, advocacy is an important element in the administrative role. And while researchers may prefer complex methods and an extended time frame for data collection and analysis, decision makers require information that can be quickly obtained and easily assimilated. These and other differences between researchers and administrators may lead administrators to perceive research data as irrelevant in their decision making (cf. Caplan, 1977; Siegel and Tucker 1985). One possible approach to this problem is for researchers to have the foresight to build data bases that ultimately will provide a resource for getting rapid and sophisticated answers to complex questions.

Although the goals of most colleges and universities include the support of research activities, administrators may fail to perceive these activities as useful in meeting their own needs for information. Therefore, the researcher must educate administrators about the potential benefits of research and must respond to the values, language, and goals of target audiences.

The Institution's Decentralized Structure

The benefits of using data available on campus have been discussed in previous sections. This task may be rendered difficult when relevant data elements are located in different sites on campus and when the data are collected or processed in such a way that it is difficult to merge with other information (Kinnick 1985). Some additional expenses could be incurred as well if data must be recoded or rekeyed. Such problems can almost always be solved if sufficient time is allowed and if top administrators communicate the importance of the effort to those who manage the data.

Another problem can arise from the decentralized nature of the university: The decentralized structure of most schools means that no one office or department is responsible for student outcomes (Ewell 1983). Support from top administrators, especially incentives for collection or application of data about outcomes, can overcome this barrier.

Faculty Resistance

Resistance from faculty is often cited as a reason that assessments of outcomes are inappropriate for a particular institution (Ewell 1985). Faculty may fear a negative evaluation or may believe that assessments of outcomes will not accurately measure the educational process. Recent research (Astin and Ayala 1987) suggests that resistance from faculty is a normal part of any attempt to implement such assessments. It is to be expected but it can be effectively dealt with. Barriers erected by faculty can be overcome by involving faculty in the research, by differentiating assessments of outcomes from teaching evaluations, and by using multiple measures to compensate for the limitations of individual instruments.

Cost

Even when decision makers believe in the value of such assessment, institutional research is one of many programs competing for limited funds and administrators may be unable or unwilling to financially support the research program. Again, support from top administrators and early education and involvement of key audiences increase the likelihood that the assessment will be funded. Costs can be reduced by using data already available on campus (Ewell 1985).

Timing and Follow-through

Late delivery of research is among the most common reasons for data's underuse (Kinnick 1985). This situation should be avoided at all costs, because it not only reduces (or eliminates) the usefulness of the current project but also decreases the likelihood of decision makers' support for future projects.

Underuse may also result if the researcher fails to conduct any follow-up activities after the final report is released. Such activities may take many forms—releasing additional memos and analyses, requesting feedback from target audiences, or participating in implementation activities, for example. Without such activities, decision makers are likely to be distracted by other, more visible issues, and findings will be neglected.

Academic Games

A number of "academic games" can be observed in committee meetings at most colleges—rationalization, passing the buck, obfuscation, co-optation, recitation, and displacement/projection (Astin 1976). One of the purposes of such games is to relieve committee members of responsibility for action; the games in this way act as barriers to utilization. Researchers can use both direct and indirect approaches to end the games and maintain control of the discussion.

Paradoxes of Guidelines for Utilization

Applying the information provided in this monograph poses several challenges, including reconciling recommendations that appear to be contradictory. This section briefly describes some of these apparent conflicts.

Rational Versus Irrational Decision Making

Applied research assumes that decision making is rational—that administrators assess situations, identify problems, generate and evaluate potential solutions, and implement the "best" alternative. In reality, however, decision making may proceed along highly subjective, unsystematic, and even irrational lines (McClintock 1984; Weick 1979; Weiss 1988). Under such circumstances "legitimating" uses of research may be more likely to occur than "instrumental" uses. Researchers must weigh the risks of their research being misrepresented or distorted against the risks of its being ignored altogether.

Involvement Versus Control

The emphasis of action research on involving target audiences in the research process may threaten the traditional objectivity and neutrality of researchers. As researchers try to understand and appeal to the values of decision makers, they risk "co-optation" (Dawson and D'Amico 1985). Similarly, the researcher walks a thin line between profiting from the involvement of decision makers and losing control of the project (Siegel and Tucker 1985). Opponents of a project might criticize the research as partisan if researchers have worked too closely with target audiences.

Democracy Versus Competition in Decision Making

The "democratic" decision-making process characteristic of action research may conflict with competitive norms found in many colleges (Buhl and Lindquist 1981). The participatory process recommended by most action researchers will be ineffective if decision making is perceived as a competitive situation in which one person wins and another loses. When such norms are firmly entrenched, the researcher must strive to create a safe setting for open discussion with target audiences.

Involvement Versus Timeliness

While the benefits of involving target audiences in the research have been discussed at length, it should be pointed out that such a process may significantly slow down the progress of the research. It takes time to schedule meetings, to consult with various stakeholders, and to respond to their feedback. Further, most decision makers are very busy people who can invest only a limited amount of time in the effort. Because late delivery of this data is a major barrier to utilization, the researcher must either be prepared to start the process early or balance time pressure against political pressure.

Methodological Rigor Versus Time and Cost

While comparative, longitudinal studies that conform to established standards of quasi-experimental design, use multiple measures, and supplement quantitative findings with qualitative data are desirable, they are also expensive and time consuming. The obvious rejoinder to this objection is that assessments that fail to accurately respond to the research questions are hard to justify, regardless of their cost or "efficiency." Researchers may have to decide which methodological tradeoffs are least damaging, however (cf. Cook and Campbell 1979).

Technical Credibility Versus Readability

The brief reports recommended by many researchers (for example, Ewell 1983; Forrest 1981; Palola and Lehmann 1976) do not include room for detailed descriptions of research methods. Academic audiences, however, may be unwilling to accept the findings without such information. The additional bulk created by including this information, on the other hand, may deter decision makers from reading the report.

Researcher's Objectivity Versus Advocacy

Action research places the researcher in the role of advocate as well as technician, although writers disagree about the most effective methods of advocacy (see the previous discussion on research recommendations). Institutional researchers must face another dilemma: If they act as advocates in one situation, might that limit their credibility in another? When researchers become politically active, will decision makers trust their information on a continuing basis? If researchers decide not to enter the political arena, however, will their data be misrepresented or neglected?

Introduction and Overview: From Classroom Assessment to Classroom Research

Thomas A. Angelo

For a decade now, higher education in the United States has been engaged in a process of self-reflection and reform. Nearly everyone involved agrees that the quality of teaching and learning should be improved. Most educators agree educational quality can be improved, and that by basing teaching practice more solidly on research findings from psychology and education, faculty could help hasten that improvement. Nonetheless, despite fifty years of inquiry into teaching and learning in college, the gap between research and teaching is still a chasm that is rarely bridged. Why has this large body of research, much of it good, had to so little effect on the practice of college teaching?

Faculty often accuse educational researchers of failing to address the practical, day-to-day needs of classroom teachers. They charge that too many researchers are more interested in publishing their findings in obscure academic journals read by a handful of colleagues than in applying those findings to improve the education of large numbers of students. Researchers counter that their job is to seek verifiable answers to general questions, not to figure out the specific applications of their findings to particular classrooms. They point out that the faculty, who are the group most capable of adapting and applying the fruits of research, are at best uninterested in research findings and at worst openly resistant to change.

But while this exercise in blame-fixing continues, the critical questions remain unanswered. How can the strengths of research and teaching be joined to improve learning in the classroom? How can higher education close, or at least narrow, the research-teaching gap?

In 1986, in an effort to narrow this long-standing gap between research and practice, K. Patricia Cross proposed a novel way to engage faculty in the systematic, disciplined study of teaching and learning in their own classrooms. She called this approach *Classroom Research*. Cross, Conner Professor of Higher Education at the University of California, Berkeley, envisions Classroom Research as a way to "reduce the distance between researchers and practitioners to zero" (Cross and Angelo, 1988, p. 2) by encouraging faculty to investigate questions that arise in their own teaching. Since these Classroom Researchers seek to answer discipline-specific questions of their own choosing they are much more likely to apply what they discover to improve learning in their own classrooms. In this "action-oriented," applied form of inquiry, researcher and teacher are one and the same person, and the research-practice gap disappears.

Comparing Classroom Research and Traditional Research

Because the word *research* in the term *Classroom Research* carries with it a heavy load of connotations, it is useful to clarify the concept. Traditional educational research seeks to discover and validate general laws of teaching and learning. For that reason, it usually requires sophisticated knowledge of research design, sampling techniques, and statistical analysis. The purpose of Classroom Research, on the other hand, is to provide faculty with information and insights into what, how, and how well their particular students are learning in their specific courses. Classroom Researchers then use the information and insights gained to inform and improve their teaching.

To successfully carry out Classroom Research, college teachers need expert knowledge in their disciplines, an understanding of their students' characteristics and needs, good analytic and problem-solving skills, and a lasting commitment to improving student learning. In sum, then, though relatively few faculty have the specialized skills required for educational research, nearly all college faculty have the potential to use Classroom Research to their own and their students' advantage.

The following quotation, by the educator most responsible for developing the concept, clearly summarizes the what and why of Classroom Research: "The purpose of classroom research is to contribute to the professionalization of teaching, to provide the knowledge, understanding, and insights that will sensitize teachers to the struggles of students to learn. Classroom research consists of any systematic inquiry designed and conducted for the purpose of increasing insight and understanding of the relationships between teaching and learning" (Cross, 1990, p. 136).

The faculty projects described in this chapter, and several others described in detail in Part Two, illustrate this definition of Classroom Research. Despite the fact that all good teachers elicit feedback and use the responses informally to help them adjust their teaching, most faculty have had little or no experience in systematically studying student learning. Therefore, to get off to a successful start in Classroom Research, many faculty have learned and benefited from a simple, well-structured approach known as Classroom Assessment.

Defining Classroom Assessment

The word *assessment*, much like the term *research*, is subject to a range of interpretations, and so it is important to clarify its meaning here in relation to Classroom Assessment. Cross (1989, p. 4, original emphasis) draws the following useful distinctions: "Most people think of assessment as a *large-scale* testing program, conducted at *institutional or state* levels, usually by *measurement experts*, to determine what students *have* learned in *college*. Classroom Assessment questions almost every working word of that definition. A definition of Classroom Assessment looks more like this: Classroom Assessment consists of *small-scale* assessments conducted *continuously* in college classrooms by discipline-based *teachers* to determine what students *are* learning in *that class*." In addition, the purpose of many large-scale assessment programs is primarily to provide accountability, and only secondarily and indirectly to improve learning. The primary purpose of Classroom Assessment, by contrast, is to improve learning directly by providing teachers with the kind of feedback they need to inform their instructional decisions.

How Faculty Get Started: Classroom Assessment Techniques

Most faculty start by trying quick and easy one-shot projects designed to discover what and how much their students are learning. These first-stage Classroom Research efforts are known as Classroom Assessment projects, and the tools faculty use to gather limited, focused feedback on student learning are known as Classroom Assessment Techniques (CATs).

The "One-Minute Paper" is a good example of a simple, quick CAT that has been used to good advantage by hundreds of college teachers in all disciplines. The One-Minute Paper, originally developed by a physics professor at UC Berkeley (Wilson, 1986), asks students to respond anonymously to the following two questions at the end of the class period: (1) What is the most important thing you learned in class today? and (2) What question remains uppermost in your mind? By quickly scanning students' responses, the teacher can make accurately focused adjustments in the following class to capitalize on what students have already learned well and to clear up confusions that can impede further learning.

One of the guiding aphorisms of Classroom Research is "Adapt, don't adopt," and faculty have repeatedly demonstrated their creativity in doing just that. For example, Frederick Mosteller, distinguished professor of statistics at Harvard, adapted and further streamlined the One-Minute Paper. He reported getting very useful feedback simply by asking students to answer one question: "What was the 'muddiest point' in my lecture today?" (Mosteller, 1989, p. 15). Faculty from many disciplines are now experimenting with the "Muddiest Point" technique and, in turn, further adapting it to fit their needs.

In the following chapter, and throughout Part Two of this volume, you will read examples of simple CATs applied in a variety of courses. All of the authors whose work appears in this section began by using simple CATs, and most continue to use them as elements of or in addition to their more elaborate Classroom Research projects. Many of the techniques mentioned in the chapters that follow are drawn from Cross and Angelo's *Classroom Assessment Techniques: A Handbook for Faculty* (1988) and have been adapted by the authors to fit their specific disciplines and students. The chapters by Kort, Cottell, and Walker, for example, all include examples of creative adaptations of CATs from the *Handbook*. But other techniques have diverse origins or were developed by the authors themselves. The chapters by Olmsted and by Obler and her colleagues illustrate several "homegrown" assessment techniques.

Classroom Assessment Techniques, Tests, and Teaching Techniques

Initially, faculty are prone to confuse CATs with the tests and quizzes they use to evaluate student learning—or with familiar teaching techniques. Unlike tests or quizzes, however, CATs are ungraded and usually anonymous. The purpose of Classroom Assessments is to quickly assess the whole class's learning in order to adjust instruction, not to evaluate the achievement of an individual student in order to assign a grade. Put another way, if the primary purpose of tests and quizzes is to classify learners, the aim of Classroom Assessment is to understand and improve learning.

While CATs are not tests, neither are they simply teaching techniques. CATs are meant to be used between teaching and testing, to find out how well students are doing in time to help them improve. All faculty use teaching techniques as a means to achieve their instructional goals. Classroom Researchers use CATs to find out how well they are achieving those goals. If we view teaching and testing as two legs of an instructional "tripod," then Classroom Assessment is a third leg that can provide more stability and reliability to the platform, making it better able to support learning.

From Classroom Assessment to Classroom Research: Three Examples

Classroom Assessment can be a useful, easy first step in Classroom Research, but it is only one approach—one set of tools—for studying the effects of teaching on learning. As mentioned earlier, many teachers who began by occasionally using simple CATs have gone on to design and carry out systematic semester- or year-long studies of student learning. These comprehensive, integrated inquiries are examples of true Classroom Research, whether or not they make use of Classroom Assessment.

In this volume, for instance, Nakaji's use of interviews, learning-style questionnaires, and videotaping to study visualization is a case in point. The Classroom Research project he describes did not incorporate any simple CATs, although he reports using them regularly in his classes. Like all good Classroom Researchers, however, Nakaji used insights gained from his inquiry to adjust his teaching in order to improve student learning. He took what he learned from the students back to the students by effectively incorporating explicit instruction on how to visualize into his physics courses.

In another case, a nursing professor who was concerned that her students' low self-confidence was interfering with their learning in clinical settings designed a multistage Classroom Research project to test her assumptions. In the course of her year-long study, she discovered that the students with the lowest self-reported confidence levels were often engaging in negative "self talk." Through this negative self-talk, her students were subconsciously sabotaging their performance and learning. The nursing instructor used this feedback to make the students explicitly aware of their "self-programming" and to teach them ways to engage in positive self-talk. In other words, once she and the students understood what was going on, they were able to gain more control over the learning process.

As a third example of Classroom Research, a philosophy professor wondered whether her introductory-level logic courses were really teaching students to think critically. Over the course of a semester, she used a number of simple CATs to probe students' concepts of "critical thinking" and to assess how well the logic class was developing their skills. She found, in a nutshell, that even though students liked and valued her course, they viewed critical thinking as something quite apart from formal logic and, not surprisingly, felt that the course had done little or nothing to improve what they thought of as useful critical thinking skills. These findings led her to incorporate instruction in "everyday logic" and practice in a wider variety of critical thinking approaches into the course.

At this point, it may be useful to summarize the relationship between Classroom Assessment and Classroom Research as a part-whole, or subset-set, relationship. Classroom Assessment is one method within a larger approach, Classroom Research, much as the lecture method is one approach to teaching. Thus, Classroom Assessment and Classroom Research differ in scope, not in kind.

The Bottom Line: Costs and Benefits of Classroom Research

In the three-year life span of the Classroom Research Project, Cross and I had many opportunities to learn firsthand what faculty considered the pros and cons of this approach. The feedback we received from participants, whether through informal focus groups or written surveys, consistently fell into the same patterns. For those readers who are considering trying this approach, it may be helpful to know in advance what their experienced colleagues see as the costs and benefits of Classroom Research.

Costs of Participating in Classroom Research. There are three kinds of costs that Classroom Researchers mention as potentially significant. The first is the amount of time that assessment and related activities take. The second involves potential threats to adequate coverage of material. The third is the relatively high tolerance for ambiguity and lack of closure sometimes necessitated by this type of assessment.

Time. The most frequently mentioned "cost" associated with using Classroom Research is time. Obviously, it does take some class time to use even the simplest CAT and some out-of-class time to analyze the feedback and prepare a response. Techniques like the Muddiest Point or One-Minute

Paper require very little time to implement and respond to, but the more elaborate the assessment, the more time required. Most of the teachers involved in the Classroom Research Project also met regularly with other faculty to discuss their experiences and share findings and insights. These meetings, which they found very valuable, also took time.

Coverage. A related but distinct cost concerns the perceived threat to coverage of course material. Faculty engaged in Classroom Assessment frequently found that students were not learning as much, as well, or as quickly as they had previously assumed. Faced with such feedback from a large segment of the class, teachers had to decide how to respond. When a CAT revealed that much of the class had not learned a critical concept or skill, the instructor had to decide whether it was best to review, go more slowly, stop and re-teach the material—or to go ahead and hope students would somehow get it later. We found that many teachers were concerned, and legitimately so, that responding to the results of their assessments might limit the amount of course content they could teach.

There is, of course, no single, simple answer to this dilemma. Many teachers strongly felt it was incumbent on them to "cover the material," even if many students were clearly not learning it. Other participants disagreed, arguing that it was more worthwhile in the long run to teach less but better. While the use of Classroom Assessment obviously does not create these "content gaps" between what students have learned and what teachers expect them to learn, it does bring the coverage issue to the foreground. As faculty awareness of this teaching-learning gap grew, so did the perception that this problematic discovery was an inevitable cost of engaging in the process.

Closure. Even the simplest Classroom Assessments sometimes raise more questions about student learning than they answer. For all that psychologists and cognitive scientists have discovered in general about human learning in the last century, we still know very little about how students acquire the particular knowledge and skills demanded by specific disciplines. When faculty carry out Classroom Research, they are exploring exactly those largely uncharted territories.

Therefore, it is not too surprising that novice Classroom Researchers sometimes find students' feedback baffling and are unsure how best to respond. In most cases, not even the cognitive scientists and educational psychologists who devote their careers to these matters could provide the "right" answers. Some faculty who had never ventured beyond their roles as content experts, however, found it initially uncomfortable to proceed without an immediate response.

Some participants also found it disconcerting to discover the wide range of diversity of preparation, understanding, and interpretation that exists beneath the surface in almost any college classroom. These participants noted, understandably, that it is frustrating not to get complete, comprehensible feedback every time a CAT is used. They also found it troubling when their instructional responses to student feedback did not fully solve the problems raised.

For some college teachers with a strong need for closure, the ongoing nature of Classroom Research was a psychological cost. For many other participants, however, its open-ended nature was a highly motivating intellectual challenge.

Benefits of Participating in Classroom Research. The participants in campus Classroom Research programs were quite clear that the benefits of engaging in this approach far outweighed the costs. The three most frequently mentioned benefits of participation are explained below.

Collegiality. The single most frequently mentioned benefit of Classroom Research was one neither Cross nor I would have predicted. Over and over again, faculty participants said that they benefited most from meeting and working with other colleagues. They valued the opportunities provided by on-campus Classroom Research programs to engage in clearly focused discussions on teaching and learning with colleagues and to collaborate on projects aimed at understanding and improving the quality of student learning.

While faculty can practice Classroom Research independently and in isolation, most have not. Instead, many of those who have enjoyed the greatest success with Classroom Research have been members of campus groups. The chapters in Part Three report on colleges with active, successful Classroom Research programs, and Stetson and Berry and others highlight the importance of supporting collegiality.

Positive Student Response. Many faculty are unprepared for the enthusiasm with which students respond to their requests for feedback on their learning. When the students know that data are being gathered to help them learn better, and not simply to grade them, they are usually not only willing but anxious to participate in Classroom Assessments. Many faculty have reported higher levels of student-faculty interaction and more active classroom participation as outcomes. It appears that most students enjoy and appreciate responding to Classroom Assessments if the instructor makes the purpose and outcomes of the assessments explicit and clearly uses the results to improve classroom learning. Kort, Olmsted, Nakaji, and Cottell all comment on their students' positive responses.

Intellectual Excitement and Renewal. Most of the participants in our project were veteran faculty members, professors at mid-career or beyond. Most of them were also teaching in institutions where there were relatively few opportunities or incentives to carry out traditional disciplinary research.

Many of these experienced college teachers found a new outlet for their intellectual energies in Classroom Research. They spoke of being "revitalized" and "challenged" by the opportunities this approach afforded them to apply their disciplinary inquiry skills to follow-up questions about teaching and learning in their courses. This volume contains many examples of tangible results of the intellectual excitement generated by faculty and administrators engaged in Classroom Research.

Summary

Classroom Research is the patient, systematic study of student learning by disciplinary faculty in their classrooms. It is aimed at producing insights and understanding that can improve teaching and learning. Classroom Assessment is one simple, practical approach to Classroom Research. Classroom Assessment provides faculty with tools and researches for getting feedback early and often on the effects of their teaching on student learning. Faculty then use that feedback to inform and improve instruction. Classroom Assessment Techniques, simple tools for collecting feedback on student learning, are meant to complement, not substitute for, teaching techniques and tests.

When asked to reflect on the costs and benefits of using Classroom Research and Classroom Assessment, faculty with a year or more experience in this approach report that getting useful feedback on student learning does require additional time, sometimes leads them to reconsider the amount of content that students can learn and they can cover in a single course, and may raise questions for which they have no immediate responses.

However, the same experienced Classroom Researchers also clearly indicate that the benefits of this approach outweigh the costs. They report many intellectual, practical, and personal benefits from cooperating with colleagues through structured Classroom Research programs on their campuses. They note increased student participation and active learning in class as well as increased faculty-student interaction. Finally, faculty also mention a heightening of their own intellectual interest in teaching and learning as a result of engaging in Classroom Research.

References

Cross, K. P. "What's in That Black Box?, or, How Do We Know What Students are Learning?" Howard R. Bowen Lecture at the Claremont Graduate School, Claremont, California, Nov. 8, 1989.

Cross, K. P. "Classroom Research: Helping Professors Learn More about Teaching and Learning," in P. Seldin and Associates, *How Administrators Can Improve Teaching: Moving from Talk to Action in Higher Education*. San Francisco: Jossey-Bass, 1990.

Cross, K. P., and Angelo, T. A. *Classroom Assessment Techniques: A Handbook for Faculty*. Ann Arbor, Mich.: National Center for Research to Improve Postsecondary Teaching and Learning, 1988.

Mosteller, F. "The 'Muddiest Point in the Lecture' as a Feedback Device." *On Teaching and Learning: The Journal of the Harvard-Danforth Center*, 1989, 3, 10–21.

Wilson, R. C. "Improving Faculty Teaching: Effective Use of Student Evaluations and Consultants." *Journal of Higher Education*, 1986, 57, 196–211.

Assessment and the Way We Work

PAT HUTCHINGS

• • •

Work With Students

The best account I've heard of how assessment changes the way we work with students comes from a faculty member from a community college, a teacher of writing, who wrote to the AAHE Assessment Forum to say, "Assessment means to me, asking whether my students are learning what I think I'm teaching."

As I say, I like that question very much; it puts in a nutshell many of the insights I was coming to at Alverno that first year. But there are other questions that might be cited here as well. They'll sound familiar to you, I think.

- What do I have to do to get an A?

- Why do we have to do this paper?

- Why don't you just tell us what you're looking for?

- Where is this course going, anyway?

- Do we have to know this?

Those are, of course, students' questions—and not, I'd like to propose, the questions of grumblers only, but of *good* students who quite reasonably want to know what's expected of them and where things are going; and they're questions, too, of students who could be a whole lot *better* if they understood the answers. They're questions that assessment speaks to very directly, as the following two examples show.

The first is a project supported by the Fund for the Improvement of Postsecondary Education (FIPSE) being undertaken by 10 (and over the next two years 20, and then 30) community colleges in California, all part of LARC, the Learning Assessment Retention Consortium that began several years ago to collaborate on the assessment of entry-level skills. This past year a number of LARC institutions got interested in looking not just at entering abilities but at outcomes down the line. And they wanted to look at "outcomes" in a way that took advantage of faculty's interest in and commitment to teaching. What they turned to is K. Patricia Cross's concept of Classroom Assessment.

I visited the group earlier this spring and got to hear them talk with one another about what happens when faculty and students engage in the small-scale, in-class assessment methods that Pat and her colleague Tom Angelo have proposed.

715

716 Assessment and Program Evaluation

There was, for instance, the chemistry professor from Cuesta College who confessed to the group that though he was an experienced teacher (and obviously one who cared a lot about students), he was feeling like a beginner with this assessment stuff, not sure that he was "doing it right.". . . But the more he and his colleagues talked, the clearer it was that something important was happening that was changing the way these faculty were working with students.

Like several others in the group, this professor was using the "one-minute paper," where students write briefly at the end of the class about what they understood that day, and what they're still not clear about. And he talked to the group about what he was learning about his students— about how they think about the problems he assigns, where they get stuck, where breakthroughs occur. "I just never knew this much about my students' thinking," he told us. Wanting to understand more, I asked him, "So, the power of Classroom Assessment is in giving you more information about students. Is that right?" And he paused and said, "Well, yes, it's information. But really, you know, the bigger difference is that I never thought to *ask* these questions before."

At the risk of putting words in this fine man's mouth, I can't help but note that he was having the same insight I had at Alverno as I worked at my syllabus that first semester—that as soon as you ask, as assessment does, Are students getting it?, you're also asking yourself to be much clearer about what that *it* is, what you expect, where you're aiming... and the whole enterprise gets more purposeful and focused. That line of thinking isn't an easy one; it's not one most of us were ever trained to undertake. But it sure can change the way faculty and students work together.

Faculty at SUNY-Fredonia (my second example) have come, I think, to a similar conclusion.

For several years now, with FIPSE funding, Fredonia has been assessing a new general-education program and they've chosen to go the local route in all cases, with faculty-designed exams to cover a variety of cross-cutting, general-education outcomes. I think that's a right idea, and when I visited there several years ago it looked like things were going well, and so I was dying to read, as I finally did this winter, their final report to FIPSE. In that report they set forth what they've learned—and equally interesting, what they didn't learn.

They didn't, for instance, ever learn the Truth about their students. In fact, much of their work at the outset entailed discussion—and I dare say heated debate—about the soundness of this and that instrument, pilot testing, whether the results could be compared this way or that, what was valid, what not . . . with the result, as I say, that no Truth was learned. What faculty *did* learn was that whether the score was 37 or 43 (a debate that can go forever), students weren't doing as well in "reflexive thinking" as faculty thought they should. That is, students were taking and passing individual courses all right, but they weren't seeing connections; they couldn't put the pieces together.

The solution? No doubt there were (and should be) several. But interestingly, one of their next steps at Fredonia is more assessment. Faculty are now working to develop a portfolio approach to assessment that will give them more in-depth information about each student's ability to put the pieces together, but also—and here's the beauty of the thing—help the student *develop* that ability.

Portfolios are kept by students themselves and include work done through the four—or whatever—years. The first piece, done at entry and used for advising, is "My History as a Learner," an essay where the student is asked (i.e., told that at Fredonia they will be *expected*) to self-reflect, to be conscious of what they do as learners. Intermediate pieces in the portfolio are, I believe, pulled from various course settings; the final entry is an essay in which students look back on all that work and are asked to put the pieces together, addressing, in particular, questions about how general education is connected to the major.

It is, as I say, a way of gathering very rich information about students. More important, it's a method that's for teaching first, assessment second . . . or that blurs the difference. Finally, it's a method that recognizes that the coherence of the curriculum has to reside not only in *our* neat schemes but in the student's ability to make connections and create coherence, an ability that can be attended to, focused on as an expectation, taught for, assessed, and improved.

These accounts of work being done in the LARC group and at Fredonia risk making things seem smoother than they are: People from the institutions in question may, I'm aware, be squirming in the audience. My intent is not to suggest that they've somehow got things righter than the rest of the world but to say instead that I *do* see in both projects (and in many more featured at this conference) some ways of thinking that have the potential to change the way we work with students . . . by making learning the test of teaching; by nudging us into a clearer view of that learning; by finding ways to communicate that view to students, to let them know, through statements in syllabi and through the assignments and assessments we give, what we expect, that we expect a lot, that we and they are going to meet those expectations.

By way of summary to this section on the way we work with students, I offer a comment that my colleague Barbara Wright, director of the AAHE Assessment Forum, made recently in response to a draft of something I was writing. I was getting heated up over the fact that the burden for learning so often falls so exclusively on students. "Students responsible for learning, . . ." Barbara wrote in the margin (I could imagine her eyebrow cocking). "Not a bad idea." It isn't, and assessment, if you will, agrees. It speaks to a shared responsibility between faculty and students. It calls on us to create conditions in which students can carry out that responsibility, where they don't have to ask, Where is this course going? What are you looking for? What am I learning here, anyway?

Work With One Another

Stories about how we work with students are, of course, also stories about how we work with one another. In fact, Pat Cross has remarked that something she didn't anticipate about Classroom Assessment—one attraction of which would be that it could be done alone—is that faculty no sooner get into asking the kinds of questions the LARC faculty were excited about, than they want to talk to and hear from colleagues who, it turns out, are also interested in those questions . . . and dying to talk about them.

What we see in those cases and on scores of campuses is one of assessment's most powerful and in many cases immediate effects: the prompting of a conversation about student learning that otherwise takes place not at all, or only on the most sporadic basis, or in ways that have little chance of finding their way into institutional decision making.

I'm thinking here of a hundred stories I've heard. From a faculty member in the art history department at the University of Tennessee-Knoxville, for instance. She said it was only when faced with assessment—in this case a state-mandated requirement to examine the outcomes of the major—that faculty in her department "for the first time sat down and talked with one another," not altogether happily, mind you, about what goes on in their respective classes, what's covered and (one hopes) uncovered, what the aims of various courses are, what assignments are given . . . all of that otherwise behind-the-doors stuff that assessment opens onto.

And I think about a man I met during a visit to the University of Connecticut. An English professor, far from convinced that assessment was the best thing in town, who said he's stuck with the work of the assessment committee because it is "the one place on campus where there was a serious conversation about student learning going on."

And I think about Harvard. Some of you may know the Harvard assessment story from the NY *Times*—the front page no less—where a report on the Harvard Assessment Seminars appeared a few months ago. Or better yet you may know it from the May *AAHE Bulletin,* where editor Ted Marchese interviews the convener of those seminars, Richard Light.

It's work that goes back to 1986, when Harvard president Derek Bok urged in his book *Higher Learning* that every college "study the learning process and assess the effects of its programs." To that end, on his own campus, he asked Richard Light, a faculty member in the Kennedy School and the Graduate School of Education, to convene a seminar on undergraduate learning—to which more than 100 faculty and administrators were soon drawn.

Interestingly, the story of the seminars, which were held over three years and still go on, is very similar to that of the LARC Classroom Assessment project. Though there have been "findings" in the Harvard picture, its seminars are best described as "faculty inquiries into student learning."

For example, participants took on questions about the impact of the size of groups in which students study, which led to several experiments conducted by faculty with their own students that showed that students who study in groups of four to six do better academically than students studying alone.

They looked too—at the urging of student participants in the seminars—at questions of gender, and discovered that women students at Harvard have an experience rather different from men's.

In the *Bulletin* interview, Ted Marchese says to Dick Light, Well, now, that's all very nice— these findings about gender and about study in groups—but it certainly isn't news. Light has a great comeback (exactly the one Ted was after, I suspect): "Newness," Light replies, "is hardly the goal here; we're after locally useful information and small but steady increments of improvement." He knows, he says, "that similar findings, some from earlier decades, exist in the library, but there is a power, an immediacy, that comes out of your own discoveries." The upshot is that long-time, long-tenured faculty are now talking to one another about how students learn, and doing things as a result that they didn't do two years ago—among them Pat Cross's "one-minute paper."

The point? It's not that Harvard has made some quantum leap forward in quality; it's that assessment has helped create an occasion to take up, collectively, questions about learning and the conditions under which it can occur best.

At Harvard, UTK, UConn, and scores of other campuses, assessment has changed the way we work by getting us talking to one another, across all kinds of lines and boundaries, coming to clearer, more collective visions of our aims and purposes, asking questions together about whether we're achieving those purposes and how we might do better.

Alverno is an interesting footnote here: By my lights, one of the most important things Alverno has done—more important than any single assessment innovation the college is admired for—is to set aside Friday afternoons for faculty to work together on questions of teaching and learning . . . questions prompted and then illuminated by assessment.

The Culture of Assessment

Thinking about assessment's impact on the way we work with students and with one another, we come to a deeper question, one about the kind of culture—the conditions—in which our best work can go forward. What kind of culture is that? What habits of mind and deeper structures make the work called for by assessment work?

In some ways I think this Assessment Conference is an answer to that question. As I've gone from session to session over the last three days, I've been struck that underlying what many of you are doing in the name of assessment is . . . what shall I call it? . . . a view of the world, a subtext, a vision of what our institutions might be like, a set of educational values. Assessment is not, I've come to believe, just a set of methods; not a technology to be plugged in anywhere toward any end.

It is (and this was my point in beginning with Alverno) an enactment of a set of beliefs about the kind of work that matters on our campuses. Here are three:

1. *That teaching is to be taken seriously and rewarded.*

   The issue of rewards may appear to be the more pointed one here, but let me pause for a moment on "taking teaching seriously"—the title, not incidentally, of a keynote address Pat Cross delivered at AAHE's 1986 National Conference. It is, I think, no accident that the spokesperson for "taking teaching seriously" also speaks for

Classroom Assessment. Assessment is a way of enacting a greater seriousness about teaching; it also challenges us, I think, to look harder at what it would mean to be really serious about teaching.

I think, for instance, of a piece that appeared a year and a half ago in *Change* magazine, entitled "Claiming Ourselves as Teachers." In it, Diane Gillespie, a faculty member from the University of Nebraska, argues that public discourse about teaching is scarce and indeed thin because teaching itself has been privatized, pushed off into the margins of work. To be caught talking in public about teaching is, she says, "like discovering at a formal dinner that you're eating someone else's salad."

Gillespie's account of things is no doubt more true on some campuses than others—more likely to be true, one supposes, on research university campuses like her own. But what's worrisome is the possibility that it might be true even on the many more campuses that identify themselves as "teaching institutions," a label that seems too often to mean an absence of research but not necessarily the *presence* of sophisticated conversation about or inquiry into teaching and learning.

What would that presence look like? It would look, I think, a lot like assessment at Harvard and SUNY-Fredonia and the LARC institutions: more conversation about teaching and learning, more *well-informed* and *collective* conversation that has a home in the institution.

The amount and character of discourse about teaching is one sign of the seriousness with which it is regarded. Another is rewards. A colleague here in D.C., Christine Young, recently wrote to me, "Until evidence of teaching effectiveness is taken seriously as a criterion for hiring, promotion, tenure, and merit raises, those faculty members who take teaching (and therefore assessment) seriously may continue to function at the margins."

That's a hard statement and a true one. If you follow assessment to its logical conclusion and ask what it's after—more student learning is a simple version of the answer—you come precisely to Young's point. Assessment will be an add-on, a marginal thing, until we reward teaching.

Interestingly, a method that's caught on in a big way (it was on this conference program prominently) for purposes of student assessment may be promising as well when it comes to evaluating teaching. I'm talking about portfolios, in this case "the teaching portfolio." We don't yet have the perfect formula for exactly what materials, what documents, could most usefully be displayed in a teaching portfolio. But the *fact* of the thing, a collection of evidence of teaching effectiveness—work samples—put on the table in the context of faculty evaluation, is already powerful. And the act of assembling evidence—like the fact of assessment itself—is likely to prompt better thought about how good teaching can be known and documented and rewarded, and what the institution *means* by "good teaching."

The issue of rewards for teaching gets a further, interesting spin when looked at in the light of assessment. As things now stand, all the rewards run to the individual. Assessment, with its principle of collective responsibility for student learning, implies a need for collective rewards. And, in fact, at Rhode Island College with assistance from FIPSE, *departments* that demonstrate gains in student learning receive modest but significant rewards, such as increased travel funds or new equipment. That may be the proverbial exception that proves the rule; it's also very suggestive in thinking about assessment and how it might shape—reshape rather radically in this case—the conditions in which we do our work.

2. *That assessment not only values teaching, it has a view of learning.*

If you look at what's being done in the name of assessment on many campuses today, you see an emerging view of learning: What matters in this view is not just what students know but what they can *do* with what they know. What's at stake is the capacity to *perform*, to put what one knows into practice. And this focus on performance implies asking not just how much (seat time or credit hours) but how *good* (where all parties understand what constitutes "good").

This conception of learning as performance has yet a larger aim. Assessment presumes a kind of learning in which students—knowing what is expected of them—can with practice over time become their own best assessors. The object here is graduates who know their own strengths and weaknesses, can set and pursue goals, who monitor their own progress and learn from experience. There's considerable evidence now that students who are self-conscious about their processes as learners are better learners, that they learn more easily and deeply, and that their learning lasts. The fashionable label for the skills in question here is "metacognitive," but whatever you call them they represent a kind of learning that speaks to a belief that learning is personally liberating, self-empowering, and for *all* students.

3. *Finally, that the culture of assessment is one in which we not only aim toward a particular kind of learning but hold ourselves accountable for it; where accountability is not a dirty word (what "they" want), but part and parcel of the way we work.*

Most of the talk about accountability so far has been about that which runs from the institution to the state. A few years ago you heard this talked about mainly in terms of reporting requirements, comparing scores, and so forth. More recently, and largely because of the work of Peter Ewell, institutions are finding more constructive ways to think about this kind of accountability. But those that are taking assessment seriously have a different and additional slant on accountability, as well. While recognizing obligations to external publics, they want to look inside to deeper-running responsibilities.

A first of these runs from the institution to its students. Accountability here means delivering an education equal to that promised in recruitment, to the student's investment (not only of money but of time and effort), and to the demands of the student's postcollegiate life.

A second kind of accountability implied by assessment is that of students for their own learning. A number of institutions are now teaching students to "self-assess," to diagnose their own progress, to take responsibility for it, to ask the "what-it-adds-up-to" question of *themselves* as learners.

Third, and most important, there's the accountability educators have to one another, in our teaching and related work, on mutually agreed upon purposes and promises. This is the professional obligation that goes with the autonomy that faculty have traditionally enjoyed; it invites many ways of working with students, but asks also that the work each of us does individually contributes to the larger aims we've agreed upon together.

Seen this way, improvement and accountability—the oft-cited tension behind assessment—are, if ends of a continuum, ends that come around and meet.

Themes for the Future

By way of summary, let me begin—presumptuously perhaps—by making a point of behalf of all of us here who are faculty members... one that comes, in fact, from a letter I recently received from a faculty member from SUNY-Fredonia who's been involved in the work I described earlier. "I am concerned," Patrick Courts writes, "that assessment has become a self-regressive project concerned primarily with itself—concerned with more and better assessment but little beyond that. Personally, I have little use for it unless we allow the voices of those assessed to be heard." That's a right and timely caution. It's one AAHE tried to keep in mind when putting this conference together; it's one to keep a constant eye on in the future.

Second, we need more leadership for assessment. From top-level administrators we need the kind of leadership that expresses itself through rewards and incentives. And those need to be for assessment itself (designing and doing it) but also, more important, for the ends we want assessment to serve: better teaching and learning. But we need leadership that goes beyond "good management" here. Too often assessment is seen as an administrative problem to be solved with administrative responses. What we need is educational leadership. Ideas about learning. And we need that from administrators and from faculty and, yes, from students too.

Third, we need assessment that follows from the ways we think about learning, the kinds of learning we value. We need to get clear about what those are. And if, as I've argued, we value not just disembodied facts and knowledge but what students can do and what they know, we need assessments that call for and document those abilities. This, I take it, is what Grant Wiggins has in mind when he talks about "authentic assessment," assessment "composed of tasks we value," assessment that is "standards-setting."

Finally, we need more than assessment to get where we need to go—that is, to more and better student learning. This, in my view, is the single most important point to be learned from Alverno. Over and over I've been asked, Has assessment actually improved things at Alverno? How do you know? That's a complicated question, but *one* relevant answer is that the growth in student learning that Alverno has been able to document is a function not of any *one* thing but of a powerful culture of learning; a consistency and clarity of purpose; teaching aimed at that purpose; a sense of responsibility to students (and *by* students); a sophisticated, institutionwide conversation about learning; and a view of teaching as a valued professional activity.

Assessment—I think my Alverno colleagues would agree with me here—is essential to all of the above, but it's also part of a bigger picture. What's at stake is not assessment but the larger ways we work.

Assessment and TQM:
In Search of Convergence

PETER T. EWELL

Both supporters and critics have drawn parallels between Total Quality Management (TQM) and the current assessment movement in higher education. Assessment practitioners, while intrigued by TQM, are frequently put off by its obvious linguistic and methodological links to industrial production processes that appear to have little to do with teaching and learning. New converts to TQM within the academy, in turn, have been critical of assessment because it appears to rely exclusively on "inspection at the end point" as a lever for quality improvement. Because proponents on both sides are enthusiastic about their own approaches, they sometimes do not listen to one another carefully, nor do they often watch what the practitioners of the other approach actually do. The result, I believe, obscures important lessons both sides might learn from a linking of these two powerful and basically allied approaches.

My purpose in this chapter is to address this condition in three ways. First, I want to demonstrate some clear conceptual parallels between the two approaches. TQM and assessment have similar objectives and origins. What divides them, I believe, is a peculiar set of historical circumstances surrounding public accountability in higher education. Second, I want to show how evolving assessment practice at the institutional and unit level is consistent with the best tenets of TQM. Assessment has taught us hard lessons about the need to collect information on both processes and outcomes. The need to link assessment information directly with the academic workplace—that is, with individual units and classrooms—is an equally hard lesson. Moreover, emerging assessment practice also now emphasizes "hearing the student's voice"—a welcome, though somewhat belated, embodiment of customer consciousness. All three trends make the emerging practice of assessment far different at present from its popular early image of end-point standardized testing. Finally, both assessment and TQM, as mechanisms for academic improvement, face some substantial common obstacles. If either is to prosper, each must systematically recognize and address these obstacles.

Assessment as a "Quality Movement"

The emergence of assessment as a national phenomenon in higher education is generally marked by the publication of two national reports: *Involvement in Learning* (National Institute of Education, 1984) and *Integrity in the College Curriculum* (Association of American Colleges, 1985). Both called for reform, including major changes in curricular coverage and coherence. In this sense the two differ little in content from similar bouts of reconceptualization that have afflicted American undergraduate education. But both reports also called for a fresh look at the undergraduate product—particularly at the array of knowledge, skills, and attitudes that all recipients of the baccalaureate should possess in common. Embedded in this admonition was something new: that regular feedback about performance was a key to improvement. At the individual level, considerable research about the dynamics of active learning backed this proposition (Astin, 1977, 1985). At the institutional level, the implied argument about assessment was more radical: Information about results, if gathered frequently at all levels of the organization, might guide a continuous process of organizational learning. The resulting "self-regarding institution" (Ewell, 1984) is infused with information about performance at all levels, thus constantly monitoring and improving its own overall performance.

But assessment, like TQM, also arose in part from a perception of crisis. Members of the National Institute of Education's (NIE's) study group, for example, were well aware that they were following in the footsteps of significant and far more critical reviews of elementary and secondary education, such as that issued by the U.S. Department of Education (1983). At the same time, higher education could no longer ignore complaints from business and industry about the declining quality of baccalaureate graduates. By 1986, the momentum of external reform had reached higher education. Reports by the Education Commission of the States (ECS) (1986) and the National Governors' Association (NGA) (1986) signaled government's growing unwillingness to remain on the sidelines with respect to undergraduate quality.

Government also saw assessment as a major component of reform. The ECS and NGA reports argued for gathering evidence at the institutional level to guide continuous improvement. But they also called for institutions to report statistics that would tell potential student "customers" what they might expect to gain from colleges and universities and that would assure the public that higher education was managing public investment well. As a result, the reports encouraged states to develop and deploy assessment initiatives that could both stimulate local reform and provide increased accountability. Because of the latter requirement, however, such systems tended by nature to emphasize assessment by inspection. In many cases, reports proposed standardized testing and included institutional comparisons as a part of the assessment program design.

Today's assessment movement is complicated largely because of these two different origins, one within higher education and the other external. Both advocated the same set of techniques—as a "market reaction" by state government to declining customer satisfaction and as an internal improvement tool by colleges and universities to help make a better product. For the most part, the typical current pattern of state initiatives avoids the implied contradictions of these two agendas. Rather than calling for uniform outcomes testing, as was largely the case in kindergarten through twelfth-grade education, the majority of current higher education assessment mandates are decentralized and enabling (Ewell, Finney, and Lenth, 1990). State authorities require institutions to develop local assessment programs suited to their own diverse missions and student clienteles and to report results periodically. Within broadly established guidelines, authorities allow many assessment methodologies provided that they generate understandable evidence of effectiveness for their respective constituencies. State authorities are often aware, to a surprising extent, of the need to avoid "micro-management" in developing such policies (Ewell, 1990). In this sense, they strongly subscribe to current quality management theory. But current evidence suggests that their patience is also limited; if institutions do not take the initiative in developing appropriate local reforms, state authorities feel that they have no choice but to deploy stronger, more centralized assessment methods to address the "crisis."

The state, for better or worse, remains the primary buyer of public higher education's product. As such, it in many ways plays the role the market plays in private industry by providing the overriding stimulus for unit adaptation and reform. State-mandated assessment represents both a market signal to colleges and universities from its primary (though often its most unrecognized) customer and a critical tool for local improvement. Given these dual motives, it is no wonder that college and university officials are often confused about how to approach the task of assessment.

But whatever the state's agenda, local assessment may prove valuable to institutions. In the best case, represented currently by such states as Virginia and Washington, state authorities will welcome and support local efforts at self-improvement. In the worst case, state-mandated testing for quality control (currently exemplified by Florida's College Level Academic Skills Test), local assessment may still be useful as a tool for quality improvement to meet externally established standards for product quality.

Convergence in Practice: Some Parallels

Emerging "best practice" in assessment, I believe, has much in common with the admonitions of TQM. Best practice, of course, has not as yet become common practice. Because most institutions currently engaging in assessment are doing so primarily to comply with state mandates, approaches that emphasize end-point inspection and purely quantitative criteria tend to predominate. More subtly, under these conditions assessment becomes the concern of administrators rather than faculty—particularly, as in states such as Virginia or Tennessee, where dollars are at stake.

Regardless of its external stimulus, moreover, a natural evolution of institutional assessment practice often occurs. Many first explore standardized testing alternatives because they are both readily available and apparently credible; few faculty are initially willing to invest the level of effort required to develop the kinds of course-embedded methods essential for guiding continuous instructional improvement. Only after experiencing the limitations of test-based assessment is the institution often willing to try alternative approaches. At institutions such as King's College (Wilkes-Barre, Pennsylvania), Northeast Missouri State University, State University of New York at Plattsburg, or the University of Tennessee at Knoxville—all of which have been practicing assessment for five years or more—initially established end-point testing is now complemented by a growing range of input and behavioral measures.

Three trends in particular now characterize emerging best practice in assessment, and all, I believe, are consistent with the tenets of TQM. First, comprehensive assessment programs rely increasingly on systematic process indicators to make sense of observed outcomes. Second, assessment relies increasingly on naturalistic settings as the locus for information gathering. Finally, a trend is growing in assessment toward simple techniques that enable line faculty to gather and use information directly about how their classrooms are actually functioning.

Rediscovering Process. Early attempts to assess instructional outcomes in higher education rested strongly on the assumption that instructional processes were uniform. The critical job was to document results in a systematic and comparable way—a substantially neglected task up to that point. The primary methodological paradigm for assessment in this period was the psychological experiment: causally linking planned and systematic variations in treatment conditions to observed differences in outcomes. Trying to make sense of obtained results, however, quickly made it clear that enormous and unknown variations in "treatment" were probably most responsible for differences in outcomes. We cannot treat instructional processes in colleges and universities simply as assigned conditions in a stable experimental design.

To some extent, this obvious "discovery" was an artifact of procedure. In developing assessments, conventional wisdom held it necessary to begin with a clear statement of intended outcomes. Without a common set of instructional goals, assessment was impossible in principle. Most college faculty had never engaged in goal making of this kind; often, in fact, they found reaching such an agreement more controversial even than measuring outcomes. For many, the resulting discussions themselves provided new insights into optimal program design (Banta and Moffett, 1987). After faculty had agreed on goals, however, it quickly became legitimate to ask who was teaching which of them, where, how, and at the same time raise behavioral questions about the ways in which the curricula on paper actually were acted out.

Current assessment practice, in response to these concerns, is devoting particular attention to collecting information about instructional process. One approach documents patterns of student course taking. Because the majority of current college curricula are choice-based and because most computerized student records systems are exclusively term-oriented, institutions often have remarkably little knowledge of their "behavioral curricula"—the actual sequence of courses taken to fulfill requirements. In the absence of such knowledge, of course, meaningful interpretation of outcomes is problematic. The construction of "curricular maps" as a part of this process is roughly equivalent to the common and essential TQM exercise of flowcharting (Ewell and Lisensky, 1988). Investigating the behavioral curriculum corresponds to TQM's necessary next step of documenting the actual flow of work. Basic tools here are transcript analysis and longitudinal student record files. In the first case, analysis is retrospective and often reveals substantial deviation in practice from intended catalogue design (Zemsky, 1989; Ratcliffe and Associates, 1990). Longitudinal tracking systems represent a more active alternative oriented toward continuous behavioral monitoring. To date, they have enjoyed their greatest success in community college settings, particularly in the improvement of placement and remediation practices (Adelman, Ewell, and Grable, 1989). In common with industrial experience, institutions in the latter case have often discovered that nothing is wrong with their current placement and remediation policies but that deficiencies occur because no one is actually following these policies.

Another process focus involves documenting student and instructor behavior. Research on student retention (and increasingly on student learning and development as well) has convincingly established that behavior factors such as student involvement (Astin, 1985), quality of effort (Pace, 1984), and substantive direct interaction with faculty members outside a classroom setting (Terenzini and Pascarella, 1977) can be at least as important as curricular design in explaining successful outcomes. As a result, many institutions are experimenting with techniques that gather information directly from students about their use of time and about their in- and out-of-class behaviors and from faculty members about their teaching practices (Gamson and Poulsen, 1989). A widely used vehicle for gathering such information is the traditional end-of-course questionnaire generally used for faculty evaluation. Increasingly, institutions are adding items to these questionnaires that tap such factors as time on task (for example, the student's amount of out-of-class preparation per week), active learning (for example, the number of times the student actively raised questions in class, the number of times the student discussed class material with the instructor or peers, or whether the student sought out additional material on the topic from the library or other sources), or high standards (for example, whether or not students felt challenged by the course or felt they did their best). Other recent approaches center on directly investigating effective student and classroom behaviors. A recent example is the work of the Harvard Assessment Seminar that established the value of such practices as group study and frequent instructor feedback (Light, 1990).

A third trend is increased attention to establishing the concrete connections that occur across courses in a curriculum. Curricular engineering generally assumes a structure of implied or actual prerequisites for successful performance in a sequence of courses. But to what extent are learnings in a given course successfully applied in another, often after a lapse of several terms? Since we often teach basic skills, in general, without attempts to link them to the problem settings where they will most likely be used, answers to this question are particularly important. Before and after exercises to help assess the core course sequence at King's College are an example of how cross-course connections of this kind establish and improve course sequencing (Farmer, 1988). At the beginning of second-year core courses, for example, the exercises ask students to respond to questions explicitly designed to tap general skills taught at an earlier point in the sequence but cast in an alien setting. Where these transitions are not occurring, faculty are encouraged to work together to develop the appropriate skills in the needed context.

Do not read assessment's growing emphasis on process information of this kind as an abandonment of outcomes. Rather, the premise is to establish a reasonable set of baseline measures that can consistently monitor the overall quality of the instructional product. But we now recognize that outcome measures are only the beginning of a process that requires additional highly disaggregated information about how and where learning takes place, as well as an active set of local intervention mechanisms for incremental improvement. Moreover, as the next section will explore, outcome measures themselves have changed. No longer are they strictly oriented toward endpoint testing; rather, they are now often embedded within the process, offering the opportunity for continuous improvement.

Using Naturalistic Inquiry in Assessment. Many early examples of assessment emphasized the use of standardized examinations. In the popular value-added rubric, for example, comparing end-point scores to entry scores assumes that any difference is due to instruction. In the more common examples of single-point testing, moreover, the objective is as much to certify the standard of the educational product as it is to improve practice. With both types of testing, assessment can be a costly external process that is imposed on the educational process and manifested in the form of specially designated test days and purpose-built instruments.

Recently, however, assessment practice has undergone a transformation similar to that experienced by program evaluation in the midseventies (Shapiro 1986). Rather than relying on externally imposed measurement devices outside the classroom, assessment is becoming more naturalistic (Guba and Lincoln, 1981)—embedded directly within the processes that it seeks to understand. This recent evolution of practice is consistent with the tenets of TQM in two important ways. First, assessment is not for the most part a costly extra step imposed on the process from without and adding little value. Curriculum-embedded assessment, as practiced at Alverno College, for example (Mentkowski and Doherty, 1984), uses assessment techniques to make general inferences about process effectiveness and to correct detected deficiencies on the line before the process is over. Second, embedded assessment takes place at the level of practice. When assessment information is gathered through the creative use of existing classroom examinations and exercises, the results are seen in their appropriate context and are thus made immediately meaningful and applicable for faculty.

Three recent trends in naturalistic assessment are particularly noteworthy as parallels to TQM. The first involves identifying and exploiting a network of existing points of contact with students as appropriate vehicles for assessment. Rather than relying on specially constructed testing points to gather information, this approach emphasizes more effective utilization of existing but underutilized data-collection opportunities. Among these are registration and orientation, end-of-course teaching evaluation surveys, and existing student surveys—as well as a range of unobtrusive data-gathering devices. Consistent with TQM, often the first step is to flowchart the current process to identify all the points at which information about students is currently collected. The resulting map is not only valuable in planning the substance of assessment but the flowchart can also help to increase the efficiency of assessment substantially. Indeed, several colleges have found that this audit process results in net gains in informational efficiency—particularly with respect to student surveys—because the audit process typically uncovers so many duplicate and badly designed data collection practices (Ewell and Lisensky, 1988).

A second practice, strongly resembling TQM's use of sampling, is to examine periodically examples of actual student work. The classic example is the portfolio that generally evaluates writing skills but that extends to other skill domains as well. To be successful, one must collect portfolios systematically, and the portfolios must contain similar kinds of student products: papers, essay test question responses, lab reports, or defined projects. Viewing the process as a regrading of large numbers of previously evaluated pieces of work subjects it to many of the same criticisms that TQM makes of other inspections. In fact, large numbers of institutions are currently experiencing enormous increases in assessment workload through the use of portfolios, precisely because they have not fully thought through the intended purposes. One of the most promising alternatives to mass portfolio collection is to choose work samples on a median performance basis. Under this methodology, administrators request instructors to forward for evaluation only the work of the median performer on each exercise; the result is a valuable periodic snapshot of assessed average performance across the curriculum.

A third naturalistic assessment practice consistent with TQM involves harnessing the faculty's own grading process to yield additional information more useful for instructional improvement. Course-embedded assessment, as practiced in general education at Kean College of New Jersey, for example, rests on the careful design of common essay items for periodic inclusion in course final examinations. Normally the faculty grades these items, but they also read a sample collectively, using an explicit scoring guide designed to detect overall patterns of strength and weakness. As a result of the scoring exercise, faculty course teams can determine how to address apparent weaknesses more systematically.

All three manifestations of naturalistic assessment have in common the assumption that the most useful information for improving practice is that which is most closely rooted in the processes it seeks to inform. Assessment has moved strongly in this direction not just because such practices are more acceptable to faculty members than are standardized tests but also because they are more applicable and informative. Carrying this logic to its extreme, however, implies that assessment will focus on individual classrooms, and this injunction has resulted in the assessment approaches, described next, that most strongly resemble TQM.

Using Assessment as Classroom Research. If naturalistic assessment calls attention to TQM's injunction that the best information is rooted in the operation of real, local processes, the emerging classroom research movement emphasizes TQM's equally important requirement that the workers themselves collect quality control information continuously. This enables individual instructors to help manage and direct their own instruction through an array of classroom feedback devices (Cross and Angelo, 1988). Advocates of classroom research believe that its potential to transform practice far exceeds that of more centralized, formal assessment procedures, both because individual faculty members manage it themselves and because it focuses largely on obtaining process information that faculty will find far less threatening than information about outcomes (Cross, 1990).

Like the control charts managed by individual production workers under TQM (Walton, 1986), the hallmark of classroom research techniques is their simplicity. While the techniques may require consistency in their application over time to be effective, faculty do not need a statistical or measurement background in order to use them. The most well-known example is the minute paper, intended to be administered to students at the end of every class period—a device that also recognizes the need for instructors to receive continuous customer feedback. The most common variant asks students to respond to two questions: What is the most important thing that you learned today, and what is the single thing that after today still is most unclear to you? The instructor collects the anonymous responses to the questions to help target instruction for the subsequent class period. Considerable experience with this technique (to this point primarily in community colleges) indicates that it can make a substantial contribution to instructor awareness about the effectiveness of presented material and, in contrast to the traditional end-of-course questionnaire, it makes this contribution in time to make a difference.

Most classroom research techniques are similar to the minute paper in their concentration on monitoring classroom process. Some, however, provide classroom counterparts for other familiar tools of statistical quality control. (For a description of these basic tools, see Appendix A.) Student work samples on comparable exercises, if collected systematically over time, are analogous to run charts. A psychology professor at the College of William and Mary in Virginia, for instance, has used the median performance sampling technique for many years to monitor performance on key exercises (H. Friedman, personal communication, April 25, 1988). In using this technique, he looks explicitly for what TQM practitioners would label "special causes" to account for deviations from expected patterns. Analogous to the Pareto chart, moreover, is the systematic classification of student errors—used primarily in such disciplines as math and the physical sciences. Under this technique, instructors, while grading a test or exercise, record the typical mistakes that students make and then reorder those mistakes in terms of frequency of occurrence. The potential of these techniques to change markedly both the teaching process and the obtained results is demonstrated convincingly by the success of such recent efforts as the New Jersey Algebra Project (Pine, 1988).

Unfortunately, integrated efforts such as these are extremely rare, and given the emphasis on individual experiment and decentralization inherent in classroom research, they are likely to remain so. For despite their admirable resemblance to TQM's techniques at the lowest level, classroom research lacks an equivalent infrastructure to support wider institution improvement. Particularly missing are attempts to monitor cross-course connections and the use of common tools across a range of similar courses. Both these situations would violate the presumption of individual faculty sovereignty that classroom research practice, for all its value, has so far left untouched.

This last observation highlights the fact that without an overarching philosophy of improvement, assessment remains an uncertain mechanism for change. Partly this is because the wider implications for practice of the trends noted here remain largely unsupported. As the first trend has shown, both outcomes and process information are needed, particularly at the level of curricular managers who must make decisions constantly about where and how to intervene, but information of this kind also requires a systematic data base, consciously designed for the purpose and actively managed by information professionals as an institutional resource. As the second trend implies, we greatly need outcomes information that matches the actual contexts and settings in which learning takes place. Naturalistic assessment to some degree fulfills this requirement, but techniques such as portfolio analysis have proved both costly and time consuming when implemented on too broad a scale or for too many purposes. As for the third trend, classroom-level monitoring tools are indispensable for continuous improvement, and we are discovering their feasibility and benefits across a wide range of institutional settings. But we rarely support systematic faculty training, and their use of classroom monitoring tools is by definition non-cumulative with respect to curricular issues. Clearly, these tools are useful for improving individual classrooms, but they are unlikely in themselves to improve joint products significantly. As in the case of TQM in industry, without significant increases in organizational commitment, we are not likely to overcome these obstacles quickly.

The Need for Commitment

Assessment as a national movement is now approximately five years old—old enough for us to draw some lessons about what is needed to make it work as an agent of institutional change. For the most part, these lessons are not surprising. Indeed, they parallel the organizational requirements for information-based change previously documented in fields such as program evaluation and organizational studies (Shapiro, 1986; Ewell, 1989). More strikingly, they also parallel those factors identified as critical in case studies of the successful application of TQM in industry (Walton, 1986). Unfortunately, most often, we lack the required conditions in colleges and universities.

One such requirement is full commitment to the process on the part of executive-level leadership. All too often, assessment does not enjoy such commitment and is seen as an auxiliary enterprise. Partly this is a residual result of mandates: Assessment is constructed as a compliance function much like any other form of accountability reporting. A more general lack of commitment to undergraduate teaching is partly responsible: In large numbers of institutions (including those whose primary mission is teaching), other agendas preoccupy top administration. As a result, the majority of institutions that practice assessment do not make it part of an overall, coordinated, institutional improvement strategy.

This sad condition is manifested in many ways. One is the fact that to date, most collected assessment results remain underutilized. While some classroom-level or departmental utilization will occur among interested faculty, institutional mechanisms are rarely in place to ensure regular and effective incorporation of results in decision making. Where such mechanisms are present, they are often simplistic or, indeed, directly antithetical to other important quality improvement principles. A good example is performance funding in Tennessee, where small differences in obtained scores—well outside the institutions' control and often well within the measurement-error limits of the instruments used—can cause notable differences in institutional dollar rewards (Banta, 1988). Another common manifestation is lack of integration among assessment functions, across departments, or, more significantly, between academic and student affairs. We tend to treat assessment in each area as a separate activity, and an institutional body or office rarely is responsible for integrating findings or for making broad recommendations about articulation and improvement. While excellent examples of such bridges do exist (for example, the living-learning communities currently under experiment at several institutions), they are far from widespread. Linkages are even more infrequent with critical support services such as facilities and equipment maintenance, parking, bursar and financial services, and registration or records—all of which also contribute to student success. In all too many institutions, these functions remain worlds unto themselves, and in the absence of vigorous, top-level leadership to span organizational boundaries they are likely to remain so.

A major contributing cause of the problem is simple turnover. It is no coincidence that the institutions most recognized for best practice in assessment also have stable, committed, top-level leadership. Alverno College, Kean College of New Jersey, Northeast Missouri State University, King's College, and the University of Tennessee at Knoxville all developed their successful assessment efforts over many years in a stable administrative environment. In several of these institutions, the tenure of chief executive and academic administration exceeded fifteen years. As in industry, such long tenure among chief executives is rare in American colleges and universities. But it is critical to making a long-term improvement process work.

An even greater obstacle to success is the general lack in higher education institutions of a meaningful, organized staff development function. If assessment is to fulfill its potential as a unit- and classroom-level tool for improvement, we must train faculty and line staff in its use and interpretation. More important, we must train them in the teaching techniques that research and experience have shown to be effective. Faculty development in most institutions is currently far from the standard required to make assessment locally meaningful. In most cases it is voluntary, and those who most need training are not generally those who will request it. Often those who view faculty development negatively need it the most. At best, faculty see such activities as peripheral and, at worst, remedial. Such attitudes render voluntary participation even more unlikely.

Interestingly, this situation is far from universal. In the United Kingdom, for example, all new faculty in polytechnic institutions engage in a formal process of staff development coordinated by a well-supported and visible staff training unit. Members of the staff development unit visit classes and work with instructors to improve their teaching practice on an ongoing basis. Staff training in these institutions not only benefits individual instructors but also serves as a visible reminder of the institution's commitment to continuous instructional improvement.

A final obstacle to success is perhaps the most difficult to overcome: sheer lack of perceived urgency regarding the need to change. Despite considerable rhetoric over the past decade, undergraduate instructional improvement is not a core issue at most colleges and universities. Promotion and tenure decisions remain focused largely on research at most four-year public institutions. At the same time, state funding formulas remain rooted in a cost-per-credit approach that does little beyond encouraging unplanned enrollment growth. The irony is that many—perhaps most—

faculty believe in effective teaching and want to do a better job. But little in the organizational culture of most colleges and universities today supports and develops this inclination into an effective focus for change.

At a number of pioneering campuses, assessment has provided this focus and has in this sense proved far more than just a mechanism for gathering disembodied evidence about outcomes. But in a far greater number, assessment has not yet had this effect because the incentives for change are too few. In industry, TQM arose largely as a response to a real crisis of competitiveness and profitability. For better or worse, higher education feels no parallel crisis as yet—though the public and its elected officials are, I believe, becoming increasingly restless. Guided by the proven principles of TQM, assessment can help institutions to develop a mechanism for responding in advance to the challenges that many think are coming. Acting now, as the experience of industry has shown, is a far better strategy than waiting for change to be dictated by circumstances.

References

Adelman, S. I., Ewell, P. T., and Grable, J. R. "LONESTAR: Texas's Voluntary Tracking and Developmental Education Evaluation System." In T. H. Bers (ed.), *Using Student Tracking Systems Effectively*. New Directions for Community Colleges, no. 66. San Francisco: Jossey-Bass, 1989.

Association of American Colleges. *Integrity in the College Curriculum: A Report to the Academic Community*. Washington, D.C.: Association of American Colleges, 1985.

Astin, A. W. *Four Critical Years: Effects of College on Beliefs, Attitudes, and Knowledge*. San Francisco: Jossey-Bass, 1977.

Astin, A W. *Achieving Educational Excellence: A Critical Assessment of Priorities and Practices in Higher Education*. San Francisco: Jossey-Bass, 1985.

Banu, T. W. "Assessment as an Instrument of State Funding Policy." In T. W. Banta (ed.), *Implementing Outcomes Assessment: Promise and Perils*. New Directions for Institutional Research, no. 59. San Francisco: Jossey-Bass, 1988.

Banu, T. W., and Moffett, M. S. "Performance Funding in Tennessee: Stimulus for Program Improvement." In D. F. Halpern (ed.), *Student Outcomes Assessment: What Institutions Stand to Gain*. New Directions for Higher Education, no. 59. San Francisco: Jossey-Bass, 1987.

Cross, K. P. "Collaborative Classroom Assessment." Address delivered at the Fifth American Association for Higher Education Conference on Assessment in Higher Education, Washington, D.C., June 27, 1990.

Cross, K. P., and Angelo, T. A. *Classroom Assessment Techniques: A Handbook for Faculty*. Ann Arbor: National Center for Research to Improve Postsecondary Teaching and Learning, University of Michigan, 1988.

Education Commission of the States. *Transforming the State Role in Undergraduate Education: Time for a Different View*. Denver, Colo.: Education Commission of the States, 1986.

Ewell, P T. *The Self-Regarding Institution: Information for Excellence*. Boulder, Colo.: National Center for Higher Education Management Systems, 1984.

Ewell, P. T. "Information for Decision: What's the Use?" In P. T. Ewell (ed.), *Enhancing Information Use in Decision Making*. New Directions for Institutional Research, no. 64. San Francisco: Jossey-Bass, 1989.

Ewell, P. T. *Assessment and the "New Accountability": A Challenge for Higher Education's Leadership.* Denver, Colo.: Education Commission of the States, 1990.

Ewell, P T., Finney, J. E., and Lenth, C. "Filling in the Mosaic: The Emerging Pattern of State-Based Assessment." *AAHE Bulletin,* 1990, 42 (8), 3–7.

Ewell, P. T., and Lisensky, R. P. *Assessing Institutional Effectiveness: Redirecting the Self-Study Process.* Washington, D.C.: Consortium for the Advancement of Private Higher Education, 1988.

Farmer, D. W. *Enhancing Student Learning: Emphasizing Essential Student Competencies in Academic Programs.* Wilkes-Barre, Penn: King's College. 1988.

Gamson, Z. F., and Poulsen, S. J. "Inventories of Good Practice: The Next Step for the Seven Principles for Good Practice in Undergraduate Education." *AAHE Bulletin,* 1989, 42 (9), 7–8.

Guba, E. G., and Lincoln, Y. S. *Effective Evaluation: Improving the Usefulness of Evaluation Results Through Responsive and Naturalistic Approaches.* San Francisco: Jossey-Bass, 1981.

Light, R. J. *The Harvard Assessment Seminars: Explorations with Students and Faculty About Teaching, Learning, and Student Life.* Cambridge, Mass.: Harvard Graduate School of Education and Kennedy School of Government, 1990.

Mentkowski, M., and Doherty, A. *Careering After College: Establishing the Validity of Abilities Learned in College for Later Careering and Performance.* Milwaukee, Wisc.: Alverno Publications, 1984.

National Governors' Association. *Time for Results: The Governors' 1991 Report on Education.* Washington, D.C.: National Governors' Association, 1986.

National Institute of Education, Study Group on the Conditions of Excellence in American Higher Education. *Involvement in Learning: Realizing the Potential of American Higher Education.* Washington, D.C.: U.S. Government Printing Office, 1984.

Pace, C. R. *Measuring the Quality of College Student Experiences.* Los Angeles: Higher Education Research Institute, University of California at Los Angeles, 1984.

Pine, C. "Student Preparedness in Math: An Interview with Charles Pine." *AAHE Bulletin,* 1988, 41(1), 3–6.

Ratcliffe, J. L., and Associates. *Determining the Effect of Different Coursework Patterns on the General Learned Abilities of College Students.* Working Paper OR 90-524. Ames: Research Institute for Studies in Education at Iowa State University and University Park Center for the Study of Higher Education at Pennsylvania State University, 1990.

Shapiro, J. Z. "Evaluation Research and Educational Decision Making." In J. C. Smart (ed.), *Higher Education: Handbook of Theory and Research.* Vol. II. New York: Agathon, 1986.

Terenzini, P T., and Pascarella, E. T. "Voluntary Freshman Attrition and Patterns of Social and Academic Integration in a University: A Test of a Conceptual Model." *Research in Higher Education,* 1977, 6(1), 25–43.

U.S. Department of Education, National Commission on Excellence in Education. *A Nation at Risk: The Imperative for Educational Reform.* Washington, D.C.: U.S. Government Printing Office, 1983.

Walton, M. *The Deming Management Method.* New York: Putnam, 1986.

Zemsky, R. *Structure and Coherence: Measuring the Undergraduate Curriculum.* Philadelphia: Institute for Research on Higher Education, University of Pennsylvania, 1989.

Information for Decision:
What's the Use?

PETER T. EWELL

Institutional researchers are not alone in lamenting the indifference with which decision makers commonly receive the fruits of their labors. As action researchers they share these concerns with a much wider community, many members of which have paid considerable attention to seeking out the reasons for this phenomenon. The most important investigations have probably been those in the field of social program evaluation and in particular in the literature on the utilization of evaluation results. What can we learn from these investigations that we can use to inform the practice of institutional research? With a few caveats, the answer is a great deal, first in broadening our conceptions of the ways in which information is actually used by administrators, then in directing our attention to key factors that affect how and whether information is used. This chapter reviews these two topics, noting some prior treatments of the utilization of institutional research and grounding these discussions in the experience of the wider evaluation tradition.

Institutional Research as Program Evaluation: Parallels and Differences

Like institutional research, program evaluation as a profession can be traced to the early sixties. Large-scale federal programming and the rise of so-called scientific management techniques, such as PPBS and MBO (first in the Defense Department, later in various social service agencies), created both a need to determine what was working and a new set of tools that could be used to find out. Based largely on classic quasi-experimental techniques drawn from social psychology (Campbell and Stanley, 1966), the result was a profusion of program impact studies in fields as diverse as primary education, social welfare, distributed health care, and prison reform. However, by the early 1970s, program evaluators were becoming concerned. Too often, "bad" programs seemed to expand, while "good" ones were ignored. In short, nobody seemed to be listening. The result was what Shapiro (1986) has aptly termed "the deconstruction of program evaluation" (p. 166). Practicing evaluators, such as Stufflebeam (1971) and Stake (1978), began advocating the rejection of study designs that stressed outcomes measurement and experimental controls and promoting more flexible—often "naturalistic"—assessments of process (Guba and Lincoln, 1981). At the same time, evaluators began explicitly and critically examining what was meant by the expression *using results* and discussing proactive strategies designed to promote greater utilization (Patton, 1978).

In drawing lessons from these discussions, institutional researchers must be aware of both identities and differences between the evaluator's profession and their own. Certainly, the two have common roots in their use of empirical, often quantitative, techniques and in their conviction that the results obtained should directly guide managerial action. Moreover, they share a strong conviction about the special role of the action researcher in the decision process, a role that must be accountable both to the decisional needs of the organization served and to the professional standards of research. In their traditional assignments, both evaluation researchers and institutional researchers must maintain independence; they must recognize and subscribe to Saupe's (1981, p. 8) maxim that, "just as the results of the research will seldom be the sole determinant of the decision, so the desired decision cannot be allowed to bias the nature of the research."

The organizational context of the institutional researcher is considerably more organic and flexible than that of the program evaluator. First, the primary unit of analysis for an institutional researcher is only rarely an identifiable program and its intended effects. As a result, such goal-based methods as explicit hypothesis testing or quasi-experiment, which constitute the core of traditional evaluation practice, are rarely applicable in higher education. Even in such areas as academic program review, where in principle goal-based techniques are appropriate, formal studies of program effectiveness remain rare. Most review processes instead employ an alternative evaluation paradigm stressing descriptive data and peer judgment over explicit outcomes measurement (Wilson, 1987).

Moreover, in contrast to the program evaluator, the institutional researcher is an insider. With respect to information use, this means that at the very least, there are considerably more opportunities. Information-laden communication with decision makers is more likely to be continuous and informal and, in the evaluator's language, more formative than summative. Moreover, much of the substance of this communication is likely to be about operations and not outcomes—the real world of decision makers. Supplying needed operating data reliably on a day-to-day basis thus puts the institutional researcher in a much better position than the program evaluator to communicate data-based decisional recommendations when the occasion arises. Most important, routine contact gives the institutional researcher an invaluable opportunity to become familiar with the tastes and traits of particular decision makers and the organization culture within which they operate. While data gathering of this kind is typically informal, it is often formalized in institutional research discussions as "appraising the needs of decision makers" (Adams, 1977) or "assessing the climate for change" (Buhl and Lindquist, 1981), and it can become as important as primary data gathering in an overall action research strategy. At the extreme, this perspective suggests a proactive change agent role for institutional research reflecting sensitivity to organizational dynamics and emphasizing strategies for promoting information-based action recommendations internally (Terrass and Pomrenke, 1981).

A review of the major findings from the literature on evaluation utilization suggests that the implications of these role differences for institutional research are two. First, for the institutional researcher, organizational and perceptual barriers to information use are fewer and less explicit. Lessons on how to promote communication by increasing issue relevance and the attention paid to data presentation will consequently have enhanced probabilities of success. Second, because the information exchange between institutional researchers and decision makers is more continuous, information use can take many different forms. The forms documented in the evaluation literature may consequently help institutional research practitioners to recognize and promote alternative uses when they do occur and to provide decision makers with the kinds of information most suited to such uses.

Concepts of Information Use

For better or for worse, most formal treatments of the role of information in decision making are based upon a rational model of organizational process. According to this model, those who make decisions seek information in order to clarify the probable consequences of the available courses of action. While information cannot make the decision, it can reduce uncertainty about the alternatives that show the greatest possibility of benefit while incurring the least cost (Raiffa, 1968).

The rational model remains compelling, and, as in other information-based professions, it tends to dominate formal constructions of both program evaluation (Weiss, 1972) and institutional research (Saupe, 1981). In essence, it has three implications. First, information professionals supply decision-relevant information but do not themselves participate in decisions. Second, information professionals are expected to try to supply complete and accurate information about the problem at hand. Third, information professionals are expected to be value-neutral in their approach both to gathering information and to presenting it. In combination, the effect of these three attributes is to render the role of the information professional transparent in any given decision. If decision-makers are rational, the information itself may have considerable impact on the outcome of a particular decision. The manner of form in which it is supplied is not a factor.

Nevertheless, it is well known that decision making in higher education, as in other complex organizational settings, does not really work this way. First, different kinds of institutional cultures can encompass quite different conceptions of what constitutes useful information. For example, Chaffee (1983) describes four alternative decision-making models—formal/rational, collegial, bureaucratic, and political—and outlines their distinct information requirements. Second, regardless of the institutional setting, the rational use of information is constrained in multiple ways. Ewell and Chaffee (1984) identify four such constraints in college and university settings: constraints imposed by incomplete information, constraints imposed by politics, constraints imposed by organizational culture, and constraints imposed by the symbolic need for the institution to take unambiguous action. Such dynamics are particularly observable in the histories of explicit information utilization projects in higher education. In one such multi-institutional project intended to test the applicability of detailed resource allocation and management information, utilization depended largely upon establishing perceived linkages between such information and visible unit-level problems (Baldridge and Tierney, 1979). In another project that attempted to apply information on student learning and development to curricular decisions, utilization was often blocked by differences among disciplinary cultures and by resulting symbolic properties of the information provided (Astin, 1976).

Multiple definitions of utilization began to arise in the evaluation literature when it was realized that policymakers were ignoring the majority of large-scale quasi-experimental studies conducted in the mid seventies—a condition described by Guba and Lincoln (1981) as "the tragedy of nonuse" (p. 3). One response was to sharpen conceptions of how evaluation results actually entered the decision process. For example, Leviton and Boruch (1983) proposed to distinguish between *impact*— utilization that actually affected the outcome of a decision—and *use*—activities that did not necessarily affect the outcome of a decision. Distinctions of this kind reflected emerging evidence about how decision makers actually reacted to the findings of large-scale evaluations. For example, one empirical study of the ways in which evaluation results were used in federal health policy found that a major theme was the reduction of uncertainly among decision makers faced by complexity (Patton and Associates, 1977). But, beyond noting that the rational paradigm of utilization rarely applies, evaluators have not achieved consensus on what alternative notions of use might look like (Shapiro, 1986). As the current debate between Weiss and Patton on utilization illustrates, they have also not agreed on the degree to which conceptions of use can vary across kinds of decision makers and decision-making communities (Smith and Chircop, 1989).

On what alternative conceptions of the way decision makers use the information that they are given can we base these discussions? Four are worth noting. Each implies a somewhat different approach to data collection and transmission.

Use of Information to Identify Problems. Rather than assessing the particular decisional consequences of a set of known alternatives, information may simply be used to signal the fact that a problem exists. In goal-based evaluation, some approaches stressing this kind of utilization are termed *discrepancy evaluation* (Yavarsky, 1976). These approaches generally involve the formal comparison of the performance targets that were hoped for and the results that were obtained. In institutional research, as Saupe (1981) points out, this effect may often result from the routine provision of descriptive information. In essence, problem identification has to do with the detection of anomalies. Consequently, it requires information that quite clearly signals the differences between what was expected and what was found. This first implies a need for comparative presentation, with a standard supplied by past history (trends over time), by the performance of other similar units or entities (peer comparisons), or by expressed expectations. In the last case, formal "expectations exercises," in which decision makers are asked to supply a profile of the numbers that they expect a given data collection instrument to obtain before it is administered, can be particularly useful. Problem identification also implies a need for simplicity in presentation. Only a few key indicators can be used to highlight discrepancy, and these must be presented in such a way that major differences are readily apparent. Graphic presentation may be particularly effective here.

Use of Information to Set a Context for Decision. Considerable research on business decision making indicates that decision makers place more reliance on suggestive than on decisive information systems (Churchman, 1975). The objective of a suggestive system is to place a given decision in its proper context, to outline its basic parameters, and, most important, to define the ways in which it affects and depends on other parts of the organization. Information of this kind is rarely sufficient for making a particular decision, but it can provide a basic contextual foundation that informs a range of related decisions and the links among them. In the research on evaluation utilization, such use is often termed *conceptual use* (Rich, 1977). It influences the way in which decision makers think about a problem or issue, but it is not identifiably used to inform particular decisions. Its manifestations are most often found in naturalistic evaluations, which attempt to document holistic processes and activities as fully as possible as they occur. In higher education, information for context setting is most often encountered in discussions of strategic planning or program review. Supplying it effectively will generally imply considerable integration and interpretation—often requiring the grouping of quite disparate kinds of information drawn from many sources around a common issue or problem (Kinnick, 1985). Because it attempts to capture holistic processes or experiences, information strategies best suited to context setting often involve substantial discussion of implications from multiple perspectives and considerable use of verbatim testimony from those experiencing the institution in different ways.

Use of Information to Induce Action. Beyond its use in clarifying the consequences of particular decisions, concrete information can help in the process of coming to a decision. Organizational theorists, such as Simon (1957), have highlighted this effect by observing that confusion between empirical and value questions is a particular obstacle to closure in decision processes in which many parties are involved. In such situations, the addition of concrete data about the problem under discussion may provide a degree of closure that goes far beyond the informational value of the data. In program evaluation, Patton (1978) has noted that decisional outcomes may already be largely decided by the time concrete evaluative information becomes available. Its prime effect is therefore to increase the confidence of the decision makers and consequently their willingness to act. Under such conditions, sensitivity analysis may be particularly helpful as an informational strategy. By supplying the probable range of variation in an available result and by indicating that it lies far from the point that would lead to a different decision, information professionals can often help policymakers come to closure. Approaches stressing multiple advocacy (Ewell and Chaffee, 1984), in which differing contenders use available information to build complete alternative cases, may also increase the confidence of decision makers by ensuring that all points of view have been covered adequately.

Use of Information to Promote or Legitimize a Decision. Once a particular decision has been taken, concrete information can become a powerful mechanism for selling the decision to those whose cooperation is needed in order to carry it out. This use reflects the contention that mobilizing support, not decision making itself, is the premier managerial activity and that information designed to promote the rationality of action rather than the rationality of decisions may therefore be most useful to practicing managers (Brunsson, 1982). The effectiveness of information supplied in this role may have nothing immediate to do with either its accuracy or its bearing on the problem at hand. Rather, the information serves as a symbol that the decision was well taken and makes it possible for opposing parties to cooperate by removing the need for one side to back down. Some of the power of explicit information to accomplish this feat undoubtedly has to do with our distinctive cultural reverence for numbers. Part of it has to do with a collective organizational ethic, which is particularly prevalent in higher education, that basing action on systematically collected information signals a serious, rational approach to decision (Feldman and March, 1981). In the evaluation literature, such usage, which has been termed *symbolic* (King and Thompson, 1981), is deemed an inevitable by-product of operating in a political environment. In higher education, it is particularly apparent in external accountability reporting, a form of activity increasingly characteristic of institutional research. The essence of this category of information use is to maintain organizational and leader credibility. As a result, its prime implication for informational strategy is to ensure face validity in the methods used and in forms of presentation. Particular problems here may be caused by the use of survey sampling or of complex statistical techniques, as decision makers, based on their own experiences, often do not believe the results produced by these methods (Ewell, 1988, Schmidtlein, 1977).

Table 1 summarizes these four conceptions of information use and highlights their broad implications for information strategy. By tailoring the content and format of the information supplied to its anticipated use, institutional researchers can anticipate greater policy benefit.

Factors Affecting Information Use

In the evaluation tradition, information use is generally modeled as a communications process between a professional evaluator who supplies information and a program manager who receives it. Factors promoting effective information use are therefore most often those associated with any communications process: attributes of sender and receiver, the channels used, and the organizational or cultural context within which the communication takes place. Thus, Rich (1981) proposes a two-community paradigm in accounting for the nonuse of evaluation results. Evaluators come from a rational social scientific perspective, while decision makers come from a pragmatic,

Table 1
Conceptions of Information Use

Information Use	Essential Processes for Decision	Appropriate Informational Strategies
Rational decision making	Assessing consequences of alternative courses of action	Cost-benefit Explicit recommendations with reasons for each
Problem identification	Detecting anomalies	Comparative trend reporting Key indicators Graphic presentation Expectations exercises
Context setting	Making holistic connections Systematizing experience	Face-to-face communication Verbatim records Scenario building
Inducing action	Closing further discussion Enhancing decision makers' confidence	Multiple advocacy Sensitivity analysis
Selling decisions	Establishing wide credibility	Face validity

political perspective. Most instances of nonuse therefore can be traced to a communications breakdown between these two quite different perceptual worlds. Shapiro (1986) carries this logic a step further by reviewing the contending metaphors of evaluation, which range from the familiar conceptions of evaluation as information production and organizational strategy—both of which focus on rationality and purposive utilization of information—to less familiar conceptions, such as evaluation as political philosophy (emphasizing the political values of those undertaking evaluation) and evaluation as research paradigm (emphasizing their disciplinary backgrounds in the various social sciences). Both arguments emphasize that utilization is largely a process of cross-cultural communication.

Shapiro (1986) outlines the history of empirical attempts to determine the factors responsible for evaluation utilization by presenting case histories of particular evaluations that attempt to follow the impact of results on subsequent decisions. Other approaches focus on decision makers, organizations, and issues: in the first instance attempting through interviews to determine the ways in which different kinds of decision makers think about information, in the second attempting a parallel analysis of the role of information in the life cycle of a particular organization, and in the third following the development of a particular issue and noting the points at which information enters the discussion. Finally, an intriguing handful of studies has been simulation based—artificially varying such attributes as visible evaluator qualifications, information formats (for example, the use of technical jargon), and other variables explicitly drawn from communications theory (Braskamp and Brown, 1980).

The modeling of information utilization as a communications process is also a strong attribute of discussions directed toward improvement of the utilization of institutional research. For example, Schmidtlein (1977) strongly echoes the two cultures perspective of evaluators in his contention that higher education policymakers and information suppliers live in different conceptual worlds and that the former are therefore inclined to be suspicious of the latter. Sheehan's three hats theory (1977) is similar in that it explicitly considers the differing roles and resulting communications problems among decision makers, analysts, and information technicians. Although empirical attempts to understand information use in higher education are more circumscribed, they also are largely organized around such factors. For example, in examining the process of using information on student outcomes in a multi-institutional demonstration project, Kinnick (1985) distinguishes between technical and organizational obstacles to utilization and treats both as modifiers to an otherwise unimpeded flow of information between researchers and decision makers.

Figure 1
Key Factors in Information Use

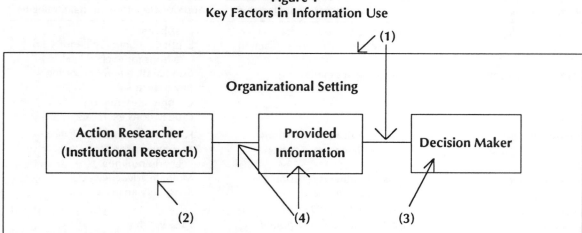

Figure 1, which models utilization as a communications process, summarizes four key factors related to information use that can be drawn from these discussions.

Key Factors:

(1)   Organizational characteristics
        Structure of power
        Organizational culture
        Structure of communication
(2)   Researcher characteristics
(3)   Decision maker characteristics
(4)   Informational characteristics
        Information content
        Medium/format

Organizational Characteristics. One difficulty with the two-community theory, Shapiro (1986) argues, is its assumption that perfect communication leads automatically to effective information use. This assumption ignores the fact that bureaucracies routinely process and interpret information before it is used and that this processing may decisively shape its implications (Rich, 1981). Here, the realization that information is only one ingredient in the decision process and that constituency satisfaction and a smooth flow of operations are paramount managerial concerns is critically important. The dominance of such concerns can decisively influence the impact of evaluation information. For example, one major finding of simulation studies on evaluation utilization is that results are rarely used (or even recognized) at organizational levels higher than the levels at which they were generated (Lazarsfeld and Reitz, 1975) and that they typically do not cross vertical reporting lines within an organization. In higher education, this finding may have particular bearing on the location of institutional research in the reporting structure. Moreover, as Schmidtlein (1977) points out, governance structures in higher education typically mean that decision making is more diffuse and likely to be based on collegial processes. As a result, institutional researchers may need to pay particular attention to group dynamics and the use of information in group settings.

Researcher Characteristics. Patton's work on utilization-focused evaluation (1978) pays considerable attention to positive personal characteristics of the evaluator, which include an open, approachable interpersonal style and a maximum of informal communication. Others stress that the evaluator needs to assess the interests, preferences, and styles of decision makers carefully from the outset of the evaluation process. When the information professional is in a permanent staff role, as he or she is in institutional research, the importance of personal characteristics is amplified (Hogan, 1981). Moreover, in group decision-making situations, the need for strong verbal and interpersonal skills becomes paramount.

Decision Maker Characteristics. While the two-community theory emphasizes differences between the cultures and values of decision makers and information professionals, studies of information utilization also reveal considerable differences in the way in which individual decision makers perceive and interpret the same information. Some differences can be traced to the differing cognitive styles of individual decision makers, while others may be the result of differing backgrounds and training (McKenney and Keen, 1974). Because most administrators in higher education were once academics, major differences of this kind may be due to original disciplinary training. Thus, administrators with varying disciplinary backgrounds may have different notions of appropriate standards of evidence for supplied information that are based upon fundamentally different notions of epistemology (Mayo and Kallio, 1983; Mitroft, 1982). For institutional research, these findings suggest that the perceptions of decision makers need to be determined—particularly with respect to the language used—before results are communicated. They also suggest the possibility that different types of individuals can be deliberately induced to play particular informational roles in a group decision-making process (Astin, 1976).

Information Characteristics. Both the content and inherent properties of the information affect utilization. Not surprisingly, simulation studies suggest that results that confirm the preconceptions of decision makers are the most likely to be listened to. In one such study, simulated evaluation findings that agreed with the initial perceptions of administrators were accepted, while those that disagreed with initial perceptions were returned with methodological comments (Eaton, 1956). Not surprisingly, utilization studies emphasize the need for data that are perceived to be of high technical quality (Shapiro, 1986). Furthermore, they suggest that the visual forms in which data are presented can have a considerable impact on credibility (Newman, Brown, and Braskamp, 1980). Summarizing the most frequently encountered technical obstacles to the use of information on student outcomes, Kinnick (1985) notes the excessive bulk of reports, the tendency to organize presentations around discrete data collection efforts rather than around issues or problems, lack of data integrity, lack of face validity, inadequate timeliness, and limited data interpretability. Strategies for overcoming these obstacles in the realm of data communication included graphic presentation, iterative release of information to stimulate a "data dialogue," and redundant data presentation strategies.

Projecting the experience of utilization in program evaluation onto higher education, Shapiro (1986) concludes that the type of information most likely to be used is descriptive and indicative—precisely the sort of data typically generated by institutional research. By concentrating on supplying such data effectively, institutional researchers can ensure a continuing place in decision making. Guided by the experience of evaluation, they can then flexibly and selectively exploit available local opportunities for rendering particular decisions more rational.

References

Adams, C. R. (ed.). *Appraising Information Needs of Decision Makers.* New Directions for Institutional Research, no. 15. San Francisco: Jossey-Bass, 1977.

Astin, A. W. *Academic Gamesmanship.* New York: Praeger, 1976.

Baldridge, J. V., and Tierney, M. L. *New Approaches to Management.* San Francisco: Jossey-Bass, 1979.

Braskamp, L. A., and Brown, R. E. *Utilization of Evaluation Information.* New Directions for Program Evaluation, no. 5. San Francisco: Jossey-Bass, 1980.

Brunsson, N. "The Irrationality of Action and Action Rationality: Decisions, Ideologies, and Organizational Actions." *Journal of Management Studies,* 1982, *19* (1), 29–44.

Buhl, L. C., and Lindquist, J. "Academic Improvement Through Action Research." In J. Lindquist (ed.), *Increasing the Use of Institutional Research.* New Directions for Institutional Research, no. 32. San Francisco: Jossey-Bass, 1981.

Campbell, D. T., and Stanley, J. C. *Experimental and Quasi-Experimental Designs for Research.* Chicago: Rand McNally, 1966.

Chaffee, E. E. *Rational Decision Making in Higher Education.* Boulder, Colo.: National Center for Higher Education Management Systems, 1983.

Churchman, C. W. "What Is Information for Policy Making?" In M. Kochen (ed.), *Information for Action: From Knowledge to Wisdom.* New York: Academic Press, 1975.

Eaton, J. "Symbolic and Substantive Evaluation Research." *Administrative Science Quarterly,* 1956, *21,* 53–56.

Ewell, P. T. "Implementing Assessment: Some Organizational Issues." In T. W. Banta (ed.), *Implementing Outcomes Assessment: Promise and Perils*. New Directions for Institutional Research, no. 59. San Francisco: Jossey-Bass, 1988.

Ewell, P. T., and Chaffee, E. E. "Promoting the Effective Use of Information in Decision Making." Paper presented at the 24th annual forum of the Association for Institutional Research, Fort Worth, May 1984.

Feldman, M. S., and March, J. G. "Information in Organizations as Signal and Symbol." *Administrative Science Quarterly*, 1981, *26*, 171–186.

Guba, E. G., and Lincoln, Y. S. *Effective Evaluation: Improving the Usefulness of Evaluation Results Through Responsive and Naturalistic Approaches*. San Francisco: Jossey-Bass, 1981.

Hogan, T. P. "The Wisconsin Evaluation Project." In J. Lindquist (ed.), *Increasing the Use of Institutional Research*. New Directions for Institutional Research, no. 32. San Francisco: Jossey-Bass, 1981.

King, J. A., and Thompson, B. "A Nationwide Survey of Administrators' Perceptions of Evaluation." Paper presented at the annual meeting of the American Educational Research Association, Los Angeles, 1981.

Kinnick, M. "Increasing the Use of Student Outcomes Information." In P. T. Ewell (ed.), *Assessing Educational Outcomes*. New Directions for Institutional Research, no. 47. San Francisco: Jossey-Bass, 1985.

Lazarsfeld, P. F., and Reitz, J. G. *An Introduction to Applied Sociology*. New York: Elsevier, 1975.

Leviton, L. C., and Boruch, R. F. "Contributions of Evaluation to Educational Programs and Policy." *Evaluation Review*, 1983, *7*, 563–598.

McKenney, J. L., and Keen, P.G.W. "How Managers' Minds Work." *Harvard Business Review*, 1975, *52*, 79–90.

Mayo, M., and Kallio, R. E. "Effective Use of Modes in the Decision Process: Theory Grounded in Three Case Studies." *AIR Professional File*, 1983, *15*, unpaged.

Mitroff, I. I. "Secure Versus Insecure Forms of Knowing in University Settings: Two Archetypes of Inquiry." *Journal of Higher Education*, 1982, *53*(6), 640–655.

Newman, D. L., Brown, R. D., and Braskamp, L. A. "Communication Theory and the Utilization of Evaluation." In L. A. Braskamp and R. Brown (eds.), *Utilization of Evaluation Information*. New Directions for Program Evaluation, no. 5. San Francisco: Jossey-Bass, 1980.

Patton, M. Q. *Utilization-Focused Evaluation*. Newbury Park, Calif.: Sage, 1978.

Patton, M. Q., and Associates. "In Search of Impact: An Analysis of the Utilization of Federal Health Evaluation Research." In C. H. Weiss (ed.), *Using Social Science Research on Public Policy Making*. Lexington, Mass.: Heath, 1977.

Raiffa, H. *Decision Analysis*. Reading, Mass.: Addison-Wesley, 1968.

Rich, R. F. "Uses of Social Science Information by Federal Bureaucrats: Knowledge for Understanding Versus Knowledge for Action." In C. H. Weiss (ed.), *Using Social Science Research in Public Policy Making*. Lexington, Mass.: Heath, 1977.

Rich, R. F. *Social Science Information and Public Policy Making*. San Francisco: Jossey-Bass, 1981.

Saupe, J. L. *The Functions of Institutional Research*. Tallahassee, Fla.: Association for Institutional Research, 1981.

Schmidtlein, F. A. "Information Systems and Concepts of Higher Education Governance." In C. R. Adams (ed.), *Appraising Information Needs of Decision Makers*. New Directions for Institutional Research, no. 15. San Francisco: Jossey-Bass, 1977.

Shapiro, J. Z. "Evaluation Research and Educational Decision Making." In J. C. Smart (ed.), *Higher Education: Handbook of Theory and Research*. Vol. 2. New York: Agathon Press, 1986.

Sheehan, B. S. "Reflections on the Effectiveness of Informational Support for Decision Makers." In C. R. Adams (ed.), *Appraising Information Needs of Decision Makers*. New Directions for Institutional Research, no. 15. San Francisco: Jossey-Bass, 1977.

Simon, H. A. *Administrative Behavior*. (2nd ed.) New York: Free Press, 1957.

Smith, N. L., and Chircop, S. "The Weiss-Patton Debate: Illumination of the Fundamental Concepts." *Evaluation Practice*, 1989, *10* (2), 5–13.

Stake, R. E. "The Case Study Method in Social Inquiry." *Educational Researcher*, 1978, *7*, 5–8.

Stufflebeam, D. L. "The Relevance of the CIPP Evaluation Model for Educational Accountability." *Journal of Research and Development in Education*, 1971, *5*, 19–25.

Terrass, S., and Pomrenke, V. "The Institutional Research as Change Agent." In J. Lindquist (ed.), *Increasing the Use of Institutional Research*. New Directions for Institutional Research, no. 32. San Francisco: Jossey-Bass, 1981.

Weiss, C. H. *Evaluation Research*. Englewood Cliffs, N.J.: Prentice-Hall, 1972.

Wilson, R. F. "Program Evaluation in Higher Education." In J. A. Muffo and G. W. McLaughlin (eds.), *A Primer on Institutional Research*. Tallahassee, Fla.: Association for Institutional Research, 1987.

Yavarsky, D. K. *Discrepancy Evaluation: A Practitioner's Guide*. Charlottesville: University of Virginia, 1976.

Linking Program Reviews to Institutional Assessment, Accreditation, and Planning

Robert J. Barak and Barbara E. Breier

In the preceding chapters we have described the essential steps in developing, conducting, and evaluating a program review and discussed the various perspectives that stakeholders share regarding the outcomes of the review process. Here we consider the ways in which program reviews interact with other institutional processes, the relationships between program review, accreditation, assessment, and planning, and the future role of program review in higher education.

Program reviews do not occur in a vacuum. Regardless of the purpose of program review, political, social, and economic concerns will affect the outcomes of the process. The object of program reviews is not to eliminate these effects. By its very nature, the program review often heightens awareness of the review's outcomes. Thus it is necessary to remember that a successful program review depends on adherence to the guiding principles outlined in Chapter One:

- Fairness: All programs must be evaluated objectively if results are to be meaningful.

- Comprehensiveness: All aspects of all programs at all levels must be reviewed.

- Timeliness: All programs must be reviewed on a regular, predetermined basis.

- Communication: Throughout the entire process, people involved in the review and key figures in the institution must be kept fully informed of the review and its results.

- Objectivity: The design of the process and the selection of personnel must ensure as much objectivity as possible.

- Credibility: The process must be perceived as being fair and equitable to all programs.

- Utility: The results of the program review must be used in the planning and budgeting of the institution.

Program reviews are not the only institutional evaluation process. Almost all institutions today are also involved in accreditation and assessment procedures. Successful program reviews build on these institutional activities and share responsibility for developing an overall institutional plan for the future. The links between program review, accreditation, assessment, and planning are discussed in the following sections.

Accreditation

One of the most widely established evaluation processes on most campuses is that of accreditation by an outside agency. The accreditation process has for over seventy years served higher education well. Institutions have voluntarily joined one of the six regional accrediting bodies and fifty-eight specialized accrediting agencies in order to confirm the quality of their academic offerings.

There are similarities between the accreditation process and program review. First, both processes require some form of self-study, some type of on-site visit, some form of evaluation report, and, finally, some type of recommendations. In fact, these two processes could be carried out simultaneously if the timing and schedules could be coordinated. Second, both accreditation and program reviews frequently use the same type of data to measure institutional operations. While different accreditation agencies use different terminology and data sets, most of the data needed for accreditation purposes are also used in program review activities as illustrated in Table 10.

Table 10 indicates that the data needs of both accreditation and program review can be divided into descriptive and judgmental categories. Descriptive data include average salaries of faculty, student credit hours, and cost per student credit hour. As illustrated in Table 10, three of the categories are identical in program review and accreditation. In two categories, average salaries and cost per student credit hour, simple calculations can be done on data gathered in the program review to derive the necessary information for accreditation. In the judgmental category, all of the data listed are used in program review and can be inferred from data used for accreditation.

As institutions experience multiple evaluations from both accrediting agencies and program reviews, the collection and reporting of the data described in Table 10 become time-consuming and unmanageable. Efforts have therefore been initiated to develop a basic set of data to assess the current state of an institution or program. In 1985 a joint project funded by the Ford Foundation for this purpose resulted in *A Common Language for Postsecondary Accreditation* (Christal and Jones, 1985), which presented a common set of data definitions used in accreditation activities. These definitions have not, however, been widely accepted by the accrediting agencies because each accrediting body prefers its own classifications. Continued efforts are needed to encourage accred-

Table 10
Comparison of Sample Program Review and Accreditation Data

Category of Data	Used for Program Review?	Used for Accreditation?
Descriptive		
• Average salaries	Yes	Can be calculated
• Direct operating expenses	Yes	Yes
• Student credit hours	Yes	Yes
• Number of graduates	Yes	Yes
• Cost/student credit hour	Yes	Can be calculated
Judgmental		
• Adequacy of facilities	Yes	Inferred
• Adequacy of support staff	Yes	Inferred
• Adequacy of competitive salary	Yes	Inferred
• Assessment of leadership	Yes	Inferred
• Peer ratings	Yes	Inferred

iting agencies to adopt standard data elements and to incorporate them into program reviews. Since most program reviews are institutionally developed, the process can easily be adjusted to conform to accreditation definitions.

Several institutions and at least two states, Pennsylvania and Maryland, are considering combining their program reviews with accreditation visits. Such efforts can result in a considerable savings of time and resources, but several important differences between these two processes should be considered. The first concerns the purposes of the reviews. Accreditation studies are typically formative reviews aimed at program improvement and attempt to measure what has already occurred against some predetermined standards. Recently, regional accreditation agencies have begun to require outcome measures and comparison of what an institution *says* it is with what it is in practice. A program review, by contrast, depending on its purpose, may focus on program improvement or termination and may therefore be either formative or summative. A second difference between program review and accreditation studies is the issue of cost-effectiveness. Accreditation studies do not address this issue. Since most program reviews, particularly summative ones, do raise questions regarding a program's efficiency as well as its effectiveness, linking the program review with budgeting gives it a dimension beyond that of an accreditation visit.

Efforts to combine program reviews with accreditation processes have been seen in several areas. Representatives from the Council on Postsecondary Accreditation, a specialized accrediting body, an evaluation expert, and one of the authors held a symposium recently to find ways in which program review and accreditation could join efforts to reduce the burdens on institutions (Breier, 1988). A notable example of such cooperation has occurred in teacher education. Under a major redesign of the National Council for Accreditation of Teacher Education (NCATE) initiated in 1986, state departments of education can now apply to NCATE for program approval status. Once status has been granted, the NCATE review can satisfy the state department's review as well. As of September 1988, fourteen of the fifty state departments of education had been granted program approval status (Kunkel, 1988). For teacher education programs in those states, duplication of program reviews has been lessened and evaluation is now done with nationally recognized standards.

Assessment

Largely as a result of the accountability issue, institutions are now assessing student outcomes in a multitude of ways. Recent studies indicate that approximately two-thirds of the states and all six of the regional accrediting agencies are involved to some extent in institutional outcomes (Banta, 1989a). Assessment of student outcomes can be defined as "any activity from the simplest to the most complicated directed at reaching a judgment" (Manning, 1986). Assessment commonly refers to the evaluation activities colleges and universities undertake to assess their students' achievement.

Originally assessment began as a means of determining what students had learned from a common core of knowledge or whether students had gained certain competencies. These early efforts resulted in pilot programs in competency-based learning such as the one at Alverno College. While assessment efforts differ from program to program, campus to campus, and state to state, there has been, in recent years, a decided shift in the assessment movement from student outcomes to program outcomes (Cook, 1989, p. 2). This shift has created areas that, like accreditation studies, can be included as part of program review activities. For example, the University of Illinois at Urbana-Champaign has a multifaceted assessment approach that includes the Council of Program Evaluation (COPE). The survey instrument is designed to measure students' opinions and satisfaction with various aspects of their departments. This information is compared with other departmental data such as the unit's administration, its national reputation, and historical data on tenure, promotion, courses, and budget. Units are reviewed on a cyclical basis (Gray, 1989). Such assessment efforts can easily be fit into the ongoing program reviews at any institution and can enhance both processes.

While there are standardized assessment instruments such as the ACT examinations, the College Outcome Measures Project (COMP), and, more recently, the Academic Profile and Educational Assessment Series (EAS), many institutions are developing their own instruments for measuring what a student has learned during the course of a college career. These individualized efforts give rise to more opportunities for sharing data between assessment and program review activities. Program assessments can be designed so that the information gathered during that process becomes one of the criteria for the program review.

An example of collaboration between assessment and program review is found at the University of Tennessee, Knoxville. Banta (1989b) reports that one of the humanities departments used assessment data in a self-study which then enabled the department to pinpoint the strengths, weaknesses, and future direction for the department. External reviewers confirmed the conclusions, and recommendations were made to further strengthen the department.

Assessment should be made as much a part of the program review as possible. But like accreditation, assessment has not been tied to planning and budgeting and therefore falls short of a review process in forming judgments about a program. In some states, such as Illinois and Ohio, assessment processes are being encouraged as part of program review and statewide planning. Such encouragement will assist in institutionalizing assessment and integrating it into ongoing processes. Community colleges, in particular, have had difficulty in conducting assessments due to limited resources and wide variations in students and programs. McIntyre (1989) notes that only if assessment is tied to institutional planning, review, and accreditation can community colleges hope to benefit from their efforts. A good starting point for integrating assessment data into the planning and budgeting process is to include them as a criterion for the program review. Thus student outcome data become one measure of program effectiveness, which in turn is one criterion in a program review's data set. As colleges and universities become more experienced in assessment, the natural integration of assessment and program review will occur.

Planning

The role of program review as a subprocess of strategic planning has been described as that aspect in which the internal strengths and weaknesses are assessed (Keller, 1983) and internal capabilities are determined (Caruthers and Lott, 1981), thus contributing to an overall assessment of an institution that leads to a strategic plan.

Program review, while useful in identifying academic strengths and weaknesses, makes numerous other contributions to a strategic planning process:

- Helps contribute to overall institutional quality
- Helps provide for institutional accountability (improved public relations)
- Helps determine institutional strengths and weaknesses
- Helps provide guidance for program improvement
- Helps assess the institution's competitive advantage
- Helps define the institution's mission
- Helps give faculty, administration, and board of trustees a sense of good stewardship
- Helps in budget allocation and reallocation
- Helps identify institutional priorities
- Helps contribute to the institution's overall effectiveness

In all of these ways, the program review can have a varied and complex relationship to an institution's strategic planning process. The specific impact of strategic planning on these dimensions may be positive or negative.

Since program review is a subprocess of planning, it is not surprising that the relation between the two, according to our survey responses, is primarily a one-way relationship. As we have just seen, program reviews can make several contributions to the planning effort, whereas planning contributes overall strategy guidance to the review process. Strategic planning provides the overall framework within which program review, as a tactical aspect of planning, is developed and implemented.

In examining the relationship between program review and strategic planning (including budgeting) in various institutions, four patterns can be identified: (1) no relationship, (2) linkage, (3) integrated, and (4) program review as a driving force. The first pattern shows no relationship between program review and planning. This pattern has the advantage of being purely formative. That is, the review is for the exclusive use of the participants for the purpose of program improvement; no one outside the unit uses the results for planning and budgeting. While this relationship (or nonrelationship) apparently exists in a few institutions, it is hard to believe there is no interaction between program review and the other management processes, since even self-improvement reviews are bound to produce requests for additional resources, which by their very nature establish a relationship with planning and budgeting. Nonetheless in a few institutions the relationship is so remote that the respondents claim it does not exist as a matter of institutional policy, management process, or tradition.

In the second pattern there appears to be linkage between program review and planning. Here planning, program review, and budgeting are related, though usually in informal ways. As one respondent explained: "The provost, who is responsible for the program reviews, also participates in the planning and budgeting process and will, on occasion, draw upon the reviews in making planning and budgeting decisions . . . usually with respect to those programs which stand out in the reviews as being exceptionally poor or exceptionally in need of additional resources." The linkage between program review and planning is generally less positive than in other patterns, primarily because of its inconsistent application, which is often viewed in such negative terms as "political," "showing favoritism," "subjective," and "punitive." The fact that it is applied only selectively (as the previous quote suggests) is perhaps the biggest liability of this pattern. The linkage pattern also appears to blur the purpose of the reviews, which is claimed to be program improvement. Concerns about a "hidden agenda" are frequently raised in many institutions having this pattern of relationship. Those who obtain additional resources are, of course, not as likely to raise questions as those whose programs have been hurt in the planning and budgeting processes. On the positive side; this approach allows a greater degree of flexibility for administrators. As one administrator noted: "The key administrators can use their own judgment and expertise in its use."

A third pattern is evidenced at institutions where program review is integrated with planning and budgeting. This pattern has the advantage of consistency between the review efforts for each program, and the purposes of the review are usually clearly known within the institution (or at least they ought to be). For whatever reasons, faculty appear to be more knowledgeable about planning, budgeting, and review in institutions using this approach. Because of the clear relationship to budgeting and planning, a program's financial aspects undergo greater scrutiny in the reviews. In institutions using this approach, the reviews are but one element of the planning and budgeting processes, along with other factors such as accreditation reports. The disadvantages of this approach include a tendency for the program's proponents to be less than candid in their appraisals because negative comments might be used to cut back the program or even eliminate it. This appears to be especially true where the program's faculty have primary responsibility for conducting the review, although the tendency to be less than candid is even reported where outside consultants have the primary recommending role. Similarly, there is also a slight tendency for the reviews to be overly positive (especially in the self-study materials prepared by the program faculty).

In the fourth pattern, the program review is a major driving force for the planning and budgeting process. Because of the pivotal role it plays in institutions having this pattern, the program review takes on much greater importance within the institution. Thus considerable stress may be associated with the reviews. Some think this is beneficial because "it forces attention on qualitative improvement," while others feel it distorts attention from program quality to "program review quality." As one respondent noted: "Quality reviews become synonymous with a quality program, and this can be pure foolishness." Even in institutions with this type of pattern, the program review is rarely the only piece of evidence considered in planning and budgeting (although the review is seldom ignored). The primary advantages of this pattern have been described as follows: "The basis of decision making is well known because the review reports are public information available for all to see" and "It reduces the subjectivity of the planning and budgeting process."

Regardless of the pattern that institutions follow with respect to program reviews, it is clear that the process will not remain static. As faculty and administrators change and as the institution's environment requires it, the process of program review will grow to fit the needs of the higher education community.

The Promise of Program Reviews

As colleges and universities move into the next decade, we see the program review becoming far more institutionalized than at present. The program review, along with assessment and accreditation, will become part of the routine institutional processes resulting in improved programs and greater effectiveness. These three processes are all part of strategic planning and represent different aspects of the overall evaluation. Faculty and departments will regard program reviews as much a part of everyday life as book orders. Administrators will use the results of program reviews as readily as they now study their enrollment data.

As colleges and universities begin to institutionalize the program review, they will become more efficient in reviewing programs, refining data collection, and streamlining the process. Institutions will find new ways to share data and will, in fact, collect data on students and programs at far more regular intervals. Using natural built-in data collection points, program reviews will occur on a continuous, not a five-year, cycle. Reports will be prepared in a matter of weeks, and administrators and faculty will know far more readily the status of their programs within an institution.

The program review, when done successfully, can lead to the improved efficiency and effectiveness of higher education. Coupled with an active strategic planning process, institutions can map their futures in ways that will ensure their continued growth and development. The challenge for higher education in the twenty-first century is to respond to its environment. The program review is one of the tools faculty and administrators can utilize in guaranteeing a successful response.

Summary

The program review is only one of the many activities that occur on college campuses every year. These activities are shaped and guided by other ongoing processes including accreditation studies, assessment, and planning and budgeting. Administrators will use the data collection and study phases of the accreditation and assessment efforts as part of their program review activities. Good communication between these activities is essential, therefore, and can be facilitated by centralizing these efforts in one office.

The contributions of the program review to planning and budgeting are numerous. Since the program review is a subprocess of strategic planning, it is important that it be successful. In previous chapters we have described the essential steps in developing, conducting, and evaluating a program review. If the principles suggested in this book are applied and evaluated, a successful program review will result.

PART VI

Evaluating the Assessment or Program Evaluation

Introduction

Since assessment is most profitably viewed as an ongoing process, the evaluation of that process can provide valuable information to guide future assessment activity. Evaluations can illuminate the quality of assessment information, impact on teaching and learning, unexpected side-effects both good and bad, cost/benefit ratio, effect on morale, and effect on student access. This information provides an institution or unit the opportunity to build on the positive aspects and to avoid or minimize the negative aspects in the ongoing assessment process.

Several selections provide important principles or standards by which an assessment should be conducted. Ory applies the *Standards of the Joint Committee* to the context of assessment as guidance for its conduct. The *Standards* were developed by representatives from several professional associations of audition and psychology. Principles specifically for assessment were developed under the auspices of the **American Association for Higher Education Assessment Forum.**

Additional sets of principles or standards reflect thinking in the regional accrediting agencies. The characteristics of an assessment program encouraged by the North Central Association are provided by **Doherty** and **Patton. The Western Association of Schools and Colleges** has also developed an extensive set of principles as guidance for its members.

Principles of Good Practice in Assessment

Western Association of Schools and Colleges

The purpose of these "Principles of Good Practice" is to provide guidance for institutions preparing self studies and other reports under the revised Commission Standards, as well as to evaluation teams conducting visits. The "Principles" are non-binding. They are not intended to be narrowly prescriptive; instead they are intended to give helpful information to institutions regarding current "best practice." The Commission continues to encourage each institution to use assessment techniques in addressing the issue of effectiveness in its own way, consistent with its own distinctive instructional mission and clientele.

The "Principles" focus on the areas of emphasis highlighted in the preceding section. Suggestions are provided on how institutions might present their assessment efforts in reports to the Commission, as well as specific guidelines for four Standards: Standard 2.C, 4.B.2, 4.F.5, and 7.A. In each case, the discussion includes a) a brief overview of assessment issues within the particular domain addressed by the Standard and b) a set of principles of good practice to broadly direct implementation of the Standard. By presenting separate discussions of each Standard, the Commission does not mean to imply that "institutional effectiveness" consists solely of discrete components that should be addressed individually. It is intended, rather, that the evidence of effectiveness presented under each Standard be broadly consistent and reflect mutually reinforcing themes within the self study as a whole.

Standard 2.C: Institutional Effectiveness

This Standard is intended to provide overall direction for an institution's assessment and evaluation efforts. It is placed in Standard 2 to reflect the *institutional* character of assessment, and to reflect the need to focus on the *use* of assessment by linking it to institutional and program planning and improvement. In essence, Standard 2.C calls for the institution to possess:

a) an overall plan, or set of plans, for assessment at the institution, which includes a census of what data are collected and how they are to be disseminated and used, and also establishes the working definition of assessment to suit institutional needs and interests;

b) a visible, regular, and technically sound array of mechanisms for gathering evidence about issues of importance at the institution;

c) a process for involving faculty, particularly in designing assessments related to student learning and achievement; and

d) a visible and meaningful link between the collection of evidence and institutional decision making.

Principles of Good Practice

Principles of good practice under this Standard can be grouped into two distinct categories.

Information Resources and Processes. In order to address Standard 2.C, institutions need to review the available information resources that will be used to provide the "evidence base" for institutional effectiveness. This review will include regularly collected data, such as registration, completion and retention records, as well as scheduled but more periodic efforts such as alumni studies or cognitive assessments. (Appendix II provides information on data sources commonly used in this regard.) In assembling and maintaining this "data base," the following principles apply:

Responsibility for assembling and interpreting information about institutional effectiveness is clearly defined. In most cases, such information will be assembled from a wide range of institutional sources. Some office or individual at the institution should know what data are available, how and when they are collected, and how they can be accessed for further analysis. Equally important is identifying those who will interpret the information and disseminate it to those who will use it to improve the institution. An office of institutional research is not required, and the actual collection of data may be distributed throughout the institution.

Whenever possible, existing information sources are used. While the self-study process provides the occasion for some new data collection, the case for institutional effectiveness should not rest primarily on "one-shot" information-gathering intended solely to meet the needs of accreditation. Founding the case for effectiveness on regularly collected existing information is efficient and serves as a visible indicator that the institution is committed to the assessment process.

Information Utilization

Information on effectiveness visibly accompanies information on costs and operations in formal institutional planning, evaluation, and resource allocation processes. Institutions should be able to clearly point to the presentation of such evidence in regularly used data formats or in narratives associated with such processes as strategic or long-range planning, program review (both academic and non-academic), or unit budgeting.

Information dissemination within the institution is linked to generally recognized campus issues or problems or to identified institutional goals. Data collection efforts should not be treated as ends in themselves. Instead, they should be visibly linked to shared goals or recognized issues as they are reported to the campus community. Ideally, such reporting should require an action response on the part of affected campus units.

Information should be linked to decisions or improvements.

Appendix III provides an example of how an institution might use assessment to work through a particular issue or problem.

Writing Reports on Assessment

The goal of the Commission's assessment initiative is to create a "culture of evidence," i.e., a culture within the institution that welcomes critical questions about institutional performance and uses data in response to such questions. While the Commission is calling for specific sections of reports to discuss institutional assessment efforts, the entire body of reports to the Commission should include, where appropriate, underlying data to support assertions made throughout the document. The separate section on assessment, particularly within a self study, should address the following topics:

> *What is the institutional sensitivity about assessment issues?* How much awareness is there within the institution about the role and value of assessment?

> *How has assessment been defined to address institutional needs?* Are institutional assessment activities consistent with this definition?

> *Describe model assessment projects recently completed or underway and evaluate their design and impact.*

> *Describe the overall institutional plan of assessment or efforts to develop such a plan.* How is assessment being incorporated into general education and program review processes? How are student experiences being assessed?

> *What have been the most notable successes in assessment? What has the institution learned from unsuccessful assessment efforts?* Is there widespread dissemination, discussion and use of assessment reports? How effectively are faculty involved?

> *How effectively is assessment linked to program and institutional planning and to improvement efforts of the institution?*

This section under Standard 2.C should provide an overview of assessment throughout the institution. Other sections of the self-study report, especially those dealing with diversity issues, general education, program review and the co-curricular environment should comment on as well as reflect the use of assessment data. The use of data throughout the institutional report is itself some indication of the extent to which a culture of evidence exists at the institution.

Standard 4.B: Evaluation of General Education

Standard 4 sets forth a number of substantive requirements for the general education component of the baccalaureate. For example, Standard 4.B.2 enumerates several common outcomes for all undergraduate programs. Standard 4.B.3 calls for upper division general education offerings. Standard 4.B.4 calls for a clear rationale for the general education program; the establishment of criteria for reviewing and approving courses counted in satisfaction of general education requirements as well as a minimum number of units required of all students in general education; assessment of the success of the general education program in meeting its stated goals; and the use of assessment results in improving the general education program. And Standard 4.B.6 expects breadth in the general education program from three broad domains of knowledge.

As an example, Standard 4.B.2 indicates a common set of goals to be attained by an institution's general education program. They include a) oral and written communication, b) quantitative skills,

c) the habit of critical analysis of data and argument, and d) an appreciation of cultural diversity. Institutions should consider setting such goals at two levels: First, establishing the basic level of competence in written communication and quantitative skill for students to engage in collegiate level work. (See Standard 4.B. 10, which calls for the faculty of the institution, as a whole, to establish minimum standards for student competency in written communication and quantitative skills.) Institutions should be able to demonstrate that adequate diagnostic procedures are implemented and that students receive necessary support to reach preparedness for collegiate study. A second set of goals would be the competence level desired of *all* graduates of the institution, regardless of the student's major. Assessment methodology can assist in determining if both levels have been attained—basic competence as well as the achievement of general education program goals.

Assessment of the general education program should include efforts to: a) establish that these skills and attributes are *taught* in the institution's general education curriculum; b) establish that students *experience* the curriculum as designed (especially in distribution-based curricula where considerable choice among courses is possible); and c) establish that students *possess* the desired skills and attributes by the conclusion of their academic programs.

While only the last of these activities involves "outcomes assessment," evidence of all three is necessary to make a case for effectiveness. Presentation of appropriate evidence addressing the first two, however, might appropriately occur at any point within the institution's response to Standard 4. In addition, special attention should be paid to not only how the institution is responding to the goal of "appreciation of cultural diversity," but also what evidence exists that the institution's outcomes are being accomplished in this area. Treatment of this topic might be presented as a part of a response to Standard 4 or Standard 1.B.

In general, four major types of data collection can be employed:

a) "Curriculum-embedded" approaches are assessment techniques that are built directly into existing general education courses in the form of specially designed examination questions and performance assessments, or additional evaluation of existing samples of student performance produced as part of regular course work. In the latter case, "portfolio" or "secondary reading" techniques are employed to assess curricular goal attainment using defined criteria.

b) Student self-reports consist of questionnaire or interview items designed to elicit a respondent's own assessment of development in particular goal areas. They can apply to values as well as cognitive goals, and are often administered to alumni as well as to current students. Existing course evaluation processes also are useful vehicles for administering such items.

c) Existing record information such as registration records or records of library usage can be useful in establishing patterns of exposure to experiences that are intended to achieve general education goals. For distribution-based curricula, for example, transcript analyses to establish how particular requirements are met can be revealing.

d) Standardized examinations are usually administered to samples of students at the end of the senior or sophomore year. In most cases, only group scores are provided and can be used comparatively with appropriate national norm groups. Examples include the ACT-COMP, ACT-CAAP, ETS "Academic Profile," ETS CLEP examinations, and a range of commercially available collegiate basic skills examinations.

Principles of Good Practice

Principles of good practice for assessing the effectiveness of general education are intended to apply across all types of general education goals—cognitive, affective, or behavioral. They are also applicable to the assessment of particular major fields within the undergraduate program, addressed under Standard 4.F.5.

> *Multiple sources of evidence are used wherever possible.* No method currently available for determining the attainment of most skills and attributes identified as goals of general education is sufficiently reliable in itself to constitute a basis for judgment. While exhaustive coverage of all domains independently is not required, institutions should in general use at least two quite different data sources (e.g., a "portfolio" evaluation and a self-report through questionnaire) to gather evidence about the effectiveness of general education.

> *What is assessed is broadly consistent with what is taught.* In essence, institutions need to carefully match the coverage of the assessment instruments or techniques employed with the main areas of emphasis in their general education programs. Use of available standardized examinations should be critically evaluated in this regard: Does the coverage of the examination really match what the institution purports to teach?

> *Assessment and evidence-gathering practices are developed and applied largely by teaching faculty.* Faculty should be aware of the assessment process and should be involved in the choice of what is assessed and how assessment is accomplished. Assessment should not be viewed as an administrative exercise divorced from the curriculum itself.

> *Evidence obtained and presented allows sufficient disaggregation so that the performance of different kinds of students can be identified.* In general, a simple statement of overall attainment or an aggregate score will be less useful in guiding improvement efforts than results broken down by appropriate student subpopulations. Appropriate breakdowns will vary with the institution's clientele, but will probably include demographic and race/ethnic groups, entering ability groups, and groups based on choice of major field. Special care should be taken to avoid misuse of data to create overbroad conclusions about different groups.

> *Assessment allows, wherever possible, direct feedback to participating students.* The design of some assessment techniques (such as standardized tests or the use of cross-sectional sampling techniques) disallows individual feedback, and such approaches should not be ruled out on these grounds alone. But as primary "stakeholders" in the evaluation, students might be individually informed of their performance and counseled about improvement. Institutions will want to avoid situations where students have no perceived reason to participate and thus may be unmotivated to perform.

Standard 4.F.5:
Program Review

In essence, the Standard asks institutions to engage in a comprehensive program review process for all academic programs, and to build such reviews on "current qualitative and quantitative data which attempt to assess strengths and weaknesses in achieving program purposes and projected outcomes." This includes programs and departments at the undergraduate and graduate levels. In addition to such traditional ingredients of program review as program need, clientele, resources required, and a curricular review, an institution must address the academic outcomes of the program. Methods for assessing the outcomes of individual academic programs are similar to those used in general education, but considerable variety among the approaches employed by different programs should be both encouraged and expected. Among the types of evidence about program outcomes that might be appropriate are the following:

a) senior or alumni follow-up information on attitudes toward the program's strengths and weaknesses, self-reported growth and development, and career plans;

b) results of comprehensive examinations (either standardized tests such as ETS GRE or Major Field Achievement examinations or faculty-designed examinations);

c) results of certification or licenser examinations taken as a prerequisite for professional practice;

d) placement studies indicating the types of jobs obtained and career paths experienced by program graduates; or

e) testimony of employers or experts in the discipline on the observed capabilities of program graduates.

As in the case of general education, evidence drawn from such sources is most effective when used in combination. Meaningful academic planning also requires that "outcomes" information of this kind be fully integrated with "input" (e.g. data on student characteristics) and "process" information (e.g. data on teaching effectiveness, library usage, etc.) as a part of the review.

Principles of Good Practice

Principles of good practice on the overall conduct of reviews concern properties of the review process itself. Principles on the achievement of projected outcomes concern the assessment of program-level results.

Conduct of Reviews

Reviews are systematic. In essence, this principle means that the review process should be a recognized, distinct process that is formally identified in some way. It also means that standards should be uniformly applied with respect to process; though essentially a self study, for example, all programs need to be subject to the same kinds of review questions.

Reviews are regular. This principle calls for reviews to examine programs periodically over time. Once is not sufficient. Nor is it sufficient to examine programs only at the point where visible problems occur.

Reviews are comprehensive. Comprehensiveness can be interpreted in two ways. First, the review process should be applied to all programs, not just those selected because of problematic performance. Second, the process embraces all aspects of the program's operation, including inputs, processes, and outcomes.

Achievement of Projected Outcomes

Assessment procedures cover knowledge and skills taught throughout the program's curriculum. Coverage should not be limited to that of a single course or subfield (unless the course is an integrative "capstone" whose coverage itself is summative). Ideally, moreover, the assessment should not consist merely of an assembly of single-course outcomes but should rather reflect comprehensive knowledge and skills for the discipline or program.

Assessment procedures relate to the goals specified for the program. Standard 4.A.5 calls for degree objectives to be clearly specified in each field of study. Assessment efforts should be directed toward those areas identified as goals of the program.

Assessment procedures ; involve multiple judgments of performance. In essence, this calls for "more than the cook to taste the pudding." A single faculty member or "assessor" giving a grade is therefore insufficient. If an external examination is given (for example, a certification or licenser examination), however, multiple judgment is implied in the construction of the instrument itself.

Assessment procedures provide information on multiple dimensions of performance. In essence, this principle asks that assessment be more than simply a summative judgment of "adequacy." Resulting information should be broken down in ways consistent with the program's goals and should be useful in guiding program improvement efforts. A single grade or certification reflecting overall mastery is therefore insufficient for this purpose.

Assessment procedures involve more than simply a self-report. While students' testimony about their own development can be useful, assessment procedures should involve at least one type of evidence based on direct observation or testing of student capacities.

Standard 7.A:
Co-Curricular Educational Growth

The Standard requires institutions to provide "a curricular environment that fosters the intellectual and personal development of students." Aspects of the environment noted include: a) concern for the welfare of students; b) commitment to student academic and self-development; c) attention to ethnic, socioeconomic, and religious diversity; d) responsiveness to the special needs of a diverse student body; e) regard for the rights and responsibilities of students; and f) active understanding of the interrelated elements of the learning environment.

In addition, an institution needs to address the attainment of any additional values or curricular goals that are presented in its statement of purpose. Among these might be the values, orientations and behaviors associated with a particular religious belief or philosophy. For the most part, sources of evidence may consist of surveys or interviews with current students and alumni. Additional appropriate evidence can be drawn from available record data on student attendance at designated events or activities, or from record data indicating the institution's attempts to meet the needs of an ethnically or religiously diverse student population.

Institutional self-study discussions under this Standard have typically addressed student services and resources rather than assessing student experiences at the institution. Assessment methodology is critical to an analysis of student experience and the impact of the institution resulting from the co-curricular environment. In this section, institutions need to pay particular attention to the experiences of different student groups, such as minority and majority students, returning adult students, disabled students, etc.

Principles of Good Practice

The assessment of co-curricular experience should be governed by all principles previously noted under Standard 2.C. In addition, the following principles are applicable:

> *Assessment of co-curricular development is integrated with the assessment of academic outcomes.* In essence, this principle discourages "student affairs" assessment as a completely separate enterprise. Faculty should be involved in defining goals, and in gathering and interpreting evidence of co-curricular development. Similarly, there may be value in including student affairs personnel in assessing the effectiveness of general education. While results may be separately reported under Standard 7.A as a part of self study, it should be clear that the institution as a whole is committed to fostering any non-cognitive attributes of students that it claims as an educational purpose.

> *All assessment results (whether cognitive, affective, or behavioral) are collected and presented in a manner that reflects the diversity of the student population and the authenticity of individual student experiences.* In essence, this principle calls for the collection of information that reflects appropriate differences as well as similarities in student experience, based on such attributes as race/ethnicity, gender, or socioeconomic background. It also encourages attention to the diverse ways in which students may learn and develop, based on their own learning styles, past experiences, or psychological types. Overall, "averages" are therefore to be discouraged as the sole means of reporting assessment results.

Criterion Three and the Assessment of Student Academic Achievement

Austin Doherty and Gerald W. Patton

• • •

Characteristics of an Assessment Program

The following characteristics are offered as a framework to guide an institution's design and implementation of a program to assess student academic achievement.

1. **Flows from the institution's mission.**

   Although institutional missions include a variety of goals and purposes, central to the existence of an educational institution is the mission to educate students and ensure their academic attainment which is then expressed in the public awarding of credits and diplomas. From each institution's specific formulation of this central aspect of its mission and purposes flows the assessment program that provides evidence of academic achievement and enables the institution to use the documentation to improve its educational programs. This first characteristic, therefore, is directly related to Criterion One of North Central's four Criteria for Accreditation.

2. **Has a conceptual framework.**

   A conceptual framework is a set of principles that derives its definition and direction from the institution's mission and purposes. It provides direction for appropriate documentation and raises questions regarding the use of inappropriate documentation. Specifically, the principles should reinforce the importance of relating curriculum design, teaching, learning, and assessment. The framework should address the tendency, referred to previously, of using readily available examinations or assessments rather than creating or locating assessments specifically related to one's institutional purposes. Institutions may unwittingly attempt to assess students in areas unrelated to what they are actually required to do in their courses and academic programs. For example, an institution might test students on their problem solving ability when the development of that ability is not an explicit goal and learning experiences have not been designed to develop the ability.

   Above all, an institution's conceptual framework is shaped by insights from the integrating and synthesizing genius of its faculty and administrators. It enables the

763

institution to probe relationships between and among mission, student academic achievement, contributions of resources to this achievement, and future directions to ensure continued achievement—the four Criteria for Accreditation, which constitute North Central's conceptual framework for accreditation.

3. **Has faculty ownership/responsibility.**

Throughout this article there are numerous references to the role of faculty in the design and implementation of a program to assess student academic achievement. Given the historic responsibility of faculty in judging the academic attainment of their students for the purpose of awarding credit and diplomas, this role should be self-evident. However, at a time characterized by some confusion in education it is important to highlight this essential role of faculty. If the ultimate goal of assessment is the improvement of student learning, as North Central believes, then faculty's role and responsibility in assessment as integral to improved student learning are crucial. What form and shape this role takes is, of course, related to each institution's overall assessment design and distinctive cultural features.

4. **Has institution-wide support.**

High-level and widespread support within the institution for assessment of student academic achievement for institutional improvement is essential if faculty, staff, and students are expected to take assessment seriously. Board members, the President, and other administrators must take an appropriately active and positive role in understanding and fostering assessment goals and activities so that assessment becomes a routine way of life at the institution. Resource allocations and institutional decision-making should reflect and reinforce the importance of the assessment program at the institution.

5. **Uses multiple measures.**

Because of the variety of components involved in a full description of student academic achievement and the importance of assessing student development at various stages in the student's program, it is essential that the assessment program employ multiple measures. No one instrument is rich enough to capture the range of student achievement necessary for the institution to make a judgment regarding how well it is fulfilling its purposes in this area. And it is especially necessary for the institution to use a variety of measures as it endeavors to find ways to improve its approach to student learning. Diverse assessment approaches provide an invaluable source of information that can be channeled into the institution's planning process to improve its educational programs.

6. **Provides feedback to students and the institution.**

This characteristic and number nine—leads to improvement—are closely related. The major reason for listing them separately is to highlight both the crucial role of feedback to the student and the institution and the necessity for feedback to lead to action since North Central stresses improvement as the purpose of assessment.

Regarding feedback to students, it is important to reinforce for institutions the contribution of timely and specific feedback to student learning. Since not all assessments are constructed to provide feedback to students on the quality of their performance and how they might improve, care must be taken to ensure that among the multiple measures used some provide this necessary feedback to students. It is also the case that some assessment instruments do not provide the kind of feedback to the institution that would enable the institution to make plans to improve its curricular or teaching practices. These limitations of feedback reinforce the need for multiple measures.

7. **Is cost-effective.**

While an institution's proposed assessment program must be well designed in order to provide information for institutional improvement, the program must also be designed to obtain maximum information for expended costs in time and money. This requirement reinforces the importance of the conceptual framework in providing direction for appropriate assessment decisions. It calls on the ability of faculty and administrators to develop appropriate timelines for those projects within the overall assessment program that can be sequenced developmentally.

8. **Does not restrict or inhibit goals of access, equity, and diversity established by the institution.**

Perhaps it may not seem necessary to include this characteristic—or caution, if you wish—in this list of guidelines for a program on student academic achievement. Enough questions have been raised in public discussions, however, to warrant a brief comment.

If institutions undertake to design more sophisticated qualitative and quantitative approaches to assessment appropriate to their distinctive institutional character and student body, then educational quality and the serving of student's diverse needs and aspirations can only improve. If, however, a restricted view of what constitutes appropriate assessment measures begins to prevail, then important values that have traditionally characterized higher education may be adversely affected. It is essential, therefore, and beneficial from many perspectives, for institutions to reflect deeply on their mission and purposes and consider their implications.

9. **Leads to improvement.**

The most important point to reinforce regarding this characteristic is that North Central views assessment of student academic achievement as a means, not an end. This view is shared by faculty whose primary purpose in designing course tests, assessments, projects, papers, and the like is to determine how well the student is progressing so that both student and teacher may decide what changes, if any, need to be made to continue or improve student development.

A number of the components described in the assessment process below are recommended for serious deliberation by institutions precisely because they can lead to institutional exploration of ways to improve educational programs and practices. Especially important are the necessity of selecting appropriate indicators for the educational achievement to be assessed, the judgment of data, and the evaluation of the data within the context of the institution's mission. How faculty and administrators use the information from the assessment program to make plans and set timetables to enhance their educational programs is, in the judgment of North Central, one of the most important issues of this new assessment emphasis and is directly related to Criterion Four of the Criteria for Accreditation.

10. **Includes a process for evaluating the assessment program.**

    Like other programs in the institution, the assessment program itself needs to be evaluated. An evaluation process will determine whether the conceptual framework is sound and all components are appropriate to the institution's mission and purposes, the data gathered are being used for the intended purposes, and the primary goal of the program—the improvement of educational programs and the enhancement of student academic achievement—is being attained. Through this evaluation the institution can determine what adaptations need to be made to ensure the success of its assessment program.

Based on these observations of the centrality of institutional mission and purpose and the characteristics of an assessment program, we will conclude this article with a sketch of an assessment process.

One approach to an assessment process might include the following:

1. **A clear statement of what is to be assessed.** As indicated in the examples throughout this paper, the appropriateness of the entire assessment process rests on the clarity of definitions and specific descriptions of the academic areas the institution includes in its mission. When expectations are stated clearly and explicitly, the task of documenting their attainment is enormously simplified. This is not to say that documenting effectiveness is a simple task—it, too, is difficult. But clear statements of expectation provide the direction.

2. **Identification of components.** It is crucial to the success of an institution's assessment process that faculty determine the components of what is to be assessed. They do this by dialogue: What abilities are included in critical thinking—for example, ability to draw inferences, make relationships, discern value orientations? What disciplinary, interdisciplinary, problem-based or other frameworks characterize various majors or areas of specialization in this institution?

    These components guide curricular design and teaching, as well as assessment. They determine the nature of appropriate assessment instruments and provide a corrective to the use of inappropriate ones.

3. **Specification of indicators.** One of the most difficult questions confronting every faculty and institution is how well its students meet the academic requirements for attainment of credits and diplomas. Traditionally, faculty have developed their own means to evaluate student performance and have employed them in their courses and seminars. As an institution engages in an assessment process, it wrestles at an institutional level with questions similar to those confronting faculty at the course or department level. Will faculty judgment on senior comprehensives and writing portfolios, scores on licensing examinations, admission and transfer rates to four-year institutions for students from two-year institutions constitute sufficient indication of successful student academic achievement? What kind of feedback will most assist the student to become a responsible learner? Will various standardized test results indicate if and how well the student(s) meet the requirements referred to in #1 and #2 above even though the tests were designed for purposes other than evaluating the contribution to academic achievement of an institution's educational program? Will success in various courses with clearly delineated requirements based on #1 and #2 above constitute appropriate indicators of academic achievement?

    Because of the complexity inherent in assessing student academic achievement, data from multiple indicators will be required to ensure that the assessment process is appropriate.

4. **Collection of data.** As indicated above, institutions often have data from courses or seminars appropriate to an assessment process for the institution. But the data have not been collated at an institutional or departmental level. Drawing on insights gained in specifying appropriate indicators of student academic achievement, faculty can direct the collection of data from various sources. These could include sources within the institution—in courses and in outside-course assessments taken by students after completing sequences in general education or major areas. They could also include appropriate alumni sources.

5. **Judgment of data.** Once collected, data need to be analyzed and judged by faculty according to criteria appropriate to the designed outcome or purpose. If assessments and tests have been faculty designed, faculty will be able to judge student products and performances and evaluate student achievement based on the criteria they have established. In the process, faculty make discoveries that will lead them to improve the collection of data. For example, do student performances in problem solving meet important criteria like the identification and formulation of the problem, judgment of relevant data, willingness to take the risk of a decision? If not, there may be several reasons for this: more, and perhaps different, data are necessary; The instrument did not elicit the ability; or the teaching/learning process needs improvement. If the assessments and test have been designed externally, faculty may need to raise questions, in the evaluation process (see #6), about the meaning and significance of the data to both the institution and the students. For example, even if subscores for categories or components of an ability like critical thinking are available, how do these categories relate to the definition of the outcome set by the faculty?

6. **Evaluation related to what is to be assessed.** After the data have been analyzed and judged, it is important to raise questions about the relevance of the findings to the original purpose if these have not arisen during the process itself. For example, if the institution has used a national test to assess its distinctive program, faculty may be ambivalent in interpreting and relating the results to the specific academic purposes of the institution. If the institution has stated expectations for written and oral communication for its students but only documents the written, then what questions does this raise for the institution?

7. **Application to improvement.** Closely related to the above evaluation is the institution's need to take the important step of using the findings of the assessment process to improve the educational programs for its students. The importance of this step and its relationship to the preceding steps have been addressed above in the description of the guidelines of an assessment program. Although improvement of student academic achievement is the purpose of the entire process, it cannot be assumed that it will occur unless it is given explicit attention, planning, and implementation.

It is important to reiterate that whatever assessment program an institution develops should be a program that emanates from the faculty and administration of the institution. In designing an assessment program an institution should guard against the tendency to identify and implement an assessment model external to the institution. An institution should develop its own approach to assessment based on its mission and purposes, programs and resources, and should make its expectations regarding student academic achievement known to all concerned, including faculty, students, and the public. Once this is done, the institution and NCA can determine if the institution is, indeed, accomplishing its purposes.

Principles of Good Practice for Assessing Student Learning

THE AAHE Assessment Forum

1. **The assessment of student learning begins with educational values.**

   Assessment is not an end in itself but a vehicle for educational improvement. Its effective practice, then, begins with and enacts a vision of the kinds of learning we most value for students and strive to help them achieve. Educational values should drive not only what we choose to assess but also *how* we do so. Where questions about educational mission and values are skipped over, assessment threatens to be an exercise in measuring what's easy, rather than a process of improving what we really care about.

2. **Assessment is most effective when it reflects an understanding of learning as multidimensional, integrated, and revealed in performance over time.**

   Learning is a complex process. It entails not only what students know but what they can do with what they know; it involves not only knowledge and abilities but values, attitudes, and habits of mind that affect both academic success and performance beyond the classroom. Assessment should reflect these understandings by employing a diverse array of methods, including those that call for actual performance, using them over time so as to reveal change, growth, and increasing degrees of integration. Such an approach aims for a more complete and accurate picture of learning, and therefore firmer bases for improving our studenb' educational experience.

3. **Assessment works best when the programs it seeks to improve have clear, explicitly stated purposes.**

   Assessment is a goal-oriented process. It entails comparing educational performance with educational purposes and expectations—these derived from the institution's mission, from faculty intentions in program and course design, and from knowledge of students' own goals. Where program purposes lack specificity or agreement, assessment as a process pushes a campus toward clarity about where to aim and what standards to apply; assessment also prompts attention to where and how program goals will be taught and learned. Clear, shared, implementable goals are the cornerstone for assessment that is focused and useful.

4. **Assessment requires attention to outcomes but also and equally to the experiences that lead to those outcomes.**

    Information about outcomes is of high importance; where students "end up" matters greatly. But to improve outcomes, we need to know about student experience along the way—about the curricula, teaching, and kind of student effort that lead to particular outcomes. Assessment can help us understand which students learn best under what conditions; with such knowledge comes the capacity to improve the whole of their learning.

5. **Assessment works best when it is ongoing, not episodic.**

    Assessment is a process. whose power is cumulative. Though isolated, "one-shot" assessment can be better than none, improvement is best fostered when assessment entails a linked series of activities undertaken over time. This may mean tracking the progress of individual students, or of cohorts of students; it may mean collecting the same examples of student performance or using the same instrument semester after semester. The point is to monitor progress toward intended goals in a spirit of continuous improvement. Along the way, the assessment process itself should be evaluated and refined in light of emerging insights.

6. **Assessment fosters wider improvement when representatives from across the educational community are involved.**

    Student learning is a campus-wide responsibility, and assessment is a way of enacting that responsibility. Thus, while assessment efforts may start small, the aim over time is to involve people from across the educational community. Faculty play an especially important role, but assessment's questions can't be fully addressed without participation by student-affairs educators, librarians, administrators, and students. Assessment may also involve individuals from beyond the campus (alumni/ae, trustees, employers) whose experience can enrich the sense of appropriate aims and standards for learning. Thus understood, assessment is not a task for small groups of experts but a collaborative activity; its aim is wider, better-informed attention to student learning by all parties with a stake in its improvement.

7. **Assessment makes a difference when it begins with issues of use and illuminates questions that people really care about.**

    Assessment recognizes the value of information in the process of improvement. But to be useful, information must be connected to issues or questions that people really care about. This implies assessment approaches that produce evidence that relevant parties will find credible, suggestive, and applicable to decisions that need to be made. It means thinking in advance about how the information will be used, and by whom. The point of assessment is not to gather data and return "results"; it is a process that starts with the questions of decision-makers, that involves them in the gathering and interpreting of data, and that informs and helps guide continuous improvement.

8. **Assessment is most likely to lead to improvement when it is part of a larger set of conditions that promote change.**

    Assessment alone changes little. Its greatest contribution comes on campuses where the quality of teaching and learning is visibly valued and worked at. On such campuses, the push to improve educational performance is a visible and primary goal of leadership; improving the quality of undergraduate education is central to the institution's planning, budgeting, and personnel decisions. On such campuses, information about learning outcomes is seen as an integral part of decision making, and avidly sought.

9. **Through assessment, educators meet responsibilities to students and to the public.**

There is a compelling public stake in education. As educators, we have a responsibility to the publics that support or depend on us to provide information about the ways in which our students meet goals and expectations. But that responsibility goes beyond the reporting of such information; our deeper obligation—to ourselves, our students, and society—is to improve. Those to whom educators are accountable have a corresponding obligation to support such attempts at improvement.

Meta-Assessment:
Evaluating Assessment Activities

John C. Ory

Given the breadth and depth of assessment activity in higher education today there is a need for a set of standards to follow in its conduct. This paper briefly describes the Standards of the Joint Committee (1982) developed for educational evaluation and demonstrates theirapplication in conducting assessment and meta-assessment activities.

Several observations about the Assessment Movement in higher education prompted the writing of this paper. The first observation is the tremendous amount of interest in and conduct of assessment activities in the last five years. Evidence of this interest and activity is well documented in recent articles about the Assessment Movement (Halpern, 1987; Banta, 1988; Blumenstyk, 1988; Ewell, 1985; Gray, 1989). Cited are state legislative mandates for assessment activities, requests for assessment information by accreditation agencies, large attendances at national assessment conferences, the creation of assessment offices at many colleges and universities, and numerous books and articles published about assessment activities.

Observation number two is the movement's expanding definition of assessment. The initial focus of the current assessment movement was measuring student outcomes for the purpose of student development. Recently the scope of assessment has been expanded to include a broader view of purposes and processes. Today's campus assessment activities focus on students as well as faculty, programs, and the institution as a whole.

Explaining the shift in emphasis, Gray (1989) writes:

> The leaders of the assessment movement have realized that they must embrace a broader view of assessment because it allows them to consider an appropriately diverse set of reasons for doing assessment; it provides the framework for conducting more comprehensive, thorough, and valid assessments; and it offers a structure for including a wide group of stakeholders. (p. 1)

Driving the Assessment Movement and shaping its definition are the demands for accountability or institutional effectiveness made by state legislators, regents, university/college administrators, taxpayers, parents, and students. A poor national economy, escalating costs of higher education, and public concern over the basic skills possessed by college graduates are some of the reasons cited (Westling, 1988) for the increasing demand for accountability in higher education.

My third observation came as a result of a survey (Ory and Parker, 1989) we conducted to determine the extent of assessment activities at other large universities. We found a diverse group of individuals responsible for campus assessment activities. Assessment was the responsibility of active and retired faculty across various disciplines, campus administrators, student affairs personnel, testing office staff, management information specialists, and educational researchers.

My fourth and final observation is one I share with Barbara Davis and several colleagues trained in educational evaluation. Davis (1989) writes, "In the rush to meet external demands for assessment, those involved in assessment have overlooked what the field of evaluation can contribute to their endeavors" (p. 6). There is very little mention of evaluation theory and practice in the assessment literature, yet for those of us trained in educational evaluation there is a strange sense of déja vu as we read about the Assessment Movement.

The feverish pace required to respond to legislative mandates and the assignment of assessment responsibilities to individuals untrained in educational evaluation have resulted in the reinventing of some evaluation wheels and the making of old and familiar evaluation mistakes. For example, a common problem in assessment is the failure of faculty to accept assessment results and to use them to improve departmental curriculum. The utilization of evaluation literature (Braskamp and Brown, 1980; Patton, 1986) identifies general conditions and behaviors that promote the use of evaluation results. Many of these suggestions could be followed to encourage the use of assessment findings. Davis (1989) cites other areas of evaluation research that may be of interest to the Assessment Movement, including the existence of evaluation models, methodology for conducting case studies and naturalistic inquiry, criteria for judging merit and worth, or strategies for acknowledging and serving various stakeholders.

The purpose of this paper is to emphasize one other area of evaluation literature that should not be overlooked by the Assessment Movement. The literature on meta-evaluation, or the evaluation of an evaluation, seems pertinent given the similarity between the conditions that exist today in the Assessment Movement and those that existed in the 1960s when evaluators began to write about meta-evaluation—namely a diverse range of evaluation/assessment activities being conducted in a variety of ways by a diverse group of individuals.

Worthen and Sanders (1987) describe how in the 1960s "Evaluators began to discuss formal meta-evaluation procedures and criteria [when] writers began to suggest what constituted good and bad evaluations (for example, Scriven, 1967; Stake, 1968, 1970; Stufflebeam, 1968)" (p. 370). Evaluators were trying to help other evaluators by discussing their failures and successes and their criteria for judging both outcomes. I believe that many conversations and correspondence between evaluators in the 1960s and 1970s parallel exchanges made at last year's national assessment conferences between individuals struggling with assessment endeavors. What should we be doing? How should we be doing it? How do we know if we did a good job?

Evaluator concern for a consumer-oriented, professionally developed set of guidelines or evaluation criteria led to the development of standards for judging an evaluation. A profession-wide Joint Committee on Standards for Educational Evaluation published a set of thirty standards in 1981, called the *Standards for Evaluation of Educational Programs, Projects, and Materials* (Joint Committee, 1981). As explained in the introduction of the *Standards*, the standards were developed to provide:

> a common language to facilitate communication and collaboration in evaluation; a set of general rules for dealing with a variety of specific evaluation problems; a conceptual framework by which to study the often-consuming world of evaluation; a set of working definitions to guide research and development on the evaluation process; a public statement of the art in educational evaluation; a basis for self-regulation and accountability by professional evaluators; and an aid to developing public credibility for the educational evaluation field. Joint Committee, 1981, p. 5)

I believe if one were to replace the word *evaluation* with the word *assessment* in the above paragraph, individuals responsible for conducting campus assessments would see more clearly the relevancy of the evaluation literature to their work. Many of the problems addressed in the introduction are as troublesome for the assessment movement as they are for the field of evaluation. Given the breadth and depth of assessment activity in the nation, I believe there is a need for a set of standards to follow in its conduct. Furthermore, these standards should be used in the evaluation of our assessment efforts, or stated differently, in the conduct of a meta-assessment.

The remaining portion of this paper will briefly describe the thirty *Standards* of the Joint Committee and attempt to demonstrate their application in conducting a meta-assessment. In doing so, it is not the intent of the author to prescribe a model for conducting assessment. A reviewer of a draft of this paper provides the reasoning behind my decision, "In reading the manuscript . . . I had a feeling that something more concrete was needed in the 'comments.' After thinking about it last night I decided that I was wrong. There are too many possible paths in assessment research to begin setting out concrete recommendations and/or models."

The thirty *Standards* of the Joint Committee are divided into four major categories: utility (Does the evaluation serve practical information needs?), feasibility (Is evaluation realistic and prudent?), propriety (Does the evaluation conform to legal and ethical standards?), and accuracy (Is the evaluation technically adequate?). Following is a brief description of each standard as written by Blaine Worthen and James Sanders in their textbook *Educational Evaluation: Alternative Approaches and Practical Guidelines* (Worthen and Sanders, 1987, pp. 372–375). The descriptions have been altered by replacing the word *evaluation* with *assessment*. Along with each description is a comment on how the standard is relevant or applicable to conducting assessment activities.

A. Utility Standards

The Utility Standards are intended to ensure that an assessment will serve the practical information needs of given audiences. These standards are:

A1. Audience Identification

Description: Audiences involved in or affected by the assessment should be identified, so that their needs can be addressed.

Comment: Assessment can involve and affect a variety of on- and off-campus audiences. Generally speaking, different audiences have different needs. Audiences should be identified before planning an assessment so that their various needs can be determined and addressed. Audiences can include administrators, faculty, high school teachers, students, state boards of education, accreditation agencies, legislators, parents, and taxpayers.

A2. Evaluator Credibility

Description: The people conducting the assessment should be trustworthy and competent to perform the assessment so that their findings achieve maximum credibility and acceptance.

Comment: On many of today's campuses (Ory and Parker, 1989) assessment is being performed by many different types of individuals, including testing of office personnel, campus advisors, active and retired faculty, institutional researchers, management information specialists, and administrators. Most individuals involved in campus assessment programs are found to be trustworthy, but many are limited in their assessment skills.

It is not uncommon, for example, for a retired English professor to be asked to direct a review of a new rhetoric curriculum. The professor will be chosen on the basis of his or her content expertise, years of experience, the high regard of colleagues, and amount of available time. After conducting a successful review the professor will most likely be asked to help with other assessment activities, possibly including the assessment of student opinions about the rhetoric program or the development of placement exams. However, due to a lack of expertise in survey and testing procedures subsequent assessments may not be as successful as the first and the professor's credibility may be questioned. Conversely, situations occur wherein the credibility of a testing expert is challenged not because of lack of technical expertise but because of lack of content knowledge and/or failure to be "of the faculty."

A3. Information Scope and Selection

Description: Information collected should be of such scope and should be selected in such ways as to address pertinent questions about the object of the assessment and should be responsive to the needs and interests of specified audiences.

Comment: Not all assessment information needs to be collected "from scratch." Often the necessary data for an assessment activity already exist on a campus but in a variety of places. Assessment staff can better respond to the information needs of their audiences by being knowledgeable of all campus offices and the type of information collected and maintained by each.

A4. Evaluation Interpretation

Description. The perspectives, procedures, and rationale used to interpret the findings should be carefully described, so that the bases for value judgments are clear.

Comment: Individuals in different campus offices represent different campus perspectives. For example, student affairs personnel may conduct assessment activities with a student-consumer orientation while a faculty member may conduct assessment with a focused, discipline-based approach. A particular perspective followed in the collection and interpretation of data should be acknowledged by identifying the affiliation of the individuals conducting the assessment in the final report and by providing a statement of their perspective in the report's introduction.

A5. Report Clarity

Description: The assessment report should describe the object being assessed and its context, and the purposes, procedures, and findings of the assessment so that the audiences will readily understand what was done, why it was done, what information was obtained, what conclusions were drawn, and what recommendations were made.

Comment: Beside including the components identified above (i.e., a clear description of the program, assessment procedures, and findings) in a report of findings, individuals responsible for assessment need to be aware of the "clarity" needs of the critical audiences. Faculty audiences may be more likely to understand and accept reports containing numerical tables and statistical tests than may be a parent association or a group of legislators.

A6. Report Dissemination

Description: Assessment findings should be disseminated to clients and other right-to-know audiences, so that they can assess and use the findings.

Comment: Often evaluators and individuals responsible for assessment do not have the authority to disseminate the results to people other than those commissioning the assessment. However, when given the opportunity to do so, it should be the responsibility of the assessment personnel to see that the assessment results are placed in the hands of people who can best respond to the information. It seems that too often assessment is conducted to satisfy external mandates for the information. The assessment is completed and the information is sent to the individual or group of individuals creating the mandate. What about the potential use of the information by internal or campus audiences? How often do the faculty see retention rates, senior exit interview comments, alumni survey results, or departmental grade distributions?

A7. Report Timeliness

Description: Release of reports should be timely, so that audiences can best use the reported information.

Comment: Assessments should be conducted so the findings will be available at times when the information has greatest value and utility. Program reviews should be available at the time budgets are established; student course selection patterns or ratings of course quality should be examined prior to curriculum reviews. Timely reports should also contain "timely" information. Assessments should be completed in a reasonable amount of time such that the data examined are no more than a semester or year behind the current period. It may not be worth examining the assessment of course selection patterns if many of the courses no longer exist due to the great amount of time spent conducting the assessment.

A8. Evaluation Impact

Description: Evaluations should be planned and conducted in ways that encourage follow-through by members of the audiences.

Comment: The literature on evaluation utilization (Braskamp and Brown, 1980; Patton, 1986) is worthwhile reading for individuals who desire greater utilization of their assessment efforts. Some of the strategies for enhancing evaluation utilization or impact written about in the literature include identifying the information needs of the critical audiences, getting them involved in the design and planning of the assessment, keeping them informed about the assessment as it progresses, making assessment results easily attainable and clearly understood, and reporting assessment results in ways that suggest alternative actions for change or improvement.

B. Feasibility Standards

The feasibility standards are intended to ensure that an assessment will be realistic, prudent, diplomatic, and frugal. They are:

B1. Practical Procedures

Description: The assessment procedures should be practical, so that disruption is kept to a minimum, and that needed information can be obtained.

Comment: This standard addresses a critical issue in assessment. Many assessment activities require students to take a test or respond to an attitudinal survey outside of regular course requirements, that is, rising junior exams, senior surveys. As a consequence, assessment personnel struggle with many practical issues regarding the collection of data. How can a test be administered to several hundred or thousand students without taking up valuable class time or finding a time that all students can attend a large group meeting (e.g., evenings, weekends) or without having difficulty motivating the students to perform to the best of their ability or as honestly as possible.

B2. Political Viability

Description: The assessment should be planned and conducted with anticipation of different positions of various interest groups so that their cooperation may be obtained, and so that possible attempts by any of these groups to curtail assessment operations or to bias or misapply the results can be averted or counteracted.

Comment: Again, the literature on evaluation utilization suggests ways to use one's knowledge of political viability or the different makeup and needs of the various audiences to maximize the utilization of assessment results.

B3. Cost-Effectiveness

Description: The assessment should produce information of sufficient value to justify the resources extended.

Comment: Should minimal effort and expense be invested in projects that are completed to satisfy state or campus mandates and little else? Or should we invest as much time and money as necessary to get the maximum use out of any assessment? How often do we hear faculty complain that the money spent on assessment could be better spent improving the programs being assessed? "We all know that the students can't write. Don't waste your money finding out something that we already know. Instead, buy more English teachers!" Assessment personnel need to consider the cost of an assessment activity in light of its benefits.

C. Propriety Standards

The propriety standards are intended to ensure that an assessment will be conducted legally, ethically, and with due regard for the welfare of those involved in the assessment as well as those affected by its results. These standards are:

C1. Formal Obligation

Description: Obligations of the formal parties to an assessment (what is to be done, how, by whom, when) should be agreed to in writing, so that these parties are obligated to adhere to all conditions of the agreement or to formally renegotiate it.

Comment: The formal negotiation of an assessment contract may not be necessary because most assessment activities are conducted by internal campus personnel. However, the rationale for developing a contract or formal agreement should not be overlooked. It is often tempting once into an assessment to stretch the original boundaries of the activity and to assess or evaluate other objects. For example, faculty are often threatened by curriculum reviews because they often turn into reviews of personnel. This is not to say that assessments should fail to recognize unintended outcomes or side effects, but rather to stress that straying from the original intent of an assessment may cause political problems that undermine the credibility and acceptance of the activity.

C2. Conflict of Interest

Description: Conflict of interest, frequently unavoidable, should be dealt with openly and honestly, so that it does not compromise the assessment processes and results.

Comment: Conflicts of interest can occur because most assessments are conducted by internal campus offices. The difficulties encountered by internal versus external evaluation units have been written about in the evaluation literature (House, 1986; Scriven, 1967). Internal units do not go away after an assessment is completed and, unfortunately, negative messages are often linked to their messengers. Assessment personnel must work closely with many of the people responsible for the programs being assessed. It may be in the best interest of a particular individual or unit to refrain from conducting an assessment that may jeopardize a necessary and cooperative working relationship.

C3. Full and Frank Disclosure

Description: Oral and written assessment reports should be open, direct, and honest in their disclosure of pertinent findings, including the limitations of the assessment.

Comment: Assessments resulting in negative findings, even when conducted for state legislators and administrators, need to be reported and dealt with in an open and honest manner. A sufficient amount of data should be provided in the assessment report to enable the reader to verify the results and conclusions.

C4. Public's Right to Know

Description: The formal parties to an assessment should respect and assure the public's right to know, within the limits of other related principles and statutes, such as those dealing with public safety and the right to privacy.

Comment: Campus policy needs to be established by the campus administration and the individuals conducting assessments regarding public access to information. The policy needs to address questions like, Who has the right to know? Who has the right to refuse access to the information? or What are the proper channels for public requests for information? There is a sense of doing public good when conducting an assessment activity in higher education, especially in public institutions. It is difficult for me to think of assessment results that should not be shared with the various campus and public audiences. Obvious assessment results that should be shared with the general public include campus crime statistics, graduation rates of student athletes, or minority admissions.

C5. Rights of Human Subjects

Description: Assessments should be designed and conducted so that the rights and welfare of the human subjects are respected and protected.

Comment: Often assessments involve the testing or surveying of students to determine group rather than individual ability levels or attitudes. Promises to the student responders of anonymity or confidentiality should be honored.

C6. Human Interactions

Description: Assessment personnel should respect human dignity and worth in their interactions with other people associated with an assessment.

Comment: Any information collected during an assessment that may be personally damaging to an individual should be carefully handled whether it is pertinent to the assessment or not. Such information may be orally reported to an appropriate audience and not printed in a written report. "Off-the-record" comments should be respected and gossip should not be repeated.

C7. Balanced Reporting

Description: The assessment should be complete and fair in its presentation of strengths and weaknesses of the object under investigation so that strengths can be built on and problem areas can be addressed.

Comment: Seldom does there exist a single truth or correct perspective when conducting an assessment. Instead, multiple truths about a program, project, or activity exist in the minds of the various constituencies (Stake, 1968). It is the responsibility of assessment personnel to see that different perspectives are detected and revealed in the final report.

C8. Fiscal Responsibility

Description: Assessment allocation and expenditure of resources should reflect sound accountability procedures and otherwise be prudent and ethically responsible.

Comment: Given consistently inadequate assessment budgets, assessment personnel are used to being judicious in their spending, therefore, forcing easy compliance with this standard.

D. Accuracy Standards

The Accuracy Standards are intended to ensure that an assessment will reveal and convey technically adequate information about the features of the object being studied that determine its worth or merit. These standards are:

D1. Object Identification

Description: The object of the assessment (program, project, activity) should be sufficiently examined so that the form(s) of the object being considered in the assessment can be clearly identified.

Comment: The boundaries of a project or program need to be clearly defined prior to the conduct of an assessment. If, for example, an assessment activity is to develop new placement exams, then efforts should not be invested in evaluating the delivery of course material. Sometimes a valuable by-product of an assessment is the clarification or description of the object being studied. For example, a review of campus support services for minority students may provide the first complete listing of all campus services provided by the university, colleges, and departments.

D2. Context Analysis

Description: The context in which the program, project, or material exists should be examined in enough detail so that its likely influences on the object can be identified.

Comment: The context of the object being assessed needs to be identified to help audiences better interpret and understand the results of the study. For example, to understand data related to the effectiveness of a TA training program it is important to know certain contextual factors, such as program resources (staff, budget, and space), campus emphasis on undergraduate teaching, or willingness of faculty members and administrators to participate in the training.

D3. Described Purposes and Procedures

Description: The purposes and procedures of the assessment should be monitored and described in enough detail so that they can be identified and evaluated.

Comment: Aside from meeting an external mandate for information, the purpose of an assessment activity is not always clear. Questions such as, Why bother? or For what reason are we doing this? need to be addressed in the planning stages of an assessment and in the final report. Using a utilization of information perspective, I would argue that a purpose statement should indicate potential uses of the information. Rather than having the purpose for a junior exam in writing skills be to test junior writing ability, I would suggest that the purpose is to determine competency levels in writing and diagnose common errors that may need to be better addressed in the curriculum.

D4. Defensible Information Sources

Description: The sources of information should be described in enough detail so that the adequacy of the information can be assessed.

Comment: Depending on who you ask on a typical campus you may get different answers to the same question. As bothersome as it is, departmental, college, and campus statistics often do not match. Different formulas are used or different policies are followed in determining various campus statistics, including enrollments, progress toward a degree, grade point average, retention rate, probationary status, or FTE (full-time equivalent) staff. In addition to trying to obtain the most accurate information, assessment personnel should indicate in the final report the source of the statistics used in the study.

D5. Valid Measurement

Description: The information-gathering instruments and procedures should be chosen or developed and then implemented in ways that will assure that the interpretation arrived at is valid for the given use.

And . . .
D6. Reliable Measurement

Description: The information-gathering instruments and procedures should be chosen or developed and then implemented in ways that will assure that the information arrived at is valid for the given use.

Comment: Assessments make generous use of both standardized and locally developed instrumentation. Efforts should be made to determine the validity and reliability of an instrument either by reading available manuals and reviews of existing tests and scales or by conducting pilot studies for locally developed instruments.

D7. Systematic Data Control

Description: The data collected, processed, and reported in an assessment should be reviewed and corrected so that the results of the assessment will not be flawed.

Comment: A benefit of many campus assessments is the development of an information network. As previously stated, assessment data, or at least some portion thereof, often exist on campus prior to the conduct of an assessment. It is usually a matter of finding its location and learning how to access it. By documenting the data retrieval process there will be more systematic control of data for future assessments.

D8. Analysis of Quantitative Information

Description: Quantitative information in an assessment should be appropriately and systematically analyzed to ensure supportable interpretations.

And . . .
D9. Analysis of Qualitative Information

Description: Qualitative information in an assessment should be appropriately and systematically analyzed to ensure supportable interpretations.

Comment: Care should be taken that the procedures used to analyze data are appropriate for the questions being asked in the assessment and the type of information being collected. Statistical procedures also should be selected on their potential for being understood and perceived as credible by the intended audiences. Graphs are more readily understood by less statistically trained audiences than are tables of analyses of variance and multiple regression results. Statistical tests should be appropriate for the type of data collected (i.e., parametric versus nonparametric statistics) and sample size should provide sufficient inferential power. Statistical significance should always be interpreted with respect to the practical significance of the finding.

In recent years much has been written in the area of evaluation and the analysis of qualitative data (Guba and Lincoln, 1981; Miles and Huberman, 1984; Patton, 1987). Qualitative analyses are used to look for patterns and categories in the data that enable the reader to draw defensible conclusions about the object being studied. Or, as Brinkerhoff and others (1983) state, "to seek confirmation and consistency." However, these same authors warn us not to force consensus when dealing with contradicting and conflicting evidence.

D10. Justified Conclusions

Description: The conclusions reached in an assessment should be explicitly justified so that the audience can assess them.

Comment: A final assessment report should include a sufficient amount of valid, reliable, and credible information that not only allows readers to judge the interpretations and conclusions of the author but allows them to draw their own conclusions. Each assessment audience has a unique perspective, history, and training that may cause them to interpret the results differently from one another. However, to draw their own conclusions audiences need to have a clear understanding of how the individual conducting the assessment developed his or her conclusions.

D11. Objective Reporting

Description: The assessment procedures should provide safeguards to protect the assessment findings and reports against distortion by the personal feelings and biases of any party to the assessment.

Comment: After an assessment is completed and the final report is submitted to the client, usually a campus administrator, the author of the report has little control over the client's handling of the information. There is very little the author can do if the client wishes to change or delete findings prior to passing the report on to funding agents, legislators, or administrative boards. Individuals responsible for assessment must make it clear to their clients that it is in the best interest of the institution to accept less-than-positive findings and attempt to address their shortcomings.

Conclusions

Worthen and Sanders (1987) believe that the purpose of meta-evaluation is to help evaluation live up to its potential. Could we say the same about the reason for conducting a meta-assessment? Many assessments are not living up to their potential. Many assessments are completed to satisfy mandates from external sources such as state legislators or accrediting agencies. Often institutional compliance drives the assessment more than does the potential usefulness of the activity. Unfortunately the quality of the assessment is often of less importance than its mere completion.

Assessment has tremendous potential for improving the quality of instruction in higher education. Among other contributions, assessments can identify institutional strengths and weaknesses and indicate areas needing improvement. The *Standards* discussed in this paper can be used to help assessment reach its potential.

Individuals responsible for commissioning and conducting assessments can use the *Standards* to review assessment plans, monitor assessment activities, and evaluate completed assessments.

The *Standards* can be followed internally by the person(s) responsible for the assessment or externally by individuals who are independent of the assessment. Awareness and knowledge of the *Standards* can also make the different assessment audiences better consumers. (Brinkerhoff and colleagues, 1983, pp. 205–207 provide an excellent summary of ways to use meta-evaluation/ assessment.)

I was brought up with the notion that if something is worth doing then it is worth doing right. However, when I think about the many assessment activities being conducted today I am compelled to reverse the statement and say, "If assessment is done right, then it is worth doing." Doing assessment right means using assessment to encourage self-study and to suggest ways for institutional improvement. It means addressing the questions, "Now that the state board wants this information how can we learn about ourselves through planning the assessment? through studying the assessment process? or through analyzing the information collected?" I believe adherence to the professional standards throughout an assessment enhances our ability to answer these questions and to maximize our use of assessment efforts.

References

Banta, T. W. (1988). *Implementing Outcomes Assessment: Promise and Perils.* New Directions for Institutional Research, no. 59. San Francisco: Jossey-Bass.

Blumenstyk, G. (1988). Diversity is keynote of states' efforts to assess students' learning. *Chronicle of Higher Education,* July 20, pp. A17, A25–A26.

Braskamp, L. S., and Brown, R. D. (eds.) (1980). *Utilization of Evaluative Information.* New Directions for Program Evaluation, no. 5. San Francisco: Jossey-Bass.

Brinkerhoff, R. O., Brethower, D. M., Hluchyj, T., and Nowakowski, J. R. (1983). *Program Evaluation: A Practitioner's Guide for Trainers and Educators.* Boston: Klower-Nijhoff.

Davis, B. G. (1989). Demystifying assessment: Learning from the field of evaluation. In Peter Gray (ed.), *Achieving Assessment Goals Using Evaluation Techniques.* New Directions for Higher Education, no. 67, pp. 5–20. San Francisco: Jossey-Bass.

Ewell, P. T. (ed.) (1985). *Assessing Educational Outcomes.* New Directions for Institutional Research, no. 47. San Francisco: Jossey-Bass.

Gray, P. J. (ed.) (1989). *Achieving Assessment Goals Using Evaluation Techniques.* New Directions for Higher Education, no. 67. San Francisco: Jossey-Bass.

Guba, E. G., and Lincoln, Y. S. (1981). *Effective Evaluation: Improving the Usefulness of Evaluation Results Through Responsive and Naturalistic Approaches.* San Francisco: Jossey-Bass.

Halpern, D. F. (ed.) (1987). *Student Outcomes Assessment: What Institutions Stand to Gain.* New Directions for Higher Education, no. 59. San Francisco: Jossey-Bass.

House, E. (1986). Internal evaluation. *Evaluation Practice* 7: 63–64.

Joint Committee on Standards for Educational Evaluation (1981). *Standards for Evaluations of Educational Programs, Projects, and Materials.* New York: McGraw-Hill.

Lincoln, Y. S., and Guba, E. G. (1985). *Naturalistic Inquiry.* Newbury Park, CA: Sage.

Miles, M. B., and Huberman, A. M. (1984). *Qualitative Data Analysis: A Sourcebook of New Methods.* Beverly Hills, CA: Sage.

Ory, J. C., and Parker, S. (1989). A survey of assessment activities at large research universities. *Research in Higher Education* 30: 373–383.

Patton, M. Q. (1987). *Creative Evaluation,* 2nd ed. Newbury Park, CA: Sage.

Patton, M. Q. (1986). *Utilization-Focused Evaluation,* 2nd ed. Newbury Park, CA: Sage.

Scriven, M. (1967). The methodology of evaluation. In R. E. Stake (ed.). *Curriculum Evaluation.*

American Educational Research Association Monograph Series on Evaluation, no. 1. Chicago: Rand McNally.

Stake, R. E. (1970). Objectives, priorities, and other judgment data. *Review of Educational Research* 40(2): 181–212.

Stake, R. E. (1968). The countenance of educational evaluation. *Teachers College Record* 68: 52–540.

Stufflebeam, D. L. (1968). *Evaluation as Enlightenment for Decision Making.* Columbus, OH: Ohio State University, Evaluation Center.

Westling, J. (1988). The Assessment Movement is based on a misdiagnosis of the malaise afflicting American higher education. *Chronicle of Higher Education,* October 19, pp. B1–B2.

Worthen, B. R., and Sanders, J. R. (1987). *Educational Evaluation: Alternative Approaches and Practical Guidelines.* New York: Longman, Inc.

PART VII
Examples of Assessment and Program Evaluation

Introduction

The few examples that can be provided because of space limitations represent diverse purposes and models. **Light** reports on the Harvard Assessment Seminars that started as a series of groups exploring how students best learn rather than how much they learn, the focus of many assessment programs. The implications for improvement of teaching and learning is also the focus of the selection by **Stetson** who describes how a classroom research program was implemented at one institution. **Clark and Rice** describe the attempt at a university to interface an assessment program with a Total Quality Management program, both of which were required by external agencies.

Additional Core Readings

Aper, J.P. and Hinkle, D. E. "State Policies for Assessing Student Outcomes: A Case Study with implications for State and Institutional Authorities." *Journal of Higher Education* 62(5) (1991), pp. 539–555.

Banta, Trudy W. (Ed.). *Mahng a Difference.* San Francisco: Jossey-Bass, 1993.

Banta, T.W. and Schneider, J. A. "Using Faculty-Developed Exit Examinations to Evaluate Academic Programs." *Journal of Higher Education* 59(1) Jan/Feb 1988), pp. 69–83.

Hutchings, P. and Marchese, T. "Watching Assessment: Questions, Stories, Prospects." *Change* 22(5) (Sept/Oct 1990), pp. 12–38.

Knight, M.E., Lumsden, D. L., and Gallaro, D. *Outcomes Assessment at Kean College of New Jersey: Academic Programs, Procedures and Models;* Lanham, Maryland: University Press of America, Inc., 1991.

Light, R.J. *The Harvard Assessment Seminars, Second Report: Explorations with Students and Faculty About Teaching, Learning and Student Life.* Cambridge, Massachusetts: Harvard University, 1992.

Explorations with Students and Faculty about Teaching, Learning, and Student Life

RICHARD J. LIGHT

2. A Brief Summary of the Main Findings

A. Gender differences in college experience

Our surveys turn up several differences between men and women students. A few are dramatic, others more subtle. Young men and women are admitted by a single admissions process. They live in the same dorms, attend the same classes, and participate in the same extracurricular activities. Both men and women express high levels of satisfaction with their overall experience at Harvard. Women's satisfaction is especially high. Yet striking differences exist between what men and women want from college; how they spend their time; whom they talk to for advice; how they study; and which adults are important to them and affect them.

B. Congruence between how alumni and current undergraduates evaluate their college experience

Alumni ten years after graduation and current undergraduates respond almost identically when asked about their college experience. This similarity holds whether the question is overall satisfaction, or quality of courses, or quality of personal academic effort, or interaction with faculty, or friendships and romantic relationships. These consistent findings suggest that experiences at college leave a deep and lasting imprint on students' memories, and that students' judgments about themselves and their environment are not easily or casually revised.

C. Characteristics of highly respected courses

Students have remarkably clear and coherent ideas about what kinds of courses they appreciate and respect most. When asked for specifics, students of all sorts (strong and not so strong, women and men, whites and minorities, freshmen and seniors) list three crucial features:

a. Immediate and detailed feedback on both written and oral work.

b. High demands and standards placed upon them, but with plentiful opportunities to revise and improve their work before it receives a grade, thereby learning from their mistakes in the process.

c. Frequent checkpoints such as quizzes, tests, brief papers, or oral exams. The key idea is that most students feel they learn best when they receive frequent evaluation, combined with the opportunity to revise their work and improve it over time.

D. Many faculty members innovate, and learn a lot about how students learn best

Faculty are far more eager to innovate in their teaching and curriculum than many administrators and students imagine. Given an opportunity and the most modest incentives, many of them will introduce new curricula. They will experiment in a systematic way with both high-tech and low–tech innovations to make their teaching more effective and to enhance students' learning. When faculty members evaluate such innovations and share the results, evidence about how students learn best begins to accumulate. For example, early evidence suggests that students who work in small groups, even when interacting with high tech equipment, learn significantly more than students who work primarily alone.

E. Connections between academic performance and non-academic factors

Students' academic performance is tied closely to factors outside of classrooms. Students' patterns of seeking advice, engaging in part-time work, and participating in other college activities all connect to academic performance. Such patterns affect what courses students choose, their level of interest in these courses, the intensity of their academic involvement, their willingness to take academic risks, and their grades.

A surprising finding: faculty accessibility

There is a vague but widespread belief that many faculty members are inaccessible, or hard to get to see. Sometimes freshmen are told this before they arrive. But the data suggest that this belief is simply wrong. The overwhelming majority of faculty members, including most senior faculty, actively invite contact with students. They find many ways to involve students with their work, both formally and informally. Most faculty expect students to take some initiative. But the most modest initiative is almost always rewarded.

An unsettling finding: student reactions to who sets a tone on campus

When asked what aspect of student life at Harvard College most troubles them, many students surprised me and my colleagues by choosing to focus on how a small number of students can influence campus climate.

Some students mention the student newspaper, the *Crimson,* to illustrate this. They point out that by choosing how to portray campus news and events, a small group of writers and editors set a tone or flavor for campus life on a daily basis. The choice of how to report activities can have a strong effect—positive or negative—on students' perceptions of quality of life. This is illustrated by sharp differences between the ways freshmen and seniors describe the *Crimson*. Freshmen have uniformly high praise for the quality of writing, and few criticisms about tone. Seniors praise the writing, but point out a sharp difference between tone in past years that troubled them (carping), versus tone in the current year (constructive).

A promising direction for future work: the value of small groups to enhance students' learning

In every comparison of how much students learn when they work in small groups with how much they learn either in large groups or when they work alone, small groups show the best outcomes. Students who study in small groups do better than students studying alone. Students interacting with videodisc technology learn more when they interact in small groups than when they sit in front of a computer screen alone. Students in the physical sciences who work in small study groups are more likely both to persist and to enjoy the experience than those who study alone. These findings are based on early pilot studies, and point to a worthwhile area for future experimentation.

3. Background of the Harvard Assessment Seminars, and sources of data for this report

The impetus for our Assessment Seminars came from discussion throughout Harvard of President Bok's Annual Report issued in the spring of 1986. In this report, Bok asks why faculty and administrators at colleges and universities do not routinely engage in research, assessment, and program evaluation within their own colleges. He points out that colleges and universities provide an extraordinarily fertile ground for internal research. Faculty members understand the importance of research, and are well trained to do it. Students are learning how to do research, so they are likely to be receptive to participating in it. Bok also argues that for such work to make a truly valuable contribution, it should be designed to affect policy decisions.

Soon after this Annual Report, Bok invited me to assemble a group of colleagues to start a long-term program of research and assessment. Our group quickly developed three ground rules. These principles have endured throughout all the Seminars' activities.

First, members of the Seminars view assessment in a particular way. It is not simply, "How much do students know?" Rather, the Seminar's goal is to encourage innovation in teaching, in curriculum, in advising, and then to evaluate the effectiveness of each innovation. A key question we examine is under what conditions students learn best, both inside and outside of classrooms. Participants agree that slow but steady improvements in instruction and advising can make college ever more effective.

Second, since the Seminars are based at Harvard, much of the work inevitably takes place with students and faculty here. But including colleagues from other colleges and universities clearly broadens everyone's perspective. Many colleagues from other colleges and universities are involved as full members in all activities. A list of participants appears at the end of this report.

Third, our mode of working divides the more than one hundred participants into a series of small 'working groups.' Each group designs its own project or innovation, implements it and then evaluates it. The only constraint is that each group involve at least one faculty member, one administrator, and one student. In retrospect, this is probably the single most important decision that shapes the Seminars' successful projects. The administrators keep each group's eye on real–world policy implications of any new work. This reduces the chance that a project will become an entirely abstract research enterprise. We all want to avoid a situation in which researchers present findings only to other researchers, with no impact on teaching, curriculum, or college life. The faculty members do the main work of creating innovations in curriculum and teaching, then trying them out. And the students offer two crucial boosts. First, they help to shape instruments for interviewing other students, and after careful training they actually do interviews. Second, under close faculty supervision, they do much of the nitty-gritty analyses. To date, two undergraduate honors theses and six doctoral theses have grown out of the Seminars.

Sources of Data

The findings in this report come from many data sets. Here is a brief summary.

Data Set #1. Our biggest data is a random sample of 6 percent of all Harvard College undergraduates. Thomas Angelo, Assistant Director of the Seminars, arranged with the Harvard College Registrar to draw a random sample from all enrolled students. This resulted in a sample of 388. These students were sent a letter inviting them to participate in two in-depth interviews focusing on their academic work, part-time paid employment, extracurricular activities, and athletic commitments. Students were asked about their experiences with academic advising and contact with faculty members and other adults. Finally, students were invited to describe in detail their level of interest and commitment and the amount of time they spend on particular courses.

The response rate for this sample was 94 percent for the first round of interviews—365 out of the 388 were completed. For a second round four months later, the interviewers completed 335 interviews of the original 365 student, a 93 percent follow-up rate. Interviews were conducted by twelve students, three undergraduates and nine graduate students, each trained first individually and then as part of a group. Reliability checks were carried out, as were comparisons between interviewers to see if any interviewer was eliciting noticeably different responses from the others. No troubling variations were found in either round of interviews.

Data Set #2. A sample of 48 upperclass students were asked to keep track of how they spent their time, half hour by half hour, for two one-week periods. This was done in a fashion similar to the way attorneys keep a log of their billing hours. Students were asked to fill in these time logs with several specific categories of activities, and then were debriefed individually.

Data Set #3. A sample of 70 freshmen were asked to keep detailed time logs of how they spent their time over a two-week period. Of these, 68 agreed to participate, and they were debriefed by their freshman proctor and advisor.

Data Set #4. A sample of 50 sophomores were selected for interviews by a team of 10 graduate students. The interviewers were trained by a group of faculty members from Harvard, MIT, and Brown. The sophomores were invited to reflect on what specific parts of freshman year courses trained them to "think well" and prosper academically, and what features of courses failed to do this. These interviews raised the question of what diagnostic efforts can be initiated for sophomores with academic difficulties.

Data Set #5. Each of 14 students concentrating in the physical sciences was interviewed, in depth, by Andrea Shlipak as part of her work for an undergraduate honors thesis. Shlipak focused especially on why some students find working in math, engineering, and the sciences entirely hospitable, while others feel differently. She made a special effort to see if women reported different experiences from those of men in math and science concentrations.

Data Set #6. Leigh Weiss, for her undergraduate honors thesis, compared the experiences of 72 intercollegiate athletes with the experiences of 250 students not involved in intercollegiate athletics.

Data Set #7. Robin Worth surveyed alumni from the classes of 1957, 1967, and 1977. She received 1,400 responses from graduates of Harvard and Radcliffe. The questionnaires invited graduates to reflect on their college experience and to tie details of that experience to details of their lives today. Worth also obtained the original admissions folders for these alumni. This enabled her to link their original admissions applications to their activities and performance at Harvard/Radcliffe, and ultimately to responses about their lives today as adults in their 30s, 40s, or 50s.

Data Set #8. Kimberly Hokanson selected a sample of 673 alumni from the Harvard and Radcliffe classes of 1978,1980, and 1983. She obtained responses from this group in three categories. One was reflections on the non-academic components of their college experience—the importance of extracurricular commitments, part time work, and relationships with faculty members and other students. A second category focused on foreign languages. What languages had these recent graduates studied? How important did they consider these courses in retrospect? And what further study of languages, if any, had they undertaken after leaving Harvard? The third part of this survey invited alumni to give advice to current Harvard administrators and faculty. What academic requirements would they suggest changing, and why? What parts of their college training had they found most helpful later, and what parts had served them less well? What suggestions could these recent graduates make to strengthen academic and personal advising for current students? . . .

8. Embedding research and evaluation into ongoing university activities

Organizing and directing the Assessment Seminars has taught me lessons about both the opportunities and the pitfalls of such a venture. Integrating research on ourselves as an ongoing, routine campus activity is taking root in some parts of Harvard but not everywhere. I hope that in the next year we can extend these efforts. For now I want to share seven lessons I have learned about assessment. Colleagues at other institutions may want to learn from both our successes and our dilemmas.

Lesson 1: The importance of faculty initiative

Faculty members must assume a central role in directing assessment projects. As I invited faculty from both Harvard and the twenty other colleges, the kind of question I was asked far more than any other was, "Who will shape this enterprise? Is this a faculty initiative? Will faculty shape the investigations?"

I was a bit taken aback by these questions. I had assumed that of course the answer would be yes. But gradually I learned many members of the faculty were concerned that they might become little more than research assistants for someone else. Most faculty are busy, and most of the work in their professional life has little to do with assessment. If they can't help to shape the important questions, and can't initiate projects to help their teaching, they may not come at all. As one faculty colleague at another university put it with a smile, "Deans are free to ask any questions they want, and free to commission any research they will find useful. I just don't want to be my Dean's research assistant." We are fortunate that, at Harvard and all the other participating institutions, administrators are highly sensitive to this faculty view. They have strongly encouraged faculty members to lead *each* working group.

Lesson 2: Clarify exactly what assessment means

Assessment means different things to different people. I quickly learned how different. For example, faculty perspectives are somewhat different at public and private universities. An increasing number of state legislatures are requiring specific procedures and steps for colleges to conduct self-evaluations. Some public institutions feel under the gun to administer large-scale standardized tests to assess "what students know now." But this is not the type of question that sparks excitement at private colleges, at least those in our Seminars. Rather than defining assessment as testing what students know now, my colleagues define it as a process of evaluating and improving current programs, encouraging innovations, and then evaluating each innovation's effectiveness. The key step is systematic evaluation.

Our group quickly agreed that it is crucial to encourage and assess innovations both inside and outside of the classroom. Many faculty members are eager to improve classroom teaching, so they are especially interested in trying in-class innovations. Some are exploring ways to improve teaching effectiveness without introducing elaborate new equipment. Others are eager to use new technology, but only when they see compelling evidence that such equipment can improve students' learning. A third group feels the biggest gains in student performance will come from a sustained effort to improve academic advising, rather than from changes in classroom teaching.

It is easy to accommodate these different views. They lead to projects that turn up useful results. For example, it was suggestions from academic advisors that led to in-class experiments to get students working in small groups. And many high-tech equipment enthusiasts are surprised to learn how effective some low-tech classroom teaching devices can be. These include, for example, the one-minute paper, and videotaping students in small groups and then watching the tape with them individually.

Lesson 3: Involve students in the assessment enterprise at every step

At the outset, I did not invite any students. Since most participants in the Seminars spend much of every day teaching and working with students, I assumed they would prefer to spend this extra evening working only with colleagues. I couldn't have been more wrong. Much of the work of the Seminars—their planning, execution, and even the establishing of the importance of different possible research efforts—has been enriched enormously by student participation.

Students took great initiative. Though none were invited at first, I soon began to receive calls. These calls continue. Some are from graduate students interested in higher education as a substantive field. Others are from specialists in statistics and research design. Still others are from undergraduates who want to do their undergraduate honors theses on topics sponsored by the Seminars. It took a while, but I finally realized that many students have a genuine interest in policy research on colleges. And they are eager to do lots of the nitty-gritty work on projects—interviewing, data collection, and computer analyses. The faculty, in turn, are able to offer these students two incentives.

One incentive is modest financial support—most students need it and all appreciate it. The other incentive, far more important in the long run, is intense and careful faculty supervision. For example, ten graduate students volunteered to carry out in-depth interviews with Harvard sophomores. Their goal was to probe why some students flourish during freshman year while others, with similar SAT scores and high school grade profiles, are less productive. Professor David Riesman invited these students, together with several faculty colleagues, to his home for two evenings of training. The agenda was to learn how to interview undergraduates in a reliable and productive way. Several of these student interviewers commented to me later that the two evenings at Professor Riesman's home, working with senior faculty based at Harvard, Brown, and MIT, were not only useful, they were the two most memorable evenings of their Harvard years.

Lesson 4: Senior administrative leadership helps to get on-campus assessment started

For our Seminars, President Bok provided such leadership in two ways. First, by advocating the value of on-campus research and assessment in his annual report, he called the attention of the entire university to this work. He publicly gave it a high priority. As a result, busy faculty and administrators understood that, by participating in assessment, they could shape policy decisions in the future. By expressing publicly his hope that assessment would become an enduring activity, he conveyed to faculty members throughout the university the long-term importance of our venture.

Second, Bok made a clear statement by allocating seed money from the President's fund to the Seminars. This money got our Seminars started, funded student assistants, and created a series of dinners for our big group of participants. It is clear in retrospect that this funding emphasized the high administrative priority of the Seminars.

Lesson 5: Choose and organize projects so they can lead to real policy change

A crucial agenda item at our earliest meetings was the challenge to "identify the biggest risk we face to reduce the chance of failure." We quickly decided there is a real risk that assessment projects may become theoretical investigations, conducted by people who are disconnected from policy decisions, who then report their findings at meetings attended only by other, similar people. To reduce this risk, each project team is now encouraged to ask itself repeatedly, "What are the policy implications of our work? How can our findings improve teaching, or curricula, or advising, or student services?" Other campuses can benefit from our experience. An emphasis on gathering information that will actually improve education helps to coordinate the work of faculty and administrators to shape real change, rather than simply to create another academic publication.

Lesson 6: Have a plan for disseminating successful innovations

Research and assessment must have enough public notice on campus that good results can be adopted widely. An example from our Seminars illustrates this. Many faculty were present at a meeting focusing on assessments of teaching innovations. One particularly simple innovation—the one minute paper—was found to yield large benefits to both students and faculty. Several of the faculty members who attended subsequently discussed this finding at their own schools. Because many on the faculty know about our Seminars and its purpose to encourage and evaluate helpful tools for teaching, a receptive audience was waiting.

Lesson 7: Leaders on any campus should work to create a climate that encourages the process of innovation and evaluation, rather than only rewarding successful outcomes

What does a Dean or department chairman typically do now, if each of five faculty members comes to propose a new and different way to teach Biology? Most Deans on most campuses will say "good luck" to each of them, and indeed they will mean it. Then, after the five professors have tried out their innovations in the classroom, anyone who succeeds in improving Biology instruction may be rewarded either privately or publicly.

A critical message from the Assessment Seminars is that such administrative action doesn't do much to encourage steady and widespread improvement. If five faculty members came to you, each proposing a new and different way to teach Biology, what would you do? You might think to yourself that there is little chance all five will succeed in doing it better than the old way. Indeed, you might be delighted if just *one* of these faculty members does better than the old way, and treasure this one improvement. After all, developing new ways to teach that are demonstrably better than existing practice is not easy. Many people have thought for many years about how to teach effectively. It would be astonishing if every new idea worked well.

Might it make good sense to stimulate and encourage all five faculty members who want to innovate, and to especially emphasize the key step of putting into place a serious, scientifically valid effort to assess each new method's effectiveness? This communicates that we *honor the process* of innovation and evaluation. Most important, we cannot be dismayed if any specific innovation doesn't turn out to be a grand success. By encouraging both innovation and systematic assessment, we embark on a longer-term program of steady improvement. Such a program will inevitably include both successes and failures.

Creating such an environment can be subtle and challenging, since it is natural for most faculty members, and I include myself, to highlight new courses or teaching methods only when they work well. It is a wonderful feeling to succeed. But evidence from Harvard tells us it is possible to create a climate that rewards innovation and assessment *as a process*. This process will identify failures as well as successes. Faculty members and administrators must agree to accept this sense of two steps forward and one step back. It can lead to a remarkable upsurge in efforts to improve education for all students.

TQM and Assessment:
The North Dakota Experience

ALICE T. CLARK AND DANIEL R. RICE

Are the two "academic quality" movements of the eighties, Assessment and Total Quality Management (TQM), based on compatible and interchangeable principles and techniques? The broad and theoretical answer this question merits is beyond the scope of this paper, but the experience of one institution will be described regarding its simultaneous attempt to implement TQM at the direction of its state governing board and to fulfill North Central's accreditation expectations for assessment of knowledge.

Definition of Terms

1. While there are many definitions, assessment, according to North Central, is attention to student achievement as it is related to the purposes of the college or university. Assessment is the process of identifying the evidence of student achievement and, also, utilizing that evidence to improve instruction. Pat Hutchings, quoting an unnamed faculty member, suggested that assessment is "asking whether my students are learning what I think I'm teaching."

2. There are many definitions of Total Quality Management. A document prepared by Oregon State University contains the following definition: "TQM is a structural system for creating organization-wide participation in planning and implementing a continuous improvement process that exceeds the expectations of the customer/ client. It is built on the assumption that 90 percent of our problems are process problems, not employee problems" (Coate, 1990). TQM is an industrial/business approach that is in the early stages of implementation in higher education. Little data or research are available on the application to academics. Preliminary results indicate that most applications have been to non-academic issues (Seymour, 1991)

3. At this stage it seems that the two concepts may not be entirely interchangeable; yet, they may be compatible in some important respects.

    a) Both approaches share the goal of improved outcomes because of improved processes. (Recent thinking about assessment has moved beyond attention to outcomes only. In this respect, TQM is described as a "commitment to ceaseless improvement involving everyone" (Imai) and assessment is described as "how we work with one another"(Hutchings).

b)   Both approaches recognize the need for administrative/managerial commitment and leadership.

c)   Both approaches understand that the people closest to the work are in the best position to make improvements.

d)   Both approaches are intent upon receiving continual feedback from the customers/learners.

One Institution's Experience

The relationship between TQM and the assessment movement has been problematic at the University of North Dakota (UND). The administration has wondered: Is there, in fact, a philosophical or process barrier when the traditional approaches to assessment bump against the quality management initiatives suggested by Deming, Juran, Feigenbaum, or Crosby?[1] Or does the conflict that appears to have arisen occur more in the "eyes of the beholders" than in the theories of quality?

Academic assessment to monitor and improve student learning has been pursued in some form at UND for many years preceding the "Assessment Movement" of the mid-eighties that has achieved such unprecedented national prominence. There has not been an institutional philosophy or set of values that has formally directed the assessment practices at UND. Most departments have availed themselves of the comprehensive data base in the Institutional Research Office; but, in general, there has been very little sophistication about the statistical and analytical procedures used to evaluate courses, students, knowledge bases, and so forth. Until very recently, departments/faculty have been quite autonomous in their accountability for the assessment of the quality of their programs. Traditional measures, such as tests, surveys, board exams, term papers, and so forth, have typically been used . . . and always with integrity and responsibility. But the faculty have not always acted with a firm commitment to any university-wide comprehensive plan designed to enhance the overall quality of the university.

However, as people on the campus began to anticipate the site visit of the next decennial review of the North Central Association, they experienced apprehension about the "new expectations" for assessment of the student knowledge base. The self-study assignments generated a flurry of activity among the departments as they searched the assessment literature for more effective techniques. Additional pressures from state and national levels as well as from the Board of Higher Education in North Dakota for greater accountability further heightened the faculty pursuit of appropriate assessment procedures. The preference was clearly for traditional measures.

In 1989 the State Board of Higher Education adopted Total Quality Management for the entire North Dakota University System. Every public higher education institution in the state was required to develop a TQM plan for its campus. State-wide workshops were sponsored by the Board to begin educating system personnel at every level. Articles, tapes, and books on TQM were widely circulated.

A new chancellor was hired with the specific mandate to implement TQM across higher education in the state. Suddenly UND found itself caught in the middle of two important quality developments, both of which required strong leadership, campus consensus on goals, budgetary resources, personnel commitments, precious time from the faculty, restructuring of priorities, reorganization of governance relationships, extensive changes in attitude and "way of life," to name just a few of the impacts.

The challenge of implementing assessment and TQM together might have resolved itself comfortably at a different point in the campus's history; but TQM, coming from the top down, was viewed by UND's faculty with suspicion, apprehension, and skepticism. At one TQM faculty workshop, faculty identified 61 reasons why TQM would not work at UND. These reasons included different aspects of time, coordination, attitude, reward, communication, commitment, and focus.

The University administration faced immediate choices:

1. to work toward merging the two quality approaches, trying to overcome the faculty resistance to TQM;

2. delay TQM implementation until after the accreditation self-study was completed and the evaluation visit had been accomplished; or

3. abandon assessment in the traditional sense and use the processes of TQM to design a knowledge assessment program.

There were no restraints on the campus from either the Board of Higher Education or from North Central as to the techniques and procedures that could be used. Theoretically, both programs could lead the campus toward systematic improvementof every phase of its operation!

A Comparison of TQM and Traditional Assessment

The following chart summarizes some of the goals, points of difference, time implications, and obstacles that have influenced decision-making at UND.

Quality Improvement Using TQM	Quatlity Improvement Using Traditional Assessment
Goals	**Goals**
• Meet and exceed customer expectations.	• Enable accountability to stakeholders.
• Improved quality through customer focus.	• Improved teaching and learning.
• Unyielding and continuous improvement.	• Documentation of effectiveness.
• Improve process to serve customers better.	• Measure outcomes to improve programs and student performance.
• "A way of life."	• "How we work with one another!"
• Continuous improvement.	• Continuous improvement.
• Lower cost and increase efficiency.	• Justify costs and increase learning efficiency and student success.
Points of Difference	**Points of Difference**
• Characteristics of the improvement are shaped by the customers.	• Characteristcs of the improvement are shaped by the faculty and students.
• Management empowers all people involved from top to bottom.	• Governance is shared and/or negotiated in the process both internally and externally.
• TQM has been developed out of a business culture.	• Assessment has been developed out of an academic culture.
Time	**Time**
• Heavy and ongoing investment of time in education, training, and decision-making.	• Heavy and ongoing investment of time in setting objectives, selecting measures, and utilizing findings.
• Improved procedures by design save time.	• Improved instruction makes learning more efficient.

- Considerable lead time required to achieve significant results.
- Discounting lead time, some processes can be improved in a relatively short time, others require much longer.

- Some objectives are assessible after a brief time, others require longer time schedules.
- Comprehensive assessment is best achieved with a longitudinal approach.

Obstacles

- Business language and concepts.

- May be viewed as imposed from top.

- Extensive training required of all employees.
- Considerable initial and ongoing cost.
- Perceived as "overly structured."
- Faculty tend to work independently.

- Very mixed reactions among participants.
- Requires accommodation to academic culture.

Obstacles

- Outcomes approach unfamiliar or seen as an end in itself.
- May be viewed as required by internal or external authority.
- Training required mainly of faculty.
- Variable initial and ongoing cost.
- Confusion with "program review."
- Faculty tend to value autonomy inside their classrooms.
- Greater familiarity with the concepts.
- Accommodation to academic culture easier than to other institutional processes.

Strengths

- Processes are blamed, not people.

- Breaks down divisions in the organization.

- Improves quality.
- Reduces absenteeism.
- Satisfies customers.

- Lowers cost (long term).

- Empowers Employees

Strengths

- Results are aimed at improvement not at engendering fear.
- Brings faculty together and faculty/students together.
- Improves teaching and learning.
- Increases retention and graduation rates.
- Motivates faculty/students and satisfies stake holders
- Makes education more effective, reducing per student cost.
- Potentially empowers faculty and students.

Potential Model

We are at the early stages of attempting to develop a model that might bring TQM and assessment together in a creative combination. We are uncertain about how TQM and assessment will interface in the future. TQM experts indicate that the implementation in an organization takes from ten to twenty years.

Recommendations to Other Campuses

1. Top-down mandates will increase resistance.

2. Faculty are skeptical about "cure-alls," as they are trained to be and should be.

3. TQM comes from an industrial/business culture and must be modified to fit an academic culture.

4. Therefore, TQM is easier to implement on the business/operations side than on the academic side of higher education organizations.

5. Careful planning is essential.

6. While TQM should reduce costs in the end, it will require significant outlay of resources, especially for training, up front. Be prepared.

7. Higher education is buffeted by short-term solutions. TQM requires long-term thinking.

8 . There is "TQ" and then there is "TQ" (Deming, Juran, Crosby, and others). There are "hard-liners" and there are more adaptable advocates.

9. Attempt to bring "quality" and assessment people together rather than engage in "holy wars."

Notes

1. W. Edwards Deming, Joseph Juran, Armand Feigenbaum, and Philip Crosby.

Implementing and Maintaining a Classroom Research Program for Faculty

Nancy E. Stetson

In the fall of 1988, College of Marin (COM) was one of five colleges invited to participate in a pilot program designed to train faculty in using Classroom Research. this pilot program was part of a larger effort, sponsored by the University of California at Berkeley Classroom Research Project, to develop and make available simple, effective means for assessing and improving student learning. COM is a community college located just across the San Francisco Bay from Berkeley. Thanks in part to its proximity, it was able to work closely with the Classroom Research Project during the following two years.

Over that period, COM adapted the Berkeley project's model to its own needs and circumstances. The resulting Classroom Research program has been highly successful in training faculty in this approach, and in maintaining their involvement and enthusiasm over several semesters. This chapter has three purposes: first, to outline the development and components of COM's program in some detail; second, to discuss the effects of classroom Research on teaching and learning at the college; and third, to offer recommendations to other colleges interested in implementing Classroom Research.

Planning and Initial Implementation

COM's involvement with the Classroom Research Project's pilot program began with a planning meeting held at UC Berkeley in September 1988. The first steps in COM's program were sketched out jointly by K. Patricia Cross, project director, Thomas A. Angelo, assistant director, Myrna R. Miller, president of COM, and two of COM's vice-presidents—one of them the author of this chapter. The five of us agreed that the UC Berkeley Classroom Research Project would supply training and consulting support for COM faculty during year 1, and that COM would recruit faculty, provide on-site material support, and organize appropriate follow-up activities. From the beginning, the shared expectation was that COM would take over all aspects of the college's Classroom Research program by the beginning of year 2, in fall 1989.

Early in the fall 1988 semester, Cross accepted an invitation from Miller to speak to the COM faculty on Classroom Research, an approach that Cross had introduced in 1986 and subsequently developed through a number of articles and speeches. Forty-eight of COM's permanent full-time faculty attended the lecture. Half of them were inspired to commit themselves to learn more about the model and how they might use it to improve teaching and learning. A short time later, these volunteers attended an intensive, introductory training workshop led by Angelo.

Throughout the fall semester, these twenty-four faculty met monthly with Angelo to begin implementing the model. Their training included the use of the Teaching Goals Inventory and practice with a number of simple, generic Classroom Assessment Techniques (CATs) from the Cross and Angelo *Classroom Assessment Techniques* handbook (1988). Participating faculty also met regularly in small groups to discuss what they were encountering in the classroom as they began implementing the model. Nancy E. Stetson, vice-president for planning and development, and Lorraine Barry, director of staff and organizational development, also attended the monthly sessions so that they could prepare to replicate Angelo's workshops in the following semesters for each new group of Classroom Researchers. In spring 1989, fifteen of the original twenty-four fall 1988 Classroom Researchers continued their involvement. At Angelo's request, each second semester participant agreed to refine and "customize" two of the handbook's generic CATs or to create two new techniques specifically designed for their disciplines.

During that same semester, the vice-president, the staff development director, and a COM nursing faculty member, Terry Gesulga-Harris, enrolled in a doctoral-level course on teaching and learning in higher education. During the course, team-taught by Cross and Angelo at UC Berkeley, they developed a detailed model for implementing the Classroom Research program at COM. The campus's semester-long model includes the following seven components: (1) stipends, (2) contracts, (3) a training curriculum, (4) instructional videotapes, (5) one-on-one consultations, (6) written reports, and (7) faculty presentations and other nonmonetary recognition. Each of these seven components is explained in detail in the following paragraphs. This COM Classroom Research model was first implemented in fall 1989, and it has been repeated successfully in each of the three subsequent semesters.

Stipends

In 1988, COM applied for and received a grant from a local foundation, the Marin Community Foundation, for a Learning Outcomes project. This grant included funds to provide stipends for faculty involved in the Classroom Research program. Participating faculty members are eligible to receive stipends for Classroom Research each semester for a total of three semesters. On completing the third semester, they are encouraged to stay involved in the program without further monetary compensation.

Contracts

To receive the stipend, COM faculty were required by union contract to apply to and be selected by a committee made up of representatives of management and of the faculty union. Those selected were required to sign an agreement stipulating the conditions under which the stipend would be paid. COM also required participants to complete, sign, and submit what amounted to invoices and time cards for up to twenty-eight hours of work on their Classroom Research projects, so that the stipend could be processed through normal channels. The vice-president's office completed as much of this paperwork as possible for the participants, in order to make it relatively easy for faculty to take part in the program.

Training Curriculum

The vice-president and the director of staff and organizational development refined and adapted the original Classroom Research Project curriculum to fit the needs of COM. They developed a syllabus and session outlines for the five faculty workshops held each semester. The curriculum for the first two workshops, for new classroom researchers (NCRs), was essentially the same as that presented by Angelo in the fall 1988 and spring 1989 workshop series. That is, the first two of five workshops introduced the concept of classroom Research and taught faculty to use the Teaching Goals Inventory and a few simple CATs. During the following three workshops, the curriculum focused primarily on structured small-group discussions designed to help faculty better understand what they were experiencing as they implemented the model.

Continuing classroom researchers (CCRs that is, those who had participated in the program for one or more semesters—were invited to attend the two workshops at the beginning of each semester to talk about what they had done and what they had learned. These "local experts" were the program's most powerful recruitment tool and a critical training resource.

The curriculum for these workshops was reconsidered and revised somewhat each semester to enhance the faculty's continuing interest in and growing sophistication about teaching and learning. For instance, the "Seven Principles for Good Practice in Undergraduate Education" (Gamson and Chickering, 1987) were introduced one semester, another semester, information about learning styles was presented; and in a third, participants discussed the most recent research on teaching and learning as synthesized by McKeachie, Pintrich, Lin, and Smith (1986). The CCRs are required to join the NCRs for the final three workshops to provide continuity across semesters. As "veterans," the CCRs are encouraged to share what they have learned by actively participating in small group discussions with the NCRs. At the same time, the NCRs' enthusiasm and fresh perspectives help motivate the CCRs to stay committed.

Participants receive a detailed syllabus for the Classroom Research training program, along with a complete set of materials. The syllabus includes listings of program goals and workshop objectives, a calendar of workshop meetings and related events, information on assignments, and guidelines for reports required of those receiving stipends. The materials packet includes the Cross and Angelo handbook, a complete set of workshop handouts, and relevant reprinted articles.

Instructional Videotapes

As part of their work for the course on teaching and learning in higher education at UC Berkeley, the vice-president, the director, and the COM nursing instructor were required to develop a term project. The trio worked with other COM staff to develop a fourteen-minute videotape entitled "Teacher-Directed Classroom Research" as a visual aid to be used in the New Classroom Researcher workshops. COM also provided copies of the completed videotape to all California community colleges and, through an arrangement with Miami-Dade Community College, made the tape available at low cost to other colleges throughout the nation. Later, the Classroom Research Project at UC Berkeley contracted with COM to develop two additional videotapes. The first is a twenty-six-minute speech by Cross introducing the concept of Classroom Research, and the second is an eighteen-minute videotape entitled "Classroom Research: Empowering Teachers." These two videotapes are now being used in faculty training workshops at COM and elsewhere and are available for rental or purchase from the UC Berkeley Extension Media Services Office.

One-on-One Consultations

Each semester, all faculty participating in the COM Classroom Research program—both CCRs and NCRs—meet individually with the director of staff development to discuss their particular projects, to ask questions, and to receive assistance, if desired. These one-on-one sessions, ranging from twenty minutes to an hour in length, have proved to be a critical part of the program's success, with benefits to participants and to program leaders alike. Participants receive individual attention and often personal coaching and encouragement. The director of staff development gains a deeper understanding of the learning process faculty are going through, and of their satisfactions and frustrations.

Written Reports

Faculty receiving stipends are required to submit written progress reports and final reports on their activities to the director and the vice-president. Faculty are given a common format for these reports at the beginning of each semester. This format lets them know exactly what is expected for successful completion of the program. For example, the end-of-semester project report asks individual faculty for the following information:

1. Name

2. Title of the course on which the faculty member focused

3. Whether the instructor had taught a similar course in the same semester of the previous year (Formation that was useful in comparison studies)

4. Specific question(s) posed or teaching goal to assess

5. Reasons for choosing that question/goal to assess

6. Kind of information or feedback collected on student learning

7. Techniques used to collect the information or feedback

8. How the feedback was analyzed

9. What the faculty member learned from analyzing the feedback

10. How the project affected the faculty member's teaching in the focus class

11. Ways in which the project affected the student learning in that class

12. Evidence the faculty member could provide to support the answers to the previous two questions

13. Suggestions on how the Staff Development Office could be more helpful to participating faculty

14. The *most* enjoyable aspect of the program

15. The *least* enjoyable aspects of the program

16. What, if anything, the faculty member would do differently next time

17. Any additional comments.

Faculty Presentations and Other Nonmonetary Recognition

At the beginning of each semester, CCRs are invited to present brief oral report to their colleagues on their experiences in the Classroom Research program as part of a two-hour workshop open to all faculty. These faculty presentations serve three purposes. First, they highlight the individual Classroom Researcher's accomplishments and provide an opportunity for much-deserved recognition. Second, they give experienced Classroom Researchers an opportunity to share the knowledge, skills, and insights gained through the program with their colleagues, thereby making good ideas known throughout the college. And third, these presentations by credible colleagues introduce nonparticipating faculty members to the Classroom Research model and encourage them to become Classroom Researchers in subsequent semesters. During the first few semesters, COM also recognized the Classroom Researchers by awarding them certificates of completion during a hosted luncheon at the close of each semester.

Evaluation of the COM Model's Effectiveness

From fall 1988 through spring 1991, sixty-nine faculty members completed at least one semester in the Classroom Research program at COM. Twenty-eight were "enrolled" participants—that is, receiving stipends—for one semester; nineteen were enrolled for two semesters; and thirteen for three semesters. Nine faculty participated for four semesters, even though the fourth semester was unpaid. During the semesters they were involved in the program, these sixty-nine faculty members involved at least 3,500 of their students in Classroom Research projects.

Did the COM Classroom Research program affect teaching? Did it affect student learning? COM wanted to know. As the program has matured, the college has developed several means of collecting and analyzing data in order to begin answering these important questions.

Effects on Teaching

Most faculty who have participated in the Classroom Research program at COM for three or more semesters report that they have incorporated Classroom Research into their regular pedagogy in most, if not all, of their classes. It appeared that, after three semesters, those faculty who initially found the approach helpful were using it and would likely continue to use it.

The fifteen faculty who participated in the Classroom Research program in spring 1989 were asked how their projects had affected their teaching in the focus class. A few representative examples of these faculty self-assessments follow:

"My teaching seems more in depth. I have questioned and changed my own teaching goals. I am more aware of the needs of my students."

"Course goals are more clearly manifest in the unit instructions and tests, which I have revised in the process. Analytical critiques of student work are better focused. I am more attentive to student behavior."

"I have custom-fit my teaching toward the needs of my students whenever possible—much more than before."

"I use more examples. Go slower. Include humor. I'm more creative in methodology. More willing to try new ideas—and occasionally fail. *I think* more about the class."

"The CATs provided me with a way to systematize my evaluation of the progress of the class and thus gave me the feedback necessary to help students improve in areas where they were weak. This I did in numerous ways: I gave brief lectures, conducted class discussions on sample essays, provided exercises, encouraged revisions, held student conferences, divided the class into peer editing groups, and so on."

"I am much more aware of the importance of identifying my goals and of seeking and getting feedback about how I am doing in regard to those goals. I found myself paying a lot more attention to why I did what I did with my class and to looking at my course from a student's point of view."

In summary, experienced Classroom Researchers reported that they had incorporated Classroom Research into their normal pedagogy. They also reported that their projects immediately affected their teaching in a variety of positive ways. To determine if these changes are permanent, however, COM will need to conduct follow-up studies.

Effects on Student Learning

Each semester since spring 1989, the college's Office of Planning and Development has compared student success in the Classroom Researchers' focus classes with student success in those classes most similar to the focus classes. That is, we have compared "Classroom Research" courses with other courses taught by the same instructor in which this approach was not used, with the same course taught during the same semester the year before, at the same time of day, and the like. Two measures of student success, grades and retention rates, were compared. While Classroom Researchers often expressed their strong belief that students in classes where they were using Classroom Research were more successful than their other or previous students, there were only a few instances where COM's research could support their impressions with evidence of significantly improved class grade averages or retention rates.

There are several possible explanations for this gap between participating faculty's beliefs that students are learning more effectively and the students' actual performance on traditional indicators of academic success. The first and most obvious possibility is that Classroom Research does not improve learning—whatever other benefits it may offer. A second explanation may be that students are learning *better* but not *more* of whatever they are being tested on. Many Classroom Researchers focused their inquiries on developing metacognitive skills, critical thinking, or self-esteem, but did not test or grade students on those elements. If this second hypothesis were true, it would mean that student learning could improve in important ways without necessarily registering on the usual tests or affecting grades.

Effects on Teaching Practice

COM also attempted to assess the effect of Classroom Research on teaching practice by determining how well the Classroom Research model embodied pedagogical principles that are believed to make positive differences in student learning. Gamson and Chickering's "Seven Principles for Good Practice in Undergraduate Education" (1987), mentioned earlier, are based on a synthesis of fifty years of research on teaching and learning in higher education. COM proposed that, if Classroom Research supported one or more of the seven principles distilled from the research, it was likely to promote student learning.

Based on faculty reports, it is clear that Classroom Research methods actively involve students in learning, supporting one of the seven principles. Offering student frequent, anonymous, and ungraded opportunities to give faculty feedback about what they are learning and not learning actively involves them in their own learning. When faculty members used the student feedback to change their teaching, students had confirmation that their feedback was important and that it had a direct impact on the teaching and learning process. And by providing students with prompt, focused feedback, faculty implemented a second recognized principle of good practice. By promoting more and more academically productive student-faculty contact, this approach embodied a third of the seven principles.

Faculty who participated in the Classroom Research program reported that their projects affected students learning in the following ways:

"Students were asking more questions and were more interested in what they were doing."

"The students knew I was sincerely interested in their learning and, as the semester progressed, they became more open in discussing their ideas and reactions."

"Students seemed much more interested in the subject matter, and were eager to discuss the practical application of any theoretical material that was presented."

"I think the students in my focus class came to rely on my willingness to listen to their feedback and to try to do something in response to what they said. This empowered them and made their learning more relevant."

"Students became involved; everyone gave feedback! Students became self-conscious about what they learned and how they learned. They became aware they were an important part of the class direction or diversion. They felt more like 'partners' with the teacher.

"Based on classroom performance, I believe the students were more active in their pursuit of knowledge and more self-aware of their understanding. Additionally, they seemed very free to express suggestions, and most seemed more aware of when/where they had difficulties and sought help more-quickly."

In summary, the Office of Planning and Development found only a few instances where Classroom Research improved student success as measured by grades or retention. There were likely dozens of variables affecting both of these measures, none of which were controlled for. However, faculty reported many observable ways in which students were more actively involved in learning, received prompt feedback, and had more contact with instructors. examples of three important and well-established principles for effective student learning.

Beginning in fall 1990, COM asked Classroom Researchers to administer a pre- and post questionnaire test to the students in their focus class. The questionnaire items were based on a "Faculty Inventory" developed from the "Seven Principles for Good Practice in Under-graduate Education" previously mentioned. Over time, student responses to these pre- and post-tests may help COM more systematically determine the effects of Classroom Research on teaching and learning.

Recommendations

The model for implementing a Classroom Research program for faculty developed by COM has been very successful on many levels. To date, the program has involved sixty-nine faculty and at least 3,500 students over a six-semester period. The following are recommendations for success related to each of the seven components of the semester-long model.

Stipends. If funding is available, colleges should consider awarding stipends to Classroom Researchers. Stipends, even relatively small ones, encourage the faculty member to feel that the program is highly regarded by the administration. They also make the faculty member feel valued for his or her involvement in the program. However, depending on the institutional culture, stipends may be more or less important in motivating faculty to participate. Given our finding that the faculty required three semesters, on average, to incorporate this approach fully into their teaching, it may make sense to offer stipends for participation in the second or third semester of the project—rather than for the initial semester. In this way, faculty might be encouraged to persist long enough to fully benefit from this approach.

Contracts. An individual contract with the Classroom Researcher helps ensure that the faculty member will complete the semester-long program. When stipends are awarded, contracts are highly recommended. However, we also recommend that the faculty developer or administrator in charge make every effort to minimize "red tape." As with students, faculty appear to benefit from having clear guidelines before they agree to participate in the program. When stipends are involved, the program outline can become part of the contract between the faculty developer and the Classroom Researcher.

Training Curriculum. The need for training workshops for new Classroom Researchers probably speaks for itself. However, the need for the follow-up workshops for both new and continuing

Classroom Researchers throughout the semester may not be as obvious. One of the primary benefits of involvement in the Classroom Research program identified by faculty was having the opportunity to meet their colleagues in small, multidisciplinary groups to talk about teaching and learning. It is critical to provide focused follow-up opportunities. And, as most faculty developers already know, it is also helpful to serve participants some light refreshments and hold meetings in a pleasant, informal environment.

Instructional Videotapes. The three videotapes that were produced by COM proved very useful, both in enlisting faculty interest in Classroom Research and in training them in the model. The tapes were especially appealing to visual learners. In addition, the process of making these inhouse training tapes involved several faculty participants and highlighted and recognized their accomplishments. Making your own campus training video, however simple, can be a powerful way to engage faculty and students in the project and to generate pride in the activity.

One-on-One Consultations. Based on their program evaluations, Classroom Researchers clearly appreciated the opportunity to consult with the director of staff and organizational development between workshops, throughout the semester. This support service is time consuming, requiring, on average, about half an hour per participant per consultation, but it provided important benefits. Several instructors would have dropped out of the program, and many others would have accomplished less, without these consultations.

Written Reports. While Classroom Researchers at COM sometimes complained about having to complete written reports—much as their students do—they also admitted that writing those reports helped them analyze and synthesize what they had learned each semester from their projects. The final reports, in particular, were also very helpful to the vice-president and the director. These reports gave them feedback about what could be done to improve the management of the program. They also provided information that was helpful in seeking continued grant funding, and in de-eloping oral and written reports for national, state, and local presentations and publications about Classroom Research. To lessen the burden on faculty, audio taped interviews could be substituted for written reports.

Faculty Presentations and Other Nonmonetary Recognition. Giving Classroom Researchers opportunities to share their results "live" with their colleagues was one of the most effective ways of enlisting new faculty in the program. COM has a number of required in-service professional development days. Each semester, one morning or afternoon of professional development time was used for presentation of the oral reports on Classroom Research. Another four-hour session was also used for the required training of NCRs at the beginning of each semester. Colleges that do not have professional development time built into the schedule may have more difficulty in implementing the Classroom Research model, but it can still be done. Many colleges have scheduled workshops on Saturdays or during semester breaks; others have provided substitute teachers for faculty attending on-campus workshops.

The awarding of certificates to Classroom Researchers completing the program was discontinued after faculty indicated that they did not consider the certificates important. In retrospect, it is not too surprising that faculty with earned master's and doctoral degrees were not particularly motivated by certificates. The end-of-the semester recognition luncheon, however, retains its appeal.

Conclusion

In summary, we can offer the following general recommendations to those interested in implementing Classroom Research as part of faculty development efforts. First, plan carefully and plan for the longer term. A Classroom Research program may take three or more semesters before it begins to bear fruit. Second, offer systematic and substantive training over the course of a semester. Third, provide ongoing support for individuals and groups to encourage continued involvement.

Fourth, use faculty participants as recruiters for the program. And fifth, offer incentives, both tangible and intangible, to those who participate fully and actively.

COM believes that when students are given frequent, anonymous, and ungraded opportunities to tell instructors what they are learning and not learning in a particular class, those students are learning more actively and effectively. In addition, when instructors immediately use student feedback to modify teaching methods or course content to improve student learning, they are teaching more actively and effectively. Finally, when faculty developers and administrators organize a Classroom Research program to help instructors help students learn and then use feedback from faculty to modify the program, they are managing more actively and effectively. The Classroom Research program at COM has helped faculty and administrators come together to better achieve the college's most important goal: to improve the quality of student learning.

References

Cross, K. P., and Angelo, T. A. *Classroom Assessment Techniques: A Handbook for Faculty.* Ann Arbor, Mich.: National Center for Research to Improve Postsecondary Teaching and Learning, 1988.

Gamson, Z., and Chickering, A. "Seven Principles for Good Practice in Undergraduate Education." *AAHE Bulletin,* Mar. 1987, pp. 51–110.

McKeachie, W. J., Pintrich, P. R., Lin, Y-G, and Smith, D.A.F. *Teaching and Learning in the College Classroom.* Ann Arbor, Mich.: National Center for Research to Improve Postsecondary Teaching and Learning, 1986.

General Bibliography

Adelman, Clifford (Ed.). *Performance and Judgment: Essays on the Principles and Practice of Assessing Student Learning*. Washington, D.C.: U.S. Department of Education, 1989.

Adelman, Clifford (Ed.). *Signs and Traces: Model Indicators of College Student Learning*. Washington, D.C.: Office of Research, U.S. Department of Education, 1989.

Adelman, Clifford. "Getting Up Off The Floor: Standards and Realities in Higher Education." *AGB Reports* (July/August, 1983), pp. 13–19.

Adelman, Clifford. "To Imagine An Adverb: Concluding Notes to Adversaries and Enthusiasts." In *Assessment in American Higher Education: Issues* and *Contexts*, edited by Clifford Adelman. Washington, D.C.: OERI, 1986.

Aleamoni, L. M. (Ed). *Techniques for Evaluating and Improving Instruction, New Directions for Teaching and Learning #31*. San Francisco: Jossey Bass, 1987.

Alexander, Joanne M. and Stark, Joan S. *Focusing on Student Academic Outcomes: A Working Paper*. Ann Arbor, Michigan: The University of Michigan, National Center for Research to Improve Postsecondary Teaching and Learning, 1986.

Alkin, Marvin C. *A Guide for Evaluation Decision Makers*. Beverly Hills, California: Sage, 1985.

Alkin, Marvin C. and Fitz-Gibbon, Carol T. "Methods and Theories of Evaluating Programs." *Journal of Research and Development in Education*. 8 (Spring, 1975), pp. 2–15.

Alverno College Faculty. *Assessment at Alverno College*. Milwaukee, Wisconsin: Alverno College Productions, 1979.

American Association for Higher Education. *'93 Conference Discussion Papers*. Washington, D.C.: The Association, 1993.

American Association for Higher Education. *Assessment 1990: Understanding the Implications*. Washington, D.C.: The Association, 1990.

American Association for Higher Education. *Assessment 1990: Accreditation and Renewal*. Washington, D.C.: The Association, 1990.

American Association for Higher Education. *Principles of Good Practice for Assessing Student Learning*. Washington, DC: American Association for Higher Education, The AAHE Assessment Forum, 1992.

American Association for Higher Education. *Three Presentations: 1987*. Washington, D.C.: The Association, 1987.

American Association for Higher Education. *Three Presentations: 1988.* Washington, D.C.: The Association, 1990.

American Association for Higher Education. *Three Presentations: 1989.* Washington, D.C.: The Association, 1989.

American Association for Higher Education. *TQM: Will it Work on Campus? Seven Articles from CHANGE.* Washington, D.C.: The Association, 1993.

American Association of State Colleges and Universities. *Defining and Assessing Baccalaureate Skills: Ten Case Studies.* Washington, D.C.: The Association, 1986.

American Association of State Colleges and Universities. *Special Report: AASCU/ERIC Model Programs Inventory.* Washington, D.C.: The Association, November 3, 1989.

Anderson, Scarvia B., and Ball, Samuel. *The Profession and Practice of Program Evaluation.* San Francisco: Jossey-Bass, 1978.

Anderson, Scarvia B., Ball, Samuel, Murphy, Richard T., and Associates. *Encyclopedia of Educational Evaluation.* San Francisco: Jossey-Bass, 1975.

Angelo, Thomas A. "Introduction and Overview: From Classroom Assessment to Classroom Research." In *Classroom Research: Early Lessons from Success. New Directions for Teaching and Learning No. 46,* edited by Thomas A. Angelo. San Francisco: Jossey-Bass (Summer, 1991), pp. 7–15.

Angelo, Thomas A. (Ed.). *Classroom Research: Early Lessons from Success, New Directions for Teaching and Learning No. 46.* San Francisco: Jossey-Bass, 1991.

Angelo, Thomas A. and Cross, K. Patricia. *Classroom Assessment Techniques, (Second Edition).* San Francisco: Jossey-Bass, 1993.

Anthell, Jane H. and Casper, Irene G. "Comprehensive Evaluation Model: A Tool for the Evaluation of Nontraditional Educational Programs." *Innovative Higher Education* 11(1) (Fall/Winter, 1986).

Aper, J. P. and Hinkle, D. E. "State Policies for Assessing Student Outcomes: A Case Study with Implications for State and Institutional Authorities." *Journal of Higher Education* 62 (5) (1991), pp. 539–555.

Aper, Jeffery, Cuver, Steven M., and Hinkle, Dennis E. "Coming to Terms With the Accountability Versus Improvement Debate in Assessment." *Higher Education* 20 (1990), pp. 471–483 .

Applebaum, M.I. "Assessment Through the Major." In *Performance and Judgment: Essays on the Principles and Practice in the Assessment of College Student Learning* edited by Clifford Adelman. Washington, D.C.: U.S. Departnlent of Education, 1989, pp. 117–137.

Arns, Robert G., and Poland, William. "Changing the University Through Program Review." *Journal of Higher Education* 51(3) (1980), pp. 268–284.

Association of American Colleges. *Program Review and Educational Quality in the Major: A Faculty Handbook.* Washington, D.C.: The Association, 1991.

Astin, Alexander W. *Achieving Educational Excellence.* San Francisco: Jossey-Bass, 1988 .

Astin, Alexander W. *Assessment for Excellence: The Philosophy and Practice of Assessment and Evaluation in Higher Education.* New York: MacMillan, 1991.

Astin, Alexander W. *What Matters in College? Four Critical Years Revisited.* San Francisco: Jossey-Bass, 1992.

Astin, Alexander W., and Ayala, Frank. "A Consortial Approach to Assessment." *The Educational Record* 68 (3) (Summer, 1987), pp. 47–51.

Astin, Alexander W., Darling-Hammond, Linda, and McCabe, Robert H. *Three Presentations from the Third National Conference on Assessment in Higher Education. June 8–11, 1988, Chicago.* Washington, D.C.: American Association for Higher Education. AAHE Assessment Forum, 1989.

Atwell, Robert. "The Dangers of U.S. Intervention in Accreditation." *The Chronicle of Higher Education* (November 20 , 1991), p. A52.

Baird, Leonard (Ed.).*Assessing Student Academic and Social Progress, New Directions for Community Colleges No.18.* San Francisco: Jossey-Bass, 1977.

Baird, Leonard L. "A Map of Postsecondary Assessment." *Research in Higher Education* 28 (2) (1988), pp. 99–115.

Baird, Leonard L. "Value Added: Using Student Gains as Yardsticks of Learning." In *Assessment in American Higher Education: Issues and Contexts* edited by Clifford Adelman. Washington D.C.: OERI, pp. 205–216.

Baker, Eva L. "Critical Validity Issues in the Methodology of Higher Education Assessment." In *On Assessing the Outcomes of Higher Education: Proceedings of the 1986 ETS Invitational Conference.* Princeton, New Jersey: Educational Testing Service, 1986.

Banta Trudy and Associates. *Making a Difference: Outcomes of a Decade of Assessment in Higher Education.* San Francisco: Jossey-Bass, 1993.

Banta, Trudy (Ed.). *Implementing Outcomes Assessment: Promise and Perils, New Directions for Institutional Research No. 59.* San Francisco: Jossey-Bass, Fall, 1988.

Banta, Trudy W. "Contemporary Approaches to Assessing Student Achievement of General Education Outcomes." *The Journal of General Education* 40 (1991), pp, 203–223.

Banta, Trudy W. "Faculty-Developed Approaches to Assessing General Education Outcomes."*Assessment Update* 3 (2) (March/April, 1991), pp. 1–2, 4.

Banta, Trudy W. "Using Outcomes Assessment to Improve Educational Programs." In *Better Teaching and Learning in College: Toward More Scholarly Practice edited* by Maryellen Weimer and Robert Menges. San Francisco: Jossey-Bass, forthcoming (1994).

Banta, Trudy W. Toward a Plan for Using National Assessment to Ensure Continuous Improvement of Higher Education. *The Journal of General Education,* 42 (1) (1993), pp. 33–58.

Banta, Trudy W., Bensey, M.W., Pitts, A.M. and Matlock, R. (Eds.). *Proceedings of the Third International Conference on Assessing Quality in Higher Education.* Knoxville, Tennessee: Center for Assessment Research and Development, 1991.

Banta, Trudy W., and Pike, Gary R. "Methods for Comparing Outcomes Assessment Instruments." *Research in Higher Education* 30 (5) (1989), pp. 455–469.

Banta, Trudy W., and Schneider, Janet A. "Using FacultyDeveloped Exit Examinations to Evaluate Academic Programs." *Journal of Higher Education* 59 (1) (January/February, 1988), pp. 69–83.

Banta, Trudy W., Lambert, E. Warren, Pike, Gary R. Schmidhammer, James L., and Schneider, Janet A. "Estimated Student Score Gain on the ACT COMP Exam: Valid Tool for Institutional Assessment?" *Research in Higher Education* 27 (3) (1987), pp. 195–217.

Barak, Robert J., and Brier, Barbara E. *Successful Program Review.* San Francisco: Jossey-Bass, 1990.

Baron, John Boykoff, Forgione, Pascal D., Jr., and Moss, Marc. *Shooting at a Moving Target: Merging the National Assessment of Educational Progress and the Longitudinal Studies Program—A State Perspective*. Washington , D. C.: National Center for Education Statistics Conference, December 1986.

Benjamin, Ernst. "The Movement to Assess Students' Learning Will Institutionalize Mediocrity in Colleges. *The Chronicle of Higher Education* (July 5, 1990).

Bensoist, Howard. "The Role of Academic Program Review in University-Business Interaction." *North Central Association Quarterly* 61 (4) (1987), pp. 497–502.

Berk, Richard A., and Rossi, Peter H. *Thinking About Program Evaluation*. London: Sage Publications, 1990.

Berk, Ronald A. "A Consumer's Guide to Setting Performance Standards on Criterion-Referenced Tests." *Review of Educational Research* 56 (1) (Spring 1986), pp, 137–172.

Bickman, Leonard (Ed.). *Using Program Theory in Evaluation, New Directions for Program Evaluation No. 33*. San Francisco: Jossey-Bass, 1987.

Blumenstyk, Goldie, and Magner, Denise K. "As Assessment Draws New Converts, Backers Gather to Ask 'What works?'" *Chronicle of Higher Education*, July 11, 1990.

Bock, R. Darrell. *Instrument Design for a Combined NAEP and NELS. National Center for Education Statistics Conference.* Washington, D.C.: National Center for Education Statistics, December 1986.

Bogue, E. Grady, and Sanders, Robert L. *The Evidence for Quality: Strengthening the Tests of Academic and Administrative Effectiveness*. San Francisco: Jossey-Bass, 1992.

Bok, Derek. "Reclaiming the Public Trust." *Change* 24 (4) (July/August, 1992), pp. 13–19.

Bok, Derek. "Toward Higher Learning: The Importance of Assessing Outcomes." *Change* 18 (6) (November/December 1986), pp. 18–27.

Boli, John, Katchadourian, Herant, and Mahoney, Sally. "Analyzing Academic Records for Informed Administration: The Stanford Curriculum Study." *Journal of Higher Education* 59 (1), pp. 54–68.

Boud, David. "Assessment and the Promotion of Academic Values." *Studies in Higher Education* 15 (1) (1990).

Boyer, Carol M. and Ewell, Peter T. "State-Based Approaches to Assessment in Undergraduate Education: A Glossary and Selected References." *Higher Education Working Papers, PS–88–2.* Denver, Colorado: Education Commission of the States, 1988.

Boyer, Carol M. and Ewell, Peter T. "State-Based Case Studies of Assessment Initiatives in Undergraduate Education: Chronology of Critical Points." *Higher Education Working Papers, PS-88-3.* Denver, Colorado: Education Commission of the States, 1988.

Boyer, Ernest L., and Michael, William B. "Outcomes of College." *Review of Educational Research* 35 (4) (October, 1965), pp. 277–295.

Braskamp, Larry A. "So, What's The Use?" In *Achieving Assessment Goals Using Evaluation Techniques, New Directions for Higher Education No. 67* edited by P.J. Gray. San Francisco: Jossey-Bass, 1989, pp. 43–50.

Braskamp, Larry A., and Brown, Robert D. (Eds.). *Utilization of Evaluative Information, New Directions for Program Evaluation No. 5.* San Francisco: Jossey Bass.

Bray, Dorothy and Belcher, Marcia J. (Eds.). *Issues in Student Assessment, New Directions for Community Colleges. No. 59.* San Francisco: Jossey Bass, 1987.

Breland, Hunter M., Camp, Roberta, Jones, Robert J., Morris, Margaret M., and Rock, Donald A. *Assessing Writing Skill.* New York: College Entrance Examination Board, 1987.

Brown, Marilyn K. "Developing and Implementing a Process for the Review of Nonacademic Units." *Research in Higher Education* 30 (1) (1989), pp. 89–112.

California State University Institute for Teaching and Learning. *Student Outcomes Assessment: What Makes It Work?* California State University System, 1992.

Carpenter, C.B., and Doig, J.C. "Assessing Critical Thinking Across the Curriculum." In *Assessing Students' Learning, New Directions for Teaching and Learning No. 34* edited by J. McMillan. San Francisco: Jossey-Bass, Summer 1988, pp. 33–46.

Chaffee, Ellen E., and Sherr, Lawrence A. *Quality: Transforming Postsecondary Education, ASHE-ERIC Higher Education Reports No. 3.* Washington, D.C.: Association for the Study of Higher Education, 1992.

Claggett, C. A. "Meeting Student Outcomes Accountability Mandates: The Institutional Research Approach." *Community/Junior College Quarterly of Research and Practice* 15 (2) (1991), pp. 175–186.

Clark, A.T. and Rice, D.R. *TQM and Assessment: The North Dakota Experience.* A collection of papers on self-study and institutional improvement. Chicago, Illinois: North Central Association of Colleges and Schools, 1992, pp. 181–186.

Claxton, Charles, Murrell, Patricia H., and Porter, Martha. "Outcomes Assessment." *AGB Reports* 25 (5) (September/October, 1987), pp. 32–35.

Clayton State College. *Outcome Handbook.* Morrow, Georgia: Clayton State College, 1990.

Conrad, C., and Eagan, D. "Achieving Excellence: How Will We Know?" In *Improving Undergraduate Education in Large Universities, New Directions for Higher Education No. 66,* edited by C.H. Pazandak. San Francisco: Jossey-Bass, Summer 1989, pp. 51–63.

Conrad, Clifton F., and Blackburn, Robert T. "Program Quality in Higher Education." In *Higher Education: Handbook of Theory and Research, Volume I* edited by John Smart. New York: Agathon Press, 1986.

Conrad, Clifton F., and Blackburn, Robert T. "Research on Program Quality: A Review and Critique of the Literature." In *Higher Education: Handbook of Theory and Research, Volume I* edited by John C. Smart. New York: Agathon Press, 1985, pp. 283–308.

Conrad, Clifton F., and Wilson, Richard F. *Academic Program Reviews: Institutional Approaches, Expectations, and Controversies, ASHE/ERIC Higher Education Reports, No. 5.* Washington, D.C.: Association for the Study of Higher Education, 1985, pp. 39–65.

Cordray, David S. (Ed.). *Utilizing Prior Research in Evaluation Planning, New Directions for Program Evaluation No. 27.* San Francisco: Jossey-Bass, 1985.

Cordray, David S., and Lipsey, Mark W. *Evaluation Studies Review Annual, Volume 11.* Beverly Hills, California: Sage Publications, 1987.

Craven, Eugene C.. "Evaluating Program Performance." In *Improving Academic Management* edited by Paul Jedamus, Marvin W. Peterson, and Associates. San Francisco: Jossey-Bass, 1980, pp. 432–457.

Craven, Eugene C. (Ed.). *Academic Program Evaluation, New Directions for Institutional Research No. 27.* San Francisco: Jossey-Bass, 1980.

Cronbach, Lee J. *Designing Evaluations of Educational and Social Programs.* San Francisco: Jossey-Bass, 1982.

Cronbach, Lee J. and Associates. *Toward Reform of Program Evaluation.* San Francisco: Jossey-Bass, 1980.

Cross, K. Patricia. *Feedback in the Classroom: Making Assessment Matter.* Washington, D.C.: American Association for Higher Education, Assessment Forum, nd circa 1989.

Daughdrill, James H., Jr. "Assessment is Doing More for Higher Education Than Any Other Development in Recent History." *The Chronicle of Higher Education* (January 27, 1988).

Davis, B.G. "Demystifying Assessment: Learning from the Field of Evaluation." In *Achieving Assessment Goals Using Evaluation Techniques, New Directions for Higher Education No. 67* edited by P.J. Gray. San Francisco: Jossey-Bass, Fall 1989, pp.5–20).

Davis, Todd M., and Murrell, Patricia H. "Joint Factor Analysis of the College Student Experiences Questionnaire and the ACT COMP Objective Exam." *Research in Higher Education* 31 (5) (1980), pp. 425–44.

Doctors, Samuel I., and Wokutch, Richard E. "Social Program Evaluation: Six Models." In *Values, Ethics and Standards in Evaluation, New Directions in Program Evaluation No. 7* edited by Robert Perloff and Evelyn Perloff. San Francisco: Jossey-Bass, 1988, pp. 27–30.

Doherty, A. and Patton, G.W. "Criterion Three and the Assessment of Student Academic Achievement." *NCA Quarterly* 66 (2) (1991), pp. 406–414.

Dressel, Paul. *Handbook of Academic Evaluation.* San Francisco: Jossey-Bass, 1976.

Dumke, Glenn. "Accrediting: The Weak Link in Education Reform. *The Chronicle of Higher Education* (January 15, 1986), p. 104.

Education Commission of the States. *Assessing College Outcomes: What State Leaders Need to Know. Report No. PA–91–03.* Denver: Colorado: Education Commission of the States, 1991.

Educational Testing Service. *Assessing the Outcomes of Higher Education: Proceedings of the 1986 ETS Invitational Conference.* Princeton, New Jersey: Educational Testing Service, 1986.

Educational Testing Service. *ETS Higher Education Assessment Brochure.* Princeton, New Jersey: Educational Testing Service.

Educational Testing Service. *What Can We Learn From Performance Assessment for the Professions?* Princeton, New Jersey: Educational Testing Service, 1992.

El-Khawas, Elaine. "Colleges Reclaim the Assessment Initiative." *Educational Record* 68 (1987), pp. 54–58.

El-Khawas, Elaine. "How Are Assessment Results Being Used?" Assessment *Update* 1 (4) (Winter 1989), pp. 1–2.

El-Khawas, Elaine. *Campus Trends.* Washington, D.C.: American Council on Education (Annual).

Elman, Sandra E., and Lynton, Ernest A. Assessment *in Professional Education.* Paper given at National Conference on Assessment in Higher Education, University of South Carolina, October 1985.

Erwin, T. Dary. *Assessing Student Learning and Development.* San Francisco: Jossey-Bass, 1991.

Ewell, Peter T. "Assessment and TQM: In Search of Convergence." In *Total Quality Management in Higher Education, New Directions for Institutional Research No.71* edited by L. Sherr and D. Teeter. San Francisco: Jossey-Bass, 1991, pp. 39–52.

Ewell, Peter T. "Assessment: What's It All About." *Change* (November/December, 1985), pp. 32–35.

Ewell, Peter T. "Identifying Benefits, Costs, and Parties-at-Interest." In *Benefits and Costs of Assessment in Higher Education: A Framework for Choice Making.* Boulder, Colorado: National Center for Higher Education Management Systems, 1991.

Ewell, Peter T. "Implementing Assessment: Some Organization Issues." In *Implementing Outcomes Assessment: Promise and Perils, New Directions for Institutional Research No. 59* edited by Trudy W. Banta. San Francisco: Jossey-Bass, 1988, pp. 15–28.

Ewell, Peter T. "Institutional Characteristics and Faculty/Administrator Perceptions of Outcomes: An Exploratory Analysis." *Research in Higher Education* 30 (2) (1989), pp. 113–136.

Ewell, Peter T. (Ed.). "Putting It All Together: Four Questions for Practitioners." In *Enhancing Information Use in Decision Making, New Directions for Institutional Research, No. 64* edited by Peter T. Ewell. San Francisco: Jossey-Bass, 1989, pp. 85–90.

Ewell, Peter T. "To Capture the Ineffable: New Forms of Assessment in Higher Education." In *Review of Research in Education* edited by G. Grant. Washington, D.C.: American Educational Research Association, 1991.

Ewell, Peter T. *Assessment, Accountability and Improvement.* Washington, D.C.: American Association for Higher Education, 1987.

Ewell, Peter T. (Ed.). *Enhancing Information Use in Decision Making, New Directions for Institutional Research No. 64.* San Francisco: Jossey-Bass, 1989.

Ewell, Peter T. *Information on Student Outcomes: How to Get It and How to Use It: Executive Overview.* Boulder, Colorado: National Center for Higher Education Management System, 1983.

Ewell, Peter T. *State Policy on Assessment: The Linkage to Learning, Report No. PA 90–4.* Denver, Colorado: Education Commission of the States, 1990.

Ewell, Peter T. *The Self-Regarding Institution: Information for Excellence: Executive Overview.* Boulder, Colorado: National Center for Higher Education Management Systems, 1984.

Ewell, Peter T. "Establishing a Campus-Based Assessment Program." *In Student Outcomes Assessment: What Institutions Stand to Gain, New Directions for Higher Education No. 59* edited by Diane F. Halpern. San Francisco: Jossey-Bass, 1987, pp. 9–24.

Ewell, Peter T. "Information for Decision: What's The Use?" In *Enhancing Information Use in Decision Making, New Directions for Institutional Research, No. 64* edited by Peter T. Ewell. San Francisco: Jossey-Bass, 1989, pp. 7–19 .

Ewell, Peter T. *Assessment and the "New Accountability": A Challenge for Higher Education's Leadership.* Denver, Colorado: Education Commission of the States, 1990.

Ewell, Peter T. (Ed.). *Assessing Educational Outcomes, New Directions for Institutional Research No. 47.* San Francisco: Jossey-Bass, 1985.

Ewell, Peter T., and Boyer, Carol M. "Acting Out State–Mandated Assessment: Evidence from Five States of Higher Education." *Change* (July/August, 1988), pp. 41–47.

Ewell, Peter T., Finney, Joni, and Lenth, Charles. "Filling in the Mosaic: The Emerging Pattern of State-Based Assessment." *AAHE Bulletin* (April 1990).

Fairweather, James S., and Brown, Dennis F. "Dimensions of Academic Program Quality." The *Review of Higher Education* 14 (2) (Winter, 1991), pp. 155–176.

Feasley, Charles E. *Program Evaluation, AAHE/ERIC Higher Education Research Report No. 2.* Washington, D.C.: American Association for Higher Education, 1980.

Fetterman, D. M. (Ed.). *Qualitative Approaches to Evaluation in Education: The Silent Scientific Revolution.* New York: Praeger, 1988.

Fetterman, David M. "Conceptual Crossroads: Methods and Ethics in Ethnographic Evaluation." In *Naturalistic Evaluation, New Directions for Program Evaluation No. 3* edited by D.D. Williams. San Francisco: Jossey-Bass, 1986.

Fincher, Cameron. "Assessing Educational Outcomes: Are We Doing Good, Can We Do Better?" *IHE Newsletter. University* of Georgia: Institute of Higher Education (February 1988).

Fincher, Cameron. "Economic and Sociological Studies of Educational Effects." *The Educational Forum* (January 1979), pp. 139–151.

Fincher, Cameron. "Knowledge, Competence and Understanding as Educational Outcomes." *Research in Higher Education* 27 (3) (1987), pp. 283–288.

Fincher, Cameron. "The Measurement of Knowledge." *Research in Higher Education* 27 (1) (1987), pp. 91–94.

Finn, Chester. "What Ails Educational Research?" *Educational Researcher* 17 (1) (1988), pp. 5–8.

Fitz-Gibbon, Carol Taylor, and Morris, Lynn Lyons. *How to Design a Program Evaluation.* Beverly Hills, California: Sage Publications, 1987.

Fitz-Gibbon, Carol Taylor, and Morris, Lynn Lyons. *How to Analyze Data.* Beverly Hills, California: Sage Publications, 1987.

Fong, Bobby. "Assessing the Departmental Major." In *Assessing Students' Learning, New Directions for Teaching and Learning No. 34* edited by J. McMillan. San Francisco: Jossey-Bass, Summer 1988, pp. 71–84.

Fong, Bobby. *The External Examiner Approach to Assessment.* Washington, D.C.: American Association for Higher Education, AAHE Assessment Forum, nd (1989).

Forrest, Aubrey, and A Study Group. *Time Will Tell: Portfolio-Assisted Assessment of General Education.* Washington, D.C.: American Association of Higher Education, The AAHE Assessment Forum, 1990.

Fredericksen, J.R., and Collins, A. (1989). "A Systems Approach to Educational Testing." *Educational Leadership 9* (1989), pp. 27–32.

Freedman, Leonard. *Quality in Continuing Education.* San Francisco: Jossey-Bass, 1987.

French-Lazovik, Grace (Ed.). *Practices that Improve Teaching Evaluation, New Directions for Teaching and Learning No. 11.* San Francisco: Jossey-Bass, 1982.

Gagne, Robert M. "Learning Outcomes and Their Effects: Useful Categories of Human Performance." *American Psychologist* (April 1984), pp. 377–385.

Garcia, Mildred. "Assessing Program Effectiveness in an Institution with a Diverse Student Body." In *The Effect of Assessment on Minority Student Participation, New Directions for Institutional Research No. 65* edited by M.T. Nettles. San Francisco: Jossey-Bass. Spring 1990, pp. 69–76.

Gardiner, Lion F. *Planning for Assessment: Mission Statements, Goals, and Objectives.* New Jersey: Office of Learning Assessment, Department of Higher Education, 1989.

Gardner, D.E. "Five Evaluation Frameworks: Implications for Decision Making in Higher Education." *Journal of Higher Education* 48 (5) (1977), pp. 571–593.

George, Melvin D. "Assessing Program Quality." In *Designing Academic Program Reviews, New Directions for Higher Education No. 37* edited by Richard F. Wilson. San Francisco: Jossey-Bass, 1982.

Grant, Donald L. (Ed.). *Monitoring Ongoing Programs, New Directions for Program Evaluation No. 3.* San Francisco: Jossey-Bass, 1978.

Gray, Peter J. (Ed.). *Achieving Assessment Goals Using Evaluation Techniques, New Directions for Higher Education No 67. San Francisco: Jossey-Bass, Fall 1989.*

Greenberg, K. L. "Assessing Writing: Theory and Practice." In *Assessing Students' Learning, New Directions for Teaching and Learning No. 34* edited by J. McMillan. San Francisco: Jossey-Bass, Summer 1988, pp. 47-59.

Greer, Darryl G. "Assessment Cannot Occur in a Vacuum." *Higher Education and National Affairs.* Washington, D.C.: American Council on Education, 8/14/89 (Opinion page).

Guba, Egon G,. and Lincoln, Yvonna S. *Effective Evaluation: Improving the Usefulness of Evaluation Results Through Responsive and Naturalistic Approaches.* San Francisco: Jossey-Bass, 1985.

Guskey, Thomas R. "Learning and Evaluation." In *Improving Student Learning in College Classrooms.* Springfield: Charles C. Thomas, 1988.

Guttentag, M., and Struening, E.L. (Eds.). *Handbook of Evaluation Research* (2 volumes). Beverly Hills, California: Sage, 1975.

Hagerty, Bonnie M.K., and Stark, Joan S. "Comparing Educational Accreditation Standards in Selected Professional Fields." *Research in Higher Education* 60 (1) (1989), pp. 1–20.

Halpern, Diane F. (Ed.). *Student Outcomes Assessment: What Institutions Stand to Gain, New Directions for Higher Education No. 59.* San Francisco: Jossey-Bass, 1987.

Hanson, G. R. *The Assessment of Student Outcomes: A Review and Critique of Assessment Instruments.* Austin, Texas: University of Texas, 1989.

Hanson, Gary R. "Critical Issues in the Assessment of Value-Added in Education." In *Implementing Outcomes Assessment: Promise and Perils, New Directions for Institutional Research No. 59* edited by T.W. Banta. San Francisco: Jossey-Bass, Fall 1988, pp. 53–69.

Harcleroad, Fred F. *Accreditation: History, Process, and Problems, AAHE/ERIC Higher Education Report No. 6, 1980.*

Harcleroad, Fred F. "The Context of Academic Program Evaluation." In *Academic Program Evaluation, New Directions for Institutional Research* edited by E.C. Craven. San Francisco: Jossey-Bass, 1980, pp. 1–20.

Harris, D., and Bell, C. *Evaluating and Assessing for Learning.* New York: Nichols Publishing Company, 1986.

Harris, J. W., and Baggett, J.M. (Eds.). *Quality Question in the Academic Process.* Birmingham, Alabama: Samford University, 1992.

Harris, John. *Assessing Outcomes in Higher Education: Practical Suggestions for Getting Started.* Paper given at the National Conference on Assessment in Higher Education, University of South Carolina, October 1985.

Harris, Shanette M., and Nettles, Michael T. "Racial Differences in Student Experiences and Attitudes." *Racism on Campus: Confronting Racial Bias Through Peer Interventions, New Directions for Student Services No. 56.* San Francisco: Jossey-Bass, 1991.

Hartle, Terry W. "The Growing Interest in Measuring the Educational Achievement of College Students." In *Assessment in American Higher Education: Issues and Contexts* edited by Clifford Adelman. Washington, D.C.: Office of Educational Research and Improvement, U.S. Office of Education, 1986.

Heffernan, James M., Hutchings, Pat, and Marchese, Theodore J. *Standardized Tests and the Purposes of Assessment.* Washington, D.C.: American Association for Higher Education, AAHE Assessment Forum, nd (circa 1989).

Henderson, Marlene E., Morris, Lynn Lyons, and Fitz-Gibbon, Carol Taylor. *How to Measure Attitudes.* Beverly Hills, California: Sage Publications, 1987.

Herman, Joan L., Morris, Lynn Lyons, and Fitz-Gibbon, Carol Taylor. *Evaluator's Handbook.* Beverly Hills, California: Sage Publications, 1987.

Hexter, Holly, and Lippincott, Joan K. "Campuses and Student Assessment." *Research Briefs, Volume 1, No.8.* Washington, D.C.: American Council on Education, 1990.

House, Ernest R. "Assumptions Underlying Evaluation Models." *Educational Researcher* 7 (March 1978.), pp. 4–12.

House, Ernest R. "Trends in Evaluation." *Educational Researcher* (April 1990), pp. 24–28.

Hurtado, Sylvia, Dey, Eric L., and Astin, Alexander W. *A Preliminary Assessment of College Environmental Factors Influencing General Education Outcomes.* Paper presented at Association of American Colleges Annual Meeting, Washington, D.C. January 7, 1989.

Hutchings, P. and Marchese, T. "Watching Assessment: Questions, Stories, Prospects." *Change* 22 (5) (September/October 1990), pp. 12–38.

Hutchings, Pat, and Ruben, Elaine. "Faculty Voices on Assessment." *Change* (July/August 1988), pp. 48–55.

Hutchings, Pat, and Wurzdorff, Allen (Eds.). *Knowing and Doing: Learning Through Experiences, New Directions for Teaching and Learning. No. 35.* San Francisco: Jossey Bass, 1988.

Hutchings, Pat, Marchese, Theodore, and Wright, Barbara. *Using Assessment to Strengthen General Education.* Washington, D.C.: American Association for Higher Education, 1991.

Hutchings, Pat. "Assessment and the Way We Work." In *Assessment 1990: Understanding the Implications.* Washington, D.C.: American Association for Higher Education, AAHE Assessment Forum, June 1990, pp. 35–45.

Hutchings, Pat. *Behind Outcomes: Context and Questions for Assessment.* Washington, D.C.: American Association for Higher Education, AAHE Assessment Forum, circa 1989.

Hutchings, Patricia. *Six Stories: Implementing Successful Assessment.* Washington, D.C.: American Association for Higher Education, AAHE Assessment Forum, nd (1989).

Jacob, Evelyn. "Clarifying Qualitative Research: A Focus on Traditions." *Educational Researcher* 17 (1) (1988), pp. 16–23.

Jacobi , Maryann , Astin , Alexander W ., and Ayala , Frank Jr. *College Student Outcomes Assessment: A Talent Development Perspective, ASHE-ERIC Higher Education Reports No. 7.* Washington, D.C.: Association for the Study of Higher Education: ERIC Clearinghouse on Higher Education, 1987.

Jacobs, Luck Chester and Chase, Clinton I. *Developing and Using Tests Effectively: A Guide for Faculty.* San Francisco : Jossey-Bass, 1992 .

Jacobson, Robert L. "Efforts to Assess Students' Learning May Trivialize the B.A., Boyer Says." *Chronicle of Higher Education* (October 15, 1986).

Jaschik, Scott. "As States Weigh 'Value-Added' Tests, Northeast Missouri Offers Model." *Chronicle of Higher Education* (October 2, 1985).

Johnson, R, Prus, J., Anderson, C. J. and El-Khawas, E. "Assessing Assessment." *Higher Education Panel Reports No. 79.* Washington, D.C.: American Council on Education, 1991.

Joint Committee on Standards for Educational Evaluation. "Proprietary Standards." *Standards for Evaluation of Educational Programs, Projects and Materials.* New York: McGraw-Hill, 1981, pp. 63–96.

Joint Committee on Testing Practices. "Code of Fair Testing Practices in Education." *American Psychologist* (July 1989), pp. 1066–1067.

Jones, Calvin. *(NORC) How to Optimize and Articulate a Longitudinal and a Cross Sectional Research Program.* Washington, D. C.: National Center for Education Statistics Conference, December 1986.

Jordan, Thomas E. *Measurement and Evaluation in Higher Education: Issues and Illustrations.* London, England: The Falmer Press, 1989.

Kaagan, Stephen S. and Coley, Richard J. *State Education Indicators: Measured strides, Missing Steps.* Rutgers University: Center for Policy Research in Education, 1989.

Keimig, Ruth T. *Raising Academic Standards, ASHE/ERIC Research Report No.4.* Washington, D.C.: Association for the Study of Higher Education: ERIC Clearinghouse on Higher Education, 1983.

Kells, H. R. *Self-Study Processes: A Guide for Postsecondary Institutions.* New York: American Council on Education/ MacMillan Publishing Company, 1983.

Kemp, G.O., Jr. "Identifying, Measuring, and Integrating Competence." In *New Directions for Experiential Learning* edited by P.S. Pottinger and J. Goldsmith. San Francisco: Jossey Bass, 1979, pp. 41–52.

Kidder, Louise and Fine, Michelle "Qualitative and Quantitative Methods: When Stories Converge." In *Multiple Methods in Program Evaluation, New Directions for Program Evaluation No. 35* edited by M.M. Mark and R.I. Shotland. San Francisco: Jossey Bass, Fall 1987.

King, Jean A., Morris, Lynn Lyons, and Fitz-Gibbon, Carol Taylor. *How to Assess Program Implementation.* Beverly Hills, California: Sage Publications, 1987.

Knefelkamp, L. Lee, Ewell, Peter T., and Brown, Rexford. ThreePresentations from the Fourth National Conference onAssessment in Higher Education. Washington, D.C.: AmericanAssociation for Higher Education, AAHE Assessment Forum in Atlanta, Georgia, June 21–24, 1989.

Knight, Michael E., Lumsden, Donald L., and Gallaro, Denise (Eds.). *Outcomes Assessment at Kean College of New Jersey: Academic Programs, Procedures, and Models*. Lanham, Maryland: University Press of America, 1991.

Kuh, George D., and Randsell, G. A. "Evaluation by Discussion." *Journal of Higher Education* 51 (3) (1980), pp. 301–313.

Kuh, George D. "In Their Own Words: What Students Learn Outside the Classroom." *American Educational Research Journal* 30 (2), pp. 277–304.

Kuh, George D. *Indices of Quality in the Undergraduate Experience, AAHE/ERIC Higher Education Research Report No. 4*. Washington, D.C.: American Association for Higher Education, 1981.

League for Innovation in the Community College. *Assessing Institutional Effectiveness in Community Colleges*. Laguna Hills, California: League for Innovation in the Community College, 1990.

Lenning, Oscar T. "Use of Noncognitive Measures in Assessment." In *Implementing Outcomes Assessment: Promise and Perils, New Directions for Institutional Research No. 59* edited by Trudy W. Banta. San Francisco: Jossey-Bass, Fall 1988, pp. 41–52.

Lewis, D. R. "Costs and Benefits of Assessment: A Paradigm." In *Implementing Outcomes Assessment: Promise and Perils, New Directions for Institutional Research No. 59 edited* by Trudy W. Banta. San Francisco: Jossey-Bass, 1988. pp. 69–80

Light, Richard J. *The Harvard Assessment Seminars. Second Report: Explorations with Students and Faculty About Teaching, Learning, and Student Life*. Cambridge, Massachusetts: Harvard University, Graduate School of Education, 1992.

Light, Richard. J. *The Harvard Assessment Seminars. First Report: Explorations with Students and Faculty About Teaching, Learning and Student Life*. Cambridge, Massachusetts: Harvard University, Graduate School of Education, 1990.

Lincoln, Yvonna S. and Guba, Egon G. "But Is It Rigorous? Trustworthiness and Authenticity in Naturalistic Evaluation." In *Naturalistic Evaluation, New Directions for Program Evaluation No. 30* edited by D. D. Williams. San Francisco: Jossey-Bass, 1986, pp. 73–84.

Lincoln, Yvonna S. and Guba, Egon G. "The Distinction Between Merit and Worth in Evaluation." *Educational Evaluation and Policy Analysis* 2 (4) (July-August 1980), pp. 61–71.

Lincoln, Yvonna S., and Guba, E. G. *Naturalistic Inquiry*. Beverly Hills, California : Sage, 1985.

Linn, R.L., and Slinde, J.A. "The Determination of the Significance of Change Between Pre- and Post-Testing Periods." *Review of Educational Research* 47 (1977), pp. 121–150.

Loacker, Georgine, Cromwell, Lucy, and O'Brien, Kathleen. *Assessment in Higher Education: To Serve the Learner*. Paper given at National Conference on Assessment in Higher Education at University of South Carolina, October 1985.

Loacker, Georgine. "Faculty as a Force to Improve Instruction Through Assessment." In *Assessing Students' Learning, New Directions for Teaching and Learning No. 34* edited by J. McMillan. San Francisco: Jossey-Bass, Summer 1988.

Loveland, Edward H. (Ed.). *Measuring the Hard-to-Measure, New Directions for Program Evaluation No 6*. San Francisco: Jossey-Bass, 1980.

Madaus, George F., Stufflebeam, D.L, and Scriven, M.S. "Program Evaluation: A Historical Overview." *Evaluation Models*. Norwell, Massachusetts: Kluwer Academic Publishers, 1987, pp. 3–22.

Madaus, George F. "The Influence of Testing on the Curriculum." In *Critical Issues in Curriculum* (Eighty-seventh Yearbook of the National Society for the Study of Education) edited by L. N. Tanner. Chicago: University of Chicago Press, 1988, pp. 83–121.

Madaus, George F., and Stufflebeam, Daniel (Eds.). *Educational Evaluation: Classic Works of Ralph W. Tyler.* Boston, Massachusetts: Kluwer Publishers, 1989.

Manning, Thurston. "The Why, What and Who of Assessment: The Accrediting Perspective." *Assessing the Outcomes of Higher Education: Proceedings of the 1986 ETS Invitational Conference.* Princeton, New Jersey: Educational Testing Service, 1986, pp. 31–38.

Manns, C.L., and March, J.G. "Financial Adversity, Internal Competition and Curriculum Change in a University." *Administrative Science Quarterly* 23, pp. 541–552.

Mark, Melvin M., and Shotland, R. Lance (Eds.). *Multiple Methods in Program Evaluation, New Directions for Program Evaluation No. 35.* San Francisco: Jossey-Bass, Fall 1987.

McCabe, Robert H. "The Assessment Movement: What Next? Who Cares?" In *Three Presentations: From the Third National Conference on Assessment in Higher Education.* Washington, D.C.: American Association for Higher Education, June 1988, pp. 1–16.

McClain, Charles J. "Assessment Produces Degrees with Integrity." *Educational Record* (Winter 1987), pp. 47–52.

McGaghie, William C. "Professional Competence Evaluation." *Educational Researcher* (January/ February 1991), pp. 3–9.

McGaghie, William C. "Evaluating Competence for Professional Practice." In Curry, Lynn, Wergin, Jon F. and Associates, *Educating Professionals: Responding to New Expectations for Competence and Accountability.* San Francisco: Jossey-Bass, 1993, pp. 229–261.

McMillan, James H. (Ed.). *Assessing Students' Learning, New Directions for Teaching and Learning No. 34.* San Francisco: Jossey-Bass, 1988.

Mensel, Frank. "Growing Up-Political (Part II)". *AACJC Journal* (Feb/Mar, 1990), pp. 19–20.

Mentkowski, Marcia, and Loacker, Georgine. "Assessing and Validating the Outcomes of College." In *Assessing Educational Outcomes, New Directions for Institutional Research No. 47* edited by Peter T. Ewell. San Francisco: Jossey-Bass, September 1985.

Mentkowski, Marcia, Astin, Alexander W., Ewell, Peter T., Moran, E. Thomas, and Cross, K. Patricia. *Catching Theory Up with Practice: Conceptual Frameworks for Assessment.* Washington, D.C.: American Association for Higher Education, 1991.

Mentkowski, Marcia; "Creating a Context Where Institutional Assessment Yields Educational Improvement." *The Journal of General Education* 40 (1991), pp. 255–283.

Meredith, Vana, and Williams, Paul L. "Issues in Direct Writing Assessment: Problem Identification and Control." *Educational Leadership* 3 (1) (Spring 1984), pp. 12–18.

Messick, Samuel. "Meaning and Values in Test Validation: The Science and Ethics of Assessment." *Educational Researcher* 18 (2) (March 1989), pp. 5–11.

Millard, R.M. "Accreditation." In *Meeting the New Demand for Standards, New Directions for Higher Education No. 43* edited by J. Warren. San Francisco: Jossey-Bass, 1983, pp. 9–28.

Miller, Richard I. *The Assessment of College Performance: A Handbook of Techniques and Measures for Institutional Self-Evaluation.* San Francisco: Jossey-Bass, 1979.

Millman, J. "Designing a College Assessment." In *Performance and Judgment: Essays on Principles and Practice in the Assessment of College Student Learning* edited by Clifford Adelman. Washington, D. C.: Office of Educational Research and Improvement, U.S. Department of Education, pp. 9–38.

Mingle, James R. *Measuring the Educational Achievement of Undergraduates: State and National Developments.* Denver, Colorado: State Higher Education Executive Officers, January 1985.

Morante, Edward A. *The State of the States in Postsecondary Assessment.* Trenton, New Jersey: New Jersey Department of Higher Education, November 20, 1986.

Morris, Lynn Lyons, Fitz-Gibbon, Carol Taylor, and Lindheim, Elaine. *How to Measure Performance and Use Tests.* Beverly Hills, California: Sage Publications, 1987.

Morris, Lynn Lyons; Fitz-Gibbon, Carol Taylor, and Freeman, Marie E. *How to Communicate Evaluation Findings.* Beverly Hills, California: Sage Publications, 1987.

Mullis, Ina V.S. "Scoring Direct Writing Assessments: What Are the Alternatives?" *Educational Leadership* 3 (1) (Spring 1984), pp. 1–11.

Nettles, Michael T. *The Emergence of College Outcome Assessments: Prospects for Enhancing State Colleges and Universities.* Trenton, New Jersey: New Jersey State College Governing Boards Association, 1987.

Nettles, Michael T. "Assessing Progress in Minority Access and Achievement in American Higher Education." *Report No. PA-91-1.* Denver, Colorado: Education Commission of the States, 1991.

Nettles, Michael T. (Ed.). *The Effect of Assessment on Minority Student Participation, New Directions for Institutional Research No. 65.* San Francisco: Jossey Bass, 1990 .

Nevo, D. "The Conceptualization of Educational Evaluation: An Analytical Review of the Literature." *Review of Educational Research* 53 (1) (Spring 1983), pp. 117–128.

Nichols, J.O. and Wolff, L.A. *The Role of Institutional Researchers in Implementation of Student Outcomes Assessment or Institutional Effectiveness: Results of a National survey* (unpublished report). University of Mississippi, 1991 .

Nichols, James 0. *A Practitioner's Handbook for Institutional Effectiveness and Student Outcomes Assessment Implementation.* New York: Agathon Press, 1991.

Nichols, James 0. *The Departmental Guide to Implementation of Student Outcomes Assessment and Institutional Effectiveness.* New York: Agathon Press, 1991

Nickerson, Raymond S. "New Directions in Educational Assessment." *Educational Leadership* 18(9) (1989), pp. 3–6.

Nielsen, Robert M., and Polishook, Irwin H. "Taking a Measure of Assessment." American Federation of Teachers Higher Education Paper No. 49. *Chronicle of Higher Education.*

Norris, Stephen P. "Can We Test for Critical Thinking?" *Educational Researcher* 18 (9) (1989), pp. 21–26.

North Central Association of Colleges and Schools. *A Handbook of Accreditation.* Tempe, Arizona: North Central Association of Colleges and Schools, Commission on Institutions of Higher Education, 1992–93.

North Central Association of Colleges and Schools. *A Collection of Papers on Self-Study and Institutional Improvement.* Tempe, Arizona: North Central Association of Colleges and Schools, Commission on Institutions of Higher Education, 1989.

North Central Association of Colleges and Schools. A *Guide to Self-Study for Commission Evaluation.* Tempe, Arizona: North Central Association of Colleges and Schools, Commission on Institutions of Higher Education.

North Central Association of Colleges and Schools. *NCA Quarterly: Assessing Student Academic Achievement, Volume 66*: 2. Tempe, Arizona: North Central Association of Colleges and Schools, 1991.

Northeast Missouri State University. *In Pursuit of Degrees with Integrity: A Value Added Approach to Undergraduate* Assessment. Washington, D.C.: American Association of State Colleges and Universities, 1984.

Novak, Joseph D., and Ridley, Dennis R. *Assessing Student Learning in Light of How Students Learn.* Washington, D.C.: American Association for Higher Education. AAHE Assessment Forum, nd (1989).

Ory, John C. "Meta-Assessment: Evaluating Assessment Activities." *Research in Higher Education* 33 (4) (1992), pp. 467–481

Ory, John C. "Suggestions for Deciding Between Commercially Available and Locally Developed Assessment Instruments." *NCA Quarterly* 66 (2) (1991), pp. 451–457.

Ory, John C., and Parker, Stephanie A. "Assessment Activities at Large Research Universities." *Research in Higher Education,* 30 (4) (1989), pp. 375–385.

Pace, C. Robert. "Assessing the Undergraduate Experience." *Assessment Update* 2 (3) (Fall 1990), pp. 1–5.

Pace, C. Robert. "Perspectives and Problems in Student Outcomes Research." In *Assessing Educational Outcomes, New Directions for Institutional Research No. 47* edited by Peter T. Ewell. San Francisco: Jossey-Bass, 1985, pp. 7–18.

Pace, C. Robert. *Measuring the Outcomes of College.* San Francisco: Jossey Bass, 1979.

Parlett, Malcolm. *Introduction to Illuminative Evaluation.* Cardiff by the Sea, California: Pacific Soundings Press, 1977.

Pascarella, E.T. and Terenzini, P.T. "Methodological and Analytical Issues in Assessing the Influence of College." In E.T. Pascarella and P.T. Terenzini. *How College Affects Students: Findings and Insights from Twenty Years of Research.* San Francisco: Jossey-Bass, 1991.

Pascarella, Ernest T. "College Environmental Influences on Learning and Cognitive Development: A Critical Review and Synthesis." In John Smart (Ed.). *Higher Education: Handbook of Theory and Research. Volume 1,* 1985, pp. 1–62.

Pascarella, Ernest T. "Student-Faculty Informal Contact and College Outcomes." *Review of Educational Research* 50 (4) (Winter 1980), pp. 545–595.

Paskow, Jacqueline (Ed.). *Assessment Programs and Projects: A Directory.* Washington, D.C.: American Association for Higher Education, AAHE Assessment Forum, nd (1989).

Patton, Michael Quinn. *How to Use Qualitative Methods in Evaluation.* Beverly Hills, California: Sage Publications, 1987.

Patton, Michael Quinn. *Qualitative Evaluation Methods*. Beverly Hills, California: Sage Publications, 1980.

Pazandak, Carol (Ed.). *Improving Undergraduate Education in Large Universities, New Directions for Higher Education No. 66*, Summer 1989.

Perloff, Robert, and Perloff, Evelyn (Eds.). *Values, Ethics and Standards in Evaluation, New Directions in Program Evaluation No. 7*. San Francisco: Jossey-Bass, 1980.

Perrone, V. (Ed.). *Expanding Student Assessment*. Alexandria, Virginia: Association for Supervision and Curriculum Development, 1991.

Pettit, Joseph. "Listening to Your Alumni: One Way to Assess Academic Outcomes." *AIR Professional File, No. 41* (Summer, 1991), pp. 1–10.

Pike, Gary R. "Background, College Experiences, and the ACT-COMP Exam: Using Construct Validity to Evaluate Assessment Instruments." *The Review of Higher Education 13 (1)* (Fall 1989), pp. 91–117.

Pike, Gary R. "Lies, Damn Lies, and Statistics Revisited." *Research in Higher Education 33 (1)* (1992), pp. 71–84.

Pike, Gary R. "The Effects of Background, Coursework, and Involvement on Students' Grades and Satisfaction." *Research in Higher Education 32 (1)* (1991), pp. 15–30.

Pike, Gary R. and Phillippi, Raymond H. "Generalizability of the Differential Coursework Methodology: Relationships Between Self-Reported Coursework and Performance on the ACTCOMP Exam." *Research in Higher Education 30 (3)* (1989), pp. 245–260.

Pintrich, Paul R. *Assessing Student Progress in College: A Process-Oriented Approach to Assessment of Student Learning in Postsecondary Settings*. Paper presented at a conference sponsored by OERI, November 20, 1986. Ann Arbor, Michigan: The University of Michigan, National Center for Research to Improve Postsecondary Education.

Popham, W. James (Ed.). *Evaluation in Education*. Berkeley, California: McCutcheon, 1974.

Pratt, Cornelius B., and McLaughlin, Gerald W. "An Analysis of Predictors of College Students' Ethical Inclinations." *Research in Higher Education 30(2)* (1989), pp. 195–219.

Provus, Malcolm. *Discrepancy Evaluation for Educational Improvement and Assessment*. Berkeley, California: McCutchan, 1971.

Prus, J. and Johnson, R. *A Critical Review of Student Assessment Options*. Rock Hill, South Carolina: Winthrop College, 1992, pp. 1–17.

Ratcliff, James L. "What Can We Learn From Coursework Patterns About Improving the Undergraduate Curriculum." In *Assessment and Curriculum Reform, New Directions for Higher Education No. 80* edited by J.L. Ratcliff. San Francisco, California: Jossey-Bass, Winter 1992, pp. 5–22.

Ratcliff, James L. (Ed.). *Assessment and Curriculum Reform, New Directions for Higher Education No. 80*. San Francisco, California: Jossey Bass, Winter 1992.

Resnick, D.P. "Expansion, Quality, and Testing in American Education." In *Issues in Student Assessment, New Directions for Community Colleges No. 59* edited by D. Bray and M. Belcher. San Francisco: Jossey-Bass, Fall 1987, pp. 5–14.

Richardson, R.C., Jr. *Institutional Climate and Minority Achievement, Report No. MP-89-2*. Denver, Colorado: Education Commission of the States, 1989.

Richardson, R.C., Jr. *Focus on Minorities: Trends in Higher Education Participation and Success.* Denver, Colorado: Education Commission of the States, 1987.

Richardson, R.C., Jr. *Promoting Fair College Outcomes; Learning from the Experiences of the Past Decade.* Denver, Colorado: Education Commission of the States, 1990.

Richardson, R.C., Jr. *Serving More Diverse Students: A Contextual View.* Denver, Colorado: Education Commission of the States, 1989.

Richardson, R., Matthews, D. and Finney, J. *Improving State and Campus Environments for Quality and Diversity: A Self–Assessment.* Denver, Colorado: Education Commission of the States, 1992.

Romberg, Elaine (Ed.). *Outcomes Assessment: A Resource Book.* Washington, D.C.: American Association of Dental Schools, 1990.

Rossi, Peter H., and Freeman, Howard E. *Evaluation: A Systematic Approach (Third Edition).* Beverly Hills, California: Sage Publications, 1985.

Rossman, Jack E., and El-Khawas, Elaine. *Thinking About Assessment: Perspectives for Presidents and Chief Academic Officers.* Washington, D.C.: American Council on Education, 1987.

Rudman, Herbert C. "The Future of Testing is Now." *Educational Measurement: Issues and Practices* (1987), pp. 511 .

Rudolph, L. and Poje, D.J. "Higher Education Assessment: Don't Overlook Ethical Practices." In T. W. Banta (Ed.). *Assessment Update 3* (4) (July/August 1991), pp.4–5.

Sachse, P. "Writing Assessment in Texas." *Educational Measurement: Issues and Practices* (Summer 1984), pp. 1-11.

Sadler, D. Royce. "Evaluation and the Improvement of Academic Learning." *Journal of Higher Education* 54 (1) (January/February 1983), pp. 60–79.

Schneider, C. "Involving Faculty Members in Assessment." *Liberal Education* 74 (3) (May 1988), pp. 2–4.

Scott, Robert A. (Ed.). "Determining the Effectiveness of Campus Services." *New Directions for Institutional Research, No. 41.* San Francisco: Jossey-Bass, 1984.

Sechrest, Lee (Ed.). *Training Program Evaluators, New Directions for Program Evaluation No. 8.* San Francisco: Jossey-Bass, 1980.

Sell, G.R. "An Organizational Perspective for the Effective Practice of Assessment." In *Achieving Assessment Goals Using Evaluation Techniques, New Directions for Higher Education No. 67* edited by P.J. Gray. San Francisco: Jossey-Bass, Fall 1989, pp. 21–41.

Seymour, Daniel. "Beyond Assessment: Managing Quality in Higher Education." *Assessment Update 3 (1)* (January/February 1991), pp. 1–2, 10.

Seymour, Daniel. *Q: Causing Quality in Higher Education.* New York: MacMillan, 1991.

Shirley, Robert C., and Volkwein, J. Fredericks. "Establishing Academic Program Priorities." *Journal of Higher Education.* 49 (5) (1978), pp. 472–488.

Shulman, Lee S., Smith, Virginia B., and Stewart, Donald M. *Three Presentations from the Second National Conference on Assessment in Higher Education, June 14–17, 1987, Denver.* Washington, D.C.: American Association for Higher Education, AAHE Assessment Forum, nd (1989).

Siegler, Robert S. "Strategy, Diversity, and Cognitive Assessment." *Educational Researcher* 18 (9) (1989), pp. 15–19 .

Skolnik, Michael L. "How Academic Program Review Can Foster Intellectual Conformity and Stifle Diversity of Thought and Method." *Journal of Higher Education* 60 (6) (1989), pp. 619–643.

Smith, John K. and Heshusius, L.. "Closing Down the Conversation: The End of the Quantitative-Qualitative Debate Among Educational Inquirers." *Educational Researcher* 15 (1) (1986), pp. 4–12.

Smith, M.F. "Evaluation Utilization Revisited." In *Evaluation Utilization, New Directions for Program Evaluation No. 39* edited by J.A. McLaughlin and others. San Francisco: Jossey-Bass.

Southern Association of Colleges and Schools. *Criteria for Accreditation: Commission on Colleges, Seventh Edition,* Southern Association of Colleges and Schools, 1991.

Southern Association of Colleges and Schools. *Resource Manual on Institutional Effectiveness.* Southern Association of Colleges and Schools, Commission on Colleges, 1987.

Spangehl, Steven D. "The Push to Assess: Why It's Feared and How to Respond." *Change* (January/ February 1987), pp. 35–39.

Stage, Frances K. "College Outcomes and Student Development: Filling the Gaps." *The Review of Higher Education* 12 (3) (Spring 1989), pp. 293–304.

Stark, Joan S. "Approaches to Assessing Educational Outcomes." *Journal of Health Administration Education* 8 (2) (Spring 1990), pp. 210–226.

Stark, Joan S., and Mets, Lisa A. (Eds.). *Improving Teaching and Learning Through Research, New Directions for Institutional Research No. 57.* San Francisco: Jossey-Bass, 1988.

Stecker, Brian M., and Davis, W. Alan. *How to Focus an Evaluation.* Beverly Hills, California: Sage Publications, 1987.

Steele, Joe M. "Evaluating College Programs Using Measures of Student Achievement and Growth." *Educational Evaluation and Policy Analysis* 11 (4) (Winter 1989), pp. 357–375.

Stetson, N.E. "Implementing and Maintaining a Classroom Research Program for Faculty." In *Classroom Research: Early Lessons from Success, New Directions for Teaching and Learning No. 46* edited by Thomas A. Angelo. San Francisco: Jossey-Bass, Summer 1991, pp. 117–128.

Stufflebeam, D. L., and Webster, W.J. "An Analysis of Alternative Approaches to Evaluation." *Educational Evaluation and Policy Analysis* 2 (3) (May/June 1980), pp. 5–20.

Tan, D.L. "A Multivariate Approach to the Assessment of Quality." *Research in Higher Education* 33 (2) (1992), pp. 205–226.

Terenzini, Patrick T. "Assessment with Open Eyes: Pitfalls in Studying Student Outcomes." *Journal of Higher Education* 60 (6) (November/December, 1989), pp. 644–664.

Terenzini, Patrick T. "The Case for Unobtrusive Measures." In *Assessing the Outcomes of Higher Education: Proceedings of the 1986 ETS Invitational Conference.* Princeton, New Jersey: Educational Testing Service, 1987, pp. 47–61.

Terenzini, Patrick T., Theophilides, Christos, and Lorang, Wendell G. "Influences on Students' Perceptions of Their Academic Skills Development During College." *Journal of Higher Education* 55 (5) (September/October 1984), pp. 621–636.

Thomas, Alice M. "Consideration of the Resources Needed in an Assessment Program." *NCA Quarterly* 66 (2) (1991), pp. 430–443.

Thompson, Kenrick S. "Changes in the Values and Life-Style Preferences of University Students." *Journal of Higher Education* 52 (5) (1981), pp. 506–518.

Thompson, Kirk. *Learning at Evergreen: An Assessment of Cognitive Development, Monograph No. 1.* Washington Center for Improving the Quality of Undergraduate Education, 1991.

Tompkins, Loren D. *Those Standardized Competency Examinations: What Do They Really Tell Us About Our Student Bodies?* Paper presented at the Annual meeting of the Association for the Study of Higher Education, San Antonio, Texas, February 20-23, 1986.

Torrance, H. "Ethics and Politics in the Study of Assessment." In R. G. Burgess, *The Ethics of Educational Research* (Social Research and Educational Studies Series: 8). New York: The Falmer Press, 1989.

Turnbull, William W. "Are They Learning Anything in College?" *Change* (November/December 1985), pp. 23-26.

Twombly, Susan B., and Baumgartel, Howard J. *The Impact of Curriculum Change on Student Achievement and Persistence in a Major Research University.* Paper presented at Association for the Study of Higher Education Annual Meeting, November 1988, St. Louis, Missouri.

Tyler, Ralph W. Educational Assessment, Standards and Quality: Can We Have One Without the Others? *Educational Measurement: Issues and Practice* (Summer 1983), pp. 14-23.

Underwood, David G. "Taking Inventory: Identifying Assessment Activities." Research *in Higher Education* 32 (1) (1991), pp. 59-69.

Wallhaus, R. A. "Process Issues in State-Level Program Reviews." In *Designing Academic Program Reviews, New Directions for Higher Education No. 37* edited by R. F. Wilson. San Francisco: Jossey-Bass, 1982, pp. 75-87.

Waluconis, Carl. "Student Self-Assessment: Students Making Connections." *Assessment Update* 3 (4) (July/August 1991), pp. 1-2, 6.

Warren, Jonathan R. (Ed.). *Meeting the New Demand for Standards, New Directions for Higher Education No.43.* San Francisco: Jossey-Bass, 1983.

Warren, Jonathan. "The Blind Alley of Value Added." *AAHE Bulletin* (September 1984), pp. 10-13.

Warren, Jonathan. "Cognitive Measures in Assessing Learning." In Implementing *Outcomes Assessment: Promise and Perils, New Directions for Institutional Research No. 59* edited by Trudy W. Banta. San Francisco: Jossey-Bass, Fall 1988, pp. 29-40.

Wergin, Jon F. "Politics and Assessment in the University. " *Assessment Update* 1 (2) (Summer 1989), pp. 5-7.

Wergin, Jon F., and Braskamp, Larry A. (Eds.). *Evaluating Administrative Services and Programs, New Directions for Institutional Research, No. 56.* San Francisco: Jossey-Bass, 1987.

Western Association of Schools and Colleges. *Achieving Institutional Effectiveness Through Assessment.* Oakland, California: Western Association of Schools and Colleges, April 1992.

Wiggins, G. "The Truth May Make You Free But The Test May Keep You Imprisoned: Toward Assessing Worth of the Liberal Arts." In *Assessment 1990: Understanding the Implications.* Washington, D.C.: The AAHE Assessment Forum, 1990, pp. 17-31

Wiggins, G. *Toward One System of Education: Assessing to Improve, Not Merely Audit, Report No. MP-91-2.* Denver, Colorado: Education Commission of the States, 1991.

Wilks, Barbara and Sikes, Susan "Guide to Practical Impact Evaluation." *Innovative Higher Education* 13 (1) (Fall/Winter 1988) pp. 54-65.

Williams, David D. (Ed.). "Naturalistic Evaluation." New *Directions for Program Evaluation No. 30*. San Francisco: Jossey-Bass, 1986.

Willingham, W. W. "Research and Assessment: Tools for Change." *In Improving Undergraduate Education in Large Universities, New Directions for Higher Education No. 66* edited by C.H. Pazandak. San Francisco: Jossey-Bass, Summer 1989, pp. 27-40.

Wilson, Everett K. "Department Review for Product Improvement in Higher Education." In *Higher Education: Handbook of Theory and Research, Volume III* edited by John C. Smart. New York: Agathon Press, 1987.

Wilson, Richard F. "Critical Issues in Program Evaluation." *The Review of Higher Education 7* (2) (1984), pp. 143-157.

Witmer, David R. *The Outcomes of Higher Education*. Resources in Higher Education: ED 136 687.

Wolf, Barbara. *Handbook on Assessment Strategies: Measures of Student Learning and Program Quality*. Bloomington, Indiana: Indiana University, 1993.

Wolff, R. A. "Assessment and Accreditation: A Shotgun Marriage?" *Assessment 1990: Accreditation and Renewal*. Washington, D.C.: The AAHE Assessment Forum, 1990, pp. 118.

Wood, Lynn, and Davis, Barbara Gross. *Designing and Evaluating Higher Education Curricula. AAHE-ERIC Higher Education Research Reports, No. 8*, 1978.

Woodard, D. B., Hyman, R., von Destinon, M. and Jamison, A. "Student Affairs and Outcomes Assessment: A National Survey." *NASPA JOURNAL* 29 (1) (1991).

Worthen, B.R., and Sanders, J.R. *Educational Evaluation: Alternative Approaches and Practical Guidelines*. White Plains, New York: Longman Press, 1987.

Worthley, J.S., and Riggs, M.L. *Student Outcomes Assessment: What makes it work?: Assessment practices and experience in the California State University*. Long Beach, California: California State University Institute for Teaching and Learning, 1992.

Wright, Barbara. "So How Do We Know It Will Work: An Assessment Memoir." *AAHE Bulletin* (April 1990), pp. 14-17.

Yarbrough, Donald. *Assessing Cognitive General Education Outcomes: Conclusions from a Decade of Research on the ACT COMP Measures* (Draft). University of Iowa, Division of Psychological and Quantitative Foundations, College of Education, May 1991.

Young, Kenneth E, Chambers, Charles M., Kells, H.R., and Associates. *Understanding Accreditation*. San Francisco: Jossey-Bass, 1983.

Zemsky, Robert. *Structure and Coherence: Measuring the Undergraduate Curriculum*. Washington, D.C.: Association of American Colleges, 1989.